THE RECRUITER'S RESEARCH BLUE BOOK

A HOW-TO GUIDE
FOR RESEARCHERS,
SEARCH CONSULTANTS,
CORPORATE RECRUITERS,
SMALL BUSINESS OWNERS,
VENTURE CAPITALISTS
AND LINE EXECUTIVES

2nd
EDITION

Previously Titled
THE HANDBOOK OF EXECUTIVE SEARCH RESEARCH

ANDREA A. JUPINA

KENNEDY INFORMATION

ISBN 1-885922-75-3
2nd Edition, copyright © 2000 by Andrea Jupina
(except bylined chapters & reprinted matter)
All rights reserved.

Published by Kennedy Information, LLC
Fitzwilliam, New Hampshire
Publishers of *The Directory of Executive Recruiters*,
The Directory of Outplacement and Career Management Firms,
SearchSelect®, *Executive Recruiter News*, and *Recruiting Trends*.

KENNEDY INFORMATION
One Kennedy Place
Fitzwilliam, NH 03447
1-800-531-0007 • 1-603-585-6544
bookstore@kennedyinfo.com
www.kennedyinfo.com

Nothing in the world can take the place of persistence.

Talent will not; nothing is more common than unsuccessful men with talent.

Genius will not; unrewarded genius is almost a proverb.

Education alone will not; the world is full of educated derelicts.

Persistence and determination alone are omnipotent.

E. Joseph Cossman

CONTENTS

PART I
THE RESEARCH PROCESS

(continued next page)

PART II
THE RECRUITER'S DIRECTORY OF DIRECTORIES – PLUS WEB SITES, DATABASES & CD ROM'S

ABOUT THE AUTHOR

Andrea Jupina is the author of *The Recruiter's Research Blue Book*, formerly *The Handbook of Executive Search Research*, first published by Kennedy Information in 1992. She began her career in executive search in 1977 in the Research Department of Booz, Allen and Hamilton in New York City. In 1979, she was one of the original members of the Research Roundtable. In 1983, she established Business Research Services, a revolutionary research consultancy that was a pioneer in providing "unbundled" search services to banks and corporations.

In 1987, Ms Jupina co-founded The Stuyvesant Group International with offices in Amsterdam, The Hague, Paris, and Madrid. This business evolved into classic retained search and the name changed to Jupina & Company.

Ms. Jupina moved her search practice to the global search firm Boyden in 1993, where she became a Senior Vice President ten months later. She subsequently reactivated Jupina & Company, a provider of retained executive search services. She also creates and produces training products in cassette and new media forms. A national expert on employment related matters, she writes and speaks regularly. In her spare time she is a traveler who writes – or a writer who travels. Ms. Jupina is a graduate of Antioch College in Yellow Springs, Ohio.

FOREWORD

Throughout history, new inventions – which is the old fashioned term for "technological advances" – have changed the way we live and work. For example, the invention of the steam engine was the driving force in the Industrial Revolution. It led the way to automating tasks, the rise of factories, and a population shift from an agrarian life to living in cities, where the jobs were. As the twentieth century marked the beginning of the computer age, we can only imagine the changes this technology will bring. The options of telecommuting and home-based businesses have taken on lives of their own, ironically bringing us back, in some ways, to the way things were throughout history before the industrial revolution, when virtually everyone worked at home. In those days, almost everybody lived on a farm and worked at home because that's where the work was.

Be that as it may, since the appearance of *The Handbook of Executive Search Research* in 1992, many things about our work in recruitment have changed. The tools used to gather data, and then massage it, have become far more powerful. That said, the fundamental process that drives an executive search is still the same. We just have faster ways of screening more information.

However, we should be careful to avoid one pitfall. Just because something is automated doesn't necessarily make it better. Sometimes the old fashioned way is simpler. For example, you don't need a sophisticated data-base to eyeball a Fortune 500 list to create a target list. However wonderful electronic automation might be, computers still lack one singularly human trait. Judgment. In your gut, you can tell whether something is amiss about a candidate. I remember the first time I interviewed a candidate. I remarked to my mentor, "He seemed ok, but there was something about him that I couldn't put my finger on." She replied, "You've just put your finger on the essence of interviewing."

The more things change, the more they stay the same. This book identifies numerous new technology-based information tools. It also covers the basics that always did – and always will – drive an executive search: target list development, identification research, use of the library, sourcing and prospecting, data gathering during a phone interview, reference checking, confidentiality, plus the importance of solid documentation practices: saving useful information and then being able to find it when you need it. Perhaps the most important fundamental of recruitment is good judgment. While I don't know anyone who teaches that, I do believe that the "put yourself in the other person's shoes" school of thought can be very useful. I have attempted to intersperse this book with common sense observations and ideas throughout. The recruiting process should feel right at a gut level.

Even though the Internet presents a vastly powerful electronic want ad capability, this does not alter the driving force of executive search – and unbundled search, for that matter. That is, many companies will retain a recruitment consultant specifically because they want access to people *not* on the job market. In the old days, that population wasn't reading the want ads because they were too busy being successful and working hard. Today the same population is not posting their resumes on various Internet web sites. We must hunt for them because they aren't looking for us.

In short, this book was designed for the benefit of several types of people.

- If you're a new researcher at a recruiting organization, this "how-to" book will point you in the right direction.
- If you're starting up an executive search business, or a corporate inhouse executive search function, this book is definitely for you.
- If executive search is a new career for you, you should definitely familiarize yourself with the concepts in this book. It explains the techniques that are at the heart of product development (i.e., generating candidates) for any search. Search is probably very different from anything else you've ever done, even if your career was in human resources.
- If you are a company human resources professional buying research or "unbundled search" products, or

managing a relationship with a search firm, you should know about the techniques described in this book so that you know what to ask of your vendors.

- If you're a small business owner, a venture capitalist or a line manager who doesn't want to pay search fees, this book tells you everything to need to know to do it yourself.

The chapter on reference checking is one of my favorites. In fact, one of the top 5 search firms licensed this material for their firm's global training. Actually, I myself reread this chapter any time I must check references. It's a great refresher and I always use several questions from it. I highly recommend it for anyone about to conduct a reference check – researchers, search consultants, recruiters of any description, corporate human resources officers, and anybody else involved in a hiring decision – line managers, small business owners, and venture capitalists, to name a few.

Last but not least is the largest enhancement to this book, Part II, "The Recruiter's Directory of Directories – Plus Web Sites, Databases & CD ROM's." Over 400 pages of information has been thoroughly cross-referenced by topic for your ease of use. While Part II does contain a great deal of information, it does not list every single possible research resource you might need. This book was not designed to be a "research cookbook" with all the answers. Rather it's more like a tool kit that will empower you to find the answers you need. It's a bit like teaching you how to farm so you can grown your own food, rather than getting a free meal, which, when it's gone, it's gone.

To make a long story short, everything I write about, I've done at one time or another. This stuff works.

Andrea Jupina
January, 2000

ACKNOWLEDGEMENTS

Special thanks go to my dear friend and tenacious information getter, Elizabeth Bull, without whose eyes and ears this book would never have been the same. This work is yet another example of what technology makes possible – with a little help from my friend – because this *Blue Book* was written while I was living overseas in a developing country – with laptop in hand and the Internet Cafe down the street.

Thanks also to Anne Marie Jenkins Ecker, who earlier on, worked thoughtfully and diligently to identify additional new references while interning at Long Island University's Palmer Graduate School of Library Science. Also thanks to all the people who so generously contributed their time and ideas by writing other chapters of this book, notably Amy Bragg, Mary Anne Denniston, Richard W. Laner, Sherri Rosenberg, Jane E. Shaffer and Glenn Van Doren.

Thanks to Jim Kennedy, who originally thought my material was worthy of being published and for his countless great ideas. Thanks to George Lutjen for his wise counsel. And, as always, thanks to the terrific people at Kennedy Information, especially Carolyn Edwards.

Thanks to Erminie Rowe for originally convincing me that I should pursue a career in search. Thanks to Bob Damon and Judith Bacher, now of Spencer Stuart, for spotting me as a "green talent" and giving me a chance to prove myself at Booz, Allen, along with Bob Harmon and Sam Marcus, so that I could eventually share my knowledge in the form of this book. Thanks also to Herb Freudenberger for persuading me that I really, truly did have a work of value in the first edition, without whose encouragement this book would not exist.

Thanks to everyone who bought or used the first edition of *The Handbook of Executive Search Research*, because I wrote it so you wouldn't have to "reinvent the wheel." Thanks even to the person who stole the copy from the New York City Public Library. I consider it a compliment, because I realized that the book wouldn't have been taken unless it was valued.

Last but not least, thanks to mom and dad for teaching me the great values of honesty, integrity, decency and compassion, and for my childhood mantra, "If it's worth doing, it's worth doing well."

INTRODUCTION

There's no question that the executive search business – and allied business activities – have evolved in many new directions over the past several years. If nothing else, one can say with certainty that the future holds even more change.

There are a number of factors that have shaped this history, factors that will impact the future as well. Some of the major ones include technology and its effect on how recruitment activities are conducted, the growth of "unbundled search" as a significant new business segment in the industry, and the globalization of business. In keeping with these changes, we at Kennedy Information have addressed these issues and others in this edition of *The Recruiter's Research Blue Book*. *The Blue Book* is actually a new edition of *The Handbook of Executive Search Research*.

When *The Handbook of Executive Search Research* was first published in 1992, the Internet was barely uttered on anyone's lips. How that has changed! No doubt the Internet will continue to be one of the single most powerful forces affecting how companies hire people, including how search firms and search consultants conduct business.

For one thing, few people are truly proficient at getting exactly what they need from the Internet, quickly, without wasting a lot of time, and without wandering all over the Internet. At least not yet. But the executive recruiting marketplace cries out for better Internet products, and sooner or later, they are bound to appear. Further, as is typically the case with any new technology, the Internet should get easier to use, and over time, it should also get cheaper.

So, gazing into the future, one might say that while today only a small, elite, technically savvy group understands how to efficiently use the Internet to identify individuals NOT in the job market, in the future, virtually everybody will be able to do that. This will happen because those in the know can teach other people, and the know-how can spread at an exponential rate. Further, as more, better, and easier to use products emerge, even more people will painlessly learn these skills. This can be compared to the automobile. When my grandmother was learning how to drive a car, it was hard to operate. She had to get out of the car to crank the starter. Starting the car demanded physical strength and driving it required mechanical knowledge. There's no question about it, model T's were not as easy to drive as today's cars. In the 1920's cars were new and few people knew how to drive them. But they were very useful. They fulfilled people's needs. As cars gained in popularity, they became affordable to virtually everyone. They also became easier to operate, so much so, that literally kids can drive them today. The Internet will likely follow the same route. This is especially so as the Internet becomes available through devices everyone has, such as the television (and cable) or telephone and, hence, ubiquitous.

At the moment, the most frequent users of Internet career sites are technically sophisticated, in fields like information technology and engineering. But in the future, as the technology becomes easier to use, these sites will increasingly be used by people in all industries and functions. Use of the Internet and other computerized tools, like databases, will gain the greatest momentum fastest with younger users because they grew up with computers, went to college using them, and aren't afraid of them. Older professionals – recruiters and otherwise – who keep pace with the technology will improve their own job security.

So, new products will emerge for the active job seeker – and conversely, companies and recruiting firms that want to tap into that population. Perhaps more important, improved products of another type will also appear in the marketplace: research tools that enable recruitment professionals to find information about individuals NOT in the job market. Obviously, this is the main distinction between search and advertising for applicants: identifying qualified, interested candidates whose résumés haven't been shopped across the Internet for the whole world to see.

The point is, in the future, the time it will take to conduct research to identify passive job seekers will be reduced from weeks to days and ultimately, hours. As far back as 1989, in *Executive Recruiter News*, Spencer Stuart chairman Tom Neff foresaw, "...Eventual access to a worldwide database from briefcase or desk will ultimately shrink the candidate identification phase to one week or one day, with a corresponding greater emphasis placed on sourcing, screening, evaluation and counseling."

In addition to the effects of technology on the recruiting process, unbundled search has emerged as a force to be reckoned with in the search and recruitment industry. In the '80's, when the US economy was distresssed, the search industry shrank, many firms went out of business, and many researchers lost their jobs. Forced to go out on their own, many of these researchers discovered that they had greater professional independence, more job satisfaction, and better incomes. Thus a new business was born. In the early 1980's it was called "research." Over time, and coinciding with the growth in professional development of the consultants who provided this service, it became known as "unbundled search," particularly when products were provided directly to the company in a hiring mode.

The product that search firms sell is really a research product – information. This is the same product sold by unbundled search consultants. It's usually information about candidates and, to lesser extent, their companies. In fact, research is the equivalent of manufacturing operations because this is where the product is made. As research is the product generation function, it is critically important to the search process. Research DRIVES the search process. In other words, without research you've got no product to sell. As company recruiters, heads of human resources and even line managers have begun to understand this, they appreciate the value added that research activities can bring to their organization. Indeed, select search firms have achieved immense success based on the strength of their outstanding research functions and the impressive reports they generated.

This book provides a hands-on "how to" explanation of search and research – to the benefit of professionals in executive search (both in research and search consulting), unbundled search consultants, and corporate recruitment professionals who wish to work either with search firms or unbundled search consultants or to establish an in-house executive recruiting function.

In the final analysis, there will continue to be more competition for the corporate recruitment dollar. Competition will come from technology, search firms, unbundled search consultants, contingency recruiters, and from within companies engaged in "do it yourself search." Further, with the globalization of business, as more international searches are conducted, smaller, local recruiting firms and unbundled search consultants will also be competing for various assignments, especially those located overseas.

In the future, we will see some shifting as companies assess the advantages and disadvantages of Internet job posting sites, classic retained search, unbundled search, contingency recruiting firms, or establishing an internal search function, possibly in conjunction with unbundled search consultants. The real question recruitment firms will have to address is, how can they add value to the companies they serve? As always, the answer is in the quality of the information they provide, in other words, through research.

Here are some of the advantages and disadvantages companies will be assessing. For example, while Internet job posting sites may be relatively inexpensive, the trade off is that using them can be time consuming, especially handling the massive résumé volume, particularly those of unqualified applicants. High-end retainer firms will always have a niche at senior levels, such as board search, for example, for reasons of confidentiality, trusted working relationships and polished handling of clients, notwithstanding their high fees and expenses. Unbundled search consultants offer a much less expensive alternative to classic executive search, especially for positions in the $80,000 to $150,000 candidate salary range, but requires far more time and involvement from the company. While unbundled search usually focuses more on finding candidates, there are typically no written reports; and all the "handling" issues, appointment scheduling, negotiations and closing are the domain of the company. While establishing an internal search function, possibly in conjunction with unbundled search consultants, does save fees and offers much more control over the process, staff must be hired, massive amounts of time must be devoted to the process, and it's difficult to keep the company's name confidential.

Research is more than just important in the search process. It is critical. Because research is the equivalent of manufacturing operations, there can be no product without research. Given the intrinsic value of a quality research function, one might be puzzled as to why no search firms have yet recongnized the important contributions of the Director of Research by granting partnership to this crucial role. After all, this position is responsible for overseeing that quality products for each client assignment are generated.

In conclusion, regardless of your relationship with research, if you are involved in any way with recruitment of managers and professionals, *The Recruiter's Research Blue Book* will contribute generously to your organization.

Wayne Cooper
President & CEO
Kennedy Information

PART I:
THE RESEARCH PROCESS

CHAPTER I

The Heart And Soul Of The Whole Thing:
Search Revealed – The Research Check List

"Wow, I always thought what you did was really easy, you know, just calling up a few of your friends on your rolodex. I never realized how much work it was."

Here's a step by step check list that will guide you through any search, in any industry, in any function. Make a copy of this check list, insert it in the front of your search binder and refer to it as you go along. If you're new to executive search, this check list was especially designed for you, whether you're a researcher or a search consultant; or a company recruiter managing search firms, working with research firms, using unbundled search, or acting as an in house executive recruiter.

For more information about directories available on CD ROM or online, plus specialized directories and target list references, see Part II of this book, " The Recruiter's Directory of Directories – Plus Web Sites, Databases & CD ROM's." Because of the rapid changes in technology and the proliferation of electronic publishing, whenever you call a publisher to place an order for a hard copy directory, be sure to ask if it has recently become available on CD ROM or online.

Last but not least, much of this research can be conducted by search firms and unbundled search consultants in preparation for a new business meeting with a potential new corporate client, especially items 2, 3 and 4.

❑ 1. Be sure you understand exactly what you're looking for. Review the proposal letter and position description/specification with the person in charge of the assignment. Remember, the only dumb question is the one that isn't asked.

❑ 2. Know the company and, if possible, the corporate culture of the hiring manager's organization.

    ❑ a. Check the company's web site.

    ❑ b. Review the annual report and related material, such as the 10 (k) report, proxy statement and relevant brochures and booklets.

    ❑ c. Ask the company for promotional materials, such as a company video, a promotional CD ROM, company newsletter(s), clippings of articles, and a package of orientation materials normally given to new employees.

    ❑ d. Review the company's listing in the *Million Dollar Directory* or in *Standard and Poors,* either in hard copy or in an electronic format.

    ❑ e. Review the *Reference Book of Corporate Managements* for a thumbnail sketch of top management's backgrounds, including education and birth dates. The same information is also available in the 10 (k) report. Date of birth provides a sense of forthcoming retirements and management succession issues.

    ❑ f. Review securities analysts' reports, such as *Value Line*. This information may be available from the company's Investor Relations Department, Shareholder Relations or Public Affairs. Or ask the Office of the Chairman or CEO.

    ❑ g. Review the Dun and Bradstreet report.

    ❑ h. Go to the library for recent articles. Check the business periodicals indices, such as ABI Inform, InfoTrak, *The Wall Street Journal* and *The New York Times*. Be sure to let the librarian know what you're looking for and ask for his or her guidance.

    ❑   i.   If you work for a large management consulting firm with an executive search practice, ask for company information and materials to read. Perhaps there is a consulting study which recommended this search. Or, for example, if the search is for a marketing position, perhaps the firm conducted a marketing study.

❑   3.   Learn about the industry.

    ❑   a.   Go to the library, or call a good library. Tell the librarian what you're looking for and why.

    ❑   b.   Get acquainted with librarian's references because they are extraordinarily rich sources of information. Pay particular attention to *Business Information Sources* by Lorna Daniels, published by the University of California Press in Berkeley (510-642-4247) and distributed by Princeton Fulfillment Services, Newark, NH (800-822-6657) for $39.95.

        c.   Find out if there are any good web sites you should review, then follow up.

        ❑   Ask appropriate professional associations. Check their sites, too.

        ❑   Use a search engine such as www.yahoo.com. For a listing of search engines, see the "Search Engines" category in Part II of this book, "The Recruiter's Directory of Directories – Plus Web Sites, Databases & CD ROM's."

        ❑   Check the Ask Jeeves web site at www.askjeeves.com or www.ask.com or www.aj.com or ask.

    ❑   d.   Refer to a business library for *Standard and Poors Industry Surveys*. Also review the card catalog and periodical indices, including *The Economist, Business Week, Fortune, Forbes,* and *The Harvard Business Review*.

    ❑   e.   Review Wall Street research reports that analyze the future of similar companies in the industry.

    ❑   f.   Review your industry and function files.

    ❑   g.   Ask your colleagues if there are any particular articles or other materials you should read.

    ❑   h.   If you have access to an industry expert, ask if he or she could spend a few minutes briefing you. You might particularly have this opportunity if you work at a large company, such as a Big 5 or other management consulting firm.

❑   4.   Identify the pertinent business and professional associations and leading trade publications. Check these sources:

    ❑   a.   *Business Information Sources* by Lorna Daniells

    ❑   b.   *Encyclopedia of Associations*

    ❑   c.   *Encyclopedia of Business Information Sources*

    ❑   d.   *National Trade and Professional Associations*

    ❑   e.   *Oxbridge's Directory of Newsletters*

    ❑   f.   *Predicasts F&S Index*

    ❑   g.   If you still haven't found what you really need, a business librarian will probably know more places to look.

❑ 5. Review your list of associations with the appropriate person. Ask if any business associates are members.

❑ 6. Wherever possible, obtain association membership rosters. When telephoning an association, remember:

    ❑ a. Many associations are willing to send membership lists to non-members. Sometimes they're free. Ask.

    ❑ b. Many association membership databases can be accessed on the Internet by members only. Others are available to everyone. Check the site to find out.

    ❑ c. Find out if any business associates or friends are members willing to help you obtain information "for members only." Someone in your company might be an individual member or your company might be a corporate member.

❑ 7. In addition to association membership directories, there are many specialized directories available for purchase by the public. Refer to:

    ❑ a. *Business Information Sources* by Lorna Daniells

    ❑ b. *Directories in Print* (Gale Group)

    ❑ c. *Encyclopedia of Business Information Sources* (Gale Group)

    ❑ d. *The Guide to American Directories* (B. Klein Publications, P.O. Box 6578, Delray Beach, FL 33482, phone (561) 496-3316)

❑ 8. Rosters of attendees at trade shows and conferences can also be good resources. The company may have access to some lists. Also, potential exhibitors can sometimes obtain lists of attendees from recent events.

❑ 9. If the company is a member of The Conference Board, you can obtain excellent research materials. Further, they provide high quality library assistance on the phone, especially if you can provide step by step instructions.

❑ 10. If your company does not have a large library, you can refer to libraries at universities, graduate business schools, foreign embassies and consulates, chambers of commerce, professional associations and the government. You can also visit the library of a neighboring town. Affluent communities usually have the budget for good library resources.

❑ 11. Remember, phone books are great research tools.

    ❑ a. The yellow pages

    ❑ b. The white pages

    ❑ c. Toll free directories

    ❑ d. National phone directories on CD ROM, such as SelectPhone

    ❑ e. www.infousa is the URL to a free national phone directory on the internet

    ❑ f. Other phone directories are listed in the Telephone Books category in Part II of this book, "The Recruiter's Directory of Directories – Plus Web Sites, Databases & CD ROM's."

❑ 12. Review any pertinent prior searches for target lists, references to research materials, web sites, and sources and prospects.

❑ 13. Develop a target list. As a general rule, about 15 to 25 companies are appropriate.

    ❑ a. Review whether the NAICS (North American Industry Code System) approach is appropriate. Previously this was known as SIC research. Basically, an NAICS code or an SIC code is a four or six digit number which serves as "shorthand" for a particular industry. You can locate this research in directories, such as *Standard and Poors, Dun and Bradstreet's Million Dollar Series, Standard Directory of Advertisers,* and others. Note that the NAICS system replaced SIC (Standard Industrial classification) codes in 1997. For a comprehensive list of what's in each code, you can consult a librarian or purchase the directory.

        ❑ To order the *North American Industry Classification System (NAICS) Manual,* contact National Technical Information Service (NTIS), Technology Administration, U.S. Department of Commerce, 5285 Port Royal Road, Springfield, VA 22161. Phone orders Monday – Friday, 8 am to 8 pm Eastern Time (800) 553-NTIS (6487) or (703) 605-6000. Fax (703) 321-8547. For questions about a product or order, email info@ntis.fedworld.gov. Web Site www.ntis.gov/. Softcover NTIS Order Number PB98-136187INQ, $28.50, $57 outside the U.S., Canada and Mexico. Hard cover and electronic formats are also available.

        ❑ No doubt, it will take time for all users of SIC codes, such as publishers, to make a complete transition from the SIC system to the NAICS system. Until the transition is complete, it may be easier to use the old SIC system, which has been in place for decades.

        ❑ For an abbreviated listing of the codes, see the SIC or NAICS volumes published by Standard and Poors and *Dun and Bradstreet's Million Dollar Directory Series.*

    ❑ b. Refer to the *Standard Directory of Advertisers – Business Classifications Edition,* published by National Register Publishing, a Reed Reference Publishing Company, New Providence, New Jersey. This directory groups companies by category, such as toiletries. It's also a good source of names and titles. As print directories go, it's very conveniently organized.

    ❑ c. Refer to the *National Directory of Addresses and Telephone Numbers,* published by Omnigraphics, Inc. in Detroit.

    ❑ d. Refer to any industry surveys which rank companies. Associations are usually helpful in finding such information. Trade publications often publish such surveys and can be located in *Business Information Sources* and *The Encyclopedia of Business Information Sources.* Other business publications also publish surveys, such as *Business Week, Fortune, Forbes, Institutional Investor, The Wall Street Journal, The New York Times,* and various journals published by Crain in Chicago. A listing of Crain's trade journals and other publications appears in chapter 7, "Major Internet Web Sites" and in the Periodicals category in Part II of this book, "The Recruiter's Directory of Directories – Plus Web Sites, Databases & CD ROMs."

        ❑ The Harvard Business School's Baker Library web site is a superb resource that should be reviewed at www.library.hbs.edu/.

    ❑ e. Review any other preferred methods of creating a target list, such as using a list developed for a prior search.

❑   f.   Be sure to include target companies the hiring manager may have suggested.

❑   g.   Similarly, be sure to omit any specified companies from the target list. Be aware if there are sensitivities, such as a "ladies' and gentlemen's agreement" in which certain companies agree to refrain from recruiting from each other.

❑   h.   Consider geographic and relocation factors as early in the search as possible.

❑   i.   For technology searches, refer to *CorpTech,* published by Corporate Technologies Information Services, Inc., 12 Alfred Street, Suite 200, Woburn, MA 01801-1915, phone (800) 333-8036, (800) 454-3647, (781)-932-3900, (781) 932-3939, fax (781) 932-6335, web site www.corptech.com, email sales@corptech.com. CorpTech's web page includes links to high tech company pages.

❑ 14. Do identification research (ID research) or target company breakdowns.

❑   a.   Find out the exact title(s) the hiring manager thinks the ideal candidate will currently hold.

❑   b.   Utilize the web and directories as fully as possible.

> ❑   Visit the company web sites for names, titles, biographies and sometimes photos of employees.
>
> ❑   Be sure to review the 10 (k) report, either on-line or in hard copy, for the names, titles, career biographies, and birth dates of top management.
>
> ❑   CD ROM's and internet databases are among the most powerful research tools around. Use them as often as possible. See the *Gale Directory of Databases* (Gale Group).
>
> ❑   Contact Gale Group about how to access their directories on the internet. Gale Group, Farmington Hills, Michigan, (800) 877-GALE, www.galegroup.com.
>
> ❑   *The Directory of Corporate Affiliations* identifies divisions, subsidiaries and plant information and ensures you're looking in the right place, especially in a very large organization. It also has a Brand Name Index.
>
> ❑   General business directories, such as *Standard and Poors Register of Corporations, The Million Dollar Directory,* and *The Standard Directory of Advertisers* will provide names to get you started, especially when you're doing ID Research on the telephone. When you make an ID research call, it's much easier to verify whether someone is still an employee and still has the same title. After you've begun a conversation and established a rapport, the person is more likely to help you with more information.
>
> ❑   In order to avoid voice mail and delays in getting information, you should be prepared to spend a good deal of effort finding the extensions of human beings who answer the phone. Sometimes the company operator will help.
>
> ❑   For more information on biographical and career history data of senior management, including education, companies titles, and date of birth, refer to Dun & Bradstreet's *Reference Book of Corporate Managements,* which provides this information by company; or see *Standard and Poors Registers of Directors and Executives,* which provides similar information alphabetically by name. *American Men and Women of Science* provides similar information for scientific and research and development searches. *Martindale-Hubbel* provides

career biographies for attorneys. Refer to the "Biographies" category in Part II of this book, "The Recruiter's Directory of Directories – Plus Web Sites, Databases & CD ROM's."

❑ Alumni directories of colleges and graduate schools often cross reference names by company or geography.

❑ Company alumni directories are sometimes available, either in a published or printed format, or as an informal list. If standard references don't lead to them, try asking a source, especially one who used to work for the company. Also see the "Company Alumni" category in Part II of this book, "The Recruiter's Directory of Directories – Plus Web Sites, Databases & CD ROM's."

❑ Use company phone books or Christmas card lists if available. Sometimes a friendly source who's recently changed jobs will assist.

❑ Association directories sometimes contain photos and biographies.

❑ Annual reports sometimes contain photos, plus valuable organization information which can supplement paltry listings in other directories.

❑ c. Refer to company files to determine whether any appropriate break downs have already been done.

❑ d. If identification (ID) calling must be done, discuss with your manager the key phrase for identifying the correct functional area, for example, "the person in charge of all merger and acquisition planning."

❑ e. Use honest, ethical means for gathering the data. No rusing.

❑ f. *This step is one of the most important in your seach because it provides the documentation that's at the heart of adding value. Present your findings in an organization chart format, neatly hand sketched and clearly documented. Be sure to "plug in" any other interesting data, such as total number of employees in the department, total number of direct reports, revenues and notes, if any, about reorganizations, vacancies, rumors, and other competitive data. For a full discussion, see chapter 8, "ID Research – What It Is, What It's Not, And How To Present It."*

❑ 15. Review the results of ID calling/target company breakdowns and decide which individuals should be approached first as possible prospects.

❑ 16. Before beginning prospect calls, be prepared to handle these 6 things:

❑ Precisely at what level to prospect

❑ How to describe the position

❑ Exactly what should – and should not – be said about the organization

❑ How confidential the company's identity is

❑ How to handle questions about compensation

❑ Relocation issues

❑ 17. If appropriate, review unsolicited resumes and contact selected sources and prospects.

❑ 18. If you can access the right population through the Internet – and obtain individual email addresses – you can email a sourcing letter. It's very efficient, inexpensive and instantaneous. This can be especially effective with technology searches.

❑ 19. For a senior search, sometimes it's more appropriate to mail a confidential "sourcing letter" with a copy of the position description/personnel specifications enclosed. If you're in the search business (as opposed to a corporate recruiter), a sourcing letter can be a new business development tool because it positions your firm as handling a certain level search.

❑ 20. There are numerous Internet web sites for job seekers. While one of the main distinctions of search is that it concentrates on finding candidates *not* on the job market, it might nevertheless be appropriate to access resumes from the Internet. Refer to Part II of this book and chapter 7, "Major Internet Web Sites" for specific web site URL's and Internet recruiting books.

❑ 21. Make prospect calls and note the person called on your Sources and Prospects sheets. Document the following: date of call, source of the name, whether the source gives permission to use his or her name, level of interest and reasons, education, compensation (broken down by base and bonus), date of last raise, and other appropriate background information. *Always state the year when noting the date.*

❑ 22. Write a detailed background profile on each interested prospect. Use the "Telephone Interview Guide" in chapter 13.

❑ 23 People who have changed jobs within the 6 to 12 months or so can be excellent sources into your target companies. It's important to track this information in your company files.

❑ 24. Frequently review the status of the search with the appropriate person. Communicate any pertinent comments or new developments as you hear from prospects.

❑ 25. If you will be conducting reference checks, find out the questions the hiring manager wants asked. Remember, all your questions should be related to bona fide job requirements and matters that relate to job performance. Otherwise there is a greater vulnerability to a discrimination action. For a discussion on reference checking, see chapter 17, "So, You Thought Reference Checking Was Easy. Here's How to *Really* Check References."

❑ 26. In general, if a reference report is negative and the candidate will not be getting a job offer as a consequence, the most prudent thing to do is put *nothing* in writing. However, this is a rare situation. If you must present written reference reports, write them so that an outsider who knows nothing about the search will understand the reports. Assume the reader has no prior knowledge of jargon or acronyms – and don't use them.

❑ 27. Make sure thank you close-out notes are sent to all candidates and pertinent sources and prospects. Without exception, everyone who took the time for a personal interview should be acknowledged, either with a phone call or a letter.

❑ 28. At the close of the search, organize and file your search documentation for inclusion in the research system for future reference.

❑ 29. With the appropriate parties, evaluate your performance on this search. Then follow up for your own career advancement.

CHAPTER 2

Research Demystified – With A Flow Chart

Research. It's one of those things which, if you ask 10 people what it is, you'll get 10 different answers. At some firms, it means "identification research," or just finding names. At other organizations, research means everything from "scratch" all the way through identifying the candidates who will be introduced to the hiring manager. This includes doing ID research to find their names, calling them, gathering their background data, interviewing them on the phone, assessing whether they're qualified, and writing background profiles.

In this chapter we will take a comprehensive view of research. At your company, all or part of this chapter may be relevant, depending on the skills and experience of research staff and how you are organized. This discussion will follow the Research Flow Chart on page 10.

STEP 1

DEVELOP A TARGET LIST.

A target list, by its very definition, is always a list of *companies*. For reasons of semantics and clear communication, it's important to use the same definitions of terminology. "Target list" *never* refers to people. It always refers to the companies you are targeting for candidates. For more clarification, refer to "Target List" in chapter 3, "Recruiting Terminology."

Go to chapter 1, "The Heart and Soul of the Whole Thing – Search Revealed – The Research Checklist." Item 13 describes in detail how to develop a fine target list. It also shows to find the references you will need. You can also refer to Part II of this book, "The Recruiter's Directory of Directories – Plus Web Sites, Databases & CD ROM's" for a listing of over 30 Target List resources.

STEP 2

DO IDENTIFICATION RESEARCH.

One of the easiest ways to do identification research (ID research) is to first gather names from various directories – and anywhere else you can find names – *before* you make any phone inquiries. First, make sure you're looking in the right subsidiary or division(s), then in the right functional area or department(s) by using the *Directory of Corporate Affiliations* (in hard copy, on CD ROM or online), the annual report and/or 10(k) report. Once you've identified the functional area to search in, then find names in general business directories, preferably on CD ROM or the Internet, such as *Standard and Poors Register of Corporations, Dun and Bradstreet's Million Dollar Directory Series, Standard Directory of Advertisers,* and possibly *Hoover's Handbook*. If the search is for a senior position in a major company, check *Dun and Bradstreet's Reference Book of Corporate Managements* and the 10 (k) report for biographical information. For an international search, refer to a *Kompass* directory (www.kompass.com).

Published and Written Materials

You can locate specialized directories by reviewing librarian's references, such as the *Directory of Directories* (Gale Group, Farmington Hills, Mich., 800-877-GALE), *Guide to American Directories* (B. Klein Publications, Delray Beach, Florida, 888-859-8083 or 561-496-3316), *Business Information Sources* by Lorna Daniells (University of California Press, distributed by California Princeton Fulfillment Services, Newark, NJ, 800-822-6657), *Encyclopedia of Business Information Sources* (Gale Group), the *Encyclopedia of Associations* (Gale Group) and the *Gale Directory of Databases*. Additional directories and CD ROM's are listed in this book in Part II, "The Recruiter's Directory of Directories – Plus Web Sites, Databases & CD ROM's." Part II has been thoroughly cross referenced by subject for your convenience.

RESEARCH FLOW CHART

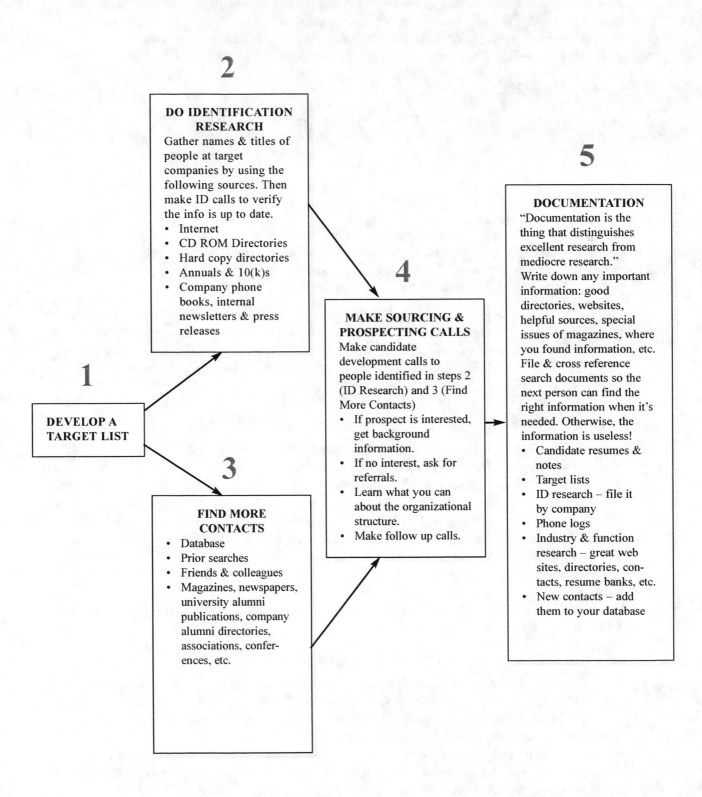

2

DO IDENTIFICATION RESEARCH
Gather names & titles of people at target companies by using the following sources. Then make ID calls to verify the info is up to date.
- Internet
- CD ROM Directories
- Hard copy directories
- Annuals & 10(k)s
- Company phone books, internal newsletters & press releases

5

DOCUMENTATION
"Documentation is the thing that distinguishes excellent research from mediocre research."
Write down any important information: good directories, websites, helpful sources, special issues of magazines, where you found information, etc. File & cross reference search documents so the next person can find the right information when it's needed. Otherwise, the information is useless!
- Candidate resumes & notes
- Target lists
- ID research – file it by company
- Phone logs
- Industry & function research – great web sites, directories, contacts, resume banks, etc.
- New contacts – add them to your database

1

DEVELOP A TARGET LIST

4

MAKE SOURCING & PROSPECTING CALLS
Make candidate development calls to people identified in steps 2 (ID Research) and 3 (Find More Contacts)
- If prospect is interested, get background information.
- If no interest, ask for referrals.
- Learn what you can about the organizational structure.
- Make follow up calls.

3

FIND MORE CONTACTS
- Database
- Prior searches
- Friends & colleagues
- Magazines, newspapers, university alumni publications, company alumni directories, associations, conferences, etc.

You can also look for names of people and their titles on the company's web site. Contact publishers for current information about which of their directories can be accessed on the Internet. Two of the most important publishers are Gale Group in Farmington Hills, Michigan (phone 800-877-GALE or web site www.galegroup.com) and R.R. Bowker in New Providence, New Jersey (phone 888-BOWKER2 (888-269-5372) and 800-323-3288, email info@bowker.com, web site www.bowker.com). As many of these resources can be expensive to purchase, you might want to check a good library, especially since Gale and Bowker's major markets are libraries.

This may seem like a lot of library research. It is. Actually, it's an investment in time that should make your telephone research much easier. This technique also assures precise, targeted ID research which will help you avoid wasted phone calls later.

Phone Research

With numerous names in hand, now you're ready to get on the phone to do some ID research. Your mission is simple. You are updating information and you need to verify that your data about these individuals is correct.

After you have reached someone on the phone and verified the information, *BE SURE TO ASK IF THERE'S ANYBODY ELSE YOU SHOULD ADD TO YOUR LIST.*

If you call a company looking for information, you will sound much more credible if you already have some information. Once someone is involved enough to help you and is already answering questions, it is much easier to obtain more information.

Needless to say, if someone asks who you are or why you are calling, it is unethical to say anything other than the truth. However, sometimes the less you say, the fewer questions will be asked. Oftentimes, if you directly ask for help and information, you will directly be given an answer. Because so many people are very busy, many will want to take care of you, get off the phone, and get back to whatever they were doing.

For more information about how to present the ID research you've gathered, see chapter 8, "ID Research – What It Is, What It Isn't, and How To Present It." It includes an example of ID research from a real, live search. The names and phone numbers have been "sanitized" to protect the innocent.

STEP 3

FIND MORE CONTACTS.

You can find more names of contacts by culling through your company's database, prior searches, association membership directories (in hard copy or on their web sites), university alumni publications (which often announce promotions and job changes), company alumni directories, company phone books, company newsletters, company press releases (which sometimes announce promotions), lists of conference attendees, articles in general business magazines, newspapers and trade publications, and so forth. You can also ask friends and co-workers for help if they used to work at a target company.

While many hiring managers are impressed when sources at Big 5 firms, law firms, and other professional services firms are asked for referrals, these sources are seldom helpful. While they are usually most knowledgeable about their client companies, we should remember that attorneys and so forth have an obligation to protect client confidentiality. In addition, because they depend on their relationships with specific people at those companies, they have a vested interest in maintaining the status quo. In other words if the client contact took a new job, it could mean a lost relationship, a lost account and lost income.

Similarly, some hiring managers are impressed when top professors at universities are sourced. This might *occasionally* yield a good referral, especially a graduating senior. Otherwise, I've always found these calls a waste of my time. The only reason I would ever pursue this avenue would be if the hiring manager specifically asked.

STEP 4

MAKE SOURCING AND PROSPECTING CALLS.

Getting Past The Secretary

If you must deal with a secretary instead of voicemail, you may find that some secretaries can be difficult when you need to leave a message. This is usually because they have strict instructions to thoroughly screen all calls. It might be less frustrating if you remember that the secretary is only doing his or her job, most likely for a busy executive frequently bombarded by nuisance calls. However, you can turn this situation into an *opportunity* to make friends with the secretary. Your call might start something like this:

"Good morning, Ms. Bossonovo's office."

"Is she there, please?"

"Who may I say is calling?"

"This is Ashley Gainer."

"What's this in reference to, Ms. Gainer?"

"It's a confidential matter. Can you please tell me, do you read all her confidential mail?"

"Yes, I do."

"Perhaps you can help me, then. I'm with the executive search firm Ryan O'Brien and Placer. We're a 12 year old firm based in Chicago with offices in London, Hong Kong and Mexico City. I'd like to ask Ms. Bosonovo's help in connection with a search we've been retained to conduct for the general manager of a division of a multinational. I'd appreciate it if you'd have her give me a call. I will only need a few minutes of her time. Can you tell me if she's in the office today?"

"No, she's not. She's traveling."

"I see. When is she expected back in the office?"

"Friday morning."

"Great. What time does she usually get in?"

"Usually around 7."

"And what time would you say is probably a good time to catch her?"

"Well, I'd say early in the morning, when she gets in, or maybe at the end of the day."

"About what time does she usually leave?"

"Rarely before 6:30, unless she goes to the gym."

"That's great. Thanks so much for your help."

"I'll make sure she gets your message."

And so forth. With this information, you can note in your calendar the day and time to make a follow up call. She will also know who you are and why you're calling.

In addition, you've already learned something important about this prospect. She works long hours. She also goes to the gym, which is another good sign.

Note that this approach is only recommended for a senior level search. In other words, it may not always be appropriate to say you're a recruiter, especially if the secretary doesn't read all the boss's confidential mail. Here are a few other techniques for dealing with an annoyingly protective secretary.

- Call before 9 a.m., before the secretary's in the office, at 12:01, when the secretary's at lunch, or after 5 p.m. Maybe the source or prospect will directly answer the phone.

- When leaving a message, say who referred you, if you were in fact referred by a person. Make sure you have permission to use the source's name.

- If you know beforehand that there's someone you really want to talk to – like a "hot prospect" – call several times, but only leave 1 or 2 messages. If your call is not returned, keep calling until the person answers his or her phone. If you get voice mail, don't leave any more messages. Just hang up. If a secretary answers, say something like, "Oh, wrong number. So sorry." Then call again later and keep trying until you reach the person directly.

- Write a polite letter asking the source for help and enclose a position description. Be sure the envelope is marked "confidential." In fact many large search firms routinely begin senior assignments with this type of mailing.

When leaving word, if you're pressed as to the nature of the call, you may wish to say, "It's a personal call."

The conversation might unfold like this:

"Does he know you?"

You simply must tell the truth! If you try to pretend you're a friend, both the boss and secretary will have a good laugh at your expense. Who do you think you're kidding?

"No, he doesn't know me, but I'm sure he'd appreciate why the call is confidential, once he knows the purpose of my call."

"He wants me to screen all his calls."

"Do you read all his confidential mail?"

"No, I don't."

"I'm sorry. I'm just not free to disclose."

Better yet, say, "It's a private matter." For all the secretary knows, you could be a divorce lawyer. It's surprising how often the person at the other end of the phone will back off. Furthermore, "private matter" doesn't necessarily imply you know each other, where a "personal" message more or less does.

After all that, you might get a call back in five minutes because the prospect figures you're probably a search consultant and is dying of curiosity!

Then, there are those people who don't call back. If there's no returned call after two messages, it's a waste of time to keep trying. Invest the time in calling a fresh, new name instead. Naturally, the exception to this is if you already know that this is a very important contact.

One final word about contacting sources and prospects. Our first responsibility is to protect their confidentiality.

The Sourcing and Prospecting Call

If you don't know beforehand whether your contact is a "source," (someone who can recommend potential candidates), or a "prospect" (a potential candidate), you might use phrases like this:

- "Do you know anyone who might be qualified and interested in an opportunity like this?"

- "Is this an opportunity which would be appropriate for someone with your background?"

- "Would you be interested in learning more about this opportunity?"

If the source has no interest, politely find out why. Is the position at the right level? Is geography a problem? Compensation? Continue your conversation with a request for a referral:

- "Perhaps you can recommend someone whose background is appropriate for this opportunity. Naturally, I'd be pleased to keep your name confidential, if you wish."

Then find out if you have permission to use the source's name. Make a note of it, either way, on your Sources and Prospects sheet.

If the source is interested in the opportunity, the source has just become a prospect! You can continue the conversation with something like this:

- "The next step would be for us to get some information on your background. We can do that while we're on the phone right now....Oh, you have to go to a meeting in 10 minutes? Well, why don't we get started and see how much we can get done. If we work really fast, we could finish."

Actually, nobody I ever talked to has finished in 10 minutes, probably because this normally succinct person is suddenly talking about his favorite subject – himself (or herself). Once the prospect has started sharing his or her background information and is psychologically involved, your follow up call will be much easier. Often the prospect will prefer finishing this conversation in the evening at home and will give you his or her phone number. Otherwise, when you call again, the prospect may have forgotten your conversation. You would have to "resell" the opportunity all over again and generally "start from scratch" with this person. "Strike while the iron is hot," as the old saying goes.

When the prospect is interested, develop a background profile using the Telephone Interview Guide in chapter 13. Be sure to get a breakdown of total compensation – base, bonus, perqs – the date of the last raise, and when the next raise is expected.

Raise dates are important information if an offer is going to be made. Naturally you will want the offer to be attractive so that it will be accepted. But if the candidate will be getting a raise anyway – and you don't know it, then the offer could turn out to be insultingly low. This scenario can be avoided by finding out the date of the last raise and when the next raise is scheduled. Also the dollar amount and percentage of the most recent raise is interesting information because it indicates how much the candidate is valued by the company.

If a prospect already has a resume prepared, or is willing to send an old resume with a handwritten update attached, that can save time. But I've always felt that a resume is a poor substitute for a phone screen. If you're screening for something specific, it may be missing from the resume. For example, I once located a candidate for an international human resources search. She was an impressive candidate and in fact ultimately received an offer. However, her resume showed *absolutely no* experience living overseas whatsoever. If the client would have seen her resume, they would have ruled her out, thinking she lacked the experience they required. In order to keep her resume brief, the candidate legitimately omitted certain information – minor details in her mind – but crucial to this search. If I had failed to engage her in a lengthy phone conversation and walk through her entire career, specifically *probing* for overseas experience, I, too, would have thought she lacked the requisite experience. If I had said, "Send me your old resume with a handwritten update attached," instead of discussing her background in detail on the phone, sure, I would have saved time. I also would have missed out on a great candidate.

That's why it's important to have a good conversation – to draw out all the relevant information. You never know what people decide to omit from their resumes, and for perfectly legitimate reasons.

Especially with resumes of senior candidates, it just isn't possible to include every single detail of a career. There's not enough room. Besides, a resume's main function is as a marketing document, to "open the door" to a meeting. If a resume is a truly comprehensive list of all career details, it can be very boring – and therefore not an effective marketing tool. So, be careful when relying on resumes for comprehensive information. It's almost impossible for anyone to fit everything on a two-page resume. That's why it's important to *talk* to people. Besides, isn't this kind of probing one of the things a company is supposed to get when it pays a large search retainer?

In addition to obtaining data that may have been omitted from a resume, another advantage of a longer phone conversation is that you can develop a much better sense of your prospect.

If the person you speak to turns out to be a source, rather than a prospect, you can:

- Ask if he or she can recommend any prospects.

- If you already have a list of names at a company, would the source rate who's good, who's an idiot (politely phrased, of course), and would they rank everyone on your list. "Out of all these names, who would you say is the best? Why do you think he's best? Who's next?" and so forth.

- Ask if the source can help you understand how the organization is structured and who the key people are.

Whenever a source refers someone, always ask for permission to use the source's name. If you realize that you're not 100% sure it's ok to use the source's name, DON'T. This could blow up and cause serious problems. It's much better to call the source back to double check that you have permission to use his or her name. The source will probably be impressed by your prudence and conscientiousness. "It's better to be safe than sorry," as the old saying goes. Better yet, if the source is sufficiently impressed, this could be your entré to developing a new client relationship.

You should also know that if you already have several names at a company, sources are usually much more forthcoming than if they must give you the names, too. This is one reason why it's important to get names from other people or from directories, CD ROM's, web sites or any other sources. Try it a few times. You'll be amazed.

You should also make a special note that former employees of companies are frequently outstanding sources, especially if they've left the company in the past 6 to 12 months. This is recent enough for their knowledge of the organization to be relatively current, yet distant enough for old feelings of loyalty to have diminished. Consequently, it's often worth the effort to track down someone who recently left the company.

Finally, one of the most important – and difficult – pieces of research to develop is an organization chart. When developing a background profile of a candidate, this is the perfect opportunity to "flesh out" the org chart, especially because reporting relationships are so relevant. You should ask your prospect for:

- His or her boss's title

- The title of that person's boss

- Titles of all direct reports of the prospect and the number of people reporting to each direct report

- Titles of all peers reporting into the same boss

Again, ask for head count information: department size, number of direct reports, revenues and so forth. These parameters are important in determining whether the prospect is at the right level.

Last but not least, whenever you connect with congenial, chatty sources, this is an opportunity to ask for all kinds of information. Of course, the best way to find a congenial, chatty source is to be equally friendly and pleasant yourself. If your source is willing to talk, keep on asking questions. She may know of some new research resources you somehow missed, such as web sites, obscure directories, trade publications or "Top 100" lists. The source might refer you to interesting reading material to help you learn more about the field. S/he might have some interesting ideas to complement your search strategy. Finally, your source might be close to industry rumors about companies that have just reorganized, which are always good places to search. If your source is a highly placed, respected name in the industry, the hiring manager should be very interested in the intelligence you've gathered. This is another way of adding value to your service.

STEP 5

DOCUMENTATION

Documentation is the thing that distinguishes excellent research from mediocre research. If your documentation is to have any value in the future, it must make sense to anybody who reads it, not just you. Besides, if you're not careful, it won't even make sense to *you* in a few months. Therefore, keep notes as if you were moving to a tropical island, never to be heard from again. The next person should be able to figure out exactly what has been done, what hasn't, the exact status of each contact and what the next steps should be. You should also state exactly where you found each name – if it was in a directory, a CD ROM, a web site (and exactly where) newspaper article, or from a person. Specify the person's name or the complete title of the directory, including date or edition.

One way to test the caliber of *your* research is to ask, "Suppose I got hit by a bus and somebody else had to pick up where I left off? How easy would it be for her to know the status of each piece of the search and what should be done next?"

Good documentation is simple. Just make a note of everything. For example, instead of writing on your sources and prospects sheet, "Not interested," say, "Not interested – wants general management opportunity." Additional data such as titles, companies, dates, education, and compensation are immensely useful. This is valuable in case the position changes, if you're reviewing an old search for names for a new assignment, or more important, if you must write a research report that summarizes your conversations with each and every contact.

Here are some pointers about documentation:

- Every document should be dated. This includes the *year.*

- In addition to keeping one complete set of search documents together, pertinent information should be copied and stored four ways:

- The first is in a file of **Company Research**. This includes org charts, identification research, web site URL's, hard copy printouts from web sites, lists of names and published company research, association membership rosters, company phone directories, annual reports, 10(k)s, company alumni directories, press releases, news clippings and articles, and any other company information. In addition, if Sources and Prospects sheets are organized by company, a copy can be filed in the company file, too.

- Second is your phone log of **Sources and Prospects** sheets for the search. This is the document that summarizes your notes of conversations with all the sources and prospects you called during the search. If possible, set up your Sources and Prospects sheets by company. This will mean that many sheets will only be partially used because you might only have one contact at a certain company, even though there's room on a page for three or four people. If you do set up your Sources and Prospects sheets according to company, it's much easier to put them in a 3 ring binder, alphabetically by company, using oak tag divider pages with ABC tabs, (such as Avery's Preprinted ABC Dividers). This approach is especially helpful if the search becomes an unusually lengthy one because it allows you to quickly check everyone you've spoken to at a given company.

  When you're complete with a particular source or prospect, you can draw a diagonal line through the left side of the source and prospect sheet. This way, when you're flipping through your sheets to review status, you can instantly see which contacts need follow up.

  What about using the computer instead of taking notes by hand? If it works for you, by all means, do it. I have personally tried using my computer instead of hard copy of Sources and Prospects forms. For me, it just created extra work because whenever a prospect would return my call, I could never get the computer screen to switch to the right place fast enough. So I'd wind up writing my notes once by hand, then later inputting them into the computer. However, at the end of the search, the computer is immensely valuable for inputting high quality, screened, proven candidate data into the company database of contacts. That kind of database is certainly an essential tool to any search firm or research consultant. However, that is obviously quite different from sourcing and prospecting sheets, which are your search work papers.

- **Candidate Backgrounds** should be filed alphabetically by name. This information is usually filed two ways. One is in the candidate's hard copy folder of notes, including the resume, notes taken during the interview, signed Permission To Check References form and so forth. Second, candidate background information should also be stored in the firm's computer database.

- **Industry and Function** files should be maintained so you can find information according to topic. This way you won't have to redo the same research next time you need to find a special directory, CD ROM, web site, professional association or industry survey. Be sure to file target lists here, too, especially the ones that are real showpieces of research.

Cross Referencing should be done, whether you use computerized files, hard copy or a combination of the two. If necessary, copy a document (such as the title page or CD ROM jacket of a great directory) and file it in all the appropriate places. For example, if a candidate provides a detailed org chart, an extra copy should also be filed in the company file.

Also, cross reference notes should be placed in files. Here's an example that might appear in your

Insurance Industry file:

> "Insurance systems – also see Arthur Andersen company file."

These notes can be written on a full 8 1/2 by 11" sheet of paper, even if it only contains one or two lines. Tiny notes will get lost, so always use a big piece of paper.

Remember, the "acid test" for good research is whether it's well documented. It must be intelligible, legible, logically organized and dated. If you can't find the information when you need it, what good is it?

For further discussion, see chapter 15, "Documentation – The Hallmark of Fabulous Research."

CONCLUSION

As a research professional, the burden is on you to ask for clarification if you're not 100% clear about what's expected. Otherwise, your boss or the hiring manager will assume that everything is fine. Furthermore, it's always better to address a problem sooner rather than later, while there's still time to do something about it. This can avert a disastrous progress report because there's time to pursue a new course of action, and time for you or your boss to manage the client's expectations.

I always expect a search to change and it usually does. In fact, if a search is not filled quickly, the likelihood of change is greater. It's only a matter of time before things change, because the one constant in life is change! Besides, hiring managers are people, and people do change their minds. Corporate changes can also affect the requirements of a search. Additionally, economic events can wreak havoc on the best laid plans. Consider the effects of war, a stock market crash, currency devaluation, or a merger, company consolidation and reorganization, plant closing or poor earnings. What all this means is that a good research consultant will always expect the unexpected. You never know when you'll need to adapt to revised specs, such as new reporting relationships, a new compensation scheme, or new objectives. This is another reason why keeping good notes is so important. It's a good way to be prepared for the unexpected.

Search is like sailing in changeable winds. You must always be ready to change course and if you're psychologically ready for this, the journey is much more fun.

CHAPTER 3

Recruiting Terminology

Every field has its own terminology. Search and recruiting are certainly no different. Search has its fair share of terms which have varied connotations and shadings of meaning, depending on who is speaking and the organization the person works for. Consider the word "sourcing," for example, or "research" and how many different meanings those words can have. Clearly it can be very confusing if two people are using the same word and it is a word that means something different to each. Because recruitment is an activity where "managing expectations" is critical to our success, it is that much more important to be communicating clearly. In any case, an outsider, such as a search consultant, a research consultant, or possibly someone from another department (like human resources) is not likely to be familiar with all the nuances of terminology – including internal acronyms – in an organization. Be that as it may, the point of this chapter is to lay the groundwork so we can establish consistency in defining some of the terms we use. Hopefully this will contribute to clear communication and greater ease in that constant challenge, "managing expectations."

Applicant. The term applicant is generally used by contingency recruiters because the individual is applying for a job. This term can be contrasted to "candidate," because retainer search firms do not represent individuals applying for jobs per se.

Blind Calling. This is another term for "rusing." Obviously it is unethical to invent a ruse or otherwise lie so that people will give you information, like names and titles of employees. To begin with, rusing was never a professional, psychologically healthy, or appropriate practice. Besides, with the growing proliferation of electronic databases and the Internet, information is increasingly accessible, rendering obsolete this disgusting technique.

Candidate. After a prospect has been interviewed in person, if he or she is still under consideration for the position and will be introduced to the company, this person has become a candidate. Very often, candidates are not on the job market. As such, they must be identified and contacted, or hunted for, so to speak. The art of research is built around this need to locate candidates not actively looking for a job.

Candidate Development. See "Sourcing and Prospecting."

Communication. A wise manager once said it best: "Good communication means good listening."

Confidentiality. Confidentiality is one of the most important aspects of conducting a search. It is unethical to fail to honor confidentiality at several levels.

- It is absolutely critical to refrain from divulging any information about a prospect or candidate to anyone except the company doing the search, especially if the individual is currently employed. Search consultants are usually accustomed to this, but sometimes a zealous hiring manager needs to be reminded that casually asking around to check somebody out is a bad idea, if not an invitation to a lawsuit. No inquiries ever should be made – by *anyone* – until the candidate has signed a release that grants permission to check references.

- Conversations with references also must be kept confidential.

- If a source refers an individual and asks for his or her name to be kept confidential, then do so. If you're not absolutely 100% sure that you have permission to use a source's name, then call the source back to double check.

- Sometimes a company's identity must be kept completely confidential, especially if a search is extremely sensitive. One example would be if a search is being conducted to replace an incumbent; and/or if it's such an important position, it could hurt the company's stock price or make the company vulnerable to a takeover if word leaked out.

If the company's identity must be kept confidential, it is not enough to just refrain from revealing the name. You must also avoid providing descriptive information that would allow someone to figure out the company's identity. The hiring manager should tell you exactly how he or she wants certain questions handled, like location, size of company, and a description of the business. If you're talking to a source or prospect who still insists on guessing, an appropriate response is, "I can neither confirm nor deny."

As a general rule, keeping the company name confidential is not only more prudent, but it's a more effective way to market an opportunity. It is also in a company's interest to keep a low profile so as to avoid feeding the rumor mill. If you wait until the interview, you still don't have to reveal the company's name if the prospect has not passed your screen.

Contingency Fee. This is a recruitment fee which is contingent on an individual being hired.

Ethics. One of my favorite candidates once said it best. "I don't ever lie, cheat, steal, intentionally hurt somebody or date somebody married." This book would be incomplete without acknowledging the importance of ethical professional behavior. In short, you know when something's right and when something's wrong. If you're thinking of doing something that would embarrass you if your parents found out, you probably shouldn't do it. Let your conscience be your guide.

Exclusivity. If you're working for a company that's using a contingency recruiting firm and you give the firm an "exclusive" for a specified period of time, you will generally get better service, (assuming you haven't negotiated too hard for a very low fee.) Usually, there's very little downside if a company gives a recruiting firm a 2 to 4 week exclusive chance to produce the successful candidate. While it may seem that if you give a contingency search to many firms, you'll cover more ground, ironically, probably very little will happen. Each firm will have little motivation to do much for you, because the likelihood of their time being wasted is so high. It becomes a race to be the first to submit the resume of the same candidate who visited several recruiting firms. Contingency recruiters devote their energy where they're most likely to make money – on exclusives.

There's something else hiring managers should know about contingency recruiting. It's not unusual for a company to call up a few contingency firms to "see what's out there." When this happens, the company has usually made no firm commitment to fill the position. Management has not yet approved filling the position. "The job is not real," and the recruiters are wasting their time. Therefore, one of the most important things a contingency recruiter must do is be able to "size up" whether a job is "real" or not. One sign of a "real job" is if the company is willing to give an exclusive.

One good way for companies and recruiting firms to create an excellent relationship is to respect each other's time for what it is – an extremely valuable asset. In other words, imagine the situation were reversed, and you were in the other person's place. How would you feel? Throughout a search, it can be extremely valuable to "put yourself in the other person's shoes," regardless of whether the other person is the candidate, the company employee, the recruiting consultant, or the researcher.

With respect to another exclusivity issue, if you are with a retainer search firm, you might be assuming that a company would not engage the services of another recruiter, contingency or otherwise, while they are paying your retainer. While this is generally true, it is more prudent to leave nothing to chance. Make sure there's language in your letter of agreement or proposal letter that assures the company will work exclusively with you on that search.

ID Research. Identification research is research conducted in order to obtain the names and titles of sources or prospects. After the names of the individuals are identified, the next level of the search activity occurs, which is sourcing and prospecting.

ID research is usually done on the phone. However, names can be identified through the use of directories, especially on CD ROM or online databases, including those on the Internet and on Intranets.

With the proliferation of extensive electronic database, over time ID phone research will need to be done less often.

Implementer is a term which applies to a senior research consultant responsible for conducting an executive search assignment in its entirety, including face-to-face interviewing. There are several differences between an implementer and a search consultant. The search consultant usually has more contact with the client company – perhaps to protect his or her relationship, since someone else is executing most of the search. A search consultant usually has an obligation to develop business for the firm, in essence, a sales quota, where an implementer is not expected to bring in new business. The third major difference is that search consultants are much better compensated. This is a classic situation in most industries, where sales performers are generally compensated more than other employees. Finally, virtually all implementers – and all researchers, for that matter – are women, although the number of female search consultants has been gradually growing at retainer search firms since the late 1970's.

The Internet is a rapidly growing electronic tool which has emerged as a fourth type of media, supplementing radio, television and print media (newspapers and magazines). When databases are available on the Internet (for example, those offered by Gale Research), they can be excellent tools for ID research. Precise data can be extracted from huge database in order to identify the names and titles of people NOT on the job market – in other words, future sources, prospects and candidates. Internet web sites are also used by job seekers and companies to find each other, something like electronic want ads with a computer matching capability. As is the case with want ads, the people who use this are actively looking for a job.

One advantage to using an Internet database is that the information is usually current. Once the Internet information is changed, everyone has instant access to it, whereas with a CD ROM, you have to get a new disk. So while an online Internet database might cost more, it should be more current.

With the right databases, you can find listings of names and titles of employees at target companies. For unusually difficult searches, you can search literature for quotes of employees at specific companies, then check their background histories on biography databases. You can also search the literature for news about reorganizations and announcements of job changes, which can reveal excellent names of sources, especially if you can locate someone who left the target company.

CD ROM's represent another powerful tool. As is typical with technology, the prices of CD ROM's and online data services should drop dramatically over time. In the future, these electronic databases will increasingly provide an alternative to using the telephone to obtain ID research.

NAICS is an acronym for North American Industry Classification System. *The North American Industry Classification System (NAICS) Manual* now replaces the *Standard Industrial Classification (SIC) Manual*. Last revised in 1987, The *SIC Manual* is still available in most business libraries. However, it is no longer published because the U.S. has implemented a new industry classification system, NAICS.

Until 1997 the *SIC Manual* had been published by The National Technical Information Service (NTIS), formerly the U.S. Government Printing Office. NTIS is the central source for government sponsored U.S. and worldwide scientific, engineering and business related information. As a self-supporting agency of the U.S. Department of Commerce's Technology Administration, NTIS covers its business and operating expenses with the sale of its products and services.

NAICS is the first North American industry classification system. It was developed by the U.S., Canada and Mexico to provide a uniform basis for statistics for all three countries, which will allow government and business analysts to compare industrial production statistics in the three North American Free Trade Agreement (NAFTA) countries. NAICS also provides for increased comparability with the International Standard Industrial Classification System (ISIC), developed and maintained by the United Nations. Both printed and CD ROM versions of the *NAICS Manual* have been available since June, 1997. These official versions include 350 new industries, definitions for each industry, tables correlating the 1997 NAICS and the 1987 SIC codes, an alphabetic list of over 18,000 business activities and the corresponding NAICS code, and a special section on What Small Businesses Need to Know About NAICS. Some new industries include specialized technology niches, such as fiber optic cable manufacturing and satellite communications. Other recognized new industries include bed and breakfast inns, environmental consulting, warehouse clubs, credit card issuers, and diet and weight reduction centers. Executive search also has been recognized as an industry, as a result of the efforts of Executive Director Emeritus of the Association of Executive Search Consultants, Sheila Avrin McLean. The ramifications of Ms. McLean's outstanding achievement are sure to benefit the search industry for years to come.

Unlike the SIC codes, which are 4 digits, the NAICS codes are 6 digits. The first 5 digits are standardized among the U.S., Canada and Mexico. However, the 6th digit may differ from country to country to accommodate different needs in individual countries. NAICS will be reviewed every five years, so classifications and information will stay current with the economy. For more information, contact the Bureau of the Census Official NAICS web page at www.census.gov/naics or send your questions by email to info@ntis.fedworld.gov.

Ordering information: Softcover version, NTIS Order Number PB98-136187INQ, $28.50, $57 outside the U.S., Canada and Mexico. Hardcover NTIS Order Number PB98-127293, $32.50, $65 outside the U.S., Canada and Mexico. CD ROM Order Number PB98-502024, single user $45, $90 outside the U.S., Canada and Mexico. Up to 5 concurrent network users $120, $240 outside the U.S., Canada and Mexico. Unlimited concurrent network users $240, $480 outside the U.S., Canada and Mexico. CD ROM includes a search capability that can access more index entries than appear in the manual plus downloadable files. Handling charge is additional.

Phone orders Monday-Friday, 8 a.m. - 8 p.m. Eastern Time (800) 553-NTIS (6487) or (703) 605-6000. Fax (703) 321-8547. For questions about a product or order, email info@ntis.fedworld.gov. Web site www.ntis.gov/. National Technical Information Service, Technology Administration, U.S. Department of Commerce, 5285 Port Royal Road, Springfield, VA 22161.

Off Limits Policy is a key issue in executive search. It refers to the recruiter agreeing to refrain from attempting to lure away employees from a client organization. Factors are the definition of "client" and time: the whole corporation (e.g., General Motors) or the division the search was done for (Chevrolet), or some even more specific entity (Truck Division, Northeast Region)...and for one year, two or possibly three.

Some large firms say they can't "afford" a strict off limits policy because it reduces the universe from which they can draw and the conversation can get complicated. Some considerations include, for example, if a client company is served by the San Francisco office or the Zurich office, how significant is the client, etc. Small firms are better able to offer "full" worldwide client protection because it really doesn't harm their business.

Regardless of whether this is considered an ethical matter or a trade practice or a business issue, it is extremely important to have it fully and mutually understood, preferably in writing, at the beginning of the recruiting engagement.

Presearch Report. Usually conducted at the beginning of the assignment, the presearch report is conducted by the search consultant to assess the organizational, operational and cultural identity of the client company. The benefit of such a report is that the more the recruiter knows about the client, the better he or she can inform sources, prospects and candidates about the opportunity. Likewise, the more the client knows about its own reality and employee perceptions, the better it is positioned to evaluate its human capital needs. The report is typically written after the recruiter has done an on-site visit and interviewed several managers and employees, including the contact person overseeing the search for the company. The presearch survey provides the client company with feedback about its organization and helps both the recruiter and the human resources manager shape the attributes and responsibilities of the company's future employee.

Progress Report. This is a formal search document which is typically reviewed in person with the hiring manager, human resources officer and other appropriate parties. It usually consists of:

- Position description

- Target List

- Summary of steps taken, including the number of sources and prospects contacted

- Detailed written profiles of the candidates to be introduced to the company, usually three to six qualified, interested individuals, all of them interviewed in person by the search consultant

Sometimes a progress report includes a detailed summary of everyone who has been contacted. Information in this research report can be organized by organization and should include: name of contact, title, organization, city and comments, specifically interest level, reasons, a background summary (from the present going backwards: all titles with dates, all companies with dates), degrees with dates, compensation (broken into base and bonus), and any remarks of interest (such as, "We're in the middle of a reorganization."). This research report should also specify a source's remarks, for example, if the Executive Director of the industry's leading professional association referred you to an individual or a job bank and you follow up. You can also state, for example, if you called a prospect, left two messages, and never received a returned call.

Proposal Letter or a letter of agreement is one of the most important documents in a recruiting engagement because it spells out the intent of the parties and, if a dispute arises, may be invoked as a contract. The proposal letter should discuss several things:

- Your "Understanding of the Situation"

- A description of the services to be provided

- A projected timetable and the "deliverables"

- A summary of the position to be filled, including expected compensation

- An "off limits" declaration that very specifically defines exactly what is "off limits"

- Terms of payment for the services to be rendered

- Cancellation clause

- Exclusivity clause, including for retained searches

Usually a position description is attached to the proposal letter. Sometimes it's appropriate to include a research plan in the proposal letter. A research plan can be as little as one brief, general paragraph. Or it could be a detailed writing sufficiently impressive as to give the writer a competitive edge in winning the business.

While it is generally preferable for both the recruiting firm and the company to sign the letter, even if only the sender signs it, it nevertheless is proof of intent. If work is commenced, there is a presumption that agreement exists. Therefore the letter is important evidence of the intent of the parties. This is your opportunity to state the fee you expect, for example, if two of your candidates are hired, or if a company sources one of your candidates and subsequently makes a hire, or if a company hires someone you introduced, say 13 months later.

Other important issues should also be addressed, such as exclusivity. Verbal agreements should be included, again, to clarify the intent of the parties. While an oral agreement is in fact a legally binding contract, the problem with enforcing it in a court of law is proof – that is, proving who said what, when, and to whom. It's definitely better to write your agreements down on paper. If an agreement is in writing, it can validly be amended *only* in writing, not orally.

Prospect. A prospect is an individual who has been contacted by phone, expresses interest in the position, and provides enough background information to ascertain that he or she is qualified for the position.

Prospecting. See "Sourcing and Prospecting."

Research (as distinguished from "ID Research"). In executive search, a standard definition of "research" really does not exist because "research" means different things to different people. However, "research" and "ID research" are two different things. "ID Research," or identification research, consists of the name, title and phone number of a possible prospect; this individual will later be contacted during a "sourcing and prospecting" call. ID research can be obtained from a directory (either published hard copy, on CD ROM or online) or from telephone research. Some researchers only do ID research and nothing more. Sometimes secretaries and administrative assistants do ID research. Some recruiters do their own ID research. Other recruiters, especially at large search firms, concentrate on selling new business and managing relationships with clients and candidates, but do little or nothing related to candidate generation.

In any case, "sourcing and prospecting" – also known as "candidate development" – is considered "research" by many people. Regardless of what you call it, candidate generation is clearly the activity that drives the business. Sourcing and prospecting is particularly crucial with retained searches because this is how you find candidates *not* on the job market.

Many people consider reference checking a "research" activity, perhaps because references are often checked by researchers. However, references are often checked by a search consultant, the corporate human resources department, or occasionally the hiring manager as well. Sometimes senior "researchers" interview candidates in person. But hardly anybody considers interviewing a research activity.

The relationship between a researcher and a search consultant can be compared to that of a paralegal and an attorney. Some paralegals are little more than secretaries while others are so knowledgeable, they are nearly practicing law. Most of the others fall somewhere in between, depending on the skills of the individual and the firm's policies on division of labor.

The point is, it can be very confusing to say, "I need research," because it can mean so many different things. It's better to be as specific as possible. Refer to the exact tasks you have in mind.

Also see Chapter 4, "So, Your Company is Thinking About Creating an Unbundled Search Function...."

Retainer Fee. Similar to a law firm, a retainer fee is paid to compensate for professional time and service, regardless of the outcome. Generally, the retainer is between 25% and 33 1/3% of the total anticipated annual compensation (including bonuses) paid in 3 equal increments: a down payment at the beginning of the assignment, the 2nd installment after 30 days, the 3rd and final installment after 60 days, adjusted upwards or downwards, depending on the actual compensation of the successful candidate. Expenses are charged in addition to the retainer fee.

Sometimes a company will actually retain a search firm to "benchmark" an internal candidate for a promotion to make sure he or she is better than "what's out there." There might even be corporate politics affecting the decision to promote from within. In any case, a search firm's relationship – and expectations – with the hiring manager must be properly managed so as to avoid disgruntlement at paying the fee.

In other words, suppose a company realizes that their internal candidate is indeed the best person for the job. However, the company cannot make this determination until they've interviewed the best talent outside the company – candidates presented by a search firm. Then, suppose that this company promotes the internal candidate and hires no one introduced by the search firm.

It is important that the company feel that value has been added. This is largely a function of good and frequent communication. The search consultant must ongoingly manage the hiring manager's expectations so that the manager is aware of the value of the information generated by a search. If it is true that information is power, then the hiring manager may need to be diplomatically reminded that your firm supplied this valuable information, information that provided the basis for promoting the internal candidate.

Many hiring managers and HR managers value high quality information (research), such as competitive information, or information about compensation practices, bonus formulas and so forth. A search firm's research staff should be taught to keep good notes on this information, which can be "anecdotal" or revealed while chatting up a relaxed candidate at home.

In addition to contingency fees and retainer fees, "modified retainer fees" are often developed quite innovatively by contingency recruiters.

Rusing. Rusing is sometimes called "blind calling" or "sourcing," which is actually an abuse of a term for a legitimate practice (see "sourcing"). Rusing is telling an untrue story to induce someone to provide information that he or she otherwise might not reveal, such as the names of everybody in the department. Rusing is unethical, unprofessional, demeaning, psychologically harmful and definitely should be avoided. The end does *not* justify the means.

SIC is an acronym for Standard Industrial Classification. It is a 4 digit number developed by the U.S. Government which is a "shorthand" expression for a specific industry. Previously all SICs were listed in *The Standard Industrial Classification Manual,* published by The National Technical Information Service (formerly the U.S. Government Printing Office). However, in 1997 *The SIC Manual* was replaced by *The North American Industry Classification System (NAICS) Manual.* The NAICS is being used by the three NAFTA (North American Free Trade Agreement) nations, Mexico, Canada and the U.S.

The *SIC Manual* was last revised in 1987 and is still available in most U.S. business libraries. *The SIC* and *NAICS Manuals* are important because they are the only unabridged references that provide complete information as to what's contained in each industry code. Sometimes an abbreviated listing of SIC or NAICS codes is sufficient, such as those which appear in *Standard and Poors* or *Dun & Bradstreet's Million Dollar Directory Series.* However, there's no substitute for the unabridged reference. See NAICS.

Source. A source is someone you call, asking for a referral of possible candidates. Sometimes a source becomes a prospect, sometimes a prospect turns out to be a source, and some people are both. If you don't know for sure whether an individual is a source or prospect, you can say something like, "I don't know whether this position is appropriate for you, but if it's not, perhaps you can recommend someone. I'd be happy to keep your name confidential, if you wish." That way you can avoid insulting someone if they're way too senior for your search.

Sourcing. Sourcing is a legitimate call to ask someone to refer a qualified candidate for the search you're conducting. The term "sourcing" should not be confused with "rusing" or "blind calling." See "Sourcing and Prospecting."

Sourcing and Prospecting. The term "sourcing and prospecting" and "candidate development" can be used interchangeably.

Here's how a sourcing and prospecting call might begin. "Hello, this is Jean DuBois of Trouver Associates. We're a 9 year old executive search firm based in New York with offices in London, Paris, Hong Kong and Mexico City. We're conducting a search for the Chief Financial Officer of a rapidly growing, aggressively positioned global company with sales over $500 million and I wanted to chat with you about it. Is this a convenient time for you to talk?"

If it is, you might continue with, "... I wanted to ask if this is something that might be appropriate and of interest to you. If it's not, perhaps you can recommend someone else. I'd be pleased to keep your name confidential, if you wish...." And so forth. Then, if the individual is interested, you might say, "Great. The next step is for us to get some background information on you." While you're on the phone, you can gather data about the person's career, following the guidelines presented in the "Telephone Interview Guide" in Chapter 13.

Target List. By its very definition, a target list is a list of companies, never names of people. If you have a list of names of people, then it is called something else, such as a list of sources and prospects, a list of contacts, or a list of candidates. In general, a target list of about 15 to 25 companies is appropriate. However, your search might generate candidates at other companies, too, resulting from referrals from sources and prospects.

Target List Research. Target list research is generally research conducted to identify leading companies within an industry. However, other criteria can further narrow your list, such as: size of the company (either in revenues or number of employees), geographic location, type of business activities or NAICS or SIC code, number of plants, types of computer systems, similar channels of distribution, size of research and development budget and so forth. Sometimes a hiring manager will be looking for other, less tangible characteristics, such as "a similar corporate culture," reputation for being a well run company, innovative use of technology, progressive human resources policies, outstanding finance function, and so on. You can often find surveys of this type of evaluative information, for example, CIO magazine's annual survey of the best chief information officers.

However, if you can't locate a certain type of survey, it might not exist. In that case, you can source experts to create your own original target list. While you're talking to the experts, one of them might know about the ideal, little-known list and you might inadvertently find "the needle in the haystack." Also, if you're working in an exotic new area of technology where no prior research has been done because the area is too new, a good librarian can help you figure out how best to use databases to create what you need. However, it should be noted that this situation would be extremely rare. Generally, a target list can be developed quite quickly. Target lists from prior searches can also be great short cuts. Finally, a thoroughly researched target list can sometimes impress a hiring manager. Information could include: Parent company, appropriate subsidiary or division, business activities and products of the targeted subsidiary or division, sales figures, number of employees, geographic location of parent, subsidiary and division, and other data, depending on the criteria that are driving the search (R&D budget figures, if available from a Business Week survey or other reference, or number of employees in a lab, for example.) Further, this analysis of divisional and subsidiary business activities can be effectively used to make sure you're searching in the right part of the organization, especially if ID research must be done. By investing time in thorough, pinpointed research at the beginning of the search, the resulting ID research will be highly precise. This "rifle shooting" approach can avoid wasting time on calls to sources in the wrong part of the organization.

URL stands for Uniform Resource Locator. The terms URL and web site address are more or less interchangeable. For example, www.technicalrecruiter.com is a URL.

According to Bryan Pfaffenberger in Introducing the Internet (Microsoft Press),

"Buried beneath each hyperlink is an address, called a Uniform Resource Locator (URL). The address specifies the document's type, its name, and its precise location on the Internet. When you click a hyperlink, your browser locates the computer on the Internet that has the document you requested. If the document is available, the browser copies the document to your computer, and your browser displays it on your screen."

On another note, if you get onto an Internet search engine to conduct an information search – in other words, to find information about a certain topic – you will learn the URL's or web sites you can visit to look for that information.

CHAPTER 4

"So, Your Company Is Thinking About Creating An Unbundled Search Function..."

"Unbundled search," sometimes referred to as "research," is an innovative service that is increasingly being purchased by company human resources departments as a less expensive way of acquiring abbreviated search services. Unbundled search provides a "no frills" alternative to full service retainer search, contingency search, and advertisements (whether in the paper or on the Internet). In general unbundled search or research services are provided by independent consultants, most of whom have been thoroughly trained in research in a retainer search environment.

A review of the Research Check List in chapter 1 will give you a sense of the specific things available from "unbundled search." Whether you want everything on the list or just part of it, there are certainly unbundling consultants available who can address any reasonable needs. One major difference between classic search and "unbundling" is that there are almost never any formal, written reports with unbundled search. This is one of the reasons it costs so much less – the report writing and production process consumes large amounts of consultant time and secretarial time. Another reason is that there is generally no overhead from fancy offices factored into the pricing.

With unbundled search, the "deliverable" is often a list of qualified, interested prospects whose backgrounds are presented in the form of handwritten notes or copies of candidate resumes, sometimes with a handwritten update attached. These prospects may have been screened on the phone but are not generally interviewed in person by the unbundled search consultant (also known as a recruiting consultant or a research consultant). The company human resources officer must do that. As they say, you get what you pay for. With unbundled search clearly there can be huge economic savings, but they do translate into much more work for the company employees.

* * * * *

Some research consultants specialize in providing services to executive search firms for hard-to-fill assignments. Often the search firms will pass their out-of-pocket research expenses directly to the corporate client. In fact, it's not unusual for a search firm to pay an unbundled search consultant about $2,000 to 3,000 for a search, *and there's a clear expectation that the consultant will find the successful candidate.* This fee usually translates to less than 10% of the total search fee for the person whose efforts ultimately determine the success or failure of the assignment. Therefore many unbundled search consultants prefer to provide services directly to the employer. Because there is more value added to the company when unbundled search consultants are directly retained by the employer, the consultant generally earns a greater fee. In addition, when an unbundled search consultant accepts a project with a search firm, in essence, the search firm acts as a "middleman" who keeps the lion's share of the fees. Clearly there is an economic advantage for an unbundled search consultant to work directly with the corporation, rather than through a search firm. It is frequently to the company's benefit, too, especially if saving fees is important.

Remember, while it is definitely possible for an employer to use research to save on search and agency fees, *there's no such thing as a free lunch.* In the beginning it will be necessary to invest time, money or both to plan the program. Later it will require considerable time and attention to properly manage the execution of each and every recruitment assignment and basically oversee each detail in the Research Check List. Time might need to be invested to get the researcher "up to speed" in a new industry or function.

If you're a corporate employer evaluating hiring additional staff to implement an unbundled search program, here are a few crucial points:

1. You absolutely must employ someone with an in depth knowledge of executive search research. This person should have been employed at a 100% retainer search firm *as a researcher.* About two years of research experience should be sufficient. It should encompass *all* aspects of research, including ID research and candidate development. This experience need not be recent, because learning research is like riding a bike: once you learn, you never forget. In fact, instead of someone who graduated college 2, 3 or 4 years ago, it may be more important to have a professionally poised person with credibility and stature who can comfortably deal with senior line executives. Because about 99% of the reseachers at search firms are women, this person will likely be female.

   Be extremely wary of hiring someone who never spent any time as a researcher *per se* at a search firm. For example, individuals who join search firms directly as search consultants are usually good sales people with smooth oral communication skills. But they often don't know how to actually develop candidates or otherwise do the legwork of conducting a search. They get the researchers to find the candidates while the consultants are managing relationships and selling new business.

   Be careful about hiring individuals who think they understand research because they were "users" of it. There's no way they can truly understand it without actually having done it themselves. This is like saying you can drive a car because you rode in one. There's no substitute for learning by doing something yourself.

2. As for compensation, employees at search firms are usually more highly compensated than in company human resources departments. If you are attempting to recruit someone from a search firm to manage your unbundled search activities, remember, *you get what you pay for.* You must be prepared to create a position at the right level, with the proper level of responsibility or Hay points, so as to offer enough compensation to attract a top performer. If you're having trouble getting management to approve a decent compensation package, they might need to be reminded that saving only one fee for a $100,000 position represents between $25,000-$33,333 *plus expenses.* The first year Bankers Trust implemented a research program, they saved over $1 million in fees. Don't be penny wise and pound foolish.

3. The hardest thing about making sourcing and prospecting calls is doing the identification (ID) research to get the names of the people you'll call. Some companies who use unbundled research "farm out" ID research projects to independent research consultants. Then, the company recruiters make the sourcing and prospecting phone calls.

4. It is relatively painless to make sourcing and prospecting calls to develop candidates. However, it *is* time consuming. Also note that if company employees make these calls, the company's name can no longer be kept confidential. Even so, this has not stopped many companies from using research, or inhouse search, such as Booz, Allen and Hamilton, the Gap and MCI. One alternative is to use an unbundled search consultant to make sourcing and prospecting calls, especially if you want to keep an employee source's name confidential. Otherwise, you should be psychologically prepared for the day when the Chairman of a competitor calls your Chairman complaining about directly "raiding" them. In fact, you might want to review this possibility with senior management *before* embarking on the program. You don't want to be the one to take the blame, so protect yourself beforehand. As usual, make sure your understandings and

agreements are in writing, even if it's a memorandum to the file that summarizes a phone call or a meeting.

5. If your company will be directly contacting competitors to make sourcing and prospecting calls, there are two situations that tend to result in complaints about "raiding" the competition. One is if you are recruiting for a large number of positions in the same department. The other is if you attract a highly valued senior executive. In these situations, it can be advantageous for an employer to use a third party consultant or firm to keep the employer's name confidential. No company needs the gossip – or a law suit. For further discussion abut related legal issues, see chapter 20, "Legal Issues In Executive Search," by Jane E. Shaffer and Richard W. Laner.

6. Here's a good rule of thumb: It usually takes about 100 conversations with sources and prospects to find the successful candidate. If the position is really wonderful, or the research is unusually easy to do, then maybe 50 conversations will suffice. If you must make more than 150 calls, there's a problem. At that point, it's important to review the position specifications, especially compensation, because the chances for a failure are high if something doesn't change.

7. Remember, there's a reason why search services are so expensive. Search only looks easy. But have you ever watched the Olympics? That looks easy, too.

Sure, a company can save a great deal in fees with a "do it yourself" in-house search or research program. But the trade-off is it's a lot of work, it takes a lot of time, and it requires the close supervision of a "hands on" manager with an eye for detail and an in depth knowledge of how the search process works. Remember, executive search and corporate recruiting are two very different things. Most company recruiters are oriented towards *interviewing* candidates. Resumes seem to magically appear on their desk – usually from ads, the Internet, agencies and search firms. On the other hand, executive search professionals are expert at doing the digging to *generate* candidates *not* on the job market. In fact corporate recruiters and executive search consultants are two very different breeds of cat, as the saying goes.

* * * * *

Virtually all research consultants or unbundling consultants charge fees on an hourly or per diem basis, which averages in excess of $60.00 per hour or $500 per day, depending on geography, expertise and experience. Simple research can cost about $40 per hour, or $300 – $325 a day. More sophisticated services can cost $100 to $150 per hour, or $1,000-$1,200 per day. It's not unusual for these consultants to work on a project basis for a lump sum fee, plus expenses. Still other companies are willing to incentivize performance by offering a percentage bonus for every candidate hired, in addition to the unbundled search consultant's regular fee – and the company still saves great sums in recruitment fees. Some of the industry's most prominent consultants who work with management to establish a recruitment strategy and develop an overall recruitment program charge $3,000 per day.

In addition to independent consultants, there are also a few small research firms in existence. For more information about the freelancers and firms comprising this cottage industry, refer to the following directory:

The Directory of Independent Research Consultants contains information on 200 contract consultants. $65. Kennedy Information, One Kennedy Place, Route 12 South, Fitzwilliam, NH 03447, (800) 531-0007, web site www.kennedyinfo.com

CHAPTER 5

The Role Of Research In The Search Process – One Scenario Among Many

By Glenn H. Van Doren, Certified Management Consultant, former Executive Director of the Association of Executive Search Consultants

Reprinted from the 1st edition, revised and updated by Andrea Jupina

This overview of the entire executive search process shows how research can be involved in each step, from proposal through actual hiring. This discussion outlines what a corporate search client can expect of the search process overall and the role of research. Similarly, it details many of the services corporate human resources officers might wish to obtain from unbundled search consultants.

Much has been written about the executive search process. Some writers call it complicated. Others describe it as mysterious and furtive. In fact the executive search process is neither complicated nor mysterious. It is a straightforward way of recruiting executive talent, based on a logical methodology and a five step procedure:

1. Defining the job

2. Identifying candidate sources

3. Identifying specific prospects

4. Interviewing and screening candidates

5. Closing the search

For the process to work, each step must be conducted in its entirety. When that happens, the search is completed to everyone's satisfaction. The client is happy because an important organizational gap has been filled; the search consultant is satisfied because a completion is a source of professional satisfaction and economic benefit; and candidates are pleased because their qualifications have passed the toughest kind of scrutiny. Candidates also realize that they have added an important new link to their career network, something that could be valuable for years to come.

The role of research in the search process is vital. Experienced researchers can be active in each of the five steps, although in some organizations their work tends to be directed at identifying candidate sources and providing a preliminary list of prospective candidates. Many researchers are involved in defining the job, either as part of the search team in initial discussions with the client, or as an advisor to the search consultant during the early stages of the assignment.

The specific role of the research consultant can – and does – vary from firm to firm. Some firms, including the larger ones, rely on their researchers to use large databases to help provide all the fundamental information needed to identify target industries, target companies, and individuals. In fact databases and computer systems are used by firms of all sizes. Surprisingly, sometimes a smaller, upstart firm will have a more sophisticated system, particularly if the firm employs many younger people who grew up with computers and are *not* afraid of them. Some firms employ researchers to do only a narrow slice of the search work. Still other firms will retain the services of contract research consultants (also known as unbundled search consultants) who are usually experienced professionals who can take almost any role that the search consultant needs, fitting their efforts to complement those of the search firm.

When a corporate executive calls a search firm for help, the need is often critical and almost always immediate. This sense of urgency runs counter to the careful and deliberate process that most search engagements require. The usual two to four months needed to complete many searches may be problematic to the company.

Yet most searches require a certain level of effort to define the position, to identify target industries and companies and to develop a list of preliminary candidates. If an extensive research library is available, the time can be shortened slightly, but the basic steps still need to be taken. While there may be a transitory temptation to shortcut the process, any time so saved will probably be expended in repairing later damage. The time invested in laying a solid research foundation in the beginning usually pays handsome dividends later on.

DEFINING THE JOB

The first major activity in the search process is defining the job. That step sets the tone for all that follows. If the job description is poorly drawn, it will produce inappropriate candidates. Knowledgeable search consultants, therefore, invest enough time in the initial step to produce a meeting of the minds between client and consultant.

Preparing a job description is the culmination of that first step where all the discussions between client and search consultant about job requirements, organizational relationships and cultural issues are crystallized. This piece of paper is, after the proposal or confirmation letter, the most important evidence of early communications between client and consultant.

The job description sets the stage for subsequent activities. Many research consultants wish to attend the client meetings during which positions are defined. In recent years, increasingly the trend has been to invite research consultants to these meetings, especially if they have extensive experience. Their contributions are valued and their knowledge of the research process helps the client develop realistic expectations. Most important, the research consultants will have a clearer understanding of the position's requirements simply by receiving the information directly from the client rather than secondhand through someone else's perceptual filters.

In most cases, the written job description should be based on:

- Discussions with the client regarding why the job is open, cultural issues, growth potential and reporting relationships

- An organization chart showing superior, subordinate and peer relationships, as validated by client discussions

- Any preliminary job write-ups prepared by the client, including specific responsibilities, compensation ranges, perquisites and other benefits, academic requirements and desired experience levels

- An understanding with the client regarding the degree of flexibility that can be exercised by the search consultant

When the research consultant does not participate in preparing this document, special caution should be taken to make sure that the write-up is clear and concise, that it has identified any special job needs or client preferences (presumably legal, non-discriminatory ones), and that it is accompanied by an adequate synopsis of the client company which can be given to prospective candidates. A client may wish to learn who will be responsible for doing most of the telephone work, including candidate development and phone screening. If research is expected to be involved in any of this, a client might request that research be present at meetings, not only to impart important information to the research consultant, but also to learn more about who will be handling a critical piece of the assignment.

RESEARCH TASK PLAN

Many researchers will prepare a formal task plan to guide them in their efforts. This plan serves as a road map in developing the proper approach to conducting research suitable to the particular assignment. The Research Check List in chapter 1 provides a detailed, comprehensive basis from which to work.

However, the task plan need not be voluminous or complicated. Its purpose is to define the various activities and sources of information for completing the research. Often the task plan, in a somewhat condensed form, will be incorporated in the proposal or confirming letter to the client.

If the search consultant is submitting a proposal to a client, the extent of effort spent in developing a preliminary research task plan will be determined by competitive circumstances. If the proposal is to be used in a "shoot out," that is, where several firms are bidding for the same search, some firms will conduct extensive research that is both detailed and impressive. This level of effort is considered appropriate in order to secure the assignment. In other circumstances, the preliminary task plan will be just that – an early effort to suggest a number of industries and entities that would be used to provide potential candidates. If the firm wins the assignment, this plan will later be expanded into a precise set of strategies and an expanded listing of industries and companies.

Another purpose of the research task plan is to provide an inventory of likely information sources that can be used in the search. Some common sources are:

1. *NAICS* (formerly *SIC*) identification of target and affinity industry groupings.

2. Publications devoted to a specific industry or a specialized portion of an industry, such as directories, journals, newsletters, survey publishers, or trade papers.

3. Professional societies, trade associations and membership organizations that can be used as conduits to target likely companies and executives, especially by using association membership rosters.

4. Academic groups, such as university alumni associations or business school placement bureaus.

5. Seminar developers and presenters who specialize in a particular industry or sub-category of an industry.

6. Knowledgeable individuals who may be prominent in a specific industry, either as participants or as observers: media people, bankers, attorneys, management consultants, accountants, etc. However, while clients are often impressed that such individuals are being sourced, as a practical matter, they are rarely good sources because of confidentiality issues.

7. Individual academics who have specialized expertise in the targeted industry. Again, these contacts might impress clients, but practically speaking, most academics tend to be too far removed from the business world to be able to recommend appropriate prospects.

In addition to the information sources, search firms usually have research libraries or accumulations of pertinent data, such as annual reports, 10(k) reports (either on the Internet or in hard copy) and clippings related to specific industries, corporations and individuals. Today's technology allows computer literate search professionals access to a wealth of information through CD ROM's and new media. Tremendous resources are available on the Internet and they are growing in number, ease of use, and power. That said, it should be noted that Internet job posting sites are similar to newspaper want ads because both basically attract people on the job market, many of them out of work. There are many other ways to use the Internet to access information about prospective candidates *not* on the job market. These techniques are taught in various Internet recruiting courses.

Once the research task plan has been developed and reviewed by all pertinent parties (search consultant, research consultant, client liaison), it can be used to guide the subsequent research efforts and to monitor progress. In some instances, estimates of time can be developed for major activities on the task list. Projected completion dates for each major task can also be developed. Occasionally this information will be plotted on a Gantt chart and used by all parties to track the performance of the project.

Most task plans consist of at least three major elements:

- Selecting likely industries

- Identifying target companies

- Sourcing for specific individuals

The first element, selecting likely industries, requires the least amount of research and search consultant time. Often, the client will specify which industries are appropriate for potential candidates. Even if the target industry is determined by the client, other related industries, or in some cases, totally unrelated industries, could be likely sources. These should be discussed with the client and, assuming there is agreement, used in the search. Sometimes a wide selection of target industries is available to broaden the pool of eventual candidates. For example, the client may believe that they already know everyone in the industry and want to look outside. This can make a search more difficult and time consuming because the parameters are so broad. Conversely, a search confined to a single industry or with otherwise very narrow specifications is usually much easier to conduct precisely because the focus is so narrow. Ironically, searches with the broadest specifications can be very difficult to execute because the search can "wander all over the place."

In the second element of the research task plan, identifying target companies, the researchers must be aware of industries dominated by one or two major companies who may be clients and are therefore "off limits" as a place to search for talent. If too many companies on the target list are clients, this could create a problem in having enough organizations open to the research consultant to legitimately search for candidates. When this situation arises, she can identify new target companies similar to the client, if not in terms of NAICS (or SIC) codes, products or services, then possibly in terms of channels of distribution, markets, manufacturing technologies, information technology, involvement in international business, or corporate culture.

The third major element of the research task plan is the description of the approach to locate specific individuals who might be appropriate candidates. This element relies on published reference books, CD ROM's, electronic databases, the Internet, Intranets, and the ability to use third parties to identify potential candidates.

IDENTIFYING CANDIDATE SOURCES

After the target industries have been selected, the research consultant starts the process of identifying specific target companies, from which potential candidates will be drawn. A number of reference sources are available for this purpose. Most in-house research departments contain at least a minimum complement of various references, including:

- *Standard and Poors Register of Corporations*

- *Dun's Billion Dollar Directory*

- *Ward's Business Directory of U.S. Private and Public Companies*

- *Directory of Corporate Affiliations*

- *Encyclopedia of Associations*

- *Moody's Industrial Manual*

- *Value Line Investment Survey*

- *Moody's Handbook of Common Stocks*

There are numerous other reference sources that could be useful in identifying target companies. In addition to these general references, there are also specialized industry directories. Some of them include the *American Financial Directory, Best's Insurance Reports, Medical Device Register, Sheldon's Retail Directory* and many others. It is fair to say that all major industry groups have one or more directories that list their members. Most search firms will not maintain a complete library of all such publications. However, firms that specialize in particular industries will typically maintain directories covering those industries. See to chapter 6, "How to Create an Executive Search Library" for more information on the most important basic references – and tips on how to find specialized references. In addition, many specialist resources are identified in Part II of this book, "The Recruiter's Directory of Directories – Plus Web Sites, Databases & CD ROM's."

There are other types of directories that can also be useful in locating target companies. These include *Directories in Print, The Oxbridge Directory of Newsletters* and the *Standard Periodical Directory*. References such as these are valuable as indirect sources of companies that could fit the targeted profile.

When identifying candidate sources, particularly the names of possible target companies, the research consultant must be able to satisfactorily answer the question: why is this company a likely target? Usually the answer pertains to industry, products, location and size. However, other considerations could be reputation, favorable operation results, R&D strength, technology or global business activities.

IDENTIFYING SPECIFIC PROSPECTS

During the process of researching target companies, the names of specific executives may surface. When this occurs, it is an added bonus for the researcher. More often, the researcher will have only the name of the company to work with. In that case, the next step is to identify names and titles of executives who are currently employed by the target companies.

Identifying qualified executives usually is the result of an identification (ID) research campaign followed up by a sourcing and prospecting campaign. ID research is the process of uncovering possible candidate names and titles. Some of these names may be quickly discarded as not suitable or outside the job description requirements. Others that appear suitable are added to a list of prospects for further investigation.

The principal purpose of an ID research call is to secure names, titles and phone numbers of individuals who appear to fit the general job criteria. At the conclusion of a typical series of ID research calls, the research consultant should have identified a number of potential candidates or prospects (who will be further investigated) and a number of additional sources. As each sequence of calls is made, a network of names is gradually constructed.

THE SOURCE CALL

The source call typically opens with recruiters or researchers identifying themselves and their organizations and asking for assistance in getting the names of prospective candidates.

Usually, the job is described, including the projected compensation range. This brief amount of information often allows the source to rule out inappropriate candidates. If the source has been previously identified as a possible candidate, there may be some discussion of this as well.

Research consultants use different techniques to get data from a source or to get prospective candidates to volunteer their own names. The specific technique is not as important as the end result – securing names through forthright and ethical means.

Most experienced research consultants make sourcing calls armed with an array of data in front of them:

- A "script" or questionnaire to be used during the source call

- The job description

- A one or two paragraph synopsis of the client company, written so as to insure anonymity, which has been approved by the client

- An organization chart of the target company, if available, or identification research, preferably in an organization chart format

- A list of individuals who have been previously identified as potential candidates

The sourcing and prospecting process is usually carried out through telephone conversations. The process starts with phone calls to several previously identified individuals who may be knowledgeable about certain industries and companies. These original sources may be association executives, trade journal editors, or business acquaintances. Or they may be individuals who have been identified by other third parties. However, generally the best sources are people you know and trust who are familiar with the population you need to identify. Other excellent sources are on a peer level with the position you are filling, for they tend to know who all the right players are and they're at the right level.

Sourcing calls can often be time consuming, depending on the circumstances, the research consultant's style and technique, and the interest and receptivity of the individual called. The overall number of calls will depend on the complexity of the search and professional judgment as to when enough names have been secured. It is not unusual to identify hundreds of potential names. One good rule of thumb is that you must generally talk to about 100 sources and prospects to develop a slate of three to six qualified, interested candidates. If you haven't achieved this after talking to 150 people, there may be a problem with the specifications. For example, the client's compensation expectations may be unreasonably low or there may be a problem with reporting relationships. If this happens, the search consultant should probably work with the client on revising the specifications. Otherwise there is a great risk that this will be the last search the firm conducts for this client.

GROUPING AND CLASSIFYING NAMES

Of course, not all identified potential candidates will have equal credentials for the job. In so far as possible, the researcher would array the names in some order of preference. Names can also be grouped into categories such as High Potential, Average, Low Potential or More Information Needed.

The purpose of arraying or grouping names is to weed out the less desirable names and to avoid wasting time with low probability prospects. Most high potential names should be further checked and screened, usually by follow up phone calls or review of documents submitted by the prospect.

Some researchers will complete their involvement in the search assignment at this stage. They will prepare a list of prospective candidates and submit them to their internal client, often the search consultant with whom they are teamed.

Sometimes this list is given to a corporate client who has contracted for "unbundled search" with the research consultant for the delivery of a given number of prospects.

For most researchers, the culmination of this phase of the search process is the preparation of a research summary. The summary is usually a document that contains at least the following:

- A synopsis of the position description, with the full description appended

- A synopsis of pertinent requirements not included in the position description

- A summary of sources used to identify prospective candidates

- A list of identified candidates

- Any preliminary recommendations pertinent to the search that could modify the remaining tasks

- A plan of action for follow up with the candidates

The research summary can vary widely in length, formality and amount of data provided. Contract research consultants who have been retained to provide a list of potential candidates sometimes view this summary report as the deliverable of their project. In these cases, the reports may be more comprehensive and detailed.

If the unbundled search consultant has been engaged to go on to the next step (interviewing and further screening of candidates), the research report may be viewed as an interim progress report. In that case, the report will be less comprehensive and may be confined to a recitation of contacts made, sources identified, total prospects considered and a final listing of preliminary candidates.

If the researcher is employed by a search firm and is working closely with a search consultant, the summary report may simply consist of a few statistics, (such as the number of sources contacted and prospects identified) and the list of candidates. In this situation, most reporting is informal and occurs during face to face discussions between the research consultant and search consultant.

INTERVIEWING AND SCREENING

The next step in the search process is to screen the list of potential candidates for appropriate fit to the company's requirements. This step is accomplished through interviews and, if an offer is about to be extended, background investigation. Not all researchers will be actively involved in interviewing and screening. Some will handle preliminary screening, some will participate in a round of interviews and some will do the obligatory background checks. Many research consultants, particularly those with extensive experience, may be active in all parts of the screening process.

Much has been written and said about the art of interviewing. Most books on consulting contain one or more chapters that describe the do's and don'ts of interviewing. Indeed, complete books are devoted to this art. Seminars are available to teach these skills, as well. Notwithstanding the available information on interviewing, many researchers are confined to providing background data for the lead consultant, rather than being actively involved in the process. Other research consultants may conduct preliminary telephone interviews to secure enough initial data to warrant keeping the prospect on a short list of potential candidates. This data then is turned over to the search consultant for follow up interviews. Still other senior research consultants, known as "implementers," conduct a search it its entirety, including face-to-face interviews.

Each candidate interview, regardless of who conducts it, is based on a background data summary. This can be used to guide the interviewer into investigating pertinent background areas. Often, the data summary is taken from the research report prepared at the conclusion of the candidate identification phase, described earlier. Sometimes the first face-to-face interview is conducted by the research consultant, although most face-to-face interviews are handled by the lead consultant, based on data provided by the research consultant.

The interview process usually consists of a number of elements:

- Setting the stage and establishing rapport with the candidate

- Describing the position in enough detail to give the candidate a reasonable understanding of the position and client environment

- Asking for further background about the candidate's career, prior experience and accomplishments, especially those that may be relevant to the position

- Assessing the candidate's fit to the position

- Determining the level of interest in the position and answering the candidate's questions

- Obtaining a signed Permission to Check References release from the candidate, including his or her social security number

- Discussing the firm's reference checking policy

- Closing the interview, often defining a next-action step to be taken, either by the search consultant or the candidate

These steps are usually based on prior interchange of data between the candidate and the researcher or search consultant. This may include resumes, position descriptions and other relevant documents.

Customarily, comprehensive references are checked only if an offer will be made. Academic claims should always be verified. If names of references are obtained before it is known that a candidate might possibly receive an offer, it is important to communicate this clearly to the candidate. Otherwise, the candidate may develop unrealistic expectations that an offer is forthcoming, which could be followed by misunderstandings or problems with "candidate handling."

Sometimes, one or two references can be safely checked early in the sequence. Many search consultants will do these independent reference checks with individuals not specifically identified by the candidate. These checks must be handled with great tact and discretion, however.

For an in-depth discussion on reference checking, see chapters 17, 18 and 19, "So, You Thought Reference Checking was Easy. Here's How to *Really* Check References," "Permission to Check References – A Sample Release Form," and "Sample Reference Check Guides."

CLOSING THE SEARCH

The last major step in the search process involves closure. This refers to final candidate presentation to the client, arranging for client interviews, and often assisting the client and candidate in negotiating a mutually agreeable final package of terms and arrangements.

Most research consultants are not involved in closing a search. Senior research consultants may be requested to participate in the preparation of the candidate submission package, often in the portion which describes the research gathered during the course of the assignment.

The final client submission contains all pertinent data needed by the client to assess the candidates. Most search consultants prefer to present more than one final candidate and, in many firms, three is considered an appropriate number. In instances where time constraints are critical, candidates may be presented sequentially as they are screened and approved for client submission. Even in these instances, the search consultant will rarely present more than four or five final candidates.

Responsibility for communicating with candidates who are not ultimately selected for the position is usually handled by the search consultant. However, responsibility for sign off contact with candidates who did not make the short list of three or four final candidates can often be assigned to the research consultant. This chore is normally handled as prospective candidates are eliminated during the interview and screening process.

If post engagement discussions are appropriate after the assignment has been closed out, the research consultant might participate. This is especially so if the assignment did not conclude with a placement but was terminated for one reason or another. Often these discussions prove valuable in reviewing the strategy, the research work plan and the general conduct of the assignment. Important lessons can be learned from such discussions and the researcher's involvement can be valuable.

Glenn H. Van Doren

Mr. Van Doren was formerly President of the Association of Executive Search Consultants, President of the Institute of Management Consultants, and a Vice President and board member of the Council of Consulting Organizations. Prior to this, he was Assistant National Director of the Management Consulting Group at Arthur Young & Company. In addition, he was that firm's National Director of Consulting Education from 1974 to 1988 and previously was partner in charge of the consulting practice with a national clientele. He has served as editorial director of the publication, The Management Advisor *and is co-author of* The Management Advisory Services Manual. *Earlier he held executive positions in industry. He is a graduate of Wayne State University in Detroit.*

CHAPTER 6

How To Create An Executive Search Library For Specialist Recruiters... And Generalists

Some people call it research. Some people call it information. Whatever you call it, it's basically the product that executive search firms sell, if you really get down to it. Research is both the means to the end and an end result as well. Consider one of the starting pieces of information for a search, the name and title of a person who should be contacted. This is certainly research, specifically identification research. Another example is organizational data, such as several names and titles of employees in a certain department at a target company. When taken a step further and arranged into an organization chart, this research becomes even more valuable. It allows a more precise selection to be made, especially when information is added to the chart, such as reporting relationships, total number of professionals in a department, number of direct reports, revenues of a business, etc. This research can be valuable to a company because it is actually *competitive information.*

The information stream gets bigger as we start adding career biographies of prospects and candidates and more competitive data – compensation information. Even a summary of a phone conversation is research, for example, "Not interested in position as a Controller. Is very focused on a position as a CFO with international responsibility for a service industry, minimum $2 billion co. Lived in Singapore 2 years." Then, there are those massive reports that list everyone who was contacted: name, title, company, location of company, and various comments, such as interest level, education, compensation, bonus formula, industry rumors, and whatever might fascinate or impress the client. These reports certainly represent the quintessential research effort.

All this research can begin with your library – which includes directories, files and your database. This chapter will explain what you need to know to build a library that will help you meet your research needs so powerfully, both you and your firm can actually generate a competitive advantage in the business.

Who Will Benefit From This Chapter

- If you're starting up an executive search business or an internal search function, you'll need to create a library. This chapter will tell you how to do it.

- If executive search is a new career for you, you should *definitely* familiarize yourself with the resources discussed in this chapter. These tools are at the heart of *product development* for any search. Search is probably very different from anything else you've ever done, even if your career was in human resources.

- If you are a company human resources professional buying research or "unbundled search" products, or managing a relationship with a search firm, you should be familiar with these resources so that you know what to ask of your vendors.

Five Easy Pieces

Broadly speaking, there are five elements of an executive search library:

1. **Publications in Hard Copy.** This includes librarian's references, general directories, specialized directories, alumni directories, newspapers, business magazines, trade journals and newsletters.

2. **Research on Electronic Media.** This includes the above references, if available, in

electronic formats, plus other databases on CD ROM, web sites, Internet databases, and other online services.

3. **Company Information**. There are three main components of company files:

- Web site information on companies

- Information published by the company, such as annual reports, 10(k) reports and proxy statements

- Identification research. Two copies of this information can be cross referenced in the files.

  - One copy can be filed with the search documents.

  - The other set can be filed by company.

4. **Industry and Function Information.**

5. **Personal Contacts.** There are 3 main types:

- *Candidates* – in the main computerized database

- *Good sources and prospects* – in the main computerized database

- Other individuals contacted for a *prior search* – noted on Sources and Prospects sheets

PUBLICATIONS IN HARD COPY

The first element of your information library is hard copy publications, including librarian's references, general directories, industry directories, alumni directories, newspapers, business magazines, trade journals and newsletters.

The second element of your library is research on electronic media. This includes electronic formats of the above, if available, plus other databases on CD ROM, Internet databases, web sites, and other online services.

If you are starting a new search practice, your search library needs will depend on whether your search practice is generalist or specialized. As you evaluate how much money to spend on these library tools, it's important to consider that if you properly invest in your library, you can free up more time of your research staff for higher level, value added tasks. Good researchers are not cheap and it's frustrating for them to waste time digging up names on the phone when it's easily and painlessly available from the right reference materials on CD ROM or available on an Internet database. You also want to avoid sending a signal that a staff member's time is not valued because that's a motivation killer – and that's one risk of skimping on research materials. If you want a mechanic to do a good job, she needs good tools. It's the same with research. If the research tools are prohibitively expensive, maybe a few trips to a good public library is the answer.

Library for a Generalist Search Practice

If your practice is a general, spanning all industries and functions, the following directories are recommended.

Librarian's References

Business Information Sources **by Lorna Daniells**

Business Information Sources by Lorna Daniells is an outstanding reference at any price. At $39.95 a copy, it's such an extraordinary value, it should have a place in every library. This is clearly one of the top three hard copy references around, and its reasonable price elevates it to first place. *Business Information Sources* provides an abundance of information routinely needed by search firms, job hunters and corporate recruiters, including general directories, specialized directories, professional associations, periodicals, industry information, international information, and much more.

Ordering information:

Business Information Sources by Lorna Daniells is published by the University of California Press (Berkeley, CA, Los Angeles, CA & Oxford, England) (510-642-4247). Orders are handled by California Princeton Fulfillment Services, P.O. Box 10769, Newark, NJ 07193-0769. (800-822-6657). $39.95.

Career X Roads

Written by Gerry Crispin and Mark Mehler, this annual directory of job and resume sites includes specialized databases for both employers and job seekers. At $22.95 it is an extraordinary value. Contact the authors for information about seminars. Web site www.careerxroads.com.

Ordering information:

Available online or by phone from distributor Kennedy Information, One Kennedy Place, Route 12 South, Fitzwilliam, NH 03447, (800) 531-0007 or 603-585-6544, fax 603-585-9555, web site www.kennedyinfo.com. Also available through from author's web site or at your local book store.

Encyclopedia of Associations: National Organizations of the U.S.

This excellent reference is one of the first places to look when beginning a new search or when looking for specialized references. It's another one of my favorite directories. It includes organizations in these categories: business, trade, environmental, agricultural, legal, governmental, engineering, technological, scientific, educational, cultural, social welfare, health and medical, public affairs, ethnic, labor unions, chambers of commerce, tourism, and others. This encyclopedia reveals each association's:

- Publications, including membership rosters and newsletters

- Dates and locations of association conferences and conventions

- Names of Executive Directors, who are usually incredible sources of industry information

- Committees

- Job and Candidate Referral banks, which can provide resumes of other industry sources and sometimes candidates

- Web site which might possibly contain a database of association members, their resumes, and/or a job matching service, all on the Internet.

Ordering information:

Encyclopedia of Associations, National Organizations of the U.S.
Volume 1,   National Organizations of the U.S., in 3 parts, $505
Volume 2,   Geographic and Executive Indexes, $390
Volume 3,   Supplement, $405

Also available on CD ROM, online on the Internet through GaleNet, through Gale's Comercial Online product, as a Custom Edition. Call publisher for prices and a catalog or see their catalog on their web site at www.galegroup.com.

Gale Group
P.O. Box 9187
Farmington Hills, MI 48333-9187
(800) 877-GALE (4253) toll free U.S. and Canada. (248) 699-GALE
Fax (800) 414-5043 and (248) 699-8061
www.galegroup.com or www.gale.com
GaleNet web site: http://galenet.gale.com

National Trade and Professional Associations of the United States

National Trade and Professional Associations of the United States (NTPA) is another reference that identifies professional associations. It is highly recommended that both this reference and Gale's *Encyclopedia of Associations* are used "back to back" because each reference contains slightly different material. At this early stage of data gathering, this information is too important to risk being incomplete. If you're looking for hard-to-find information, it's possible that one directory will lead you to the ideal solution and the other wouldn't. Check them both to be on the safe side.

Ordering information:

National Trade and Professional Associations of the United States, $129.00
Columbia Books, Inc.
1212 New York Ave., NW, Suite 330
Washington, DC 20005
(202) 898-0662 Phone
(202) 898-0775 Fax

The Encyclopedia of Business Information Sources

The Encyclopedia of Business Information Sources is another important reference, especially if you're researching materials to include in a library for a specialized search practice or if you're a generalist beginning a search in a new field. *The Encyclopedia of Business Information Sources* will lead you to specialized directories, professional associations, trade publications, newsletters, databases, Internet resources and more. It's an excellent reference and a great way to find key resources in any industry *fast*.

Ordering Information:

Encyclopedia of Business Information Sources, $330.00
Gale Group
P.O. Box 9187
Farmington Hills, MI 48333-9187
Phone (248) 699-GALE, toll free U.S. and Canada (800) 877-GALE (4253)
Fax (800) 414-5043 and (248) 699-8061
Web site www.galegroup.com or www.gale.com.

Directories in Print

Directories in Print is another amazing reference that tells you what kinds of directories are available. Directories are listed according to subject. This publication used to be titled *The Directory of Directories* but the name has been changed.

Ordering information:

Directories in Print, $489.00
Gale Group
P.O. Box 9187
Farmington Hills, MI 48333-9187

Phone (248) 699-GALE, toll free U.S. and Canada (800) 877-GALE (4253)
Fax (800) 414-5043 and (248) 699-8061
Web site www.galegroup.com or www.gale.com.

The Guide To American Directories

The Guide To American Directories is another directory of directories. Both references should be used to assure thorough research.

Ordering information:

The Guide to American Directories. $95
B. Klein Publications
P.O. Box 6578
Delray Beach, Florida 33482
(888) 859-8083 toll free
(561) 496-3316 phone
(561) 496-5546 fax

The Gale Directory of Databases

The Gale Directory of Databases Online is a GaleNet database that identifies over 12,000 international databases in various formats, including CD ROM's and online. All types of databases are listed: directories, dictionaries, software, bibliographies, bulletin boards, and technical databases. Contact Gale for price.

Ordering information:

Gale Directory of Data Bases CD ROM Online
Gale Group
P.O. Box 9187
Farmington Hills, MI 48333-9187
Phone (248) 699-GALE, toll free U.S. and Canada (800) 877-GALE (4253)
Fax (800) 414-5043 and (248) 699-8061
www.galegroup.com or www.gale.com
GaleNet web site: http://galenet.gale.com

The Gale Directory of Databases

The Gale Directory of Databases in hard copy profiles over 10,000 databases in various formats. Each entry includes producer name and contact information, description, subject, language, update frequency, geographic coverage, availability, cost, and information on software and system requirements.

Ordering information:

Gale Directory of Data Bases
Vol. 1, *Online Databases*, $260.00
Vol. 2, *CD ROM, Diskette, Magnetic Tape, Handheld & Batch Access Database Products*, $170
Both volumes $390
Gale Group
P.O. Box 9187
Farmington Hills, MI 48333-9187
Phone (248) 699-GALE, toll free U.S. and Canada (800) 877-GALE (4253)
Fax (800) 414-5043 and (248) 699-8061
Web site www.galegroup.com or www.gale.com

Standard and Poors Register of Corporations

Dun & Bradstreet's Million Dollar Directory

Both *Standard and Poors Register of Corporations* and *Dun & Bradstreet's Million Dollar Directory* are excellent references. Basically each directory provides extensive lists of companies with names and titles of management, addresses and phone numbers. Other volumes list companies geographically and by Standard Industrial Classification (SIC). (In 1998, the U.S. Government replaced the SIC system by NAICS [North American Industry Classification System], a 6 digit code instead of 4 digits). Biographical profiles of senior management appear in another volume. If you can't find what you're looking for in one directory, try the other. Or use both in tandem, if you have time.

One of the main differences between these two directories is that the *Million Dollar Directory* lists more companies, including more smaller companies and privately held companies. If you're working in an industry where there are many privately owned businesses, the *Million Dollar Directory* might be a better resource. Contact the publishers for more information on electronic formats available.

Ordering information:

Standard and Poors Register of Corporations, $799, hard copy
Distributed by: Larry Meranus Professional Publications & Services
4 Demoray Court
Pine Brook, NJ 07058
(800) MERANUS or (800) 637-2687.

Standard and Poors
A Division of The McGraw-Hill Companies
25 Broadway
New York, New York 10004
(212) 438-2000

Million Dollar Directory
Dun & Bradstreet
Three Sylvan Way, Parsippany, NJ 07054-3896
(800) 526-0651, (201) 605-6713 (Business Reference Solutions, U.S. Sales)

The North American Industry Classification System (NAICS) Manual

The *North American Industry Classification System (NAICS) Manual* now replaces the *Standard Industrial Classification (SIC) Manual.* Last revised in 1987, The SIC Manual is still available in most business libraries. An SIC is a 4 digit number that serves as a "shorthand" for a specific industry. It identifies in detail the composition of each and every SIC code, including products manufactured and specific services provided. Historically this fundamental reference has been important in researching companies by SIC because abbreviated lists of SIC codes, such as those which appear in *Standard and Poors* or *Dun & Bradstreet's Million Dollar Directory Series,* didn't always provide the level of detail needed. Until 1998 the *SIC Manual* had been published by The National Technical Information Service, formerly the U.S. Government Printing Office. NTIS is the central source for government sponsored U.S. and worldwide scientific, engineering and business related information. As a self-supporting agency of the U.S. Department of Commerce's Technology Administration, NTIS covers its business and operating expenses with the sale of its products and services.

NAICS is the first North American industry classification system. It was developed by the U.S., Canada and Mexico to provide comparable statistics for all three countries. This will allow government and business analysts to uniformly compare industrial production statistics in the three North American Free Trade Agreement (NAFTA) countries. NAICS also provides for increased comparability with the International Standard Industrial Classification System (ISIC), developed and maintained by the United Nations.

Unlike the SIC codes, which are 4 digits, the NAICS codes are 6 digits. The first 5 digits are standardized among the U.S., Canada and Mexico. However, the 6th digit may differ from country to country to accommodate different needs in individual countries. NAICS will be reviewed every five years, so classifications and information will stay current with the economy. For more information, contact the Bureau of the Census Official NAICS web page at www.census.gov/naics or send your questions by email to info@ntis.fedworld.gov.

Ordering information:

Softcover version, NTIS Order Number PB98-136187INQ, $28.50, $57 outside the U.S., Canada and Mexico. Hardcover NTIS Order Number PB98-127293, $32.50, $65 outside the U.S., Canada and Mexico. CD ROM Order Number PB98-502024, single user $45, 90 outside the U.S., Canada and Mexico. Up to 5 concurrent network users $120, $240 outside the U.S., Canada and Mexico. Unlimited concurrent network users $240, $480 outside the U.S., Canada and Mexico. CD ROM includes a search capability that includes access to more index entries than appear in the manual plus downloadable files.

Handling charge is additional.

National Technical Information Service
Technology Administration
U.S. Department of Commerce
5285 Port Royal Road, Springfield, VA 22161
(800) 553-NTIS (6487) or (703) 605-6000
Fax (703) 321-8547
www.ntis.gov/.
Email: info@ntis.fedworld.gov

The Standard Directory of Advertisers

The Standard Directory of Advertisers is another general directory which can be used the same way as *Standard and Poors Register of Corporations* and *The Million Dollar Directory,* with a few added bonuses.

The Classified Edition of *The Standard Directory of Advertisers* is especially helpful. It groups companies according to product category. Examples of some classifications are "Apparel 2 – Men's and Boys' Wear," "Heating and Air Conditioning," "Cosmetics and Toiletries," and "Aviation and Aerospace." The Classified Edition of *The Standard Directory of Advertisers* can be a very convenient source of research because both your target list of companies and the corresponding names and titles of management all appear together, in the same Classification. This is important if you must ever rely on research books in hard copy.

The Standard Directory of Advertisers also publishes a special volume called *The Standard Directory of Advertisers Tradename Index.* You can use the *Tradename Index* if you know the brand name of a product and need to find the company that manufactures it.

Call about availability on CD ROM and price.

Ordering information:
The Standard Directory of Advertisers, Classified Edition, $629.95
National Register Publishing

Reed Elsevier – New Providence
121 Chanlon Road, New Providence, NJ 07974
(800) 521-8110
(908) 464-6800
(908) 665-6688 to place an order
Fax (800) 836-7736
www.redbooks.com or www.marquiswhoswho.com

Note: The publisher's catalog states, "If you're dissatisfied for any reason, simply return the product within 30 days for a full refund." If the price is prohibitively high, remember your local library.

The Directory of Corporate Affiliations

The Directory of Corporate Affiliations or *Who Owns Whom* provides detailed information about the subsidiaries and divisions of companies, such as plant locations, joint ventures, a brief description of the subsidiary or division, a partial listing of names and titles, location, phone number, and sometimes revenues or number of employees.[1] It's an excellent reference. In fact it's one of my favorites.

The Directory of Corporate Affiliations consists of 5 volumes, including U.S. companies, both publicly and privately held, foreign companies, both publicly and privately held, and indices. It also has a **Brand Name Index.**

Ordering information:

Directory of Corporate Affiliations or Who Owns Whom, $1,029.95/5 volumes
National Register Publishing
Reed Elsevier – New Providence
121 Chanlon Road, New Providence, NJ 07974
(800) 521-8110
(908) 464-6800
(908) 665-6688 to place an order
Fax (800) 836-7736
www.redbooks.com or www.marquiswhoswho.com

---

1 FREE INFORMATION

If *The Directory of Corporate Affiliations* does not provide all the information you want and the company is privately held, there's plenty of free information available! Just call the company and ask for the annual report and the 10(k) report. Or check their web site. If a company is publicly held (in other words, if you can buy their stock), the Securities and Exchange Commission (SEC) requires, as a matter of law, that every year each company publishes an Annual Report, 10(k) Report and a Proxy Statement. They're outstanding sources of information about divisions and subsidiaries, strategy, future plans, finances, organizational structure, backgrounds of top management (the 10(k) even reveals their ages), and litigation that could materially affect the company's financial performance. As a matter of law, the proxy statement even reveals the compensation of the 4 highest paid executives in the company! You can find out whether the company has an 800 number by calling toll free information (800-555-1212). You can also look up the phone number in one of these directories:

Standard and Poors Register of Corporations

Dun and Bradstreet's Million Dollar Directory

The Standard Directory of Advertisers

National Directory of Addresses and Telephone Numbers

In addition, most privately held companies will also send information if you ask for it.

Publisher's catalog states, "If you're dissatisfied for any reason, simply return the product within 30 days for a full refund." If the price is prohibitively high, remember your local library.

The Directory of Corporate Affiliations is also available in CD-ROM and online through Knight-Ridder Information's DIALOG Service. For more information, call (800) 334-2564 or (800) 3-DIALOG.

HOW TO DEVELOP A LIBRARY FOR A SPECIALIZED SEARCH PRACTICE

If your specialty is technology, you should be familiar with *The CorpTech Directory of Technology Companies*. It's available in hard copy, Regional Guides, on PC floppy diskette, and on CD ROM. *CorpTech EXPLORE Database* is an outstanding reference that was awarded Best CD-ROM Directory by the National Directory Publishing Association. One click moves you from the CD ROM Database to Internet information on the same company. *CorpTech* also provides other sophisticated but reasonably priced automated services (and quantity discounts) with their customized data-on-demand service, which uses up to 30 search parameters. You can save a tremendous amount of time researching relatively small, emerging new companies in various high technology niches and obtain names, titles and even mailing address labels. If *CorpTech* is too expensive to purchase, go to the library.

Ordering information:

CorpTech
Corporate Technology Information Services, Inc.
12 Alfred Street, Suite 200
Woburn, MA 01801-1915
(800) 333-8036
(781) 932-3100
(781) 932-3939
Fax (781) 932-6335
Email: sales@corptech.com
http://www.corptech.com

CorpTech EXPLORE Silver Database CD ROM, $2,495, (including free soft cover CorpTech Directory worth $745).

CorpTech EXPLORE Gold Database CD ROM, $5,995 offers an export capability, extended company history and has hyperlinks to news services to aid company research, such as Reuters and PR Newswire. Both Silver and Gold CD's have links to company web sites.

CorpTech print directories are available for $795 hard cover, $745 soft cover.

CorpTech regional directories are available in print for $225 (soft cover only). Regional Explore Gold CD's are $995 each and Explore Silver are $795 each.

Industry specific products segmented into 17 different industries are also available on CD ROM. Each industry costs $995, except computer software, which is very large and counts as two industries. The 17 industry segments are: factory automation, biotechnology, chemicals, computer hardware, defense, energy, environmental, manufacturing, advanced materials, medical, pharmaceuticals, photonics, computer software, subassemblies and components, test and measurement companies, telecommunications & Internet, and transportation.

* * * * *

Regardless of your specialty, you can find virtually every directory and membership roster in your niche by using the librarian's references discussed in this chapter. Additional references and web sites are identified in Part II of this book, "The Recruiter's Directory of Directories – Plus Web Sites, Databases & CD ROM's."

In addition to finding resources by looking them them up in a directory or on the Internet, you can call knowledgeable people who can help you. First, identify contacts in the appropriate industries and functions, such as in the *Encyclopedia of Associations, Business Information Sources* (Daniells) and the *Encyclopedia of Business Information Sources*. Then, call these contacts and ask them to recommend web sites, directories, trade journals, CD ROM's, and other people you should contact.

- Look up specialized directories listed in the librarians' references listed in this chapter.

- Use the librarians' references to identify trade organizations and trade publications.

- Go to a large business library and examine the appropriate references.

- While you're at the library in person, ask the librarian for recommendations.

- Call other librarians and ask for recommendations for your collection, such as:

  - a business reference librarian at a public library

  - the head librarian at a corporation that's an industry leader

  - a professor at a graduate school of Library Science

  - a business reference librarian at a graduate school of business, such as Harvard or Stanford

  - a librarian at a large professional association. For more information, contact the American Library Association (ALA), 50 East Huron Street, Chicago, IL 60611, (800) 545-2433; (800) 545-2444 in Illinois; (800) 545-2455 in Canada; or the Special Libraries Association (SLA) which includes business libraries. Special Libraries Association, 1700 18th Street, NW, Washington, DC 20009, (202) 234-4700.

- As you are looking for libraries to visit, in addition to public libraries, remember that these types of organizations often have libraries: universities, graduate schools of business, corporations, banks and investment banks, professional associations, outplacement firms, chambers of commerce, embassies and consulates, The Conference Board in New York City and the government.

- Ask your friends – and their friends – and other contacts in the industry what professional associations they belong to, what trade papers they're familiar with, and whether they know about any directories or web sites.

Keep asking for information and you will eventually uncover virtually everything available in your specialized niche. You'll know when you're finished because you'll continuously be referred to the same information again and again.

COMPANY INFORMATION

The third element of your library is company information. You should **cross reference** select information and file it in your Company Files. If you're a specialist and frequently recruit from the same company, you might want to keep copies (of names and titles) from multiple directories in one file for that company. This information could be obtained from a directory, such as *Standard and Poors Register of Corporations*, either CD ROM or a print out. Other information for a company file could include ID Research, or hard copy of appropriate information on a company web site, including names, titles, biographies and even photographs; and top management's biographical data that the government requires be included in all 10(k) reports. This way you'll conveniently have a lot of information about important target companies in one place. Again, this should be done selectively because it might not be a good use of your time to do it for every single company.

A great deal of information is available in additional sources, such as:

- Company alumni directories

- Company telephone directories, if you are able to obtain them

- Company newsletters, if it's possible to obtain copies

- College and university alumni newspapers

- Trade journal announcements of promotions, job changes and company changes, including the *New York Times,* "Who's News" in the *Wall Street Journal* and other major papers

- Lists of attendees at conferences, assuming there's enough information to make it easy to locate and contact the desired individuals

- Information from computerized searches of newspaper and trade journal articles. Your local business reference librarian can guide you in conducting these automated searches. Be sure to ask about ABI Inform, InfoTrak, Lexis, Nexis, and web sites, such as www.cnn.com, www.nytimes.com, www.latimes.com and www.wsj.com *(CNN, The New York Times, The Los Angeles Times* and *The Wall Street Journal).* When you ask for help, make sure you let the librarian know specifically why you need the information, because he or she may know some good shortcuts or new references.

- If you have time, experiment with the Ask Jeeves web site at www.askjeeves.com or www.ask.com or www.aj.com or ask.

- While it may be very time consuming, you may wish to check search engines, such as Yahoo at www.yahoo.com or excite at www.excite.com. For a listing of search engine URL's, refer to the "Search Engines" category in Part II of this book, "The Recruiter's Directory of Directories – Plus Web Sites, Databases & CD ROM's."

INDUSTRY AND FUNCTION FILES

Industry and function files are the fourth element of your library. You might find good research when you least expect it, perhaps browsing on the Internet or a newspaper, magazine, conference flyer, theater program, on movie credits or even an invitation to a fund raising event. It might quote important industry sources, list names and titles, or be "Top 10" or "The 100 Largest" surveys, such as:

- The top research analysts on Wall Street

- The best chief financial officers in the United States

- The leading manufacturers of specialty chemicals, commercial stoves, or any other product

- Companies that are the most savvy users of technology

- The most successful manufacturers, designers or retailers of the season's hottest fashions

- Organizations noted for their progressive human resources policies and practices

- The highest return on assets ratios, etc.

- The highest ratios of sales to research and development expenditures

- The best paid CEO's in America

- The 10 worst managed companies in the country

Naturally, anytime this information crosses your path, you should save it for your library files. Remember, "There's no such thing as a coincidence," because the moment you throw one of these lists out, you'll need it!

The best way to set up industry and function files is to keep it simple. It could mean using one or two filing cabinet drawers. You might also have ancillary information in the computer. It's generally advisable to keep "industry" files together with "function" files. This way you only have to look for information in one place instead of two.

Sometimes using a computer is overkill because it's easier to put an article or top 100 list into a file folder than to use the computer. A filing cabinet might even be easier than using a CD ROM because then you won't have to search the CD to find the article. Remember, old technology is not necessarily bad technology. It's just old. Some things get old because they were good enough to last a long time. Then they become classics! In any case, whether you decide to use a manual system or a computer system or both together, remember the KISS principle – Keep It Simple, Stupid.

The important thing is to be able to find information when you need it. Because if you can't, the information is useless.

This could mean putting one piece of paper in a file folder, such as the title page of a directory. Or place a hand written note in one file to cross reference where a survey is filed, especially if it is appropriate for several areas. There are 3 things to remember whenever you do this:

1. Use a large piece of paper, 8-1/2" x 11". Otherwise, it could get lost. It doesn't matter if there are only a few words on it. If you can't find the note when you need it, it might as well not be there.

2. Get in the habit of dating every piece of paper you put in the file. In fact, get in the habit of dating every piece of paper you use during a search.

3. Always include the year as part of the date.

A few final comments about your classification system for industry and function files are in order. Finance can be considered both an industry and a function. Depending on how much work you do in the area, it might be appropriate to break down this category into more specialized components, such as "Financial Function – Chief Financial Officers, Controllers, Treasurers," "Banking – Investment," "Banking – Investment, International," or "Banking – Commercial," to name just a few areas. The finance industry is huge and it may be appropriate to have many narrow, specific categories. The same can be said of many other areas, such as technology, electronics, information technology, or marketing. Further, certain functions vary widely from one industry to another, for example research or operations. Your particular needs will depend on how much you specialize in a given area.

A Good Rule of Thumb

Generally speaking, information more than two years old has limited value. In fact, a directory or any names and titles that are two years old are so hard to work with, it's usually more cost-efficient to buy new information or to start doing new ID research from scratch. This is because so many people will have changed jobs and it's very time consuming to locate them. Sometimes locating a current title and phone number can only be achieved after expending a *ridiculous* amount of time, far more than should be devoted to such an effort, especially when you consider the hourly value of a researcher's time.

However, before you decide to throw out an old list, publication or CD ROM, consider keeping it around so that you will have enough information to track down a new, updated list next time you need one. If you're cleaning files, make sure you keep a few pages of information, printed out from a CD or photocopied from a print reference, such as:

- the table of contents

- the title page

- publisher, address, phone number, web site

- sample of one or two pages that show what kind of information the resource contains

- Web site URL, if applicable

Be judicious about discarding everything! In other words, be sure you keep enough information around so you won't have to completely research the same thing from scratch again – like the name and publisher of a terrific directory, or the URL of a free online association membership list.

Target lists are another matter. For one thing, they don't become outdated as quickly. They can also be recycled, in whole or in part, for similar searches. Just be sure to double check that none of the companies have merged or have new parents companies. Also, if you had to do original research in order to invent an exotic target list – because nothing similar had ever been published – do save that. It takes very little space anyway.

PERSONAL CONTACTS DATABASE

Last but not least is the fifth element of your library, personal contacts.

The truth is, you never know whether you'll find the successful candidate through research or through a personal referral. In fact, sometimes you'll be surprised that the opposite of what you expect is what actually materializes. Therefore, it's important to cover both avenues – personal contacts and research.

Sometimes your industry contacts will be very knowledgeable about associations, directories, and special surveys in trade publications. Even so, it's best to rely on doing thorough research yourself. If you do good research, you'll soon sound very knowledgeable about the industry and will project an aura of credibility, which is important.

Sourcing well placed contacts is very important in conducting a search. If you don't already have a database, you will probably be developing one. For further discussion, see chapter 16, "'Setting up a Database – Garbage in, Garbage Out'."

Conclusion

In summary, the following reference materials, either in hard copy or electronic formats, provide the backbone for a generalist search library.

- ❑ *Business Information Sources* by Lorna Daniells

- ❑ *Encyclopedia of Associations*

- ❑ *National Trade and Professional Associations of the United States*

- ❑ *Career X Roads* by Gerry Crispin and Mark Mehler

- ❑ *The Encyclopedia of Business Information Sources*

- ❑ *Directories in Print*

- ❑ *The Guide to American Directories*

- ❑ *The Gale Directory of Databases*

- ❑ *Standard and Poors Register of Corporations*

- ❑ *Dun & Bradstreet Million Dollar Directory*

- ❑ *Standard Industrial Classification Manual*

- ❑ *Standard Directory of Advertisers*

- ❑ *Directory of Corporate Affiliations*

- ❑ and optionally *CorpTech Directory of Technology Companies*

To identify appropriate references for a specialist recruiting library, conduct research using the following resources. Be sure to check Part II of this book, "The Recruiter's Directory of Directories – Plus Web Sites, Databases & CD ROM's" for additional materials.

- ❑ *Business Information Sources* by Lorna Daniells

- ❑ *Career X Roads* by Gerry Crispin and Mark Mehler

- ❑ *Encyclopedia of Associations*

- ❑ *National Trade and Professional Associations of the United States*

- ❑ *The Encyclopedia of Business Information Sources*

- ❑ *Directories in Print*

- ❑ *The Guide to American Directories*

- ❑ *The Gale Directory of Databases*

CHAPTER 7

This chapter is organized into three major sections. The first is Major Internet Web Sites for Recruiters and Researchers. At the end it lists search engine URLs and the web sites for all the specialized trade journals published by the excellent publisher, Crain Communications. The second section is "Web Sites to Publishers of Directories and Databases and Related Web Sites." The third section is "Books of Web sites."

1. Major Internet Web Sites for Recruiters and Researchers

Here is a good cross section of URL's (Uniform Resource Locators) for company recruiters, executive search and unbundled search professionals and contingency recruiters and personnel agencies:

www.abbott.com/career/index.htm – This is the URL for the Career Pages for Abbott Laboratories. Their main web site is http://www.abbot.com. Check the sites of other companies for additional career opportunities.

www.airsdirectory.com – This is the URL for AIRS – Advanced Internet Recruitment Strategies. AIRS is a firm which provides training for recruiters who use the Internet as a recruiting tool. For more information contact AIRS, 1790 Franklin Street, Berkeley, CA 94702, phone (800) 336-6360, fax (888) 997-5559. Their web site contains many excellent free helpful resources.

www.amazon.com – This is the web site for a large online bookstore which gives discounts.

www.asianet.com – This site matches Pacific Rim positions with individuals who speak Asian languages.

www.askjeeves.com or **www.ask.com** or **www.aj.com** – Ask Jeeves a question. For example, if you ask Jeeves, "How can I find a job?" or "How can I find candidates for an engineering job?" Jeeves has an answer! Actually, there's very little you can't ask Jeeves. This web site can also be used for targeted email. How-to details are discussed in *The Internet Recruiting Edge* by Barbara Ling @ http://www.barbaraling.com.

www.asktheheadhunter.com – This is the web site for the book, *Ask The Headhunter,* a book that can effectively be used by both job hunters and interviewers, by Nick Corcodilos, email northbridge@sprintmail.com. According to Tom Peters, it is "a powerful hiring tool no manager can afford to miss" and it "shreds some of our most basic assumptions about the way to hire top people." Published by Penguin Putnam, New York, $14.95, the book is available from the web site and at bookstores. Corcodilos and his client, Merrill Lynch's Vice President of Global Staffing, were jointly featured in a discussion about changes in corporate recruiting and hiring practices in a segment on "Opportunity Knocks," a CNBC special on Executive Search. To purchase this 5 hour video, contact CNBC or Corcodilos.

www.aviationtoday.com – This is the web site for *Phillips Aviation Today,* published by Phillips Business Information, Inc., A Phillips Publishing International Company, 120 Seven Locks Road, Potomac, MD 20854, (301) 340-1520, (301) 340-7788, (800) 777-5006, Internet pbi@phillips.com, web site www.phillips.com.

www.barbaraling.com – This is the web site for the book *The Internet Recruiting Edge* by Barbara Ling. Linked to this site is AIRS, a collection of Internet recruiting tools and recruiting seminars; and author Bill Radin's site.

www.bookwire.com – For information about publishing and research, the *Publishers Weekly* web site at http://www.bookwire.com serves consumers and publishing professionals. Bowker's *Publishers Weekly's* web site includes a searchable database of current author tour information, links to all book-related web sites, Industry Classifieds, and Book Wire Insider Direct, a subscription daily e-mail news service, and more.

www.boston.com – This is the site for the *Boston Globe's* online access to their newspaper ads.

www.bowker.com – This large research publisher's web site includes an online product catalog, ordering information, electronic publishing, Internet databases, CD ROM's, online subscription and site licensing databases, press releases, career opportunities, and more. Many of their references are accessible through this web site, such as *Books in Print Plus Canadian Edition, Ulrich's on Disc, German Books In Print, German Books Out of Print, International Books in Print PLUS, Italian Books in Print, Yearbook of International Organizations PLUS, Ulrich's International Periodicals Directory, The Software Encyclopedia, Bowker's Complete Video Directory, American Book Publishing Record.* Visit the web site for more information.

www.businessweek.com/careers/right.htm – *Business Week's* Internet Career Center offers a free, confidential service for job seekers, advertising that's cheaper than a want ad, and a job posting service if you're an employer.

www.career.com – Career.com links employers and candidates throughout the world. Heart's goals for www.career.com are to provide *free* job seeker assistance and to offer employers an effective way to reach qualified job seekers. Most positions are in Engineering, IT and marketing and usually range between $30,000 and $75,000. The site was launched in 1993 and developed by Heart Advertising Network, Los Altos, California.

www.careermag.com – A comprehensive site for both recruiters and job seekers, including articles for job hunters, on campus, diversity and funny work stores sent in by readers.

www.careermosaic.com – Career Mosaic is a major recruitment web site that spends millions of dollars in advertising to draw traffic to this site. CareerMosaic features a jobs database; newsgroups for jobs, college connection, online job fairs, employer job postings; company information and more. CareerMosaic was ranked as one of the top five "Sites Offering the Best Overall Support for Job Seekers" by the *National Business Employment Weekly*. The site was developed by Bernard Hodes Advertising in New York and went online in 1994.

www.careerpath.com – This site was ranked as one of the top five "Sites Offering the Best Overall Support for Job-Seekers" by the *National Business Employment Weekly*. CareerPath.com puts the help wanted sections of over 70 U.S. newspapers into one database. Job hunters can post their resumes *free*. Companies must pay a fee to access resumes. The web site claims, "Powered by the nation's leading newspapers and employers, CareerPath.com has the Web's largest number of the most current job listings." Launched in 1995, the site was developed by a consortium of media companies – Knight-Ridder, The New York Times, the Time Mirror Company, the Tribune Company, the Washington Post, Cox Interactive Media, Gannett Company and Hearst Corp.

www.careers.computerworld.com – This is a computer industry career web site.

www.careers.wsj.com – This *Wall Street Journal* web site includes Job Seek, Who's Hiring, Career Columnists, Salaries & Profiles, The Salary Calculator™, Job Hunting Advice, Succeeding at Work, HR Issues, Executive Recruiters, Working Globally, College Connection, Starting a Business, Career Bookstore and more.

www.careerxroads.com – This is the web site for the book *CareerXRoads* by Gerry Crispin and Mark Mehler. It is a directory to the best job, resume and career management sites on the world wide web.

www.ceweekly.com – This site for *Contract Employment Weekly* lists engineering and information systems positions, for both recruiters and job seekers. Contract Employment Weekly Online is a service of C.E. Publications, Inc., P.O. Box 3006, Bothell, WA 98041-3006. (425) 806-5200, Fax (425) 806-5585, email publisher@ceweekly.com.

www.clickit.com – "Access Business Online" Brings Buyers and Sellers Together on the Internet, including Executive Job Network, Capital Sources, Trade Announcements, Professional Services, Top 100 World Business Charts, International Buyer-Seller, Company Profiles, BizWiz! Search Engine, Web Emporium Web Site Development, Classifieds, Corporate News Net, Wall Street and World Wide Finance, Market News & Business Connections, and more.

www.cnn.com – CNN's impressive web site contains Big Yellow Search Books to find Businesses, people, global directories and The Directory Store™. It also contains a "search the net" capability with InfoSeek. InfoSeek has a Business Channel with business resources and small businesses and a Careers Channel.

www.cyberhound.com – This is the site to CYBERHOUND® ONLINE, a guide to finding and retrieving significant sites on the Internet. It has a search engine and 75 search delimiters. It adds thousands of site reviews monthly. Visit the site to try it out free. For more information, call the Gale Group at (800) 877-GALE.

www.datamation.com – This winner of the Jesse H. Neal Award is a web site for IT executives and professionals. Provides targeted daily computer news, IT Executive Job Pavilion, Management Benchmarking Application (MBA), technology workbench, back issues from Datamation and comprehensive links to IT vendors and other online resources. It is a Cahners Business Information web site.

www.dbm.com/jobguide – This is the web site of DBM, an outplacement firm. It is "the best Internet recruiting starting point" according to the Tiburon Group, a Chicago based firm that provides "Strategic Internet Recruiting Solutions Consultants and Trainers." Tiburon Group, phone (773) 907-8330, Fax (773) 907-9481, email getajob@tiburongroup.com, web site www.tiburongroup.com.

www.decalumni.com – This is the web site for alumni of Digital Equipment Corp. It includes a directory.

www.the-dma.or – This is the site of the Direct Marketing Association, 1120 Avenue of the Americas, New York, NY 10036-6700, (212) 768-7277, fax (212) 302-6714. It features the DMA Job Bank, Online Bookstore, Seminars, Conferences. Their membership directory is available to members.

www.eagleview.com – Eagleview presents Select Candidate™ Network for job seekers and employers and other information for Data General alumni.

www.ectoday.com – This is the web site that contains the latest electronic commerce industry news. For more information, contact: Phillips Business Information, Inc., A Phillips Publishing International Company, 120 Seven Locks Road, Potomac, MD 20854, (301) 340-1520, (301) 340-7788, (800) 777-5006, Internet pbi@phillips.com, web site www.phillips.com.

www.ejobs.com – This is a job site for positions in high technology, electronics and semiconductors.

www.electronic-jobs.com – This is another job site for positions in technology, electronics and semiconductors.

www.emheadlines.com – This site is an entertainment business headline news service from Cahners Business Information. It covers Film, Television, Books, Technology, Music, Nielsen Ratings, Domestic Box Office, Bestseller List.

www.emory.edu/CAREER/index.html – This is Emory University's Career Paradise web site, with modules for alumni, students and employers.

www.espan.com – E-Span's web site includes "The Right Person for the Job" and "The Right Job for the Person," job listings, resume posting, career library, job match downloading and more.

www.europages.com – This is the site to a business directory of over 500,000 European firms in Deutsch, English, Espanol, Français & Italiano. Modules include Search for Companies, Company Catalogues, Business Information, Yellow Pages in Europe, Search by Product/Service, Thematic Search or by Company Name. Other information includes address, phone, fax, products, turnover, Europages' Daily Business News, European trade fairs, Chambers of Commerce in Europe, European patent offices, Official international organisations, and European standardization bodies.

www.excite.com – This URL contains a search engine and an excellent career site.

www.execunet.com – Exec-U-Net is a subscription service, listing executive level positions by search firms and a few companies for positions at $100,000 or more. Candidates tend to be high quality, perhaps because of the cost.

www.galegroup.com – This is the web site to publisher Gale Group, formerly Gale Research, one of the largest providers of research references serving the search industry, recruiting and libraries. At the time of this writing, the predecessor web site for Gale Research, www.gale.com, contains different information from www.galegroup.com.

www.gale.com – This is the original web site to publisher Gale Research, prior to their merger with Information Access Company and Primary Source Media which resulted in the company's name changing to The Gale Group.

www.galenet.gale.com – This is the web site used to access Gale Group's directories, for a fee.

www.helpwanted.co – This is a web site for free posting and searching of all content for job seekers, employers and agencies.

www.iccweb.com – This is the site to Internet Career Connection, an employment matching service, including Federal Government employment.

www.infousa.com – This is the web site to a free national phone directory from SelectPhone, a CD ROM phone directory produced by Pro CD, Inc., Omaha, Nebraska.

www.interbiznet.com/hrstart.html – This is the URL to the Electronic Recruiting News web site. It includes the Recruiters Internet Survival Guide and recruiting seminars information.

www.jobhunt.com – JOBHUNT is a Meta-list of On-line Job-Search Resources and Services for recruiters and jobhunters. It includes: The Online Career Center, Career Mosaic, Career Net, Job Web, Standard Job Hunt List, Americas Job Bank, Best Jobs in the USA, Career Web, College Grad Job Hunter, JobOptions (www.joboptions.com, formerly E-span Interactive Employment Network), Job Trak, The Internet Job Locator, The Monster Board, Virtual Job Fair. It also offers the capability of searching by state and local newspapers. New Items (less than a week old) are highlighted, as are "Outstanding Job Resources."

www.job-hunt.org – This site provides on-line job search resources and services identifies jobs resources and ranks the outstanding ones. It is linked to Career Paradise of Emory University

Career Center (www.emory.edu/CAREER/index.html), featuring a "Colossal List" or Career Links and Hiring Express pages. It's given high marks for both its content and humorous presentation.

www.jobnet.org – This Canadian web site includes "Looking for a career in financial services?" Scotiabank online recruiting, Jobnet and Alumnet.

www.jobtrak.com – Jobtrak is a career service network for college students, alumni, college career staff and employers. JOBTRAK CORPORATION, Los Angeles, CA, (310) 474-3377, (800) 999-8725, fax (310) 475-7912.

www.kennedyinfo.com – The web site of publisher Kennedy Information (Fitzwilliam, New Hampshire) includes newsletters, books, research reports, training materials, directories, and surveys for executive recruiting, human resources, outplacement, management consulting and executive job seekers. Resources include *Executive Recruiter News, Recruiting Trends, The Directory of Executive Recruiters, The International Directory of Executive Recruiters, The Directory of Legal Recruiters, The Directory of Outplacement Firms, The Directory of Temporary Placement Firms for Executives, Managers and Professionals* and Executive Recruiters' Bookstore. (800) 531-0007, (603) 585-6544.

www.kompass.com – Kompass's web site contains a searchable database that encompasses over 60 countries, 2.5 million executive names, information on 1.5 million companies, 19 million key product references, and 370,000 trade and brand names. At the time of this writing, Kompass is available in English and French. Deutsch, Espanol and Italiano will soon be available.

www.latimes.com – This is the URL to the comprehensive *Los Angeles Times* web site.

www.mediacorp2.com/ – This is the site to *Canada Employment Weekly*. It includes The Career Bookstore for Canadian career books, Talent Available to market yourself to Canadian recruiters and search firms, Canadian Directory of Search Firms, and Who's Hiring for a list of Canada's top employers. www.mediacorp2.com/cds/findex.html sells the *Canadian Directory of Search Firms*, in French and English. It contains over 1,700 search firms and 3,000 recruitment professionals, 70 occupational categories, a geographic index, and a Who's Who Index. $39.95, ISBN 0-9681447-1-3. To locate the *Canadian Directory of Search Firms*, go to www.netjobs.com. Send questions or comments to info@netjobs.com, NetJobs Information Services @JOBNET, 103 Wright Street, Richmond Hill, ON L4C 4A3, CANADA, (800) 367-6563 or (905) 770-0829, fax (905) 770-5024.

www.monster.com – This is the URL for the popular Monster Board web site. The Monster Board was ranked as one of the top 5 "Best General-Purpose Sites" by *National Business Employment Weekly*. It is a major recruitment web site that spends millions of dollars in advertising to attract traffic to this site. Features include Job search in the U.S., International or by Companies, Career Center Events, Recruiters' Center, Seminars, Post a Job, *free* online recruitment seminar. It also offers special links for human resources, health care, technology and entry level positions. Toll free phone number (800) MONSTER. The Monster Board, PO Box 586, Framingham, MA 01704-0586. The site developer is TMP Worldwide, New York, New York and has been online since 1994.

www.monsterhr.com – This is the site to the Monster Board: Human Resources careers on the web. Enter your job profile and have job listings automatically downloaded to your Email. International opportunities in Canada are classified by Canada overall, then Alberta, British Columbia, Newfoundland, Ontario and Quebec.

www.nationjob.com – Nationjob Network Online Jobs Database offers "Search for a Job Now (no email required)," "Search for a Company" and "Directory of all Companies." P.J. Scout service is a "(P) ersonal (J)ob Scout service that's "like having a friend shop for a job for you." Fill in a form and PJ will send you information on jobs you might be interested in. Information on salary comparisons, moving costs, relocation information, insurance calculator and more. NationJob Inc., 601 SW 9th Street, Suites J&K, Des Moines, IA 50309, (800) 292-7731.

www.nehra.com – This is the URL to the Northeast Human Resources Association's web site.

www.netjobs.com – This site is reportedly Canada's premiere employment web site. It includes Internet Career Centre for employers and job seekers. Overseas Jobs Express, Personal Computer Training. Email info@netjobs.com. Linked to www.jobnet.org.

www.netshare.com – This is the URL for NETSHARE 2000, a confidential for-fee career management service designed for executives, companies and recruiters that posts senior level positions on the Internet daily. Salary usually exceeds $100,000 but is sometimes in the $75,000 range. Their ad claims, "A best search site"...*FORTUNE Magazine* and "Best of the Best"...*CareerXRoads*. NETSHARE 2000 was developed by Netshare, Inc., Novato, California and went online in 1995. (800) 241-5642, email netshare@netshare.com.

www.nytimes.com – This is *The New York Times* web site.

www.occ.com – This is the URL for the On Line Career Center, one of the Internet's first online recruitment sites, launched in 1993. It is a major recruitment web site that spends millions of dollars in advertising to drive traffic to the site. This is a major site that was developed by William O Warren, who has received honors for his pioneering work in the development of Internet Recruiting. This web site allows you to enter your job profile and have job listings automatically downloaded to your Email. Send questions to webmaster@occ.com. www.occ.com was rated by the National Business Employment Weekly as one of the top 5 sites in 3 different categories: "Sites Offering the Best Overall Support for Job Seekers," "Sites Offering the Best Job-Search Support" and "Sites Offering the Best Career Resources for Job Seekers." Openings are mainly in engineering, information technology and sales and marketing. The site developer is TMP Worldwide, New York, New York.

www.reedref.com – This site presents a current catalog for all Reed Reference Publishing companies for both print and electronic references for National Register Publishing, R.R. Bowker, Bowker-Saur, KG Saur, Marquis Who's Who, Martindale-Hubbell and Lexis-Nexis Business Information. At the time of this writing, this catalog is searchable by name, subject, publisher and keyword. To check new offerings, visit individual publisher pages. *Free product demos* of CD ROM's can be downloaded for for experimentation and some sample pages – and even entire chapters – and are available for unlimited viewing. The web site also includes a constantly updated menu of special discounts which are available only on the web site. Ask about the growing number of RRP databases accessible via the Internet on subscription or for a usage based price, such as the *Martindale-Hubbell Law Directory*. For more information visit Bowker Reed Reference's web site at www.reedref.com or www.bowker.com or contact corporate offices, 121 Chanlon Road, New Providence, NJ 07974, (800) 521-8110, (800) 323-3288, Fax (908) 665-3528.

www.ritesite.com – This is the web site to the book, *Rites of Passage at $100,000+* by John Lucht.

www.rtp.org – This is the home page for Research Triangle Park, North Carolina including a directory of companies in the Park. Includes listing of companies according to research specialization, appropriate for target list development.

www.sec.gov/edgarhp.htm – This is the site to the EDGAR Database of corporate information from the Securities & Exchange Commission database of corporate information. It contains About the SEC, Investor Assistance & Complaints, EDGAR Database, SEC Digest & Statements,

Current SEC Rulemaking, Enforcement Division, Small Business Information, Other Sites to Visit.

www.shrm.org/jobs/ – The Society for Human Resource Management site is linked to www.career.mosaic./com. It also includes Membership Directory Online, which only can be accessed by members.

www.sireport.com – This is the site to the Staffing Industry Report.

www.technicalrecruiter.com – This is an excellent starting point for a large number of specialized sites, such as ProjectManager.com and SoftwareEngineer.com.

www.thomasregister.com – This site provides information on U.S. and Canadian manufacturing firms.

www.tiburongroup.com – This is the web site to the Tiburon Group in Chicago, an Internet Recruitment Training and Strategy firm, which is affiliated with the respected AIRS group. They are also a recruiting firm. Phone (773) 907-8330, Fax (773) 907-9481, email getajob@tiburongroup.com.

www.townline.com/working/ – This site encompasses job listings from 113 community newspapers. It also has job profiles that can automatically be downloaded to your email.

www.wageweb.com – This is the site to the Salary Survey Data Online.

www.washingtonpost.com – The Washington Post's web site contains excellent career resources.

www.world.hire.com – World Hire Online is a web site with job listings mainly in engineering, information technology and "senior management," usually in the $50,000 to $100,000 range. The site was developed by World.Hire, Austin, Texas and was launched in 1996. World Hire also features a Job profile notification and the Recruiter™ web site product. Some sample recruiter sites include www.coastalcorp.com, www.eds.com, www.ibm.com.

www.web sitez.com – This is the URL to a web site that assists in finding any web address in the world.

www.whois.net – This site can help you find your own domain or look up a web site.

www.yahoo.com – This site contains an excellent search engine and career resources.

www.555-1212.com – This is the Internet Domain name registration service and directory of phone and email listings for businesses and individuals.

http://199.233.99.2/neerc/ – The NEERC is small organization of search consultants and heads of human resources. The group meets 4 times a year in Waltham, Massachusetts. Their web site includes a listing of members, including some photos. In an effort to remain as egalitarian as possible, there are no officers. As there is no contact person per se, you may get in touch with anyone on the web site. http://199.233.99.2/neerc/

http://member.aol.com/uncleroy22/prime.htm – This is the URL to the Prime Computer/ Computervision alumni web site.

SEARCH ENGINES

Yahoo! (http://www.yahoo.com)

Lycos (http://www.lycos.com)

AltaVista (http://www.AltaVista.com)

Excite (http://www.excite.com)

Dejanews (http://www.dejanews.com)

HotBot (http://www.HotBot.com)

Inference (http://www.inference.com/infind)

Infoseek (http://www.infoseek.com)

Nerd World (http://www.NerdWorld.com)

Netfind (http://www.netfind.com)

Northern Light (http://www.northernlight.com)

Opentext (http://www.pinstripe.opentext.com/)

Webcrawler (http://webcrawler.com)

WEB SITES OF TRADE PUBLICATIONS FROM CRAIN COMMUNICATIONS

www.AdAge.com

www.autoweek.com

www.businessinsurance.com

www.crainschicagobusiness.com

www.crainscleveland.com

www.crainsdetroit.com

www.crainsny.com

emonline.com

www.investmentnews.com

www.modernhealthcare.com

www.pionline.com

www.plasticsnews.com

www.rcrnews.com

www.rubbernews.com

www.tirebusiness.com

www.wastenews.com

www.globalwirelessnews.com

Crain Communications has offices in Chicago, New York, Akron, Boston, Cleveland, Detroit, the Florida Keys, Los Angeles, Nashville, San Francisco, Washington, DC, plus London and Tokyo. For more information, contact the New York office at (212) 210-0100, Chicago at (312) 337-7700 or customer service toll free at (800) 678-9595.

II. Web Sites To Publishers of Directories and Databases and Related Web Sites

In addition to the information below, if you wish to locate more publishers and their web sites, refer to the *Literary Market Place* on publisher R.R. Bowker's web site at www.bowker.com. Remember, another research option is to go to the "Ask Jeeves" web site at www.askjeeves.com, www.ask.com, www.aj.com or ask.

www.amazon.com is a large bookstore web site. At the time of this writing they offer discounts up to 40%.

www.ambest.com is the insurance industry web site for A.M. Best Company. It includes publications and services, a web services resources center, employment, plus sites for Best's Safety Directory, and Attorneys and Adjusters.

www.askjeeves.com or www.ask.com is an easy site to use. You can ask any type of question in plain English. Visit the site and try it for fun! If you ask Jeeves, "How can I find a job?" or "How can I find candidates for an engineering job?" Jeeves has an answer! Actually, there's very little you CAN'T ask Jeeves. The Ask Jeeves site includes Hoover's Career Center, which consists of Job Search Tools (monster.com, CareerMosaic,wsj.com careers, hotjobs, Westech's Virtual Job Fair and joboptions), Career Links and Career Research Links. Hoover's Career Center contains much additional information, including extensive relocation data, such as cost of living comparisons, etc. You can also subscribe to Hoover's and access their directories on the Internet.

www.bookwire.com is the web site for *Publishers Weekly*. It is an important web site that serves both publishing industry professionals and consumers with information about publishing and research. Bowker's *Publishers Weekly* web site includes a searchable database of current author tour information, links to all book-related web sites, industry classifieds, and Book Wire Insider Direct, a subscription daily e-mail news service, and more.

www.bowker.com is the web site for this major research publisher. The site includes Flagship Products and Services, an online Product Catalog, Electronic Publishing products including CD ROM's, Internet Databases, and Online Subscription and Site Licensing Databases; press releases, career opportunities, and more. Many of their references are accessible through this web site, such as *Books in Print Plus Canadian Edition, Ulrich's on Disc, German Books In Print, German Books Out of Print, International Books in Print PLUS, Italian Books in Print, Yearbook of International Organizations PLUS, Ulrich's International Periodicals Directory, The Software Encyclopedia, Bowker's Complete Video Directory, American Book Publishing Record.* Visit the web site for more information. At this web site you can also search-free-*Book Out of Print* database. At this site you can also search free Bowker's *Library Resource Guide – Internet Edition*, a directory of library services and suppliers which is drawn from Bowker's *American Library Directory*. At www.bowker.com you can also access a free online directory from *Literary Market Place*, including hundreds of services and suppliers to the book publishing community – ad agencies, publicists, typesetters, printers and more.

www.cahners.com is the web site for Cahners Business Information.

www.corptech.com is the site for CorpTech Technology Company Information, including directories, guides, databases, mailing lists, and reports customized from the CorpTech Database.

www.cpsnet.com is the site for the healthcare industry CPS Communications, Inc. They publish the *Pharmaceutical Marketers Directory, Healthcare News Net,* a daily online publication, and the trade publication *Medical Marketing and Media.*

www.csgis.com is one of the URLs to Chain Store Guide Information Services. Another is www. d-net.com/csgis.

www.dialog.com is the web site to The Dialog Corporation, "the world's largest online information company."

www.dnbmdd.com is the web site to the *Dun & Bradstreet Million Dollar Directory*. Their database provides information on over one million leading public and private U.S. companies.

www.d-net.com/csgis is one of the URLs to Chain Store Guide Information Services. Another is www.csgis.com.

www.fairchildpub.com and www.fairchildbooks.com are web sites to Fairchild Publications, publisher of the New York City fashion trade paper *Women's Wear Daily* and other apparel industry publications.

www.galegroup.com is the web site to publisher Gale Group, formerly Gale Research, one of the largest providers of research references serving the search industry, recruiting and libraries. At the time of this writing, the predecessor web site for Gale Research, www.gale.com, contains different information from www.galegroup.com.

www.gale.com is the original web site to publisher Gale Research, prior to their merger with Information Access Company and Primary Source Media which resulted in the company's name changing to The Gale Group.

www.galenet.gale.com is the web site used to access Gale Group's directories, for a fee.

www.greyhouse.com is the URL for Grey House Publishing in Lakeville, Connecticut, publisher of *The Directory of Business Information Resources, Associations, Newsletters, Magazines and Tradeshows*.

www.harrisinfo.com is the URL to the web site of the publisher of technology directories, Harris InfoSource International, 2057 Aurora Road, Twinsburg, OH 44087-1999, (800) 888-5900, fax (800) 643-5997.

www.iliterarymarketplace.com is the URL for *International Literary Market Place*'s Internet database, which is available by subscription from R.R. Bowker. For more information, see Bowker's site at www.bowker.com.

www.kennedyinfo.com is the web site for publisher Kennedy Information. It includes books, newsletters, training materials, directories, and surveys for executive recruiting, human resources, outplacement, management consulting and job seekers. (800) 531-0007, (603) 585-6544.

www.kompass.com is the URL to Kompass's web site. It contains a searchable database that encompasses over 60 countries, 2.5 million executive names, information on 1.5 million companies, 19 million key product references, and 370,000 trade and brand names. At the time of this writing, Kompass is available in English and French. Inquire to find out when Deutsch, Espanol and Italiano be available.

www.literarymarketplace.com is the URL for *Literary Market Place*'s Internet database, which is available by subscription from R.R. Bowker. Bowker's web site at www.bowker.com also contains a partial free online directory taken directly from the pages of *Literary Market Place*.

www.lexis-nexis.com is the URL to the Lexis-Nexis web site.

www.macmillan.com is the URL to Macmillan's web site. It contains sections on science, technical, medical, college academic Professional, School books and ELT, magazines, general books, electronic publishing and associated companies, including Scientific American

www.manufacturersnews.com is the web site to Manufacturers' News, Inc., publisher of geographic and manufacturing directories, both U.S. and foreign.

www.mhbizlink.com is the web site address for the major Canadian publisher Maclean Hunter. Among other things, it has links to 30 business publications. For more information call them in Toronto at (416) 596-5000.

www.mmdaccess.com is the web site to financial publisher Money Market Directories, Inc., a division of Standard & Poors, which is a division of McGraw Hill.

www.nelnet.com is the URL to Nelson Information's web site. It includes Manager Hires, Job Bank, Nelson's Products, Investment Manager Listings, World's Best Money Managers, M&A News and more.

www.ntis.gov/ is the web site for National Technical Information Service, formerly called the U.S. Government Printing Office. NTIS published the *Standard Industrial Classification (SIC) Manual* until it had been replaced by the *North American Industry Code System (NAICS) Manual* in 1997. National Technical Information Service, Technology Administration, U.S. Department of Commerce, Springfield, VA 22161. Phone orders Monday-Friday, 8 am - 8 pm Eastern Time (800) 553-NTIS (6487) or (703) 605-6000. NTIS is the central source for government sponsored U.S. and worldwide scientific, engineering and business related information. As a self-supporting agency of the U.S. Department of Commerce's Technology Administration, NTIS covers its business and operating expenses with the sale of its products and services. For questions about a product or order, email info@ntis.fedworld.gov.

www.oryxpress.com is the web site to Oryx Press, publisher of librarian directories. Browse the site by subject, titles, and authors.

www.phillips.com is the web site to Phillips Business Information, Inc. It contains product catalogs for aviation, defense, electronic commerce, energy/oil and gas, finance, health, marketing/public relations, media, new media/Internet, politics/public policy, satellite, security, telecommunications. Subscription web site to Aviation Today, Communications Today, Defense Daily Network, Electronic Commerce Today, Fabian Investment Resources, Richard E. Bank's Profitable Investing, Telecom Web, Wireless Today. Phillips Subsidiaries are Phillips Publishing Inc., Phillips Business Information, Hart Publications, and Eagle Publishing.

www.reedref.com presents a current catalog for all Reed Reference Publishing companies for both print and electronic references – National Register Publishing, R.R. Bowker, Bowker-Saur, K.G. Saur, Marquis Who's Who, Martindale-Hubbell and Lexis-Nexis Business Information. At the time of this writing, this catalog is searchable by name, subject, publisher and keyword. To check new offerings, visit individual publisher pages. *Free product demos of CD ROM's* can be downloaded for for experimentation and some sample pages – and even entire chapters – and are available for unlimited viewing. The web site also includes a constantly updated menu of special discounts which are available only on the web site. Ask about the growing number of RRP databases accessible via the Internet on subscription or for a usage based price, such as the *Martindale-Hubbell Law Directory*. For more information visit Bowker Reed Reference's web site at www.reedref.com or www.bowker.com or contact corporate offices, 121 Chanlon Road, New Providence, NJ 07974, (800) 521-8110, (800) 323-3288, Fax (908) 665-3528, email info@bowker.com or webmaster@www.reedref.com.

www.tfp.bankinfo.com is the web site to banking industry publisher Thomson Financial Publishing.

www.thomasregister.com is the web site to Thomas' Register.

www.umi.com is the web site to publisher UMI in Ann Arbor, Michigan, the highly respected publisher of large databases of periodicals and other library references, especially electronic references. UMI publishes the important databases *ABI Inform, ABI Global,* and *Books on Demand, Magazines, Newspapers and Collections Online* which consists of 19,000 titles. UMI is a Bell and Howell company.

www.uniworldbp.com is the web site to a publisher of U.S.-International company directories.

www.ziff-davis.com is the web site to computer magazine publisher Ziff-Davis, a Softbank Company.

III. Books of Web Sites

CareerXRoads, by Gerry Crispin and Mark Mehler, is an annual directory of job and resume sites. At the time of this writing the number of sites has more than tripled in two years to over 1,000 sites. It includes specialized databases for job seekers and employers. $22.95. Order online or by phone from distributor Kennedy Information, One Kennedy Place, Route 12 South, Fitzwilliam, NH 03447, (800) 531-0007, (603) 585-6544, web site www.kennedyinfo.com. Also available through from author's web site or at your local book store.

Cyberhound® Online is a guide to finding and retrieving significant sites on the Internet. It has a search engine and 75 search delimiters. It adds thousands of site reviews monthly. To try it out free, go to the world wide web at http://www.cyberhound.com. For pricing and ordering information, call Gale Research at (800) 877-GALE.

Cyberhound's® Guide to Companies on the Internet reviews over 2,000 corporate sites, including major companies as well as those in the information industry, software and hardware developers and networking and telecommunications companies. It also includes a user's guide, a directory of specialized business we sites, a bibliography of Internet products, and a glossary of Internet terms. At the time of this writing 1st edition (1996) available from Gale for $79, reduced from $95. Published by Euromonitor (England). Distributed by Gale Group, P.O. Box 9187, Farmington Hills, MI 48333-9187. Toll free U.S. and Canada (800) 877-GALE (4253) and (248) 699-GALE, fax (800) 414-5043 and (248) 699-8061, Internet orders galeord@galegroup.com, web site www.galegroup.com or www.gale.com. All Gale Group products are available on approval. Contact Gale for details.

Cyberhound's® Guide to Internet Discussion Groups contains over 4,000 Internet listservs and news groups and a subject and master index, such as computer know-how groups, such as the virus Computer Newsgroup (comp.virus), health information groups, and social interaction groups. $79. Gale Group, P.O. Box 9187, Farmington Hills, MI 48333-9187. Toll free U.S. and Canada (800) 877-GALE (4253) and (248) 699-GALE, fax (800) 414-5043 and (248) 699-8061, Internet orders galeord@galegroup.com, web site www.galegroup.com or www.gale.com. All Gale Group products are available on approval. Contact Gale for details.

Cyberhound's® Guide to Internet Libraries will guide you to online information including site descriptions and reviews of over 2,000 libraries, including contact information, mainfiles/subfiles, holdings information, subscriptions, services, how to access, information on special collections, OPAC addresses, plus a bibliography, a glossary of Internet terms, White Pages and two indexes. $79. Gale Group, P.O. Box 9187, Farmington Hills, MI 48333-9187. Toll free U.S. and Canada (800) 877-GALE (4253) and (248) 699-GALE, fax (800) 414-5043 and (248) 699-8061, Internet orders galeord@galegroup.com, web site www.galegroup.com or www.gale.com. All Gale Group products are available on approval. Contact Gale for details.

Cyberhound's® Guide to People on the Internet is organized into three sections. (1) *Who's Who Online identifies 1,000 online directories, databases and membership listings.* For example, it lists Architects in Canada, Attorney Finder, Famous Left-Handers, and The Missing Persons

Pages. (2) White Pages provides and alphabetical listing of 3,000 business professionals who are accessible by email. Other information includes area of expertise, personal and professional affiliation and company information. (3) Personal Web Sites are organized alphabetically by name. 1,500 pages of people in the news in business, entertainment, and sports. $79. Gale Group, P.O. Box 9187, Farmington Hills, MI 48333-9187. Toll free U.S. and Canada (800) 877-GALE (4253) and (248) 699-GALE, fax (800) 414-5043 and (248) 699-8061, Internet orders galeord@galegroup.com, web site www.galegroup.com or www.gale.com. All Gale Group products are available on approval. Contact Gale for details.

Cyberhound's® Guide to Publications on the Internet provides fully indexed information on over 3,000 Internet publications. Covers the World Wide Web, Gopher, Telnet and FTP sites that make online publication available to the public. $79. Gale Group, P.O. Box 9187, Farmington Hills, MI 48333-9187. Toll free U.S. and Canada (800) 877-GALE (4253) and (248) 699-GALE, fax (800) 414-5043 and (248) 699-8061, Internet orders galeord@galegroup.com, web site www.galegroup.com or www.gale.com. All Gale Group products are available on approval. Contact Gale for details.

Gale Guide to Internet Databases, formerly titled *Cyberhound's® Guide to Internet Databases*, identifies over 5,000 Internet databases. $115. Gale Group, P.O. Box 9187, Farmington Hills, MI 48333-9187. Toll free U.S. and Canada (800) 877-GALE (4253) and (248) 699-GALE, fax (800) 414-5043 and (248) 699-8061, Internet orders galeord@galegroup.com, web site www.galegroup.com or www.gale.com. All Gale Group products are available on approval. Contact Gale for details.

Internet Recruiting Edge by Barbara Ling is a comprehensive collection of research assembled over a two year period. Developed for the novice and experienced Internet recruiter alike, and with a foreword by Tony Byrne, topics include: Where, Oh Where, is my Candidate Now? Does the Internet Really Benefit Businesses? Phones Still Work, But Don't Buy a Mansion if You Only Need a Cottage, How to Find Candidates on the Internet, Non-Traditional Resources, Before You Begin – A Primer on Internet Culture – Netiquette, Beginner Candidate Location Skills, Resume Banks, Search Engine Basics, The Joy of Bookmarks, The Art of Job Posting, Sleuthing for Company Directories, Finding Employee Directories, Finding Executive Biographies, Alumni Organizations, Forums and Bulletin Boards, Internet Classifieds, Online E-zines (magazines), Professional Organizations, Colleges, Metasearch at Highway 61, Realistic Goals Before You Begin Your Own Recruiter Web Site, Perilous Pitfalls, How To Buy Your Recruiter Business Site, Locating Good Web Site Designers, Your Site is Designed – Now What? How To Market A Recruiter Web Site, 14 Killer Web Site Search Engine Visibility Tips, and more. $149. Order by visiting the web site http://www.barbaraling.com or call (732) 563-1464.

Jobhunting on the Internet by Richard Nelson Bolles, Ten Speed Press, P.O. Box 7123, Berkeley, CA 94707. Among other things, this book provides a small but reasonably complete listing of Internet URLS (Uniform Resource Locators) with a short description of the contents of each. By the author of the classic *What Color is Your Parachute*?

Recruiters' Internet Survival Guide by John Sumser, author of the 1996 Electronic Recruiting Index, rated over 500 recruiting web sites and analyzed Internet recruiting issues. The Recruiters' Internet Survival Guide, published by Staffing Industry Resources, $89.50. To view the table of contents or to order a copy, go to web site www.interbiznet.com or contact IBN (Internet Business Network) in Mill Valley, CA.

World Directory of Business Information Web Sites provides full details on over 1,500 free business web sites, including information such as online surveys, top company rankings, company information, brand information, market research reports and trade association statistics. $590. Published by Euromonitor (England). Distributed by Gale Group, P.O. Box 9187, Farmington Hills, MI 48333-9187. Toll free U.S. and Canada (800) 877-GALE (4253) and (248) 699-GALE, fax (800) 414-5043 and (248) 699-8061, Internet orders galeord@galegroup.com, web site www.galegroup.com or www.gale.com. All Gale Group products are available on approval. Contact Gale for details.

CHAPTER 8

Identification Research – What It Is, What It Isn't and How to Present It

A Conversation About the Art of Presenting Identification Research
What It Is and Isn't, and a Real Live Sample from an Actual Search

This chapter is essential reading for anyone new to search or research – search consultants, research consultants, corporate users of 'unbundled search' and search firm clients who want a better hands-on understanding of the search process. It clarifies 'research' and explains what's appropriate to expect from ID research, what's not, and why.

This discussion will focus on three things. The first question is, what is Identification Research, or ID research? Conversely the second question is, what *isn't* ID Research? Our definition will also reveal the specific types of information that are – and are not – considered ID Research. For example, should you expect ID Research to provide the name and title of a potential contact? (Yes.) What else? What about the phone number? (Yes.) Is information about education considered ID research? (No.) Compensation? (No.)

Third, we will present a real, live example of ID research conducted for an actual search. Fictitious names were used for reasons of confidentiality. At the end of this chapter, this ID research is presented in an organization chart format. That's the best way to display ID research. Because one picture is worth a thousand words.

Research – it's one of those words that means different things to different people. Even within the recruiting community, if you ask 10 different people what research means, you'll get 10 different answers. To some of them, research encompasses everything from "scratch" all the way through finding the three to six finalist candidates presented to the hiring manager. This includes calling sources and prospects, describing the career opportunity, obtaining background information and interviewing them on the phone (and in some cases, interviewing them in person) and then writing the candidate report for the client.

To others, research consists only of finding names and titles of people who should be called. This type of research used to be called "book research." Today that might translate to "electronic database research." Generally, this is referred to as Identification Research ("ID Research") because the research consultant *identifies* the names of the individuals who will later be called to discuss the search.

Overriding Consideration

The whole idea of ID research is to gather sufficient data so that the recruiter or researcher can select names of people to call. In other words, we need to know which people have the right job titles. Basically, ID research consists of the names of people, their titles, phone numbers, and related organizational information – enough so that we can make a good, educated guess that this individual *probably* is now employed in the right kind of position, in the right division or subsidiary or department, at one of the companies on the search target list.

REALLY GOOD ID RESEARCH
WHAT KIND OF INFORMATION DOES IT TAKE?

Put the following information into a hand sketched organization chart. You can use the ID research worksheet in chapter 11, "Blank Forms You Can Use."

- ❑ PERSON'S NAME

- ❑ NICKNAME. DOES RICHARD GO BY RICH, RICK, DICK OR "J.R."? OR HIS MIDDLE NAME, WALLY?

- ❑ TITLE

- ❑ PHONE NUMBER, INCLUDING DIRECT DIAL NUMBER AND/OR EXTENSION

- ❑ MAIN SWITCHBOARD NUMBER

   AS MUCH ORG CHART DATA AS POSSIBLE:

- ❑ NAME OF DEPARTMENT, DIVISION, SUBSIDIARY, ETC.

- ❑ BOSS'S TITLE AND NAME

- ❑ TITLES OF PEERS AND NAMES

- ❑ NUMBER OF PEOPLE IN THE PERSON'S ORGANIZATION (BOTH DIRECT REPORTS & TOTAL REPORTS)

- ❑ OTHER HEAD COUNTS. HOW MANY PEOPLE ARE IN THE DEPARTMENT, HOW MANY REPORT TO THE SAME BOSS, HOW MANY PEERS DOES THIS PERSON HAVE? BE SURE TO DISTINGUISH BETWEEN PROFESSIONALS & SECRETARIES, ETC. SPECIFY IF HEAD COUNT IS AN ESTIMATE.

- ❑ HARD COPY OF DIRECTORY INFO SHOULD BE ATTACHED. BE SURE TO INCLUDE THE EXACT TITLE AND YEAR OF PUBLICATION.

The following should also be noted at the top of the research:

- ❑ LOCATION OF CORPORATE HEADQUARTERS OR COUNTRY HEADQUARTERS

- ❑ PHONE NUMBER

- ❑ TOLL FREE NUMBERS, IF ANY

- ❑ SPECIFY IF THERE ARE ANY REALLY GOOD PLACES TO GET INFORMATION, SUCH AS:

  - A GOOD WEB SITE
  - A PHONE NUMBER OR NAME TO CALL FOR ORGANIZATIONAL INFO
  - A PHONE NUMBER OR NAME TO CALL FOR TITLES
  - A DEPARTMENT THAT WILL SEND INFORMATION: NEWS CLIPPINGS, BROCHURES, LISTS OF PLANTS & OTHER FACILITIES, 10(K) REPORTS OR ANNUAL REPORTS

Be sure to note if you've located an org chart, whether it's published in an annual report, a brochure, or if you received one from a candidate – or if an interviewer was able to construct an org chart from information provided during a candidate interview. However, you should realize that obtaining an organization chart is a rare and exciting event, so don't expect it to happen every day.

Make sure each Research Worksheet identifies any special references you're using, such as web sites and directories, including the year. For your convenience, a blank ID Research Worksheet appears in chapter 11, "Blank Forms You Can Use."

Your research should document where every name came from ("per 2000 Standard & Poors," "per switchboard," "per Ms. Chris Bickford's secy Bev," etc.) If the research came from a directory or a CD ROM, be absolutely sure to specify the year or edition. Next time someone looks at this research, he or she will know how old the information is.

If you're figuring out how an organization is put together and you have the names of six people and you believe there are five more, make a note saying so, i.e., that Jenny Penny's secretary Lenny said so-and-so on such-and-such a date. If you believe that you already have the right name(s), make a note with an asterisk (*) and say why you think that's the right name to call, and why you think it's not a good investment of your time to get the other five names. When you find out how many people are in an organization, make sure you know how many are professionals and how many are clericals. If you happen to learn that two are summer interns, make a note of that.

If someone casually mentions that he or she doesn't know who's in charge now because of a retirement, vacancy, promotion, reorganization, merger, or whatever, this is PURE GOLD! Write it down! If there's a vacancy, it could be a new business opportunity if you're with a search or research firm. If there's upheaval or change, this is a strong signal that top notch people may be unusually interested in an overture for a new position. It's very important and valuable research, the kind of competitive information which *adds value* to the search.

* * * * *

What ID Research is *Not*

The following data is *not* considered ID Research. This information[1] is usually generated during a "sourcing and prospecting" call, which is also known as a "candidate development" call:

- Education

- Number of years in the company

- Number of years in the position

- Compensation

- Prior companies worked for

- Age or birthdate

---

[1] Sometimes it's better to conduct electronic research to obtain some of this data. For example, in a research and development search you can look up names of scientists or department heads in a directory of labs, such as *The Directory of American Research and Technology,* and then look up their biographies in *American Men and Women of Science.* There are also numerous biographical databases and Who's Who volumes, the *Dun and Bradstreet Reference Book of Corporate Managements*, and similar directories and databases. But first you must identify the person's name, either from a directory, an electronic reference, or a phone call. Therefore, while this research is sometimes appropriate before sourcing and prospecting calls are made, it is not considered ID research per se. Refer to "Biographies" and "Who's Who" in Part II of this book, "The Recruiter's Directory of Directories – Plus Web Sites, Databases & CD ROM's."

ID research should render names of likely prospects for the search so as to avoid wasting calls to people with inappropriate jobs. We want to identify PROSPECTS, that is, individuals with the right qualifications and background, NOT SOURCES, because they are always at least one step removed from prospects, which is what we really want.

The research should be written so that anyone who reads it can select the right names without having to ask the researcher any questions. Good research documentation is crystal clear to anyone who reads it. This means that any abbreviations or acronyms should be defined on each and every sheet of paper where they appear.

Two Main Points

In summary, there are two main things to remember when you're conducting identification research.

1. SET THE INFORMATION UP LIKE AN ORGANIZATION CHART.

- Plug in as much information as possible so that the recruiter can look at the ID research and select names to call of prospects who are right "on target" for the position. There are two advantages to this:

    - You can avoid wasting time calling an inappropriate individual.

    - You want to avoid making too many candidate development calls within a given department. For example, if there are only five people in the department, including the department head, an awkward situation could develop if you call more than one person. You never know whether someone will recognize your name or whether two friends in the department will compare notes about your call.

        Precise, "rifle shooting" ID research can reduce the possibility of wasting phone calls to inappropriate individuals *and* spare the embarrassment arising from blanketing a department with phone messages.

        However, there's something far more important than being embarrassed when half the department thinks that a recruiter is on a "fishing expedition." A breach of confidentiality in an executive search is a serious matter. Your reputation is on the line. In fact, there could even be legal ramifications. So, be judicious when deciding which individuals you will contact.

        This is another reason why comprehensive notes are important. For example, it should be documented if a secretary is shared and by whom, and what phone numbers the secretary covers.

2. DOCUMENT EVERYTHING CLEARLY.

Write down everything so that if you got hit by a bus tomorrow, the person who picked up where you left off would be able to understand exactly where you left off, exactly what you were thinking and why, and what the next steps should be.

* * * * *

There is one exception to the rule that educational data is *not* ID research, and that is if you use a school alumni directory as your source of names. Sometimes a search is *driven* by educational credentials. For example, an MBA from a top school may be an ironclad requirement for joining a first tier general management consulting firm. In that case, you can use graduate business school alumni directories, such as the Harvard or Wharton directories, to look for names, year of degree and company. However, except for something like this, this is usually too time consuming to be worth the effort, unless you can access the directory electronically. Also, if you know that there are only two or three schools which produce the graduates you need, you can refer to alumni magazines and newspapers which publish announcements of promotions and job changes.

If you're involved with campus recruiting and professionals with about 2-5 years of experience, you can utilize

- Resume books of graduating MBA's at top schools. This project offers a long term pay off, especially if your search needs are specialized: build a computer database, year after year, selectively inputting information from these resumes, coding them according to their interests, such as Management Consulting Club, Corporate Finance Club, and so forth. A record might consist of:

  > Name
  > Address (which might be parents' address),
  > Undergraduate degree, school and year
  > Graduate degree, school and year
  > Date of birth
  > Functional interest (e.g., management consulting club member)
  > Outstanding accomplishments, awards, or publications and pre-business school career experience.

If you regularly update your database, either through a mailing or after a phone conversation, this information will quickly become more complete and as such, will grow in value.

- Campus recruiting records have tremendous value. Companies spend a great deal of time and money doing campus recruiting and it's a shame to fail to maximize that investment. Highly select information can be incorporated into a "farm team" database that keeps track of candidates who did well during the campus interview but, for one reason or another, did not join the company. These individuals already have a relationship with your company and who knows when circumstances will change? Their skills will broaden and deepen with experience and they could become future candidates. They can also be great sources. When you're building your candidate database, remember to create campus recruiting fields, such as "Campus Candidate/Year," "Offer made and declined/Year" and/or "Farm Team."

In fact, the more you invest in building a database, the less you'll need to rely on ID Research at the beginning of a search to learn the names of people you should contact. The future of search will be increasingly technology driven. Those recruiters who utilize technology first will have the advantage of an early start in gaining a competitive advantage overall. For example, one thing that can reduce the reliance on ID Research is a database of company alumni. What's great about this is you already know the prospects had worked at a particular company. If they have no interest in your search, they might refer other people from their former company. If you have a list of names, they will be more likely to provide comments. Remember to ask the source to rank the people on your list, too. Ask, "Who's the best one," "Why?" and so forth.

For more information about web site, online databases, and CD ROM's, refer to Part II of this book, "The Recruiter's Directory of Directories – Plus Web Sites, Databases & CD ROM's."

SUMMARY

One of the most important things in conducting a search is *getting to the right person*. The reason ID research is so important is that's how most of the "legwork" is done to figure out where that person will be located – and what is his or her name, title and phone number.

One picture is worth a thousand words. The best way to present ID research is to use an organization chart format. Insert all relevant information. Use footnotes if appropriate.

Write up the information so that it's clear and completely understandable in case you're not available to interpret what you've written. For that matter, make sure you will understand your own notes six months from now, long after you've forgotten everything that's fresh in your mind at this moment.

When you're writing up your research, *be sure to allow enough space* so that the information is easy to read. If one page isn't enough, use two or three. Be sure to number your pages, for example, "Two's Company, Page 1 of 3." Do *not* cram information just to save space – that's a real nightmare to read, especially to someone who needs reading glasses. When presenting org chart data, "nesting" the charts can be a good technique. For example, if you need to understand what the marketing organization looks like, the first org chart might show a CEO with 5 boxes reporting to the position, something like this:

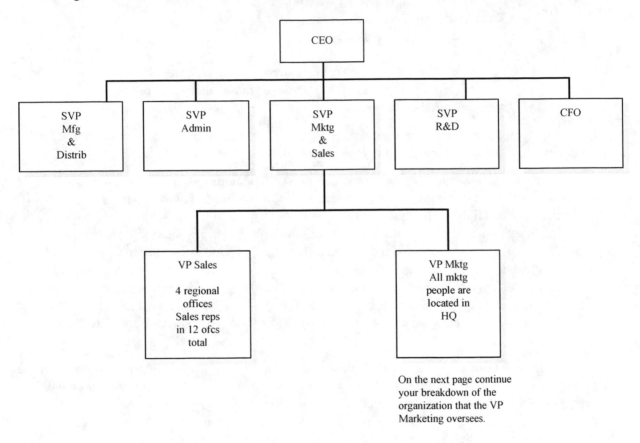

On the next page continue your breakdown of the organization that the VP Marketing oversees.

This type of research presentation shows how the individual prospects fit into the big picture. If all your ID research won't comfortably fit on one page, continue on the next page with a "nested" organization chart.

Also note, in large corporations, there are often several different organizations where you might find people with similar functional duties, for example at the corporate level vs. in an operating company.

* * * * *

The third part of this chapter consists of an example of ID research which was conducted for a search in private placements. However, fictitious names and phone numbers have been used for reasons of confidentiality. Sample presentations of ID research are shown for five companies.

These samples illustrate the principles discussed in this chapter and demonstrate how different types of findings can be written up.

Incidentally, as research goes, this was rather time consuming and as such, quite expensive. This information was presented to the client company as part of an unbundled search project. Line managers and the human resources officer at the company reviewed the ID research, commented about what they knew about whom, and participated in the process of selecting names for candidate development calls. Subsequently a slate of candidates was developed, to the great satisfaction of the company. The overall fees to the company were about one-third that of a retained search or contingency assignment. At the same time, the unbundling consultant earned about four times more by working directly for the company than if she would have done basically the same thing for a search firm.

It should be noted that this sample is a better example of what is *possible*, given sufficient time and budget, rather than an example of what is *typical*. Customarily, ID research is much less elaborate. But, as usual, there is a trade off. While you might save time and money on ID Research, a more senior person could wind up wasting time by sourcing and prospecting people who are clearly inappropriate. They could be so far removed from the search specs that, however willing sources might be to offer names, they simply don't know the right types of people.

Regardless of whether you are with a search firm or a company purchasing unbundled search products, neither one of you can afford to waste time contacting prospects who come nowhere near to matching your specs. In conclusion, ID research is an investment. As with any good investment, the payoff is well worth the time and the money spent in the beginning, when the foundation is laid.

SAMPLE PRESENTATION OF ID RESEARCH
PRIVATE PLACEMENTS
ORGANIZATION INFORMATION
BIG APPLE LIFE INSURANCE COMPANY
NEW YORK, NY
(555) 555-6000

The area that handles Private Placements at Big Apple Life is broken down below. A total of about 20 people work with private placements. The person responsible for private placement activity at Big Apple Life is:

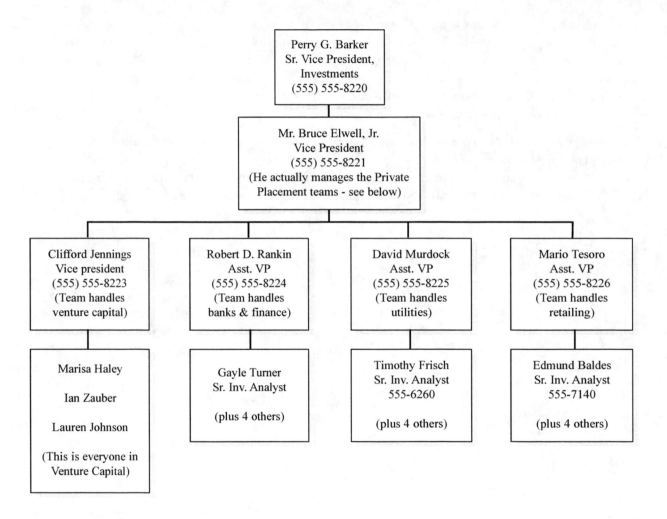

Note: Above per the secretary who works for all of the above people. Her name is Nancy: 555-8227

*Be sure to note the month/year
this research was done.*

SAMPLE PRESENTATION OF ID RESEARCH
PRIVATE PLACEMENTS
ORGANIZATION INFORMATION
BRIGHT LIGHTS INSURANCE COMPANY
NEW YORK, NY
(555) 555-6500

The department that handles Private Placements seems very small here. There are only four people. They are:

Abbot Bearden
VP, Securities
(555) 555-6558

Note: According to Abbot's sec'y, Diane, he is the "head guy" in Private Placements. It's not clear, however, whether or not the following VP's report to Abbot, since they all have the same title.

Louise M. Rudolph
VP, Securities
555-6573

Mark Falstad
VP, Securities
555-6559

Stewart Springer
VP, Securities
555-6552

Note: It's possible that Stewart could be the replacement for Glenda Case (who was hired away to join our company last fall). Stewart was not listed in the 1999 Corporate Finance Sourcebook whereas Glenda was.

Above per Abbot Bearden's secretary, Diane.

Be sure to note the month/year this research was done.

SAMPLE PRESENTATION OF ID RESEARCH
PRIVATE PLACEMENTS
ORGANIZATION INFORMATION
COSMOPOLITAN LIFE INSURANCE COMPANY
NEW YORK, NY
(555) 555-1277

The Private Placement activity at Cosmopolitan Life takes place in the Corporate Investment Department. The person with overall responsibility for Private Placement activity appears to be:

Mr. David F. Beals
Executive Vice President –
Corporate Investment Department
(555) 555-4239

Mr. Daniel Merrit
Sr. Vice President
(555) 555-4240
(appears he does Private Placements in oil and gas; his secy would not say how many people work with him or who they are)

Mr. Theodore Russo
Vice President
(555) 555-4241
(secy, Mary says Ted is in charge of Private Placements working with general industries)

Mr. Stephen Williams
Vice President
(555) 555-4242
(secy, Fran says that Williams does work with Private Placements in public utilities and has 3 people who work with him. But she could not give their names.)

In his group are:

Mr. David Shields
Asst. VP
(555) 555-4243

Mr. Steven Lowenthal
Asst. VP
(555) 555-4244

Ms. Kathleen Ryan
Sr. Investment Analyst
(555) 555-4245

Mr. Vince Ottenburg
Investment Analyst
(555) 555-4246

Five Financial Analysts

Ms. Lois West
Mr. Gregory Adams
Mr. Morris Macke
Mr. Mark Wright
Mr. Thomas Krist

Be sure to note the month/year this research was done.

Note: *1999 Corporate Finance Sourcebook says that Russo handles USA-Northeast region. There may well be more "head honchos" reporting to Beals but getting information was almost impossible and Russo's secretary was the only one who would provide any information. This is an example of being "stonewalled."*

SAMPLE PRESENTATION OF ID RESEARCH
PRIVATE PLACEMENTS
ORGANIZATION INFORMATION
ESMERADA INSURANCE COMPANY (PAGE 1 OF 5)
NEW YORK, NY
(555) 555-6700

This company seems, so far, to be the most complex as far as private placements go. We spoke with a Research Associate in the Portfolio Management department (Ms. Barbara Hardin (555) 555-6720) who gave us an overview of how the Private Placement activity is set up here.

There are many people in different areas/departments of the company who work with Private Placements. They basically fall into three separate areas of the company:

A. Portfolio Management
B. Corporate Finance Department
C. Esmerada Capital Inc.

Note: *According to Barbara and a few secretaries we eventually spoke with, the hierarchy in these departments of Esmerada is as follows:*

1) Managing Director (equivalent of a "full" VP in a bank)
2) Vice President – Corporate Finance (a significant notch below Managing Dir.)
3) Senior Associate
4) Associate
5) Analysts (They may not always be called analysts, but this level is the equivalent of analysts.)

Sometimes there are also Directors and Investment Managers somewhere between Managing Directors and Analysts, depending on the departmental structure.

A. Portfolio Management Department

Barbara said that these people are mostly portfolio managers and handle private placements as well as public transactions. (It seems that these people do the private placements that go through a third party, i.e. an investment bank rather than making direct deals with the companies themselves.)

Barbara gave us some names of the portfolio managers in this department.

Mr. Pat Martino, Managing Director
Mr. Keith Reed, Managing Director
Mr. Richard Talmadge, Managing Director
Mr. Jack Randall, Managing Director
Mr. Reggie Moody, Managing Director
Mr. Tom Morris, Investment Manager

Be sure to note the month/year
this research was done.

B. Corporate Finance Department

According to Barbara Hardin, the people in this department are the ones who "do the actual private placement deals." And according to one of the secretaries in this area, these people handle "direct placements." So, it seems that these are the ones who make private placement deals directly with the companies rather than going through a third party. There are two groups within the Corporate Finance Department, each of which is broken down into two teams of anywhere from 6-20 people.

1) Captial Markets Group
2) Financial Services Group

The Capital Markets Group is headed by:

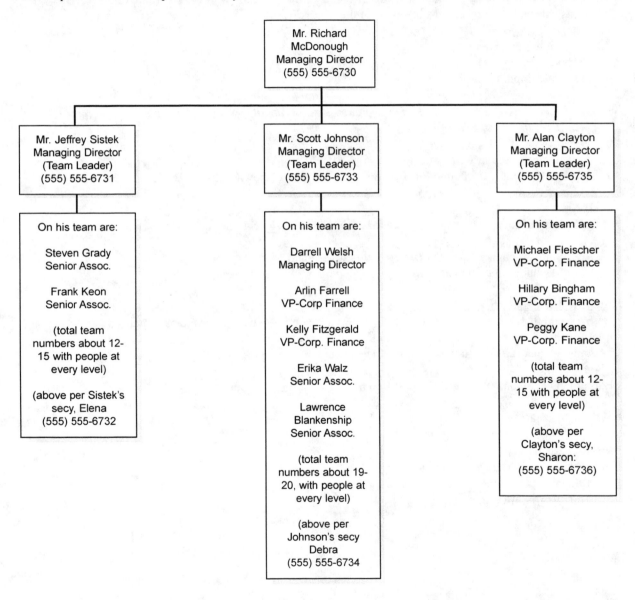

Be sure to note the month/year this research was done.

The Financial Services Group is headed by:

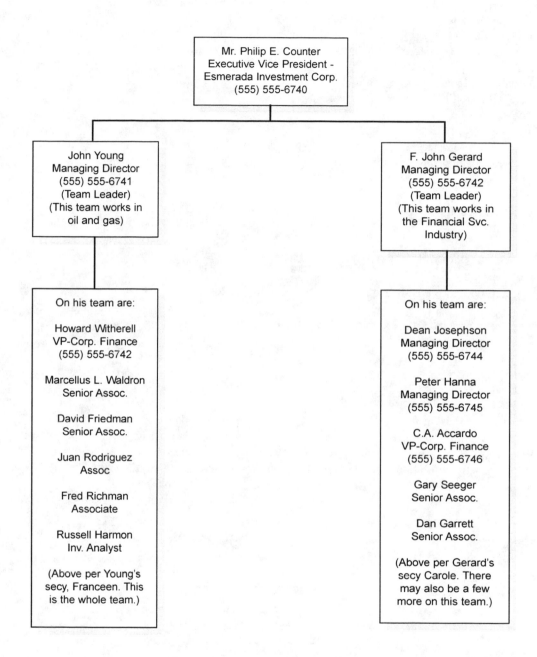

```
                    ┌─────────────────────────────┐
                    │      Mr. Philip E. Counter   │
                    │   Executive Vice President - │
                    │   Esmerada Investment Corp.  │
                    │        (555) 555-6740        │
                    └─────────────────────────────┘
```

Mr. Philip E. Counter
Executive Vice President -
Esmerada Investment Corp.
(555) 555-6740

John Young
Managing Director
(555) 555-6741
(Team Leader)
(This team works in
oil and gas)

F. John Gerard
Managing Director
(555) 555-6742
(Team Leader)
(This team works in
the Financial Svc.
Industry)

On his team are:

Howard Witherell
VP-Corp. Finance
(555) 555-6742

Marcellus L. Waldron
Senior Assoc.

David Friedman
Senior Assoc.

Juan Rodriguez
Assoc

Fred Richman
Associate

Russell Harmon
Inv. Analyst

(Above per Young's
secy, Franceen. This
is the whole team.)

On his team are:

Dean Josephson
Managing Director
(555) 555-6744

Peter Hanna
Managing Director
(555) 555-6745

C.A. Accardo
VP-Corp. Finance
(555) 555-6746

Gary Seeger
Senior Assoc.

Dan Garrett
Senior Assoc.

(Above per Gerard's
secy Carole. There
may also be a few
more on this team.)

According to John Young's secy, Franceen, the Capital Markets Group and the Financial Services Group used to be one merged unit. So, some of the people in the Financial Services Group may still be listed at the switchboard as being in the Capital Markets Group. Franceen said that the two groups recently "disconnected" from each other and now function as two separate entities within the Corporate Finance Department. Also, according to Jeffrey Sistek's secretary in the Capital Markets Group, the 3 teams in the Capital Markets Group do not specialize in a particular industry. So it's not clear as to how/why they're broken down the way they are.

Be sure to note the month/year
this research was done.

C. Esmerada Capital, Inc.

According to Barbara Hardin, a Research Associate in the Portfolio Management department, this group is more removed from the main organization of Esmerada but it does engage in a substantial amount of Private Placement Activity. It's largely a regional network based at corporate headquarters. Barbara referred us to:

Mr. George Reitherman
Corporate VP-Liability and Risk Management
(555) 555-6750

Mr. Reitherman's secretary, Claire, gave us a rough idea of which "pieces" of Esmerada Capital are involved with private placements in the New York metropolitan area. They are:

1. New York Regional Office
    Esmerada Capital Corp.
    Wall St.
    25th Floor
    New York, New York 10000

2. Special Industries East office is located at corporate headquarters.

The New York Regional Office is headed by:

Mr. Barry Briskin
Regional VP
(555) 555-6760

According to Mr. Briskin's secretary, the New York office of Esmerada Corp. has only 9 people in it. They do work with private placements but it is only one of many things that they are involved with. She would not give out the names of these 9 people. She did refer us to another Private Placement Group within Esmerada – which deals strictly with private placements. Joan, the group's secy said that it's headed by:

PRIVATE PLACEMENT GROUP

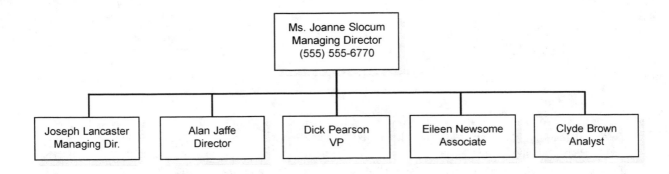

*Be sure to note the month/year
this research was done.*

The Special Industries-East office also works with private placements and is headed by:

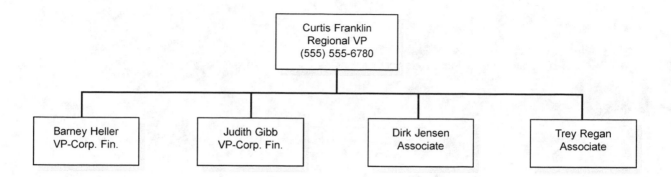

Above per Franklin's secretary, Andrea.

There are also a Special Industries – Central and a Special Industries – West offices set up similar to the Eastern region office shown above.

Be sure to note the month/year this research was done.

SAMPLE PRESENTATION OF ID RESEARCH
PRIVATE PLACEMENTS
ORGANIZATION INFORMATION
MAESTRO INSURANCE AND INVESTING COMPANY
NEW YORK, NY
(555) 555-8000

Private placements activity at Maestro is headed by:

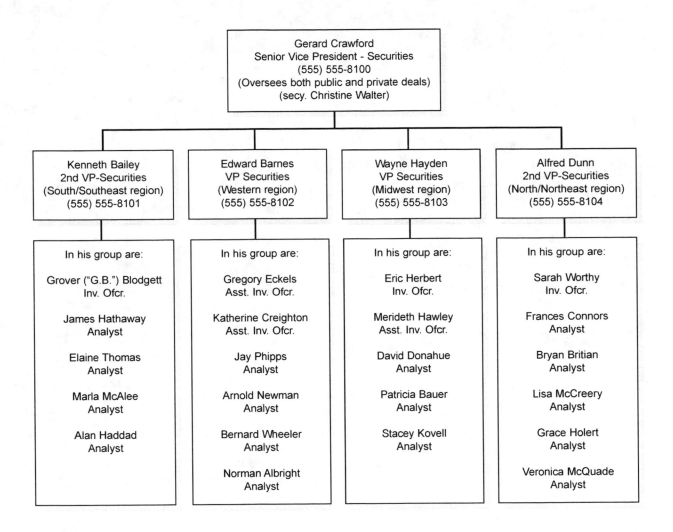

All of the above information per Anita, Alfred Dunn's secretary. She said there is also a person named Patrick Heffernan, an Assistant Investment Officer, who works independent of the above teams with high yield bonds (she also mentioned something about junk bonds but it was not clear.)

Training Pointer: Note that Grover Blodgett uses his nickname, G.B. So when you call him, ask to speak to G.B., because if you ask for Grover, it's a "dead give away" that you don't know him.

Be sure to note the month/year
this research was done.

CHAPTER 9

How To Identify Plant Locations

❏ 1.　Refer to "Manufacturing – Plant Locations," on page 246 in Part II of this book, "The Recruiter's Directory of Directories – Plus Web Sites, Databases & CD ROM's."

❏ 2.　Review annual reports.

❏ 3.　Review 10(k) reports.

❏ 4.　When calling the company to request the annual report and 10(k), also ask for any other lists or brochures which specify where plants are located, or other information you might need, such as product line information.

❏ 5.　Review the *Directory of Corporate Affiliations* for divisions and subsidiaries. Plant information is often listed, too: plant size (sales/number of employees), products, NAICS or SIC codes and name of Plant Manager.

❏ 6.　Review state directories published by Manufacturers' News, Inc. in Evanston, Illinois, (888) 752-5200), email info@manufacturersnews.com, web site www. manufacturersnews.com.

❏ 7.　Contact local chambers of commerce. Call information for the phone number of the chamber of commerce in the location of interest. Or review the Chambers of Commerce category in Part II of this book.

❏ 8.　Local telephone directories frequently list plant locations.

❏ 9.　Check a national phone directory, such as SelectPhone, manufactured by Pro CD, Inc, Omaha (800 992-3766) and their web site at www.infousa.com.

❏ 10.　Call or visit the library, especially if this seems to be taking too long.

❏ 11.　Call and ask the switchboard, the secretary to the CEO, or the secretary to a senior manufacturing executive, such as the VP Operations, Director of Manufacturing, or Plant Manager.

❏ 12.　For information about international companies, refer to Kompass directories, published by Cahners Business Information, 121 Chanlon Road, New Providence, NJ 07974, (908) 771-8785, email marketaccess@cahners.com, web sites www.kompass.com and www.cahners.com. Headquarters: Cahners Business Information, 275 Washington Street, Newton, MA 02158-1630, (617) 558-4663 or (617) 964-3030, fax (617) 558-4700.

❏ 13.　For information about Canadian companies, refer to Scott's Directories, 1450 Don Mills Road, Don Mills, Ontario, M3B 2X7, CANADA, (416) 442-2291, (416) 932-9555, (888) 709-9907. Montréal area: Scott's Directories, 3300 Cote Verde, Suite 410 Ville St. Laurent, Quebec H4B 2B7 CANADA (514) 339-1397, (800) 363-1327. Publisher's email scotts@southam.ca.

❏ 14.　Use a search engine on the Internet or query www.askjeeves.com. See the Search Engines category in Part II of this book, "The Recruiter's Directory of Directories – Plus Web Sites, Databases & CD ROM's."

CHAPTER 10

Hunting For A Needle In A Haystack

HOW TO FIND INFORMATION ON PRIVATELY HELD COMPANIES

Here's a brief check list of places to look for hard-to-find information about privately held companies. Remember, web sites, online databases and CD ROM's can be supplemented by hard copy directories and other printed information.

❑ 1. Go online. Check the company's web site. Many companies, especially technology companies, have impressive sites. Some companies even provide biographical information about their employees. You can also use various search engines to look for information, such as:

> Yahoo! (www.yahoo.com)
>
> Lycos (www.lycos.com)
>
> AltaVista (www.AltaVista.com)
>
> Excite (www.excite.com)

For more search engines, see the Search Engines category in Part II of this book.

❑ 2. Find out if the company has a toll free number by calling (800) 555-1212 in the U.S. Or look up the number on a national phone directory on CD ROM, available at your local software shop, or from a catalog. Or call national information. Call the company and say you want to request some information. Remember, just because the company is privately held, don't make the mistake of assuming that they don't publish an annual report. Some companies do. The Sales Department and company librarians are professionally oriented towards being helpful and providing information, so they can be very good places to get information. Or call the office of the Chairman or the President. Their administrative assistants are usually very well informed about the company and they are generally knowledgeable and polite. If you call when they're not too busy, they can be extremely helpful.

At first you can ask the switchboard – or whoever the computer connects you to – if they have an annual report or any other information they can send. If you can manage to get connected to a human being, you could say some thing like this. "Hi, maybe you can help me.[1] I'm looking for some information about your company and I imagine that because you're privately held, you don't publish an annual report. I wonder if there's something else you might be able to send me, maybe some brochures, or something like that." Then, prompt the person with specific ideas. When you mention the right thing, they might respond, "Oh, yeah, I forgot we had that." Items to mention include: "product information, a list of your plant locations, an old company newsletter, a

---

[1] Psychologically there seems to be something compelling about asking for help. Many people are very responsive when someone expresses a need for help, directly and specifically, such as "Can you help me with this?" How do you react whenever someone asks for help? Whenever you're looking for information, sometimes "Can you help me?" are the magic words, particularly if the person can spare a few minutes. This could be because some people are brought up to be helpful and nice and responsive to other people's needs. Other people might get off on the sense of one-upsmanship and power because it might be considered "weak" to need help. (Actually, it's quite the opposite of weak to marshal additional resources!) In any case, if all else fails, you can arrange to call someone back if he or she is too busy the first time you call, especially if you think s/he or she has the information you need.

promotional CD ROM about the company, maybe some news clippings or something like that. Or maybe you have some ideas...."

☐ 3. If the company will send you their news clippings, that could save some research time. You can also go to the library and conduct a literature search about the company. If you find one or two stories that describe a reorganization, you can use this to start piecing together the ultimate corporate puzzle: the organization chart! When you go to the library, be sure to ask about these periodicals databases, such as ABI Inform.

Also check the general business press, including:

❏ *The Wall Street Journal* and

❏ *The New York Times.*

You can also search hundreds of trade publications with:

❏ *Predicasts F&S Index*

Other options are:

❏ DIALOG

❏ LEXIS-NEXIS

Make sure you ask the librarian for advice. There are all kinds of new products available, especially as technology changes so rapidly.

☐ 4. Refer to various general directories – on CD ROM, online, or in hard copy – that include information on both publicly held and privately held companies, such as:

❏ *Million Dollar Directory* (Dun & Bradstreet)

❏ *Directory of Corporate Affiliations* (National Register Publications/Reed)

❏ *Corporate Affiliations PLUS CD ROM* (Reed Electronic)

❏ *Standard Directory of Advertisers* (National Register Publishing/Reed)

❏ *Companies International CD ROM* (Gale Research)

❏ *Standard & Poors Register of Corporations* (Standard and Poors/McGraw Hill)

❏ 5. Refer to the Privately Held Companies section in Part II of this book, "The Recruiter's Directory of Directories – Plus Web Sites, Databases & CD ROM's."

❏ 6. Geographic directories, such as state directories, often include privately held companies. The largest distributor of state directories is Manufacturers' News, Inc. in Evanston, Illinois, (888) 752-5200), email info@manufacturersnews.com, web site www.manufacturersnews.com.

❏ Additional geographic company research can be obtained from Chambers of Commerce. Call information for the phone number of the Chamber of Commerce in the location of interest. Also refer to the Chambers of Commerce category in Part II of this book.

❏ 7. Crain Publications often provide excellent information about niche companies. Their surveys of industry leaders also tend to contain information on privately held companies, particularly in year end issues of geographic papers, such as *Crain New York, Crain Chicago Business, Crain Cleveland, Crain in Detroit.* For a complete list of their 23 trade journals, refer to Periodicals in Part II of this book. Crain Communications, Inc. is headquartered in Chicago with offices in major cities throughout the U.S. plus London and Tokyo. New York location: 220 East 42nd Street, New York, NY 10017, (212) 210-0100, Customer Service (800) 678-9595.

❑ 8. Industry specific directories sometimes include information about privately held companies, such as *The Corporate Finance Sourcebook* (National Register Publishing, New Providence, NJ, 800-521-8110 or 908-464-6800) for various financial services industries. Here are some references to review in order to identify specialized directories: *The Encyclopedia of Associations* (Gale Group, Farmington Hills, Michigan, 800-877-GALE or 248-699-GALE), *Directories in Print* (Gale Group), *The Encyclopedia of Business Information Sources* (Gale Group), *Business Information Sources* (by Lorna Daniells, California Princeton Fulfillment Services, Newark, NJ, 800-822-6657). Also, be sure to check the industry category in "The Recruiter's Directory of Directories – Plus Web Sites, Databases & CD ROM's" in Part II of this book.

❑ 9. Get a Dun & Bradstreet report on the company (sometimes called a D&B or a D&B credit report.) In addition to information about a company's credit worthiness and history of how quickly they pay their bills, other important data is provided, including information about management, their names, titles, background information, and other data about locations and business activities the company is engaged in. Ask your company's Chief Financial Officer, Controller, Treasurer, your stock broker, your banker or your local library. This information is available on a subscription basis and if the cost for a report on one company proves prohibitively expensive, perhaps you have a friend in banking or finance whose company already subscribes to the service. You can also obtain a D&B credit report for a fee by contacting the Harvard Business School's Baker Library in Boston. Ask for the Reference Desk. Web site www.library.hbs.edu/.

❑ 10. Certain industries, such as investment banking and management consulting, tend to be privately held. Trade publications and industry newsletters often contain information about promotions and career moves. Specialized industry directories are also valuable, such as:

> ❑ *Directory of Management Consultants* published by Kennedy Information, Fitzwilliam, NH, (800) 531-0007, (603) 585-6544, www.kennedyinfo.com.
>
> ❑ *Corporate Finance Sourcebook* published by National Register Publishing, a Reed Elsevier company, New Providence, NJ, (800) 521-8110, www.redbooks. com.
>
> ❑ Specialized Wall Street directories published by Nelson Information, Port Chester, New York (800) 333-6357, (914) 937-8400, www.nelnet.com.
>
> ❑ Surveys conducted by industry publications, such as those in the respected Institutional Investor, can also be excellent.

❑ 11. Students at The Harvard Business School gather data and publish it for their own job hunting purposes. The Management Consulting Club publishes one book and The Corporate Finance Club publishes another. Basically, the major firms provide descriptions of their businesses, strategic focus, size, contact information and other important data.

> It usually requires some detective work to track it down, but it's worth the effort. Call the Harvard Business School in Boston. The switchboard operators should know which students are in charge of these clubs and they'll give you their phone numbers and other contact information, such as a web site or mailing address. If all

else fails, try a search engine or the Ask Jeeves web site at www.askjeeves.com, www.ask.com or www.aj.com or ask.

❑ 12. Be sure to use the resources identified in "The Recruiter's Directory of Directories" in Part II of this book. You will find directories containing information on privately held companies, both in the U.S. and abroad, databases which you can search for news media coverage in magazines, trade journals and newspapers, and trade associations whose librarians or executive directors can provide other leads.

It's possible to get sidetracked because the information you're finding can be very interesting. Be careful to avoid getting swamped by the sheer abundance of the information available. Do remember one thing when you're doing any research, whether it's for privately held companies or otherwise. Know when to stop. You should stop looking for information when you have enough to work with. Otherwise, you can wind up doing research for the sake of research because there's so much information available, and some of it is fascinating. So remember to stay focused.

CHAPTER 11

Blank Forms You Can Use

The forms in this section are included for you to photocopy and use at your convenience. Several types of forms are included.

Basically, ID Research Worksheets should be used instead of a regular pad of paper when you're taking notes while doing ID research on the phone. The worksheet is set up to make good documentation easy. In other words, important repetitive information will automatically appear on every page of your notes. This will be valuable next time you need to review old research from a similar recruiting assignment.

Here's a good documentation trick that saves time, too. Take one blank ID Research Worksheet and make a master copy – fill in the top right corner. Also add the complete title of any directory/ies or great web sites you're using. Be sure to state the year or edition of the directory, so you know how old the information is next time you refer to it. Then make about 30 or 40 photocopies of the master Research Worksheet to keep handy for taking notes. For a detailed discussion on how to write up and present your ID research, see chapter 8, "Identification Research – What It Is, What It Isn't, And How To Present It."

Two very similar ID Research Worksheets are in this chapter. Since it is a good discipline to present your findings in as much of an org chart format as possible, one of the worksheets has the first box already drawn in. Except for this, the other ID Research Worksheet is identical.

Two virtually identical Sources and Prospects sheets are also included. The vertical form has room for 4 names while the horizontal one has room for 3. My personal preference is the 3 person form because it allows more space for notes. These Sources and Prospects sheets have been modified to allow additional space for the several phone numbers, email addresses and web sites that technology has brought to our lives.

Speaking of technology, there's no question that computers are great, if not essential, for storing and massaging information. But despite my dependence on them, (translation: a love-hate relationship), when I'm the phone, I still mainly rely on note taking by hand. This is because I can never seem to get to the right computer record fast enough! So I grab my three ring binder – full of forms that I've already set up for that search. I like 3 ring binders because they're hard to lose on a cluttered desk. I use a different color binder for each search, which is a big help when a prospect returns my call and I need to find the right notes fast.

As with ID Research Worksheets, it's a good idea to make a master Sources and Prospects sheet for each search. Fill in the basic information at the top. You can also add the *year* on the top left corner. Then make a supply of photocopies to keep handy as phone calls come in.

Here's another trick with Sources and Prospects sheets: when you've completed your conversation with an individual on your list, draw a single diagonal line through that person's box. This way you won't waste a lot of time reading the same notes over and over because you can see at a glance that no follow up is needed.

As for the specific kind of notes that can be written on Sources and Prospects sheets, first, you should note your attempts to reach the person. Second, you should provide enough data so that a future review of this information will reveal whether the person should be contacted. For example:

"12/4/00 – LW." Left word on December 4, 2000

"4/5/00 – Busy 2x. 4/6/00, 9:15 am – No ans." Phone was busy despite 2 attempts to call on April 5, 2000. No answer on April 6 at 9:15 am."

"8/6/00 – Traveling til 8/8. LW w/secy Lynn. Best time to call – early am, 7:30 on." It's good to get in the habit of finding out the best time to reach your contact, if at all possible, i.e., if a human being answers the phone. Also, if a voice mail announcement provides that information, absolutely write it down!

"7/1/00 – On vac til 7/9 per VM – contact Jennifer Wood x2790 if emerg." Sometimes a voice mail (VM) announcement provides very useful information. Not only do you know when to call this person back, you also have another name to research. Is Jennifer a secretary or the Director of Marketing? Call the company switchboard for her title or possibly check their web site. While you're talking to the switchboard, see what else you can find out.

After you've made contact, include a thumbnail sketch on your Sources and Prospects sheet, assuming the prospect is interested and had time to provide background data. Your notes should include: date joined the company (month and year), all titles at the company and dates of those titles, education and years of degrees, prior companies with all titles and dates, compensation (both base and bonus and anything else, like a car). If prospects decline to state their current compensation, ask what their *requirements* are. Here are a few more examples:

"Wants min $150 K base + bonus + options."

"No int – dual career marriage & spouse won't relo."

"No int – 2 kids in HS, 16 & 17. Won't relo."

"V. int – dept just reorg."

"No int now – boss just retired. Thinks he's in line for promo. Poss try again later?"

"Guessed client (but I did not confirm or deny). Said no int if co is "An Offer You Can't Refuse Contracting" because of reputation.

"No int – sounds great but says he's now making more than co wants to pay. Is open to an exploratory meeting for future."

In other words, if a prospect is *not* interested, it's very important to note why, for two reasons. First, if there's a problem filling the position, it's important to know why people have no interest. If nothing else, it proves you've been doing your job. Second, if the specs are revised – for example, if the compensation is increased – you can avoid calling everybody again because the information you need is in your notes.

One final word of caution about what you write down. Because it is possible the government or a plaintiff could subpoena your working papers in a discrimination suit, be sure the wording in all your notes is appropriate. In general, specify the facts and write down exact quotations. It is more prudent to note exactly what the person said, rather than "sounds like a moron." If you write, "Said this company is wasting its time with this venture because of...," you have factual data to review with the client, rather than a subjective opinion with nothing to support it.

ID Research Worksheet

CLIENT _____

JOB NO. _____

TITLE _____

DATE _____

NAME _____

COMPANY _____ DIV/SUB OF _____

LOCATION _____ REVENUE $ _____ NO. EMPLOYEES _____

TELEPHONE (____) _____ NAICS/SIC _____

TOLL FREE PHONE (____) _____ EMAIL/WEBSITE _____

DIRECTORY/IES:

SOURCES IF ANY:

INDUSTRY/PRODUCTS/COMMENTS:

ID Research Worksheet With Org Chart

CLIENT _____

JOB NO. _____

TITLE _____

DATE _____

NAME _____

COMPANY _____ DIV/SUB OF _____

LOCATION _____ REVENUE $ _____ NO. EMPLOYEES _____

TELEPHONE ( ) _____ NAICS/SIC _____

TOLL FREE PHONE ( ) _____ EMAIL/WEBSITE _____

DIRECTORY/IES:

SOURCES IF ANY:

INDUSTRY/PRODUCTS/COMMENTS:

Sources and Prospects

CLIENT		POSITION	CONTRACT NO.
NO. NAME C S		SOURCE	
TITLE			
COMPANY			
ADDRESS			
BUSINESS PHONE	HOME PHONE		
FAX	CELL/CAR		
EMAIL	WEBSITE		
NO. NAME C S		SOURCE	
TITLE			
COMPANY			
ADDRESS			
BUSINESS PHONE	HOME PHONE		
FAX	CELL/CAR		
EMAIL	WEBSITE		
NO. NAME C S		SOURCE	
TITLE			
COMPANY			
ADDRESS			
BUSINESS PHONE	HOME PHONE		
FAX	CELL/CAR		
EMAIL	WEBSITE		
NO. NAME C S		SOURCE	
TITLE			
COMPANY			
ADDRESS			
BUSINESS PHONE	HOME PHONE		
FAX	CELL/CAR		
EMAIL	WEBSITE		

Sources and Prospects

YEAR:

CLIENT				POSITION			ACCOUNT NO.
NO.	NAME			SOURCE			DATE CLOSED
TITLE							
COMPANY			CLIENT?				
ADDRESS							
BUSINESS TELEPHONE		HOME PHONE					
NO.	NAME			SOURCE			DATE CLOSED
TITLE							
COMPANY			CLIENT?				
ADDRESS							
BUSINESS TELEPHONE		HOME PHONE					
NO.	NAME			SOURCE			DATE CLOSED
TITLE							
COMPANY			CLIENT?				
ADDRESS							
BUSINESS TELEPHONE		HOME PHONE					

THE RECRUITER'S RESEARCH BLUE BOOK by Andrea Jupina

Candidate Profile

DATE	CONSULTANT		❏ DELETE ❏ NEW ❏ UPDATE ❏ RESERVE	**RETENTION** ❏ 5 YRS. ❏ 3 YRS. ❏ I YR.	❏ **SOURCE** ❏ **PROSPECT** ❏ **INTERVIEWED**	❏ REFERENCE ❏ PRESENTED ❏ PLACED ❏ NCP
SEARCH						

NAME LAST FIRST MI				

STREET	CITY	STATE/COUNTRY	ZIP	LOCATION

HOME PHONE	OFFICE PHONE	SOURCE OF NAME	YES	NO
DOB MO/DAY/YR				

EDUCATION (COLLEGE, YEAR, DEGREE/MAJOR)	CITIZENSHIP	AFFIRM ACTION
	INT'L EXP. G ME ASIAN LA EUR O	
	LANGUAGES	
CERTIFICATIONS (INC. YR.)	COMMENTS	

PRESENT CO.	
DIVISION	LOCATION
JOB TITLE	REPORTS TO
BASE SALARY EST $ E CIRCLE	BONUS	PERKS
DATES: MO/YR TO	

PREVIOUS CO.	
DIVISION	LOCATION
JOB TITLE	REPORTS TO
DATES: MO/YR TO	LAST COMP

PREVIOUS CO.	
DIVISION	LOCATION
JOB TITLE	REPORTS TO
DATES: MO/YR TO	LAST COMP

BEST SUITED FOR		SOURCE INFO I.
SUMMARY COMMENTS		2.
		3.

Alternative to Source And Prospect Sheets

Alphabetical cards by person's name filed on a rolodex-style spindle.

A separate spindle for each search assignment.

Different color cards for each search, along with a code or number for the search assignment.

This approach makes it much easier to handle returned phone calls from prospects whose names you don't recognize right away.

THE RECRUITER'S RESEARCH BLUE BOOK by Andrea Jupina

Active Search Assignments

PROPRIETARY INFORMATION

STATUS CODES:
1. New search
2. Satisfactory progress to date
3. Placement anticipated shortly
4. Need candidate and/or suggestions
5. Search in abeyance

UNIT/REGION	POSITION TITLE	SPECIFICATION	STAFF	STATUS

Completed Search Assignments

PROPRIETARY INFORMATION

UNIT/REGION	POSITION TITLE	background/explanation	STAFF	STATUS

THE RECRUITER'S RESEARCH BLUE BOOK by Andrea Jupina

CHAPTER 12

Sample Script for a Sourcing & Prospecting Call

Below are notes one researcher used to pitch a job to sources and prospects. Using a "script" like this is a big help if you're nervous at the beginning of a new search. Your "cheat sheet" might be handwritten with bullets and in big block letters, or you might word process one. It should be easy for you to follow, something like index cards when you're giving a speech. After a while you won't need to look at your script, but it's nice to have for those calls that straggle in as a search winds down and you need a quick memory refresher. It's also good documentation to attach to the formal specs in the final file.

DIRECTOR OF STRATEGIC HUMAN RESOURCES PLANNING

• Well regarded, highly profitable $multibillion service co.

> Co. has been doing well, should double in size in next 5 yrs.

> A nice guy – helpful – constructive kind of mgmt. style. (Right person won't be hard driving, super ambitious type who'll be chomping at the bit for promotion in 2 yrs.)

> Businesses are service driven. So people are more important here than a co. intensive in equip., technology or money.

> Co. has a reputation for organizing around people rather than pushing them into boxes on the org chart.

• Staff job, #2 slot, reports to VP Human Resources Planning & Dev. No direct reports. Dotted line w/Div. head of HR. Newly created position.

> Need a technician, a doer, w/good analytical skills.

• Fantastic opportunity. Co. is growing (1) by running its businesses well & (2) by acquisition.

> Good way for a comp pro to broaden to a personnel generalist.

• Responsibilities: Everything in HR except labor rels & training.

> Develop a strategic HR plan parallel to corp. bus plan

> 1. Install comp plng/benefits systems which tie into bottom line

> 2. Develop effective incentive programs

> 3. Need a working knowledge of succession planning

• Following per annual report:

> 3 main businesses: lodging, food service, entertainment. (Also in hotel mgmt. business – aids cash flow, requires less investment.)

> Founded 1927 as family business. Now over $3 billion.

> Lodging – past 5 yrs. sales grew 26% & operating income up 19% & no. of hotel rooms has doubled.

> Last year operating income rose 13% & sales rose 27%, even in a yr. of poor economy w/most cos. cutting back on bus travel. Simultaneously built 20 new hotels, which normally take 1 yr. to become established in the marketplace.

CHAPTER 13

Telephone Interview Guide

Today's date

Company/dates employed

Business company is in

Size of company

    Revenues and/or number of employees

    If this information is sensitive, ask for a "ballpark" range

Subsidiary/Division/Group/Department or other unit

    (Especially important in a large organization such as a bank or multi-billion $ company)

All titles at each company

Dates of each title

Reporting relationships

    Title person reports to

    Titles of direct reports and total number of employees managed

    Titles of peers (i.e., who reports to the same boss?)

Responsibilities and accomplishments

    Quantify accomplishments if possible. Measuring accomplishments tells not only what s/he did but how well.

    For example: % of sales quota attained and dollar volume

    Amount of money saved or revenue growth

    Increase in market share

    Profit growth

Why change jobs?

Education

    Schools/years/degrees

    Academic honors & distinctions/high grades

    Specify if evening program – this is usually a sign of a very hardworking person

Compensation

    Base

    Bonus – How much was last year's ($ and % of base)

        What's it based on?

        Is there a formula?

Pension/profit sharing

Savings plan

Car

Other perqs

Total package

When is next salary review?

When was last raise?

How much was it? ($ and %)

Resume?

Full name/nickname

Home address

Home phone number/best time to call/latest time it's convenient

Business phone number

Email address(es)

Do you have a web site?

Fax number – ok to transmit confidential communications?

Car phone? Cell phone?

Availability for an interview – Any trips planned to this area? When?

Feelings about relocation

Interest level/objections/issues

If s/he's only lukewarm, ask, "What would it take for us to seriously discuss this position?"

Always thank the person for his or her time and help.

CHAPTER 14

How to Track Down People Who Have Moved

Ask the switchboard, "Do you know where I can find Joe Allen?" Use this exact phrase – it doesn't reveal you don't know whether he's been transferred or has left the company altogether.

If that doesn't work, then ask the identical question again:

* Former secretary

* Someone else in the old department – a friend who might know, or his or her former boss

* Person who took his or her place

* Personnel records

Sometimes people will say, "He doesn't work here any more." This doesn't necessarily mean he's left the *company*, only that department. However, if you learn he has definitely left the company and you say you're an executive recruiter, people will often give a number or address. But before you reveal you're a recruiter, be sure the prospect is no longer a *company* employee. Exercise good judgment in explaining the purpose of your call. Remember, you have an obligation to protect the person's confidentiality.

If they won't give any information, ask if you can leave a message. Can someone call the prospect and ask him or her to call you back.

You can also ask if they will forward a letter. Send it to the attention of the person you talked to. Otherwise, it may not be worth the time, unless you know for sure that the contact is an important one. If you're not sure, ask somone.

Try using a search engine, such as Yahoo at www.yahoo.com, to get an email address or a street address.

Try calling an old home phone number.

* Maybe s/he still lives there

* A recording may give a new number

Look in the phone book for the phone number.

Check a national phone directory on CD-ROM, such as SelectPhone, published by Pro CD, Inc., Omaha, Nebraska (800) 922-3766. Their web site at www.infousa.com provides free US directory assistance.

Call or write the college alumni association. Most schools keep very good records for fundraising purposes. Try the undergraduate school first.

If you can't reach the prospect by phone, write a letter or send an email and ask him or her to call.

Look in the phone book for the address. You can verify the address is correct by matching the phone number with the address. This works well with a common name, like Smith. If the person has moved, the Post Office will forward mail for six months.

Call information for the home phone number and address:

"Do you have a listing for James Smith? I'm not sure what street it's on."

"I have a listing for a James T. Smith on Fairview."

"Yes, that's it."

"666-2222."

"Can you tell me what number on Fairview that is?"

"We don't give out that information."

Now call Information again:

"Do you have a listing for James T. Smith on Fairview?"

"666-2222."

"Can you tell me what number on Fairview?"

"34."

"And is that Fairview Street or Avenue?"

"That's Fairview Street."

"And do you have the zip code?"

If the operator can't provide the zip code, call the U.S. Postal Service free, 24 hours a day, at 800-ASK-USPS.

Even with computerized information operators, you can hold until a live operator returns and then ask your questions. If this doesn't work the first time, try again and maybe you'll connect with a nicer operator.

Check a biographical database, especially if the person is senior or prominent. Refer to Biography and "Who's Who" in Part II of this book.

CHAPTER 15

Documentation: The Hallmark of Fabulous Research

"What's the difference between research that's really terrific and mediocre research? Documentation." Manager Staff Selection, Booz, Allen and Hamilton

Your notes of sources and prospects' comments should be thorough and specific, especially if a problem may be surfacing. For example, if you suspect the client is offering too low a compensation package, then gather facts to prove your point and cover yourself. Wherever appropriate, ask sources and prospects, "What would it take for you to seriously consider a position with our client?" Then ask for compensation and break it into all its components – base, bonus, car, stock options, stock grants, etc. – so that all the pieces add up to the total package. Be sure you also know the person's title and the size of the organization. Otherwise this compensation data will lack the "framework" which will give it real meaning.

Be sure to make a note if someone is a good source – or if they sound really good. This way your research will be a real asset next time you're handling a similar search...or if your client changes his mind and you must re-evaluate the calls you've already made.

If a prospect sounds good but isn't interested, find out what it would take to get him or her interested – compensation, responsibilities, opportunities, job satisfaction, and whatever else is important. *Be sure to write it down.*

As management consultants, it's our job to provide clients with meaningful information so they can then make intelligent decisions. For example, the client may eventually realize that they really need a "heavy hitter" and decide to upgrade the job. But first they would probably want to review a good deal of data which supports this move.

This is why you should take complete notes: to protect yourself, to have the material to write a report and to be prepared for the unexpected. Clients are people, they change their minds, and more often than not the specs will change.

MORE COMMENTS ON DOCUMENTATION:
ADVICE FOR THE AMBITIOUS RESEARCHER

When you're talking to a knowledgeable source or prospect, pretend you're the line manager who's running the business, and take notes accordingly. For example, what information might be helpful to your client, not only in making a hiring decision, but in *running the business* as well? Sometimes you'll access outstanding, hard-to-obtain information. You and your client really ought to benefit from your phone skills. This is called *adding value*.

Valuable information could include:

*   Trends in compensation

*   Compensation formulas, especially in fields where incentives and bonuses are important

*   Organizational data, rumors, industry trends, information about organizations, mergers, companies for sale, plans to enter or sell businesses

Be sure to note the date, and ALWAYS, ALWAYS, ALWAYS show the year. Also show the source of the information – name, title, and company – so you'll have a frame of reference. The easiest way to do this is to keep track of everything on your sources and prospects sheets.

Documentation is especially important if problems arise with the search because of circumstances which are outside a researcher's control (for example, compensation or location). Thorough documentation will show both how good a job you're doing and can also pave the way for an innovative solution. This brings to mind an old saying: If you want to be successful, you have to make your boss look good.

In fact, a senior researcher or a consultant can offer an interesting "twist" to the data-gathering phase of search. In all likelihood, few search professionals have considered the similarity between search research and qualitative market research. However, in both cases one interviews knowledgeable sources and prospects to gather specific types of information. But a word of caution: this additional data gathering can be an extremely time consuming activity and absolutely should be discussed with your boss beforehand. Also, your boss should know what kind of information is appropriate to present to the client, if any, and will help you focus on the key questions to ask.

But getting back to the main point, if your sources and prospects are making the same remarks over and over, it's important to make a note of it. This way, if you must go back to the client with a report that the compensation package needs to be increased, you can do more than say, "Oh, everybody says the money's too low." You can specifically say who thinks so – including titles and companies – ideally with information about their current compensation, plus how much it would take to seriously talk about the job. And, if the client does upgrade, then you have some real candidates. Your boss looks good...and so do you.

REMEMBER, SPECS CAN CHANGE. This is a *rule* in search and if you think it's the exception, you'll make yourself crazy – fast. By keeping good notes, you'll be prepared for the unexpected and will make your own life much easier.

Suppose you're working on a search and you think there might be a problem with the position. You're an experienced researcher and your gut tells you that by this time you'd normally have more candidates than you do. You've been hearing some of these things repeatedly:

"I'm not interested in general management responsibility unless there's stock or equity."

"I don't want to relocate to the Midwest."

"I'm only interested in a job on the West Coast."

"Your client is not in a growth industry and I don't think they can offer the kind of long range opportunities I want."

"I'm extremely happy and no amount of money could induce me to leave."

"You'll never find anybody any good for that kind of money. Your client should upgrade the job and pay a heavy hitter to really do it right. Pat Green would be perfect."

"It sounds kind of interesting but I would never consider it unless sales also reported to me."

"I think you have an impossible search to fill. That's really two jobs you're talking about and your client should realize that you really need to structure this into two positions."

OK, so now what do you do?

1. THINK POSITIVE. This means offer alternative ways to solve the problem. Pretend you are the client. What would you want to know, and what would you want to do if you were in charge? What information would you need to support that move? What would really make sense? Keep in mind all the business issues and constraints *from the client's point of view.*

2. Keep detailed records of who said what. This will be important in supporting your recommendations. And the client will probably be most interested – if not surprised – to know what his

colleagues think. This can be very effective if some of your contacts are considered real "heavyweights" in the business. In fact your client may know them either personally or by reputation, and this may lend even more credibility to your recommendations.

One final comment about what you put in writing. Do be candid and complete. Deal with specific facts, not generalizations. For example, note, "The first thing he asked about was benefits," not "Sounds like a jerk." There are two reasons for this. First, the second statement contains less information than the first one – obviously he's a jerk. Second, we should always expect the unexpected, especially in terms of a possible audit by governmental authorities that might arise in connection with a discrimination complaint against a client or your firm. So if you document your work as though it will be carefully scrutinized, you're doing great research.

After all, if the information isn't written down, there's no research to refer to. Therefore, documentation is at the heart of a researcher's function. It's really documentation that makes the difference between an outstanding researcher and a mediocre one. So don't be lazy about writing things down. It's really worth the extra investment of time.

No matter how you look at it, if you keep track of what sources and prospects are saying, it sure can't hurt. And it can save the day if the client starts asking a lot of questions about a difficult search.

ORGANIZATION OF SEARCH WORK PAPERS

Prior to beginning a search, the work papers can be organized into a 3-ring binder using manila indexed divider pages into the following sections:

Specs and Notes

Target List and Supporting Data

Research Worksheets (1 worksheet for each target company) (See *Saving Search Documents* below)

Sources and Prospect Sheets (See *Saving Search Documents*)

Resumes/Backgrounds/Notes/Correspondence

References

File labels should be detailed for future reference. For example:

Client/Title/Month and Year

Description of Contents (e.g., Target List and Supporting Data)

SAVING SEARCH DOCUMENTS

Function and Industry Files

When reading business publications, you'll likely come across an industry survey or a reference to a directory or web site that could be useful in the future. This information should be filed for future referral. Eventually it can save considerable time in developing target lists, especially unusual ones. If everyone in the office contributes, this can grow into an effective and cost efficient research tool.

Of course, standard resources should also be obtained, such as the *Fortune 500 Directory*, the *Business Week Corporate Scoreboard*, *Advertising Age's Top 100 Brands*, and other surveys.

Company Files

At the close of a search, two sets of research worksheets should be filed:

   One set should be filed with all the other search papers, and

   The other worksheets should be filed in alphabetical company files for future reference.

Other company information can be integrated into the company files, such as annual reports, 10(k)'s, proxy statements, WHO'S NEWS clippings, articles, company newsletters, and photocopied company listings from miscellaneous directories, such as the *Directory Of Corporate Affiliations*.

Names of good sources and web sites should also be noted.

Company files should be reviewed at the beginning of a new search prior to the identification phase, since having a name can help make it easier to obtain more information.

CHAPTER 16

Setting up a Database or "Garbage In, Garbage Out"

Here are some guidelines for setting up a database of contacts, specifically sources, prospects and candidates. The first area of discussion concerns software. The second relates to the specific fields of information appropriate for each record.

As you are designing your database, remember the KISS principle. Keep it simple, stupid.

SOFTWARE

Consider these features when evaluating database software or applications packages. Remember, the database software that came loaded onto your computer might provide the ideal solution.

1. First and foremost, invest time to determine your needs. Be as specific as possible. Otherwise, if you don't know in the beginning what you expect, how will you know whether your database system is a success? In other words, what parameters will you use to evaluate the system?

2. Does it work? How easy is it to use?

3. How much time does it take to learn? How much time and money will you have to invest in training? Are there any good, easy-to-understand training materials available, such as CD ROM's, videos, text books, or documentation from the publisher? How dependent will you be on expensive training consultants? Are any group or classroom training seminars available, such as at computer stores? Are there any good seminars that travel around the country that are presented in hotels?

4. How well is the software supported? Is there a "Help" function built into it, and if so, how good is it? Will you have a systems expert in your office who can solve a problem every time something goes wrong, or will you have to get on the phone yourself? How long will you have to hold? Is there a toll free number or will you have to pay for long distance calls? How good is their telephone technical support? How much does it cost to subscribe for phone support? As you factor these costs into the price, remember the value of your time, too.

5. Does the package include features you don't want or need? If so, is the purchase still a good value?

6. Do you need to print address labels? How easy is this to set up? Is it easier to use a typewriter?

7. Do you need a mail merge capability, for example, for marketing mailings, company announcements, newsletters, surveys, or to send position specifications to sources and prospects?

8. How fast is the system?

9. How many records is it designed to manage efficiently? How many records do you think your database will eventually contain?

10. Is there a limit to the maximum number of characters each field will accept?

RECORD DESIGN

If you are designing a customized database, here are fields of data to include in each record. This information has been taken from a real, live database which has been refined and revised for several years:

Date

Name Title – Mr., Ms., Dr., etc. This precedes the first name in letter headings and address labels.

First Name

Middle Initial

Last Name – Information such as Jr., III or Ph.D. can be added to this field, as it should not interfere with the sort function.

Salutation – Do you want the letter to begin, Dear Joe, or Dear Dr. Frankenstein?

Job Title

Division

Company

Address 1

Address 2

Address 3

City & State

Zip

Country – It's a good idea to input the country name in solid capitals, especially if you'll be using your database for address labels or envelopes.

Be sure to allow plenty of space for multiple phone numbers, email addresses and so forth. Consider the impact of technological changes in the next few years and plan a few extra fields that may be needed for new information.

Office Phone

Office Fax

Office Email

Home Phone

Home Fax

Home Email

Web Site 1

Web Site 2

Car Phone

Cell Phone

Pager

Misc. Phone 1

Misc Phone 2

Education

Languages

International – Specify countries or regions.

Functions & Industries

SIC's/NAICS – Recently the U.S. Government replaced its Standard Industrial Classification (SIC) system with the North American Industry Code System (NAICS)

Marital Status & Names – Specify name of spouse & children. Kids' ages are especially important in case of relocation.

Birthdate

Compensation – You can usually set this up to add the total. Other fields should include: Base, Bonus, Car, Other, Total Comp, Comp Info Date, Date of Last Raise.

How Known

Comments – If you will be limited by the number of characters this field will accept, you might want to create a "Comments Cont." field in case you need extra space. There's nothing more frustrating than a system which restricts you from including important information! "Comments" should be a large field with room for a lot of information, such as prior companies and titles, and anything else you think is relevant. For example, you might want to select sources from a certain company or with a certain title.

Mark – You can use this field to mark a record, say with an X, symbols, an abbreviation or the date, to make it easier to select a group of records.

A NOTE ABOUT HOME ADDRESS

With respect to home address, you basically have two choices. You can design a larger record, and keep one record per person.

The second alternative might sound strange at first, but there's actually a good reason for it. You can omit home address fields altogether in the design of the record. If you do have home address information, simply make a second record for this information. The benefit is, if you are printing address labels or doing mail merges, you only need to select one set of fields.

If you expect to use this database for mail merges, envelopes and address labels, it may actually be easier to design the record to completely omit home address information. Otherwise, every time you do a mailing, you will have select two batches of records, once for business addresses and once for home addresses. It can be both cumbersome and time consuming to review the database twice for business and home address information.

However, if you do decide to design a record that contains home address fields per se, be sure to allow an extra field in case it's needed for long addresses, foreign addresses or for the name of a building, such as an apartment complex or a gated residence community.

Home Address 1

Home Address 2

Home Address 3

Home City & State

Home Zip

Home Country

GARBAGE IN, GARBAGE OUT – YOUR DATABASE MUST BE PROPERLY CODED

If the information in your database is to have any value, it must be accurate.

If the records in your system are incorrectly coded – for example, if the wrong functions or SIC/NAICS codes have been assigned, your searches for these records will fail to produce the contacts you're really looking for.

The only way to avoid this problem is to make sure the records are properly coded. While this is sometimes viewed as a low level clerical function, an attitude adjustment throughout the organization is in order here. This work is very important!

Someone with an in depth business understanding of industries, functions, and SIC/NAICS codes must oversee this activity. The SIC Manual or the NAICS Manual must be referred to. Someone needs to be accountable for the result, to have "pride of ownership" so that this task is done correctly. The manager must be charged with double checking the accuracy of how records are coded, or else the system loses value. What good is the information if it's inaccurate? If people are miscoded and don't turn up when you do a database search to identify contacts, why bother?

Finally, one way to minimize tedium with this task is to regularly work on it for small amounts of time. Maybe setting aside the first 30 minutes of every day will be sufficient.

OTHER WAYS TO KEEP YOUR RECORDS CURRENT

Whenever you send first class mail, make sure "Address Correction Requested" appears as the last line of your return address. If the address has changed within the past six months, the Post Office will return mail, noting the new address. Otherwise, if the mail is forwarded and you don't receive a reply, you won't know the new address, or possibly even that the address has changed!

If you do frequent mailings, you will automatically receive updated address information.

Your company might want to send surveys to track career progress, raises, and address changes of people in the database.

If you're having trouble locating someone, university alumni organizations usually have current addresses on its graduates. This information is very important for their fund raising purposes and they usually make a point of keeping their records current.

You might also obtain updated information on a person on the Internet, such as Yahoo's People Search, or through a national phone directory on the Internet or on CD ROM, or through national information on the telephone.

Finally, if your information about a person is two years old or more, it's more time-efficient to conduct new research from scratch than it is to track down that individual. However, there is one exception, and that is if you know the person, you have a relationship, and the relationship is valuable. You should definitely be prepared to invest considerable time in the detective work – perhaps as much as one to two hours or more.

CONCLUSION

Your database is only as good as the information in it. Therefore, it's critical to be selective about the individuals included. Remember, it takes time to keep information current, and time is money. Consider what it will cost to pay clerical help to update files. More important, consider the value of your own time, if you need to get involved with this yourself. Therefore, avoid clogging up the system with contacts of marginal value. Also remember the importance of correctly coding contacts' background information, such as industries, functions, and SIC or NAICS codes. Because if you can't find the right contacts when you need them, they have no value. In other words, garbage in, garbage out.

CHAPTER 17

So, You Thought Reference Checking Was Easy. Here's How to *Really* Check References

Reference checking is customarily one of the final steps in recruiting. References are generally checked immediately prior to extending an offer. This is because it takes time to thoroughly conduct a reference check.

It makes no sense to check multiple references for several individuals earlier in the search. It's an inefficient use of time and it creates unnecessary work. This invites "rushing" the process and taking short cuts to get all that work done fast enough. The result can be a hiring mistake, superficial reference reports, and the opportunity for someone to defensively say, "But I checked the references..."

If a reference check is to uncover any in depth information, it takes *time* to develop a rapport and win the trust of references. Otherwise, a ten minute conversation is most likely to yield remarks like, "He's a great guy," because most references don't want to jeopardize a candidate's chance for a job offer. It takes probing, "reading between the lines," a feel for voice intonation and "pregnant pauses" and possibly a "sixth sense" to determine whether a reference is glossing over the truth or conveniently "forgetting" any negatives. Besides, it could take a while to figure out if there's any relevant history between a candidate and a reference. This is one reason why many people would rather not delegate the reference checks – so they can "read" the references themselves.

On the other hand, some people don't believe in checking references at all. One manager said, "I always go with my gut feel about people. Once I had a secretary and I really wanted to get rid of her. I knew she was looking for another job and one day somebody called to check her out. I gave her a fabulous reference and generally lied through my teeth. She got the job. So I don't believe in references myself. Somebody else could do the same thing to me with someone they want to get rid of but are afraid to fire."

Even so, references should always be checked as a matter of self-preservation and protecting yourself. Imagine your vulnerability if you were involved with a bad hire and the references *hadn't* been contacted! Reference checking represents a due diligence step in which there's little downside, particularly if written reports contain nothing negative, or if there are no written reports at all. However, it should be emphasized that your sense of a candidate should take priority over even the most glowing reference report. If you're hesitating about hiring a particular individual, you'll probably make a mistake if you hire him or her. When in doubt, don't.

You could also find that many employers have a policy of verifying only titles held, dates of employment and compensation. It's not unusual to be "stonewalled" like this, to receive virtually no information, if you contact the personnel department. There are a few legal implications of this. One is that companies are protecting themselves from lawsuits for defamation and violation of privacy. So the less they say, the safer they are. That attitude is prevalent in most companies' human resources policies. In addition, as a matter of public interest the courts often favor an individual's right to work. Otherwise, the government could wind up with more people on unemployment or other forms of welfare.

Sometime it's appropriate to meet a reference in person, especially if the position is important. Ideally, the meeting should be unrushed and in a relaxed setting, such as over lunch, dinner, cocktails or perhaps at a weekend social event, such as golf or sailing. There are at least two advantages to this. One is that a face to face meeting should help establish a better rapport and trust. The second is, it signals to the reference that his or her opinion is so important, you are taking the time and trouble to be physically present. A face to face meeting with a reference usually should induce a higher degree of candor in the reference. Plus, sometimes a few drinks can lubricate the truth out of someone. A face to face meeting with a reference is also an excellent opportunity to establish a relationship with an important contact. If you're with a search firm or you are an unbundled search consultant, this could be a new business opportunity. If you were a CEO, and a consultant was willing to spend a day on the golf course with you to check out a former manager, would you be impressed?

In addition, an overseas phone call to a reference can sometimes generate a great degree of honesty. I once spent over 45 minutes really probing a reticent reference in England. Finally he confided, "Well, this must be very important if you're willing to go to the expense of an overseas call. The least I can do is give you my honest opinion. To answer your question, do I feel your candidate has what it takes to be a future CEO, I must unfortunately say I don't believe he's got it." This was a remarkable admission! Especially from someone in a culture where it is considered extremely rude to say anything but the nicest, most polite things about another person. This information was an incredible value relative to the cost of the phone call.

Reference checking is an activity that can be handled by any number of professionals. If an executive search firm is conducting a search, references will be checked by either a senior researcher or the search consultant. Sometimes a senior partner will want to speak to the references, especially if the reference is a senior executive who could potentially become a new client. At a company, sometimes the hiring manager or someone in the personnel department will check references, especially if he or she wants to speak directly to the reference.

The purpose of this chapter is to show you how to find out the real story when you conduct a reference check. This chapter will be valuable to a hiring managers, human resources professionals, researchers at search firms, executive recruiters, unbundled search consultants, and entrepreneurs and venture capitalists who like to do their own hiring.

THE FIRST STEP

As soon as possible, get *written* permission to check references. Do this as soon as possible, preferably at the end of the interview when you will have decided, "This one's a candidate." See chapter 18 for a sample release.

THE NEXT STEP

Refresh yourself on the art of reference checking. This chapter is the best mini-course around. As a matter of fact, I wrote this chapter, and I always read it before I check references. It really works!

THE STEP AFTER THAT

After I've reviewed this material, I always prepare a Reference Check Guide. That's a list of the individualized questions to be discussed with each reference. This chapter will show you how to tailor a Reference Check Guide for a candidate's references. Remember, each search is different and so is each company's corporate culture. In fact, there can be tremendous variation from one department to another within the same company! Consequently, there can be variation in each Reference Check Guide, especially if you are checking references for more than one candidate for the same position.

No matter how much reference checking experience you might have, it's still very helpful to conduct your reference check using an easy to read guide. This is important for a number of reasons:

1. Reference checking is a skill that gets "rusty" when it's not used. Having a list in front of you will allow you to start your interview more comfortably and confidently.

2. References are usually extremely busy people. They don't usually expect to devote the amount of time a thorough reference check requires, which can be 30 to 45 minutes or longer. It's

important to be prepared with a list of good, relevant questions, rather than get "stuck" about an important question on the tip of your tongue. You want to avoid appearing disorganized or unprepared.

3. When a reference returns your call and you're in the middle of another project, having a list of questions helps you switch gears quickly and efficiently, assuring that you'll cover all the necessary material.

As an added bonus, checking references can offer new business opportunities, since many references are senior executives in a position to approve search business. In fact, an impressive Reference Check Guide could even be used as a marketing tool.

A FEW WORDS ABOUT PERMISSION TO CHECK REFERENCES

The moment you think someone might possibly be a candidate, you should get his or her written permission to check references and the social security number. When it's time to check references, you will avoid the inconvenience and lost time of faxing confidential forms back and forth, no doubt while the hiring manager is impatient to make an offer and close the deal.

A secretary could always insert a blank "permission to check references" release form into each candidate's file, prior to the interview. That way, there will always be a reminder.

It's important to manage candidates' expectations. If they provide permission to check references, they may think that they are closer to getting an offer than they really are. Be forthright with your candidates. It's not fair to get their hopes up and then to disappoint them. How would you feel if the situation were reversed? You could say something like, "We routinely ask our candidates to give us permission to check references so we have it in the file. It saves both of us time later on. Of course, if we're going to check references, we'll get in touch with you so you give us their names. It's premature for you to give us that information now, though."

As a courtesy to the candidates, you should let them know when their references should expect to be called. Most candidates already know this, but just to be sure, I always recommend they alert their references to expect a call. Not only is it polite, it also gives the references a chance to think about what they want to say. This can be important with a former employer who hasn't seen the candidate in years.

At the end of this chapter is a sample Permission To Check References release. If you're thinking of using it, have an attorney review it first.

THE REFERENCE CHECK PROCESS

After the candidate has granted written permission to check references, the next step is to verify educational background. You will need the candidate's social security number, year of graduation and other information. You or your secretary should call the school and they will advise if it's necessary to submit a written request. If the switchboard operator has trouble figuring out the right person to connect you to, ask for the Registrar's office. If you can conduct a degree check on the phone, be sure to note the name of the person you spoke to and the date. Always note the year when dating any item.

Be sure to allow plenty of lead time. Sometimes it takes several weeks for an answer. Some schools require a written request and otherwise won't release information over the phone or by fax or email.

Next, prepare your Reference Check Guide. It should include the basic areas you wish to cover plus specific questions you want to ask. Each search is different, and so is each candidate. Your guide should take into account the requirements of the position and any particular concerns the hiring manager may have about the candidate.

A FEW BASICS

A few examples of reference check guides appear at the end of the chapter.

When leaving a message for a reference, state your name and firm and that you're calling to conduct a reference check. Never leave the name of the candidate as this can be a violation of his or her privacy. Suppose someone walks by and sees the candidate's name on the message slip? Never assume that voicemail is confidential because you never know when someone's secretary will pick up voicemail. We absolutely have a strict responsibility to protect the candidate's identity at all times, all the more so with someone *not* on the job market.

When you reach the reference on the phone, introduce yourself and state the purpose of your call.

If you plan to conduct a really thorough, in depth reference check, as a courtesy to the reference, let him or her know that you will need at least 30 minutes. In fact many such conversations last an hour or longer. If you catch the reference at a bad time, make an appointment and schedule the phone call. Otherwise, it could take days or weeks to reconnect, especially if one of you travels. Some references actually prefer being called at home in the evening.

Emphasize that everything will be kept confidential.

Describe the position. Remember, we are gathering information to get a handle on how well a candidate will perform in a specific job, in a certain working environment, and dealing with particular personalities.

It's important to establish the reference's relationship to the candidate. In general a superior whom the candidate directly reported to is the best reference. However, in a search where managerial skills are important, it can be extremely useful to interview the "consumer" of the manager's skill, that is, subordinates who reported to the manager. Certainly they can provide a perspective about their boss that superiors can't. Likewise, peers are frequently in a position to comment candidly about the candidate's real feelings about what was going on at the company, for a peer is the most likely to be a friend as well.

Speaking of personal references, these are not good contacts, unless there is also a business relationship. Besides, what kind of a friend would say something negative to a reference?

QUESTIONS

Nature of Their Relationship and Credibility of the Reference

What was the nature of the reference's relationship to the candidate? Was it business, personal, or both? When did they meet? How? If they worked together, was there a reporting relationship? Was the reference a superior, peer, or a subordinate? If there was no direct reporting relationship, in what capacity did they work together? What was the nature of their last contact? When was it? How often are they in touch?

What was the reference's title and responsibilities at the time the two worked together? When was this?

What is the reference's current title? What are his or her responsibilities? This is important information because it helps establish the reference's credibility. For example, suppose the reference was previously the Corporate Controller and is currently the President of the company. If the search is for a marketing position, the reference's comments should be weighed in the appropriate context, since a controller might not be in the best position to offer insight about the candidate's success potential in certain aspects of the job.

Ask the reference to describe the business, revenues, number of employees, lines of business, and anything else about the business that can be an important measure of the candidate's accomplishments.

(For example, for a sales manager one such parameter might be the amount of sales growth and whether this growth can be attributed to a price increase or real growth in the number of units sold.)

If the reference was a boss, what kind of an employee was the candidate? How did s/he perform? What was it like to manage him or her?

If the reference was a peer, how did s/he compete?

If the reference was a subordinate, what kind of a boss was the candidate? Comment on the candidate's skills as a manager – interpersonally, as a motivator, in terms of fairness, consistency, willingness to go to bat for his or her people, keeping promises, and developing staff.

Strengths and Weaknesses

Ask the reference to comment on strengths and weaknesses, keeping in mind the candidate's relationship with the reference. This is an important question which should always be asked, regardless of the candidate or the search.

In some cases it might be preferable to ask this question less directly. For example, instead of asking about "weaknesses," you could say, "As we look to manage this person, what areas should we concentrate on developing?" Otherwise, a reference might be reluctant to reveal any shortcomings for fear of hurting the candidate's chances of getting an offer.

Throughout your conversation, pay attention to the demeanor of the reference. Does he or she sound fair and objective, with no hidden agenda? Does the reference sound like a self-important idiot or an overly political user of people? Bear this in mind in assessing the validity of the reference's remarks. Do you feel like the reference isn't being completely forthright, or might be holding something back? If so, you might see how he or she responds to, "I keep getting this feeling that you're not telling me everything, that there's something else." Do you suspect that the reference might have a vendetta against the candidate? That could require several extra calls to "blind references" to sort out what is really going on. Remember our friend, the reference who lied so he wouldn't have to fire his secretary.

Open and Close Ended Questions

Ask open ended questions. Don't lead the reference by asking close ended questions, that is, ones which can be answered yes or no. For example don't ask, "Is he a good manager?" Instead say, "Please describe his skills as a manager," or "What's she like as a manager?" Then probe, probe, probe. When the reference makes a general statement, ask, "Why do you say that? Can you give me an example?" We need facts, ideally the kind of information which can be connected to performance.

For instance, you might say to a reference, "You just said that the candidate was an excellent sales manager. Why do you say that? Can you give me an example?"

The reference might answer, "Before Kathy became Region Manager, sales were off and morale was terrible. Most of us were pretty unhappy because we thought our sales commission plan wasn't fair. Actually, the more we sold, the more our percentage shrank! But when Kathy joined the department, it didn't take long to figure out that she was really a terrific person. She's smart. It was obvious she cared about people. She's fun to be with. She's a really great manager, a fabulous motivator, and a straight shooter. And she listens, she really listens.

She was smart enough to see that our commission plan was lose-lose. She knew we felt we weren't paid fairly if we worked extra hard, and that meant that the company was the ultimate loser. She had some great ideas about how to keep costs under control. One of the things Kathy did was ask for our thoughts about a new commissions plan. She wanted to know what we thought would give us an incentive to perform, what would really reward performance. Her management style is basically participative, and that's how she got a lot of her ideas. Well, she collected our ideas, added a few of her own, and then proposed to top management a new commission plan. And she had the savvy to shepherd the new plan through the political mine field in corporate. It took a while, but she hung in there and it was finally approved. She's so smart! She knew her success depended on us, and it's paid off nicely for everyone – us, her and the company. All the good people are making lots more money now. Sales are up 46% over last year, and this is without a price increase. She's very well thought of here...I'd sure hate to see her go."

"You mentioned that the sales reps felt the old commissions plan was unfair. Why is the new plan so much better? What's the difference? Is there a formula?"

"Sure. Actually, the brilliance of Kathy's proposal was in its simplicity. Here's how it works..."

This example shows that reference checking can provide an opportunity to gather information that can be valuable to a hiring manager, in this case, detailed information about how the competition is compensating its sales force.

Open Ended Questions

The Importance of Asking for Examples...and Facts

The following is a list of some specific areas which can be probed, using open ended questioning techniques, such as, "Why do you say that?" and, "Can you give an example?" A specific example can provide the facts of a situation. Knowing the facts then allows us to independently make our own assessments, rather than totally depending on a reference's judgments, opinions and biases.

Some Open Ended Questions

Remember to ask for examples (including factual details) when interviewing references about the following, especially if they are important areas of concern:

Technical skills

Ability to work with customers

Knowledge of the industry

Product knowledge

Potential to grown into more responsibility (be specific)

New business development skills

Political skills

Interpersonal skills

Negotiating skills

Values and ethics

Maturity

Team player

Skills as a manager of people

What motivates him/her?

What do you think is important to the candidate? In his or her career? In life overall?

Why has the candidate changed jobs in the past? This is another important question, especially if there are any gaps in employment or if there's any controversy surrounding a candidate's departure from a company.

Why do you think the candidate is interested in this opportunity?

Assuming you had an appropriate position, would you rehire the candidate?

Is there anything else we should know about the candidate? Personal life, work habits, alcohol, drugs, gambling, running around, anything an employer would be concerned about that could interfere with job performance? This is an excellent question to ask near the end of your interview as it covers anything your exhaustive list of questions may have missed. This is another question which should always be asked.

Do you know of anyone else qualified to confidentially comment about the candidate? This question is extremely important, because it will lead you to "blind" references. Presumably the references given to you by the candidate will be positive. But the most valuable, candid information sometimes comes from those not provided by the candidate. Again, carefully consider the source in evaluating a reference's remarks. Remember, references are important, but they aren't God. They're just references.

Final Question

The following is a good closing question for wrapping up the reference check:

"Overall, what kind of a recommendation would you give for this particular position?" Sometimes it's helpful to ask the reference to rate this on a scale of 1 to 10, especially if you feel the reference is being vague. If the reply is not a 10, be sure to ask, "Why not?"

Some references don't believe in ever giving anybody a 10, just as some teachers don't believe in giving an A, which means perfect, and nobody's perfect. If this is the case with the reference, it's important to note that this is his or her value system.

At the conclusion of the conversation, be sure to thank the reference for being so generous with his or her time.

HONESTY

Obviously, it's important to verify that the candidate has told the truth. Besides conducting a degree check, you should also "spot check" the following:

Titles

The dates they were held

Reporting relationships

Responsibilities

Promotions

Accomplishments

Why the candidate left the company

Whether the candidate resigned or was fired

However, make sure that the reference is both credible and in a position to know the answers to your questions. For example, while personnel departments will generally release very little information, they should be willing to verify some of this information. Also, bear in mind that some references simply may not remember all this detail, especially if their relationship goes back several years. In that case, you should ask for the name of someone else in a better position to provide verification. Be sure to ask for permission to use the reference's name.

In the course of conducting a reference check, we have an obligation to thoroughly exercise due diligence to ascertain that the candidate has indeed been honest. Naturally, if even the slightest discrepancy turns up, or if we have a "hunch" that something is amiss, further investigation is appropriate until any doubts have been resolved.

THE TRUTH, THE WHOLE TRUTH, AND NOTHING BUT THE TRUTH
FERRETING OUT THE NEGATIVES

Understandably, most references have no desire to say anything that will hurt a candidate's chances of getting a job offer. Consequently, it takes a great deal of effort to develop rapport with a reference so that he or she feels comfortable discussing all the candidate's strengths and weaknesses. This is one reason why a good reference check takes so long – it takes a while for people to feel enough trust to open up – especially to a stranger on the phone. For this reason, a face to face interview with a reference is sometimes appropriate.

If you're a corporate employee working with contingency recruiters, you might want to make sure you're getting objective information from references, either by conducting the reference check yourself or by retaining an expert who can do this for you. Some successful venture capital firms use contingency firms to recruit executives for their start up companies, and then retain independent consultants, such as unbundled search consultants, to check references on a per diem fee basis. This avoids an economic conflict of interest because the consultant who checks references is earning a guaranteed fee, regardless of whether the candidate is placed.

The point is not to cast aspersions on the reference checking capability of recruiting firms – certainly any quality firm understands that it's not in their best interest to generate a fee by placing the wrong person in the job – especially if they value long term client relationships. But it is important to understand what motivates each kind of firm, to "get inside their head," so to speak, so that you can make sure your interests are protected. One good test is whether all parties share the same goals. Again, a real desire for a long term relationship is very important.

The main purpose of reference checking is avoiding a hiring mistake. This is largely achieved by gathering good information, both intellectual and emotional. This also means "reading between the lines," paying attention to your "gut instinct," and listening carefully to what's said and what's omitted. In other words, is a candidate being "condemned by faint praise?" How enthusiastic is the reference? What kinds of information does he or she volunteer about the candidate? Reference reports should be accurate, candid, detailed and thorough.

Since it's human nature to "come up short" in one way or another, a reference check that reveals no shortcomings isn't really complete.

In fact, a reference report which discloses some negatives is not only more "reality-based," it can actually help an employer manage the employee.

Obviously, some searches are more critical than others. For example, the success of a new start up company hinges on hiring the right top management. In this situation, it's generally more important to dig really hard to ferret out as much as possible about a candidate. Naturally, some of the most important details are the negatives...precisely what references are reluctant to disclose in the first place, for fear of ruining the candidate's chances of a job offer. It's only human to want to be honest, but not to say so much that it's damaging. So references have a tendency to hold back on bad news, unless someone can draw it out.

Of course the idea is not to conduct a "witch hunt" but simply to avoid any surprises after the candidate's in the job. It's like buying a house and knowing beforehand that you'll need a new kitchen.

If you need to check references, here are some questions you might ask to determine whether to do the work internally or use an outside professional, such as a provider of "unbundled search" services:

1. Are the motivations and goals of the person conducting the reference checks "in sync" with yours? Is his or her goal to find out as much information as possible...to provide good service needed to nurture a long term relationship...or is it just to close the search quickly and collect a fee?

2. Does the "reference checker" have time to do a thorough, deeply probing reference check?

3. Can you get a written report if you need one? What's the "down side" to doing this internally? Is there enough time to do this? Assume that it takes as much time to write the report as it does to gather the information, plus extra time for word processing, corrections and proof reading.

4. Is the person conducting the reference checks skilled and experienced? For example, in some ways reference checking is similar to conducting an interview, especially in drawing information out of reluctant people and knowing how to "read" it. If a line executive is contemplating conducting reference checks, does he or she have a record of being a good judge of "horse flesh" that's backed up by a history of consistently making good hiring decisions? If not, that's not likely to change now, and it will be important to have a strong person jointly working on the reference checks.

5. Are there any political sensitivities that make it advantageous to use the services of an outside vendor?

6. Should you use outside help to assure confidentiality...either yours or the candidate's?

Conclusion

In summary, whenever you check references, first, obtain the candidate's social security number and written permission to check references. This should be done as soon as possible, preferably at the end of the interview, while the candidate is still in the office. Second, refresh yourself on how to conduct a reference check by rereading this chapter or listening to the cassette tape "Uncovering the Truth – How to Really Check References." Third, write a Reference Check Guide – a list of all the areas you want to cover – so you're prepared for references who return your calls when you're in the middle of another project. Finally, as you interview the reference, ask mainly open ended questions. Get specific examples whenever generalizations are made by asking questions like, "Why do you say that?" and "Can you give me an example?" Probe for details. Be sure you can explain 100% of what a reference says because if the hiring manager asks, "What does he mean by that?" and you don't know, you'll look like an idiot. It is a mistake to assume that someone else knows more than you do about terminology or technical jargon. They usually don't. Make sure you understand it so you can explain it. Make sure everything makes sense to you. Because the buck stops with you.

There are several questions which should always be asked. Always ask about greatest strengths and weakness. Follow up with questions like, "Is there anything else?" and "Is that all?" Ask about accomplishments and "How did s/he do that?" Get specific examples. Probe. Find out why the candidate changed jobs. Absolutely be sure to ask if the reference would rehire the candidate. Towards the end of the interview, be sure you ask, "Is there anything about the candidate that we should know that we haven't covered yet?" Finally, be sure to ask, "Do you know anyone else who knows the candidate well enough to confidentially comment? Of course, we will keep your name confidential." Last but not least, remember to thank references for their time.

In conclusion, an employer should be able to make a reasonable, informed decision about hiring a candidate. Everyone's life will be a lot easier if there are no unpleasant surprises after the candidate is hired. Astute interviewing, good listening and thorough reference checking should reveal any tendencies that might need to be managed. When someone is hired, there should be no surprises. That's what's important about full disclosure. It's not that you expect somebody to be perfect, it's that your eyes are open and you are aware of what's in the package. Because a candidate who is a "10" in one setting might be less than that if there's bad chemistry or a poor match with the corporate culture. That's why it's important to "listen to your gut" and to assess candidates through other means than references.

However, candidates also have rights, and a considerable body of law protects them with respect to privacy and third party inquiry. Since laws vary from one state to another, getting legal advice is strongly recommended.

One final word. Reference checks are important. But you should never second guess your feelings about a candidate because of something a reference said. Don't ever let a reference's remarks override your instincts, especially if the candidate will be working for you. And don't ever let a glowing reference report persuade you to hire someone your otherwise wouldn't. Because even if references are right about how wonderful a candidate is, the combination of bad chemistry and "self-fulfilling prophecy" are the seeds of disaster, regardless of all the wonderful things references might say.

The Ideal Reference Refresher

For your convenience, a reasonably priced cassette tape of this chapter is available from the publisher. Don't waste time reading when you can listen to a tape on the way to work or at the gym. For more information about "Uncovering the Truth – How to Really *Check References," call Kennedy Information at (800) 531-0007.*

CHAPTER 18

Permission to Check References

A Sample Release Form

Candidate's name

Street Address

City, State, Zip

I, (*name of candidate*), authorize all persons, including but not limited to schools, companies, corporations, credit bureaus and law enforcement agencies, to supply any information concerning my background to employees of (*name of employer company*), (*name of firm conducting reference checks*), and any organizations owned by or affiliated with either.

Name of Candidate _____

Social Security Number _____

Date_____

Note: Since laws vary from state to state, seek the advice of local legal counsel before using this form.

CHAPTER 19

Sample Reference Check Guides

Director of Development

For a Private University

Emphasize that everything will be kept confidential

Describe position

Nature of their relationship – work, personal friendship, or both

1 or 2 questions to verify the resume's true, e.g., titles, dates, and best of all, accomplishments (including dollar amounts and other numbers)

Strengths and weaknesses, both personal and professional

Open ended questions. ("Please comment on...")

Fund raising skills

Management skills

How would s/he go about conveying to subordinates who's in charge, especially in a setting where there's been a lot of turnover and change?

Rehire?

Anything else we should know?

Overall, what kind of recommendation would you give for this particular position (1-10)?

Emphasize that everything will be kept confidential.

Describe position

Nature of their relationship

Business, social, or both? If business, was there a reporting relationship or were they peers...or something else?

Relationships with people

How does he handle a difficult situation?

> For example, if he feels his job is on the line...or he's lost credibility...or has been reprimanded by his boss...what would he do? Would he go home and yell at the wife and kids, fire a subordinate, buy an expensive car, withdraw, drink at lunch, or something else? What?

Political skills

How's his head for financial data, e.g.:

> Glance at operating data and spot a problem right away?

> If spend $10 K on new equipment, quickly calculate how long it will take to realize return on investment?

CEO potential (Rate on a scale of 1-10)

Rehire?

Anything else we should know – personal life, work habits

Overall recommendation for this particular position (1-10)

Emphasize that everything will be kept confidential.

Describe position

Nature of their relationship – business, personal or both?

If business, what was reporting relationship, if any?

Comment on how he runs a business

What kind of a manager is he?

How does he motivate people?

Relationships with people (probe, probe, probe!)

How does he deal with a difficult boss?

How opinionated is he?

How flexible?

How sensitive to people from another culture?

How tenacious? Stubborn?

Communication skills?

Creativity

Functional skills

Marketing

Operations/technical

Analytical skills

Finance

Anything else we should know? Personal life, work habits

Rehire (for appropriate job)?

Overall recommendation for this particular position

Anyone else we could confidentially speak to?

Sample Reference Check Guide for a "Controversial" Candidate
President & Chief Operating Officer
Venture Capital Start Up Company in Retail Services

Emphasize that everything will be kept completely confidential.

Describe position

Nature of relationship

How long?

Business, personal, or both?

Last contact?

What's reference currently doing?

Strengths and weaknesses

Functional strengths and weaknesses overall

Rate how you think he'd handle acquisitions (overall on a scale of 1-10)

Nose for a good deal

The numbers

Sizing up the people situation

Negotiating skills

What kind of a manager is he?

Hiring & firing

Team building

How does he motivate people?

How would subordinates rank his fairness as a boss?

    Willingness to go to bat for his people

    Keep promises

    Develop staff

Give an example of how he handled a difficult, sensitive, people problem

Is he a "bull in a china shop?"

What kind of a guy his he? Psychological makeup

Hobbies, interests

What's he like socially?

What motivates him? What's really important to him in life?

How has he changed since he got married?

Interpersonal skills (1-10)

Does he have perfectionist tendencies? (Distinguish between high standards vs. excessive pursuit of detail/paralysis by analysis)

Flexibility

How does he handle change?

Values and ethics

Maturity

How was he different in the earlier years of his career, say from age 20-40, compared to now?

Political skills

Critically important question – Why'd he leave his last job? What's he been doing since he left?

What do you figure his enemies would say about him? Why?

Why do you think he's interested in this opportunity?

Anything else we should know about him that could affect his performance? Personal life, work habits, alcohol, drugs, gambling, running around?

Anyone else qualified to comment about him?

Overall recommendation for this particular position (1-10)? Why not a 10?

CHAPTER 20

Legal Issues In Executive Search

By Jane E. Shaffer and Richard W. Laner

From crafting the job description on through telephone and face-to-face interviewing, legal booby traps abound and search professionals should be aware of the risks to themselves personally as well as to search firm and company.

INTRODUCTION

It used to be rare for executives to sue their employers. But that was before the rash of corporate takeovers and mergers, where suddenly more and more executives were phased out, retired early or were simply fired. As a result, there is more alienation and bitterness: executives increasingly have retreated from loyal company-oriented behavior and turned to self-protection and security.

Employment discrimination laws for search firms are in large part identical to the employment discrimination laws for corporate employers. Conducting an executive search today requires a basic knowledge of Title VII of the Civil Rights Act of 1964, Executive Order 11246, the Age Discrimination in Employment Act, The Americans with Disabilities Act, Fair Labor Standards Act, Fair Credit Reporting Act, tortious interference with contract, negligent hiring, defamation laws as well as state and local laws. Moreover, the Nuremberg rules apply to search firms, too, that is, they cannot exonerate themselves from liability merely by claiming "we were just following our client's orders." A search firm can be sued and found liable just as any other employer. In fact, it risks being sued by an applicant for either improper recruiting procedures or for failing to refer the applicant to the client, or both; as a co-defendant with its client by a rejected applicant or an unhappy employee; an by the client itself for negligence in the selection process, or for failing to reveal certain information learned during that process.

This chapter reviews the legal risks that search firms face at the different steps of the selection process, and it is important for search researchers and other recruiting professionals to be aware of these risks.

DEFINING THE JOB CRITERIA

It is critical to be cautious. Discrimination suits need to be defended from the moment a job search is received. What is the job? What criteria will be used to get candidates? The burden is on both the search firm and its client to justify the criteria that will be used. The criteria must be job related, that is, necessary for the proper performance of the job. Unfortunately, it is difficult to articulate the requirements for a good executive. For that reason, many high level employment decisions end up being made on intangible subjective discretionary factors such as "leadership ability," "ability to fit in," "confidence," or simply, "I feel good about him." Generally, using these subjective criteria alone is not discriminatory. However, significant legal liability may arise if the only applicants that meet these subjective criteria of "fitting in" are white males under the age of 40.

This risk cannot be avoided by simply setting objective criteria such as *years of experience* or *educational level*. These apparently "neutral" requirements may result in excluding minorities or other protected groups from the job search. For example, if women have only been permitted to work in a particular field for the last five years and the job criteria requires ten years of experience, those criteria have effectively eliminated all women. This may be non-discriminatory if the search firm and its client are able to justify that ten years of experience is truly *necessary* to perform the job properly. However, if the ten years is merely a *preference* and a person is capable of performing the job with only five years of experience, setting ten years as a criteria could be discriminatory.

Since a search firm can be held legally liable, it should not blindly accept the criteria set by its client. Instead, it should be part of the process, or at least, review the criteria carefully to make certain that they are necessary and meaningful to the performance of the job. Articulate the criteria with as much objectivity as possible.

A search firm may be faced with a situation where its client's desires and its legal responsibilities are in conflict. It is clear that if a search firm accepts a job in which a client requests that only males or only white applicants be referred, the search firm is as liable as the client for intentional discrimination. The Equal Employment Opportunity Commission ("EEOC") Regulations specifically provide: "An employment agency that receives a job order containing an unlawful sex specification will share responsibility with the employer placing a job order if the agency fills the order knowing that the sex specification is not based upon a bona fide occupational qualification ("BFOQ"). 29 C.F.R. S1604.6(b). This issue becomes more complicated when a client requests that a search firm refer only minority or only female candidates because it wishes to increase the number of minority or women executives in a company. Although this is a noble endeavor, it constitutes *illegal* reverse discrimination. The EEOC has held that "exclusive referrals" are *only* permissible if there is a court ordered hiring plan, or if there is a BFOQ.

This does not mean that a search firm cannot aid in the implementation of an employer's affirmation action obligations. A search firm can make "specific efforts" to recruit minority and female applicants. There is nothing illegal about referring a greater number of women or minorities for a position as long as the search firm also refers all qualified male and non-minority candidates. If such a request is received, the sensible thing to do is to advise the client that a special effort will be made to refer women and/or minorities but, of course, *all* qualified applicants will be referred in a non-discriminatory manner.

RECRUITMENT

It is important to note that the plaintiff in a discrimination suit does not need to show an *intent* to discriminate, merely a discriminatory *result* or *effect*. Statistical evidence of the number of people interviewed, rejected or accepted, compared to the population in the area of a search can and will be used against the recruiter. For example, if 15% of the people in the search area are black and 45% are women, yet all of the managers and executives that are referred to the prospective employer are white males, there is a strong presumptive statistical case of discrimination.

1. Tortious Interference with Contract

America's free enterprise system permits a company to hire the best employees it can, either through its own efforts or by employing an executive search firm. This is true whether the potential employees are currently working for another employer or not. The privilege of fair competition, as it is known, even includes the right to offer higher salaries to lure away a competitor's employees. However, that privilege does *not* protect a search firm that uses unfair methods to hire competitor's employees, or hires them with the hope of injuring the competitor. The search firm and its client could be sued by the competitor for any resulting damages, under the legal theory of "tortious interference with contract." Under this theory, the outsider is liable to the employer for causing an employee to breach his or her employment contract because, in the eyes of the law, when two parties enter a contract, each has a legally protected interest in the other's performance.

If a search firm knowingly assists a client in "raiding" a competitor for the improper purpose of harming the competitor, or by using improper means during the process, the search firm could be charged with conspiracy or wrongful interference with the employment contract.

This is a very broad and undefined area of law. However, the legal elements of intentional interference with contract have been established in many states as follows:

1. The existence of a valid and enforceable contract between the employee and the former employer;

2. Awareness of the contractual relationship by the new employer or search firm;

3. Intentional and unjustified inducement of a breach of that contract;

4. A subsequent breach of the contract caused by the company's or the search firm's wrongful conduct; and

5. Damages resulting from the breach of contract.

The second element can be misleading. A search firm cannot avoid liability by not asking the candidate about an employment contract. Under the law, knowledge of facts that would lead a reasonable person to believe that such a contract exists is sufficient to find that the person is aware of the contract itself. The most troubling aspect of this legal theory is that there are no set rules as to what types of action constitute tortious interference. That is because the legality of the actions depends upon the "intent" of the person or company doing the recruiting. For example, recruiting an employee from a client's top competitor with the "intent" to hurt that competitor would be tortious interference. Yet, recruiting that same employee may be perfectly legal if the fact that he or she worked for the competitor never entered into the decision process and the person was just one of several candidates for the job. There is often a very fine line between the two situations, making it difficult for either side to prove its case.

Although there are no set rules as to what is tortious interference, a look at what has been found to be tortious interference in the past gives us some guidelines. It is relatively clear that the presence of a malicious motive, a sense of spite or a desire to harm the former employer are indicative of interference with the contract. Also, the use of threats, economic coercion, misrepresentation, bribery, falsehood or any other illegal act in an effort to induce the employee to breach the contract is tortious. Courts have also found that it is improper interference to entice away another company's employees solely for the purpose of taking them away from *that* employer. Similarly, it's improper to entice away an employee for the purpose of enhancing a new company's opportunities at the expense of the former company's opportunities.

To properly assess the risk of legal liability, the employment contract in question must be reviewed. The contract that contains a restrictive covenant, such as a non-compete agreement, is more likely to result in litigation – particularly if employment with the new company would violate that non-compete covenant. In such a situation, an attorney should be consulted to determine the likelihood that the non-compete covenant is enforceable.

If the contract is for no specific period of time, or if there is no written contract, the employee will probably be considered an "at-will" employee who is free to quit his or her job at any time. The general rule is that a contract that is terminable at-will is ordinarily not protected as long as the interference by the outsider is based on a legitimate business purpose and no improper means are used. However, this area of law varies from state to state. For example, Illinois courts have held that the fact that the employment is at-will is "immaterial to whether there exists a valid contractual relationship or prospective business relationship in tortious interference actions. Plaintiff need know only that both parties would have been willing and desirous of continuing the employment relationship for an indefinite period of time."

THE INTERVIEW

The actual interview with new applicants may be the single area most likely to lead to claims against a company or a search firm. Everyone has an initial reaction to either liking or disliking an applicant. However, the tendency to waive some criteria because the applicant is so good in other respects must be overcome. As difficult as it may seem, search firms must attempt to limit the arbitrariness or subjectivity used in hiring executives to avoid charges of discrimination. One method is to develop a list of questions that are asked of each applicant for a certain position. Failure to ask the same questions of all the applicants places your objectivity under suspicion. There is also a tendency to ask certain questions to only some groups. For example, a facially neutral question such as: "Are you willing to travel" is non-discriminatory if it is asked of all applicants. However, it becomes potentially discriminatory if it is asked only of female applicants. Following a checklist will help avoid this situation.

Although federal law does not spell out exactly what can and cannot be asked during an interview, there are some areas that are generally thought to imply bias, such as questions about children, pregnancy, military discharge or arrests. In addition, many state and local laws have specific restrictions on questions that can be asked during the interview. For example, New York and several other states prohibit questions about an applicant's arrest record.

An interviewer should ask the following questions to help develop a non-discriminatory list:

Would the question be necessary to judge the individual's competence to perform the job?

Could it have a disproportionate affect on minority groups?

How can the use of such information be defended?

Can an informed decision be made about this person if the answer to this question is not known?

If the answers to these questions indicate illegality, the question should be deleted or restructured so it becomes legal. That is done by deciding exactly what is wanted to be known about the applicant. For example, a recruiter may be concerned that a woman may leave a job to raise a family. The natural tendency is for the recruiter to ask "Do you plan on getting married?", "Do you have children?", or "Do you plan on having children?" However, these questions are potentially discriminatory and do not provide the information being sought. That is, the fact that a person has children or does not have children will not answer the question of whether they will be at work every day. Instead, the recruiter should ask the direct question. For example, "Our client is planning on investing several years of training in whomever takes this position; therefore, they are looking for someone that will make a long term commitment to the Company. Is there any reason you might not stay with us for the next few years?" Or, "What are your career objectives?" Or, "Where do you see yourself in five years?" These questions address the real issue and are non-discriminatory.

BACKGROUND INVESTIGATIONS

In a growing number of reported cases across the country, employers are being sued under the trot of "negligent hiring" by persons claiming that they were injured by an employee. The claim is that the employer knew or should have known that the employee was not fit for the particular job; thus, the injury involved was foreseeable. Typically, this liability is based on the employer's failure to perform an adequate reference check or to verify previous employment. A search firm that is involved in such a hiring or background investigation, may also be brought into such a lawsuit.

As a general rule, to find liability, the claimant must prove *at least* that: (1) the injury or harm was foreseeable; (2) that the employee who caused the injury was unfit for the job; (3) the employer's hiring and retention of the unfit employee was the proximate cause of the plaintiff's injury; and (4) the employer knew or should have known of the employee's unfitness.

Negligent hiring claims initially evolved from a clear cut situation, such as an early claim in which a woman was murdered by a man hired by her landlord to paint her apartment. The landlord had employed the painter without ever checking his references and then provided him with a key to the woman's apartment. After the murder, it was discovered that the man previously had been committed to a hospital for the criminally insane. In this case, the direct relationship between the employer's negligence and the claimant was clear. However, as these claims increased, the courts expanded the right to sue to a point where the cases are no longer as clear cut.

The tougher claims to anticipate are those where a less than thorough investigation was conducted, or, the information was learned in the investigation but the recruiter did not recognize the potential risk. These difficult cases often are decided simply on what the court determines to be the employer's duty in the particular situation. The courts typically find a direct link between the type of job applied for and the extent of the duty to research the applicant's background. The more public contact and opportunity to take advantage of others involved with the employee's job, the greater the duty to investigate the applicant's background. Thus, a criminal records check may not be expected for a file clerk but it may be expected for a top executive. Executives are often in positions where they may abuse their authority or improperly influence people. Executives are also privy to confidential information that could aid them in the commission of a crime.

The risk of negligent hiring claims is countered by the additional legal risks involved with background investigations such as invasion of privacy and libel claims. Therefore, it is important that a reasonable investigation be make, without going beyond the accepted standards. Resumes should not be relied upon alone as they can be written to cover gaps in employment. Each candidate should complete an application form or the recruiter must devise another method to assure that uniform data is collected on each candidate. A background investigation should include, at a minimum, a review and verification of he documents and information supplied by the applicant. First, all diplomas, degrees, licenses and prior jobs should be documented. All gaps in employment history should be questioned and verified. An investigation should not be limited to just those persons listed as references; names of other individuals that may be able to supply information about the candidate should be sought from the references supplied.

To help keep the background investigation within legal limits to avoid charges of libel or invasion of privacy, the recruiter should make sure that all questions are job related. The probe should not go further than is necessary. Each candidate should sign a waiver that permits both the employer and the search firm to investigate his/her background and releases the references and former employers to answer questions.

Whether additional information is needed is dependent upon two factors: (1) the information obtained in the first part of the investigation; and (2) the job being applied for. Any information obtained that raises doubt must be investigated further. The greater the need for trustworthiness, honesty and competence in the job, the more reasonable it becomes to do additional background checks such as criminal records, newspaper or magazine articles, and credit reports. If this type of investigation is conducted, state and local laws should be reviewed to determine their applicability. The recruiter must comply with the federal Fair Credit Reporting Act (15 U.S.C. 1681) when this information is obtained through a consumer reporting agency. The FCRA requires the employee's written authorization for the investigation in a "stand alone" document, as well as several additional notice requirements before any adverse employment action is taken based upon the report.

A paper trail should be made to verify that a reasonable investigation was made. Everything should be put in writing. For example, notes should be kept on any explanation given by an applicant for gaps in employment; the names of persons spoken to should be recorded; all refusals of information or access to records should be documented.

The recruiter must also take appropriate safeguards to assure that the data that is obtained is accurate and relevant, that is, was it attained through legal sources; is it legal to use the information; and can it be verified. To protect against claims of discrimination, the investigatory information used in the hiring process needs to be related to the applicant's ability to properly and safely perform the job. Therefore, it is important to be thorough enough to see the complete picture. An applicant should not be categorically rejected because it is learned that (s)he was an alcoholic. More information is needed – for example, the risk of hiring a practicing alcoholic that is known to have fits of violence. Of course, the decisions are not always as straightforward. Therefore, if anything questionable is revealed during the investigation, the information about the applicant should be reviewed by an attorney familiar with employment law to assure that its use complies with the applicable state and federal laws.

TESTING

Since discharging employees has become a greater legal risk to employers, many are turning to pre-employment testing in the hopes of avoiding problem employees. Although testing job applicants poses fewer risks that testing current employees, its renewed popularity has created greater legal interest.

Equal Employment Opportunity laws restrict applicant and employee testing that have an adverse impact upon people of a particular age, race, color, religion, sex or national origin. Moreover, the Americans with Disabilities Act prohibits the use of qualification standards, employment tests, or selection criteria that tend to screen out individuals with disabilities, unless the standard is job related and consistent with business necessity.

The Equal Employment Opportunity Commission's "Uniform Guidelines for Employment Selection Procedures" expressly authorize the use of "professionally developed" scored tests. However, the guidelines also expressly prohibit the use of any test that may have an adverse impact on a protected group. Adverse impact is *generally* defined as a circumstance in which a protected group is found to pass the test at a rate less than 80% of an unprotected group. If the test is shown to have an adverse impact, the employer must prove that the test is job related and/or required by business necessity. Absent proof of adverse impact, most courts have held that there is no duty to validate a test.

However, a validation study will be required to defend a claim of adverse impact. Waiting until after the fact to find out if the test is discriminatory is a serious legal risk. Therefore, only validated tests should be administered. For further protection, an indemnification guarantee from the test vendor should be obtained; confidentiality of test results should be protected; and the recommended test procedures should be followed *exactly*.

Restrictions on pre-employment testing can be found in many laws. There are federal statutes such as the Americans with Disabilities Act that specifically states that pre-employment physicals *cannot* be given until an offer of emplyment has been made. There are also state constitutional issues, such as whether pre-employment tests violate the applicant's right to privacy. There may also be state statutes; for example, Massachusetts prohibits the use of paper and pencil honesty tests. Thus, it is crucial that all federal, state and local laws be reviewed prior to administering any pre-employment test.

PERSONAL LIABILITY

At least 28 states and the District of Columbia have provisions in their anti-discrimination statutes that confer liability upon those that "aid and abet" in the violation of the law. There have not been many cases interpreting these "aiding and abetting" statutes. However, they can be used to hold third party companies and individuals liable for enabling another company to discriminate in the employment process. For example, an employee recovered damages from her employer and from its insurance company because her health insurance did not cover normal pregnancies. The insurance company attempted to defend itself by claiming that it had no intent to discriminate. It offered the company a policy that included normal pregnancy coverage, but the company chose not to take it. The court rejected this argument because Colorado's aiding and abetting statute does not require intent. Instead, it found liability merely on the basis that the insurance company's conduct *assisted the company in furtherance of its illegal acts.*

In addition, California recently added a provision to its state code that makes it unlawful for an employment agency to fail to take all reasonable steps necessary to prevent discrimination and harassment from occurring. It appears at this point that state agencies are awaiting more specific guidelines from the courts in this area. However, search firms and individual recruiters should be aware of this potential cause of action and the fact that it may grow as plaintiffs attempt to reach deep pocket defendants who were previously insulated from liability.

Jane E. Shaffer

Jane E. Shaffer is a partner with the law firm of Laner, Muchin, Dombrow, Becker, Levin and Tominberg, Ltd. She represents management in a variety of employment-related matters, including employment discrimination, wage and hour, affirmative action, as well as in collective bargaining negotiations, contract drafting and interpretation, grievance handling and unfair labor practice matters. Ms. Shaffer's prior experience in the Corporate Human Resources Department of A.C. Nielsen Company provides her with practical insight that she uses in helping clients to develop and implement effective programs to avoid employment litigation and disputes. Her prevention oriented services include auditing personnel policies and practices, conducting supervisory training, drafting effective employee communications and manuals, reviewing sensitive discharges and preparing severance agreements.

Ms. Shaffer received her Bachelor of Business Administration from the University of Michigan and her law degree from Loyola University of Chicago School of Law. While in law school, Ms. Shaffer served as a Senior Member of the Law Journal Staff and was listed in Who's Who Among American Law Students.

Richard W. Laner

Richard W. Laner serves as "of counsel" to Laner, Muchin, Dombrow, Becker, Levin and Tominberg, Ltd., a law firm that concentrates in the representation of management in labor-management employment relations. He has over forty years experience in labor management relations law.

Mr. Laner is a member and past chairman of The Chicago Bar Associaton's Labor Law Committee. He has served as special labor counsel to the Mayor of the City of Chicago and acted as a special labor counsel and chief negotiator for the Chicago Board of Education and the Chicago Housing Authority.

Mr. Laner received his law degree from Northwestern University School of Law, where he was elected to the Order of the Coif. He was a member of the editorial board of the Northwestern Law Review.

CHAPTER 21

Unbundling The Search Process

By Mary Anne Denniston

I continue to be stunned by comments made years ago by a newly appointed Recruiting VP from a major bank during a particularly spirited panel discussion on the use and misuse of executive search in corporate America. We were debating the relative merits of knowing who was actually executing the day to day aspects of search engagement. He said, with great fervor, "If I am buying a Mercedes, why would I spend any time worrying about what's under the hood; I'm paying someone else to do that for me." As a corporate recruiter with roots in executive search research I was astounded; it had not occurred to me that anyone, given the option, would choose not to know.

I have been truly blessed in my work. I have fallen into an industry that never ceases to fascinate me, doing work I am passionate about. We have grown up together, the executive search business and I; times and business climates have dictated that we continually invent and reinvent ourselves, our services and our delivery. When I entered the search field in the late 1970's, the role of research in the search process was in the earliest stages of a metamorphosis that has changed the industry forever. Prior to this time, research was primarily a library function often performed by trained librarians providing library type research services. As the search business itself became more competitive, there arose a need for individuals who could play a more hands-on role in the search process. Researchers began to develop candidates in addition to developing job descriptions and target lists. It was a learning process for everyone. Search consultants were more than a little leery about delegating key responsibilities, but the increased emphasis on business development afforded them little choice. Corporate clients were unaware of the changes. In the early days it was virtually unheard of for a researcher to have client contact.

Competition in the industry continued to grow and with it, the business development demands on search consultants escalated. Concurrently the role of the researcher broadened. Researchers were primarily young women in those days. As our experience and responsibilities grew, so did we. In time many among us married; then the children followed. The desire, and to a degree a sense of obligation to "have it all, to do it all", made flexibility a priority. The executive search industry of the mid-to-late 80's was not an industry with a great deal of bench strength. As a result, when a number of researchers opted to become independent, in order to have more control of the work/family balance, firms were willing – if not always eager – to accommodate them. Researchers became more confident in their capabilities and more aware of how critical their role as consultants had become. Within search firms the distinction between business developers and search executors was becoming more accepted and defined. Salaries increased, as did the fees for independent contractors.

While the search community was adjusting to its new dynamic, researcher visibility increased dramatically. Direct contact with the corporate client was no longer the rare exception; it was the norm. At the same time, search clients, particularly corporate human resources officers, were becoming more discriminating in their requirements for the search firms they retained. Contract researchers or unbundled search consultants, as they had become known, recognized that the market for their services was not confined to the search community, but included corporate America as well. Individuals such as myself, who had elected to apply my skills within a corporate environment, were eager to introduce and facilitate the application of unbundled search. While not as widely applied as the classic executive search process from which it has evolved, unbundled search has a dedicated and increasingly growing following.

Unbundled search can be thought of as "search a la carte." It takes a product that is traditionally

---

considered a package and breaks it into the individual pieces that together have become known as an executive search. The most obvious difference is in the pricing; unbundled search is generally billed on time and expense rather than a fixed fee based on a percentage of the compensation package, as is the case with most retained search firms.

Unbundled search consultants, like their search firm counterparts, may be specialists or generalists. Some work for only corporate clients, some only for search firms, others serve both. Most tend to be sole proprietors or have established strategic alliances with one or two other consultants in order to share the costs of administrative support, broaden service offerings and/or retain the benefits of professional camaraderie that can be lacking when one works entirely alone. Unbundled search consultants offer a variety of services relating to the search process; many offer the full range of services from candidate identification, candidate development, face to face interviewing, through referencing. Other unbundled search consultants concentrate on one or two parts of the process, candidate identification, or candidate development or referencing only. Recently, a select few individuals have developed an expertise in Internet recruiting. This vehicle is destined to be an increasingly fertile source of both candidates and information for those who know how to access it effectively.

Effectively utilizing unbundled search requires that the individual retaining the services be ready, willing and able to take an active role in the process. This has a great deal of appeal for an increasing number of individuals charged with responsibility for recruiting talent; it has decidedly less appeal for those whose sole focus is the successful outcome of a specific engagement. Those undaunted by the hands-on elements of employing an unbundled approach to recruiting will find that it is not only cost effective, but exceedingly flexible as well. You pay for and receive what you need. If, for example, you are interested in who does business process reengineering consulting in Atlanta, you can get just that. If billing is on a time and expense basis, multiple hires do not result in multiple fees.

Since the unbundled search consultant and the individual retaining the service are in effect partnering on the engagements, issues affecting the successful outcome tend to be identified and addressed earlier. Candidates are more often than not introduced as they are developed rather than as a unit at a formal progress meeting. This is very helpful in ensuring that everyone is on the same page right from the very beginning. The ability to set flexible budgets can be extremely appealing in those instances where a business wants to test the waters or is toying with multiple position profiles. Twenty to thirty hours of targeted work is generally enough to get a reasonable picture of what is out there and provide sufficient information to make an informed decision as to whether continuing in a particular direction is warranted. The cost to retain twenty to thirty hours of targeted work is generally less than the cost of placing a newspaper display ad in most major markets.

Those already familiar with the benefits of unbundling the search process need no additional incentive to continue. Hopefully those who have not had experience to date will be motivated to apply it within their own organizations.

Mary Anne Denniston

Mary Anne Denniston has been in the search field for 22 years, first as a search firm researcher, most recently as an independent recruiting consultant. In the interim her career was spent at Booz, Allen and Hamilton, KMPG Peat Marwick, and Bankers Trust. Currently Ms. Denniston is providing strategic recruiting consulting services to both Fortune 500 and entrepreneurial companies. Here she speaks with perspective about the history of search research, issues around unbundling the search process and her own experiences as a researcher. She is based in Bronxville, New York.

CHAPTER 22

Company Considerations – Executive Search Or Unbundled Search

Reasons for Retaining an Executive Search Firm

- The consultant can totally focus his or her efforts on a particular task or objective.

- Professional executive recruiters are experts at locating, assessing, and attracting top-flight management talent.

- A search professional allows top management to focus on what it does best – manage the business.

- An executive recruiter provides third-party objectivity – and does not have to live with the same political consequences.

- Use of a third party can minimize ill feelings among competitors who might otherwise "raid" each other directly, or whose Chairmen might start complaining to your boss.

- The consultant can approach potential candidates from a firm's competitors without revealing the company's name.

- The confidentiality of the candidate can be protected. This is especially important if the candidate is not on the job market. Otherwise, a quality candidate who's not on the market might decline to speak to a directly to a competitor.

- The search can be kept confidential *within* the company. This can be crucial if an incumbent holds an important position and a replacement must be identified before the incumbent can be terminated.

- In a retained executive search, the focus is to find people *not* on the market – that is, people the client normally would not have access to.

- A search consultant offers the ability to work with a search committee and bring it to consensus on the selection of a candidate.

- Search is sometimes used as a means of evaluating an internal candidate against the best possible outside talent – especially individuals *not* on the market.

Reasons for Retaining an Unbundled Search Consultant

- The consultant can totally focus his or her efforts on a particular task or objective.

- Professional unbundled search consultants and research consultants are experts at locating and attracting top-flight management talent.

- A recruitment professional provides third-party objectivity – and does not have to live with the same political consequences.

- Use of a third party can minimize ill feelings among competitors who might otherwise "raid" each other directly, or whose Chairmen might start complaining to your boss.

- The consultant can approach potential candidates from a firm's competitors without revealing the company's name.

- The confidentiality of the candidate can be protected. This is especially important if the candidate is not on the job market. Otherwise, a quality candidate who's not on the market might decline to speak to a directly to a competitor.

- The search can be kept confidential *within* the company. This can be crucial if an incumbent holds an important position and a replacement must be identified before the incumbent can be terminated.

- With unbundled search or research the focus is to find people *not* on the market – that is, people the client normally would not have access to.

- Unbundled search is much less expensive than executive search. However, typically there are no formal written reports, no formal candidate write-ups, no in-person interviews of candidates, and no fancy offices with high overhead.

- With unbundled search the company must have greater hands on involvement in the process. This gives the company more control of the process, but it also demands vastly more time.

What A Corporate Client Should Look for in a Recruitment Consultant

- Integrity and ethics

- A genuine desire to build long term relationships with clients

- Quality research – thoroughness, attention to detail, accurate data gathering, good notes, timely follow-up, and tenacity when the going gets tough

- The ability and willingness to pitch in and actually develop candidates to back up research's efforts

- Well written, clear presentations that don't waste your time

- A high quality list of candidates that the search executive is able to generate

- Thorough reference checking

- Good interviewing skills; making sure that the client gets no surprises

- Providing a successful interface between the client and the candidate in closing the search, and avoiding having the candidate and client becoming involved in hard negotiating that can generate ill feelings

- Comfort level with the search executive in terms of personal compatibility, style, chemistry, etc.

- Timely completion of search (3 months is normally the minimum), depending on difficulty

- Clear understanding of the search firm's off limits policy. Exactly what is the definition of a "client" – is it the entire company, or is it just your subsidiary, division, group or department?

- In the beginning, an agreement as to under what, if any, circumstances is the firm is willing to recruit a replacement if someone hired doesn't work out? How long must a placement stay in a position for a client to get a "fair shake" considering that the position was actually filled? For example, if somebody quits the first month, or after six months, clearly the search was not properly filled. But after 18 months, that's another matter. But suppose a client changes his mind about promised stock options that were part of the deal? Suppose someone quits after 11 months? 12 months? 13 months?

What a Recruitment Consultant Should Look for in a Corporate Client

- Honesty, full disclosure and open communication

    - ❏ Description of the position and the reason for the opening

    - ❏ The person to whom position reports, and those reporting to it

    - ❏ Environment/culture of the organization

    - ❏ Pitfalls – why might one candidate succeed and another one fail?

    - ❏ Compensation

    - ❏ Information about the organization – its history, its present, its future

    - ❏ Relevant competitive information

    - ❏ Future plans that could affect the position. For example, if you're recruiting a new head of human resources and you're planning to execute a massive layoff, full, confidential disclosure is appropriate, even if it means a signed confidentiality agreement during the interview process.

- Prompt follow up

    - ❏ When a search consultant calls, unreturned phone calls are not only discourteous, it's behavior that says the search unimportant.

    - ❏ When there are long delays with candidate follow up, a good candidate who would otherwise be interested might withdraw from the search. A good rule of thumb is, how would *you* feel if you were in the candidate's shoes?

- Trust

Obviously, trust mutually benefits both parties. One would expect it would grow from a long term relationship. The company should be able to trust the judgment and integrity of the consultant. Likewise, the consultant should be able to trust the integrity of the client. In addition, it is practically impossible for a consultant to do a good job for a company if the company, for some reason, has a "hidden agenda." If there is, in fact, "bad news," a good consultant can handle the situation so as to preserve confidentiality and at the same time – with the company's advance permission – reveal this information to the selected candidate in the course of psychologically preparing him or her to succeed with the challenges.

Otherwise, failing to disclose the "bad news" is not only unethical, it is an invitation to making a bad hire. It makes as much sense as going for therapy to get help with a problem, and then lying to the therapist.

CHAPTER 23

Excerpts From *On Target,* The Newsletter of The Executive Search Roundtable

HOW TO MANAGE THE SEARCH CONSULTANT YOU'RE WORKING WITH

By Sherri L. Rosenberg, Bedford, New York

In my six years as a Director of Research, I learned that there is nothing more critical to a researcher's success and sanity as being able to effectively manage the consultant with whom you're working on a search. Now that I have made the transition to the consulting side, I see more than ever how important it is.

So, I offer the following advice, from the perspective of someone who's been on both sides of the fence. The helpful hints that follow should assist any researcher in managing the search process more effectively and hopefully, they will also help you manage those impossible consultants with greater ease.

Now that I, too, have been an impossible consultant, I understand what may sometimes cause that impossible behavior. However, we all know that there are some consultants out there whose impossible behavior cannot be attributed entirely to circumstances, and that is all the more reason we need to manage up as effectively and delicately as we can.

❑ **Communicate!** It is the key to any successful relationship. During the search process, encourage the flow of information in both directions. Do this formally or informally, verbally or on paper – whatever works best for you and the consultant.

❑ **Create a "team relationship" with the search consultant.** At my firm, we create that relationship formally, by writing a search plan at the beginning of an assignment. This document details the strategy that will be used in solving the assignment (e.g. how you will interrogate your database, what target companies you will look at, what other sources of information will be used, and who will be making which calls.) It also details who will be doing the work (consultants and researchers each get their assignments), and when each specific task will be complete. This document then becomes a contract between the team members; everyone is clear about expectations and deadlines. This enhances communication and can be helpful in identifying any misconceptions on who will be doing what, when.

❑ **Be in control.** If things are not going well on an assignment, and you are having trouble finding or attracting the right candidates, let the consultant know as soon as possible. Nothing can be more frustrating for a consultant than thinking everything is okay, and then finding out three weeks into a search that there are problems. If you are doing your work, you should never be defensive about not having candidates. The search may need to be redirected, or the consultant may need to go back to the client to discuss the stumbling blocks you're encountering (issues related to compensation, reporting structure, etc.) Help that consultant manage his/her client as effectively as possible by providing solid information. Be aggressive and don't let the consultant come to you screaming for candidates. Manage the relationship and ask for help. If you're on top of things and communicating effectively with the consultant, you should never find yourself in a defensive position.

Realize that a search cannot be conducted, or successfully completed, without research. You are an integral part of the process and professional member of the team. Be on top of the process and manage your consultants.

R-E-S-P-E-C-T (And How to Earn it)

by Amy Bragg

Some search consultants, to the chagrin of researchers who work for them, do not view the research function as an integral, or even important, part of the search process. Many consultants simply are not aware of all that research can do for them, and some are reluctant to give up what they perceive as the business development or relationship building aspects of doing everything themselves. Still others may harbor a somewhat chauvinistic attitude when it comes to a relatively junior person doing the "same work" as a seasoned practitioner. In short, consultants who feel this way generally have lots of reasons for why research should *not* be involved, and zero reasons for why they should. So, what can you do to inject content into your job when the people for whom you work are not encouraging you to assume greater responsibility?

First, I think it's important to realize that, generally speaking, people who stagnate in their jobs often have only themselves to blame. I think we have a tendency as researchers in this business to place too much of the burden of responsibility for our professional development on the shoulders of our bosses. Having once been an underutilized researcher myself, and later a manager of researchers who wanted more responsibility, I swiftly concluded that hanging around waiting for people to discover our keen minds and unlimited potential, while grousing about our disinterested bosses, was (and is) a waste of time.

We should all follow the standard advice about dressing, speaking and acting the part, but keep in mind that results matter most in the search business. Few consultants (even those who are research-friendly) care very much about how those results are achieved, so don't waste your time regaling anybody (except your colleagues in research) with tales of how you got from Point A to Point B. Instead, start to think like a consultant and be prepared to devote a lot of time and effort, beyond what you currently expend, toward the goal of enriching your job.

Be creative, have courage, work smart and take the initiative. Only the most hardened consultants (the Death Row variety) could fail to acknowledge a truly valuable contribution made in a time of crisis, which is why I recommend the "valiant effort" as the best attention-getting device. Helping to pull the fat out of the fire will position you as a simpatico, consultant-like entity who can be depended upon to produce.

Pick your spots carefully, don't ever promise more than you can deliver, and make sure your first forays are successful. For instance, don't offer to write a candidate presentation for a consultant who may secretly doubt your ability to walk and chew gum simultaneously if you flunked English in college. As a manager, I found that changing the mind set of the consulting staff toward research was a dirty job, but someone had to do it. My strategy going in was to let actions speak louder than words and take no prisoners when it came to the performance of my department. "Good enough" in my mind was simply not good enough.

I began by choosing two very busy partners, who also happened to be the most open-minded of the lot, and I encouraged them to use as much research as I could possibly afford to give them. I paired those partners with the most competent, hard-working researchers (myself and one other), thereby ensuring that the first efforts were the best efforts. I discovered that as these partners began to rave publicly about the terrific results they had achieved by using research in a more pro-active manner, and as their billings gradually increased as a result of their ability to handle more searches at once, suddenly, there were a lot of partners in my office volunteering to "experiment" in a similar fashion.

The largest problem I encountered during this period of transformation was staffing. Keeping up with the increasing demand for research services while controlling the quality of the product meant that, for the first two years, I did a lot of search work myself. Furthermore, I had inherited a department comprised of people who had not been trained in newfangled (some thought heretical) research techniques, and the kind of work I was expecting of them was a lot different than what they had been hired to do. Fortunately, attrition took its toll within the first six months or so, and I was able to hire people I felt would excel in the environment I wanted to create.

My objective was to engender confidence in the ability of research to perform tasks which, up until that time, had been solely the domain of the consulting staff. Therefore, my first hire was critical, and I chose someone whose ability and work ethic I trusted implicitly. This person became the cornerstone of the department.

CHAPTER 24

Philosophy of Executive Search

Some years ago I began writing down the things that captured the essence of my approach to the whole process of executive search. Here they are:

- There is no substitute for quality – in our business or yours.

- Executive search can affect people's lives and we take that responsibility seriously. After all, most people spend the majority of their waking hours working.

- We have a serious ethical responsibility to protect the confidentiality of candidates, especially those not actively on the job market.

- The client's identity must be kept confidential for as long as possible, normally until the candidate has been interviewed in person. Even so, the client's name is only released to appropriate candidates.

- It is critical to keep our word to sources and references when we say their identities ill be kept confidential. In fact, it is critical to keep our word, period.

- Search is a process that is driven by research...because without candidates, you've got nothing.

- It's not right to let clients think their work isn't being farmed out when it is.

- Chemistry and a comfort level with the people in the organization are crucially important factors in predicting the success of a candidate.

- It is completely and totally unacceptable to ever misrepresent a situation to a candidate. Besides, you're more likely to find a candidate who thrives on challenges if the true situation is disclosed.

- One of the best ways to develop business is to do an outstanding job with the searches you have so that satisfied clients will give repeat business and refer new clients.

- We keep our client list small because long term relationships with a small number of select clients is a good thing. For one thing, repeat business means we're spending our time serving clients rather than marketing. A small client roster also means we have more places available to search for talent ethically.

- We will not recruit candidates from client organizations for two years after the completion of any search assignment.

- The end does not justify the means. It simply is wrong to ever misrepresent yourself in order to obtain information. Likewise, delegating your work to someone lower in the organization with a "do whatever you have to do to get the information" attitude – and then looking the other way – does not absolve you of responsibility. If you and the team you oversee can't get the information you need by ethical means, you're in the wrong business.

CHAPTER 25

Professional Associations And Roundtables – Including Research, Recruitment and an Array of Human Resources Activities

Here is a listing of varied human resources associations that includes executive search and research professional associations. As for the "roundtables," some are loosely formed "ad hoc" groups that are not formal organizations. However, their presence is noteworthy and a contact is provided. At the time of this writing, contact and officer information was current. However, it may require a bit of detective work to locate people as their employment relationships or independent consultant status may change.

AMERICAN COMPENSATION ASSOCIATION (ACA)
14040 North Northsight Boulevard
Scottsdale, AZ 85260
(480) 951-9191
(480) 483-8352 Fax
www.acaonline.org
wnichols@acaonline.org
Wally Nichols, Executive Director

AMERICAN SOCIETY FOR TRAINING & DEVELOPMENT (ASTD)
Box 1443
1640 King Street
Alexandria, VA 22313-2043
(703) 683-8100
(703) 683-8103 Fax
www.astd.org
Greta Kotler, Interim President

ASSOCIATION OF CAREER MANAGEMENT FIRMS INTERNATIONAL (ACMFI)
Formerly Association of Outplacement Consulting Firms International (AOCFI)
1200 19th Street NW
Suite 300
Washington, DC 20036
(202) 857-1185
(202) 857-4579 Fax
Faye Malarkey, Manager

ASSOCIATION OF EXECUTIVE SEARCH CONSULTANTS (AESC)
500 Fifth Avenue
Suite 930
New York, New York 10110
(212) 398-9556
(212) 398-9560 Fax
www.aesc.org
nd@aesc.org
Peter Felix, President
Nancy DeKoven, Director of Administration and Programs

ATLANTA RESEARCH ROUNDTABLE
PRESIDENT, Anne Swartz, SpencerStuart
VICE PRESIDENT, Kathryn Allen, Leadersonline.com, Heidrick & Struggles
SECRETARY, Helen Neely Smith, FutureStep.com, Korn/Ferry International
TREASURER, Eric Handler, W. L. Handler & Associates

CHICAGO RESEARCH ROUNDTABLE
CHAIR, Maureen Hale
Hale Associates
1816 North Sedgwick Street
Chicago, IL 60614
(312) 337-3288
(312) 337-3451 Fax

FIRST VICE PRESIDENT & TREASURER, Mary Molony
Heidrick & Struggles
233 South Wacker Drive
Suite 7000
Chicago, IL 60606
(312) 496-1000
mkm@h-s.com

DALLAS-FT. WORTH AREA RESEARCH ROUNDTABLE
CONTACTS:
Ginnie Bellville
P.O. Box 816042
Dallas, TX 75381
(972) 394-3310
ginnie_b2@hotmail.com

Jane Norris Roberts
P.O. Box 701
Rockwall, TX 75087
(972) 771-0493
JaneNorrisRoberts@email.msn.com

EMPLOYEE RELOCATION COUNCIL (ERC)
1720 N Street NW
Washington, DC 20036
(202) 857-0857
(202) 467-4012 Fax
ww.erc.org
H. Cris Collie, Executive Vice President

EMPLOYMENT MANAGEMENT ASSOCIATION (EMA)
SOCIETY FOR HUMAN RESOURCE MANAGEMENT
1800 Duke Street
Alexandria, VA 22314
(800) 283-7476
Rebecca Hastings, Manager, Employment Management
    Association Operations, extension 6076
rhastings@shrm.org
www.shrm.org

The Employment Management Association (EMA) is part of the Society of Human Resource Management (SHRM). You must be a member of SHRM to join the EMA. At the time of this writing, EMA regions are located in Charlotte, NC, Cleveland/Akron, Washington, D.C. Metro, Boston Metro, Dallas/Fort Worth, Chicago, Milwaukee, Phoenix and Philadelphia/Delaware Valley.

THE EXECUTIVE SEARCH ROUNDTABLE
P.O. Box 3565
Grand Central Station
New York, NY 10163
(212) 439-4630
www.esroundtable.org

The Executive Search Roundtable – originally named The Research Roundtable – was the first search research association established. Based in New York City, its original members were research professionals at Booz, Allen & Hamilton's Executive Personnel Services and other major retainer search firms. The author, then at Booz, Allen, was one of those members. Established in 1979, "The Research Roundtable" was the first organization to conduct an executive compensation survey of search research professionals. Since that time, the organization has provided a forum for discussing various topics related to search, research and unbundled search, client management, small business ownership, growth and development and so forth. Training is also periodically provided. With approximately 400 members at the time of this writing, about half are search firm employees and half independent research and recruitment consultants. While most members are from the New York tri-state area, members from other parts of the country are welcomed and there are a few members from abroad.

HUMAN RESOURCE CERTIFICATION INSTITUTE (HRCI)

1800 Duke Street
Alexandria, VA 22314
(800) 283-7476
(703) 548-3440
(703) 836-0367 Fax
www.shrm.org
losey@shrm.org
Michael R. Losey, President

Formerly the ASPA Accreditation Institute, HRCI is affiliated with the Society for Human Resources Management (SHRM).

HUMAN RESOURCE PLANNING SOCIETY (HRPS)

317 Madison Avenue
Suite 1509
New York, NY 10017
(212) 490-6387
(212) 682-6851 Fax
www.hrps.org
wclever@hrps.org
Walt Clever, Executive Director

INDEPENDENT EDUCATIONAL SERVICES (IES)

1101 King Street
Suite 305
Alexandria, VA 22314
(800) 257-5102
(703) 548-9700
(703) 548-7171 Fax
www.ies_search.org
info@ies_search.org
John W. Sanders, President

INTERNATIONAL ASSOCIATION OF CORPORATE AND PROFESSIONAL RECRUITERS (IACPR)

1001 Green Bay Road, #308
Winnetka, IL 60093
(847) 441-1644 National Headquarters
(847) 441-7551 Fax
www.iacpr.org
iacpr@aol.com
Susan Roberts, Executive Director

PRESIDENT OF ALL IACPR CHAPTERS, Michael S. Mimnaugh
SONY
550 Madison Avenue, 33rd Floor
New York, NY 10022

INTERNATIONAL PERSONNEL MANAGEMENT ASOCIATION (IPMA)
1617 Duke Street
Alexandria, VA 22314
(703) 549-7100
(703) 684-0948 Fax
www.ipma_hr.org
Neil Reichenberg, Executive Director

INSTITUTE FOR INTERNATIONAL HUMAN RESOURCES (IIHR)
1800 Duke Street
Alexandria, VA 22314
(800) 283-7476
(703) 548-3440
(703) 836-0367 Fax
www.shrm.org
losey@shrm.org
Michael Losey, President and CEO

The IIHR is an affiliate of the Society of Human Resources Management (SHRM).

**MARYLAND ASSOCIATION OF PROFESSIONAL RECRUITMENT CONSULTANTS
(MAPRC)**
10751 Falls Road
Lutherville, MD 21093
(410) 339-7673
(410) 823-0146 Fax
www.maprc.org
Tbrindisi@aol.com
Tom Brindisi, President

NATIONAL ASSOCIATION OF EXECUTIVE RECRUITERS (NAER)
20 North Wacker Drive
Suite 2262
Chicago, IL 60606
(312) 701-0744
(312) 630-9882 Fax
Susan Roberts, Executive Director

This organization of executive recruitment and search specialist firms, among other things, conducts educational programs and owners' roundtables and makes available group insurance coverage.

NATIONAL ASSOCIATION OF PERSONNEL SERVICES (NAPS)
3133 Mount Vernon Avenue
Alexandria, VA 22305
(703) 684-0180
(703) 684-0071 Fax
www.napsweb.org
Dianne Callis, President

NATIONAL ASSOCIATION OF PUBLIC SECTOR EQUAL OPPORTUNITY OFFICERS (NAPSEO)

c/o Sharon Ofuani
City of Tallahassee Equal Opportunity Dept.
300 South Adams Street
Tallahassee, FL 32301
(850) 891-8290
ofuanis@mail.ci.tlh.fl.us

Membership is comprised of equal employment opportunity officers and coordinators, human resources managers, employee relations directors, attorneys, legislators, consultants, community relations specialists and other related professionals in the public sector.

NATIONAL HUMAN RESOURCES ASSOCIATION

6767 W. Greenfield Ave.
Milwaukee, WI 53214
(414) 453-7499
(414) 475-5959 Fax
www.humanresources.org
nhra@globaldialog.com
Linda Lee, President

Formerly named the International Association of Personnel Women (IAPW), the mandate of this organization is serving human resources executives in business, industry, education and government.

NEW ENGLAND EXECUTIVE RESOURCES COUNCIL (NEERC)

The NEERC is a small organization of search consultants and heads of human resources. The group meets four times a year in Waltham, Massachusetts. Their web site includes a listing of members, including some photos. In an effort to remain as egalitarian as possible, there are no officers. As there is no contact person per se, you may get in touch with anyone on the web site. http://199.233.99.2/neerc/

PHILADELPHIA RESEARCH ROUNDTABLE

At the time of this writing the Philadelphians appear to be inactive. If you wish to make contact, we suggest you call one of the major firms.

PROFIT SHARING COUNCIL OF AMERICA (PSCA) and
PROFIT SHARING RESEARCH FOUNDATION (PSRF)
10 South Riverside
No. 1610
Chicago, IL 60606
(312) 441-8550
(312) 441-8559 Fax
www.psca.org
psca@psca.org
David L. Wray, President, Profit Sharing Council of America and Executive Director, Profit Sharing Research Foundation.

Among other things, the Research Foundation studies the potential of profit sharing programs in dealing with human and economic issues, such as motivation, inflation, productivity, industrial relations, quality of life, and retirement income.

SAN FRANCISCO BAY AREA RESEARCH ASSOCIATION
CONTACTS:
Janice Litvin
Micro Search
3527 Mt. Diablo Blvd.
Suite 280
Lafayette, CA 94549
(925) 937-4080
(925) 937-4082 Fax
jlitvin@microsearchsf.com

SOCIETY FOR HUMAN RESOURCE MANAGEMENT (SHRM)
1800 Duke Street
Alexandria, VA 22314
(800) 283-7476
(703) 548-3440
(703) 836-0367 Fax
www.shrm.org
losey@shrm.org
Michael R. Losey, SPHR, CEO

Formerly named the American Society for Personnel Administration (ASPA), this major multinational association has over 50 state groups, over 400 local groups, a staff of about 100 people, and a multi-million dollar budget. They offer a certification program through the Human Resource Certification Institute.

SOUTHERN CALIFORNIA RESEARCH ROUNDTABLE
CONTACTS:
Ginny Simonds
The Simonds Group
4002 Pine Avenue
Long Beach, CA 90807
(562) 424-3020
(562) 989-1200 Fax
vsimonds@yahoo.com

Lucille Pearson
Global Resources Ltd.
P.O. Box 3675
Rolling Hills Estates, CA 90274
(310) 544-7144
(310) 544-7148 Fax
lucille@grlltd.com

WASHINGTON, DC RESEARCH ROUNDTABLE
CONTACT:
Mike Andrews
Korn/Ferry International, Suite 800
900 19th Street NW
Washington, DC 20006
(202) 822-9444
(202) 822-8127 Fax
mikeandrews@kornferry.com

CHAPTER 26

Association Of Executive Search Consultants, Inc.

Code Of Ethics And Professional Practice Guidelines

NOTE: This information was provided by AESC.

INTRODUCTION TO CODE OF ETHICS AND
PROFESSIONAL PRACTICE GUIDELINES

The Association of Executive Search Consultants (AESC) is an association of leading retained executive search consulting firms worldwide. Dating from its inception in 1959, the AESC has sought to promote high standards of professionalism among retained executive search consultants. In furtherance of this aim, AESC adopted a Code of Ethics in 1977, and a set of Professional Practice Guidelines in 1984. In 1996, with the advice of a panel of AESC member firm leaders and outside experts, the AESC revised and updated both the Code and the Professional Practice Guidelines to reflect important developments in the profession and the business environment.

"Retained executive search consulting" is a specialized form of senior-level management consulting, conducted through an exclusive engagement and on a predetermined retainer fee basis. Its purpose is to assist executives of a client organization in defining executive positions, identifying well-qualified and motivated candidates, and selecting those best suited through comprehensive, quality assured search processes.

Executive search is widely recognized as an indispensable service to organizations worldwide and is generally built on relationships rather than discrete transactions. The services provided by executive search consultants are an integral part of the process of building and maintaining corporate, nonprofit and government clients. Like professionals in the fields of law, public accounting and general management consulting, executive search consultants have a profound influence on the organizations they serve.

AESC and its members recognize that outstanding professional service rests on the quality and integrity of relationships with clients, candidates, employees and the public. Executive search consulting firms depend on all of these groups for their continuing success, and to each group they have important responsibilities.

Clients

AESC members are partners with their clients in a consultative process aimed at selecting organizational leaders. As "leadership" can have many meanings, the professional search consultant identifies the client's specific needs and unique culture as essential elements in recruiting appropriate leaders for client organizations.

Candidates

AESC members maintain professional relationships with candidates and treat them with respect at all times. AESC members regard honesty, objectivity, accuracy and confidentiality as fundamental to their relationships with candidates.

Consultants

AESC members strive to attract and develop their own talent, building the knowledge and experience that will guide the profession into the future. Recognizing the importance of training and education to this process, AESC members provide opportunities for consultants, research professionals and other staff to improve their skills and capabilities. AESC and its member firms are partners in professional development.

The Public

AESC members understand the importance of public trust in the executive search profession. Professional search consultants stay abreast of socio-economic developments in the communities they serve and recognize the need to respond to contemporary developments such as changing demographics, new technologies and changes in the employment relationship. AESC's mission includes understanding these changes and taking constructive positions on public policy issues that affect the executive search profession, client organizations and the public.

The AESC's updated Code of Ethics clarifies the fundamental principles that guide executive search consultants in performing their duties and conducting their relationships with these constituencies. The Professional Practice Guidelines represent the AESC's view of contemporary best practices that exemplify the standards of professionalism expected of executive search consultants into the 21st Century. Underlying these principles and best practices is the expectation that AESC members will articulate and define clearly for clients the terms of their relationship and the members' commitment to perform their work professionally.

CODE OF ETHICS

The Association of Executive Search Consultants, Inc. (AESC) is a worldwide association of retained executive search consulting firms. In order to perform their duties responsibly, AESC member firms are guided by the following ethical principles, which reflect fundamental values of the retained executive search consulting profession. The AESC is committed to educating its members about the application of these principles.

AESC members will:

Professionalism: conduct their activities in a manner that reflects favorably on the profession.

Integrity: conduct their business activities with integrity and avoid conduct that is deceptive or misleading.

Competence: perform all search consulting assignments competently, and with an appropriate degree of knowledge, thoroughness and urgency.

Objectivity: exercise objective and impartial judgment in each search consulting assignment, giving due consideration to all relevant facts.

Accuracy: strive to be accurate in all communications with clients and candidates and encourage them to exchange relevant and accurate information.

Conflicts of Interest: avoid, or resolve through disclosure and waiver, conflicts of interest.

Confidentiality: respect confidential information entrusted to them by clients and candidates.

Loyalty: serve their clients loyally and protect client interests when performing assignments.

Equal Opportunity: support equal opportunity in employment and objectively evaluate all qualified candidates.

Public Interest: conduct their activities with respect for the public interest.

PROFESSIONAL PRACTICE GUIDELINES

Preamble

The Association of Executive Search Consultants (AESC) strives to enhance the professionalism of its members. Accordingly, AESC has developed the following Professional Practice Guidelines to assist AESC member firms in their business relationships with clients, candidates and the public. As the profession evolves and adapts to developments in business practices, technology and law, the AESC may amend these Guidelines.

Relationships between AESC Members and Their Clients

AESC members are partners with their clients in a consultative process aimed at selecting organizational leaders. The success of these partnerships depends on excellence in client service. The following guidelines describe the processes and professional practices that contribute to outstanding client service.

Accepting Client Assignments

Outstanding client service begins with a full understanding of the client organization, its business needs and the position to be filled. An AESC member should:

Accept only those assignments that a member is qualified to undertake on the basis of the member's knowledge of the client's needs and the member's ability to perform the specific assignment.

Accept only those assignments that will not adversely affect the member's objectivity, loyalty and integrity.

Disclose to present and prospective clients information known to the member about relationships, circumstances or interests that might create actual or potential conflicts of interest, and accept potential assignments only if all affected parties have expressly agreed to waive any conflict.

Disclose to present and prospective clients limitations arising through service to other clients that may affect the member's ability to perform the search assignment.

Base acceptances on an understanding that, among other things, defines the scope and character of the services to be provided; the identity of the client organization; the period, if any, during which the member will not recruit from the defined client organization; and the fees and expenses to be charged for the services rendered.

Discuss with the client when advertising is required by law or is a recommended strategy for the particular search assignment.

Performing Client Assignments

Members should serve their clients with integrity and objectivity, making every effort to conduct search consulting activities on the basis of impartial consideration of relevant facts. Specifically, an AESC member should:

Conduct an appropriate search for qualified candidates.

Advise the client promptly, and offer alternative courses of action if it becomes apparent that no qualified candidates can be presented, or that the length of the search will differ considerably from that originally specified.

Present information about the client, the position, and the candidate honestly and factually, and include reservations that are pertinent and important to an assignment.

Withdraw from the assignment if a member determines that a client has characterized its organization falsely or misled candidates, provided the situation is not rectified.

Thoroughly evaluate potential candidates, including:

    in-depth interviews in person or by video conferencing,

    verification of credentials, and

    careful assessment of the candidate's strengths and weaknesses, before presenting candidates for client interviews.

Complete thorough reference checks and transmit these references to the client.

Advise the client if advertising becomes necessary.

Avoid the voluntary presentation of resumes in the absence of an existing client relationship.

Preserving the Confidentiality of Client Information

AESC members should use their best efforts to protect confidential information concerning their clients. Specifically, a member should:

Use such confidential information received from clients only for purposes of conducting the assignment.

Disclose such confidential client information only to those individuals within the firm or to potential candidates who have a need to know the information.

Not use such confidential information for personal gain, nor provide inside information to third parties for their personal gain.

Avoiding Conflicts of Interest

AESC members should protect their integrity, objectivity and loyalty by avoiding conflicts of interest with their clients. For example, a member should:

Refuse or withdraw from an assignment upon learning of conditions that impair the member's ability to perform services properly, including conflicts of interest that may arise during the assignment (unless all affected parties expressly agree to waive the conflict).

Inform clients of business or personal relationships with candidates that might affect or appear to affect the member's objectivity in conducting the assignment.

Not accept payment for assisting an individual in securing employment.

Avoid knowingly presenting simultaneously, without disclosure to clients, the same candidate to more than one client.

Relationships between AESC Members and Candidates

Although a member's primary relationship is with the client, member firms seek also to establish professional relationships with candidates. These relationships should be characterized by honesty, objectivity, accuracy and respect for confidentiality. In building such relationships, a member should:

Provide candidates with relevant and accurate information about the client organization and the position.

Present to clients accurate and relevant information about candidates, and otherwise maintain the confidentiality of information provided by prospective and actual candidates.

Encourage candidates to provide accurate information about their qualifications. Upon learning that a candidate has misled the client or member regarding his or her qualifications, the member should reject the candidate, unless the client, candidate and member agree that the candidacy should continue following disclosure of the facts.

Advise prospects and candidates of the status and disposition of their candidacies in a timely fashion.

Consider whether an individual's permission is needed before sharing his or her background information with a client and secure permission as necessary (permission should always be obtained if an executive's "resume" is submitted).

Advise candidates of any limitations on a member firm's ability to advance them as candidates in future searches.

Relationships between AESC Members and Their Contractors

AESC members sometimes rely on contractors and subcontractors to assist in the search process. A member should:

Avoid contractors and subcontractors whose practices are inconsistent with the standards of professionalism expected of AESC members.

Encourage its contractors and subcontractors to adhere to the Code of Ethics and Professional Practice Guidelines.

Relationships between AESC Members and the Public

AESC members should recognize the importance of public trust and confidence in their profession and seek to serve their clients in a manner consistent with the public interest. Therefore, a member should:

Observe the principles of equal opportunity in employment and avoid unlawful discrimination against qualified candidates.

Promote and advertise member firm services in a professional and accurate manner.

Conduct relations with the media so as to reflect favorably upon the AESC, clients and the executive search consulting profession.

PART II:
THE RECRUITER'S DIRECTORY
OF DIRECTORIES
Plus Web Sites, Databases and CD ROM's

INTRODUCTION TO PART II:
DIRECTORIES, WEB SITES, DATABASES &
CD ROM'S BY CATEGORY

Previously APPENDIX 3 – A BROAD OVERVIEW OF SEARCH REFERENCES
in *The Handbook of Executive Search Research*

WHO CAN BENEFIT FROM THIS INFORMATION

"Not for Recruiters Only"

While this section of the book was initially conceived *by* a search professional *for* other search professionals – especially researchers – many other people can benefit from it. This includes anybody who – for any reason whatsoever – needs to locate the right person with the right title, in the right industry, in the right company, in the exact right division or subsidiary of the organization. Here's who can use this information to great advantage:

- **Sales professionals** who need to identify a finely honed list of *qualified* good leads to avoid wasting time prospecting the wrong individuals

- **Job hunters** who need to identify a precisely targeted list of potential future bosses, who then can be contacted directly, thereby avoiding being screened out by the personnel department

- **Company recruiters, inhouse search consultants and users of "unbundled search"** who are taking a more aggressive, proactive, hands – on approach to conducting their own searches and who want to control the process more effectively and save on recruiting fees at the same time

- **"Do-it-yourself" recruiters,** such as **small business owners, venture capitalists and department heads** who need to hire someone *not* on the job market without paying for recruiting fees, newspaper advertisements or Internet recruiting fees. Actually, Internet job posting sites are the electronic equivalent of want ads. So while these sites can generate more responses faster, they also generate more unqualified responses faster.

Great, you might be thinking, if Internet job posting sites don't offer the solution, how do I figure out who the precise right contacts are? You can start by looking them up in the directories, online databases or on web sites identified in this section of the book. Next, make some telephone calls to verify that you have identified the right individuals. For example, "Can you please confirm that Mr. Warbucks is still the Chief Financial Officer?" or "Can you please help me – is Ms. Innovata still in charge of new product development? . . . She is? . . . Great. Can you help me understand what aspect – is that R&D or more marketing oriented? . . . Oh, that's *doctor* Innovata and she's in the lab . . ." and so forth.

Finally, while you are doing your research, both using these references and on the phone, you will probably turn up some other interesting information. Some of your best leads can be developed this way, so be sure to follow them up.

In conclusion, there's no question that you can save a considerable sum in recruiting fees and ad expenses by acting as a do-it-yourself search consultant. If you decide to pursue that route, this book tells you virtually everything you need to know. But that said, having spent my career on both sides of the fence, in corporate recruiting and as a search consultant, there's no question that you get what you pay for. If you do decide to take the "do-it-yourself" search route, be prepared to devote a great deal of time to the effort. Ask:

- How much time you can afford to divert away from your "real" job to act as a search consultant?

- How long can you truly afford to wait to fill the position? In other words, how much is it costing you, both in terms of lost revenue and intangible costs?

Then consider the potential disaster of making a bad hire and weigh the costs of that – again, in terms of economics and stress to you – versus the cost of recruiting fees.

Beware if you're tempted to think the search business is easy. The Olympics look easy, too!

*   *   *   *   *

DIGGING FOR GOLD –
HOW TO USE THESE DIRECTORIES AND DATABASES FOR ID RESEARCH

This section, The Recruiter's Directory of Directories – Plus Web Sites, Databases & CD ROM's, identifies major directories,[1] CD ROM's, online databases and Internet web sites that recruiters and researchers need. You can use this information in two ways.

(1) The easiest way is to directly locate ID research (identification research) is in books or databases. Again, ID research is the names and titles you need in order to make sourcing and prospecting calls. Then, once you have the names, you can look for background information in your favorite biographical database (see "Biographies").

(2) Second, you can refer to these names and titles in references if you need to make phone calls to complete your ID research. When you're on the phone, if you already sound knowledgeable about the company, people are more likely to help you with the information you need. Again, you need their help to make sure you're reaching the right people. Sometimes you will need to talk to more than one person, such as a switchboard operator, to obtain the following data:

> Name
> Title
> Company
> Subsidiary or Division
> Department Name
> Location
> Phone Number
> Email address

Here's how to use directories for ID research:

First, get your target list of companies. If you don't already have one, make one. See "The Research Check List" in chapter 1 if you need help. Also, look up the "Target List Development" category in this section of the book.

Second, check the web sites of your target companies. If you're lucky, a web site will provide complete ID research for that target company, including names, titles, phone numbers, career summaries and sometimes email and photos! Presumably, web information will be up–to–the–minute accurate, but if you have any doubts, you can make a phone call to confirm it.

Now you're ready to use the resources in this section to start making a list of names and titles of people at each target company. Find a good directory, the annual report, 10(k), or company research in your files. Then, call the company and verify two things: that these individuals are still employees and that they still hold the same titles. (Remember, "He doesn't work here anymore," could mean that the person changed divisions or departments.) Once you've engaged the person in conversation, it's much easier to ask for additional information. Sometimes a simple question can be very effective, such as, "Is there anybody else?" especially if you're updating your list.

---

[1]Throughout this section, "directories" refers to all formats—hard copy, CD ROM's and online databases, including those on the Internet.

Of course, you should never stoop to using a ruse to obtain information. Just ask your question straight out. It's surprising how few people seem concerned about your reasons for needing information. If you can't conduct telephone ID research legitimately, don't. Your alternatives are to rely on directories and electronic sources of data for names and titles, and to ask sources to recommend candidates. You can get the names of sources in directories, from your files, from other sources, from executive directors of professional associations, or from job banks, lists of conference attendees, company phone books, company alumni directories, association membership rosters, announcements of job changes and promotions in trade journals, college and business school alumni magazines, or *The Wall Street Journal* "Who's News," and so forth. The main thing, however, is to *source at the right level,* in other words, talk to people who will recommend their peers. Peers tend to know each other. However, managers usually don't want to lose their best people and will seldom nominate them for a search. In fact, sometimes they'll be very sly about recommending someone they want to get rid of, such as a problem subordinate, or a superior blocking his or her career path!

Here is one of the most powerful sourcing techniques in the business. People who have changed jobs in the past 6 to 12 months can be superb sources of names at their old company. When you find such a source – and it won't be very often – find your list of ID research for that company. Be sure to ask for comments about those individuals – and identify them by name. Most important, ask for a ranking of who's best. This usually works well because while a source may be reluctant to volunteer that much information, if you already have some names, the source will usually be more willing to answer your questions. Remember to make assurances that all remarks will be kept completely confidential. A short thank you note is a nice idea, too, especially if you want to build a relationship with an excellent source for future help.

FREE INFORMATION
ANNUAL REPORTS, 10(K) REPORTS AND PROXY STATEMENTS

It's a good discipline to automatically call your target companies to request Annual Reports, 10(k)s, Proxies, and other information immediately, the moment the search begins. This is because this data is important, fundamental, crucial for laying a solid research foundation. Its absence could slow the progress of your search. It's best to get into the habit of calling for it right away, unless web access is faster and easier. This task could easily be delegated to a secretary or a student intern, if there's available time. You can look up the phone numbers in STANDARD AND POORS or another large general directory, or call toll free information (800-555-1212). Make sure you're calling corporate headquarters. While you're on the phone, also ask if the company can send "any other brochures or fact books or lists of locations, like plant locations, or anything like that." Alternatively, you may prefer to go online for the information. However, hard copy is portable and you can always take it home and peruse through it with a glass of wine in the evening, if you're so inclined. Or review it while waiting for a train or plane. You don't have that option with the Internet.

When the Annuals, 10(k)s and Proxies arrive, you don't necessarily have to read every word, but a good researcher will scan them, possibly with a highlighter pen, so you have an idea of what's there – and also to uncover hidden treasures! It's truly amazing what some companies will disclose, but you have to look to find it. In any case, the Annuals, 10(k)s and Proxies will likely prove a valuable reference at some point, especially if somebody is "stonewalling" you – that is, giving you no information. Incidentally, the Securities and Exchange Commission (SEC), as a matter of law, requires all publicly held companies to file these documents annually. Here's what you can expect to find in them:

Annual Reports provide valuable organizational information, division and subsidiary data, locations, names, titles, revenues, numbers of employees, discussions about strategy and growth plans, and sometimes even photos of employees.

10(k) Reports are required to disclose names and titles of senior management, each executive's number of years with the company and a career summary, and his or her age. Age is relevant because shareholders have a right to know when key managers might be approaching retirement, which could materially affect the performance of the company. 10(k)s often provide plant locations and define a company's lines of businesses. They must also state if anything could adversely affect the company's performance or stock price, for example, a major law suit or pending environmental expenses.

Proxy Statements are required to disclose the compensation paid to the four highest paid executives. Proxies also provide detailed background information on the Board of Directors.

You can obtain hard copy of the Annual, 10(k) and Proxy free by calling the company. Most companies post these reports on their web sites. This information is also available electronically for a fee – or free at a public library. As these services are constantly changing, you can find out the best databases by calling a library. If your local library can't help, make a long distance call. Try the library at one of the top graduate schools of business, or the Conference Board in New York City, or a library at a major city or in a wealthy town with a generous library budget.

*   *   *   *   *

If you're conducting a senior level search, directories will probably provide the names you need. But if the search is for a more junior position, directories might fail to provide names and titles at the appropriate level. Does this mean you should abandon directories? Absolutely not! Directories provide a brilliant starting point for research and make the task immensely simpler than calling up a company cold because you will already have at least one name to refer to in your conversation. For example, suppose a directory reveals the name of a manager in the right area for your search. Even if you need the name of a direct report a level lower in the organization, it's much easier to get this highly precise information by using a directory first, then calling the switchboard or someone else in the company to verify the accuracy of the information you already have.

Remember, when we refer to ID research, all we're talking about is the name and title of the person – that's all. Before we can make a sourcing and prospecting call, first we have to know who to call. If you must dig deeper into the organization to identify the right names, consider this. Again, when you call a company asking for information, if you show that you already know something about the company, the person you're talking to will be much more likely to provide information. You've done your homework and you have much more credibility. This is very different from showing up "empty handed," so to speak.

In summary, you can look up names and titles in directories, the company's web site, the Annual Report, your database and your files. Remember, in order to determine that you're prospecting at the right level, you need to know the size of the organization, either in revenues or number of employees. For example, a Manager of a $5 billion company is senior to a Director of a $100 million company. Sometimes you can piece ID research together into a reasonably accurate hypothesis for an organization chart. Like the pieces of a puzzle, start with information from company web sites, directories, the Annual Report, or 10(k). To make sure you're at the right level, be sure to factor in quantitative information: any numbers relating to size, revenues, number of employees in a department or division, number of direct reports, size of research and development budget, and any other measures that turn up in your research. Then, call the company and confirm these names and titles. Adopt a pleasant, chatty tone. Be friendly, strike up a conversation and ask for more information. Try simple, direct questions, like "Is there anybody else?" or, "Oh, I guess that's his boss." Keep asking questions until you have the information you need. And remember to say thank you.

*   *   *   *   *

I. CATEGORIES

Here is a master list of the categories used to classify the references in THE RECRUITER'S DIRECTORY OF DIRECTORIES—PLUS WEB SITES, DATABASES & CD ROM'S.

II. DIRECTORIES, WEB SITES, DATABASES & CD ROM'S BY CATEGORY

Note: If your company is considering investing in some of these resources, remember that most publishers sell books "on approval." In other words, they allow a free trial period—frequently 30 days—after which you can return the resource for a full refund. For more information, call the publisher. Another alternative is to use the library. If you are looking for a specific reference, call the library first. If they don't have it, they might be able to help you find it in another library. Be sure to tell them why you are looking for that reference, because they might know of something else that will meet your needs.

A note about fax numbers: Because fax numbers can change so frequently, it is strongly recommended that you verify beforehand that you will be sending a fax to the best location.

A

Accounting

AMERICAN INSTITUTE OF CERTIFIED PUBLIC ACCOUNTANTS (AICPA) is a major professional association which can provide information about surveys, directories and so forth. For more information about this and other accounting organizations, refer to one of the references listed under "References—Librarian" such as BUSINESS INFORMATION SOURCES by Lorna Daniells, ENCYCLOPEDIA OF BUSINESS INFORMATION SOURCES, and the ENCYCLOPEDIA OF ASSOCIATIONS. Or contact the AICPA, Harborside Financial Center, 201 Plaza Three, Jersey City, NJ 07311-3881. (201) 938-3000. www.aicpa.org.

CORPORATE FINANCE SOURCEBOOK—THE GUIDE TO MAJOR INVESTMENT SOURCES AND RELATED FINANCIAL SERVICES contains over 13,000 names of executives at 3,700 organizations that, broadly speaking, supply growth capital to businesses or are service firms, such as US venture capital lenders, private lenders, commercial finance and factoring, pension managers, master trusts and other sources. Names of key management are included. A special section details public offerings of the past 3 years and mergers and acquisitions over $100 million. $575. If the price is prohibitively high, remember your local library. National Register Publishing, Reed Elsevier-New Providence, 121 Chanlon Road, New Providence, NJ 07974, (800) 521-8110, fax (800) 836-7736, web site www.redbooks.com or www.marquiswhoswho.com. "If, for any reason whatsoever, your order does not fully meet your expectations, simply return the product within 30 days for a prompt, complete, unquestioned refund," as stated in Catalog of Biographical and Professional References of publisher Marquis Who's Who/National Register Publishing.

D & B DIRECTORY OF SERVICE COMPANIES is a directory with information on 50,000 US service businesses, including privately held companies, in these sectors: accounting, auditing and bookkeeping, advertising and public relations, architecture and engineering, consumer services, executive search, health, hospitality, management consulting, motion pictures, repair, research, social services and law. Listings include key executives' names and titles, address, phone, sales volume, number of employees, parent company and location, and more. Companies listed employ 50 or more people. Information is listed alphabetically and is cross-referenced geographically and by industry classification. Updated annually. For prices call Dun & Bradstreet at (800) 526-0651. For more information contact Dun & Bradstreet, Business Reference Solutions, Three Sylvan Way, Parsippany, New Jersey 07054. Email dnbmdd@mail.dnb.com. Web site http://www.dnbmdd.com.

FINANCIAL SERVICES CANADA is a handbook of banks, non-depository institutions, stock exchange and brokers, investment management, mutual funds, insurance, accountants, government agencies, financial associations and more, including contact numbers, name, title, organization, phone, fax, email, web site, and cellular. $199 for book, $299 for CD ROM, $399 for both. Ordering information: Copp Clark Professional, 200 Adelaide Street West, 3rd floor, Toronto, ON M5H 1W7 CANADA. Email orders@mail.CanadaInfo.com. Web site http://www.coppclark.com. For additional information contact: IHS Canada, Micromedia Limited, 20 Victoria Street, Toronto, Ontario M5C 2N8 CANADA, (800) 387-2689, (416) 362-5211, fax (416) 362-6161, email info@micromedia.on.ca.

www.accountingjobs.com or Accounting and Finance Jobs, was developed by AccountingNet of Seattle in a joint venture with Career Mosaic. Launched in 1997, this site specializes in accounting and finance positions, mainly in the $30,000-50,000 range.

www.careermosaic.com is the URL for a major recruitment web site that spends millions of dollars in advertising to draw traffic to this site. CareerMosaic features a jobs database; newsgroups for jobs, college connection, online job fairs, employer job postings; company information and more. CareerMosaic was ranked as one of the top 5 "Sites Offering the Best Overall Support for Job Seekers" by the *National Business Employment Weekly*. The site was developed Bernard Hodes Advertising in New York and went online in 1994.

Adoption

THE ADOPTION DIRECTORY provides the names of agencies and individuals to contact and a range of other information and three indexes. $65.00. Gale Group, P.O. Box 9187, Farmington Hills, MI 48333-9187. Toll free US and Canada (800) 877-GALE (4253) and (248) 699-GALE, fax (800) 414-5043 and (248) 699-8061, Internet orders galeord@galegroup.com, web site www.galegroup.com or www.gale.com. All Gale Group products are available on approval. Contact Gale for details.

Advertising

ADVERTISER AND AGENCY RED BOOKS PLUS CD ROM combines all the information in THE STANDARD DIRECTORY OF ADVERTISERS, THE STANDARD DIRECTORY OF ADVERTISING AGENCIES and THE STANDARD DIRECTORY OF INTERNATIONAL ADVERTISERS AND AGENCIES. Information is searchable by 25 fields, including company name, personal name, job title/function, product type, product/account name, city, state, zip or country, area code, revenues, number of employees, outside ad agency and even type of computer hardware. Contains professional association information. Available for Windows and Macintosh. Updated quarterly. 1 year subscription $1,295. If the price is prohibitively high, remember your local library. National Register Publishing, Reed Elsevier-New Providence, 121 Chanlon Road, New Providence, NJ 07974, (800) 521-8110, fax (800) 836-7736, web site www.redbooks.com or www.marquiswhoswho.com. "If, for any reason whatsoever, your order does not fully meet your expectations, simply return the product within 30 days for a prompt, complete, unquestioned refund," as stated in Catalog of Biographical and Professional References of publisher Marquis Who's Who/National Register Publishing.

ADVERTISING AGE is a weekly trade paper. Inquire about their 100 Leading National Advertisers issue, an annual survey which identifies names and titles of employees at large consumer marketing companies. 1 year subscription $109, 2 years $175. web site www.adage.com. Crain Communications, Inc. is headquartered in Chicago with offices in major cities throughout the US, plus London, Tokyo and Frankfurt. New York location: 220 East 42nd Street, New York, NY 10017, (212) 210-0100, Circulation (800) 678-9595.

ASIAN ADVERTISING, MARKETING AND MEDIA HANDBOOK lists information about advertising agencies, newspaper and magazine publishers and market research companies. Published by Euromonitor (England), at $470 (1st edition), it had been exclusively distributed by Gale Group. At the time of this writing, Gale no longer carries it. For more information, contact Euromonitor or Gale or refer to BOOKS IN PRINT. This reference might also be available in the library.

CO-OP ADVERTISING PROGRAMS SOURCEBOOK identifies over 5,300 co-op programs in 52 product classifications. This sourcebook includes all the essentials of any co-op plan, including eligible media, program timing, qualifying products and trademarks, participation data, claim information and contact information. $479 for 2 volume set. If the price is prohibitively high, remember your local library. National Register Publishing, Reed Elsevier-New Providence, 121 Chanlon Road, New Providence, NJ 07974, (800) 521-8110, fax (800) 836-7736, web site www.redbooks.com or www.marquiswhoswho.com. "If, for any reason whatsoever, your order does not fully meet your expectations, simply return the product within 30 days for a prompt, complete, unquestioned refund," as stated in Catalog of Biographical and Professional References of publisher Marquis Who's Who/National Register Publishing.

COMPLETE MARQUIS WHO'S WHO ON CD ROM is a compilation of literally all 19 Marquis Who's Who that have appeared in print since 1985, including living and deceased people. WHO'S WHO IN AMERICA®, WHO'S WHO IN THE WORLD®, WHO'S WHO IN AMERICAN EDUCATION®, WHO'S

WHO IN AMERICAN LAW®, WHO'S WHO IN AMERICAN NURSING®, WHO'S WHO IN MEDICINE AND HEALTHCARE®, WHO'S WHO IN FINANCE AND INDUSTRY®, WHO'S WHO IN SCIENCE AND ENGINEERING®, WHO'S WHO IN THE EAST®, WHO'S WHO IN THE MIDWEST®, WHO'S WHO IN THE SOUTH AND SOUTHWEST®, WHO'S WHO IN THE WEST®, WHO'S WHO OF AMERICAN WOMEN®, WHO'S WHO IN ADVERTISING®, WHO'S WHO OF EMERGING LEADERS IN AMERICA®, WHO'S WHO IN ENTERTAINMENT®, WHO'S WHO AMONG HUMAN SERVICES PROFESSIONALS®. One year subscription with semi-annual updates $995. National Register Publishing, Reed Elsevier-New Providence, 121 Chanlon Road, New Providence, NJ 07974, (800) 521-8110, fax (800) 836-7736, web site www.marquiswhoswho.com or www.redbooks.com. "If, for any reason whatsoever, your order does not fully meet your expectations, simply return the product within 30 days for a prompt, complete, unquestioned refund," as stated in Catalog of Biographical and Professional References of publisher Marquis Who's Who/National Register Publishing.

CREATIVE HANDBOOK is a portfolio and a directory of creative services, published annually. Call publisher for prices. Cahners Business Information, 34-35 Newman Street, London W1P 3PD England. (011) 44-171-637-3663, fax (011) 44-171-580-5559. Headquarters: Cahners Business Information, 275 Washington Street, Newton, MA 02158-1630, (617) 558-4663 or (617) 964-3030, fax (617) 558-4700, email marketaccess@cahners.com. Web sites www.cahners.com or www.chilton.net.

CREATIVITY is a monthly trade publication. Crain Communications, Inc. is headquartered in Chicago with offices in major cities throughout the US, plus London, Tokyo and Frankfurt. New York location: 220 East 42nd Street, New York, NY 10017, (212) 210-0100, Circulation (800) 678-9595. Annual subscription $49.

D&B DIRECTORY OF SERVICE COMPANIES is a directory with information on 50,000 US service businesses, including privately held companies, in these sectors: accounting, auditing and bookkeeping, advertising and public relations, architecture and engineering, consumer services, executive search, health, hospitality, management consulting, motion pictures, repair, research, social services and law. Listings include key executives' names and titles, address, phone, sales volume, number of employees, parent company and location, and more. Companies listed employ 50 or more people. Information is listed alphabetically and is cross-referenced geographically and by industry classification. Updated annually. For prices call Dun & Bradstreet at (800) 526-0651. For more information contact Dun & Bradstreet, Business Reference Solutions, Three Sylvan Way, Parsippany, New Jersey 07054. Email dnbmdd@mail.dnb.com. Web site http://www.dnbmdd.com.

DIRECT MARKETING MARKET PLACE lists over 4,000 direct marketing companies, organized into numerous categories: associations, catalogs, continuity programs, credit card companies, list brokers, market researchers, computer & fulfillment services, creative sources, ad agencies, copywriters, art services and photographers. Also included are geographic indexes, direct marketing publications, telemarketers, printers and lettershops. $239.95. If the price is prohibitively high, remember your local library. National Register Publishing, Reed Elsevier-New Providence, 121 Chanlon Road, New Providence, NJ 07974, (800) 521-8110, fax (800) 836-7736, web site www.redbooks.com or www.marquiswhoswho.com. "If, for any reason whatsoever, your order does not fully meet your expectations, simply return the product within 30 days for a prompt, complete, unquestioned refund," as stated in Catalog of Biographical and Professional References of publisher Marquis Who's Who/National Register Publishing.

LATIN AMERICAN ADVERTISING, MARKETING & MEDIA SOURCEBOOK, published by Euromonitor (England), at $470 (1st edition), had been exclusively distributed in the USA, Canada and Australia by Gale Group. At the time of this writing, Gale no longer carries it. For more information, contact Euromonitor or Gale or refer to BOOKS IN PRINT or INTERNATIONAL BOOKS IN PRINT. This reference might also be available in the library.

LITERARY MARKET PLACE, "The Directory of the American Book Publishing Industry With Industry Yellow Pages" is an excellent 3 volume directory with comprehensive information on US book publishers; imprints, subsidiaries and distributors; book trade acquisitions and mergers, small presses, Canadian book publishers, micropublishers, US electronic publishers, electronic publishing consultants, electronic publishing products and services, editorial services, literary agents, illustrations agents, US agents and offices of foreign publishers, lecture agents, specialized advertising and public relations firms, direct mail specialists, mailing list brokers and services, book review syndicates, book review and index journals and services, book exhibits, book clubs, book lists and catalogs, book importers and exporters, book producers, translators, artists, photographers, stock photo agencies, associations, book trade events and conferences, awards, contents and grants, reference books for the trade, magazines for the trade, a toll free directory of publishers, magazine and newspaper publicity, radio and television publicity, book manufacturing services, book distributors and sales representatives, and wholesalers. $189.95.

LITERARY MARKET PLACE ON DISC, previously titled LITERARY MARKET PLACE PLUS CD ROM, one year subscription $297.00.

LITERARY MARKET PLACE—INTERNET EDITION, www.literarymarketplace.com, is available by subscription.

INTERNATIONAL LITERARY MARKET PLACE Internet database can be directly accessed at www.iliterarymarketplace.com. It is also linked to the US domestic LITERARY MARKET PLACE web site at www.literarymarketplace.com. Contact the publisher for subscription price. INTERNATIONAL LITERARY MARKET PLACE, hard copy $189.95.

R.R. Bowker (a unit of Cahners Business Information), 121 Chanlon Road, New Providence, NJ 07974 USA, Phone (888) BOWKER2 (888-269-5372) & (800) 323-3288, fax (908) 508-7696, email info@bowker.com, web www.bowker.com. Canada—R.R. Bowker, Markham, Ontario, phone (888) BOWKER9 & (905) 415-5837, fax (905) 479-6266. German speaking Europe—K.G. Saur Verlag, Munich, Germany, phone 49-89-76902-232, fax 49-89-76902-250, email 100730.1341@compuserve.com, web www.saur.de/home.htm. Rest of Europe incl. United Kingdom plus Africa & Asia—Bowker-Saur, W. Sussex, UK, phone 44-1342-326-972, fax 44-1342-335-612, email customer@bowker-saur.co.uk, web www.bowker-saur.com/service/. Australia/New Zealand—Thorpe, Port Melbourne, Victoria, Australia, phone 61-03-9-245-7370, fax 61-03-9-245-7395, email customer.service@thorpe.com.au, web www.thorpe.com.au. Technical support for CD ROMs (800) 323-3288, fax 908) 665-3528, email techsupport@bowker.com.

PHARMACEUTICAL MARKETERS DIRECTORY is a well organized directory that contains many names and titles and other information, including a listing of specialized professional associations. Published annually. $162.50. CPS COMMUNICATIONS, INC., 7200 West Camino Real, Suite 215, Boca Raton, FL 33433, (561) 368-9301, sales office (203) 778-1463, email pmd@cpsnet.com, web site http://www.cpsnet.com.

STANDARD DIRECTORY OF ADVERTISING AGENCIES, also referred to as the "Red Book," is a comprehensive directory of the advertising agency business, generally including extensive listings of executives, especially in management, media, account services, creative and production. It also reveals the names of each agency's corporate clients. A CyberAgency Section lists agencies involved with web design and development and a special "Who Owns Whom" section listing agency subsidiaries. $599. If the price is prohibitively high, remember your local library. THE STANDARD DIRECTORY OF ADVERTISING AGENCIES is also available on CD ROM under the title ADVERTISER AND AGENCY RED BOOKS PLUS. National Register Publishing, Reed Elsevier-New Providence, 121 Chanlon Road, New Providence, NJ 07974, (800) 521-8110, fax (800) 836-7736, web site www.marquiswhoswho.com or www.redbooks.com. "If, for any reason whatsoever, your order does not fully meet your expectations, simply return the product within 30 days for a prompt, complete, unquestioned refund," as stated in Catalog of Biographical and Professional References of publisher Marquis Who's Who/National Register Publishing.

STANDARD DIRECTORY OF INTERNATIONAL ADVERTISERS & AGENCIES covers the advertising industry in over 120 countries, including 1,700 companies and 2,000 agencies. Listings include names and titles of key executives. $539. If the price is prohibitively high, remember your local library. National Register Publishing, Reed Elsevier-New Providence, 121 Chanlon Road, New Providence, NJ 07974, (800) 521-8110, fax (800) 836-7736, web site www.redbooks.com or www.marquiswhoswho.com. "If, for any reason whatsoever, your order does not fully meet your expectations, simply return the product within 30 days for a prompt, complete, unquestioned refund," as stated in Catalog of Biographical and Professional References of publisher Marquis Who's Who/National Register Publishing.

Aerospace

WORLD AVIATION DIRECTORY AND BUYER'S GUIDE is available as a hard copy directory, on CD ROM and as an Internet database. Some companies on the Internet even have email and web site links. Print directory $275, 2 issues per year; CD ROM $995. Published by Aviation Week, a Division of The McGraw-

Hill Companies. McGraw Hill, Print Division, PO Box 629, Hightstown, NJ 08520, (800) 525-5003. McGraw Hill, Other Media Division (202) 383-2420, (800) 551-2015, extension 4. Web site: www.wadaviation.com.

Africa

See Arab, International

AFRICAN BOOKS IN PRINT, $400, published by Bowker-Saur. R.R. Bowker (a unit of Cahners Business Information), 121 Chanlon Road, New Providence, NJ 07974 USA, Phone (888) BOWKER2 (888-269-5372) & (800) 323-3288, fax (908) 508-7696, email info@bowker.com, web www.bowker.com. Canada—R.R. Bowker, Markham, Ontario, phone (888) BOWKER9 & (905) 415-5837, fax (905) 479-6266. German speaking Europe—K.G. Saur Verlag, Munich, Germany, phone 49-89-76902-232, fax 49-89-76902-250, email 100730.1341@compuserve.com, web www.saur.de/home.htm. Rest of Europe incl. United Kingdom plus Africa & Asia—Bowker-Saur, W. Sussex, UK, phone 44-1342-326-972, fax 44-1342-335-612, email customer@bowker-saur.co.uk, web www.bowker-saur.com/service/. Australia/New Zealand—Thorpe, Port Melbourne, Victoria, Australia, phone 61-03-9-245-7370, fax 61-03-9-245-7395, email customer.service@thorpe.com.au, web www.thorpe.com.au. Technical support for CD ROMs (800) 323-3288, fax 908) 665-3528, email techsupport@bowker.com.

DIRECTORY OF AMERICAN FIRMS OPERATING IN FOREIGN COUNTRIES, REGIONAL EDITION—AFRICA. Includes Algeria, Angola, Benin, Botswana, Burkina Faso, Burundi, Cameroon, Central African Republic, Chad, Congo, Dem. Republic of Congo, Djibouti, Egypt, Ethiopia, Gabon, Gambia, Ghana, Guinea, Ivory Coast, Kenya Lesotho, Liberia, Libya, Madagascar, Malawi, Mali, Mauritius, Morocco, Mozambique, Namibia, Nigeria, Reunion, Senengal, Seychelles, Sierra Leone, South Africa, Sudan, Swaziland, Tanzania, Tunisia, Uganda, Zambia, Zimbabwe. $59. Uniworld Business Publications, Inc., 257 Central Park West, Suite 10A, New York, NY 10024-4110, (212) 496-2448, fax (212) 769-0413, email uniworldbp@aol.com. Web site: http://www.uniworldbp.com.

DIRECTORY OF FOREIGN FIRMS OPERATING IN THE UNITED STATES, REGIONAL EDITION—AFRICA, including Egypt, Ivory Coast, Morocco, Nigeria, South Africa. $29. Uniworld Business Publications, Inc., 257 Central Park West, Suite 10A, New York, NY 10024-4110, (212) 496-2448, fax (212) 769-0413, email uniworldbp@aol.com. Web site: http://www.uniworldbp.com.

KOMPASS is described by the publisher as "the world's most comprehensive global database of companies, products and services for manufacturing and engineering professionals in print, on CD ROM and on the Internet." It contains company and product information for companies in all lines of business, including manufacturing and industrial sectors. Each company listing includes name, address, phone number, management names, business descriptions, and industry and product listings. Kompass's web site is www.kompass.com. Call publisher for prices and information on country directories. Cahners Business Information, 121 Chanlon Road, New Providence, NJ 07974, (908) 771-8785, fax (908) 665-8755, email hholmes@reedref.com. Headquarters: Cahners Business Information, 275 Washington Street, Newton, MA 02158-1630, (617) 558-4663 or (617) 964-3030, fax (617) 558-4700, email marketaccess@cahners.com, web sites www.cahners.com or www.chilton.net.

MAJOR COMPANIES OF AFRICA SOUTH OF THE SAHARA identifies 22,000 contacts at over 6,000 companies in 42 countries, including 1,700 in South Africa alone. $530. CD ROMs available. Published by Graham & Whiteside Ltd., Tuition House, 5-6 Francis Grove, London SW19 4DT, England. Web site http://www.major-co-data.com. Email sales@major-co-data.com. Distributed by: Larry Meranus Professional Publications & Services, 4 Demoray Court, Pine Brook, NJ 07058, (800) MERANUS or (800) 637-2687. Also distributed by Gale Group, P.O. Box 9187, Farmington Hills, MI 48333-9187. Toll free US and Canada (800) 877-GALE (4253) and (248) 699-GALE, fax (800) 414-5043 and (248) 699-8061, Internet orders galeord@galegroup.com, web site www.galegroup.com or www.gale.com. All Gale Group products are available on approval. Contact Gale for details.

Countries include: Angola, Benin, Botswana, Burkina Faso, Burundi, Cameroon, Cape Verde, Central Africa Republic, Chad, Comoros, The Congo, Democratic Republic of the Congo, Equatorial Guinea, Ethiopia, Gabon, The Gambia, Ghana, Guinea, Guinea Bissau, Ivory Coast, Kenya, Lesotho, Liberia, Madagascar,

Malawi, Mali, Mauritius, Mozambique, Namibia, Niger, Nigeria, Rwanda, Sao Tome & Principe, Senegal, Seychelles, Sierra Leone, Swaziland, Tanzania, Togo, Uganda, Zambia, Zimbabwe.

MAJOR COMPANIES SERIES ON CD ROM consists of Graham & Whiteside's annual directories of major international companies. All six directories reside on one disk. After payment, you'll receive a security code to access the region(s) you select. This Windows™ based CD can navigate by company name, company locations, executive names, business activity and more. Free demo CD ROM is available. Regions also available separately for Europe, Central & Eastern Europe, the Far East and Australasia, the Arab World, Africa, and Latin America. For prices and availability, contact the Gale Group, P.O. Box 9187, Farmington Hills, MI 48333-9187. Toll free US and Canada (800) 877-GALE (4253) and (248) 699-GALE, fax (800) 414-5043 and (248) 699-8061, Internet orders galeord@galegroup.com, web site www.galegroup.com or www.gale.com. All Gale Group products are available on approval. Contact Gale for details.

Airlines

CONSUMER REPORTS TRAVEL LETTER is published by Consumers Union, a nonprofit independent organization providing consumers with information and advice on goods, services, health and personal finance. No advertising is accepted. $39/year subscription. Single copy $5. Flash By Fax releases late breaking news that would otherwise miss CONSUMER REPORTS TRAVEL LETTER. It also reveals short term deals on travel, especially airfare. To order Flash By Fax, call 800-559-8905 for 12 issues @ $25 per year. For more information contact Consumer Reports Travel Letter, Ed Perkins, Editor, Consumers Union, 101 Truman Avenue, Yonkers, NY 10703-1057, (800) 234-1970, (914) 378-2740.

REGIONAL AIRLINE DIRECTORY is also available on CD. Phillips Business Information, Inc., a Phillips Publishing International Company, 120 Seven Locks Road, Potomac, MD 20854, (301) 340-1520, (301) 340-7788, (800) 777-5006, Internet pbi@phillips.com, web site www.phillips.com.

www.aeps.com/aeps/aepshm.html is the URL for the Aviation Employee Placement Service. Positions generally range from $30,000 to $100,000 and mostly include pilots, mechanics and management. Developed by Sysops, Inc. in Fort Lauderdale, Florida, the site was established in 1995.

Alaska

ALASKA INDUSTRIAL DIRECTORY contains information on 600 companies. $39 directory, $115 database. Database Publishing Company, PO Box 70024, Anaheim, CA 92825, (800) 888-8434, (714) 778-6400, email sales@databasepublishing.com.

Alumni

See *Company Alumni* and *University Alumni*

Apparel

See *Retail*

ADVERTISER AND AGENCY RED BOOKS PLUS CD ROM combines all the information in THE STANDARD DIRECTORY OF ADVERTISERS, THE STANDARD DIRECTORY OF ADVERTISING AGENCIES and THE STANDARD DIRECTORY OF INTERNATIONAL ADVERTISERS AND AGENCIES. Information is searchable by 25 fields, including company name, personal name, job title/function, product type, product/account name, city, state, zip or country, area code, revenues, number of employees, outside ad agency and even type of computer hardware. Contains professional association information. Available for Windows and Macintosh. Updated quarterly. 1 year subscription $1,295. If the price is prohibitively high, remember your local library. National Register Publishing, Reed Elsevier-New Providence, 121 Chanlon Road, New Providence, NJ 07974, (800) 521-8110, fax (800) 836-7736, web site www.redbooks.com or www.marquiswhoswho.com. "If, for any reason whatsoever, your order does not fully meet your expectations, simply return the product within 30 days for a prompt, complete, unquestioned

refund," as stated in Catalog of Biographical and Professional References of publisher Marquis Who's Who/National Register Publishing.

FAIRCHILD PUBLICATIONS publishes a number of fashion and retail publications, such as FAIRCHILD'S TEXTILE AND APPAREL FINANCIAL DIRECTORY, which provides information about a range of textile and garment manufacturers. Published annually. $85. Fairchild also publishes industry trade publications, such as WOMEN'S WEAR DAILY (www.wwd.com) and numerous specialized apparel industry directories, such as FASHION RESOURCE DIRECTORY, DIRECTORY OF BRAND NAME APPAREL MANUFACTURERS (which includes buyers), and APPAREL INDUSTRY SOURCEBOOK (which also includes buyers). Fairchild also publishes material for specialized retail niches, such as supermarkets, shoes, etc. For more information, contact Fairchild Books, 7 West 34th Street, New York, NY 10001, (212) 630-3880, (800) 247 6622, email fpwebmaster@fairchildpub.com, web site www.fairchildpub.com or www.fairchildbooks.com.

SHELDON'S RETAIL DIRECTORY OF THE US AND CANADA is published by Phelon, Sheldon & Marsar, 1364 Georgetowne Circle, Sarasota, FL 34232-2048, (941) 342-7990, fax (941) 342-7994, who also publish numerous retail and apparel directories. For more information contact the Reference Desk at the Baker Library, Harvard Business School in Boston, in connection with the Advisor Database. Web site www.library.hbs.edu/.

STANDARD DIRECTORY OF ADVERTISERS Business Classifications Edition is an excellent general directory that organizes companies by a wide range of product categories. A few examples include "Apparel 2—Men's and Boys' Wear," "Heating and Air Conditioning," "Cosmetics and Toiletries," and "Aviation and Aerospace." This directory lists names and titles of key officers, revenues and other information. It is available in a geographic edition for the same price. This directory is comprised of over 24,000 companies that annually spend over $200,000 on advertising. It represents a reasonable place to look for hard-to-find information about privately held companies, especially those that heavily advertise their products. It is a good place to look for names if STANDARD AND POORS and the MILLION DOLLAR DIRECTORY fail to yield the names you need. Finally, the Classified Edition of THE STANDARD DIRECTORY OF ADVERTISERS can be a very convenient source of research because both your target list of companies and the corresponding names and titles of management all appear together, in the same Classification. This is important if you still rely on research books in hard copy. THE STANDARD DIRECTORY OF ADVERTISERS also publishes a special volume called THE STANDARD DIRECTORY OF ADVERTISERS TRADENAME INDEX. You can use the TRADENAME INDEX if you know the brand name of a product and need to find the company that manufactures it. In addition, this directory contains an Associations section which identifies marketing oriented associations.

$599 hard copy. If the price is prohibitively high, remember your local library. THE STANDARD DIRECTORY OF ADVERTISERS is also available on CD ROM under the title ADVERTISER AND AGENCY RED BOOKS PLUS. It is available in Windows® and Macintosh® formats. National Register Publishing, Reed Elsevier-New Providence, 121 Chanlon Road, New Providence, NJ 07974, (800) 521-8110, fax (800) 836-7736, web site www.redbooks.com or www.marquiswhoswho.com. "If, for any reason whatsoever, your order does not fully meet your expectations, simply return the product within 30 days for a prompt, complete, unquestioned refund," as stated in Catalog of Biographical and Professional References of publisher Marquis Who's Who/National Register Publishing.

Arab

DIRECTORY OF AMERICAN FIRMS OPERATING IN FOREIGN COUNTRIES, REGIONAL EDITION—THE ARABIC COUNTRIES. Includes Algeria, Bahrain, Egypt, Jordan, Kuwait, Lebanon, Morocco, Oman, Qatar, Saudi Arabia, Sudan, Syria, Tunisia, United Arab Emirates, West Bank, Yemen. $49. Ordering information: Uniworld Business Publications, Inc., 257 Central Park West, Suite 10A, New York, NY 10024-4110, (212) 496-2448, fax (212) 769-0413, email uniworldbp@aol.com. Web site: http://www.uniworldbp.com.

DIRECTORY OF AMERICAN FIRMS OPERATING IN FOREIGN COUNTRIES, REGIONAL EDITION—NEAR & MIDDLE EAST & ARABIC COUNTRIES COMBINED, $59. Ordering information: Uniworld Business Publications, Inc., 257 Central Park West, Suite 10A, New York, NY 10024-

4110, (212) 496-2448, fax (212) 769-0413, email uniworldbp@aol.com. Web site: http://www.uniworldbp.com.

MAJOR COMPANIES OF THE ARAB WORLD identifies 34,000 senior executives in 7,000 companies in 20 Arab countries. $870. Also available on CD ROM. Published by Graham & Whiteside Ltd., Tuition House, 5-6 Francis Grove, London SW19 4DT, England. Web site http://www.major-co-data.com. Email sales@major-co-data.com. Distributed by: Larry Meranus Professional Publications & Services, 4 Demoray Court, Pine Brook, NJ 07058, (800) MERANUS or (800) 637-2687. Also distributed by Gale Group, P.O. Box 9187, Farmington Hills, MI 48333-9187. Toll free US and Canada (800) 877-GALE (4253) and (248) 699-GALE, fax (800) 414-5043 and (248) 699-8061, Internet orders galeord@galegroup.com, web site www.galegroup.com or www.gale.com. All Gale Group products are available on approval. Contact Gale for details.

MAJOR COMPANIES SERIES ON CD ROM consists of Graham & Whiteside's annual directories of major international companies. All six directories reside on one disk. After payment, you'll receive a security code to access the region(s) you select. This Windows™ based CD can navigate by company name, company locations, executive names, business activity and more. Free demo CD ROM is available. Regions also available separately for Europe, Central & Eastern Europe, the Far East and Australasia, the Arab World, Africa, and Latin America. For prices and availability, contact the Gale Group, P.O. Box 9187, Farmington Hills, MI 48333-9187. Toll free US and Canada (800) 877-GALE (4253) and (248) 699-GALE, fax (800) 414-5043 and (248) 699-8061, Internet orders galeord@galegroup.com, web site www.galegroup.com or www.gale.com. All Gale Group products are available on approval. Contact Gale for details.

MAJOR FINANCIAL INSTITUTIONS OF THE ARAB WORLD provides contacts and information on over 1,000 top financial institutions in the Arab world. US distributor: Larry Meranus Professional Publications & Services, 4 Demoray Court, Pine Brook, NJ 07058, (800) MERANUS or (800) 637-2687. Published by Graham & Whiteside Ltd., Tuition House, 5-6 Francis Grove, London SW19 4DT, England. Web site http://www.major-co-data.com. Email sales@major-co-data.com.

WHO'S WHO IN THE ARAB WORLD contains 6,000 biographies from 19 Arab countries. $340. Published by Publitec Publications, Beirut. Distributed to libraries in the US and Canada by Gale Group, P.O. Box 9187, Farmington Hills, MI 48333-9187. Toll free US and Canada (800) 877-GALE (4253) and (248) 699-GALE, fax (800) 414-5043 and (248) 699-8061, Internet orders galeord@galegroup.com, web site www.galegroup.com or www.gale.com. All Gale Group products are available on approval. Contact Gale for details.

Architecture

ADVERTISER AND AGENCY RED BOOKS PLUS CD ROM combines all the information in THE STANDARD DIRECTORY OF ADVERTISERS, THE STANDARD DIRECTORY OF ADVERTISING AGENCIES and THE STANDARD DIRECTORY OF INTERNATIONAL ADVERTISERS AND AGENCIES. Information is searchable by 25 fields, including company name, personal name, job title/function, product type, product/account name, city, state, zip or country, area code, revenues, number of employees, outside ad agency and even type of computer hardware. Contains professional association information. Available for Windows and Macintosh. Updated quarterly. 1 year subscription $1,295. If the price is prohibitively high, remember your local library. National Register Publishing, Reed Elsevier-New Providence, 121 Chanlon Road, New Providence, NJ 07974, (800) 521-8110, fax (800) 836-7736, web site www.redbooks.com or www.marquiswhoswho.com. "If, for any reason whatsoever, your order does not fully meet your expectations, simply return the product within 30 days for a prompt, complete, unquestioned refund," as stated in Catalog of Biographical and Professional References of publisher Marquis Who's Who/National Register Publishing.

D&B DIRECTORY OF SERVICE COMPANIES is a directory with information on 50,000 US service businesses, including privately held companies, in these sectors: accounting, auditing and bookkeeping, advertising and public relations, architecture and engineering, consumer services, executive search, health, hospitality, management consulting, motion pictures, repair, research, social services and law. Listings include key executives' names and titles, address, phone, sales volume, number of employees, parent company and location, and more. Companies listed employ 50 or more people. Information is listed alphabetically and is cross-referenced geographically and by industry classification. Updated annually. For prices call Dun &

Bradstreet at (800) 526-0651. For more information contact Dun & Bradstreet, Business Reference Solutions, Three Sylvan Way, Parsippany, New Jersey 07054. Email dnbmdd@mail.dnb.com. Web site http://www.dnbmdd.com.

STANDARD DIRECTORY OF ADVERTISERS Business Classifications Edition is an excellent general directory that organizes companies by a wide range of product categories. A few examples include "Apparel 2—Men's and Boys' Wear," "Heating and Air Conditioning," "Cosmetics and Toiletries," and "Aviation and Aerospace." This directory lists names and titles of key officers, revenues and other information. It is available in a geographic edition for the same price. This directory is comprised of over 24,000 companies that annually spend over $200,000 on advertising. It represents a reasonable place to look for hard-to-find information about privately held companies, especially those that heavily advertise their products. It is a good place to look for names if STANDARD AND POORS and the MILLION DOLLAR DIRECTORY fail to yield the names you need. Finally, the Classified Edition of THE STANDARD DIRECTORY OF ADVERTISERS can be a very convenient source of research because both your target list of companies and the corresponding names and titles of management all appear together, in the same Classification. This is important if you still rely on research books in hard copy.

THE STANDARD DIRECTORY OF ADVERTISERS also publishes a special volume called THE STANDARD DIRECTORY OF ADVERTISERS TRADENAME INDEX. You can use the TRADENAME INDEX if you know the brand name of a product and need to find the company that manufactures it. In addition, this directory contains an Associations section which identifies marketing oriented associations. $599 hard copy. If the price is prohibitively high, remember your local library. THE STANDARD DIRECTORY OF ADVERTISERS is also available on CD ROM under the title ADVERTISER AND AGENCY RED BOOKS PLUS. It is available in Windows® and Macintosh® formats. National Register Publishing, Reed Elsevier-New Providence, 121 Chanlon Road, New Providence, NJ 07974, (800) 521-8110, fax (800) 836-7736, web site www.redbooks.com or www.marquiswhoswho.com. "If, for any reason whatsoever, your order does not fully meet your expectations, simply return the product within 30 days for a prompt, complete, unquestioned refund," as stated in Catalog of Biographical and Professional References of publisher Marquis Who's Who/National Register Publishing.

Argentina

See International, South America, Latin America

DIRECTORY OF AMERICAN FIRMS OPERATING IN FOREIGN COUNTRIES, REGIONAL EDITION—ARGENTINA. $29. Uniworld Business Publications, Inc., 257 Central Park West, Suite 10A, New York, NY 10024-4110, (212) 496-2448, fax (212) 769-0413, email uniworldbp@aol.com. Web site: http://www.uniworldbp.com.

DIRECTORY OF AMERICAN FIRMS OPERATING IN FOREIGN COUNTRIES, REGIONAL EDITION—ARGENTINA, BRAZIL, CHILE. $59. Uniworld Business Publications, Inc., 257 Central Park West, Suite 10A, New York, NY 10024-4110, (212) 496-2448, fax (212) 769-0413, email uniworldbp@aol.com. Web site: http://www.uniworldbp.com.

Arts

AMERICAN ART DIRECTORY provides information about national and regional art organizations, museums, libraries and associations in the US and Canada, art schools in the US and Canada, plus listings of museums abroad, art schools abroad, state arts councils, state directors and supervisors of art education, art magazines, art editors and critics, scholarships and fellowships, open exhibitions, and traveling exhibition booking agencies, plus a personnel index. $210. If the price is prohibitively high, remember your local library. National Register Publishing, Reed Elsevier-New Providence, 121 Chanlon Road, New Providence, NJ 07974, (800) 521-8110, fax (800) 836-7736, web site www.redbooks.com or www.marquiswhoswho.com. "If, for any reason whatsoever, your order does not fully meet your expectations, simply return the product within 30 days for a prompt, complete, unquestioned refund," as stated in Catalog of Biographical and Professional References of publisher Marquis Who's Who/National Register Publishing.

BALTIMORE/ANNAPOLIS is a guide to over 2,000 organizations and institutions. Chapters include government, business, education, medicine/health, arts and culture, community affairs and more. $65. Columbia Books, Inc., 1212 New York Avenue, NW, Suite 330, Washington, DC 20005, (212) 898-0662.

BOWKER BIOGRAPHICAL DIRECTORY is comprised of the electronic equivalents of AMERICAN MEN AND WOMEN OF SCIENCE™, WHO'S WHO IN AMERICAN ART™ and WHO'S WHO IN AMERICAN POLITICS™. It is available in electronic database formats from Reed Reference. Entries include past and current career details, publications, education, research interests, languages, personal and family information and more. Available online through Knight-Ridder Information, Inc., (DIALOG file number 236) and on LEXIS™—NEXIS™ (American Men and Women of Science Library: People; busref, file AMSCI). For more information visit Bowker Reed Reference's web site at http://www.reedref.com or contact: Bowker Reed Reference Electronic Publishing, 121 Chanlon Road, New Providence, NJ 07974 USA, Phone (800) 323-3288, Fax (908) 665-3528, email info@bowker.com.

CANADIAN ALMANAC AND DIRECTORY includes abbreviations, associations and societies, broadcasting and communications, business statistics, church and religious organizations, commerce and finance, cultural directory, education directory, electoral districts, foreign and international contacts, geographic information, government directory, government quick reference, health and hospitals, historical and general information, legal and judicial directory, postal information, tourism and transportation. The Almanac also includes web sites of significant institutions in business, communications, and the arts, a "Who's Who" of key officials and organizations on the Canadian information highway and up-to-date provincial and territorial election results. Indexed by titles and keyword. $249 US. Inquire about CD ROM availability. Published by IHS Canada, Micromedia Limited, 20 Victoria Street, Toronto, Ontario M5C 2N8 CANADA, (800) 387-2689, (416) 362-5211, fax (416) 362-6161, email info@micromedia.on.ca. Distributed in the US by the Gale Group, P.O. Box 9187, Farmington Hills, MI 48333-9187. Toll free US and Canada (800) 877-GALE (4253) and (248) 699-GALE, fax (800) 414-5043 and (248) 699-8061, Internet orders galeord@galegroup.com, web site www.galegroup.com or www.gale.com. All Gale Group products are available on approval. Contact Gale for details.

INTERNATIONAL DIRECTORY OF THE ARTS contains information on artists, museums, publishers, conservation authorities, auctioneers, collectors, art dealers, academics, antique dealers and publications. 175 countries are covered. $275. By K.G. Saur. To order contact R.R. Bowker (a unit of Cahners Business Information), 121 Chanlon Road, New Providence, NJ 07974 USA, Phone (888) BOWKER2 (888-269-5372) & (800) 323-3288, fax (908) 508-7696, email info@bowker.com, web www.bowker.com. Canada—R.R. Bowker, Markham, Ontario, phone (888) BOWKER9 & (905) 415-5837, fax (905) 479-6266. German speaking Europe—K.G. Saur Verlag, Munich, Germany, phone 49-89-76902-232, fax 49-89-76902-250, email 100730.1341@compuserve.com, web www.saur.de/home.htm. Rest of Europe incl. United Kingdom plus Africa & Asia—Bowker-Saur, W. Sussex, UK, phone 44-1342-326-972, fax 44-1342-335-612, email customer@bowker-saur.co.uk, web www.bowker-saur.com/service/. Australia/New Zealand—Thorpe, Port Melbourne, Victoria, Australia, phone 61-03-9-245-7370, fax 61-03-9-245-7395, email customer.service@thorpe.com.au, web www.thorpe.com.au. Technical support for CD ROMs (800) 323-3288, fax 908) 665-3528, email techsupport@bowker.com.

INTERNATIONAL DIRECTORY OF ARTS AND MUSEUMS OF THE WORLD CD-ROM, $525. R.R. Bowker (a unit of Cahners Business Information), 121 Chanlon Road, New Providence, NJ 07974 USA, Phone (888) BOWKER2 (888-269-5372) & (800) 323-3288, fax (908) 508-7696, email info@bowker.com, web www.bowker.com. Canada—R.R. Bowker, Markham, Ontario, phone (888) BOWKER9 & (905) 415-5837, fax (905) 479-6266. German speaking Europe—K.G. Saur Verlag, Munich, Germany, phone 49-89-76902-232, fax 49-89-76902-250, email 100730.1341@compuserve.com, web www.saur.de/home.htm. Rest of Europe incl. United Kingdom plus Africa & Asia—Bowker-Saur, W. Sussex, UK, phone 44-1342-326-972, fax 44-1342-335-612, email customer@bowker-saur.co.uk, web www.bowker-saur.com/service/. Australia/New Zealand—Thorpe, Port Melbourne, Victoria, Australia, phone 61-03-9-245-7370, fax 61-03-9-245-7395, email customer.service@thorpe.com.au, web www.thorpe.com.au. Technical support for CD ROMs (800) 323-3288, fax 908) 665-3528, email techsupport@bowker.com.

SONGWRITERS' MARKET edited by Cindy Laufenberg is a how-to book for songwriters. It includes these chapters: Music Print Publishers comprised of companies that print sheet music; Record Companies; Record Producers; Managers and Booking Agents; Advertising, Audiovisual and Commercial Music Firms;

Play Producers and Publishers; and Organizations. $21.95. Published by Writer's Digest. Distributed by SPIN (Songwriter Products, Ideas & Necessities), 345 Sprucewood Road, Lake Mary, FL 32746-5917. (800) 800-487-SPIN, (407) 321-3702. Email rsfspin@aol.com. Web site http://members.aol.com/rsfspin.

WASHINGTON identifies 4,500 organizations and institutions in Washington DC and 22,000 key people in them. Includes government, business, education, medicine/health, community affairs, art/culture and others. $85. Columbia Books, Inc., 1212 New York Avenue, NW, Suite 330, Washington, DC 20005, (212) 898-0662.

WHO'S WHO IN AMERICAN ART, $210. National Register Publishing, Reed Elsevier-New Providence, 121 Chanlon Road, New Providence, NJ 07974, (800) 521-8110, fax (800) 836-7736, web site www.marquiswhoswho.com or www.redbooks.com. "If, for any reason whatsoever, your order does not fully meet your expectations, simply return the product within 30 days for a prompt, complete, unquestioned refund," as stated in Catalog of Biographical and Professional References of publisher Marquis Who's Who/National Register Publishing.

WHO'S WHO IN ART contains 3,000 brief biographies. $120 Published by Art Trade Press. Distributed by Gale Group, P.O. Box 9187, Farmington Hills, MI 48333-9187. Toll free US and Canada (800) 877-GALE (4253) and (248) 699-GALE, fax (800) 414-5043 and (248) 699-8061, Internet orders galeord@galegroup.com, web site www.galegroup.com or www.gale.com. All Gale Group products are available on approval. Contact Gale for details.

Asia

See International

ASIA IMAGE is a monthly magazine for creative professionals in broadcast, production and post-production industries in Asia. Contact publisher for price. Cahners Business Information, 58A Smith Street, Singapore 058962, (011) 65 223-8823, fax (011) 65-220-5015, email jonnypim@pacific.net.sg. Headquarters: Cahners Business Information, 275 Washington Street, Newton, MA 02158-1630, (617) 558-4663 or (617) 964-3030, fax (617) 558-4700, email marketaccess@cahners.com. Web sites www.cahners.com or www.chilton.net.

ASIA PACIFIC SATELLITE INDUSTRY DIRECTORY, Phillips Business Information, Inc., a Phillips Publishing International Company, 120 Seven Locks Road, Potomac, MD 20854, (301) 340-1520, (301) 340-7788, (800) 777-5006, Internet pbi@phillips.com, web site www.phillips.com.

ASIAN ADVERTISING, MARKETING AND MEDIA HANDBOOK lists information about advertising agencies, newspaper and magazine publishers and market research companies. Published by Euromonitor (England), at $470 (1st edition), it had been exclusively distributed by Gale Group. At the time of this writing, Gale no longer carries it. For more information, contact Euromonitor or Gale or refer to Books in Print. This reference might also be available in the library.

ASIAN HOTELIER is a hospitality trade newspaper with an emphasis on the People's Republic of China's hotel development. Produced in English and Chinese. 11 issues per year. Contact publisher for price. Cahners Business Information, 19/F, 8 Commercial Tower, 8 Sun Yip Street, Chaiwan, Hong Kong, (011) 852-2965-1555, fax (011) 852-2976-0706, email hotelier@hk.super.net. Headquarters: Cahners Business Information, 275 Washington Street, Newton, MA 02158-1630, (617) 558-4663 or (617) 964-3030, fax (617) 558-4700, email marketaccess@cahners.com. Web sites www.cahners.com or www.chilton.net.

CATALOG OF INSTITUTIONAL RESEARCH REPORTS (GLOBAL EDITION) tracks over 15,000 monthly investment research reports published by Wall Street's European and Pacific counterparts in over 500 research firms worldwide. Reports are listed alphabetically by company and by research firm. This information is best used for target list research, or your own personal investing. Published ten times per year. $125 per year. Nelson Information, P.O. Box 591, Port Chester, NY 10573 USA. (800) 333-6357, Phone outside the US (914) 937-8400, Fax (914) 937-8590, web site http://www.nelnet.com.

DIRECTORY OF AMERICAN FIRMS OPERATING IN FOREIGN COUNTRIES, REGIONAL EDITION —ASIA. Includes Bangladesh, Brunei, Cambodia, China, Hong Kong, India, Indonesia, Japan, Korea, Laos, Macau, Malaysia, Mongolia, Myanmar, Nepal, Pakistan, Philippines, Singapore, Sri Lanka, Taiwan, Thailand, Vietnam. $119. Ordering information: Uniworld Business Publications, Inc., 257 Central

Park West, Suite 10A, New York, NY 10024-4110, (212) 496-2448, fax (212) 769-0413, email uniworldbp@aol.com. Web site: http://www.uniworldbp.com.

DIRECTORY OF AMERICAN FIRMS OPERATING IN FOREIGN COUNTRIES, REGIONAL EDITION— SOUTH ASIA. Includes Bangladesh, India, Myanmar, Nepal, Pakistan, Sri Lanka. $39. Ordering information: Uniworld Business Publications, Inc., 257 Central Park West, Suite 10A, New York, NY 10024-4110, (212) 496-2448, fax (212) 769-0413, email uniworldbp@aol.com. Web site: http://www.uniworldbp.com.

DIRECTORY OF AMERICAN FIRMS OPERATING IN FOREIGN COUNTRIES, REGIONAL EDITION—SOUTHEAST ASIA. Includes Brunei, Cambodia, Indonesia, Laos, Malaysia, Philippines, Singapore, Thailand, Vietnam, $69. Ordering information: Uniworld Business Publications, Inc., 257 Central Park West, Suite 10A, New York, NY 10024-4110, (212) 496-2448, fax (212) 769-0413, email uniworldbp@aol.com. Web site: http://www.uniworldbp.com.

DIRECTORY OF AMERICAN FIRMS OPERATING IN FOREIGN COUNTRIES, REGIONAL EDITION—CHINA GROUP. Includes China, Hong Kong, Singapore, Taiwan, Macau. $79. Uniworld Business Publications, Inc., 257 Central Park West, Suite 10A, New York, NY 10024-4110, (212) 496-2448, fax (212) 769-0413, email uniworldbp@aol.com. Web site: http://www.uniworldbp.com.

DIRECTORY OF CONSUMER BRANDS AND THEIR OWNERS provides information on 50,000 brands in 56 countries and detailed information about the companies that own and manage them. Asia Pacific edition $990. Latin America edition $990. Eastern Europe edition $990. Europe edition $1,190 for 2 volumes. Published by Euromonitor (England). Distributed by Gale Group, P.O. Box 9187, Farmington Hills, MI 48333-9187. Toll free US and Canada (800) 877-GALE (4253) and (248) 699-GALE, fax (800) 414-5043 and (248) 699-8061, Internet orders galeord@galegroup.com, web site www.galegroup.com or www.gale.com. All Gale Group products are available on approval. Contact Gale for details.

DIRECTORY OF FOREIGN FIRMS OPERATING IN THE UNITED STATES, REGIONAL EDITION—ASIA. Includes China, Hong Kong, India, Indonesia, Japan, Korea, Malaysia, Pakistan, Philippines, Singapore, Taiwan, Thailand. $79. Uniworld Business Publications, Inc., 257 Central Park West, Suite 10A, New York, NY 10024-4110, (212) 496-2448, fax (212) 769-0413, email uniworldbp@aol.com. Web site: http://www.uniworldbp.com.

DIRECTORY OF MAJOR COMPANIES IN SOUTH EAST ASIA covers over 1,500 indigenous and multinational companies, including in Brunei, Hong Kong, Indonesia, Malaysia, Philippines, Singapore, South Korea, Taiwan and Thailand. It is cross referenced by business activities. $550. Published by Euromonitor (England). Distributed by Gale Group, P.O. Box 9187, Farmington Hills, MI 48333-9187. Toll free US and Canada (800) 877-GALE (4253) and (248) 699-GALE, fax (800) 414-5043 and (248) 699-8061, Internet orders galeord@galegroup.com, web site www.galegroup.com or www.gale.com. All Gale Group products are available on approval. Contact Gale for details. Also see Major Companies of the Far East and Australasia.

EDN ASIA is a monthly magazine for electronics engineers and managers in Asia's original equipment manufacturing market. Call publisher for price. EDN/Cahners Business Information, 19/F, 8 Commercial Tower, 8 Sun Yip Street, Chaiwan, Hong Kong, (011) 852-2965-1555, fax (011) 852-2976-0706, email chriseverett@rebi.com.hk, URL www.cahners.com/mainmag/ednas.htm. Headquarters: EDN Worldwide Editorial, 275 Washington Street, Newton, MA 02158-1630, (617) 558-4454 or (617) 964-3030, fax (617) 558-4470, URL www.ednmag.com.

ELECTRONIC BUSINESS ASIA is a monthly magazine for business management in electronics, computers and systems companies. Call publisher for prices. Cahners Business Information, 19/f, 8 Commercial Tower, 8 Sun Yip Street, Chaiwan, Hong Kong, (011) 852-2965-1555, fax (011)852-2976-0706, email msavery@rebi.com.hk, URL www.cahners.com/mainmag/eba.htm. Headquarters: Cahners Business Information, 275 Washington Street, Newton, MA 02158-1630 (617) 558-4663 or (617) 964-3030, fax (617) 558-4700, email marketaccess@cahners.com. Web sites www.cahners.com or www.chilton.net.

EUROMONITOR DIRECTORY OF ASIAN COMPANIES provides information about 5,000 major companies in Asia and a ranking of the top 100 companies, excluding financial institutions. Each country chapter includes a listing of the top 50 companies. $550. Published by Euromonitor (England). Distributed by Gale Group, P.O. Box 9187, Farmington Hills, MI 48333-9187. Toll free US and Canada (800) 877-GALE (4253) and (248) 699-GALE, fax (800) 414-5043 and (248) 699-8061, Internet orders

galeord@galegroup.com, web site www.galegroup.com or www.gale.com. All Gale Group products are available on approval. Contact Gale for details.

KEY BUSINESS DIRECTORY OF FOREIGN COMPANIES WITH ASEAN OFFICES contains information on 3,000 active foreign-owned companies in Asia. Dun & Bradstreet, Business Reference Solutions, Three Sylvan Way, Parsippany, NJ 07054 USA. (800) 526-0651. Email dnbmdd@mail.dnb.com. Web site http://www.dnbmdd.com.

KEY BUSINESS DIRECTORY OF MALAYSIA contains information of 2,500 companies with at least 50 employees and revenues over $18 million. Dun & Bradstreet, Business Reference Solutions, Three Sylvan Way, Parsippany, NJ 07054 USA. (800) 526-0651. Email dnbmdd@mail.dnb.com. Web site http://www.dnbmdd.com.

KOMPASS is described by the publisher as "the world's most comprehensive global database of companies, products and services for manufacturing and engineering professionals in print, on CD ROM and on the Internet." It contains company and product information for companies in all lines of business, including manufacturing and industrial sectors. Each company listing includes name, address, phone number, management names, business descriptions, and industry and product listings. Kompass's web site is www.kompass.com. Call publisher for prices and information on country directories. Cahners Business Information, 121 Chanlon Road, New Providence, NJ 07974, (908) 771-8785, fax (908) 665-8755, email hholmes@reedref.com. Headquarters: Cahners Business Information, 275 Washington Street, Newton, MA 02158-1630, (617) 558-4663 or (617) 964-3030, fax (617) 558-4700, email marketaccess@cahners.com, web sites www.cahners.com or www.chilton.net.

MAJOR CHEMICAL & PETROCHEMICAL COMPANIES OF THE FAR EAST & AUSTRALASIA provides information on over 1,100 companies. $415. US distributor: Larry Meranus Professional Publications & Services, 4 Demoray Court, Pine Brook, NJ 07058, (800) MERANUS or (800) 637-2687. Published by Graham & Whiteside Ltd., Tuition House, 5-6 Francis Grove, London SW19 4DT, England. Web site http://www.major-co-data.com. Email sales@major-co-data.com.

MAJOR COMPANIES OF ASIA presents contact information on 4,000 major companies in the region. $395, 1st edition, published by Graham & Whiteside Ltd., England. Distributed by Gale Group. Also see Major Companies of the Far East and Australasia. Gale Group, P.O. Box 9187, Farmington Hills, MI 48333-9187. Toll free US and Canada (800) 877-GALE (4253) and (248) 699-GALE, fax (800) 414-5043 and (248) 699-8061, Internet orders galeord@galegroup.com, web site www.galegroup.com or www.gale.com. All Gale Group products are available on approval. Contact Gale for details.

MAJOR COMPANIES OF SOUTH WEST ASIA provides names of 39,000 contacts at 6,000 companies, description of business activities, brand names and trademarks, branches and subsidiaries, number of employees, date of establishment, and three indexes. Countries included are Bangladesh, Bhutan, Iran, Nepal, Pakistan, Sri Lanka and Turkey. Hardback directory $450. Standard CD ROM $675. Premium CD ROM $1,150. CD ROMs are published quarterly. US distributor: Larry Meranus Professional Publications & Services, 4 Demoray Court, Pine Brook, NJ 07058, (800) MERANUS or (800) 637-2687. Published by Graham & Whiteside Ltd., Tuition House, 5-6 Francis Grove, London SW19 4DT, England. Web site http://www.major-co-data.com. Email sales@major-co-data.com.

MAJOR COMPANIES OF THE FAR EAST AND AUSTRALASIA identifies 68,000 senior executives at 12,000 key Asia Pacific companies in 20 countries. Published by Graham & Whiteside Ltd., Tuition House, 5-6 Francis Grove, London SW19 4DT, England. Web site http://www.major-co-data.com. Email sales@major-co-data.com.

$1,450 for all three volumes
    Volume 1: South East Asia, $560
    Volume 2: East Asia, $560
    Volume 3: Australia and New Zealand, $365

CD ROM, updated quarterly, is also available. Distributed by: Larry Meranus Professional Publications & Services, 4 Demoray Court, Pine Brook, NJ 07058, (800) MERANUS or (800) 637-2687. Or by Gale Group, P.O. Box 9187, Farmington Hills, MI 48333-9187. Toll free US and Canada (800) 877-GALE (4253) and (248) 699-GALE, fax (800) 414-5043 and (248) 699-8061, Internet orders galeord@galegroup.com, web site

www.galegroup.com or www.gale.com. All Gale Group products are available on approval. Contact Gale for details.

MAJOR COMPANIES SERIES ON CD ROM consists of Graham & Whiteside's annual directories of major international companies. All six directories reside on one disk. After payment, you'll receive a security code to access the region(s) you select. This Windows™ based CD can navigate by company name, company locations, executive names, business activity and more. Free demo CD ROM is available. Regions also available separately for Europe, Central & Eastern Europe, the Far East and Australasia, the Arab World, Africa, and Latin America. For prices and availability, contact the Gale Group, P.O. Box 9187, Farmington Hills, MI 48333-9187. Toll free US and Canada (800) 877-GALE (4253) and (248) 699-GALE, fax (800) 414-5043 and (248) 699-8061, Internet orders galeord@galegroup.com, web site www.galegroup.com or www.gale.com. All Gale Group products are available on approval. Contact Gale for details.

MAJOR ENERGY COMPANIES OF THE FAR EAST & AUSTRALASIA provides information on over 500 leading energy companies in the Asia Pacific, $415. US distributor: Larry Meranus Professional Publications & Services, 4 Demoray Court, Pine Brook, NJ 07058, (800) MERANUS or (800) 637-2687. Published by Graham & Whiteside Ltd., Tuition House, 5-6 Francis Grove, London SW19 4DT, England. Web site http://www.major-co-data.com. Email sales@major-co-data.com.

MAJOR FINANCIAL INSTITUTIONS OF THE FAR EAST & AUSTRALASIA contains information on over 1,500 Asia/Pacific financial institutions. $450. US distributor: Larry Meranus Professional Publications & Services, 4 Demoray Court, Pine Brook, NJ 07058, (800) MERANUS or (800) 637-2687. Published by Graham & Whiteside Ltd., Tuition House, 5-6 Francis Grove, London SW19 4DT, England. Web site http://www.major-co-data.com. Email sales@major-co-data.com.

MAJOR FOOD & DRINK COMPANIES OF THE FAR EAST & AUSTRALASIA provides information on over 1,100 top food and beverage (alcoholic and non-alcoholic) organizations in the Asia Pacific region. $415. US distributor: Larry Meranus Professional Publications & Services, 4 Demoray Court, Pine Brook, NJ 07058, (800) MERANUS or (800) 637-2687. Published by Graham & Whiteside Ltd., Tuition House, 5-6 Francis Grove, London SW19 4DT, England. Web site http://www.major-co-data.com. Email sales@major-co-data.com.

MAJOR TELECOMMUNICATIONS COMPANIES OF THE FAR EAST & AUSTRALASIA contains information on 1,000 top telecommunications companies and their Asia Pacific equipment suppliers. $415. US distributor: Larry Meranus Professional Publications & Services, 4 Demoray Court, Pine Brook, NJ 07058, (800) MERANUS or (800) 637-2687. Published by Graham & Whiteside Ltd., Tuition House, 5-6 Francis Grove, London SW19 4DT, England. Web site http://www.major-co-data.com. Email sales@major-co-data.com.

POLLUTION ENGINEERING INTERNATIONAL is a magazine for environmental professionals in Asia and Europe, published 4 times a year. Call publisher for price. Cahners Business Information, 1350 East Touhy Avenue, Des Plaines, IL 60018-5080, (847) 390-2752, fax (847) 390-2636, URL www.pollutioneng.com. Headquarters: Cahners Business Information, 275 Washington Street, Newton, MA 02158-1630, (617) 558-4663 or (617) 964-3030, fax (617) 558-4700, email marketaccess@cahners.com. Web sites www.cahners.com or www.chilton.net.

TELEVISION ASIA is a Singapore based publication that covers the Asian television industry. Call publisher for prices. Cahners Business Information, 58A Smith Street, Singapore 058962, (011) 65-223-8823, fax (011) 65-220-5015, email jonnypim@pacific.net.sg and rschatz@cahners.com, URL home1.pacific.net.sg/~tvasia. Headquarters: Cahners Business Information, 275 Washington Street, Newton, MA 02158-1630, (617) 558-4663 or (617) 964-3030, fax (617) 558-4700, email marketaccess@cahners.com. Web sites www.cahners.com or www.chilton.net.

WHO OWNS WHOM DIRECTORY by Dun & Bradstreet is a six volume set containing information on the structure and ownership of 320,000 company affiliates and subsidiaries of over 23,000 companies worldwide. It is available in four regional editions: Australia and the Far East, North America, UK/Ireland, and Continental Europe. Published annually. For prices and ordering information as well as information about more worldwide corporate linkage products from D&B WORLDBASE, D&B's global database of 42 million records in over 200 countries, contact Dun & Bradstreet at (800) 526-0651, Dun & Bradstreet, Business Reference Solutions, Three Sylvan Way, Parsippany, NJ 07054. Email dnbmdd@mail.dnb.com. Web site http://www.dnbmdd.com

www.asianet.com is the address to a web site that matches Pacific Rim positions with individuals who speak Asian languages.

Asia-Pacific

See Pacific

Associations

While there are many references cited in this section, an asterisk (*) indicates preferred sources that can be used first. In addition to general references which identify a wide range of associations across a broad spectrum of industries and functions, specialized directories with association information are also included here.

ADVERTISER AND AGENCY RED BOOKS PLUS CD ROM combines all the information in THE STANDARD DIRECTORY OF ADVERTISERS, THE STANDARD DIRECTORY OF ADVERTISING AGENCIES and THE STANDARD DIRECTORY OF INTERNATIONAL ADVERTISERS AND AGENCIES. Information is searchable by 25 fields, including company name, personal name, job title/function, product type, product/account name, city, state, zip or country, area code, revenues, number of employees, outside ad agency and even type of computer hardware. Contains professional association information. Available for Windows and Macintosh. Updated quarterly. 1 year subscription $1,295. If the price is prohibitively high, remember your local library. National Register Publishing, Reed Elsevier-New Providence, 121 Chanlon Road, New Providence, NJ 07974, (800) 521-8110, fax (800) 836-7736, web site www.redbooks.com or www.marquiswhoswho.com. "If, for any reason whatsoever, your order does not fully meet your expectations, simply return the product within 30 days for a prompt, complete, unquestioned refund," as stated in Catalog of Biographical and Professional References of publisher Marquis Who's Who/National Register Publishing.

ASSOCIATIONS CANADA, previously titled DIRECTORY OF ASSOCIATIONS IN CANADA, provides information on a $1 billion economic sector, including information on conferences, publications, mailing lists and more. $289 Canadian in print, $389 Canadian for CD ROM, and $489 Canadian for both. Published annually by Micromedia Ltd., 20 Victoria Street, Toronto, ON. (800) 387-2689, (416) 362-5211, email info@micromedia.on.ca, web site www.micromedia.on.ca.

ASSOCIATIONS UNLIMITED ONLINE is available on the Internet through GaleNet. You can subscribe to any of the several databases comprising ASSOCIATIONS UNLIMITED, including:

- NATIONAL ORGANIZATIONS OF THE US DATABASE

- REGIONAL, STATE AND LOCAL ORGANIZATIONS DATABASE

- INTERNATIONAL ORGANIZATIONS DATABASE

- ASSOCIATIONS MATERIALS DATABASE

- GOVERNMENT NONPROFIT ORGANIZATIONS DATABASE

For more information on available databases and pricing, contact Gale Group, P.O. Box 9187, Farmington Hills, MI 48333-9187. Toll free US and Canada (800) 877-GALE (4253) and (248) 699-GALE, fax (800) 414-5043 and (248) 699-8061, Internet orders galeord@galegroup.com, web site www.galegroup.com or www.gale.com. All Gale Group products are available on approval. Contact Gale for details.

*BUSINESS INFORMATION SOURCES by Lorna Daniells is an outstanding reference at any price. At $39.95 a copy, it's such an extraordinary value, it should have a place in every library. This is clearly one of the top three hard copy references around, and its reasonable price elevates it to first place. BUSINESS INFORMATION SOURCES provides a wealth of information routinely needed by search firms, job hunters and corporate recruiters, including general directories, specialized directories, professional associations, periodicals, industry information, international information, and much more. $39.95. Ordering information: Business Information Sources by Lorna Daniells, is published by the University of California Press (Berkeley, CA, Los Angeles, CA & Oxford, England) (510-642-4247). Orders are handled by California Princeton Fulfillment Services, P.O. Box 10769, Newark, NJ 07193-0769. (800-822-6657).

CANADIAN ALMANAC AND DIRECTORY includes abbreviations, associations and societies, broadcasting and communications, business statistics, church and religious organizations, commerce and finance, cultural directory, education directory, electoral districts, foreign and international contacts, geographic information, government directory, government quick reference, health and hospitals, historical and general information, legal and judicial directory, postal information, tourism and transportation. The Almanac also includes web sites of significant institutions in business, communications, and the arts, a "Who's Who" of key officials and organizations on the Canadian information highway and up-to-date provincial and territorial election results. Indexed by titles and keyword. $249 US. Inquire about CD ROM availability. Published by IHS Canada, Micromedia Limited, 20 Victoria Street, Toronto, Ontario M5C 2N8 CANADA, (800) 387-2689, (416) 362-5211, fax (416) 362-6161, email info@micromedia.on.ca. Distributed in the US by the Gale Group, P.O. Box 9187, Farmington Hills, MI 48333-9187. Toll free US and Canada (800) 877-GALE (4253) and (248) 699-GALE, fax (800) 414-5043 and (248) 699-8061, Internet orders galeord@galegroup.com, web site www.galegroup.com or www.gale.com. All Gale Group products are available on approval. Contact Gale for details.

CANADIAN BUSINESS AND ECONOMICS: A GUIDE TO SOURCES OF INFORMATION lists information by subject, including books, periodicals and services. Fully indexed and thoroughly cross referenced. Price reduced to $39.95 for 1992 edition. Canada Library Association, 200 Elgin Street, Suite 602, Ottawa, Ontario K2P 1L5 CANADA, (613) 232-9625, fax (613) 563-9895, Internet: bj491@freenet.carleton.ca.

CANADIAN SOURCEBOOK provides listings of libraries, resource centers, associations, societies, labour unions and media outlets, plus names and addresses of government officials, industry associations, financial institutions and social and cultural societies. $197. Special discounts available for combined purchases. Southam Information Products Ltd, 1450 Don Mills Road, Don Mills, Ontario M3B 2X7 CANADA, (800) 668-2374, (416) 445-6641, (416) 442-2122, web site www.southam.com.

CHAIN STORE GUIDE'S CHAIN RESTAURANT OPERATORS CD-ROM. allows you to conduct data searches from five topic screens: 1. Personnel by title, 2. Personnel by functional area, 3. Restaurant type (cafeteria, dinnerhouse, fast food, family restaurant, in-store feeder, table cloth), 4. Menu type (Greek, German, health food, ice cream, etc.) You can also make selections based on geography or the size of a company (number of units and/or sales). Contains information about professional associations. Several output options are available, including mailing labels, and electronic formats (such as DBASE, ASCII, text) for mail merge customization. $995 including companion directory. If the price is prohibitively high, remember your local library. Ordering information: Chain Store Guide Information Services, 3922 Coconut Palm Drive, Tampa, FL 33619. (800) 927-9292, (813) 664-6800, (813) 627-6822, (800) 289-6822. http://www.d-net.com/csgis or http://www.csgis.com.

DIRECT MARKETING MARKET PLACE lists over 4,000 direct marketing companies, organized into numerous categories: associations, catalogs, continuity programs, credit card companies, list brokers, market researchers, computer & fulfillment services, creative sources, ad agencies, copywriters, art services and photographers. Also included are geographic indexes, direct marketing publications, telemarketers, printers and lettershops. $239.95. If the price is prohibitively high, remember your local library. National Register Publishing, Reed Elsevier-New Providence, 121 Chanlon Road, New Providence, NJ 07974, (800) 521-8110, fax (800) 836-7736, web site www.redbooks.com or www.marquiswhoswho.com. "If, for any reason whatsoever, your order does not fully meet your expectations, simply return the product within 30 days for a prompt, complete, unquestioned refund," as stated in Catalog of Biographical and Professional References of publisher Marquis Who's Who/National Register Publishing.

DIRECTORY OF BUSINESS INFORMATION RESOURCES, ASSOCIATIONS, NEWSLETTERS, MAGAZINES AND TRADESHOWS, published by Grey House Publishing, Pocket Knife Square, Lakeville, CT 06039, $199. (800) 562-2139, (860) 435-0868, web site www.greyhouse.com or books@il.com.

DIRECTORY OF CHAIN RESTAURANT OPERATORS describes 3-or-more unit chain restaurant companies in the U.S. and Canada operating or franchising restaurants, cafeterias, contract and industrial feeders. Hotel/motel companies controlling three or more restaurants within hotels and 3 or more foodservice operations are profiled, as well as food units in drug chains, general merchandise chains and discount stores. Key personnel, a listing of major trade associations and a trade show calendar are also included. An index to the top 100 restaurants is also included and is a valuable tool for target list development. An industry profile as provided by the National Restaurant Association is also included. Updated annually. $290. Chain Store Guide Information Services, 3922 Coconut Palm Drive, Tampa, FL 33619. (800) 927-9292, (813) 664-6800, (813) 627-6822, (800) 289-6822. http://www.d-net.com/csgis or http://www.csgis.com.

DIRECTORY OF DRUG STORE AND HBC CHAINS identifies over 1,800 drug retailers in the U.S. and Canada operating over 45,000 stores including drug, HBC, cosmetic, deep discount, home health care, discount, and grocery stores/supermarket chains with pharmacies, mass merchants with pharmacies, deep discount chains, and wholesale drug companies. It includes names and titles of key personnel, a listing of major trade associations and a trade show calendar. It also provides indexes to top drug retailers, top drug wholesalers, top grocery chains and top discount chains. $290. Chain Store Guide Information Services, 3922 Coconut Palm Drive, Tampa, FL 33619. (800) 927-9292, (813) 664-6800, (813) 627-6822, (800) 289-6822. http://www.d-net.com/csgis or http://www.csgis.com.

DIRECTORY OF FOODSERVICE DISTRIBUTORS lists U.S. and Canadian companies with at least $500,000 in sales to foodservice, food equipment, supply and full-line distributors. Each offers more than one product line and no more than 95% of its food distribution sales volume comes from self-manufactured merchandise. Key personnel and major buying/marketing groups, trade associations and a trade show calendar are also included. $290. Chain Store Guide Information Services, 3922 Coconut Palm Drive, Tampa, FL 33619. (800) 927-9292, (813) 664-6800, (813) 627-6822, (800) 289-6822. http://www.d-net.com/csgis or http://www.csgis.com

DIRECTORY OF HAZARDOUS WASTE SERVICES contains information on over 1,500 Canadian hazardous waste management companies with information on hazardous waste consultants, waste treatment and disposal outlets, equipment manufacturers, laboratory services, drum reconditioners, spill cleanup firms, hazwaste recyclers, associations, key government contacts, liquid waste haulers, lawyers specializing in environmental law, and environmental libraries. $115. Special discounts available for combined purchases. Published by Southam Information Products Ltd, 1450 Don Mills Road, Don Mills, Ontario M3B 2X7 CANADA, (800) 668-2374. In Toronto 442-2122. Web site www.southam.com.

DIRECTORY OF HIGH VOLUME INDEPENDENT RESTAURANTS lists nearly 6,000 independent restaurants in the U.S. with at least $1 million in annual sales. A companion to the Chain Restaurant Operators directory, this guide identifies independent restaurants with one or two units that are part of a national chain but purchase separately. This directory lists key executives and buyers, major trade associations and a trade show calendar. $290. Chain Store Guide Information Services, 3922 Coconut Palm Drive, Tampa, FL 33619. (800) 927-9292, (813) 664-6800, (813) 627-6822, (800) 289-6822. http://www.d-net.com/csgis or http://www.csgis.com.

DIRECTORY OF SINGLE UNIT SUPERMARKET OPERATORS lists 7,000 independent (single unit) supermarket operators/grocery retailers with sales of at least $1 million. names and titles of key personnel. It also identifies major trade associations and a trade show calendar. $280. Chain Store Guide Information Services, 3922 Coconut Palm Drive, Tampa, FL 33619. (800) 927-9292, (813) 664-6800, (813) 627-6822, (800) 289-6822. http://www.d-net.com/csgis or http://www.csgis.com

DIRECTORY OF SUPERMARKET, GROCERY AND CONVENIENCE STORE CHAINS describes and indexes over 2,300 supermarket chains with $2 million in annual sales. It covers supermarkets, superstores, club stores, gourmet supermarkets and combo stores in the U.S. and Canada, plus a special section profiling 1,700 convenience store chains. It includes an index to the top 200 supermarket chains and the top 100 convenience store chains, which is a valuable tool for target list development. It also lists over 29,000 key executives, buyers and administrative personnel. The directory also lists major trade associations and a trade show calendar. $300. Chain Store Guide Information Services, 3922 Coconut Palm Drive, Tampa, FL 33619. (800) 927-9292, (813) 664-6800, (813) 627-6822, (800) 289-6822. http://www.d-net.com/csgis or http://www.csgis.com.

DIRECTORY OF WHOLESALE GROCERY lists wholesale grocers' headquarters, divisions and branches, both in the US and Canada. All companies listed are required to sell a multi-line of products to the supermarket, convenience store, discount and drug industries. It includes names and titles of personnel, a listing of major trade associations and a trade show calendar. It also provides an index to the top 100 wholesale grocers, which is a valuable tool for target list development. $300. Chain Store Guide Information

Services, 3922 Coconut Palm Drive, Tampa, FL 33619. (800) 927-9292, (813) 664-6800, (813) 627-6822, (800) 289-6822. http://www.d-net.com/csgis or http://www.csgis.com

ENCYCLOPEDIA OF ASSOCIATIONS: INTERNATIONAL ORGANIZATIONS includes nearly 20,000 multinational and national organizations in foreign countries, including US based associations with multinational membership. Entries also include email addresses, web sites and bulletin board addresses, lobbying activities, and publication and convention information. Indexed by geography, keyword and executives. $595 for 2 volume set. Also available in CD ROM. Database available via commercial online service. Gale Group, P.O. Box 9187, Farmington Hills, MI 48333-9187. Toll free US and Canada (800) 877-GALE (4253) and (248) 699-GALE, fax (800) 414-5043 and (248) 699-8061, Internet orders galeord@galegroup.com, web site www.galegroup.com or www.gale.com. All Gale Group products are available on approval. Contact Gale for details.

*ENCYCLOPEDIA OF ASSOCIATIONS: NATIONAL ORGANIZATIONS OF THE US. This superb reference is one of the first places you should look when beginning a new recruiting assignment or when looking for specialized references of any type. The keyword index makes this comprehensive reference easy to use, even in hard copy. For over 23,000 nonprofit professional associations with a national scope, this encyclopedia reveals:

- Publications, including membership rosters and newsletters

- Dates and locations of association conferences and conventions

- Names of Executive Directors, who are usually incredible sources of industry information if you call and speak to them

- Committees

- Job and candidate referral banks, which can provide resumes of other industry sources and sometimes candidates

- It includes organizations in these categories: business, trade, environmental, agricultural, legal, governmental, engineering, technological, scientific, educational, cultural, social welfare, health & medical, public affairs, ethnic, labor unions, chambers of commerce, tourism, & others.

Volume 1, Organizations of the US, $505
Volume 2, Geographic and Executive Indexes, $390
Volume 3, Supplement, $405

Gale Group, P.O. Box 9187, Farmington Hills, MI 48333-9187. Toll free US and Canada (800) 877-GALE (4253) and (248) 699-GALE, fax (800) 414-5043 and (248) 699-8061, Internet orders galeord@galegroup.com, web site www.galegroup.com or www.gale.com. All Gale Group products are available on approval. Contact Gale for details.

ENCYCLOPEDIA OF ASSOCIATIONS: REGIONAL, STATE AND LOCAL ORGANIZATIONS. The information in this directory is not duplicated anywhere in ENCYCLOPEDIA OF ASSOCIATIONS. Over 100,000 nonprofit organizations are included in this directory. $585 for 5 volume set or $140 per individual volume. Also available on CD ROM and online on the Internet through a GaleNet subscription.

Volume 1, Great Lakes States (Illinois, Indiana, Michigan, Minnesota, Ohio, Wisconsin)
Volume 2, Northeastern States (Connecticut, Maine, Massachusetts, New Hampshire, New Jersey, New York, Pennsylvania, Rhode Islands, Vermont)
Volume 3, Southern and Middle Atlantic States (Including Puerto Rico and the Virgin Islands) (Alabama, Delaware, Washington, DC, Florida, Georgia, Kentucky, Maryland, Mississippi, North Carolina, Puerto Rico, South Carolina, Tennessee, Virginia, West Virginia, Virgin Islands)
Volume 4, South Central and Great Plains States (Arkansas, Iowa, Kansas, Louisiana, Missouri, Nebraska, North Dakota, Oklahoma, South Dakota, Texas)
Volume 5, Western States (Alaska, Arizona, California, Colorado, Guam, Hawaii, Idaho, Montana, Nevada, New Mexico, Oregon, Utah, Washington, Wyoming)

Gale Group, P.O. Box 9187, Farmington Hills, MI 48333-9187. Toll free US and Canada (800) 877-GALE (4253) and (248) 699-GALE, fax (800) 414-5043 and (248) 699-8061, Internet orders

galeord@galegroup.com, web site www.galegroup.com or www.gale.com. All Gale Group products are available on approval. Contact Gale for details.

*ENCYCLOPEDIA OF BUSINESS INFORMATION SOURCES** will lead you to specialized directories, professional associations, trade publications, newsletters, databases, Internet resources and more. It's an excellent reference and a great way to find key resources in any industry fast. $330. Gale Group, P.O. Box 9187, Farmington Hills, MI 48333-9187. Toll free US and Canada (800) 877-GALE (4253) and (248) 699-GALE, fax (800) 414-5043 and (248) 699-8061, Internet orders galeord@galegroup.com, web site www.galegroup.com or www.gale.com. All Gale Group products are available on approval. Contact Gale for details.

FINANCIAL SERVICES CANADA is a handbook of banks, non-depository institutions, stock exchange and brokers, investment management, mutual funds, insurance, accountants, government agencies, financial associations and more, including contact numbers, name, title, organization, phone, fax, email, web site, and cellular. $199 for book, $299 for CD ROM, $399 for both. Ordering information: Copp Clark Professional, 200 Adelaide Street West, 3rd floor, Toronto, ON M5H 1W7 CANADA. Email orders@mail.CanadaInfo.com. Web site http://www.coppclark.com. For additional information contact: IHS Canada, Micromedia Limited, 20 Victoria Street, Toronto, Ontario M5C 2N8 CANADA, (800) 387-2689, (416) 362-5211, fax (416) 362-6161, email info@micromedia.on.ca.

GALE BUSINESS RESOURCES ONLINE provides modules on US Industry (over 200,000 companies) and International Industry (over 200,000 companies), including public and privately held companies, brands, business rankings, trade and professional associations, company histories, merger information, and more. Comprehensive records include company name, officers' names and titles, SIC/NAICS codes and more. GALE BUSINESS RESOURCES is available online on the Internet through GaleNet.

For information on pricing, contact: Gale Group, P.O. Box 9187, Farmington Hills, MI 48333-9187. Toll free US and Canada (800) 877-GALE (4253) and (248) 699-GALE, fax (800) 414-5043 and (248) 699-8061, Internet orders galeord@galegroup.com, web site www.galegroup.com or www.gale.com. All Gale Group products are available on approval. Contact Gale for details.

GaleNet is an online resource on the Internet that provides an integrated, one-step access to the most frequently used Gale databases, such as GALE'S READY REFERENCE SHELF ONLINE. As GaleNet's capabilities are constantly changing and being upgraded, contact the publisher for details and prices. Gale Group, P.O. Box 9187, Farmington Hills, MI 48333-9187. Toll free US and Canada (800) 877-GALE (4253) and (248) 699-GALE, fax (800) 414-5043 and (248) 699-8061, Internet orders galeord@galegroup.com, web site www.galegroup.com or www.gale.com. All Gale Group products are available on approval. Contact Gale for details.

GALE'S READY REFERENCE SHELF ONLINE is a GaleNet Internet resource that provides integrated access to databases covering national, regional, state, local and international associations, publishers, newspapers and periodicals, directories, newsletters, online databases, portable databases, database products and vendors, special libraries and research centers. Information is included from numerous Gale databases, among them THE ENCYCLOPEDIA OF ASSOCIATIONS, PUBLISHERS DIRECTORY, GALE DIRECTORY OF PUBLICATIONS AND BROADCAST MEDIA and several others. If it is prohibitively expensive, locate a library with with this resource. Gale Group, P.O. Box 9187, Farmington Hills, MI 48333-9187. Toll free US and Canada (800) 877-GALE (4253) and (248) 699-GALE, fax (800) 414-5043 and (248) 699-8061, Internet orders galeord@galegroup.com, web site www.galegroup.com or www.gale.com. All Gale Group products are available on approval. Contact Gale for details.

LITERARY MARKET PLACE, "The Directory of the American Book Publishing Industry With Industry Yellow Pages" is an excellent 3 volume directory with comprehensive information on US book publishers; imprints, subsidiaries and distributors; book trade acquisitions and mergers, small presses, Canadian book publishers, micropublishers, US electronic publishers, electronic publishing consultants, electronic publishing products and services, editorial services, literary agents, illustrations agents, US agents and offices of foreign publishers, lecture agents, specialized advertising and public relations firms, direct mail specialists, mailing list brokers and services, book review syndicates, book review and index journals and services, book exhibits, book clubs, book lists and catalogs, book importers and exporters, book producers, translators, artists, photographers, stock photo agencies, associations, book trade events and conferences, awards, contents and grants, reference books for the trade, magazines for the trade, a toll free directory of publishers, magazine and newspaper publicity, radio and television publicity, book manufacturing services, book distributors and sales representatives, and wholesalers. $189.95.

LITERARY MARKET PLACE ON DISC, previously titled LITERARY MARKET PLACE PLUS CD ROM, one year subscription $297.00.

LITERARY MARKET PLACE—INTERNET EDITION, www.literarymarketplace.com, is available by subscription.

INTERNATIONAL LITERARY MARKET PLACE Internet database can be directly accessed at www.iliterarymarketplace.com. It is also linked to the US domestic LITERARY MARKET PLACE web site at www.literarymarketplace.com. Contact the publisher for subscription price. INTERNATIONAL LITERARY MARKET PLACE, hard copy $189.95.

R.R. Bowker (a unit of Cahners Business Information), 121 Chanlon Road, New Providence, NJ 07974 USA, Phone (888) BOWKER2 (888-269-5372) & (800) 323-3288, fax (908) 508-7696, email info@bowker.com, web www.bowker.com. Canada—R.R. Bowker, Markham, Ontario, phone (888) BOWKER9 & (905) 415-5837, fax (905) 479-6266. German speaking Europe—K.G. Saur Verlag, Munich, Germany, phone 49-89-76902-232, fax 49-89-76902-250, email 100730.1341@compuserve.com, web www.saur.de/home.htm. Rest of Europe incl. United Kingdom plus Africa & Asia—Bowker-Saur, W. Sussex, UK, phone 44-1342-326-972, fax 44-1342-335-612, email customer@bowker-saur.co.uk, web www.bowker-saur.com/service/. Australia/New Zealand—Thorpe, Port Melbourne, Victoria, Australia, phone 61-03-9-245-7370, fax 61-03-9-245-7395, email customer.service@thorpe.com.au, web www.thorpe.com.au. Technical support for CD ROMs (800) 323-3288, fax 908) 665-3528, email techsupport@bowker.com.

MEMBERSHIP DIRECTORIES FOR PROFESSIONAL ASSOCIATIONS are frequently published, either in hard copy or on an Internet web site. If a membership directory is not accessible on the web site, you might want to purchase a hard copy from the association. However, some associations refuse to sell their membership rosters to non-members. Some even preclude recruiters from becoming members. As a last resort, if an association membership directory is not online, you might need to borrow a copy from a member. Of course, that can be a bit of a "Catch 22," because how can you find a member if you don't have the membership list? Just keep asking everybody you talk to.

If you're having trouble locating an association's web site address (URL), you can always look them up in a directory. If the web site address isn't in the directory, sometimes it's easier to make a phone call and ask for the web site. You can also go to www.web sitez.com to get an organization's URLs.

One way to identify membership directories is to look up associations in a directory, such as Lorna Daniell's BUSINESS INFORMATION SOURCES (University of California Press, Berkeley, Los Angeles and Oxford England/Princeton Fulfillment Services, Newark, NJ), ENCYCLOPEDIA OF ASSOCIATIONS (Gale Group, Farmington Hills, MI) or NATIONAL TRADE AND PROFESSIONAL ASSOCIATIONS (Columbia Books, Washington, DC).

You can call the association and ask them to send information about becoming a member. If you don't want them to know the name of your company, ask them to send the information to your home address. While you're chatting, and before you give your name, make a casual inquiry about whether their membership roster is available for sale to non-members. If it's not, find out their requirements for joining, specifically whether recruiters are precluded.

NATION'S RESTAURANT NEWS is a 30 year old newsweekly of the foodservice industry. For info about subscriptions and customer service, call 800-447-7133. URL: www.nrn.com or http://www.d-net.com/csgis or http://www.csgis.com. Chain Store Guide Information Services, 3922 Coconut Palm Drive, Tampa, FL 33619.

*NATIONAL TRADE AND PROFESSIONAL ASSOCIATIONS OF THE UNITED STATES is a major directory of associations. It includes 7,600 national trade associations, professional societies and labor unions cross referenced by subject. Also includes publications, convention schedule, membership and staff size, and budget. $129. Colombia Books, Washington, DC.

PHARMACEUTICAL MARKETERS DIRECTORY is a well organized directory that contains many names and titles and other information, including a listing of specialized professional associations. Published annually. $162.50. CPS COMMUNICATIONS, INC., 7200 West Camino Real, Suite 215, Boca Raton, FL 33433, (561) 368-9301, sales office (203) 778-1463, email pmd@cpsnet.com, web site http://www.cpsnet.com.

SMALL BUSINESS SOURCEBOOK encompasses comprehensive information on small businesses, including professional associations, training sources, small business investment companies, over 400 Internet databases, publications, awards and honors, company and personal email addresses. $325 for 2 vol. set. Gale Group, P.O. Box 9187, Farmington Hills, MI 48333-9187. Toll free US and Canada (800) 877-GALE (4253) and (248) 699-GALE, fax (800) 414-5043 and (248) 699-8061, Internet orders galeord@galegroup.com, web site www.galegroup.com or www.gale.com. All Gale Group products are available on approval. Contact Gale for details.

STANDARD DIRECTORY OF ADVERTISERS Business Classifications Edition is an excellent general directory that organizes companies by a wide range of product categories. A few examples include "Apparel 2—Men's and Boys' Wear," "Heating and Air Conditioning," "Cosmetics and Toiletries," and "Aviation and Aerospace." This directory lists names and titles of key officers, revenues and other information. It is available in a geographic edition for the same price. This directory is comprised of over 24,000 companies that annually spend over $200,000 on advertising. It represents a reasonable place to look for hard-to-find information about privately held companies, especially those that heavily advertise their products. It is a good place to look for names if STANDARD AND POORS and the MILLION DOLLAR DIRECTORY fail to yield the names you need. Finally, the Classified Edition of THE STANDARD DIRECTORY OF ADVERTISERS can be a very convenient source of research because both your target list of companies and the corresponding names and titles of management all appear together, in the same Classification. This is important if you still rely on research books in hard copy. THE STANDARD DIRECTORY OF ADVERTISERS also publishes a special volume called THE STANDARD DIRECTORY OF ADVERTISERS TRADENAME INDEX. You can use the TRADENAME INDEX if you know the brand name of a product and need to find the company that manufactures it. In addition, this directory contains an Associations section which identifies marketing oriented associations.

$599 hard copy. If the price is prohibitively high, remember your local library. THE STANDARD DIRECTORY OF ADVERTISERS is also available on CD ROM under the title ADVERTISER AND AGENCY RED BOOKS PLUS. It is available in Windows® and Macintosh® formats. National Register Publishing, Reed Elsevier-New Providence, 121 Chanlon Road, New Providence, NJ 07974, (800) 521-8110, fax (800) 836-7736, web site www.redbooks.com or www.marquiswhoswho.com. "If, for any reason whatsoever, your order does not fully meet your expectations, simply return the product within 30 days for a prompt, complete, unquestioned refund," as stated in Catalog of Biographical and Professional References of publisher Marquis Who's Who/National Register Publishing.

STATE AND REGIONAL ASSOCIATIONS OF THE UNITED STATES identifies over 7,000 state and regional associations in the US. Information is cross referenced by subject, state, budget and chief executive and includes publications, convention schedule, membership/ staff size and budget. $79. Columbia Books, Inc., 1212 New York Avenue, NW, Suite 330, Washington, DC 20005, (212) 898-0662.

TELECOMMUNICATIONS DIRECTORY includes information on over 2,500 national and international communications systems and services, including providers of telephone lines, local area networks, teleconferencing, videotext and teletext, electronic mail, facsimile, Internet access, voicemail, satellite and electronic transactional services. Also includes associations, a glossary, and four indexes. $400. Gale Group, P.O. Box 9187, Farmington Hills, MI 48333-9187. Toll free US and Canada (800) 877-GALE (4253) and (248) 699-GALE, fax (800) 414-5043 and (248) 699-8061, Internet orders galeord@galegroup.com, web site www.galegroup.com or www.gale.com. All Gale Group products are available on approval. Contact Gale for details.

THOMSON BANK DIRECTORY is a five volume set of commercial banking directories, worldwide. Listings include head office and branch offices, address, phone, phone and fax, names of key decision makers, the past 2 years of structural changes (such as mergers, name changes and closings), central banks and trade associations. Published twice a year. For more information contact (800) 321-3373, Thomson Financial Publishing, 4709 West Golf Road, Skokie, IL 60076-1253. Web site @ tfp.bankinfo.com.

WASHINGTON identifies 4,500 organizations and institutions in Washington DC and 22,000 key people in them. Includes government, business, education, medicine/health, community affairs, art/culture and others. $85. Columbia Books, Inc., 1212 New York Avenue, NW, Suite 330, Washington, DC 20005, (212) 898-0662.

WORLD DIRECTORY OF MARKETING INFORMATION SOURCES identifies market research companies, online databases, directories and marketing journals for every major consumer market in 75 countries. $595. Published by Euromonitor (England). Distributed by Gale Group, P.O. Box 9187, Farmington Hills, MI 48333-9187. Toll free US and Canada (800) 877-GALE (4253) and (248) 699-GALE, fax (800) 414-5043 and (248) 699-8061, Internet orders galeord@galegroup.com, web site www.galegroup.com or www.gale.com. All Gale Group products are available on approval. Contact Gale for details.

WORLD DIRECTORY OF TRADE AND BUSINESS ASSOCIATIONS profiles 3,000 trade and business associations globally, including finance, general business and industry, advertising, marketing and major consumer markets. Entries include web site addresses and publications. $595. Published by Euromonitor (England). Distributed by Gale Group, P.O. Box 9187, Farmington Hills, MI 48333-9187. Toll free US and Canada (800) 877-GALE (4253) and (248) 699-GALE, fax (800) 414-5043 and (248) 699-8061, Internet orders galeord@galegroup.com, web site www.galegroup.com or www.gale.com. All Gale Group products are available on approval. Contact Gale for details.

WORLD GUIDE TO SCIENTIFIC ASSOCIATIONS AND LEARNED SOCIETIES encompasses international, national and regional associations in science, culture and technology. From K.G. Saur, $300. R.R. Bowker (a unit of Cahners Business Information), 121 Chanlon Road, New Providence, NJ 07974 USA, Phone (888) BOWKER2 (888-269-5372) & (800) 323-3288, fax (908) 508-7696, email info@bowker.com, web www.bowker.com. Canada—R.R. Bowker, Markham, Ontario, phone (888) BOWKER9 & (905) 415-5837, fax (905) 479-6266. German speaking Europe—K.G. Saur Verlag, Munich, Germany, phone 49-89-76902-232, fax 49-89-76902-250, email 100730.1341@compuserve.com, web www.saur.de/home.htm. Rest of Europe incl. United Kingdom plus Africa & Asia—Bowker-Saur, W. Sussex, UK, phone 44-1342-326-972, fax 44-1342-335-612, email customer@bowker-saur.co.uk, web www.bowker-saur.com/service/. Australia/New Zealand—Thorpe, Port Melbourne, Victoria, Australia, phone 61-03-9-245-7370, fax 61-03-9-245-7395, email customer.service@thorpe.com.au, web www.thorpe.com.au. Technical support for CD ROMs (800) 323-3288, fax 908) 665-3528, email techsupport@bowker.com.

WORLD GUIDE TO TRADE ASSOCIATIONS edited by Michael Zils includes key personnel, publications, a translation of the name in English, information that reflects the structure of Eastern Europe and the former USSR, a German-English concordance of subject areas and other data. From K.G. Saur. 2 volume set $650. R.R. Bowker (a unit of Cahners Business Information), 121 Chanlon Road, New Providence, NJ 07974 USA, Phone (888) BOWKER2 (888-269-5372) & (800) 323-3288, fax (908) 508-7696, email info@bowker.com, web www.bowker.com. Canada—R.R. Bowker, Markham, Ontario, phone (888) BOWKER9 & (905) 415-5837, fax (905) 479-6266. German speaking Europe—K.G. Saur Verlag, Munich, Germany, phone 49-89-76902-232, fax 49-89-76902-250, email 100730.1341@compuserve.com, web www.saur.de/home.htm. Rest of Europe incl. United Kingdom plus Africa & Asia—Bowker-Saur, W. Sussex, UK, phone 44-1342-326-972, fax 44-1342-335-612, email customer@bowker-saur.co.uk, web www.bowker-saur.com/service/. Australia/New Zealand—Thorpe, Port Melbourne, Victoria, Australia, phone 61-03-9-245-7370, fax 61-03-9-245-7395, email customer.service@thorpe.com.au, web www.thorpe.com.au. Technical support for CD ROMs (800) 323-3288, fax 908) 665-3528, email techsupport@bowker.com.

YEARBOOK OF INTERNATIONAL ORGANIZATIONS is a 4 volume directory of non-profit organizations, commercial associations, business groups, conferences, religious orders and intergovernmental bodies. From K.G. Saur. $1,170 for 4 volumes.

YEARBOOK OF INTERNATIONAL ORGANIZATIONS PLUS is a CD ROM which was described by American Reference Books Annual as "The most comprehensive coverage of international organizations." This CD consolidates THE YEARBOOK OF INTERNATIONAL ORGANIZATIONS and WHO'S WHO IN INTERNATIONAL ORGANIZATIONS. It encompasses intergovernmental and national organizations, conferences and religious orders and fraternities. Search criteria include organization name, fields of activity, titles of publications, links to other organizations and more. User languages are English, German, French and Dutch. MS-DOS, Windows and Macintosh compatibility. From K.G. Saur. Updated annually. 1 year subscription $1,318.

R.R. Bowker (a unit of Cahners Business Information), 121 Chanlon Road, New Providence, NJ 07974 USA, Phone (888) BOWKER2 (888-269-5372) & (800) 323-3288, fax (908) 508-7696, email info@bowker.com, web www.bowker.com. Canada—R.R. Bowker, Markham, Ontario, phone (888) BOWKER9 & (905) 415-

5837, fax (905) 479-6266. German speaking Europe—K.G. Saur Verlag, Munich, Germany, phone 49-89-76902-232, fax 49-89-76902-250, email 100730.1341@compuserve.com, web www.saur.de/home.htm. Rest of Europe incl. United Kingdom plus Africa & Asia—Bowker-Saur, W. Sussex, UK, phone 44-1342-326-972, fax 44-1342-335-612, email customer@bowker-saur.co.uk, web www.bowkcr-saur.com/service/. Australia/New Zealand—Thorpc, Port Melbourne, Victoria, Australia, phone 61-03-9-245-7370, fax 61-03-9-245-7395, email customer.service@thorpe.com.au, web www.thorpe.com.au. Technical support for CD ROMs (800) 323-3288, fax 908) 665-3528, email techsupport@bowker.com.

Australia

See Pacific, International

AUSTRALIAN BOOKS IN PRINT, published by Thorpe, $130. Also available on CD ROM. R.R. Bowker (a unit of Cahners Business Information), 121 Chanlon Road, New Providence, NJ 07974 USA, Phone (888) BOWKER2 (888-269-5372) & (800) 323-3288, fax (908) 508-7696, email info@bowker.com, web www.bowker.com. Canada—R.R. Bowker, Markham, Ontario, phone (888) BOWKER9 & (905) 415-5837, fax (905) 479-6266. German speaking Europe—K.G. Saur Verlag, Munich, Germany, phone 49-89-76902-232, fax 49-89-76902-250, email 100730.1341@compuserve.com, web www.saur.de/home.htm. Rest of Europe incl. United Kingdom plus Africa & Asia—Bowker-Saur, W. Sussex, UK, phone 44-1342-326-972, fax 44-1342-335-612, email customer@bowker-saur.co.uk, web www.bowker-saur.com/service/. Australia/New Zealand—Thorpe, Port Melbourne, Victoria, Australia, phone 61-03-9-245-7370, fax 61-03-9-245-7395, email customer.service@thorpe.com.au, web www.thorpe.com.au. Technical support for CD ROMs (800) 323-3288, fax 908) 665-3528, email techsupport@bowker.com.

AUSTRALIA'S TOP 500 COMPANIES. Dun & Bradstreet, Business Reference Solutions, Three Sylvan Way, Parsippany, NJ 07054 USA. (800) 526-0651. Email dnbmdd@mail.dnb.com. Web site http://www.dnbmdd.com.

BOOKSELLERS DIRECTORY (AUSTRALIAN), from Thorpe, $30. R.R. Bowker (a unit of Cahners Business Information), 121 Chanlon Road, New Providence, NJ 07974 USA, Phone (888) BOWKER2 (888-269-5372) & (800) 323-3288, fax (908) 508-7696, email info@bowker.com, web www.bowker.com. Canada—R.R. Bowker, Markham, Ontario, phone (888) BOWKER9 & (905) 415-5837, fax (905) 479-6266. German speaking Europe—K.G. Saur Verlag, Munich, Germany, phone 49-89-76902-232, fax 49-89-76902-250, email 100730.1341@compuserve.com, web www.saur.de/home.htm. Rest of Europe incl. United Kingdom plus Africa & Asia—Bowker-Saur, W. Sussex, UK, phone 44-1342-326-972, fax 44-1342-335-612, email customer@bowker-saur.co.uk, web www.bowker-saur.com/service/. Australia/New Zealand—Thorpe, Port Melbourne, Victoria, Australia, phone 61-03-9-245-7370, fax 61-03-9-245-7395, email customer.service@thorpe.com.au, web www.thorpe.com.au. Technical support for CD ROMs (800) 323-3288, fax 908) 665-3528, email techsupport@bowker.com.

BUSINESS WHO'S WHO OF AUSTRALIA contains 20,000 privately held companies in Australia. Dun & Bradstreet, Business Reference Solutions, Three Sylvan Way, Parsippany, NJ 07054 USA. (800) 526-0651. Email dnbmdd@mail.dnb.com. Web site http://www.dnbmdd.com.F

DIRECTORY OF AMERICAN FIRMS OPERATING IN FOREIGN COUNTRIES, REGIONAL EDITION—AUSTRALIA GROUP. Includes Australia, New Zealand, Fiji French Polynesia, Guam, New Caledonia, New Guinea, North Mariana Island, Palau, Papua, Polynesia. Ordering information: Uniworld Business Publications, Inc., 257 Central Park West, Suite 10A, New York, NY 10024-4110, (212) 496-2448, fax (212) 769-0413, email uniworldbp@aol.com. Web site: http://www.uniworldbp.com.

DIRECTORY OF AUSTRALIAN PUBLISHERS & DISTRIBUTORS, published by Thorpe, $60. R.R. Bowker (a unit of Cahners Business Information), 121 Chanlon Road, New Providence, NJ 07974 USA, Phone (888) BOWKER2 (888-269-5372) & (800) 323-3288, fax (908) 508-7696, email info@bowker.com, web www.bowker.com. Canada—R.R. Bowker, Markham, Ontario, phone (888) BOWKER9 & (905) 415-5837, fax (905) 479-6266. German speaking Europe—K.G. Saur Verlag, Munich, Germany, phone 49-89-76902-232, fax 49-89-76902-250, email 100730.1341@compuserve.com, web www.saur.de/home.htm. Rest of Europe incl. United Kingdom plus Africa & Asia—Bowker-Saur, W. Sussex, UK, phone 44-1342-326-972, fax 44-1342-335-612, email customer@bowker-saur.co.uk, web www.bowker-saur.com/service/.

Australia/New Zealand—Thorpe, Port Melbourne, Victoria, Australia, phone 61-03-9-245-7370, fax 61-03-9-245-7395, email customer.service@thorpe.com.au, web www.thorpe.com.au. Technical support for CD ROMs (800) 323-3288, fax 908) 665-3528, email techsupport@bowker.com.

DIRECTORY OF FOREIGN FIRMS OPERATING IN THE UNITED STATES, REGIONAL EDITION—AUSTRALIA GROUP. Includes Australia and New Zealand. $29. Uniworld Business Publications, Inc., 257 Central Park West, Suite 10A, New York, NY 10024-4110, (212) 496-2448, fax (212) 769-0413, email uniworldbp@aol.com. Web site: http://www.uniworldbp.com.

JOBSON'S MINING YEAR BOOK contains information on 600 of Australia and New Zealand's leading mining, petroleum and exploration companies. Dun & Bradstreet, Business Reference Solutions, Three Sylvan Way, Parsippany, NJ 07054 USA. (800) 526-0651. Email dnbmdd@mail.dnb.com. Web site http://www.dnbmdd.com.

JOBSON'S YEAR BOOK OF PUBLIC COMPANIES OF AUSTRALIA AND NEW ZEALAND contains information on over 2,000 public and private companies and their executives. Dun & Bradstreet, Business Reference Solutions, Three Sylvan Way, Parsippany, NJ 07054 USA. (800) 526-0651. Email dnbmdd@mail.dnb.com. Web site http://www.dnbmdd.com.

KOMPASS is described by the publisher as "the world's most comprehensive global database of companies, products and services for manufacturing and engineering professionals in print, on CD ROM and on the Internet." It contains company and product information for companies in all lines of business, including manufacturing and industrial sectors. Each company listing includes name, address, phone number, management names, business descriptions, and industry and product listings. Kompass's web site is www.kompass.com. Call publisher for prices and information on country directories. Cahners Business Information, 121 Chanlon Road, New Providence, NJ 07974, (908) 771-8785, fax (908) 665-8755, email hholmes@reedref.com. Headquarters: Cahners Business Information, 275 Washington Street, Newton, MA 02158-1630, (617) 558-4663 or (617) 964-3030, fax (617) 558-4700, email marketaccess@cahners.com, web sites www.cahners.com or www.chilton.net.

MAJOR CHEMICAL & PETROCHEMICAL COMPANIES OF THE FAR EAST & AUSTRALASIA provides information on over 1,100 companies. $415. US distributor: Larry Meranus Professional Publications & Services, 4 Demoray Court, Pine Brook, NJ 07058, (800) MERANUS or (800) 637-2687. Published by Graham & Whiteside Ltd., Tuition House, 5-6 Francis Grove, London SW19 4DT, England. Web site http://www.major-co-data.com. Email sales@major-co-data.com.

MAJOR COMPANIES OF THE FAR EAST AND AUSTRALASIA identifies 68,000 senior executives at 12,000 key Asia Pacific companies in 20 countries. Published by Graham & Whiteside Ltd., Tuition House, 5-6 Francis Grove, London SW19 4DT, England. Web site http://www.major-co-data.com. Email sales@major-co-data.com.

$1,450 for all three volumes

Volume 1: South East Asia, $560
Volume 2: East Asia, $560
Volume 3: Australia and New Zealand, $365

CD ROM, updated quarterly, is also available. Distributed by: Larry Meranus Professional Publications & Services, 4 Demoray Court, Pine Brook, NJ 07058, (800) MERANUS or (800) 637-2687. Or by Gale Group, P.O. Box 9187, Farmington Hills, MI 48333-9187. Toll free US and Canada (800) 877-GALE (4253) and (248) 699-GALE, fax (800) 414-5043 and (248) 699-8061, Internet orders galeord@galegroup.com, web site www.galegroup.com or www.gale.com. All Gale Group products are available on approval. Contact Gale for details.

MAJOR COMPANIES SERIES ON CD ROM consists of Graham & Whiteside's annual directories of major international companies. All six directories reside on one disk. After payment, you'll receive a security code to access the region(s) you select. This Windows™ based CD can navigate by company name, company locations, executive names, business activity and more. Free demo CD ROM is available. Regions also available separately for Europe, Central & Eastern Europe, the Far East and Australasia, the Arab World, Africa, and Latin America. For prices and availability, contact the Gale Group, P.O. Box 9187, Farmington

Hills, MI 48333-9187. Toll free US and Canada (800) 877-GALE (4253) and (248) 699-GALE, fax (800) 414-5043 and (248) 699-8061, Internet orders galeord@galegroup.com, web site www.galegroup.com or www.gale.com. All Gale Group products are available on approval. Contact Gale for details.

MAJOR ENERGY COMPANIES OF THE FAR EAST & AUSTRALASIA provides information on over 500 leading energy companies in the Asia Pacific, $415. US distributor: Larry Meranus Professional Publications & Services, 4 Demoray Court, Pine Brook, NJ 07058, (800) MERANUS or (800) 637-2687. Published by Graham & Whiteside Ltd., Tuition House, 5-6 Francis Grove, London SW19 4DT, England. Web site http://www.major-co-data.com. Email sales@major-co-data.com.

MAJOR FINANCIAL INSTITUTIONS OF THE FAR EAST & AUSTRALASIA contains information on over 1,500 Asia/Pacific financial institutions. $450. US distributor: Larry Meranus Professional Publications & Services, 4 Demoray Court, Pine Brook, NJ 07058, (800) MERANUS or (800) 637-2687. Published by Graham & Whiteside Ltd., Tuition House, 5-6 Francis Grove, London SW19 4DT, England. Web site http://www.major-co-data.com. Email sales@major-co-data.com.

MAJOR FOOD & DRINK COMPANIES OF THE FAR EAST & AUSTRALASIA provides information on over 1,100 top food and beverage (alcoholic and non-alcoholic) organizations in the Asia Pacific region. $415. US distributor: Larry Meranus Professional Publications & Services, 4 Demoray Court, Pine Brook, NJ 07058, (800) MERANUS or (800) 637-2687. Published by Graham & Whiteside Ltd., Tuition House, 5-6 Francis Grove, London SW19 4DT, England. Web site http://www.major-co-data.com. Email sales@major-co-data.com.

MAJOR TELECOMMUNICATIONS COMPANIES OF THE FAR EAST & AUSTRALASIA contains information on 1,000 top telecommunications companies and their Asia Pacific equipment suppliers. $415. US distributor: Larry Meranus Professional Publications & Services, 4 Demoray Court, Pine Brook, NJ 07058, (800) MERANUS or (800) 637-2687. Published by Graham & Whiteside Ltd., Tuition House, 5-6 Francis Grove, London SW19 4DT, England. Web site http://www.major-co-data.com. Email sales@major-co-data.com.

WHO OWNS WHOM DIRECTORY by Dun & Bradstreet is a six volume set containing information on the structure and ownership of 320,000 company affiliates and subsidiaries of over 23,000 companies worldwide. It is available in four regional editions: Australia and the Far East, North America, UK/Ireland, and Continental Europe. Published annually. For prices and ordering information as well as information about more worldwide corporate linkage products from D&B WORLDBASE, D&B's global database of 42 million records in over 200 countries, contact Dun & Bradstreet at (800) 526-0651, Dun & Bradstreet, Business Reference Solutions, Three Sylvan Way, Parsippany, NJ 07054. Email dnbmdd@mail.dnb.com. Web site http://www.dnbmdd.com

www.whitepages.com.au/ is the web site address for Australian white pages. I found it by first going to www.askjeeves.com and asking "How can I find someone in Australia?"

Austria

See Europe, International

AUSTRIA'S 10,000 LARGEST contains tables, ranking, key decision makers and standard business information. Text in German. Dun & Bradstreet, Business Reference Solutions, Three Sylvan Way, Parsippany, NJ 07054 USA. (800) 526-0651. Email dnbmdd@mail.dnb.com. Web site http://www.dnbmdd.com.

Automobile

ADVERTISER AND AGENCY RED BOOKS PLUS CD ROM combines all the information in THE STANDARD DIRECTORY OF ADVERTISERS, THE STANDARD DIRECTORY OF ADVERTISING AGENCIES and THE STANDARD DIRECTORY OF INTERNATIONAL ADVERTISERS AND AGENCIES. Information is searchable by 25 fields, including company name, personal name, job title/function, product type, product/account name, city, state, zip or country, area code, revenues, number of employees, outside ad agency and even type of computer hardware. Contains professional association information. Available for Windows and Macintosh. Updated quarterly. 1 year subscription $1,295. If the price is prohibitively high, remember your local library. National Register Publishing, Reed Elsevier-New Providence, 121 Chanlon Road, New Providence, NJ 07974, (800) 521-8110, fax (800) 836-7736, web site www.redbooks.com or www.marquiswhoswho.com. "If, for any reason whatsoever, your order does not fully meet your expectations, simply return the product within 30 days for a prompt, complete, unquestioned refund," as stated in Catalog of Biographical and Professional References of publisher Marquis Who's Who/National Register Publishing.

AUTOMOTIVE NEWS is a weekly trade publication. Crain Communications, Inc. is headquartered in Chicago with offices in major cities throughout the US plus London, Tokyo and Frankfurt. New York location: 220 East 42nd Street, New York, NY 10017, (212) 210-0100, Circulation (800) 678-9595. Annual subscription $104, 2 years $187.

AUTOWEEK is a weekly trade publication. Crain Communications, Inc. is headquartered in Chicago with offices in major cities throughout the US plus London, Tokyo and Frankfurt. New York location: 220 East 42nd Street, New York, NY 10017, (212) 210-0100, Circulation (800) 678-9595. Annual subscription $32, 2 years $56. Web site www.autoweek.com.

STANDARD DIRECTORY OF ADVERTISERS Business Classifications Edition is an excellent general directory that organizes companies by a wide range of product categories. A few examples include "Apparel 2—Men's and Boys' Wear," "Heating and Air Conditioning," "Cosmetics and Toiletries," and "Aviation and Aerospace." This directory lists names and titles of key officers, revenues and other information. It is available in a geographic edition for the same price. This directory is comprised of over 24,000 companies that annually spend over $200,000 on advertising. It represents a reasonable place to look for hard-to-find information about privately held companies, especially those that heavily advertise their products. It is a good place to look for names if STANDARD AND POORS and the MILLION DOLLAR DIRECTORY fail to yield the names you need. Finally, the Classified Edition of THE STANDARD DIRECTORY OF ADVERTISERS can be a very convenient source of research because both your target list of companies and the corresponding names and titles of management all appear together, in the same Classification. This is important if you still rely on research books in hard copy. THE STANDARD DIRECTORY OF ADVERTISERS also publishes a special volume called THE STANDARD DIRECTORY OF ADVERTISERS TRADENAME INDEX. You can use the TRADENAME INDEX if you know the brand name of a product and need to find the company that manufactures it. In addition, this directory contains an Associations section which identifies marketing oriented associations.

$599 hard copy. If the price is prohibitively high, remember your local library. THE STANDARD DIRECTORY OF ADVERTISERS is also available on CD ROM under the title ADVERTISER AND AGENCY RED BOOKS PLUS. It is available in Windows® and Macintosh® formats. National Register Publishing, Reed Elsevier-New Providence, 121 Chanlon Road, New Providence, NJ 07974, (800) 521-8110, fax (800) 836-7736, web site www.redbooks.com or www.marquiswhoswho.com. "If, for any reason whatsoever, your order does not fully meet your expectations, simply return the product within 30 days for a prompt, complete, unquestioned refund," as stated in Catalog of Biographical and Professional References of publisher Marquis Who's Who/National Register Publishing.

TIRE BUSINESS is a biweekly trade publication. Crain Communications, Inc. is headquartered in Chicago with offices in major cities throughout the US plus London, Tokyo and Frankfurt. New York location: 220 East 42nd Street, New York, NY 10017, (212) 210-0100, Circulation (800) 678-9595. Annual subscription $59, two years $108. Web site www.tirebusiness.com

Aviation

ADVERTISER AND AGENCY RED BOOKS PLUS CD ROM combines all the information in THE STANDARD DIRECTORY OF ADVERTISERS, THE STANDARD DIRECTORY OF ADVERTISING AGENCIES and THE STANDARD DIRECTORY OF INTERNATIONAL ADVERTISERS AND AGENCIES. Information is searchable by 25 fields, including company name, personal name, job title/function, product type, product/account name, city, state, zip or country, area code, revenues, number of employees, outside ad agency and even type of computer hardware. Contains professional association information. Available for Windows and Macintosh. Updated quarterly. 1 year subscription $1,295. If the price is prohibitively high, remember your local library. National Register Publishing, Reed Elsevier-New Providence, 121 Chanlon Road, New Providence, NJ 07974, (800) 521-8110, fax (800) 836-7736, web site www.redbooks.com or www.marquiswhoswho.com. "If, for any reason whatsoever, your order does not fully meet your expectations, simply return the product within 30 days for a prompt, complete, unquestioned refund," as stated in Catalog of Biographical and Professional References of publisher Marquis Who's Who/National Register Publishing.

PHILLIPS BUSINESS INFORMATION provides information in newsletters, magazines, directories and on multiple web sites covering a range of topics, such as magazine products, telecommunications and cable products, satellite products, media, new media and Internet products, marketing and public relations products, financial technology and electronic commerce, aviation and defense products. For more information, contact: Phillips Business Information, Inc., a Phillips Publishing International Company, 120 Seven Locks Road, Potomac, MD 20854, (301) 340-1520, (301) 340-7788, (800) 777-5006, Internet pbi@phillips.com, web site www.phillips.com.

STANDARD DIRECTORY OF ADVERTISERS Business Classifications Edition is an excellent general directory that organizes companies by a wide range of product categories. A few examples include "Apparel 2—Men's and Boys' Wear," "Heating and Air Conditioning," "Cosmetics and Toiletries," and "Aviation and Aerospace." This directory lists names and titles of key officers, revenues and other information. It is available in a geographic edition for the same price. This directory is comprised of over 24,000 companies that annually spend over $200,000 on advertising. It represents a reasonable place to look for hard-to-find information about privately held companies, especially those that heavily advertise their products. It is a good place to look for names if STANDARD AND POORS and the MILLION DOLLAR DIRECTORY fail to yield the names you need. Finally, the Classified Edition of THE STANDARD DIRECTORY OF ADVERTISERS can be a very convenient source of research because both your target list of companies and the corresponding names and titles of management all appear together, in the same Classification. This is important if you still rely on research books in hard copy. THE STANDARD DIRECTORY OF ADVERTISERS also publishes a special volume called THE STANDARD DIRECTORY OF ADVERTISERS TRADENAME INDEX. You can use the TRADENAME INDEX if you know the brand name of a product and need to find the company that manufactures it. In addition, this directory contains an Associations section which identifies marketing oriented associations.

$599 hard copy. If the price is prohibitively high, remember your local library. THE STANDARD DIRECTORY OF ADVERTISERS is also available on CD ROM under the title ADVERTISER AND AGENCY RED BOOKS PLUS. It is available in Windows® and Macintosh® formats. National Register Publishing, Reed Elsevier-New Providence, 121 Chanlon Road, New Providence, NJ 07974, (800) 521-8110, fax (800) 836-7736, web site www.redbooks.com or www.marquiswhoswho.com. "If, for any reason whatsoever, your order does not fully meet your expectations, simply return the product within 30 days for a prompt, complete, unquestioned refund," as stated in Catalog of Biographical and Professional References of publisher Marquis Who's Who/National Register Publishing.

WORLD AVIATION DIRECTORY AND BUYER'S GUIDE is available as a hard copy directory, on CD ROM and as an Internet database. Some companies on the Internet even have email and web site links. Print directory $275, 2 issues per year; CD ROM $995. Published by Aviation Week, a Division of The McGraw-Hill Companies. McGraw Hill, Print Division, PO Box 629, Hightstown, NJ 08520, (800) 525-5003. McGraw Hill, Other Media Division (202) 383-2420, (800) 551-2015, extension 4. Web site: www.wadaviation.com.

www.aviationtoday.com is the web site for PHILLIPS AVIATION TODAY, published by Phillips Business Information, Inc., a Phillips Publishing International Company, 120 Seven Locks Road, Potomac, MD 20854, (301) 340-1520, (301) 340-7788, (800) 777-5006, Internet pbi@phillips.com, web site www.phillips.com.

Awards

AWARDS, HONORS & PRIZES provides an alphabetical listing of the organizations giving the awards. Specifies organization, award and subject indexes and email addresses. $450 for two volume set, $255 per single volume.

Volume 1, US and Canada, $228
Volume 2, International and Foreign, $255

Gale Group, P.O. Box 9187, Farmington Hills, MI 48333-9187. Toll free US and Canada (800) 877-GALE (4253) and (248) 699-GALE, fax (800) 414-5043 and (248) 699-8061, Internet orders galeord@galegroup.com, web site www.galegroup.com or www.gale.com. All Gale Group products are available on approval. Contact Gale for details.

INTERNATIONAL FOUNDATION DIRECTORY includes national foundations located in 50 countries. Includes institutions which either operate internationally or offer fellowships or similar awards to applicants from outside its own country, or operate within its own national territory on a scale large enough to establish its international importance. $210. Published by Europa Publications. Distributed by Gale Group, P.O. Box 9187, Farmington Hills, MI 48333-9187. Toll free US and Canada (800) 877-GALE (4253) and (248) 699-GALE, fax (800) 414-5043 and (248) 699-8061, Internet orders galeord@galegroup.com, web site www.galegroup.com or www.gale.com. All Gale Group products are available on approval. Contact Gale for details.

INTERNATIONAL WHO'S WHO OF WOMEN lists 4,000 women, including well known figures and women who have recently come to the forefront of their fields. Information includes woman's nationality, date and place of birth, education, family, career history and present position, honors, awards, publications, and contact information. $390. Published by Europa. Distributed by Gale Group, P.O. Box 9187, Farmington Hills, MI 48333-9187. Toll free US and Canada (800) 877-GALE (4253) and (248) 699-GALE, fax (800) 414-5043 and (248) 699-8061, Internet orders galeord@galegroup.com, web site www.galegroup.com or www.gale.com. All Gale Group products are available on approval. Contact Gale for details.

LITERARY MARKET PLACE, "The Directory of the American Book Publishing Industry With Industry Yellow Pages" is an excellent 3 volume directory with comprehensive information on US book publishers; imprints, subsidiaries and distributors; book trade acquisitions and mergers, small presses, Canadian book publishers, micropublishers, US electronic publishers, electronic publishing consultants, electronic publishing products and services, editorial services, literary agents, illustrations agents, US agents and offices of foreign publishers, lecture agents, specialized advertising and public relations firms, direct mail specialists, mailing list brokers and services, book review syndicates, book review and index journals and services, book exhibits, book clubs, book lists and catalogs, book importers and exporters, book producers, translators, artists, photographers, stock photo agencies, associations, book trade events and conferences, awards, contents and grants, reference books for the trade, magazines for the trade, a toll free directory of publishers, magazine and newspaper publicity, radio and television publicity, book manufacturing services, book distributors and sales representatives, and wholesalers. $189.95.

LITERARY MARKET PLACE ON DISC, previously titled LITERARY MARKET PLACE Plus CD ROM, one year subscription $297.00.

LITERARY MARKET PLACE—INTERNET EDITION, www.literarymarketplace.com, is available by subscription.

INTERNATIONAL LITERARY MARKET PLACE Internet database can be directly accessed at www.iliterarymarketplace.com. It is also linked to the US domestic LITERARY MARKET PLACE web site at www.literarymarketplace.com. Contact the publisher for subscription price. INTERNATIONAL LITERARY MARKET PLACE, hard copy $189.95.

R.R. Bowker (a unit of Cahners Business Information), 121 Chanlon Road, New Providence, NJ 07974 USA, Phone (888) BOWKER2 (888-269-5372) & (800) 323-3288, fax (908) 508-7696, email info@bowker.com, web www.bowker.com. Canada—R.R. Bowker, Markham, Ontario, phone (888) BOWKER9 & (905) 415-5837, fax (905) 479-6266. German speaking Europe—K.G. Saur Verlag, Munich, Germany, phone 49-89-76902-232, fax 49-89-76902-250, email 100730.1341@compuserve.com, web www.saur.de/home.htm. Rest of Europe incl. United Kingdom plus Africa & Asia—Bowker-Saur, W. Sussex, UK, phone 44-1342-326-972, fax 44-1342-335-612, email customer@bowker-saur.co.uk, web www.bowker-saur.com/service/. Australia/New Zealand—Thorpe, Port Melbourne, Victoria, Australia, phone 61-03-9-245-7370, fax 61-03-9-245-7395, email customer.service@thorpe.com.au, web www.thorpe.com.au. Technical support for CD ROMs (800) 323-3288, fax 908) 665-3528, email techsupport@bowker.com.

PROFESSIONAL CAREERS SOURCEBOOK directs users to career information sources related to specific professions, such as civil engineering, psychology, law, public relations, dance and choreography and more. It includes information on general career and test guides, professional associations, standards and certification agencies, educational directories and programs, awards and scholarships, basic reference guides, handbooks and more, including a master index. $99. Gale Group, P.O. Box 9187, Farmington Hills, MI 48333-9187. Toll free US and Canada (800) 877-GALE (4253) and (248) 699-GALE, fax (800) 414-5043 and (248) 699-8061, Internet orders galeord@galegroup.com, web site www.galegroup.com or www.gale.com. All Gale Group products are available on approval. Contact Gale for details.

SMALL BUSINESS SOURCEBOOK encompasses comprehensive information on small businesses, including professional associations, training sources, small business investment companies, over 400 Internet databases, publications, awards and honors, company and personal email addresses. $325 for 2 vol. set. Gale Group, P.O. Box 9187, Farmington Hills, MI 48333-9187. Toll free US and Canada (800) 877-GALE (4253) and (248) 699-GALE, fax (800) 414-5043 and (248) 699-8061, Internet orders galeord@galegroup.com, web site www.galegroup.com or www.gale.com. All Gale Group products are available on approval. Contact Gale for details.

B

Baltimore/Annapolis

BALTIMORE/ANNAPOLIS is a guide to over 2,000 organizations and institutions. Chapters include government, business, education, medicine/health, arts and culture, community affairs and more. $65. Columbia Books, Inc., 1212 New York Avenue, NW, Suite 330, Washington, DC 20005, (212) 898-0662.

Banking

See Credit Unions, Finance—International, Investment Banking, Mortgage Banking, Mutual Funds, Securities, Thrifts

AMERICAN BANKERS ASSOCIATION (ABA) publishes numerous specialized banking journals and otherwise provides a wealth of information, especially lists of leading firms engaged in various banking.activities, such as correspondent banking, second mortgages, credit card operations, mortgage servicing, foreign banks in the US, and so forth. AMERICAN BANKERS ASSOCIATION, 1120 Connecticut Ave. NW, Washington, DC 20036, (202) 663-5000, Fax (202) 663-7533, web site www.aba.com.

AMERICAN FINANCIAL DIRECTORY consists of five desktop volumes of banks, bank holding companies, savings and Loan Associations and Major Credit Unions in the US, Canada and Mexico. It includes information on head office and branch offices, names of key decision makers, phone and fax numbers, financial summaries, and structural changes such as mergers, name changes and closings. Published twice a year. For more information contact (800) 321-3373, Thomson Financial Publishing, 4709 West Golf Road, Skokie, IL 60076-1253. Web site@tfp.bankinfo.com.

AMERICAN FINANCIAL DIRECTORY CUSTOMIZED DIRECTORIES are available for any state or combination of states for banks, bank holding companies, savings and loans and major credit unions. For more information contact (800) 321-3373, Thomson Financial Publishing, 4709 West Golf Road, Skokie, IL 60076-1253. Web site@tfp.bankinfo.com.

AMERICAN FINANCIAL DIRECTORY REGIONAL DIRECTORIES include banks, bank holding companies, savings and loan associations and major credit unions. Published twice a year.

- **SOUTHERN BANKERS DIRECTORY** covers Alabama, Arkansas, District of Columbia, Florida, Georgia, Kentucky, Louisiana, Maryland, Mississippi, North Carolina, South Carolina, Tennessee, Virginia and West Virginia. Published twice a year.

- **GOLDEN STATES FINANCIAL DIRECTORY** includes Alaska, Arizona, California, Colorado, Hawaii, Idaho, Montana, Nevada, New Mexico, Oregon, Utah, Washington, and Wyoming. Published twice a year.

- **UPPER MIDWEST FINANCIAL DIRECTORY** includes Michigan, Minnesota, Montana, North Dakota, South Dakota and Wisconsin. Published once a year.

- **SOUTHWESTERN FINANCIAL DIRECTORY** includes Arkansas, Louisiana, New Mexico, Oklahoma and Texas. Published twice a year.

For more information contact (800) 321-3373, Thomson Financial Publishing, 4709 West Golf Road, Skokie, IL 60076-1253. Web site @ tfp.bankinfo.com.

BANK AUTOMATION NEWS, Phillips Business Information, Inc., a Phillips Publishing International Company, 120 Seven Locks Road, Potomac, MD 20854, (301) 340-1520, (301) 340-7788, (800) 777-5006, Internet pbi@phillips.com, web site www.phillips.com.

CENTRAL BANK & MINISTRY OF FINANCE YEARBOOK. For more information contact Larry Meranus Professional Publications & Services, 4 Demoray Court, Pine Brook, NJ 07058, (800) MERANUS or (800) 637-2687. Distributed in England by EUROMONEY Books, Plymbridge Distributors Limited, Estover, Plymouth PL6 7PZ, England. Phone 44 (0) 171 779-8955. Fax 44 (0) 171 779-8541.

CORPORATE FINANCE SOURCEBOOK—THE GUIDE TO MAJOR INVESTMENT SOURCES AND RELATED FINANCIAL SERVICES contains over 13,000 names of executives at 3,700 organizations that, broadly speaking, supply growth capital to businesses or are service firms, such as US venture capital lenders, private lenders, commercial finance and factoring, pension managers, master trusts and other sources. Names of key management are included. A special section details public offerings of the past 3 years and mergers and acquisitions over $100 million. $575. If the price is prohibitively high, remember your local library. National Register Publishing, Reed Elsevier-New Providence, 121 Chanlon Road, New Providence, NJ 07974, (800) 521-8110, fax (800) 836-7736, web site www.redbooks.com or www.marquiswhoswho.com. "If, for any reason whatsoever, your order does not fully meet your expectations, simply return the product within 30 days for a prompt, complete, unquestioned refund," as stated in Catalog of Biographical and Professional References of publisher Marquis Who's Who/National Register Publishing.

DIRECTORY OF TRUST BANKING, an official publication of the American Bankers Association, is a one volume directory that identifies banks and private trust companies in the Unites States. Listings include trust officer names and functional responsibilities, address, fax and phone, financial information outlining scope and amount of trust activity in collective investment funds, investment instruments used, discretionary and non-discretionary assets and corporate funds, plus national and state rankings and a summary of mergers. Published annually. For more information contact (800) 321-3373, Thomson Financial Publishing, 4709 West Golf Road, Skokie, IL 60076-1253. Web site @ tfp.bankinfo.com.

DUN & BRADSTREET AND GALE INDUSTRY REFERENCE HANDBOOKS offer a line of industry-specific sourcebooks which include key companies in the industry, ranked lists of companies, professional associations, trade shows and conferences, mergers and acquisitions, consultants who service those industries, information sources, and more. 6 volume set $495. Also available individually for $99: Pharmaceuticals, Health and Medical Services, Computers and Software, Banking and Finance, Telecommunications, Agriculture and Food, Insurance, Construction, Entertainment, Hospitality. First edition December, 1999. Gale Group, P.O. Box 9187, Farmington Hills, MI 48333-9187. Toll free US and Canada (800) 877-GALE (4253) and (248) 699-GALE, fax (800) 414-5043 and (248) 699-8061, Internet orders galeord@galegroup.com, web site www.galegroup.com or www.gale.com. All Gale Group products are available on approval. Contact Gale for details.

EUROMONEY BANK REGISTER is a detailed directory of the world's leading financial institutions and a comprehensive guide to "who's who" in global capital markets. This directory lists senior executives, investment and commercial bankers, traders, analysts, support and legal staff. Expanded coverage of Asia, central Europe and eastern Europe and Latin America is provided. Available in print or CD ROM. The print version of The EUROMONEY Bank Register is comprehensively indexed alphabetically and by city. It also contains rankings of the top banks. The read only version of the CD ROM provides full access to the entire database. However, by disabling the print and export functions, the result is a lower cost alternative to the full version. A 14 day free trial is available with the CD ROM.

Print Directory, USA, US $493 or 297 pounds sterling
Print Directory, UK, Europe, Rest of World US $493 or 297 pounds sterling
Read Only Version CD ROM US $1,250 or 750 pounds sterling
Full Version CD ROM US $3,000 or 1,750 pounds sterling

Ordering information: Larry Meranus Professional Publications & Services, 4 Demoray Court, Pine Brook, NJ 07058, (800) MERANUS or (800) 637-2687. Distributed in England by EUROMONEY Books, Plymbridge Distributors Limited, Estover, Plymouth PL6 7PZ, England. Phone 44 (0) 171 779-8955 for a free demo disk. Fax 44 (0) 171 779-8541.

FINANCIAL SERVICES CANADA is a handbook of banks, non-depository institutions, stock exchange and brokers, investment management, mutual funds, insurance, accountants, government agencies, financial associations and more, including contact numbers, name, title, organization, phone, fax, email, web site, and cellular. $199 for book, $299 for CD ROM, $399 for both. Ordering information: Copp Clark Professional, 200 Adelaide Street West, 3rd floor, Toronto, ON M5H 1W7 CANADA. Email orders@mail.CanadaInfo.com. Web site http://www.coppclark.com. For additional information contact: IHS Canada, Micromedia Limited, 20 Victoria Street, Toronto, Ontario M5C 2N8 CANADA, (800) 387-2689, (416) 362-5211, fax (416) 362-6161, email info@micromedia.on.ca.

FINANCIAL TIMES, the London daily business journal and a subsidiary of Pearson, can be subscribed to in major US cities by calling its New York City office at (800) 628-8088 or faxing (212) 308-2397. Web site www.ft.com.

FINANCIAL TIMES TOP BANKS list can be obtained by calling the FINANCIAL TIMES in London, England (from the USA) at (011) 44 171 896-2274, (011) 44 171 873-4211. Faxes (011) 44 171 896-2371 & (011) 44 171 873-3595. Web site www.ft.com.

JAPAN FINANCIAL DIRECTORY NEW YORK is published by Nikkin America, Inc., 445 Fifth Avenue, Suite 27D, New York, NY 10016, (212) 679-0196. $195 hard copy. It can also be purchased at Asahiya, the Japanese bookstore at the corner of Vanderbilt and 45th Street, near Grand Central Station in Manhattan. Check other major cities for an Asahiya book store near you.

MAJOR FINANCIAL INSTITUTIONS OF EUROPE contains information on some 1,600 financial institutions in western Europe. $450. US distributor: Larry Meranus Professional Publications & Services, 4 Demoray Court, Pine Brook, NJ 07058, (800) MERANUS or (800) 637-2687. Published by Graham & Whiteside Ltd., Tuition House, 5-6 Francis Grove, London SW19 4DT, England. Web site http://www.major-co-data.com. Email sales@major-co-data.com.

MAJOR FINANCIAL INSTITUTIONS OF THE ARAB WORLD provides contacts and information on over 1,000 top financial institutions in the Arab world. US distributor: Larry Meranus Professional Publications & Services, 4 Demoray Court, Pine Brook, NJ 07058, (800) MERANUS or (800) 637-2687. Published by Graham & Whiteside Ltd., Tuition House, 5-6 Francis Grove, London SW19 4DT, England. Web site http://www.major-co-data.com. Email sales@major-co-data.com.

MAJOR FINANCIAL INSTITUTIONS OF THE FAR EAST & AUSTRALASIA contains information on over 1,500 Asia/Pacific financial institutions. $450. US distributor: Larry Meranus Professional Publications & Services, 4 Demoray Court, Pine Brook, NJ 07058, (800) MERANUS or (800) 637-2687. Published by Graham & Whiteside Ltd., Tuition House, 5-6 Francis Grove, London SW19 4DT, England. Web site http://www.major-co-data.com. Email sales@major-co-data.com.

MAJOR FINANCIAL INSTITUTIONS OF THE WORLD provides information on over 7,500 of the largest financial institutions globally. $890. US distributor: Larry Meranus Professional Publications & Services, 4 Demoray Court, Pine Brook, NJ 07058, (800) MERANUS or (800) 637-2687. Published by Graham & Whiteside Ltd., Tuition House, 5-6 Francis Grove, London SW19 4DT, England. Web site http://www.major-co-data.com. Email sales@major-co-data.com.

POLK NORTH AMERICAN FINANCIAL INSTITUTIONS DIRECTORY includes information on banks, savings and loan associations and major credit unions in North America, including head office and branch offices,names of key decision makers, address, phone and fax, financial summaries, maps, and structural changes such as mergers, name changes, and closings. Published twice a year. For more information contact (800) 321-3373, Thomson Financial Publishing, 4709 West Golf Road, Skokie, IL 60076-1253. Web site @ tfp.bankinfo.com.

POLK WORLD BANK DIRECTORY includes information on worldwide banks, including the top 1,000 banks in the US. Listings include names of key decision makers, address, phone and fax, financial summaries, branch information, maps, and structural changes such as mergers, name changes, and closings, and discontinued banks with explanations. Published annually. For more information contact (800) 321-3373, Thomson Financial Publishing, 4709 West Golf Road, Skokie, IL 60076-1253. Web site @ tfp.bankinfo.com.

THOMSON BANK DIRECTORY is a five volume set of commercial banking directories, worldwide. Listings include head office and branch offices, address, phone, phone and fax, names of key decision makers, the past 2 years of structural changes (such as mergers, name changes and closings), central banks and trade associations. Published twice a year. For more information contact (800) 321-3373, Thomson Financial Publishing, 4709 West Golf Road, Skokie, IL 60076-1253. Web site @ tfp.bankinfo.com.

www.americanbanker.com/careerzone or American Banker Online was launched in 1998 by American Banker, New York, New York.

www.jobnet.org is a Canadian web site.that features "Looking for a career in financial services?" Scotiabank online recruiting, Jobnet and Alumnet.

Belgium

See Europe, International

PENSION FUNDS AND THEIR ADVISERS provides information on the top 2,000 pension funds in the United Kingdom, plus major funds of Japan, Belgium, France, Germany, Ireland, The Netherlands and Switzerland. This Directory is the only source in the US that monitors the growth of assets in the international market. Information includes internal and external fund management contacts, major US and Canadian pension funds and money managers, major European and Japanese pension funds and their advisors. It also includes comprehensive listings of 900 advisors to the pension fund industry including financial advisers, accountants, actuaries and pension fund consultants, pension administrators, insurance companies, attorneys, computer services, global custody, pension trustees, pension /financial recruitment consultants, investment research, associations and professional groups, and publications. $310. Published by A.P. Information Services, Ltd. Marketed exclusively in North America MONEY MARKET DIRECTORIES INC./STANDARD AND POORS, 320 East Main Street, Charlottesville, VA 22902, http://www.mmdaccess.com, (800) 446-2810, (804) 977-1450.

TOP 25,000 COMPANIES OF BELGIUM AND LUXEMBOURG contains information on 25,000 companies. Text in English, Dutch and French. Dun & Bradstreet, Business Reference Solutions, Three Sylvan Way, Parsippany, NJ 07054 USA. (800) 526-0651. Email dnbmdd@mail.dnb.com. Web site http://www.dnbmdd.com.

Bermuda

See Caribbean, International

DIRECTORY OF FOREIGN FIRMS OPERATING IN THE UNITED STATES, REGIONAL EDITION—SOUTH/CENTRAL AMERICA & THE CARIBBEAN. Includes Argentina, Bermuda, Bolivia, Brazil, Chile, Colombia, Costa Rica, Dominican Republic, Guatemala, Mexico, Panama, Paraguay, Peru, Uruguay, Venezuela. $39. Uniworld Business Publications, Inc., 257 Central Park West, Suite 10A, New York, NY 10024-4110, (212) 496-2448, fax (212) 769-0413, email uniworldbp@aol.com. Web site: http://www.uniworldbp.com.

Beverages

ADVERTISER AND AGENCY RED BOOKS PLUS CD ROM combines all the information in THE STANDARD DIRECTORY OF ADVERTISERS, THE STANDARD DIRECTORY OF ADVERTISING AGENCIES and THE STANDARD DIRECTORY OF INTERNATIONAL ADVERTISERS AND AGENCIES. Information is searchable by 25 fields, including company name, personal name, job title/function, product type, product/account name, city, state, zip or country, area code, revenues, number of employees, outside ad agency and even type of computer hardware. Contains professional association information. Available for Windows and Macintosh. Updated quarterly. 1 year subscription $1,295. If the price is prohibitively high, remember your local library. National Register Publishing, Reed Elsevier-New Providence, 121 Chanlon Road, New Providence, NJ 07974, (800) 521-8110, fax (800) 836-7736, web site www.redbooks.com or www.marquiswhoswho.com. "If, for any reason whatsoever, your order does not fully meet your expectations, simply return the product within 30 days for a prompt, complete, unquestioned refund," as stated in Catalog of Biographical and Professional References of publisher Marquis Who's Who/National Register Publishing.

EUROPEAN DRINKS MARKETING DIRECTORY provides information on over 1,600 drink manufacturers and over 750 retail and wholesale distributors in Western and Eastern Europe. Includes a directory of 1,500 information sources. $425. Published by Euromonitor (England). Distributed by Gale Group, P.O. Box 9187, Farmington Hills, MI 48333-9187. Toll free US and Canada (800) 877-GALE (4253) and (248) 699-GALE, fax (800) 414-5043 and (248) 699-8061, Internet orders galeord@galegroup.com, web site www.galegroup.com or www.gale.com. All Gale Group products are available on approval. Contact Gale for details.

MAJOR FOOD & DRINK COMPANIES OF EUROPE provides information on 2,100 major companies in food and beverages (alcoholic and non-alcoholic) in Western Europe. $450. US distributor: Larry Meranus Professional Publications & Services, 4 Demoray Court, Pine Brook, NJ 07058, (800) MERANUS or (800) 637-2687. Published by Graham & Whiteside Ltd., Tuition House, 5-6 Francis Grove, London SW19 4DT, England. Web site http://www.major-co-data.com. Email sales@major-co-data.com.

MAJOR FOOD & DRINK COMPANIES OF THE WORLD provides information on nearly 6,000 major food and drink companies in the world. $830 or 460 pounds sterling. US distributor: Larry Meranus Professional Publications & Services, 4 Demoray Court, Pine Brook, NJ 07058, (800) MERANUS or (800) 637-2687. Published by Graham & Whiteside Ltd., Tuition House, 5-6 Francis Grove, London SW19 4DT, England. Web site http://www.major-co-data.com. Email sales@major-co-data.com.

MODERN BREWERY AGE—BLUE BOOK is an annual publication about the microbrewery industry. For more information contact the Baker Library at the Harvard Business School in Boston, in connection with the Advisor Database, web site www.library.hbs.edu/.

STANDARD DIRECTORY OF ADVERTISERS Business Classifications Edition is an excellent general directory that organizes companies by a wide range of product categories. A few examples include "Apparel 2—Men's and Boys' Wear," "Heating and Air Conditioning," "Cosmetics and Toiletries," and "Aviation and Aerospace." This directory lists names and titles of key officers, revenues and other information. It is available in a geographic edition for the same price. This directory is comprised of over 24,000 companies that annually spend over $200,000 on advertising. It represents a reasonable place to look for hard-to-find information about privately held companies, especially those that heavily advertise their products. It is a good place to look for names if STANDARD AND POORS and the MILLION DOLLAR DIRECTORY fail to yield the names you need. Finally, the Classified Edition of THE STANDARD DIRECTORY OF ADVERTISERS can be a very convenient source of research because both your target list of companies and the corresponding names and titles of management all appear together, in the same Classification. This is important if you still rely on research books in hard copy. THE STANDARD DIRECTORY OF ADVERTISERS also publishes a special volume called THE STANDARD DIRECTORY OF ADVERTISERS TRADENAME INDEX. You can use the TRADENAME INDEX if you know the brand name of a product and need to find the company that manufactures it. In addition, this directory contains an Associations section which identifies marketing oriented associations.

$599 hard copy. If the price is prohibitively high, remember your local library. THE STANDARD DIRECTORY OF ADVERTISERS is also available on CD ROM under the title ADVERTISER AND AGENCY RED BOOKS PLUS. It is available in Windows® and Macintosh® formats. National Register

Publishing, Reed Elsevier-New Providence, 121 Chanlon Road, New Providence, NJ 07974, (800) 521-8110, fax (800) 836-7736, web site www.redbooks.com or www.marquiswhoswho.com. "If, for any reason whatsoever, your order does not fully meet your expectations, simply return the product within 30 days for a prompt, complete, unquestioned refund," as stated in Catalog of Biographical and Professional References of publisher Marquis Who's Who/National Register Publishing.

WORLD DRINKS MARKETING DIRECTORY, $990. Published by Euromonitor (England). Distributed by Gale Group, P.O. Box 9187, Farmington Hills, MI 48333-9187. Toll free US and Canada (800) 877-GALE (4253) and (248) 699-GALE, fax (800) 414-5043 and (248) 699-8061, Internet orders galeord@galegroup.com, web site www.galegroup.com or www.gale.com. All Gale Group products are available on approval. Contact Gale for details.

Biographies

See Who's Who

ABRIDGED BIOGRAPHY AND GENEALOGY MASTER INDEX contains 2.2 million citations from 266 reference works. $432 for 3 volume set. Gale Group, P.O. Box 9187, Farmington Hills, MI 48333-9187. Toll free US and Canada (800) 877-GALE (4253) and (248) 699-GALE, fax (800) 414-5043 and (248) 699-8061, Internet orders galeord@galegroup.com, web site www.galegroup.com or www.gale.com. All Gale Group products are available on approval. Contact Gale for details.

AMERICAN MEN AND WOMEN OF SCIENCE provides detailed biographical information on over 100,000 US and Canadian scientists. This information is very useful for searches in research and development and other areas, because you can review the individual's background, titles, and degrees with dates,before you ever place a phone call. 8 volume set $900. AMERICAN MEN & WOMEN OF SCIENCE (AMWS Online) is also available online on a "pay as you go" basis through The Dialog Corporation, DIALOG file no. 236, Subfile: AMWS, or through LEXIS-NEXIS using NEXIS Library : BUSREF, File Name: AMSCI. Call Bowker for more information including availability of American Men and Women of Science on CD ROM.

R.R. Bowker (a unit of Cahners Business Information), 121 Chanlon Road, New Providence, NJ 07974 USA, Phone (888) BOWKER2 (888-269-5372) & (800) 323-3288, fax (908) 508-7696, email info@bowker.com, web www.bowker.com. Canada—R.R. Bowker, Markham, Ontario, phone (888) BOWKER9 & (905) 415-5837, fax (905) 479-6266. German speaking Europe—K.G. Saur Verlag, Munich, Germany, phone 49-89-76902-232, fax 49-89-76902-250, email 100730.1341@compuserve.com, web www.saur.de/home.htm. Rest of Europe incl. United Kingdom plus Africa & Asia—Bowker-Saur, W. Sussex, UK, phone 44-1342-326-972, fax 44-1342-335-612, email customer@bowker-saur.co.uk, web www.bowker-saur.com/service/. Australia/New Zealand—Thorpe, Port Melbourne, Victoria, Australia, phone 61-03-9-245-7370, fax 61-03-9-245-7395, email customer.service@thorpe.com.au, web www.thorpe.com.au. Technical support for CD ROMs (800) 323-3288, fax 908) 665-3528, email techsupport@bowker.com.

BIO-BASE is a microfiche version of BIOGRAPHY AND GENEALOGY MASTER INDEX. It is updated annually and cumulated from its inception every five years. $285. Gale Group, P.O. Box 9187, Farmington Hills, MI 48333-9187. Toll free US and Canada (800) 877-GALE (4253) and (248) 699-GALE, fax (800) 414-5043 and (248) 699-8061, Internet orders galeord@galegroup.com, web site www.galegroup.com or www.gale.com. All Gale Group products are available on approval. Contact Gale for details.

BIOGRAPHY AND GENEALOGY MASTER INDEX provides citations to biographical articles appearing in 127 editions and volumes of 70 biographical dictionaries and who's whos. Citations indicate when a portrait is included with the biography. $360. Also available online. Gale Group, P.O. Box 9187, Farmington Hills, MI 48333-9187. Toll free US and Canada (800) 877-GALE (4253) and (248) 699-GALE, fax (800) 414-5043 and (248) 699-8061, Internet orders galeord@galegroup.com, web site www.galegroup.com or www.gale.com. All Gale Group products are available on approval. Contact Gale for details.

BIOGRAPHY INDEX is an index to biographical information in periodicals, current books of individual and collective biography, obituaries, including those of national interest in *The New York Times* and biographical passages in nonbiographical books, such as business books. Portraits are noted when they appeared with indexed material. $190/year US and Canada, $220 other countries. For further information contact: H.W.

Wilson Company, 950 University Avenue, Bronx, New York 10452, Phones (800) 367-6770 & (718) 588-8400, Fax (718) 590-1617 & (800) 590-1617, email: ordernow@info.hwwilson.com.

BIOGRAPHY RESOURCE CENTER is a comprehensive online biographical reference database. It contains information on figures from both the past and present in various fields, including business. While it it primarily designed for purchase by libraries, you could also contact the publisher, the Gale Group, P.O. Box 9187, Farmington Hills, MI 48333-9187. Toll free US and Canada (800) 877-GALE (4253) and (248) 699-GALE, fax (800) 414-5043 and (248) 699-8061, Internet orders galeord@galegroup.com, web site www.galegroup.com or www.gale.com. All Gale Group products are available on approval. Contact Gale for details.

BOWKER BIOGRAPHICAL DIRECTORY is comprised of the electronic equivalents of AMERICAN MEN AND WOMEN OF SCIENCE™, WHO'S WHO IN AMERICAN ART™ and WHO'S WHO IN AMERICAN POLITICS™. It is available in electronic database formats from Reed Reference. Entries include past and current career details, publications, education, research interests, languages, personal and family information and more. Available online through Knight-Ridder Information, Inc., (DIALOG file number 236) and on LEXIS™—NEXIS™ (American Men and Women of Science Library: People; busref, file AMSCI). For more information visit Bowker Reed Reference's web site at http://www.reedref.com or contact: Bowker Reed Reference Electronic Publishing, 121 Chanlon Road, New Providence, NJ 07974 USA, Phone (800) 323-3288, Fax (908) 665-3528, email info@bowker.com.

COMPLETE MARQUIS WHO'S WHO ON CD ROM is a compilation of literally all 19 Marquis Who's Who that have appeared in print since 1985, including living and deceased people. WHO'S WHO IN AMERICA®, WHO'S WHO IN THE WORLD®, WHO'S WHO IN AMERICAN EDUCATIONS®, WHO'S WHO IN AMERICAN LAW®, WHO'S WHO IN AMERICAN NURSING®, WHO'S WHO IN MEDICINE AND HEALTHCARE®, WHO'S WHO IN FINANCE AND INDUSTRY®, WHO'S WHO IN SCIENCE AND ENGINEERING®, WHO'S WHO IN THE EAST®, WHO'S WHO IN THE MIDWEST®, WHO'S WHO IN THE SOUTH AND SOUTHWEST®, WHO'S WHO IN THE WEST®, WHO'S WHO OF AMERICAN WOMEN®, WHO'S WHO IN ADVERTISING®, WHO'S WHO OF EMERGING LEADERS IN AMERICA®, WHO'S WHO IN ENTERTAINMENT®, WHO'S WHO AMONG HUMAN SERVICES PROFESSIONALS®. One year subscription with semi-annual updates $995. National Register Publishing, Reed Elsevier-New Providencc, 121 Chanlon Road, New Providence, NJ 07974, (800) 521-8110, fax (800) 836-7736, web site www.marquiswhoswho.com or www.redbooks.com. "If, for any reason whatsoever, your order does not fully meet your expectations, simply return the product within 30 days for a prompt, complete, unquestioned refund," as stated in Catalog of Biographical and Professional References of publisher Marquis Who's Who/National Register Publishing.

CORPORATE GIVING DIRECTORY lists the 1,000 largest corporate foundations and corporate direct giving programs in the USA. It includes listings of the executives in Corporate Affairs, Public Relations and Marketing who manage their companies' giving programs. It also provides biographical data and provides links between the organization's leaders and trustees, donors, officers and directors. $440. Gale Group, P.O. Box 9187, Farmington Hills, MI 48333-9187. Toll free US and Canada (800) 877-GALE (4253) and (248) 699-GALE, fax (800) 414-5043 and (248) 699-8061, Internet orders galeord@galegroup.com, web site www.galegroup.com or www.gale.com. All Gale Group products are available on approval. Contact Gale for details.

CURRENT BIOGRAPHY is a monthly review of biographical articles about names in the news. It's also available on CD ROM. $62/year US and Canada, $72 other countries. Ordering information: Cumulative Book Index, H.W. Wilson Co., 950 University Avenue, Bronx, NY 10452, (800) 367-6770, (718) 588-8400.

CYBERHOUND'S® GUIDE TO PEOPLE ON THE INTERNET is organized into three sections. (1) Who's Who Online identifies 1,000 online directories, databases and membership listings. For example, it lists Architects in Canada, Attorney Finder, Famous Left-Handers, and The Missing Persons Pages. (2) White Pages provides and alphabetical listing of 3,000 business professionals who are accessible by email. Other information includes area of expertise, personal and professional affiliation and company information. (3) Personal Web Sites are organized alphabetically by name. 1,500 pages of people in the news in business, entertainment, and sports. $79. Gale Group, P.O. Box 9187, Farmington Hills, MI 48333-9187. Toll free US and Canada (800) 877-GALE (4253) and (248) 699-GALE, fax (800) 414-5043 and (248) 699-8061, Internet orders galeord@galegroup.com, web site www.galegroup.com or www.gale.com. All Gale Group products are available on approval. Contact Gale for details.

D&B MILLION DOLLAR DATABASE is an online database on the Internet. Users can access information on more than one million small, mid-sized and large companies, with minimum revenues of $1 million. Searches can be conducted by 22 criteria, including as geographic location, sales volume, number of employees, industry classification. Each company includes up to 30 executive names and titles and biographical data that includes education, work history and birth date. For prices call Dun & Bradstreet at (800) 526-0651. For more information contact Dun & Bradstreet, Business Reference Solutions, Three Sylvan Way, Parsippany, New Jersey 07054. Email dnbmdd@mail.dnb.com. Web site http://www.dnbmdd.com.

D&B MILLION DOLLAR DISC is a CD ROM which covers over 240,000 public and private companies, compared to either 160,000 or 50,000 in the two versions of the MILLION DOLLAR DIRECTORY in hard copy. In addition, this CD ROM also contains BIOGRAPHICAL information on key executives. Searches can be conducted by company name, industry, size of company, geography, executive name, key word, and executive business backgrounds. Companies listed have sales of at least $ million or more than 100 employees. Branch locations have more than 500 employees. Both are updated annually. D&B MILLION DOLLAR DISC PLUS is a similar CD ROM with more expansive coverage, including 400,000 companies—both privately held and public—compared to 240,000 in the MILLION DOLLAR DISC. It includes companies with at least 50 employees or revenues of $3 million. For prices call Dun & Bradstreet at (800) 526-0651. For more information contact Dun & Bradstreet, Business Reference Solutions, Three Sylvan Way, Parsippany, New Jersey 07054. Email dnbmdd@mail.dnb.com. Web site http://www.dnbmdd.com.

DIRECTORY OF AMERICAN SCHOLARS contains current biographies of over 30,000 scholars in the humanities. Volume 1, History. Volume 2, English, Speech and Drama. Volume 3, Foreign Languages, Linguistics and Philology. Volume 4, Philosophy, Religion and Law. $450 for 5 Volume set. Individual volumes $135. Gale Group, P.O. Box 9187, Farmington Hills, MI 48333-9187. Toll free US and Canada (800) 877-GALE (4253) and (248) 699-GALE, fax (800) 414-5043 and (248) 699-8061, Internet orders galeord@galegroup.com, web site www.galegroup.com or www.gale.com. All Gale Group products are available on approval. Contact Gale for details.

DIRECTORY OF INTERNATIONAL CORPORATE GIVING IN AMERICA AND ABROAD profiles over 650 companies that give in the U.S. and overseas, including biographical informational on corporate and giving program officers, such as year and place of birth, university, and corporate and nonprofit affiliations. Section I provides information on funding activities of 477 foreign-owned companies in the US. Section II contains information on international funding activities of 195 US headquartered companies. 18 cross referenced indexes. $215. Gale Group, P.O. Box 9187, Farmington Hills, MI 48333-9187. Toll free US and Canada (800) 877-GALE (4253) and (248) 699-GALE, fax (800) 414-5043 and (248) 699-8061, Internet orders galeord@galegroup.com, web site www.galegroup.com or www.gale.com. All Gale Group products are available on approval. Contact Gale for details.

FOUNDATION REPORTER provides information on grants made by the top 1,000 private foundations in the US. It includes biographical data on foundations officers and directors. $400. Gale Group, P.O. Box 9187, Farmington Hills, MI 48333-9187. Toll free US and Canada (800) 877-GALE (4253) and (248) 699-GALE, fax (800) 414-5043 and (248) 699-8061, Internet orders galeord@galegroup.com, web site www.galegroup.com or www.gale.com. All Gale Group products are available on approval. Contact Gale for details.

MD SELECT is an Electronic Canadian Medical Directory endorsed by the Canadian Medical Association. It lists over 50,000 physicians. Information can be searched by these fields: physician name, phone, hospital affiliation, hospital bed size, hospital type, medical specialty, degrees, honors, certified specialty, subspecialty, primary interest, gender, year of graduation, University/Country of graduation, appointments, fellowships, and languages spoken. $495. THE CANADIAN MEDICAL DIRECTORY in hard copy costs $175. Published annually. Special discounts available for combined purchases. Published by Southam Information Products Ltd, 1450 Don Mills Road, Don Mills, Ontario M3B 2X7 CANADA, (800) 668-2374. In Toronto 442-2122. Web site www.southam.com.

NEW CAREER MAKERS by John Sibbald provides profiles on 250 leading individuals in the retained executive search business. $28. Ordering information: Kennedy Information, One Kennedy Place, Route 12

South, Fitzwilliam, NH 03447, phone (800) 531-0007 or 603-585-6544, fax 603-585-9555, email bookstore@kennedyinfo.com, web site www.kennedyinfo.com.

O'DWYER'S DIRECTORY OF PR EXECUTIVES provides biographical data about over 8,000 public relations professionals, including job and educational backgrounds, plus business addresses and phone numbers, cross referenced by employers. This directory encompasses almost all the organizations in O'DWYER'S DIRECTORY OF PR FIRMS AND O'DWYER'S DIRECTORY OF CORPORATE COMMUNICATIONS. $120. J.R O'Dwyer Co., Inc., 271 Madison Avenue, New York, New York 10157-0160. Phone (212) 679-2471. Fax (212) 683-2750.

PROFILES OF AMERICAN LABOR UNIONS, formerly titled American Directory of Organized Labor, outlines nearly 300 national labor unions. It includes information on bargaining agreements and biographies of over 170 past and present union officials, nearly 800 current bargaining agreements and over 500 employers and their addresses. It is indexed by industry, geography and key officials. $285. Gale Group, P.O. Box 9187, Farmington Hills, MI 48333-9187. Toll free US and Canada (800) 877-GALE (4253) and (248) 699-GALE, fax (800) 414-5043 and (248) 699-8061, Internet orders galeord@galegroup.com, web site www.galegroup.com or www.gale.com. All Gale Group products are available on approval. Contact Gale for details.

REFERENCE BOOK OF CORPORATE MANAGEMENTS is a three volume directory which details the professional histories of the principal officers and directors of over 12,000 US companies. Listings include key executives' names and titles, present positions, year of birth, colleges attended, degrees earned and dates, prior positions with other companies, titles and dates, military background and more. Information is presented alphabetically by company and is cross referenced geographically and by industry classification. It also lists principal officers and directors alphabetically, as well as by the colleges they attended and their military affiliations. Updated annually. For prices call Dun & Bradstreet at (800) 526-0651. For more information contact Dun & Bradstreet, Business Reference Solutions, Three Sylvan Way, Parsippany, New Jersey 07054. Email dnbmdd@mail.dnb.com. Web site http://www.dnbmdd.com.

SCITECH REFERENCE PLUS CD ROM contains directory information, 125,000 biographies of US and Canadian scientists and engineers from AMERICAN MEN AND WOMEN OF SCIENCE, listings for over 8,000 laboratories from the DIRECTORY OF AMERICAN RESEARCH AND TECHNOLOGY, and information from THE DIRECTORY OF CORPORATE AFFILIATIONS (including public, private and international companies) of leading US and international technology firms and their subsidiaries. It also contains 60,000 records on science/technology and medical serials from ULRICH'S INTERNATIONAL PERIODICALS DIRECTORY. Searches can be conducted by SIC, year founded, activity, education, employees, institution/company, city, state or country, memberships/honors, product description, personal statistics, personal title, research area, revenue. Updated annually. 1 year subscription $995, 3 years 2,836, excluding discounts. For more information visit Bowker Reed Reference's web site at http://www.reedref.com or contact: Bowker Reed Reference Electronic Publishing, 121 Chanlon Road, New Providence, NJ 07974 USA, Phone (800) 323-3288, Fax (908) 665-3528, email info@bowker.com.

STANDARD AND POORS REGISTER OF CORPORATIONS, DIRECTORS AND EXECUTIVES.
Volume 1, Corporations, contains complete listings for 75,000 companies (including large subsidiaries), specifically names, titles, phone numbers, number of employees, annual sales, main products, and SIC/NAICS codes. Volume 2, Directors and Executives alphabetically lists 70,000 key managers with biographical data. Volume 3, Corporate Family Index is useful for locating a company's parent, subsidiaries, divisions and affiliates; also contains an index of companies by state and major cities. Published annually. Hardback directory, $799. Available in CD ROM. Call for price. Published by Standard & Poors Corporation, New York, New York. Distributed by: Larry Meranus Professional Publications & Services, 4 Demoray Court, Pine Brook, NJ 07058, (800) MERANUS or (800) 637-2687.

WHO'S WEALTHY IN AMERICA provides information on nearly 110,000 of the richest Americans. Information includes address and sometimes phone, plus data on political contributions, real estate holdings, insider stock holdings, education and lifestyle indicators. $460 for 2 volume set. Gale Group, P.O. Box 9187, Farmington Hills, MI 48333-9187. Toll free US and Canada (800) 877-GALE (4253) and (248) 699-GALE, fax (800) 414-5043 and (248) 699-8061, Internet orders galeord@galegroup.com, web site www.galegroup.com or www.gale.com. All Gale Group products are available on approval. Contact Gale for details.

WHO'S WHO IN AMERICA, $525. National Register Publishing, Reed Elsevier-New Providence, 121 Chanlon Road, New Providence, NJ 07974, (800) 521-8110, fax (800) 836-7736, web site www.marquiswhoswho.com or www.redbooks.com. "If, for any reason whatsoever, your order does not fully meet your expectations, simply return the product within 30 days for a prompt, complete, unquestioned refund," as stated in Catalog of Biographical and Professional References of publisher Marquis Who's Who/National Register Publishing.

WHO'S WHO IN THE WORLD, $379.95. National Register Publishing, Reed Elsevier-New Providence, 121 Chanlon Road, New Providence, NJ 07974, (800) 521-8110, fax (800) 836-7736, web site www.marquiswhoswho.com or www.redbooks.com. "If, for any reason whatsoever, your order does not fully meet your expectations, simply return the product within 30 days for a prompt, complete, unquestioned refund," as stated in Catalog of Biographical and Professional References of publisher Marquis Who's Who/National Register Publishing.

10(K) Reports are required, as a matter of law, to provide summary career data, including age, of top management of publicly traded companies. Call the company for a free copy.

Biotechnology

CORPTECH DIRECTORY OF TECHNOLOGY COMPANIES is available in hard copy, Regional Guides, on PC disk, and on CD ROM. CorpTech EXPLORE Database is an outstanding reference that was awarded Best CD-ROM Directory by the National Directory Publishing Association. One click moves you from the CD ROM Database to Internet information on the same company. CorpTech also provides other sophisticated but reasonably priced automated services. You can save a tremendous amount of time researching relatively small, emerging new companies in various high technology niches and obtain names, titles and mailing address labels. CorpTech EXPLORE Database CD ROM $2,450 (including free soft cover CorpTech Directory worth $545). Ordering Information: CorpTech, Corporate Technology Information Services, Inc., 12 Alfred Street, Suite 200, Woburn, MA 01801-1915. (800) 333-8036, (781) 932-3100, (781) 932-3939. Fax (781) 932-6335. Email sales@corptech.com. Web site http://www.corptech.com.

DIRECTORY OF BIOTECHNOLOGY COMPANIES, published by A-Gee Associates, 7770 Regents Road, No. 113-525, San Diego, CA 92122, fax (619) 453-8283.

DIRECTORY OF CALIFORNIA TECHNOLOGY COMPANIES identifies over 33,000 executive names and titles at over 12,000 companies, including research labs, telecommunications, biotechnology and software. Published annually by Database Publishing, PO Box 70024, Anaheim, CA 92825/1590 South Lewis Street, Anaheim, CA 92805. (800) 888-8434, (714) 778-6400, web site www.databasepublishing.com, email sales@databasepublishing.com. Directory $145, complete CD ROM $645, CD ROM one-year lease $425. Also distributed by Manufacturers' News, Inc., (888) 752-5200, 1633 Central Street, Evanston, IL 60201-1569. Email info@manufacturersnews.com. Web site www.manufacturersnews.com.

PHARMACEUTICAL MARKETERS DIRECTORY is a well organized directory that contains many names and titles and other information, including a listing of specialized professional associations. Published annually. $162.50. CPS COMMUNICATIONS, INC., 7200 West Camino Real, Suite 215, Boca Raton, FL 33433, (561) 368-9301, sales office (203) 778-1463, email pmd@cpsnet.com, web site http://www.cpsnet.com.

www.bio.com is the URL for Bio Online. Most positions are for research chemists, biochemists and in clinical development and are usually in the $40,000 to $75,000 range. Developed by Vitadata Corp, Berkeley, California, the site went online in 1993.

Board of Directors

CORPORATE GIVING DIRECTORY lists the 1,000 largest corporate foundations and corporate direct giving programs in the USA. It includes listings of the executives in Corporate Affairs, Public Relations and Marketing who manage their companies' giving programs. It also provides biographical data and provides links between the organization's leaders and trustees, donors, officers and directors. $440. Gale Group, P.O. Box 9187, Farmington Hills, MI 48333-9187. Toll free US and Canada (800) 877-GALE (4253) and (248) 699-GALE, fax (800) 414-5043 and (248) 699-8061, Internet orders galeord@galegroup.com, web site www.galegroup.com or www.gale.com. All Gale Group products are available on approval. Contact Gale for details.

PROXY STATEMENTS must be filed with the Securities and Exchange Commission every year by all publicly held companies. Proxy statements are most useful for obtaining compensation information about senior management, specifically the four highest paid executives. Proxy statements also contain background information and sometimes photos of a company's directors. If you are calling to request a proxy, you might want to also get an annual report and a 10(k), because they're all free. Just call the company switchboard and say you'd like to request a copy of an annual report, a 10(k) and a proxy.

Boston

See New England Category

Brands

ADVERTISER AND AGENCY RED BOOKS PLUS CD ROM combines all the information in THE STANDARD DIRECTORY OF ADVERTISERS, THE STANDARD DIRECTORY OF ADVERTISING AGENCIES and THE STANDARD DIRECTORY OF INTERNATIONAL ADVERTISERS AND AGENCIES. Information is searchable by 25 fields, including company name, personal name, job title/function, product type, product/account name, city, state, zip or country, area code, revenues, number of employees, outside ad agency and even type of computer hardware. Contains professional association information. Available for Windows and Macintosh. Updated quarterly. 1 year subscription $1,295. If the price is prohibitively high, remember your local library. National Register Publishing, Reed Elsevier-New Providence, 121 Chanlon Road, New Providence, NJ 07974, (800) 521-8110, fax (800) 836-7736, web site www.redbooks.com or www.marquiswhoswho.com. "If, for any reason whatsoever, your order does not fully meet your expectations, simply return the product within 30 days for a prompt, complete, unquestioned refund," as stated in Catalog of Biographical and Professional References of publisher Marquis Who's Who/National Register Publishing.

BRANDS AND THEIR COMPANIES lists brands alphabetically with company names and addresses included in the yellow pages section. $805 for 3 volumes. Database also available via commercial online service. Gale Group, P.O. Box 9187, Farmington Hills, MI 48333-9187. Toll free US and Canada (800) 877-GALE (4253) and (248) 699-GALE, fax (800) 414-5043 and (248) 699-8061, Internet orders galeord@galegroup.com, web site www.galegroup.com or www.gale.com. All Gale Group products are available on approval. Contact Gale for details.

COMPANIES AND THEIR BRANDS is a rearrangement of Brands and Their Companies, alphabetically sorted by manufacturers, distributors and importers. Each company's brands, trademarks and trade names are included. $530 for 2 volume set. Gale Group, P.O. Box 9187, Farmington Hills, MI 48333-9187. Toll free US and Canada (800) 877-GALE (4253) and (248) 699-GALE, fax (800) 414-5043 and (248) 699-8061, Internet orders galeord@galegroup.com, web site www.galegroup.com or www.gale.com. All Gale Group products are available on approval. Contact Gale for details.

CORPORATE AFFILIATIONS PLUS CD ROM consolidates information in all five volumes of THE DIRECTORY OF CORPORATE AFFILIATIONS, including publicly held and privately held companies in the US and internationally, and AMERICA'S CORPORATE FINANCE DIRECTORY. This CD provides "family tree" overviews for each company with the reporting structure. It also contains information on 15,000 parent companies in the US and abroad, records on over 100,000 subsidiaries, divisions, plants and joint ventures, names and titles of over 250,000 employees, revenue figures and more. Information can be searched by 29 criteria, such as location, SIC or NAICS codes, sales, number of employees, net worth, pension assets and more. Updated quarterly. 1 year subscription $1,995, available for both Windows and Macintosh. If the price is prohibitively high, remember your local library. National Register Publishing, Reed Elsevier-New Providence, 121 Chanlon Road, New Providence, NJ 07974, (800) 521-8110, fax (800) 836-7736, web site www.redbooks.com or www.marquiswhoswho.com. "If, for any reason whatsoever, your order does not fully meet your expectations, simply return the product within 30 days for a prompt, complete, unquestioned refund," as stated in Catalog of Biographical and Professional References of publisher Marquis Who's Who/National Register Publishing.

DIRECTORY OF CONSUMER BRANDS AND THEIR OWNERS provides information on 50,000 brands in 56 countries and detailed information about the companies that own and manage them. Asia Pacific edition $990. Latin America edition $990. Eastern Europe edition $990. Europe edition $1,190 for 2 volumes. Published by Euromonitor (England). Distributed by Gale Group, P.O. Box 9187, Farmington Hills, MI 48333-9187. Toll free US and Canada (800) 877-GALE (4253) and (248) 699-GALE, fax (800) 414-5043 and (248) 699-8061, Internet orders galeord@galegroup.com, web site www.galegroup.com or www.gale.com. All Gale Group products are available on approval. Contact Gale for details.

DIRECTORY OF CORPORATE AFFILIATIONS OR WHO OWNS WHOM is a superb directory which can help you decipher the organizational structure of a company. This directory provides detailed information about all parent companies, subsidiaries and divisions, plus plant locations, joint ventures, a brief description of the subsidiary or division, a partial listing of names and titles, location, phone number, and sometimes revenues or number of employees. THE DIRECTORY OF CORPORATE AFFILIATIONS provides a comprehensive "family tree" listing that lays out the corporate hierarchy to provide a picture of the structure of companies, subsidiaries, affiliates & divisions. It includes companies with revenues of at least $10 million and reveals division and subsidiary reporting relationships down to the sixth level. It provides information on 8,500 privately held companies. For US companies it details complex multinational relationships and joint ventures. For additional names and titles of key executives in subsidiaries & divisions, refer to another directory such as STANDARD & POORS, THE STANDARD DIRECTORY OF ADVERTISERS, or a specialized industry directory. THE DIRECTORY OF CORPORATE AFFILIATIONS consists of 5 volumes, including US Public Companies, US Private Companies, International Companies (both public and private), and indices. It also contains a Brand Name Index. The CD ROM version of this directory is titled Corporate Affiliations Plus.

*Note: If THE DIRECTORY OF CORPORATE AFFILIATIONS does not provide all the organization structure information you want and the company is publicly held, there's an abundance of **free** information available! Check the company's web site or call them for an annual report and 10(k). Even if the company is privately held, they will usually send information if you ask for it. The more specific your request, the more likely you are to get what you need, for example, a list of all company locations, a list of plant locations, or product information.*

Ordering information: $1,029.95/5 volumes, excluding discounts. If the price is prohibitively high, remember your local library. National Register Publishing, Reed Elsevier-New Providence, 121 Chanlon Road, New Providence, NJ 07974, (800) 521-8110, fax (800) 836-7736, web site www.redbooks.com or www.marquiswhoswho.com. "If, for any reason whatsoever, your order does not fully meet your expectations, simply return the product within 30 days for a prompt, complete, unquestioned refund," as stated in Catalog of Biographical and Professional References of publisher Marquis Who's Who/National Register Publishing.

GALE BUSINESS RESOURCES ONLINE provides modules on US Industry (over 200,000 companies) and International Industry (over 200,000 companies), including public and privately held companies, brands, business rankings, trade and professional associations, company histories, merger information, and more. Comprehensive records include company name, officers' names and titles, SIC/NAICS codes and more. GALE BUSINESS RESOURCES is available online on the Internet through GaleNet.

For information on pricing, contact: Gale Group, P.O. Box 9187, Farmington Hills, MI 48333-9187. Toll free US and Canada (800) 877-GALE (4253) and (248) 699-GALE, fax (800) 414-5043 and (248) 699-8061, Internet orders galeord@galegroup.com, web site www.galegroup.com or www.gale.com. All Gale Group products are available on approval. Contact Gale for details.

STANDARD DIRECTORY OF ADVERTISERS Business Classifications Edition is an excellent general directory that organizes companies by a wide range of product categories. A few examples include "Apparel 2—Men's and Boys' Wear," "Heating and Air Conditioning," "Cosmetics and Toiletries," and "Aviation and Aerospace." This directory lists names and titles of key officers, revenues and other information. It is available in a geographic edition for the same price. This directory is comprised of over 24,000 companies that annually spend over $200,000 on advertising. It represents a reasonable place to look for hard-to-find information about privately held companies, especially those that heavily advertise their products. It is a good place to look for names if STANDARD AND POORS and the MILLION DOLLAR DIRECTORY fail to yield the names you need. Finally, the Classified Edition of THE STANDARD DIRECTORY OF ADVERTISERS can be a very convenient source of research because both your target list of companies and the corresponding names and titles of management all appear together, in the same Classification. This is important if you still rely on research books in hard copy. THE STANDARD DIRECTORY OF ADVERTISERS also publishes a special volume called THE STANDARD DIRECTORY OF ADVERTISERS TRADENAME INDEX. You can use the TRADENAME INDEX if you know the brand name of a product and need to find the company that manufactures it. In addition, this directory contains an Associations section which identifies marketing oriented associations.

$599 hard copy. If the price is prohibitively high, remember your local library. THE STANDARD DIRECTORY OF ADVERTISERS is also available on CD ROM under the title ADVERTISER AND AGENCY RED BOOKS PLUS. It is available in Windows® and Macintosh® formats. National Register Publishing, Reed Elsevier-New Providence, 121 Chanlon Road, New Providence, NJ 07974, (800) 521-8110, fax (800) 836-7736, web site www.redbooks.com or www.marquiswhoswho.com. "If, for any reason whatsoever, your order does not fully meet your expectations, simply return the product within 30 days for a prompt, complete, unquestioned refund," as stated in Catalog of Biographical and Professional References of publisher Marquis Who's Who/National Register Publishing.

WORLD DIRECTORY OF BUSINESS INFORMATION WEB SITES provides full details on over 1,500 free business web sites, including information such as online surveys, top company rankings, company information, brand information, market research reports and trade association statistics. $590. Published by Euromonitor (England). Distributed by Gale Group, P.O. Box 9187, Farmington Hills, MI 48333-9187. Toll free US and Canada (800) 877-GALE (4253) and (248) 699-GALE, fax (800) 414-5043 and (248) 699-8061, Internet orders galeord@galegroup.com, web site www.galegroup.com or www.gale.com. All Gale Group products are available on approval. Contact Gale for details.

www.kompass.com is the web site for the highly respected Kompass country directories and databases. This web site contains a searchable database that encompasses over 60 countries, 2.5 million executive names, information on 1.5 million companies, 19 million key product references, and 370,000 trade and brand names. At the time of this writing, Kompass is available in English and French. Deutsch, Espanol and Italiano will soon be available.

Brazil

See International, South America, Latin America

DIRECTORY OF AMERICAN FIRMS OPERATING IN FOREIGN COUNTRIES, REGIONAL EDITION—BRAZIL. $39. Uniworld Business Publications, Inc., 257 Central Park West, Suite 10A, New York, NY 10024-4110, (212) 496-2448, fax (212) 769-0413, email uniworldbp@aol.com. Web site: http://www.uniworldbp.com.

DIRECTORY OF AMERICAN FIRMS OPERATING IN FOREIGN COUNTRIES, REGIONAL EDITION—ARGENTINA, BRAZIL, CHILE. $59. Uniworld Business Publications, Inc., 257 Central Park West, Suite 10A, New York, NY 10024-4110, (212) 496-2448, fax (212) 769-0413, email uniworldbp@aol.com. Web site: http://www.uniworldbp.com.

Bulletin Boards

See Internet Category

CYBERHOUND'S® GUIDE TO INTERNET DISCUSSION GROUPS contains over 4,000 Internet listservs and news groups and a subject and master index, such as computer know-how groups, such as the virus Computer Newsgroup (comp.virus), health information groups, and social interaction groups. $79. Gale Group, P.O. Box 9187, Farmington Hills, MI 48333-9187. Toll free US and Canada (800) 877-GALE (4253) and (248) 699-GALE, fax (800) 414-5043 and (248) 699-8061, Internet orders galeord@galegroup.com, web site www.galegroup.com or www.gale.com. All Gale Group products are available on approval. Contact Gale for details.

ENCYCLOPEDIA OF ASSOCIATIONS: INTERNATIONAL ORGANIZATIONS includes nearly 20,000 multinational and national organizations in foreign countries, including US based associations with multinational membership. Entries also include email addresses, web sites and bulletin board addresses, lobbying activities, and publication and convention information. Indexed by geography, keyword and executives. $595 for 2 volume set. Also available in CD ROM. Database available via commercial online service. Gale Group, P.O. Box 9187, Farmington Hills, MI 48333-9187. Toll free US and Canada (800) 877-GALE (4253) and (248) 699-GALE, fax (800) 414-5043 and (248) 699-8061, Internet orders galeord@galegroup.com, web site www.galegroup.com or www.gale.com. All Gale Group products are available on approval. Contact Gale for details.

INTERNET RECRUITING EDGE by Barbara Ling is a comprehensive collection of research assembled over a two year period. Developed for the novice and experienced Internet recruiter alike, and with a foreword by Tony Byrne, topics include: Where, Oh Where, is my Candidate Now?, Does the Internet Really Benefit Businesses? Phones Still Work, But Don't Buy a Mansion if You Only Need a Cottage, How to Find Candidates on the Internet, Non-Traditional Resources, Before You Begin—A Primer on Internet Culture—Netiquette, Beginner Candidate Location Skill, Resume Banks, Search Engine Basics, The Joy of Bookmarks, The Art of Job Posting, Sleuthing for Company Directories, Finding Employee Directories, Finding Executive Biographies, Alumni Organizations, Forums and Bulletin Boards, Internet Classifieds, Online E-zines (magazines), Professional Organizations, Colleges, Metasearch at Highway 61, Realistic Goals Before You Begin Your Own Recruiter Web site, Perilous Pitfalls, How To Buy Your Recruiter Business Site, Locating Good Web Site Designers, Your Site is Designed—Now What? How To Market A Recruiter Web Site, 14 Killer Web Site Search Engine Visibility Tips, and more. $149. Order by visiting the web site http://www.barbaraling.com or call (732) 563-1464.

www.airsdirectory.com is the URL for AIRS—Advanced Internet Recruitment Strategies. AIRS is a firm which provides training for recruiters who use the Internet as a recruiting tool. For more information contact AIRS, 1790 Franklin Street, Berkeley, CA 94702, phone (800) 336-6360, fax (888) 997-5559. Their web site contains many excellent free helpful resources.

Business Planning

See Planning

C

Cable

See Television

ADVERTISER AND AGENCY RED BOOKS PLUS CD ROM combines all the information in THE STANDARD DIRECTORY OF ADVERTISERS, THE STANDARD DIRECTORY OF ADVERTISING AGENCIES and the STANDARD DIRECTORY OF INTERNATIONAL ADVERTISERS AND AGENCIES. Information is searchable by 25 fields, including company name, personal name, job title/function, product type, product/account name, city, state, zip or country, area code, revenues, number of employees, outside ad agency and even type of computer hardware. Contains professional association information. Available for Windows and Macintosh. Updated quarterly. 1 year subscription $1,295. If the price is prohibitively high, remember your local library. National Register Publishing, Reed Elsevier-New Providence, 121 Chanlon Road, New Providence, NJ 07974, (800) 521-8110, fax (800) 836-7736, web site www.redbooks.com or www.marquiswhoswho.com. "If, for any reason whatsoever, your order does not fully meet your expectations, simply return the product within 30 days for a prompt, complete, unquestioned refund," as stated in Catalog of Biographical and Professional References of publisher Marquis Who's Who/National Register Publishing.

BACON'S RADIO/TV/CABLE DIRECTORY is a two volume set that identifies all US national and regional networks, all US broadcast stations, management and news executives, radio and TV syndicators, including programming staff, detailed show listings, over 100,000 names of contacts, an index of show subjects and more. $275. Ordering information: Call (800) 621-0561, (800) 753-6675. Bacon's Information, Inc., a K-III Communications Company, 332 South Michigan Avenue, Chicago, IL 60604. Satisfaction guaranteed or a full refund within 30 days.

BROADCASTING AND CABLE YEARBOOK contains information on radio, TV and cable including information about trade associations, trade shows, broadcasting education, awards, industry related books, magazines, videos and more. Also includes information of direct broadcast satellites, Multichannel Multipoint Distribution Services (MMDS), wireless cable companies and more. $179.95. R.R. Bowker (a unit of Cahners Business Information), 121 Chanlon Road, New Providence, NJ 07974 USA, Phone (888) BOWKER2 (888-269-5372) & (800) 323-3288, fax (908) 508-7696, email info@bowker.com, web www.bowker.com. Canada—R.R. Bowker, Markham, Ontario, phone (888) BOWKER9 & (905) 415-5837, fax (905) 479-6266. German speaking Europe—K.G. Saur Verlag, Munich, Germany, phone 49-89-76902-232, fax 49-89-76902-250, email 100730.1341@compuserve.com, web www.saur.de/home.htm. Rest of Europe incl. United Kingdom plus Africa & Asia—Bowker-Saur, W. Sussex, UK, phone 44-1342-326-972, fax 44-1342-335-612, email customer@bowker-saur.co.uk, web www.bowker-saur.com/service/. Australia/New Zealand—Thorpe, Port Melbourne, Victoria, Australia, phone 61-03-9-245-7370, fax 61-03-9-245-7395, email customer.service@thorpe.com.au, web www.thorpe.com.au. Technical support for CD ROMs (800) 323-3288, fax 908) 665-3528, email techsupport@bowker.com.

CABLE BLUE BOOK, Phillips Business Information, Inc., a Phillips Publishing International Company, 120 Seven Locks Road, Potomac, MD 20854, (301) 340-1520, (301) 340-7788, (800) 777-5006, Internet pbi@phillips.com, web site www.phillips.com.

CABLE EUROPE, Phillips Business Information, Inc., a Phillips Publishing International Company, 120 Seven Locks Road, Potomac, MD 20854, (301) 340-1520, (301) 340-7788, (800) 777-5006, Internet pbi@phillips.com, web site www.phillips.com.

CABLE INDUSTRY DIRECTORY, Phillips Business Information, Inc., a Phillips Publishing International Company, 120 Seven Locks Road, Potomac, MD 20854, (301) 340-1520, (301) 340-7788, (800) 777-5006, Internet pbi@phillips.com, web site www.phillips.com.

CABLE TV & TELECOM YEARBOOK (UK), Phillips Business Information, Inc., a Phillips Publishing International Company, 120 Seven Locks Road, Potomac, MD 20854, (301) 340-1520, (301) 340-7788, (800) 777-5006, Internet pbi@phillips.com, web site www.phillips.com.

GALE DIRECTORY OF PUBLICATIONS AND BROADCAST MEDIA identifies key personnel, feature editors and more at radio and TV stations and cable companies. $615 for 5 volume set. Gale Group, P.O. Box 9187, Farmington Hills, MI 48333-9187. Toll free US and Canada (800) 877-GALE (4253) and (248) 699-GALE, fax (800) 414-5043 and (248) 699-8061, Internet orders galeord@galegroup.com, web site www.galegroup.com or www.gale.com. All Gale Group products are available on approval. Contact Gale for details.

GALE DIRECTORY OF PUBLICATIONS AND BROADCAST MEDIA ONLINE is a GaleNet resource on the Internet that includes information on 64,000 newspapers, periodicals, newsletters, industry directories, television and radio stations, including names of key personnel. Contact the library to access this reference free. For pricing and ordering information, contact: Gale Group, P.O. Box 9187, Farmington Hills, MI 48333-9187. Toll free US and Canada (800) 877-GALE (4253) and (248) 699-GALE, fax (800) 414-5043 and (248) 699-8061, Internet orders galeord@galegroup.com, web site www.galegroup.com or www.gale.com. All Gale Group products are available on approval. Contact Gale for details.

PHILLIPS BUSINESS INFORMATION provides information in newsletters, magazines, directories and on multiple web sites covering a range of topics, such as magazine products, telecommunications and cable products, satellite products, media, new media and Internet products, marketing and public relations products, financial technology and electronic commerce, aviation and defense products. For more information, contact: Phillips Business Information, Inc., a Phillips Publishing International Company, 120 Seven Locks Road, Potomac, MD 20854, (301) 340-1520, (301) 340-7788, (800) 777-5006, Internet pbi@phillips.com, web site www.phillips.com.

STANDARD DIRECTORY OF ADVERTISERS Business Classifications Edition is an excellent general directory that organizes companies by a wide range of product categories. A few examples include "Apparel 2—Men's and Boys' Wear," "Heating and Air Conditioning," "Cosmetics and Toiletries," and "Aviation and

Aerospace." This directory lists names and titles of key officers, revenues and other information. It is available in a geographic edition for the same price. This directory is comprised of over 24,000 companies that annually spend over $200,000 on advertising. It represents a reasonable place to look for hard-to-find information about privately held companies, especially those that heavily advertise their products. It is a good place to look for names if STANDARD AND POORS and the MILLION DOLLAR DIRECTORY fail to yield the names you need. Finally, the Classified Edition of THE STANDARD DIRECTORY OF ADVERTISERS can be a very convenient source of research because both your target list of companies and the corresponding names and titles of management all appear together, in the same Classification. This is important if you still rely on research books in hard copy. THE STANDARD DIRECTORY OF ADVERTISERS also publishes a special volume called THE STANDARD DIRECTORY OF ADVERTISERS TRADENAME INDEX. You can use the TRADENAME INDEX if you know the brand name of a product and need to find the company that manufactures it. In addition, this directory contains an Associations section which identifies marketing oriented associations.

$599 hard copy. If the price is prohibitively high, remember your local library. THE STANDARD DIRECTORY OF ADVERTISERS is also available on CD ROM under the title ADVERTISER AND AGENCY RED BOOKS PLUS. It is available in Windows® and Macintosh® formats. National Register Publishing, Reed Elsevier-New Providence, 121 Chanlon Road, New Providence, NJ 07974, (800) 521-8110, fax (800) 836-7736, web site www.redbooks.com or www.marquiswhoswho.com. "If, for any reason whatsoever, your order does not fully meet your expectations, simply return the product within 30 days for a prompt, complete, unquestioned refund," as stated in Catalog of Biographical and Professional References of publisher Marquis Who's Who/National Register Publishing.

STANDARD RATE AND DATA PUBLICATIONS includes "Radio Advertising Source" and "Television and Cable Source" and direct marketing information. $354 annual subscription. Standard Rate and Data Service, Inc., 3004 Glenview Road, Wilmette, IL 60091, (708) 441-2210 in Illinois, (800) 323-4601.

TELEVISION INTERNATIONAL is a magazine for cable TV, radio, satellite and interactive multimedia industries around the world. Call publisher for price. Cahners Business Information, 245 West 17th Street, New York, NY 10011-5300, (212) 337-6944, fax (212) 337-6948, email jonnypim@pacific.net.sg and rschatz@cahners.com, URL www.cahners.com/mainmag/bci.htm. Headquarters: Cahners Business Information, 275 Washington Street, Newton, MA 02158-1630, (617) 558-4663 or (617) 964-3030, fax (617) 558-4700, email marketaccess@cahners.com. Web sites www.cahners.com or www.chilton.net.

WHO'S WHO IN CABLE & SATELLITE EUROPE, Phillips Business Information, Inc., a Phillips Publishing International Company, 120 Seven Locks Road, Potomac, MD 20854, (301) 340-1520, (301) 340-7788, (800) 777-5006, Internet pbi@phillips.com, web site www.phillips.com.

WHO'S WHO IN CABLE & SATELLITE (UK), Phillips Business Information, Inc., a Phillips Publishing International Company, 120 Seven Locks Road, Potomac, MD 20854, (301) 340-1520, (301) 340-7788, (800) 777-5006, Internet pbi@phillips.com, web site www.phillips.com.

California

BACON'S CALIFORNIA MEDIA DIRECTORY presents more in-depth coverage than their main directories, including statewide print and broadcast coverage of daily and community newspapers, state bureaus of US dailies, regional business and general interest magazines, broadcast networks, stations, syndicators and programming, detailed editorial staff listings at all outlets, freelance journalists, including "editorial pitching profiles," phone, fax, email and home page. $195. Ordering information: Call (800) 621-0561, (800) 753-6675. Bacon's Information, Inc., a K-III Communications Company, 332 South Michigan Avenue, Chicago, IL 60604. Satisfaction guaranteed or a full refund within 30 days.

CALIFORNIA INTERNATIONAL TRADE REGISTER identifies 24,000 contacts at over 7,000 companies engaged in import/export, manufacturing, wholesaling, freight forwarding, custom brokerage and trading companies. Published annually by Database Publishing. Directory $129. Complete CD ROM $545, CD ROM one year lease $365. Distributed by Manufacturers' News, Inc., (888) 752-5200, 1633 Central Street, Evanston, IL 60201-1569. Email info@manufacturersnews.com. Web site www.manufacturersnews.com.

CALIFORNIA PINPOINT DATABASES ON CD ROM *use the same information as the* **CALIFORNIA MANUFACTURERS AND CALIFORNIA WHOLESALERS AND SERVICE COMPANIES REGISTERS.** It averages from 2 to slightly over 3 executive names per company, depending on the database. Data includes company name, phone, fax, toll free numbers, web sites, email addresses, sales, plant size, products manufactured, up to 6 SIC or NAICS codes, up to 10 executive names, public or private status.

NORTHERN CALIFORNIA BUSINESS DATABASE, $595
SOUTHERN CALIFORNIA BUSINESS DATABASE, $595
CALIFORNIA MANUFACTURERS DATABASE, $595
CALIFORNIA MANUFACTURERS, 20+ EMPLOYEES, $429
CALIFORNIA WHOLESALERS AND SERVICE COMPANIES, $595
CALIFORNIA TOP COMPANIES, 100+ EMPLOYEES, $429
CALIFORNIA BUSINESS DATABASE, $995
CALIFORNIA TECHNOLOGY COMPANIES DATABASE, $425
CALIFORNIA EXPORTERS AND IMPORTERS, $365
CALIFORNIA AGRICULTURAL EXPORTERS, $195
ALAMEDA COUNTY DATABASE, $215
CONTRA COSTA COUNTY DATABASE, $215
LOS ANGELES COUNTY DATABASE, $429
ORANGE COUNTY DATABASE, $235
SAN DIEGO COUNTY DATABASE, $215
SAN FRANCISCO COUNTY DATABASE, $215
SAN MATEO COUNTY DATABASE, $215
SANTA CLARA COUNTY DATABASE, $215

For more information and a catalog, contact Database Publishing Company, PO Box 70024, Anaheim, CA 92825, (800) 888-8434, (714) 778-6400, email sales@databasepublishing.com.

DIRECTORY OF CALIFORNIA TECHNOLOGY COMPANIES identifies over 33,000 executive names and titles at over 12,000 companies, including research labs, telecommunications, biotechnology and software. Published annually by Database Publishing, PO Box 70024, Anaheim, CA 92825/1590 South Lewis Street, Anaheim, CA 92805. (800) 888-8434, (714) 778-6400, web site www.databasepublishing.com, email sales@databasepublishing.com. Directory $145, complete CD ROM $645, CD ROM one-year lease $425. Also distributed by Manufacturers' News, Inc., (888) 752-5200, 1633 Central Street, Evanston, IL 60201-1569. Email info@manufacturersnews.com. Web site www.manufacturersnews.com.

DIRECTORY OF CALIFORNIA WHOLESALERS AND SERVICE COMPANIES identifies over 85,000 names and titles of executives at some 34,000 non-manufacturing firms, such as wholesalers, transportation, telecommunications, video production and software, including web sites and email addresses. Annual directory published by Database Publishing, $169. Complete CD ROM $925, One year CD ROM lease, $595. Distributed by Manufacturers' News, Inc., (888) 752-5200, 1633 Central Street, Evanston, IL 60201-1569. Email info@manufacturersnews.com. Web site www.manufacturersnews.com.

NORTHERN CALIFORNIA BUSINESS DIRECTORY & BUYERS GUIDE identifies over 57,000 names and titles of executives at some 24,000 manufacturing and service companies in 45 counties. Published annually be Database Publishing. Directory $169, CD ROM complete $925, CD ROM with 50 or more employees $395, CD ROM one-year lease $595. Distributed by Manufacturers' News, Inc., (888) 752-5200, 1633 Central Street, Evanston, IL 60201-1569. Email info@manufacturersnews.com. Web site www.manufacturersnews.com.

PARKER DIRECTORY ON CD ROM identifies addresses, phone and fax numbers for over 85,000 practicing attorneys in California, including descriptions of over 7,000 firms, plus information on judicial districts, judges and other court personnel. Searches can be conducted for attorneys, legal services, suppliers and consultants, such as court reporters and process servers. Available for Windows and Macintosh. One year subscription $99, excluding discounts. Call for information on Windows and Macintosh capability. For more information visit Bowker Reed Reference's web site at http://www.reedref.com or contact: Bowker Reed Reference Electronic Publishing, 121 Chanlon Road, New Providence, NJ 07974 USA, Phone (800) 323-3288, Fax (908) 665-3528, email info@bowker.com.

SOUTHERN CALIFORNIA BUSINESS DIRECTORY & BUYERS GUIDE identifies 78,000 executives by name and title at some 31,000 manufacturing and service companies in 13 counties, including web sites and email addresses. Published annually by Database Publishing. Directory $169, Complete CD ROM $925, CD ROM with 50 or more employees $495, CD ROM one-year lease $595. Distributed by Manufacturers' News, Inc., (888) 752-5200, 1633 Central Street, Evanston, IL 60201-1569. Email info@manufacturersnews.com. Web site www.manufacturersnews.com.

Campus Recruiting

AFRICAN AMERICANS INFORMATION DIRECTORY identifies over 5,200 organizations, publications, institutions, agencies and programs, including a new chapter on scholarships, fellowships and loans. This information on scholarships and fellowships could possibly be used to identify top candidates for college and MBA recruiting. $85. Gale Group, P.O. Box 9187, Farmington Hills, MI 48333-9187. Toll free US and Canada (800) 877-GALE (4253) and (248) 699-GALE, fax (800) 414-5043 and (248) 699-8061, Internet orders galeord@galegroup.com, web site www.galegroup.com or www.gale.com. All Gale Group products are available on approval. Contact Gale for details.

ALUMNI DIRECTORIES. Sometimes school directories (graduate and undergraduate) cross-reference names of people according to company. When the directory is so organized, it can be a useful recruiting tool, for example, if you're looking for an MSEE employed by a certain company. If you want to buy a directory, you will usually need the help of a graduate because most schools will only sell directories to their alumni. If you work for a big company, there's usually a graduate around willing to either lend you a directory, or will help you buy one. Actually, it's usually as simple as getting the graduate's permission to use his or her name to order the directory. Then YOU can order the directory, send a company check with your order, and have the directory mailed to the company, to your office address c/o the graduate. This way the graduate doesn't have to go to any trouble. Historically the alumni directories for the graduate schools of business at Harvard and Wharton have been well organized, from a recruiting research standpoint. To find out if an alumni directory is available in a CD ROM, ask a graduate, or call the alumni office directly.

BLACK AMERICAN COLLEGES AND UNIVERSITIES reviews 118 institutions that were founded primarily for African Americans and/or possess predominantly black enrollments. This reference can be used to identify target schools for campus recruiting purposes. $70. Gale Group, P.O. Box 9187, Farmington Hills, MI 48333-9187. Toll free US and Canada (800) 877-GALE (4253) and (248) 699-GALE, fax (800) 414-5043 and (248) 699-8061, Internet orders galeord@galegroup.com, web site www.galegroup.com or www.gale.com. All Gale Group products are available on approval. Contact Gale for details.

PETERSON'S GRADSEARCH is a GaleNet database that provide access to graduate school and professional programs in over 31,000 graduate academic departments. If your recruiting is driven by highly specific educational credentials, you can use this database to identify the schools that produce the graduates you're looking for. Once your targeted graduate program has been identified, you can then contact the placement office at the school, if you're recruiting new graduates. If you're recruiting for more senior positions, or looking for a job yourself, you can contact the alumni office to locate job seekers with the right credentials. You could also review alumni publications, which often publish announcements about promotions and job changes, which can be valuable ID research and which will also lead you to sources and prospects NOT on the job market.

www.careermosaic.com is the URL for a major recruitment web site that spends millions of dollars in advertising to draw traffic to this site. CareerMosaic features a jobs database; newsgroups for jobs, college connection, online job fairs, employer job postings; company information and more. CareerMosaic was ranked as one of the top 5 "Sites Offering the Best Overall Support for Job Seekers" by the *National Business Employment Weekly*. The site was developed Bernard Hodes Advertising in New York and went online in 1994.

www.careers.wsj.com is the *Wall Street Journal*'s web site. It focuses on positions for middle and senior management including financial positions at $75,000 and up. This web site is among those that encompass senior executive positions. Other features includes Job Seek, Who's Hiring, Career Columnists, Salaries & Profiles, The Salary Calculator™, Job Hunting Advice, Succeeding at Work, HR Issues, Executive Recruiters, Working Globally, College Connection, Starting a Business, Career Bookstore and more. Content from The National Employment Business Weekly is also featured. The site was developed by Dow Jones & Company, Inc., Princeton, New Jersey and was established in 1997.

www.emory.edu/CAREER/index.html is Emory University's Career Paradise web site, with modules for alumni, students and employers. It is an excellent resource that should not be missed.

www.job-hunt.org is an on-line job search resources and services that identifies jobs resources and ranks the outstanding ones. It is linked to Career Paradise of Emory University Career Center (www.emory.edu/CAREER/index.html), featuring a "Colossal List" or Career Links and Hiring Express pages. It's given high marks for both its content and humorous presentation.

www.jobtrak.com is the web site for the Career service network for college students, alumni, college career staff and employers. JOBTRAK was ranked as one of the top 5 "Best Specialty Sites" by the *National Business Employment Weekly.* JOBTRAK has established relationships with college and university career offices, MBA programs and alumni associations. Most salaries range between $30,000 and $50,000. The site developer is JOBTRAK CORPORATION, Los Angeles, CA, (310) 474-3377, (800) 999-8725, fax (310) 475-7912. The site has been online since 1995.

www.monster.com is the URL for the popular Monster Board web site. The Monster Board was ranked as one of the top 5 "Best General-Purpose Sites" by the *National Business Employment Weekly.* It is a major recruitment web site that spends millions of dollars in advertising to attract traffic to this site. Features include Job search in the US, International or by Companies, Career Center Events, Recruiters' Center, Seminars, Post a Job, free online recruitment seminar. It also offers special links for human resources, health care, technology and entry level positions. Toll free phone number (800) MONSTER. The Monster Board, PO Box 586, Framingham, MA 01704-0586. The site developer is TMP Worldwide, New York, New York and has been online since 1994.

Canada

AMERICAN ART DIRECTORY provides information about national and regional art organizations, museums, libraries and associations in the US and Canada, art schools in the US and Canada, plus listings of museums abroad, art schools abroad, state arts councils, state directors and supervisors of art education, art magazines, art editors and critics, scholarships and fellowships, open exhibitions, and traveling exhibition booking agencies, plus a personnel index. $210. If the price is prohibitively high, remember your local library. National Register Publishing, Reed Elsevier-New Providence, 121 Chanlon Road, New Providence, NJ 07974, (800) 521-8110, fax (800) 836-7736, web site www.redbooks.com or www.marquiswhoswho.com. "If, for any reason whatsoever, your order does not fully meet your expectations, simply return the product within 30 days for a prompt, complete, unquestioned refund," as stated in Catalog of Biographical and Professional References of publisher Marquis Who's Who/National Register Publishing.

AMERICAN FINANCIAL DIRECTORY consists of five desktop volumes of banks, bank holding companies, savings and Loan Associations and Major Credit Unions in the US, Canada and Mexico. It includes information on head office and branch offices, names of key decision makers, phone and fax numbers, financial summaries, and structural changes such as mergers, name changes and closings. Published twice a year. For more information contact (800) 321-3373, Thomson Financial Publishing, 4709 West Golf Road, Skokie, IL 60076-1253. Web site @ tfp.bankinfo.com.

AMERICAN LIBRARY DIRECTORY is available in hard copy and electronic database formats. It identifies 36,000 general and specialized libraries in the US, Canada and Mexico. Searches can be conducted by 40 general information search criteria, further refined with 50 more fields related to the specific collections and services.

AMERICAN LIBRARY DIRECTORY ON DISC, one year subscription $423.

AMERICAN LIBRARY DIRECTORY ONLINE can be accessed by contacting Bowker or Knight-Ridder Information, Inc., Mountainview, California, (800) 334-2564 or (800) 3-DIALOG. Refer to DIALOG file number 460.

LIBRARY RESOURCE GUIDE—INTERNET EDITION is a free Internet directory of library services and suppliers which is drawn from Bowker's American Library Directory. Log on at www.bowker.com or call for more information.

R.R. Bowker (a unit of Cahners Business Information), 121 Chanlon Road, New Providence, NJ 07974 USA, Phone (888) BOWKER2 (888-269-5372) & (800) 323-3288, fax (908) 508-7696, email info@bowker.com, web www.bowker.com. Canada—R.R. Bowker, Markham, Ontario, phone (888) BOWKER9 & (905) 415-5837, fax (905) 479-6266. German speaking Europe—K.G. Saur Verlag, Munich, Germany, phone 49-89-76902-232, fax 49-89-76902-250, email 100730.1341@compuserve.com, web www.saur.de/home.htm. Rest of Europe incl. United Kingdom plus Africa & Asia—Bowker-Saur, W. Sussex, UK, phone 44-1342-326-972, fax 44-1342-335-612, email customer@bowker-saur.co.uk, web www.bowker-saur.com/service/. Australia/New Zealand—Thorpe, Port Melbourne, Victoria, Australia, phone 61-03-9-245-7370, fax 61-03-9-245-7395, email customer.service@thorpe.com.au, web www.thorpe.com.au. Technical support for CD ROMs (800) 323-3288, fax 908) 665-3528, email techsupport@bowker.com.

AMERICAN MEN AND WOMEN OF SCIENCE provides detailed biographical information on over 100,000 US and Canadian scientists. This information is very useful for searches in research and development and other areas, because you can review the individual's background, titles, and degrees with dates, before you ever place a phone call. 8 volume set $900. AMERICAN MEN & WOMEN OF SCIENCE (AMWS Online) is also available online on a "pay as you go" basis through The Dialog Corporation, DIALOG file no. 236, Subfile: AMWS, or through LEXIS-NEXIS using NEXIS Library: BUSREF, File Name: AMSCI. Call Bowker for more information including availability of American Men and Women of Science on CD ROM.

R.R. Bowker (a unit of Cahners Business Information), 121 Chanlon Road, New Providence, NJ 07974 USA, Phone (888) BOWKER2 (888-269-5372) & (800) 323-3288, fax (908) 508-7696, email info@bowker.com, web www.bowker.com. Canada—R.R. Bowker, Markham, Ontario, phone (888) BOWKER9 & (905) 415-5837, fax (905) 479-6266. German speaking Europe—K.G. Saur Verlag, Munich, Germany, phone 49-89-76902-232, fax 49-89-76902-250, email 100730.1341@compuserve.com, web www.saur.de/home.htm. Rest of Europe incl. United Kingdom plus Africa & Asia—Bowker-Saur, W. Sussex, UK, phone 44-1342-326-972, fax 44-1342-335-612, email customer@bowker-saur.co.uk, web www.bowker-saur.com/service/. Australia/New Zealand—Thorpe, Port Melbourne, Victoria, Australia, phone 61-03-9-245-7370, fax 61-03-9-245-7395, email customer.service@thorpe.com.au, web www.thorpe.com.au. Technical support for CD ROMs (800) 323-3288, fax 908) 665-3528, email techsupport@bowker.com.

ASSOCIATIONS CANADA, previously titled DIRECTORY OF ASSOCIATIONS IN CANADA, provides information on a $1 billion economic sector, including information on conferences, publications, mailing lists and more. $289 Canadian in print, $389 Canadian for CD ROM, and $489 Canadian for both. Published annually by Micromedia Ltd., 20 Victoria Street, Toronto, ON. (800) 387-2689, (416) 362-5211, email info@micromedia.on.ca, web site www.micromedia.on.ca.

AWARDS, HONORS & PRIZES provides an alphabetical listing of the organizations giving the awards. Specifies organization, award and subject indexes and email addresses. $450 for two volume set, $255 per single volume.

    Volume 1, US and Canada, $228
    Volume 2, International and Foreign, $255

Gale Group, P.O. Box 9187, Farmington Hills, MI 48333-9187. Toll free US and Canada (800) 877-GALE (4253) and (248) 699-GALE, fax (800) 414-5043 and (248) 699-8061, Internet orders galeord@galegroup.com, web site www.galegroup.com or www.gale.com. All Gale Group products are available on approval. Contact Gale for details.

BEST'S INSURANCE REPORTS, LIFE/HEALTH CANADA contains information on over 100 life/health companies that are licensed to operate in Canada. $295. To order call (908) 439-2200, ext. 5742, A.M. Best Company, Ambest Road, Oldwick, NJ 08858, fax (908) 439-3296, web site http://www.ambest.com.

BIOGRAPHY INDEX is an index to biographical information in periodicals, current books of individual and collective biography, obituaries, including those of national interest in *The New York Times* and biographical passages in nonbiographical books, such as business books. Portraits are noted when they appeared with indexed material. $190/year US and Canada, $220 other countries. For further information contact: H.W. Wilson Company, 950 University Avenue, Bronx, New York 10452, Phones (800) 367-6770 & (718) 588-8400, Fax (718) 590-1617 & (800) 590-1617, email: ordernow@info.hwwilson.com.

BOOK TRADE IN CANADA/L'INDUSTRIE DU LIVRE AU CANADA is an annual publication. For further information contact: Ampersand Communications, Inc., 5606 Scobie Crescent, Manotick, ON K4M 1B7, CANADA.

BOOKS IN CANADA is a monthly publication which reviews 300-400 new Canadian books each year. It provides an inexpensive way to learn about new resources in Canada. It is available by subscription ($22.98/year) and is sold at newsstands and in bookstores ($3.95 per issue).

Ordering information:

BOOKS IN CANADA
Canadian Review of Books Ltd.
427 Mt. Pleasant Road
Toronto, ON M4S 2L8 CANADA
(416) 489-4755 Phone

BOOKS IN PRINT ON DISC, Canadian Edition, annual subscription $599. R.R. Bowker (a unit of Cahners Business Information), 121 Chanlon Road, New Providence, NJ 07974 USA, Phone (888) BOWKER2 (888-269-5372) & (800) 323-3288, fax (908) 508-7696, email info@bowker.com, web www.bowker.com. Canada—R.R. Bowker, Markham, Ontario, phone (888) BOWKER9 & (905) 415-5837, fax (905) 479-6266. German speaking Europe—K.G. Saur Verlag, Munich, Germany, phone 49-89-76902-232, fax 49-89-76902-250, email 100730.1341@compuserve.com, web www.saur.de/home.htm. Rest of Europe incl. United Kingdom plus Africa & Asia—Bowker-Saur, W. Sussex, UK, phone 44-1342-326-972, fax 44-1342-335-612, email customer@bowker-saur.co.uk, web www.bowker-saur.com/service/. Australia/New Zealand—Thorpe, Port Melbourne, Victoria, Australia, phone 61-03-9-245-7370, fax 61-03-9-245-7395, email customer.service@thorpe.com.au, web www.thorpe.com.au. Technical support for CD ROMs (800) 323-3288, fax 908) 665-3528, email techsupport@bowker.com.

BUSINESS ORGANIZATIONS, AGENCIES AND PUBLICATIONS DIRECTORY contains 32 chapters including information on Canada, business information sources, web sites, and local chambers of commerce. $415. Gale Group, P.O. Box 9187, Farmington Hills, MI 48333-9187. Toll free US and Canada (800) 877-GALE (4253) and (248) 699-GALE, fax (800) 414-5043 and (248) 699-8061, Internet orders galeord@galegroup.com, web site www.galegroup.com or www.gale.com. All Gale Group products are available on approval. Contact Gale for details.

CANADIAN ALMANAC AND DIRECTORY includes abbreviations, associations and societies, broadcasting and communications, business statistics, church and religious organizations, commerce and finance, cultural directory, education directory, electoral districts, foreign and international contacts, geographic information, government directory, government quick reference, health and hospitals, historical and general information, legal and judicial directory, postal information, tourism and transportation. The Almanac also includes web sites of significant institutions in business, communications, and the arts, a "Who's Who" of key officials and organizations on the Canadian information highway and up-to-date provincial and territorial election results. Indexed by titles and keyword. $249 US. Inquire about CD ROM availability. Published by IHS Canada, Micromedia Limited, 20 Victoria Street, Toronto, Ontario M5C 2N8 CANADA, (800) 387-2689, (416) 362-5211, fax (416) 362-6161, email info@micromedia.on.ca. Distributed in the US by the Gale Group, P.O. Box 9187, Farmington Hills, MI 48333-9187. Toll free US and Canada (800) 877-GALE (4253) and (248) 699-GALE, fax (800) 414-5043 and (248) 699-8061, Internet orders galeord@galegroup.com, web site www.galegroup.com or www.gale.com. All Gale Group products are available on approval. Contact Gale for details.

CANADIAN ASSOCIATION FOR INFORMATION SCIENCE, University of Toronto, 140 St. George Street, Toronto, ON M5S 1A1 CANADA, (416) 978-8876.

CANADIAN BUSINESS AND ECONOMICS: A GUIDE TO SOURCES OF INFORMATION lists information by subject, including books, periodicals and services. Fully indexed and thoroughly cross referenced. Price reduced to $39.95 for 1992 edition. Canada Library Association, 200 Elgin Street, Suite 602, Ottawa, Ontario K2P 1L5 CANADA, (613) 232-9625, fax (613) 563-9895, Internet: bj491@freenet.carleton.ca.

CANADIAN BUSINESS MAGAZINE publishes an Annual Top 500.

CANADIAN COMPANY HANDBOOK is published by Micromedia Ltd., 20 Victoria Street, Toronto, ON. For information about pricing, or their demand document center CANCORP, contact (800) 387-2689, (416) 362-5211, email info@micromedia.on.ca, web site www.micromedia.on.ca.

CANADIAN COMPUTER RESELLER is a trade publication which annually produces the RESELLER REFERENCE GUIDE for $50. Published by by Maclean Hunter in Toronto. For more information call them in Toronto at (416) 596-5000. Web site www.mhbizlink.com.

CANADIAN DENTAL DIRECTORY provides alphabetical and geographic listings of certified Canadian dentists in Canada. $119. Special discounts available for combined purchases. Published by Southam Information Products Ltd, 1450 Don Mills Road, Don Mills, Ontario M3B 2X7 CANADA, (800) 668-2374. In Toronto 442-2122. Web site www.southam.com.

CANADIAN DIRECTORY OF SEARCH FIRMS, in French and English, lists over 1,700 search firms and 3,000 recruitment professionals. 70 occupational categories, geographic index, and a Who's Who Index. $39.95, ISBN 0-9681447-1-3. To locate the CANADIAN DIRECTORY OF SEARCH FIRMS, go to www.netjobs.com or ask your favorite bookstore to look it up in BOOKS IN PRINT.

CANADIAN ELECTRONIC COMMERCE DIRECTORY, Phillips Business Information, Inc., a Phillips Publishing International Company, 120 Seven Locks Road, Potomac, MD 20854, (301) 340-1520, (301) 340-7788, (800) 777-5006, Internet pbi@phillips.com, web site www.phillips.com.

CANADA EMPLOYMENT WEEKLY'S URL is www.mediacorp2.com/. It features The Career Bookstore for Canadian Career Books, Talent Available to Market Yourself to Canadian Recruiters and Search Firms, Canadian Directory of Search Firms, and Who's Hiring for a list of Canada's top employers. www.mediacorp2.com/cdsf/index.html leads you directly to the Canadian Directory of Search Firms and the Career Bookstore—"Quality Canadian Career Books" including GET WIRED, YOU'RE HIRED, "the definitive Canadian guide to job hunting in Canada."

CANADIAN ENVIRONMENTAL DIRECTORY identifies government departments, companies and organizations concerned with environmental issues, plus contact names, publications, activities, programs, research laboratories, universities and college environmental programs, conferences and trade shows, lawyers, journalists, book and periodical information, and more. Available in directory or CD ROM formats. For pricing and ordering information, contact: IHS Canada, Micromedia Limited, 20 Victoria Street, Toronto, Ontario M5C 2N8 CANADA, (800) 387-2689, (416) 362-5211, fax (416) 362-6161, email info@micromedia.on.ca.

CANADIAN GROCER is a trade publication which produces CANADIAN GROCER WHO'S WHO. Published by Maclean Hunter in Toronto. For more information call them in Toronto at (416) 596-5000. Web site www.mhbizlink.com.

CANADIAN HEALTH FACILITIES DIRECTORY provides detailed information on Canadian hospitals, nursing homes, health clinics, university medical facilities, medical associations, government departments and more. $175. Special discounts available for combined purchases. Published by Southam Information Products Ltd, 1450 Don Mills Road, Don Mills, Ontario M3B 2X7 CANADA, (800) 668-2374. In Toronto 442-2122. Web site www.southam.com.

CANADIAN LIBRARIES provides information on over 6,000 active Canadian libraries, resources centers, business information centers, professional associations, regional library systems, library schools, library technical programs, and archives. Names, titles, telephone numbers and email addresses of key personnel are included. It is updated annually. $185 directory, $350 stand alone CD ROM. Ordering information: IHS Canada, Micromedia Limited, 20 Victoria Street, Toronto, Ontario M5C 2N8 CANADA, (800) 387-2689, (416) 362-5211, fax (416) 362-6161, email info@micromedia.on.ca.

CANADIAN LIBRARY ASSOCIATION is located at Suite 602, 200 Elgin Street, Ottawa, ON K2P 1L5, (613) 232-9625. Their online catalog can be viewed on their web site, www.cla.amlibs.ca and should indicate when an update will be available for their 1992 edition of CANADIAN BUSINESS AND ECONOMICS, A GUIDE TO SOURCES OF INFORMATION.

CANADIAN MINES HANDBOOK contains information on over 2,300 Canadian mining companies, mines and advanced projects, including key contact names, mine and site addresses, and 60 pages of mining area maps. $62. Special discounts available for combined purchases. For more information on Energy Information Services, call Calgary office (403) 244-6111. Published by Southam Information Products Ltd,

1450 Don Mills Road, Don Mills, Ontario M3B 2X7 CANADA, (800) 668-2374. In Toronto 442-2122. Web site www.southam.com.

CANADIAN MINESCAN is a diskette version of the CANADIAN MINES HANDBOOK. Information is available on over 2,500 Canadian mining companies, mines, advanced projects, smelters, refineries and the DIRECTORY OF KEY INDUSTRY CONTACTS.

Free demo disk available. $156. Special discounts available for combined purchases. For more information on Energy Information Services, call Calgary office (403) 244-6111. Published by Southam Information Products Ltd, 1450 Don Mills Road, Don Mills, Ontario M3B 2X7 CANADA, (800) 668-2374. In Toronto 442-2122. Web site www.southam.com.

CANADIAN MINING JOURNAL is a leading exploration and mining journal in Canada. Published six times a year, it announces executive appointments, provides information on corporate developments, rates Canada's major mining companies, and includes news on mills and metallurgical plants. Annual subscription $34 Canada, $49 US, $34 Foreign. Special discounts available for combined purchases. For more information on Energy Information Services, call Calgary office (403) 244-6111. Published by Southam Information Products Ltd, 1450 Don Mills Road, Don Mills, Ontario M3B 2X7 CANADA, (800) 668-2374. In Toronto 442-2122. Web site www.southam.com.

CANADIAN PERIODICAL INDEX is the standard bilingual resource to over 400 French and English journals, including more than 30 American titles, including 80 business journals. 11 issues per year plus an annual edition. For pricing and ordering information, call Gale Canada at (800) 701-9130.

CANADIAN PHARMACISTS DIRECTORY lists over 18,000 Canadian pharmacists, drug information centers, poison control centres, pharmaceutical suppliers, drug wholesalers, related universities, drug store head offices, pharmaceutical associations, chain drug stores, and brand name/generic pharmaceutical companies. $119 prepaid, $149 plus $5 shipping and handling if billed. Special discounts available for combined purchases. Published by Southam Information Products Ltd, 1450 Don Mills Road, Don Mills, Ontario M3B 2X7 CANADA, (800) 668-2374. In Toronto 442-2122. Web site www.southam.com.

CANADIAN PUBLISHERS DIRECTORY is issued semi-annually and includes information about Canadian book publishers in addition to that found in "Canadian Book Publishers" in volume 1 of LITERARY MARKET PLACE. For further information contact: Quill & Quire, Quill & Quire Magazine, 70 The Esplanade, 4th floor, Toronto, ON M5E 1R2, CANADA.

CANADIAN SOURCEBOOK provides listings of libraries, resource centers, associations, societies, labour unions and media outlets, plus names and addresses of government officials, industry associations, financial institutions and social and cultural societies. $197. Special discounts available for combined purchases. Southam Information Products Ltd, 1450 Don Mills Road, Don Mills, Ontario M3B 2X7 CANADA, (800) 668-2374, (416) 445-6641, (416) 442-2122, web site www.southam.com.

CHAIN STORE GUIDE'S CHAIN RESTAURANT OPERATORS CD-ROM allows you to conduct data searches from five topic screens: 1. Personnel by title, 2. Personnel by functional area, 3. Restaurant type (cafeteria, dinnerhouse, fast food, family restaurant, in-store feeder, table cloth), 4. Menu type (Greek, German, health food, ice cream, etc.) You can also make selections based on geography or the size of a company (number of units and/or sales). Contains information about professional associations. Several output options are available, including mailing labels, and electronic formats (such as DBASE, ASCII, text) for mail merge customization. $995 including companion directory. If the price is prohibitively high, remember your local library. Ordering information: Chain Store Guide Information Services, 3922 Coconut Palm Drive, Tampa, FL 33619. (800) 927-9292, (813) 664-6800, (813) 627-6822, (800) 289-6822. http://www.d-net.com/csgis or http://www.csgis.com.

CHAIN STORE GUIDE'S DATABASE MARKETING DIVISION can customize databases in these industries: Supermarket, department stores, discount department stores, drug stores. Your made-to-order database can include one or several of the named industries and the criteria of your ideal "customer" or search prospect. Information is available on a 3.5" diskette for IBM-PC, Apple Macintosh and DBF, ASCII, comma delimited and others. Mailing labels are also available or you can generate your own labels from a 3.5" diskette. For pricing or ordering information contact Chain Store Guide Information Services, 3922 Coconut

Palm Drive, Tampa, FL 33619. (800) 927-9292, (813) 664-6800, (813) 627-6822, (800) 289-6822. http://www.d-net.com/csgis or http://www.csgis.com.

COMPANIES INTERNATIONAL CD-ROM contains comprehensive financial and contact data for over 300,000 public and privately held companies in 180 countries including the Commonwealth of Independent States, Mexico, Canada and Japan. Companies can be located by company name, product or industry, location, or a combination. This reference can also be used for target lists development for international companies, including privately held companies. $2,995. Gale Group, P.O. Box 9187, Farmington Hills, MI 48333-9187. Toll free US and Canada (800) 877-GALE (4253) and (248) 699-GALE, fax (800) 414-5043 and (248) 699-8061, Internet orders galeord@galegroup.com, web site www.galegroup.com or www.gale.com. All Gale Group products are available on approval. Contact Gale for details.

COMPUTING, HI-TECH AND TELECOMMUNICATIONS CAREER HANDBOOK, published by Canadian publisher Marskell. Web site www.marskell.com.

CURRENT BIOGRAPHY is a monthly review of biographical articles about names in the news. It's also available on CD ROM. $62/year US and Canada, $72 other countries. Ordering information: Cumulative Book Index, H.W. Wilson Co., 950 University Avenue, Bronx, NY 10452, (800) 367-6770, (718) 588-8400.

CYBERHOUND'S® GUIDE TO PEOPLE ON THE INTERNET is organized into three sections. (1) Who's Who Online identifies 1,000 online directories, databases and membership listings. For example, it lists Architects in Canada, Attorney Finder, Famous Left-Handers, and The Missing Persons Pages. (2) White Pages provides and alphabetical listing of 3,000 business professionals who are accessible by email. Other information includes area of expertise, personal and professional affiliation and company information. (3) Personal Web Sites are organized alphabetically by name. 1,500 pages of people in the news in business, entertainment, and sports. $79. Gale Group, P.O. Box 9187, Farmington Hills, MI 48333-9187. Toll free US and Canada (800) 877-GALE (4253) and (248) 699-GALE, fax (800) 414-5043 and (248) 699-8061, Internet orders galeord@galegroup.com, web site www.galegroup.com or www.gale.com. All Gale Group products are available on approval. Contact Gale for details.

D&B CANADIAN KEY BUSINESS DIRECTORY contains information on Canada's top 20,000 companies, both publicly and privately held, with at least $20 million in sales and over 100 employees. Information includes multiple executive names and titles, sales revenue in Canadian dollars, number of employees, address and phone numbers, lines of business, and SIC or NAICS codes. Contains explanations in both English and French. Published annually. For prices call Dun & Bradstreet at (800) 526-0651. For more information contact Dun & Bradstreet, Business Reference Solutions, Three Sylvan Way, Parsippany, NJ 07054. Email dnbmdd@mail.dnb.com. Web site http://www.dnbmdd.com.

DAILY OIL BULLETIN is the leading trade paper for the Canadian oil and gas industry. Includes announcements of staff appointments. $891 annual subscription. Free two week trial subscription is available. Special discounts available for combined purchases. For more information on Energy Information Services, call Calgary office (403) 244-6111. Published by Southam Information Products Ltd, 1450 Don Mills Road, Don Mills, Ontario M3B 2X7 CANADA, (800) 668-2374. In Toronto 442-2122. Web site www.southam.com.

DIALOG® is the oldest and largest online information service, comprised of over 470 databases from an array of disciplines, including business, US and international news, patents and trademarks, science and technology and consumer news. DIALOG SELECT provides a web based guided search service with access to 250 DIALOG databases for people with little or no database search expertise. It is designed to meet the specific information needs of professional end users in the technology, pharmaceutical, legal, consumer product and media industries. DIALOG@SITE is an intranet-based service providing access to the current DIALOG ONDISC™ CD ROM collection, using Internet browser capabilities. Companies will have wide access to an array of fields, such as business, science, technology, medicine and law through their local Intranet. DIALOG is a service mark of the Dialog Corporation and is exclusively distributed in Canada by Infomart Dialog Limited. For subscriptions and rate information for all services in Canada, contact Infomart Dialog Limited at (416) 442-2198 or (800) 668-9215. In the US call Dialog (Knight Ridder Information, Inc.) in Mountain View, California at (800) 3-DIALOG, web site www.dialog.com.

DIRECTORY OF AMERICAN FIRMS OPERATING IN FOREIGN COUNTRIES, REGIONAL EDITION—NORTH AMERICA. $69. Uniworld Business Publications, Inc., 257 Central Park West, Suite

10A, New York, NY 10024-4110, (212) 496-2448, fax (212) 769-0413, email uniworldbp@aol.com. Web site: http://www.uniworldbp.com.

DIRECTORY OF CANADIAN LIBRARY AND INFORMATION SCIENCE CONSULTANTS is a national Canadian directory of library and library related consultants. $29.95. Canada Library Association, 200 Elgin Street, Suite 602, Ottawa, Ontario K2P 1L5 CANADA, (613) 232-9625, fax (613) 563-9895, Internet: bj491@freenet.carleton.ca.

DIRECTORY OF CHAIN RESTAURANT OPERATORS describes 3-or-more unit chain restaurant companies in the U.S. and Canada operating or franchising restaurants, cafeterias, contract and industrial feeders. Hotel/motel companies controlling three or more restaurants within hotels and 3 or more foodservice operations are profiled, as well as food units in drug chains, general merchandise chains and discount stores. Key personnel, a listing of major trade associations and a trade show calendar are also included. An index to the top 100 restaurants is also included and is a valuable tool for target list development. An industry profile as provided by the National Restaurant Association is also included. Updated annually. $290. Chain Store Guide Information Services, 3922 Coconut Palm Drive, Tampa, FL 33619. (800) 927-9292, (813) 664-6800, (813) 627-6822, (800) 289-6822. http://www.d-net.com/csgis or http://www.csgis.com.

DIRECTORY OF DRUG STORE AND HBC CHAINS identifies over 1,800 drug retailers in the U.S. and Canada operating over 45,000 stores including drug, HBC, cosmetic, deep discount, home health care, discount, and grocery stores/supermarket chains with pharmacies, mass merchants with pharmacies, deep discount chains, and wholesale drug companies. It includes names and titles of key personnel, a listing of major trade associations and a trade show calendar. It also provides indexes to top drug retailers, top drug wholesalers, top grocery chains and top discount chains. $290. Chain Store Guide Information Services, 3922 Coconut Palm Drive, Tampa, FL 33619. (800) 927-9292, (813) 664-6800, (813) 627-6822, (800) 289-6822. http://www.d-net.com/csgis or http://www.csgis.com.

DIRECTORY OF FOODSERVICE DISTRIBUTORS lists U.S. and Canadian companies with at least $500,000 in sales to foodservice, food equipment, supply and full-line distributors. Each offers more than one product line and no more than 95% of its food distribution sales volume comes from self-manufactured merchandise. Key personnel and major buying/marketing groups, trade associations and a trade show calendar are also included. $290. Chain Store Guide Information Services, 3922 Coconut Palm Drive, Tampa, FL 33619. (800) 927-9292, (813) 664-6800, (813) 627-6822, (800) 289-6822. http://www.d-net.com/csgis or http://www.csgis.com

DIRECTORY OF FOREIGN FIRMS OPERATING IN THE UNITED STATES, REGIONAL EDITION—NORTH AMERICA. Includes Canada and Mexico. $39. Uniworld Business Publications, Inc., 257 Central Park West, Suite 10A, New York, NY 10024-4110, (212) 496-2448, fax (212) 769-0413, email uniworldbp@aol.com. Web site: http://www.uniworldbp.com.

DIRECTORY OF HAZARDOUS WASTE SERVICES contains information on over 1,500 Canadian hazardous waste management companies with information on hazardous waste consultants, waste treatment and disposal outlets, equipment manufacturers, laboratory services, drum reconditioners, spill cleanup firms, hazwaste recyclers, associations, key government contacts, liquid waste haulers, lawyers specializing in environmental law, and environmental libraries. $115. Special discounts available for combined purchases. Published by Southam Information Products Ltd, 1450 Don Mills Road, Don Mills, Ontario M3B 2X7 CANADA, (800) 668-2374. In Toronto 442-2122. Web site www.southam.com.

DIRECTORY OF SUPERMARKET, GROCERY AND CONVENIENCE STORE CHAINS describes and indexes over 2,300 supermarket chains with $2 million in annual sales. It covers supermarkets, superstores, club stores, gourmet supermarkets and combo stores in the U.S. and Canada, plus a special section profiling 1,700 convenience store chains. It includes an index to the top 200 supermarket chains and the top 100 convenience store chains, which is a valuable tool for target list development. It also lists over 29,000 key executives, buyers and administrative personnel. The directory also lists major trade associations and a trade show calendar. $300. Chain Store Guide Information Services, 3922 Coconut Palm Drive, Tampa, FL 33619. (800) 927-9292, (813) 664-6800, (813) 627-6822, (800) 289-6822. http://www.d-net.com/csgis or http://www.csgis.com.

DIRECTORY OF WHOLESALE GROCERY lists wholesale grocers' headquarters, divisions and branches, both in the US and Canada. All companies listed are required to sell a multi-line of products to the supermarket, convenience store, discount and drug industries. It includes names and titles of personnel, a listing of major trade associations and a trade show calendar. It also provides an index to the top 100 wholesale grocers, which is a valuable tool for target list development. $300. Chain Store Guide Information Services, 3922 Coconut Palm Drive, Tampa, FL 33619. (800) 927-9292, (813) 664-6800, (813) 627-6822, (800) 289-6822. http://www.d-net.com/csgis or http://www.csgis.com.

DUN'S BUSINESS LOCATOR® CANADA contains primary information on 700,000 Canadian companies on one disk. Dun & Bradstreet, Business Reference Solutions, Three Sylvan Way, Parsippany, NJ 07054 USA. (800) 526-0651. Email dnbmdd@mail.dnb.com. Web site http://www.dnbmdd.com.

ELECTRONICS MANUFACTURERS DIRECTORY contains information on 17,000 US companies and nearly 2,000 Canadian companies. A total of 68,000 names and titles are included. Available as a directory and database. For pricing and more information, contact distributor Database Publishing Company, PO Box 70024, Anaheim, CA 92825, (800) 888-8434, (714) 778-6400, email sales@databasepublishing.com. Also contact Harris InfoSource, 2057 East Aurora Road, Twinsburg, OH 44087-1999, (330) 425-9000, (800) 888-5900, www.HarrisInfo.com.

ENCYCLOPEDIA OF ASSOCIATIONS: INTERNATIONAL ORGANIZATIONS includes nearly 20,000 multinational and national organizations in foreign countries, including US based associations with multinational membership. Entries also include email addresses, web sites and bulletin board addresses, lobbying activities, and publication and convention information. Indexed by geography, keyword and executives. $595 for 2 volume set. Also available in CD ROM. Database available via commercial online service. Gale Group, P.O. Box 9187, Farmington Hills, MI 48333-9187. Toll free US and Canada (800) 877-GALE (4253) and (248) 699-GALE, fax (800) 414-5043 and (248) 699-8061, Internet orders galeord@galegroup.com, web site www.galegroup.com or www.gale.com. All Gale Group products are available on approval. Contact Gale for details.

FINANCIAL SERVICES CANADA, formerly titled GUIDE TO THE CANADIAN FINANCIAL SERVICES INDUSTRY, is now published by Micromedia Ltd., 20 Victoria Street, Toronto, ON. $249 Canadian print, $349 Canadian for CD ROM, $399 Canadian for both. For information about their demand document center CANCORP, contact (800) 387-2689, (416) 362-5211, email info@micromedia.on.ca, web site www.micromedia.on.ca.

FOREIGN EMBASSIES OR CONSULATES sometimes have library resources from their countries located in foreign countries. For example, there is a superb Canadian library in New York City. For more information, refer to a directory of libraries listed in the "Libraries" section, or ask a librarian. If you do call the embassy or consulate, make sure you speak with a knowledgeable person so as to avoid misinformation. You might ask, "May I please speak to someone who is an expert about libraries?"

GALE DIRECTORY OF PUBLICATIONS AND BROADCAST MEDIA ONLINE is a GaleNet resource on the Internet that includes information on 64,000 newspapers, periodicals, newsletters, industry directories, television and radio stations, including names of key personnel. Contact the library to access this reference free. For pricing and ordering information, contact: Gale Group, P.O. Box 9187, Farmington Hills, MI 48333-9187. Toll free US and Canada (800) 877-GALE (4253) and (248) 699-GALE, fax (800) 414-5043 and (248) 699-8061, Internet orders galeord@galegroup.com, web site www.galegroup.com or www.gale.com. All Gale Group products are available on approval. Contact Gale for details.

GOVERNMENT RESEARCH DIRECTORY identifies over 4,300 research labs and programs of the U.S. and Canadian federal governments. $510. Gale Group, P.O. Box 9187, Farmington Hills, MI 48333-9187. Toll free US and Canada (800) 877-GALE (4253) and (248) 699-GALE, fax (800) 414-5043 and (248) 699-8061, Internet orders galeord@galegroup.com, web site www.galegroup.com or www.gale.com. All Gale Group products are available on approval. Contact Gale for details.

GOVERNMENTS CANADA is published by Micromedia Ltd., 20 Victoria Street, Toronto, ON. For information about pricing, or their demand document center CANCORP, contact (800) 387-2689, (416) 362-5211, email info@micromedia.on.ca, web site www.micromedia.on.ca.

GREATER TORONTO BUSINESS DIRECTORY is a 2 volume directory which identifies over 56,000 executive names and titles at some 30,000 companies. Volume 1 is comprised of Metropolitan Toronto engaged in contracting, jobbers, transportation, law, finance and retail. Volume 2, Metro Toronto Boundary covers surrounding Toronto from Brampton to Richmond Hill to Whitby. $249 for both volumes, $141 apiece. Published annually by Scott's Directories. Distributed by Manufacturers' News, Inc., (888) 752-5200, 1633 Central Street, Evanston, IL 60201-1569. Email info@manufacturersnews.com. Web site www.manufacturersnews.com.

GUIDE TO CANADIAN MANUFACTURERS contains information on Canada's top 44,000 manufacturing companies. Dun & Bradstreet, Business Reference Solutions, Three Sylvan Way, Parsippany, NJ 07054 USA. (800) 526-0651. Email dnbmdd@mail.dnb.com. Web site http://www.dnbmdd.com.

HARRIS ELECTRONICS MANUFACTURERS DATABASE, also available as a directory, is published in cooperation with the Electronics Representatives Association and the National Electronic Distributors Association. It contains information on over 20,000 US electronics manufacturing firms and over 2,500 Canadian electronics manufacturers, including names of about 68,000 American executives and 5,500 Canadian executives. Selectory $595. Selectory multi-user (LAN) version $1,190. Directory, updated annually, $255. Ordering information: Harris InfoSource International, 2057 Aurora Road, Twinsburg, OH 44087-1999, (800) 888-5900, fax (800) 643-5997, web site http://www.harrisinfo.com.

INDUSTRY CANADA's Library can be reached at (613) 954-2728. Orders can be placed by calling (613) 947-5194. For more information, see their "Strategis Department" "Canadian Company Capabilities" web site at www.strategis.ic.gc.ca. Strategis's mandate is to print virtually any kind of information you want on Canadian companies. Their Help Desk number is (800) 328-6189. There are virtually no more updated print versions of information as all updates are now online.

INFOMART DIRECT is a satellite service produced by Infomart Dialog Limited that delivers consolidated news feeds and provides full text print and broadcast sources to the end-user's office computer or LAN. Sources include Canadian daily newspapers, Canadian and international newswire services, including Southam News, Canada NewsWire, and Agence-France Presse, select television broadcast transcripts from major Canadian networks, CBC and CTV, industry trade publications, including Daily Oil Bulletin, Eco/Log Week, Canadian Underwriter, Canadian Business and Marketing Magazine. For Subscriptions and rate information, contact Infomart Dialog Limited at (416) 442-2198 or (800) 668-9215. DIALOG is a service mark of the Dialog Corporation.

INFOMART ON CD is available to CD ROM subscribers from IHS Micromedia Ltd. A full range of Canadian daily newspapers is available on both the KIOSK and VOYAGEUR platforms. KIOSK offers coverage for The Daily News (Halifax), The Gazette (Montréal), Ottawa Citizen, Toronto Star, Toronto Sun, The Spectator (Hamilton), Calgary Herald, Edmonton Journal, The Province (Vancouver), Vancouver Sun, The Financial Post and broadcast news transcripts. On the VOYAGEUR platform, Canadian NewsDisc is available as a complete package, either quarterly or monthly. For Subscriptions and rate information, contact Infomart Dialog Limited at (416) 442-2198 or (800) 668-9215. DIALOG is a service mark of the Dialog Corporation.

INFORMATION IN CANADA—A DIRECTORY OF ELECTRONIC AND SUPPORT RESOURCES provides electronic information on information resources, consultants and information brokers, library based online research services, library automation software, computer accessible library catalogues and a directory of information industry services, plus a large section on databases produced in Canada. Price reduced to $49.95 for 1996 edition. Canada Library Association, 200 Elgin Street, Suite 602, Ottawa, Ontario K2P 1L5 CANADA, (613) 232-9625, fax (613) 563-9895,web site www.cla.amlibs.ca includes an online catalog. Email bj491@freenet.carleton.ca.

JAPANESE AFFILIATED COMPANIES IN THE US AND CANADA lists companies operating in North America whose ownership is at least 10% Japanese. Includes key personnel and chief products. $260. Published by the Japanese External Trade Organization (JETRO). JETRO is headquartered in Japan and has offices in major cities in the US, including Atlanta, Chicago, Dallas, Denver, Houston, Los Angeles, New York and San Francisco. If this reference is no longer being distributed by the Gale Group, contact JETRO. Gale Group, P.O. Box 9187, Farmington Hills, MI 48333-9187. Toll free US and Canada (800) 877-GALE (4253) and (248) 699-GALE, fax (800) 414-5043 and (248) 699-8061, Internet orders galeord@galegroup.com, web site www.galegroup.com or www.gale.com. All Gale Group products are available on approval. Contact Gale for details.

KOMPASS is described by the publisher as "the world's most comprehensive global database of companies, products and services for manufacturing and engineering professionals in print, on CD ROM and on the

Internet." It contains company and product information for companies in all lines of business, including manufacturing and industrial sectors. Each company listing includes name, address, phone number, management names, business descriptions, and industry and product listings. Kompass's web site is www.kompass.com. Call publisher for prices and information on country directories. Cahners Business Information, 121 Chanlon Road, New Providence, NJ 07974, (908) 771-8785, fax (908) 665-8755, email hholmes@reedref.com. Headquarters: Cahners Business Information, 275 Washington Street, Newton, MA 02158-1630, (617) 558-4663 or (617) 964-3030, fax (617) 558-4700, email marketaccess@cahners.com, web sites www.cahners.com or www.chilton.net.

LITERARY MARKET PLACE, "The Directory of the American Book Publishing Industry With Industry Yellow Pages" is an excellent 3 volume directory with comprehensive information on US book publishers; imprints, subsidiaries and distributors; book trade acquisitions and mergers, small presses, Canadian book publishers, micropublishers, US electronic publishers, electronic publishing consultants, electronic publishing products and services, editorial services, literary agents, illustrations agents, US agents and offices of foreign publishers, lecture agents, specialized advertising and public relations firms, direct mail specialists, mailing list brokers and services, book review syndicates, book review and index journals and services, book exhibits, book clubs, book lists and catalogs, book importers and exporters, book producers, translators, artists, photographers, stock photo agencies, associations, book trade events and conferences, awards, contents and grants, reference books for the trade, magazines for the trade, a toll free directory of publishers, magazine and newspaper publicity, radio and television publicity, book manufacturing services, book distributors and sales representatives, and wholesalers. $189.95.

LITERARY MARKET PLACE ON DISC, previously titled LITERARY MARKET PLACE PLUS CD ROM, one year subscription $297.00.

LITERARY MARKET PLACE—INTERNET EDITION, www.literarymarketplace.com, is available by subscription.

INTERNATIONAL LITERARY MARKET PLACE Internet database can be directly accessed at www.iliterarymarketplace.com. It is also linked to the US domestic LITERARY MARKET PLACE web site at www.literarymarketplace.com. Contact the publisher for subscription price. INTERNATIONAL LITERARY MARKET PLACE, hard copy $189.95.

R.R. Bowker (a unit of Cahners Business Information), 121 Chanlon Road, New Providence, NJ 07974 USA, Phone (888) BOWKER2 (888-269-5372) & (800) 323-3288, fax (908) 508-7696, email info@bowker.com, web www.bowker.com. Canada—R.R. Bowker, Markham, Ontario, phone (888) BOWKER9 & (905) 415-5837, fax (905) 479-6266. German speaking Europe—K.G. Saur Verlag, Munich, Germany, phone 49-89-76902-232, fax 49-89-76902-250, email 100730.1341@compuserve.com, web www.saur.de/home.htm. Rest of Europe incl. United Kingdom plus Africa & Asia—Bowker-Saur, W. Sussex, UK, phone 44-1342-326-972, fax 44-1342-335-612, email customer@bowker-saur.co.uk, web www.bowker-saur.com/service/. Australia/New Zealand—Thorpe, Port Melbourne, Victoria, Australia, phone 61-03-9-245-7370, fax 61-03-9-245-7395, email customer.service@thorpe.com.au, web www.thorpe.com.au. Technical support for CD ROMs (800) 323-3288, fax 908) 665-3528, email techsupport@bowker.com.

MARTINDALE-HUBBELL LAW DIRECTORY ON CD ROM contains biographies for over 700,000 attorneys in the US and Canada, at law firms and in house counsel. Searches can be conducted by name/firm, country, state, county, city, birth year, first college, year of graduation, law school, year of graduation, bar, admission year, biography text, languages, job titles, firm size, legal specialties and more. Updated quarterly. (Martindale-Hubbell listing subscribers should call for additional discount information.) CD ROM 1 year subscription $995, 3 years $2,445, excluding discounts. This directory is also available in electronic database formats, online through LEXIS® (Library Name: MARHUB, File Name: ALLDIR) and NEXIS® (Library Name: PEOPLE, File Name: MHPROF). For more information visit Bowker Reed Reference's web site at http://www.reedref.com or contact: Bowker Reed Reference Electronic Publishing, 121 Chanlon Road, New Providence, NJ 07974 USA, Phone (800) 323-3288, Fax (908) 665-3528, email info@bowker.com.

MD SELECT is an Electronic Canadian Medical Directory endorsed by the Canadian Medical Association. It lists over 50,000 physicians. Information can be searched by these fields: physician name, phone, hospital affiliation, hospital bed size, hospital type, medical specialty, degrees, honors, certified specialty, subspecialty, primary interest, gender, year of graduation, University/Country of graduation, appointments, fellowships, and languages spoken. $495. THE CANADIAN MEDICAL DIRECTORY in hard copy costs $175 Published annually. Special discounts available for combined purchases. Published by Southam Information Products Ltd, 1450 Don Mills Road, Don Mills, Ontario M3B 2X7 CANADA, (800) 668-2374. In Toronto 442-2122. Web site www.southam.com.

MICROMEDIA, the Toronto publisher, publishes a legal directory. For more information, contact Micromedia Ltd., 20 Victoria Street, Toronto, ON, (800) 387-2689, (416) 362-5211, email info@micromedia.on.ca, web site www.micromedia.on.ca.

MUTUAL FUNDS SOURCEBOOK provides information on 1,300 Canadian mutual funds. However, it is impossible to determine from the publisher's catalog whether this directory includes names of personnel. $350 per year, $150 book. Special discounts available for combined purchases. Published by Southam Information Products Ltd, 1450 Don Mills Road, Don Mills, Ontario M3B 2X7 CANADA, (800) 668-2374. In Toronto 442-2122. Web site www.southam.com.

NATIONAL FACULTY DIRECTORY provides names, departmental affiliations and institutional addresses of academic professionals, listing over 670,000 teaching faculty at 3,600 US colleges and universities and at 240 Canadian institutions that use primarily English m\teaching materials. $755. Information compiled by CMG Information Services. Distributed by Gale Group, P.O. Box 9187, Farmington Hills, MI 48333-9187. Toll free US and Canada (800) 877-GALE (4253) and (248) 699-GALE, fax (800) 414-5043 and (248) 699-8061, Internet orders galeord@galegroup.com, web site www.galegroup.com or www.gale.com. All Gale Group products are available on approval. Contact Gale for details.

NATION'S RESTAURANT NEWS is a 30 year old newsweekly of the foodservice industry. For info about subscriptions and customer service, call 800-447-7133. URL: www.nrn.com or http://www.d-net.com/csgis or http://www.csgis.com. Chain Store Guide Information Services, 3922 Coconut Palm Drive, Tampa, FL 33619.

NICKLE'S CANADIAN OIL REGISTER (COR)—CONTACTS is a diskette on Maximizer, a contact management software. It includes 3,500 companies in 15 business sectors and 17,000 names and titles for over 1,000 product and service categories. COR—CONTACTS (OIL AND GAS PRODUCERS) $395. COR—CONTACTS (SERVICE COMPANIES) $595. COR—CONTACTS (PRODUCTS SOURCING) $495. Special discounts available for combined purchases. For more information on Energy Information Services, call Calgary office (403) 244-6111. Published by Southam Information Products Ltd, 1450 Don Mills Road, Don Mills, Ontario M3B 2X7 CANADA, (800) 668-2374. In Toronto 442-2122. Web site www.southam.com.

NICKLE'S CANADIAN OIL REGISTER is a directory that provides names of key personnel and other information on 4,500 Canadian companies in these industry categories: exploration and production companies, service and supply companies, data processors, consultants, engineers, financial and investment companies, leasebrokers and land agents, geophysical contractors, oil well drilling contractors, oil well servicing contractors, pipeline and power distributors, refiners and processors, transportation and construction companies, government departments, agencies and industry associations. Includes a Who's Who section that identifies over 24,000 key management, engineering and technical personnel. $175. Published annually. Special discounts available for combined purchases. For more information on Energy Information Services, call Calgary office (403) 244-6111. Published by Southam Information Products Ltd, 1450 Don Mills Road, Don Mills, Ontario M3B 2X7 CANADA, (800) 668-2374. In Toronto 442-2122. Web site www.southam.com.

NORTH AMERICAN ELECTRONICS MANUFACTURERS contains information on over 19,000 Canadian and US electronics companies. Directory $395, Selectory $895. Scott's Directories, Toronto area: 1450 Don Mills Road, Don Mills, Ontario, M3B 2X7, CANADA, (416) 442-2291, (416) 932-9555, (888) 709-9907. Montréal area: Scott's Directories, 3300 Cote Verde, Suite 410 Ville St.-Laurent, Quebec H4B 2B7 CANADA (514) 339-1397, (800) 363-1327. Publisher's email scotts@southam.ca.

NORTHERN MINER is a weekly newspaper that covers the worldwide activities of all North American Based mining companies. It includes information on company profiles, mergers, career opportunities, a professional directory, a diamond drillers directory, industry news and much more. Annual subscription in Canada $87, US $87, foreign $130 (surface mail or $288 (airmail). Online subscription rates for newspaper subscribers: $60 Canadian, $42 US, $60 Canadian collars for foreign. Online subscription rates for newspaper non-subscribers: $144 Canadian, $108 US, $144 Canadian dollars for foreign. Northern Miner Home Page www.northernminer.com. Special discounts available for combined purchases. For more information on Energy Information Services, call Calgary office (403) 244-6111. Published by Southam Information Products Ltd, 1450 Don Mills Road, Don Mills, Ontario M3B 2X7 CANADA, (800) 668-2374. In Toronto 442-2122. Web site www.southam.com.

ONTARIO RECYCLING RESOURCEBOOK—HOW TO COMPLY WITH THE 3RS REGULATIONS contains an extensive directory of companies and organizations which are users of recyclable materials. It also lists waste reduction consultants and Ontario municipalities with their material bans and recycling coordinators. Free copy of the "Waste Audit Workbook" with your paid order. $79. Special discounts available for combined purchases. Published by Southam Information Products Ltd, 1450 Don Mills Road, Don Mills, Ontario M3B 2X7 CANADA, (800) 668-2374. In Toronto 442-2122. Web site www.southam.com.

OWNERSHIP STRUCTURES OF PRINCIPAL PETROLEUM COMPANIES IN CANADA documents "who owns whom" in the Canadian Petroleum industry. Includes directors and key officers and a list of major oil patch takeovers since 1976. $177. Special discounts available for combined purchases. For more information on Energy Information Services, call Calgary office (403) 244-6111. Published by Southam Information Products Ltd, 1450 Don Mills Road, Don Mills, Ontario M3B 2X7 CANADA, (800) 668-2374. In Toronto 442-2122. Web site www.southam.com.

PENSION FUNDS AND THEIR ADVISERS provides information on the top 2,000 pension funds in the United Kingdom, plus major funds of Japan, Belgium, France, Germany, Ireland, The Netherlands and Switzerland. This Directory is the only source in the US that monitors the growth of assets in the international market. Information includes internal and external fund management contacts, major US and Canadian pension funds and money managers, major European and Japanese pension funds and their advisors. It also includes comprehensive listings of 900 advisors to the pension fund industry including financial advisers, accountants, actuaries and pension fund consultants, pension administrators, insurance companies, attorneys, computer services, global custody, pension trustees, pension /financial recruitment consultants, investment research, associations and professional groups, and publications. $310. Published by A.P. Information Services, Ltd. Marketed exclusively in North America MONEY MARKET DIRECTORIES INC./STANDARD AND POORS, 320 East Main Street, Charlottesville, VA 22902, http://www.mmdaccess.com, (800) 446-2810, (804) 977-1450.

POLK NORTH AMERICAN FINANCIAL INSTITUTIONS DIRECTORY includes information on banks, savings and loan associations and major credit unions in North America, including head office and branch offices,names of key decision makers, address, phone and fax, financial summaries, maps, and structural changes such as mergers, name changes, and closings. Published twice a year. For more information contact (800) 321-3373, Thomson Financial Publishing, 4709 West Golf Road, Skokie, IL 60076-1253. Web site @ tfp.bankinfo.com.

PUBLISHERS DIRECTORY contains information about 20,000 US and Canadian publishers, including small, independent presses and companies which provide electronic formats. Entries include email addresses. $357. Gale Group, P.O. Box 9187, Farmington Hills, MI 48333-9187. Toll free US and Canada (800) 877-GALE (4253) and (248) 699-GALE, fax (800) 414-5043 and (248) 699-8061, Internet orders galeord@galegroup.com, web site www.galegroup.com or www.gale.com. All Gale Group products are available on approval. Contact Gale for details.

PULP AND PAPER ANNUAL AND DIRECTORY contains an index of companies, divisions and subsidiaries, plus information on 3 sectors: pulp, paper and board manufacturing sector, supply sector and support sector. Includes information on key contacts, mills and recycling companies. Canada $95, USA and foreign $115. Special discounts available for combined purchases. Published by Southam Information Products Ltd, 1450 Don Mills Road, Don Mills, Ontario M3B 2X7 CANADA, (800) 668-2374. In Toronto 442-2122. Web site www.southam.com.

REFERENCE AND RESEARCH BOOK NEWS provides prompt information about new books and CD ROMs of interest to reference librarians and users of reference materials. 8 issues per year, 900 books and

CD's reviewed per issue. $100/institutions, $80/individuals US and Canada, $115/foreign. Ordering information: REFERENCE & RESEARCH BOOK NEWS, 5600 NE Hassalo Street, Portland, OR 97213, (503) 281-9230, email: booksnews@booknews. com, http://www.books.com//booknews.

REFERENCE CANADA is a comprehensive information source. For more information call (613) 941-4823 or the Reference Librarian at the Ottawa Public Library at (613) 598-4008.

RESEARCH CENTERS DIRECTORY describes programs, facilities, publications,educational efforts and services of North America's leading nonprofit research institutes. It includes a personal name index that lists center directors and other contacts. Subject, geographic and master indexes are also included. Booklist's review described this as "an extremely valuable reference tool." $548 for a two volume set. Database also available via commercial online service. Gale Group, P.O. Box 9187, Farmington Hills, MI 48333-9187. Toll free US and Canada (800) 877-GALE (4253) and (248) 699-GALE, fax (800) 414-5043 and (248) 699-8061, Internet orders galeord@galegroup.com, web site www.galegroup.com or www.gale.com. All Gale Group products are available on approval. Contact Gale for details.

SCOTT'S CANADA DIRECTORIES profile over 60,000 facilities and identify over 120,000 executive names in Canada. The following directories are available and are updated annually:

> SCOTT'S ONTARIO MANUFACTURERS, $209
> SCOTT'S QUEBEC MANUFACTURERS, $189
> SCOTT'S WESTERN INDUSTRIAL EDITION, including Manitoba, Saskatchewan, Alberta and British Columbia, $169
> SCOTT'S ATLANTIC INDUSTRIAL EDITION, including Prince Edward Island, Nova Scotia, New Brunswick, $129.

Distributed by Manufacturers' News, Inc., (888) 752-5200, 1633 Central Street, Evanston, IL 60201-1569. Email info@manufacturersnews.com. Web site www.manufacturersnews.com.

SCOTT'S DIRECTORIES publishes a number of well respected Canadian directories. Most directories are available in print and in their SELECTORY® format. There are two Selectory® products, Selectory® Prospector and the Selectory® Profiler. Both Prospector and Profiler offer an identical search capability, which can be done using any combination of up to 25 categories, including: by executive titles, products, SIC or NAICS codes, city, province, region, area code, plant size, revenues, number of employees, company name, executive name, year established, and others. However, only the Prospector provides these 3 additional features: printing mailing labels, doing unlimited data transfers, and merging its data with MSWORD, EXCEL, Act!, WordPerfect, Lotus and other programs. Therefore, Selectory® Profiler is more appropriate for a recruiters' needs. Further, Profiler is considerably less expensive than Prospector. A free Selectory demo disk is available.At the time of this writing, the following Scott's Selectory® products are available:

Title	Profiler/ Prospector Price	Book, if available
SCOTT'S ATLANTIC INDUSTRIAL SELECTORY	$299/495	$175
SCOTT'S QUEBEC MANUFACTURERS SELECTORY	$399/795	$260
SCOTT'S QUEBEC INDUSTRIAL SELECTORY	$499/995	
SCOTT'S GREATER MONTREAL BUSINESS SELECTORY	$349/695	$220
SCOTT'S ONTARIO MANUFACTURERS SELECTORY	$549/1,095	$295
SCOTT'S ONTARIO INDUSTRIAL SELECTORY	$699/1,595	
SCOTT'S ONTARIO (ALL) SELECTORY	$699/1,995	
SCOTT'S GREATER TORONTO BUSINESS SELECTORY	$649/1,195	$195 per vol.
SCOTT'S WESTERN INDUSTRIAL SELECTORY	$499/895	$240
SCOTT'S CANADIAN DISTRIBUTION SELECTORY	$599/995	
CENTRAL CANADA DISTRIBUTION DIRECTORY	$199	
SCOTT'S NATIONAL MANUFACTURERS SELECTORY	$1,299/2,695	
SCOTT'S NATIONAL MANUFACTURERS SELECTORY	$799/1,695	
SCOTT'S NATIONAL INDUSTRIAL SELECTORY	$1,699/$3,695	
SCOTT'S CUSTOM SELECTORY	NA/$Minimum $500 for 2,500 names	

For more information contact Scott's Directories, Toronto area: 1450 Don Mills Road, Don Mills, Ontario, M3B 2X7, CANADA, (416) 442-2291, (416) 932-9555, (888) 709-9907. Montréal area: Scott's Directories, 3300 Cote Verde, Suite 410 Ville St.-Laurent, Quebec H4B 2B7 CANADA (514) 339-1397, (800) 363-1327. Publisher's email scotts@southam.ca.

SciTECH REFERENCE PLUS CD ROM contains directory information, 125,000 biographies of US and Canadian scientists and engineers from AMERICAN MEN AND WOMEN OF SCIENCE, listings for over 8,000 laboratories from the DIRECTORY OF AMERICAN RESEARCH AND TECHNOLOGY, and information from THE DIRECTORY OF CORPORATE AFFILIATIONS (including public, private and international companies) of leading US and international technology firms and their subsidiaries. It also contains 60,000 records on science/technology and medical serials from ULRICH'S INTERNATIONAL PERIODICALS DIRECTORY. Searches can be conducted by SIC, year founded, activity, education, employees, institution/company, city, state or country, memberships/honors, product description, personal statistics, personal title, research area, revenue. Updated annually. 1 year subscription $995, 3 years 2,836, excluding discounts. For more information visit Bowker Reed Reference's web site at http://www.reedref.com or contact: Bowker Reed Reference Electronic Publishing, 121 Chanlon Road, New Providence, NJ 07974 USA, Phone (800) 323-3288, Fax (908) 665-3528, email info@bowker.com.

SCOTT'S DIRECTORY OF CANADIAN MUNICIPALITIES is a new directory that contains information on municipalities, cities, towns and villages, including addresses, phone numbers, web sites and email addresses, and names and titles of senior administrative staff. Directory $99, Canadian Municipalities Select $149.For more information contact Scott's Directories, Toronto area: 1450 Don Mills Road, Don Mills, Ontario, M3B 2X7, CANADA, (416) 442-2291, (416) 932-9555, (888) 709-9907. Montréal area: Scott's Directories, 3300 Cote Verde, Suite 410 Ville St.-Laurent, Quebec H4B 2B7 CANADA (514) 339-1397, (800) 363-1327. Publisher's email scotts@southam.ca.

SCOTT'S DIRECTORY OF CANADIAN SCHOOLS contains information on over 16,000 private and public schools, school boards, colleges, universities, native schools, special needs schools, vocational schools and departments of education, plus names of key contacts, including principals, librarians and guidance counselors. Book $127, diskette $547. Special discounts available for combined purchases. Published by Southam Information Products Ltd, 1450 Don Mills Road, Don Mills, Ontario M3B 2X7 CANADA, (800) 668-2374. In Toronto 442-2122. Web site www.southam.com.

SCOTT'S GOVERNMENT INDEX DIRECTORY identifies key officials in the federal and provincial departments, agencies, boards, commissions and Crown corporations in Canada. Listings include name, title, address, phone number, fax, email. Updated quarterly. $197 in print. For more information contact Scott's Directories, Toronto area: 1450 Don Mills Road, Don Mills, Ontario, M3B 2X7, CANADA, (416) 442-2291, (416) 932-9555, (888) 709-9907. Montréal area: Scott's Directories, 3300 Cote Verde, Suite 410 Ville St.-Laurent, Quebec H4B 2B7 CANADA (514) 339-1397, (800) 363-1327. Publisher's email scotts@southam.ca. For information about an $497 electronic version updated four times a year, contact Southam Information Products Ltd, 1450 Don Mills Road, Don Mills, Ontario M3B 2X7 CANADA, (800) 668-2374. In Toronto 442-2122. Web site www.southam.com.

SHELDON'S RETAIL DIRECTORY OF THE US AND CANADA is published by Phelon, Sheldon & Marsar, 1364 Georgetowne Circle, Sarasota, FL 34232-2048, (941) 342-7990, fax (941) 342-7994, who also publish numerous retail and apparel directories. For more information contact the Reference Desk at the Baker Library, Harvard Business School in Boston, in connection with the Advisor Database. Web site www.library.hbs.edu/.

STANDARD PERIODICAL DIRECTORY consists of 85,000 American and Canadian periodicals referenced by 250 subjects. Includes new online index and title index. $895. Also available on CD ROM. Published by Oxbridge. Distributed by Gale Group, P.O. Box 9187, Farmington Hills, MI 48333-9187. Toll free US and Canada (800) 877-GALE (4253) and (248) 699-GALE, fax (800) 414-5043 and (248) 699-8061, Internet orders galeord@galegroup.com, web site www.galegroup.com or www.gale.com. All Gale Group products are available on approval. Contact Gale for details.

STANDARD PERIODICAL DIRECTORY ON CD-ROM encompasses 75,000 North American publications, vastly simplifying research in consumer magazines, trade journals, newspapers, yearbooks, museum publications, ethnic publications and more. Contact Gale for prices. Gale Group, P.O. Box 9187, Farmington Hills, MI 48333-9187. Toll free US and Canada (800) 877-GALE (4253) and (248) 699-GALE, fax (800) 414-5043 and (248) 699-8061, Internet orders galeord@galegroup.com, web site www.galegroup.com or www.gale.com. All Gale Group products are available on approval. Contact Gale for details.

SUPERMARKET, GROCERY AND CONVENIENCE STORE CHAINS CD-ROM can conduct data searches from five topic screens: 1. Personnel by title, 2. Personnel by functional area, 3. Listing type (branch office, corporate office, divisional office, headquarters, location, managed care div, regional office, subsidiary, warehouse), 4. Stores operated (superstores, supermarkets, convenience, warehouse, combo stores, gourmet supermarkets, stores w/gas), 5. Specialty departments (e.g., auto supplies, automatic teller machines, beer, books/magazines, floral/horticulture,gourmet/specialty foods, greeting cards, in-store bakeries, in-store banking, in-store restaurant, lawn & garden, liquor, nutrition center, et al.). You can also make selections based on geography or the size of a company (number of units and/or sales). Several output options are available, including mailing labels, and electronic formats (such as DBASE, ASCII, text) for mail merge customization. $795, including companion directory. If the price is prohibitively high, remember your local library. Chain Store Guide Information Services, 3922 Coconut Palm Drive, Tampa, FL 33619. (800) 927-9292, (813) 664-6800, (813) 627-6822, (800) 289-6822. http://www.d-net.com/csgis or http://www.csgis.com.

WHO OWNS WHOM DIRECTORY by Dun & Bradstreet is a six volume set containing information on the structure and ownership of 320,000 company affiliates and subsidiaries of over 23,000 companies worldwide. It is available in four regional editions: Australia and the Far East, North America, UK/Ireland, and Continental Europe. Published annually. For prices and ordering information as well as information about more worldwide corporate linkage products from D&B WORLDBASE, D&B's global database of 42 million records in over 200 countries, contact Dun & Bradstreet at (800) 526-0651, Dun & Bradstreet, Business Reference Solutions, Three Sylvan Way, Parsippany, NJ 07054. Email dnbmdd@mail.dnb.com. Web site http://www.dnbmdd.com

www.bowker.com is the web site for this major research publisher. It includes Flagship Products and Services, an online Product Catalog, Electronic Publishing products including CD ROMs, Internet Databases, and Online Subscription and Site Licensing Databases; press releases, career opportunities, and more. Many of their references are accessible through this web site, such as BOOKS IN PRINT PLUS CANADIAN EDITION, ULRICH'S ON DISC, GERMAN BOOKS IN PRINT, GERMAN BOOKS OUT OF PRINT, INTERNATIONAL BOOKS IN PRINT PLUS, ITALIAN BOOKS IN PRINT, YEARBOOK OF INTERNATIONAL ORGANIZATIONS PLUS, ULRICH'S INTERNATIONAL PERIODICALS DIRECTORY, THE SOFTWARE ENCYCLOPEDIA, BOWKER'S COMPLETE VIDEO DIRECTORY, AMERICAN BOOK PUBLISHING RECORD. Visit the web site for more information.

www.careerexchange.com is a web site for North American job seekers developed by CorpNet InfoHub, Ltd., Vancouver, BC, Canada. Launched in 1996, its People-Match capability notifies the user of jobs through email. Most positions are in high technology, engineering, sales and marketing and are primarily in the $40,000 to $75,000 range.

www.jobnet.org is a Canadian web site.that features "Looking for a career in financial services?" Scotiabank online recruiting, Jobnet and Alumnet.

www.kompass.com is the web site for the highly respected Kompass country directories and databases. This web site contains a searchable database that encompasses over 60 countries, 2.5 million executive names, information on 1.5 million companies, 19 million key product references, and 370,000 trade and brand names. At the time of this writing, Kompass is available in English and French. Deutsch, Espanol and Italiano will soon be available.

www.medhunters.com is a healthcare jobhunting site developed by Helen Ziegler and Associates, Inc., Toronto, Canada. Worldwide positions are posted for doctors, nurses and therapists, encompassing a broad range of salaries. The site has been online since 1997.

www.mhbizlink.com is the web site address for the major Canadian publisher Maclean Hunter. Among other things, it links to 30 business publications. For more information call them in Toronto at (416) 596-5000.

www.monsterhr.com is the URL for The Monster Board: Human Resources careers on the web. Enter your job profile and have job listings automatically downloaded to your Email. International opportunities in Canada are classified by Canada overall, then Alberta, British Columbia, Newfoundland, Ontario and Quebec.

www.netjobs.com is the URL to Canada's premiere employment web site. It features Internet Career Centre for employers and job seekers, Overseas Jobs Express, and Personal Computer Training. Email info@netjobs.com. Linked to www.jobnet.org.

www.nickles.com/ is the web site for Nickel's Energy Web site. It provides access to over 18,000 articles published in the DAILY OIL BULLETIN, company profiles linked to news articles, a weekly synopsis of key developments in Canadian energy markets, classified ads, and energy information sources. For more information on Energy Information Services, call Calgary office (403) 244-6111. Published by Southam Information Products Ltd, 1450 Don Mills Road, Don Mills, Ontario M3B 2X7 CANADA, (800) 668-2374. In Toronto 442-2122. Web site www.southam.com.

www.thomasregister.com is the URL for Thomas' Register, which provides information Information on US and Canadian manufacturing firms.

Caribbean

See Puerto Rico, Virgin Islands, International

DIRECTORY OF AMERICAN FIRMS OPERATING IN FOREIGN COUNTRIES, REGIONAL EDITION—CARIBBEAN ISLANDS. Includes Anguilla, Antigua, Aruba, Bahamas, Barbados, Bermuda, British West Indies, Cayman Islands, Dominican Republic, Grenada, Haiti, Jamaica, Netherlands Antilles, Trinidad & Tobago, Turks & Caicos. $39. Uniworld Business Publications, Inc., 257 Central Park West, Suite 10A, New York, NY 10024-4110, (212) 496-2448, fax (212) 769-0413, email uniworldbp@aol.com. Web site: http://www.uniworldbp.com.

DIRECTORY OF FOREIGN FIRMS OPERATING IN THE UNITED STATES, REGIONAL EDITION—SOUTH/CENTRAL AMERICA & THE CARIBBEAN. Includes Argentina, Bermuda, Bolivia, Brazil, Chile, Colombia, Costa Rica, Dominican Republic, Guatemala, Mexico, Panama, Paraguay, Peru, Uruguay, Venezuela. $39. Uniworld Business Publications, Inc., 257 Central Park West, Suite 10A, New York, NY 10024-4110, (212) 496-2448, fax (212) 769-0413, email uniworldbp@aol.com. Web site: http://www.uniworldbp.com.

MAJOR COMPANIES OF LATIN AMERICA AND THE CARIBBEAN lists information on 7,500 companies in Latin America and South America and the Caribbean, including description of company activities, brand names, over 35,000 names of key executives and financial data, plus three indexes, mainly for target list development. $765. Available in CD ROM. Distributed by Larry Meranus Professional Publications & Services, 4 Demoray Court, Pine Brook, NJ 07058, (800) MERANUS or (800) 637-2687. Also distributed by Gale Group, P.O. Box 9187, Farmington Hills, MI 48333-9187. Toll free US and Canada (800) 877-GALE (4253) and (248) 699-GALE, fax (800) 414-5043 and (248) 699-8061, Internet orders galeord@galegroup.com, web site www.galegroup.com or www.gale.com. All Gale Group products are available on approval. Contact Gale for details. Published by Graham & Whiteside Ltd., Tuition House, 5-6 Francis Grove, London SW19 4DT, England. Web site http://www.major-co-data.com. Email sales@major-co-data.com.

Cassettes

WORDS ON CASSETTE is the only complete guide to audio cassette collections with location, ordering and pricing information, running times, content summaries and rental availability, an index to authors, readers and performers. Published annually. Cahners Business Information, 121 Chanlon Road, New Providence, NJ 07974, (908) 777-8669, (888) 269-5372, fax (908) 508-7696, email marin.mixon@bowker.com, URL www.bowker.com. Headquarters: Cahners Business Information, 275 Washington Street, Newton, MA 02158-1630, (617) 558-4663 or (617) 964-3030, fax (617) 558-4700, email marketaccess@cahners.com. Web sites www.cahners.com or www.chilton.net.

Central Europe

See International, Europe

DIRECTORY OF AMERICAN FIRMS OPERATING IN FOREIGN COUNTRIES, REGIONAL EDITION—EUROPE, ALL. $169. Ordering information: Uniworld Business Publications, Inc., 257 Central Park West, Suite 10A, New York, NY 10024-4110, (212) 496-2448, fax (212) 769-0413, email uniworldbp@aol.com. Web site: http://www.uniworldbp.com.

MAJOR COMPANIES OF CENTRAL AND EASTERN EUROPE AND THE COMMONWEALTH OF INDEPENDENT STATES identifies some 38,000 executives at 8,000 major business organizations in 24 countries in Eastern and Central Europe and the former Soviet Republics (CIS). Includes three indexes. $980. Also available in CD ROM. Published by Graham & Whiteside Ltd., Tuition House, 5-6 Francis Grove, London SW19 4DT, England. Web site http://www.major-co-data.com. Email sales@major-co-data.com. Distributed by: Larry Meranus Professional Publications & Services, 4 Demoray Court, Pine Brook, NJ 07058, (800) MERANUS or (800) 637-2687. Also distributed by Gale Group, P.O. Box 9187, Farmington Hills, MI 48333-9187. Toll free US and Canada (800) 877-GALE (4253) and (248) 699-GALE, fax (800) 414-5043 and (248) 699-8061, Internet orders galeord@galegroup.com, web site www.galegroup.com or www.gale.com. All Gale Group products are available on approval. Contact Gale for details.

MAJOR COMPANIES SERIES ON CD ROM consists of Graham & Whiteside's annual directories of major international companies. All six directories reside on one disk. After payment, you'll receive a security code to access the region(s) you select. This Windows™ based CD can navigate by company name, company locations, executive names, business activity and more. Free demo CD ROM is available. Regions also available separately for Europe, Central & Eastern Europe, the Far East and Australasia, the Arab World, Africa, and Latin America. For prices and availability, contact the Gale Group, P.O. Box 9187, Farmington Hills, MI 48333-9187. Toll free US and Canada (800) 877-GALE (4253) and (248) 699-GALE, fax (800) 414-5043 and (248) 699-8061, Internet orders galeord@galegroup.com, web site www.galegroup.com or www.gale.com. All Gale Group products are available on approval. Contact Gale for details.

MAJOR TELECOMMUNICATIONS COMPANIES OF EUROPE contains information and contacts for 1,100 major telecommunications companies and their equipment suppliers in western Europe, central Europe and eastern Europe. $415. US distributor: Larry Meranus Professional Publications & Services, 4 Demoray Court, Pine Brook, NJ 07058, (800) MERANUS or (800) 637-2687. Published by Graham & Whiteside Ltd., Tuition House, 5-6 Francis Grove, London SW19 4DT, England. Web site http://www.major-co-data.com. Email sales@major-co-data.com.

CD ROM

If you've identified a database on CD ROM that will make your job easier but the price is prohibitively high, remember your local library. If you're having trouble locating a library with that particular database, perhaps the librarian can check another library for you. Besides a public library, a library at a corporation, embassy, professional association, university or school might be able to help you. Alternatively, maybe the publisher of the database can help locate a library which has it. The publisher should know who their customers are and it is actually to their benefit to help you. After all, as a user of their products, you are creating a demand in the marketplace. If the people at the toll free number can't help you, you're probably calling too low in the organization. Make a point of finding the phone number of corporate headquarters. Call someone senior enough to have the sophistication to understand why demand for their product is a good reason to help you, such as the Vice President or Senior Vice President of Sales and Marketing or even the CEO or Chairman.

CD-ROM'S IN PRINT contains information on over 11,000 CD's, including subject indexes. It also lists information for nearly 4,000 publishing and distribution companies. LIBRARY JOURNAL'S review describes CD-ROM'S IN PRINT as "The starting point for those who choose CD-ROM titles." $155. Gale Group, P.O. Box 9187, Farmington Hills, MI 48333-9187. Toll free US and Canada (800) 877-GALE (4253) and (248) 699-GALE, fax (800) 414-5043 and (248) 699-8061, Internet orders galeord@galegroup.com, web site www.galegroup.com or www.gale.com. All Gale Group products are available on approval. Contact Gale for details.

DIRECTORIES IN PRINT identifies over 15,000 directories (local, regional, national and international) which are organized in 26 subject chapters. An alternate formats index includes directories in online databases, CD ROM, diskettes, microfiche and mailing labels and lists. $489 for 2 volumes. Gale Group, P.O. Box 9187, Farmington Hills, MI 48333-9187. Toll free US and Canada (800) 877-GALE (4253) and (248) 699-GALE, fax (800) 414-5043 and (248) 699-8061, Internet orders galeord@galegroup.com, web site www.galegroup.com or www.gale.com. All Gale Group products are available on approval. Contact Gale for details.

GALE DIRECTORY OF DATABASES identifies over 12,000 international databases available in a variety of formats including online, CD ROM, diskette, and others. Entries include producer name, description, subject, language, cost, update frequency, geographic coverage. Volume 1, Online Databases, $260. Volume 2, CD-ROM, Diskette, Magnetic Tape, Handheld and Batch Access Database Products, $170. Both volumes $390. ONLINE MAGAZINE described this as "An excellent directory of online databases." Gale Group, P.O. Box 9187, Farmington Hills, MI 48333-9187. Toll free US and Canada (800) 877-GALE (4253) and (248) 699-GALE, fax (800) 414-5043 and (248) 699-8061, Internet orders galeord@galegroup.com, web site www.galegroup.com or www.gale.com. All Gale Group products are available on approval. Contact Gale for details.

GALE DIRECTORY OF DATABASES ONLINE is a GaleNet database on the Internet that identifies over 12,000 international databases in various formats, including CD ROM, diskettes, online and others. Check your local library for free access or contact Gale for annual subscription rates. Gale Group, P.O. Box 9187, Farmington Hills, MI 48333-9187. Toll free US and Canada (800) 877-GALE (4253) and (248) 699-GALE, fax (800) 414-5043 and (248) 699-8061, Internet orders galeord@galegroup.com, web site www.galegroup.com or www.gale.com. All Gale Group products are available on approval. Contact Gale for details.

GALE'S READY REFERENCE SHELF ONLINE is a GaleNet Internet resource that provides integrated access to databases covering national, regional, state, local and international associations, publishers, newspapers and periodicals, directories, newsletters, online databases, portable databases, database products and vendors, special libraries and research centers. Information is included from numerous Gale databases, among them THE ENCYCLOPEDIA OF ASSOCIATIONS, PUBLISHERS DIRECTORY, GALE DIRECTORY OF PUBLICATIONS AND BROADCAST MEDIA and several others. If it is prohibitively expensive, locate a library with with this resource. Gale Group, P.O. Box 9187, Farmington Hills, MI 48333-9187. Toll free US and Canada (800) 877-GALE (4253) and (248) 699-GALE, fax (800) 414-5043 and (248) 699-8061, Internet orders galeord@galegroup.com, web site www.galegroup.com or www.gale.com. All Gale Group products are available on approval. Contact Gale for details.

REFERENCE AND RESEARCH BOOK NEWS provides prompt information about new books and CD ROMs of interest to reference librarians and users of reference materials. 8 issues per year, 900 books and CD's reviewed per issue. $100/institutions, $80/individuals US and Canada, $115/foreign. Ordering information: REFERENCE & RESEARCH BOOK NEWS, 5600 NE Hassalo Street, Portland, OR 97213, (503) 281-9230, email: booksnews@booknews. com, http://www.books.com//booknews.

Chambers of Commerce

One of the fastest and easiest ways to locate a chamber of commerce is to call information. However, numerous directories are also available.

AMERICAN CHAMBERS OF COMMERCE are established in most countries with which the US has diplomatic relations, for example the American Chamber of Commerce in The Netherlands, located in the Dutch capital, The Hague. The US DEPARTMENT OF COMMERCE has established chamber of commerce offices in foreign countries to stimulate American business activity abroad. For more information as to location, ask a librarian, check the phone book of a country's capital or other major cities, ask the consulate or embassy, the US Department of Commerce, look in a reference listed in the chambers of commerce section, ask another chamber of commerce, or search the Internet.

BUSINESS ORGANIZATIONS, AGENCIES AND PUBLICATIONS DIRECTORY contains 32 chapters including information on Canada, business information sources, web sites, and local chambers of commerce. $415. Gale Group, P.O. Box 9187, Farmington Hills, MI 48333-9187. Toll free US and Canada (800) 877-GALE (4253) and (248) 699-GALE, fax (800) 414-5043 and (248) 699-8061, Internet orders

galeord@galegroup.com, web site www.galegroup.com or www.gale.com. All Gale Group products are available on approval. Contact Gale for details.

ENCYCLOPEDIA OF ASSOCIATIONS: INTERNATIONAL ORGANIZATIONS includes nearly 20,000 multinational and national organizations in foreign countries, including US based associations with multinational membership. Entries also include email addresses, web sites and bulletin board addresses, lobbying activities, and publication and convention information. Indexed by geography, keyword and executives. $595 for 2 volume set. Also available in CD ROM. Database available via commercial online service. Gale Group, P.O. Box 9187, Farmington Hills, MI 48333-9187. Toll free US and Canada (800) 877-GALE (4253) and (248) 699-GALE, fax (800) 414-5043 and (248) 699-8061, Internet orders galeord@galegroup.com, web site www.galegroup.com or www.gale.com. All Gale Group products are available on approval. Contact Gale for details.

ENCYCLOPEDIA OF ASSOCIATIONS: NATIONAL ORGANIZATIONS OF THE US. This superb reference is one of the first places you should look when beginning a new recruiting assignment or when looking for specialized references of any type. The keyword index makes this comprehensive reference easy to use, even in hard copy. For over 23,000 nonprofit professional associations with a national scope, this encyclopedia reveals:

- Publications, including membership rosters and newsletters

- Dates and locations of association conferences and conventions

- Names of Executive Directors, who are usually incredible sources of industry information if you call and speak to them

- Committees

- Job and candidate referral banks, which can provide resumes of other industry sources and sometimes candidates

- It includes organizations in these categories: business, trade, environmental, agricultural, legal, governmental, engineering, technological, scientific, educational, cultural, social welfare, health & medical, public affairs, ethnic, labor unions, chambers of commerce, tourism, & others.

    Volume 1, National Organizations of the US, $505
    Volume 2, Geographic and Executive Indexes, $390
    Volume 3, Supplement, $405

Gale Group, P.O. Box 9187, Farmington Hills, MI 48333-9187. Toll free US and Canada (800) 877-GALE (4253) and (248) 699-GALE, fax (800) 414-5043 and (248) 699-8061, Internet orders galeord@galegroup.com, web site www.galegroup.com or www.gale.com. All Gale Group products are available on approval. Contact Gale for details.

ENCYCLOPEDIA OF ASSOCIATIONS: REGIONAL, STATE AND LOCAL ORGANIZATIONS. The information in this directory is not duplicated anywhere in ENCYCLOPEDIA OF ASSOCIATIONS. Over 100,000 nonprofit organizations are included in this directory. $585 for 5 volume set or $140 per individual volume. Also available on CD ROM and online on the Internet through a GaleNet subscription.

    Volume 1, Great Lakes States (Illinois, Indiana, Michigan, Minnesota, Ohio, Wisconsin)
    Volume 2, Northeastern States (Connecticut, Maine, Massachusetts, New Hampshire, New Jersey, New
            York, Pennsylvania, Rhode Islands, Vermont)
    Volume 3, Southern and Middle Atlantic States (Including Puerto Rico and the Virgin Islands) (Alabama,
            Delaware, Washington, DC, Florida, Georgia, Kentucky, Maryland, Mississippi, North
            Carolina, Puerto Rico, South Carolina, Tennessee, Virginia, West Virginia, Virgin Islands)
    Volume 4, South Central and Great Plains States (Arkansas, Iowa, Kansas, Louisiana, Missouri,
            Nebraska, North Dakota, Oklahoma, South Dakota, Texas)
    Volume 5, Western States (Alaska, Arizona, California, Colorado, Guam, Hawaii, Idaho, Montana,
            Nevada, New Mexico, Oregon, Utah, Washington, Wyoming)

Gale Group, P.O. Box 9187, Farmington Hills, MI 48333-9187. Toll free US and Canada (800) 877-GALE (4253) and (248) 699-GALE, fax (800) 414-5043 and (248) 699-8061, Internet orders galeord@galegroup.com, web site www.galegroup.com or www.gale.com. All Gale Group products are available on approval. Contact Gale for details.

Chain Stores

See Retail

CANADIAN PHARMACISTS DIRECTORY lists over 18,000 Canadian pharmacists, drug information centers, poison control centres, pharmaceutical suppliers, drug wholesalers, related universities, drug store head offices, pharmaceutical associations, chain drug stores, and brand name/generic pharmaceutical companies. $119 prepaid, $149 plus $5 shipping and handling if billed. Special discounts available for combined purchases. Published by Southam Information Products Ltd, 1450 Don Mills Road, Don Mills, Ontario M3B 2X7 CANADA, (800) 668-2374. In Toronto 442-2122. Web site www.southam.com.

CHAIN STORE GUIDE'S DATABASE MARKETING DIVISION can customize databases in these industries: Supermarket, department stores, discount department stores, drug stores. Your made-to-order database can include one or several of the named industries and the criteria of your ideal "customer" or search prospect. Information is available on a 3.5" diskette for IBM-PC, Apple Macintosh and DBF, ASCII, comma delimited and others. Mailing labels are also available or you can generate your own labels from a 3.5" diskette. For pricing or ordering information contact Chain Store Guide Information Services, 3922 Coconut Palm Drive, Tampa, FL 33619. (800) 927-9292, (813) 664-6800, (813) 627-6822, (800) 289-6822. http://www.d-net.com/csgis or http://www.csgis.com.

DIRECTORY OF DRUG STORE AND HBC CHAINS identifies over 1,800 drug retailers in the U.S. and Canada operating over 45,000 stores including drug, HBC, cosmetic, deep discount, home health care, discount, and grocery stores/supermarket chains with pharmacies, mass merchants with pharmacies, deep discount chains, and wholesale drug companies. It includes names and titles of key personnel, a listing of major trade associations and a trade show calendar. It also provides indexes to top drug retailers, top drug wholesalers, top grocery chains and top discount chains. $290. Chain Store Guide Information Services, 3922 Coconut Palm Drive, Tampa, FL 33619. (800) 927-9292, (813) 664-6800, (813) 627-6822, (800) 289-6822. http://www.d-net.com/csgis or http://www.csgis.com.

DIRECTORY OF SUPERMARKET, GROCERY AND CONVENIENCE STORE CHAINS describes and indexes over 2,300 supermarket chains with $2 million in annual sales. It covers supermarkets, superstores, club stores, gourmet supermarkets and combo stores in the U.S. and Canada, plus a special section profiling 1,700 convenience store chains. It includes an index to the top 200 supermarket chains and the top 100 convenience store chains, which is a valuable tool for target list development. It also lists over 29,000 key executives, buyers and administrative personnel. The directory also lists major trade associations and a trade show calendar. $300. Chain Store Guide Information Services, 3922 Coconut Palm Drive, Tampa, FL 33619. (800) 927-9292, (813) 664-6800, (813) 627-6822, (800) 289-6822. http://www.d-net.com/csgis or http://www.csgis.com.

SUPERMARKET, GROCERY AND CONVENIENCE STORE CHAINS CD-ROM can conduct data searches from five topic screens: 1. Personnel by title, 2. Personnel by functional area, 3. Listing type (branch office, corporate office, divisional office, headquarters, location, managed care div, regional office, subsidiary, warehouse), 4. Stores operated (superstores, supermarkets, convenience, warehouse, combo stores, gourmet supermarkets, stores w/gas), 5. Specialty departments (e.g., auto supplies, automatic teller machines, beer, books/magazines, floral/horticulture,gourmet/specialty foods, greeting cards, in-store bakeries, in-store banking, in-store restaurant, lawn & garden, liquor, nutrition center, et al.). You can also make selections based on geography or the size of a company (number of units and/or sales). Several output options are available, including mailing labels, and electronic formats (such as DBASE, ASCII, text) for mail merge customization. $795, including companion directory. If the price is prohibitively high, remember your local library. Chain Store Guide Information Services, 3922 Coconut Palm Drive, Tampa, FL 33619. (800) 927-9292, (813) 664-6800, (813) 627-6822, (800) 289-6822. http://www.d-net.com/csgis or http://www.csgis.com.

Chemicals

See Commercial Development

COMMERCIAL DEVELOPMENT AND MARKETING ASSOCIATION (CDMA) was formed by a merger of the COMMERCIAL DEVELOPMENT ASSOCIATION (CDA) and the CHEMICAL MANAGEMENT AND RESEARCH ASSOCIATION (CMRA). The CDA's membership directory had been a superb resource that included biographies and photos. You might need the assistance of a member in order to obtain a copy, or borrow one. COMMERCIAL DEVELOPMENT AND MARKETING ASSOCIATION, 1850 M Street, Suite 700, Washington, DC 20036, (202) 721-4110, www.cdmaonline.org.

MAJOR CHEMICAL & PETROCHEMICAL COMPANIES OF EUROPE contains information on 1,800 companies in 19 western European countries. $450. US distributor: Larry Meranus Professional Publications & Services, 4 Demoray Court, Pine Brook, NJ 07058, (800) MERANUS or (800) 637-2687. Published by Graham & Whiteside Ltd., Tuition House, 5-6 Francis Grove, London SW19 4DT, England. Web site http://www.major-co-data.com. Email sales@major-co-data.com.

MAJOR CHEMICAL & PETROCHEMICAL COMPANIES OF THE FAR EAST & AUSTRALASIA provides information on over 1,100 companies. $415. US distributor: Larry Meranus Professional Publications & Services, 4 Demoray Court, Pine Brook, NJ 07058, (800) MERANUS or (800) 637-2687. Published by Graham & Whiteside Ltd., Tuition House, 5-6 Francis Grove, London SW19 4DT, England. Web site http://www.major-co-data.com. Email sales@major-co-data.com.

MAJOR CHEMICAL & PETROCHEMICAL COMPANIES OF THE WORLD provides information on 6,500 companies. $830. US distributor: Larry Meranus Professional Publications & Services, 4 Demoray Court, Pine Brook, NJ 07058, (800) MERANUS or (800) 637-2687. Published by Graham & Whiteside Ltd., Tuition House, 5-6 Francis Grove, London SW19 4DT, England. Web site http://www.major-co-data.com. Email sales@major-co-data.com.

PLASTICS NEWS is a weekly trade publication. Crain Communications, Inc. is headquartered in Chicago with offices in major cities throughout the US, plus London, Tokyo and Frankfurt. New York location: 220 East 42nd Street, New York, NY 10017, (212) 210-0100, Circulation (800) 678-9595. Annual subscription $59. Web site www.plasticsnews.com.

RUBBER & PLASTICS NEWS is a biweekly trade publication. Crain Communications, Inc. is headquartered in Chicago with offices in major cities throughout the US plus London, Tokyo and Frankfurt. New York location: 220 East 42nd Street, New York, NY 10017, (212) 210-0100, Circulation (800) 678-9595. Annual subscription $69, two years $126. Web site www.rubbernews.com.

Chicago

See Illinois

CRAIN CHICAGO BUSINESS is a weekly trade publication. Look for special issues with surveys and lists of top companies by industry. Crain Communications, Inc. is headquartered in Chicago with offices in major cities throughout the US plus London, plus Tokyo and Frankfurt. New York location: 220 East 42nd Street, New York, NY 10017, (212) 210-0100, Circulation (800) 678-9595. Annual subscription $89, two years $155.

ILLINOIS COUNTY BUSINESS DATABASES & DIRECTORIES are published every two years and combine detailed profiles from the ILLINOIS MANUFACTURERS DIRECTORY and the companion ILLINOIS SERVICES DIRECTORY. All directories contains executive names and titles and other information. These editions are available:

- CHICAGO BUSINESS DIRECTORY, $129, Complete CD ROM $545, CD ROM with 100 or more employees $225. CD ROMs with 20 or more employees and 50 or more employees are also available.

- SUBURBAN COOK COUNTY BUSINESS DIRECTORY, $158, Complete CD ROM $695, CD ROM with 100 or more employees $260. CD ROMs with 10 or more employees, 20 or more employees and 50 or more employees are also available.

- DUPAGE COUNTY BUSINESS DIRECTORY, $94, Complete CD ROM $445. Abbreviated CD ROMs are also available.

- KANE COUNTY BUSINESS DIRECTORY, $49, Complete CD ROM $295. Abbreviated CD ROMs are also available.

- LAKE COUNTY BUSINESS DIRECTORY, $59. Complete CD ROM $325. Abbreviated CD ROMs are also available.

- McHENRY COUNTY BUSINESS DIRECTORY, $39, Complete CD ROM $195. Abbreviated CD ROMs are also available.

- WILL COUNTY BUSINESS DIRECTORY, $35, Complete CD ROM $195. Abbreviated CD ROMs are also available.

Distributed by Manufacturers' News, Inc., (888) 752-5200, 1633 Central Street, Evanston, IL 60201-1569. Email info@manufacturersnews.com. Web site www.manufacturersnews.com.

www.crainschicagobusiness.com is the web site for *Crain Chicago Business*. Crain Communications, Inc. is headquartered in Chicago with offices in major cities throughout the US, plus London, Tokyo and Frankfurt. New York location: 220 East 42nd Street, New York, NY 10017, (212) 210-0100, Circulation (800) 678-9595.

Chile

See *International, South America, Latin America*

DIRECTORY OF AMERICAN FIRMS OPERATING IN FOREIGN COUNTRIES, REGIONAL EDITION—ARGENTINA, BRAZIL, CHILE. $59. Uniworld Business Publications, Inc., 257 Central Park West, Suite 10A, New York, NY 10024-4110, (212) 496-2448, fax (212) 769-0413, email uniworldbp@aol.com. Web site: http://www.uniworldbp.com.

China

See *People's Republic of China, International, Asia, Hong Kong*

Cleveland

CRAIN CLEVELAND is a weekly trade publication. Look for special issues with surveys and lists of top companies by industry. Crain Communications, Inc. is headquartered in Chicago with offices in major cities throughout the US plus London, Tokyo and Frankfurt. New York location: 220 East 42nd Street, New York, NY 10017, (212) 210-0100, Circulation (800) 678-9595. Annual subscription $49, two years $87. Web site www.crainscleveland.com.

College Alumni

See *University Alumni*

College Recruiting

See *Campus Recruiting*

Commercial Development

COMMERCIAL DEVELOPMENT AND MARKETING ASSOCIATION (CDMA) was formed by a merger of the COMMERCIAL DEVELOPMENT ASSOCIATION (CDA) and the CHEMICAL MANAGEMENT AND RESEARCH ASSOCIATION (CMRA). The CDA's membership directory had been a superb resource that included biographies and photos. You might need the assistance of a member in order to obtain a copy, or borrow one. COMMERCIAL DEVELOPMENT AND MARKETING ASSOCIATION, 1850 M Street, Suite 700, Washington, DC 20036, (202) 721-4110, www.cdmaonline.org.

Commonwealth of Independent States

COMPANIES INTERNATIONAL CD-ROM contains comprehensive financial and contact data for over 300,000 public and privately held companies in 180 countries including the Commonwealth of Independent States, Mexico, Canada and Japan. Companies can be located by company name, product or industry, location, or a combination. This reference can also be used for target lists development for international companies, including privately held companies. $2,995. Gale Group, P.O. Box 9187, Farmington Hills, MI 48333-9187. Toll free US and Canada (800) 877-GALE (4253) and (248) 699-GALE, fax (800) 414-5043 and (248) 699-8061, Internet orders galeord@galegroup.com, web site www.galegroup.com or www.gale.com. All Gale Group products are available on approval. Contact Gale for details.

DIRECTORY OF AMERICAN FIRMS OPERATING IN FOREIGN COUNTRIES, REGIONAL EDITION—EUROPE, EASTERN. Includes Albania, Armenia, Azerbaijan, Belarus, Bulgaria, Croatia, Czech Republic, Estonia, Hungary, Kazakhstan, Latvia, Lithuania, Macedonia, Poland, Romania, Russia, Slovakia, Slovenia, Turkmenistan, Ukraine, Uzbekistan, Yugoslavia. $49. Uniworld Business Publications, Inc., 257 Central Park West, Suite 10A, New York, NY 10024-4110, (212) 496-2448, fax (212) 769-0413, email uniworldbp@aol.com. Web site: http://www.uniworldbp.com.

EUROPEAN R&D PLUS DATABASE ON CD ROM is a consolidation of the DIRECTORY OF EUROPEAN RESEARCH AND DEVELOPMENT and WHO'S WHO IN EUROPEAN RESEARCH AND DEVELOPMENT. It covers over 20,000 labs, both commercial and academic, in 36 countries including all the European former Soviet Republics. Searches can be conducted by over 20 fields in over 600 scientific disciplines. Information is available about over 100,000 people, including senior researchers, research managers and consultants, including: name, career data, current position, education, publications, research scope, current activities, nationality, languages and more. From Bowker-Saur. Updated annually. 1 year subscription $1,595, excluding discounts. For more information visit Bowker Reed Reference's web site at http://www.reedref.com or contact: Bowker Reed Reference Electronic Publishing, 121 Chanlon Road, New Providence, NJ 07974 USA, Phone (800) 323-3288, Fax (908) 665-3528, email info@bowker.com.

MAJOR COMPANIES OF CENTRAL AND EASTERN EUROPE AND THE COMMONWEALTH OF INDEPENDENT STATES identifies some 38,000 executives at 8,000 major business organizations in 24 countries in Eastern and Central Europe and the former Soviet Republics (CIS). Includes three indexes. $980. Also available in CD ROM. Published by Graham & Whiteside Ltd., Tuition House, 5-6 Francis Grove, London SW19 4DT, England. Web site http://www.major-co-data.com. Email sales@major-co-data.com. Distributed by: Larry Meranus Professional Publications & Services, 4 Demoray Court, Pine Brook, NJ 07058, (800) MERANUS or (800) 637-2687. Also distributed by Gale Group, P.O. Box 9187, Farmington Hills, MI 48333-9187. Toll free US and Canada (800) 877-GALE (4253) and (248) 699-GALE, fax (800) 414-5043 and (248) 699-8061, Internet orders galeord@galegroup.com, web site www.galegroup.com or www.gale.com. All Gale Group products are available on approval. Contact Gale for details.

WORLD GUIDE TO TRADE ASSOCIATIONS edited by Michael Zils includes key personnel, publications, a translation of the name in English, information that reflects the structure of Eastern Europe and the former USSR, a German-English concordance of subject areas and other data. From K.G. Saur. 2 volume set $650. R.R. Bowker (a unit of Cahners Business Information), 121 Chanlon Road, New Providence, NJ 07974 USA, Phone (888) BOWKER2 (888-269-5372) & (800) 323-3288, fax (908) 508-7696, email info@bowker.com, web www.bowker.com. Canada—R.R. Bowker, Markham, Ontario, phone (888) BOWKER9 & (905) 415-5837, fax (905) 479-6266. German speaking Europe—K.G. Saur Verlag, Munich, Germany, phone 49-89-76902-232, fax 49-89-76902-250, email 100730.1341@compuserve.com, web www.saur.de/home.htm. Rest of Europe incl. United Kingdom plus Africa & Asia—Bowker-Saur, W. Sussex, UK, phone 44-1342-326-972, fax 44-1342-335-612, email customer@bowker-saur.co.uk, web www.bowker-saur.com/service/. Australia/New Zealand—Thorpe, Port Melbourne, Victoria, Australia, phone 61-03-9-245-7370, fax 61-03-9-245-7395, email customer.service@thorpe.com.au, web www.thorpe.com.au. Technical support for CD ROMs (800) 323-3288, fax 908) 665-3528, email techsupport@bowker.com.

Communications

See Corporate Communications, Telecommunications

Community Affairs

See Social Services

Company Alumni

Directories of former employees of various companies are available, such as for IBM, Proctor and Gamble, McKinsey & Company and Booz, Allen & Hamilton. In some cases, such as for Booz, Allen and McKinsey, they are only available to former employees, so the best way to get one is to borrow a copy from a friendly alumnus/a. In other cases, as for IBM, the alumni directory is available to anyone who wishes to buy it (contact the ex-IBM Corporation in Garland, Texas. See Company Alumni Category for more information). At the time of this writing, very little is known about how to obtain a copy of a P&G alumni directory, except there are reports that one does exist. However, one way to research finding it would be to check Directories in Print and other librarians references, to ask your local business librarian, to ask sources and prospects who previously worked for P&G, to source librarians and other employees at consumer marketing professional associations, or possibly source the librarians at the Harvard Business School's Baker Library, which is an excellent source of consumer marketing information.

IBM ALUMNI DIRECTORY can be purchased by contacting Bob McGrath, Ex-IBM Corporation, 2713 Foxboro Drive, Garland, TX 75044-2819, phone (972) 761-0000 or (972) 414-0046. At the time of this writing, 3 versions of the directory are available: (1) alphabetically by name, $60, (2) cross referenced by company, zip code, title, with email if available but no phone numbers, $125 and (3) the edition most useful for executive recruiters which includes home and business phones and up to 9 previous positions since leaving IBM, $295.

PRIME COMPUTER AND COMPUTERVISION'S COMPANY ALUMNI WEB SITE URL'S are http://member.aol.com/uncleroy22/prime.htm and http://members.xoom.com/uncleroy/prime.htm

www.decalumni.com is the web site for alumni of Digital Equipment Corp. It includes a directory.

Company Research

See Chapter 6, "How To Create An Executive Search Library."
See References—General, Privately Held Companies

ADVERTISER AND AGENCY RED BOOKS PLUS CD ROM combines all the information in THE STANDARD DIRECTORY OF ADVERTISERS, THE STANDARD DIRECTORY OF ADVERTISING AGENCIES and THE STANDARD DIRECTORY OF INTERNATIONAL ADVERTISERS AND AGENCIES. Information is searchable by 25 fields, including company name, personal name, job title/function, product type, product/account name, city, state, zip or country, area code, revenues, number of employees, outside ad agency and even type of computer hardware. Contains professional association information. Available for Windows and Macintosh. Updated quarterly. 1 year subscription $1,295. If the price is prohibitively high, remember your local library. National Register Publishing, Reed Elsevier-New Providence, 121 Chanlon Road, New Providence, NJ 07974, (800) 521-8110, fax (800) 836-7736, web site www.redbooks.com or www.marquiswhoswho.com. "If, for any reason whatsoever, your order does not fully meet your expectations, simply return the product within 30 days for a prompt, complete, unquestioned refund," as stated in Catalog of Biographical and Professional References of publisher Marquis Who's Who/National Register Publishing.

ANNUAL REPORTS. Get the company phone number by calling toll free information (800-555-1212) or looking in a general directory such as STANDARD AND POORS, THE STANDARD DIRECTORY OF ADVERTISERS or NATIONAL DIRECTORY OF ADDRESSES AND TELEPHONE NUMBERS. Say you're calling to request a copy of an Annual Report, a 10(k) Report and a Proxy Statement. This information is FREE and you might as well ask for everything as long as you're on the phone. Note that while publicly held companies are legally required to file these documents with the Securities and Exchange Commission (SEC) every year, privately held companies are not. However, sometimes private companies produce annual reports or other brochures, lists of locations and so forth. You can also ask the Public Affairs department for news clippings or other information. Sales representatives are usually willing to send product information.

While it is possible to review annual reports on line, sometimes on a company's web site or using a specialized database, it may be easier to review hard copy, which is a quick phone call away. Hard copy is easy to mark up and it's portable. You can read it commuting on a bus or train or while you're waiting at the dentist's office.

Annual Reports sometimes contain photos of management, organization charts, lists of all locations, including plants; lists of divisions and subsidiaries, names and titles of management, sometimes at surprisingly junior levels; and almost always provide an explanation of how the company is organized. 10(k) Reports, as a matter of law, are required to identify senior management, their ages and brief background histories; to describe the business activities and products of the company; and to disclose any pending activities which could materially affect the company's financial performance, for example, the potential of an unfavorable outcome in a lawsuit. Proxy Statements are required to reveal the compensation of the four highest paid executives, backgrounds of the Directors of the company, and details about stock ownership and pension plans.

These materials are immensely valuable in analyzing whether you're searching in the part of an organization. This information is often more reliable than anything you will find in a directory or on a CD ROM because the company wrote it themselves and you are obtaining information firsthand, directly from the source. In fact, it could be the same source used by publishers of directories and CD ROMs.

Note: The Securities and Exchange Commission (SEC) legally requires all publicly held companies (that is, any companies that sell their stock) to publish an Annual Report, a 10(k) Report and a Notice of Annual Meeting and Proxy Statement (commonly called the "proxy statement" or just the "proxy.") However, privately held companies are not required to publish such information. Even so, some closely held companies do publish an annual report or an annual review, although they can be difficult to obtain. Sometimes the easiest way to do this is to ask for information from a friend who works there. Or if you work near the company, drop by in person and ask a receptionist for company literature.

BACON'S INFORMATION provides a news clipping and analysis service which can be used to monitor competitive news, to conduct topic research, or to track "pickup" of press releases. For more information, call BACON'S CLIPPING BUREAU to inquire about ExpressClips (same day coverage of top media in key markets), Electronic Clipping (database retrieval of transcripts from a wide selection of publications), International Clipping (coverage for specific countries worldwide) and Clip Analysis Reports (for a review of your own press coverage). (800) 621-0561, (800) 753-6675. Bacon's Information, Inc., a K-III Communications Company, 332 South Michigan Avenue, Chicago, IL 60604.

CANADIAN COMPANY HANDBOOK is published by Micromedia Ltd., 20 Victoria Street, Toronto, ON. For information about pricing, or their demand document center CANCORP, contact (800) 387-2689, (416) 362-5211, email info@micromedia.on.ca, web site www.micromedia.on.ca.

COMPANIES INTERNATIONAL CD-ROM contains comprehensive financial and contact data for over 300,000 public and privately held companies in 180 countries including the Commonwealth of Independent States, Mexico, Canada and Japan. Companies can be located by company name, product or industry, location, or a combination. This reference can also be used for target lists development for international companies, including privately held companies. $2,995. Gale Group, P.O. Box 9187, Farmington Hills, MI 48333-9187. Toll free US and Canada (800) 877-GALE (4253) and (248) 699-GALE, fax (800) 414-5043 and (248) 699-8061, Internet orders galeord@galegroup.com, web site www.galegroup.com or www.gale.com. All Gale Group products are available on approval. Contact Gale for details.

CYBERHOUND'S® GUIDE TO COMPANIES ON THE INTERNET reviews over 2,000 corporate sites, including major companies as well as those in the information industry, software and hardware developers and networking and telecommunications companies. It also includes a user's guide, a directory of specialized business we sites, a bibliography of Internet products, and a glossary of Internet terms. At the time of this writing 1st edition (1996) available from Gale for $79, reduced from $95. Published by Euromonitor

---

(England). Distributed by Gale Group, P.O. Box 9187, Farmington Hills, MI 48333-9187. Toll free US and Canada (800) 877-GALE (4253) and (248) 699-GALE, fax (800) 414-5043 and (248) 699-8061, Internet orders galeord@galegroup.com, web site www.galegroup.com or www.gale.com. All Gale Group products are available on approval. Contact Gale for details.

D&B MARKETING INFORMATION BASE contains marketing information on 10,000,000 companies. Every month it is updated, reflecting some 500,000 changes: new business additions, CEO CHANGES and address changes. Information on senior management changes is particularly valuable to job hunters and search firms is an indicator of change, which could mean hiring activity, and/or a need for executive search services. Organizations in transition are generally good places to recruit because quality talent may be unhappy with the politics of the new organization. With respect to the execution of an executive search, this information can be best utilized to develop a list of target companies. Then, names and titles can be identified using another database or through traditional ID research. This technique could be used for an extremely difficult recruiting assignment. For example, finding companies in turmoil could provide a good place to search for candidates eager for a change. Selections are delivered on tape, cartridge, diskette or hard copy. For prices call Dun & Bradstreet at (800) 526-0651. For more information contact Dun & Bradstreet, Business Reference Solutions, Three Sylvan Way, Parsippany, New Jersey 07054. Email dnbmdd@mail.dnb.com. Web site http://www.dnbmdd.com.

D&B MILLION DOLLAR DATABASE is an online database on the Internet. Users can access information on more than one million small, mid-sized and large companies, with minimum revenues of $1 million. Searches can be conducted by 22 criteria, including as geographic location, sales volume, number of employees, industry classification. Each company includes up to 30 executive names and titles and biographical data that includes education, work history and birth date. For prices call Dun & Bradstreet at (800) 526-0651. For more information contact Dun & Bradstreet, Business Reference Solutions, Three Sylvan Way, Parsippany, New Jersey 07054. Email dnbmdd@mail.dnb.com. Web site http://www.dnbmdd.com.

GALE BUSINESS RESOURCES ONLINE provides modules on US Industry (over 200,000 companies) and International Industry (over 200,000 companies), including public and privately held companies, brands, business rankings, trade and professional associations, company histories, merger information, and more. Comprehensive records include company name, officers' names and titles, SIC/NAICS codes and more. GALE BUSINESS RESOURCES is available online on the Internet through GaleNet. For information on pricing, contact: Gale Group, P.O. Box 9187, Farmington Hills, MI 48333-9187. Toll free US and Canada (800) 877-GALE (4253) and (248) 699-GALE, fax (800) 414-5043 and (248) 699-8061, Internet orders galeord@galegroup.com, web site www.galegroup.com or www.gale.com. All Gale Group products are available on approval. Contact Gale for details.

HOOVER'S HANDBOOK OF AMERICAN BUSINESS provides information on 500 companies, including contacts, products, brand names, key competitors, and a brief history. Published annually. $29.95 softcover, $39.95 hardcover. The Reference Press, Inc., 6448 Highway 209 East, Suite E104, Austin, TX 78723, (512) 454-7778. Hoover's directories can also be accessed on the Internet by going to the Ask Jeeves web site at www.askjeeves.com. A subscription fee is charged for the service.

HOOVER'S HANDBOOK OF WORLD BUSINESS contains information on 200 companies, including contact information, products, key competitors, and a brief history. Published annually. $27.95 soft cover, $37.95 hard cover. The Reference Press, Inc., 6448 Highway 209 East, Suite E104, Austin, TX 78723, (512) 454-7778. Hoover's directories can also be accessed on the Internet by going to the Ask Jeeves web site at www.askjeeves.com. A subscription fee is charged for the service.

INDUSTRY CANADA's Library can be reached at (613) 954-2728. Orders can be placed by calling (613) 947-5194. For more information, see their "Strategis Department" "Canadian Company Capabilities" web site at www.strategis.ic.gc.ca. Strategis's mandate is to print virtually any kind of information you want on Canadian companies. Their Help Desk number is (800) 328-6189. There are virtually no more updated print versions of information as all updates are now online.

INFORMATION SOURCES was an award winning directory published by the Gale Group in partnership with the Information Industry Association (IIA). At the time of this writing, the IIA has merged with the Software Publishers Association (SPA) to form the newly named Software and Information Industry Association (SIIA).

This directory provides information for the 550 member companies of the Information Industry Association. Entries include company name, address, phone, names of executives, regional offices, trade and brand names and description of products and services. Indexed by product, personal name, trade name, geography, parent company, international, and niche markets. The directory also identifies publishers, database producers, online services, telecommunications and network providers, system integrators and many others. $125. Contact Gale for information as to when an updated directory will be available. In the meantime, visit the Software and Information Industry's web site at www.siia.net to see their membership roster.

Gale Group, P.O. Box 9187, Farmington Hills, MI 48333-9187. Toll free US and Canada (800) 877-GALE (4253) and (248) 699-GALE, fax (800) 414-5043 and (248) 699-8061, Internet orders galeord@galegroup.com, web site www.galegroup.com or www.gale.com. All Gale Group products are available on approval. Contact Gale for details.

Software & Information Industry Association (SIIA), formerly the Software Publishers Association (SPA) and Information Industry Association (IIA) is located at 1730 M Street, NW, Washington, DC 20036, (202) 452-1600, www.siia.net.

INTERNATIONAL DIRECTORY OF COMPANY HISTORIES. While this directory provides few names and titles, it could be useful as a new business development tool. It provides historical backgrounds of 2,000 companies—potential new clients about whom you should be familiar prior to making a new business presentation. $175 per volume. 25 volumes in print at the time of this writing. If it is not feasible to purchase these reference materials, visit your local library. If they don't have the reference you need, they may have a sharing agreement with another library. Published by Gale Group, P.O. Box 9187, Farmington Hills, MI 48333-9187. Toll free US and Canada (800) 877-GALE (4253) and (248) 699-GALE, fax (800) 414-5043 and (248) 699-8061, Internet orders galeord@galegroup.com, web site www.galegroup.com or www.gale.com. All Gale Group products are available on approval. Contact Gale for details.

PRIME COMPUTER AND COMPUTERVISION'S COMPANY ALUMNI WEB SITE URL'S are http://member.aol.com/uncleroy22/prime.htm and http://members.xoom.com/uncleroy/prime.htm

KOMPASS is described by the publisher as "the world's most comprehensive global database of companies, products and services for manufacturing and engineering professionals in print, on CD ROM and on the Internet." It contains company and product information for companies in all lines of business, including manufacturing and industrial sectors. Each company listing includes name, address, phone number, management names, business descriptions, and industry and product listings. Kompass's web site is www.kompass.com. Call publisher for prices and information on country directories. Cahners Business Information, 121 Chanlon Road, New Providence, NJ 07974, (908) 771-8785, fax (908) 665-8755, email hholmes@reedref.com. Headquarters: Cahners Business Information, 275 Washington Street, Newton, MA 02158-1630, (617) 558-4663 or (617) 964-3030, fax (617) 558-4700, email marketaccess@cahners.com, web sites www.cahners.com or www.chilton.net.

MAJOR COMPANIES SERIES ON CD ROM consists of Graham & Whiteside's annual directories of major international companies. All six directories reside on one disk. After payment, you'll receive a security code to access the region(s) you select. This Windows™ based CD can navigate by company name, company locations, executive names, business activity and more. Free demo CD ROM is available. Regions also available separately for Europe, Central & Eastern Europe, the Far East and Australasia, the Arab World, Africa, and Latin America. For prices and availability, contact the Gale Group, P.O. Box 9187, Farmington Hills, MI 48333-9187. Toll free US and Canada (800) 877-GALE (4253) and (248) 699-GALE, fax (800) 414-5043 and (248) 699-8061, Internet orders galeord@galegroup.com, web site www.galegroup.com or www.gale.com. All Gale Group products are available on approval. Contact Gale for details.

NATIONAL DIRECTORY OF ADDRESSES AND TELEPHONE NUMBERS contains addresses and phone numbers for major US companies, arranged alphabetically and by SIC or NAICS codes. Includes special information on hotels, banks, government information, area codes for US cities, transportation, colleges and more. Published annually. $95. Omnigraphics, Inc., Penobscot Building, Detroit, Michigan 48226, (313) 961-1340.

NATIONAL E-MAIL AND FAX DIRECTORY provides over 180,000 fax numbers for US companies, organizations and government agencies, cross referenced by subject. $126. Gale Group, P.O. Box 9187, Farmington Hills, MI 48333-9187. Toll free US and Canada (800) 877-GALE (4253) and (248) 699-GALE,

fax (800) 414-5043 and (248) 699-8061, Internet orders galeord@galegroup.com, web site www.galegroup.com or www.gale.com. All Gale Group products are available on approval. Contact Gale for details.

NELSON FINANCIAL DATABASE provides comprehensive information on the global institutional investment market. Information formatted to your precise needs is available from Nelson Information Mailing List & Customized Database service. The NELSON FINANCIAL DATABASE is comprised of:

> 30,000 executives at investment management firms
> 11,000 executives at research firms
> 100,000 executives at public companies
> 40,000 executives at plan sponsors
> 3,000 executives at pension fund consulting firms
> 24,000 executives at institutional real estate firms
> 4,000 executives at technology based vendors

The database also consists of extensive investment information, including money manager performance, peer group analysis, special surveys and more. For customers who with to use Nelson's information in their own systems, Nelson will supply customized data export, using all or any data items. Mailing lists are also available for direct marketers.For more information, contact Nelson Mailing List & Customized Database Services, P.O. Box 591, Port Chester, NY 10573 USA. (800) 333-6357, Phone outside the US (914) 937-8400, Fax (914) 937-8590, web site http://www.nelnet.com.

NEW YORK TIMES can be researched for company information.

ORGANIZATION CHARTS is a working collection of 200 power structures of a diverse range of companies—large and small, international and local, public and private, for profit and not for profit. $150. At the time of this writing, this reference was last published in 1996. Contact the publisher for information about an updated edition. Gale Group, P.O. Box 9187, Farmington Hills, MI 48333-9187. Toll free US and Canada (800) 877-GALE (4253) and (248) 699-GALE, fax (800) 414-5043 and (248) 699-8061, Internet orders galeord@galegroup.com, web site www.galegroup.com or www.gale.com. All Gale Group products are available on approval. Contact Gale for details.

SELECTPHONE is a national telephone directory on CD ROM. They offer a range of products at different prices. For more information, call them at (800) 992-3766 or visit their web site at www.infousa.com. SelectPhone is a product of Pro CD, Inc., 5711 South 86th Circle, Omaha, NE 68127.

STANDARD DIRECTORY OF ADVERTISERS Business Classifications Edition is an excellent general directory that organizes companies by a wide range of product categories. A few examples include "Apparel 2—Men's and Boys' Wear," "Heating and Air Conditioning," "Cosmetics and Toiletries," and "Aviation and Aerospace." This directory lists names and titles of key officers, revenues and other information. It is available in a geographic edition for the same price. This directory is comprised of over 24,000 companies that annually spend over $200,000 on advertising. It represents a reasonable place to look for hard-to-find information about privately held companies, especially those that heavily advertise their products. It is a good place to look for names if STANDARD AND POORS and the MILLION DOLLAR DIRECTORY fail to yield the names you need. Finally, the Classified Edition of THE STANDARD DIRECTORY OF ADVERTISERS can be a very convenient source of research because both your target list of companies and the corresponding names and titles of management all appear together, in the same Classification. This is important if you still rely on research books in hard copy. THE STANDARD DIRECTORY OF ADVERTISERS also publishes a special volume called THE STANDARD DIRECTORY OF ADVERTISERS TRADENAME INDEX. You can use the TRADENAME INDEX if you know the brand name of a product and need to find the company that manufactures it. In addition, this directory contains an Associations section which identifies marketing oriented associations.

$599 hard copy. If the price is prohibitively high, remember your local library. THE STANDARD DIRECTORY OF ADVERTISERS is also available on CD ROM under the title ADVERTISER AND AGENCY RED BOOKS PLUS. It is available in Windows® and Macintosh® formats. National Register Publishing, Reed Elsevier-New Providence, 121 Chanlon Road, New Providence, NJ 07974, (800) 521-8110, fax (800) 836-7736, web site www.redbooks.com or www.marquiswhoswho.com. "If, for any reason whatsoever, your order does not fully meet your expectations, simply return the product within 30 days for a prompt, complete, unquestioned refund," as stated in Catalog of Biographical and Professional References of publisher Marquis Who's Who/National Register Publishing.

STANDARD DIRECTORY OF ADVERTISING AGENCIES, also referred to as the "Red Book," is a comprehensive directory of the advertising agency business, generally including extensive listings of executives, especially in management, media, account services, creative and production. It also reveals the names of each agency's corporate clients. A CyberAgency Section lists agencies involved with Web design and development and a special "Who Owns Whom" section listing agency subsidiaries. $599. If the price is prohibitively high, remember your local library. THE STANDARD DIRECTORY OF ADVERTISING AGENCIES is also available on CD ROM under the title ADVERTISER AND AGENCY RED BOOKS PLUS. National Register Publishing, Reed Elsevier-New Providence, 121 Chanlon Road, New Providence, NJ 07974, (800) 521-8110, fax (800) 836-7736, web site www.marquiswhoswho.com or www.redbooks.com. "If, for any reason whatsoever, your order does not fully meet your expectations, simply return the product within 30 days for a prompt, complete, unquestioned refund," as stated in Catalog of Biographical and Professional References of publisher Marquis Who's Who/National Register Publishing.

STANDARD AND POORS REGISTER OF CORPORATIONS, DIRECTORS AND EXECUTIVES. Volume 1, Corporations, contains complete listings for 75,000 companies (including large subsidiaries), specifically names, titles, phone numbers, number of employees, annual sales, main products, and SIC/NAICS codes. Volume 2, Directors and Executives alphabetically lists 70,000 key managers with biographical data. Volume 3, Corporate Family Index is useful for locating a company's parent, subsidiaries, divisions and affiliates; also contains an index of companies by state and major cities. Published annually. Hardback directory, $799. Available in CD ROM. Call for price. Published by Standard & Poors Corporation, New York, New York. Distributed by: Larry Meranus Professional Publications & Services, 4 Demoray Court, Pine Brook, NJ 07058, (800) MERANUS or (800) 637-2687.

STATE MANUFACTURING DIRECTORIES and US regional geographic directories published by Harris are available for all US states as hard copy directories or in electronic Selectory® formats. With Selectory® information is searchable from 25 fields and generates an easy-to-read report containing: company, address, location, county, phone, fax, toll free number, Internet address, a listing of personnel with titles, SIC/NAICS codes, product description, products, number of employees, per cent employment change, sales range, plant size, foreign trade, year established, private or public ownership, and experian credit score. This information could either provide an alternative to "identification research" calls, or offer an excellent place to begin the verification calls of ID research. If time is money, you can access a tremendous amount of precise information quickly with electronic references, such as this one or many others. One attractive feature of Harris's products is that they are relatively inexpensive. Here are a few sample prices: Directories and databases are available for all US states: Alabama $79 directory, $349 database. Arizona $90 directory, $475 database. Arkansas $69 directory, $325 database, Ohio $159 directory, $725 database. New Jersey $99 directory, $595 database. The most expensive is California, $169 directory, $925 database. The least expensive are Delaware and Washington, DC each one at $39 for directory, $149 for database.

Contact Harris for a sample Harris Profile Report. For exact pricing, a catalog and other information, call distributor Scott's Directories, Toronto area: 1450 Don Mills Road, Don Mills, Ontario, M3B 2X7, CANADA, (888) 709-9907, (416) 442-2291, (416) 932-9555. Montréal area: Scott's Directories, 3300 Cote Verde, Suite 410 Ville St.-Laurent, Quebec H4B 2B7 CANADA (514) 339-1397, (800) 363-1327, email scotts@southam.ca. Publisher Harris InfoSource, 2057 East Aurora Road, Twinsburg, OH 44087-1999, (330) 425-9000, (800) 888-5900, www.HarrisInfo.com.

SURVEILLANT: ACQUISITIONS & COMMENTARY FOR INTELLIGENCE & SECURITY PROFESSIONALS publishes SURVEILLANT, a book alert newsletter reviews over 250 new books per issue in these areas: competitor and business intelligence, tradecraft, technology-transfer, military intelligence, espionage, covert actions, security and counterintelligence, psychological warfare, propaganda, disinformation, deception, cryptology, guerrilla warfare, terrorism, resistance movements, aerial and space reconnaissance, science, histories or accounts of FBI, CIA, NSA, MOSSAD and other intelligence agencies and personal memoirs. $18 per issue, annual subscription $110 US, $120 Canada, $140 foreign. Ordering information: SURVEILLANT, Suite 165, 2020 Pennsylvania Ave. NW, Washington, DC 20006-1846. (202) 797-1234, email: reviews@surveillant.com.

VALUE LINE INVESTMENT SURVEY is considered one of the most respected investment surveys around, particularly for their analysis of future prospects of the publicly held companies they follow. Also analyzes industries. Value Line Investment Survey, 220 East 42nd Street, New York, NY 10017-5891. Available as a Windows® CD ROM or a 3.5" disk covering 1,700 stocks, 2 month trial, $55. 1 year subscription $595. Covering 5,000+ stocks, 2 month trial $95, 1 year subscription $995. Call (800) 535-9648, ext. 2751. Call (800) 634-3583 for pricing about other products, including Mutual Fund Survey, Options, Convertibles, Over-the-Counter Special Situations, and hard copy of the Value Line Investment Survey and Value Line Investment Survey Expanded.

WALKER'S CORPORATE DIRECTORY OF US PUBLIC COMPANIES contains information on 10,000 publicly held companies, including names of key executives. Hard cover directory $360, CD ROM $595, both together $765. Kennedy Information, One Kennedy Place, Route 12 South, Fitzwilliam, NH 03447, phone (800) 531-0007 or 603-585-6544, fax 603-585-9555, email bookstore@kennedyinfo.com, web site www.kennedyinfo.com.

WALL STREET JOURNAL, New York, New York, can be researched for company information.

WARD'S BUSINESS DIRECTORY OF U.S. PRIVATE AND PUBLIC COMPANIES provides information on over 120,000 US companies, over 90% of them privately held. Volumes 1-3 contain company information. Volume 4 lists companies geographically and ranks the top 1,000 privately held companies and the top 1,000 employers. Volume 5 ranks private and public companies by sales within SIC or NAICS code. Volumes 6-7 contain state rankings by sales within SIC or NAICS. Also includes ranking of the top 100 privately held companies, the top publicly held companies and the top 100 employers for each state. Volume 8 ranks sales within the 6 digit NAICS (North American Industry Classification System which replaced the SIC code system). It sorts companies by cross-national agreements between the US, Canada and Mexico. Vols. 1-8, $2,515. Vols. 1-5, $2,125. Vols. 1-4, $1,880. Vol 5, $950. Vols. 6-7, $950. Vol 8, $640. Gale Group, P.O. Box 9187, Farmington Hills, MI 48333-9187. Toll free US and Canada (800) 877-GALE (4253) and (248) 699-GALE, fax (800) 414-5043 and (248) 699-8061, Internet orders galeord@galegroup.com, web site www.galegroup.com or www.gale.com. All Gale Group products are available on approval. Contact Gale for details.

WORLD DIRECTORY OF BUSINESS INFORMATION WEB SITES provides full details on over 1,500 free business web sites, including information such as online surveys, top company rankings, company information, brand information, market research reports and trade association statistics. $590. Published by Euromonitor (England). Distributed by Gale Group, P.O. Box 9187, Farmington Hills, MI 48333-9187. Toll free US and Canada (800) 877-GALE (4253) and (248) 699-GALE, fax (800) 414-5043 and (248) 699-8061, Internet orders galeord@galegroup.com, web site www.galegroup.com or www.gale.com. All Gale Group products are available on approval. Contact Gale for details.

www.abbott.com/career/index.htm is the Career pages web site for Abbott Laboratories. Check other company web sites for career opportunities at the company of your choice.

www.askjeeves.com or **www.ask.com** or **www.aj.com** or **ask**. If you ask Jeeves, "How can I find a job" or "How can I find candidates for an engineering job?" Jeeves has an answer! (Actually, there's very little you CAN'T ask Jeeves.) The Ask Jeeves site includes HOOVER'S CAREER CENTER, which consists of Job Search Tools (monster.com, CareerMosaic,wsj.com careers, hotjobs, westech's virtual job fair and joboptions), Career Links and Career Research Links. Hoover's Career Center contains much additional information, including extensive RELOCATION data, such as cost of living comparisons, etc. You can also subscribe to **Hoover**'s and access their directories on the Internet.

www.decalumni.com is the web site for alumni of Digital Equipment Corp. It includes a directory.

www.europages.com is a web site of a business directory of over 500,000 European firms. In Deutsch, English, Espanol, Français & Italiano. Features include Search for Companies, Company Catalogues, Business Information, Yellow Pages in Europe. Search by Product/Service, Thematic Search or by Company Name. Address, phone, fax, products, turnover. Europages' Daily Business News, European Trade Fairs, Chambers of Commerce in Europe, European Patent Offices, Official International Organisations, European Standardization Bodies.

www.galegroup.com is the web site to publisher Gale Research, one of the largest providers of research for search, recruiting and libraries.

www.infousa.com provides free US national directory assistance.

www.kompass.com is the web site for the highly respected Kompass country directories and databases. This web site contains a searchable database that encompasses over 60 countries, 2.5 million executive names, information on 1.5 million companies, 19 million key product references, and 370,000 trade and brand names. At the time of this writing, Kompass is available in English and French. Deutsch, Espanol and Italiano will soon be available.

www.nytimes.com is the URL for *The New York Times* web site.

www.sec.gov/edgarhp.htm is the URL to the EDGAR Database of corporate information from the Securities & Exchange Commission, a database of corporate information. Features include: About the SEC, Investor Assistance & Complaints, EDGAR Database, SEC Digest & Statements, Current SEC Rulemaking, Enforcement Division, Small Business Information, Other sites to visit.

www.thomasregister.com is the URL for Thomas' Register, which provides information Information on US and Canadian manufacturing firms.

Compensation

AMERICAN COST OF LIVING SURVEY provides cost and expense data for 455 American cities and metropolitan areas. Includes housing, transportation, food, clothing and other consumer goods, utilities, insurance, entertainment, taxes, education and more. $160, 2nd edition, 1995. Contact publisher to find out when next edition will be available. Gale Group, P.O. Box 9187, Farmington Hills, MI 48333-9187. Toll free US and Canada (800) 877-GALE (4253) and (248) 699-GALE, fax (800) 414-5043 and (248) 699-8061, Internet orders galeord@galegroup.com, web site www.galegroup.com or www.gale.com. All Gale Group products are available on approval. Contact Gale for details.

AMERICAN ELECTRONICS ASSOCIATION annually publishes the AEA DIRECTORY for $175. With 18 regional groups, this association conducts networking programs for industry executives, and provides information on compensation surveys and employee benefits plans, among other things. For more information contact: American Electronics Association (AEA), 5201 Great America Parkway, Suite 520, PO Box 54990, Santa Clara, CA 95056, (408) 987-4200.

AMERICAN SALARIES AND WAGES SURVEY presents salary data about occupation, industry, location; low, mid and high figures. Contact publisher for date of latest information and scheduled updates. $120. Gale Group, P.O. Box 9187, Farmington Hills, MI 48333-9187. Toll free US and Canada (800) 877-GALE (4253) and (248) 699-GALE, fax (800) 414-5043 and (248) 699-8061, Internet orders galeord@galegroup.com, web site www.galegroup.com or www.gale.com. All Gale Group products are available on approval. Contact Gale for details.

PERKS AND PARACHUTES: NEGOTIATING YOUR EXECUTIVE EMPLOYMENT CONTRACT is a manual on senior executive employment agreements, non-compete agreements, termination agreements and so forth. It includes sample agreements and negotiating strategies, plus twelve different samples of agreements. $105 by Priority Mail available from Kenneth J. Cole, Publisher, The Recruiting & Search Report, P.O. Box 9433, Panama City Beach, FL 32417. (850) 235-3733, fax (850) 233-9695 Email jcole9433@aol.com.

PR NEWS ANNUAL SALARY SURVEY AND EXCLUSIVE GUIDE TO EXECUTIVE RECRUITERS, Phillips Business Information, Inc., a Phillips Publishing International Company, 120 Seven Locks Road, Potomac, MD 20854, (301) 340-1520, (301) 340-7788, (800) 777-5006, Internet pbi@phillips.com, web site www.phillips.com.

PROXY STATEMENTS must be filed with the Securities and Exchange Commission every year by all publicly held companies. Proxy statements are most useful for obtaining compensation information about senior management, specifically the four highest paid executives. Proxy statements also contain background information and sometimes photos of a company's directors. If you are calling to request a proxy, you might want to also get an annual report and a 10(k), because they're all free. Just call the company switchboard and say you'd like to request a copy of an annual report, a 10(k) and a proxy.

TOP EXECUTIVE COMPENSATION is published annually. $30 for members, $120 for non-members. The Conference Board, 845 Third Avenue, New York, New York 10022, (212) 339-0345.

WORLD COST OF LIVING SURVEY includes information such as child care, education, health care, utilities and other areas for major cities around the world. It is a useful resource for companies relocating employees to determine appropriate levels of compensation adjustment and for individuals considering a move abroad. $240. Gale Group, P.O. Box 9187, Farmington Hills, MI 48333-9187. Toll free US and Canada (800) 877-GALE (4253) and (248) 699-GALE, fax (800) 414-5043 and (248) 699-8061, Internet orders galeord@galegroup.com, web site www.galegroup.com or www.gale.com. All Gale Group products are available on approval. Contact Gale for details.

www.careers.wsj.com is the *Wall Street Journal*'s web site. It focuses on positions for middle and senior management including financial positions at $75,000 and up. This web site is among those that encompass senior executive positions. Other features includes Job Seek, Who's Hiring, Career Columnists, Salaries & Profiles, The Salary Calculator™, Job Hunting Advice, Succeeding at Work, HR Issues, Executive Recruiters, Working Globally, College Connection, Starting a Business, Career Bookstore and more. Content from The National Employment Business Weekly is also featured. The site was developed by Dow Jones & Company, Inc., Princeton, New Jersey and was established in 1997.

www.nationjob.com is the web site for NationJob Network Online Jobs Database. NationJob, Inc. was ranked as one of the top 5 sites in two different categories by the *National Business Employment Weekly*: "Sites Offering the Best Job-Search Support" and "Best General Purpose Sites." The site offers "Search for a Job Now (no email required)," "Search for a Company" and "Directory of all Companies." P.J. Scout service is a "(P)ersonal (J)ob Scout service that's "like having a friend shop for a job for you." Fill in a form and PJ will send you info on jobs you might be interested in. Information on salary comparisons, moving costs, relocation info, insurance calculator and more. NationJob Inc., 601 SW 9th Street, Suites J&K, Des Moines, IA 50309, (800) 292-7731. The site developer is NationJob, Inc.

www.wageweb.com is the URL for the Salary Survey Data Online web site.

Computer Systems

See Information Technology, Software, Telecommunications
See Software

Conferences

See Trade Shows

ASSOCIATIONS CANADA, previously titled DIRECTORY OF ASSOCIATIONS IN CANADA, provides information on a $1 billion economic sector, including information on conferences, publications, mailing lists and more. $289 Canadian in print, $389 Canadian for CD ROM, and $489 Canadian for both. Published annually by Micromedia Ltd., 20 Victoria Street, Toronto, ON. (800) 387-2689, (416) 362-5211, email info@micromedia.on.ca, web site www.micromedia.on.ca.

ENCYCLOPEDIA OF ASSOCIATIONS: INTERNATIONAL ORGANIZATIONS includes nearly 20,000 multinational and national organizations in foreign countries, including US based associations with multinational membership. Entries also include email addresses, web sites and bulletin board addresses, lobbying activities, and publication and convention information. Indexed by geography, keyword and executives. $595 for 2 volume set. Also available in CD ROM. Database available via commercial online service. Gale Group, P.O. Box 9187, Farmington Hills, MI 48333-9187. Toll free US and Canada (800) 877-GALE (4253) and (248) 699-GALE, fax (800) 414-5043 and (248) 699-8061, Internet orders galeord@galegroup.com, web site www.galegroup.com or www.gale.com. All Gale Group products are available on approval. Contact Gale for details.

ENCYCLOPEDIA OF ASSOCIATIONS: NATIONAL ORGANIZATIONS OF THE US. This superb reference is one of the first places you should look when beginning a new recruiting assignment or when looking for specialized references of any type. The keyword index makes this comprehensive reference easy to use, even in hard copy. For over 23,000 nonprofit professional associations with a national scope, this encyclopedia reveals:

- Publications, including membership rosters and newsletters

- Dates and locations of association conferences and conventions

- Names of Executive Directors, who are usually incredible sources of industry information if you call and speak to them

- Committees

- Job and candidate referral banks, which can provide resumes of other industry sources and sometimes candidates

- It includes organizations in these categories: business, trade, environmental, agricultural, legal, govern mental, engineering, technological, scientific, educational, cultural, social welfare, health & medical, public affairs, ethnic, labor unions, chambers of commerce, tourism, & others.

  Volume 1, National Organizations of the US, $505
  Volume 2, Geographic and Executive Indexes, $390
  Volume 3, Supplement, $405

Gale Group, P.O. Box 9187, Farmington Hills, MI 48333-9187. Toll free US and Canada (800) 877-GALE (4253) and (248) 699-GALE, fax (800) 414-5043 and (248) 699-8061, Internet orders galeord@galegroup.com, web site www.galegroup.com or www.gale.com. All Gale Group products are available on approval. Contact Gale for details.

ENCYCLOPEDIA OF ASSOCIATIONS: REGIONAL, STATE AND LOCAL ORGANIZATIONS. The information in this directory is not duplicated anywhere in ENCYCLOPEDIA OF ASSOCIATIONS. Over 100,000 nonprofit organizations are included in this directory. $585 for 5 volume set or $140 per individual volume. Also available on CD ROM and online on the Internet through a GaleNet subscription.

  Volume 1, Great Lakes States (Illinois, Indiana, Michigan, Minnesota, Ohio, Wisconsin)
  Volume 2, Northeastern States (Connecticut, Maine, Massachusetts, New Hampshire, New Jersey, New York, Pennsylvania, Rhode Islands, Vermont)
  Volume 3, Southern and Middle Atlantic States (Including Puerto Rico and the Virgin Islands) (Alabama, Delaware, Washington, DC, Florida, Georgia, Kentucky, Maryland, Mississippi, North Carolina, Puerto Rico, South Carolina, Tennessee, Virginia, West Virginia, Virgin Islands)
  Volume 4, South Central and Great Plains States (Arkansas, Iowa, Kansas, Louisiana, Missouri, Nebraska, North Dakota, Oklahoma, South Dakota, Texas)
  Volume 5, Western States (Alaska, Arizona, California, Colorado, Guam, Hawaii, Idaho, Montana, Nevada, New Mexico, Oregon, Utah, Washington, Wyoming)

Gale Group, P.O. Box 9187, Farmington Hills, MI 48333-9187. Toll free US and Canada (800) 877-GALE (4253) and (248) 699-GALE, fax (800) 414-5043 and (248) 699-8061, Internet orders galeord@galegroup.com, web site www.galegroup.com or www.gale.com. All Gale Group products are available on approval. Contact Gale for details.

LITERARY MARKET PLACE, "The Directory of the American Book Publishing Industry With Industry Yellow Pages" is an excellent 3 volume directory with comprehensive information on US book publishers; imprints, subsidiaries and distributors; book trade acquisitions and mergers, small presses, Canadian book publishers, micropublishers, US electronic publishers, electronic publishing consultants, electronic publishing products and services, editorial services, literary agents, illustrations agents, US agents and offices of foreign publishers, lecture agents, specialized advertising and public relations firms, direct mail specialists, mailing list brokers and services, book review syndicates, book review and index journals and services, book exhibits, book clubs, book lists and catalogs, book importers and exporters, book producers, translators, artists, photographers, stock photo agencies, associations, book trade events and conferences, awards, contents and grants, reference books for the trade, magazines for the trade, a toll free directory of publishers, magazine and newspaper publicity, radio and television publicity, book manufacturing services, book distributors and sales representatives, and wholesalers. $189.95.

LITERARY MARKET PLACE ON DISC, previously titled LITERARY MARKET PLACE PLUS CD ROM, one year subscription $297.00.

LITERARY MARKET PLACE—INTERNET EDITION, www.literarymarketplace.com, is available by subscription.

INTERNATIONAL LITERARY MARKET PLACE Internet database can be directly accessed at www.iliterarymarketplace.com. It is also linked to the US domestic LITERARY MARKET PLACE web site at www.literarymarketplace.com. Contact the publisher for subscription price. INTERNATIONAL LITERARY MARKET PLACE, hard copy $189.95.

R.R. Bowker (a unit of Cahners Business Information), 121 Chanlon Road, New Providence, NJ 07974 USA, Phone (888) BOWKER2 (888-269-5372) & (800) 323-3288, fax (908) 508-7696, email info@bowker.com, web www.bowker.com. Canada—R.R. Bowker, Markham, Ontario, phone (888) BOWKER9 & (905) 415-5837, fax (905) 479-6266. German speaking Europe—K.G. Saur Verlag, Munich, Germany, phone 49-89-76902-232, fax 49-89-76902-250, email 100730.1341@compuserve.com, web www.saur.de/home.htm. Rest of Europe incl. United Kingdom plus Africa & Asia—Bowker-Saur, W. Sussex, UK, phone 44-1342-326-972, fax 44-1342-335-612, email customer@bowker-saur.co.uk, web www.bowker-saur.com/service/. Australia/New Zealand—Thorpe, Port Melbourne, Victoria, Australia, phone 61-03-9-245-7370, fax 61-03-9-245-7395, email customer.service@thorpe.com.au, web www.thorpe.com.au. Technical support for CD ROMs (800) 323-3288, fax 908) 665-3528, email techsupport@bowker.com.

NATIONAL TRADE AND PROFESSIONAL ASSOCIATIONS OF THE UNITED STATES is a major directory of associations. It includes 7,600 national trade associations, professional societies and labor unions cross referenced by subject. Also includes publications, convention schedule, membership and staff size, and budget. $129. Colombia Books, Washington, DC.

STATE AND REGIONAL ASSOCIATIONS OF THE UNITED STATES identifies over 7,000 state and regional associations in the US. Information is cross referenced by subject, state, budget and chief executive and includes publications, convention schedule, membership/ staff size and budget. $79. Columbia Books, Inc., 1212 New York Avenue, NW, Suite 330, Washington, DC 20005, (212) 898-0662.

YEARBOOK OF INTERNATIONAL ORGANIZATIONS is a 4 volume directory of non-profit organizations, commercial associations, business groups, conferences, religious orders and intergovernmental bodies. From K.G. Saur. $1,170 for 4 volumes.

YEARBOOK OF INTERNATIONAL ORGANIZATIONS PLUS is a CD ROM which was described by American Reference Books Annual as "The most comprehensive coverage of international organizations." This CD consolidates THE YEARBOOK OF INTERNATIONAL ORGANIZATIONS and WHO'S WHO IN INTERNATIONAL ORGANIZATIONS. It encompasses intergovernmental and national organizations, conferences and religious orders and fraternities. Search criteria include organization name, fields of activity, titles of publications, links to other organizations and more. User languages are English, German, French and Dutch. MS-DOS, Windows and Macintosh compatibility. From K.G. Saur. Updated annually. 1 year subscription $1,318.

R.R. Bowker (a unit of Cahners Business Information), 121 Chanlon Road, New Providence, NJ 07974 USA, Phone (888) BOWKER2 (888-269-5372) & (800) 323-3288, fax (908) 508-7696, email info@bowker.com, web www.bowker.com. Canada—R.R. Bowker, Markham, Ontario, phone (888) BOWKER9 & (905) 415-5837, fax (905) 479-6266. German speaking Europe—K.G. Saur Verlag, Munich, Germany, phone 49-89-76902-232, fax 49-89-76902-250, email 100730.1341@compuserve.com, web www.saur.de/home.htm. Rest of Europe incl. United Kingdom plus Africa & Asia—Bowker-Saur, W. Sussex, UK, phone 44-1342-326-972, fax 44-1342-335-612, email customer@bowker-saur.co.uk, web www.bowker-saur.com/service/. Australia/New Zealand—Thorpe, Port Melbourne, Victoria, Australia, phone 61-03-9-245-7370, fax 61-03-9-245-7395, email customer.service@thorpe.com.au, web www.thorpe.com.au. Technical support for CD ROMs (800) 323-3288, fax 908) 665-3528, email techsupport@bowker.com.

Connecticut

www.tristatejobs.com is the URL for Tri-State Jobs, a site for positions in New York, New Jersey and Connecticut. Many positions are for programmers, engineers and managers, often in the $50,000 to $100,000 range. The site was developed by Tri-State Jobs, Southbury, Connecticut and went online in 1997.

Consulting

See Management Consulting, Health Care Consulting

LITERARY MARKET PLACE, The Directory of the American Book Publishing Industry With Industry Yellow Pages" is an excellent 3 volume directory with comprehensive information on US book publishers; imprints, subsidiaries and distributors; book trade acquisitions and mergers, small presses, Canadian book publishers, micropublishers, US electronic publishers, electronic publishing consultants, electronic publishing products and services, editorial services, literary agents, illustrations agents, US agents and offices of foreign publishers, lecture agents, specialized advertising and public relations firms, direct mail specialists, mailing list brokers and services, book review syndicates, book review and index journals and services, book exhibits, book clubs, book lists and catalogs, book importers and exporters, book producers, translators, artists, photographers, stock photo agencies, associations, book trade events and conferences, awards, contents and grants, reference books for the trade, magazines for the trade, a toll free directory of publishers, magazine and newspaper publicity, radio and television publicity, book manufacturing services, book distributors and sales representatives, and wholesalers. LITERARY MARKET PLACE $189.95. INTERNATIONAL LITERARY MARKET PLACE $189.95. LITERARY MARKET PLACE PLUS CD ROM $295.00. Ordering information: R.R. Bowker, New Providence, New Jersey. Phone (800) 521-8110, Fax (908) 665-2898. http://www.bowker.com

Consumer Affairs

CONSUMER SOURCEBOOK includes over 15,000 programs and services available to the general public at little or no cost. Services are provided by federal, state, county and local governments, agencies, and organizations and associations. Consumer affairs and customer service departments for corporations are also listed as well as publications. $265.00. Gale Group, P.O. Box 9187, Farmington Hills, MI 48333-9187. Toll free US and Canada (800) 877-GALE (4253) and (248) 699-GALE, fax (800) 414-5043 and (248) 699-8061, Internet orders galeord@galegroup.com, web site www.galegroup.com or www.gale.com. All Gale Group products are available on approval. Contact Gale for details.

Consumer Marketing

See Marketing Category, Toiletries Category and Pharmaceuticals

ADVERTISER AND AGENCY RED BOOKS PLUS CD ROM combines all the information in THE STANDARD DIRECTORY OF ADVERTISERS, THE STANDARD DIRECTORY OF ADVERTISING AGENCIES and THE STANDARD DIRECTORY OF INTERNATIONAL ADVERTISERS AND AGENCIES. Information is searchable by 25 fields, including company name, personal name, job title/function, product type, product/account name, city, state, zip or country, area code, revenues, number of employees, outside ad agency and even type of computer hardware. Contains professional association information. Available for Windows and Macintosh. Updated quarterly. 1 year subscription $1,295. If the price is prohibitively high, remember your local library. National Register Publishing, Reed Elsevier-New Providence, 121 Chanlon Road, New Providence, NJ 07974, (800) 521-8110, fax (800) 836-7736, web site www.redbooks.com or www.marquiswhoswho.com. "If, for any reason whatsoever, your order does not fully meet your expectations, simply return the product within 30 days for a prompt, complete, unquestioned refund," as stated in Catalog of Biographical and Professional References of publisher Marquis Who's Who/National Register Publishing.

ADVERTISING AGE is a weekly trade paper. Inquire about their 100 Leading National Advertisers issue, an annual survey which identifies names and titles of employees at large consumer marketing companies. 1 year subscription $109, 2 years $175. web site www.adage.com. Crain Communications, Inc. is headquartered in Chicago with offices in major cities throughout the US plus London, Tokyo and Frankfurt. New York location: 220 East 42nd Street, New York, NY 10017, (212) 210-0100, Circulation (800) 678-9595.

DIRECTORIES OF FORMER EMPLOYEES OF VARIOUS COMPANIES are available, such as for IBM, Proctor and Gamble, McKinsey & Company and Booz, Allen & Hamilton. In some cases, such as for Booz, Allen and McKinsey, they are only available to former employees, so the best way to get one is to borrow a copy from a friendly alumnus/a. In other cases, as for IBM, the alumni directory is available to anyone who wishes to buy it (contact the ex-IBM Corporation in Garland, Texas. See Company Alumni Category for more information). At the time of this writing, very little is known about how to obtain a copy of a P&G alumni directory, except there are reports that one does exist. However, one way to research finding it would be to check Directories in Print and other librarians references, to ask your local business librarian, to ask sources and prospects who previously worked for P&G, to source librarians and other employees at consumer marketing professional associations, or possibly source the librarians at the Harvard Business School's Baker Library, which is an excellent source of consumer marketing information.

DIRECTORY OF CONSUMER BRANDS AND THEIR OWNERS provides information on 50,000 brands in 56 countries and detailed information about the companies that own and manage them. Asia Pacific edition $990. Latin America edition $990. Eastern Europe edition $990. Europe edition $1,190 for 2 volumes. Published by Euromonitor (England). Distributed by Gale Group, P.O. Box 9187, Farmington Hills, MI 48333-9187. Toll free US and Canada (800) 877-GALE (4253) and (248) 699-GALE, fax (800) 414-5043 and (248) 699-8061, Internet orders galeord@galegroup.com, web site www.galegroup.com or www.gale.com. All Gale Group products are available on approval. Contact Gale for details.

HARVARD BUSINESS SCHOOL'S BAKER LIBRARY in Boston provides an outstanding consumer marketing web site at www.library.hbs.edu/. This web site identifies extensive sources of information on consumer marketing, including retail both for job hunters and researchers. It includes associations, membership directories, information on direct mail, public relations, corporate communications, online direct mail and online Dun and Bradstreet Credit Reports.

While the access to the web site itself is free and available to anyone, access to the CAREER ADVISOR database is available only to current Harvard Business School students and Harvard Business School Alumni Advisors (Harvard Business School alumni who have agreed to serve as Career advisors to current students and other alumni). The Advisor Database can be searched by industry, geography, job function, job title, year of graduation and company name. In addition, Reference Librarians at the Harvard Business School can conduct searches for a fee. Hundreds of databases are available. Ask at the Reference Desk for more information. For example, Dun & Bradstreet's Credit Reports are a lucrative source of information about privately held companies.

MAJOR MARKETING CAMPAIGNS ANNUAL summarizes 100 major marketing programs of the prior year, including what worked, what didn't and why. $125. Gale Group, P.O. Box 9187, Farmington Hills, MI 48333-9187. Toll free US and Canada (800) 877-GALE (4253) and (248) 699-GALE, fax (800) 414-5043 and (248) 699-8061, Internet orders galeord@galegroup.com, web site www.galegroup.com or www.gale.com. All Gale Group products are available on approval. Contact Gale for details.

MODERN BREWERY AGE—BLUE BOOK is an annual publication about the microbrewery industry. For more information contact the Baker Library at the Harvard Business School in Boston, in connection with the Advisor Database, web site www.library.hbs.edu/.

STANDARD DIRECTORY OF ADVERTISERS Business Classifications Edition is an excellent general directory that organizes companies by a wide range of product categories. A few examples include "Apparel 2—Men's and Boys' Wear," "Heating and Air Conditioning," "Cosmetics and Toiletries," and "Aviation and Aerospace." This directory lists names and titles of key officers, revenues and other information. It is available in a geographic edition for the same price. This directory is comprised of over 24,000 companies that annually spend over $200,000 on advertising. It represents a reasonable place to look for hard-to-find information about privately held companies, especially those that heavily advertise their products. It is a good place to look for names if STANDARD AND POORS and the MILLION DOLLAR DIRECTORY fail to yield the names you need. Finally, the Classified Edition of THE STANDARD DIRECTORY OF ADVERTISERS can be a very convenient source of research because both your target list of companies and the corresponding names and titles of management all appear together, in the same Classification. This is important if you still rely on research books in hard copy. THE STANDARD DIRECTORY OF ADVERTISERS also publishes a special volume called THE STANDARD DIRECTORY OF ADVERTISERS TRADENAME INDEX. You can use the TRADENAME INDEX if you know the brand name of a product and need to find the company that manufactures it. In addition, this directory contains an Associations section which identifies marketing oriented associations.

$599 hard copy. If the price is prohibitively high, remember your local library. THE STANDARD DIRECTORY OF ADVERTISERS is also available on CD ROM under the title ADVERTISER AND AGENCY RED BOOKS PLUS. It is available in Windows® and Macintosh® formats. National Register Publishing, Reed Elsevier-New Providence, 121 Chanlon Road, New Providence, NJ 07974, (800) 521-8110, fax (800) 836-7736, web site www.redbooks.com or www.marquiswhoswho.com. "If, for any reason whatsoever, your order does not fully meet your expectations, simply return the product within 30 days for a prompt, complete, unquestioned refund," as stated in Catalog of Biographical and Professional References of publisher Marquis Who's Who/National Register Publishing.

STANDARD DIRECTORY OF ADVERTISING AGENCIES, also referred to as the "Red Book," is a comprehensive directory of the advertising agency business, generally including extensive listings of executives, especially in management, media, account services, creative and production. It also reveals the names of each agency's corporate clients. A CyberAgency Section lists agencies involved with Web design and development and a special "Who Owns Whom" section listing agency subsidiaries. $599. If the price is prohibitively high, remember your local library. THE STANDARD DIRECTORY OF ADVERTISING AGENCIES is also available on CD ROM under the title ADVERTISER AND AGENCY RED BOOKS PLUS. National Register Publishing, Reed Elsevier-New Providence, 121 Chanlon Road, New Providence, NJ 07974, (800) 521-8110, fax (800) 836-7736, web site www.marquiswhoswho.com or www.redbooks.com. "If, for any reason whatsoever, your order does not fully meet your expectations, simply return the product within 30 days for a prompt, complete, unquestioned refund," as stated in Catalog of Biographical and Professional References of publisher Marquis Who's Who/National Register Publishing.

STANDARD DIRECTORY OF INTERNATIONAL ADVERTISERS & AGENCIES covers the advertising industry in over 120 countries, including 1,700 companies and 2,000 agencies. Listings include names and titles of key executives. $539. If the price is prohibitively high, remember your local library. National Register Publishing, Reed Elsevier-New Providence, 121 Chanlon Road, New Providence, NJ 07974, (800) 521-8110, fax (800) 836-7736, web site www.redbooks.com or www.marquiswhoswho.com. "If, for any reason whatsoever, your order does not fully meet your expectations, simply return the product within 30 days for a prompt, complete, unquestioned refund," as stated in Catalog of Biographical and Professional References of publisher Marquis Who's Who/National Register Publishing.

WORLD FOOD MARKETING DIRECTORY. $990. Published by Euromonitor (England). Distributed by Gale Group, P.O. Box 9187, Farmington Hills, MI 48333-9187. Toll free US and Canada (800) 877-GALE (4253) and (248) 699-GALE, fax (800) 414-5043 and (248) 699-8061, Internet orders galeord@galegroup.com, web site www.galegroup.com or www.gale.com. All Gale Group products are available on approval. Contact Gale for details.

WORLD DIRECTORY OF BUSINESS INFORMATION LIBRARIES identifies 2,500 major business libraries in 145 countries whose collections are oriented towards consumer markets. $590. Published by Euromonitor (England). Distributed by Gale Group, P.O. Box 9187, Farmington Hills, MI 48333-9187. Toll free US and Canada (800) 877-GALE (4253) and (248) 699-GALE, fax (800) 414-5043 and (248) 699-8061, Internet orders galeord@galegroup.com, web site www.galegroup.com or www.gale.com. All Gale Group products are available on approval. Contact Gale for details.

WORLD DRINKS MARKETING DIRECTORY, $990. Published by Euromonitor (England). Distributed by Gale Group, P.O. Box 9187, Farmington Hills, MI 48333-9187. Toll free US and Canada (800) 877-GALE (4253) and (248) 699-GALE, fax (800) 414-5043 and (248) 699-8061, Internet orders galeord@galegroup.com, web site www.galegroup.com or www.gale.com. All Gale Group products are available on approval. Contact Gale for details.

www.library.hbs.edu/ is the URL for the Harvard Business School Baker Library, which contains free excellent information on consumer marketing, retail, associations, membership directories, direct mail, public relations, corporate communications, online direct mail and more. Dun and Bradstreet Credit Reports can also be accessed. In addition, for a fee, reference librarians can conduct online searches from any of several hundred databases. See "Harvard Business School's Baker Library" above.

Contract Consulting Positions

See Temporary

Convenience Stores

DIRECTORY OF SUPERMARKET, GROCERY AND CONVENIENCE STORE CHAINS describes and indexes over 2,300 supermarket chains with $2 million in annual sales. It covers supermarkets, superstores, club stores, gourmet supermarkets and combo stores in the U.S. and Canada, plus a special section profiling 1,700 convenience store chains. It includes an index to the top 200 supermarket chains and the top 100 convenience store chains, which is a valuable tool for target list development. It also lists over 29,000 key executives, buyers and administrative personnel. The directory also lists major trade associations and a trade show calendar. $300. Chain Store Guide Information Services, 3922 Coconut Palm Drive, Tampa, FL 33619. (800) 927-9292, (813) 664-6800, (813) 627-6822, (800) 289-6822. http://www.d-net.com/csgis or http://www.csgis.com.

SUPERMARKET, GROCERY AND CONVENIENCE STORE CHAINS CD-ROM can conduct data searches from five topic screens: 1. Personnel by title, 2. Personnel by functional area, 3. Listing type (branch office, corporate office, divisional office, headquarters, location, managed care div, regional office, subsidiary, warehouse), 4. Stores operated (superstores, supermarkets, convenience, warehouse, combo stores, gourmet supermarkets, stores w/gas), 5. Specialty departments (e.g., auto supplies, automatic teller machines, beer, books/magazines, floral/horticulture,gourmet/specialty foods, greeting cards, in-store bakeries, in-store banking, in-store restaurant, lawn & garden, liquor, nutrition center, et al.). You can also make selections based on geography or the size of a company (number of units and/or sales). Several output options are available, including mailing labels, and electronic formats (such as DBASE, ASCII, text) for mail merge customization. $795, including companion directory. If the price is prohibitively high, remember your local library. Chain Store Guide Information Services, 3922 Coconut Palm Drive, Tampa, FL 33619. (800) 927-9292, (813) 664-6800, (813) 627-6822, (800) 289-6822. http://www.d-net.com/csgis or http://www.csgis.com.

Corporate Affiliations

See Subsidiaries and Organization Charts

AMERICA'S CORPORATE FAMILIES & INTERNATIONAL AFFILIATES is comprised of two volumes of US subsidiaries, divisions and branches and one volume of some 3,000 foreign ultimate parent companies and their 11,000 US subsidiaries and nearly 3,000 US ultimate parent corporations and their 18,000 foreign subsidiaries. Published annually. The International Affiliates (Volume 3) lists US companies with their foreign subsidiaries and foreign ultimates with their US subsidiaries. In addition to listing US and foreign ultimates with their family members alphabetically, all companies are cross-referenced geographically and by industry classification. Updated annually For prices call Dun & Bradstreet at (800) 526-0651. For more information contact Dun & Bradstreet, Business Reference Solutions, Three Sylvan Way, Parsippany, New Jersey 07054. Email dnbmdd@mail.dnb.com. Web site http://www.dnbmdd.com.

CORPORATE AFFILIATIONS PLUS CD ROM consolidates information in all five volumes of THE DIRECTORY OF CORPORATE AFFILIATIONS, including publicly held and privately held companies in the US and internationally, and AMERICA'S CORPORATE FINANCE DIRECTORY. This CD provides "family tree" overviews for each company with the reporting structure. It also contains information on 15,000 parent companies in the US and abroad, records on over 100,000 subsidiaries, divisions, plants and joint ventures, names and titles of over 250,000 employees, revenue figures and more. Information can be searched by 29 criteria, such as location, SIC or NAICS codes, sales, number of employees, net worth, pension assets and more. Updated quarterly. 1 year subscription $1,995, available for both Windows and Macintosh. If the price is prohibitively high, remember your local library. National Register Publishing, Reed Elsevier-New Providence, 121 Chanlon Road, New Providence, NJ 07974, (800) 521-8110, fax (800) 836-7736, web site www.redbooks.com or www.marquiswhoswho.com. "If, for any reason whatsoever, your order does not fully meet your expectations, simply return the product within 30 days for a prompt, complete, unquestioned refund," as stated in Catalog of Biographical and Professional References of publisher Marquis Who's Who/National Register Publishing.

DIRECTORY OF CORPORATE AFFILIATIONS OR WHO OWNS WHOM is a superb directory which can help you decipher the organizational structure of a company. This directory provides detailed information about all parent companies, subsidiaries and divisions, plus plant locations, joint ventures, a brief description of the subsidiary or division, a partial listing of names and titles, location, phone number, and sometimes revenues or number of employees. THE DIRECTORY OF CORPORATE AFFILIATIONS provides a comprehensive "family tree" listing that lays out the corporate hierarchy to provide a picture of the structure of companies, subsidiaries, affiliates & divisions. It includes companies with revenues of at least $10 million and reveals division and subsidiary reporting relationships down to the sixth level. It provides information on 8,500 privately held companies. For US companies it details complex multinational relationships and joint ventures. For additional names and titles of key executives in subsidiaries & divisions, refer to another directory such as STANDARD & POORS, THE STANDARD DIRECTORY OF ADVERTISERS, or a specialized industry directory. THE DIRECTORY OF CORPORATE AFFILIATIONS consists of 5 volumes, including US Public Companies, US Private Companies, International Companies (both public and private), and indices. It also contains a Brand Name Index. The CD ROM version of this directory is titled Corporate Affiliations Plus.

Note: If THE DIRECTORY OF CORPORATE AFFILIATIONS does not provide all the organization structure information you want and the company is publicly held, there's an abundance of free information available! Check the company's web site or call them for an annual report and 10(k). Even if the company is privately held, they will usually send information if you ask for it. The more specific your request, the more likely you are to get what you need, for example, a list of all company locations, a list of plant locations, or product information.

Ordering information: $1,029.95/5 volumes, excluding discounts. If the price is prohibitively high, remember your local library. National Register Publishing, Reed Elsevier-New Providence, 121 Chanlon Road, New Providence, NJ 07974, (800) 521-8110, fax (800) 836-7736, web site www.redbooks.com or www.marquiswhoswho.com. "If, for any reason whatsoever, your order does not fully meet your expectations, simply return the product within 30 days for a prompt, complete, unquestioned refund," as stated in Catalog of Biographical and Professional References of publisher Marquis Who's Who/National Register Publishing.

OWNERSHIP STRUCTURES OF PRINCIPAL PETROLEUM COMPANIES IN CANADA documents "who owns whom" in the Canadian Petroleum industry. Includes directors and key officers and a list of major oil patch takeovers since 1976. $177. Special discounts available for combined purchases. For more information on Energy Information Services, call Calgary office (403) 244-6111. Published by Southam Information Products Ltd, 1450 Don Mills Road, Don Mills, Ontario M3B 2X7 CANADA, (800) 668-2374. In Toronto 442-2122. Web site www.southam.com.

SciTECH REFERENCE PLUS CD ROM contains directory information, 125,000 biographies of US and Canadian scientists and engineers from AMERICAN MEN AND WOMEN OF SCIENCE, listings for over 8,000 laboratories from the DIRECTORY OF AMERICAN RESEARCH AND TECHNOLOGY, and information from THE DIRECTORY OF CORPORATE AFFILIATIONS (including public, private and international companies) of leading US and international technology firms and their subsidiaries. It also contains 60,000 records on science/technology and medical serials from ULRICH'S INTERNATIONAL PERIODICALS DIRECTORY. Searches can be conducted by SIC, year founded, activity, education, employees, institution/company, city, state or country, memberships/honors, product description, personal statistics, personal title, research area, revenue. Updated annually. 1 year subscription $995, 3 years 2,836, excluding discounts. For more information visit Bowker Reed Reference's web site at http://www.reedref.com or contact: Bowker Reed Reference Electronic Publishing, 121 Chanlon Road, New Providence, NJ 07974 USA, Phone (800) 323-3288, Fax (908) 665-3528, email info@bowker.com.

WHO OWNS WHOM DIRECTORY by Dun & Bradstreet is a six volume set containing information on the structure and ownership of 320,000 company affiliates and subsidiaries of over 23,000 companies worldwide. It is available in four regional editions: Australia and the Far East, North America, UK/Ireland, and Continental Europe. Published annually. For prices and ordering information as well as information about more worldwide corporate linkage products from D&B WORLDBASE, D&B's global database of 42 million records in over 200 countries, contact Dun & Bradstreet at (800) 526-0651, Dun & Bradstreet, Business Reference Solutions, Three Sylvan Way, Parsippany, NJ 07054. Email dnbmdd@mail.dnb.com. Web site http://www.dnbmdd.com.

www.reedref.com presents a current catalog for all Reed Reference Publishing companies for both print and electronic references—National Register Publishing, R.R. Bowker, Bowker-Saur, KG Saur, Marquis Who's Who, Martindale-Hubbell and Lexis-Nexis Business Information. At the time of this writing, this catalog is searchable by name, subject, publisher and keyword. To check new offerings, visit individual publisher pages. Free product demos of CD ROM'S can be downloaded for for experimentation and some sample pages—and even entire chapters—and are available for unlimited viewing. The web site also includes a constantly updated menu of special discounts which are available only on the web site. Ask about the growing number of RRP databases accessible via the Internet on subscription or for a usage based price, such as the MARTINDALE-HUBBELL LAW DIRECTORY. For more information visit Bowker Reed Reference's web site at www.reedref.com or www.bowker.com or contact corporate offices, 121 Chanlon Road, New Providence, NJ 07974, (800) 521-8110, (800) 323-3288, fax (908) 665-3528, email info@bowker.com or webmaster@www.reedref.com.

Corporate Communications

O'DWYER'S DIRECTORY OF CORPORATE COMMUNICATIONS lists over 10,000 public relations professionals in companies, trade associations and the government, including foreign embassies, cross referenced by industry. $110. J.R O'Dwyer Co., Inc., 271 Madison Avenue, New York, New York 10157-0160. Phone (212) 679-2471. Fax (212) 683-2750.

O'DWYER'S DIRECTORY OF PR EXECUTIVES provides biographical data about over 8,000 public relations professionals, including job and educational backgrounds, plus business addresses and phone numbers, cross referenced by employers. This directory encompasses almost all the organizations in O'DWYER'S DIRECTORY OF PR FIRMS AND O'DWYER'S DIRECTORY OF CORPORATE COMMUNICATIONS. $120. J.R O'Dwyer Co., Inc., 271 Madison Avenue, New York, New York 10157-0160. Phone (212) 679-2471. Fax (212) 683-2750.

Corporate Finance

See Investment Banking

Corporate Giving

CORPORATE GIVING DIRECTORY lists the 1,000 largest corporate foundations and corporate direct giving programs in the USA. It includes listings of the executives in Corporate Affairs, Public Relations and Marketing who manage their companies' giving programs. It also provides biographical data and provides links between the organization's leaders and trustees, donors, officers and directors. $440. Gale Group, P.O. Box 9187, Farmington Hills, MI 48333-9187. Toll free US and Canada (800) 877-GALE (4253) and (248) 699-GALE, fax (800) 414-5043 and (248) 699-8061, Internet orders galeord@galegroup.com, web site www.galegroup.com or www.gale.com. All Gale Group products are available on approval. Contact Gale for details.

DIRECTORY OF CORPORATE AND FOUNDATION GIVERS identifies 4,500 private foundations and 3,500 corporate giving programs, 1,500 corporate foundations and 2,000 corporate direct givers. Includes biographical data and nine indexes. The largest listing of corporate giving data available. $260 for 2 volume set. Gale Group, P.O. Box 9187, Farmington Hills, MI 48333-9187. Toll free US and Canada (800) 877-GALE (4253) and (248) 699-GALE, fax (800) 414-5043 and (248) 699-8061, Internet orders galeord@galegroup.com, web site www.galegroup.com or www.gale.com. All Gale Group products are available on approval. Contact Gale for details.

DIRECTORY OF INTERNATIONAL CORPORATE GIVING IN AMERICA AND ABROAD profiles over 650 companies that give in the U.S. and overseas, including biographical informational on corporate and giving program officers, such as year and place of birth, university, and corporate and nonprofit affiliations. Section I provides information on funding activities of 477 foreign-owned companies in the US. Section II contains information on international funding activities of 195 US headquartered companies. 18 cross referenced indexes. $215. Gale Group, P.O. Box 9187, Farmington Hills, MI 48333-9187. Toll free US and Canada (800) 877-GALE (4253) and (248) 699-GALE, fax (800) 414-5043 and (248) 699-8061, Internet orders galeord@galegroup.com, web site www.galegroup.com or www.gale.com. All Gale Group products are available on approval. Contact Gale for details.

FC FAX is the Foundation Center's free fax-on-demand service, available 24 hours a day. You can request a complete menu of Foundation center documents which will be forwarded to the fax number of your choice. FC FAX: (212) 807-2577. For more information contact The Foundation Center, 79 Fifth Avenue, New York, NY 10003-3076, (212) 620-4230, (212) 807-3690. Web site www.fdncenter.org.

FC SEARCH is the Foundation Center's Database on CD ROM. It includes information in THE FOUNDATION DIRECTORY (PARTS 1, 2 AND SUPPLEMENT), GUIDE TO US FOUNDATIONS: THEIR TRUSTEES, OFFICERS AND DONORS, NATIONAL DIRECTORY OF CORPORATE GIVING, THE FOUNDATION GRANTS INDEX and THE FOUNDATION GRANTS INDEX QUARTERLY. Information can be searched from 21 search fields, including Trustees, Officers and Donors. FC SEARCH also offers the capability of linking to web sites of over 400 grantmakers. For more information contact The Foundation Center, 79 Fifth Avenue, New York, NY 10003-3076, (212) 620-4230, (212) 807-3690. Web site www.fdncenter.org.

FOUNDATION CENTER maintains two databases on DIALOG, one with information about grantmakers, the other on the grants they distribute. For more information about the Foundation Center's databases on DIALOG (Files 26 and 27), contact DIALOG at (800) 334-2564. For more information about these databases, call the Foundation Center's DIALOG Support Staff in New York at (212) 807-3690.

FOUNDATION CENTER publishes a number of specialized directories, such as GUIDE TO US FOUNDATIONS, NATIONAL DIRECTORY OF CORPORATE GIVING, CORPORATE FOUNDATION PROFILES, NATIONAL DIRECTORY OF GRANTMAKING PUBLIC CHARITIES, WHO GETS GRANTS—FOUNDATION GRANTS TO NONPROFIT ORGANIZATIONS, NATIONAL GUIDE TO FUNDING FOR THE ENVIRONMENT AND ANIMAL WELFARE, NATIONAL GUIDE TO FUNDING IN RELIGION, NATIONAL GUIDE TO FUNDING FOR WOMEN AND GIRLS, NATIONAL GUIDE TO FUNDING FOR INFORMATION TECHNOLOGY, NATIONAL GUIDE TO FUNDING FOR LIBRARIES AND INFORMATION SERVICES, THE FOUNDATION CENTER'S GUIDE TO GRANTSEEKING ON THE WEB, NEW YORK STATE FOUNDATIONS, DIRECTORY OF MISSOURI GRANTMAKERS, GUIDE TO GREATER WASHINGTON D.C. GRANTMAKERS, NATIONAL GUIDE TO FUNDING FOR ELEMENTARY AND SECONDARY EDUCATION, NATIONAL GUIDE TO FUNDING FOR COMMUNITY DEVELOPMENT, NATIONAL GUIDE TO FUNDING IN HIGHER EDUCATION, EDUCATION GRANT GUIDE, NATIONAL GUIDE TO FUNDING IN ARTS AND CULTURE, GUIDE TO FUNDING FOR INTERNATIONAL AND FOREIGN PROGRAMS, INTERNATIONAL GRANTMAKING: A REPORT ON US FOUNDATION TRENDS, NATIONAL GUIDE TO FUNDING IN SUBSTANCE ABUSE, AIDS FUNDING—A GUIDE TO GIVING BY FOUNDATIONS AND CHARITABLE ORGANI-ZATIONS, NATIONAL GUIDE TO FUNDING IN HEALTH, NATIONAL GUIDE TO FUNDING FOR CHILDREN, YOUTH AND FAMILIES, THE FOUNDATION GRANTS INDEX and more. Most of these directories cost under $100. For more information contact The Foundation Center, 79 Fifth Avenue, New York, NY 10003-3076, (212) 620-4230, (212) 807-3690. Web site www.fdncenter.org includes catalog of publications.

GRANTS ON DISC provides information that pinpoints funders of over 300,000 grants. Windows version, $695 building price annual subscription. Gale Group, P.O. Box 9187, Farmington Hills, MI 48333-9187. Toll free US and Canada (800) 877-GALE (4253) and (248) 699-GALE, fax (800) 414-5043 and (248) 699-8061, Internet orders galeord@galegroup.com, web site www.galegroup.com or www.gale.com. All Gale Group products are available on approval. Contact Gale for details.

PHILANTHROPY NEWS DIGEST (PND), the Foundation Center's award winning weekly online journal, is available free. To subscribe, go the web site http://www.fdncenter.org/phil/philmain.html. Enter your email address and click on the "Add me!" button. If you do not have web access, you can still receive free weekly issues of PND by email. To subscribe, send an email to listserv@lists.fdncenter.org with the words SUBSCRIBE PND-1 <YOUR NAME> in the body of the message. For more information contact The Foundation Center, 79 Fifth Avenue, New York, NY 10003-3076, (212) 620-4230, (212) 807-3690. Web site www.fdncenter.org.

NATIONAL DIRECTORY OF CORPORATE PUBLIC AFFAIRS identifies some 14,000 people who manage public affairs and government affairs programs of nearly 2,000 corporations. This directory also includes Washington area offices, corporate foundation/giving programs, federal and state lobbyists and outside contract lobbyists. Indexed by subject and geography. $95. Columbia Books, Inc., 1212 New York Avenue, NW, Suite 330, Washington, DC 20005, (212) 898-0662.

Credit Unions

AMERICAN FINANCIAL DIRECTORY consists of five desktop volumes of banks, bank holding companies, savings and Loan Associations and Major Credit Unions in the US, Canada and Mexico. It includes information on head office and branch offices, names of key decision makers, phone and fax numbers, financial summaries, and structural changes such as mergers, name changes and closings. Published twice a year. For more information contact (800) 321-3373, Thomson Financial Publishing, 4709 West Golf Road, Skokie, IL 60076-1253. Web site @ tfp.bankinfo.com.

AMERICAN FINANCIAL DIRECTORY CUSTOMIZED DIRECTORIES are available for any state of combination of states for banks, bank holding companies, savings and loans and major credit unions. For more information contact (800) 321-3373, Thomson Financial Publishing, 4709 West Golf Road, Skokie, IL 60076-1253. Web site @ tfp.bankinfo.com.

AMERICAN FINANCIAL DIRECTORY REGIONAL DIRECTORIES include banks, bank holding companies, savings and loan associations and major credit unions. Published twice a year.

- SOUTHERN BANKERS DIRECTORY covers Alabama, Arkansas, District of Columbia, Florida, Georgia, Kentucky, Louisiana, Maryland, Mississippi, North Carolina, South Carolina, Tennessee, Virginia and West Virginia. Published twice a year.

- GOLDEN STATES FINANCIAL DIRECTORY includes Alaska, Arizona, California, Colorado, Hawaii, Idaho, Montana, Nevada, New Mexico, Oregon, Utah, Washington, and Wyoming. Published twice a year.

- UPPER MIDWEST FINANCIAL DIRECTORY includes Michigan, Minnesota, Montana, North Dakota, South Dakota and Wisconsin. Published once a year.

- SOUTHWESTERN FINANCIAL DIRECTORY includes Arkansas, Louisiana, New Mexico, Oklahoma and Texas. Published twice a year.

For more information contact (800) 321-3373, Thomson Financial Publishing, 4709 West Golf Road, Skokie, IL 60076-1253. Web site @ tfp.bankinfo.com.

POLK NORTH AMERICAN FINANCIAL INSTITUTIONS DIRECTORY includes information on banks, savings and loan associations and major credit unions in North America, including head office and branch offices,names of key decision makers, address, phone and fax, financial summaries, maps, and structural changes such as mergers, name changes, and closings. Published twice a year. For more information contact (800) 321-3373, Thomson Financial Publishing, 4709 West Golf Road, Skokie, IL 60076-1253. Web site @ tfp.bankinfo.com.

THOMSON CREDIT UNION DIRECTORY identifies credit unions in the US. Listings include names of key decision makers. addresses. phone and fax numbers, branch offices, number of employees.head office and branch offices,names of key decision makers, address, phone and fax, financial summaries, maps, and structural changes such as mergers, name changes, and closings. Published twice a year. For more information contact (800) 321-3373, Thomson Financial Publishing, 4709 West Golf Road, Skokie, IL 60076-1253. Web site @ tfp.bankinfo.com.

D

Databases

Also see Internet

If you've identified an electronic database that will make your job easier but the price is prohibitively high, remember your local library. If you're having trouble locating a library with that particular database, perhaps the librarian can check another library for you. Besides a public library, a library at a corporation, embassy, professional association, university or school might be able to help you. Alternatively, maybe the publisher of the database can help locate a library which has it. The publisher should know who their customers are and it is actually to their benefit to help you. After all, as a user of their products, you are creating a demand in the marketplace. If the people at the toll free number can't help you, you're probably calling too low in the organization. Make a point of finding the phone number of corporate headquarters. Call a senior person, such as the Vice President or Senior Vice President of Sales and Marketing or even the CEO or Chairman. He or she—and often the secretary—should understand why a need for their product is a good reason to help you. For one thing, it signals a marketing opportunity.

ABI GLOBAL and **ABI INFORM** are highly respected databases published by UMI in Ann Arbor, Michigan, a Bell and Howell company. Available in CD ROM and online, ABI allows you to search massive amounts of periodical literature. If you must conduct a literature search for anything, this is one of the first places you should look. Some libraries, such as the New York City Public Library, offer **free courses** in how to use ABI and other databases. Call your local library for more information. Ordering information: UMI, 300 North Zeeb Road, Ann Arbor, Michigan 48106 (800) 521-0600, Sales (800) 521-3042, email: pprice@umi.com.

ASSOCIATIONS UNLIMITED ONLINE is available on the Internet through GaleNet. You can subscribe to any of the several databases comprising ASSOCIATIONS UNLIMITED, including:

- NATIONAL ORGANIZATIONS OF THE US DATABASE
- REGIONAL, STATE AND LOCAL ORGANIZATIONS DATABASE
- INTERNATIONAL ORGANIZATIONS DATABASE
- ASSOCIATIONS MATERIALS DATABASE
- GOVERNMENT NONPROFIT ORGANIZATIONS DATABASE

For more information on available databases and pricing, contact Gale Group, P.O. Box 9187, Farmington Hills, MI 48333-9187. Toll free US and Canada (800) 877-GALE (4253) and (248) 699-GALE, fax (800) 414-5043 and (248) 699-8061, Internet orders galeord@galegroup.com, web site www.galegroup.com or www.gale.com. All Gale Group products are available on approval. Contact Gale for details.

CAHNERS BUSINESS LISTS provides business-to-business lists and databases that include nearly 200 industry-leading business publications, directories, trade show and travel publications. For more information, contact Cahners Business Information, Vice President General Manager, 1350 East Touhy Avenue, Des Plaines, IL 60018, (847) 390-2361, fax (847) 390-2779, email directmarketing@cahners.com, URL www.relists.com. Headquarters: Cahners Business Information, 275 Washington Street, Newton, MA 02158-1630, (617) 558-4663 or (617) 964-3030, fax (617) 558-4700, email marketaccess@cahners.com. Web sites www.cahners.com or www.chilton.net.

CD-ROM'S IN PRINT contains information on over 11,000 CD's, including subject indexes. It also lists information for nearly 4,000 publishing and distribution companies. LIBRARY JOURNAL'S review describes CD-ROM'S IN PRINT as "The starting point for those who choose CD-ROM titles." $155. Gale Group, P.O. Box 9187, Farmington Hills, MI 48333-9187. Toll free US and Canada (800) 877-GALE (4253) and (248) 699-GALE, fax (800) 414-5043 and (248) 699-8061, Internet orders galeord@galegroup.com, web site www.galegroup.com or www.gale.com. All Gale Group products are available on approval. Contact Gale for details.

DIALOG® is the oldest and largest online information service, comprised of over 470 databases from an array of disciplines, including business, US and international news, patents and trademarks, science and technology and consumer news. DIALOG SELECT provides a web based guided search service with access to 250 DIALOG databases for people with little or no database search expertise. It is designed to meet the specific information needs of professional end users in the technology, pharmaceutical, legal, consumer product and media industries. DIALOG@SITE is an intranet-based service providing access to the current DIALOG ONDISC™ CD ROM collection, using Internet browser capabilities. Companies will have wide access to an array of fields, such as business, science, technology, medicine and law through their local Intranet. DIALOG is a service mark of the Dialog Corporation and is exclusively distributed in Canada by Infomart Dialog Limited. For subscriptions and rate information for all services in Canada, contact Infomart Dialog Limited at (416) 442-2198 or (800) 668-9215. In the US call Dialog (Knight Ridder Information, Inc.) in Mountain View, California at (800) 3-DIALOG, web site www.dialog.com.

DIRECTORIES IN PRINT identifies over 15,000 directories (local, regional, national and international) which are organized in 26 subject chapters. An alternate formats index includes directories in online databases, CD ROM, diskettes, microfiche and mailing labels and lists. $489 for 2 volumes. Gale Group, P.O. Box 9187, Farmington Hills, MI 48333-9187. Toll free US and Canada (800) 877-GALE (4253) and (248) 699-GALE, fax (800) 414-5043 and (248) 699-8061, Internet orders galeord@galegroup.com, web site www.galegroup.com or www.gale.com. All Gale Group products are available on approval. Contact Gale for details.

ENCYCLOPEDIA OF BUSINESS INFORMATION SOURCES will lead you to specialized directories, professional associations, trade publications, newsletters, databases, Internet resources and more. It's an excellent reference and a great way to find key resources in any industry fast. $330. Gale Group, P.O. Box 9187, Farmington Hills, MI 48333-9187. Toll free US and Canada (800) 877-GALE (4253) and (248) 699-GALE, fax (800) 414-5043 and (248) 699-8061, Internet orders galeord@galegroup.com, web site www.galegroup.com or www.gale.com. All Gale Group products are available on approval. Contact Gale for details.

GALE GROUP provides an extensive offering of Internet databases through GaleNet, such as GALE'S READY REFERENCE SHELF ONLINE. As these products are constantly changing and being upgraded, contact the publisher for details and prices. Gale Group, P.O. Box 9187, Farmington Hills, MI 48333-9187. Toll free US and Canada (800) 877-GALE (4253) and (248) 699-GALE, fax (800) 414-5043 and (248) 699-8061, Internet orders galeord@galegroup.com, web site www.galegroup.com or www.gale.com. All Gale Group products are available on approval. Contact Gale for details.

The Gale Group's publications are available on GaleNet's customized Internet databases. For more information and a possible free trial, contact a sales representative at The Gale Group, P.O. Box 9187, Farmington Hills, MI 48333-9187. Toll free US and Canada (800) 877-GALE (4253) and (248) 699-GALE, fax (800) 414-5043 and (248) 699-8061, web site www.galegroup.com or www.gale.com.

GALE DIRECTORY OF DATABASES identifies over 12,000 international databases available in a variety of formats including online, CD ROM, diskette, and others. Entries include producer name, description, subject, language, cost, update frequency, geographic coverage. Volume 1, Online Databases, $260. Volume 2, CD-ROM, Diskette, Magnetic Tape, Handheld and Batch Access Database Products, $170. Both volumes $390. ONLINE MAGAZINE described this as "An excellent directory of online databases." Gale Group, P.O. Box 9187, Farmington Hills, MI 48333-9187. Toll free US and Canada (800) 877-GALE (4253) and (248) 699-GALE, fax (800) 414-5043 and (248) 699-8061, Internet orders galeord@galegroup.com, web site www.galegroup.com or www.gale.com. All Gale Group products are available on approval. Contact Gale for details.

GALE DIRECTORY OF DATABASES ONLINE is a GaleNet database on the Internet that identifies over 12,000 international databases in various formats, including CD ROM, diskettes, online and others. Check your local library for free access or contact Gale for annual subscription rates. Gale Group, P.O. Box 9187, Farmington Hills, MI 48333-9187. Toll free US and Canada (800) 877-GALE (4253) and (248) 699-GALE, fax (800) 414-5043 and (248) 699-8061, Internet orders galeord@galegroup.com, web site www.galegroup.com or www.gale.com. All Gale Group products are available on approval. Contact Gale for details.

GALE GUIDE TO INTERNET DATABASES, formerly titled CYBERHOUND'S GUIDE TO INTERNET DATABASES, identifies over 5,000 Internet databases. $115. Gale Group, P.O. Box 9187, Farmington Hills, MI 48333-9187. Toll free US and Canada (800) 877-GALE (4253) and (248) 699-GALE, fax (800) 414-5043 and (248) 699-8061, Internet orders galeord@galegroup.com, web site www.galegroup.com or www.gale.com. All Gale Group products are available on approval. Contact Gale for details.

GaleNet is an online resource on the Internet that provides an integrated, one-step access to the most frequently used Gale databases, such as GALE'S READY REFERENCE SHELF ONLINE. As GaleNet's capabilities are constantly changing and being upgraded, contact the publisher for details and prices. Gale Group, P.O. Box 9187, Farmington Hills, MI 48333-9187. Toll free US and Canada (800) 877-GALE (4253) and (248) 699-GALE, fax (800) 414-5043 and (248) 699-8061, Internet orders galeord@galegroup.com, web site www.galegroup.com or www.gale.com. All Gale Group products are available on approval. Contact Gale for details.

GALE'S READY REFERENCE SHELF ONLINE is a GaleNet Internet resource that provides integrated access to databases covering national, regional, state, local and international associations, publishers, newspapers and periodicals, directories, newsletters, online databases, portable databases, database products and vendors, special libraries and research centers. Information is included from numerous Gale databases, among them THE ENCYCLOPEDIA OF ASSOCIATIONS, PUBLISHERS DIRECTORY, GALE DIRECTORY OF PUBLICATIONS AND BROADCAST MEDIA and several others. If it is prohibitively expensive, locate a library with with this resource. Gale Group, P.O. Box 9187, Farmington Hills, MI 48333-9187. Toll free US and Canada (800) 877-GALE (4253) and (248) 699-GALE, fax (800) 414-5043 and (248) 699-8061, Internet orders galeord@galegroup.com, web site www.galegroup.com or www.gale.com. All Gale Group products are available on approval. Contact Gale for details.

HARVARD BUSINESS SCHOOL'S BAKER LIBRARY in Boston provides an outstanding consumer marketing web site at www.library.hbs.edu/. This web site identifies extensive sources of information on consumer marketing, including retail, both for job hunters and researchers. It includes associations, membership directories, information on direct mail, public relations, corporate communications, online direct mail and online Dun and Bradstreet Credit Reports.

While the access to the web site itself is free and available to anyone, access to the CAREER ADVISOR database is available only to current Harvard Business School students and Harvard Business School Alumni Advisors (Harvard Business School alumni who have agreed to serve as Career advisors to current students and other alumni). The Advisor Database can be searched by industry, geography, job function, job title, year of graduation and company name. In addition, **Reference Librarians at the Harvard Business School can conduct searches for a fee.** Hundreds of databases are available. Ask at the Reference Desk for more information. For example, Dun & Bradstreet's Credit Reports are a lucrative source of information about privately held companies.

INFORMATION IN CANADA—A DIRECTORY OF ELECTRONIC AND SUPPORT RESOURCES provides electronic information on information resources, consultants and information brokers, library based online research services, library automation software, computer accessible library catalogues and a directory of information industry services, plus a large section on databases produced in Canada. Price reduced to $49.95 for 1996 edition. Canada Library Association, 200 Elgin Street, Suite 602, Ottawa, Ontario K2P 1L5 CANADA, (613) 232-9625, fax (613) 563-9895,web site www.cla.amlibs.ca includes an online catalog. Email bj491@freenet.carleton.ca.

KENNEDY INFORMATION has databases of management consulting firms and their key principals, North American and international executive recruiters, temporary placement firms, venture capital firms and out-placement firms. Kennedy Information, One Kennedy Place, Route 12 South, Fitzwilliam, NH 03447, phone (800) 531-0007 or 603-585-6544, fax 603-585-9555, email bookstore@kennedyinfo.com, web site www.kennedyinfo.com.

NELSON FINANCIAL DATABASE provides comprehensive information on the global institutional investment market. Information formatted to your precise needs is available from Nelson Information Mailing List & Customized Database service. The NELSON FINANCIAL DATABASE is comprised of:

    30,000 executives at investment management firms
    11,000 executives at research firms
    100,000 executives at public companies
    40,000 executives at plan sponsors
    3,000 executives at pension fund consulting firms
    24,000 executives at institutional real estate firms
    4,000 executives at technology based vendors

The database also consists of extensive investment information, including money manager performance, peer group analysis, special surveys and more. For customers who with to use Nelson's information in their own systems, Nelson will supply customized data export, using all or any data items. Mailing lists are also available for direct marketers. For more information, contact Nelson Mailing List & Customized Database Services, P.O. Box 591, Port Chester, NY 10573 USA. (800) 333-6357, Phone outside the US (914) 937-8400, Fax (914) 937-8590, web site http://www.nelnet.com.

NELSON INVESTMENT MANAGEMENT NETWORK, also known as Nelnet, is an Internet database (www.nelnet.com) that provides comprehensive information on over 3,000 worldwide institutional investment management firms on 9,500 products and 45,000 professionals. Nelnet users can access without charge the World's Best Money Managers, Nelson's industry standard performance rankings, Manager Hires, which managers were hired by which plan sponsors; Job bank, the investment industry's free *online employment service;* and useful Industry Analyses. Investment Managers can launch their own Nelnet Web site for $100 a month. Users can access Nelnet free. www.nelnet.com. For more information, contact Nelson Information, P.O. Box 591, Port Chester, NY 10573 USA. (800) 333-6357, Phone outside the US (914) 937-8400, Fax (914) 937-8590, web site http://www.nelnet.com.

O'DWYER'S PR SERVICES REPORT is the largest monthly public relations magazine. It is a source of information about databases, among other things. $40 J.R O'Dwyer Co., Inc., 271 Madison Avenue, New York, New York 10157-0160. Phone (212) 679-2471. Fax (212) 683-2750.

PENSIONSCOPE DATASYSTEMS is a database service from MONEY MARKET DIRECTORIES, a division of STANDARD AND POORS. Their database will help you select key decision makers in the pension funds, pension service companies, institutional asset managers, and the nonprofit marketplaces of public and private foundations, endowments and health service organizations. Selections can be based on job function, asset size, type of organization or plan, and geographic location. Selected information available as labels, printouts on index cards or sheets of paper, on magnetic tape, or on disk (minimum $500 order). For more information call STANDARD AND POORS, a division of McGraw-Hill, MONEY MARKET DIRECTORIES, INC., 320 East Main Street, Charlottesville, VA 22902, http://www.mmaccess.com, (800) 446-2810, (804) 977-1450.

Publishers Web Sites. Refer to the web site of your favorite publisher(s) for up-to-the-minute information on new electronic database products, such as directories. For URLs see Publishers Web Sites category or call the publisher, preferably on their toll free number (if they have one).

SMALL BUSINESS SOURCEBOOK encompasses comprehensive information on small businesses, including professional associations, training sources, small business investment companies, over 400 Internet databases, publications, awards and honors, company and personal email addresses. $325 for 2 vol. set. Gale Group, P.O. Box 9187, Farmington Hills, MI 48333-9187. Toll free US and Canada (800) 877-GALE (4253) and (248) 699-GALE, fax (800) 414-5043 and (248) 699-8061, Internet orders galeord@galegroup.com, web site www.galegroup.com or www.gale.com. All Gale Group products are available on approval. Contact Gale for details.

www.bowker.com is the web site for this major research publisher. It includes Flagship Products and Services, an online Product Catalog, Electronic Publishing products including CD ROMs, Internet Databases, and Online Subscription and Site Licensing Databases; press releases, career opportunities, and more. Many of their references are accessible through this web site, such as BOOKS IN PRINT PLUS CANADIAN EDITION, ULRICH'S ON DISC, GERMAN BOOKS IN PRINT, GERMAN BOOKS OUT OF PRINT, INTERNATIONAL BOOKS IN PRINT PLUS, ITALIAN BOOKS IN PRINT, YEARBOOK OF INTERNATIONAL ORGANIZATIONS PLUS, ULRICH'S INTERNATIONAL PERIODICALS DIRECTORY, THE SOFTWARE ENCYCLOPEDIA, BOWKER'S COMPLETE VIDEO DIRECTORY, AMERICAN BOOK PUBLISHING RECORD. Visit the web site for more information.

www.library.hbs.edu/ is the URL for the Harvard Business School Baker Library, which contains free excellent information on consumer marketing, retail, associations, membership directories, direct mail, public relations, corporate communications, online direct mail and more. Dun and Bradstreet Credit Reports can also be accessed. In addition, for a fee, reference librarians can conduct online searches from any of several hundred databases. See "Harvard Business School's Baker Library" above.

Databases—Resume and Job Matching

See Jobhunters' Resources, Recruiting. Also see Web Sites.

CareerXRoads, by Gerry Crispin and Mark Mehler, is an annual directory of job and resume sites. At the time of this writing the number of sites has more than tripled in two years to over 1,000 sites. It includes specialized databases for job seekers and employers. $22.95. Order online or by phone from distributor Kennedy Information, One Kennedy Place, Route 12 South, Fitzwilliam, NH 03447, phone (800) 531-0007 or 603-585-6544, fax 603-585-9555, email bookstore@kennedyinfo.com, web site www.kennedyinfo.com. Also available through from author's web site or at your local book store.

Defense

Also see Government Contractors

CORPTECH DIRECTORY OF TECHNOLOGY COMPANIES is available in hard copy, Regional Guides, on PC floppy diskette, and on CD ROM. CORPTECH EXPLORE DATABASE is an outstanding reference that was awarded Best CD-ROM Directory by the National Directory Publishing Association. One click moves you from the CD ROM Database to the company's Internet web site. CORPTECH also provides other sophisticated but reasonably priced automated services (and quantity discounts) with their customized data-on-demand service, which uses up to 30 search parameters. You can save a tremendous amount of time researching relatively small, emerging new companies in various high technology niches and obtain names, titles and even mailing address labels. If CORPTECH is too expensive to purchase, go to the library.

- CORPTECH EXPLORE SILVER DATABASE CD ROM, $2,495 (including free soft cover CorpTech Directory worth $745).
- CORPTECH EXPLORE GOLD DATABASE CD ROM, $5,995 offers an export capability, extended company history and has hyperlinks to news services to aid company research, such as Reuters and PR Newswire. Both Silver and Gold CD's have links to company web sites.
- CORPTECH print directories are available for $795 hard cover, $745 soft cover.
- CORPTECH regional directories are available in print for $225 (soft cover only). Regional Explore Gold CD's are $995 each and Explore Silver are $795 each.

Industry specific directories segmented into 17 different industries are also available on CD ROM. Each industry costs $995, except computer software, which is very large and counts as two industries. The 17 industry segments are: factory automation, biotechnology, chemicals, computer hardware, **defense,** energy, environmental, manufacturing, advanced materials, medical, pharmaceuticals, photonics, computer software, subassemblies and components, test and measurement companies, telecommunications & Internet, and transportation.

Ordering Information: CORPTECH, Corporate Technology Information Services, Inc., 12 Alfred Street, Suite 200, Woburn, MA 01801-1915. (800) 333-8036, (800) 454-3647, (781) 932-3100, (781) 932-3939. Fax (781) 932-6335. Email sales@corptech.com. Web site www.corptech.com.

PHILLIPS BUSINESS INFORMATION provides information in newsletters, magazines, directories and on multiple web sites covering a range of topics, such as magazine products, telecommunications and cable products, satellite products, media, new media, new media and Internet products, marketing and public relations products, financial technology and electronic commerce, aviation and defense products. For more information, contact: Phillips Business Information, Inc., a Phillips Publishing International Company, 120 Seven Locks Road, Potomac, MD 20854, (301) 340-1520, (301) 340-7788, (800) 777-5006, Internet pbi@phillips.com, web site www.phillips.com.

WORLD AVIATION DIRECTORY AND BUYER'S GUIDE is available as a hard copy directory, on CD ROM and as an Internet database. Some companies on the Internet even have email and web site links. Print directory $275, 2 issues per year; CD ROM $995. Published by Aviation Week, a Division of The McGraw-Hill Companies. McGraw-Hill, Other Media Division (202) 383-2420, (800) 551-2015, extension 4. Web site: www.wadaviation.com.

www.aviationtoday.com is the web site for PHILLIPS AVIATION TODAY, published by Phillips Business Information, Inc., a Phillips Publishing International Company, 120 Seven Locks Road, Potomac, MD 20854, (301) 340-1520, (301) 340-1520, (301) 340-7788, (800) 777-5006, Internet pbi@phillips.com, web site www.phillips.com.

Delaware

www.jobnet.com was ranked as one of the top 5 "Best Specialty Sites" by the *National Business Employment Weekly*. jobnet.com specializes in positions located in southeastern Pennsylania and neighboring areas of New Jersey and Delaware. The site was developed by Online Opportunities, Malvern, Pennsylvania and has been online since 1992.

Denmark

See Scandinavia, Europe, International

DENMARK'S TOP 10,000 COMPANIES provides business information and rankings by sales and gross profit. Dun & Bradstreet, Business Reference Solutions, Three Sylvan Way, Parsippany, NJ 07054 USA. (800) 526-0651. Email dnbmdd@mail.dnb.con. Web site http://www.dnbmdd.com.

Department Stores

Also see Retail

ADVERTISER AND AGENCY RED BOOKS PLUS CD ROM combines all the information in THE STANDARD DIRECTORY OF ADVERTISERS, THE STANDARD DIRECTORY OF ADVERTISING AGENCIES and THE STANDARD DIRECTORY OF INTERNATIONAL ADVERTISERS AND AGENCIES. Information is searchable by 25 fields, including company name, personal name, job title/function, product type, product/account name, city, state, zip or country, area code, revenues, number of employees, outside ad agency and even type of computer hardware. Contains professional association information. Available for Windows and Macintosh. Updated quarterly. 1 year subscription $1,295. If the price is prohibitively high, remember your local library. National Register Publishing, Reed Elsevier-New Providence, 121 Chanlon Road, New Providence, NJ 07974, (800) 521-8110, fax (800) 836-7736, web site www.redbooks.com or www.marquiswhoswho.com. "If, for any reason whatsoever, your order does not fully meet your expectations, simply return the product within 30 days for a prompt, complete, unquestioned refund," as stated in Catalog of Biographical and Professional References of publisher Marquis Who's Who/National Register Publishing.

CHAIN STORE GUIDE'S DATABASE MARKETING DIVISION can customize databases in these industries: Supermarket, department stores, discount department stores, drug stores. Your made-to-order database can include one or several of the named industries and the criteria of your ideal "customer" or search prospect. Information is available on a 3.5" diskette for IBM-PC, Apple Macintosh and DBF, ASCII, comma delimited and others. Mailing labels are also available or you can generate your own labels from a 3.5" diskette. For pricing or ordering information contact Chain Store Guide Information Services, 3922 Coconut Palm Drive, Tampa, FL 33619. (800) 927-9292, (813) 664-6800, (813) 627-6822, (800) 289-6822. http://www.d-net.com/csgis or http://www.csgis.com.

SHELDON'S RETAIL DIRECTORY OF THE US AND CANADA is published by Phelon, Sheldon & Marsar in Florida, (941) 342-7990, fax (941) 342-7994, who also publish numerous retail and apparel directories. For more information contact the Reference Desk at the Baker Library, Harvard Business School in Boston, in connection with the Advisor Database. Web site www.library.hbs.edu/.

STANDARD DIRECTORY OF ADVERTISERS Business Classifications Edition is an excellent general directory that organizes companies by a wide range of product categories. A few examples include "Apparel 2—Men's and Boys' Wear," "Heating and Air Conditioning," "Cosmetics and Toiletries," and "Aviation and Aerospace." This directory lists names and titles of key officers, revenues and other information. It is available in a geographic edition for the same price. This directory is comprised of over 24,000 companies that annually spend over $200,000 on advertising. It represents a reasonable place to look for hard-to-find information about privately held companies, especially those that heavily advertise their products. It is a good place to look for names if STANDARD AND POORS and the MILLION DOLLAR DIRECTORY fail to yield the names you need. Finally, the Classified Edition of THE STANDARD DIRECTORY OF ADVERTISERS can be a very convenient source of research because both your target list of companies and the corresponding names and titles of management all appear together, in the same Classification. This is important if you still rely on research books in hard copy. THE STANDARD DIRECTORY OF ADVERTISERS also publishes a special volume called THE STANDARD DIRECTORY OF ADVERTISERS TRADENAME INDEX. You can use the TRADENAME INDEX if you know the brand name of a product and need to find the company that manufactures it. In addition, this directory contains an Associations section which identifies marketing oriented associations.

$599 hard copy. If the price is prohibitively high, remember your local library. THE STANDARD DIRECTORY OF ADVERTISERS is also available on CD ROM under the title ADVERTISER AND AGENCY RED BOOKS PLUS. It is available in Windows® and Macintosh® formats. National Register Publishing, Reed Elsevier-New Providence, 121 Chanlon Road, New Providence, NJ 07974, (800) 521-8110, fax (800) 836-7736, web site www.redbooks.com or www.marquiswhoswho.com. "If, for any reason whatsoever, your order does not fully meet your expectations, simply return the product within 30 days for a prompt, complete, unquestioned refund," as stated in Catalog of Biographical and Professional References of publisher Marquis Who's Who/National Register Publishing.

Detroit

CRAIN DETROIT is a weekly trade publication. Look for special issues with surveys and lists of top companies by industry. Crain Communications, Inc. is headquartered in Chicago with offices in major cities throughout the US plus London and Tokyo. New York location: 220 East 42nd Street, New York, NY 10017, (212) 210-0100, Customer Service (800) 678-9595. Annual subscription $49, two years $84. Web site www.crainsdetroit.com.

Development and Fundraising

Also see Foundations

CONSULTANTS AND CONSULTING ORGANIZATIONS DIRECTORY identifies consultants in over 400 specialties within 14 general areas. Includes finance, computers, fundraising and others. $620 for 2 volumes. Gale Group, P.O. Box 9187, Farmington Hills, MI 48333-9187. Toll free US and Canada (800) 877-GALE (4253) and (248) 699-GALE, fax (800) 414-5043 and (248) 699-8061, Internet orders galeord@galegroup.com, web site www.galegroup.com or www.gale.com. All Gale Group products are available on approval. Contact Gale for details.

COUNCIL FOR THE ADVANCEMENT AND SUPPORT OF HIGHER EDUCATION (CASE) MEMBERSHIP DIRECTORY provides a comprehensive listing of administrators at colleges and universities. Members are entitled to one free copy and can purchase additional copies for $49 each. Non-members' price is $349. Council for the Advancement and Support of Higher Education, 11 Dupont Circle NW, Suite 400, Washington, DC 20036, (202) 328-5900, web site www.case.org.

FC SEARCH is the Foundation Center's Database on CD ROM. It includes information in THE FOUNDATION DIRECTORY (PARTS 1, 2 AND SUPPLEMENT), GUIDE TO US FOUNDATIONS: THEIR TRUSTEES, OFFICERS AND DONORS, NATIONAL DIRECTORY OF CORPORATE GIVING, THE FOUNDATION GRANTS INDEX and THE FOUNDATION GRANTS INDEX QUARTERLY. Information can be searched from 21 search fields, including Trustees, Officers and Donors. FC SEARCH also offers the capability of linking to web sites of over 400 grantmakers. For more information contact The Foundation Center, 79 Fifth Avenue, New York, NY 10003-3076, (212) 620-4230, (212) 807-3690. Web site www.fdncenter.org.

FOUNDATION CENTER publishes a number of specialized directories, such as GUIDE TO US FOUNDATIONS, NATIONAL DIRECTORY OF CORPORATE GIVING, CORPORATE FOUNDATION

PROFILES, NATIONAL DIRECTORY OF GRANTMAKING PUBLIC CHARITIES, WHO GETS GRANTS—FOUNDATION GRANTS TO NONPROFIT ORGANIZATIONS, NATIONAL GUIDE TO FUNDING FOR THE ENVIRONMENT AND ANIMAL WELFARE, NATIONAL GUIDE TO FUNDING IN RELIGION, NATIONAL GUIDE TO FUNDING FOR WOMEN AND GIRLS, NATIONAL GUIDE TO FUNDING FOR INFORMATION TECHNOLOGY, NATIONAL GUIDE TO FUNDING FOR LIBRARIES AND INFORMATION SERVICES, THE FOUNDATION CENTER'S GUIDE TO GRANTSEEKING ON THE WEB, NEW YORK STATE FOUNDATIONS, DIRECTORY OF MISSOURI GRANTMAKERS, GUIDE TO GREATER WASHINGTON D.C. GRANTMAKERS, NATIONAL GUIDE TO FUNDING FOR ELEMENTARY AND SECONDARY EDUCATION, NATIONAL GUIDE TO FUNDING FOR COMMUNITY DEVELOPMENT, NATIONAL GUIDE TO FUNDING IN HIGHER EDUCATION, EDUCATION GRANT GUIDE, NATIONAL GUIDE TO FUNDING IN ARTS AND CULTURE, GUIDE TO FUNDING FOR INTERNATIONAL AND FOREIGN PROGRAMS, INTERNATIONAL GRANTMAKING: A REPORT ON US FOUNDATION TRENDS, NATIONAL GUIDE TO FUNDING IN SUBSTANCE ABUSE, AIDS FUNDING—A GUIDE TO GIVING BY FOUNDATIONS AND CHARITABLE ORGANI-ZATIONS, NATIONAL GUIDE TO FUNDING IN HEALTH, NATIONAL GUIDE TO FUNDING FOR CHILDREN, YOUTH AND FAMILIES, THE FOUNDATION GRANTS INDEX and more. Most of these directories cost under $100. For more information contact The Foundation Center, 79 Fifth Avenue, New York, NY 10003-3076, (212) 620-4230, (212) 807-3690. Web site www.fdncenter.org includes catalog of publications.

MONEY MARKET DIRECTORY OF TAX-EXEMPT ORGANIZATIONS provides information on private foundations, hospitals and other health service organizations, church related service groups, schools, associations, civic leagues and fraternal beneficiary organizations. Names are provided for over 6,000 senior investment officers, 3000 secondary investment officers, 4,800 presidents and principals, over 4,000 Chairmen, 12,500 trustees and board officers, 600 in house managers, 900 benefits managers, 900 chief human resources officers, 700 chief operating officers and 300 directors of development. $440. Published by STANDARD AND POORS, a division of McGraw-Hill, MONEY MARKET DIRECTORIES, INC., 320 East Main Street, Charlottesville, VA 22902, http://www.mmdaccess.com, (800) 446-2810, (804) 977-1450.

PHILANTHROPY NEWS DIGEST (PND), the Foundation Center's award winning weekly online journal, is available free. To subscribe, go the web site http://www.fdncenter.org/phil/philmain.html. Enter your email address and click on the "Add me!" button. If you do not have web access, you can still receive free weekly issues of PND by email. To subscribe, send an email to listserv@lists.fdncenter.org with the words SUBSCRIBE PND-1 <YOUR NAME> in the body of the message. For more information contact The Foundation Center, 79 Fifth Avenue, New York, NY 10003-3076, (212) 620-4230, (212) 807-3690. Web site www.fdncenter.org.

Direct Mail

CAHNERS BUSINESS LISTS provides business-to-business lists and databases that include nearly 200 industry-leading business publications, directories, trade show and travel publications. For more information, contact Cahners Business Information, Vice President General Manager, 1350 East Touhy Avenue, Des Plaines, IL 60018, (847) 390-2361, fax (847) 390-2779, email directmarketing@cahners.com, URL www.relists.com. Headquarters: Cahners Business Information, 275 Washington Street, Newton, MA 02158-1630, (617) 558-4663 or (617) 964-3030, fax (617) 558-4700, email marketaccess@cahners.com. Web sites www.cahners.com or www.chilton.net.

DIRECT MARKETING ASSOCIATION, INC. ANNUAL DIRECTORY OF MEMBERS is not available to non-members. DMA members are entitled to one free copy and may purchase additional copies at $40 apiece. Membership directory database can also be accessed on the Internet at www.the-dma.org. Direct Marketing Association, 1120 Avenue of the Americas, New York, NY 10036-6700, (212) 768-7277, fax (212) 302-6714.

DIRECT MARKETING MARKET PLACE lists over 4,000 direct marketing companies, organized into numerous categories: associations, catalogs, continuity programs, credit card companies, list brokers, market researchers, computer & fulfillment services, creative sources, ad agencies, copywriters, art services and photographers. Also included are geographic indexes, direct marketing publications, telemarketers, printers and lettershops. $239.95. If the price is prohibitively high, remember your local library. National Register Publishing, Reed Elsevier-New Providence, 121 Chanlon Road, New Providence, NJ 07974, (800) 521-8110, fax (800) 836-7736, web site www.redbooks.com or www.marquiswhoswho.com. "If, for any reason whatsoever, your order does not fully meet your expectations, simply return the product within 30 days for a prompt, complete, unquestioned refund," as stated in Catalog of Biographical and Professional References of publisher Marquis Who's Who/National Register Publishing.

LITERARY MARKET PLACE, "The Directory of the American Book Publishing Industry With Industry Yellow Pages" is an excellent 3 volume directory with comprehensive information on US book publishers; imprints, subsidiaries and distributors; book trade acquisitions and mergers, small presses, Canadian book publishers, micropublishers, US electronic publishers, electronic publishing consultants, electronic publishing products and services, editorial services, literary agents, illustrations agents, US agents and offices of foreign publishers, lecture agents, specialized advertising and public relations firms, direct mail specialists, mailing list brokers and services, book review syndicates, book review and index journals and services, book exhibits, book clubs, book lists and catalogs, book importers and exporters, book producers, translators, artists, photographers, stock photo agencies, associations, book trade events and conferences, awards, contents and grants, reference books for the trade, magazines for the trade, a toll free directory of publishers, magazine and newspaper publicity, radio and television publicity, book manufacturing services, book distributors and sales representatives, and wholesalers. $189.95.

LITERARY MARKET PLACE ON DISC, previously titled LITERARY MARKET PLACE PLUS CD ROM, one year subscription $297.00.

LITERARY MARKET PLACE—INTERNET EDITION, www.literarymarketplace.com, is available by subscription.

INTERNATIONAL LITERARY MARKET PLACE Internet database can be directly accessed at www.iliterarymarketplace.com. It is also linked to the US domestic LITERARY MARKET PLACE web site at www.literarymarketplace.com. Contact the publisher for subscription price.

INTERNATIONAL LITERARY MARKET PLACE, hard copy $189.95.

R.R. Bowker (a unit of Cahners Business Information), 121 Chanlon Road, New Providence, NJ 07974 USA, Phone (888) BOWKER2 (888-269-5372) & (800) 323-3288, fax (908) 508-7696, email info@bowker.com, web www.bowker.com. Canada—R.R. Bowker, Markham, Ontario, phone (888) BOWKER9 & (905) 415-5837, fax (905) 479-6266. German speaking Europe—K.G. Saur Verlag, Munich, Germany, phone 49-89-76902-232, fax 49-89-76902-250, email 100730.1341@compuserve.com, web www.saur.de/home.htm. Rest of Europe incl. United Kingdom plus Africa & Asia—Bowker-Saur, W. Sussex, UK, phone 44-1342-326-972, fax 44-1342-335-612, email customer@bowker-saur.co.uk, web www.bowker-saur.com/service/. Australia/New Zealand—Thorpe, Port Melbourne, Victoria, Australia, phone 61-03-9-245-7370, fax 61-03-9-245-7395, email customer.service@thorpe.com.au, web www.thorpe.com.au. Technical support for CD ROMs (800) 323-3288, fax (908) 665-3528, email techsupport@bowker.com.

MAIL ORDER BUSINESS DIRECTORY provides information on over 9,000 of the most active mail order and catalog houses. $75.00. Available on computer disc and mailing labels. B. Klein Publications, P.O. Box 6578, Delray Beach, Florida 33482. Phone (888) 859-8083, (561) 496-3316, fax (561) 496-5546.

NATIONAL DIRECTORY OF CATALOGS includes over 7,000 catalogs and their producers, products, printers and circulation and list managers. It's organized by product in 78 areas. $395. Published by Oxbridge Communications, Inc. At the time of this writing, distributor Gale Group was no longer selling this reference, which was in its 7th edition. However, Gale advised it might possibly be available directly from the publisher. Refer to "Publishing Industry" for BOOKS IN PRINT or BOOKS OUT OF PRINT or LITERARY MARKET PLACE or INTERNATIONAL LITERARY MARKET PLACE for information about the publisher.

STANDARD RATE AND DATA PUBLICATIONS includes "Radio Advertising Source" and "Television and Cable Source" and direct marketing information. $354 annual subscription. Standard Rate and Data Service, Inc., 3004 Glenview Road, Wilmette, IL 60091, (708) 441-2210 in Illinois, (800) 323-4601.

www.the-dma.org is the web site for the Direct Marketing Association, 1120 Avenue of the Americas, New York, NY 10036-6700, (212) 768-7277, fax (212) 302-6714. It feature the DMA Job Bank, Online Bookstore, Seminars, Conferences. Membership directory is available to members.

Direct Marketing

See Direct Mail

Directories

Also see Associations and References—Librarian

While there are many references cited in this section, an asterisk (*) indicates preferred sources that can be used first.

*BUSINESS INFORMATION SOURCES by Lorna Daniells is an outstanding reference at any price. At $39.95 a copy, it's such an extraordinary value, it should have a place in every library. This is clearly one of the top three hard copy references around, and its reasonable price elevates it to first place. BUSINESS INFORMATION SOURCES provides a wealth of information routinely needed by search firms, job hunters and corporate recruiters, including general directories, specialized directories, professional associations, periodicals, industry information, international information, and much more. $39.95. Ordering information: BUSINESS INFORMATION SOURCES by Lorna Daniells, is published by the University of California Press (Berkeley, CA, Los Angeles, CA & Oxford, England) (510-642-4247). Orders are handled by California Princeton Fulfillment Services, P.O. Box 10769, Newark, NJ 07193-0769. (800-822-6657).

CYBERHOUND'S® GUIDE TO PEOPLE ON THE INTERNET is organized into three sections. (1) WHO'S WHO ONLINE identifies 1,000 online directories, databases and membership listings. For example, it lists Architects in Canada, Attorney Finder, Famous Left-Handers, and The Missing Persons Pages. (2) White Pages provides an alphabetical listing of 3,000 business professionals who are accessible by email. Other information includes area of expertise, personal and professional affiliation and company information. (3) Personal Web Sites are organized alphabetically by name. 1,500 pages of people in the news in business, entertainment, and sports. $79. Gale Group, P.O. Box 9187, Farmington Hills, MI 48333-9187. Toll free US and Canada (800) 877-GALE (4253) and (248) 699-GALE, fax (800) 414-5043 and (248) 699-8061, Internet orders galeord@galegroup.com, web site www.galegroup.com or www.gale.com. All Gale Group products are available on approval. Contact Gale for details.

*DIRECTORIES IN PRINT identifies over 15,000 directories (local, regional, national and international) which are organized in 26 subject chapters. An alternate formats index includes directories in online databases, CD ROM, diskettes, microfiche and mailing labels and lists. $489 for 2 volumes. Gale Group, P.O. Box 9187, Farmington Hills, MI 48333-9187. Toll free US and Canada (800) 877-GALE (4253) and (248) 699-GALE, fax (800) 414-5043 and (248) 699-8061, Internet orders galeord@galegroup.com, web site www.galegroup.com or www.gale.com. All Gale Group products are available on approval. Contact Gale for details.

ENCYCLOPEDIA OF ASSOCIATIONS: INTERNATIONAL ORGANIZATIONS includes nearly 20,000 multinational and national organizations in foreign countries, including US based associations with multinational membership. Entries also include email addresses, web sites and bulletin board addresses, lobbying activities, and publication and convention information. Indexed by geography, keyword and executives. $595 for 2 volume set. Also available in CD ROM. Database available via commercial online service. Gale Group, P.O. Box 9187, Farmington Hills, MI 48333-9187. Toll free US and Canada (800) 877-GALE (4253) and (248) 699-GALE, fax (800) 414-5043 and (248) 699-8061, Internet orders galeord@galegroup.com, web site www.galegroup.com or www.gale.com. All Gale Group products are available on approval. Contact Gale for details.

*ENCYCLOPEDIA OF ASSOCIATIONS: NATIONAL ORGANIZATIONS OF THE US. This superb reference is one of the first places you should look when beginning a new recruiting assignment or when looking for specialized references of any type. The keyword index makes this comprehensive reference easy to use, even in hard copy. For over 23,000 nonprofit professional associations with a national scope, this encyclopedia reveals:

- Publications, including membership rosters and newsletters
- Dates and locations of association conferences and conventions

- Names of Executive Directors, who are usually incredible sources of industry information if you call and speak to them
- Committees
- Job and candidate referral banks, which can provide resumes of other industry sources and sometimes candidates
- It includes organizations in these categories: business, trade, environmental, agricultural, legal, governmental, engineering, technological, scientific, educational, cultural, social welfare, health & medical, public affairs, ethnic, labor unions, chambers of commerce, tourism, & others.

Volume 1, National Organizations of the US, $505
Volume 2, Geographic and Executive Indexes, $390
Volume 3, Supplement, $405

Gale Group, P.O. Box 9187, Farmington Hills, MI 48333-9187. Toll free US and Canada (800) 877-GALE (4253) and (248) 699-GALE, fax (800) 414-5043 and (248) 699-8061, Internet orders galeord@galegroup.com, web site www.galegroup.com or www.gale.com. All Gale Group products are available on approval. Contact Gale for details.

ENCYCLOPEDIA OF ASSOCIATIONS: REGIONAL, STATE AND LOCAL ORGANIZATIONS. The information in this directory is *not* duplicated anywhere in ENCYCLOPEDIA OF ASSOCIATIONS. Over 100,000 nonprofit organizations are included in this directory. $585 for 5 volume set or $140 per individual volume. Also available on CD ROM and online on the Internet through a GaleNet subscription.

Volume 1, Great Lakes States (Illinois, Indiana, Michigan, Minnesota, Ohio, Wisconsin)
Volume 2, Northeastern States (Connecticut, Maine, Massachusetts, New Hampshire, New Jersey, New York, Pennsylvania, Rhode Islands, Vermont)
Volume 3, Southern and Middle Atlantic States (Including Puerto Rico and the Virgin Islands) (Alabama, Delaware, Washington, DC, Florida, Georgia, Kentucky, Maryland, Mississippi, North Carolina, Puerto Rico, South Carolina, Tennessee, Virginia, West Virginia, Virgin Islands)
Volume 4, South Central and Great Plains States (Arkansas, Iowa, Kansas, Louisiana, Missouri, Nebraska, North Dakota, Oklahoma, South Dakota, Texas)
Volume 5, Western States (Alaska, Arizona, California, Colorado, Guam, Hawaii, Idaho, Montana, Nevada, New Mexico, Oregon, Utah, Washington, Wyoming)

Gale Group, P.O. Box 9187, Farmington Hills, MI 48333-9187. Toll free US and Canada (800) 877-GALE (4253) and (248) 699-GALE, fax (800) 414-5043 and (248) 699-8061, Internet orders galeord@galegroup.com, web site www.galegroup.com or www.gale.com. All Gale Group products are available on approval. Contact Gale for details.

*ENCYCLOPEDIA OF BUSINESS INFORMATION SOURCES will lead you to specialized directories, professional associations, trade publications, newsletters, databases, Internet resources and more. It's an excellent reference and a great way to find key resources in any industry *fast.* $330. Gale Group, P.O. Box 9187, Farmington Hills, MI 48333-9187. Toll free US and Canada (800) 877-GALE (4253) and (248) 699-GALE, fax (800) 414-5043 and (248) 699-8061, Internet orders galeord@galegroup.com, web site www.galegroup.com or www.gale.com. All Gale Group products are available on approval. Contact Gale for details.

GUIDE TO AMERICAN DIRECTORIES, $95. B. Klein Publications, P.O. Box 6578, Delray Beach, Florida 33482. Phone (888) 859-8083, (561) 496-3316, fax (561) 496-5546.

B. KLEIN PUBLICATIONS, publisher of THE GUIDE TO AMERICAN DIRECTORIES, will send a free catalog of their other publications. Call B. Klein Publications, Phone (888) 859-8083, (561) 496-3316, fax (561) 496-5546. Address: P. O. Box 6578, Delray Beach, Florida 33482.

MEMBERSHIP DIRECTORIES FOR PROFESSIONAL ASSOCIATIONS are frequently published, either in hard copy or on an Internet web site. If a membership directory is not accessible on the web site, you might want to purchase a hard copy from the association. However, some associations refuse to sell their membership rosters to non-members. Some even preclude recruiters from becoming members. As a last resort, if an association membership directory is not online, you might need to borrow a copy from a member.

Of course, that can be a bit of a "Catch 22," because how can you find a member if you don't have the membership list? Just keep asking everybody you talk to.

If you're having trouble locating an association's web site address (URL), you can always look them up in a directory. If the web site address isn't in the directory, sometimes it's easier to make a phone call and ask for the web site. You can also go to www.web sitez.com to get an organization's URLs.

One way to identify membership directories is to look up associations in a directory, such as Lorna Daniells' BUSINESS INFORMATION SOURCES (University of California Press, Berkeley, Los Angeles and Oxford England/Princeton Fulfillment Services, Newark, NJ), ENCYCLOPEDIA OF ASSOCIATIONS (Gale Group, Farmington Hills, MI) or NATIONAL TRADE AND PROFESSIONAL ASSOCIATIONS (Columbia Books, Washington, DC).

You can call the association and ask them to send information about becoming a member. If you don't want them to know the name of your company, ask them to send the information to your home address. While you're chatting, and before you give your name, make a casual inquiry about whether their membership roster is available for sale to non-members. If it's not, find out their requirements for joining, specifically whether recruiters are precluded.

PUBLISHERS WEB SITES. Refer to the web site of your favorite publisher(s) for up-to-the-minute information on new electronic database products, such as directories. For URLs see Publishers Web Sites category or call the publisher, preferably on their toll free number (if they have one).

Discount Stores

CHAIN STORE GUIDE'S DATABASE MARKETING DIVISION can customize databases in these industries: Supermarket, department stores, discount department stores, drug stores. Your made-to-order database can include one or several of the named industries and the criteria of your ideal "customer" or search prospect. Information is available on a 3.5" diskette for IBM-PC, Apple Macintosh and DBF, ASCII, comma delimited and others. Mailing labels are also available or you can generate your own labels from a 3.5" diskette. For pricing or ordering information contact Chain Store Guide Information Services, 3922 Coconut Palm Drive, Tampa, FL 33619. (800) 927-9292, (813) 664-6800, (813) 627-6822, (800) 289-6822. http://www.d-net.com/csgis or http://www.csgis.com.

CANADIAN PHARMACISTS DIRECTORY lists over 18,000 Canadian pharmacists, drug information centers, poison control centres, pharmaceutical suppliers, drug wholesalers, related universities, drug store head offices, pharmaceutical associations, chain drug stores, and brand name/generic pharmaceutical companies. $119 prepaid, $149 plus $5 shipping and handling if billed. Special discounts available for combined purchases. Published by Southam Information Products Ltd, 1450 Don Mills Road, Don Mills, Ontario M3B 2X7 CANADA, (800) 668-2374. In Toronto 442-2122. Web site www.southam.com.

DIRECTORY OF DRUG STORE AND HBC CHAINS identifies over 1,800 drug retailers in the U.S. and Canada operating over 45,000 stores including drug, HBC, cosmetic, deep discount, home health care, discount, and grocery stores/supermarket chains with pharmacies, mass merchants with pharmacies, deep discount chains, and wholesale drug companies. It includes names and titles of key personnel, a listing of major trade associations and a trade show calendar. It also provides indexes to top drug retailers, top drug wholesalers, top grocery chains and top discount chains. $290. Chain Store Guide Information Services, 3922 Coconut Palm Drive, Tampa, FL 33619. (800) 927-9292, (813) 664-6800, (813) 627-6822, (800) 289-6822. http://www.d-net.com/csgis or http://www.csgis.com.

Diversity

Also see Associations, Campus Recruiting, Women

AFRICAN AMERICANS INFORMATION DIRECTORY identifies over 5,200 organizations, publications, institutions, agencies and programs, including a new chapter on scholarships, fellowships and loans. This information on scholarships and fellowships could possibly be used to identify top candidates for college and MBA recruiting. $85. Gale Group, P.O. Box 9187, Farmington Hills, MI 48333-9187. Toll free US and Canada (800) 877-GALE (4253) and (248) 699-GALE, fax (800) 414-5043 and (248) 699-8061,

Internet orders galeord@galegroup.com, web site www.galegroup.com or www.gale.com. All Gale Group products are available on approval. Contact Gale for details.

BLACK AMERICAN COLLEGES AND UNIVERSITIES reviews 118 institutions that were founded primarily for African Americans and/or possess predominantly black enrollments. This reference can be used to identify target schools for campus recruiting purposes. $70. Gale Group, P.O. Box 9187, Farmington Hills, MI 48333-9187. Toll free US and Canada (800) 877-GALE (4253) and (248) 699-GALE, fax (800) 414-5043 and (248) 699-8061, Internet orders galeord@galegroup.com, web site www.galegroup.com or www.gale.com. All Gale Group products are available on approval. Contact Gale for details.

ENCYCLOPEDIA OF ASSOCIATIONS: INTERNATIONAL ORGANIZATIONS includes nearly 20,000 multinational and national organizations in foreign countries, including US based associations with multinational membership. Entries also include email addresses, web sites and bulletin board addresses, lobbying activities, and publication and convention information. Indexed by geography, keyword and executives. $595 for 2 volume set. Also available in CD ROM. Database available via commercial online service. Gale Group, P.O. Box 9187, Farmington Hills, MI 48333-9187. Toll free US and Canada (800) 877-GALE (4253) and (248) 699-GALE, fax (800) 414-5043 and (248) 699-8061, Internet orders galeord@galegroup.com, web site www.galegroup.com or www.gale.com. All Gale Group products are available on approval. Contact Gale for details.

ENCYCLOPEDIA OF ASSOCIATIONS: NATIONAL ORGANIZATIONS OF THE US. This superb reference is one of the first places you should look when beginning a new recruiting assignment or when looking for specialized references of any type. The keyword index makes this comprehensive reference easy to use, even in hard copy. For over 23,000 nonprofit professional associations with a national scope, this encyclopedia reveals:

- Publications, including membership rosters and newsletters
- Dates and locations of association conferences and conventions
- Names of Executive Directors, who are usually incredible sources of industry information if you call and speak to them
- Committees
- Job and candidate referral banks, which can provide resumes of other industry sources and sometimes candidates
- It includes organizations in these categories: business, trade, environmental, agricultural, legal, governmental, engineering, technological, scientific, educational, cultural, social welfare, health & medical, public affairs, ethnic, labor unions, chambers of commerce, tourism, & others.

  Volume 1, National Organizations of the US, $505
  Volume 2, Geographic and Executive Indexes, $390
  Volume 3, Supplement, $405

Gale Group, P.O. Box 9187, Farmington Hills, MI 48333-9187. Toll free US and Canada (800) 877-GALE (4253) and (248) 699-GALE, fax (800) 414-5043 and (248) 699-8061, Internet orders galeord@galegroup.com, web site www.galegroup.com or www.gale.com. All Gale Group products are available on approval. Contact Gale for details.

ENCYCLOPEDIA OF ASSOCIATIONS: REGIONAL, STATE AND LOCAL ORGANIZATIONS. The information in this directory is *not* duplicated anywhere in ENCYCLOPEDIA OF ASSOCIATIONS. Over 100,000 nonprofit organizations are included in this directory. $585 for 5 volume set or $140 per individual volume. Also available on CD ROM and online on the Internet through a GaleNet subscription.

  Volume 1, Great Lakes States (Illinois, Indiana, Michigan, Minnesota, Ohio, Wisconsin)
  Volume 2, Northeastern States (Connecticut, Maine, Massachusetts, New Hampshire, New Jersey, New York, Pennsylvania, Rhode Islands, Vermont)
  Volume 3, Southern and Middle Atlantic States (Including Puerto Rico and the Virgin Islands) (Alabama, Delaware, Washington, DC, Florida, Georgia, Kentucky, Maryland, Mississippi, North Carolina, Puerto Rico, South Carolina, Tennessee, Virginia, West Virginia, Virgin Islands)
  Volume 4, South Central and Great Plains States (Arkansas, Iowa, Kansas, Louisiana, Missouri, Nebraska, North Dakota, Oklahoma, South Dakota, Texas)

Volume 5, Western States (Alaska, Arizona, California, Colorado, Guam, Hawaii, Idaho, Montana, Nevada, New Mexico, Oregon, Utah, Washington, Wyoming)

Gale Group, P.O. Box 9187, Farmington Hills, MI 48333-9187. Toll free US and Canada (800) 877-GALE (4253) and (248) 699-GALE, fax (800) 414-5043 and (248) 699-8061, Internet orders galeord@galegroup.com, web site www.galegroup.com or www.gale.com. All Gale Group products are available on approval. Contact Gale for details.

HISPANIC AMERICANS INFORMATION DIRECTORY provides information on over 5,000 Hispanic organizations, Hispanic publishers, bilingual education and Hispanic studies programs, related government agencies and Hispanic owned businesses. Includes alphabetical and subject indexes. American Reference Books Annual's review of this stated, "This excellent publication is recommended for all libraries." $85. Gale Group, P.O. Box 9187, Farmington Hills, MI 48333-9187. Toll free US and Canada (800) 877-GALE (4253) and (248) 699-GALE, fax (800) 414-5043 and (248) 699-8061, Internet orders galeord@galegroup.com, web site www.galegroup.com or www.gale.com. All Gale Group products are available on approval. Contact Gale for details.

NATIONAL DIRECTORY OF MINORITY OWNED BUSINESS FIRMS includes government contracting experience and other information. $275. Published by Business Research Services. Distributed by Gale Group, P.O. Box 9187, Farmington Hills, MI 48333-9187. Toll free US and Canada (800) 877-GALE (4253) and (248) 699-GALE, fax (800) 414-5043 and (248) 699-8061, Internet orders galeord@galegroup.com, web site www.galegroup.com or www.gale.com. All Gale Group products are available on approval. Contact Gale for details.

NATIVE AMERICANS INFORMATION DIRECTORY identifies nearly 4,500 organizations, publications, institutions, agencies, programs and services. Includes name and keyword indexes. $95. Gale Group, P.O. Box 9187, Farmington Hills, MI 48333-9187. Toll free US and Canada (800) 877-GALE (4253) and (248) 699-GALE, fax (800) 414-5043 and (248) 699-8061, Internet orders galeord@galegroup.com, web site www.galegroup.com or www.gale.com. All Gale Group products are available on approval. Contact Gale for details.

SMALL BUSINESS SOURCING FILE contains information on more than 250,000 small businesses with an emphasis on minority-owned and women-owned businesses. For prices call Dun & Bradstreet at (800) 526-0651. For more information contact Dun & Bradstreet, Business Reference Solutions, Three Sylvan Way, Parsippany, NJ 07054. Email dnbmdd@mail.dnb.com. Web site http://www.dnbmdd.com.

STANDARD PERIODICAL DIRECTORY consists of 85,000 American and Canadian periodicals referenced by 250 subjects. Includes new online index and title index. $895. Also available on CD ROM. Published by Oxbridge. Distributed by Gale Group, P.O. Box 9187, Farmington Hills, MI 48333-9187. Toll free US and Canada (800) 877-GALE (4253) and (248) 699-GALE, fax (800) 414-5043 and (248) 699-8061, Internet orders galeord@galegroup.com, web site www.galegroup.com or www.gale.com. All Gale Group products are available on approval. Contact Gale for details.

STANDARD PERIODICAL DIRECTORY ON CD-ROM encompasses 75,000 North American publications, vastly simplifying research in consumer magazines, trade journals, newspapers, yearbooks, museum publications, ethnic publications and more. Contact Gale for prices. Gale Group, P.O. Box 9187, Farmington Hills, MI 48333-9187. Toll free US and Canada (800) 877-GALE (4253) and (248) 699-GALE, fax (800) 414-5043 and (248) 699-8061, Internet orders galeord@galegroup.com, web site www.galegroup.com or www.gale.com. All Gale Group products are available on approval. Contact Gale for details.

WHO'S WHO AMONG AFRICAN AMERICANS contains information on 20,000 people including figures in business, the arts, sports, and religion. Includes geographic and occupational indexes. $165. Gale Group, P.O. Box 9187, Farmington Hills, MI 48333-9187. Toll free US and Canada (800) 877-GALE (4253) and (248) 699-GALE, fax (800) 414-5043 and (248) 699-8061, Internet orders galeord@galegroup.com, web site www.galegroup.com or www.gale.com. All Gale Group products are available on approval. Contact Gale for details.

WHO'S WHO AMONG ASIAN AMERICANS contains information including career information and addresses for nearly 6,000 people. Also includes occupation, geographic and ethnic/cultural heritage indexes and and obituary section. $85. Gale Group, P.O. Box 9187, Farmington Hills, MI 48333-9187. Toll free US and Canada (800) 877-GALE (4253) and (248) 699-GALE, fax (800) 414-5043 and (248) 699-8061, Internet orders galeord@galegroup.com, web site www.galegroup.com or www.gale.com. All Gale Group products are available on approval. Contact Gale for details.

WHO'S WHOM AMONG HISPANIC AMERICANS contains biographical data on over 11,000 people from a broad range of professions. Includes occupation, geographic and ethnic/cultural heritage indexes. $100. Gale Group, P.O. Box 9187, Farmington Hills, MI 48333-9187. Toll free US and Canada (800) 877-GALE (4253) and (248) 699-GALE, fax (800) 414-5043 and (248) 699-8061, Internet orders galeord@galegroup.com, web site www.galegroup.com or www.gale.com. All Gale Group products are available on approval. Contact Gale for details.

www.blackworld.com/careers.htm is the URL for Blackworld Career Center, a site jointly developed by Blackworld Internet Directory in Oakland, California and CareerMosaic. The site, launched in 1998, provides resources for African Americans and other ethnic groups worldwide.

Divisions

See Subsidiaries

Drug Stores

CANADIAN PHARMACISTS DIRECTORY lists over 18,000 Canadian pharmacists, drug information centers, poison control centres, pharmaceutical suppliers, drug wholesalers, related universities, drug store head offices, pharmaceutical associations, chain drug stores, and brand name/generic pharmaceutical companies. $119 prepaid, $149 plus $5 shipping and handling if billed. Special discounts available for combined purchases. Published by Southam Information Products Ltd, 1450 Don Mills Road, Don Mills, Ontario M3B 2X7 CANADA, (800) 668-2374. In Toronto 442-2122. Web site www.southam.com.

CHAIN STORE GUIDE'S DATABASE MARKETING DIVISION can customize databases in these industries: Supermarket, department stores, discount department stores, drug stores. Your made-to-order database can include one or several of the named industries and the criteria of your ideal "customer" or search prospect. Information is available on a 3.5" diskette for IBM-PC, Apple Macintosh and DBF, ASCII, comma delimited and others. Mailing labels are also available or you can generate your own labels from a 3.5" diskette. For pricing or ordering information contact Chain Store Guide Information Services, 3922 Coconut Palm Drive, Tampa, FL 33619. (800) 927-9292, (813) 664-6800, (813) 627-6822, (800) 289-6822. http://www.d-net.com/csgis or http://www.csgis.com.

DIRECTORY OF DRUG STORE AND HBC CHAINS identifies over 1,800 drug retailers in the U.S. and Canada operating over 45,000 stores including drug, HBC, cosmetic, deep discount, home health care, discount, and grocery stores/supermarket chains with pharmacies, mass merchants with pharmacies, deep discount chains, and wholesale drug companies. It includes names and titles of key personnel, a listing of major trade associations and a trade show calendar. It also provides indexes to top drug retailers, top drug wholesalers, top grocery chains and top discount chains. $290. Chain Store Guide Information Services, 3922 Coconut Palm Drive, Tampa, FL 33619. (800) 927-9292, (813) 664-6800, (813) 627-6822, (800) 289-6822. http://www.d-net.com/csgis or http://www.csgis.com.

Drugs

See Pharmaceuticals. Also see Biotechnology, Wholesale Drugs

E

Eastern Europe

See Commonwealth of Independent States, International, Europe

DIRECTORY OF AMERICAN FIRMS OPERATING IN FOREIGN COUNTRIES, REGIONAL EDITION—EUROPE, EASTERN. Includes Albania, Armenia, Azerbaijan, Belarus, Bulgaria, Croatia, Czech Republic, Estonia, Hungary, Kazakhstan, Latvia, Lithuania, Macedonia, Poland, Romania, Russia, Slovakia, Slovenia, Turkmenistan, Ukraine, Uzbekistan, Yugoslavia. $49. Uniworld Business Publications, Inc., 257 Central Park West, Suite 10A, New York, NY 10024-4110, (212) 496-2448, fax (212) 769-0413, email uniworldbp@aol.com. Web site: http://www.uniworldbp.com.

DIRECTORY OF AMERICAN FIRMS OPERATING IN FOREIGN COUNTRIES, REGIONAL EDITION—EUROPE, ALL. $169. Ordering information: Uniworld Business Publications, Inc., 257 Central Park West, Suite 10A, New York, NY 10024-4110, (212) 496-2448, fax (212) 769-0413, email uniworldbp@aol.com. Web site: http://www.uniworldbp.com.

DIRECTORY OF CONSUMER BRANDS AND THEIR OWNERS provides information on 50,000 brands in 56 countries and detailed information about the companies that own and manage them. Asia Pacific edition $990. Latin America edition $990. Eastern Europe edition $990. Europe edition $1,190 for 2 volumes. Published by Euromonitor (England). Distributed by Gale Group, P.O. Box 9187, Farmington Hills, MI 48333-9187. Toll free US and Canada (800) 877-GALE (4253) and (248) 699-GALE, fax (800) 414-5043 and (248) 699-8061, Internet orders galeord@galegroup.com, web site www.galegroup.com or www.gale.com. All Gale Group products are available on approval. Contact Gale for details.

DIRECTORY OF FOREIGN FIRMS OPERATING IN THE UNITED STATES, REGIONAL EDITION—EUROPE, ALL. Includes Austria, Belgium, Czech Republic, Denmark, England, Finland, France, Germany, Greece, Iceland, Ireland, Italy, Luxembourg, Netherlands, Norway, Poland, Portugal, Romania, Russia, Scotland, Slovenia, Spain, Sweden, Switzerland. $119. Uniworld Business Publications, Inc., 257 Central Park West, Suite 10A, New York, NY 10024-4110, (212) 496-2448, fax (212) 769-0413, email uniworldbp@aol.com. Web site: http://www.uniworldbp.com.

EASTERN EUROPE: A DIRECTORY AND SOURCEBOOK identifies major sources of marketing information, independent and government organizations, and details on leading companies. $590. Published by Euromonitor (England). Distributed by Gale Group, P.O. Box 9187, Farmington Hills, MI 48333-9187. Toll free US and Canada (800) 877-GALE (4253) and (248) 699-GALE, fax (800) 414-5043 and (248) 699-8061, Internet orders galeord@galegroup.com, web site www.galegroup.com or www.gale.com. All Gale Group products are available on approval. Contact Gale for details.

EUROPEAN DRINKS MARKETING DIRECTORY provides information on over 1,600 drink manufacturers and over 750 retail and wholesale distributors in Western and Eastern Europe. Includes a directory of 1,500 information sources. $425. Published by Euromonitor (England). Distributed by Gale Group, P.O. Box 9187, Farmington Hills, MI 48333-9187. Toll free US and Canada (800) 877-GALE (4253) and (248) 699-GALE, fax (800) 414-5043 and (248) 699-8061, Internet orders galeord@galegroup.com, web site www.galegroup.com or www.gale.com. All Gale Group products are available on approval. Contact Gale for details.

KOMPASS is described by the publisher as "the world's most comprehensive global database of companies, products and services for manufacturing and engineering professionals in print, on CD ROM and on the Internet." It contains company and product information for companies in all lines of business, including manufacturing and industrial sectors. Each company listing includes name, address, phone number, management names, business descriptions, and industry and product listings. Kompass's web site is www.kompass.com. Call publisher for prices and information on country directories. Cahners Business Information, 121 Chanlon Road, New Providence, NJ 07974, (908) 771-8785, fax (908) 665-8755, email hholmes@reedref.com. Headquarters: Cahners Business Information, 275 Washington Street, Newton, MA 02158-1630, (617) 558-4663 or (617) 964-3030, fax (617) 558-4700, email marketaccess@cahners.com, web sites www.cahners.com or www.chilton.net.

MAJOR COMPANIES OF CENTRAL AND EASTERN EUROPE AND THE COMMONWEALTH OF INDEPENDENT STATES identifies some 38,000 executives at 8,000 major business organizations in 24 countries in Eastern and Central Europe and the former Soviet Republics (CIS). Includes three indexes. $980. Also available in CD ROM. Published by Graham & Whiteside Ltd., Tuition House, 5-6 Francis Grove, London SW19 4DT, England. Web site http://www.major-co-data.com. Email sales@major-co-data.com. Distributed by: Larry Meranus Professional Publications & Services, 4 Demoray Court, Pine Brook, NJ 07058, (800) MERANUS or (800) 637-2687. Also distributed by Gale Group, P.O. Box 9187, Farmington Hills, MI 48333-9187. Toll free US and Canada (800) 877-GALE (4253) and (248) 699-GALE, fax (800) 414-5043 and (248) 699-8061, Internet orders galeord@galegroup.com, web site www.galegroup.com or www.gale.com. All Gale Group products are available on approval. Contact Gale for details.

MAJOR COMPANIES SERIES ON CD ROM consists of Graham & Whiteside's annual directories of major international companies. All six directories reside on one disk. After payment, you'll receive a security code to access the region(s) you select. This Windows™ based CD can navigate by company name, company locations, executive names, business activity and more. Free demo CD ROM is available. Regions also available separately for Europe, Central & Eastern Europe, the Far East and Australasia, the Arab World, Africa, and Latin America. For prices and availability, contact the Gale Group, P.O. Box 9187, Farmington Hills, MI 48333-9187. Toll free US and Canada (800) 877-GALE (4253) and (248) 699-GALE, fax (800) 414-5043 and (248) 699-8061, Internet orders galeord@galegroup.com, web site www.galegroup.com or www.gale.com. All Gale Group products are available on approval. Contact Gale for details.

MAJOR TELECOMMUNICATIONS COMPANIES OF EUROPE contains information and contacts for 1,100 major telecommunications companies and their equipment suppliers in western Europe, central Europe and eastern Europe. $415. US distributor: Larry Meranus Professional Publications & Services, 4 Demoray Court, Pine Brook, NJ 07058, (800) MERANUS or (800) 637-2687. Published by Graham & Whiteside Ltd., Tuition House, 5-6 Francis Grove, London SW19 4DT, England. Web site http://www.major-co-data.com. Email sales@major-co-data.com.

WORLD GUIDE TO TRADE ASSOCIATIONS edited by Michael Zils includes key personnel, publications, a translation of the name in English, information that reflects the structure of Eastern Europe and the former USSR, a German-English concordance of subject areas and other data. From K.G. Saur. 2 volume set $650. R.R. Bowker (a unit of Cahners Business Information), 121 Chanlon Road, New Providence, NJ 07974 USA, Phone (888) BOWKER2 (888-269-5372) & (800) 323-3288, fax (908) 508-7696, email info@bowker.com, web www.bowker.com. Canada—R.R. Bowker, Markham, Ontario, phone (888) BOWKER9 & (905) 415-5837, fax (905) 479-6266. German speaking Europe—K.G. Saur Verlag, Munich, Germany, phone 49-89-76902-232, fax 49-89-76902-250, email 100730.1341@compuserve.com, web www.saur.de/home.htm. Rest of Europe incl. United Kingdom plus Africa & Asia—Bowker-Saur, W. Sussex, UK, phone 44-1342-326-972, fax 44-1342-335-612, email customer@bowker-saur.co.uk, web www.bowker-saur.com/service/. Australia/New Zealand—Thorpe, Port Melbourne, Victoria, Australia, phone 61-03-9-245-7370, fax 61-03-9-245-7395, email customer.service@thorpe.com.au, web www.thorpe.com.au. Technical support for CD ROMs (800) 323-3288, fax (908) 665-3528, email techsupport@bowker.com.

Education

Also see Higher Education

AMERICAN ART DIRECTORY provides information about national and regional art organizations, museums, libraries and associations in the US and Canada, art schools in the US and Canada, plus listings of museums abroad, art schools abroad, state arts councils, state directors and supervisors of art education, art magazines, art editors and critics, scholarships and fellowships, open exhibitions, and traveling exhibition booking agencies, plus a personnel index. $210. If the price is prohibitively high, remember your local library. National Register Publishing, Reed Elsevier-New Providence, 121 Chanlon Road, New Providence, NJ 07974, (800) 521-8110, fax (800) 836-7736, web site www.redbooks.com or www.marquiswhoswho.com. "If, for any reason whatsoever, your order does not fully meet your expectations, simply return the product within 30 days for a prompt, complete, unquestioned refund," as stated in Catalog of Biographical and Professional References of publisher Marquis Who's Who/National Register Publishing.

AWARDS, HONORS & PRIZES provides an alphabetical listing of the organizations giving the awards. Specifies organization, award and subject indexes and email addresses. $450 for two volume set, $255 per single volume.

> Volume 1, US and Canada, $228
> Volume 2, International and Foreign, $255

Gale Group, P.O. Box 9187, Farmington Hills, MI 48333-9187. Toll free US and Canada (800) 877-GALE (4253) and (248) 699-GALE, fax (800) 414-5043 and (248) 699-8061, Internet orders galeord@galegroup.com, web site www.galegroup.com or www.gale.com. All Gale Group products are available on approval. Contact Gale for details.

BALTIMORE/ANNAPOLIS is a guide to over 2,000 organizations and institutions. Chapters include government, business, education, medicine/health, arts and culture, community affairs and more. $65. Columbia Books, Inc., 1212 New York Avenue, NW, Suite 330, Washington, DC 20005, (212) 898-0662.

CANADIAN ALMANAC AND DIRECTORY includes abbreviations, associations and societies, broadcasting and communications, business statistics, church and religious organizations, commerce and finance, cultural directory, education directory, electoral districts, foreign and international contacts, geographic information, government directory, government quick reference, health and hospitals, historical and general information, legal and judicial directory, postal information, tourism and transportation. The Almanac also includes web sites of significant institutions in business, communications, and the arts, a "Who's Who" of key officials and organizations on the Canadian information highway and up-to-date provincial and territorial election results. Indexed by titles and keyword. $249 US. Inquire about CD ROM availability. Published by IHS Canada, Micromedia Limited, 20 Victoria Street, Toronto, Ontario M5C 2N8 CANADA, (800) 387-2689, (416) 362-5211, fax (416) 362-6161, email info@micromedia.on.ca. Distributed in the US by the Gale Group, P.O. Box 9187, Farmington Hills, MI 48333-9187. Toll free US and Canada (800) 877-GALE (4253) and (248) 699-GALE, fax (800) 414-5043 and (248) 699-8061, Internet orders galeord@galegroup.com, web site www.galegroup.com or www.gale.com. All Gale Group products are available on approval. Contact Gale for details.

CERTIFICATION AND ACCREDITATION PROGRAMS DIRECTORY describes 1,600 certification programs and details over 200 accrediting organizations. It contains information on certification eligibility and the procedures for national voluntary certification and accreditation programs that denote skill level, professionalism, accomplishment and excellence. $99. Gale Group, P.O. Box 9187, Farmington Hills, MI 48333-9187. Toll free US and Canada (800) 877-GALE (4253) and (248) 699-GALE, fax (800) 414-5043 and (248) 699-8061, Internet orders galeord@galegroup.com, web site www.galegroup.com or www.gale.com. All Gale Group products are available on approval. Contact Gale for details.

COUNCIL FOR THE ADVANCEMENT AND SUPPORT OF HIGHER EDUCATION (CASE) MEMBERSHIP DIRECTORY provides a comprehensive listing of administrators at colleges and universities. Members are entitled to one free copy and can purchase additional copies for $49 each. Non-members' price is $349. Council for the Advancement and Support of Higher Education, 11 Dupont Circle NW, Suite 400, Washington, DC 20036, (202) 328-5900, web site www.case.org.

DIRECTORY OF AMERICAN SCHOLARS contains current biographies of over 30,000 scholars in the humanities. Volume 1, History. Volume 2, English, Speech and Drama. Volume 3 Foreign Languages, Linguistics and Philology. Volume 4, Philosophy, Religion and Law. $450 for 5 volume set. Individual volumes $135. Gale Group, P.O. Box 9187, Farmington Hills, MI 48333-9187. Toll free US and Canada (800) 877-GALE (4253) and (248) 699-GALE, fax (800) 414-5043 and (248) 699-8061, Internet orders galeord@galegroup.com, web site www.galegroup.com or www.gale.com. All Gale Group products are available on approval. Contact Gale for details.

EDUCATIONAL RANKINGS ANNUAL presents 3,500 national, regional, local and international lists and complete source citations if you need additional research. $199. Gale Group, P.O. Box 9187, Farmington Hills, MI 48333-9187. Toll free US and Canada (800) 877-GALE (4253) and (248) 699-GALE, fax (800) 414-5043 and (248) 699-8061, Internet orders galeord@galegroup.com, web site www.galegroup.com or www.gale.com. All Gale Group products are available on approval. Contact Gale for details.

ENCYCLOPEDIA OF ASSOCIATIONS: INTERNATIONAL ORGANIZATIONS includes nearly 20,000 multinational and national organizations in foreign countries, including US based associations with multinational membership. Entries also include email addresses, web sites and bulletin board addresses, lobbying activities, and publication and convention information. Indexed by geography, keyword and executives. $595 for 2 volume set. Also available in CD ROM. Database available via commercial online service. Gale Group, P.O. Box 9187, Farmington Hills, MI 48333-9187. Toll free US and Canada (800) 877-GALE (4253) and (248) 699-GALE, fax (800) 414-5043 and (248) 699-8061, Internet orders galeord@galegroup.com, web site www.galegroup.com or www.gale.com. All Gale Group products are available on approval. Contact Gale for details.

ENCYCLOPEDIA OF ASSOCIATIONS: NATIONAL ORGANIZATIONS OF THE US. This superb reference is one of the first places you should look when beginning a new recruiting assignment or when looking for specialized references of any type. The keyword index makes this comprehensive reference easy to use, even in hard copy. For over 23,000 nonprofit professional associations with a national scope, this encyclopedia reveals:

- Publications, including membership rosters and newsletters
- Dates and locations of association conferences and conventions
- Names of Executive Directors, who are usually incredible sources of industry information if you call and speak to them
- Committees
- Job and candidate referral banks, which can provide resumes of other industry sources and sometimes candidates
- It includes organizations in these categories: business, trade, environmental, agricultural, legal, governmental, engineering, technological, scientific, educational, cultural, social welfare, health & medical, public affairs, ethnic, labor unions, chambers of commerce, tourism, & others.

Volume 1, National Organizations of the US, $505
Volume 2, Geographic and Executive Indexes, $390
Volume 3, Supplement, $405

Gale Group, P.O. Box 9187, Farmington Hills, MI 48333-9187. Toll free US and Canada (800) 877-GALE (4253) and (248) 699-GALE, fax (800) 414-5043 and (248) 699-8061, Internet orders galeord@galegroup.com, web site www.galegroup.com or www.gale.com. All Gale Group products are available on approval. Contact Gale for details.

ENCYCLOPEDIA OF ASSOCIATIONS: REGIONAL, STATE AND LOCAL ORGANIZATIONS. The information in this directory is *not* duplicated anywhere in ENCYCLOPEDIA OF ASSOCIATIONS. Over 100,000 nonprofit organizations are included in this directory. $585 for 5 volume set or $140 per individual volume. Also available on CD ROM and online on the Internet through a GaleNet subscription.

Volume 1, Great Lakes States (Illinois, Indiana, Michigan, Minnesota, Ohio, Wisconsin)
Volume 2, Northeastern States (Connecticut, Maine, Massachusetts, New Hampshire, New Jersey, New York, Pennsylvania, Rhode Islands, Vermont)
Volume 3, Southern and Middle Atlantic States (Including Puerto Rico and the Virgin Islands) (Alabama, Delaware, Washington, DC, Florida, Georgia, Kentucky, Maryland, Mississippi, North Carolina, Puerto Rico, South Carolina, Tennessee, Virginia, West Virginia, Virgin Islands)
Volume 4, South Central and Great Plains States (Arkansas, Iowa, Kansas, Louisiana, Missouri, Nebraska, North Dakota, Oklahoma, South Dakota, Texas)
Volume 5, Western States (Alaska, Arizona, California, Colorado, Guam, Hawaii, Idaho, Montana, Nevada, New Mexico, Oregon, Utah, Washington, Wyoming)

Gale Group, P.O. Box 9187, Farmington Hills, MI 48333-9187. Toll free US and Canada (800) 877-GALE (4253) and (248) 699-GALE, fax (800) 414-5043 and (248) 699-8061, Internet orders galeord@galegroup.com, web site www.galegroup.com or www.gale.com. All Gale Group products are available on approval. Contact Gale for details.

SCHOLARSHIPS, FELLOWSHIPS AND LOANS identifies 3,700 sources of education-related financial aid and awards at all levels of study. It includes a summary of programs sponsored by the federal government and a state listing of agencies. $175. Gale Group, P.O. Box 9187, Farmington Hills, MI 48333-9187. Toll free US and Canada (800) 877-GALE (4253) and (248) 699-GALE, fax (800) 414-5043 and (248) 699-8061, Internet orders galeord@galegroup.com, web site www.galegroup.com or www.gale.com. All Gale Group products are available on approval. Contact Gale for details.

SCOTT'S DIRECTORY OF CANADIAN SCHOOLS contains information on over 16,000 private and public schools, school boards, colleges, universities, native schools, special needs schools, vocational schools and departments of education, plus names of key contacts, including principals, librarians and guidance counselors. Book $127, diskette $547. Special discounts available for combined purchases. Published by Southam Information Products Ltd, 1450 Don Mills Road, Don Mills, Ontario M3B 2X7 CANADA, (800) 668-2374. In Toronto 442-2122. Web site www.southam.com.

WASHINGTON identifies 4,500 organizations and institutions in Washington DC and 22,000 key people in them. Includes government, business, education, medicine/health, community affairs, art/culture and others. $85. Columbia Books, Inc., 1212 New York Avenue, NW, Suite 330, Washington, DC 20005, (212) 898-0662.

WHO'S WHO IN AMERICAN EDUCATION, $159.95, first time standing order $143.95, Marquis Who's Who, 121 Chanlon Road, New Providence, NJ 07974, (800) 521-8110.

WORLD GUIDE TO SCIENTIFIC ASSOCIATIONS AND LEARNED SOCIETIES encompasses international, national and regional associations in science, culture and technology. From K.G. Saur, $300. R.R. Bowker (a unit of Cahners Business Information), 121 Chanlon Road, New Providence, NJ 07974 USA, Phone (888) BOWKER2 (888-269-5372) & (800) 323-3288, fax (908) 508-7696, email info@bowker.com, web www.bowker.com. Canada—R.R. Bowker, Markham, Ontario, phone (888) BOWKER9 & (905) 415-5837, fax (905) 479-6266. German speaking Europe—K.G. Saur Verlag, Munich, Germany, phone 49-89-76902-232, fax 49-89-76902-250, email 100730.1341@compuserve.com, web www.saur.de/home.htm. Rest of Europe incl. United Kingdom plus Africa & Asia—Bowker-Saur, W. Sussex, UK, phone 44-1342-326-972, fax 44-1342-335-612, email customer@bowker-saur.co.uk, web www.bowker-saur.com/service/. Australia/New Zealand—Thorpe, Port Melbourne, Victoria, Australia, phone 61-03-9-245-7370, fax 61-03-9-245-7395, email customer.service@thorpe.com.au, web www.thorpe.com.au. Technical support for CD ROMs (800) 323-3288, fax (908) 665-3528, email techsupport@bowker.com.

www.jobsingovernment.com contains job postings for positions in government, education and the public sector. Many positions are in city administration, engineering and public safety, often in the $30,000 to $50,000 range. Jobs In Government has been online since 1996.

www.umn.edu/apn or Academic Position Network is a web site that lists positions for faculty, professional and administrative staff, including librarians, in academia. The site was developed by Academic Position Network in Blaine, Minnesota and established in 1996.

Educational Credentials

ALUMNI DIRECTORIES. Sometimes school directories (graduate and undergraduate) cross-reference names of people according to company. When the directory is so organized, it can be a useful recruiting tool, for example, if you're looking for an MSEE employed by a certain company. If you want to buy a directory, you will usually need the help of a graduate because most schools will only sell directories to their alumni. If you work for a big company, there's usually a graduate around willing to either lend you a directory, or will help you buy one. Actually, it's usually as simple as getting the graduate's permission to use his or her name to order the directory. Then YOU can order the directory, send a company check with your order, and have the directory mailed to the company, to your office address c/o the graduate. This way the graduate doesn't have to go to any trouble. Historically the alumni directories for the graduate schools of business at Harvard and Wharton have been well organized, from a recruiting research standpoint. To find out if an alumni directory is available in a CD ROM, ask a graduate, or call the alumni office directly.

PETERSON'S GRADSEARCH is a GaleNet database that provide access to graduate school and professional programs in over 31,000 graduate academic departments. If your recruiting is driven by highly specific educational credentials, you can use this database to identify the schools that produce the graduates you're looking for. Once your targeted graduate program has been identified, you can then contact the placement office at the school, if you're recruiting new graduates. If you're recruiting for more senior positions, or looking for a job yourself, you can contact the alumni office to locate job seekers with the right credentials. You could also review alumni publications, which often publish announcements about promotions and job changes, which can be valuable ID research and which will also lead you to sources and prospects NOT on the job market.

Electronic Commerce

CANADIAN ELECTRONIC COMMERCE DIRECTORY, Phillips Business Information, Inc., a Phillips Publishing International Company, 120 Seven Locks Road, Potomac, MD 20854, (301) 340-1520, (301) 340-7788, (800) 777-5006, Internet pbi@phillips.com, web site www.phillips.com.

ELECTRONIC COMMERCE DIRECTORY, Phillips Business Information, Inc., a Phillips Publishing International Company, 120 Seven Locks Road, Potomac, MD 20854, (301) 340-1520, (301) 340-7788, (800) 777-5006, Internet pbi@phillips.com, web site www.phillips.com.

www.ectoday.com is the web site that contains the latest industry news for Electronic Commerce. For more information, contact: Phillips Business Information, Inc., a Phillips Publishing International Company, 120 Seven Locks Road, Potomac, MD 20854, (301) 340-1520, (301) 340-7788, (800) 777-5006, Internet pbi@phillips.com, web site www.phillips.com.

Electronics

Also see Engineering, Information Technology, Software and Technology.

AMERICAN ELECTRONICS ASSOCIATION annually publishes the AEA DIRECTORY for $175. With 18 regional groups, this association conducts networking programs for industry executives, and provides information on compensation surveys and employee benefits plans, among other things. For more information contact: American Electronics Association (AEA), 5201 Great America Parkway, Suite 520, PO Box 54990, Santa Clara, CA 95056, (408) 987-4200.

ASIAN AMERICAN MANUFACTURERS ASSOCIATION (AAMA) publishes an annual Membership Directory and a newsletter which contains new member listings and employment listings. It also publishes ASIAN AMERICAN ENTREPRENEURS AND EXECUTIVES OF PUBLIC COMPANIES IN THE HIGH TECH INDUSTRY. Membership is comprised of Asian American manufacturers of technology products, such as computers, microprocessors, semiconductors, biotech, software and electronics equipment. Presents an annual award for entrepreneurship. For more information contact Asian American Manufacturers Association (AAMA), 39120 Argonaut Way, #309, Freemont, CA 94538-1398, (925) 461-0800.

CORPTECH DIRECTORY OF TECHNOLOGY COMPANIES is available in hard copy, Regional Guides, on PC floppy diskette, and on CD ROM. CORPTECH EXPLORE DATABASE is an outstanding reference that was awarded Best CD-ROM Directory by the National Directory Publishing Association. One click moves you from the CD ROM Database to the company's Internet web site. CORPTECH also provides other sophisticated but reasonably priced automated services (and quantity discounts) with their customized data-on-demand service, which uses up to 30 search parameters. You can save a tremendous amount of time researching relatively small, emerging new companies in various high technology niches and obtain names, titles and even mailing address labels. If CORPTECH is too expensive to purchase, go to the library.

- CORPTECH EXPLORE SILVER DATABASE CD ROM, $2,495 (including free soft cover CorpTech Directory worth $745).
- CORPTECH EXPLORE GOLD DATABASE CD ROM, $5,995 offers an export capability, extended company history and has hyperlinks to news services to aid company research, such as Reuters and PR Newswire. Both Silver and Gold CD's have links to company web sites.
- CORPTECH print directories are available for $795 hard cover, $745 soft cover.
- CORPTECH regional directories are available in print for $225 (soft cover only). Regional Explore Gold CD's are $995 each and Explore Silver are $795 each.

Industry specific directories segmented into 17 different industries are also available on CD ROM. Each industry costs $995, except computer software, which is very large and counts as two industries. The 17 industry segments are: factory automation, biotechnology, chemicals, computer hardware, **defense,** energy, environmental, manufacturing, advanced materials, medical, pharmaceuticals, photonics, computer software, subassemblies and components, test and measurement companies, telecommunications & Internet, and transportation.

Ordering Information: CORPTECH, Corporate Technology Information Services, Inc., 12 Alfred Street, Suite 200, Woburn, MA 01801-1915. (800) 333-8036, (800) 454-3647, (781) 932-3100, (781) 932-3939. Fax (781) 932-6335. Email sales@corptech.com. Web site www.corptech.com.

EDN is a trade journal published 26 times a year with information on electronic products, technology and design techniques for engineers and engineering managers. Call publisher for price. EDN Worldwide Editorial, 275 Washington Street, Newton, MA 02158-1630, (617) 558-4454 or (617) 964-3030, fax (617) 558-4470, URL www.ednmag.com.

EDN ASIA is a monthly magazine for electronics engineers and managers in Asia's original equipment manufacturing market. Call publisher for price. EDN/Cahners Business Information, 19/F, 8 Commercial Tower, 8 Sun Yip Street, Chaiwan, Hong Kong, (011) 852-2965-1555, fax (011) 852-2976-0706, email chriseverett@rebi.com.hk, URL www.cahners.com/mainmag/ednas.htm. Headquarters: EDN Worldwide Editorial, 275 Washington Street, Newton, MA 02158-1630, (617) 558-4454 or (617) 964-3030, fax (617) 558-4470, URL www.ednmag.com.

EDN CHINA is a monthly magazine for China's electronic original equipment manufacturers. Call publisher for price. EDN China/Cahners Business Information, 10th floor, STIP Building, 22 Bai Wan Zhuang Road, Beijing, China, (011) 8610-6832-7920, fax (011) 8610-6832-8356, email ednc@public3.bta.net.cn, URL www.cahners.com/mainmag/ednc.htm. Headquarters: EDN Worldwide Editorial, 275 Washington Street, Newton, MA 02158-1630, (617) 558-4454 or (617) 964-3030, fax (617) 558-4470, URL www.ednmag.com.

EDN EUROPE is a monthly magazine for electronics engineers and managers in Europe's original equipment manufacturing area. Call publisher for price. EDN Europe/Cahners Business Information, P.O. Box 377, Norwich NR14 6UQ, England, (011) 44 1508 528-435, fax (011) 44-1508 528-430, email ttobeck@edn.cahners.com, mike.hancock@rbi.co.uk, URL www.ednmag.com. Headquarters: EDN Worldwide Editorial, 275 Washington Street, Newton, MA 02158-1630, (617) 558-4454 or (617) 964-3030, fax (617) 558-4470, URL www.ednmag.com.

ELECTRONIC BUSINESS ASIA is a monthly magazine for business management in electronics, computers and systems companies. Call publisher for prices. Cahners Business Information, 19/f, 8 Commercial Tower, 8 Sun Yip Street, Chaiwan, Hong Kong, (011) 852-2965-1555, fax (011) 852-2976-0706, email msavery@rebi.com.hk, URL www.cahners.com/mainmag/eba.htm. Headquarters: Cahners Business Information, 275 Washington Street, Newton, MA 02158-1630. (617) 558-4663 or (617) 964-3030, fax (617) 558-4700, email marketaccess@cahners.com. Web sites www.cahners.com or www.chilton.net.

ELECTRONICS INDUSTRY TELEPHONE DIRECTORY (EITD) is an industry phone directory that lists over 30,000 company locations and 3,000 product types in the electronics industry. Published annually. Available in hard copy for $55 from Harris InfoSource, 2057 East Aurora Road, Twinsburg, OH 44087-1999, (330) 425-9000, (800) 888-5900, www.HarrisInfo.com. Also available from Cahners Business Information, 201 King of Prussia Road, Radnor, PA 19089, (610) 964-4345, fax (610) 964-4348, email jbreck@chilton.net, URL www.ecnmag.com/eitd. Headquarters: Cahners Business Information, 275 Washington Street, Newton, MA 02158-1630, (617) 558-4663 or (617) 964-3030, fax (617) 558-4700, email marketaccess@cahners.com. Web sites www.cahners.com or www.chilton.net.

ELECTRONICS MANUFACTURERS DIRECTORY contains information on 17,000 US companies and nearly 2,000 Canadian companies. A total of 68,000 names and titles are included. Available as a directory and database. For pricing and more information, contact distributor Database Publishing Company, PO Box 70024, Anaheim, CA 92825, (800) 888-8434, (714) 778-6400, email sales@databasepublishing.com. Also contact Harris InfoSource, 2057 East Aurora Road, Twinsburg, OH 44087-1999, (330) 425-9000, (800) 888-5900, www.HarrisInfo.com.

ELSEVIER ADVANCED TECHNOLOGY is a leading supplier of Electronics industry information. They publish a CD-ROM of a complete database of electronic companies in Europe, developed in conjunction with THE EUROPEAN ELECTRONICS DIRECTORY: COMPONENTS AND SUB-ASSEMBLIES AND SYSTEMS AND APPLICATIONS. Elsevier also publishes yearbooks, directories, market research reports and industrial journals, technical handbooks and newsletters, such as PROFILE OF THE WORLDWIDE TELECOMMUNICATIONS INDUSTRY, PROFILE OF THE WORLDWIDE CAPACITOR INDUSTRY, PROFILE OF THE WORLDWIDE SEMICONDUCTOR INDUSTRY, and PROFILE OF THE EUROPEAN CONNECTOR INDUSTRY. For more information contact: Elsevier Advanced Technology, P.O. Box 150, Kidlington, Oxford, OX5 1AS, England. Phone (44) (0) 1865 843-848, fax (44) (0) 1865 843-971.

EUROPEAN ELECTRONICS DATABASE ON CD ROM is available for $790 from Harris InfoSource, 2057 East Aurora Road, Twinsburg, OH 44087-1999, (330) 425-9000, (800) 888-5900, www.HarrisInfo.com.

EUROPEAN ELECTRONICS DIRECTORY (COMPONENTS AND SUB-ASSEMBLIES) is available as a directory for $410 from Harris InfoSource, 2057 East Aurora Road, Twinsburg, OH 44087-1999, (330) 425-9000, (800) 888-5900, www.HarrisInfo.com.

EUROPEAN ELECTRONICS DIRECTORY (SYSTEMS AND APPLICATIONS) is available as a directory for $399 from Harris InfoSource, 2057 East Aurora Road, Twinsburg, OH 44087-1999, (330) 425-9000, (800) 888-5900, www.HarrisInfo.com.

HARRIS ELECTRONICS MANUFACTURERS DATABASE, also available as a directory, is published in cooperation with the Electronics Representatives Association and the National Electronic Distributors Association. It contains information on over 20,000 US electronics manufacturing firms and over 2,500 Canadian electronics manufacturers, including names of about 68,000 American executives and 5,500 Canadian executives. Selectory $595. Selectory multi-user (LAN) version $1,190. Directory, updated annually, $255. Ordering information: Harris InfoSource International, 2057 Aurora Road, Twinsburg, OH 44087-1999, (800) 888-5900, fax (800) 643-5997, web site http://www.harrisinfo.com.

INFORMATION INDUSTRY DIRECTORY tracks companies that produce electronic systems, services and products, including database producers, CD ROM and other optical publishing products and services, Internet accessible services, online host services, transactional services and more. Entries include contact information and email address, thorough description of organization systems and more. $605 for 2 volumes. Database available via commercial online service. Gale Group, P.O. Box 9187, Farmington Hills, MI 48333-9187. Toll free US and Canada (800) 877-GALE (4253) and (248) 699-GALE, fax (800) 414-5043 and (248) 699-8061, Internet orders galeord@galegroup.com, web site www.galegroup.com or www.gale.com. All Gale Group products are available on approval. Contact Gale for details.

NORTH AMERICAN ELECTRONICS MANUFACTURERS contains information on over 19,000 Canadian and US electronics companies. Directory $395, Selectory $895. Scott's Directories, Toronto area: 1450 Don Mills Road, Don Mills, Ontario, M3B 2X7, CANADA, (416) 442-2291, (416) 932-9555, (888) 709-9907. Montréal area: Scott's Directories, 3300 Cote Verde, Suite 410 Ville St.-Laurent, Quebec H4B 2B7 CANADA (514) 339-1397, (800) 363-1327. Publisher's email scotts@southam.ca.

PHILLIPS BUSINESS INFORMATION provides information in newsletters, magazines, directories and on multiple web sites covering a range of topics, such as magazine products, telecommunications and cable products, satellite products, media, new media and Internet products, marketing and public relations products, financial technology and electronic commerce, aviation and defense products. For more information, contact: Phillips Business Information, Inc., a Phillips Publishing International Company, 120 Seven Locks Road, Potomac, MD 20854, (301) 340-1520, (301) 340-7788, (800) 777-5006, Internet pbi@phillips.com, web site www.phillips.com.

SOFTWARE AND INFORMATION INDUSTRY ASSOCIATION (SIIA), 1730 M Street NW, Washington, DC 20036 was formed by a merger with the Information Industry Association (IIA) and the Software Publishers Association (SPA). (202) 452-1600. Visit their web site at www.siia.net to access their online membership directory free.

WHO'S WHO IN TESTING & MONITORING, Phillips Business Information, Inc., a Phillips Publishing International Company, 120 Seven Locks Road, Potomac, MD 20854, (301) 340-1520, (301) 340-7788, (800) 777-5006, Internet pbi@phillips.com, web site www.phillips.com.

www.careermosaic.com is the URL for a major recruitment web site that spends millions of dollars in advertising to draw traffic to this site. CareerMosaic features a jobs database; newsgroups for jobs, college connection, online job fairs, employer job postings; company information and more. CareerMosaic was ranked as one of the top 5 "Sites Offering the Best Overall Support for Job Seekers" by the *National Business Employment Weekly*. The site was developed Bernard Hodes Advertising in New York and went online in 1994.

www.ejobs.com—This is a job site for positions in high technology, electronics and semiconductors.

www.electronic-jobs.com—This is another job site for positions in technology, electronics and semiconductors.

Energy

See Environment, Petroleum

CORPTECH DIRECTORY OF TECHNOLOGY COMPANIES is available in hard copy, Regional Guides, on PC floppy diskette, and on CD ROM. CORPTECH EXPLORE DATABASE is an outstanding reference that was awarded Best CD-ROM Directory by the National Directory Publishing Association. One click moves you from the CD ROM Database to the company's Internet web site. CORPTECH also provides other sophisticated but reasonably priced automated services (and quantity discounts) with their customized data-on-demand service, which uses up to 30 search parameters. You can save a tremendous amount of time researching relatively small, emerging new companies in various high technology niches and obtain names, titles and even mailing address labels. If CORPTECH is too expensive to purchase, go to the library.

- CORPTECH EXPLORE SILVER DATABASE CD ROM, $2,495 (including free soft cover CorpTech Directory worth $745).
- CORPTECH EXPLORE GOLD DATABASE CD ROM, $5,995 offers an export capability, extended company history and has hyperlinks to news services to aid company research, such as Reuters and PR Newswire. Both Silver and Gold CD's have links to company web sites.
- CORPTECH print directories are available for $795 hard cover, $745 soft cover.
- CORPTECH regional directories are available in print for $225 (soft cover only). Regional Explore Gold CD's are $995 each and Explore Silver are $795 each.

Industry specific directories segmented into 17 different industries are also available on CD ROM. Each industry costs $995, except computer software, which is very large and counts as two industries. The 17 industry segments are: factory automation, biotechnology, chemicals, computer hardware, defense, **energy,** environmental, manufacturing, advanced materials, medical, pharmaceuticals, photonics, computer software, subassemblies and components, test and measurement companies, telecommunications & Internet, and transportation.

Ordering Information: CORPTECH, Corporate Technology Information Services, Inc., 12 Alfred Street, Suite 200, Woburn, MA 01801-1915. (800) 333-8036, (800) 454-3647, (781) 932-3100, (781) 932-3939. Fax (781) 932-6335. Email sales@corptech.com. Web site www.corptech.com.

FINANCIAL TIMES ENERGY YEARBOOKS: MINING contains full contact details, financial and operating information, and details about subsidiaries, affiliates, property and operations for about 800 mining companies globally. $320. Published by Financial Times Energy. Distributed by Gale Group, P.O. Box 9187, Farmington Hills, MI 48333-9187. Toll free US and Canada (800) 877-GALE (4253) and (248) 699-GALE, fax (800) 414-5043 and (248) 699-8061, Internet orders galeord@galegroup.com, web site www.galegroup.com or www.gale.com. All Gale Group products are available on approval. Contact Gale for details.

FINANCIAL TIMES ENERGY YEARBOOKS: OIL AND GAS provides narrative, production and financial information for over 800 major oil and gas companies, including full contact details. It also includes major oil and gas brokers and traders, industry associations, and outlines all parent, subsidiary and associate companies. $320. Published by Financial Times Energy. Distributed by Gale Group, P.O. Box 9187, Farmington Hills, MI 48333-9187. Toll free US and Canada (800) 877-GALE (4253) and (248) 699-GALE, fax (800) 414-5043 and (248) 699-8061, Internet orders galeord@galegroup.com, web site www.galegroup.com or www.gale.com. All Gale Group products are available on approval. Contact Gale for details.

MAJOR ENERGY COMPANIES OF EUROPE presents information on over 1,200 companies in 20 European countries. $415. US distributor: Larry Meranus Professional Publications & Services, 4 Demoray Court, Pine Brook, NJ 07058, (800) MERANUS or (800) 637-2687. Published by Graham & Whiteside Ltd., Tuition House, 5-6 Francis Grove, London SW19 4DT, England. Web site http://www.major-co-data.com. Email sales@major-co-data.com.

MAJOR ENERGY COMPANIES OF THE FAR EAST & AUSTRALASIA provides information on over 500 leading energy companies in the Asia Pacific, $415. US distributor: Larry Meranus Professional Publications & Services, 4 Demoray Court, Pine Brook, NJ 07058, (800) MERANUS or (800) 637-2687. Published by Graham & Whiteside Ltd., Tuition House, 5-6 Francis Grove, London SW19 4DT, England. Web site http://www.major-co-data.com. Email sales@major-co-data.com.

MAJOR ENERGY COMPANIES OF THE WORLD provides information on over 3,500 leading energy companies. $830. US distributor: Larry Meranus Professional Publications & Services, 4 Demoray Court, Pine Brook, NJ 07058, (800) MERANUS or (800) 637-2687. Published by Graham & Whiteside Ltd., Tuition House, 5-6 Francis Grove, London SW19 4DT, England. Web site http://www.major-co-data.com. Email sales@major-co-data.com.

Engineering

Also see Aerospace, Electronics, Technology, Telecommunications

AMERICAN CHEMICAL SOCIETY is a major professional society of chemists and chemical engineers with a budget of over $250 million dollars. It operates an employment clearinghouse, offers career guidance counseling and maintains a speakers bureau, among other things. A description of their services, libraries, computer services, publications and committees appears in THE ENCYCLOPEDIA OF ASSOCIATIONS. For more information contact them at 1155 16th Street NW, Washington, DC, 20036, (800) 227-5558 or (202) 872-4600.

COMPLETE MARQUIS WHO'S WHO ON CD ROM is a compilation of literally all 19 Marquis Who's Who that have appeared in print since 1985, including living and deceased people. WHO'S WHO IN AMERICA®, WHO'S WHO IN THE WORLD®, WHO'S WHO IN AMERICAN EDUCATIONS®, WHO'S WHO IN AMERICAN LAW®, WHO'S WHO IN AMERICAN NURSING®, WHO'S WHO IN MEDICINE AND HEALTHCARE®, WHO'S WHO IN FINANCE AND INDUSTRY®, **WHO'S WHO IN SCIENCE AND ENGINEERING®,** WHO'S WHO IN THE EAST®, WHO'S WHO IN THE MIDWEST®, WHO'S WHO IN THE SOUTH AND SOUTHWEST®, WHO'S WHO IN THE WEST®, WHO'S WHO OF AMERICAN WOMEN®, WHO'S WHO IN ADVERTISING®, WHO'S WHO OF EMERGING LEADERS IN AMERICA®, WHO'S WHO IN ENTERTAINMENT®, WHO'S WHO AMONG HUMAN SERVICES PROFESSIONALS®. One year subscription with semi-annual updates $995. National Register Publishing, Reed Elsevier-New Providence, 121 Chanlon Road, New Providence, NJ 07974, (800) 521-8110, fax (800) 836-7736, web site www.marquiswhoswho.com or www.redbooks.com. "If, for any reason whatsoever, your order does not fully meet your expectations, simply return the product within 30 days for a prompt, complete, unquestioned refund," as stated in Catalog of Biographical and Professional References of publisher Marquis Who's Who/National Register Publishing.

CORPTECH DIRECTORY OF TECHNOLOGY COMPANIES is available in hard copy, Regional Guides, on PC floppy diskette, and on CD ROM. CORPTECH EXPLORE DATABASE is an outstanding reference that was awarded Best CD-ROM Directory by the National Directory Publishing Association. One click moves you from the CD ROM Database to the company's Internet web site. CORPTECH also provides other sophisticated but reasonably priced automated services (and quantity discounts) with their customized data-on-demand service, which uses up to 30 search parameters. You can save a tremendous amount of time researching relatively small, emerging new companies in various high technology niches and obtain names, titles and even mailing address labels. If CORPTECH is too expensive to purchase, go to the library.

- CORPTECH EXPLORE SILVER DATABASE CD ROM, $2,495 (including free soft cover CorpTech Directory worth $745).

- CORPTECH EXPLORE GOLD DATABASE CD ROM, $5,995 offers an export capability, extended company history and has hyperlinks to news services to aid company research, such as Reuters and PR Newswire. Both Silver and Gold CD's have links to company web sites.
- CORPTECH print directories are available for $795 hard cover, $745 soft cover.
- CORPTECH regional directories are available in print for $225 (soft cover only). Regional Explore Gold CD's are $995 each and Explore Silver are $795 each.

Industry specific directories segmented into 17 different industries are also available on CD ROM. Each industry costs $995, except computer software, which is very large and counts as two industries. The 17 industry segments are: factory automation, biotechnology, chemicals, computer hardware, defense, energy, environmental, manufacturing, advanced materials, medical, pharmaceuticals, photonics, computer software, subassemblies and components, test and measurement companies, telecommunications & Internet, and transportation.

Ordering Information: CORPTECH, Corporate Technology Information Services, Inc., 12 Alfred Street, Suite 200, Woburn, MA 01801-1915. (800) 333-8036, (800) 454-3647, (781) 932-3100, (781) 932-3939. Fax (781) 932-6335. Email sales@corptech.com. Web site www.corptech.com.

D&B DIRECTORY OF SERVICE COMPANIES is a directory with information on 50,000 US service businesses, including privately held companies, in these sectors: accounting, auditing and bookkeeping, advertising and public relations, architecture and engineering, consumer services, executive search, health, hospitality, management consulting, motion pictures, repair, research, social services and law. Listings include key executives' names and titles, address, phone, sales volume, number of employees, parent company and location, and more. Companies listed employ 50 or more people. Information is listed alphabetically and is cross-referenced geographically and by industry classification. Updated annually. For prices call Dun & Bradstreet at (800) 526-0651. For more information contact Dun & Bradstreet, Business Reference Solutions, Three Sylvan Way, Parsippany, New Jersey 07054. Email dnbmdd@mail.dnb.com. Web site http://www.dnbmdd.com.

ENCYCLOPEDIA OF ASSOCIATIONS: INTERNATIONAL ORGANIZATIONS includes nearly 20,000 multinational and national organizations in foreign countries, including US based associations with multinational membership. Entries also include email addresses, web sites and bulletin board addresses, lobbying activities, and publication and convention information. Indexed by geography, keyword and executives. $595 for 2 volume set. Also available in CD ROM. Database available via commercial online service. Gale Group, P.O. Box 9187, Farmington Hills, MI 48333-9187. Toll free US and Canada (800) 877-GALE (4253) and (248) 699-GALE, fax (800) 414-5043 and (248) 699-8061, Internet orders galeord@galegroup.com, web site www.galegroup.com or www.gale.com. All Gale Group products are available on approval. Contact Gale for details.

ENCYCLOPEDIA OF ASSOCIATIONS: NATIONAL ORGANIZATIONS OF THE US. This superb reference is one of the first places you should look when beginning a new recruiting assignment or when looking for specialized references of any type. The keyword index makes this comprehensive reference easy to use, even in hard copy. For over 23,000 nonprofit professional associations with a national scope, this encyclopedia reveals:

- Publications, including membership rosters and newsletters
- Dates and locations of association conferences and conventions
- Names of Executive Directors, who are usually incredible sources of industry information if you call and speak to them
- Committees
- Job and candidate referral banks, which can provide resumes of other industry sources and sometimes candidates
- It includes organizations in these categories: business, trade, environmental, agricultural, legal, governmental, engineering, technological, scientific, educational, cultural, social welfare, health & medical, public affairs, ethnic, labor unions, chambers of commerce, tourism, & others.

Volume 1, National Organizations of the US, $505

Volume 2, Geographic and Executive Indexes, $390

Volume 3, Supplement, $405

Gale Group, P.O. Box 9187, Farmington Hills, MI 48333-9187. Toll free US and Canada (800) 877-GALE (4253) and (248) 699-GALE, fax (800) 414-5043 and (248) 699-8061, Internet orders galeord@galegroup.com, web site www.galegroup.com or www.gale.com. All Gale Group products are available on approval. Contact Gale for details.

ENCYCLOPEDIA OF ASSOCIATIONS: REGIONAL, STATE AND LOCAL ORGANIZATIONS. The information in this directory is *not* duplicated anywhere in ENCYCLOPEDIA OF ASSOCIATIONS. Over 100,000 nonprofit organizations are included in this directory. $585 for 5 volume set or $140 per individual volume. Also available on CD ROM and online on the Internet through a GaleNet subscription.

Volume 1, Great Lakes States (Illinois, Indiana, Michigan, Minnesota, Ohio, Wisconsin)
Volume 2, Northeastern States (Connecticut, Maine, Massachusetts, New Hampshire, New Jersey, New York, Pennsylvania, Rhode Islands, Vermont)
Volume 3, Southern and Middle Atlantic States (Including Puerto Rico and the Virgin Islands) (Alabama, Delaware, Washington, DC, Florida, Georgia, Kentucky, Maryland, Mississippi, North Carolina, Puerto Rico, South Carolina, Tennessee, Virginia, West Virginia, Virgin Islands)
Volume 4, South Central and Great Plains States (Arkansas, Iowa, Kansas, Louisiana, Missouri, Nebraska, North Dakota, Oklahoma, South Dakota, Texas)
Volume 5, Western States (Alaska, Arizona, California, Colorado, Guam, Hawaii, Idaho, Montana, Nevada, New Mexico, Oregon, Utah, Washington, Wyoming)

Gale Group, P.O. Box 9187, Farmington Hills, MI 48333-9187. Toll free US and Canada (800) 877-GALE (4253) and (248) 699-GALE, fax (800) 414-5043 and (248) 699-8061, Internet orders galeord@galegroup.com, web site www.galegroup.com or www.gale.com. All Gale Group products are available on approval. Contact Gale for details.

ENCYCLOPEDIA OF PHYSICAL SCIENCES AND ENGINEERING INFORMATION SOURCES covers over 600 subjects such as chemistry, geology, physics, civil engineering plus new areas of technology such as CD ROM, cybernetics, hazardous material, space shuttle and others. Each subject includes a bibliography of live, print and electronic sources of information. $165. Gale Group, P.O. Box 9187, Farmington Hills, MI 48333-9187. Toll free US and Canada (800) 877-GALE (4253) and (248) 699-GALE, fax (800) 414-5043 and (248) 699-8061, Internet orders galeord@galegroup.com, web site www.galegroup.com or www.gale.com. All Gale Group products are available on approval. Contact Gale for details.

SciTECH REFERENCE PLUS CD ROM contains directory information, 125,000 biographies of US and Canadian scientists and engineers from AMERICAN MEN AND WOMEN OF SCIENCE, listings for over 8,000 laboratories from the DIRECTORY OF AMERICAN RESEARCH AND TECHNOLOGY, and information from THE DIRECTORY OF CORPORATE AFFILIATIONS (including public, private and international companies) of leading US and international technology firms and their subsidiaries. It also contains 60,000 records on science/technology and medical serials from ULRICH'S INTERNATIONAL PERIODICALS DIRECTORY. Searches can be conducted by SIC, year founded, activity, education, employees, institution/company, city, state or country, memberships/honors, product description, personal statistics, personal title, research area, revenue. Updated annually. 1 year subscription $995, 3 years 2,836, excluding discounts. For more information visit Bowker Reed Reference's web site at http://www.reedref.com or contact: Bowker Reed Reference Electronic Publishing, 121 Chanlon Road, New Providence, NJ 07974 USA, Phone (800) 323-3288, Fax (908) 665-3528, email info@bowker.com.

WHO'S WHO IN SCIENCE AND ENGINEERING, $259.95. National Register Publishing, Reed Elsevier-New Providence, 121 Chanlon Road, New Providence, NJ 07974, (800) 521-8110, fax (800) 836-7736, web site www.marquiswhoswho.com or www.redbooks.com. "If, for any reason whatsoever, your order does not fully meet your expectations, simply return the product within 30 days for a prompt, complete, unquestioned refund," as stated in Catalog of Biographical and Professional References of publisher Marquis Who's Who/National Register Publishing.

WORLD AVIATION DIRECTORY AND BUYER'S GUIDE is available as a hard copy directory, on CD ROM and as an Internet database. Some companies on the Internet even have email and web site links. Print directory $275, 2 issues per year; CD ROM $995. Published by Aviation Week, a Division of The McGraw-Hill Companies. McGraw Hill, Print Division, PO Box 629, Hightstown, NJ 08520, (800) 525-5003.

McGraw Hill, Other Media Division (202) 383-2420, (800) 551-2015, extension 4. Web site: www.wadaviation.com.

www.bestjobsusa.com or Best Jobs U.S.A. is a site mainly for information technology, sales and engineering positions usually in the $50,000 to $100,000 range. Launched in 1996, the site was developed by Recourse Communications, Inc., West Palm Beach, Florida.

www.careeravenue.com or Career Avenue lists positions mainly in information technology, management and engineering, mostly in the $50,000 to $100,000 range. The site was established in 1996 and developed by Internet Advertising, Inc., San Antonio, Texas.

www.careerexchange.com is a web site for North American job seekers developed by CorpNet InfoHub, Ltd., Vancouver, BC, Canada. Launched in 1996, its People-Match capability notifies the user of jobs through email. Most positions are in high technology, engineering, sales and marketing and are primarily in the $40,000 to $75,000 range.

www.ceweekly.com is the URL for Contract Employment Weekly, a site for the temporary technical industry. Positions are mainly in information technology, engineering and technical and are mostly in the $40,000 to $75,000 range. The site was developed by C.E. Publications, Inc., Bothell, Washington and has been online since 1994. Contract Employment Weekly Online is a service of C.E. Publications, Inc., P.O. Box 3006, Bothell, WA 98041-3006. (425) 806-5200, Fax (425) 806-5585, email publisher@ceweekly.com.

www.engineeringjobs.com is a web site mainly for mechanical, electrical, industrial and computer engineers. The site was developed by EngineeringJobs, El Cerrito, California and launched in 1996.

www.net-temps.com or Net-Temps Job Posting Service was ranked as one of the top 5 "Sites Offering the Best Job-Search Support" by the *National Business Employment Weekly*. Many positions are in information systems, engineering, and sales and marketing, often in the $50,000 to $100,000 range. The site was developed by Net-Temps, Inc., Tyngsboro, Massachusetts and went online in 1996.

www.occ.com is the URL for the On Line Career Center, one of the Internet's first online recruitment sites, launched in 1993. It is a major recruitment web site that spends millions of dollars in advertising to drive traffic to the site. This is a major site that was developed by William O Warren, who has received honors for his pioneering work in the development of Internet Recruiting. This web site allows you to enter your job profile and have job listings automatically downloaded to your Email. Questions to webmaster@occ.com. www.occ.com was rated by the *National Business Employment Weekly* as one of the top 5 sites in 3 different categories: "Sites Offering the Best Overall Support for Job Seekers," "Sites Offering the Best Job-Search Support" and "Sites Offering the Best Career Resources for Job Seekers." Openings are mainly in engineering, information technology and sales and marketing. The site developer is TMP Worldwide, New York, New York.

www.passportaccess.com is a site with many positions in computers and engineering, many of them in the $50,000 to $100,000 range. The site was developed by PassportAccess, Inc., Lafayette, California and was established in 1995.

www.technicalrecruiter.com is a web site which is an excellent starting point for a large number of specialized technology sites, such as ProjectManager.com and SoftwareEngineer.com and others.

www.world.hire.com is the URL for World Hire Online, a web site with job listings mainly in engineering, information technology and "senior management," usually in the $50,000 to $100,000 range. The site was developed by World.Hire, Austin, Texas and was launched in 1996.

England

See Europe, International

BRITISH BUSINESS RANKINGS ranks the top 500 employers. It is a companion to **KEY BRITISH ENTERPRISES.** Dun & Bradstreet, Business Reference Solutions, Three Sylvan Way, Parsippany, NJ 07054 USA. (800) 526-0651. Email dnbmdd@mail.dnb.com. Web site http://www.dnbmdd.com.

CABLE TV & TELECOM YEARBOOK (UK), Phillips Business Information, Inc., a Phillips Publishing International Company, 120 Seven Locks Road, Potomac, MD 20854, (301) 340-1520, (301) 340-7788, (800) 777-5006, Internet pbi@phillips.com, web site www.phillips.com.

CREATIVE HANDBOOK is a portfolio and a directory of creative services, published annually. Call publisher for prices. Cahners Business Information, 34-35 Newman Street, London W1P 3PD England. (011) 44-171-637-3663, fax (011) 44-171-580-5559. Headquarters: Cahners Business Information, 275 Washington Street, Newton, MA 02158-1630, (617) 558-4663 or (617) 964-3030, fax (617) 558-4700, email marketaccess@cahners.com. Web sites www.cahners.com or www.chilton.net.

CTI PLUS (CURRENT TECHNOLOGY INDEX) is a technology index database enhanced with the **SUPERTECH ABSTRACTS** database. CTI PLUS covers 320 technical and applied science journals from the US and the UK. Topics covered include general technology, industrial health and safety, ergonomics, electronics, applied optics, heat, machine vision, natural language processing, pattern recognition, computer architecture, neural networks, computer integrated manufacturing, computer graphics, simulation, robot research, engineering, applied acoustics, power transmission, civil engineering, town planning, transport technology, military technology, fishing, mining, chemical engineering, radiochemistry, photochemistry, inorganic and organic chemistry, coatings, textile manufacturing, photography, packaging and more. If you're doing a search in an exotic new area of technology, this library index will lead you to the right organizations. You can conduct a literature search to determine which companies are engaged in cutting edge research, or to locate people who have been quoted. From Bowker-Saur. Updated quarterly. 1 year subscription $1,495, excluding discounts. For more information visit Bowker Reed Reference's web site at http://www.reedref.com or contact: Bowker Reed Reference Electronic Publishing, 121 Chanlon Road, New Providence, NJ 07974 USA, Phone (800) 323-3288, Fax (908) 665-3528, email info@bowker.com.

DIRECTORY OF AMERICAN FIRMS OPERATING IN FOREIGN COUNTRIES, REGIONAL EDITION—EUROPE, WESTERN, $159. Uniworld Business Publications, Inc., 257 Central Park West, Suite 10A, New York, NY 10024-4110, (212) 496-2448, fax (212) 769-0413, email uniworldbp@aol.com. Web site: http://www.uniworldbp.com.

DIRECTORY OF FOREIGN FIRMS OPERATING IN THE UNITED STATES, REGIONAL EDITION—EUROPE, ALL. Includes Austria, Belgium, Czech Republic, Denmark, England, Finland, France, Germany, Greece, Iceland, Ireland, Italy, Luxembourg, Netherlands, Norway, Poland, Portugal, Romania, Russia, Scotland, Slovenia, Spain, Sweden, Switzerland. $119. Uniworld Business Publications, Inc., 257 Central Park West, Suite 10A, New York, NY 10024-4110, (212) 496-2448, fax (212) 769-0413, email uniworldbp@aol.com. Web site: http://www.uniworldbp.com.

DIRECTORY OF FOREIGN FIRMS OPERATING IN THE UNITED STATES, REGIONAL EDITION—BRITISH ISLES. Includes England, Ireland, Scotland. $59. Ordering information: Uniworld Business Publications, Inc., 257 Central Park West, Suite 10A, New York, NY 10024-4110, (212) 496-2448, fax (212) 769-0413, email uniworldbp@aol.com. Web site: http://www.uniworldbp.com.

FINANCIAL TIMES, the London daily business journal and a subsidiary of Pearson, can be subscribed to in major US cities by calling its New York City office at (800) 628-8088 or faxing (212) 308-2397. Web site www.ft.com.

FT 500 Expanded Book Version is a listing of the top 500 UK and European companies, ranked by market capitalization and published by the FINANCIAL TIMES. It contains the names of the CEO or Chairman, address, phone and fax. 29.95 pounds sterling. Also available on disk, 171 896-2744. For more information contact FT 500, FT Publishing, Financial Times, Number One Southwark Bridge, London SE1 9HL, England. Phone from the US (011) 44 171 873-3000 or (011) 44 171 873-4211. Fax from US (011) 44 171 873 3595, web site http://www.FT.com.

http://taps.com is a web site for people looking for contract and permanent positions in the United Kingdom and Europe. Positions are mainly in information technology, mostly in the $20,000 to $50,000 range. TAPS.COM was developed by Internet Appointments, Ltd., London, England and was launched in 1996.

KEY BRITISH ENTERPRISES contains information on 50,000 large and medium-size companies. Dun & Bradstreet, Business Reference Solutions, Three Sylvan Way, Parsippany, NJ 07054 USA. (800) 526-0651. Email dnbmdd@mail.dnb.com. Web site http://www.dnbmdd.com.

MAJOR COMPANIES OF EUROPE is a 4 volume edition containing 194,000 names of contacts at 24,000 companies in all 20 western European countries. Vol. 1 —Austria, Belgium, Denmark, Ireland, Finland, France. Vol. 2—Germany, Greece, Italy, Liechtenstein, Luxembourg. Vol. 3—The Netherlands, Norway, Portugal, Spain, Sweden, Switzerland. Vol. 4—United Kingdom. $1,700 for 4 volume set. $535 per volume. CD ROM, updated quarterly, is also available. Published by Graham & Whiteside Ltd., Tuition House, 5-6 Francis Grove, London SW19 4DT, England. Web site http://www.major-co-data.com. Email sales@major-co-data.com. Distributed by: Larry Meranus Professional Publications & Services, 4 Demoray Court, Pine Brook, NJ 07058, (800) MERANUS or (800) 637-2687. Also distributed by Gale Group, P.O. Box 9187, Farmington Hills, MI 48333-9187. Toll free US and Canada (800) 877-GALE (4253) and (248) 699-GALE, fax (800) 414-5043 and (248) 699-8061, Internet orders galeord@galegroup.com, web site www.galegroup.com or www.gale.com. All Gale Group products are available on approval. Contact Gale for details.

PENSION FUNDS AND THEIR ADVISERS provides information on the top 2,000 pension funds in the United Kingdom, plus major funds of Japan, Belgium, France, Germany, Ireland, The Netherlands and Switzerland. This Directory is the only source in the US that monitors the growth of assets in the international market. Information includes internal and external fund management contacts, major US and Canadian pension funds and money managers, major European and Japanese pension funds and their advisors. It also includes comprehensive listings of 900 advisors to the pension fund industry including financial advisers, accountants, actuaries and pension fund consultants, pension administrators, insurance companies, attorneys, computer services, global custody, pension trustees, pension /financial recruitment consultants, investment research, associations and professional groups, and publications. $310. Published by A.P. Information Services, Ltd. Marketed exclusively in North America MONEY MARKET DIRECTORIES INC./STANDARD AND POORS, 320 East Main Street, Charlottesville, VA 22902, http://www.mmdaccess.com, (800) 446-2810, (804) 977-1450.

UNITED KINGDOM'S 10,000 LARGEST provides rankings on sales, profits, profit margins, manufacturing, distribution and by assets. Dun & Bradstreet, Business Reference Solutions, Three Sylvan Way, Parsippany, NJ 07054 USA. (800) 526-0651. Email dnbmdd@mail.dnb.com. Web site http://www.dnbmdd.com.

WHITAKER'S BOOKS IN PRINT (BRITISH), $740. R.R. Bowker (a unit of Cahners Business Information), 121 Chanlon Road, New Providence, NJ 07974 USA, Phone (888) BOWKER2 (888-269-5372) & (800) 323-3288, fax (908) 508-7696, email info@bowker.com, web www.bowker.com. Canada—R.R. Bowker, Markham, Ontario, phone (888) BOWKER9 & (905) 415-5837, fax (905) 479-6266. German speaking Europe—K.G. Saur Verlag, Munich, Germany, phone 49-89-76902-232, fax 49-89-76902-250, email 100730.1341@compuserve.com, web www.saur.de/home.htm. Rest of Europe incl. United Kingdom plus Africa & Asia—Bowker-Saur, W. Sussex, UK, phone 44-1342-326-972, fax 44-1342-335-612, email customer@bowker-saur.co.uk, web www.bowker-saur.com/service/. Australia/New Zealand—Thorpe, Port Melbourne, Victoria, Australia, phone 61-03-9-245-7370, fax 61-03-9-245-7395, email customer.service@thorpe.com.au, web www.thorpe.com.au. Technical support for CD ROMs (800) 323-3288, fax 908) 665-3528, email techsupport@bowker.com.

WHO OWNS WHOM DIRECTORY by Dun & Bradstreet is a six volume set containing information on the structure and ownership of 320,000 company affiliates and subsidiaries of over 23,000 companies worldwide. It is available in four regional editions: Australia and the Far East, North America, UK/Ireland, and Continental Europe. Published annually. For prices and ordering information as well as information about more worldwide corporate linkage products from D&B WORLDBASE, D&B's global database of 42 million records in over 200 countries, contact Dun & Bradstreet at (800) 526-0651, Dun & Bradstreet, Business Reference Solutions, Three Sylvan Way, Parsippany, NJ 07054. Email dnbmdd@mail.dnb.com. Web site http://www.dnbmdd.com.

WHO'S WHO IN CABLE & SATELLITE (UK), Phillips Business Information, Inc., a Phillips Publishing International Company, 120 Seven Locks Road, Potomac, MD 20854, (301) 340-1520, (301) 340-7788, (800) 777-5006, Internet pbi@phillips.com, web site www.phillips.com.

WILLINGS PRESS GUIDE identifies UK and international print media, including national and regional newspapers, magazines, and periodicals. It specifies 30,000 titles, contact names, summary of contents, and more. Volume 1, United Kingdom. Volume 2, International. $350 for 2 volume set or $275 per individual volume. Published by Hollis Directories Ltd. Distributed by Gale Group, P.O. Box 9187, Farmington Hills, MI 48333-9187. Toll free US and Canada (800) 877-GALE (4253) and (248) 699-GALE, fax (800) 414-5043 and (248) 699-8061, Internet orders galeord@galegroup.com, web site www.galegroup.com or www.gale.com. All Gale Group products are available on approval. Contact Gale for details.

www.europages.com is a web site of a business directory of over 500,000 European firms. In Deutsch, English, Espanol, Français & Italiano. Features include Search for Companies, Company Catalogues, Business Information, Yellow Pages in Europe. Search by Product/Service, Thematic Search or by Company Name. Address, phone, fax, products, turnover. Europages' Daily Business News, European Trade Fairs, Chambers of Commerce in Europe, European Patent Offices, Official International Organisations, European Standardization Bodies

YEARBOOK OF INTERNATIONAL ORGANIZATIONS is a 4 volume directory of nonprofit organizations, commercial associations, business groups, conferences, religious orders and intergovernmental bodies. From K.G. Saur. $1,170 for 4 volumes.

YEARBOOK OF INTERNATIONAL ORGANIZATIONS PLUS is a CD ROM which was described by American Reference Books Annual as "The most comprehensive coverage of international organizations." This CD consolidates THE YEARBOOK OF INTERNATIONAL ORGANIZATIONS and WHO'S WHO IN INTERNATIONAL ORGANIZATIONS. It encompasses intergovernmental and national organizations, conferences and religious orders and fraternities. Search criteria include organization name, fields of activity, titles of publications, links to other organizations and more. User languages are English, German, French and Dutch. MS-DOS, Windows and Macintosh compatibility. From K.G. Saur. Updated annually. 1 year subscription $1,318.

R.R. Bowker (a unit of Cahners Business Information), 121 Chanlon Road, New Providence, NJ 07974 USA, Phone (888) BOWKER2 (888-269-5372) & (800) 323-3288, fax (908) 508-7696, email info@bowker.com, web www.bowker.com. Canada—R.R. Bowker, Markham, Ontario, phone (888) BOWKER9 & (905) 415-5837, fax (905) 479-6266. German speaking Europe—K.G. Saur Verlag, Munich, Germany, phone 49-89-76902-232, fax 49-89-76902-250, email 100730.1341@compuserve.com, web www.saur.de/home.htm. Rest of Europe incl. United Kingdom plus Africa & Asia—Bowker-Saur, W. Sussex, UK, phone 44-1342-326-972, fax 44-1342-335-612, email customer@bowker-saur.co.uk, web www.bowker-saur.com/service/. Australia/New Zealand—Thorpe, Port Melbourne, Victoria, Australia, phone 61-03-9-245-7370, fax 61-03-9-245-7395, email customer.service@thorpe.com.au, web www.thorpe.com.au. Technical support for CD ROMs (800) 323-3288, fax (908) 665-3528, email techsupport@bowker.com.

Entertainment

WHO'S WHO IN ENTERTAINMENT, $259.95. National Register Publishing, Reed Elsevier-New Providence, 121 Chanlon Road, New Providence, NJ 07974, (800) 521-8110, fax (800) 836-7736, web site www.marquiswhoswho.com or www.redbooks.com. "If, for any reason whatsoever, your order does not fully meet your expectations, simply return the product within 30 days for a prompt, complete, unquestioned refund," as stated in Catalog of Biographical and Professional References of publisher Marquis Who's Who/National Register Publishing.

Entrepreneurs

ASIAN AMERICAN MANUFACTURERS ASSOCIATION (AAMA) publishes an annual Membership Directory and a newsletter which contains new member listings and employment listings. It also publishes ASIAN AMERICAN ENTREPRENEURS AND EXECUTIVES OF PUBLIC COMPANIES IN THE HIGH TECH INDUSTRY. Membership is comprised of Asian American manufacturers of technology products, such as computers, microprocessors, semiconductors, biotech, software and electronics equipment. Presents an annual award for entrepreneurship. For more information contact Asian American Manufacturers Association (AAMA), 39120 Argonaut Way, #309, Freemont, CA 94538-1398, (925) 461-0800.

BUSINESS PLANS HANDBOOK is a collection of real business plans prepared by entrepreneurs searching for small business funding in North America. 25 actual plans are presented across a broad spectrum of businesses in manufacturing, retail and service industries. Company identities have been changed to protect confidentiality. $125. Gale Group, P.O. Box 9187, Farmington Hills, MI 48333-9187. Toll free US and Canada (800) 877-GALE (4253) and (248) 699-GALE, fax (800) 414-5043 and (248) 699-8061, Internet orders galeord@galegroup.com, web site www.galegroup.com or www.gale.com. All Gale Group products are available on approval. Previous volumes are available. Contact Gale for details.

ENCYCLOPEDIA OF EMERGING INDUSTRIES provides information on industries that are pioneering new technologies, introducing breakthrough marketing strategies or executing new innovative ways of serving new markets. Each industry profile includes the current size and situation of the industry, a technological overview, leading companies, references to further reading and more. It covers technologies from artificial intelligence to voice recognition systems, marketing initiatives from coffee houses to super-sized movie theater complexes; and service industry ventures from AIDS testing to home health care. $270. Gale Group, P.O. Box 9187, Farmington Hills, MI 48333-9187. Toll free US and Canada (800) 877-GALE (4253) and (248) 699-GALE, fax (800) 414-5043 and (248) 699-8061, Internet orders galeord@galegroup.com, web site www.galegroup.com or www.gale.com. All Gale Group products are available on approval. Contact Gale for details.

ENCYCLOPEDIA OF SMALL BUSINESS provides entrepreneurs with how-to information on business plan creation, financing, financial planning, market analysis, sales strategy, tax planning, succession plans and more. $395 for 2 volume set. Gale Group, P.O. Box 9187, Farmington Hills, MI 48333-9187. Toll free US and Canada (800) 877-GALE (4253) and (248) 699-GALE, fax (800) 414-5043 and (248) 699-8061, Internet orders galeord@galegroup.com, web site www.galegroup.com or www.gale.com. All Gale Group products are available on approval. Contact Gale for details.

INC. is a magazine written for entrepreneurs and small businesses. Their INC. 500 list of the 500 most rapidly growing businesses is an excellent resource. INC. Magazine, 38 Commercial Wharf, Boston, MA 02110, (800) 978-1800, (617) 248-8000, www.inc.com. To search for articles, go to www.inc.com/search.

NATIONAL CORPORATE TECHNOLOGY DIRECTORY is a 4 volume set that profiles over 35,000 technology manufacturers. Includes information on 3,000 product categories, details of operating units, and toll free phone numbers. Most of these companies are "small," with under 1,000 employees. $545 soft cover, $595 hard cover. Regional Directories are also available, although the national directory does contain more detailed information. Regional directories are available for: Northern New England, Eastern Lakes, New York Metro, New Jersey & the Delaware Valley, Mid-Atlantic, Southeast, Central, Great Lakes, Midwest, Southwest, Northwest, Northern California, Southern California. $175 per regional directory. Diskettes are also available. Call for price and availability. Ordering information: Harris InfoSource International, 2057 Aurora Road, Twinsburg, OH 44087-1999, (800) 888-5900, fax (800) 643-5997, web site http://www.harrisinfo.com.

SMALL BUSINESS SOURCEBOOK encompasses comprehensive information on small businesses, including professional associations, training sources, small business investment companies, over 400 Internet databases, publications, awards and honors, company and personal email addresses. $325 for 2 vol. set. Gale Group, P.O. Box 9187, Farmington Hills, MI 48333-9187. Toll free US and Canada (800) 877-GALE (4253) and (248) 699-GALE, fax (800) 414-5043 and (248) 699-8061, Internet orders galeord@galegroup.com, web site www.galegroup.com or www.gale.com. All Gale Group products are available on approval. Contact Gale for details.

www.careers.wsj.com is the *Wall Street Journal*'s web site. It focuses on positions for middle and senior management including financial positions at $75,000 and up. This web site is among those that encompass senior executive positions. Other features includes Job Seek, Who's Hiring, Career Columnists, Salaries & Profiles, The Salary Calculator™, Job Hunting Advice, Succeeding at Work, HR Issues, Executive Recruiters, Working Globally, College Connection, Starting a Business, Career Bookstore and more. Content from The National Employment Business Weekly is also featured. The site was developed by Dow Jones & Company, Inc., Princeton, New Jersey and was established in 1997.

Environment

CANADIAN ENVIRONMENTAL DIRECTORY identifies government departments, companies and organizations concerned with environmental issues, plus contact names, publications, activities, programs, research laboratories, universities and college environmental programs, conferences and trade shows, lawyers, journalists, book and periodical information, and more. Available in directory or CD ROM formats. For pricing and ordering information, contact: IHS Canada, Micromedia Limited, 20 Victoria Street, Toronto,

Ontario M5C 2N8 CANADA, (800) 387-2689, (416) 362-5211, fax (416) 362-6161, email info@micromedia.on.ca.

CORPTECH DIRECTORY OF TECHNOLOGY COMPANIES is available in hard copy, Regional Guides, on PC floppy diskette, and on CD ROM. CORPTECH EXPLORE DATABASE is an outstanding reference that was awarded Best CD-ROM Directory by the National Directory Publishing Association. One click moves you from the CD ROM Database to the company's Internet web site. CORPTECH also provides other sophisticated but reasonably priced automated services (and quantity discounts) with their customized data-on-demand service, which uses up to 30 search parameters. You can save a tremendous amount of time researching relatively small, emerging new companies in various high technology niches and obtain names, titles and even mailing address labels. If CORPTECH is too expensive to purchase, go to the library.

- CORPTECH EXPLORE SILVER DATABASE CD ROM, $2,495 (including free soft cover CorpTech Directory worth $745).
- CORPTECH EXPLORE GOLD DATABASE CD ROM, $5,995 offers an export capability, extended company history and has hyperlinks to news services to aid company research, such as Reuters and PR Newswire. Both Silver and Gold CD's have links to company web sites.
- CORPTECH print directories are available for $795 hard cover, $745 soft cover.
- CORPTECH regional directories are available in print for $225 (soft cover only). Regional Explore Gold CD's are $995 each and Explore Silver are $795 each.

Industry specific directories segmented into 17 different industries are also available on CD ROM. Each industry costs $995, except computer software, which is very large and counts as two industries. The 17 industry segments are: factory automation, biotechnology, chemicals, computer hardware, defense, energy, **environmental,** manufacturing, advanced materials, medical, pharmaceuticals, photonics, computer software, subassemblies and components, test and measurement companies, telecommunications & Internet, and transportation.

Ordering Information: CORPTECH, Corporate Technology Information Services, Inc., 12 Alfred Street, Suite 200, Woburn, MA 01801-1915. (800) 333-8036, (800) 454-3647, (781) 932-3100, (781) 932-3939. Fax (781) 932-6335. Email sales@corptech.com. Web site www.corptech.com.

DIRECTORY OF HAZARDOUS WASTE SERVICES contains information on over 1,500 Canadian hazardous waste management companies with information on hazardous waste consultants, waste treatment and disposal outlets, equipment manufacturers, laboratory services, drum reconditioners, spill cleanup firms, hazwaste recyclers, associations, key government contacts, liquid waste haulers, lawyers specializing in environmental law, and environmental libraries. $115. Special discounts available for combined purchases. Published by Southam Information Products Ltd, 1450 Don Mills Road, Don Mills, Ontario M3B 2X7 CANADA, (800) 668-2374. In Toronto 442-2122. Web site www.southam.com.

ENCYCLOPEDIA OF ASSOCIATIONS: INTERNATIONAL ORGANIZATIONS includes nearly 20,000 multinational and national organizations in foreign countries, including US based associations with multinational membership. Entries also include email addresses, web sites and bulletin board addresses, lobbying activities, and publication and convention information. Indexed by geography, keyword and executives. $595 for 2 volume set. Also available in CD ROM. Database available via commercial online service. Gale Group, P.O. Box 9187, Farmington Hills, MI 48333-9187. Toll free US and Canada (800) 877-GALE (4253) and (248) 699-GALE, fax (800) 414-5043 and (248) 699-8061, Internet orders galeord@galegroup.com, web site www.galegroup.com or www.gale.com. All Gale Group products are available on approval. Contact Gale for details.

ENCYCLOPEDIA OF ASSOCIATIONS: NATIONAL ORGANIZATIONS OF THE US. This superb reference is one of the first places you should look when beginning a new recruiting assignment or when looking for specialized references of any type. The keyword index makes this comprehensive reference easy to use, even in hard copy. For over 23,000 nonprofit professional associations with a national scope, this encyclopedia reveals:

- Publications, including membership rosters and newsletters
- Dates and locations of association conferences and conventions

- Names of Executive Directors, who are usually incredible sources of industry information if you call and speak to them
- Committees
- Job and candidate referral banks, which can provide resumes of other industry sources and sometimes candidates
- It includes organizations in these categories: business, trade, environmental, agricultural, legal, governmental, engineering, technological, scientific, educational, cultural, social welfare, health & medical, public affairs, ethnic, labor unions, chambers of commerce, tourism, & others.

> Volume 1, National Organizations of the US, $505
> Volume 2, Geographic and Executive Indexes, $390
> Volume 3, Supplement, $405

Gale Group, P.O. Box 9187, Farmington Hills, MI 48333-9187. Toll free US and Canada (800) 877-GALE (4253) and (248) 699-GALE, fax (800) 414-5043 and (248) 699-8061, Internet orders galeord@galegroup.com, web site www.galegroup.com or www.gale.com. All Gale Group products are available on approval. Contact Gale for details.

ENCYCLOPEDIA OF ASSOCIATIONS: REGIONAL, STATE AND LOCAL ORGANIZATIONS. The information in this directory is *not* duplicated anywhere in ENCYCLOPEDIA OF ASSOCIATIONS. Over 100,000 nonprofit organizations are included in this directory. $585 for 5 volume set or $140 per individual volume. Also available on CD ROM and online on the Internet through a GaleNet subscription.

> Volume 1, Great Lakes States (Illinois, Indiana, Michigan, Minnesota, Ohio, Wisconsin)
> Volume 2, Northeastern States (Connecticut, Maine, Massachusetts, New Hampshire, New Jersey, New York, Pennsylvania, Rhode Islands, Vermont)
> Volume 3, Southern and Middle Atlantic States (Including Puerto Rico and the Virgin Islands) (Alabama, Delaware, Washington, DC, Florida, Georgia, Kentucky, Maryland, Mississippi, North Carolina, Puerto Rico, South Carolina, Tennessee, Virginia, West Virginia, Virgin Islands)
> Volume 4, South Central and Great Plains States (Arkansas, Iowa, Kansas, Louisiana, Missouri, Nebraska, North Dakota, Oklahoma, South Dakota, Texas)
> Volume 5, Western States (Alaska, Arizona, California, Colorado, Guam, Hawaii, Idaho, Montana, Nevada, New Mexico, Oregon, Utah, Washington, Wyoming)

Gale Group, P.O. Box 9187, Farmington Hills, MI 48333-9187. Toll free US and Canada (800) 877-GALE (4253) and (248) 699-GALE, fax (800) 414-5043 and (248) 699-8061, Internet orders galeord@galegroup.com, web site www.galegroup.com or www.gale.com. All Gale Group products are available on approval. Contact Gale for details.

ENVIRONMENT ENCYCLOPEDIA AND DIRECTORY identifies organizations, publications, research programs, projects and key people and provides a list of relevant periodicals. $385. Gale Group, P.O. Box 9187, Farmington Hills, MI 48333-9187. Toll free US and Canada (800) 877-GALE (4253) and (248) 699-GALE, fax (800) 414-5043 and (248) 699-8061, Internet orders galeord@galegroup.com, web site www.galegroup.com or www.gale.com. All Gale Group products are available on approval. Contact Gale for details.

ONTARIO RECYCLING RESOURCEBOOK—HOW TO COMPLY WITH THE 3RS REGULATIONS contains an extensive directory of companies and organizations which are users of recyclable materials. It also lists waste reduction consultants and Ontario municipalities with their material bans and recycling coordinators. *Free* copy of the "Waste Audit Workbook" with your paid order. $79. Special discounts available for combined purchases. Published by Southam Information Products Ltd, 1450 Don Mills Road, Don Mills, Ontario M3B 2X7 CANADA, (800) 668-2374. In Toronto 442-2122. Web site www.southam.com.

POLLUTION ENGINEERING INTERNATIONAL is a magazine for environmental professionals in Asia and Europe, published 4 times a year. Call publisher for price. Cahners Business Information, 1350 East Touhy Avenue, Des Plaines, IL 60018-5080, (847) 390-2752, fax (847) 390-2636, URL www.pollutioneng.com. Headquarters: Cahners Business Information, 275 Washington Street, Newton, MA

02158-1630, (617) 558-4663 or (617) 964-3030, fax (617) 558-4700, email marketaccess@cahners.com. Web sites www.cahners.com or www.chilton.net.

PULP AND PAPER ANNUAL AND DIRECTORY contains an index of companies, divisions and subsidiaries, plus information on 3 sectors: pulp, paper and board manufacturing sector, supply sector and support sector. Includes information on key contacts, mills and recycling companies. Canada $95, USA and foreign $115. Special discounts available for combined purchases. Published by Southam Information Products Ltd, 1450 Don Mills Road, Don Mills, Ontario M3B 2X7 CANADA, (800) 668-2374. In Toronto 442-2122. Web site www.southam.com.

WASTE NEWS is a weekly trade publication. Crain Communications, Inc. is headquartered in Chicago with offices in major cities throughout the US plus London and Tokyo. New York location: 220 East 42nd Street, New York, NY 10017, (212) 210-0100, Customer Service (800) 678-9595. Annual subscription $38, two years $69. Web site www.wastenews.com

Ethical Drugs

See Biotechnology and Pharmaceuticals

Europe

See International, Eastern Europe, Central Europe, Commonwealth of Independent States, and individual countries by name

BACON'S INTERNATIONAL MEDIA DIRECTORY identifies over 28,000 Western European publications and their editors, including business, trade and consumer magazines, national newspapers by country, mailing address, phone, fax and telex, Magazine editorial profiles, and translation requirements by country. $275. Ordering information: Call (800) 621-0561, (800) 753-6675. Bacon's Information, Inc., a K-III Communications Company, 332 South Michigan Avenue, Chicago, IL 60604. Satisfaction guaranteed or a full refund within 30 days.

CABLE EUROPE, Phillips Business Information, Inc., a Phillips Publishing International Company, 120 Seven Locks Road, Potomac, MD 20854, (301) 340-1520, (301) 340-7788, (800) 777-5006, Internet pbi@phillips.com, web site www.phillips.com.

CATALOG OF INSTITUTIONAL RESEARCH REPORTS (GLOBAL EDITION) tracks over 15,000 monthly investment research reports published by Wall Street's European and Pacific counterparts in over 500 research firms worldwide. Reports are listed alphabetically by company and by research firm. This information is best used for target list research, or your own personal investing. Published ten times per year. $125 per year. Nelson Information, P.O. Box 591, Port Chester, NY 10573 USA. (800) 333-6357, Phone outside the US (914) 937-8400, Fax (914) 937-8590, web site http://www.nelnet.com.

CD EUROPA contains comprehensive financial and operational data on 130,000 public and private companies in 20 European countries. Dun & Bradstreet, Business Reference Solutions, Three Sylvan Way, Parsippany, NJ 07054 USA. (800) 526-0651. Email dnbmdd@mail.dnb.com. Web site http://www.dnbmdd.com.

DIRECTORY OF AMERICAN FIRMS OPERATING IN FOREIGN COUNTRIES, REGIONAL EDITION—EUROPE, ALL. $169. Ordering information: Uniworld Business Publications, Inc., 257 Central Park West, Suite 10A, New York, NY 10024-4110, (212) 496-2448, fax (212) 769-0413, email uniworldbp@aol.com. Web site: http://www.uniworldbp.com.

DIRECTORY OF AMERICAN FIRMS OPERATING IN FOREIGN COUNTRIES, REGIONAL EDITION—EUROPE, EASTERN. Includes Albania, Armenia, Azerbaijan, Belarus, Bulgaria, Croatia, Czech Republic, Estonia, Hungary, Kazakhstan, Latvia, Lithuania, Macedonia, Poland, Romania, Russia, Slovakia, Slovenia, Turkmenistan, Ukraine, Uzbekistan, Yugoslavia. $49. Uniworld Business Publications, Inc., 257 Central Park West, Suite 10A, New York, NY 10024-4110, (212) 496-2448, fax (212) 769-0413, email uniworldbp@aol.com. Web site: http://www.uniworldbp.com.

DIRECTORY OF AMERICAN FIRMS OPERATING IN FOREIGN COUNTRIES, REGIONAL EDITION—EUROPE, WESTERN, $159. Uniworld Business Publications, Inc., 257 Central Park West, Suite 10A, New York, NY 10024-4110, (212) 496-2448, fax (212) 769-0413, email uniworldbp@aol.com. Web site: http://www.uniworldbp.com.

DIRECTORY OF CONSUMER BRANDS AND THEIR OWNERS provides information on 50,000 brands in 56 countries and detailed information about the companies that own and manage them. Asia Pacific edition $990. Latin America edition $990. Eastern Europe edition $990. Europe edition $1,190 for 2 volumes. Published by Euromonitor (England). Distributed by Gale Group, P.O. Box 9187, Farmington Hills, MI 48333-9187. Toll free US and Canada (800) 877-GALE (4253) and (248) 699-GALE, fax (800) 414-5043 and (248) 699-8061, Internet orders galeord@galegroup.com, web site www.galegroup.com or www.gale.com. All Gale Group products are available on approval. Contact Gale for details.

DIRECTORY OF FOREIGN FIRMS OPERATING IN THE UNITED STATES, REGIONAL EDITION—EUROPE, ALL. Includes Austria, Belgium, Czech Republic, Denmark, England, Finland, France, Germany, Greece, Iceland, Ireland, Italy, Luxembourg, Netherlands, Norway, Poland, Portugal, Romania, Russia, Scotland, Slovenia, Spain, Sweden, Switzerland. $119. Uniworld Business Publications, Inc., 257 Central Park West, Suite 10A, New York, NY 10024-4110, (212) 496-2448, fax (212) 769-0413, email uniworldbp@aol.com. Web site: http://www.uniworldbp.com.

DIRECTORY OF FOREIGN FIRMS OPERATING IN THE UNITED STATES, REGIONAL EDITION—EUROPE, EXCLUDING THE BRITISH ISLES. $109. Uniworld Business Publications, Inc., 257 Central Park West, Suite 10A, New York, NY 10024-4110, (212) 496-2448, fax (212) 769-0413, email uniworldbp@aol.com. Web site: http://www.uniworldbp.com.

EDN EUROPE is a monthly magazine for electronics engineers and managers in Europe's original equipment manufacturing area. Call publisher for price. EDN Europe/Cahners Business Information, P.O. Box 377, Norwich NR14 6UQ, England, (011) 44 1508 528-435, fax (011) 44-1508 528-430, email ttobeck@edn.cahners.com, mike.hancock@rbi.co.uk, URL www.ednmag.com. Headquarters: EDN Worldwide Editorial, 275 Washington Street, Newton, MA 02158-1630, (617) 558-4454 or (617) 964-3030, fax (617) 558-4470, URL www.ednmag.com.

ELSEVIER ADVANCED TECHNOLOGY is a leading supplier of Electronics industry information. They publish a CD-ROM of a complete database of electronic companies in Europe, developed in conjunction with THE EUROPEAN ELECTRONICS DIRECTORY: COMPONENTS AND SUB-ASSEMBLIES AND SYSTEMS AND APPLICATIONS. Elsevier also publishes yearbooks, directories, market research reports and industrial journals, technical handbooks and newsletters, such as PROFILE OF THE WORLDWIDE TELECOMMUNICATIONS INDUSTRY, PROFILE OF THE WORLDWIDE CAPACITOR INDUSTRY, PROFILE OF THE WORLDWIDE SEMICONDUCTOR INDUSTRY, and PROFILE OF THE EUROPEAN CONNECTOR INDUSTRY. For more information contact: Elsevier Advanced Technology, P.O. Box 150, Kidlington, Oxford, OX5 1AS, England. Phone (44) (0) 1865 843-848, fax (44) (0) 1865 843-971.

EUROPE'S MAJOR COMPANIES DIRECTORY provides information on 6,000 leading companies in 16 European countries, including banking, retail and utilities. Details ownership, subsidiaries, key personnel, main operations, main products and brand names, and when available retail outlets and number of employees. $590. Published by Euromonitor (England). Distributed by Gale Group, P.O. Box 9187, Farmington Hills, MI 48333-9187. Toll free US and Canada (800) 877-GALE (4253) and (248) 699-GALE, fax (800) 414-5043 and (248) 699-8061, Internet orders galeord@galegroup.com, web site www.galegroup.com or www.gale.com. All Gale Group products are available on approval. Contact Gale for details.

EUROPE'S MEDIUM SIZED COMPANIES DIRECTORY profiles 6,500 of the "next largest" companies, beginning where EUROPE'S MAJOR COMPANIES DIRECTORY leaves off. It includes key personnel, ownership, subsidiaries, main products and brands, revenues, outlets and trading names, number of employees and more. $590. Published by Euromonitor (England). Distributed by Gale Group, P.O. Box 9187, Farmington Hills, MI 48333-9187. Toll free US and Canada (800) 877-GALE (4253) and (248) 699-GALE, fax (800) 414-5043 and (248) 699-8061, Internet orders galeord@galegroup.com, web site www.galegroup.com or www.gale.com. All Gale Group products are available on approval. Contact Gale for details.

EUROPEAN DIRECTORY OF RETAILERS AND WHOLESALERS includes information on some 3,000 European retailers and wholesalers, including a directory of information sources. $790. Published by Euromonitor (England). Distributed by Gale Group, P.O. Box 9187, Farmington Hills, MI 48333-9187. Toll free US and Canada (800) 877-GALE (4253) and (248) 699-GALE, fax (800) 414-5043 and (248) 699-8061, Internet orders galeord@galegroup.com, web site www.galegroup.com or www.gale.com. All Gale Group products are available on approval. Contact Gale for details.

EUROPEAN DRINKS MARKETING DIRECTORY provides information on over 1,600 drink manufacturers and over 750 retail and wholesale distributors in Western and Eastern Europe. Includes a directory of 1,500 information sources. $425. Published by Euromonitor (England). Distributed by Gale Group, P.O. Box 9187, Farmington Hills, MI 48333-9187. Toll free US and Canada (800) 877-GALE (4253) and (248) 699-GALE, fax (800) 414-5043 and (248) 699-8061, Internet orders galeord@galegroup.com, web site www.galegroup.com or www.gale.com. All Gale Group products are available on approval. Contact Gale for details.

EUROPEAN ELECTRONICS DATABASE ON CD ROM is available for $790 from Harris InfoSource, 2057 East Aurora Road, Twinsburg, OH 44087-1999, (330) 425-9000, (800) 888-5900, www.HarrisInfo.com.

EUROPEAN ELECTRONICS DIRECTORY (COMPONENTS AND SUB-ASSEMBLIES) is available as a directory for $410 from Harris InfoSource, 2057 East Aurora Road, Twinsburg, OH 44087-1999, (330) 425-9000, (800) 888-5900, www.HarrisInfo.com.

EUROPEAN ELECTRONICS DIRECTORY (SYSTEMS AND APPLICATIONS) is available as a directory for $399 from Harris InfoSource, 2057 East Aurora Road, Twinsburg, OH 44087-1999, (330) 425-9000, (800) 888-5900, www.HarrisInfo.com.

EUROPEAN MARKETING DATABASE CD contains information on the top 750,000 businesses in 17 European countries. Dun & Bradstreet, Business Reference Solutions, Three Sylvan Way, Parsippany, NJ 07054 USA. (800) 526-0651. Email dnbmdd@mail.dnb.com. Web site http://www.dnbmdd.com.

EUROPEAN R&D PLUS DATABASE ON CD ROM is a consolidation of the DIRECTORY OF EUROPEAN RESEARCH AND DEVELOPMENT and WHO'S WHO IN EUROPEAN RESEARCH AND DEVELOPMENT. It covers over 20,000 labs, both commercial and academic, in 36 countries including all the European former Soviet Republics. Searches can be conducted by over 20 fields in over 600 scientific disciplines. Information is available about over 100,000 people, including senior researchers, research managers and consultants, including: name, career data, current position, education, publications, research scope, current activities, nationality, languages and more. From Bowker-Saur. Updated annually. 1 year subscription $1,595, excluding discounts. For more information visit Bowker Reed Reference's web site at http://www.reedref.com or contact: Bowker Reed Reference Electronic Publishing, 121 Chanlon Road, New Providence, NJ 07974 USA, Phone (800) 323-3288, Fax (908) 665-3528, email info@bowker.com.

EUROPEAN TELECOMMUNICATIONS, Phillips Business Information, Inc., a Phillips Publishing International Company, 120 Seven Locks Road, Potomac, MD 20854, (301) 340-1520, (301) 340-7788, (800) 777-5006, Internet pbi@phillips.com, web site www.phillips.com.

FT 500 Expanded Book Version is a listing of the top 500 UK and European companies, ranked by market capitalization and published by the FINANCIAL TIMES. It contains the names of the CEO or Chairman, address, phone and fax. 29.95 pounds sterling. Also available on disk, 171 896-2744. For more information contact FT 500, FT Publishing, Financial Times, Number One Southwark Bridge, London SE1 9HL, England. Phone from the US (011) 44 171 873-3000 or (011) 44 171 873-4211. Fax from US (011) 44 171 873 3595, web site http://www.FT.com.

GERMAN BOOKS IN PRINT—VERZEICHNIS LIEFERBARER BUCHER (VLB) contains information on all German language books, videos, audiocassettes, software and bibles from publishers in Germany, the former East Germany, Austria, Switzerland and elsewhere. From K.G. Saur. $650.

GERMAN BOOKS IN PRINT ON CD-ROM (VLB-AKTUELL), one year subscription $1,440. R.R. Bowker (a unit of Cahners Business Information), 121 Chanlon Road, New Providence, NJ 07974 USA, Phone (888) BOWKER2 (888-269-5372) & (800) 323-3288, fax (908) 508-7696, email info@bowker.com, web www.bowker.com. Canada—R.R. Bowker, Markham, Ontario, phone (888) BOWKER9 & (905) 415-

5837, fax (905) 479-6266. German speaking Europe—K.G. Saur Verlag, Munich, Germany, phone 49-89-76902-232, fax 49-89-76902-250, email 100730.1341@compuserve.com, web www.saur.de/home.htm. Rest of Europe incl. United Kingdom plus Africa & Asia—Bowker-Saur, W. Sussex, UK, phone 44-1342-326-972, fax 44-1342-335-612, email customer@bowker-saur.co.uk, web www.bowker-saur.com/service/. Australia/New Zealand—Thorpe, Port Melbourne, Victoria, Australia, phone 61-03-9-245-7370, fax 61-03-9-245-7395, email customer.service@thorpe.com.au, web www.thorpe.com.au. Technical support for CD ROMs (800) 323-3288, fax 908) 665-3528, email techsupport@bowker.com.

http://taps.com is a web site for people looking for contract and permanent positions in the United Kingdom and Europe. Positions are mainly in information technology, mostly in the $20,000 to $50,000 range. TAPS.COM was developed by Internet Appointments, Ltd., London, England and was launched in 1996.

KOMPASS is described by the publisher as "the world's most comprehensive global database of companies, products and services for manufacturing and engineering professionals in print, on CD ROM and on the Internet." It contains company and product information for companies in all lines of business, including manufacturing and industrial sectors. Each company listing includes name, address, phone number, management names, business descriptions, and industry and product listings. Kompass's web site is www.kompass.com. Call publisher for prices and information on country directories. Cahners Business Information, 121 Chanlon Road, New Providence, NJ 07974, (908) 771-8785, fax (908) 665-8755, email hholmes@reedref.com. Headquarters: Cahners Business Information, 275 Washington Street, Newton, MA 02158-1630, (617) 558-4663 or (617) 964-3030, fax (617) 558-4700, email marketaccess@cahners.com, web sites www.cahners.com or www.chilton.net.

MAJOR CHEMICAL & PETROCHEMICAL COMPANIES OF EUROPE contains information on 1,800 companies in 19 western European countries. $450. US distributor: Larry Meranus Professional Publications & Services, 4 Demoray Court, Pine Brook, NJ 07058, (800) MERANUS or (800) 637-2687. Published by Graham & Whiteside Ltd., Tuition House, 5-6 Francis Grove, London SW19 4DT, England. Web site http://www.major-co-data.com. Email sales@major-co-data.com.

MAJOR COMPANIES OF CENTRAL AND EASTERN EUROPE AND THE COMMONWEALTH OF INDEPENDENT STATES identifies some 38,000 executives at 8,000 major business organizations in 24 countries in Eastern and Central Europe and the former Soviet Republics (CIS). Includes three indexes. $980. Also available in CD ROM. Published by Graham & Whiteside Ltd., Tuition House, 5-6 Francis Grove, London SW19 4DT, England. Web site http://www.major-co-data.com. Email sales@major-co-data.com. Distributed by: Larry Meranus Professional Publications & Services, 4 Demoray Court, Pine Brook, NJ 07058, (800) MERANUS or (800) 637-2687. Also distributed by Gale Group, P.O. Box 9187, Farmington Hills, MI 48333-9187. Toll free US and Canada (800) 877-GALE (4253) and (248) 699-GALE, fax (800) 414-5043 and (248) 699-8061, Internet orders galeord@galegroup.com, web site www.galegroup.com or www.gale.com. All Gale Group products are available on approval. Contact Gale for details.

MAJOR COMPANIES OF EUROPE is a 4 volume edition containing 194,000 names of contacts at 24,000 companies in all 20 western European countries. Vol. 1 —Austria, Belgium, Denmark, Ireland, Finland, France. Vol. 2—Germany, Greece, Italy, Liechtenstein, Luxembourg. Vol. 3—The Netherlands, Norway, Portugal, Spain, Sweden, Switzerland. Vol. 4—United Kingdom. $1,700 for 4 volume set. $535 per volume. CD ROM, updated quarterly, is also available. Published by Graham & Whiteside Ltd., Tuition House, 5-6 Francis Grove, London SW19 4DT, England. Web site http://www.major-co-data.com. Email sales@major-co-data.com. Distributed by: Larry Meranus Professional Publications & Services, 4 Demoray Court, Pine Brook, NJ 07058, (800) MERANUS or (800) 637-2687. Also distributed by Gale Group, P.O. Box 9187, Farmington Hills, MI 48333-9187. Toll free US and Canada (800) 877-GALE (4253) and (248) 699-GALE, fax (800) 414-5043 and (248) 699-8061, Internet orders galeord@galegroup.com, web site www.galegroup.com or www.gale.com. All Gale Group products are available on approval. Contact Gale for details.

MAJOR COMPANIES SERIES ON CD ROM consists of Graham & Whiteside's annual directories of major international companies. All six directories reside on one disk. After payment, you'll receive a security code to access the region(s) you select. This Windows™ based CD can navigate by company name, company locations, executive names, business activity and more. *Free demo CD ROM* is available. Regions also available separately for Europe, Central & Eastern Europe, the Far East and Australasia, the Arab World, Africa, and Latin America. For prices and availability, contact the Gale Group, P.O. Box 9187, Farmington

Hills, MI 48333-9187. Toll free US and Canada (800) 877-GALE (4253) and (248) 699-GALE, fax (800) 414-5043 and (248) 699-8061, Internet orders galeord@galegroup.com, web site www.galegroup.com or www.gale.com. All Gale Group products are available on approval. Contact Gale for details.

MAJOR ENERGY COMPANIES OF EUROPE presents information on over 1,200 companies in 20 European countries. $415. US distributor: Larry Meranus Professional Publications & Services, 4 Demoray Court, Pine Brook, NJ 07058, (800) MERANUS or (800) 637-2687. Published by Graham & Whiteside Ltd., Tuition House, 5-6 Francis Grove, London SW19 4DT, England. Web site http://www.major-co-data.com. Email sales@major-co-data.com.

MAJOR FINANCIAL INSTITUTIONS OF EUROPE contains information on some 1,600 financial institutions in western Europe. $450. US distributor: Larry Meranus Professional Publications & Services, 4 Demoray Court, Pine Brook, NJ 07058, (800) MERANUS or (800) 637-2687. Published by Graham & Whiteside Ltd., Tuition House, 5-6 Francis Grove, London SW19 4DT, England. Web site http://www.major-co-data.com. Email sales@major-co-data.com.

MAJOR FOOD & DRINK COMPANIES OF EUROPE provides information on 2,100 major companies in food and beverages (alcoholic and non-alcoholic) in Western Europe. $450. US distributor: Larry Meranus Professional Publications & Services, 4 Demoray Court, Pine Brook, NJ 07058, (800) MERANUS or (800) 637-2687. Published by Graham & Whiteside Ltd., Tuition House, 5-6 Francis Grove, London SW19 4DT, England. Web site http://www.major-co-data.com. Email sales@major-co-data.com.

MAJOR TELECOMMUNICATIONS COMPANIES OF EUROPE contains information and contacts for 1,100 major telecommunications companies and their equipment suppliers in western Europe, central Europe and eastern Europe. $415. US distributor: Larry Meranus Professional Publications & Services, 4 Demoray Court, Pine Brook, NJ 07058, (800) MERANUS or (800) 637-2687. Published by Graham & Whiteside Ltd., Tuition House, 5-6 Francis Grove, London SW19 4DT, England. Web site http://www.major-co-data.com. Email sales@major-co-data.com.

PENSION FUNDS AND THEIR ADVISERS provides information on the top 2,000 pension funds in the United Kingdom, plus major funds of Japan, Belgium, France, Germany, Ireland, The Netherlands and Switzerland. This Directory is the only source in the US that monitors the growth of assets in the international market. Information includes internal and external fund management contacts, major US and Canadian pension funds and money managers, major European and Japanese pension funds and their advisors. It also includes comprehensive listings of 900 advisors to the pension fund industry including financial advisers, accountants, actuaries and pension fund consultants, pension administrators, insurance companies, attorneys, computer services, global custody, pension trustees, pension /financial recruitment consultants, investment research, associations and professional groups, and publications. $310. Published by A.P. Information Services, Ltd. Marketed exclusively in North America MONEY MARKET DIRECTORIES INC./STANDARD AND POORS, 320 East Main Street, Charlottesville, VA 22902, http://www.mmdaccess.com, (800) 446-2810, (804) 977-1450.

POLLUTION ENGINEERING INTERNATIONAL is a magazine for environmental professionals in Asia and Europe, published 4 times a year. Call publisher for price. Cahners Business Information, 1350 East Touhy Avenue, Des Plaines, IL 60018-5080, (847) 390-2752, fax (847) 390-2636, URL www.pollutioneng.com. Headquarters: Cahners Business Information, 275 Washington Street, Newton, MA 02158-1630, (617) 558-4663 or (617) 964-3030, fax (617) 558-4700, email marketaccess@cahners.com. Web sites www.cahners.com or www.chilton.net.

TELEVISION EUROPE is a London based publication that covers the European television industry. Call publisher for price. Cahners Business Information, 6 Bell Yard, London WC2 A1EJ, England, (011) 44 171 520-5285, fax (011) 44 171 520-5226, email jonnypim@pacific.net.sg and rschatz@cahners.com. Headquarters: Cahners Business Information, 275 Washington Street, Newton, MA 02158-1630, (617) 558-4663 or (617) 964-3030, fax (617) 558-4700, email marketaccess@cahners.com. Web sites www.cahners.com or www.chilton.net.

WHO OWNS WHOM DIRECTORY by Dun & Bradstreet is a six volume set containing information on the structure and ownership of 320,000 company affiliates and subsidiaries of over 23,000 companies worldwide. It is available in four regional editions: Australia and the Far East, North America, UK/Ireland, and Continental Europe. Published annually. For prices and ordering information as well as information about more worldwide corporate linkage products from D&B WORLDBASE, D&B's global database of 42 million records in over 200 countries, contact Dun & Bradstreet at (800) 526-0651, Dun & Bradstreet, Business Reference Solutions, Three Sylvan Way, Parsippany, NJ 07054. Email dnbmdd@mail.dnb.com. Web site http://www.dnbmdd.com.

WHO'S WHO IN CABLE & SATELLITE EUROPE, Phillips Business Information, Inc., a Phillips Publishing International Company, 120 Seven Locks Road, Potomac, MD 20854, (301) 340-1520, (301) 340-7788, (800) 777-5006, Internet pbi@phillips.com, web site www.phillips.com.

WHO'S WHO IN UK MULTIMEDIA, Phillips Business Information, Inc., a Phillips Publishing International Company, 120 Seven Locks Road, Potomac, MD 20854, (301) 340-1520, (301) 340-7788, (800) 777-5006, Internet pbi@phillips.com, web site www.phillips.com.

www.europages.com is a web site of a business directory of over 500,000 European firms. In Deutsch, English, Espanol, Français & Italiano. Features include Search for Companies, Company Catalogues, Business Information, Yellow Pages in Europe. Search by Product/Service, Thematic Search or by Company Name. Address, phone, fax, products, turnover. Europages' Daily Business News, European Trade Fairs, Chambers of Commerce in Europe, European Patent Offices, Official International Organisations, European Standardization Bodies.

Executive Recruiting

See Executive Search

Executive Search

Also see Research—Executive Search

ASSOCIATION OF EXECUTIVE SEARCH CONSULTANTS MEMBERSHIP DIRECTORY identifies the premier retainer search firms and includes over 100 firms, including addresses of all locations around the world. Cost to non-members is $35.00. AESC, 230 Park Avenue, Suite 1549, New York, NY 10169-0005, (212) 949-9556.

CANADA EMPLOYMENT WEEKLY'S URL is www.mediacorp2.com/. It features The Career Bookstore for Canadian Career Books, Talent Available to Market Yourself to Canadian Recruiters and Search Firms, Canadian Directory of Search Firms, and Who's Hiring for a list of Canada's top employers. www.mediacorp2.com/cdsf/index.html leads you directly to the Canadian Directory of Search Firms and the Career Bookstore—"Quality Canadian Career Books" including GET WIRED, YOU'RE HIRED, "the definitive Canadian guide to job hunting in Canada."

CANADIAN DIRECTORY OF SEARCH FIRMS, in French and English, lists over 1,700 search firms and 3,000 recruitment professionals. 70 occupational categories, geographic index, and a Who's.Who Index. $39.95, ISBN 0-9681447-1-3. To locate the CANADIAN DIRECTORY OF SEARCH FIRMS, go to www.netjobs.com or ask your favorite bookstore to look it up in BOOKS IN PRINT.

D&B DIRECTORY OF SERVICE COMPANIES is a directory with information on 50,000 US service businesses, including privately held companies, in these sectors: accounting, auditing and bookkeeping, advertising and public relations, architecture and engineering, consumer services, *executive search,* health, hospitality, management consulting, motion pictures, repair, research, social services and law. Listings include key executives' names and titles, address, phone, sales volume, number of employees, parent company and location, and more. Companies listed employ 50 or more people. Information is listed alphabetically and is cross-referenced geographically and by industry classification. Updated annually. For prices call Dun & Bradstreet at (800) 526-0651. For more information contact Dun & Bradstreet, Business Reference Solutions, Three Sylvan Way, Parsippany, New Jersey 07054. Email dnbmdd@mail.dnb.com. Web site http://www.dnbmdd.com.

DIRECTORY OF EXECUTIVE RECRUITERS profiles over 5,000 firms in 7,000 locations with over 12,800 individual recruiters listed. It is cross-referenced according to retainer vs. contingency firms, job functions, industries, geography and recruiter specialities. Available in paperback $47.95, hardcover (with more details on each firm) $179.95, on CD as SearchSelect® $245.00, in label or list form for selected categories or on the web. A companion publication, KENNEDY'S POCKET GUIDE TO WORKING WITH EXECUTIVE RECRUITERS is a 150-page assemblage of 30 chapters by the experts themselves, plus a Lexicon of Executive Recruiting. $9.95. Kennedy Information, One Kennedy Place, Route 12 South, Fitzwilliam, NH 03447, phone (800) 531-0007 or 603-585-6544, fax 603-585-9555, email bookstore@kennedyinfo.com, web site www.kennedyinfo.com.

DIRECTORY OF INDEPENDENT RESEARCH CONSULTANTS contains information on 200 contract consultants. Jobhunters who are sending resumes to search firms might also want to include research consultants. They are often indistinguishable from search consultants because the roles of both can be so similar. In addition, at a search firm, a researcher customarily conducts the first screen of a resume, regardless of whom it's addressed to. Further, it's not unusual for these consultants to be directly retained by corporations purchasing "unbundled search" services, which basically means a less expensive "no frills" search product. This means that independent research consultants represent another third party avenue for job hunters, in addition to executive search firms and contingency recruiting firms. $65. Ordering information: Published by Kennedy Information, One Kennedy Place, Route 12 South, Fitzwilliam, NH 03447, phone (800) 531-0007 or 603-585-6544, fax 603-585-9555, email bookstore@kennedyinfo.com, web site www.kennedyinfo.com.

EXECUTIVE RECRUITER NEWS is a monthly executive search industry newsletter with profiles of search firms, interviews with recruiters and clients, statistics on the executive search profession, firm management techniques for staff development, compensation, marketing and client relationships. $197/yr. Published by Kennedy Information, One Kennedy Place, Route 12 South, Fitzwilliam, NH 03447, phone (800) 531-0007 or 603-585-6544, fax 603-585-9555, email bookstore@kennedyinfo.com, web site www.kennedyinfo.com.

EXECUTIVE SEARCH RESEARCH DIRECTORY (ESRD) provides information on over 350 contract research consultants, including descriptions of research services provided, fees, experience, where trained, areas of concentration, and unusual capabilities, including 26 freelancers with an Internet specialty. Cross referenced by over 300 specialties. $88 postpaid. Ordering information: Kenneth J. Cole, Publisher, The Recruiting & Search Report, P.O. Box 9433, Panama City Beach, FL 32417. (850) 235-3733, fax (850) 233-9695. Email jcole9433@aol.com.

NEW CAREER MAKERS by John Sibbald provides profiles on 250 leading individuals in the retained executive search business. $28. Ordering information: Kennedy Information, One Kennedy Place, Route 12 South, Fitzwilliam, NH 03447, phone (800) 531-0007 or 603-585-6544, fax 603-585-9555, email bookstore@kennedyinfo.com, web site www.kennedyinfo.com.

NEW ENGLAND EXECUTIVE RESOURCES COUNCIL, whose URL is http://199.233.99.2/neerc/, is a small organization of search consultants and heads of human resources. The group meets 4 times a year in Waltham Massachusetts. Their web site includes a listing of members, including some photos. In an effort to remain as egalitarian as possible, there are no officers. As ther is no contact person *per se,* you may get in touch with anyone on the web site. http://199.233.99.2/neerc/

PR NEWS ANNUAL SALARY SURVEY AND EXCLUSIVE GUIDE TO EXECUTIVE RECRUITERS, Phillips Business Information, Inc., a Phillips Publishing International Company, 120 Seven Locks Road, Potomac, MD 20854, (301) 340-1520, (301) 340-7788, (800) 777-5006, Internet pbi@phillips.com, web site www.phillips.com.

RECRUITING TRENDS is a monthly newsletter that provides strategies and tactics for creating and maintaining a competitive work force. Practical guidance on college recruiting, finding "in demand" talent, interviewing, diversity, legal issues, reference checking, managing cost-per-hire expenses. $179. Published by Kennedy Information, One Kennedy Place, Route 12 South, Fitzwilliam, NH 03447, phone (800) 531-0007 or 603-585-6544, fax 603-585-9555, email bookstore@kennedyinfo.com, web site www.kennedyinfo.com.

SPECIFICATION SHEET ANALYSIS is a collection of 245 different sets of actual search specifications from senior executive retainer searches. These specifications offer insights into major firm retainer search methodology and specification creation. Especially useful to contingency firms evolving towards retained search. Full catalog of specifications available by fax upon request. $125 for any 25 specifications.

Ordering information: Kenneth J. Cole, Publisher, The Recruiting & Search Report, P.O. Box 9433, Panama City Beach, FL 32417. (850) 235-3733, fax (850) 233-9695 Email jcole9433@aol.com.

UNCOVERING THE TRUTH—HOW TO *REALLY* CHECK REFERENCES is a cassette by Andrea Jupina that completely covers the art of reference checking in 30 minutes. It's an excellent refresher that really gets your mental juices flowing before you begin to interview references—ideal for line managers, search firms, small business owners, and anyone who needs to know the *real* story—*without* a lawsuit. $15.95 plus shipping & handling. Available from Jupina by email order at andreajupina@yahoo.com and from Kennedy Information, One Kennedy Place, Route 12 South, Fitzwilliam, NH 03447, phone (800) 531-0007 or 603-585-6544, fax 603-585-9555, email bookstore@kennedyinfo.com, web site www.kennedyinfo.com.

www.careers.wsj.com is the *Wall Street Journal*'s web site. It focuses on positions for middle and senior management including financial positions at $75,000 and up. This web site is among those that encompass senior executive positions. Kennedy Information's executive recruiter database is available there. Other features include Job Seek, Who's Hiring, Career Columnists, Salaries & Profiles, The Salary Calculator™, Job Hunting Advice, Succeeding at Work, HR Issues, Executive Recruiters, Working Globally, College Connection, Starting a Business, Career Bookstore and more. Content from The National Employment Business Weekly is also featured. The site was developed by Dow Jones & Company, Inc., Princeton, New Jersey and was established in 1997.

www.nehra.com is the URL for the Northeast Human Resources Association web site, which is largely comprised of executive search consultants.

F

Factories

See Manufacturing—Plant Locations Category

Factoring

CORPORATE FINANCE SOURCEBOOK—THE GUIDE TO MAJOR INVESTMENT SOURCES AND RELATED FINANCIAL SERVICES contains over 13,000 names of executives at 3,700 organizations that, broadly speaking, supply growth capital to businesses or are service firms, such as US venture capital lenders, private lenders, commercial finance and factoring, pension managers, master trusts and other sources. Names of key management are included. A special section details public offerings of the past 3 years and mergers and acquisitions over $100 million. $575. If the price is prohibitively high, remember your local library. National Register Publishing, Reed Elsevier-New Providence, 121 Chanlon Road, New Providence, NJ 07974, (800) 521-8110, fax (800) 836-7736, web site www.redbooks.com or www.marquiswhoswho.com. "If, for any reason whatsoever, your order does not fully meet your expectations, simply return the product within 30 days for a prompt, complete, unquestioned refund," as stated in Catalog of Biographical and Professional References of publisher Marquis Who's Who/National Register Publishing.

Fax Numbers

MEXICO BUSINESS COMMUNICATIONS AND FAX DIRECTORY or CD lists over 11,000 businesses, over 5,000 associations and chambers of commerce, plus a listing of Mexican government departments and Canadian and US embassies and consulates in Mexico. Section 1 lists government offices. Section 2 lists businesses alphabetically by company. Section 3 lists companies by business category. A listing of city codes, maps, historical information and a list of the top 100 companies in Mexico is also included. Published annually. Directory $179.95, CD $229.95. Ordering information: Scott's Directories, Toronto area: 1450 Don Mills Road, Don Mills, Ontario, M3B 2X7, CANADA, (888) 709-9907, (416) 442-2291, (416) 932-9555. Montréal area: Scott's Directories, 3300 Cote Verde, Suite 410 Ville St.-Laurent, Quebec H4B 2B7 CANADA (514) 339-1397, (800) 363-1327, email scotts@southam.ca.

NATIONAL E-MAIL AND FAX DIRECTORY provides over 180,000 fax numbers for US companies, organizations and government agencies, cross referenced by subject. $126. Gale Group, P.O. Box 9187, Farmington Hills, MI 48333-9187. Toll free US and Canada (800) 877-GALE (4253) and (248) 699-GALE, fax (800) 414-5043 and (248) 699-8061, Internet orders galeord@galegroup.com, web site www.galegroup.com or www.gale.com. All Gale Group products are available on approval. Contact Gale for details.

Federal Government

See Government—Federal

Finance

See Accounting, Banking, Investment Management

AMERICA'S CORPORATE FINANCE DIRECTORY provides a financial profile of the US's leading 5,000 public and private companies. It includes information about the company's pension plan, names of contacts, and a listing of over 17,000 wholly owned US subsidiaries. The title appears previously to have been The Corporate Finance Bluebook. $585. If the price is prohibitively high, remember your local library. National Register Publishing, Reed Elsevier-New Providence, 121 Chanlon Road, New Providence, NJ 07974, (800) 521-8110, fax (800) 836-7736, web site www.redbooks.com or www.marquiswhoswho.com. "If, for any reason whatsoever, your order does not fully meet your expectations, simply return the product within 30 days for a prompt, complete, unquestioned refund," as stated in Catalog of Biographical and Professional References of publisher Marquis Who's Who/National Register Publishing.

COMPLETE MARQUIS WHO'S WHO ON CD ROM is a compilation of literally all 19 Marquis Who's Who that have appeared in print since 1985, including living and deceased people. WHO'S WHO IN AMERICA®, WHO'S WHO IN THE WORLD®, WHO'S WHO IN AMERICAN EDUCATIONS®, WHO'S WHO IN AMERICAN LAW®, WHO'S WHO IN AMERICAN NURSING®, WHO'S WHO IN MEDICINE AND HEALTHCARE®, WHO'S WHO IN FINANCE AND INDUSTRY®, WHO'S WHO IN SCIENCE AND ENGINEERING®, WHO'S WHO IN THE EAST®, WHO'S WHO IN THE MIDWEST®, WHO'S WHO IN THE SOUTH AND SOUTHWEST®, WHO'S WHO IN THE WEST®, WHO'S WHO OF AMERICAN WOMEN®, WHO'S WHO IN ADVERTISING®, WHO'S WHO OF EMERGING LEADERS IN AMERICA®, WHO'S WHO IN ENTERTAINMENT®, WHO'S WHO AMONG HUMAN SERVICES PROFESSIONALS®. One year subscription with semi-annual updates $995. National Register Publishing, Reed Elsevier-New Providence, 121 Chanlon Road, New Providence, NJ 07974, (800) 521-8110, fax (800) 836-7736, web site www.marquiswhoswho.com or www.redbooks.com. "If, for any reason whatsoever, your order does not fully meet your expectations, simply return the product within 30 days for a prompt, complete, unquestioned refund," as stated in Catalog of Biographical and Professional References of publisher Marquis Who's Who/National Register Publishing.

CONSULTANT DIRECTORY profiles the top 400 consulting organizations that specifically serve the pension and investment industries. Includes career biographical information, including education, number of years with the firm, specialties, employment history, direct dial phone number and email address. $295. Published by STANDARD AND POORS, a division of McGraw-Hill, MONEY MARKET DIRECTORIES, INC., 320 East Main Street, Charlottesville, VA 22902, http://www.mmdaccess.com, (800) 446-2810, (804) 977-1450.

CONSULTANTS AND CONSULTING ORGANIZATIONS DIRECTORY identifies consultants in over 400 specialties within 14 general areas. Includes finance, computers, fundraising and others. $620 for 2 volumes. Gale Group, P.O. Box 9187, Farmington Hills, MI 48333-9187. Toll free US and Canada (800) 877-GALE (4253) and (248) 699-GALE, fax (800) 414-5043 and (248) 699-8061, Internet orders galeord@galegroup.com, web site www.galegroup.com or www.gale.com. All Gale Group products are available on approval. Contact Gale for details.

CORPORATE FINANCE SOURCEBOOK—THE GUIDE TO MAJOR INVESTMENT SOURCES AND RELATED FINANCIAL SERVICES contains over 13,000 names of executives at 3,700 organizations that, broadly speaking, supply growth capital to businesses, such as venture capital lenders, private lenders, commercial finance and factoring, pension managers, master trusts. Names of key management are included. A special section details public offerings of the past 3 years and mergers and acquisitions over $100 million. $499.95 hard copy, excluding discounts. NRP's catalog states, "If you're dissatisfied for any reason, simply return the product within 30 days for a full refund." If the price is prohibitively high, remember your local library. Available in book, online, magnetic tape, and in mailing list formats. For more information contact: National Register Publishing, 121 Chanlon Road, New Providence, NJ 07974 USA, (800) 521-8110, http://www.lexis-nexis.com. For information about online access, call LEXIS®—NEXIS® Online Services, Mountainview, CA at (800) 346-9759; for mailing lists call Cahners Direct Marketing Services at (800) 323-4958; all other inquiries (800) 521-8110.

DIRECTORY OF REGISTERED INVESTMENT ADVISORS identifies over 9,000 CEO's, 7,000 Investment Officers, 10,000 Portfolio Managers, 6,000 Directors of Research and Research Analysts, 2,800 Traders and Trading Managers, and 1,200 Directors of Operations/Chief Financial Officers, plus web sites and personal email addresses. The directory also includes a section on mutual funds for over 4,000 funds at 375 firms, including the name of the person responsible for managing the fund, 1,3 and 5 year returns, benchmark comparisons, and more. DIRECTORY OF REGISTERED INVESTMENT ADVISORS with 4 Regional editions, $475. The Directory with no regional editions, $395. Published by STANDARD AND POORS, a division of McGraw-Hill, MONEY MARKET DIRECTORIES, INC., 320 East Main Street, Charlottesville, VA 22902, http://www.mmdaccess.com, (800) 446-2810, (804) 977-1450.

FINANCIAL EXECUTIVES INSTITUTE (FEI) provides a resume matching service for its members, who are senior financial executives, and employers and search firms. The cost is minimal or nil. For more information, contact the Financial Executive Institute. They can be located in the Encyclopedia of Associations or Lorna Daniells' BUSINESS INFORMATION SOURCES or another librarians' reference. Or call your local business librarian. Or ask a senior financial executive, such as a corporate controller or chief financial officer who would likely be a member. The FEI also publishes a membership directory which cross references members by company. However, it is only available to members, so you will have to borrow a copy from a member. It can be used to identify names of contacts, either for recruiting purposes, or for job hunters networking.The FEI is one of many professional associations that provides its members with this type of service.

FINANCIAL SERVICES CANADA is a handbook of banks, non-depository institutions, stock exchange and brokers, investment management, mutual funds, insurance, accountants, government agencies, financial associations and more, including contact numbers, name, title, organization, phone, fax, email, web site, and cellular. $199 for book, $299 for CD ROM, $399 for both. Ordering information: Copp Clark Professional, 200 Adelaide Street West, 3rd floor, Toronto, ON M5H 1W7 CANADA. Email orders@mail.CanadaInfo.com. Web site http://www.coppclark.com. For additional information contact: IHS Canada, Micromedia Limited, 20 Victoria Street, Toronto, Ontario M5C 2N8 CANADA, (800) 387-2689, (416) 362-5211, fax (416) 362-6161, email info@micromedia.on.ca.

INSTITUTIONAL INVESTOR publishes excellent surveys of various Wall Street industries. Generally one survey appears in each monthly issue, including names of contacts. Annual subscription $325. INSTITUTIONAL INVESTOR, 488 Madison Avenue, New York, NY 10022, (212) 303-3300.

INVESTMENT NEWS is a weekly trade publication. Crain Communications, Inc. is headquartered in Chicago with offices in major cities throughout the US plus London, Tokyo and Frankfurt. New York location: 220 East 42nd Street, New York, NY 10017, (212) 210-0100, Circulation (800) 678-9595. Annual subscription $38. Web site www.investmentnews.com.

MAJOR FINANCIAL INSTITUTIONS OF EUROPE contains information on some 1,600 financial institutions in western Europe. $450. US distributor: Larry Meranus Professional Publications & Services, 4 Demoray Court, Pine Brook, NJ 07058, (800) MERANUS or (800) 637-2687. Published by Graham & Whiteside Ltd., Tuition House, 5-6 Francis Grove, London SW19 4DT, England. Web site http://www.major-co-data.com. Email sales@major-co-data.com.

MAJOR FINANCIAL INSTITUTIONS OF THE ARAB WORLD provides contacts and information on over 1,000 top financial institutions in the Arab world. US distributor: Larry Meranus Professional Publications & Services, 4 Demoray Court, Pine Brook, NJ 07058, (800) MERANUS or (800) 637-2687.

Published by Graham & Whiteside Ltd., Tuition House, 5-6 Francis Grove, London SW19 4DT, England. Web site http://www.major-co-data.com. Email sales@major-co-data.com.

MAJOR FINANCIAL INSTITUTIONS OF THE FAR EAST & AUSTRALASIA contains information on over 1,500 Asia/Pacific financial institutions. $450. US distributor: Larry Meranus Professional Publications & Services, 4 Demoray Court, Pine Brook, NJ 07058, (800) MERANUS or (800) 637-2687. Published by Graham & Whiteside Ltd., Tuition House, 5-6 Francis Grove, London SW19 4DT, England. Web site http://www.major-co-data.com. Email sales@major-co-data.com.

MAJOR FINANCIAL INSTITUTIONS OF THE WORLD provides information on over 7,500 of the largest financial institutions globally. $890. US distributor: Larry Meranus Professional Publications & Services, 4 Demoray Court, Pine Brook, NJ 07058, (800) MERANUS or (800) 637-2687. Published by Graham & Whiteside Ltd., Tuition House, 5-6 Francis Grove, London SW19 4DT, England. Web site http://www.major-co-data.com. Email sales@major-co-data.com.

MONEY MARKET DIRECTORY OF PENSION FUNDS AND THEIR INVESTMENT MANAGERS provides plan sponsor profiles, including firm name, address, phone and fax, senior investment officers, names of other key personnel and decision makes including in house asset manager, officer handling inquiries from money managers, officer who evaluates money managers, officer who handles responses to requests for proposals, benefits administrator, chief human resources officer, investor relations officer, corporate cash manager, director of development for endowments some direct dial phone numbers and personal email addresses. The Directory also profiles investment management firms that invest pension assets and investment manager consultant firms. Published by STANDARD AND POORS, a division of McGraw-Hill, MONEY MARKET DIRECTORIES, INC., 320 East Main Street, Charlottesville, VA 22902, http://www.mmdaccess.com, (800) 446-2810, (804) 977-1450. Regional Directories also available. $995 per copy MONEY MARKET DIRECTORY, $150 per additional REGIONAL DIRECTORY.

MONEY MARKET DIRECTORY OF TAX-EXEMPT ORGANIZATIONS provides information on private foundations, hospitals and other health service organizations, church related service groups, schools, associations, civic leagues and fraternal beneficiary organizations. Names are provided for over 6,000 senior investment officers, 3000 secondary investment officers, 4,800 presidents and principals, over 4,000 Chairmen, 12,500 trustees and board officers, 600 in house managers, 900 benefits managers, 900 chief human resources officers, 700 chief operating officers and 300 directors of development. $440. Published by STANDARD AND POORS, a division of McGraw-Hill, MONEY MARKET DIRECTORIES, INC., 320 East Main Street, Charlottesville, VA 22902, http://www.mmdaccess.com, (800) 446-2810, (804) 977-1450.

NELSON FINANCIAL DATABASE provides comprehensive information on the global institutional investment market. Information formatted to your precise needs is available from Nelson Information Mailing List & Customized Database service. The NELSON FINANCIAL DATABASE is comprised of:

    30,000 executives at investment management firms
    11,000 executives at research firms
    100,000 executives at public companies
    40,000 executives at plan sponsors
    3,000 executives at pension fund consulting firms
    24,000 executives at institutional real estate firms
    4,000 executives at technology based vendors

The database also consists of extensive investment information, including money manager performance, peer group analysis, special surveys and more. For customers who with to use Nelson's information in their own systems, Nelson will supply customized data export, using all or any data items. Mailing lists are also available for direct marketers.For more information, contact Nelson Mailing List & Customized Database Services, P.O. Box 591, Port Chester, NY 10573 USA. (800) 333-6357, Phone outside the US (914) 937-8400, Fax (914) 937-8590, web site http://www.nelnet.com.

PENSIONSCOPE DATASYSTEMS is a database service from MONEY MARKET DIRECTORIES, a division of STANDARD AND POORS. Their database will help you select key decision makers in the pension funds, pension service companies, institutional asset managers, and the nonprofit marketplaces of public and private foundations, endowments and health service organizations. Selections can be based on job function, asset size, type of organization or plan, and geographic location. Selected information available as labels, printouts on index cards or sheets of paper, on magnetic tape, or on disk (minimum $500 order). For more information call STANDARD AND POORS, a division of McGraw-Hill, MONEY MARKET DIRECTORIES, INC., 320 East Main Street, Charlottesville, VA 22902, http://www.mmdaccess.com, (800) 446-2810, (804) 977-1450.

RETAIL BROKER-DEALER DIRECTORY identifies key personnel, number of employees and representatives, product sales mix, areas of specialization, commission payout levels, clearing firm, technology providers, total revenues, and capital. It is indexed by company, by distribution channel and by geographic location. $270. Ordering information: Securities Data Publishing, 40 West 57th Street, 11th Floor, New York, NY 10019, (212) 765-5311, (800) 455-5844. At the time of this writing, Investment Dealers Digest has been purchased by Securities Data Publishing, a division of Thomson Financial Publishers.

WHO'S WHO IN FINANCE AND INDUSTRY, $279.95. National Register Publishing, Reed Elsevier-New Providence, 121 Chanlon Road, New Providence, NJ 07974, (800) 521-8110, fax (800) 836-7736, web site www.marquiswhoswho.com or www.redbooks.com. "If, for any reason whatsoever, your order does not fully meet your expectations, simply return the product within 30 days for a prompt, complete, unquestioned refund," as stated in Catalog of Biographical and Professional References of publisher Marquis Who's Who/National Register Publishing.

www.accountingjobs.com or Accounting and Finance Jobs, was developed by AccountingNet of Seattle in a joint venture with Career Mosaic. Launched in 1997, this site specializes in accounting and finance positions, mainly in the $30,000-50,000 range.

www.americasemployers.com or America's Employers is a site mainly for positions in technology, finance and sales at approximately $50,000 to $100,000. Launched in 1995, it was developed by Career Relocation Corp of America in Armonk, New York.

www.careermosaic.com is the URL for a major recruitment web site that spends millions of dollars in advertising to draw traffic to this site. CareerMosaic features a jobs database; newsgroups for jobs, college connection, online job fairs, employer job postings; company information and more. CareerMosaic was ranked as one of the top 5 "Sites Offering the Best Overall Support for Job Seekers" by the *National Business Employment Weekly*. The site was developed Bernard Hodes Advertising in New York and went online in 1994.

www.careers.wsj.com is the *Wall Street Journal*'s web site. It focuses on positions for middle and senior management including financial positions at $75,000 and up. This web site is among those that encompass senior executive positions. Other features includes Job Seek, Who's Hiring, Career Columnists, Salaries & Profiles, The Salary Calculator™, Job Hunting Advice, Succeeding at Work, HR Issues, Executive Recruiters, Working Globally, College Connection, Starting a Business, Career Bookstore and more. Content from The National Employment Business Weekly is also featured. The site was developed by Dow Jones & Company, Inc., Princeton, New Jersey and was established in 1997.

www.LatPro.com is the URL for Latin America's Professional Network, a site for experienced Spanish and Portuguese bilingual professionals. Many job postings are for positions in sales and marketing, finance and information technology, often in the $50,000 to $100,000 range. The site was developed by Latin America's Professional Network, Miami, Florida and was launched in 1997.

www.nelnet.com is the URL for Wall Street and financial publisher Nelson Information, P.O. Box 591, Port Chester, NY 10573 USA. (800) 333-6357, phone outside the US (914) 937-8400, fax (914) 937-8590.

www.usresume.com is the URL for US Resume, a site that lists many positions in computers, sales and finance, usually in the $50,000 to $100,000 range. The site was developed by Market 2000 Corp, Sparkill, New York and went online in 1996.

Finance—International

AMERICA'S CORPORATE FAMILIES & INTERNATIONAL AFFILIATES is comprised of two volumes of US subsidiaries, divisions and branches and one volume of some 3,000 foreign ultimate parent companies and their 11,000 US subsidiaries and nearly 3,000 US ultimate parent corporations and their 18,000 foreign subsidiaries. Published annually. The International Affiliates (Volume 3) lists US companies with their foreign subsidiaries and foreign ultimates with their US subsidiaries. In addition to listing US and foreign ultimates with their family members alphabetically, all companies are cross-referenced geographically and by industry classification. Updated annually For prices call Dun & Bradstreet at (800) 526-0651. For more information contact Dun & Bradstreet, Business Reference Solutions, Three Sylvan Way, Parsippany, New Jersey 07054. Email dnbmdd@mail.dnb.com. Web site http://www.dnbmdd.com.

CENTRAL BANK & MINISTRY OF FINANCE YEARBOOK. For more information contact Larry Meranus Professional Publications & Services, 4 Demoray Court, Pine Brook, NJ 07058, (800) MERANUS or (800) 637-2687. Distributed in England by EUROMONEY Books, Plymbridge Distributors Limited, Estover, Plymouth PL6 7PZ, England. Phone 44 (0) 171 779-8955. Fax 44 (0) 171 779-8541.

CORPORATE AFFILIATIONS PLUS CD ROM consolidates information in all five volumes of THE DIRECTORY OF CORPORATE AFFILIATIONS, including publicly held and privately held companies in the US and internationally, and AMERICA'S CORPORATE FINANCE DIRECTORY. This CD provides "family tree" overviews for each company with the reporting structure. It also contains information on 15,000 parent companies in the US and abroad, records on over 100,000 subsidiaries, divisions, plants and joint ventures, names and titles of over 250,000 employees, revenue figures and more. Information can be searched by 29 criteria, such as location, SIC or NAICS codes, sales, number of employees, net worth, pension assets and more. Updated quarterly. 1 year subscription $1,995, available for both Windows and Macintosh. If the price is prohibitively high, remember your local library. National Register Publishing, Reed Elsevier-New Providence, 121 Chanlon Road, New Providence, NJ 07974, (800) 521-8110, fax (800) 836-7736, web site www.redbooks.com or www.marquiswhoswho.com. "If, for any reason whatsoever, your order does not fully meet your expectations, simply return the product within 30 days for a prompt, complete, unquestioned refund," as stated in Catalog of Biographical and Professional References of publisher Marquis Who's Who/National Register Publishing.

EUROMARKETS ISSUERS DIRECTORY. For more information contact Larry Meranus Professional Publications & Services, 4 Demoray Court, Pine Brook, NJ 07058, (800) MERANUS or (800) 637-2687. Distributed in England by EUROMONEY Books, Plymbridge Distributors Limited, Estover, Plymouth PL6 7PZ, England. Phone 44 (0) 171 779-8955. Fax 44 (0) 171 779-8541.

EUROMONEY BANK REGISTER is a detailed directory of the world's leading financial institutions and a comprehensive guide to "who's who" in global capital markets. This directory lists senior executives, investment and commercial bankers, traders, analysts, support and legal staff. Expanded coverage of Asia, central Europe and eastern Europe and Latin America is provided. Available in print or CD ROM. The print version of The EUROMONEY Bank Register is comprehensively indexed alphabetically and by city. It also contains rankings of the top banks. The read only version of the CD ROM provides full access to the entire database. However, by disabling the print and export functions, the result is a lower cost alternative to the full version. A 14 day free trial is available with the CD ROM.

> Print Directory, USA, US $493 or 297 pounds sterling
> Print Directory, UK, Europe, Rest of World US $493 or 297 pounds sterling
> Read Only Version CD ROM US $1,250 or 750 pounds sterling
> Full Version CD ROM US $3,000 or 1,750 pounds sterling

Ordering information: Larry Meranus Professional Publications & Services, 4 Demoray Court, Pine Brook, NJ 07058, (800) MERANUS or (800) 637-2687. Distributed in England by EUROMONEY Books, Plymbridge Distributors Limited, Estover, Plymouth PL6 7PZ, England. Phone 44 (0) 171 779-8955 for a free demo disk. Fax 44 (0) 171 779-8541.

GUIDE TO GLOBAL M&A. For more information contact Larry Meranus Professional Publications & Services, 4 Demoray Court, Pine Brook, NJ 07058, (800) MERANUS or (800) 637-2687. Distributed in England by EUROMONEY Books, Plymbridge Distributors Limited, Estover, Plymouth PL6 7PZ, England. Phone 44 (0) 171 779-8955. Fax 44 (0) 171 779-8541.

JAPAN FINANCIAL DIRECTORY NEW YORK is published by Nikkin America, Inc., 445 Fifth Avenue, Suite 27D, New York, NY 10016, (212) 679-0196. $195 hard copy. It can also be purchased at Asahiya, the

Japanese bookstore at the corner of Vanderbilt and 45th Street, near Grand Central Station in Manhattan. Check other major cities for an Asahiya book store near you.

Financial Services

See Banking, Finance, Insurance, Investment Management, Pension Funds, Real Estate, Thrifts, Venture Capital

CANADIAN SOURCEBOOK provides listings of libraries, resource centers, associations, societies, labour unions and media outlets, plus names and addresses of government officials, industry associations, financial institutions and social and cultural societies. $197. Special discounts available for combined purchases. Southam Information Products Ltd, 1450 Don Mills Road, Don Mills, Ontario M3B 2X7 CANADA, (800) 668-2374, (416) 445-6641, (416) 442-2122, web site www.southam.com.

CORPORATE FINANCE SOURCEBOOK—THE GUIDE TO MAJOR INVESTMENT SOURCES AND RELATED FINANCIAL SERVICES contains over 13,000 names of executives at 3,700 organizations that, broadly speaking, supply growth capital to businesses, such as venture capital lenders, private lenders, commercial finance and factoring, pension managers, master trusts. Names of key management are included. A special section details public offerings of the past 3 years and mergers and acquisitions over $100 million. $499.95 hard copy, excluding discounts. NRP's catalog states, "If you're dissatisfied for any reason, simply return the product within 30 days for a full refund." If the price is prohibitively high, remember your local library. Available in book, online, magnetic tape, and in mailing list formats. For more information contact: National Register Publishing, 121 Chanlon Road, New Providence, NJ 07974 USA, (800) 521-8110, http://www.lexis-nexis.com. For information about online access, call LEXIS®—NEXIS® Online Services, Mountainview, CA at (800) 346-9759; for mailing lists call Cahners Direct Marketing Services at (800) 323-4958; all other inquiries (800) 521-8110.

FINANCIAL SERVICES CANADA, formerly titled GUIDE TO THE CANADIAN FINANCIAL SERVICES **INDUSTRY**, is now published by Micromedia Ltd., 20 Victoria Street, Toronto, ON. $249 Canadian print, $349 Canadian for CD ROM, $399 Canadian for both. For information about their demand document center CANCORP, contact (800) 387-2689, (416) 362-5211, email info@micromedia.on.ca, web site www.micromedia.on.ca.

INSTITUTIONAL INVESTOR publishes excellent surveys of various Wall Street industries. Generally one survey appears in each monthly issue, including names of contacts. Annual subscription $325. INSTITUTIONAL INVESTOR, 488 Madison Avenue, New York, NY 10022, (212) 303-3300.

JAPAN FINANCIAL DIRECTORY NEW YORK is published by Nikkin America, Inc., 445 Fifth Avenue, Suite 27D, New York, NY 10016, (212) 679-0196. $195 hard copy. It can also be purchased at Asahiya, the Japanese bookstore at the corner of Vanderbilt and 45th Street, near Grand Central Station in Manhattan. Check other major cities for an Asahiya book store near you.

Finland

See Scandinavia, International, Europe

Food

ADVERTISER AND AGENCY RED BOOKS PLUS CD ROM combines all the information in THE STANDARD DIRECTORY OF ADVERTISERS, THE STANDARD DIRECTORY OF ADVERTISING AGENCIES and THE STANDARD DIRECTORY OF INTERNATIONAL ADVERTISERS AND AGENCIES. Information is searchable by 25 fields, including company name, personal name, job title/function, product type, product/account name, city, state, zip or country, area code, revenues, number of employees, outside ad agency and even type of computer hardware. Contains professional association information. Available for Windows and Macintosh. Updated quarterly. 1 year subscription $1,295. If the price is prohibitively high, remember your local library. National Register Publishing, Reed Elsevier-New Providence, 121 Chanlon Road, New Providence, NJ 07974, (800) 521-8110, fax (800) 836-7736, web site www.redbooks.com or www.marquiswhoswho.com. "If, for any reason whatsoever, your order does not fully meet your expectations, simply return the product within 30 days for a prompt, complete, unquestioned refund," as stated in Catalog of Biographical and Professional References of publisher Marquis Who's Who/National Register Publishing.

DUN & BRADSTREET AND GALE INDUSTRY REFERENCE HANDBOOKS offer a line of industry-specific sourcebooks which include key companies in the industry, ranked lists of companies, professional associations, trade shows and conferences, mergers and acquisitions, consultants who service those industries, information sources, and more. 6 volume set $495. Also available individually for $99: Pharmaceuticals, Health and Medical Services, Computers and Software, Banking and Finance, Telecommunications, Agriculture and Food, Insurance, Construction, Entertainment, Hospitality. First edition available December, 1999. Gale Group, P.O. Box 9187, Farmington Hills, MI 48333-9187. Toll free US and Canada (800) 877-GALE (4253) and (248) 699-GALE, fax (800) 414-5043 and (248) 699-8061, Internet orders galeord@galegroup.com, web site www.galegroup.com or www.gale.com. All Gale Group products are available on approval. Contact Gale for details.

MAJOR FOOD & DRINK COMPANIES OF EUROPE provides information on 2,100 major companies in food and beverages (alcoholic and non-alcoholic) in Western Europe. $450. US distributor: Larry Meranus Professional Publications & Services, 4 Demoray Court, Pine Brook, NJ 07058, (800) MERANUS or (800) 637-2687. Published by Graham & Whiteside Ltd., Tuition House, 5-6 Francis Grove, London SW19 4DT, England. Web site http://www.major-co-data.com. Email sales@major-co-data.com.

MAJOR FOOD & DRINK COMPANIES OF THE WORLD provides information on nearly 6,000 major food and drink companies in the world. $830 or 460 pounds sterling. US distributor: Larry Meranus Professional Publications & Services, 4 Demoray Court, Pine Brook, NJ 07058, (800) MERANUS or (800) 637-2687. Published by Graham & Whiteside Ltd., Tuition House, 5-6 Francis Grove, London SW19 4DT, England. Web site http://www.major-co-data.com. Email sales@major-co-data.com.

STANDARD DIRECTORY OF ADVERTISERS Business Classifications Edition is an excellent general directory that organizes companies by a wide range of product categories. A few examples include "Apparel 2—Men's and Boys' Wear," "Heating and Air Conditioning," "Cosmetics and Toiletries," and "Aviation and Aerospace." This directory lists names and titles of key officers, revenues and other information. It is available in a geographic edition for the same price. This directory is comprised of over 24,000 companies that annually spend over $200,000 on advertising. It represents a reasonable place to look for hard-to-find information about privately held companies, especially those that heavily advertise their products. It is a good place to look for names if STANDARD AND POORS and the MILLION DOLLAR DIRECTORY fail to yield the names you need. Finally, the Classified Edition of THE STANDARD DIRECTORY OF ADVERTISERS can be a very convenient source of research because both your target list of companies and the corresponding names and titles of management all appear together, in the same Classification. This is important if you still rely on research books in hard copy. THE STANDARD DIRECTORY OF ADVERTISERS also publishes a special volume called THE STANDARD DIRECTORY OF ADVERTISERS TRADENAME INDEX. You can use the TRADENAME INDEX if you know the brand name of a product and need to find the company that manufactures it. In addition, this directory contains an Associations section which identifies marketing oriented associations.

$599 hard copy. If the price is prohibitively high, remember your local library. THE STANDARD DIRECTORY OF ADVERTISERS is also available on CD ROM under the title ADVERTISER AND AGENCY RED BOOKS PLUS. It is available in Windows® and Macintosh® formats. National Register Publishing, Reed Elsevier-New Providence, 121 Chanlon Road, New Providence, NJ 07974, (800) 521-8110, fax (800) 836-7736, web site www.redbooks.com or www.marquiswhoswho.com. "If, for any reason whatsoever, your order does not fully meet your expectations, simply return the product within 30 days for a prompt, complete, unquestioned refund," as stated in Catalog of Biographical and Professional References of publisher Marquis Who's Who/National Register Publishing.

WORLD FOOD MARKETING DIRECTORY. $990. Published by Euromonitor (England). Distributed by Gale Group, P.O. Box 9187, Farmington Hills, MI 48333-9187. Toll free US and Canada (800) 877-GALE (4253) and (248) 699-GALE, fax (800) 414-5043 and (248) 699-8061, Internet orders galeord@galegroup.com, web site www.galegroup.com or www.gale.com. All Gale Group products are available on approval. Contact Gale for details.

Foodservice

DIRECTORY OF FOODSERVICE DISTRIBUTORS lists U.S. and Canadian companies with at least $500,000 in sales to foodservice, food equipment, supply and full-line distributors. Each offers more than one product line and no more than 95% of its food distribution sales volume comes from self-manufactured merchandise. Key personnel and major buying/marketing groups, trade associations and a trade show calendar are also included. $290. Chain Store Guide Information Services, 3922 Coconut Palm Drive, Tampa, FL 33619. (800) 927-9292, (813) 664-6800, (813) 627-6822, (800) 289-6822. http://www.d-net.com/csgis or http://www.csgis.com

Foundations

See Corporate Giving

AMERICA'S NEW FOUNDATIONS identifies nearly 3,000 private, corporate and community foundations created since 1988. Includes officers and directors and other information, including newly established foundations. $191. Gale Group, P.O. Box 9187, Farmington Hills, MI 48333-9187. Toll free US and Canada (800) 877-GALE (4253) and (248) 699-GALE, fax (800) 414-5043 and (248) 699-8061, Internet orders galeord@galegroup.com, web site www.galegroup.com or www.gale.com. All Gale Group products are available on approval. Contact Gale for details.

DIRECTORY OF CORPORATE AND FOUNDATION GIVERS identifies 4,500 private foundations and 3,500 corporate giving programs, 1,500 corporate foundations and 2,000 corporate direct givers. Includes biographical data and nine indexes. The largest listing of corporate giving data available. $260 for 2 volume set. Gale Group, P.O. Box 9187, Farmington Hills, MI 48333-9187. Toll free US and Canada (800) 877-GALE (4253) and (248) 699-GALE, fax (800) 414-5043 and (248) 699-8061, Internet orders galeord@galegroup.com, web site www.galegroup.com or www.gale.com. All Gale Group products are available on approval. Contact Gale for details.

FC FAX is the Foundation Center's free fax-on-demand service, available 24 hours a day. You can request a complete menu of Foundation center documents which will be forwarded to the fax number of your choice. FC FAX: (212) 807-2577. For more information contact The Foundation Center, 79 Fifth Avenue, New York, NY 10003-3076, (212) 620-4230, (212) 807-3690. Web site www.fdncenter.org.

FC SEARCH is the Foundation Center's Database on CD ROM. It includes information in THE FOUNDATION DIRECTORY (PARTS 1, 2 AND SUPPLEMENT), GUIDE TO US FOUNDATIONS: THEIR TRUSTEES, OFFICERS AND DONORS, NATIONAL DIRECTORY OF CORPORATE GIVING, THE FOUNDATION GRANTS INDEX and THE FOUNDATION GRANTS INDEX QUARTERLY. Information can be searched from 21 search fields, including Trustees, Officers and Donors. FC SEARCH also offers the capability of linking to web sites of over 400 grantmakers. For more information contact The Foundation Center, 79 Fifth Avenue, New York, NY 10003-3076, (212) 620-4230, (212) 807-3690. Web site www.fdncenter.org.

FOUNDATION 1000 provides names and affiliations, and other information, of the 1,000 wealthiest foundations in the USA. $295, Order Code F10006. Ordering information: The Foundation Center, 79 Fifth Avenue, New York, NY 10003-3076, (212) 620-4230, (212) 807-3690, web site www.fdncenter.org.

FOUNDATION CENTER maintains two databases on DIALOG, one with information about grantmakers, the other on the grants they distribute. For more information about the Foundation Center's databases on DIALOG (Files 26 and 27), contact DIALOG at (800) 334-2564. For more information about these databases, call the Foundation Center's DIALOG Support Staff in New York at (212) 807-3690.

FOUNDATION CENTER provides library services and disseminates current information on foundation and corporate giving through their national collections in New York City and Washington, DC, through field offices in Atlanta, Cleveland and San Francisco, and through their network of over 200 libraries in all 50 states and abroad. With these resources, grant seekers have free access to core Center publications and a wide range of books, periodicals and research in connection with foundations and philanthropy. Services include reference librarian assistance, free orientations, and microform and photocopying facilities. For more information call or visit the National Collections in New York (212) 620-4230 or Washington, DC (202) 331-

1400. Or contact Field Offices in San Francisco (415) 397-0902, Cleveland (216) 861-1934, or Atlanta (404) 880-0094. The Foundation Center, 79 Fifth Avenue, New York, NY 10003-3076. Web site http://www.fdncenter.org includes their catalog of publications.

FOUNDATION CENTER publishes a number of specialized directories, such as GUIDE TO US FOUNDATIONS, NATIONAL DIRECTORY OF CORPORATE GIVING, CORPORATE FOUNDATION PROFILES, NATIONAL DIRECTORY OF GRANTMAKING PUBLIC CHARITIES, WHO GETS GRANTS—FOUNDATION GRANTS TO NONPROFIT ORGANIZATIONS, NATIONAL GUIDE TO FUNDING FOR THE ENVIRONMENT AND ANIMAL WELFARE, NATIONAL GUIDE TO FUNDING IN RELIGION, NATIONAL GUIDE TO FUNDING FOR WOMEN AND GIRLS, NATIONAL GUIDE TO FUNDING FOR INFORMATION TECHNOLOGY, NATIONAL GUIDE TO FUNDING FOR LIBRARIES AND INFORMATION SERVICES, THE FOUNDATION CENTER'S GUIDE TO GRANTSEEKING ON THE WEB, NEW YORK STATE FOUNDATIONS, DIRECTORY OF MISSOURI GRANTMAKERS, GUIDE TO GREATER WASHINGTON D.C. GRANTMAKERS, NATIONAL GUIDE TO FUNDING FOR ELEMENTARY AND SECONDARY EDUCATION, NATIONAL GUIDE TO FUNDING FOR COMMUNITY DEVELOPMENT, NATIONAL GUIDE TO FUNDING IN HIGHER EDUCATION, EDUCATION GRANT GUIDE, NATIONAL GUIDE TO FUNDING IN ARTS AND CULTURE, GUIDE TO FUNDING FOR INTERNATIONAL AND FOREIGN PROGRAMS, INTERNATIONAL GRANTMAKING: A REPORT ON US FOUNDATION TRENDS, NATIONAL GUIDE TO FUNDING IN SUBSTANCE ABUSE, AIDS FUNDING—A GUIDE TO GIVING BY FOUNDATIONS AND CHARITABLE ORGANI-ZATIONS, NATIONAL GUIDE TO FUNDING IN HEALTH, NATIONAL GUIDE TO FUNDING FOR CHILDREN, YOUTH AND FAMILIES, THE FOUNDATION GRANTS INDEX and more. Most of these directories cost under $100. For more information contact The Foundation Center, 79 Fifth Avenue, New York, NY 10003-3076, (212) 620-4230, (212) 807-3690. Web site www.fdncenter.org includes catalog of publications.

FOUNDATION REPORTER provides information on grants made by the top 1,000 private foundations in the US. It includes biographical data on foundations officers and directors. $400. Gale Group, P.O. Box 9187, Farmington Hills, MI 48333-9187. Toll free US and Canada (800) 877-GALE (4253) and (248) 699-GALE, fax (800) 414-5043 and (248) 699-8061, Internet orders galeord@galegroup.com, web site www.galegroup.com or www.gale.com. All Gale Group products are available on approval. Contact Gale for details.

GRANTS ON DISC provides information that pinpoints funders of over 300,000 grants. Windows version, $695 building price annual subscription. Gale Group, P.O. Box 9187, Farmington Hills, MI 48333-9187. Toll free US and Canada (800) 877-GALE (4253) and (248) 699-GALE, fax (800) 414-5043 and (248) 699-8061, Internet orders galeord@galegroup.com, web site www.galegroup.com or www.gale.com. All Gale Group products are available on approval. Contact Gale for details.

INTERNATIONAL FOUNDATION DIRECTORY includes national foundations located in 50 countries. Includes institutions which either operate internationally or offer fellowships or similar awards to applicants from outside its own country, or operate within its own national territory on a scale large enough to establish its international importance. $210. Published by Europa Publications. Distributed by Gale Group, P.O. Box 9187, Farmington Hills, MI 48333-9187. Toll free US and Canada (800) 877-GALE (4253) and (248) 699-GALE, fax (800) 414-5043 and (248) 699-8061, Internet orders galeord@galegroup.com, web site www.galegroup.com or www.gale.com. All Gale Group products are available on approval. Contact Gale for details.

MONEY MARKET DIRECTORY OF TAX-EXEMPT ORGANIZATIONS provides information on private foundations, hospitals and other health service organizations, church related service groups, schools, associations, civic leagues and fraternal beneficiary organizations. Names are provided for over 6,000 senior investment officers, 3000 secondary investment officers, 4,800 presidents and principals, over 4,000 Chairmen, 12,500 trustees and board officers, 600 in house managers, 900 benefits managers, 900 chief human resources officers, 700 chief operating officers and 300 directors of development. $440. Published by STANDARD AND POORS, a division of McGraw-Hill, MONEY MARKET DIRECTORIES, INC., 320 East Main Street, Charlottesville, VA 22902, http://www.mmdaccess.com, (800) 446-2810, (804) 977-1450.

PHILANTHROPY NEWS DIGEST (PND), the Foundation Center's award winning weekly online journal, is available free. To subscribe, go the web site http://www.fdncenter.org/phil/philmain.html. Enter your email address and click on the "Add me!" button. If you do not have web access, you can still receive free weekly issues of PND by email. To subscribe, send an email to listserv@lists.fdncenter.org with the words SUBSCRIBE PND-1 <YOUR NAME> in the body of the message. For more information contact The Foundation Center, 79 Fifth Avenue, New York, NY 10003-3076, (212) 620-4230, (212) 807-3690. Web site www.fdncenter.org.

NATIONAL DIRECTORY OF CORPORATE PUBLIC AFFAIRS identifies some 14,000 people who manage public affairs and government affairs programs of nearly 2,000 corporations. This directory also includes Washington area offices, corporate foundation/giving programs, federal and state lobbyists and outside contract lobbyists. Indexed by subject and geography. $95. Columbia Books, Inc., 1212 New York Avenue, NW, Suite 330, Washington, DC 20005, (212) 898-0662.

WORLD GUIDE TO FOUNDATIONS edited by Michael Zils identifies over 20,000 foundations, key personnel, publications and more in 112 countries. $225. R.R. Bowker (a unit of Cahners Business Information), 121 Chanlon Road, New Providence, NJ 07974 USA, Phone (888) BOWKER2 (888-269-5372) & (800) 323-3288, fax (908) 508-7696, email info@bowker.com, web www.bowker.com. Canada—R.R. Bowker, Markham, Ontario, phone (888) BOWKER9 & (905) 415-5837, fax (905) 479-6266. German speaking Europe—K.G. Saur Verlag, Munich, Germany, phone 49-89-76902-232, fax 49-89-76902-250, email 100730.1341@compuserve.com, web www.saur.de/home.htm. Rest of Europe incl. United Kingdom plus Africa & Asia—Bowker-Saur, W. Sussex, UK, phone 44-1342-326-972, fax 44-1342-335-612, email customer@bowker-saur.co.uk, web www.bowker-saur.com/service/. Australia/New Zealand—Thorpe, Port Melbourne, Victoria, Australia, phone 61-03-9-245-7370, fax 61-03-9-245-7395, email customer.service@thorpe.com.au, web www.thorpe.com.au. Technical support for CD ROMs (800) 323-3288, fax 908) 665-3528, email techsupport@bowker.com.

www.fdncenter.org is the web site to the Foundation Center. This site provides grant makers, grant seekers, researchers, policy makers and the general public with 24 hour access to information about the philanthropic community. This site provides links to over 280 foundations, a catalog of their publications you can order online, seminars you can register for, a proposal writing course, an online library with librarians who will respond to your email questions within 48 hours, online orientations to the grant seeking process (both for individuals and for nonprofit organizations), a review of the latest funding trends, the location of the nearest Cooperating Collection where you can use the Foundation Center's publications and CD ROM, and more. The Foundation Center, 79 Fifth Avenue, New York, NY 10003-3076, (212) 620-4230.

Fundraising

See Development and Fundraising

France

See Europe, International

DIRECTORY OF AMERICAN FIRMS OPERATING IN FOREIGN COUNTRIES, REGIONAL EDITION—FRANCE, $59. Ordering information: Uniworld Business Publications, Inc., 257 Central Park West, Suite 10A, New York, NY 10024-4110, (212) 496-2448, fax (212) 769-0413, email uniworldbp@aol.com. Web site: http://www.uniworldbp.com.

DIRECTORY OF FOREIGN FIRMS OPERATING IN THE UNITED STATES, REGIONAL EDITION—FRANCE. $39. Ordering information: Uniworld Business Publications, Inc., 257 Central Park West, Suite 10A, New York, NY 10024-4110, (212) 496-2448, fax (212) 769-0413, email uniworldbp@aol.com. Web site: http://www.uniworldbp.com.

FRANCE'S 30,000 TOP COMPANIES contains information on companies with revenue over $4 million. Text in French. Dun & Bradstreet, Business Reference Solutions, Three Sylvan Way, Parsippany, NJ 07054 USA. (800) 526-0651. Email dnbmdd@mail.dnb.com. Web site http://www.dnbmdd.com.

www.europages.com is a web site of a business directory of over 500,000 European firms. In Deutsch, English, Espanol, Français & Italiano. Features include Search for Companies, Company Catalogues,

Business Information, Yellow Pages in Europe. Search by Product/Service, Thematic Search or by Company Name. Address, phone, fax, products, turnover. Europages' Daily Business News, European Trade Fairs, Chambers of Commerce in Europe, European Patent Offices, Official International Organisations, European Standardization Bodies.

www.kompass.com is the web site for the highly respected Kompass country directories and databases. This web site contains a searchable database that encompasses over 60 countries, 2.5 million executive names, information on 1.5 million companies, 19 million key product references, and 370,000 trade and brand names. At the time of this writing, Kompass is available in English and French. Deutsch, Espanol and Italiano will soon be available.

YEARBOOK OF INTERNATIONAL ORGANIZATIONS is a 4 volume directory of non-profit organizations, commercial associations, business groups, conferences, religious orders and intergovernmental bodies. From K.G. Saur. $1,170 for 4 volumes.

YEARBOOK OF INTERNATIONAL ORGANIZATIONS PLUS is a CD ROM which was described by American Reference Books Annual as "The most comprehensive coverage of international organizations." This CD consolidates THE YEARBOOK OF INTERNATIONAL ORGANIZATIONS and WHO'S WHO IN INTERNATIONAL ORGANIZATIONS. It encompasses intergovernmental and national organizations, conferences and religious orders and fraternities. Search criteria include organization name, fields of activity, titles of publications, links to other organizations and more. User languages are English, German, French and Dutch. MS-DOS, Windows and Macintosh compatibility. From K.G. Saur. Updated annually. 1 year subscription $1,318.

R.R. Bowker (a unit of Cahners Business Information), 121 Chanlon Road, New Providence, NJ 07974 USA, Phone (888) BOWKER2 (888-269-5372) & (800) 323-3288, fax (908) 508-7696, email info@bowker.com, web www.bowker.com. Canada—R.R. Bowker, Markham, Ontario, phone (888) BOWKER9 & (905) 415-5837, fax (905) 479-6266. German speaking Europe—K.G. Saur Verlag, Munich, Germany, phone 49-89-76902-232, fax 49-89-76902-250, email 100730.1341@compuserve.com, web www.saur.de/home.htm. Rest of Europe incl. United Kingdom plus Africa & Asia—Bowker-Saur, W. Sussex, UK, phone 44-1342-326-972, fax 44-1342-335-612, email customer@bowker-saur.co.uk, web www.bowker-saur.com/service/. Australia/New Zealand—Thorpe, Port Melbourne, Victoria, Australia, phone 61-03-9-245-7370, fax 61-03-9-245-7395, email customer.service@thorpe.com.au, web www.thorpe.com.au. Technical support for CD ROMs (800) 323-3288, fax 908) 665-3528, email techsupport@bowker.com.

G

General References

See References—General. Also see Chapter 6, "How To Create An Executive Search Library"

Geographic References (USA)

See state or city in the US. Also see International, Chambers of Commerce, country name (e.g., Canada), continent (Europe, Asia, South America, Africa or Australia) or region (e.g., Latin America). Also see International for a listing of large general references that include all countries.

ADVERTISER AND AGENCY RED BOOKS PLUS CD ROM combines all the information in THE STANDARD DIRECTORY OF ADVERTISERS, THE STANDARD DIRECTORY OF ADVERTISING AGENCIES and THE STANDARD DIRECTORY OF INTERNATIONAL ADVERTISERS AND AGENCIES. Information is searchable by 25 fields, including company name, personal name, job title/function, product type, product/account name, city, state, zip or country, area code, revenues, number of employees, outside ad agency and even type of computer hardware. Contains professional association information. Available for Windows and Macintosh. Updated quarterly. 1 year subscription $1,295. If the price is prohibitively high, remember your local library. National Register Publishing, Reed Elsevier-New Providence, 121 Chanlon Road, New Providence, NJ 07974, (800) 521-8110, fax (800) 836-7736, web site www.redbooks.com or www.marquiswhoswho.com. "If, for any reason whatsoever, your order does not fully meet your expectations, simply return the product within 30 days for a prompt, complete, unquestioned refund," as stated in Catalog of Biographical and Professional References of publisher Marquis Who's Who/National Register Publishing.

AMERICAN FINANCIAL DIRECTORY CUSTOMIZED DIRECTORIES are available for any state of combination of states for banks, bank holding companies, savings and loans and major credit unions. For more information contact (800) 321-3373, Thomson Financial Publishing, 4709 West Golf Road, Skokie, IL 60076-1253. Web site @ tfp.bankinfo.com.

AMERICAN FINANCIAL DIRECTORY REGIONAL DIRECTORIES include banks, bank holding companies, savings and loan associations and major credit unions. Published twice a year.

- SOUTHERN BANKERS DIRECTORY covers Alabama, Arkansas, District of Columbia, Florida, Georgia, Kentucky, Louisiana, Maryland, Mississippi, North Carolina, South Carolina, Tennessee, Virginia and West Virginia. Published twice a year.
- GOLDEN STATES FINANCIAL DIRECTORY includes Alaska, Arizona, California, Colorado, Hawaii, Idaho, Montana, Nevada, New Mexico, Oregon, Utah, Washington, and Wyoming. Published twice a year.
- UPPER MIDWEST FINANCIAL DIRECTORY includes Michigan, Minnesota, Montana, North Dakota, South Dakota and Wisconsin. Published once a year.
- SOUTHWESTERN FINANCIAL DIRECTORY includes Arkansas, Louisiana, New Mexico, Oklahoma and Texas. Published twice a year.

For more information contact (800) 321-3373, Thomson Financial Publishing, 4709 West Golf Road, Skokie, IL 60076-1253. Web site @ tfp.bankinfo.com.

ASSOCIATIONS often have local and regional chapters. If you are conducting a search with geographic parameters, contact the appropriate associations and ask whether they have local and regional chapters. To identify suitable professional and trade associations, use the references listed in the Associations Category, such as The Encyclopedia of Associations, National Trade and Professional Associations, Business Information Sources (Lorna Daniells), or The Encyclopedia of Business Information Sources.

BUSINESS INFORMATION SOURCES by Lorna Daniells is an outstanding reference at any price. At $39.95 a copy, it's such an extraordinary value, it should have a place in every library. This is clearly one of the top three hard copy references around, and its reasonable price elevates it to first place. Business Information Sources provides a wealth of information routinely needed by search firms, job hunters and corporate recruiters, including general directories, specialized directories, professional associations, periodicals, industry information, international information, information by geographic location, and much more. $39.95. Ordering information: Business Information Sources by Lorna Daniells, is published by the University of California Press (Berkeley, CA, Los Angeles, CA & Oxford, England) (510-642-4247). Orders are handled by California Princeton Fulfillment Services, P.O. Box 10769, Newark, NJ 07193-0769. (800-822-6657).

CORPTECH DIRECTORY OF TECHNOLOGY COMPANIES is available in hard copy, Regional Guides, on PC disk, and on CD ROM. CorpTech EXPLORE Database is an outstanding reference that was awarded Best CD-ROM Directory by the National Directory Publishing Association. One click moves you from the CD ROM Database to Internet information on the same company. CorpTech also provides other sophisticated but reasonably priced automated services. You can save a tremendous amount of time researching relatively small, emerging new companies in various high technology niches and obtain names, titles and mailing address labels. CorpTech EXPLORE Database CD ROM $2,450 (including free soft cover CorpTech Directory worth $545). Ordering Information: CorpTech, Corporate Technology Information Services, Inc., 12 Alfred Street, Suite 200, Woburn, MA 01801-1915. (800) 333-8036, (781) 932-3100, (781) 932-3939. Fax (781) 932-6335. Email sales@corptech.com. Web site http://www.corptech.com.

D&B INDUSTRIAL GUIDE—THE METAL WORKING DIRECTORY contains information about 75,000 original equipment manufacturers, metalworking plants, metal distributors, machine tools/metalworking machinery distributors for locations with at least 20 people. Listings include plant name, key executives' names and titles, principal manufacturing processes, plant square footage, number of employees and more. Volumes 1 & 2 list plants geographically by state and city. Volume 3 lists companies alphabetically and by industry classification. Updated annually. For prices call Dun & Bradstreet at (800) 526-0651. For more information contact Dun & Bradstreet, Business Reference Solutions, Three Sylvan Way, Parsippany, New Jersey 07054. Email dnbmdd@mail.dnb.com. Web site http://www.dnbmdd.com.

D&B MILLION DOLLAR DATABASE is an online database on the Internet. Users can access information on more than one million small, mid-sized and large companies, with minimum revenues of $1 million. Searches can be conducted by 22 criteria, including as geographic location, sales volume, number of employees, industry classification. Each company includes up to 30 executive names and titles and biographical data that includes education, work history and birth date. For prices call Dun & Bradstreet at (800) 526-0651. For more information contact Dun & Bradstreet, Business Reference Solutions, Three Sylvan Way, Parsippany, New Jersey 07054. Email dnbmdd@mail.dnb.com. Web site http://www.dnbmdd.com.

D&B MILLION DOLLAR DIRECTORY is a hard copy 5 volume reference that contains profiles on 160,000 public and private US companies. Information is listed alphabetically, geographically and by industry classification. In order to be listed, the company must be a headquarters or single location and must satisfy one of these three requirements: 250 or more employees at that location; $revenues of at least $25 million; tangible net worth of at least $500,000. Entries include key executives' names and titles, parent company and location, sales volume, address, phone number and more. THE D&B MILLION DOLLAR DIRECTORY TOP 50,000 COMPANIES is an abridged version of the MILLION DOLLAR DIRECTORY. Both are updated annually. For prices call Dun & Bradstreet at (800) 526-0651. For more information contact Dun & Bradstreet, Business Reference Solutions, Three Sylvan Way, Parsippany, New Jersey 07054. Email dnbmdd@mail.dnb.com. Web site http://www.dnbmdd.com.

D&B MILLION DOLLAR DISC is a CD ROM which covers over 240,000 public and private companies, compared to either 160,000 or 50,000 in the two versions of the MILLION DOLLAR DIRECTORY in hard copy. In addition, this CD ROM also contains BIOGRAPHICAL information on key executives. Searches can be conducted by company name, industry, size of company, geography, executive name, key word, and executive business backgrounds. Companies listed have sales of at least $ million or more than 100 employees. Branch locations have more than 500 employees. Both are updated annually. D&B MILLION DOLLAR DISC PLUS is a similar CD ROM with more expansive coverage, including 400,000 companies—both privately held and public—compared to 240,000 in the MILLION DOLLAR DISC. It includes companies with at least 50 employees or revenues of $3 million. For prices call Dun & Bradstreet at (800) 526-0651. For more information contact Dun & Bradstreet, Business Reference Solutions, Three Sylvan Way, Parsippany, New Jersey 07054. Email dnbmdd@mail.dnb.com. Web site http://www.dnbmdd.com.

D&B REGIONAL BUSINESS DIRECTORIES are available for each of fifty-four metropolitan areas. Each three-volume set provides profiles on 20,000 companies, including hard-to-find information on privately held companies. Listings include key executives' names and titles, number of employees at location, sales volume, address, phone number, line of business, parent company, year established, and more. Each directory is cross referenced alphabetically and by industry classification. Updated annually. D&B REGIONAL BUSINESS DISK is a CD ROM which provides up to ten names and titles per company. Searches can be conducted by company name, industry, size of company, geography, executive name and key word. Unmetered and updated bi-annually. For prices call Dun & Bradstreet at (800) 526-0651. For more information contact Dun & Bradstreet, Business Reference Solutions, Three Sylvan Way, Parsippany, New Jersey 07054. Email dnbmdd@mail.dnb.com. Web site http://www.dnbmdd.com.

ENCYCLOPEDIA OF BUSINESS INFORMATION SOURCES will lead you to specialized directories, professional associations, trade publications, newsletters, databases, Internet resources and more. It's an excellent reference and a great way to find key resources in any industry fast. $330. Gale Group, P.O. Box 9187, Farmington Hills, MI 48333-9187. Toll free US and Canada (800) 877-GALE (4253) and (248) 699-GALE, fax (800) 414-5043 and (248) 699-8061, Internet orders galeord@galegroup.com, web site www.galegroup.com or www.gale.com. All Gale Group products are available on approval. Contact Gale for details.

ENCYCLOPEDIA OF ASSOCIATIONS: NATIONAL ORGANIZATIONS OF THE US. This superb reference is one of the first places you should look when beginning a new recruiting assignment or when looking for specialized references of any type. The keyword index makes this comprehensive reference easy to use, even in hard copy. For over 23,000 nonprofit professional associations with a national scope, this encyclopedia reveals:

- Publications, including membership rosters and newsletters
- Dates and locations of association conferences and conventions
- Names of Executive Directors, who are usually incredible sources of industry information if you call and speak to them
- Committees
- Job and candidate referral banks, which can provide resumes of other industry sources and sometimes candidates
- It includes organizations in these categories: business, trade, environmental, agricultural, legal, governmental, engineering, technological, scientific, educational, cultural, social welfare, health & medical, public affairs, ethnic, labor unions, chambers of commerce, tourism, & others.

> Volume 1, National Organizations of the US, $505
> Volume 2, Geographic and Executive Indexes, $390
> Volume 3, Supplement, $405

Gale Group, P.O. Box 9187, Farmington Hills, MI 48333-9187. Toll free US and Canada (800) 877-GALE (4253) and (248) 699-GALE, fax (800) 414-5043 and (248) 699-8061, Internet orders galeord@galegroup.com, web site www.galegroup.com or www.gale.com. All Gale Group products are available on approval. Contact Gale for details.

ENCYCLOPEDIA OF ASSOCIATIONS: REGIONAL, STATE AND LOCAL ORGANIZATIONS. The information in this directory is not duplicated anywhere in ENCYCLOPEDIA OF ASSOCIATIONS. Over 100,000 nonprofit organizations are included in this directory. $585 for 5 volume set or $140 per individual volume. Also available on CD ROM and online on the Internet through a GaleNet subscription.

> Volume 1, Great Lakes States (Illinois, Indiana, Michigan, Minnesota, Ohio, Wisconsin)
> Volume 2, Northeastern States (Connecticut, Maine, Massachusetts, New Hampshire, New Jersey, New York, Pennsylvania, Rhode Islands, Vermont)
> Volume 3, Southern and Middle Atlantic States (Including Puerto Rico and the Virgin Islands) (Alabama, Delaware, Washington, DC, Florida, Georgia, Kentucky, Maryland, Mississippi, North Carolina, Puerto Rico, South Carolina, Tennessee, Virginia, West Virginia, Virgin Islands)
> Volume 4, South Central and Great Plains States (Arkansas, Iowa, Kansas, Louisiana, Missouri, Nebraska, North Dakota, Oklahoma, South Dakota, Texas)
> Volume 5, Western States (Alaska, Arizona, California, Colorado, Guam, Hawaii, Idaho, Montana, Nevada, New Mexico, Oregon, Utah, Washington, Wyoming)

Gale Group, P.O. Box 9187, Farmington Hills, MI 48333-9187. Toll free US and Canada (800) 877-GALE (4253) and (248) 699-GALE, fax (800) 414-5043 and (248) 699-8061, Internet orders galeord@galegroup.com, web site www.galegroup.com or www.gale.com. All Gale Group products are available on approval. Contact Gale for details.

MANUFACTURERS DIRECTORIES and CD ROM'S distributed by Manufacturers' News, Inc. are available for every state of the union plus the metropolitan New York area. They are published by Manufacturers' News, Database Publishing, Commerce Register, Pick Publications. Directory prices generally range between $50 and $165, depending on the size of the directory. Close out prices on old directories are also available. Virtually all directories are published annually. CD ROMs are available with "complete" information, or for 10 or more employees, 20 or more employees, 50 or more employees, or 100 or more employees. CD prices range between $100 for information on plants with over 100 employees for a small state, up to $745 for a complete disk for a large state. Includes names and titles of key executives, plant square footage, number of employees, product, SIC, distribution area. "EZ Select" CD ROMs are another CD ROM option. It allows you to search by 11 fields, including company size, type of industry, and geographic criteria, job function and title. EZ Select CD ROMs cost between approximately $175-$400, depending on the size of the database. EZ Select Disks are also available. For more information contact Manufacturers' News,

Inc., (888) 752-5200, 1633 Central Street, Evanston, IL 60201-1569. Email info@manufacturersnews.com. Web site www.manufacturersnews.com.

STANDARD AND POORS REGISTER OF CORPORATIONS, DIRECTORS AND EXECUTIVES.
Volume 1, Corporations, contains complete listings for 75,000 companies (including large subsidiaries), specifically names, titles, phone numbers, number of employees, annual sales, main products, and SIC/NAICS codes. Volume 2, Directors and Executives alphabetically lists 70,000 key managers with biographical data. Volume 3, Corporate Family Index is useful for locating a company's parent, subsidiaries, divisions and affiliates; also contains an index of companies by state and major cities. Published annually. Hardback directory, $799. Available in CD ROM. Call for price. Published by Standard & Poors Corporation, New York, New York. Distributed by: Larry Meranus Professional Publications & Services, 4 Demoray Court, Pine Brook, NJ 07058, (800) MERANUS or (800) 637-2687.

STANDARD DIRECTORY OF ADVERTISERS is available in a Geographic Edition and a Business Classifications Edition. In both editions it lists names and titles of key officers, revenues and other information. This directory is comprised of over 24,000 companies that annually spend over $200,000 on advertising. It represents a reasonable place to look for hard-to-find information about privately held companies, especially those that heavily advertise their products. It is a good place to look for names if STANDARD AND POORS and the MILLION DOLLAR DIRECTORY fail to yield the names you need. THE STANDARD DIRECTORY OF ADVERTISERS also publishes a special volume called THE STANDARD DIRECTORY OF ADVERTISERS TRADENAME INDEX. You can use the TRADENAME INDEX if you know the brand name of a product and need to find the company that manufactures it. In addition, this directory contains an Associations section which identifies marketing oriented associations.

$629.95 hard copy, excluding discounts. NRP's catalog states, "If you're dissatisfied for any reason, simply return the product within 30 days for a full refund." If the price is prohibitively high, remember your local library.

Available in book, CD ROM, online, magnetic tape, and in mailing list formats. For more information contact: National Register Publishing, 121 Chanlon Road, New Providence, NJ 07974 USA, (800) 521-8110, (908) 464-6800, http://www.lexis-nexis.com. For information about online access, call LEXIS®—NEXIS® Online Services, Mountainview, CA at (800) 346-9759; for mailing lists call Cahners Direct Marketing Services at (800) 323-4958; all other inquiries (800) 521-8110 or web site http://www.reedref.com.

STATE AND REGIONAL ASSOCIATIONS OF THE UNITED STATES identifies over 7,000 state and regional associations in the US. Information is cross referenced by subject, state, budget and chief executive and includes publications, convention schedule, membership/ staff size and budget. $79. Columbia Books, Inc., 1212 New York Avenue, NW, Suite 330, Washington, DC 20005, (212) 898-0662.

STATE MANUFACTURING DIRECTORIES and US regional geographic directories published by Harris are available for all US states as hard copy directories or in electronic Selectory® formats. With Selectory® information is searchable from 25 fields and generates an easy-to-read report containing: company, address, location, county, phone, fax, toll free number, Internet address, a listing of personnel with titles, SIC/NAICS codes, product description, products, number of employees, per cent employment change, sales range, plant size, foreign trade, year established, private or public ownership, and experian credit score. This information could either provide an alternative to "identification research" calls, or offer an excellent place to begin the verification calls of ID research. If time is money, you can access a tremendous amount of precise information quickly with electronic references, such as this one or many others. One attractive feature of Harris's products is that they are relatively inexpensive. Here are a few sample prices: Directories and databases are available for all US states: Alabama $79 directory, $349 database. Arizona $90 directory, $475 database. Arkansas $69 directory, $325 database, Ohio $159 directory, $725 database. New Jersey $99 directory, $595 database. The most expensive is California, $169 directory, $925 database. The least expensive are Delaware and Washington, DC each one at $39 for directory, $149 for database.

Contact Harris for a sample Harris Profile Report. For exact pricing, a catalog and other information, call distributor Scott's Directories, Toronto area: 1450 Don Mills Road, Don Mills, Ontario, M3B 2X7, CANADA, (888) 709-9907, (416) 442-2291, (416) 932-9555. Montréal area: Scott's Directories, 3300 Cote Verde, Suite 410 Ville St.-Laurent, Quebec H4B 2B7 CANADA (514) 339-1397, (800) 363-1327, email scotts@southam.ca. Publisher Harris InfoSource, 2057 East Aurora Road, Twinsburg, OH 44087-1999, (330) 425-9000, (800) 888-5900, www.HarrisInfo.com.

U.S. MANUFACTURERS DATABASE™ ON CD ROM is a comprehensive database that profiles 340,000 manufacturing establishments and contains names and titles of 600,000 CEO's, owners and key executives (This averages to less than 2 names for each of the 340 manufacturing establishments.) This CD ROM can print mailing labels and company profiles. Information can be searched by 24 different fields, including zip code, and 5,500 product categories. National edition (100 or more employees) $1,795. Regional editions (100 or more employees) for the Midwest, South Central and Southeast, $695 each. Northeast regional edition (100 or more employees) $695. West regional edition (100 or more employees) $429. State directories are also available for western states. For more information and a catalog, contact Database Publishing Company, PO Box 70024, Anaheim, CA 92825, (800) 888-8434, (714) 778-6400, email sales@databasepublishing.com.

WARD'S BUSINESS DIRECTORY OF U.S. PRIVATE AND PUBLIC COMPANIES provides information on over 120,000 US companies, over 90% of them privately held. Volumes 1-3 contain company information. Volume 4 lists companies geographically and ranks the top 1,000 privately held companies and the top 1,000 employers. Volume 5 ranks private and public companies by sales within SIC or NAICS code. Volumes 6-7 contain state rankings by sales within SIC or NAICS. Also includes ranking of the top 100 privately held companies, the top publicly held companies and the top 100 employers for each state. Volume 8 ranks sales within the 6 digit NAICS (North American Industry Classification System which replaced the SIC code system). It sorts companies by cross-national agreements between the US, Canada and Mexico. Vols. 1-8, $2,515. Vols. 1-5, $2,125. Vols. 1-4, $1,880. Vol 5, $950. Vols. 6-7, $950. Vol 8, $640. Gale Group, P.O. Box 9187, Farmington Hills, MI 48333-9187. Toll free US and Canada (800) 877-GALE (4253) and (248) 699-GALE, fax (800) 414-5043 and (248) 699-8061, Internet orders galeord@galegroup.com, web site www.galegroup.com or www.gale.com. All Gale Group products are available on approval. Contact Gale for details.

WHO'S WHO IN THE EAST, $289.95. National Register Publishing, Reed Elsevier-New Providence, 121 Chanlon Road, New Providence, NJ 07974, (800) 521-8110, fax (800) 836-7736, web site www.marquiswhoswho.com or www.redbooks.com. "If, for any reason whatsoever, your order does not fully meet your expectations, simply return the product within 30 days for a prompt, complete, unquestioned refund," as stated in Catalog of Biographical and Professional References of publisher Marquis Who's Who/National Register Publishing.

WHO'S WHO IN THE MIDWEST, $269.95. National Register Publishing, Reed Elsevier-New Providence, 121 Chanlon Road, New Providence, NJ 07974, (800) 521-8110, fax (800) 836-7736, web site www.marquiswhoswho.com or www.redbooks.com. "If, for any reason whatsoever, your order does not fully meet your expectations, simply return the product within 30 days for a prompt, complete, unquestioned refund," as stated in Catalog of Biographical and Professional References of publisher Marquis Who's Who/National Register Publishing.

WHO'S WHO IN THE SOUTH AND SOUTHWEST, $259.95. National Register Publishing, Reed Elsevier-New Providence, 121 Chanlon Road, New Providence, NJ 07974, (800) 521-8110, fax (800) 836-7736, web site www.marquiswhoswho.com or www.redbooks.com. "If, for any reason whatsoever, your order does not fully meet your expectations, simply return the product within 30 days for a prompt, complete, unquestioned refund," as stated in Catalog of Biographical and Professional References of publisher Marquis Who's Who/National Register Publishing.

WHO'S WHO IN THE WEST, $272.95. National Register Publishing, Reed Elsevier-New Providence, 121 Chanlon Road, New Providence, NJ 07974, (800) 521-8110, fax (800) 836-7736, web site www.marquiswhoswho.com or www.redbooks.com. "If, for any reason whatsoever, your order does not fully meet your expectations, simply return the product within 30 days for a prompt, complete, unquestioned refund," as stated in Catalog of Biographical and Professional References of publisher Marquis Who's Who/National Register Publishing.

www.careerpath.com was ranked as one of the top 5 "Sites Offering the Best Overall Support for Job-Seekers" by the *National Business Employment Weekly*. CareerPath.com puts the help wanted sections of over 70 US newspapers into one database. Job hunters can post their resumes free. Companies must pay a fee to access resumes. The web site claims, "Powered by the nation's leading newspapers and employers,

CareerPath.com has the Web's largest number of the most current job listings." Launched in 1995, the site was developed by a consortium of media companies—Knight-Ridder, *The New York Times*, the Time Mirror Company, the Tribune Company, the Washington Post, Cox Interactive Media, Gannett Company and Hearst Corp.

www.excite.com/careers or Excite Careers Network was ranked as one of the top 5 "Sites Offering the Best Overall Support for Job Seekers" by the *National Business Employment Weekly*. Many positions are in IT, engineering and management, often in the $50,000 to $100,000 range. The site, online since 1995, was developed by Excite Inc., the search engine, Redwood City, California.

www.townonline.com/working or Town Online Working is the web site to various community newspapers, including 13 in New England. In addition to job listings, it also has a job profile with the capability of automatically downloading to your Email. Town Online Working was ranked as one of the top 5 "Sites Offering the Best Career Resources for Job Seekers" by the *National Business Employment Weekly*. Many positions are administrative, management and blue collar, often paying in the teens up to $30,000. The site developer is the Community Newspaper Company, Needham, Massachusetts and was established in 1996.

Germany

See Europe, International

DIRECTORY OF AMERICAN FIRMS OPERATING IN FOREIGN COUNTRIES, REGIONAL EDITION—GERMANY, $59. Ordering information: Uniworld Business Publications, Inc., 257 Central Park West, Suite 10A, New York, NY 10024-4110, (212) 496-2448, fax (212) 769-0413, email uniworldbp@aol.com. Web site: http://www.uniworldbp.com.

DIRECTORY OF FOREIGN FIRMS OPERATING IN THE UNITED STATES, REGIONAL EDITION—GERMANY. $59. Ordering information: Uniworld Business Publications, Inc., 257 Central Park West, Suite 10A, New York, NY 10024-4110, (212) 496-2448, fax (212) 769-0413, email uniworldbp@aol.com. Web site: http://www.uniworldbp.com.

GERMAN BOOKS IN PRINT—VERZEICHNIS LIEFERBARER BUCHER (VLB) contains information on all German language books, videos, audiocassettes, software and bibles from publishers in Germany, the former East Germany, Austria, Switzerland and elsewhere. From K.G. Saur. $650.

GERMAN BOOKS IN PRINT ON CD-ROM (VLB-AKTUELL), one year subscription $1,440. R.R. Bowker (a unit of Cahners Business Information), 121 Chanlon Road, New Providence, NJ 07974 USA, Phone (888) BOWKER2 (888-269-5372) & (800) 323-3288, fax (908) 508-7696, email info@bowker.com, web www.bowker.com. Canada—R.R. Bowker, Markham, Ontario, phone (888) BOWKER9 & (905) 415-5837, fax (905) 479-6266. German speaking Europe—K.G. Saur Verlag, Munich, Germany, phone 49-89-76902-232, fax 49-89-76902-250, email 100730.1341@compuserve.com, web www.saur.de/home.htm. Rest of Europe incl. United Kingdom plus Africa & Asia—Bowker-Saur, W. Sussex, UK, phone 44-1342-326-972, fax 44-1342-335-612, email customer@bowker-saur.co.uk, web www.bowker-saur.com/service/. Australia/New Zealand—Thorpe, Port Melbourne, Victoria, Australia, phone 61-03-9-245-7370, fax 61-03-9-245-7395, email customer.service@thorpe.com.au, web www.thorpe.com.au. Technical support for CD ROMs (800) 323-3288, fax 908) 665-3528, email techsupport@bowker.com.

PENSION FUNDS AND THEIR ADVISERS provides information on the top 2,000 pension funds in the United Kingdom, plus major funds of Japan, Belgium, France, Germany, Ireland, The Netherlands and Switzerland. This Directory is the only source in the US that monitors the growth of assets in the international market. Information includes internal and external fund management contacts, major US and Canadian pension funds and money managers, major European and Japanese pension funds and their advisors. It also includes comprehensive listings of 900 advisors to the pension fund industry including financial advisers, accountants, actuaries and pension fund consultants, pension administrators, insurance companies, attorneys, computer services, global custody, pension trustees, pension /financial recruitment consultants, investment research, associations and professional groups, and publications. $310. Published by A.P. Information Services, Ltd. Marketed exclusively in North America MONEY MARKET DIRECTORIES

INC./STANDARD AND POORS, 320 East Main Street, Charlottesville, VA 22902, http://www.mmdaccess.com, (800) 446-2810, (804) 977-1450.

WORLD GUIDE TO TRADE ASSOCIATIONS edited by Michael Zils includes key personnel, publications, a translation of the name in English, information that reflects the structure of Eastern Europe and the former USSR, a German-English concordance of subject areas and other data. From K.G. Saur. 2 volume set $650. R.R. Bowker (a unit of Cahners Business Information), 121 Chanlon Road, New Providence, NJ 07974 USA, Phone (888) BOWKER2 (888-269-5372) & (800) 323-3288, fax (908) 508-7696, email info@bowker.com, web www.bowker.com. Canada—R.R. Bowker, Markham, Ontario, phone (888) BOWKER9 & (905) 415-5837, fax (905) 479-6266. German speaking Europe—K.G. Saur Verlag, Munich, Germany, phone 49-89-76902-232, fax 49-89-76902-250, email 100730.1341@compuserve.com, web www.saur.de/home.htm. Rest of Europe incl. United Kingdom plus Africa & Asia—Bowker-Saur, W. Sussex, UK, phone 44-1342-326-972, fax 44-1342-335-612, email customer@bowker-saur.co.uk, web www.bowker-saur.com/service/. Australia/New Zealand—Thorpe, Port Melbourne, Victoria, Australia, phone 61-03-9-245-7370, fax 61-03-9-245-7395, email customer.service@thorpe.com.au, web www.thorpe.com.au. Technical support for CD ROMs (800) 323-3288, fax 908) 665-3528, email techsupport@bowker.com.

www.bowker.com is the web site for this major research publisher. It includes Flagship Products and Services, an online Product Catalog, Electronic Publishing products including CD ROMs, Internet Databases, and Online Subscription and Site Licensing Databases; press releases, career opportunities, and more. Many of their references are accessible through this web site, such as BOOKS IN PRINT PLUS CANADIAN EDITION, ULRICH'S ON DISC, GERMAN BOOKS IN PRINT, GERMAN BOOKS OUT OF PRINT, INTERNATIONAL BOOKS IN PRINT PLUS, ITALIAN BOOKS IN PRINT, YEARBOOK OF INTERNATIONAL ORGANIZATIONS PLUS, ULRICH'S INTERNATIONAL PERIODICALS DIRECTORY, THE SOFTWARE ENCYCLOPEDIA, BOWKER'S COMPLETE VIDEO DIRECTORY, AMERICAN BOOK PUBLISHING RECORD. Visit the web site for more information.

www.europages.com is a web site of a business directory of over 500,000 European firms. In Deutsch, English, Espanol, Français & Italiano. Features include Search for Companies, Company Catalogues, Business Information, Yellow Pages in Europe. Search by Product/Service, Thematic Search or by Company Name. Address, phone, fax, products, turnover. Europages' Daily Business News, European Trade Fairs, Chambers of Commerce in Europe, European Patent Offices, Official International Organisations, European Standardization Bodies.

www.kompass.com is the web site for the highly respected Kompass country directories and databases. This web site contains a searchable database that encompasses over 60 countries, 2.5 million executive names, information on 1.5 million companies, 19 million key product references, and 370,000 trade and brand names. At the time of this writing, Kompass is available in English and French. Deutsch, Espanol and Italiano will soon be available.

YEARBOOK OF INTERNATIONAL ORGANIZATIONS is a 4 volume directory of non-profit organizations, commercial associations, business groups, conferences, religious orders and intergovernmental bodies. From K.G. Saur. $1,170 for 4 volumes.

YEARBOOK OF INTERNATIONAL ORGANIZATIONS PLUS is a CD ROM which was described by American Reference Books Annual as "The most comprehensive coverage of international organizations." This CD consolidates THE YEARBOOK OF INTERNATIONAL ORGANIZATIONS and WHO'S WHO IN INTERNATIONAL ORGANIZATIONS. It encompasses intergovernmental and national organizations, conferences and religious orders and fraternities. Search criteria include organization name, fields of activity, titles of publications, links to other organizations and more. User languages are English, German, French and Dutch. MS-DOS, Windows and Macintosh compatibility. From K.G. Saur. Updated annually. 1 year subscription $1,318.

R.R. Bowker (a unit of Cahners Business Information), 121 Chanlon Road, New Providence, NJ 07974 USA, Phone (888) BOWKER2 (888-269-5372) & (800) 323-3288, fax (908) 508-7696, email info@bowker.com, web www.bowker.com. Canada—R.R. Bowker, Markham, Ontario, phone (888) BOWKER9 & (905) 415-5837, fax (905) 479-6266. German speaking Europe—K.G. Saur Verlag, Munich, Germany, phone 49-89-76902-232, fax 49-89-76902-250, email 100730.1341@compuserve.com, web www.saur.de/home.htm. Rest of Europe incl. United Kingdom plus Africa & Asia—Bowker-Saur, W. Sussex, UK, phone 44-1342-326-972, fax 44-1342-335-612, email customer@bowker-saur.co.uk, web www.bowker-saur.com/service/. Australia/New Zealand—Thorpe, Port Melbourne, Victoria, Australia, phone 61-03-9-245-7370, fax 61-03-9-245-7395, email customer.service@thorpe.com.au, web www.thorpe.com.au. Technical support for CD ROMs (800) 323-3288, fax 908) 665-3528, email techsupport@bowker.com.

Government

CANADIAN ALMANAC AND DIRECTORY includes abbreviations, associations and societies, broadcasting and communications, business statistics, church and religious organizations, commerce and finance, cultural directory, education directory, electoral districts, foreign and international contacts, geographic information, government directory, government quick reference, health and hospitals, historical and general information, legal and judicial directory, postal information, tourism and transportation. The Almanac also includes web sites of significant institutions in business, communications, and the arts, a "Who's Who" of key officials and organizations on the Canadian information highway and up-to-date provincial and territorial election results. Indexed by titles and keyword. $249 US. Inquire about CD ROM availability. Published by IHS Canada, Micromedia Limited, 20 Victoria Street, Toronto, Ontario M5C 2N8 CANADA, (800) 387-2689, (416) 362-5211, fax (416) 362-6161, email info@micromedia.on.ca. Distributed in the US by the Gale Group, P.O. Box 9187, Farmington Hills, MI 48333-9187. Toll free US and Canada (800) 877-GALE (4253) and (248) 699-GALE, fax (800) 414-5043 and (248) 699-8061, Internet orders galeord@galegroup.com, web site www.galegroup.com or www.gale.com. All Gale Group products are available on approval. Contact Gale for details.

CANADIAN ENVIRONMENTAL DIRECTORY identifies government departments, companies and organizations concerned with environmental issues, plus contact names, publications, activities, programs, research laboratories, universities and college environmental programs, conferences and trade shows, lawyers, journalists, book and periodical information, and more. Available in directory or CD ROM formats. For pricing and ordering information, contact:: IHS Canada, Micromedia Limited, 20 Victoria Street, Toronto, Ontario M5C 2N8 CANADA, (800) 387-2689, (416) 362-5211, fax (416) 362-6161, email info@micromedia.on.ca.

FINANCIAL SERVICES CANADA is a handbook of banks, non-depository institutions, stock exchange and brokers, investment management, mutual funds, insurance, accountants, government agencies, financial associations and more, including contact numbers, name, title, organization, phone, fax, email, web site, and cellular. $199 for book, $299 for CD ROM, $399 for both. Ordering information: Copp Clark Professional, 200 Adelaide Street West, 3rd floor, Toronto, ON M5H 1W7 CANADA. Email orders@mail.CanadaInfo.com. Web site http://www.coppclark.com. For additional information contact: IHS Canada, Micromedia Limited, 20 Victoria Street, Toronto, Ontario M5C 2N8 CANADA, (800) 387-2689, (416) 362-5211, fax (416) 362-6161, email info@micromedia.on.ca.

NATIONAL E-MAIL AND FAX DIRECTORY provides over 180,000 fax numbers for US companies, organizations and government agencies, cross referenced by subject. $126. Gale Group, P.O. Box 9187, Farmington Hills, MI 48333-9187. Toll free US and Canada (800) 877-GALE (4253) and (248) 699-GALE, fax (800) 414-5043 and (248) 699-8061, Internet orders galeord@galegroup.com, web site www.galegroup.com or www.gale.com. All Gale Group products are available on approval. Contact Gale for details.

SCOTT'S DIRECTORY OF CANADIAN MUNICIPALITIES is a new directory that contains information on municipalities, cities, towns and villages, including addresses, phone numbers, web sites and email addresses, and names and titles of senior administrative staff. Directory $99, Canadian Municipalities Select $149.For more information contact Scott's Directories, Toronto area: 1450 Don Mills Road, Don Mills, Ontario, M3B 2X7, CANADA, (416) 442-2291, (416) 932-9555, (888) 709-9907. Montréal area: Scott's Directories, 3300 Cote Verde, Suite 410 Ville St.-Laurent, Quebec H4B 2B7 CANADA (514) 339-1397, (800) 363-1327. Publisher's email scotts@southam.ca.

SCOTT'S GOVERNMENT INDEX DIRECTORY identifies key officials in the federal and provincial departments, agencies, boards, commissions and Crown corporations in Canada. Listings include name, title, address, phone number, fax, email. Updated quarterly. $197 in print. For more information contact Scott's Directories, Toronto area: 1450 Don Mills Road, Don Mills, Ontario, M3B 2X7, CANADA, (416) 442-2291,

(416) 932-9555, (888) 709-9907. Montréal area: Scott's Directories, 3300 Cote Verde, Suite 410 Ville St.-Laurent, Quebec H4B 2B7 CANADA (514) 339-1397, (800) 363-1327. Publisher's email scotts@southam.ca. For information about an $497 electronic version updated four times a year, contact Southam Information Products Ltd, 1450 Don Mills Road, Don Mills, Ontario M3B 2X7 CANADA, (800) 668-2374. In Toronto 442-2122. Web site www.southam.com.

SUBJECT DIRECTORY OF SPECIAL LIBRARIES presents the alphabetically organized contents of the DIRECTORY OF SPECIAL LIBRARIES AND INFORMATION CENTERS. It consists of 3 subject volumes and is organized by subject.

> Volume 1, Business, Government and Law Libraries
> Volume 2, Computers, Engineering and Science Libraries
> Volume 3, Health Science Libraries

$875 for 3 volume set. Available individually at $340 per volume. Gale Group, P.O. Box 9187, Farmington Hills, MI 48333-9187. Toll free US and Canada (800) 877-GALE (4253) and (248) 699-GALE, fax (800) 414-5043 and (248) 699-8061, Internet orders galeord@galegroup.com, web site www.galegroup.com or www.gale.com. All Gale Group products are available on approval. Contact Gale for details.

WORLDWIDE GOVERNMENT DIRECTORY identifies top level foreign government offices and officials in 196 countries. It includes state agencies and state-owned corporations and defines hierarchical arrangements of state structures. $368. Published by Keesing's Worldwide and distributed by the Gale Group, P.O. Box 9187, Farmington Hills, MI 48333-9187. Toll free US and Canada (800) 877-GALE (4253) and (248) 699-GALE, fax (800) 414-5043 and (248) 699-8061, Internet orders galeord@galegroup.com, web site www.galegroup.com or www.gale.com. All Gale Group products are available on approval. Contact Gale for details.

www.jobsingovernment.com contains job postings for positions in government, education and the public sector. Many positions are in city administration, engineering and public safety, often in the $30,000 to $50,000 range. Jobs In Government has been online since 1996.

Government Contractors

CBDISK is available a free sample PC disk. It contains information about government contract and subcontract opportunities in all product and service areas. It is updated every week. Available from Government Data Publications, Inc., 1155 Connecticut Avenue, NW, Washington, DC 20077-6106.

GOVERNMENT CONTRACTS DIRECTORY contains government contract listings for a fiscal year, organized by product category, then broken down alphabetically. Each listing includes name and address of contractor, agency, description of material, quantity, contract number and amount. Published annually. $89.50 Ordering Information: Government Data Publications, Inc., 1155 Connecticut Avenue, NW, Washington, DC 20077-6106.

NATIONAL DIRECTORY OF MINORITY OWNED BUSINESS FIRMS includes government contracting experience and other information. $275. Published by Business Research Services. Distributed by Gale Group, P.O. Box 9187, Farmington Hills, MI 48333-9187. Toll free US and Canada (800) 877-GALE (4253) and (248) 699-GALE, fax (800) 414-5043 and (248) 699-8061, Internet orders galeord@galegroup.com, web site www.galegroup.com or www.gale.com. All Gale Group products are available on approval. Contact Gale for details.

NATIONAL DIRECTORY OF WOMAN-OWNED BUSINESS FIRMS includes government contracting experience and other information. $275.Gale Group, P.O. Box 9187, Farmington Hills, MI 48333-9187. Toll free US and Canada (800) 877-GALE (4253) and (248) 699-GALE, fax (800) 414-5043 and (248) 699-8061, Internet orders galeord@galegroup.com, web site www.galegroup.com or www.gale.com. All Gale Group products are available on approval. Contact Gale for details.

R&D CONTRACTS MONTHLY is the monthly counterpart of the annual UNIQUE THREE-IN-ONE RESEARCH AND DEVELOPMENT DIRECTORY. $49.50 on CD ROM. Ordering Information: Government Data Publications, Inc., 1155 Connecticut Avenue, NW, Washington, DC 20077-6106.

UNIQUE THREE-IN-ONE RESEARCH AND DEVELOPMENT DIRECTORY, details research and development government contracts awarded over the prior 12 months. Each listing includes awardee, address, agency, description of work, amount of contract, and more. Directory I contains alphabetical information by awardee. Directory II contains geographical information by awarding agency. Directory III is organized by the nature of the research. It identifies the latest developments in materials, techniques and processes in every field of industrial and scientific endeavor, programs whose production contracts are likely to expire, areas where advanced research is being conducted, and the names of organizations specializing in specific technical areas. Published annually since 1959. $49.50 ON CD ROM. Ordering Information: Government Data Publications, Inc., 1155 Connecticut Avenue, NW, Washington, DC 20077-6106.

Government—Federal

ENCYCLOPEDIA OF GOVERNMENTAL ADVISORY ORGANIZATIONS identifies the activities and personnel of groups and committees that advise the President of the United States and various departments and bureaus. $605. Gale Group, P.O. Box 9187, Farmington Hills, MI 48333-9187. Toll free US and Canada (800) 877-GALE (4253) and (248) 699-GALE, fax (800) 414-5043 and (248) 699-8061, Internet orders galeord@galegroup.com, web site www.galegroup.com or www.gale.com. All Gale Group products are available on approval. Contact Gale for details.

GOVERNMENT RESEARCH DIRECTORY identifies over 4,300 research labs and programs of the U.S. and Canadian federal governments. $510. Gale Group, P.O. Box 9187, Farmington Hills, MI 48333-9187. Toll free US and Canada (800) 877-GALE (4253) and (248) 699-GALE, fax (800) 414-5043 and (248) 699-8061, Internet orders galeord@galegroup.com, web site www.galegroup.com or www.gale.com. All Gale Group products are available on approval. Contact Gale for details.

www.fedjobs.com provides assistance to people seeking a position with the federal government, including in the Judiciary and Congressional branches, and the United Nations. Many positions are in computers, engineering and medical, with salaries often in the $30,000 to $50,000 range. The site was developed by Federal Research Service, Inc., Vienna, Virginia and was launched in 1996.

www.hrsjobs.com is the URL for HRS Federal Job Search, a site that emails notifications about announced federal vacancies that match subscribers' requirements. Many positions are computer-related, clerical and professional, often in the $30,000 to $50,000 range. The site was developed by HRS Automated Solutions, Vienna, Virginia and was launched in 1997.

www.iccweb.com is the web site for Internet Career Connection, an employment matching service with a special section for US Federal Government employment. Internet Career Connection was developed by Gonyea & Associates, Inc., New Port Richey, Florida and launched in 1995. Features include Help Wanted-USA, the Worldwide Resume Bank and Government JOBS Central. Many positions include engineering, computer technology and business. While candidates do pay a fee to post their resumes, employers can view resumes free.

www.sec.gov/edgarhp.htm is the URL to the EDGAR Database of corporate information from the Securities & Exchange Commission, a database of corporate information. Features include: About the SEC, Investor Assistance & Complaints, EDGAR Database, SEC Digest & Statements, Current SEC Rulemaking, Enforcement Division, Small Business Information, Other sites to visit.

Government Organizations

See International Associations, Lobbyists

ASSOCIATIONS UNLIMITED ONLINE is available on the Internet through GaleNet. You can subscribe to any of the several databases comprising ASSOCIATIONS UNLIMITED, including:

• NATIONAL ORGANIZATIONS OF THE US DATABASE

• REGIONAL, STATE AND LOCAL ORGANIZATIONS DATABASE

• INTERNATIONAL ORGANIZATIONS DATABASE

- ASSOCIATIONS MATERIALS DATABASE

- GOVERNMENT NONPROFIT ORGANIZATIONS DATABASE

For more information on available databases and pricing, contact Gale Group, P.O. Box 9187, Farmington Hills, MI 48333-9187. Toll free US and Canada (800) 877-GALE (4253) and (248) 699-GALE, fax (800) 414-5043 and (248) 699-8061, Internet orders galeord@galegroup.com, web site www.galegroup.com or www.gale.com. All Gale Group products are available on approval. Contact Gale for details.

CANADIAN SOURCEBOOK provides listings of libraries, resource centers, associations, societies, labour unions and media outlets, plus names and addresses of government officials, industry associations, financial institutions and social and cultural societies. $197. Special discounts available for combined purchases. Southam Information Products Ltd, 1450 Don Mills Road, Don Mills, Ontario M3B 2X7 CANADA, (800) 668-2374, (416) 445-6641, (416) 442-2122, web site www.southam.com.

ENCYCLOPEDIA OF ASSOCIATIONS: INTERNATIONAL ORGANIZATIONS includes nearly 20,000 multinational and national organizations in foreign countries, including US based associations with multinational membership. Entries also include email addresses, web sites and bulletin board addresses, lobbying activities, and publication and convention information. Indexed by geography, keyword and executives. $595 for 2 volume set. Also available in CD ROM. Database available via commercial online service. Gale Group, P.O. Box 9187, Farmington Hills, MI 48333-9187. Toll free US and Canada (800) 877-GALE (4253) and (248) 699-GALE, fax (800) 414-5043 and (248) 699-8061, Internet orders galeord@galegroup.com, web site www.galegroup.com or www.gale.com. All Gale Group products are available on approval. Contact Gale for details.

ENCYCLOPEDIA OF ASSOCIATIONS: NATIONAL ORGANIZATIONS OF THE US. This superb reference is one of the first places you should look when beginning a new recruiting assignment or when looking for specialized references of any type. The keyword index makes this comprehensive reference easy to use, even in hard copy. For over 23,000 nonprofit professional associations with a national scope, this encyclopedia reveals:

- Publications, including membership rosters and newsletters

- Dates and locations of association conferences and conventions

- Names of Executive Directors, who are usually incredible sources of industry information if you call and speak to them

- Committees

- Job and candidate referral banks, which can provide resumes of other industry sources and sometimes candidates

- It includes organizations in these categories: business, trade, environmental, agricultural, legal, governmental, engineering, technological, scientific, educational, cultural, social welfare, health & medical, public affairs, ethnic, labor unions, chambers of commerce, tourism, & others.

  Volume 1, National Organizations of the US, $505
  Volume 2, Geographic and Executive Indexes, $390
  Volume 3, Supplement, $405

Gale Group, P.O. Box 9187, Farmington Hills, MI 48333-9187. Toll free US and Canada (800) 877-GALE (4253) and (248) 699-GALE, fax (800) 414-5043 and (248) 699-8061, Internet orders galeord@galegroup.com, web site www.galegroup.com or www.gale.com. All Gale Group products are available on approval. Contact Gale for details.

ENCYCLOPEDIA OF ASSOCIATIONS: REGIONAL, STATE AND LOCAL ORGANIZATIONS. The information in this directory is not duplicated anywhere in ENCYCLOPEDIA OF ASSOCIATIONS. Over 100,000 nonprofit organizations are included in this directory. $585 for 5 volume set or $140 per individual volume. Also available on CD ROM and online on the Internet through a GaleNet subscription.

  Volume 1, Great Lakes States (Illinois, Indiana, Michigan, Minnesota, Ohio, Wisconsin)

Volume 2, Northeastern States (Connecticut, Maine, Massachusetts, New Hampshire, New Jersey, New York, Pennsylvania, Rhode Islands, Vermont)

Volume 3, Southern and Middle Atlantic States (Including Puerto Rico and the Virgin Islands) (Alabama, Delaware, Washington, DC, Florida, Georgia, Kentucky, Maryland, Mississippi, North Carolina, Puerto Rico, South Carolina, Tennessee, Virginia, West Virginia, Virgin Islands)

Volume 4, South Central and Great Plains States (Arkansas, Iowa, Kansas, Louisiana, Missouri, Nebraska, North Dakota, Oklahoma, South Dakota, Texas)

Volume 5, Western States (Alaska, Arizona, California, Colorado, Guam, Hawaii, Idaho, Montana, Nevada, New Mexico, Oregon, Utah, Washington, Wyoming)

Gale Group, P.O. Box 9187, Farmington Hills, MI 48333-9187. Toll free US and Canada (800) 877-GALE (4253) and (248) 699-GALE, fax (800) 414-5043 and (248) 699-8061, Internet orders galeord@galegroup.com, web site www.galegroup.com or www.gale.com. All Gale Group products are available on approval. Contact Gale for details.

GOVERNMENTS CANADA is published by Micromedia Ltd., 20 Victoria Street, Toronto, ON. For information about pricing, or their demand document center CANCORP, contact (800) 387-2689, (416) 362-5211, email info@micromedia.on.ca, web site www.micromedia.on.ca.

WASHINGTON identifies 4,500 organizations and institutions in Washington DC and 22,000 key people in them. Includes government, business, education, medicine/health, community affairs, art/culture and others. $85. Columbia Books, Inc., 1212 New York Avenue, NW, Suite 330, Washington, DC 20005, (212) 898-0662.

YEARBOOK OF INTERNATIONAL ORGANIZATIONS is a 4 volume directory of non-profit organizations, commercial associations, business groups, conferences, religious orders and intergovernmental bodies. From K.G. Saur. $1,170 for 4 volumes.

YEARBOOK OF INTERNATIONAL ORGANIZATIONS PLUS is a CD ROM which was described by American Reference Books Annual as "The most comprehensive coverage of international organizations." This CD consolidates THE YEARBOOK OF INTERNATIONAL ORGANIZATIONS and WHO'S WHO IN INTERNATIONAL ORGANIZATIONS. It encompasses intergovernmental and national organizations, conferences and religious orders and fraternities. Search criteria include organization name, fields of activity, titles of publications, links to other organizations and more. User languages are English, German, French and Dutch. MS-DOS, Windows and Macintosh compatibility. From K.G. Saur. Updated annually. 1 year subscription $1,318.

R.R. Bowker (a unit of Cahners Business Information), 121 Chanlon Road, New Providence, NJ 07974 USA, Phone (888) BOWKER2 (888-269-5372) & (800) 323-3288, fax (908) 508-7696, email info@bowker.com, web www.bowker.com. Canada—R.R. Bowker, Markham, Ontario, phone (888) BOWKER9 & (905) 415-5837, fax (905) 479-6266. German speaking Europe—K.G. Saur Verlag, Munich, Germany, phone 49-89-76902-232, fax 49-89-76902-250, email 100730.1341@compuserve.com, web www.saur.de/home.htm. Rest of Europe incl. United Kingdom plus Africa & Asia—Bowker-Saur, W. Sussex, UK, phone 44-1342-326-972, fax 44-1342-335-612, email customer@bowker-saur.co.uk, web www.bowker-saur.com/service/. Australia/New Zealand—Thorpe, Port Melbourne, Victoria, Australia, phone 61-03-9-245-7370, fax 61-03-9-245-7395, email customer.service@thorpe.com.au, web www.thorpe.com.au. Technical support for CD ROMs (800) 323-3288, fax 908) 665-3528, email techsupport@bowker.com.

Grocery

CANADIAN GROCER is a trade publication which produces CANADIAN GROCER WHO'S WHO. Published by Maclean Hunter in Toronto. For more information call them in Toronto at (416) 596-5000. Web site www.mhbizlink.com.

DIRECTORY OF SUPERMARKET, GROCERY AND CONVENIENCE STORE CHAINS describes and indexes over 2,300 supermarket chains with $2 million in annual sales. It covers supermarkets, superstores, club stores, gourmet supermarkets and combo stores in the U.S. and Canada, plus a special section profiling 1,700 convenience store chains. It includes an index to the top 200 supermarket chains and the top 100 convenience store chains, which is a valuable tool for target list development. It also lists over 29,000 key executives, buyers and administrative personnel. The directory also lists major trade associations and a trade show calendar. $300. Chain Store Guide Information Services, 3922 Coconut Palm Drive, Tampa, FL 33619. (800) 927-9292, (813) 664-6800, (813) 627-6822, (800) 289-6822. http://www.d-net.com/csgis or http://www.csgis.com.

DIRECTORY OF WHOLESALE GROCERY lists wholesale grocers' headquarters, divisions and branches, both in the US and Canada. All companies listed are required to sell a multi-line of products to the supermarket, convenience store, discount and drug industries. It includes names and titles of personnel, a listing of major trade associations and a trade show calendar. It also provides an index to the top 100 wholesale grocers, which is a valuable tool for target list development. $300. Chain Store Guide Information Services, 3922 Coconut Palm Drive, Tampa, FL 33619. (800) 927-9292, (813) 664-6800, (813) 627-6822, (800) 289-6822. http://www.d-net.com/csgis or http://www.csgis.com.

SUPERMARKET BUSINESS is a monthly trade magazine provides information about key trade events, trends, and research findings. Supermarket Business Week is a weekly news fax with highlights of the week's key developments in the supermarket business. Call (201) 833-1900 for subscription information. Remember to find out if there are any back issues with the specific information you need—or an annual index. Ordering information: Chain Store Guide Information Services, 3922 Coconut Palm Drive, Tampa, FL 33619. (800) 927-9292, (813) 664-6800, (813) 627-6822, (800) 289-6822. http://www.d-net.com/csgis or http://www.csgis.com.

SUPERMARKET, GROCERY AND CONVENIENCE STORE CHAINS CD-ROM can conduct data searches from five topic screens: 1. Personnel by title, 2. Personnel by functional area, 3. Listing type (branch office, corporate office, divisional office, headquarters, location, managed care div, regional office, subsidiary, warehouse), 4. Stores operated (superstores, supermarkets, convenience, warehouse, combo stores, gourmet supermarkets, stores w/gas), 5. Specialty departments (e.g., auto supplies, automatic teller machines, beer, books/magazines, floral/horticulture,gourmet/specialty foods, greeting cards, in-store bakeries, in-store banking, in-store restaurant, lawn & garden, liquor, nutrition center, et al.). You can also make selections based on geography or the size of a company (number of units and/or sales). Several output options are available, including mailing labels, and electronic formats (such as DBASE, ASCII, text) for mail merge customization. $795, including companion directory. If the price is prohibitively high, remember your local library. Chain Store Guide Information Services, 3922 Coconut Palm Drive, Tampa, FL 33619. (800) 927-9292, (813) 664-6800, (813) 627-6822, (800) 289-6822. http://www.d-net.com/csgis or http://www.csgis.com.

Guam

See Pacific, International

DIRECTORY OF AMERICAN FIRMS OPERATING IN FOREIGN COUNTRIES, REGIONAL EDITION—AUSTRALIA GROUP. Includes Australia, New Zealand, Fiji French Polynesia, Guam, New Caledonia, New Guinea, North Mariana Island, Palau, Papua, Polynesia. Ordering information: Uniworld Business Publications, Inc., 257 Central Park West, Suite 10A, New York, NY 10024-4110, (212) 496-2448, fax (212) 769-0413, email uniworldbp@aol.com. Web site: http://www.uniworldbp.com.

ENCYCLOPEDIA OF ASSOCIATIONS: REGIONAL, STATE AND LOCAL ORGANIZATIONS. The information in this directory is not duplicated anywhere in ENCYCLOPEDIA OF ASSOCIATIONS. Over 100,000 nonprofit organizations are included in this directory. $585 for 5 volume set or $140 per individual volume. Also available on CD ROM and online on the Internet through a GaleNet subscription.

Volume 1, Great Lakes States (Illinois, Indiana, Michigan, Minnesota, Ohio, Wisconsin)

Volume 2, Northeastern States (Connecticut, Maine, Massachusetts, New Hampshire, New Jersey, New York, Pennsylvania, Rhode Islands, Vermont)

Volume 3, Southern and Middle Atlantic States (Including Puerto Rico and the Virgin Islands) (Alabama, Delaware, Washington, DC, Florida, Georgia, Kentucky, Maryland, Mississippi, North Carolina, Puerto Rico, South Carolina, Tennessee, Virginia, West Virginia, Virgin Islands)

Volume 4, South Central and Great Plains States (Arkansas, Iowa, Kansas, Louisiana, Missouri, Nebraska, North Dakota, Oklahoma, South Dakota, Texas)

Volume 5, Western States (Alaska, Arizona, California, Colorado, Guam, Hawaii, Idaho, Montana, Nevada, New Mexico, Oregon, Utah, Washington, Wyoming)

Gale Group, P.O. Box 9187, Farmington Hills, MI 48333-9187. Toll free US and Canada (800) 877-GALE (4253) and (248) 699-GALE, fax (800) 414-5043 and (248) 699-8061, Internet orders galeord@galegroup.com, web site www.galegroup.com or www.gale.com. All Gale Group products are available on approval. Contact Gale for details.

H

Hawaii

See Pacific

HAWAII INDUSTRIAL DIRECTORY contains information on 800 companies. $39 directory, $115 database. Database Publishing Company, PO Box 70024, Anaheim, CA 92825, (800) 888-8434, (714) 778-6400, email sales@databasepublishing.com.

Health and Beauty Aids

See Toiletries

Health Care

See Health Care Consulting, Health Care—Hospitals and Medical Centers, Nursing, Medical, Physicians

DUN & BRADSTREET AND GALE INDUSTRY REFERENCE HANDBOOKS offer a line of industry-specific sourcebooks which include key companies in the industry, ranked lists of companies, professional associations, trade shows and conferences, mergers and acquisitions, consultants who service those industries, information sources, and more. 6 volume set $495. Also available individually for $99: Pharmaceuticals, Health and Medical Services, Computers and Software, Banking and Finance, Telecommunications, Agriculture and Food, Insurance, Construction, Entertainment, Hospitality. First edition available December, 1999. Gale Group, P.O. Box 9187, Farmington Hills, MI 48333-9187. Toll free US and Canada (800) 877-GALE (4253) and (248) 699-GALE, fax (800) 414-5043 and (248) 699-8061, internet orders galeord@galegroup.com, web site www.galegroup.com or www.gale.com. All Gale Group products are available on approval. Contact Gale for details.

CANADIAN ALMANAC AND DIRECTORY includes abbreviations, associations and societies, broadcasting and communications, business statistics, church and religious organizations, commerce and finance, cultural directory, education directory, electoral districts, foreign and international contacts, geographic information, government directory, government quick reference, health and hospitals, historical and general information, legal and judicial directory, postal information, tourism and transportation. The Almanac also includes web sites of significant institutions in business, communications, and the arts, a "Who's Who" of key officials and organizations on the Canadian information highway and up-to-date provincial and territorial election results. Indexed by titles and keyword. $249 US. Inquire about CD ROM availability. Published by IHS Canada, Micromedia Limited, 20 Victoria Street, Toronto, Ontario M5C 2N8 CANADA, (800) 387-2689, (416) 362-5211, fax (416) 362-6161, email info@micromedia.on.ca. Distributed in the US by the Gale Group, P.O. Box 9187, Farmington Hills, MI 48333-9187. Toll free US and Canada (800) 877-GALE (4253) and (248) 699-GALE, fax (800) 414-5043 and (248) 699-8061, internet orders galeord@galegroup.com, web site www.galegroup.com or www.gale.com. All Gale Group products are available on approval. Contact Gale for details.

COMPLETE MARQUIS WHO'S WHO ON CD ROM is a compilation of literally all 19 Marquis Who's Who that have appeared in print since 1985, including living and deceased people. WHO'S WHO IN AMERICA®, WHO'S WHO IN THE WORLD®, WHO'S WHO IN AMERICAN EDUCATIONS®, WHO'S WHO IN AMERICAN LAW®, WHO'S WHO IN AMERICAN NURSING®, WHO'S WHO IN MEDICINE

AND HEALTHCARE®, WHO'S WHO IN FINANCE AND INDUSTRY®, WHO'S WHO IN SCIENCE AND ENGINEERING®, WHO'S WHO IN THE EAST®, WHO'S WHO IN THE MIDWEST®, WHO'S WHO IN THE SOUTH AND SOUTHWEST®, WHO'S WHO IN THE WEST®, WHO'S WHO OF AMERICAN WOMEN®, WHO'S WHO IN ADVERTISING®, WHO'S WHO OF EMERGING LEADERS IN AMERICA®, WHO'S WHO IN ENTERTAINMENT®, WHO'S WHO AMONG HUMAN SERVICES **PROFESSIONALS®.** One year subscription with semi-annual updates $995. National Register Publishing, Reed Elsevier-New Providence, 121 Chanlon Road, New Providence, NJ 07974, (800) 521-8110, fax (800) 836-7736, web site www.marquiswhoswho.com or www.redbooks.com. "If, for any reason whatsoever, your order does not fully meet your expectations, simply return the product within 30 days for a prompt, complete, unquestioned refund," as stated in Catalog of Biographical and Professional References of publisher Marquis Who's Who/National Register Publishing.

D&B DIRECTORY OF SERVICE COMPANIES is a directory with information on 50,000 US service businesses, including privately held companies, in these sectors: accounting, auditing and bookkeeping, advertising and public relations, architecture and engineering, consumer services, executive search, health, hospitality, management consulting, motion pictures, repair, research, social services and law. Listings include key executives' names and titles, address, phone, sales volume, number of employees, parent company and location, and more. Companies listed employ 50 or more people. Information is listed alphabetically and is cross-referenced geographically and by industry classification. Updated annually. For prices call Dun & Bradstreet at (800) 526-0651. For more information contact Dun & Bradstreet, Business Reference Solutions, Three Sylvan Way, Parsippany, New Jersey 07054. Email dnbmdd@mail.dnb.com. Web site http://www.dnbmdd.com.

ENCYCLOPEDIA OF ASSOCIATIONS: INTERNATIONAL ORGANIZATIONS includes nearly 20,000 multinational and national organizations in foreign countries, including US based associations with multinational membership. Entries also include email addresses, web sites and bulletin board addresses, lobbying activities, and publication and convention information. Indexed by geography, keyword and executives. $595 for 2 volume set. Also available in CD ROM. Database available via commercial online service. Gale Group, P.O. Box 9187, Farmington Hills, MI 48333-9187. Toll free US and Canada (800) 877-GALE (4253) and (248) 699-GALE, fax (800) 414-5043 and (248) 699-8061, internet orders galeord@galegroup.com, web site www.galegroup.com or www.gale.com. All Gale Group products are available on approval. Contact Gale for details.

ENCYCLOPEDIA OF ASSOCIATIONS: NATIONAL ORGANIZATIONS OF THE US. This superb reference is one of the first places you should look when beginning a new recruiting assignment or when looking for specialized references of any type. The keyword index makes this comprehensive reference easy to use, even in hard copy. For over 23,000 nonprofit professional associations with a national scope, this encyclopedia reveals:

• Publications, including membership rosters and newsletters

• Dates and locations of association conferences and conventions

• Names of Executive Directors, who are usually incredible sources of industry information if you call and speak to them

• Committees

• Job and candidate referral banks, which can provide resumes of other industry sources and sometimes candidates

• It includes organizations in these categories: business, trade, environmental, agricultural, legal, governmental, engineering, technological, scientific, educational, cultural, social welfare, health & medical, public affairs, ethnic, labor unions, chambers of commerce, tourism, & others.

Volume 1, National Organizations of the US, $505
Volume 2, Geographic and Executive Indexes, $390
Volume 3, Supplement, $405

Gale Group, P.O. Box 9187, Farmington Hills, MI 48333-9187. Toll free US and Canada (800) 877-GALE (4253) and (248) 699-GALE, fax (800) 414-5043 and (248) 699-8061, internet orders

galeord@galegroup.com, web site www.galegroup.com or www.gale.com. All Gale Group products are available on approval. Contact Gale for details.

ENCYCLOPEDIA OF ASSOCIATIONS: REGIONAL, STATE AND LOCAL ORGANIZATIONS. The information in this directory is not duplicated anywhere in ENCYCLOPEDIA OF ASSOCIATIONS. Over 100,000 nonprofit organizations are included in this directory. $585 for 5 volume set or $140 per individual volume. Also available on CD ROM and online on the internet through a GaleNet subscription.

Volume 1, Great Lakes States (Illinois, Indiana, Michigan, Minnesota, Ohio, Wisconsin)

Volume 2, Northeastern States (Connecticut, Maine, Massachusetts, New Hampshire, New Jersey, New York, Pennsylvania, Rhode Islands, Vermont)

Volume 3, Southern and Middle Atlantic States (Including Puerto Rico and the Virgin Islands) (Alabama, Delaware, Washington, DC, Florida, Georgia, Kentucky, Maryland, Mississippi, North Carolina, Puerto Rico, South Carolina, Tennessee, Virginia, West Virginia, Virgin Islands)

Volume 4, South Central and Great Plains States (Arkansas, Iowa, Kansas, Louisiana, Missouri, Nebraska, North Dakota, Oklahoma, South Dakota, Texas)

Volume 5, Western States (Alaska, Arizona, California, Colorado, Guam, Hawaii, Idaho, Montana, Nevada, New Mexico, Oregon, Utah, Washington, Wyoming)

Gale Group, P.O. Box 9187, Farmington Hills, MI 48333-9187. Toll free US and Canada (800) 877-GALE (4253) and (248) 699-GALE, fax (800) 414-5043 and (248) 699-8061, internet orders galeord@galegroup.com, web site www.galegroup.com or www.gale.com. All Gale Group products are available on approval. Contact Gale for details.

ENCYCLOPEDIA OF MEDICAL ORGANIZATIONS AND AGENCIES identifies public and private agencies concerned with medical information, funding, research, education, planning, advocacy, advice and service. Entries provide contact and descriptive information, including name and keyword indexes and subject cross-index. $249. Gale Group, P.O. Box 9187, Farmington Hills, MI 48333-9187. Toll free US and Canada (800) 877-GALE (4253) and (248) 699-GALE, fax (800) 414-5043 and (248) 699-8061, internet orders galeord@galegroup.com, web site www.galegroup.com or www.gale.com. All Gale Group products are available on approval. Contact Gale for details.

HEALTHCARE NEWS NET, whose URL is http://cpsnet.com, is web site which includes a daily online news service from CPS COMMUNICATIONS, Publisher of the Pharmaceutical Marketers Directory. News is presented in eight areas: Headline news, Industry News, Product News, Media News, People On The Move, Agency Assignments, New Companies and Locations, and Information & Resources. Another part of CPSNET is JobMart, a confidential Internet career advertising service which costs $180 to list a 90 word ad for 90 days. http://cpsnet.com. For more information contact CPS COMMUNICATIONS, INC., 7200 West Camino Real, Suite 215, Boca Raton, FL 33433, (561) 368-9301, sales office (203) 778-1463, email webmaster@cpsnet.com, web site http://www.cpsnet.com.

HEALTH CARE SERVICES DIRECTORY provides information on over 65,000 US providers of health and rehabilitation services in 50 different categories. Includes homecare, rehab, eldercare, addiction, hospice, mental health, AIDS and more. Available in regional editions and a national edition. For pricing and more information, contact Database Publishing Company, PO Box 70024, Anaheim, CA 92825, (800) 888-8434, (714) 778-6400, email sales@databasepublishing.com.

MEDICAL AND HEALTH INFORMATION DIRECTORY identifies organizations, agencies, institutions, services and information sources in medicine and health related fields. It includes approximately 20,000 organizations, 11,000 libraries, publications and electronic resources and 27,000 health service providers. Volume 1, Organizations, Agencies and Institutions. Volume 2, Publications, Libraries and Other Information Resources. Volume 3 Health Services. 3 volume set $590. $245 per volume. Gale Group, P.O. Box 9187, Farmington Hills, MI 48333-9187. Toll free US and Canada (800) 877-GALE (4253) and (248) 699-GALE, fax (800) 414-5043 and (248) 699-8061, internet orders galeord@galegroup.com, web site www.galegroup.com or www.gale.com. All Gale Group products are available on approval. Contact Gale for details.

MEDICAL MARKETING & MEDIA (MM&M) is a trade publication available in hard copy or online. "People on the Move" provides career announcements and sometimes photos. Career & Salary Surveys are also available. www.cpsnet.com. For more information contact CPS COMMUNICATIONS, INC., 7200 West Camino Real, Suite 215, Boca Raton, FL 33433, (561) 368-9301, sales office (203) 778-1463, email webmaster@cpsnet.com, web site http://www.cpsnet.com.

MODERN HEALTHCARE is a weekly trade publication. Crain Communications, Inc. is headquartered in Chicago with offices in major cities throughout the US plus London, Tokyo and Frankfurt. New York location: 220 East 42nd Street, New York, NY 10017, (212) 210-0100, Circulation (800) 678-9595. Annual subscription $125, two years $200. Web site www.modernhealthcare.com.

PHARMACEUTICAL MARKETERS DIRECTORY is a well organized directory that contains many names and titles and other information, including a listing of specialized professional associations. Published annually. $162.50. CPS COMMUNICATIONS, INC., 7200 West Camino Real, Suite 215, Boca Raton, FL 33433, (561) 368-9301, sales office (203) 778-1463, email pmd@cpsnet.com, web site http://www.cpsnet.com.

WHO'S WHO IN MEDICINE AND HEALTHCARE, $249.95. National Register Publishing, Reed Elsevier-New Providence, 121 Chanlon Road, New Providence, NJ 07974, (800) 521-8110, fax (800) 836-7736, web site www.marquiswhoswho.com or www.redbooks.com. "If, for any reason whatsoever, your order does not fully meet your expectations, simply return the product within 30 days for a prompt, complete, unquestioned refund," as stated in Catalog of Biographical and Professional References of publisher Marquis Who's Who/National Register Publishing.

www.abbott.com/career/index.htm is the Career pages web site for Abbott Laboratories. Check other company web sites for career opportunities at the company of your choice.

www.careermosaic.com is the URL for a major recruitment web site that spends millions of dollars in advertising to draw traffic to this site. CareerMosaic features a jobs database; newsgroups for jobs, college connection, online job fairs, employer job postings; company information and more. CareerMosaic was ranked as one of the top 5 "Sites Offering the Best Overall Support for Job Seekers" by the *National Business Employment Weekly.* The site was developed Bernard Hodes Advertising in New York and went online in 1994.

www.medhunters.com is a healthcare jobhunting site developed by Helen Ziegler and Associates, Inc., Toronto, Canada. Worldwide positions are posted for doctors, nurses and therapists, encompassing a broad range of salaries. The site has been online since 1997.

www.monster.com is the URL for the popular Monster Board web site. The Monster Board was ranked as one of the top 5 "Best General-Purpose Sites" by the *National Business Employment Weekly.* It is a major recruitment web site that spends millions of dollars in advertising to attract traffic to this site. Features include Job search in the US, International or by Companies, Career Center Events, Recruiters' Center, Seminars, Post a Job, free online recruitment seminar. It also offers special links for human resources, health care, technology and entry level positions. Toll free phone number (800) MONSTER. The Monster Board, PO Box 586, Framingham, MA 01704-0586. The site developer is TMP Worldwide, New York, New York and has been online since 1994.

Health Care Consulting

DIRECTORY OF MANAGEMENT CONSULTANTS provides accurate information on over 1,300 management consulting firms, specialties, key principals, revenues, fees, geographic information, professional associations, and advice on selecting consultants. $106.95. Kennedy Information, One Kennedy Place, Route 12 South, Fitzwilliam, NH 03447, phone (800) 531-0007 or 603-585-6544, fax 603-585-9555, email bookstore@kennedyinfo.com, web site www.kennedyinfo.com.

Health Care—Hospitals and Medical Centers

BEST HOSPITALS IN AMERICA describes nearly 400 top rated medical facilities in the USA. Written from the patient's point of view, it includes a history of each institution, highly rated services, special programs and facilities, well-known specialists, admissions policies and contact information. Best utilized for target list development or possibly a search in hospital admissions. $40. Gale Group, P.O. Box 9187, Farmington Hills, MI 48333-9187. Toll free US and Canada (800) 877-GALE (4253) and (248) 699-GALE,

fax (800) 414-5043 and (248) 699-8061, internet orders galeord@galegroup.com, web site www.galegroup.com or www.gale.com. All Gale Group products are available on approval. Contact Gale for details.

CANADIAN HEALTH FACILITIES DIRECTORY provides detailed information on Canadian hospitals, nursing homes, health clinics, university medical facilities, medical associations, government departments and more. $175. Special discounts available for combined purchases. Published by Southam Information Products Ltd, 1450 Don Mills Road, Don Mills, Ontario M3B 2X7 CANADA, (800) 668-2374. In Toronto 442-2122. Web site www.southam.com.

CRAIN NEW YORK. For a ranking of top Health Maintenance Organizations and Hospitals in New York, contact Crain New York for a copy of their Top Business Lists issue, or ask your librarian. Crain also publishes Crain Chicago, Crain Cleveland and Crain Detroit. Crain Communications, Inc. is headquartered in Chicago with offices in major cities throughout the US plus London, Tokyo and Frankfurt. New York location: 220 East 42nd Street, New York, NY 10017, (212) 210-0100, Circulation (800) 678-9595.

High Net Worth Individuals

See Wealth

Higher Education

AFRICAN AMERICANS INFORMATION DIRECTORY identifies over 5,200 organizations, publications, institutions, agencies and programs, including a new chapter on scholarships, fellowships and loans. This information on scholarships and fellowships could possibly be used to identify top candidates for college and MBA recruiting. $85. Gale Group, P.O. Box 9187, Farmington Hills, MI 48333-9187. Toll free US and Canada (800) 877-GALE (4253) and (248) 699-GALE, fax (800) 414-5043 and (248) 699-8061, internet orders galeord@galegroup.com, web site www.galegroup.com or www.gale.com. All Gale Group products are available on approval. Contact Gale for details.

BLACK AMERICAN COLLEGES AND UNIVERSITIES reviews 118 institutions that were founded primarily for African Americans and/or possess predominantly black enrollments. This reference can be used to identify target schools for campus recruiting purposes. $70. Gale Group, P.O. Box 9187, Farmington Hills, MI 48333-9187. Toll free US and Canada (800) 877-GALE (4253) and (248) 699-GALE, fax (800) 414-5043 and (248) 699-8061, internet orders galeord@galegroup.com, web site www.galegroup.com or www.gale.com. All Gale Group products are available on approval. Contact Gale for details.

COMPLETE MARQUIS WHO'S WHO ON CD ROM is a compilation of literally all 19 Marquis Who's Who that have appeared in print since 1985, including living and deceased people. WHO'S WHO IN AMERICA®, WHO'S WHO IN THE WORLD®, WHO'S WHO IN AMERICAN EDUCATIONS®, WHO'S WHO IN AMERICAN LAW®, WHO'S WHO IN AMERICAN NURSING®, WHO'S WHO IN MEDICINE AND HEALTHCARE®, WHO'S WHO IN FINANCE AND INDUSTRY®, WHO'S WHO IN SCIENCE AND ENGINEERING®, WHO'S WHO IN THE EAST®, WHO'S WHO IN THE MIDWEST®, WHO'S WHO IN THE SOUTH AND SOUTHWEST®, WHO'S WHO IN THE WEST®, WHO'S WHO OF AMERICAN WOMEN®, WHO'S WHO IN ADVERTISING®, WHO'S WHO OF EMERGING LEADERS IN AMERICA®, WHO'S WHO IN ENTERTAINMENT®, WHO'S WHO AMONG HUMAN SERVICES PROFESSIONALS®. One year subscription with semi-annual updates $995. National Register Publishing, Reed Elsevier-New Providence, 121 Chanlon Road, New Providence, NJ 07974, (800) 521-8110, fax (800) 836-7736, web site www.marquiswhoswho.com or www.redbooks.com. "If, for any reason whatsoever, your order does not fully meet your expectations, simply return the product within 30 days for a prompt, complete, unquestioned refund," as stated in Catalog of Biographical and Professional References of publisher Marquis Who's Who/National Register Publishing.

HIGHER EDUCATION DIRECTORY provides an extensive list of names and titles of administrative officers and staff at colleges and universities. It is an excellent resource for higher education searches. $55.00. Ordering information: Higher Education Publications, Inc., 6400 Arlington Blvd., Suite 648, Falls Church, VA 22042, (703) 532-2300, fax (703) 532-2305, email info@hepinc.com, web site http://www.hepinc.com.

NATIONAL FACULTY DIRECTORY provides names, departmental affiliations and institutional addresses of academic professionals, listing over 670,000 teaching faculty at 3,600 US colleges and universities and at 240 Canadian institutions that use primarily English m\teaching materials. $755. Information compiled by CMG Information Services. Distributed by Gale Group, P.O. Box 9187, Farmington Hills, MI 48333-9187. Toll free US and Canada (800) 877-GALE (4253) and (248) 699-GALE, fax (800) 414-5043 and (248) 699-8061, internet orders galeord@galegroup.com, web site www.galegroup.com or www.gale.com. All Gale Group products are available on approval. Contact Gale for details.

SCOTT'S DIRECTORY OF CANADIAN SCHOOLS contains information on over 16,000 private and public schools, school boards, colleges, universities, native schools, special needs schools, vocational schools and departments of education, plus names of key contacts, including principals, librarians and guidance counselors. Book $127, diskette $547. Special discounts available for combined purchases. Published by Southam Information Products Ltd, 1450 Don Mills Road, Don Mills, Ontario M3B 2X7 CANADA, (800) 668-2374. In Toronto 442-2122. Web site www.southam.com.

www.jobtrak.com is the web site for the Career service network for college students, alumni, college career staff and employers. JOBTRAK was ranked as one of the top 5 "Best Specialty Sites" by the *National Business Employment Weekly*. JOBTRAK has established relationships with college and university career offices, MBA programs and alumni associations. Most salaries range between $30,000 and $50,000. The site developer is JOBTRAK CORPORATION, Los Angeles, CA, (310) 474-3377, (800) 999-8725, fax (310) 475-7912. The site has been online since 1995.

www.umn.edu/apn or Academic Position Network is a web site that lists positions for faculty, professional and administrative staff, including librarians, in academia. The site was developed by Academic Position Network in Blaine, Minnesota and established in 1996.

Holland

See Netherlands

Hong Kong

See Asia, International, China

CHINA: A DIRECTORY AND SOURCEBOOK includes information on 800 of China's and Hong Kong's companies, rankings for the top 50 companies, and over 500 information sources, both national and international. $595. Published by Euromonitor (England). Distributed by Gale Group, P.O. Box 9187, Farmington Hills, MI 48333-9187. Toll free US and Canada (800) 877-GALE (4253) and (248) 699-GALE, fax (800) 414-5043 and (248) 699-8061, internet orders galeord@galegroup.com, web site www.galegroup.com or www.gale.com. All Gale Group products are available on approval. Contact Gale for details.

DIRECTORY OF AMERICAN FIRMS OPERATING IN FOREIGN COUNTRIES, REGIONAL EDITION—CHINA GROUP. Includes China, Hong Kong, Singapore, Taiwan, Macau. $79. Uniworld Business Publications, Inc., 257 Central Park West, Suite 10A, New York, NY 10024-4110, (212) 496-2448, fax (212) 769-0413, email uniworldbp@aol.com. Web site: http://www.uniworldbp.com.

DIRECTORY OF FOREIGN FIRMS OPERATING IN THE UNITED STATES, REGIONAL EDITION—CHINA GROUP. Includes China, Hong Kong, Singapore, Taiwan. $29. Uniworld Business Publications, Inc., 257 Central Park West, Suite 10A, New York, NY 10024-4110, (212) 496-2448, fax (212) 769-0413, email uniworldbp@aol.com. Web site: http://www.uniworldbp.com.

DUN'S GUIDE TO KEY DECISION MAKERS IN HONG KONG identifies some 8,000 directors and senior executives at 1,500 businesses in Hong Kong—an average of two names per company. Also provides information on presence in the People's Republic of China. All companies listed have annual sales of at least$200 million or total employees of 150 or more. Published annually. For prices call Dun & Bradstreet at (800) 526-0651. For more information contact Dun & Bradstreet, Business Reference Solutions, Three Sylvan Way, Parsippany, NJ 07054. Email dnbmdd@mail.dnb.com. Web site http://www.dnbmdd.com.

DUN'S MARKET GUIDE: SMALL TO MEDIUM SIZE BUSINESSES IN HONG KONG identifies 30,000 companies in Hong Kong with 50 or fewer employees in seven industries: Construction, Finance, Insurance and Real Estate, Manufacturing, Retail Trade, Services, Transportation, and Wholesale Trade. However, as the only name this directory provides is that of the CEO, this reference is best used for Target List Development. For prices call Dun & Bradstreet at (800) 526-0651. For more information contact Dun & Bradstreet, Business Reference Solutions, Three Sylvan Way, Parsippany, NJ 07054. Email dnbmdd@mail.dnb.com. Web site http://www.dnbmdd.com.

Hospitals

See Health Care—Hospitals and Medical Centers

Hospitality

See Hotels, Restaurants, Tourism

DUN & BRADSTREET AND GALE INDUSTRY REFERENCE HANDBOOKS offer a line of industry-specific sourcebooks which include key companies in the industry, ranked lists of companies, professional associations, trade shows and conferences, mergers and acquisitions, consultants who service those industries, information sources, and more. 6 volume set $495. Also available individually for $99: Pharmaceuticals, Health and Medical Services, Computers and Software, Banking and Finance, Telecommunications, Agriculture and Food, Insurance, Construction, Entertainment, Hospitality. First edition available December, 1999. Gale Group, P.O. Box 9187, Farmington Hills, MI 48333-9187. Toll free US and Canada (800) 877-GALE (4253) and (248) 699-GALE, fax (800) 414-5043 and (248) 699-8061, internet orders galeord@galegroup.com, web site www.galegroup.com or www.gale.com. All Gale Group products are available on approval. Contact Gale for details.

D&B DIRECTORY OF SERVICE COMPANIES is a directory with information on 50,000 US service businesses, including privately held companies, in these sectors: accounting, auditing and bookkeeping, advertising and public relations, architecture and engineering, consumer services, executive search, health, hospitality, management consulting, motion pictures, repair, research, social services and law. Listings include key executives' names and titles, address, phone, sales volume, number of employees, parent company and location, and more. Companies listed employ 50 or more people. Information is listed alphabetically and is cross-referenced geographically and by industry classification. Updated annually. For prices call Dun & Bradstreet at (800) 526-0651. For more information contact Dun & Bradstreet, Business Reference Solutions, Three Sylvan Way, Parsippany, New Jersey 07054. Email dnbmdd@mail.dnb.com. Web site http://www.dnbmdd.com.

Hotels

ADVERTISER AND AGENCY RED BOOKS PLUS CD ROM combines all the information in THE STANDARD DIRECTORY OF ADVERTISERS, THE STANDARD DIRECTORY OF ADVERTISING AGENCIES and THE STANDARD DIRECTORY OF INTERNATIONAL ADVERTISERS AND AGENCIES. Information is searchable by 25 fields, including company name, personal name, job title/function, product type, product/account name, city, state, zip or country, area code, revenues, number of employees, outside ad agency and even type of computer hardware. Contains professional association information. Available for Windows and Macintosh. Updated quarterly. 1 year subscription $1,295. If the price is prohibitively high, remember your local library. National Register Publishing, Reed Elsevier-New Providence, 121 Chanlon Road, New Providence, NJ 07974, (800) 521-8110, fax (800) 836-7736, web site www.redbooks.com or www.marquiswhoswho.com. "If, for any reason whatsoever, your order does not fully meet your expectations, simply return the product within 30 days for a prompt, complete, unquestioned refund," as stated in Catalog of Biographical and Professional References of publisher Marquis Who's Who/National Register Publishing.

ASIAN HOTELIER is a hospitality trade newspaper with an emphasis on the PRC's hotel development. Produced in English and Chinese. 11 issues per year. Contact publisher for price. Cahners Business

Information, 19/F, 8 Commercial Tower, 8 Sun Yip Street, Chaiwan, Hong Kong, (011) 852-2965-1555, fax (011) 852-2976-0706, email hotelier@hk.super.net. Headquarters: Cahners Business Information, 275 Washington Street, Newton, MA 02158-1630, (617) 558-4663 or (617) 964-3030, fax (617) 558-4700, email marketaccess@cahners.com. Web sites www.cahners.com or www.chilton.net.

CONSUMER REPORTS TRAVEL LETTER is published by Consumers Union, a nonprofit independent organization providing consumers with information and advice on goods, services, health and personal finance. No advertising is accepted. $39/year subscription. Single copy $5. Flash By Fax releases late breaking news that would otherwise miss Consumer Reports Travel Letter. It also reveals short term deals on travel, especially airfare. To order Flash By Fax, call 800-559-8905 for 12 issues @ $25 per year. For more information contact Consumer Reports Travel Letter, Ed Perkins, Editor, Consumers Union, 101 Truman Avenue, Yonkers, NY 10703-1057, (800) 234-1970, (914) 378-2740.

STANDARD DIRECTORY OF ADVERTISERS Business Classifications Edition is an excellent general directory that organizes companies by a wide range of product categories. A few examples include "Apparel 2—Men's and Boys' Wear," "Heating and Air Conditioning," "Cosmetics and Toiletries," and "Aviation and Aerospace." This directory lists names and titles of key officers, revenues and other information. It is available in a geographic edition for the same price. This directory is comprised of over 24,000 companies that annually spend over $200,000 on advertising. It represents a reasonable place to look for hard-to-find information about privately held companies, especially those that heavily advertise their products. It is a good place to look for names if STANDARD AND POORS and the MILLION DOLLAR DIRECTORY fail to yield the names you need. Finally, the Classified Edition of THE STANDARD DIRECTORY OF ADVERTISERS can be a very convenient source of research because both your target list of companies and the corresponding names and titles of management all appear together, in the same Classification. This is important if you still rely on research books in hard copy. THE STANDARD DIRECTORY OF ADVERTISERS also publishes a special volume called THE STANDARD DIRECTORY OF ADVERTISERS TRADENAME INDEX. You can use the TRADENAME INDEX if you know the brand name of a product and need to find the company that manufactures it. In addition, this directory contains an Associations section which identifies marketing oriented associations.

$599 hard copy. If the price is prohibitively high, remember your local library. THE STANDARD DIRECTORY OF ADVERTISERS is also available on CD ROM under the title ADVERTISER AND AGENCY RED BOOKS PLUS. It is available in Windows® and Macintosh® formats. National Register Publishing, Reed Elsevier-New Providence, 121 Chanlon Road, New Providence, NJ 07974, (800) 521-8110, fax (800) 836-7736, web site www.redbooks.com or www.marquiswhoswho.com. "If, for any reason whatsoever, your order does not fully meet your expectations, simply return the product within 30 days for a prompt, complete, unquestioned refund," as stated in Catalog of Biographical and Professional References of publisher Marquis Who's Who/National Register Publishing.

TRAVEL LETTER, published by Consumer Reports, reports that substantial savings on hotels are available by using a hotel broker or by joining a half-price hotel program. Each program offers varying additional discounts (if any) on airfares, car rentals, cruises, admissions to visitor attractions, and so forth. One large hotel broker and six discount hotel programs are listed below, ranked by quality and value:

- HRN is a large hotel broker. There's no need to join a program to use their services. (800) 380-7666.

- Entertainment Publications, publisher of HOTEL & TRAVEL ULTIMATE SAVINGS DIRECTORY ranks number 1 in total North American and worldwide locations. $62.95. (800) 445-4137.

- ENCORE, (800) 444-9800. $49.95

- ITC-50, (800) 987-6216, $49.00

- PRIVILEGE CARD, (800) 236-9732, www.privilegecard.com $80.90.

- GREAT AMERICAN TRAVELER also offers discounts on condominium rentals through Condolink and 50% off greens fees at golf courses through its Golf Access program. (800) 548-2812. Web site www.memberweb.com. Portfolio Package $99.95 for the first year, $49.95 for renewals.

- QUEST is sometimes available at a discount through associations, charge cards and so forth. (800) 742-3543, $99.00

For more information, contact Consumer Reports Travel Letter, Ed Perkins, Editor, Consumers Union, 101 Truman Avenue, Yonkers, NY 10703-1057, (800) 234-1970, (914) 378-2740. Refer to March, 1997 issue, pages 52-56.

www.hospitalitynet.nl is the URL for Hospitality Net, a site developed by Hospitality Net BV in Maastricht, The Netherlands. It connects job hunters and employers in the hospitality and restaurant industries worldwide for positions mostly in the $30,000 to $50,000 range. The site was established in 1995.

Human Resources

Also see Compensation, Databases—Resume and Job Matching, Executive Search, Jobhunters Resources, Outplacement, Recruiting, Research— Executive Search, Training

AWARDS, HONORS & PRIZES provides an alphabetical listing of the organizations giving the awards. Specifies organization, award and subject indexes and email addresses. $450 for two volume set, $255 per single volume.

Volume 1, US and Canada, $228
Volume 2, International and Foreign, $255

Gale Group, P.O. Box 9187, Farmington Hills, MI 48333-9187. Toll free US and Canada (800) 877-GALE (4253) and (248) 699-GALE, fax (800) 414-5043 and (248) 699-8061, internet orders galeord@galegroup.com, web site www.galegroup.com or www.gale.com. All Gale Group products are available on approval. Contact Gale for details.

DIRECTORY OF OUTPLACEMENT FIRMS provides information on over 350 firms, staff size, revenues, fees, key principals, feature articles and statistics. $129.95. Kennedy Information, One Kennedy Place, Route 12 South, Fitzwilliam, NH 03447, phone (800) 531-0007 or 603-585-6544, fax 603-585-9555, email bookstore@kennedyinfo.com, web site www.kennedyinfo.com.

HUMAN RESOURCE MANAGEMENT NEWS (HRMN) is a twice-monthly newsletter encompassing HR news and analysis, trends and technology. Annual subscription US and Canada $295.00. Kennedy Information, One Kennedy Place, Route 12 South, Fitzwilliam, NH 03447, phone (800) 531-0007 or 603-585-6544, fax 603-585-9555, email bookstore@kennedyinfo.com, web site www.kennedyinfo.com.

PROFESSIONAL ASSOCIATIONS for human resources, recruitment and research are listed in chapter 25.

SELECT GUIDE TO HUMAN RESOURCE EXECUTIVES, $149, Hunt Scanlon Publishing, 2 Pickwick Plaza, Greenwich, CT 06830, (800) 477-1199, (203) 629-3629, web site www.hunt-scanlon.com.

www.it-ta.com is the URL for the ITTA Connection, a site developed by the Information Technology Talent Association in Scottsdale, Arizona. Many positions are in IT, engineering and recruiting, often at the $50,000 to $100,000 range. The site went online in 1995.

www.kennedyinfo.com is the web site for publisher Kennedy Information. It includes books, newsletters, training materials, directories, and surveys for executive recruiting, human resources, outplacement, management consulting and job seekers. (800) 531-0007 or (603) 585-6544.

www.monster.com is the URL for the popular Monster Board web site. The Monster Board was ranked as one of the top 5 "Best General-Purpose Sites" by the *National Business Employment Weekly.* It is a major recruitment web site that spends millions of dollars in advertising to attract traffic to this site. Features include Job search in the US, International or by Companies, Career Center Events, Recruiters' Center, Seminars, Post a Job, free online recruitment seminar. It also offers special links for human resources, health care, technology and entry level positions. Toll free phone number (800) MONSTER. The Monster Board, PO Box 586, Framingham, MA 01704-0586. The site developer is TMP Worldwide, New York, New York and has been online since 1994.

www.monsterhr.com is the URL for The Monster Board: Human Resources careers on the web. Enter your job profile and have job listings automatically downloaded to your Email. International opportunities in Canada are classified by Canada overall, then Alberta, British Columbia, Newfoundland, Ontario and Quebec.

www.nehra.com is the URL for the Northeast Human Resources Association web site, which is largely comprised of executive search consultants.

www.shrm.org/jobs/ is the web site for the Society for Human Resource Management site. It is linked to the major recruitment web site www.career.mosaic./com. It also includes Membership Directory Online, which only can be accessed by members.

I

Illinois

ILLINOIS COUNTY BUSINESS DATABASES & DIRECTORIES are published every two years and combine detailed profiles from the ILLINOIS MANUFACTURERS DIRECTORY and the companion ILLINOIS SERVICES DIRECTORY. All directories contains executive names and titles and other information. These editions are available:

- CHICAGO BUSINESS DIRECTORY, $129, Complete CD ROM $545, CD ROM with 100 or more employees $225. CD ROMs with 20 or more employees and 50 or more employees are also available.

- SUBURBAN COOK COUNTY BUSINESS DIRECTORY, $158, Complete CD ROM $695, CD ROM with 100 or more employees $260. CD ROMs with 10 or more employees, 20 or more employees and 50 or more employees are also available.

- DUPAGE COUNTY BUSINESS DIRECTORY, $94, Complete CD ROM $445. Abbreviated CD ROMs are also available.

- KANE COUNTY BUSINESS DIRECTORY, $49, Complete CD ROM $295. Abbreviated CD ROMs are also available.

- LAKE COUNTY BUSINESS DIRECTORY, $59. Complete CD ROM $325. Abbreviated CD ROMs are also available.

- McHENRY COUNTY BUSINESS DIRECTORY, $39, Complete CD ROM $195. Abbreviated CD ROMs are also available.

- WILL COUNTY BUSINESS DIRECTORY, $35, Complete CD ROM $195. Abbreviated CD ROMs are also available.

Distributed by Manufacturers' News, Inc., (888) 752-5200, 1633 Central Street, Evanston, IL 60201-1569. Email info@manufacturersnews.com. Web site www.manufacturersnews.com.

ILLINOIS SERVICES DIRECTORY is a companion to the ILLINOIS MANUFACTURERS DIRECTORY. It provides information on service firms such as distributors, financial institutions, transportation, advertising, medical services, including 71,000 names for 28,000 businesses. $179. CD ROM prices range from $250 for companies with at least 100 employees up to $995 for the complete disk. Annual directory $179. Published and distributed by Manufacturers' News, Inc., (888) 752-5200, 1633 Central Street, Evanston, IL 60201-1569. Email info@manufacturersnews.com. Web site www.manufacturersnews.com.

Import Export

CALIFORNIA INTERNATIONAL TRADE REGISTER identifies 24,000 contacts at over 7,000 companies engaged in import/export, manufacturing, wholesaling, freight forwarding, custom brokerage and trading companies. Published annually by Database Publishing. Directory $129. Complete CD ROM $545, CD ROM one year lease $365. Distributed by Manufacturers' News, Inc., (888) 752-5200, 1633 Central

Street, Evanston, IL 60201-1569. Email info@manufacturersnews.com. Web site www.manufacturersnews.com.

DUN'S DIRECTORY OF MAJOR CORPORATIONS IN PEOPLE'S REPUBLIC OF CHINA is a two volume set with information on 20,000 major corporations in the PRC. Business categories include financial institutions, foreign invested enterprises, importers/exporters, and manufacturers. Over 80% of the corporations listed have more than 50 employees. Because only one executive name is provided per company, this reference is most suitable for target list development. However, once you've developed a target list, you can consult a business librarian as to the best way to conduct an electronic literature search to obtain names and other information. Better yet, make some telephone inquiries to PRC experts to locate research in English published in Asia. Listings in DUN'S DIRECTORY OF MAJOR CORPORATIONS IN PEOPLE'S REPUBLIC OF CHINA are presented alphabetically within four main business categories and cross-referenced by province, industry and company name in English. In English and Chinese. Published annually. For prices call Dun & Bradstreet at (800) 526-0651. For more information contact Dun & Bradstreet, Business Reference Solutions, Three Sylvan Way, Parsippany, NJ 07054. Email dnbmdd@mail.dnb.com. Web site http://www.dnbmdd.com.

India

See Asia, International

DIRECTORY OF AMERICAN FIRMS OPERATING IN FOREIGN COUNTRIES, REGIONAL EDITION —ASIA. Includes Bangladesh, Brunei, Cambodia, China, Hong Kong, India, Indonesia, Japan, Korea, Laos, Macau, Malaysia, Mongolia, Myanmar, Nepal, Pakistan, Philippines, Singapore, Sri Lanka, Taiwan, Thailand, Vietnam. $119 Ordering information: Uniworld Business Publications, Inc., 257 Central Park West, Suite 10A, New York, NY 10024-4110, (212) 496-2448, fax (212) 769-0413, email uniworldbp@aol.com. Web site: http://www.uniworldbp.com.

DIRECTORY OF AMERICAN FIRMS OPERATING IN FOREIGN COUNTRIES, REGIONAL EDITION—SOUTH ASIA. Includes Bangladesh, India, Myanmar, Nepal, Pakistan, Sri Lanka. $39. Ordering information: Uniworld Business Publications, Inc., 257 Central Park West, Suite 10A, New York, NY 10024-4110, (212) 496-2448, fax (212) 769-0413, email uniworldbp@aol.com. Web site: http://www.uniworldbp.com.

DIRECTORY OF FOREIGN FIRMS OPERATING IN THE UNITED STATES, REGIONAL EDITION—ASIA. Includes China, Hong Kong, India, Indonesia, Japan, Korea, Malaysia, Pakistan, Philippines, Singapore, Taiwan, Thailand. $79. Uniworld Business Publications, Inc., 257 Central Park West, Suite 10A, New York, NY 10024-4110, (212) 496-2448, fax (212) 769-0413, email uniworldbp@aol.com. Web site: http://www.uniworldbp.com.

KEY BUSINESS DIRECTORY OF INDIA contains information on 4,000 leading companies in India. Dun & Bradstreet, Business Reference Solutions, Three Sylvan Way, Parsippany, NJ 07054 USA. (800) 526-0651. Email dnbmdd@mail.dnb.com. Web site http://www.dnbmdd.com.

Indonesia

KEY BUSINESS DIRECTORY OF INDONESIA/PHILIPPINES/THAILAND contains information on 4,000 companies with more than 50 employees. Dun & Bradstreet, Business Reference Solutions, Three Sylvan Way, Parsippany, NJ 07054 USA. (800) 526-0651. Email dnbmdd@mail.dnb.com. Web site http://www.dnbmdd.com.

Information Systems

See Information Technology

Information Technology

ADVERTISER AND AGENCY RED BOOKS PLUS CD ROM combines all the information in THE STANDARD DIRECTORY OF ADVERTISERS, THE STANDARD DIRECTORY OF ADVERTISING AGENCIES and THE STANDARD DIRECTORY OF INTERNATIONAL ADVERTISERS AND AGENCIES. Information is searchable by 25 fields, including company name, personal name, job title/function, product type, product/account name, city, state, zip or country, area code, revenues, number of employees, outside ad agency and even type of computer hardware. Contains professional association information. Available for Windows and Macintosh. Updated quarterly. 1 year subscription $1,295. If the price is prohibitively high, remember your local library. National Register Publishing, Reed Elsevier-New Providence, 121 Chanlon Road, New Providence, NJ 07974, (800) 521-8110, fax (800) 836-7736, web site www.redbooks.com or www.marquiswhoswho.com. "If, for any reason whatsoever, your order does not fully meet your expectations, simply return the product within 30 days for a prompt, complete, unquestioned refund," as stated in Catalog of Biographical and Professional References of publisher Marquis Who's Who/National Register Publishing.

AMERICAN ELECTRONICS ASSOCIATION annually publishes the AEA DIRECTORY for $175. With 18 regional groups, this association conducts networking programs for industry executives, and provides information on compensation surveys and employee benefits plans, among other things. For more information contact: American Electronics Association (AEA), 5201 Great America Parkway, Suite 520, PO Box 54990, Santa Clara, CA 95056, (408) 987-4200.

ASIAN AMERICAN MANUFACTURERS ASSOCIATION (AAMA) publishes an annual Membership Directory and a newsletter which contains new member listings and employment listings. It also publishes ASIAN AMERICAN ENTREPRENEURS AND EXECUTIVES OF PUBLIC COMPANIES IN THE HIGH TECH INDUSTRY. Membership is comprised of Asian American manufacturers of technology products, such as computers, microprocessors, semiconductors, biotech, software and electronics equipment. Presents an annual award for entrepreneurship. For more information contact Asian American Manufacturers Association (AAMA), 39120 Argonaut Way, #309, Freemont, CA 94538-1398, (925) 461-0800.

BACON'S COMPUTER & HI-TECH MEDIA DIRECTORY identifies 6,500 contacts at 1,900 print and broadcast outlets, serving computers, data management, software, the Internet, electronics, telecommunications and more. $225. Ordering information: Call (800) 621-0561, (800) 753-6675. Bacon's Information, Inc., a K-III Communications Company, 332 South Michigan Avenue, Chicago, IL 60604. Satisfaction guaranteed or a full refund within 30 days.

BANK AUTOMATION NEWS, Phillips Business Information, Inc., a Phillips Publishing International Company, 120 Seven Locks Road, Potomac, MD 20854, (301) 340-1520, (301) 340-7788, (800) 777-5006, Internet pbi@phillips.com, web site www.phillips.com.

CANADIAN COMPUTER RESELLER is a trade publication which annually produces the RESELLER REFERENCE GUIDE for $50. Published by by Maclean Hunter in Toronto. For more information call them in Toronto at (416) 596-5000. Web site www.mhbizlink.com.

"The Best Web Sites For Job Hunters" was the cover story in the *National Business Employment Weekly* November 15-21, 1998 issue. It surveyed and reviewed 70 web sites which had been profiled in their publication during the previous year. To see a copy, try the library.

Over 60 of the 70 surveyed web sites have been included in this book. Web sites with lower compensation positions have been omitted, and most of those were in computer related areas. However, all the web sites which received top rankings were included, regardless of compensation range, especially sites in out-of-the-ordinary niches.

COMPUTING, HI-TECH AND TELECOMMUNICATIONS CAREER HANDBOOK, published by Canadian publisher The Marskell Group, Inc., 19 Redstone Path, Etobicoke (Toronto), Ontario M9C 1Y7, Canada, (416) 620-1940, Fax (416) 620-9335. Email contacts: Computing—computer@marskell.com, Health Care—health@marskell.com, Marketing—marketing@marskell.com, Marskell Group—Kmarskel.com. Web site www.marskell.com.

CONSULTANTS AND CONSULTING ORGANIZATIONS DIRECTORY identifies consultants in over 400 specialties within 14 general areas. Includes finance, computers, fundraising and others. $620 for 2 volumes. Gale Group, P.O. Box 9187, Farmington Hills, MI 48333-9187. Toll free US and Canada (800) 877-GALE (4253) and (248) 699-GALE, fax (800) 414-5043 and (248) 699-8061, internet orders galeord@galegroup.com, web site www.galegroup.com or www.gale.com. All Gale Group products are available on approval. Contact Gale for details.

CORPTECH DIRECTORY OF TECHNOLOGY COMPANIES is available in hard copy, Regional Guides, on PC disk, and on CD ROM. CorpTech EXPLORE Database is an outstanding reference that was awarded Best CD-ROM Directory by the National Directory Publishing Association. One click moves you from the CD ROM Database to Internet information on the same company. CorpTech also provides other sophisticated but reasonably priced automated services. You can save a tremendous amount of time researching relatively small, emerging new companies in various high technology niches and obtain names, titles and mailing address labels. CorpTech EXPLORE Database CD ROM $2,450 (including free soft cover CorpTech Directory worth $545). Ordering Information: CorpTech, Corporate Technology Information Services, Inc., 12 Alfred Street, Suite 200, Woburn, MA 01801-1915. (800) 333-8036, (781) 932-3100, (781) 932-3939. Fax (781) 932-6335. Email sales@corptech.com. Web site http://www.corptech.com.

CYBERHOUND'S® GUIDE TO COMPANIES ON THE INTERNET reviews over 2,000 corporate sites, including major companies as well as those in the information industry, software and hardware developers and networking and telecommunications companies. It also includes a user's guide, a directory of specialized business we sites, a bibliography of Internet products, and a glossary of Internet terms. At the time of this writing 1st edition (1996) available from Gale for $79, reduced from $95. Published by Euromonitor (England). Distributed by Gale Group, P.O. Box 9187, Farmington Hills, MI 48333-9187. Toll free US and Canada (800) 877-GALE (4253) and (248) 699-GALE, fax (800) 414-5043 and (248) 699-8061, internet orders galeord@galegroup.com, web site www.galegroup.com or www.gale.com. All Gale Group products are available on approval. Contact Gale for details.

DATA SOURCES. Volume 1, "Hardware" is comprised of 11,000 manufacturers of computers systems, graphics equipment, PC expansion boards, modems, LAN products, multiplexers, printers, disk and tape equipment, and terminals. Volume 2, :Software" is comprised of over 70,000 products including data communications and telecommunications software, database management systems software, software utilities and other application software packages. Listings include corporate officers, company name, address, phone, gross revenues, number of employees, products, and year established. Information is presented by function, then alphabetically with indexes by company, product, and a master subject index. Published semi-annually. $495 per year. Also available on CD ROM. Ordering information: DATA SOURCES, Information Access Company, One Park Avenue, New York, NY 10016, (800) 546-1223 and (212) 503-5398, fax (212) 502 5800.

DUN & BRADSTREET AND GALE INDUSTRY REFERENCE HANDBOOKS offer a line of industry-specific sourcebooks which include key companies in the industry, ranked lists of companies, professional associations, trade shows and conferences, mergers and acquisitions, consultants who service those industries, information sources, and more. 6 volume set $495. Also available individually for $99: Pharmaceuticals, Health and Medical Services, Computers and Software, Banking and Finance, Telecommunications, Agriculture and Food, Insurance, Construction, Entertainment, Hospitality. First edition available December, 1999. Gale Group, P.O. Box 9187, Farmington Hills, MI 48333-9187. Toll free US and Canada (800) 877-GALE (4253) and (248) 699-GALE, fax (800) 414-5043 and (248) 699-8061, internet orders galeord@galegroup.com, web site www.galegroup.com or www.gale.com. All Gale Group products are available on approval. Contact Gale for details.

EMPLOYMENT MARKETPLACE featured several articles on Internet Recruiting in the Winter 1998 issues. While the information is particularly appropriate for contingency recruiters, especially in technology and information systems, there is also valuable information and ideas for the retained search community. Articles include "Evaluating Employment Internet Sites" by William O. Warren, founder and president of Online Career Center, the Internet's first online recruitment site, (317) 293-6499, http://www.occ.com. "Internet Recruiting—Real Possibilities" by Bob Mhoon, President of the Manx Group, Inc., Arlington Texas. Mhoon is an IT recruiter who provides Internet recruiting training programs and IT candidate profile directories. (817) 784-6775, email bobmhoon@onramp.net. "How We Billed an Extra $100,000 by Using the Internet" by Scott Allen, a Technical Recruiter for Emerald Resource Group in Cleveland, (216) 518-4048, email sfa@emeraldresourcegroup.com.

According to Bob Mhoon, President of The Manx Group in Arlington, Texas, "A fundamental problem facing recruiters who want to learn how to effectively use the Internet is simply that no one has a map leading to all of the available resources and tools. Then, even though common Internet tools have user instructions, the tricks to effective recruiting applications must often be learned through trial and error. Difficulties are compounded when generic Internet training programs frustrate recruiters who want sessions focused on their real needs. The Internet is such a new phenomenon that Internet trainers who also have a recruiting background are in short supply."

Ordering information: Call to request back issues. $26 annual subscription, 4 issues, Employment Marketplace, PO Box 31112, St. Louis, MO 63131, (314) 569-3095, fax (314) 458-4955.

EUROPEAN ELECTRONICS DIRECTORY (SYSTEMS AND APPLICATIONS) is available as a directory for $399 from Harris InfoSource, 2057 East Aurora Road, Twinsburg, OH 44087-1999, (330) 425-9000, (800) 888-5900, www.HarrisInfo.com.

http://taps.com is a web site for people looking for contract and permanent positions in the United Kingdom and Europe. Positions are mainly in information technology, mostly in the $20,000 to $50,000 range. TAPS.COM was developed by Internet Appointments, Ltd., London, England and was launched in 1996.

IBM ALUMNI DIRECTORY can be purchased by contacting Bob McGrath, Ex-IBM Corporation, 2713 Foxboro Drive, Garland, TX 75044-2819, phone (972) 761-0000 or (972) 414-0046. At the time of this writing, 3 versions of the directory are available: (1) alphabetically by name, $60, (2) cross referenced by company, zip code, title, with email if available but no phone numbers, $125 and (3) the edition most useful for executive recruiters which includes home and business phones and up to 9 previous positions since leaving IBM, $295.

INFORMATION INDUSTRY DIRECTORY tracks companies that produce electronic systems, services and products, including database producers, CD ROM and other optical publishing products and services, Internet accessible services, online host services, transactional services and more. Entries include contact information and email address, thorough description of organization systems and more. $605 for 2 volumes. Database available via commercial online service. Gale Group, P.O. Box 9187, Farmington Hills, MI 48333-9187. Toll free US and Canada (800) 877-GALE (4253) and (248) 699-GALE, fax (800) 414-5043 and (248) 699-8061, internet orders galeord@galegroup.com, web site www.galegroup.com or www.gale.com. All Gale Group products are available on approval. Contact Gale for details.

INFORMATION INDUSTRY ASSOCIATION (IIA) merged with the Software Publishers Association (SPA) to form the Software and Information Industry Association (SIIA). As with many other professional associations, you can access their membership directory online free by going to their web site, www.siia.net. Software and Information Industry Association, 1730 M Street, NW, Washington, DC 20036, (202) 452-1600, www.siia.net.

INFORMATION SOURCES was an award winning directory published by the Gale Group in partnership with the Information Industry Association (IIA). At the time of this writing, the IIA has merged with the Software Publishers Association (SPA) to form the newly named Software and Information Industry Association (SIIA).

This directory provides information for the 550 member companies of the Information Industry Association. Entries include company name, address, phone, names of executives, regional offices, trade and brand names and description of products and services. Indexed by product, personal name, trade name, geography, parent company, international, and niche markets. The directory also identifies publishers, database producers, online services, telecommunications and network providers, system integrators and many others. $125. Contact Gale for information as to when an updated directory will be available. In the meantime, visit the Software and Information Industry's web site at www.siia.net to see their membership roster.

Gale Group, P.O. Box 9187, Farmington Hills, MI 48333-9187. Toll free US and Canada (800) 877-GALE (4253) and (248) 699-GALE, fax (800) 414-5043 and (248) 699-8061, internet orders galeord@galegroup.com, web site www.galegroup.com or www.gale.com. All Gale Group products are available on approval. Contact Gale for details.

Software & Information Industry Association (SIIA), formerly the Software Publishers Association (SPA) and Information Industry Association (IIA) is located at 1730 M Street, NW, Washington, DC 20036, (202) 452-1600, www.siia.net.

INFORMATION TECHNOLOGY ASSOCIATION OF AMERICA (ITAA) MEMBERSHIP DIRECTORY) is an annual directory which covers 11,000 members, mainly in the US with limited international coverage. Listings include, company name, address, phone, fax, names of executives, number of employees, company descriptions, products and services. Indexed geographically, by services provided, software application, hardware, and vertical markets served. It is available to non-members for $100. For more information contact Information Technology Association of America (ITAA), 1616 North Fort Myer Drive, Suite 1300, Arlington, VA 22209, (703) 522-5055, Fax (525-2279. Email can be accessed through their web site, www.itaa.org.

PRIME COMPUTER AND COMPUTERVISION'S COMPANY ALUMNI WEB SITE URL'S are http://member.aol.com/uncleroy22/prime.htm and http://members.xoom.com/uncleroy/prime.htm.

SOFTWARE AND INFORMATION INDUSTRY ASSOCIATION (SIIA), 1730 M Street NW, Washington, DC 20036 was formed by a merger with the Information Industry Association (IIA) and the Software Publishers Association (SPA). (202) 452-1600. Visit their web site at www.siia.net to access their online membership directory free.

STANDARD DIRECTORY OF ADVERTISERS Business Classifications Edition is an excellent general directory that organizes companies by a wide range of product categories. A few examples include "Apparel 2—Men's and Boys' Wear," "Heating and Air Conditioning," "Cosmetics and Toiletries," and "Aviation and Aerospace." This directory lists names and titles of key officers, revenues and other information. It is available in a geographic edition for the same price. This directory is comprised of over 24,000 companies that annually spend over $200,000 on advertising. It represents a reasonable place to look for hard-to-find information about privately held companies, especially those that heavily advertise their products. It is a good place to look for names if STANDARD AND POORS and the MILLION DOLLAR DIRECTORY fail to yield the names you need. Finally, the Classified Edition of THE STANDARD DIRECTORY OF ADVERTISERS can be a very convenient source of research because both your target list of companies and the corresponding names and titles of management all appear together, in the same Classification. This is important if you still rely on research books in hard copy. THE STANDARD DIRECTORY OF ADVERTISERS also publishes a special volume called THE STANDARD DIRECTORY OF ADVERTISERS TRADENAME INDEX. You can use the TRADENAME INDEX if you know the brand name of a product and need to find the company that manufactures it. In addition, this directory contains an Associations section which identifies marketing oriented associations.

$599 hard copy. If the price is prohibitively high, remember your local library. THE STANDARD DIRECTORY OF ADVERTISERS is also available on CD ROM under the title ADVERTISER AND AGENCY RED BOOKS PLUS. It is available in Windows® and Macintosh® formats. National Register Publishing, Reed Elsevier-New Providence, 121 Chanlon Road, New Providence, NJ 07974, (800) 521-8110, fax (800) 836-7736, web site www.redbooks.com or www.marquiswhoswho.com. "If, for any reason whatsoever, your order does not fully meet your expectations, simply return the product within 30 days for a prompt, complete, unquestioned refund," as stated in Catalog of Biographical and Professional References of publisher Marquis Who's Who/National Register Publishing.

www.ajb.dni.us is the URL for America's Job Bank. It was ranked as one of the top 5 "Sites Offering the Best Job-Search Support" by the *National Business Employment Weekly.* Launched in 1995, the site was developed by the U.S. Department of Labor and state employment/unemployment offices. Most openings were originally listed with a state department of labor and are mainly in the $30,000 to $50,000 range. Many positions are in information technology, administrative and production and manufacturing.

www.bestjobsusa.com or Best Jobs U.S.A. is a site mainly for information technology, sales and engineering positions usually in the $50,000 to $100,000 range. Launched in 1996, the site was developed by Recourse Communications, Inc., West Palm Beach, Florida.

www.careeravenue.com or Career Avenue lists positions mainly in information technology, management and engineering, mostly in the $50,000 to $100,000 range. The site was established in 1996 and developed by Internet Advertising, Inc., San Antonio, Texas.

www.careermosaic.com is the URL for a major recruitment web site that spends millions of dollars in advertising to draw traffic to this site. CareerMosaic features a jobs database; newsgroups for jobs, college connection, online job fairs, employer job postings; company information and more. CareerMosaic was ranked as one of the top 5 "Sites Offering the Best Overall Support for Job Seekers" by the *National Business Employment Weekly*. The site was developed Bernard Hodes Advertising in New York and went online in 1994.

www.careers.computerworld.com offers a "Career Search" capability, a free "Resume Database" and posting service for candidates, and various services for recruiters, including workshops and conferences, online and in print.

www.ceweekly.com is the URL for Contract Employment Weekly, a site for the temporary technical industry. Positions are mainly in information technology, engineering and technical and are mostly in the $40,000 to $75,000 range. The site was developed by C.E. Publications, Inc., Bothell, Washington and has been online since 1994. Contract Employment Weekly Online is a service of C.E. Publications, Inc., P.O. Box 3006, Bothell, WA 98041-3006. (425) 806-5200, Fax (425) 806-5585, email publisher@ceweekly.com.

www.computerwork.com is a specialized site for computer positions with a national web site and sites for Colorado, the Midwest, Minnesota and New England. Developed by Internet Association Group, Inc., Jacksonville, Florida, Computerwork.com has been online since 1996.

www.datamation.com is the web site for IT executives and professionals. It provides targeted daily computer news, IT Executive Job Pavilion, Management Benchmarking Application (MBA), technology workbench, back issues from Datamation and comprehensive links to IT vendors and other online resources. This web site is the winner of the Jesse H. Neal Award and is a Cahners Business Information web site.

www.dice.com or DICE was ranked as one of the top 5 "Best Specialty Sites" by the *National Business Employment Weekly*. DICE specializes in information technology and high technology positions. One of the oldest employment sites on the internet, DICE only accepts positions from recruiting firms. The site was developed by is D&L Online, Inc., Des Moines, Iowa and was launched in 1990.

www.eagleview.com is the web site for Eagleview, which presents the Select Candidate™ Network for job seekers and employers, including computer industry positions.

www.infospace.com is the URL for Classifieds/Jobs at Infospace, Inc., a site with many positions in computers, engineering and marketing, often in the $50,000 to $100,000 range. The site was developed by Infospace, Inc., Redmond, Washington and was launched in 1996.

www.it-ta.com is the URL for the ITTA Connection, a site developed by the Information Technology Talent Association in Scottsdale, Arizona. Many positions are in IT, engineering and recruiting, often at the $50,000 to $100,000 range. The site went online in 1995.

www.jobcenter.com is the URL for JobCenter Employment Services, Inc., a site with many job postings in IT, programming and sales and marketing, often in the $30,000 to $100,000 range. The site was developed by JobCenter Employment Services, Inc., Skaneateles, New York and was launched in 1995.

www.joblynx.com is a site that connects recruiters with people seeking full time, part time and contract positions at all levels, starting at $50,000 and exceeding $100,000. Many positions are posted in IT, management and sales and marketing. The site was developed by JobLynx, Green Bay, Wisconsin. It was launched in 1996.

www.LatPro.com is the URL for Latin America's Professional Network, a site for experienced Spanish and Portuguese bilingual professionals. Many job postings are for positions in sales and marketing, finance and information technology, often in the $50,000 to $100,000 range. The site was developed by Latin America's Professional Network, Miami, Florida and was launched in 1997.

www.net-temps.com or Net-Temps Job Posting Service was ranked as one of the top 5 "Sites Offering the Best Job-Search Support" by the *National Business Employment Weekly*. Many positions are in information systems, engineering, and sales and marketing, often in the $50,000 to $100,000 range. The site was developed by Net-Temps, Inc., Tyngsboro, Massachusetts and went online in 1996.

www.occ.com is the URL for the On Line Career Center, one of the Internet's first online recruitment sites, launched in 1993. It is a major recruitment web site that spends millions of dollars in advertising to drive traffic to the site. This is a major site that was developed by William O Warren, who has received honors for his pioneering work in the development of Internet Recruiting. This web site allows you to enter your job profile and have job listings automatically downloaded to your Email. Questions to webmaster@occ.com. www.occ.com was rated by the *National Business Employment Weekly* as one of the top 5 sites in 3 different categories: "Sites Offering the Best Overall Support for Job Seekers," "Sites Offering the Best Job-Search Support" and "Sites Offering the Best Career Resources for Job Seekers." Openings are mainly in engineering, information technology and sales and marketing. The site developer is TMP Worldwide, New York, New York.

www.passportaccess.com is a site with many positions in computers and engineering, many of them in the $50,000 to $100,000 range. The site was developed by PassportAccess, Inc., Lafayette, California and was established in 1995.

www.recruitersonline.com is the URL for Recruiters Online Network, a free web site that allows recruiters to post open positions at various online locations and maintain private resume database for members. Most positions are in information technology, management and software. Positions usually range from $50,000 to over $100,000. The site was developed by Recruiters Online Network, Inc., Plano, Texas and was established in 1995.

www.selectjobs.com was ranked as one of the top 5 "Best Specialty Sites" by the *National Business Employment Weekly*. SelectJOBS specializes in computer industry positions. Many job postings are for database administrators, programmer/analysts, and system/network engineers. salary often ranges between $40,000 and $75,000. The site was developed by SelectJOBS, Fort Lauderdale, Florida and was established in 1996.

www.technicalrecruiter.com is a web site which is an excellent starting point for a large number of specialized technology sites, such as ProjectManager.com and SoftwareEngineer.com and others.

www.usresume.com is the URL for US Resume, a site that lists many positions in computers, sales and finance, usually in the $50,000 to $100,000 range. The site was developed by Market 2000 Corp, Sparkill, New York and went online in 1996.

www.vjf.com is the URL for Westech Virtual Job Fair. It was ranked as one of the top 5 "Best Specialty Sites" by the *National Business Employment Weekly*. Westech Virtual Job Fair specializes in high tech positions which are listed by the companies. The site developer is Westech Expo Corp in Santa Clara, California, one of the largest sponsors of career fairs in the US. The site went online in 1994.

www.world.hire.com is the URL for World Hire Online, a web site with job listings mainly in engineering, information technology and "senior management," usually in the $50,000 to $100,000 range. The site was developed by World.Hire, Austin, Texas and was launched in 1996.

Institutional Investing

See Investment Management, Investment Research, Pension Funds, Real Estate

DIRECTORY OF PLAN SPONSORS/NELSONS PLAN SPONSORS contains comprehensive information on the pension and endowment industry, including key executives, investment style, level of risk, current investment interest, externally and internally managed funds, investment managers used, consultants and more. Includes 8,500 corporate sponsors, 2,700 endowments and foundations, 1,600 unions, 1,000 hospitals and 900 public /government funds. Available in two versions, alphabetically by sponsor name and geographically by metropolitan area. Published annually. $495. Nelson Information, P.O. Box 591, Port Chester, NY 10573 USA. (800) 333-6357, Phone outside the US (914) 937-8400, Fax (914) 937-8590, web site http://www.nelnet.com.

INSTITUTIONAL INVESTOR publishes excellent surveys of various Wall Street industries. Generally one survey appears in each monthly issue, including names of contacts. Annual subscription $325. INSTITU-TIONAL INVESTOR, 488 Madison Avenue, New York, NY 10022, (212) 303-3300.

INSTITUTIONAL MARKETPLACE CD ROM is a relational database the provides information on 14,000 plan sponsors, 3,400 institutional money managers, 400 pension fund consultants, and 80,000 key business executives in those organizations. Updated quarterly, IBM compatible PC required. Free demo disk available. For more information contact Nelson Information, P.O. Box 591, Port Chester, NY 10573 USA. (800) 333-6357, Phone outside the US (914) 937-8400, Fax (914) 937-8590, web site http://www.nelnet.com.

NELSON FINANCIAL DATABASE provides comprehensive information on the global institutional investment market. Information formatted to your precise needs is available from Nelson Information Mailing List & Customized Database service. The NELSON FINANCIAL DATABASE is comprised of:

30,000 executives at investment management firms
11,000 executives at research firms
100,000 executives at public companies
40,000 executives at plan sponsors
3,000 executives at pension fund consulting firms
24,000 executives at institutional real estate firms
4,000 executives at technology based vendors

The database also consists of extensive investment information, including money manager performance, peer group analysis, special surveys and more. For customers who with to use Nelson's information in their own systems, Nelson will supply customized data export, using all or any data items. Mailing lists are also available for direct marketers.For more information, contact Nelson Mailing List & Customized Database Services, P.O. Box 591, Port Chester, NY 10573 USA. (800) 333-6357, Phone outside the US (914) 937-8400, Fax (914) 937-8590, web site http://www.nelnet.com.

www.nelnet.com is the URL for Wall Street and financial publisher Nelson Information, P.O. Box 591, Port Chester, NY 10573 USA. (800) 333-6357, phone outside the US (914) 937-8400, fax (914) 937-8590.

www.mmdaccess.com is the URL for Money Market Directories, Inc., 320 East Main Street, Charlottesville, VA 22902, (800) 446-2810, (804) 977-1450. Owned by Standard & Poors, a division of McGraw Hill.

Instrumentation, Medical

See Medical Devices

Insurance

ADVERTISER AND AGENCY RED BOOKS PLUS CD ROM combines all the information in THE STANDARD DIRECTORY OF ADVERTISERS, THE STANDARD DIRECTORY OF ADVERTISING AGENCIES and THE STANDARD DIRECTORY OF INTERNATIONAL ADVERTISERS AND AGENCIES. Information is searchable by 25 fields, including company name, personal name, job title/function, product type, product/account name, city, state, zip or country, area code, revenues, number of employees, outside ad agency and even type of computer hardware. Contains professional association information. Available for Windows and Macintosh. Updated quarterly. 1 year subscription $1,295. If the price is prohibitively high, remember your local library. National Register Publishing, Reed Elsevier-New Providence, 121 Chanlon Road, New Providence, NJ 07974, (800) 521-8110, fax (800) 836-7736, web site www.redbooks.com or www.marquiswhoswho.com. "If, for any reason whatsoever, your order does not fully meet your expectations, simply return the product within 30 days for a prompt, complete, unquestioned refund," as stated in Catalog of Biographical and Professional References of publisher Marquis Who's Who/National Register Publishing.

BEST'S INSURANCE REPORTS, INTERNATIONAL contain the same information as Best's Insurance Reports P/C and L/H. Information on over 1,100 companies in over 60 countries is included. $695. Also available on CD ROM for $1,195 including free printed volumes of Best's Insurance Reports, Best's Pocket

Key Rating Guide, and toll-free technical support. To order call (908) 439-2200, ext. 5742. For a free CD ROM demo call (908) 439-2200 ext. 5184. A.M. Best Company, Ambest Road, Oldwick, NJ 08858, fax (908) 439-3296, web site http://www.ambest.com.

BEST'S INSURANCE REPORTS, LIFE/HEALTH CANADA contains information on over 100 life/health companies that are licensed to operate in Canada. $295. To order call (908) 439-2200, ext. 5742, A.M. Best Company, Ambest Road, Oldwick, NJ 08858, fax (908) 439-3296, web site http://www.ambest.com.

BEST'S INSURANCE REPORTS, PROPERTY/CASUALTY AND LIFE/HEALTH contain extensive information, including names and titles of management on over 3,000 property/casualty insurers and 1,750 life/health US insurers. $695. Also available on CD ROM for $1,195, including free printed volumes of Best's Insurance Reports, Best's Pocket Key Rating Guide, and toll-free technical support. To order call (908) 439-2200, ext. 5742. For a free CD ROM demo call (908) 439-2200 ext. 5184. A.M. Best Company, Ambest Road, Oldwick, NJ 08858, fax (908) 439-3296, web site http://www.ambest.com.

BUSINESS INSURANCE is a weekly trade publication. Crain Communications, Inc. is headquartered in Chicago with offices in major cities throughout the US plus London, Tokyo and Frankfurt. New York location: 220 East 42nd Street, New York, NY 10017, (212) 210-0100, Circulation (800) 678-9595. Annual subscription $87, two years $149. Web site www.businessinsurance.com.

DUN & BRADSTREET AND GALE INDUSTRY REFERENCE HANDBOOKS offer a line of industry-specific sourcebooks which include key companies in the industry, ranked lists of companies, professional associations, trade shows and conferences, mergers and acquisitions, consultants who service those industries, information sources, and more. 6 volume set $495. Also available individually for $99: Pharmaceuticals, Health and Medical Services, Computers and Software, Banking and Finance, Telecommunications, Agriculture and Food, Insurance, Construction, Entertainment, Hospitality. First edition available December, 1999. Gale Group, P.O. Box 9187, Farmington Hills, MI 48333-9187. Toll free US and Canada (800) 877-GALE (4253) and (248) 699-GALE, fax (800) 414-5043 and (248) 699-8061, internet orders galeord@galegroup.com, web site www.galegroup.com or www.gale.com. All Gale Group products are available on approval. Contact Gale for details.

FINANCIAL SERVICES CANADA is a handbook of banks, non-depository institutions, stock exchange and brokers, investment management, mutual funds, insurance, accountants, government agencies, financial associations and more, including contact numbers, name, title, organization, phone, fax, email, web site, and cellular. $199 for book, $299 for CD ROM, $399 for both. Ordering information: Copp Clark Professional, 200 Adelaide Street West, 3rd floor, Toronto, ON M5H 1W7 CANADA. Email orders@mail.CanadaInfo.com. Web site http://www.coppclark.com. For additional information contact: IHS Canada, Micromedia Limited, 20 Victoria Street, Toronto, Ontario M5C 2N8 CANADA, (800) 387-2689, (416) 362-5211, fax (416) 362-6161, email info@micromedia.on.ca.

INSURANCE ALMANAC provides names and titles and other information. A very good reference. $115. Underwriter Printing and Publishing Company, 50 East Palisades Avenue, Englewood, NJ 07631, (201) 569-8808, (800) 526-4700.

STANDARD DIRECTORY OF ADVERTISERS Business Classifications Edition is an excellent general directory that organizes companies by a wide range of product categories. A few examples include "Apparel 2—Men's and Boys' Wear," "Heating and Air Conditioning," "Cosmetics and Toiletries," and "Aviation and Aerospace." This directory lists names and titles of key officers, revenues and other information. It is available in a geographic edition for the same price. This directory is comprised of over 24,000 companies that annually spend over $200,000 on advertising. It represents a reasonable place to look for hard-to-find information about privately held companies, especially those that heavily advertise their products. It is a good place to look for names if STANDARD AND POORS and the MILLION DOLLAR DIRECTORY fail to yield the names you need. Finally, the Classified Edition of THE STANDARD DIRECTORY OF ADVERTISERS can be a very convenient source of research because both your target list of companies and the corresponding names and titles of management all appear together, in the same Classification. This is important if you still rely on research books in hard copy. THE STANDARD DIRECTORY OF ADVERTISERS also publishes a special volume called THE STANDARD DIRECTORY OF ADVERTISERS TRADENAME INDEX. You can use the TRADENAME INDEX if you know the brand name of a product and need to find the company

that manufactures it. In addition, this directory contains an Associations section which identifies marketing oriented associations.

$599 hard copy. If the price is prohibitively high, remember your local library. THE STANDARD DIRECTORY OF ADVERTISERS is also available on CD ROM under the title ADVERTISER AND AGENCY RED BOOKS PLUS. It is available in Windows® and Macintosh® formats. National Register Publishing, Reed Elsevier-New Providence, 121 Chanlon Road, New Providence, NJ 07974, (800) 521-8110, fax (800) 836-7736, web site www.redbooks.com or www.marquiswhoswho.com. "If, for any reason whatsoever, your order does not fully meet your expectations, simply return the product within 30 days for a prompt, complete, unquestioned refund," as stated in Catalog of Biographical and Professional References of publisher Marquis Who's Who/National Register Publishing.

WHO'S WHO IN INSURANCE provides biographical information. $115. Underwriter Printing and Publishing Company, 50 East Palisades Avenue, Englewood, NJ 07631, (201) 569-8808, (800) 526-4700.

WHO'S WHO IN RISK MANAGEMENT. $65. Underwriter Printing and Publishing Company, 50 East Palisades Avenue, Englewood, NJ 07631, (201) 569-8808, (800) 526-4700.

www.careermosaic.com is the URL for a major recruitment web site that spends millions of dollars in advertising to draw traffic to this site. CareerMosaic features a jobs database; newsgroups for jobs, college connection, online job fairs, employer job postings; company information and more. CareerMosaic was ranked as one of the top 5 "Sites Offering the Best Overall Support for Job Seekers" by the *National Business Employment Weekly.* The site was developed Bernard Hodes Advertising in New York and went online in 1994.

International

See Canada. Also refer to country name, continent (South America, Europe, Asia, Australia, Africa) or region (Arab, Latin America, Pacific). Also see Finance—International.

Items with an asterisk (*) are large general references that are especially recommended for researching companies in most countries outside the USA.

ADVERTISER AND AGENCY RED BOOKS PLUS CD ROM combines all the information in THE STANDARD DIRECTORY OF ADVERTISERS, THE STANDARD DIRECTORY OF ADVERTISING AGENCIES and THE STANDARD DIRECTORY OF INTERNATIONAL ADVERTISERS AND AGENCIES. Information is searchable by 25 fields, including company name, personal name, job title/function, product type, product/account name, city, state, zip or country, area code, revenues, number of employees, outside ad agency and even type of computer hardware. Contains professional association information. Available for Windows and Macintosh. Updated quarterly. 1 year subscription $1,295. If the price is prohibitively high, remember your local library. National Register Publishing, Reed Elsevier-New Providence, 121 Chanlon Road, New Providence, NJ 07974, (800) 521-8110, fax (800) 836-7736, web site www.redbooks.com or www.marquiswhoswho.com. "If, for any reason whatsoever, your order does not fully meet your expectations, simply return the product within 30 days for a prompt, complete, unquestioned refund," as stated in Catalog of Biographical and Professional References of publisher Marquis Who's Who/National Register Publishing.

AMERICAN CHAMBERS OF COMMERCE are established in most countries with which the US has diplomatic relations, for example the American Chamber of Commerce in The Netherlands, located in the Dutch capital, The Hague. The US DEPARTMENT OF COMMERCE has established chamber of commerce offices in foreign countries to stimulate American business activity abroad. For more information as to location, ask a librarian, check the phone book of a country's capital or other major cities, ask the consulate or embassy, the US Department of Commerce, look in a reference listed in the chambers of commerce section, ask another chamber of commerce, or search the Internet.

AMERICAN JOBS ABROAD is a guide to over 800 US firms and organizations that employ Americans abroad in 110 countries. While this directory provides considerable information for a job seeker, it can also be used to identify American target companies operating in foreign countries. Regardless of whether the ideal candidate will be a local or an American, once you have identified who the target companies are, you can then conduct ID research to identify sources and prospects. $65. Gale Group, P.O. Box 9187, Farmington Hills, MI 48333-9187. Toll free US and Canada (800) 877-GALE (4253) and (248) 699-GALE, fax (800) 414-5043 and (248) 699-8061, internet orders galeord@galegroup.com, web site www.galegroup.com or www.gale.com. All Gale Group products are available on approval. Contact Gale for details.

ASSOCIATIONS UNLIMITED ONLINE is available on the Internet through GaleNet. You can subscribe to any of the several databases comprising ASSOCIATIONS UNLIMITED, including:

- NATIONAL ORGANIZATIONS OF THE US DATABASE

- REGIONAL, STATE AND LOCAL ORGANIZATIONS DATABASE

- INTERNATIONAL ORGANIZATIONS DATABASE

- ASSOCIATIONS MATERIALS DATABASE

- GOVERNMENT NONPROFIT ORGANIZATIONS DATABASE

For more information on available databases and pricing, contact Gale Group, P.O. Box 9187, Farmington Hills, MI 48333-9187. Toll free US and Canada (800) 877-GALE (4253) and (248) 699-GALE, fax (800) 414-5043 and (248) 699-8061, internet orders galeord@galegroup.com, web site www.galegroup.com or www.gale.com. All Gale Group products are available on approval. Contact Gale for details.

AWARDS, HONORS & PRIZES provides an alphabetical listing of the organizations giving the awards. Specifies organization, award and subject indexes and email addresses. $450 for two volume set, $255 per single volume.

Volume 1, US and Canada, $228

Volume 2, International and Foreign, $255

Gale Group, P.O. Box 9187, Farmington Hills, MI 48333-9187. Toll free US and Canada (800) 877-GALE (4253) and (248) 699-GALE, fax (800) 414-5043 and (248) 699-8061, internet orders galeord@galegroup.com, web site www.galegroup.com or www.gale.com. All Gale Group products are available on approval. Contact Gale for details.

BEST'S INSURANCE REPORTS, INTERNATIONAL contain the same information as Best's Insurance Reports P/C and L/H. Information on over 1,100 companies in over 60 countries is included. $695. Also available on CD ROM for $1,195 including free printed volumes of Best's Insurance Reports, Best's Pocket Key Rating Guide, and toll-free technical support. To order call (908) 439-2200, ext. 5742. For a free CD ROM demo call (908) 439-2200 ext. 5184. A.M. Best Company, Ambest Road, Oldwick, NJ 08858, fax (908) 439-3296, web site http://www.ambest.com.

BOWKER/WHITAKER GLOBAL BOOKS IN PRINT ON DISC includes the entire databases of Books in Print (US and Canada), Whitaker's BookBank (UK) and International Books in Print (Continental Europe, Africa, Asia and Latin America), Australian and New Zealand Books in Print (Australia, New Zealand and the Oceanic states). 1 year subscription $2,055.

R.R. Bowker (a unit of Cahners Business Information), 121 Chanlon Road, New Providence, NJ 07974 USA, Phone (888) BOWKER2 (888-269-5372) & (800) 323-3288, fax (908) 508-7696, email info@bowker.com, web www.bowker.com. Canada—R.R. Bowker, Markham, Ontario, phone (888) BOWKER9 & (905) 415-5837, fax (905) 479-6266. German speaking Europe—K.G. Saur Verlag, Munich, Germany, phone 49-89-76902-232, fax 49-89-76902-250, email 100730.1341@compuserve.com, web www.saur.de/home.htm. Rest of Europe incl. United Kingdom plus Africa & Asia—Bowker-Saur, W. Sussex, UK, phone 44-1342-326-972, fax 44-1342-335-612, email customer@bowker-saur.co.uk, web www.bowker-saur.com/service/. Australia/New Zealand—Thorpe, Port Melbourne, Victoria, Australia, phone 61-03-9-245-7370, fax 61-03-9-245-7395, email customer.service@thorpe.com.au, web www.thorpe.com.au. Technical support for CD ROMs (800) 323-3288, fax 908) 665-3528, email techsupport@bowker.com.

BUSINESS INFORMATION SOURCES by Lorna Daniells is an outstanding reference at any price. At $39.95 a copy, it's such an extraordinary value, it should have a place in every library. This is clearly one of the top three hard copy references around, and its reasonable price elevates it to first place. Business Information Sources provides a wealth of information routinely needed by search firms, job hunters and corporate recruiters, including general directories, specialized directories, professional associations, periodicals, industry information, international information, information by geographic location, and much more. $39.95. Ordering information: Business Information Sources by Lorna Daniells, is published by the University of California Press (Berkeley, CA, Los Angeles, CA & Oxford, England) (510-642-4247). Orders are handled by California Princeton Fulfillment Services, P.O. Box 10769, Newark, NJ 07193-0769. (800-822-6657).

CELLULAR WORLDWIDE DIRECTORY, Phillips Business Information, Inc., a Phillips Publishing International Company, 120 Seven Locks Road, Potomac, MD 20854, (301) 340-1520, (301) 340-7788, (800) 777-5006, Internet pbi@phillips.com, web site www.phillips.com.

*COMPANIES INTERNATIONAL CD-ROM contains comprehensive financial and contact data for over 300,000 public and privately held companies in 180 countries including the Commonwealth of Independent States, Mexico, Canada and Japan. Companies can be located by company name, product or industry, location, or a combination. This reference can also be used for target lists development for international companies, including privately held companies. $2,995. Gale Group, P.O. Box 9187, Farmington Hills, MI 48333-9187. Toll free US and Canada (800) 877-GALE (4253) and (248) 699-GALE, fax (800) 414-5043 and (248) 699-8061, internet orders galeord@galegroup.com, web site www.galegroup.com or www.gale.com. All Gale Group products are available on approval. Contact Gale for details.

*CORPORATE AFFILIATIONS PLUS CD ROM consolidates information in all five volumes of THE DIRECTORY OF CORPORATE AFFILIATIONS, including publicly held and privately held companies in the US and internationally, and AMERICA'S CORPORATE FINANCE DIRECTORY. This CD provides "family tree" overviews for each company with the reporting structure. It also contains information on 15,000 parent companies in the US and abroad, records on over 100,000 subsidiaries, divisions, plants and joint ventures, names and titles of over 250,000 employees, revenue figures and more. Information can be searched by 29 criteria, such as location, SIC or NAICS codes, sales, number of employees, net worth, pension assets and more. Updated quarterly. 1 year subscription $1,995, available for both Windows and Macintosh. If the price is prohibitively high, remember your local library. National Register Publishing, Reed Elsevier-New Providence, 121 Chanlon Road, New Providence, NJ 07974, (800) 521-8110, fax (800) 836-7736, web site www.redbooks.com or www.marquiswhoswho.com. "If, for any reason whatsoever, your order does not fully meet your expectations, simply return the product within 30 days for a prompt, complete, unquestioned refund," as stated in Catalog of Biographical and Professional References of publisher Marquis Who's Who/National Register Publishing.

CRAIGHEAD'S INTERNATIONAL BUSINESS, TRAVEL AND RELOCATION GUIDE TO 81 COUNTRIES provides information about the business practices, economies, customs, communications, tours and attractions plus maps. $695 for 3 volumes. Data compiled by Craighead Publications. Gale Group, P.O. Box 9187, Farmington Hills, MI 48333-9187. Toll free US and Canada (800) 877-GALE (4253) and (248) 699-GALE, fax (800) 414-5043 and (248) 699-8061, internet orders galeord@galegroup.com, web site www.galegroup.com or www.gale.com. All Gale Group products are available on approval. Contact Gale for details.

*D&B PRINCIPAL INTERNATIONAL BUSINESSES DIRECTORY is the international companion to the MILLION DOLLAR DIRECTORY SERIES. It provides information on over 50,000 leading companies outside the US. Listings are presented geographically and are cross-referenced alphabetically and by industry classifications. Updated annually. D&B PRINCIPAL INTERNATIONAL BUSINESSES DISC SERIES is a CD ROM is available in three levels of coverage. THE PRINCIPAL INTERNATIONAL BUSINESSES DISC—BASIC provides information on 70,000 leading companies outside the US, based on total number of employees. PRINCIPAL INTERNATIONAL BUSINESSES DISC—EXPANDED covers 220,000 companies outside the US. PRINCIPAL INTERNATIONAL BUSINESSES DISC—EXPANDED PLUS provides information on 450,000 companies outside the US. Searches can be conducted by company name, industry, size of company, geography, chief executive name, key word and line of business. For prices call Dun & Bradstreet at (800) 526-0651. For more information contact Dun & Bradstreet, Business

Reference Solutions, Three Sylvan Way, Parsippany, NJ 07054. Email dnbmdd@mail.dnb.com. Web site http://www.dnbmdd.com.

DIRECTORIES IN PRINT identifies over 15,000 directories (local, regional, national and international) which are organized in 26 subject chapters. An alternate formats index includes directories in online databases, CD ROM, diskettes, microfiche and mailing labels and lists. $489 for 2 volumes. Gale Group, P.O. Box 9187, Farmington Hills, MI 48333-9187. Toll free US and Canada (800) 877-GALE (4253) and (248) 699-GALE, fax (800) 414-5043 and (248) 699-8061, internet orders galeord@galegroup.com, web site www.galegroup.com or www.gale.com. All Gale Group products are available on approval. Contact Gale for details.

DIRECTORY OF AMERICAN FIRMS OPERATING IN FOREIGN COUNTRIES lists over 2,500 American companies and 18,500 Foreign subsidiaries, affiliates or branches in 132 countries. Companies can be looked up by name in volume 1 and by country in volumes 2 and 3. Listings include name and US address of firm, Phone and fax numbers of US headquarters, CEO and other executive names such as personnel officer and foreign officer, principal product or service, number of employees, countries where foreign affiliates are located. $220. Ordering information: Uniworld Business Publications, Inc., 257 Central Park West, Suite 10A, New York, NY 10024-4110, (212) 496-2448, fax (212) 769-0413, email uniworldbp@aol.com. Web site: http://www.uniworldbp.com.

*DIRECTORY OF CORPORATE AFFILIATIONS OR WHO OWNS WHOM is a superb directory which can help you decipher the organizational structure of a company. This directory provides detailed information about all parent companies, subsidiaries and divisions, plus plant locations, joint ventures, a brief description of the subsidiary or division, a partial listing of names and titles, location, phone number, and sometimes revenues or number of employees. THE DIRECTORY OF CORPORATE AFFILIATIONS provides a comprehensive "family tree" listing that lays out the corporate hierarchy to provide a picture of the structure of companies, subsidiaries, affiliates & divisions. It includes companies with revenues of at least $10 million and reveals division and subsidiary reporting relationships down to the sixth level. It provides information on 8,500 privately held companies. For US companies it details complex multinational relationships and joint ventures. For additional names and titles of key executives in subsidiaries & divisions, refer to another directory such as Standard & Poors, THE STANDARD DIRECTORY OF ADVERTISERS, or a specialized industry directory. THE DIRECTORY OF CORPORATE AFFILIATIONS consists of 5 volumes, including US Public Companies, US Private Companies, *International Companies (both public and private),* and indices. It also contains a Brand Name Index. The CD ROM version of this directory is titled Corporate Affiliations Plus.

Ordering information: $1,029.95/5 volumes, excluding discounts. If the price is prohibitively high, remember your local library. National Register Publishing, Reed Elsevier-New Providence, 121 Chanlon Road, New Providence, NJ 07974, (800) 521-8110, fax (800) 836-7736, web site www.redbooks.com or www.marquiswhoswho.com. "If, for any reason whatsoever, your order does not fully meet your expectations, simply return the product within 30 days for a prompt, complete, unquestioned refund," as stated in Catalog of Biographical and Professional References of publisher Marquis Who's Who/National Register Publishing.

DIRECTORY OF FOREIGN FIRMS OPERATING IN THE UNITED STATES identifies over 2,000 foreign firms plus some 4,000 US affiliates from 71 countries. Includes name of parent foreign firm and address, principal products or service, name and address of American subsidiary, CEO, affiliate or branch, principal product, number of employees, phone and fax, percentage of foreign ownership. $200. Uniworld Business Publications, Inc., 257 Central Park West, Suite 10A, New York, NY 10024-4110, (212) 496-2448, fax (212) 769-0413, email uniworldbp@aol.com. Web site: http://www.uniworldbp.com.

DIRECTORY OF INTERNATIONAL CORPORATE GIVING IN AMERICA AND ABROAD profiles over 650 companies that give in the U.S. and overseas, including biographical informational on corporate and giving program officers, such as year and place of birth, university, and corporate and nonprofit affiliations. Section I provides information on funding activities of 477 foreign-owned companies in the US. Section II contains information on international funding activities of 195 US headquartered companies. 18 cross referenced indexes. $215. Gale Group, P.O. Box 9187, Farmington Hills, MI 48333-9187. Toll free US and Canada (800) 877-GALE (4253) and (248) 699-GALE, fax (800) 414-5043 and (248) 699-8061, internet orders galeord@galegroup.com, web site www.galegroup.com or www.gale.com. All Gale Group products are available on approval. Contact Gale for details.

DIRECTORY OF INVESTMENT RESEARCH/NELSON'S INVESTMENT RESEARCH profiles over 9,000 US companies and 13,000 non-US public companies, including 100,000 key corporate executives. This directory also identifies which securities analysts cover which stocks for over 22,000 stocks worldwide. Complete analyst coverage is presented for over 750 research firms, representing 1,000 offices and over 9,000 securities analysts. Published annually. $535. Nelson Information, P.O. Box 591, Port Chester, NY 10573 USA. (800) 333-6357, Phone outside the US (914) 937-8400, Fax (914) 937-8590, web site http://www.nelnet.com.

DIRECTORY OF SPECIAL LIBRARIES AND INFORMATION CENTERS includes over 23,000 libraries and information centers, including libraries associated with the general fields of science and engineering, medicine, law, art, religion and social sciences and humanities, plus expanded international coverage. $815 for 3 volume set. Also available individually.

Volume 1: Directory of Special Libraries and Information Centers, 2 book set, $580
Volume 2: Geographic and Personnel Indexes $479. Gale Group, P.O. Box 9187, Farmington Hills, MI 48333-9187. Toll free US and Canada (800) 877-GALE (4253) and (248) 699-GALE, fax (800) 414-5043 and (248) 699-8061, internet orders galeord@galegroup.com, web site www.galegroup.com or www.gale.com. All Gale Group products are available on approval. Contact Gale for details.

ELSEVIER ADVANCED TECHNOLOGY is a leading supplier of Electronics industry information. They publish a CD-ROM of a complete database of electronic companies in Europe, developed in conjunction with THE EUROPEAN ELECTRONICS DIRECTORY: COMPONENTS AND SUB-ASSEMBLIES AND SYSTEMS AND APPLICATIONS. Elsevier also publishes yearbooks, directories, market research reports and industrial journals, technical handbooks and newsletters, such as PROFILE OF THE WORLDWIDE **TELECOMMUNICATIONS INDUSTRY, PROFILE OF THE WORLDWIDE CAPACITOR INDUSTRY, PROFILE OF THE WORLDWIDE SEMICONDUCTOR INDUSTRY,** and PROFILE OF THE EUROPEAN CONNECTOR INDUSTRY. For more information contact: Elsevier Advanced Technology, P.O. Box 150, Kidlington, Oxford, OX5 1AS, England. Phone (44) (0) 1865 843-848, fax (44) (0) 1865 843-971.

ENCYCLOPEDIA OF ASSOCIATIONS: INTERNATIONAL ORGANIZATIONS includes nearly 20,000 multinational and national organizations in foreign countries, including US based associations with multinational membership. Entries also include email addresses, web sites and bulletin board addresses, lobbying activities, and publication and convention information. Indexed by geography, keyword and executives. $595 for 2 volume set. Also available in CD ROM. Database available via commercial online service. Gale Group, P.O. Box 9187, Farmington Hills, MI 48333-9187. Toll free US and Canada (800) 877-GALE (4253) and (248) 699-GALE, fax (800) 414-5043 and (248) 699-8061, internet orders galeord@galegroup.com, web site www.galegroup.com or www.gale.com. All Gale Group products are available on approval. Contact Gale for details.

ENCYCLOPEDIA OF BUSINESS INFORMATION SOURCES will lead you to specialized directories, professional associations, trade publications, newsletters, databases, Internet resources and more. It's an excellent reference and a great way to find key resources in any industry fast. $330. Gale Group, P.O. Box 9187, Farmington Hills, MI 48333-9187. Toll free US and Canada (800) 877-GALE (4253) and (248) 699-GALE, fax (800) 414-5043 and (248) 699-8061, internet orders galeord@galegroup.com, web site www.galegroup.com or www.gale.com. All Gale Group products are available on approval. Contact Gale for details.

FINANCIAL TIMES ENERGY YEARBOOKS: MINING contains full contact details, financial and operating information, and details about subsidiaries, affiliates, property and operations for about 800 mining companies globally. $320. Published by Financial Times Energy. Distributed by Gale Group, P.O. Box 9187, Farmington Hills, MI 48333-9187. Toll free US and Canada (800) 877-GALE (4253) and (248) 699-GALE, fax (800) 414-5043 and (248) 699-8061, internet orders galeord@galegroup.com, web site www.galegroup.com or www.gale.com. All Gale Group products are available on approval. Contact Gale for details.

FINANCIAL TIMES ENERGY YEARBOOKS: OIL AND GAS provides narrative, production and financial information for over 800 major oil and gas companies, including full contact details. It also includes major oil and gas brokers and traders, industry associations, and outlines all parent, subsidiary and associate companies. $320. Published by Financial Times Energy. Distributed by Gale Group, P.O. Box 9187, Farmington Hills, MI 48333-9187. Toll free US and Canada (800) 877-GALE (4253) and (248) 699-GALE, fax (800) 414-5043 and (248) 699-8061, internet orders galeord@galegroup.com, web site www.galegroup.com or www.gale.com. All Gale Group products are available on approval. Contact Gale for details.

FINANCIAL TIMES, the London daily business journal and a subsidiary of Pearson, can be subscribed to in major US cities by calling its New York City office at (800) 628-8088 or faxing (212) 308-2397. Web site www.ft.com.

FINANCIAL TIMES TOP BANKS list can be obtained by calling the FINANCIAL TIMES in London, England (from the USA) at (011) 44 171 896-2274, (011) 44 171 873-4211. Faxes (011) 44 171 896-2371 & (011) 44 171 873-3595. Web site www.ft.com.

FOREIGN EMBASSIES OR CONSULATES sometimes have library resources from their countries located in foreign countries. For example, there is a superb Canadian library in New York City. For more information, refer to a directory of libraries listed in the "Libraries" section, or ask a librarian. If you do call the embassy or consulate, make sure you speak with a knowledgeable person so as to avoid misinformation. You might ask, "May I please speak to someone who is an expert about libraries?"

FT 500 Expanded Book Version is a listing of the top 500 UK and European companies, ranked by market capitalization and published by the FINANCIAL TIMES. It contains the names of the CEO or Chairman, address, phone and fax. 29.95 pounds sterling. Also available on disk, 171 896-2744. For more information contact FT 500, FT Publishing, Financial Times, Number One Southwark Bridge, London SE1 9HL, England. Phone from the US (011) 44 171 873-3000 or (011) 44 171 873-4211. Fax from US (011) 44 171 873 3595, web site http://www.FT.com.

*GALE BUSINESS RESOURCES ONLINE provides modules on US Industry (over 200,000 companies) and International Industry (over 200,000 companies), including public and privately held companies, brands, business rankings, trade and professional associations, company histories, merger information, and more. Comprehensive records include company name, officers' names and titles, SIC/NAICS codes and more. GALE BUSINESS RESOURCES is available online on the Internet through GaleNet.

For information on pricing, contact: Gale Group, P.O. Box 9187, Farmington Hills, MI 48333-9187. Toll free US and Canada (800) 877-GALE (4253) and (248) 699-GALE, fax (800) 414-5043 and (248) 699-8061, internet orders galeord@galegroup.com, web site www.galegroup.com or www.gale.com. All Gale Group products are available on approval. Contact Gale for details.

*GALE DIRECTORY OF DATABASES identifies over 12,000 international databases available in a variety of formats including online, CD ROM, diskette, and others. Entries include producer name, description, subject, language, cost, update frequency, geographic coverage. Volume 1, Online Databases, $260. Volume 2, CD-ROM, Diskette, Magnetic Tape, Handheld and Batch Access Database Products, $170. Both volumes $390. ONLINE MAGAZINE described this as "An excellent directory of online databases." Gale Group, P.O. Box 9187, Farmington Hills, MI 48333-9187. Toll free US and Canada (800) 877-GALE (4253) and (248) 699-GALE, fax (800) 414-5043 and (248) 699-8061, internet orders galeord@galegroup.com, web site www.galegroup.com or www.gale.com. All Gale Group products are available on approval. Contact Gale for details.

*GALE DIRECTORY OF DATABASES ONLINE is a GaleNet database on the Internet that identifies over 12,000 international databases in various formats, including CD ROM, diskettes, online and others. Check your local library for free access or contact Gale for annual subscription rates. Gale Group, P.O. Box 9187, Farmington Hills, MI 48333-9187. Toll free US and Canada (800) 877-GALE (4253) and (248) 699-GALE, fax (800) 414-5043 and (248) 699-8061, internet orders galeord@galegroup.com, web site www.galegroup.com or www.gale.com. All Gale Group products are available on approval. Contact Gale for details.

GALE'S READY REFERENCE SHELF ONLINE is a GaleNet Internet resource that provides integrated access to databases covering national, regional, state, local and international associations, publishers, newspapers and periodicals, directories, newsletters, online databases, portable databases, database products and vendors, special libraries and research centers. Information is included from numerous Gale databases, among them THE ENCYCLOPEDIA OF ASSOCIATIONS, PUBLISHERS DIRECTORY, GALE DIRECTORY OF PUBLICATIONS AND BROADCAST MEDIA and several others. If it is prohibitively expensive, locate a library with with this resource. Gale Group, P.O. Box 9187, Farmington Hills, MI 48333-9187. Toll free US and Canada (800) 877-GALE (4253) and (248) 699-GALE, fax (800) 414-5043 and (248) 699-8061, internet orders galeord@galegroup.com, web site www.galegroup.com or www.gale.com. All Gale Group products are available on approval. Contact Gale for details.

*HOOVER'S HANDBOOK OF WORLD BUSINESS contains information on 200 companies, including contact information, products, key competitors, and a brief history. Published annually. $27.95 soft cover, $37.95 hard cover. The Reference Press, Inc., 6448 Highway 209 East, Suite E104, Austin, TX 78723, (512) 454-7778. Hoover's directories can also be accessed on the Internet by going to the Ask Jeeves web site at www.askjeeves.com. A subscription fee is charged for the service.

INTERNATIONAL BOOK TRADE DIRECTORY contains detailed listings for booksellers, bookstores, and wholesalers worldwide. From K.G. Saur, $360. R.R. Bowker (a unit of Cahners Business Information), 121 Chanlon Road, New Providence, NJ 07974 USA, Phone (888) BOWKER2 (888-269-5372) & (800) 323-3288, fax (908) 508-7696, email info@bowker.com, web www.bowker.com. Canada—R.R. Bowker, Markham, Ontario, phone (888) BOWKER9 & (905) 415-5837, fax (905) 479-6266. German speaking Europe—K.G. Saur Verlag, Munich, Germany, phone 49-89-76902-232, fax 49-89-76902-250, email 100730.1341@compuserve.com, web www.saur.de/home.htm. Rest of Europe incl. United Kingdom plus Africa & Asia—Bowker-Saur, W. Sussex, UK, phone 44-1342-326-972, fax 44-1342-335-612, email customer@bowker-saur.co.uk, web www.bowker-saur.com/service/. Australia/New Zealand—Thorpe, Port Melbourne, Victoria, Australia, phone 61-03-9-245-7370, fax 61-03-9-245-7395, email customer.service@thorpe.com.au, web www.thorpe.com.au. Technical support for CD ROMs (800) 323-3288, fax 908) 665-3528, email techsupport@bowker.com.

INTERNATIONAL BOOKS IN PRINT, from K.G. Saur, $795.

INTERNATIONAL BOOKS IN PRINT PLUS, one year subscription, $1,303. R.R. Bowker (a unit of Cahners Business Information), 121 Chanlon Road, New Providence, NJ 07974 USA, Phone (888) BOWKER2 (888-269-5372) & (800) 323-3288, fax (908) 508-7696, email info@bowker.com, web www.bowker.com. Canada—R.R. Bowker, Markham, Ontario, phone (888) BOWKER9 & (905) 415-5837, fax (905) 479-6266. German speaking Europe—K.G. Saur Verlag, Munich, Germany, phone 49-89-76902-232, fax 49-89-76902-250, email 100730.1341@compuserve.com, web www.saur.de/home.htm. Rest of Europe incl. United Kingdom plus Africa & Asia—Bowker-Saur, W. Sussex, UK, phone 44-1342-326-972, fax 44-1342-335-612, email customer@bowker-saur.co.uk, web www.bowker-saur.com/service/. Australia/New Zealand—Thorpe, Port Melbourne, Victoria, Australia, phone 61-03-9-245-7370, fax 61-03-9-245-7395, email customer.service@thorpe.com.au, web www.thorpe.com.au. Technical support for CD ROMs (800) 323-3288, fax 908) 665-3528, email techsupport@bowker.com.

INTERNATIONAL DIRECTORY OF BUSINESS INFORMATION SOURCES AND SERVICES contains information on over 4,000 organizations which produce and provide business information in 50 countries. $185 . Published by Euromonitor (England). At the time of this writing, while distributor Gale Group was no longer selling this reference, the sales representative indicated it might be available directly from the publisher. For more information check Books in Print or International Books in Print.

INTERNATIONAL DIRECTORY OF EXECUTIVE RECRUITERS profiles 1,600 recruiting firms with names of over 2,800 recruiters in 60 countries. The directory is arranged by country and indexed by functions, industries, firm names and key principals. Also included are introductory articles $149.00. Published by Kennedy Information, One Kennedy Place, Route 12 South, Fitzwilliam, NH 03447, phone (800) 531-0007 or 603-585-6544, fax 603-585-9555, email bookstore@kennedyinfo.com, web site www.kennedy.com.

INTERNATIONAL DIRECTORY OF THE ARTS contains information on artists, museums, publishers, conservation authorities, auctioneers, collectors, art dealers, academics, antique dealers and publications. 175 countries are covered. $275. By K.G. Saur. To order contact R.R. Bowker (a unit of Cahners Business Information), 121 Chanlon Road, New Providence, NJ 07974 USA, Phone (888) BOWKER2 (888-269-5372) & (800) 323-3288, fax (908) 508-7696, email info@bowker.com, web www.bowker.com. Canada—R.R. Bowker, Markham, Ontario, phone (888) BOWKER9 & (905) 415-5837, fax (905) 479-6266. German speaking Europe—K.G. Saur Verlag, Munich, Germany, phone 49-89-76902-232, fax 49-89-76902-250, email 100730.1341@compuserve.com, web www.saur.de/home.htm. Rest of Europe incl. United Kingdom plus Africa & Asia—Bowker-Saur, W. Sussex, UK, phone 44-1342-326-972, fax 44-1342-335-612, email customer@bowker-saur.co.uk, web www.bowker-saur.com/service/. Australia/New Zealand—Thorpe, Port Melbourne, Victoria, Australia, phone 61-03-9-245-7370, fax 61-03-9-245-7395, email customer.service@thorpe.com.au, web www.thorpe.com.au. Technical support for CD ROMs (800) 323-3288, fax 908) 665-3528, email techsupport@bowker.com.

INTERNATIONAL LEADS reviews works dealing with librarianship in countries other than the USA, with international library and information science agencies and activities. Members $10 per year, non-members $12. Formerly American Library Association, International Relations Round Table. Ordering information: International Leads, International Relations Round Table, International Relations Office, 50 East Huron Street, Chicago, IL 60611, (800) 545-2433, (312) 280-3200, email: robert.p.doyle@ala.org.

INTERNATIONAL LITERARY MARKET PLACE contains information on major publishers, book trade organizations, reference books, literary agents, book manufacturers, book clubs, translation agencies and related groups. $189.95 INTERNATIONAL LITERARY MARKET PLACE can also be accessed on the internet, directly at www.iliterarymarketplace.com or through a link at the domestic US LITERARY MARKET PLACE site at www.literarymarketplace.com. R.R. Bowker (a unit of Cahners Business Information), 121 Chanlon Road, New Providence, NJ 07974 USA, Phone (888) BOWKER2 (888-269-5372) & (800) 323-3288, fax (908) 508-7696, email info@bowker.com, web www.bowker.com. Canada—R.R. Bowker, Markham, Ontario, phone (888) BOWKER9 & (905) 415-5837, fax (905) 479-6266. German speaking Europe—K.G. Saur Verlag, Munich, Germany, phone 49-89-76902-232, fax 49-89-76902-250, email 100730.1341@compuserve.com, web www.saur.de/home.htm. Rest of Europe incl. United Kingdom plus Africa & Asia—Bowker-Saur, W. Sussex, UK, phone 44-1342-326-972, fax 44-1342-335-612, email customer@bowker-saur.co.uk, web www.bowker-saur.com/service/. Australia/New Zealand—Thorpe, Port Melbourne, Victoria, Australia, phone 61-03-9-245-7370, fax 61-03-9-245-7395, email customer.service@thorpe.com.au, web www.thorpe.com.au. Technical support for CD ROMs (800) 323-3288, fax 908) 665-3528, email techsupport@bowker.com.

INTERNATIONAL RESEARCH CENTERS DIRECTORY identifies government, university, independent, nonprofit and commercial research and development facilities in nearly 125 countries. Entries include English and foreign name of center, email addresses, personal contact, organizational affiliates, staff, description of research program, publications, services and more. Master, subject and country indexes are included. Booklist's review described this as "A useful contribution to the reference shelf of international directories." $470. Database also available via commercial online service. Gale Group, P.O. Box 9187, Farmington Hills, MI 48333-9187. Toll free US and Canada (800) 877-GALE (4253) and (248) 699-GALE, fax (800) 414-5043 and (248) 699-8061, internet orders galeord@galegroup.com, web site www.galegroup.com or www.gale.com. All Gale Group products are available on approval. Contact Gale for details.

INTERNATIONAL WHO'S WHO contains 20,000 biographies. $340. Published by Europa. Distributed in the US and Canada by Gale Group, P.O. Box 9187, Farmington Hills, MI 48333-9187. Toll free US and Canada (800) 877-GALE (4253) and (248) 699-GALE, fax (800) 414-5043 and (248) 699-8061, internet orders galeord@galegroup.com, web site www.galegroup.com or www.gale.com. All Gale Group products are available on approval. Contact Gale for details.

INTERNATIONAL WHO'S WHO OF WOMEN lists 4,000 women, including well known figures and women who have recently come to the forefront of their fields. Information includes woman's nationality, date and place of birth, education, family, career history and present position, honors, awards, publications, and contact information. $390. Published by Europa. Distributed by Gale Group, P.O. Box 9187, Farmington Hills, MI 48333-9187. Toll free US and Canada (800) 877-GALE (4253) and (248) 699-GALE, fax (800) 414-5043 and (248) 699-8061, internet orders galeord@galegroup.com, web site www.galegroup.com or www.gale.com. All Gale Group products are available on approval. Contact Gale for details.

*KOMPASS is described by the publisher as "the world's most comprehensive global database of companies, products and services for manufacturing and engineering professionals in print, on CD ROM and on the Internet." It contains company and product information for companies in all lines of business, including manufacturing and industrial sectors. Each company listing includes name, address, phone number, management names, business descriptions, and industry and product listings. Kompass's web site is www.kompass.com. Call publisher for prices and information on country directories. Cahners Business Information, 121 Chanlon Road, New Providence, NJ 07974, (908) 771-8785, fax (908) 665-8755, email hholmes@reedref.com. Headquarters: Cahners Business Information, 275 Washington Street, Newton, MA 02158-1630, (617) 558-4663 or (617) 964-3030, fax (617) 558-4700, email marketaccess@cahners.com, web sites www.cahners.com or www.chilton.net.

LITERARY MARKET PLACE, "The Directory of the American Book Publishing Industry With Industry Yellow Pages" is an excellent 3 volume directory with comprehensive information on US book publishers; imprints, subsidiaries and distributors; book trade acquisitions and mergers, small presses, Canadian book publishers, micropublishers, US electronic publishers, electronic publishing consultants, electronic publishing products and services, editorial services, literary agents, illustrations agents, US agents and offices of foreign publishers, lecture agents, specialized advertising and public relations firms, direct mail specialists, mailing list brokers and services, book review syndicates, book review and index journals and services, book exhibits, book clubs, book lists and catalogs, book importers and exporters, book producers, translators, artists, photographers, stock photo agencies, associations, book trade events and conferences, awards, contents and grants, reference books for the trade, magazines for the trade, a toll free directory of publishers, magazine and newspaper publicity, radio and television publicity, book manufacturing services, book distributors and sales representatives, and wholesalers. $189.95.

LITERARY MARKET PLACE ON DISC, previously titled LITERARY MARKET PLACE PLUS CD ROM, one year subscription $297.00.

LITERARY MARKET PLACE—INTERNET EDITION, www.literarymarketplace.com, is available by subscription.

INTERNATIONAL LITERARY MARKET PLACE Internet database can be directly accessed at www.iliterarymarketplace.com. It is also linked to the US domestic LITERARY MARKET PLACE web site at www.literarymarketplace.com. Contact the publisher for subscription price. INTERNATIONAL LITERARY MARKET PLACE, hard copy $189.95.

R.R. Bowker (a unit of Cahners Business Information), 121 Chanlon Road, New Providence, NJ 07974 USA, Phone (888) BOWKER2 (888-269-5372) & (800) 323-3288, fax (908) 508-7696, email info@bowker.com, web www.bowker.com. Canada—R.R. Bowker, Markham, Ontario, phone (888) BOWKER9 & (905) 415-5837, fax (905) 479-6266. German speaking Europe—K.G. Saur Verlag, Munich, Germany, phone 49-89-76902-232, fax 49-89-76902-250, email 100730.1341@compuserve.com, web www.saur.de/home.htm. Rest of Europe incl. United Kingdom plus Africa & Asia—Bowker-Saur, W. Sussex, UK, phone 44-1342-326-972, fax 44-1342-335-612, email customer@bowker-saur.co.uk, web www.bowker-saur.com/service/. Australia/New Zealand—Thorpe, Port Melbourne, Victoria, Australia, phone 61-03-9-245-7370, fax 61-03-9-245-7395, email customer.service@thorpe.com.au, web www.thorpe.com.au. Technical support for CD ROMs (800) 323-3288, fax 908) 665-3528, email techsupport@bowker.com.

MAJOR CHEMICAL & PETROCHEMICAL COMPANIES OF THE WORLD provides information on 6,500 companies. $830. US distributor: Larry Meranus Professional Publications & Services, 4 Demoray Court, Pine Brook, NJ 07058, (800) MERANUS or (800) 637-2687. Published by Graham & Whiteside Ltd., Tuition House, 5-6 Francis Grove, London SW19 4DT, England. Web site http://www.major-co-data.com. Email sales@major-co-data.com.

*****MAJOR COMPANIES SERIES ON CD ROM** consists of Graham & Whiteside's annual directories of major international companies. All six directories reside on one disk. After payment, you'll receive a security code to access the region(s) you select. This Windows™ based CD can navigate by company name, company locations, executive names, business activity and more. Free demo CD ROM is available. Regions also available separately for Europe, Central & Eastern Europe, the Far East and Australasia, the Arab World, Africa, and Latin America. For prices and availability, contact the Gale Group, P.O. Box 9187, Farmington Hills, MI 48333-9187. Toll free US and Canada (800) 877-GALE (4253) and (248) 699-GALE, fax (800) 414-5043 and (248) 699-8061, internet orders galeord@galegroup.com, web site www.galegroup.com or www.gale.com. All Gale Group products are available on approval. Contact Gale for details.

MAJOR FOOD & DRINK COMPANIES OF THE WORLD provides information on nearly 6,000 major food and drink companies in the world. $830 or 460 pounds sterling. US distributor: Larry Meranus

Professional Publications & Services, 4 Demoray Court, Pine Brook, NJ 07058, (800) MERANUS or (800) 637-2687. Published by Graham & Whiteside Ltd., Tuition House, 5-6 Francis Grove, London SW19 4DT, England. Web site http://www.major-co-data.com. Email sales@major-co-data.com.

MAJOR TELECOMMUNICATIONS COMPANIES OF THE WORLD—INCLUDING MAJOR INTERNET COMPANIES provides information on 3,700 companies, including 600 international companies involved in the Internet. $830. US distributor: Larry Meranus Professional Publications & Services, 4 Demoray Court, Pine Brook, NJ 07058, (800) MERANUS or (800) 637-2687. Published by Graham & Whiteside Ltd., Tuition House, 5-6 Francis Grove, London SW19 4DT, England. Web site http://www.major-co-data.com. Email sales@major-co-data.com.

NELSON FINANCIAL DATABASE provides comprehensive information on the global institutional investment market. Information formatted to your precise needs is available from Nelson Information Mailing List & Customized Database service. The NELSON FINANCIAL DATABASE is comprised of:

30,000 executives at investment management firms
11,000 executives at research firms
100,000 executives at public companies
40,000 executives at plan sponsors
3,000 executives at pension fund consulting firms
24,000 executives at institutional real estate firms
4,000 executives at technology based vendors

The database also consists of extensive investment information, including money manager performance, peer group analysis, special surveys and more. For customers who with to use Nelson's information in their own systems, Nelson will supply customized data export, using all or any data items. Mailing lists are also available for direct marketers.For more information, contact Nelson Mailing List & Customized Database Services, P.O. Box 591, Port Chester, NY 10573 USA. (800) 333-6357, Phone outside the US (914) 937-8400, Fax (914) 937-8590, web site http://www.nelnet.com.

NELSON INVESTMENT MANAGEMENT NETWORK, also known as Nelnet, is an Internet database (www.nelnet.com) that provides comprehensive information on over 3,000 worldwide institutional investment management firms on 9,500 products and 45,000 professionals. Nelnet users can access without charge the World's Best Money Managers, Nelson's industry standard performance rankings, Manager Hires, which managers were hired by which plan sponsors; Job bank, the investment industry's free online employment service; and useful Industry Analyses. Investment Managers can launch their own Nelnet Web site for $100 a month. Users can access Nelnet free. www.nelnet.com. For more information, contact Nelson Information, P.O. Box 591, Port Chester, NY 10573 USA. (800) 333-6357, Phone outside the US (914) 937-8400, Fax (914) 937-8590, web site http://www.nelnet.com.

POLK WORLD BANK DIRECTORY includes information on worldwide banks, including the top 1,000 banks in the US. Listings include names of key decision makers, address, phone and fax, financial summaries, branch information, maps, and structural changes such as mergers, name changes, and closings, and discontinued banks with explanations. Published annually. For more information contact (800) 321-3373, Thomson Financial Publishing, 4709 West Golf Road, Skokie, IL 60076-1253. Web site @ tfp.bankinfo.com.

PUBLISHING MARKET PLACE REFERENCE PLUS CD ROM contains information from the LITERARY MARKET PLACE, INTERNATIONAL LITERARY MARKET PLACE, the AMERICAN LIBRARY DIRECTORY and the WORLD GUIDE TO LIBRARIES, plus 32,000 listings for bookstores and book dealers listed in the AMERICAN BOOK TRADE DIRECTORY, over 100,000 companies listed in PUBLISHERS, DISTRIBUTORS AND WHOLESALERS plus information from the BOWKER ANNUAL LIBRARY AND BOOK TRADE ALMANAC. Includes contact information and the ability to generate customized mailing lists and print labels for publishers, libraries and book dealers. This same mailing list information could be used to develop a list of prospects to contact. Can be searched by keyword, company/institution, personal name, position, subject, titles, conference/meeting, membership, and more. Updated annually. 1 year subscription $895, 3 years $2,551, excluding discounts. For more information visit Bowker Reed Reference's web site at http://www.reedref.com or contact: Bowker Reed Reference Electronic Publishing, 121 Chanlon Road, New Providence, NJ 07974 USA, Phone (800) 323-3288, Fax (908) 665-3528, email info@bowker.com.

RESEARCH CENTERS AND SERVICES DIRECTORY ONLINE is a GaleNet database on the Internet which includes three types of R&D centers around the world—US research centers, international research centers and government research centers, including nonprofit research centers, commercial labs, international institutes, government experiment stations, university research parks, in the areas of agriculture, environment, engineering, physical and earth sciences, labor and industrial relations, and education. Available by subscription or at a library. 1 user $1,575 per year, 2 users $2,835 annually. Call publisher for additional pricing information. Gale Group, P.O. Box 9187, Farmington Hills, MI 48333-9187. Toll free US and Canada (800) 877-GALE (4253) and (248) 699-GALE, fax (800) 414-5043 and (248) 699-8061, internet orders galeord@galegroup.com, web site www.galegroup.com or www.gale.com. All Gale Group products are available on approval. Contact Gale for details.

SciTECH REFERENCE PLUS CD ROM contains directory information, 125,000 biographies of US and Canadian scientists and engineers from AMERICAN MEN AND WOMEN OF SCIENCE, listings for over 8,000 laboratories from the DIRECTORY OF AMERICAN RESEARCH AND TECHNOLOGY, and information from THE DIRECTORY OF CORPORATE AFFILIATIONS (including public, private and international companies) of leading US and international technology firms and their subsidiaries. It also contains 60,000 records on science/technology and medical serials from ULRICH'S INTERNATIONAL PERIODICALS DIRECTORY. Searches can be conducted by SIC, year founded, activity, education, employees, institution/company, city, state or country, memberships/honors, product description, personal statistics, personal title, research area, revenue. Updated annually. 1 year subscription $995, 3 years 2,836, excluding discounts. For more information visit Bowker Reed Reference's web site at http://www.reedref.com or contact: Bowker Reed Reference Electronic Publishing, 121 Chanlon Road, New Providence, NJ 07974 USA, Phone (800) 323-3288, Fax (908) 665-3528, email info@bowker.com.

STANDARD DIRECTORY OF INTERNATIONAL ADVERTISERS & AGENCIES covers the advertising industry in over 120 countries, including 1,700 companies and 2,000 agencies. Listings include names and titles of key executives. $539. If the price is prohibitively high, remember your local library. National Register Publishing, Reed Elsevier-New Providence, 121 Chanlon Road, New Providence, NJ 07974, (800) 521-8110, fax (800) 836-7736, web site www.redbooks.com or www.marquiswhoswho.com. "If, for any reason whatsoever, your order does not fully meet your expectations, simply return the product within 30 days for a prompt, complete, unquestioned refund," as stated in Catalog of Biographical and Professional References of publisher Marquis Who's Who/National Register Publishing.

TELEVISION INTERNATIONAL is a magazine for cable TV, radio, satellite and interactive multimedia industries around the world. Call publisher for price. Cahners Business Information, 245 West 17th Street, New York, NY 10011-5300, (212) 337-6944, fax (212) 337-6948, email jonnypim@pacific.net.sg and rschatz@cahners.com, URL www.cahners.com/mainmag/bci.htm. Headquarters: Cahners Business Information, 275 Washington Street, Newton, MA 02158-1630, (617) 558-4663 or (617) 964-3030, fax (617) 558-4700, email marketaccess@cahners.com. Web sites www.cahners.com or www.chilton.net.

"THE LIST" is Cahners Business Information catalog. The former Reed Travel Group has merged with Cahners and Chilton to form Cahners Business Information. For every publication in "The List," publishers and editors' names are identified, with address, phone number and email. It also provides a superb description of every periodical they publish—including many serving the travel industry—with local contact information Publications are located throughout the US and in foreign countries. Free. Cahners Business Information, 275 Washington Street, Newton, MA 02158-1630, (617) 558-4663 or (617) 964-3030, fax (617) 558-4700, email marketaccess@cahners.com. Web sites www.cahners.com or www.chilton.net.

TRADE SHOWS WORLDWIDE—AN INTERNATIONAL DIRECTORY OF EVENTS, FACILITIES AND SUPPLIERS profiles over 8,000 trade shows, some 5,000 trade show organizers, over 1,200 convention centers plus exhibit builders, transportations firms industry suppliers, professional associations, consultants, and published sources of industry information. Three sections cover hotel/motel systems, visitor and convention bureaus and world trade centers. $277. Gale Group, P.O. Box 9187, Farmington Hills, MI 48333-9187. Toll free US and Canada (800) 877-GALE (4253) and (248) 699-GALE, fax (800) 414-5043 and (248) 699-8061, internet orders galeord@galegroup.com, web site www.galegroup.com or www.gale.com. All Gale Group products are available on approval. Contact Gale for details.

ULRICH'S INTERNATIONAL PERIODICALS DIRECTORY is available in electronic database formats. It contains information on every active and ceased global periodical, annual, irregular publication, plus thousands of newspapers. You can retrieve citations for over 900 subjects. Information is available for current titles of publications, title changes, and translated titles. Contains names, addresses and phone numbers for 80,000 publishers from 200 countries. $469.95 for 5 volume set. ULRICH'S ON DISC encompasses ULRICH'S INTERNATIONAL PERIODICALS DATABASE and contains information on over 210,000 periodicals, annuals and irregulars, both active and ceased, plus newspapers, including foreign and US topical newspapers and international general interest dailies and weeklies. It also includes information on over 90,000 publishers in over 200 countries, including the new states of the former Soviet Union, Czechoslovakia and Yugoslavia. One year subscription $650. ULRICH'S INTERNATIONAL PERIODICALS DIRECTORY— INTERNET EDITION, is available by subscription at www.ulrichsweb.com. ULRICH'S ONLINE is available from Bowker or through Knight-Ridder Information, Inc. (DIALOG file 480), OVID Technologies, Inc., LEXIS®—NEXIS® (Library: BUSREF, File Name: ULRICH) and through SilverPlatter Information, Inc. for a subscription online. For more information contact R.R. Bowker (a unit of Cahners Business Information), 121 Chanlon Road, New Providence, NJ 07974 USA, Phone (888) BOWKER2 (888-269-5372) & (800) 323-3288, fax (908) 508-7696, email info@bowker.com, web www.bowker.com. Canada—R.R. Bowker, Markham, Ontario, phone (888) BOWKER9 & (905) 415-5837, fax (905) 479-6266. German speaking Europe—K.G. Saur Verlag, Munich, Germany, phone 49-89-76902-232, fax 49-89-76902-250, email 100730.1341@compuserve.com, web www.saur.de/home.htm. Rest of Europe incl. United Kingdom plus Africa & Asia—Bowker-Saur, W. Sussex, UK, phone 44-1342-326-972, fax 44-1342-335-612, email customer@bowker-saur.co.uk, web www.bowker-saur.com/service/. Australia/New Zealand—Thorpe, Port Melbourne, Victoria, Australia, phone 61-03-9-245-7370, fax 61-03-9-245-7395, email customer.service@thorpe.com.au, web www.thorpe.com.au. Technical support for CD ROMs (800) 323-3288, fax 908) 665-3528, email techsupport@bowker.com.

UMI is a respected publisher (including databases) whose catalog of Books on Demand, Magazines, Newspapers and Collections, consisting of 19,000 titles, is on line. For more information, go to their Home page and then to the Support Center for pricing. www.umi.com. Email: pprice@umi.com. UMI, 300 North Zeeb Road, Ann Arbor, Michigan 48106 (800) 521-0600, Sales (800) 521-3042, email: pprice@umi.com

WASHINGTON REPRESENTATIVES—Who Does What For Whom in The Nation's Capital identifies over 17,000 lobbyists, public and government affairs representatives and special interest advocates in Washington, DC. Includes foreign agent registration numbers and federal lobbyist indicators. Listings are organized by client and by representative and are indexed by subject/ industry and foreign interest. $95. Columbia Books, Inc., 1212 New York Avenue, NW, Suite 330, Washington, DC 20005, (212) 898-0662.

*WHO OWNS WHOM DIRECTORY by Dun & Bradstreet is a six volume set containing information on the structure and ownership of 320,000 company affiliates and subsidiaries of over 23,000 companies worldwide. It is available in four regional editions: Australia and the Far East, North America, UK/Ireland, and Continental Europe. Published annually. For prices and ordering information as well as information about more worldwide corporate linkage products from D&B WORLDBASE, D&B's global database of 42 million records in over 200 countries, contact Dun & Bradstreet at (800) 526-0651, Dun & Bradstreet, Business Reference Solutions, Three Sylvan Way, Parsippany, NJ 07054. Email dnbmdd@mail.dnb.com. Web site http://www.dnbmdd.com.

WHO'S WHO IN INTERNATIONAL AFFAIRS contains over 7,000 biographies of individuals in politics, trade, diplomats, international academics, civil servants, delegates to international bodies, judges, elected officials, bankers and scientists. $425. Published by Europa. Distributed by the Gale Group, P.O. Box 9187, Farmington Hills, MI 48333-9187. Toll free US and Canada (800) 877-GALE (4253) and (248) 699-GALE, fax (800) 414-5043 and (248) 699-8061, internet orders galeord@galegroup.com, web site www.galegroup.com or www.gale.com. All Gale Group products are available on approval. Contact Gale for details.

WHO'S WHO IN THE WORLD, $379.95. National Register Publishing, Reed Elsevier-New Providence, 121 Chanlon Road, New Providence, NJ 07974, (800) 521-8110, fax (800) 836-7736, web site www.marquiswhoswho.com or www.redbooks.com. "If, for any reason whatsoever, your order does not fully meet your expectations, simply return the product within 30 days for a prompt, complete, unquestioned refund," as stated in Catalog of Biographical and Professional References of publisher Marquis Who's Who/National Register Publishing.

*WORLD BUSINESS RANKINGS ANNUAL is modeled after Gale's award-winning BUSINESS RANKINGS ANNUAL. It provides 2,500 "top 10" ranked lists and references the sources of information. $189. Gale Group, P.O. Box 9187, Farmington Hills, MI 48333-9187. Toll free US and Canada (800) 877-GALE (4253) and (248) 699-GALE, fax (800) 414-5043 and (248) 699-8061, internet orders galeord@galegroup.com, web site www.galegroup.com or www.gale.com. All Gale Group products are available on approval. Contact Gale for details.

WORLD COSMETICS AND TOILETRIES DIRECTORY includes products in fragrances, skincare, oral hygiene, shower additives, baby care and more. $990. Published by Euromonitor (England). Distributed by Gale Group, P.O. Box 9187, Farmington Hills, MI 48333-9187. Toll free US and Canada (800) 877-GALE (4253) and (248) 699-GALE, fax (800) 414-5043 and (248) 699-8061, internet orders galeord@galegroup.com, web site www.galegroup.com or www.gale.com. All Gale Group products are available on approval. Contact Gale for details.

WORLD COST OF LIVING SURVEY includes information such as child care, education, health care, utilities and other areas for major cities around the world. It is a useful resource for companies relocating employees to determine appropriate levels of compensation adjustment and for individuals considering a move abroad. $240. Gale Group, P.O. Box 9187, Farmington Hills, MI 48333-9187. Toll free US and Canada (800) 877-GALE (4253) and (248) 699-GALE, fax (800) 414-5043 and (248) 699-8061, internet orders galeord@galegroup.com, web site www.galegroup.com or www.gale.com. All Gale Group products are available on approval. Contact Gale for details.

WORLD DIRECTORY OF BUSINESS INFORMATION LIBRARIES identifies 2,500 major business libraries in 145 countries whose collections are oriented towards consumer markets. $590. Published by Euromonitor (England). Distributed by Gale Group, P.O. Box 9187, Farmington Hills, MI 48333-9187. Toll free US and Canada (800) 877-GALE (4253) and (248) 699-GALE, fax (800) 414-5043 and (248) 699-8061, internet orders galeord@galegroup.com, web site www.galegroup.com or www.gale.com. All Gale Group products are available on approval. Contact Gale for details.

WORLD DIRECTORY OF MARKETING INFORMATION SOURCES identifies market research companies, online databases, directories and marketing journals for every major consumer market in 75 countries. $595. Published by Euromonitor (England). Distributed by Gale Group, P.O. Box 9187, Farmington Hills, MI 48333-9187. Toll free US and Canada (800) 877-GALE (4253) and (248) 699-GALE, fax (800) 414-5043 and (248) 699-8061, internet orders galeord@galegroup.com, web site www.galegroup.com or www.gale.com. All Gale Group products are available on approval. Contact Gale for details.

WORLD DIRECTORY OF TRADE AND BUSINESS ASSOCIATIONS profiles 3,000 trade and business associations globally, including finance, general business and industry, advertising, marketing and major consumer markets. Entries include web site addresses and publications. $595. Published by Euromonitor (England). Distributed by Gale Group, P.O. Box 9187, Farmington Hills, MI 48333-9187. Toll free US and Canada (800) 877-GALE (4253) and (248) 699-GALE, fax (800) 414-5043 and (248) 699-8061, internet orders galeord@galegroup.com, web site www.galegroup.com or www.gale.com. All Gale Group products are available on approval. Contact Gale for details.

WORLD DRINKS MARKETING DIRECTORY, $990. Published by Euromonitor (England). Distributed by Gale Group, P.O. Box 9187, Farmington Hills, MI 48333-9187. Toll free US and Canada (800) 877-GALE (4253) and (248) 699-GALE, fax (800) 414-5043 and (248) 699-8061, internet orders galeord@galegroup.com, web site www.galegroup.com or www.gale.com. All Gale Group products are available on approval. Contact Gale for details.

WORLD FOOD MARKETING DIRECTORY. $990. Published by Euromonitor (England). Distributed by Gale Group, P.O. Box 9187, Farmington Hills, MI 48333-9187. Toll free US and Canada (800) 877-GALE (4253) and (248) 699-GALE, fax (800) 414-5043 and (248) 699-8061, internet orders galeord@galegroup.com, web site www.galegroup.com or www.gale.com. All Gale Group products are available on approval. Contact Gale for details.

WORLD GUIDE TO FOUNDATIONS edited by Michael Zils identifies over 20,000 foundations, key personnel, publications and more in 112 countries. $225. R.R. Bowker (a unit of Cahners Business

Information), 121 Chanlon Road, New Providence, NJ 07974 USA, Phone (888) BOWKER2 (888-269-5372) & (800) 323-3288, fax (908) 508-7696, email info@bowker.com, web www.bowker.com. Canada—R.R. Bowker, Markham, Ontario, phone (888) BOWKER9 & (905) 415-5837, fax (905) 479-6266. German speaking Europe—K.G. Saur Verlag, Munich, Germany, phone 49-89-76902-232, fax 49-89-76902-250, email 100730.1341@compuserve.com, web www.saur.de/home.htm. Rest of Europe incl. United Kingdom plus Africa & Asia—Bowker-Saur, W. Sussex, UK, phone 44-1342-326-972, fax 44-1342-335-612, email customer@bowker-saur.co.uk, web www.bowker-saur.com/service/. Australia/New Zealand—Thorpe, Port Melbourne, Victoria, Australia, phone 61-03-9-245-7370, fax 61-03-9-245-7395, email customer.service@thorpe.com.au, web www.thorpe.com.au. Technical support for CD ROMs (800) 323-3288, fax 908) 665-3528, email techsupport@bowker.com.

WORLD GUIDE TO LIBRARIES, from K.G. Saur, $425. R.R. Bowker (a unit of Cahners Business Information), 121 Chanlon Road, New Providence, NJ 07974 USA, Phone (888) BOWKER2 (888-269-5372) & (800) 323-3288, fax (908) 508-7696, email info@bowker.com, web www.bowker.com. Canada—R.R. Bowker, Markham, Ontario, phone (888) BOWKER9 & (905) 415-5837, fax (905) 479-6266. German speaking Europe—K.G. Saur Verlag, Munich, Germany, phone 49-89-76902-232, fax 49-89-76902-250, email 100730.1341@compuserve.com, web www.saur.de/home.htm. Rest of Europe incl. United Kingdom plus Africa & Asia—Bowker-Saur, W. Sussex, UK, phone 44-1342-326-972, fax 44-1342-335-612, email customer@bowker-saur.co.uk, web www.bowker-saur.com/service/. Australia/New Zealand—Thorpe, Port Melbourne, Victoria, Australia, phone 61-03-9-245-7370, fax 61-03-9-245-7395, email customer.service@thorpe.com.au, web www.thorpe.com.au. Technical support for CD ROMs (800) 323-3288, fax 908) 665-3528, email techsupport@bowker.com.

WORLD GUIDE TO TRADE ASSOCIATIONS edited by Michael Zils includes key personnel, publications, a translation of the name in English, information that reflects the structure of Eastern Europe and the former USSR, a German-English concordance of subject areas and other data. From K.G. Saur. 2 volume set $650. R.R. Bowker (a unit of Cahners Business Information), 121 Chanlon Road, New Providence, NJ 07974 USA, Phone (888) BOWKER2 (888-269-5372) & (800) 323-3288, fax (908) 508-7696, email info@bowker.com, web www.bowker.com. Canada—R.R. Bowker, Markham, Ontario, phone (888) BOWKER9 & (905) 415-5837, fax (905) 479-6266. German speaking Europe—K.G. Saur Verlag, Munich, Germany, phone 49-89-76902-232, fax 49-89-76902-250, email 100730.1341@compuserve.com, web www.saur.de/home.htm. Rest of Europe incl. United Kingdom plus Africa & Asia—Bowker-Saur, W. Sussex, UK, phone 44-1342-326-972, fax 44-1342-335-612, email customer@bowker-saur.co.uk, web www.bowker-saur.com/service/. Australia/New Zealand—Thorpe, Port Melbourne, Victoria, Australia, phone 61-03-9-245-7370, fax 61-03-9-245-7395, email customer.service@thorpe.com.au, web www.thorpe.com.au. Technical support for CD ROMs (800) 323-3288, fax 908) 665-3528, email techsupport@bowker.com.

WORLD RETAIL DIRECTORY profiles over 2,600 retailers in 15 sectors, including in Latin America, Eastern Europe and Asia. $990. Published by Euromonitor (England). Distributed by Gale Group, P.O. Box 9187, Farmington Hills, MI 48333-9187. Toll free US and Canada (800) 877-GALE (4253) and (248) 699-GALE, fax (800) 414-5043 and (248) 699-8061, internet orders galeord@galegroup.com, web site www.galegroup.com or www.gale.com. All Gale Group products are available on approval. Contact Gale for details.

WORLD TOURISM DIRECTORY identifies associations, institutions, authorities, services and information centers associated with the travel trade. Produced in conjunction with the World Tourism Organization, this directory identifies sources in over 330 countries and territories. Volume 1—Europe, Volume 2—The Americas, Volume 3—Africa, Middle East, Asia and Oceania. From K.G. Saur. $185 per volume.

R.R. Bowker (a unit of Cahners Business Information), 121 Chanlon Road, New Providence, NJ 07974 USA, Phone (888) BOWKER2 (888-269-5372) & (800) 323-3288, fax (908) 508-7696, email info@bowker.com, web www.bowker.com. Canada—R.R. Bowker, Markham, Ontario, phone (888) BOWKER9 & (905) 415-5837, fax (905) 479-6266. German speaking Europe—K.G. Saur Verlag, Munich, Germany, phone 49-89-76902-232, fax 49-89-76902-250, email 100730.1341@compuserve.com, web www.saur.de/home.htm. Rest of Europe incl. United Kingdom plus Africa & Asia—Bowker-Saur, W. Sussex, UK, phone 44-1342-326-972, fax 44-1342-335-612, email customer@bowker-saur.co.uk, web www.bowker-saur.com/service/. Australia/New Zealand—Thorpe, Port Melbourne, Victoria, Australia, phone 61-03-9-245-7370, fax 61-03-9-

245-7395, email customer.service@thorpe.com.au, web www.thorpe.com.au. Technical support for CD ROMs (800) 323-3288, fax 908) 665-3528, email techsupport@bowker.com.

*WORLDWIDE BRANCH LOCATIONS OF MULTINATIONAL COMPANIES focuses on some 500 multinationals and nearly 20,000 plants, branch offices and subsidiaries worldwide and NOT headquartered in the USA. It's organized geographically. Indexes include names of facilities and parent companies, SIC, and a geographic listing of parent companies by country. $200. Ordering information: Gale Research, P.O. Box 33477, Detroit, MI 48232-5477. Phone (800) 877-GALE, Fax (800) 414-5043 will be responded to within 48 hours. Internet orders: galeord@galegroup.com, CompuServe email: 72203.1552, web site http://www.galegroup.com, GaleNet web site address @http://galenet.galegroup.com.

WORLDWIDE GOVERNMENT DIRECTORY identifies top level foreign government offices and officials in 196 countries. It includes state agencies and state-owned corporations and defines hierarchical arrangements of state structures. $368. Published by Keesing's Worldwide and distributed by the Gale Group, P.O. Box 9187, Farmington Hills, MI 48333-9187. Toll free US and Canada (800) 877-GALE (4253) and (248) 699-GALE, fax (800) 414-5043 and (248) 699-8061, internet orders galeord@galegroup.com, web site www.galegroup.com or www.gale.com. All Gale Group products are available on approval. Contact Gale for details.

www.bowker.com is the web site for this major research publisher. It includes Flagship Products and Services, an online Product Catalog, Electronic Publishing products including CD ROMs, Internet Databases, and Online Subscription and Site Licensing Databases; press releases, career opportunities, and more. Many of their references are accessible through this web site, such as BOOKS IN PRINT PLUS CANADIAN EDITION, ULRICH'S ON DISC, GERMAN BOOKS IN PRINT, GERMAN BOOKS OUT OF PRINT, INTERNATIONAL BOOKS IN PRINT PLUS, ITALIAN BOOKS IN PRINT, YEARBOOK OF INTERNATIONAL ORGANIZATIONS PLUS, ULRICH'S INTERNATIONAL PERIODICALS DIRECTORY, THE SOFTWARE ENCYCLOPEDIA, BOWKER'S COMPLETE VIDEO DIRECTORY, AMERICAN BOOK PUBLISHING RECORD. Visit the web site for more information.

www.careers.wsj.com is the *Wall Street Journal*'s web site. It focuses on positions for middle and senior management including financial positions at $75,000 and up. This web site is among those that encompass senior executive positions. Other features includes Job Seek, Who's Hiring, Career Columnists, Salaries & Profiles, The Salary Calculator™, Job Hunting Advice, Succeeding at Work, HR Issues, Executive Recruiters, Working Globally, College Connection, Starting a Business, Career Bookstore and more. Content from The National Employment Business Weekly is also featured. The site was developed by Dow Jones & Company, Inc., Princeton, New Jersey and was established in 1997.

www.galegroup.com is the web site to publisher Gale Research, one of the largest providers of research for search, recruiting and libraries.

www.hospitalitynet.nl is the URL for Hospitality Net, a site developed by Hospitality Net BV in Maastricht, The Netherlands. It connects job hunters and employers in the hospitality and restaurant industries worldwide for positions mostly in the $30,000 to $50,000 range. The site was established in 1995.

www.kompass.com is the web site for the highly respected Kompass country directories and databases. This web site contains a searchable database that encompasses over 60 countries, 2.5 million executive names, information on 1.5 million companies, 19 million key product references, and 370,000 trade and brand names. At the time of this writing, Kompass is available in English and French. Deutsch, Espanol and Italiano will soon be available.

www.monster.com is the URL for the popular Monster Board web site. The Monster Board was ranked as one of the top 5 "Best General-Purpose Sites" by the *National Business Employment Weekly*. It is a major recruitment web site that spends millions of dollars in advertising to attract traffic to this site. Features include Job search in the US, International or by Companies, Career Center Events, Recruiters' Center, Seminars, Post a Job, free online recruitment seminar. It also offers special links for human resources, health care, technology and entry level positions. Toll free phone number (800) MONSTER. The Monster Board, PO Box 586, Framingham, MA 01704-0586. The site developer is TMP Worldwide, New York, New York and has been online since 1994.

www.reedref.com presents a current catalog for all Reed Reference Publishing companies for both print and electronic references—National Register Publishing, R.R. Bowker, Bowker-Saur, KG Saur, Marquis Who's Who, Martindale-Hubbell and Lexis-Nexis Business Information. At the time of this writing, this catalog is searchable by name, subject, publisher and keyword. To check new offerings, visit individual publisher pages. Free product demos of CD ROM'S can be downloaded for for experimentation and some sample pages—and even entire chapters—and are available for unlimited viewing. The web site also includes a constantly updated menu of special discounts which are available only on the web site. Ask about the growing number of RRP databases accessible via the Internet on subscription or for a usage based price, such as the MARTINDALE-HUBBELL LAW DIRECTORY. For more information visit Bowker Reed Reference's web site at www.reedref.com or www.bowker.com or contact corporate offices, 121 Chanlon Road, New Providence, NJ 07974, (800) 521-8110, (800) 323-3288, fax (908) 665-3528, email info@bowker.com or webmaster@www.reedref.com.

YEARBOOK OF INTERNATIONAL ORGANIZATIONS is a 4 volume directory of non-profit organizations, commercial associations, business groups, conferences, religious orders and intergovernmental bodies. From K.G. Saur. $1,170 for 4 volumes.

YEARBOOK OF INTERNATIONAL ORGANIZATIONS PLUS is a CD ROM which was described by American Reference Books Annual as "The most comprehensive coverage of international organizations." This CD consolidates THE YEARBOOK OF INTERNATIONAL ORGANIZATIONS and WHO'S WHO IN INTERNATIONAL ORGANIZATIONS. It encompasses intergovernmental and national organizations, conferences and religious orders and fraternities. Search criteria include organization name, fields of activity, titles of publications, links to other organizations and more. User languages are English, German, French and Dutch. MS-DOS, Windows and Macintosh compatibility. From K.G. Saur. Updated annually. 1 year subscription $1,318.

R.R. Bowker (a unit of Cahners Business Information), 121 Chanlon Road, New Providence, NJ 07974 USA, Phone (888) BOWKER2 (888-269-5372) & (800) 323-3288, fax (908) 508-7696, email info@bowker.com, web www.bowker.com. Canada—R.R. Bowker, Markham, Ontario, phone (888) BOWKER9 & (905) 415-5837, fax (905) 479-6266. German speaking Europe—K.G. Saur Verlag, Munich, Germany, phone 49-89-76902-232, fax 49-89-76902-250, email 100730.1341@compuserve.com, web www.saur.de/home.htm. Rest of Europe incl. United Kingdom plus Africa & Asia—Bowker-Saur, W. Sussex, UK, phone 44-1342-326-972, fax 44-1342-335-612, email customer@bowker-saur.co.uk, web www.bowker-saur.com/service/. Australia/New Zealand—Thorpe, Port Melbourne, Victoria, Australia, phone 61-03-9-245-7370, fax 61-03-9-245-7395, email customer.service@thorpe.com.au, web www.thorpe.com.au. Technical support for CD ROMs (800) 323-3288, fax 908) 665-3528, email techsupport@bowker.com.

Internet

See Databases, Search Engines, and Web Sites—Books of URLs for Recruiters & Jobhunters

If you've identified an electronic database on the Internet that will make your job easier but the price is prohibitively high, check your local library. If you're having trouble locating a library with that particular database, perhaps the librarian can check another library for you. Besides a public library, a library at a corporation, embassy, professional association, university or school might be able to help you. Alternatively, maybe the publisher of the database can help locate a library which has it. The publisher should know who their customers are and it is actually to their benefit to help you. After all, as a user of their products, you are creating a demand in the marketplace. If the people at the toll free number can't help you, you're probably calling too low in the organization. Make a point of finding the phone number of corporate headquarters. Call someone senior enough to have the sophistication to understand why demand for their product is a good reason to help you, such as the Vice President or Senior Vice President of Sales and Marketing or even the CEO or Chairman.

ASSOCIATIONS UNLIMITED ONLINE is available on the Internet through GaleNet. You can subscribe to any of the several databases comprising ASSOCIATIONS UNLIMITED, including:

- NATIONAL ORGANIZATIONS OF THE US DATABASE

- REGIONAL, STATE AND LOCAL ORGANIZATIONS DATABASE

- INTERNATIONAL ORGANIZATIONS DATABASE

- ASSOCIATIONS MATERIALS DATABASE

- GOVERNMENT NONPROFIT ORGANIZATIONS DATABASE

For more information on available databases and pricing, contact Gale Group, P.O. Box 9187, Farmington Hills, MI 48333-9187. Toll free US and Canada (800) 877-GALE (4253) and (248) 699-GALE, fax (800) 414-5043 and (248) 699-8061, internet orders galeord@galegroup.com, web site www.galegroup.com or www.gale.com. All Gale Group products are available on approval. Contact Gale for details.

BOOKS IN PRINT is the only complete record of in-print, out-of-print and forthcoming books published or distributed in the US. For up-to-the-minute current information on INTERNET references and Internet Databases and Internet web sites available, use this reference. It should be available at a public library or in a good book store. Published annually. 9 volume set, $550. BOOKS IN PRINT ON DISC is available in Windows, MS-DOS and Macintosh. Annual subscription $550.

BOOKS IN PRINT INTERNET EDITION at www.booksinprint.com is available by subscription. Log on or call for details.

BOOKS IN PRINT ONLINE is available through the Dialog Corporation, Ovid Technologies, Inc. and LEXIS ®-NEXIS® on a "pay-as-you-go" basis. Contact the publisher for details. BOOKS OUT OF PRINT INTERNET EDITION can be searched free at www.bowker.com. R.R. Bowker (a unit of Cahners Business Information), 121 Chanlon Road, New Providence, NJ 07974 USA, Phone (888) BOWKER2 (888-269-5372) & (800) 323-3288, fax (908) 508-7696, email info@bowker.com, web www.bowker.com. Canada—R.R. Bowker, Markham, Ontario, phone (888) BOWKER9 & (905) 415-5837, fax (905) 479-6266. German speaking Europe—K.G. Saur Verlag, Munich, Germany, phone 49-89-76902-232, fax 49-89-76902-250, email 100730.1341@compuserve.com, web www.saur.de/home.htm. Rest of Europe incl. United Kingdom plus Africa & Asia—Bowker-Saur, W. Sussex, UK, phone 44-1342-326-972, fax 44-1342-335-612, email customer@bowker-saur.co.uk, web www.bowker-saur.com/service/. Australia/New Zealand—Thorpe, Port Melbourne, Victoria, Australia, phone 61-03-9-245-7370, fax 61-03-9-245-7395, email customer.service@thorpe.com.au, web www.thorpe.com.au. Technical support for CD ROMs (800) 323-3288, fax 908) 665-3528, email techsupport@bowker.com. Also see International Books in Print.

CANADIAN ALMANAC AND DIRECTORY includes abbreviations, associations and societies, broadcasting and communications, business statistics, church and religious organizations, commerce and finance, cultural directory, education directory, electoral districts, foreign and international contacts, geographic information, government directory, government quick reference, health and hospitals, historical and general information, legal and judicial directory, postal information, tourism and transportation. The Almanac also includes web sites of significant institutions in business, communications, and the arts, a "Who's Who" of key officials and organizations on the Canadian information highway and up-to-date provincial and territorial election results. Indexed by titles and keyword. $249 US. Inquire about CD ROM availability. Published by IHS Canada, Micromedia Limited, 20 Victoria Street, Toronto, Ontario M5C 2N8 CANADA, (800) 387-2689, (416) 362-5211, fax (416) 362-6161, email info@micromedia.on.ca. Distributed in the US by the Gale Group, P.O. Box 9187, Farmington Hills, MI 48333-9187. Toll free US and Canada (800) 877-GALE (4253) and (248) 699-GALE, fax (800) 414-5043 and (248) 699-8061, internet orders galeord@galegroup.com, web site www.galegroup.com or www.gale.com. All Gale Group products are available on approval. Contact Gale for details.

CYBERHOUND® ONLINE is a guide to finding and retrieving significant sites on the Internet. It has a search engine and 75 search delimiters. It adds thousands of site reviews monthly. To try it out free, go to the world wide web at http://www.cyberhound.com. For pricing and ordering information, call Gale Research at (800) 877-GALE.

CYBERHOUND'S® GUIDE TO COMPANIES ON THE INTERNET reviews over 2,000 corporate sites, including major companies as well as those in the information industry, software and hardware developers and networking and telecommunications companies. It also includes a user's guide, a directory of specialized business we sites, a bibliography of Internet products, and a glossary of Internet terms. At the time of this writing 1st edition (1996) available from Gale for $79, reduced from $95. Published by Euromonitor (England). Distributed by Gale Group, P.O. Box 9187, Farmington Hills, MI 48333-9187. Toll free US and Canada (800) 877-GALE (4253) and (248) 699-GALE, fax (800) 414-5043 and (248) 699-8061, internet orders galeord@galegroup.com, web site www.galegroup.com or www.gale.com. All Gale Group products are available on approval. Contact Gale for details.

CYBERHOUND'S® GUIDE TO INTERNET DISCUSSION GROUPS contains over 4,000 Internet listservs and news groups and a subject and master index, such as computer know-how groups, such as the virus Computer Newsgroup (comp.virus), health information groups, and social interaction groups. $79. Gale Group, P.O. Box 9187, Farmington Hills, MI 48333-9187. Toll free US and Canada (800) 877-GALE (4253) and (248) 699-GALE, fax (800) 414-5043 and (248) 699-8061, internet orders galeord@galegroup.com, web site www.galegroup.com or www.gale.com. All Gale Group products are available on approval. Contact Gale for details.

CYBERHOUND'S® GUIDE TO INTERNET LIBRARIES will guide you to online information including site descriptions and reviews of over 2,000 libraries, including contact information, mainfiles/subfiles, holdings information, subscriptions, services, how to access, information on special collections, OPAC addresses, plus a bibliography, a glossary of Internet terms, White Pages and two indexes. $79. Gale Group, P.O. Box 9187, Farmington Hills, MI 48333-9187. Toll free US and Canada (800) 877-GALE (4253) and (248) 699-GALE, fax (800) 414-5043 and (248) 699-8061, internet orders galeord@galegroup.com, web site www.galegroup.com or www.gale.com. All Gale Group products are available on approval. Contact Gale for details.

CYBERHOUND'S® GUIDE TO PEOPLE ON THE INTERNET is organized into three sections. (1) Who's Who Online identifies 1,000 online directories, databases and membership listings. For example, it lists Architects in Canada, Attorney Finder, Famous Left-Handers, and The Missing Persons Pages. (2) White Pages provides and alphabetical listing of 3,000 business professionals who are accessible by email. Other information includes area of expertise, personal and professional affiliation and company information. (3) Personal Web Sites are organized alphabetically by name. 1,500 pages of people in the news in business, entertainment, and sports. $79. Gale Group, P.O. Box 9187, Farmington Hills, MI 48333-9187. Toll free US and Canada (800) 877-GALE (4253) and (248) 699-GALE, fax (800) 414-5043 and (248) 699-8061, internet orders galeord@galegroup.com, web site www.galegroup.com or www.gale.com. All Gale Group products are available on approval. Contact Gale for details.

CYBERHOUND'S® GUIDE TO PUBLICATIONS ON THE INTERNET provides fully indexed information on over 3,000 Internet publications. Covers the World Wide Web, Gopher, Telnet and FTP sites that make online publication available to the public. $79. Gale Group, P.O. Box 9187, Farmington Hills, MI 48333-9187. Toll free US and Canada (800) 877-GALE (4253) and (248) 699-GALE, fax (800) 414-5043 and (248) 699-8061, internet orders galeord@galegroup.com, web site www.galegroup.com or www.gale.com. All Gale Group products are available on approval. Contact Gale for details.

D&B MILLION DOLLAR DATABASE is an online database on the Internet. Users can access information on more than one million small, mid-sized and large companies, with minimum revenues of $1 million. Searches can be conducted by 22 criteria, including as geographic location, sales volume, number of employees, industry classification. Each company includes up to 30 executive names and titles and biographical data that includes education, work history and birth date. For prices call Dun & Bradstreet at (800) 526-0651. For more information contact Dun & Bradstreet, Business Reference Solutions, Three Sylvan Way, Parsippany, New Jersey 07054. Email dnbmdd@mail.dnb.com. Web site http://www.dnbmdd.com.

EMPLOYERS' GUIDE TO RECRUITING ON THE INTERNET by Ray Schreyer and John McCarter, Impact Publications. $24.95. Available at bookstores or can be ordered on the web at www.technicalrecruiter.com.

EMPLOYMENT MARKETPLACE featured several articles on Internet Recruiting in the Winter 1998 issues. While the information is particularly appropriate for contingency recruiters, especially in technology and information systems, there is also valuable information and ideas for the retained search community. Articles include "Evaluating Employment Internet Sites" by William O. Warren, founder and president of Online Career Center, the Internet's first online recruitment site, (317) 293-6499, http://www.occ.com.

"Internet Recruiting—Real Possibilities" by Bob Mhoon, President of the Manx Group, Inc., Arlington Texas. Mhoon is an IT recruiter who provides Internet recruiting training programs and IT candidate profile directories. (817) 784-6775, email bobmhoon@onramp.net. "How We Billed an Extra $100,000 by Using the Internet" by Scott Allen, a Technical Recruiter for Emerald Resource Group in Cleveland, (216) 518-4048, email sfa@emeraldresourcegroup.com. According to Bob Mhoon, President of The Manx Group in Arlington, Texas, "A fundamental problem facing recruiters who want to learn how to effectively use the Internet is simply that no one has a map leading to all of the available resources and tools. Then, even though common Internet tools have user instructions, the tricks to effective recruiting applications must often be learned through trial and error. Difficulties are compounded when generic Internet training programs frustrate recruiters who want sessions focused on their real needs. The Internet is such a new phenomenon that Internet trainers who also have a recruiting background are in short supply." Ordering information: Call to request back issues. $26 annual subscription, 4 issues, Employment Marketplace, PO Box 31112, St. Louis, MO 63131, (314) 569-3095, fax (314) 458-4955.

ENCYCLOPEDIA OF BUSINESS INFORMATION SOURCES will lead you to specialized directories, professional associations, trade publications, newsletters, databases, Internet resources and more. It's an excellent reference and a great way to find key resources in any industry fast. $330. Gale Group, P.O. Box 9187, Farmington Hills, MI 48333-9187. Toll free US and Canada (800) 877-GALE (4253) and (248) 699-GALE, fax (800) 414-5043 and (248) 699-8061, internet orders galeord@galegroup.com, web site www.galegroup.com or www.gale.com. All Gale Group products are available on approval. Contact Gale for details.

EXECUTIVE SEARCH RESEARCH DIRECTORY (ESRD) provides information on over 350 contract research consultants, including descriptions of research services provided, fees, experience, where trained, areas of concentration, and unusual capabilities, including 26 freelancers with an Internet specialty. Cross referenced by over 300 specialties. $88 postpaid. Ordering information: Kenneth J. Cole, Publisher, The Recruiting & Search Report, P.O. Box 9433, Panama City Beach, FL 32417. (850) 235-3733, fax (850) 233-9695. Email jcole9433@aol.com.

GALE DIRECTORY OF DATABASES identifies over 12,000 international databases available in a variety of formats including online, CD ROM, diskette, and others. Entries include producer name, description, subject, language, cost, update frequency, geographic coverage. Volume 1, Online Databases, $260. Volume 2, CD-ROM, Diskette, Magnetic Tape, Handheld and Batch Access Database Products, $170. Both volumes $390. ONLINE MAGAZINE described this as "An excellent directory of online databases." Gale Group, P.O. Box 9187, Farmington Hills, MI 48333-9187. Toll free US and Canada (800) 877-GALE (4253) and (248) 699-GALE, fax (800) 414-5043 and (248) 699-8061, internet orders galeord@galegroup.com, web site www.galegroup.com or www.gale.com. All Gale Group products are available on approval. Contact Gale for details.

GALE DIRECTORY OF DATABASES ONLINE is a GaleNet database on the Internet that identifies over 12,000 international databases in various formats, including CD ROM, diskettes, online and others. Check your local library for free access or contact Gale for annual subscription rates. Gale Group, P.O. Box 9187, Farmington Hills, MI 48333-9187. Toll free US and Canada (800) 877-GALE (4253) and (248) 699-GALE, fax (800) 414-5043 and (248) 699-8061, internet orders galeord@galegroup.com, web site www.galegroup.com or www.gale.com. All Gale Group products are available on approval. Contact Gale for details.

GALE DIRECTORY OF PUBLICATIONS AND BROADCAST MEDIA identifies key personnel, feature editors and more at radio and TV stations and cable companies. $615 for 5 volume set. Gale Group, P.O. Box 9187, Farmington Hills, MI 48333-9187. Toll free US and Canada (800) 877-GALE (4253) and (248) 699-GALE, fax (800) 414-5043 and (248) 699-8061, internet orders galeord@galegroup.com, web site www.galegroup.com or www.gale.com. All Gale Group products are available on approval. Contact Gale for details.

The Gale Group's publications are available on GaleNet's customized internet databases. For more information and a possible free trial, contact a sales representative at The Gale Group, P.O. Box 9187, Farmington Hills, MI 48333-9187. Toll free US and Canada (800) 877-GALE (4253) and (248) 699-GALE, fax (800) 414-5043 and (248) 699-8061, web site www.galegroup.com or www.gale.com.

GALE GUIDE TO INTERNET DATABASES, formerly titled CYBERHOUND'S GUIDE TO INTERNET DATABASES, identifies over 5,000 internet databases. $115. Gale Group, P.O. Box 9187, Farmington Hills, MI 48333-9187. Toll free US and Canada (800) 877-GALE (4253) and (248) 699-GALE, fax (800) 414-5043 and (248) 699-8061, internet orders galeord@galegroup.com, web site www.galegroup.com or www.gale.com. All Gale Group products are available on approval. Contact Gale for details.

GaleNet is an online resource on the Internet that provides an integrated, one-step access to the most frequently used Gale databases, such as GALE'S READY REFERENCE SHELF ONLINE. As GaleNet's capabilities are constantly changing and being upgraded, contact the publisher for details and prices. Gale Group, P.O. Box 9187, Farmington Hills, MI 48333-9187. Toll free US and Canada (800) 877-GALE (4253) and (248) 699-GALE, fax (800) 414-5043 and (248) 699-8061, internet orders galeord@galegroup.com, web site www.galegroup.com or www.gale.com. All Gale Group products are available on approval. Contact Gale for details.

GALE'S READY REFERENCE SHELF ONLINE is a GaleNet Internet resource that provides integrated access to databases covering national, regional, state, local and international associations, publishers, newspapers and periodicals, directories, newsletters, online databases, portable databases, database products and vendors, special libraries and research centers. Information is included from numerous Gale databases, among them THE ENCYCLOPEDIA OF ASSOCIATIONS, PUBLISHERS DIRECTORY, GALE DIRECTORY OF PUBLICATIONS AND BROADCAST MEDIA and several others. If it is prohibitively expensive, locate a library with with this resource. Gale Group, P.O. Box 9187, Farmington Hills, MI 48333-9187. Toll free US and Canada (800) 877-GALE (4253) and (248) 699-GALE, fax (800) 414-5043 and (248) 699-8061, internet orders galeord@galegroup.com, web site www.galegroup.com or www.gale.com. All Gale Group products are available on approval. Contact Gale for details.

INTERNET ADVERTISING BUREAUS (IABs)—According to Warren O. Warren, founder and president of Online Career Center, the Internet's first online recruiting site, careful evaluation of recruiting sites is crucial to the success of your recruiting program. In order to substantiate claims made by commercial sites, ask for third party audits and forms of proof. Make sure the sites you select will provide third party audit reports from an Internet Advertising Bureau (IAB) recognized audit firm, such as Nielsen I/PRO, publishers of I/AUDIT™, a trademark of Internet Profiles Corporation. For more information, refer to Warren's article, "Evaluating Employment Internet Sites" which appeared in the Winter 1998 Employment Marketplace. Employment Marketplace, PO Box 31112, St. Louis, MO 63131, (314) 569-3095, fax (314) 458-4955.

INTERNET RECRUITING EDGE by Barbara Ling is a comprehensive collection of research assembled over a two year period. Developed for the novice and experienced Internet recruiter alike, and with a foreword by Tony Byrne, topics include: Where, Oh Where, is my Candidate Now?, Does the Internet Really Benefit Businesses? Phones Still Work, But Don't Buy a Mansion if You Only Need a Cottage, How to Find Candidates on the Internet, Non-Traditional Resources, Before You Begin—A Primer on Internet Culture—Netiquette, Beginner Candidate Location Skill, Resume Banks, Search Engine Basics, The Joy of Bookmarks, The Art of Job Posting, Sleuthing for Company Directories, Finding Employee Directories, Finding Executive Biographies, Alumni Organizations, Forums and Bulletin Boards, Internet Classifieds, Online E-zines (magazines), Professional Organizations, Colleges, Metasearch at Highway 61, Realistic Goals Before You Begin Your Own Recruiter Web site, Perilous Pitfalls, How To Buy Your Recruiter Business Site, Locating Good Web Site Designers, Your Site is Designed—Now What? How To Market A Recruiter Web Site, 14 Killer Web Site Search Engine Visibility Tips, and more. $149. Order by visiting the web site http://www.barbaraling.com or call (732) 563-1464.

JOBHUNTING ON THE INTERNET by Richard Nelson Bolles, Ten Speed Press, P.O. Box 7123, Berkeley, CA 94707. Among other things, this book provides a small but reasonably complete listing of INTERNET URL's (Uniform Resource Locators) with a short description of the contents of each. By the author of the classic WHAT COLOR IS YOUR PARACHUTE?

KENNEDY INFORMATION has databases of management consulting firms and their key principals, North American and international executive recruiters, temporary placement firms, venture capital firms and out-placement firms. Kennedy Information, One Kennedy Place, Route 12 South, Fitzwilliam, NH 03447, phone (800) 531-0007 or 603-585-6544, fax 603-585-9555, email bookstore@kennedyinfo.com, web site www.kennedyinfo.com.

MAJOR TELECOMMUNICATIONS COMPANIES OF THE WORLD—INCLUDING MAJOR INTERNET COMPANIES provides information on 3,700 companies, including 600 international companies involved in the Internet. $830. US distributor: Larry Meranus Professional Publications & Services, 4 Demoray Court, Pine Brook, NJ 07058, (800) MERANUS or (800) 637-2687. Published by Graham & Whiteside Ltd., Tuition House, 5-6 Francis Grove, London SW19 4DT, England. Web site http://www.major-co-data.com. Email sales@major-co-data.com.

NELSON INVESTMENT MANAGEMENT NETWORK, also known as Nelnet, is an Internet database (www.nelnet.com) that provides comprehensive information on over 3,000 worldwide institutional investment management firms on 9,500 products and 45,000 professionals. Nelnet users can access without charge the World's Best Money Managers, Nelson's industry standard performance rankings, Manager Hires, which managers were hired by which plan sponsors; Job bank, the investment industry's free online employment service; and useful Industry Analyses. Investment Managers can launch their own Nelnet Web site for $100 a month. Users can access Nelnet free. www.nelnet.com. For more information, contact Nelson Information, P.O. Box 591, Port Chester, NY 10573 USA. (800) 333-6357, Phone outside the US (914) 937-8400, Fax (914) 937-8590, web site http://www.nelnet.com.

PHILLIPS BUSINESS INFORMATION provides information in newsletters, magazines, directories and on multiple web sites covering a range of topics, such as magazine products, telecommunications and cable products, satellite products, media, new media and Internet products, marketing and public relations products, financial technology and electronic commerce, aviation and defense products. For more information, contact: Phillips Business Information, Inc., a Phillips Publishing International Company, 120 Seven Locks Road, Potomac, MD 20854, (301) 340-1520, (301) 340-7788, (800) 777-5006, Internet pbi@phillips.com, web site www.phillips.com.

RECRUITERS' INTERNET SURVIVAL GUIDE by John Sumser, author of the 1996 Electronic Recruiting Index, rated over 500 recruiting web sites and analyzed Internet recruiting issues. The Recruiters' Internet Survival Guide, published by Staffing Industry Resources, $89.50. To view the table of contents or to order a copy, go to web site www.interbiznet.com or contact IBN (Internet Business Network) in Mill Valley, CA.

RESEARCH CENTERS AND SERVICES DIRECTORY ONLINE is a GaleNet database on the Internet which includes three types of R&D centers around the world—US research centers, international research centers and government research centers, including nonprofit research centers, commercial labs, international institutes, government experiment stations, university research parks, in the areas of agriculture, environment, engineering, physical and earth sciences, labor and industrial relations, and education. Available by subscription or at a library. 1 user $1,575 per year, 2 users $2,835 annually. Call publisher for additional pricing information. Gale Group, P.O. Box 9187, Farmington Hills, MI 48333-9187. Toll free US and Canada (800) 877-GALE (4253) and (248) 699-GALE, fax (800) 414-5043 and (248) 699-8061, internet orders galeord@galegroup.com, web site www.galegroup.com or www.gale.com. All Gale Group products are available on approval. Contact Gale for details.

SMALL BUSINESS SOURCEBOOK encompasses comprehensive information on small businesses, including professional associations, training sources, small business investment companies, over 400 Internet databases, publications, awards and honors, company and personal email addresses. $325 for 2 vol. set. Gale Group, P.O. Box 9187, Farmington Hills, MI 48333-9187. Toll free US and Canada (800) 877-GALE (4253) and (248) 699-GALE, fax (800) 414-5043 and (248) 699-8061, internet orders galeord@galegroup.com, web site www.galegroup.com or www.gale.com. All Gale Group products are available on approval. Contact Gale for details.

www.555-1212.com is a URL for an Internet Domain name registration service and directory of phone and email listings for businesses and individuals.

www.asktheheadhunter.com is the web site for the book, ASK THE HEADHUNTER, a book that can effectively be used by both job hunters and interviewers, by Nick Corcodilos, email northbridge@sprintmail.com. According to Tom Peters, it is "a powerful hiring tool.no manager can afford to miss" and it "shreds some of our most basic assumptions about the way to hire top people." Published by Penguin Putnam, New York, $14.95 The book is available from the web site and at bookstores. Corcodilos and his client, Merrill Lynch's Vice President of Global Staffing, were jointly featured in a discussion about changes in corporate recruiting and hiring practices in a segment on "Opportunity Knocks," a CNBC special on Executive Search. To purchase this 5 hour video, contact CNBC or Corcodilos.

www.dbm.com/jobguide is an excellent comprehensive web site if you're either a recruiter looking for candidates or a job seeker. It is the "best Internet recruiting starting point" taught to recruiters by the Tiburon Group, web site http://www.tiburon group.com, a Chicago based firm that provides "Strategic Internet Recruiting Solutions Consultants and Trainers." Tiburon Group, phone (773) 907-8330, Fax (773) 907-9481, email getajob@tiburongroup.com, web site www.tiburongroup.com.

www.interbiznet.com/hrstart.html is the Electronic Recruiting News web site. It features the Recruiters Internet Survival Guide, recruiting seminars and more.

www.occ.com is the URL for the On Line Career Center, one of the Internet's first online recruitment sites, launched in 1993. It is a major recruitment web site that spends millions of dollars in advertising to drive traffic to the site. This is a major site that was developed by William O Warren, who has received honors for his pioneering work in the development of Internet Recruiting. This web site allows you to enter your job profile and have job listings automatically downloaded to your Email. Questions to webmaster@occ.com. www.occ.com was rated by the *National Business Employment Weekly* as one of the top 5 sites in 3 different categories: "Sites Offering the Best Overall Support for Job Seekers," "Sites Offering the Best Job-Search Support" and "Sites Offering the Best Career Resources for Job Seekers." Openings are mainly in engineering, information technology and sales and marketing. The site developer is TMP Worldwide, New York, New York.

www.tiburon group.com is the web site for the Tiburon Group, Inc., a Chicago based firm that provides "Strategic Internet Recruiting Solutions Consultants and Trainers." They are also a recruiting firm. Phone (773) 907-8330, Fax (773) 907-9481, email getajob@tiburongroup.com.

www.web sitez.com is the URL to a web site that assists in finding any web address in the world.

www.whois.net is the URL to a capability that allows you to find your own domain or look up a web site.

Internet Recruitment Training

AIRS—Advanced Internet Recruitment Strategies—is a firm which provides training for recruiters who use the Internet as a recruiting tool. For more information contact AIRS, 1790 Franklin Street, Berkeley, CA 94702, phone (800) 336-6360, fax (888) 997-5559. Check their web site at www.airsdirectory.com, which contains many excellent free resources.

CAREERXROADS and Cornell University have partnered to provide hands-on Internet workshops for Electronic Staffing and Human Resources and the Internet. Seminars are are scheduled for major cities across the country. For further information about conferences, call Cornell at (212) 340-2863. For information about content of conferences, call (732) 821-6652 or email mmc@careerxroads.com. Web site www.careerxroads.com

EMPLOYMENT MARKETPLACE featured several articles on Internet Recruiting in the Winter 1998 issues. While the information is particularly appropriate for contingency recruiters, especially in technology and information systems, there is also valuable information and ideas for the retained search community. Articles include "Evaluating Employment Internet Sites" by William O. Warren, founder and president of Online Career Center, the Internet's first online recruitment site, (317) 293-6499, http://www.occ.com. "Internet Recruiting—Real Possibilities" by Bob Mhoon, President of the Manx Group, Inc., Arlington Texas. Mhoon is an IT recruiter who provides Internet recruiting training programs and IT candidate profile directories. (817) 784-6775, email bobmhoon@onramp.net. "How We Billed an Extra $100,000 by Using the Internet" by Scott Allen, a Technical Recruiter for Emerald Resource Group in Cleveland, (216) 518-4048, email sfa@emeraldresourcegroup.com.

According to Bob Mhoon, President of The Manx Group in Arlington, Texas, "A fundamental problem facing recruiters who want to learn how to effectively use the Internet is simply that no one has a map leading to all of the available resources and tools. Then, even though common Internet tools have user instructions, the tricks to effective recruiting applications must often be learned through trial and error. Difficulties are compounded when generic Internet training programs frustrate recruiters who want sessions focused on their real needs. The Internet is such a new phenomenon that Internet trainers who also have a recruiting background are in short supply."

Ordering information: Call to request back issues. $26 annual subscription, 4 issues, Employment Marketplace, PO Box 31112, St. Louis, MO 63131, (314) 569-3095, fax (314) 458-4955

INTERNET BUSINESS NETWORK presents Advanced Internet Recruiting Strategies and Tactics, an intensive one day workshop led by John Sumoor, author of the RECRUITER'S INTERNET SURVIVAL GUIDE. For more information call (800) 358-2278 or fax 415-383-8676, or contact Employment Marketplace, PO Box 31112, St. Louis, MO 63131, (314) 569-3095, fax (314) 458-4955.

INTERNET RECRUITING EDGE by Barbara Ling is a comprehensive collection of research assembled over a two year period. Developed for the novice and experienced Internet recruiter alike, and with a foreword by Tony Byrne, topics include: Where, Oh Where, is my Candidate Now?, Does the Internet Really Benefit Businesses? Phones Still Work, But Don't Buy a Mansion if You Only Need a Cottage, How to Find Candidates on the Internet, Non-Traditional Resources, Before You Begin—A Primer on Internet Culture—Netiquette, Beginner Candidate Location Skill, Resume Banks, Search Engine Basics, The Joy of Bookmarks, The Art of Job Posting, Sleuthing for Company Directories, Finding Employee Directories, Finding Executive Biographies, Alumni Organizations, Forums and Bulletin Boards, Internet Classifieds, Online E-zines (magazines), Professional Organizations, Colleges, Metasearch at Highway 61, Realistic Goals Before You Begin Your Own Recruiter Web site, Perilous Pitfalls, How To Buy Your Recruiter Business Site, Locating Good Web Site Designers, Your Site is Designed—Now What? How To Market A Recruiter Web Site, 14 Killer Web Site Search Engine Visibility Tips, and more. $149. Order by visiting the web site http://www.barbaraling.com or call (732) 563-1464.

TIBURON GROUP, a certified AIRS and hire.com solutions partner, is a Chicago firm comprised of "Strategic Internet Recruiting Solutions Consultants and Trainers." They are leading industry knowledge experts on effective Internet recruiting strategies who offer hands-on seminars across the US aimed at helping companies maximize their Internet recuiting efforts. "We consult, train, or do it for our clients." For more information, contact Carl Kutsmode, Principal, Tiburon Group, Inc., 4753 North Broadway, Suite 500, Chicago, IL 60640-3700, (773) 907-8330, fax (773) 907-9481, getajob@tiburongroup.com, web sites www.tiburongroup.com and www.recruiterresources.com.

www.interbiznet.com/hrstart.html is the Electronic Recruiting News web site. It features the Recruiters Internet Survival Guide, recruiting seminars and more.

Intranet

DIALOG® is the oldest and largest online information service, comprised of over 470 databases from an array of disciplines, including business, US and international news, patents and trademarks, science and technology and consumer news. DIALOG SELECT provides a web based guided search service with access to 250 DIALOG databases for people with little or no database search expertise. It is designed to meet the specific information needs of professional end users in the technology, pharmaceutical, legal, consumer product and media industries. DIALOG@SITE is an intranet-based service providing access to the current DIALOG ONDISC™ CD ROM collection, using Internet browser capabilities. Companies will have wide access to an array of fields, such as business, science, technology, medicine and law through their local Intranet. DIALOG is a service mark of the Dialog Corporation and is exclusively distributed in Canada by Infomart Dialog Limited. For subscriptions and rate information for all services in Canada, contact Infomart Dialog Limited at (416) 442-2198 or (800) 668-9215. In the US call Dialog (Knight Ridder Information, Inc.) in Mountain View, California at (800) 3-DIALOG, web site www.dialog.com.

Investment Banking

CORPORATE FINANCE SOURCEBOOK—THE GUIDE TO MAJOR INVESTMENT SOURCES AND RELATED FINANCIAL SERVICES contains over 13,000 names of executives at 3,700 organizations that, broadly speaking, supply growth capital to businesses, such as venture capital lenders, private lenders, commercial finance and factoring, pension managers, master trusts. Names of key management are included. A special section details public offerings of the past 3 years and mergers and acquisitions over $100 million. $499.95 hard copy, excluding discounts. NRP's catalog states, "If you're dissatisfied for any reason, simply return the product within 30 days for a full refund." If the price is prohibitively high, remember your local library. Available in book, online, magnetic tape, and in mailing list formats. For more information contact: National Register Publishing, 121 Chanlon Road, New Providence, NJ 07974 USA, (800) 521-8110, http://www.lexis-nexis.com. For information about online access, call LEXIS®—NEXIS® Online Services, Mountainview, CA at (800) 346-9759; for mailing lists call Cahners Direct Marketing Services at (800) 323-4958; all other inquiries (800) 521-8110.

EUROMONEY BANK REGISTER is a detailed directory of the world's leading financial institutions and a comprehensive guide to "who's who" in global capital markets. This directory lists senior executives, investment and commercial bankers, traders, analysts, support and legal staff. Expanded coverage of Asia, central Europe and eastern Europe and Latin America is provided. Available in print or CD ROM. The print version of The EUROMONEY Bank Register is comprehensively indexed alphabetically and by city. It also contains rankings of the top banks. The read only version of the CD ROM provides full access to the entire database. However, by disabling the print and export functions, the result is a lower cost alternative to the full version. A 14 day free trial is available with the CD ROM.

> Print Directory, USA, US $493 or 297 pounds sterling
> Print Directory, UK, Europe, Rest of World US $493 or 297 pounds sterling
> Read Only Version CD ROM 750 pounds or US $1,250
> Full Version CD ROM 1,750 pounds or US $3,000

Ordering information: Larry Meranus Professional Publications & Services, 4 Demoray Court, Pine Brook, NJ 07058, (800) MERANUS or (800) 637-2687. Distributed in England by EUROMONEY Books, Plymbridge Distributors Limited, Estover, Plymouth PL6 7PZ, England. Phone 44 (0) 171 779-8955 for a free demo disk. Fax 44 (0) 171 779-8541.

GUIDE TO GLOBAL M&A. For more information contact Larry Meranus Professional Publications & Services, 4 Demoray Court, Pine Brook, NJ 07058, (800) MERANUS or (800) 637-2687. Distributed in England by EUROMONEY Books, Plymbridge Distributors Limited, Estover, Plymouth PL6 7PZ, England. Phone 44 (0) 171 779-8955. Fax 44 (0) 171 779-8541.

HARVARD BUSINESS SCHOOL students gather data and publish it for their own job hunting purposes. The Management Consulting Club publishes one fine book and The Corporate Finance Club publishes another. Basically, the major firms provide descriptions of their businesses, strategic focus, size, contact information and other important data. Since many of these companies are privately held, these resources are unusually valuable because this information could otherwise be very difficult to obtain. It usually requires some detective work to track them down, but it's worth the effort. Call the Harvard Business School in Boston. Ask the operator for contact information for either the Management Consulting Club or the Corporate Finance Club. If you coax them, you might be able to get more information than a phone number, like a mailing address, an email address or a web site.

INSTITUTIONAL INVESTOR publishes excellent surveys of various Wall Street industries. Generally one survey appears in each monthly issue, including names of contacts. Annual subscription $325. INSTITUTIONAL INVESTOR, 488 Madison Avenue, New York, NY 10022, (212) 303-3300.

Investment Management

CONSULTANT DIRECTORY profiles the top 400 consulting organizations that specifically serve the pension and investment industries. Includes career biographical information, including education, number of years with the firm, specialties, employment history, direct dial phone number and email address. $295. Published by Standard & Poors, a division of McGraw-Hill, MONEY MARKET DIRECTORIES, INC., 320 East Main Street, Charlottesville, VA 22902, http://www.mmdaccess.com, (800) 446-2810, (804) 977-1450.

DIRECTORY OF REGISTERED INVESTMENT ADVISORS identifies over 9,000 CEO's, 7,000 Investment Officers, 10,000 Portfolio Managers, 6,000 Directors of Research and Research Analysts, 2,800 Traders and Trading Managers, and 1,200 Directors of Operations/Chief Financial Officers, plus web sites and personal email addresses. The directory also includes a section on mutual funds for over 4,000 funds at 375 firms, including the name of the person responsible for managing the fund, 1,3 and 5 year returns, benchmark comparisons, and more. DIRECTORY OF REGISTERED INVESTMENT ADVISORS with 4 Regional editions, $475. The Directory with no regional editions, $395. Published by Standard & Poors, a division of

McGraw-Hill, MONEY MARKET DIRECTORIES, INC., 320 East Main Street, Charlottesville, VA 22902, http://www.mmdaccess.com, (800) 446-2810, (804) 977-1450.

FINANCIAL SERVICES CANADA is a handbook of banks, non-depository institutions, stock exchange and brokers, investment management, mutual funds, insurance, accountants, government agencies, financial associations and more, including contact numbers, name, title, organization, phone, fax, email, web site, and cellular. $199 for book, $299 for CD ROM, $399 for both. Ordering information: Copp Clark Professional, 200 Adelaide Street West, 3rd floor, Toronto, ON M5H 1W7 CANADA. Email orders@mail.CanadaInfo.com. Web site http://www.coppclark.com. For additional information contact: IHS Canada, Micromedia Limited, 20 Victoria Street, Toronto, Ontario M5C 2N8 CANADA, (800) 387-2689, (416) 362-5211, fax (416) 362-6161, email info@micromedia.on.ca.

INSTITUTIONAL INVESTOR publishes excellent surveys of various Wall Street industries. Generally one survey appears in each monthly issue, including names of contacts. Annual subscription $325. INSTITUTIONAL INVESTOR, 488 Madison Avenue, New York, NY 10022, (212) 303-3300.

INVESTMENT COMPANIES YEARBOOK is an annual directory that summarizes 12,000 funds, provides performance information, fund address, phone number, advisor, and identifies portfolio manager(s) and tenure, plus minimum investment, sales charges and more. $295. Ordering information: Securities Data Publishing, 1290 Avenue of the Americas, 36th floor, New York, NY 10104, (212) 830-9363.

INVESTMENT MANAGEMENT DIRECTORY. For more information contact Larry Meranus Professional Publications & Services, 4 Demoray Court, Pine Brook, NJ 07058, (800) MERANUS or (800) 637-2687. Distributed in England by EUROMONEY Books, Plymbridge Distributors Limited, Estover, Plymouth PL6 7PZ, England. Phone 44 (0) 171 779-8955. Fax 44 (0) 171 779-8541.

INVESTMENT NEWS is a weekly trade publication. Crain Communications, Inc. is headquartered in Chicago with offices in major cities throughout the US plus London, Tokyo and Frankfurt. New York location: 220 East 42nd Street, New York, NY 10017, (212) 210-0100, Circulation (800) 678-9595. Annual subscription $38. Web site www.investmentnews.com.

MMD ACCESS for Windows is software exclusively designed for investment management sales and marketing professionals. It identifies over 42,000 Corporate, union and government pension plan sponsors, including over 40,000 defined benefit officers and over 55,000 Defined Contribution Investment Officers and more. Published by Standard & Poors, a division of McGraw-Hill, MONEY MARKET DIRECTORIES, INC., 320 East Main Street, Charlottesville, VA 22902, http://www.mmdaccess.com, (800) 446-2810, (804) 977-1450.

MONEY MARKET DIRECTORY OF PENSION FUNDS AND THEIR INVESTMENT MANAGERS provides plan sponsor profiles, including firm name, address, phone and fax, senior investment officers, names of other key personnel and decision makes including in house asset manager, officer handling inquiries from money managers, officer who evaluates money managers, officer who handles responses to requests for proposals, benefits administrator, chief human resources officer, investor relations officer, corporate cash manager, director of development for endowments some direct dial phone numbers and personal email addresses. The Directory also profiles investment management firms that invest pension assets and investment manager consultant firms. Published by Standard & Poors, a division of McGraw-Hill, MONEY MARKET DIRECTORIES, INC., 320 East Main Street, Charlottesville, VA 22902, http://www.mmdaccess.com, (800) 446-2810, (804) 977-1450. Regional Directories also available. $995 per copy MONEY MARKET DIRECTORY, $150 per additional REGIONAL DIRECTORY.

MONEY MARKET DIRECTORY OF TAX-EXEMPT ORGANIZATIONS provides information on private foundations, hospitals and other health service organizations, church related service groups, schools, associations, civic leagues and fraternal beneficiary organizations. Names are provided for over 6,000 senior investment officers, 3000 secondary investment officers, 4,800 presidents and principals, over 4,000 Chairmen, 12,500 trustees and board officers, 600 in house managers, 900 benefits managers, 900 chief human resources officers, 700 chief operating officers and 300 directors of development. $440. Published by Standard & Poors, a division of McGraw-Hill, MONEY MARKET DIRECTORIES, INC., 320 East Main Street, Charlottesville, VA 22902, http://www.mmdaccess.com, (800) 446-2810, (804) 977-1450.

NELSON FINANCIAL DATABASE provides comprehensive information on the global institutional investment market. Information formatted to your precise needs is available from Nelson Information Mailing List & Customized Database service. The NELSON FINANCIAL DATABASE is comprised of:

30,000 executives at investment management firms

11,000 executives at research firms

40,000 executives at plan sponsors

3,000 executives at pension fund consulting firms

24,000 executives at institutional real estate firms

4,000 executives at technology based vendors

The database also consists of extensive investment information, including money manager performance, peer group analysis, special surveys and more. For customers who with to use Nelson's information in their own systems, Nelson will supply customized data export, using all or any data items. Mailing lists are also available for direct marketers.For more information, contact Nelson Mailing List & Customized Database Services, P.O. Box 591, Port Chester, NY 10573 USA. (800) 333-6357, Phone outside the US (914) 937-8400, Fax (914) 937-8590, web site http://www.nelnet.com.

NELSON INVESTMENT MANAGEMENT NETWORK, also known as Nelnet, is an Internet database (www.nelnet.com) that provides comprehensive information on over 3,000 worldwide institutional investment management firms on 9,500 products and 45,000 professionals. Nelnet users can access without charge the World's Best Money Managers, Nelson's industry standard performance rankings, Manager Hires, which managers were hired by which plan sponsors; Job bank, the investment industry's free online employment service; and useful Industry Analyses. Investment Managers can launch their own Nelnet Web site for $100 a month. Users can access Nelnet free. www.nelnet.com. For more information, contact Nelson Information, P.O. Box 591, Port Chester, NY 10573 USA. (800) 333-6357, Phone outside the US (914) 937-8400, Fax (914) 937-8590, web site http://www.nelnet.com.

NELSON'S DIRECTORY OF INVESTMENT MANAGERS identifies names of key executives at the top 2,600 investment management firms. Includes information on investment styles, asset allocations, largest holdings, stock selection processes, areas of investment emphasis, clients service, and performance results for 1,3,5 and 10 year periods for over 9,500 investment products. Published annually. $495. Nelson Information, P.O. Box 591, Port Chester, NY 10573 USA. (800) 333-6357, Phone outside the US (914) 937-8400, Fax (914) 937-8590, web site http://www.nelnet.com.

WORLD'S BEST MONEY MANAGERS is a quarterly report extracted from the Nelson Investment Manager Database that ranks the performance of investment managers in 200 categories. Portfolios are grouped according to investment style, time period and portfolio size. Results are available for 1 quarter and for 1,3, 5 and 10 years. Published quarterly. $245 per year. Nelson Information, P.O. Box 591, Port Chester, NY 10573 USA. (800) 333-6357, Phone outside the US (914) 937-8400, Fax (914) 937-8590, web site http://www.nelnet.com.

www.mmdaccess.com is the URL for Money Market Directories, Inc., 320 East Main Street, Charlottesville, VA 22902, (800) 446-2810, (804) 977-1450. Owned by Standard & Poors, a division of McGraw Hill.

www.nelnet.com is the URL for Wall Street and financial publisher Nelson Information, P.O. Box 591, Port Chester, NY 10573 USA. (800) 333-6357, phone outside the US (914) 937-8400, fax (914) 937-8590.

Investment Research

CATALOG OF INSTITUTIONAL RESEARCH REPORTS (GLOBAL EDITION) tracks over 15,000 monthly investment research reports published by Wall Street's European and Pacific counterparts in over 500 research firms worldwide. Reports are listed alphabetically by company and by research firm. This information is best used for target list research, or your own personal investing. Published ten times per year. $125 per year. Nelson Information, P.O. Box 591, Port Chester, NY 10573 USA. (800) 333-6357, Phone outside the US (914) 937-8400, Fax (914) 937-8590, web site http://www.nelnet.com.

DIRECTORY OF INVESTMENT RESEARCH/NELSON'S INVESTMENT RESEARCH profiles over 9,000 US companies and 13,000 non-US public companies, including 100,000 key corporate executives. This directory also identifies which securities analysts cover which stocks for over 22,000 stocks worldwide. Complete analyst coverage is presented for over 750 research firms, representing 1,000 offices and over 9,000 securities analysts. Published annually. $535. Nelson Information, P.O. Box 591, Port Chester, NY 10573 USA. (800) 333-6357, Phone outside the US (914) 937-8400, Fax (914) 937-8590, web site http://www.nelnet.com.

DIRECTORY OF REGISTERED INVESTMENT ADVISORS identifies over 9,000 CEO's, 7,000 Investment Officers, 10,000 Portfolio Managers, 6,000 Directors of Research and Research Analysts, 2,800 Traders and Trading Managers, and 1,200 Directors of Operations/Chief Financial Officers, plus web sites and personal email addresses. The directory also includes a section on mutual funds for over 4,000 funds at 375 firms, including the name of the person responsible for managing the fund, 1,3 and 5 year returns, benchmark comparisons, and more. DIRECTORY OF REGISTERED INVESTMENT ADVISORS with 4 Regional editions, $475. The Directory with no regional editions, $395. Published by Standard & Poors, a division of McGraw-Hill, MONEY MARKET DIRECTORIES, INC., 320 East Main Street, Charlottesville, VA 22902, http://www.mmdaccess.com, (800) 446-2810, (804) 977-1450.

INSTITUTIONAL INVESTOR publishes excellent surveys of various Wall Street industries. Generally one survey appears in each monthly issue, including names of contacts. Annual subscription $325. INSTITU-TIONAL INVESTOR, 488 Madison Avenue, New York, NY 10022, (212) 303-3300.

Ireland

See England, Europe, International

DIRECTORY OF AMERICAN FIRMS OPERATING IN FOREIGN COUNTRIES, REGIONAL EDITION—EUROPE, WESTERN, $159. Uniworld Business Publications, Inc., 257 Central Park West, Suite 10A, New York, NY 10024-4110, (212) 496-2448, fax (212) 769-0413, email uniworldbp@aol.com. Web site: http://www.uniworldbp.com.

DIRECTORY OF FOREIGN FIRMS OPERATING IN THE UNITED STATES, REGIONAL EDITION—EUROPE, ALL. Includes Austria, Belgium, Czech Republic, Denmark, England, Finland, France, Germany, Greece, Iceland, Ireland, Italy, Luxembourg, Netherlands, Norway, Poland, Portugal, Romania, Russia, Scotland, Slovenia, Spain, Sweden, Switzerland. $119. Uniworld Business Publications, Inc., 257 Central Park West, Suite 10A, New York, NY 10024-4110, (212) 496-2448, fax (212) 769-0413, email uniworldbp@aol.com. Web site: http://www.uniworldbp.com.

DIRECTORY OF FOREIGN FIRMS OPERATING IN THE UNITED STATES, REGIONAL EDITION—BRITISH ISLES. Includes England, Ireland, Scotland. $59. Ordering information: Uniworld Business Publications, Inc., 257 Central Park West, Suite 10A, New York, NY 10024-4110, (212) 496-2448, fax (212) 769-0413, email uniworldbp@aol.com. Web site: http://www.uniworldbp.com.

MAJOR COMPANIES OF EUROPE is a 4 volume edition containing 194,000 names of contacts at 24,000 companies in all 20 western European countries. Vol. 1 —Austria, Belgium, Denmark, Ireland, Finland, France. Vol. 2—Germany, Greece, Italy, Liechtenstein, Luxembourg. Vol. 3—The Netherlands, Norway, Portugal, Spain, Sweden, Switzerland. Vol. 4—United Kingdom. $1,700 for 4 volume set. $535 per volume. CD ROM, updated quarterly, is also available. Published by Graham & Whiteside Ltd., Tuition House, 5-6 Francis Grove, London SW19 4DT, England. Web site http://www.major-co-data.com. Email sales@major-co-data.com. Distributed by: Larry Meranus Professional Publications & Services, 4 Demoray Court, Pine Brook, NJ 07058, (800) MERANUS or (800) 637-2687. Also distributed by Gale Group, P.O. Box 9187, Farmington Hills, MI 48333-9187. Toll free US and Canada (800) 877-GALE (4253) and (248) 699-GALE, fax (800) 414-5043 and (248) 699-8061, internet orders galeord@galegroup.com, web site www.galegroup.com or www.gale.com. All Gale Group products are available on approval. Contact Gale for details.

PENSION FUNDS AND THEIR ADVISERS provides information on the top 2,000 pension funds in the United Kingdom, plus major funds of Japan, Belgium, France, Germany, Ireland, The Netherlands and

Switzerland. This Directory is the only source in the US that monitors the growth of assets in the international market. Information includes internal and external fund management contacts, major US and Canadian pension funds and money managers, major European and Japanese pension funds and their advisors. It also includes comprehensive listings of 900 advisors to the pension fund industry including financial advisers, accountants, actuaries and pension fund consultants, pension administrators, insurance companies, attorneys, computer services, global custody, pension trustees, pension /financial recruitment consultants, investment research, associations and professional groups, and publications. $310. Published by A.P. Information Services, Ltd. Marketed exclusively in North America MONEY MARKET DIRECTORIES INC./STANDARD AND POORS, 320 East Main Street, Charlottesville, VA 22902, http://www.mmdaccess.com, (800) 446-2810, (804) 977-1450.

WHO OWNS WHOM DIRECTORY by Dun & Bradstreet is a six volume set containing information on the structure and ownership of 320,000 company affiliates and subsidiaries of over 23,000 companies worldwide. It is available in four regional editions: Australia and the Far East, North America, UK/Ireland, and Continental Europe. Published annually. For prices and ordering information as well as information about more worldwide corporate linkage products from D&B WORLDBASE, D&B's global database of 42 million records in over 200 countries, contact Dun & Bradstreet at (800) 526-0651, Dun & Bradstreet, Business Reference Solutions, Three Sylvan Way, Parsippany, NJ 07054. Email dnbmdd@mail.dnb.com. Web site http://www.dnbmdd.com

Israel

See International, Middle East

DUN'S GUIDE TO ISRAEL contains information on the 10,000 leading companies in Israel. Text in Hebrew and English. Dun & Bradstreet, Business Reference Solutions, Three Sylvan Way, Parsippany, NJ 07054 USA. (800) 526-0651. Email dnbmdd@mail.dnb.com. Web site http://www.dnbmdd.com.

Italy

See Europe, International

DIRECTORY OF AMERICAN FIRMS OPERATING IN FOREIGN COUNTRIES, REGIONAL EDITION—ITALY, $49. Ordering information: Uniworld Business Publications, Inc., 257 Central Park West, Suite 10A, New York, NY 10024-4110, (212) 496-2448, fax (212) 769-0413, email uniworldbp@aol.com. Web site: http://www.uniworldbp.com.

DIRECTORY OF FOREIGN FIRMS OPERATING IN THE UNITED STATES, REGIONAL EDITION—ITALY. $29. Ordering information: Uniworld Business Publications, Inc., 257 Central Park West, Suite 10A, New York, NY 10024-4110, (212) 496-2448, fax (212) 769-0413, email uniworldbp@aol.com. Web site: http://www.uniworldbp.com.

ITALIAN BOOKS IN PRINT—CATALOGO DEI LIBRI IN COMMERCIO, sponsored by Associazione Italiana Editori, published by Editrice Bibliografica, 6 volumes $650. ITALIAN BOOKS IN PRINT ON CD-ROM (ALICE CD), one year subscription $1,220. R.R. Bowker (a unit of Cahners Business Information), 121 Chanlon Road, New Providence, NJ 07974 USA, Phone (888) BOWKER2 (888-269-5372) & (800) 323-3288, fax (908) 508-7696, email info@bowker.com, web www.bowker.com. Canada—R.R. Bowker, Markham, Ontario, phone (888) BOWKER9 & (905) 415-5837, fax (905) 479-6266. German speaking Europe—K.G. Saur Verlag, Munich, Germany, phone 49-89-76902-232, fax 49-89-76902-250, email 100730.1341@compuserve.com, web www.saur.de/home.htm. Rest of Europe incl. United Kingdom plus Africa & Asia—Bowker-Saur, W. Sussex, UK, phone 44-1342-326-972, fax 44-1342-335-612, email customer@bowker-saur.co.uk, web www.bowker-saur.com/service/. Australia/New Zealand—Thorpe, Port Melbourne, Victoria, Australia, phone 61-03-9-245-7370, fax 61-03-9-245-7395, email customer.service@thorpe.com.au, web www.thorpe.com.au. Technical support for CD ROMs (800) 323-3288, fax 908) 665-3528, email techsupport@bowker.com.

ITALY'S TOP 10,000 COMPANIES provides company information by export percentages, profit/loss ratios and rankings. Dun & Bradstreet, Business Reference Solutions, Three Sylvan Way, Parsippany, NJ 07054 USA. (800) 526-0651. Email dnbmdd@mail.dnb.com. Web site http://www.dnbmdd.com.

www.bowker.com is the web site for this major research publisher. It includes Flagship Products and Services, an online Product Catalog, Electronic Publishing products including CD ROMs, Internet Databases, and Online Subscription and Site Licensing Databases; press releases, career opportunities, and more. Many of their references are accessible through this web site, such as BOOKS IN PRINT PLUS CANADIAN EDITION, ULRICH'S ON DISC, GERMAN BOOKS IN PRINT, GERMAN BOOKS OUT OF PRINT, INTERNATIONAL BOOKS IN PRINT PLUS, ITALIAN BOOKS IN PRINT, YEARBOOK OF INTERNATIONAL ORGANIZATIONS PLUS, ULRICH'S INTERNATIONAL PERIODICALS DIRECTORY, THE SOFTWARE ENCYCLOPEDIA, BOWKER'S COMPLETE VIDEO DIRECTORY, AMERICAN BOOK PUBLISHING RECORD. Visit the web site for more information.

www.europages.com is a web site of a business directory of over 500,000 European firms. In Deutsch, English, Espanol, Français & Italiano. Features include Search for Companies, Company Catalogues, Business Information, Yellow Pages in Europe. Search by Product/Service, Thematic Search or by Company Name. Address, phone, fax, products, turnover. Europages' Daily Business News, European Trade Fairs, Chambers of Commerce in Europe, European Patent Offices, Official International Organisations, European Standardization Bodies.

www.kompass.com is the web site for the highly respected Kompass country directories and databases. This web site contains a searchable database that encompasses over 60 countries, 2.5 million executive names, information on 1.5 million companies, 19 million key product references, and 370,000 trade and brand names. At the time of this writing, Kompass is available in English and French. Deutsch, Espanol and Italiano will soon be available.

J

Japan

See Asia, International

ASAHIYA is a bookstore that specializes in Japanese publications. While most are popular in nature and written in Japanese, there are some directories and business publications in English, such as those from JETRO, the Japan External Trade Organization. A store is located at the corner of Vanderbilt and 45th Street, near Grand Central Station in Manhattan. Check other major cities for an Asahiya book store near you.

DIRECTORY OF AMERICAN FIRMS OPERATING IN FOREIGN COUNTRIES, REGIONAL EDITION—JAPAN AND KOREA. $59. Uniworld Business Publications, Inc., 257 Central Park West, Suite 10A, New York, NY 10024-4110, (212) 496-2448, fax (212) 769-0413, email uniworldbp@aol.com. Web site: http://www.uniworldbp.com.

DIRECTORY OF FOREIGN FIRMS OPERATING IN THE UNITED STATES, REGIONAL EDITION—JAPAN AND KOREA. $69. Uniworld Business Publications, Inc., 257 Central Park West, Suite 10A, New York, NY 10024-4110, (212) 496-2448, fax (212) 769-0413, email uniworldbp@aol.com. Web site: http://www.uniworldbp.com.

JAPAN FINANCIAL DIRECTORY NEW YORK is published by Nikkin America, Inc., 445 Fifth Avenue, Suite 27D, New York, NY 10016, (212) 679-0196. $195 hard copy. It can also be purchased at Asahiya, the Japanese bookstore at the corner of Vanderbilt and 45th Street, near Grand Central Station in Manhattan. Check other major cities for an Asahiya book store near you.

JAPAN TRADE DIRECTORY is a comprehensive reference with information on Japanese companies seeking export, import, service trade and international business opportunities. It provides data on about 2,800 companies and over 22,000 products. $340. Published by JETRO, the Japanese External Trade Organization. Distributed by Gale Group, P.O. Box 9187, Farmington Hills, MI 48333-9187. Toll free US and Canada (800)

877-GALE (4253) and (248) 699-GALE, fax (800) 414-5043 and (248) 699-8061, Internet orders galeord@galegroup.com, web site www.galegroup.com or www.gale.com. All Gale Group products are available on approval. Contact Gale for details.

JAPANESE AFFILIATED COMPANIES IN THE US AND CANADA lists companies operating in North America whose ownership is at least 10% Japanese. Includes key personnel and chief products. $260. Published by the Japanese External Trade Organization (JETRO). JETRO is headquartered in Japan and has offices in major cities in the US, including Atlanta, Chicago, Dallas, Denver, Houston, Los Angeles, New York and San Francisco. If this reference is no longer being distributed by the Gale Group, contact JETRO. Gale Group, P.O. Box 9187, Farmington Hills, MI 48333-9187. Toll free US and Canada (800) 877-GALE (4253) and (248) 699-GALE, fax (800) 414-5043 and (248) 699-8061, Internet orders galeord@galegroup.com, web site www.galegroup.com or www.gale.com. All Gale Group products are available on approval. Contact Gale for details.

JAPANESE EXTERNAL TRADE ORGANIZATION (JETRO) is headquartered in Japan and has offices in major cities in the US, including Atlanta, Chicago, Dallas, Denver, Houston, Los Angeles, New York and San Francisco. For more information about business information which they publish, contact them. New York (212) 997-0400 and (212) 220-4365.

PENSION FUNDS AND THEIR ADVISERS provides information on the top 2,000 pension funds in the United Kingdom, plus major funds of Japan, Belgium, France, Germany, Ireland, The Netherlands and Switzerland. This Directory is the only source in the US that monitors the growth of assets in the international market. Information includes internal and external fund management contacts, major US and Canadian pension funds and money managers, major European and Japanese pension funds and their advisors. It also includes comprehensive listings of 900 advisors to the pension fund industry including financial advisers, accountants, actuaries and pension fund consultants, pension administrators, insurance companies, attorneys, computer services, global custody, pension trustees, pension /financial recruitment consultants, investment research, associations and professional groups, and publications. $310. Published by A.P. Information Services, Ltd. Marketed exclusively in North America MONEY MARKET DIRECTORIES INC./STANDARD AND POORS, 320 East Main Street, Charlottesville, VA 22902, http://www.mmdaccess.com, (800) 446-2810, (804) 977-1450.

Jobhunters' Resources

See Databases—Resume and Job Matching and Web Sites

Jobhunters and recruiters often need each other, especially if you're a company recruiter, or if you work for a contingency recruiting firm or a personnel agency where most of your candidates come to you, actively looking for a job. This category of the book—Jobhunters' Resources—contains information that is especially useful for that type of recruiting because it identifies where a recruiter can find job seekers. Naturally, this information will also be valuable to jobhunters.

It should be noted that not all recruiters will necessarily need this information, especially retained search consultants whose primary mission is to identify candidates not on the job market. Basically, tapping into a web site where job hunters post their resumes is similar to the old-fashioned want ad because it generates job applicants actively on the job market. Obviously, some of these applicants will be out of work (some for good reason) while other unemployed candidates will be excellent. In addition, many employers paying handsome retainer search fees would rather see candidates who aren't looking, because, for one thing, the psychology usually is that people want something if they think they can't have it. Further, search firm clients are paying for *access* to candidates who are otherwise not available to them. That said, search firms who fail to use the Internet, electronic databases and other electronic career management tools are going the way of the buggy whip. Here are some places to start researching these electronic tools. Also refer to "Web Sites."

If you've identified an electronic database that will make your job easier but the price is prohibitively high, check your local library. If you're having trouble locating a library with that particular database, perhaps the librarian can locate another library which has the resource you need. Besides a public library, a library at a corporation, embassy, professional association, outplacement firm, university or school or the government might be able to help you. Alternatively, maybe the publisher of the database can help locate a library which has it. The publisher should know who their customers are and it is actually to their benefit to help you. After all, as a user of their products, you are creating a demand in the marketplace. If the people at the toll free number can't help you, you're probably calling too low in the organization. Make a point of finding the phone number of corporate headquarters. Call someone senior enough to have the sophistication to understand why demand for their product is a good reason to help you, such as the Vice President or Senior Vice President of Sales and Marketing or even the CEO or Chairman.

AMERICAN ELECTRONICS ASSOCIATION annually publishes the AEA DIRECTORY for $175. With 18 regional groups, this association conducts networking programs for industry executives, and provides information on compensation surveys and employee benefits plans, among other things. For more information contact: American Electronics Association (AEA), 5201 Great America Parkway, Suite 520, PO Box 54990, Santa Clara, CA 95056, (408) 987-4200.

AMERICAN JOBS ABROAD is a guide to over 800 US firms and organizations that employ Americans abroad in 110 countries. While this directory provides considerable information for a job seeker, it can also be used to identify American target companies operating in foreign countries. Regardless of whether the ideal candidate will be a local or an American, once you have identified who the target companies are, you can then conduct ID research to identify sources and prospects. $65. Gale Group, P.O. Box 9187, Farmington Hills, MI 48333-9187. Toll free US and Canada (800) 877-GALE (4253) and (248) 699-GALE, fax (800) 414-5043 and (248) 699-8061, Internet orders galeord@galegroup.com, web site www.galegroup.com or www.gale.com. All Gale Group products are available on approval. Contact Gale for details.

ASIAN AMERICAN MANUFACTURERS ASSOCIATION (AAMA) publishes an annual Membership Directory and a newsletter which contains new member listings and employment listings. It also publishes ASIAN AMERICAN ENTREPRENEURS AND EXECUTIVES OF PUBLIC COMPANIES IN THE HIGH TECH INDUSTRY. Membership is comprised of Asian American manufacturers of technology products, such as computers, microprocessors, semiconductors, biotech, software and electronics equipment. They present an annual award for entrepreneurship. For more information contact Asian American Manufacturers Association (AAMA), 39120 Argonaut Way, #309, Freemont, CA 94538-1398, (925) 461-0800.

ASSOCIATION OF EXECUTIVE SEARCH CONSULTANTS MEMBERSHIP DIRECTORY identifies the premier retainer search firms and includes over 100 firms, including addresses of all locations around the world. Cost to non-members is $35.00. AESC, 230 Park Avenue, Suite 1549, New York, NY 10169-0005, (212) 949-9556.

"The Best Web Sites For Job Hunters" was the cover story in the *National Business Employment Weekly* November 15-21, 1998 issue. It surveyed and reviewed 70 web sites which had been profiled in their publication during the previous year. To see a copy, try the library.

Over 60 of the 70 surveyed web sites have been included in this book. Web sites with lower compensation positions have been omitted, and most of those were in computer related areas. However, all the web sites which received top rankings were included, regardless of compensation range, especially sites in out-of-the-ordinary niches.

CANADA EMPLOYMENT WEEKLY'S URL is www.mediacorp2.com/. It features The Career Bookstore for Canadian Career Books, Talent Available to Market Yourself to Canadian Recruiters and Search Firms, Canadian Directory of Search Firms, and Who's Hiring for a list of Canada's top employers. www.mediacorp2.com/cdsf/index.html leads you directly to the Canadian Directory of Search Firms and the Career Bookstore—"Quality Canadian Career Books" including GET WIRED, YOU'RE HIRED, "the definitive Canadian guide to job hunting in Canada."

CANADIAN DIRECTORY OF SEARCH FIRMS, in French and English, lists over 1,700 search firms and 3,000 recruitment professionals. 70 occupational categories, geographic index, and a Who's Who Index. $39.95, ISBN 0-9681447-1-3. To locate the CANADIAN DIRECTORY OF SEARCH FIRMS, go to www.netjobs.com or ask your favorite bookstore to look it up in BOOKS IN PRINT.

CAREER GUIDE—D&B EMPLOYMENT OPPORTUNITIES DIRECTORY provides information on approximately 5,000 companies throughout the US. It contains listings for the largest employers in the US, including information for questionnaires and from the D&B information base. Information is presented alphabetically, geographically, by industry, employer branch offices, disciplines hired geographically, employers offering WORK-STUDY OR INTERNSHIP PROGRAMS and personnel consultants. Updated annually. For prices call Dun & Bradstreet at (800) 526-0651. For more information contact Dun & Bradstreet, Business Reference Solutions, Three Sylvan Way, Parsippany, New Jersey 07054. Email dnbmdd@mail.dnb.com. Web site http://www.dnbmdd.com.

CERTIFICATION AND ACCREDITATION PROGRAMS DIRECTORY describes 1,600 certification programs and details over 200 accrediting organizations. It contains information on certification eligibility and the procedures for national voluntary certification and accreditation programs that denote skill level, professionalism, accomplishment and excellence. $99. Gale Group, P.O. Box 9187, Farmington Hills, MI 48333-9187. Toll free US and Canada (800) 877-GALE (4253) and (248) 699-GALE, fax (800) 414-5043 and (248) 699-8061, Internet orders galeord@galegroup.com, web site www.galegroup.com or www.gale.com. All Gale Group products are available on approval. Contact Gale for details.

COMPUTING, HI-TECH AND TELECOMMUNICATIONS CAREER HANDBOOK, published by Canadian publisher Marskell. Web site www.marskell.com.

D&B MARKETING INFORMATION BASE contains marketing information on 10,000,000 companies. Every month it is updated, reflecting some 500,000 changes: new business additions, CEO CHANGES and address changes. Information on senior management changes is particularly valuable to job hunters and search firms is an indicator of change, which could mean hiring activity, and/or a need for executive search or unbundled search services. Organizations in transition are generally good places to recruit because quality talent may be unhappy with the politics of the new organization. With respect to the execution of an executive search, this information can be best utilized to develop a list of target companies. Then, names and titles can be identified using another database or through traditional ID research. This technique could be used for an extremely difficult recruiting assignment. For example, finding companies in turmoil could provide a good place to search for candidates eager for a change. Selections are delivered on tape, cartridge, diskette or hard copy. For prices call Dun & Bradstreet at (800) 526-0651. For more information contact Dun & Bradstreet, Business Reference Solutions, Three Sylvan Way, Parsippany, New Jersey 07054. Email dnbmdd@mail.dnb.com. Web site http://www.dnbmdd.com.

D&B MARKETPLACE DISC is a CD ROM that provides access to names, titles, addresses, SIC or NAICS codes, sales volume, number of employees, year the business was founded, phone numbers and marketing information on more than 10 million US businesses. Searches can be conducted by location, size, industry code and by business information. Mailing labels, telemarketing data and full demographic data records can be printed and exported. Available in Windows and Macintosh. Updated quarterly. For prices call Dun & Bradstreet at (800) 526-0651. For more information contact Dun & Bradstreet, Business Reference Solutions, Three Sylvan Way, Parsippany, New Jersey 07054. Email dnbmdd@mail.dnb.com. Web site http://www.dnbmdd.com.

D&B MILLION DOLLAR DATABASE is an online database on the Internet. Users can access information on more than one million small, mid-sized and large companies, with minimum revenues of $1 million. Searches can be conducted by 22 criteria, including as geographic location, sales volume, number of employees, industry classification. Each company includes up to 30 executive names and titles and biographical data that includes education, work history and birth date. For prices call Dun & Bradstreet at (800) 526-0651. For more information contact Dun & Bradstreet, Business Reference Solutions, Three Sylvan Way, Parsippany, New Jersey 07054. Email dnbmdd@mail.dnb.com. Web site http://www.dnbmdd.com.

D&B MILLION DOLLAR DISC is a CD ROM which covers over 240,000 public and private companies, compared to either 160,000 or 50,000 in the two versions of the MILLION DOLLAR DIRECTORY in hard copy. In addition, this CD ROM also contains BIOGRAPHICAL information on key executives. Searches can be conducted by company name, industry, size of company, geography, executive name, key word, and executive business backgrounds. Companies listed have sales of at least $ million or more than 100 employees. Branch locations have more than 500 employees. Both are updated annually. D&B MILLION DOLLAR DISC PLUS is a similar CD ROM with more expansive coverage, including 400,000 companies—both privately held and public—compared to 240,000 in the MILLION DOLLAR DISC. It includes companies with at least 50 employees or revenues of $3 million. For prices call Dun & Bradstreet at (800) 526-0651. For more information contact Dun & Bradstreet, Business Reference Solutions, Three Sylvan Way, Parsippany, New Jersey 07054. Email dnbmdd@mail.dnb.com. Web site http://www.dnbmdd.com.

DIRECTORY OF AMERICAN FIRMS OPERATING IN FOREIGN COUNTRIES lists over 2,500 American companies and 18,500 Foreign subsidiaries, affiliates or branches in 132 countries. Companies can be looked up by name in volume 1 and by country in volumes 2 and 3. Listings include name and US address of firm, Phone and fax numbers of US headquarters, CEO and other executive names such as personnel officer and foreign officer, principal product or service, number of employees, countries where foreign affiliates are located. $220. Ordering information: Uniworld Business Publications, Inc., 257 Central Park West, Suite 10A, New York, NY 10024-4110, (212) 496-2448, fax (212) 769-0413, email uniworldbp@aol.com. Web site: http://www.uniworldbp.com.

DIRECTORY OF EXECUTIVE RECRUITERS profiles over 5,000 firms in 7,000 locations with over 12,800 individual recruiters listed. It is cross-referenced according to retainer vs. contingency firms, job functions, industries, geography and recruiter specialities. Available in paperback $47.95, hardcover (with more details on each firm) $179.95, on CD as SearchSelect® $245.00, in label or list form for selected categories or on the web. A companion publication, KENNEDY'S POCKET GUIDE TO WORKING WITH EXECUTIVE RECRUITERS is a 150-page assemblage of 30 chapters by the experts themselves, plus a Lexicon of Executive Recruiting. $9.95. Kennedy Information, One Kennedy Place, Route 12 South, Fitzwilliam, NH 03447, phone (800) 531-0007 or 603-585-6544, fax 603-585-9555, email bookstore@kennedyinfo.com, web site www.kennedyinfo.com.

DIRECTORY OF FOREIGN FIRMS OPERATING IN THE UNITED STATES identifies over 2,000 foreign firms plus some 4,000 US affiliates from 71 countries. Includes name of parent foreign firm and address, principal products or service, name and address of American subsidiary, CEO, affiliate or branch, principal product, number of employees, phone and fax, percentage of foreign ownership. $200. Uniworld Business Publications, Inc., 257 Central Park West, Suite 10A, New York, NY 10024-4110, (212) 496-2448, fax (212) 769-0413, email uniworldbp@aol.com. Web site: http://www.uniworldbp.com.

DIRECTORY OF INDEPENDENT RESEARCH CONSULTANTS contains information on 200 contract consultants. Jobhunters who are sending resumes to search firms might also want to include research consultants. They are often indistinguishable from search consultants because the roles of both can be so similar. In addition, at a search firm, a researcher customarily conducts the first screen of a resume, regardless of whom it's addressed to. Further, it's not unusual for these consultants to be directly retained by corporations purchasing "unbundled search" services, which basically means a less expensive "no frills" search product. This means that independent research consultants represent another third party avenue for job hunters, in addition to executive search firms and contingency recruiting firms. $65. Ordering information: Kennedy Information, Kennedy Place, Route 12 South, Fitzwilliam, NH 03447, (800) 531-1026, (800) 531-0007, (603) 585-3101, web site www.kennedyinfo.com.

DIRECTORY OF LEGAL RECRUITERS, $129. Ordering information: Kennedy Information, One Kennedy Place, Route 12 South, Fitzwilliam, NH 03447, phone (800) 531-0007 or 603-585-6544, fax 603-585-9555, email bookstore@kennedyinfo.com, web site www.kennedyinfo.com.

ENCYCLOPEDIA OF ASSOCIATIONS: INTERNATIONAL ORGANIZATIONS includes nearly 20,000 multinational and national organizations in foreign countries, including US based associations with multinational membership. Entries also include email addresses, web sites and bulletin board addresses, lobbying activities, and publication and convention information. Indexed by geography, keyword and executives. $595 for 2 volume set. Also available in CD ROM. Database available via commercial online service. Gale Group, P.O. Box 9187, Farmington Hills, MI 48333-9187. Toll free US and Canada (800) 877-GALE (4253) and (248) 699-GALE, fax (800) 414-5043 and (248) 699-8061, Internet orders galeord@galegroup.com, web site www.galegroup.com or www.gale.com. All Gale Group products are available on approval. Contact Gale for details.

ENCYCLOPEDIA OF ASSOCIATIONS: NATIONAL ORGANIZATIONS OF THE US. This superb reference is one of the first places you should look when beginning a new recruiting assignment or when looking for specialized references of any type. The keyword index makes this comprehensive reference easy to use, even in hard copy. For over 23,000 nonprofit professional associations with a national scope, this encyclopedia reveals:

- Publications, including membership rosters and newsletters

- Dates and locations of association conferences and conventions

- Names of Executive Directors, who are usually incredible sources of industry information if you call and speak to them

- Committees

- Job and candidate referral banks, which can provide resumes of other industry sources and sometimes candidates

- It includes organizations in these categories: business, trade, environmental, agricultural, legal, govern mental, engineering, technological, scientific, educational, cultural, social welfare, health & medical, public affairs, ethnic, labor unions, chambers of commerce, tourism, & others.

   Volume 1, National Organizations of the US, $505
   Volume 2, Geographic and Executive Indexes, $390
   Volume 3, Supplement, $405

Gale Group, P.O. Box 9187, Farmington Hills, MI 48333-9187. Toll free US and Canada (800) 877-GALE (4253) and (248) 699-GALE, fax (800) 414-5043 and (248) 699-8061, Internet orders galeord@galegroup.com, web site www.galegroup.com or www.gale.com. All Gale Group products are available on approval. Contact Gale for details.

ENCYCLOPEDIA OF ASSOCIATIONS: REGIONAL, STATE AND LOCAL ORGANIZATIONS. The information in this directory is not duplicated anywhere in ENCYCLOPEDIA OF ASSOCIATIONS. Over 100,000 nonprofit organizations are included in this directory. $585 for 5 volume set or $140 per individual volume. Also available on CD ROM and online on the Internet through a GaleNet subscription.

   Volume 1, Great Lakes States (Illinois, Indiana, Michigan, Minnesota, Ohio, Wisconsin)
   Volume 2, Northeastern States (Connecticut, Maine, Massachusetts, New Hampshire, New Jersey, New York, Pennsylvania, Rhode Islands, Vermont)
   Volume 3, Southern and Middle Atlantic States (Including Puerto Rico and the Virgin Islands) (Alabama, Delaware, Washington, DC, Florida, Georgia, Kentucky, Maryland, Mississippi, North Carolina, Puerto Rico, South Carolina, Tennessee, Virginia, West Virginia, Virgin Islands)
   Volume 4, South Central and Great Plains States (Arkansas, Iowa, Kansas, Louisiana, Missouri, Nebraska, North Dakota, Oklahoma, South Dakota, Texas)
   Volume 5, Western States (Alaska, Arizona, California, Colorado, Guam, Hawaii, Idaho, Montana, Nevada, New Mexico, Oregon, Utah, Washington, Wyoming)

Gale Group, P.O. Box 9187, Farmington Hills, MI 48333-9187. Toll free US and Canada (800) 877-GALE (4253) and (248) 699-GALE, fax (800) 414-5043 and (248) 699-8061, Internet orders galeord@galegroup.com, web site www.galegroup.com or www.gale.com. All Gale Group products are available on approval. Contact Gale for details.

EXECUTIVE SEARCH RESEARCH DIRECTORY (ESRD) provides information on over 350 contract research consultants, including descriptions of research services provided, fees, experience, where trained, areas of concentration, and unusual capabilities, including 26 freelancers with an Internet specialty. Cross referenced by over 300 specialties. $88 postpaid. Ordering information: Kenneth J. Cole, Publisher, The Recruiting & Search Report, P.O. Box 9433, Panama City Beach, FL 32417. (850) 235-3733, fax (850) 233-9695. Email jcole9433@aol.com.

FINANCIAL EXECUTIVES INSTITUTE (FEI) provides a resume matching service for its members, who are senior financial executives, and employers and search firms. The cost is minimal or nil. For more information, contact the Financial Executive Institute. They can be located in the ENCYCLOPEDIA OF ASSOCIATIONS or Lorna Daniells' BUSINESS INFORMATION SOURCES or another librarians' reference. Or call your local business librarian. Or ask a senior financial executive, such as a corporate controller or chief financial officer who would likely be a member. The FEI also publishes a membership directory which cross references members by company. However, it is only available to members, so you will have to borrow a copy from a member. It can be used to identify names of contacts, either for recruiting purposes, or for job hunters networking. They also have a web site.

The FEI is one of many professional associations that provides its members with this type of service.

FOUNDATION CENTER provides library services and disseminates current information on foundation and corporate giving through their national collections in New York City and Washington, DC, through field offices in Atlanta, Cleveland and San Francisco, and through their network of over 200 libraries in all 50 states and abroad. With these resources, grant seekers have free access to core Center publications and a wide range of books, periodicals and research in connection with foundations and philanthropy. Services include reference librarian assistance, free orientations, and microform and photocopying facilities. For more information call or visit the National Collections in New York (212) 620-4230 or Washington, DC (202) 331-1400. Or contact Field Offices in San Francisco (415) 397-0902, Cleveland (216) 861-1934, or Atlanta (404) 880-0094. The Foundation Center, 79 Fifth Avenue, New York, NY 10003-3076. Web site http://www.fdncenter.org includes their catalog of publications.

HARVARD BUSINESS SCHOOL'S BAKER LIBRARY in Boston provides an outstanding consumer marketing web site at www.library.hbs.edu/. This web site identifies extensive sources of information on consumer marketing, including retail both for job hunters and researchers. It includes associations, membership directories, information on direct mail, public relations, corporate communications, online direct mail and online Dun and Bradstreet Credit Reports.

While access to the web site itself is free and available to anyone, access to the CAREER ADVISOR database is available only to current Harvard Business School students and Harvard Business School Alumni Advisors (Harvard Business School alumni who have agreed to serve as Career advisors to current students and other alumni). The Advisor Database can be searched by industry, geography, job function, job title, year of graduation and company name. In addition, Reference Librarians at the Harvard Business School can conduct searches for a fee. Hundreds of databases are available. Ask at the Reference Desk for more information. For example, Dun & Bradstreet's Credit Reports are a lucrative source of information about privately held companies.

HEALTHCARE NEWS NET, whose URL is http://cpsnet.com, is web site which includes a daily online news service from CPS COMMUNICATIONS, Publisher of the Pharmaceutical Marketers Directory. News is presented in eight areas: Headline news, Industry News, Product News, Media News, People On The Move, Agency Assignments, New Companies and Locations, and Information & Resources. Another part of CPSNET is JobMart, a confidential Internet career advertising service which costs $180 to list a 90 word ad for 90 days. http://cpsnet.com. For more information contact CPS COMMUNICATIONS, INC., 7200 West Camino Real, Suite 215, Boca Raton, FL 33433, (561) 368-9301, sales office (203) 778-1463, email webmaster@cpsnet.com, web site http://www.cpsnet.com.

http://taps.com is a web site for people looking for contract and permanent positions in the United Kingdom and Europe. Positions are mainly in information technology, mostly in the $20,000 to $50,000 range. TAPS.COM was developed by Internet Appointments, Ltd., London, England and was launched in 1996.

NEW ENGLAND EXECUTIVE RESOURCES COUNCIL, whose URL is http://199.233.99.2/neerc/, is an organization of primarily search consultants. The group meets in Waltham, Mass. The web site includes a listing of members, including some photos.

I COULD DO ANYTHING IF I ONLY KNEW WHAT IT WAS—HOW TO DISCOVER WHAT YOU REALLY WANT AND HOW TO GET IT, by Barbara Sher. $12.95 at bookstores.

INDUSTRY NORMS & KEY BUSINESS RATIOS is a reference that provides financial performance statistics for over 1 million public and private firms in over 800 lines of business. This statistical reference provides performance benchmarks for over 800 lines of business on over 1 million companies, both publicly and privately held. As this directory contains no names or titles, it is most appropriate for conducting industry research to develop a target list of top performing companies. Published annually. Also available on diskette. For prices call Dun & Bradstreet at (800) 526-0651. For more information contact Dun & Bradstreet, Business Reference Solutions, Three Sylvan Way, Parsippany, New Jersey 07054. Email dnbmdd@mail.dnb.com. Web site http://www.dnbmdd.com.

INC. is a magazine written for entrepreneurs and small businesses. Their INC. 500 list of the 500 most rapidly growing businesses is an excellent resource. INC. Magazine, 38 Commercial Wharf, Boston, MA 02110, (800) 978-1800, (617) 248-8000, www.inc.com. To search for articles, go to www.inc.com/search.

INTERNET RECRUITING EDGE by Barbara Ling is a comprehensive collection of research assembled over a two year period. Developed for the novice and experienced Internet recruiter alike, and with a foreword by Tony Byrne, topics include: Where, Oh Where, is my Candidate Now?, Does the Internet Really Benefit Businesses? Phones Still Work, But Don't Buy a Mansion if You Only Need a Cottage, How to Find Candidates on the Internet, Non-Traditional Resources, Before You Begin—A Primer on Internet Culture—Netiquette, Beginner Candidate Location Skill, Resume Banks, Search Engine Basics, The Joy of Bookmarks, The Art of Job Posting, Sleuthing for Company Directories, Finding Employee Directories, Finding Executive Biographies, Alumni Organizations, Forums and Bulletin Boards, Internet Classifieds, Online E-zines (magazines), Professional Organizations, Colleges, Metasearch at Highway 61, Realistic Goals Before You Begin Your Own Recruiter Web site, Perilous Pitfalls, How To Buy Your Recruiter Business Site, Locating Good Web Site Designers, Your Site is Designed—Now What? How To Market A Recruiter Web Site, 14 Killer Web Site Search Engine Visibility Tips, and more. $149. Order by visiting the web site http://www.barbaraling.com or call (732) 563-1464.

JOB HUNTER'S SOURCEBOOK lists "Sources of Job-Hunting Information by Professions and Occupations." It is alphabetically arranged by careers and lists sources of help-wanted ads, employer directories, employment agencies, placement services and electronic resources for 179 careers and email addresses and web sites. $90. Gale Group, P.O. Box 9187, Farmington Hills, MI 48333-9187. Toll free US and Canada (800) 877-GALE (4253) and (248) 699-GALE, fax (800) 414-5043 and (248) 699-8061, Internet orders galeord@galegroup.com, web site www.galegroup.com or www.gale.com. All Gale Group products are available on approval. Contact Gale for details.

JOBHUNTING ON THE INTERNET by Richard Nelson Bolles, Ten Speed Press, P.O. Box 7123, Berkeley, CA 94707. Among other things, this book provides a small but reasonably complete listing of INTERNET URL's (Uniform Resource Locators) with a short description of the contents of each. By the author of the classic WHAT COLOR IS YOUR PARACHUTE?

JOBSEEKERS GUIDE TO SOCIALLY RESPONSIBLE COMPANIES, $59.95. If this directory is not available from the publisher, you might find it in the library. Gale Group, P.O. Box 9187, Farmington Hills, MI 48333-9187. Toll free US and Canada (800) 877-GALE (4253) and (248) 699-GALE, fax (800) 414-5043 and (248) 699-8061, Internet orders galeord@galegroup.com, web site www.galegroup.com or www.gale.com. All Gale Group products are available on approval. Contact Gale for details.

MANUFACTURERS DIRECTORIES and CD ROM'S distributed by Manufacturers' News, Inc. are available for every state of the union plus the metropolitan New York area. They are published by Manufacturers' News, Database Publishing, Commerce Register, Pick Publications. Directory prices generally range between $50 and $165, depending on the size of the directory. Close out prices on old directories are also available. Virtually all directories are published annually. CD ROMs are available with "complete" information, or for 10 or more employees, 20 or more employees, 50 or more employees, or 100 or more employees. CD prices range between $100 for information on plants with over 100 employees for a small state, up to $745 for a complete disk for a large state. Includes names and titles of key executives, plant square footage, number of employees, product, SIC, distribution area. "EZ Select" CD ROMs are another CD ROM option. It allows you to search by 11 fields, including company size, type of industry, and geographic criteria, job function and title. EZ Select CD ROMs cost between approximately $175-$400, depending on the size of the database. EZ Select Disks are also available. For more information contact Manufacturers' News, Inc., (888) 752-5200, 1633 Central Street, Evanston, IL 60201-1569. Email info@manufacturersnews.com. Web site www.manufacturersnews.com.

NELSON INVESTMENT MANAGEMENT NETWORK, also known as Nelnet, is an Internet database (www.nelnet.com) that provides comprehensive information on over 3,000 worldwide institutional investment management firms on 9,500 products and 45,000 professionals. Nelnet users can access without charge the World's Best Money Managers, Nelson's industry standard performance rankings, Manager Hires, which managers were hired by which plan sponsors; Job bank, the investment industry's free online employment service; and useful Industry Analyses. Investment Managers can launch their own Nelnet Web site for $100 a month. Users can access Nelnet free. www.nelnet.com. For more information, contact Nelson Information, P.O. Box 591, Port Chester, NY 10573 USA. (800) 333-6357, Phone outside the US (914) 937-8400, Fax (914) 937-8590, web site http://www.nelnet.com.

NEW CAREER MAKERS by John Sibbald provides profiles on 250 leading individuals in the retained executive search business. $28. Ordering information: Kennedy Information, One Kennedy Place, Route 12

South, Fitzwilliam, NH 03447, phone (800) 531-0007 or 603-585-6544, fax 603-585-9555, email bookstore@kennedyinfo.com, web site www.kennedyinfo.com.

O'DWYER'S PR MARKETPLACE is a biweekly publication which lists classified want ads. $24 subscription.J.R O'Dwyer Co., Inc., 271 Madison Avenue, New York, New York 10157-0160. Phone (212) 679-2471. Fax (212) 683-2750.

PERKS AND PARACHUTES: NEGOTIATING YOUR EXECUTIVE EMPLOYMENT CONTRACT is a manual on senior executive employment agreements, non-compete agreements, termination agreements and so forth. It includes sample agreements and negotiating strategies, plus twelve different samples of agreements. $105 by Priority Mail available from Kenneth J. Cole, Publisher, The Recruiting & Search Report, P.O. Box 9433, Panama City Beach, FL 32417. (850) 235-3733, fax (850) 233-9695 Email jcole9433@aol.com.

PETERSON'S GRADSEARCH is a GaleNet database that provide access to graduate school and professional programs in over 31,000 graduate academic departments. If your recruiting is driven by highly specific educational credentials, you can use this database to identify the schools that produce the graduates you're looking for. Once your targeted graduate program has been identified, you can then contact the placement office at the school, if you're recruiting new graduates. If you're recruiting for more senior positions, or looking for a job yourself, you can contact the alumni office to locate job seekers with the right credentials. You could also review alumni publications, which often publish announcements about promotions and job changes, which can be valuable ID research and which will also lead you to sources and prospects NOT on the job market.

PROFESSIONAL AND OCCUPATIONAL LICENSING DIRECTORY provides national and state information on licensing procedures for over 500 occupations in the US, including professional and vocational careers. Cross referenced by titles. $105. Gale Group, P.O. Box 9187, Farmington Hills, MI 48333-9187. Toll free US and Canada (800) 877-GALE (4253) and (248) 699-GALE, fax (800) 414-5043 and (248) 699-8061, Internet orders galeord@galegroup.com, web site www.galegroup.com or www.gale.com. All Gale Group products are available on approval. Contact Gale for details.

PROFESSIONAL CAREERS SOURCEBOOK directs users to career information sources related to specific professions, such as civil engineering, psychology, law, public relations, dance and choreography and more. It includes information on general career and test guides, professional associations, standards and certification agencies, educational directories and programs, awards and scholarships, basic reference guides, handbooks and more, including a master index. $99. Gale Group, P.O. Box 9187, Farmington Hills, MI 48333-9187. Toll free US and Canada (800) 877-GALE (4253) and (248) 699-GALE, fax (800) 414-5043 and (248) 699-8061, Internet orders galeord@galegroup.com, web site www.galegroup.com or www.gale.com. All Gale Group products are available on approval. Contact Gale for details.

RITES OF PASSAGE AT $100,000+: The Insider's Lifetime Guide to Executive Job-Changing and Faster Career Progress by John Lucht. Published by Viceroy Press, Inc., New York, NY. Distributed to the trade in the USA by Henry Holt & Company, Inc., 115 West 18th Street, New York, NY 10011. $29.95.

SEARCH ENGINES. Here are the main search engines you can use as a starting point. Some people consider the first four better—Yahoo, Lycos, AltaVista and Excite. The remaining search engines are listed alphabetically.

Yahoo! (http://www.yahoo.com)
Lycos (http://www.lycos.com)
AltaVista (http://www.AltaVista.com)
Excite (http://www.excite.com)
Dejanews (http://www.dejanews.com)
HotBot (http://www.HotBot.com)
Inference (http://www.inference.com/infind)
Infoseek (http://www.infoseek.com)
Nerd World (http://www.NerdWorld.com)
Netfind (http://www.netfind.com)
Northern Light (http://www.northernlight.com)

Opentext (http://www.pinstripe.opentext.com/)
Webcrawler (http://webcrawler.com)

SMALL BUSINESS SOURCING FILE contains information on more than 250,000 small businesses with an emphasis on minority-owned and women-owned businesses. For prices call Dun & Bradstreet at (800) 526-0651. For more information contact Dun & Bradstreet, Business Reference Solutions, Three Sylvan Way, Parsippany, NJ 07054. Email dnbmdd@mail.dnb.com. Web site http://www.dnbmdd.com.

SPECIFICATION SHEET ANALYSIS is a collection of 245 different sets of actual search specifications from senior executive retainer searches. These specifications offer insights into major firm retainer search methodology and specification creation. Especially useful to contingency firms evolving towards retained search. Full catalog of specifications available by fax upon request. $125 for any 25 specifications. Ordering information: Kenneth J. Cole, Publisher, The Recruiting & Search Report, P.O. Box 9433, Panama City Beach, FL 32417. (850) 235-3733, fax (850) 233-9695 Email jcole9433@aol.com.

THROUGH THE BRICK WALL—How to Job Hunt in a Tight Market by Kate Wendleton. A job hunter's classic with an excellent chapter on salary negotiating. $12.95 at bookstores or www.technicalrecruiter.com.

VOCATIONAL CAREERS SOURCEBOOK was designed as a companion to Gale Research's PROFES-SIONAL CAREERS SOURCEBOOK. It covers nearly 135 careers listed in the OCCUPATIONAL OUTLOOK HANDBOOK as "vocational," that typically do not require a four year college degree, such as insurance and real estate sales, mechanics, armed forces and administrative support. Many of the information sources were selected from the more than 3,000 sources comprising the career collection of InfoPLACE, the highly regarded job and education service of Ohio's Cuyahoga County Public Library in Cleveland. $105. Gale Group, P.O. Box 9187, Farmington Hills, MI 48333-9187. Toll free US and Canada (800) 877-GALE (4253) and (248) 699-GALE, fax (800) 414-5043 and (248) 699-8061, Internet orders galeord@galegroup.com, web site www.galegroup.com or www.gale.com. All Gale Group products are available on approval. Contact Gale for details.

WHAT COLOR IS YOUR PARACHUTE by Richard Bolles. This classic has been impressively updated every year since it first appeared in 1972 and has certainly passed the test of time. "Excellent...a distinguished public service," according to Peter Drucker. Superb for both job hunters and career changers. $14.95.

WISHCRAFT by Barbara Sher. This classic is great at helping you make your dream job become a reality. Available at bookstores in paperback. $12.00.

NOTE: Also refer to "http://" under "H" above for web addresses that omit "www" in the address, such as http://taps.com.

www.accountingjobs.com or Accounting and Finance Jobs, was developed by AccountingNet of Seattle in a joint venture with Career Mosaic. Launched in 1997, this site specializes in accounting and finance positions, mainly in the $30,000-50,000 range.

www.abbott.com/career/index.htm is the Career pages web site for Abbott Laboratories. Check other company web sites for career opportunities at the company of your choice.

www.aeps.com/aeps/aepshm.html is the URL for the Aviation Employee Placement Service. Positions generally range from $30,000 to $100,000 and mostly include pilots, mechanics and management. Developed by Sysops, Inc. in Fort Lauderdale, Florida, the site was established in 1995.

www.ajb.dni.us is the URL for America's Job Bank. It was ranked as one of the top 5 "Sites Offering the Best Job-Search Support" by the *National Business Employment Weekly*. Launched in 1995, the site was developed by the U.S. Department of Labor and state employment/unemployment offices. Most openings were originally listed with a state department of labor and are mainly in the $30,000 to $50,000 range. Many positions are in information technology, administrative and production and manufacturing.

www.amazon.com is a large bookstore web site. At the time of this writing they offer discounts up to 40%.

www.americanbanker.com/careerzone or American Banker Online was launched in 1998 by American Banker, New York, New York.

www.americasemployers.com or America's Employers is a site mainly for positions in technology, finance and sales at approximately $50,000 to $100,000. Launched in 1995, it was developed by Career Relocation Corp of America in Armonk, New York.

www.asianet.com is the address to a web site that matches Pacific Rim positions with individuals who speak Asian languages.

www.askjeeves.com or **www.ask.com** or **www.aj.com** or **ask.** If you ask Jeeves, "How can I find a job" or "How can I find candidates for an engineering job?" Jeeves has an answer! (Actually, there's very little you CAN'T ask Jeeves.) The Ask Jeeves site includes HOOVER'S CAREER CENTER, which consists of Job Search Tools (monster.com, CareerMosaic,wsj.com careers, hotjobs, westech's virtual job fair and joboptions), Career Links and Career Research Links. Hoover's Career Center contains much additional information, including extensive RELOCATION data, such as cost of living comparisons, etc. You can also subscribe to Hoover's and access their directories on the Internet.

www.asktheheadhunter.com is the web site for ASK THE HEADHUNTER, a book that can effectively be used by both job hunters and interviewers, by Nick Corcodilos, email northbridge@sprintmail.com. According to Tom Peters, it is "a powerful hiring tool.no manager can afford to miss" and it "shreds some of our most basic assumptions about the way to hire top people." Published by Penguin Putnam, New York, $14.95 The book is available from the web site and at bookstores. Corcodilos and his client, Merrill Lynch's Vice President of Global Staffing, were jointly featured in a discussion about changes in corporate recruiting and hiring practices in a segment on "Opportunity Knocks," a CNBC special on Executive Search. To purchase this 5 hour video, contact CNBC or Corcodilos.

www.barnesandnoble.com is the web site for Barnes & Noble Bookstores. Discounts are available.

www.bestjobsusa.com or Best Jobs U.S.A. is a site mainly for information technology, sales and engineering positions usually in the $50,000 to $100,000 range. Launched in 1996, the site was developed by Recourse Communications, Inc., West Palm Beach, Florida.

www.bio.com is the URL for Bio Online. Most positions are for research chemists, biochemists and in clinical development and are usually in the $40,000 to $75,000 range. Developed by Vitadata Corp, Berkeley, California, the site went online in 1993.

www.blackworld.com/careers.htm is the URL for Blackworld Career Center, a site jointly developed by Blackworld Internet Directory in Oakland, California and CareerMosaic. The site, launched in 1998, provides resources for African Americans and other ethnic groups worldwide.

www.boston.com is the web site for Boston Globe online accesses the Globe's newspaper ads.

www.bowker.com is the web site for this major research publisher. It includes Flagship Products and Services, an online Product Catalog, Electronic Publishing products including CD ROMs, Internet Databases, and Online Subscription and Site Licensing Databases; press releases, career opportunities, and more. Many of their references are accessible through this web site, such as BOOKS IN PRINT PLUS CANADIAN EDITION, ULRICH'S ON DISC, GERMAN BOOKS IN PRINT, GERMAN BOOKS OUT OF PRINT, INTERNATIONAL BOOKS IN PRINT PLUS, ITALIAN BOOKS IN PRINT, YEARBOOK OF INTERNATIONAL ORGANIZATIONS PLUS, ULRICH'S INTERNATIONAL PERIODICALS DIRECTORY, THE SOFTWARE ENCYCLOPEDIA, BOWKER'S COMPLETE VIDEO DIRECTORY, AMERICAN BOOK PUBLISHING RECORD. Visit the web site for more information.

www.businessweek.com/careers/right.htm is the web site for BusinessWeek's Internet Career Center. It offers a free, confidential service for job seekers, advertising that's cheaper than a want ad, and a job posting service if you're an employer.

www.careeravenue.com or Career Avenue lists positions mainly in information technology, management and engineering, mostly in the $50,000 to $100,000 range. The site was established in 1996 and developed by Internet Advertising, Inc., San Antonio, Texas.

www.careerbuilder.com or CareerBuilder Network was ranked as one of the top 5 "Sites Offering the Best Career Resources for Job Seekers" by the *National Business Employment Weekly*. At the time of this writing, CareerBuilder is a network of over 19 different career web sites encompassing diversity, professional, industry and general career sites. Career Builder was established in 1996 and was developed by NetStart, Inc., Reston, Virginia.

www.carccr.com or Career.com links employers and candidates throughout the world. Heart's goals for www.career.com are to provide free job seeker assistance and to offer employers an effective way to reach qualified job seekers. Most positions are in Engineering, IT and marketing and usually range between $30,000 and $75,000. The site was launched in 1993 and developed by HEART Advertising Network, Los Altos, California.

www.careerexchange.com is a web site for North American job seekers developed by CorpNet InfoHub, Ltd., Vancouver, BC, Canada. Launched in 1996, its People-Match capability notifies the user of jobs through email. Most positions are in high technology, engineering, sales and marketing and are primarily in the $40,000 to $75,000 range.

www.careermag.com or CareerMagazine is a comprehensive site for both job seekers and recruiters, including articles for job hunters, on campus, diversity, and funny work stories sent in by readers. It was ranked as one of the top 5 "Sites Offering the Best Overall Support for Job Seekers" and as one of the top 5 "Sites Offering the Best Career Resources for Job Seekers" by the *National Business Employment Weekly*. The site was developed by NCS, Inc. (National Career Search) in Boulder, Colorado and established in 1994.

www.careermosaic.com is the URL for a major recruitment web site that spends millions of dollars in advertising to draw traffic to this site. CareerMosaic features a jobs database; newsgroups for jobs, college connection, online job fairs, employer job postings; company information and more. CareerMosaic was ranked as one of the top 5 "Sites Offering the Best Overall Support for Job Seekers" by the *National Business Employment Weekly*. The site was developed Bernard Hodes Advertising in New York and went online in 1994.

www.careerpath.com was ranked as one of the top 5 "Sites Offering the Best Overall Support for Job-Seekers" by the *National Business Employment Weekly*. CareerPath.com puts the help wanted sections of over 70 US newspapers into one database. Job hunters can post their resumes free. Companies must pay a fee to access resumes. The web site claims, "Powered by the nation's leading newspapers and employers, CareerPath.com has the Web's largest number of the most current job listings." Launched in 1995, the site was developed by a consortium of media companies—Knight-Ridder, *The New York Times*, the Time Mirror Company, the Tribune Company, the Washington Post, Cox Interactive Media, Gannett Company and Hearst Corp.

www.careers.wsj.com is the *Wall Street Journal*'s web site. It focuses on positions for middle and senior management including financial positions at $75,000 and up. This web site is among those that encompass senior executive positions. Other features includes Job Seek, Who's Hiring, Career Columnists, Salaries & Profiles, The Salary Calculator™, Job Hunting Advice, Succeeding at Work, HR Issues, Executive Recruiters, Working Globally, College Connection, Starting a Business, Career Bookstore and more. Content from The National Employment Business Weekly is also featured. The site was developed by Dow Jones & Company, Inc., Princeton, New Jersey and was established in 1997.

www.careersite.com sends email notification of a job match to job seekers and employers. Most positions are in engineering, marketing and sales and management, mainly in the $40,000 to $75,000 range. CareerSite was developed by CareerSite Corp., Ann Arbor Michigan and was launched in 1995.

www.ceweekly.com is the URL for Contract Employment Weekly, a site for the temporary technical industry. Positions are mainly in information technology, engineering and technical and are mostly in the $40,000 to $75,000 range. The site was developed by C.E. Publications, Inc., Bothell, Washington and has been online since 1994. Contract Employment Weekly Online is a service of C.E. Publications, Inc., P.O. Box 3006, Bothell, WA 98041-3006. (425) 806-5200, Fax (425) 806-5585, email publisher@ceweekly.com.

www.clickit.com is the web site address to "Access Business Online." Its objective is to bring Buyers and Sellers Together on the Internet. Features include Executive Job Network, Capital Sources, Trade Announcements, Professional Services, Top 100 World Business Charts, Company Profiles, International Buyer-Seller, BizWiz! Search Engine, Web Emporium Web Site Development, Classifieds, Corporate News Net, Wall Street and World Wide Finance, Market News & Business Connections, and more. However, a service fee is charged if you wish to access this information.

www.computerwork.com is a specialized site for computer positions with a national web site and sites for Colorado, the Midwest, Minnesota and New England. Developed by Internet Association Group, Inc., Jacksonville, Florida, Computerwork.com has been online since 1996.

www.computerworld offers a "Career Search" capability, a free "Resume Database" and posting service for candidates, and various services for recruiters, including workshops and conferences, online and in print.

www.cnn.com is the URL to CNN's impressive comprehensive web site. It contains Big Yellow Search Books to assist in finding businesses and people. It also features global directories, The Directory Store™and a "search the net" capability with InfoSeek. InfoSeek also has a Business Channel with business resources and small businesses, and a Careers Channel.

www.cweb.com or CareerWeb was ranked as one of the top 5 "Sites Offering the Best Career Resources for Job Seekers" as well as one of the top 5 "General Purpose Sites" by the *National Business Employment Weekly.* Its features include a career resource center and a library. The site was developed by Landmark Communications, Norfolk, Virginia and launched in 1995.

www.datamation.com is the web site for IT executives and professionals. It provides targeted daily computer news, IT Executive Job Pavilion, Management Benchmarking Application (MBA), technology workbench, back issues from Datamation and comprehensive links to IT vendors and other online resources. This web site is the winner of the Jesse H. Neal Award and is a Cahners Business Information web site.

www.dbm.com/jobguide is an excellent comprehensive web site if you're either a recruiter looking for candidates or a job seeker. It is the "best Internet recruiting starting point" taught to recruiters by the Tiburon Group, web site http://www.tiburon group.com, a Chicago based firm that provides "Strategic Internet Recruiting Solutions Consultants and Trainers." Tiburon Group, phone (773) 907-8330, Fax (773) 907-9481, email getajob@tiburongroup.com, web site www.tiburongroup.com.

www.decalumni.com is the web site for alumni of Digital Equipment Corp. It includes a directory.

www.dice.com or DICE was ranked as one of the top 5 "Best Specialty Sites" by the *National Business Employment Weekly.* DICE specializes in information technology and high technology positions. One of the oldest employment sites on the Internet, DICE only accepts positions from recruiting firms. The site was developed by is D&L Online, Inc., Des Moines, Iowa and was launched in 1990.

www.eagleview.com is the web site for Eagleview, which presents the Select Candidate™ Network for job seekers and employers, including computer industry positions.

www.emory.edu/CAREER/index.html is Emory University's Career Paradise web site, with modules for alumni, students and employers. It is an excellent resource that should not be missed.

www.employnet-inc.com is the URL for Employnet, a confidential resume database only for recruitment firms, executive search firms and placement agencies. Both recruiters and candidates pay a fee to use this service. It was developed by Employnet, Inc., New York, New York and went online in 1995.

www.EngineeringJobs.com is a web site mainly for mechanical, electrical, industrial and computer engineers. The site was developed by EngineeringJobs, El Cerrito, California and launched in 1996.

www.excite.com/careers or Excite Careers Network was ranked as one of the top 5 "Sites Offering the Best Overall Support for Job Seekers" by the *National Business Employment Weekly.* Many positions are in IT, engineering and management, often in the $50,000 to $100,000 range. The site, online since 1995, was developed by Excite Inc., the search engine, Redwood City, California.

www.execunet.com is the web site for Exec-U-Net. It is a subscription service listing executive level positions by search firms and a few companies for positions at $100,000 or more. Candidates tend to be high quality, perhaps because of the cost. The site was developed by Exec-U-Net, Norwalk, Connecticut and was launched in 1995.

www.executiveagent.com is a web site that helps executive job seekers market their skills and experience to a targeted list of executive recruiters via email. ExecutiveAgent is completely confidential as resumes go directly to the search firms.

www.fedjobs.com provides assistance to people seeking a position with the federal government, including in the Judiciary and Congressional branches, and the United Nations. Many positions are in computers, engineering and medical, with salaries often in the $30,000 to $50,000 range. The site was developed by Federal Research Service, Inc., Vienna, Virginia and was launched in 1996.

www.galegroup.com is the web site to publisher Gale Research, one of the largest providers of research for search, recruiting and libraries.

www.Headhunter.net was ranked as one of the top 5 "Best General-Purpose Sites" by the *National Business Employment Weekly.* This site claims that no job postings are over 45 days old and that their resume database protects jobhunter confidentiality. Many positions are in computers, engineering and accounting, often in the $50,000 to $100,000 range. The site was developed by HeadHunter.NET, Inc., Norcross, Georgia and went online in 1996.

www.helpwanted.com is a web site for free posting and searching of all content for job seekers, employers and agencies.

www.hospitalitynet.nl is the URL for Hospitality Net, a site developed by Hospitality Net BV in Maastricht, The Netherlands. It connects job hunters and employers in the hospitality and restaurant industries worldwide for positions mostly in the $30,000 to $50,000 range. The site was established in 1995.

www.hotjobs.com was ranked as one of the top 5 "Best General-Purpose Sites" by the *National Business Employment Weekly.* HotJobs.com limits job postings to employers only. They also offer a personal home page to people who store their resume in HotJobs.com's database. Launched in 1996, Hot Jobs was developed by HotJobs.com Ltd., New York, New York.

www.hrsjobs.com is the URL for HRS Federal Job Search, a site that emails notifications about announced federal vacancies that match subscribers' requirements. Many positions are computer-related, clerical and professional, often in the $30,000 to $50,000 range. The site was developed by HRS Automated Solutions, Vienna, Virginia and was launched in 1997.

www.iccweb.com is the web site for Internet Career Connection, an employment matching service with a special section for US Federal Government employment. Internet Career Connection was developed by Gonyea & Associates, Inc., New Port Richey, Florida and launched in 1995. Features include Help Wanted-USA, the Worldwide Resume Bank and Government JOBS Central. Many positions include engineering, computer technology and business. While candidates do pay a fee to post their resumes, employers can view resumes free.

www.infospace.com is the URL for Classifieds/Jobs at Infospace, Inc., a site with many positions in computers, engineering and marketing, often in the $50,000 to $100,000 range. The site was developed by Infospace, Inc., Redmond, Washington and was launched in 1996.

www.it-ta.com is the URL for the ITTA Connection, a site developed by the Information Technology Talent Association in Scottsdale, Arizona. Many positions are in IT, engineering and recruiting, often at the $50,000 to $100,000 range. The site went online in 1995.

www.jobcenter.com is the URL for JobCenter Employment Services, Inc., a site with many job postings in IT, programming and sales and marketing, often in the $30,000 to $100,000 range. The site was developed by JobCenter Employment Services, Inc., Skaneateles, New York and was launched in 1995.

www.jobhunt.com is a Meta-list of On-line Job-Search Resources and Services for recruiters and jobhunters. It includes: The Online Career Center, Career Mosaic, Career Net, Job Web, Standard Job Hunt List, Americas Job Bank, Best Jobs in the USA, Career Web, College Grad Job Hunter, JobOptions (www.joboptions.com, formerly E-span Interactive Employment Network), Job Trak, The Internet Job Locator, The Monster Board, Virtual Job Fair. It also offers the capability of searching by state and local newspapers. New Items (less than a week old) are highlighted, as are "Outstanding Job Resources."

www.job-hunt.org is an on-line job search resources and services that identifies jobs resources and ranks the outstanding ones. It is linked to Career Paradise of Emory University Career Center (www.emory.edu/CAREER/index.html), featuring a "Colossal List" or Career Links and Hiring Express pages. It's given high marks for both its content and humorous presentation.

www.jobnet.com was ranked as one of the top 5 "Best Specialty Sites" by the *National Business Employment Weekly.* Jobnet.com specializes in positions located in southeastern Pennsylvania and neighboring areas of New Jersey and Delaware. The site was developed by Online Opportunities, Malvern, Pennsylvania and has been online since 1992.

www.jobnet.org is a Canadian web site.that features "Looking for a career in financial services?" Scotiabank online recruiting, Jobnet and Alumnet.

www.joboptions.com is the URL for JobOptions, formerly E-Span, a site that has been online since 1991. At the time of this writing, features include "The Right Person For The Job" and "The Right Job For The Person," job listings; post resume edit resume, career library, job match download and more. Many job postings are in sales and marketing, finance and accounting and in technology. The site was developed by Gund Business Group, Indianapolis.

www.jobsingovernment.com contains job postings for positions in government, education and the public sector. Many positions are in city administration, engineering and public safety, often in the $30,000 to $50,000 range. Jobs In Government has been online since 1996.

www.jobtrak.com is the web site for the Career service network for college students, alumni, college career staff and employers. JOBTRAK was ranked as one of the top 5 "Best Specialty Sites" by the *National Business Employment Weekly.* JOBTRAK has established relationships with college and university career offices, MBA programs and alumni associations. Most salaries range between $30,000 and $50,000. The site developer is JOBTRAK CORPORATION, Los Angeles, CA, (310) 474-3377, (800) 999-8725, fax (310) 475-7912. The site has been online since 1995.

www.kennedyinfo.com is the web site for publisher Kennedy Information. It includes books, newsletters, training materials, directories, and surveys for executive recruiting, human resources, outplacement, management consulting and job seekers. (800) 531-000,or (603) 585-6544.

www.latimes.com is the URL to the comprehensive *Los Angeles Times* web site.

www.LatPro.com is the URL for Latin America's Professional Network, a site for experienced Spanish and Portuguese bilingual professionals. Many job postings are for positions in sales and marketing, finance and information technology, often in the $50,000 to $100,000 range. The site was developed by Latin America's Professional Network, Miami, Florida and was launched in 1997.

www.library.hbs.edu/ is the URL for the Harvard Business School Baker Library, which contains free excellent information on consumer marketing, retail, associations, membership directories, direct mail, public relations, corporate communications, online direct mail and more. Dun and Bradstreet Credit Reports can also be accessed. In addition, for a fee, reference librarians can conduct online searches from any of several hundred databases. See "Harvard Business School's Baker Library" above.

www.medhunters.com is a healthcare jobhunting site developed by Helen Ziegler and Associates, Inc., Toronto, Canada. Worldwide positions are posted for doctors, nurses and therapists, encompassing a broad range of salaries. The site has been online since 1997.

www.monster.com is the URL for the popular Monster Board web site. The Monster Board was ranked as one of the top 5 "Best General-Purpose Sites" by the *National Business Employment Weekly.* It is a major recruitment web site that spends millions of dollars in advertising to attract traffic to this site. Features include Job search in the US, International or by Companies, Career Center Events, Recruiters' Center, Seminars, Post a Job, free online recruitment seminar. It also offers special links for human resources, health care, technology and entry level positions. Toll free phone number (800) MONSTER. The Monster Board, PO Box 586, Framingham, MA 01704-0586. The site developer is TMP Worldwide, New York, New York and has been online since 1994.

www.monsterhr.com is the URL for The Monster Board: Human Resources careers on the web. Enter your job profile and have job listings automatically downloaded to your Email. International opportunities in Canada are classified by Canada overall, then Alberta, British Columbia, Newfoundland, Ontario and Quebec.

www.nationjob.com is the web site for NationJob Network Online Jobs Database. NationJob, Inc. was ranked as one of the top 5 sites in two different categories by the *National Business Employment Weekly:*

"Sites Offering the Best Job-Search Support" and "Best General Purpose Sites." The site offers "Search for a Job Now (no email required)," "Search for a Company" and "Directory of all Companies." P.J. Scout service is a "(P) ersonal (J)ob Scout service that's "like having a friend shop for a job for you." Fill in a form and PJ will send you info on jobs you might be interested in. Information on salary comparisons, moving costs, relocation info, insurance calculator and more. NationJob Inc., 601 SW 9th Street, Suites J&K, Des Moines, IA 50309, (800) 292-7731. The site developer is NationJob, Inc.

www.netjobs.com is the URL to Canada's premiere employment web site. It features Internet Career Centre for employers and job seekers, Overseas Jobs Express, and Personal Computer Training. Email info@netjobs.com. Linked to www.jobnet.org.

www.netshare.com is the URL for NETSHARE 2000, a confidential for-fee career management service designed for executives, companies and recruiters that posts senior level positions on the Internet daily. Salary usually exceeds $100,000 but is sometimes in the $75,000 range. Their ad claims, "A best search site"...FORTUNE Magazine and "Best of the Best"...CareerXRoads. NETSHARE 2000 was developed by Netshare, Inc., Novato, California and went online in 1995. (800) 241-5642, email netshare@netshare.com.

www.net-temps.com or Net-Temps Job Posting Service was ranked as one of the top 5 "Sites Offering the Best Job-Search Support" by the *National Business Employment Weekly*. Many positions are in information systems, engineering, and sales and marketing, often in the $50,000 to $100,000 range. The site was developed by Net-Temps, Inc., Tyngsboro, Massachusetts and went online in 1996.

www.ntes.com is the URL for the Contract Employment Connection, a web site for contract professionals in the temporary professional job market. Most positions are in engineering, computer science and management, mainly in the $50,000 to $100,000 range. The site was developed by National Technical Employment Services, Scottsboro, Alabama and was launched in 1993.

www.nytimes.com is the URL for *The New York Times* web site.

www.nzjobs.com is a recruiting and jobhunting web site for positions in New Zealand. Email: info@nzjobs.co.nz.

www.occ.com is the URL for the On Line Career Center, one of the Internet's first online recruitment sites, launched in 1993. It is a major recruitment web site that spends millions of dollars in advertising to drive traffic to the site. This is a major site that was developed by William O Warren, who has received honors for his pioneering work in the development of Internet Recruiting. This web site allows you to enter your job profile and have job listings automatically downloaded to your Email. Questions to webmaster@occ.com. www.occ.com was rated by the *National Business Employment Weekly* as one of the top 5 sites in 3 different categories: "Sites Offering the Best Overall Support for Job Seekers," "Sites Offering the Best Job-Search Support" and "Sites Offering the Best Career Resources for Job Seekers." Openings are mainly in engineering, information technology and sales and marketing. The site developer is TMP Worldwide, New York, New York.

www.passportaccess.com is a site with many positions in computers and engineering, many of them in the $50,000 to $100,000 range. The site was developed by PassportAccess, Inc., Lafayette, California and was established in 1995.

www.realbank.com serves professionals in real estate, mortgages and construction. Many positions are in the $40,000 to $75,000 range. REALBANK was developed by Realbank, Inc., New York, New York and went online in 1996.

www.recruitersonline.com is the URL for Recruiters Online Network, a free web site that allows recruiters to post open positions at various online locations and maintain private resume database for members. Most positions are in information technology, management and software. Positions usually range from $50,000 to over $100,000. The site was developed by Recruiters Online Network, Inc., Plano, Texas and was established in 1995.

www.ritesite.com is the web site for the book, RITES OF PASSAGE AT $100,000+ by John Lucht.
www.rtp.org is the home page for Research Triangle Park, North Carolina. It includes a directory of companies in the Park and listing of companies according to research specialization, appropriate for target list development.

www.sciencemag.org is the URL for Science Online, a career site which posts many positions for research scientists, research directors and post-Doctoral positions. Salary often ranges from $50,000 to $100,000. Science Online was developed by the American Association for the Advancement of Science, Washington, DC and was established in 1996.

www.selectjobs.com was ranked as one of the top 5 "Best Specialty Sites" by the *National Business Employment Weekly*. SelectJOBS specializes in computer industry positions. Many job postings are for database administrators, programmer/analysts, and system/network engineers. salary often ranges between $40,000 and $75,000. The site was developed by SelectJOBS, Fort Lauderdale, Florida and was established in 1996.

www.shrm.org/jobs/ is the web site for the Society for Human Resource Management site. It is linked to the major recruitment web site www.career.mosaic./com. It also includes Membership Directory Online, which only can be accessed by members.

www.technicalrecruiter.com is a web site which is an excellent starting point for a large number of specialized technology sites, such as ProjectManager.com and SoftwareEngineer.com and others.

www.tjobs.com is the URL for Telecommuting Jobs, which connects people to positions at home or otherwise using off site electronic facilities. Most positions are in programming, sales and writing. The site was developed by Levine Communications, Winnetka, Illinois and was launched in 1996.

www.the-dma.org is the web site for the Direct Marketing Association, 1120 Avenue of the Americas, New York, NY 10036-6700, (212) 768-7277, fax (212) 302-6714. It feature the DMA Job Bank, Online Bookstore, Seminars, Conferences. Membership directory is available to members.

www.tiburongroup.com is the web site for the Tiburon Group, Inc., a Chicago based firm that provides "Strategic Internet Recruiting Solutions Consultants and Trainers." They are also a recruiting firm and a certified AIRS and hire.com solutions partner. Phone (773) 907-8330, Fax (773) 907-9481, email getajob@tiburongroup.com.

www.townonline.com/working or Town Online Working is the web site to various community newspapers, including 13 in New England. In addition to job listings, it also has a job profile with the capability of automatically downloading to your Email. Town Online Working was ranked as one of the top 5 "Sites Offering the Best Career Resources for Job Seekers" by the *National Business Employment Weekly*. Many positions are administrative, management and blue collar, often paying in the teens up to $30,000. The site developer is the Community Newspaper Company, Needham, Massachusetts and was established in 1996.

www.tristatejobs.com is the URL for Tri-State Jobs, a site for positions in New York, New Jersey and Connecticut. Many positions are for programmers, engineers and managers, often in the $50,000 to $100,000 range. The site was developed by Tri-State Jobs, Southbury, Connecticut and went online in 1997.

www.umn.edu/apn or Academic Position Network is a web site that lists positions for faculty, professional and administrative staff, including librarians, in academia. The site was developed by Academic Position Network in Blaine, Minnesota and established in 1996.

www.usresume.com is the URL for US Resume, a site that lists many positions in computers, sales and finance, usually in the $50,000 to $100,000 range. The site was developed by Market 2000 Corp, Sparkill, New York and went online in 1996.

www.worldhire.com is the web site for World Hire. It features a Job profile notification and the Recruiter™ web site product. Some sample recruiter sites include www.coastalcorp.com, www.eds.com, www.ibm.com.

www.world.hire.com is the URL for World Hire Online, a web site with job listings mainly in engineering, information technology and "senior management," usually in the $50,000 to $100,000 range. The site was developed by World.Hire, Austin, Texas and was launched in 1996.

www.vjf.com is the URL for Westech Virtual Job Fair. It was ranked as one of the top 5 "Best Specialty Sites" by the *National Business Employment Weekly*. Westech Virtual Job Fair specializes in high tech positions which are listed by the companies. The site developer is Westech Expo Corp in Santa Clara, California, one of the largest sponsors of career fairs in the US. The site went online in 1994.

www.womenconnect.com contains job postings and editorial content from Working Woman and Working Mother magazines. Many positions are in sales, software engineering and general engineering, often in the $30,000 to $75,000 range. The site was developed by womenCONNECT.com, McLean, Virginia and has been online since 1994.

wwwyahoo.com is a site with an excellent search engine, career resources and much more.

K

Korea

See Asia, International

DIRECTORY OF AMERICAN FIRMS OPERATING IN FOREIGN COUNTRIES, REGIONAL EDITION—JAPAN AND KOREA. $59. Uniworld Business Publications, Inc., 257 Central Park West, Suite 10A, New York, NY 10024-4110, (212) 496-2448, fax (212) 769-0413, email uniworldbp@aol.com. Web site: http://www.uniworldbp.com.

DIRECTORY OF FOREIGN FIRMS OPERATING IN THE UNITED STATES, REGIONAL EDITION—JAPAN AND KOREA. $69. Uniworld Business Publications, Inc., 257 Central Park West, Suite 10A, New York, NY 10024-4110, (212) 496-2448, fax (212) 769-0413, email uniworldbp@aol.com. Web site: http://www.uniworldbp.com.

L

Labor Unions

See Unions

Laboratories

See Research and Development

Latin America

See Mexico, South America, International

DIRECTORY OF AMERICAN FIRMS OPERATING IN FOREIGN COUNTRIES, REGIONAL EDITION—CENTRAL AMERICA. Includes Belize, Costa Rica, El Salvador, Guatemala, Honduras, Nicaragua, Panama. $39. Uniworld Business Publications, Inc., 257 Central Park West, Suite 10A, New York, NY 10024-4110, (212) 496-2448, fax (212) 769-0413, email uniworldbp@aol.com. Web site: http://www.uniworldbp.com.

DIRECTORY OF CONSUMER BRANDS AND THEIR OWNERS provides information on 50,000 brands in 56 countries and detailed information about the companies that own and manage them. Asia Pacific edition $990. Latin America edition $990. Eastern Europe edition $990. Europe edition $1,190 for 2 volumes. Published by Euromonitor (England). Distributed by Gale Group, P.O. Box 9187, Farmington Hills, MI 48333-9187. Toll free US and Canada (800) 877-GALE (4253) and (248) 699-GALE, fax (800) 414-5043 and (248) 699-8061, Internet orders galeord@galegroup.com, web site www.galegroup.com or www.gale.com. All Gale Group products are available on approval. Contact Gale for details.

DIRECTORY OF FOREIGN FIRMS OPERATING IN THE UNITED STATES, REGIONAL EDITION—SOUTH/CENTRAL AMERICA & THE CARIBBEAN. Includes Argentina, Bermuda, Bolivia, Brazil, Chile, Colombia, Costa Rica, Dominican Republic, Guatemala, Mexico, Panama, Paraguay, Peru, Uruguay, Venezuela. $39. Uniworld Business Publications, Inc., 257 Central Park West, Suite 10A, New York, NY 10024-4110, (212) 496-2448, fax (212) 769-0413, email uniworldbp@aol.com. Web site: http://www.uniworldbp.com.

LATIN AMERICA: A DIRECTORY AND SOURCEBOOK contains thousands of information sources and detailed profiles of major commercial organizations. $590. Published by Euromonitor (England). Distributed by Gale Group, P.O. Box 9187, Farmington Hills, MI 48333-9187. Toll free US and Canada (800) 877-GALE (4253) and (248) 699-GALE, fax (800) 414-5043 and (248) 699-8061, Internet orders galeord@galegroup.com, web site www.galegroup.com or www.gale.com. All Gale Group products are available on approval. Contact Gale for details.

LATIN AMERICAN ADVERTISING, MARKETING & MEDIA SOURCEBOOK, published by Euromonitor (England), at $470 (1st edition), had been exclusively distributed in the USA, Canada and Australia by Gale Group. At the time of this writing, Gale no longer carries it. For more information, contact Euromonitor or Gale or refer to Books in Print or International Books in Print. This reference might also be available in the library.

LATIN AMERICAN SATELLITE DIRECTORY, Phillips Business Information, Inc., a Phillips Publishing International Company, 120 Seven Locks Road, Potomac, MD 20854, (301) 340-1520, (301) 340-7788, (800) 777-5006, Internet pbi@phillips.com, web site www.phillips.com.

MAJOR COMPANIES OF LATIN AMERICA AND THE CARIBBEAN lists information on 7,500 companies in Latin America and South America and the Caribbean, including description of company activities, brand names, over 35,000 names of key executives and financial data, plus three indexes, mainly for target list development. $765. Available in CD ROM. Distributed by Larry Meranus Professional Publications & Services, 4 Demoray Court, Pine Brook, NJ 07058, (800) MERANUS or (800) 637-2687. Also distributed by Gale Group, P.O. Box 9187, Farmington Hills, MI 48333-9187. Toll free US and Canada (800) 877-GALE (4253) and (248) 699-GALE, fax (800) 414-5043 and (248) 699-8061, Internet orders galeord@galegroup.com, web site www.galegroup.com or www.gale.com. All Gale Group products are available on approval. Contact Gale for details. Published by Graham & Whiteside Ltd., Tuition House, 5-6 Francis Grove, London SW19 4DT, England. Web site http://www.major-co-data.com. Email sales@major-co-data.com.

MAJOR COMPANIES SERIES ON CD ROM consists of Graham & Whiteside's annual directories of major international companies. All six directories reside on one disk. After payment, you'll receive a security code to access the region(s) you select. This Windows™ based CD can navigate by company name, company locations, executive names, business activity and more. Free demo CD ROM is available. Regions also available separately for Europe, Central & Eastern Europe, the Far East and Australasia, the Arab World, Africa, and Latin America. For prices and availability, contact the Gale Group, P.O. Box 9187, Farmington Hills, MI 48333-9187. Toll free US and Canada (800) 877-GALE (4253) and (248) 699-GALE, fax (800) 414-5043 and (248) 699-8061, Internet orders galeord@galegroup.com, web site www.galegroup.com or www.gale.com. All Gale Group products are available on approval. Contact Gale for details.

www.kompass.com is the web site for the highly respected Kompass country directories and databases. This web site contains a searchable database that encompasses over 60 countries, 2.5 million executive names, information on 1.5 million companies, 19 million key product references, and 370,000 trade and brand names. At the time of this writing, Kompass is available in English and French. Deutsch, Espanol and Italiano will soon be available.

www.LatPro.com is the URL for Latin America's Professional Network, a site for experienced Spanish and Portuguese bilingual professionals. Many job postings are for positions in sales and marketing, finance and information technology, often in the $50,000 to $100,000 range. The site was developed by Latin America's Professional Network, Miami, Florida and was launched in 1997.

Law

CANADIAN ALMANAC AND DIRECTORY includes abbreviations, associations and societies, broadcasting and communications, business statistics, church and religious organizations, commerce and finance, cultural directory, education directory, electoral districts, foreign and international contacts, geographic information, government directory, government quick reference, health and hospitals, historical and general information, legal and judicial directory, postal information, tourism and transportation. The Almanac also includes web sites of significant institutions in business, communications, and the arts, a "Who's Who" of key officials and organizations on the Canadian information highway and up-to-date provincial and territorial election results. Indexed by titles and keyword. $249 US. Inquire about CD ROM availability. Published by IHS Canada, Micromedia Limited, 20 Victoria Street, Toronto, Ontario M5C 2N8 CANADA, (800) 387-2689, (416) 362-5211, fax (416) 362-6161, email info@micromedia.on.ca. Distributed in the US by the Gale Group, P.O. Box 9187, Farmington Hills, MI 48333-9187. Toll free US and Canada (800) 877-GALE (4253) and (248) 699-GALE, fax (800) 414-5043 and (248) 699-8061, Internet orders galeord@galegroup.com, web site www.galegroup.com or www.gale.com. All Gale Group products are available on approval. Contact Gale for details.

COMPLETE MARQUIS WHO'S WHO ON CD ROM is a compilation of literally all 19 Marquis Who's Who that have appeared in print since 1985, including living and deceased people. WHO'S WHO IN AMERICA®, WHO'S WHO IN THE WORLD®, WHO'S WHO IN AMERICAN EDUCATIONS®, WHO'S WHO IN AMERICAN LAW®, WHO'S WHO IN AMERICAN NURSING®, WHO'S WHO IN MEDICINE AND HEALTHCARE®, WHO'S WHO IN FINANCE AND INDUSTRY®, WHO'S WHO IN SCIENCE AND ENGINEERING®, WHO'S WHO IN THE EAST®, WHO'S WHO IN THE MIDWEST®, WHO'S WHO IN THE SOUTH AND SOUTHWEST®, WHO'S WHO IN THE WEST®, WHO'S WHO OF AMERICAN WOMEN®, WHO'S WHO IN ADVERTISING®, WHO'S WHO OF EMERGING LEADERS IN AMERICA®, WHO'S WHO IN ENTERTAINMENT®, WHO'S WHO AMONG HUMAN SERVICES PROFESSIONALS®. One year subscription with semi-annual updates $995. National Register Publishing, Reed Elsevier-New Providence, 121 Chanlon Road, New Providence, NJ 07974, (800) 521-8110, fax (800) 836-7736, web site www.marquiswhoswho.com or www.redbooks.com. "If, for any reason whatsoever, your order does not fully meet your expectations, simply return the product within 30 days for a prompt, complete, unquestioned refund," as stated in Catalog of Biographical and Professional References of publisher Marquis Who's Who/National Register Publishing.

CYBERHOUND'S® GUIDE TO PEOPLE ON THE INTERNET is organized into three sections. (1) Who's Who Online identifies 1,000 online directories, databases and membership listings. For example, it lists Architects in Canada, Attorney Finder, Famous Left-Handers, and The Missing Persons Pages. (2) White Pages provides and alphabetical listing of 3,000 business professionals who are accessible by email. Other information includes area of expertise, personal and professional affiliation and company information. (3) Personal Web Sites are organized alphabetically by name. 1,500 pages of people in the news in business, entertainment, and sports. $79. Gale Group, P.O. Box 9187, Farmington Hills, MI 48333-9187. Toll free US and Canada (800) 877-GALE (4253) and (248) 699-GALE, fax (800) 414-5043 and (248) 699-8061, Internet orders galeord@galegroup.com, web site www.galegroup.com or www.gale.com. All Gale Group products are available on approval. Contact Gale for details.

D&B DIRECTORY OF SERVICE COMPANIES is a directory with information on 50,000 US service businesses, including privately held companies, in these sectors: accounting, auditing and bookkeeping, advertising and public relations, architecture and engineering, consumer services, executive search, health, hospitality, management consulting, motion pictures, repair, research, social services and law. Listings include key executives' names and titles, address, phone, sales volume, number of employees, parent company and location, and more. Companies listed employ 50 or more people. Information is listed alphabetically and is cross-referenced geographically and by industry classification. Updated annually. For prices call Dun & Bradstreet at (800) 526-0651. For more information contact Dun & Bradstreet, Business Reference Solutions, Three Sylvan Way, Parsippany, New Jersey 07054. Email dnbmdd@mail.dnb.com. Web site http://www.dnbmdd.com.

DIRECTORY OF AMERICAN SCHOLARS contains current biographies of over 30,000 scholars in the humanities. Volume 1, History. Volume 2, English, Speech and Drama. Volume 3 Foreign Languages, Linguistics and Philology. Volume 4, Philosophy, Religion and Law. $450 for 5 volume set. Individual volumes $135. Gale Group, P.O. Box 9187, Farmington Hills, MI 48333-9187. Toll free US and Canada (800) 877-GALE (4253) and (248) 699-GALE, fax (800) 414-5043 and (248) 699-8061, Internet orders galeord@galegroup.com, web site www.galegroup.com or www.gale.com. All Gale Group products are available on approval. Contact Gale for details.

DIRECTORY OF LEGAL RECRUITERS, $129. Kennedy Information, One Kennedy Place, Route 12 South, Fitzwilliam, NH 03447, phone (800) 531-0007 or 603-585-6544, fax 603-585-9555, email bookstore@kennedyinfo.com, web site www.kennedyinfo.com.

ENCYCLOPEDIA OF ASSOCIATIONS: INTERNATIONAL ORGANIZATIONS includes nearly 20,000 multinational and national organizations in foreign countries, including US based associations with multinational membership. Entries also include email addresses, web sites and bulletin board addresses, lobbying activities, and publication and convention information. Indexed by geography, keyword and executives. $595 for 2 volume set. Also available in CD ROM. Database available via commercial online service. Gale Group, P.O. Box 9187, Farmington Hills, MI 48333-9187. Toll free US and Canada (800) 877-GALE (4253) and (248) 699-GALE, fax (800) 414-5043 and (248) 699-8061, Internet orders galeord@galegroup.com, web site www.galegroup.com or www.gale.com. All Gale Group products are available on approval. Contact Gale for details.

ENCYCLOPEDIA OF ASSOCIATIONS: NATIONAL ORGANIZATIONS OF THE US. This superb reference is one of the first places you should look when beginning a new recruiting assignment or when looking for specialized references of any type. The keyword index makes this comprehensive reference easy to use, even in hard copy. For over 23,000 nonprofit professional associations with a national scope, this encyclopedia reveals:

- Publications, including membership rosters and newsletters

- Dates and locations of association conferences and conventions

- Names of Executive Directors, who are usually incredible sources of industry information if you call and speak to them

- Committees

- Job and candidate referral banks, which can provide resumes of other industry sources and sometimes candidates

- It includes organizations in these categories: business, trade, environmental, agricultural, legal, governmental, engineering, technological, scientific, educational, cultural, social welfare, health & medical, public affairs, ethnic, labor unions, chambers of commerce, tourism, & others.

    Volume 1, National Organizations of the US, $505
    Volume 2, Geographic and Executive Indexes, $390
    Volume 3, Supplement, $405

Gale Group, P.O. Box 9187, Farmington Hills, MI 48333-9187. Toll free US and Canada (800) 877-GALE (4253) and (248) 699-GALE, fax (800) 414-5043 and (248) 699-8061, Internet orders galeord@galegroup.com, web site www.galegroup.com or www.gale.com. All Gale Group products are available on approval. Contact Gale for details.

ENCYCLOPEDIA OF ASSOCIATIONS: REGIONAL, STATE AND LOCAL ORGANIZATIONS. The information in this directory is not duplicated anywhere in ENCYCLOPEDIA OF ASSOCIATIONS. Over 100,000 nonprofit organizations are included in this directory. $585 for 5 volume set or $140 per individual volume. Also available on CD ROM and online on the Internet through a GaleNet subscription.

    Volume 1, Great Lakes States (Illinois, Indiana, Michigan, Minnesota, Ohio, Wisconsin)
    Volume 2, Northeastern States (Connecticut, Maine, Massachusetts, New Hampshire, New Jersey, New York, Pennsylvania, Rhode Islands, Vermont)
    Volume 3, Southern and Middle Atlantic States (Including Puerto Rico and the Virgin Islands) (Alabama, Delaware, Washington, DC, Florida, Georgia, Kentucky, Maryland, Mississippi, North Carolina, Puerto Rico, South Carolina, Tennessee, Virginia, West Virginia, Virgin Islands)

Volume 4, South Central and Great Plains States (Arkansas, Iowa, Kansas, Louisiana, Missouri, Nebraska, North Dakota, Oklahoma, South Dakota, Texas)

Volume 5, Western States (Alaska, Arizona, California, Colorado, Guam, Hawaii, Idaho, Montana, Nevada, New Mexico, Oregon, Utah, Washington, Wyoming)

Gale Group, P.O. Box 9187, Farmington Hills, MI 48333-9187. Toll free US and Canada (800) 877-GALE (4253) and (248) 699-GALE, fax (800) 414-5043 and (248) 699-8061, Internet orders galeord@galegroup.com, web site www.galegroup.com or www.gale.com. All Gale Group products are available on approval. Contact Gale for details.

Ordering info: Gale Research, P.O. Box 33477, Detroit, MI 48232-5477. (800) 877-GALE, Fax (800) 414-5043 will be responded to within 48 hours. Internet orders: galeord@galegroup.com, CompuServe email: 72203.1552, web site http://www.galegroup.com, GaleNet web site address @http://galenet.galegroup.com.

EUROMONEY BANK REGISTER is a detailed directory of the world's leading financial institutions and a comprehensive guide to "who's who" in global capital markets. This directory lists senior executives, investment and commercial bankers, traders, analysts, support and legal staff. Expanded coverage of Asia, central Europe and eastern Europe and Latin America is provided. Available in print or CD ROM. The print version of The EUROMONEY Bank Register is comprehensively indexed alphabetically and by city. It also contains rankings of the top banks. The read only version of the CD ROM provides full access to the entire database. However, by disabling the print and export functions, the result is a lower cost alternative to the full version. A 14 day free trial is available with the CD ROM.

Print Directory, USA, US $493 or 297 pounds sterling
Print Directory, UK, Europe, Rest of World US $493 or 297 pounds sterling
Read Only Version CD ROM 750 pounds or US $1,250
Full Version CD ROM 1,750 pounds or US $3,000

Ordering information: Larry Meranus Professional Publications & Services, 4 Demoray Court, Pine Brook, NJ 07058, (800) MERANUS or (800) 637-2687. Distributed in England by EUROMONEY Books, Plymbridge Distributors Limited, Estover, Plymouth PL6 7PZ, England. Phone 44 (0) 171 779-8955 for a free demo disk. Fax 44 (0) 171 779-8541.

MARTINDALE-HUBBELL LAW DIRECTORY ON CD ROM contains biographies for over 700,000 attorneys in the US and Canada, at law firms and in house counsel. Searches can be conducted by name/firm, country, state, county, city, birth year, first college, year of graduation, law school, year of graduation, bar, admission year, biography text, languages, job titles, firm size, legal specialties and more. Updated quarterly. (Martindale-Hubbell listing subscribers should call for additional discount information.) CD ROM 1 year subscription $995, 3 years $2,445, excluding discounts. This directory is also available in electronic database formats, online through LEXIS® (Library Name: MARHUB, File Name: ALLDIR) and NEXIS® (Library Name: PEOPLE, File Name: MHPROF). For more information visit Bowker Reed Reference's web site at http://www.reedref.com or contact: Bowker Reed Reference Electronic Publishing, 121 Chanlon Road, New Providence, NJ 07974 USA, Phone (800) 323-3288, Fax (908) 665-3528, email info@bowker.com.

MICROMEDIA, the Toronto publisher, publishes a legal directory. For more information, contact Micromedia Ltd., 20 Victoria Street, Toronto, ON, (800) 387-2689, (416) 362-5211, email info@micromedia.on.ca, web site www.micromedia.on.ca.

PARKER DIRECTORY ON CD ROM identifies addresses, phone and fax numbers for over 85,000 practicing attorneys in California, including descriptions of over 7,000 firms, plus information on judicial districts, judges and other court personnel. Searches can be conducted for attorneys, legal services, suppliers and consultants, such as court reporters and process servers. Available for Windows and Macintosh. One year subscription $99, excluding discounts. Call for information on Windows and Macintosh capability. For more information visit Bowker Reed Reference's web site at http://www.reedref.com or contact: Bowker Reed Reference Electronic Publishing, 121 Chanlon Road, New Providence, NJ 07974 USA, Phone (800) 323-3288, Fax (908) 665-3528, email info@bowker.com.

WHO'S WHO IN AMERICAN LAW, $285. WHO'S WHO IN AMERICAN LAW ON CD ROM is also available. Call publisher for price. National Register Publishing, Reed Elsevier-New Providence, 121 Chanlon Road, New Providence, NJ 07974, (800) 521-8110, fax (800) 836-7736, web site www.marquiswhoswho.com or www.redbooks.com. "If, for any reason whatsoever, your order does not fully meet your expectations, simply return the product within 30 days for a prompt, complete, unquestioned refund," as stated in Catalog of Biographical and Professional References of publisher Marquis Who's Who/National Register Publishing.

www.fedjobs.com provides assistance to people seeking a position with the federal government, including in the Judiciary and Congressional branches, and the United Nations. Many positions are in computers, engineering and medical, with salaries often in the $30,000 to $50,000 range. The site was developed by Federal Research Service, Inc., Vienna, Virginia and was launched in 1996.

Lebanon

See International, Arab, Middle East

WHO'S WHO IN LEBANON contains 2,000 biographies plus essays on economics and demographics. Published by Publitec Publications, Beirut. Distributed exclusively to libraries in the US and Canada by Gale. $168. Gale Group, P.O. Box 9187, Farmington Hills, MI 48333-9187. Toll free US and Canada (800) 877-GALE (4253) and (248) 699-GALE, fax (800) 414-5043 and (248) 699-8061, Internet orders galeord@galegroup.com, web site www.galegroup.com or www.gale.com. All Gale Group products are available on approval. Contact Gale for details.

Libraries

AMERICAN LIBRARY ASSOCIATION (ALA), 50 East Huron Street, Chicago, IL 60611, (800) 545-2433, in Illinois (800) 545-2444, in Canada (800) 545-2455. Annually publishes the ALA Handbook of Organization and Membership Directory, which provides information about the ALA's divisions, committees, round tables and discussion groups. The major divisions of the ALA are:

* REFERENCE AND ADULT SERVICES DIVISION (RASD) publishes RQ. Committees include Business Reference Sources Committee, Reference Sources Committee, Adult Library Materials Committee, and Reference Tools Advisory Committee (which provides assistance to publishers of reference titles). Other sections include Machine-Assisted Reference Section and History Section.

* ASSOCIATION OF COLLEGE AND RESEARCH LIBRARIES (ACRL) is the largest group within the ALA. It publishes CHOICE, COLLEGE & RESEARCH LIBRARIES, COLLEGE & RESEARCH LIBRARIES NEWS, RARE BOOKS AND MANUSCRIPTS LIBRARIANSHIP.

* PUBLIC LIBRARY ASSOCIATION (PLA) consists of the Metropolitan Libraries Section, Community Information Section, and Armed Forces Library Section. PLA publishes PUBLIC LIBRARIES.

* ASSOCIATION FOR LIBRARY COLLECTIONS AND TECHNICAL SERVICES (ALCTS) publishes LIBRARY RESOURCES AND TECHNICAL SERVICES.

* AMERICAN ASSOCIATION OF SCHOOL LIBRARIANS (AASL) publishes SCHOOL LIBRARY MEDIA QUARTERLY.

AMERICAN LIBRARY DIRECTORY is available in hard copy and electronic database formats. It identifies 36,000 general and specialized libraries in the US, Canada and Mexico. Searches can be conducted by 40 general information search criteria, further refined with 50 more fields related to the specific collections and services.

AMERICAN LIBRARY DIRECTORY ON DISC, one year subscription $423.

AMERICAN LIBRARY DIRECTORY ONLINE can be accessed by contacting Bowker or Knight-Ridder Information, Inc., Mountainview, California, (800) 334-2564 or (800) 3-DIALOG. Refer to DIALOG file number 460.

LIBRARY RESOURCE GUIDE—INTERNET EDITION is a free Internet directory of library services and suppliers which is drawn from Bowker's American Library Directory. Log on at www.bowker.com or call for more information. R.R. Bowker (a unit of Cahners Business Information), 121 Chanlon Road, New

Providence, NJ 07974 USA, Phone (888) BOWKER2 (888-269-5372) & (800) 323-3288, fax (908) 508-7696, email info@bowker.com, web www.bowker.com. Canada—R.R. Bowker, Markham, Ontario, phone (888) BOWKER9 & (905) 415-5837, fax (905) 479-6266. German speaking Europe—K.G. Saur Verlag, Munich, Germany, phone 49-89-76902-232, fax 49-89-76902-250, email 100730.1341@compuserve.com, web www.saur.de/home.htm. Rest of Europe incl. United Kingdom plus Africa & Asia—Bowker-Saur, W. Sussex, UK, phone 44-1342-326-972, fax 44-1342-335-612, email customer@bowker-saur.co.uk, web www.bowker-saur.com/service/. Australia/New Zealand—Thorpe, Port Melbourne, Victoria, Australia, phone 61-03-9-245-7370, fax 61-03-9-245-7395, email customer.service@thorpe.com.au, web www.thorpe.com.au. Technical support for CD ROMs (800) 323-3288, fax 908) 665-3528, email techsupport@bowker.com.

AMERICAN LIBRARY GUIDE identifies collections, books, library networks, and trade organizations. Published annually. Contact publisher for price. Cahners Business Information, 121 Chanlon Road, New Providence, NJ 07974, (908) 665-2801, 888-269-5372, www.bowker.com. Headquarters: Cahners Business Information, 275 Washington Street, Newton, MA 02158-1630, (617) 558-4663 or (617) 964-3030, fax (617) 558-4700, email marketaccess@cahners.com. Web sites www.cahners.com or www.chilton.net.

BOWKER ANNUAL LIBRARY AND BOOK TRADE ALMANAC is a directory that provides budget, Internet, legislation, industry event and research information. Published annually. Call publisher for price. Cahners Business Information, 121 Chanlon Road, New Providence, NJ 07074, (908) 665-2804, (888) 269-5372, URL www.bowker.com. Headquarters: Cahners Business Information, 275 Washington Street, Newton, MA 02158-1630, (617) 558-4663 or (617) 964-3030, fax (617) 558-4700, email marketaccess@cahners.com. Web sites www.cahners.com or www.chilton.net.

CANADIAN LIBRARIES provides information on over 6,000 active Canadian libraries, resources centers, business information centers, professional associations, regional library systems, library schools, library technical programs, and archives. Names, titles, telephone numbers and email addresses of key personnel are included. It is updated annually. $185 directory, $350 stand alone CD ROM. Ordering information: IHS Canada, Micromedia Limited, 20 Victoria Street, Toronto, Ontario M5C 2N8 CANADA, (800) 387-2689, (416) 362-5211, fax (416) 362-6161, email info@micromedia.on.ca.

CANADIAN LIBRARY ASSOCIATION is located at Suite 602, 200 Elgin Street, Ottawa, ON K2P 1L5, (613) 232-9625. Their online catalog can be viewed on their web site, www.cla.amlibs.ca and should indicate when an update will be available for their 1992 edition of CANADIAN BUSINESS AND ECONOMICS, A GUIDE TO SOURCES OF INFORMATION. CANADIAN BUSINESS AND ECONOMICS: A GUIDE TO SOURCES OF INFORMATION lists information by subject, including books, periodicals and services. Fully indexed and thoroughly cross referenced. Price reduced to $39.95 for 1992 edition. Canada Library Association, 200 Elgin Street, Suite 602, Ottawa, Ontario K2P 1L5 CANADA, (613) 232-9625, fax (613) 563-9895, Internet: bj491@freenet.carleton.ca.

CANADIAN SOURCEBOOK provides listings of libraries, resource centers, associations, societies, labour unions and media outlets, plus names and addresses of government officials, industry associations, financial institutions and social and cultural societies. $197. Special discounts available for combined purchases. Southam Information Products Ltd, 1450 Don Mills Road, Don Mills, Ontario M3B 2X7 CANADA, (800) 668-2374, (416) 445-6641, (416) 442-2122, web site www.southam.com.

CYBERHOUND'S® GUIDE TO INTERNET LIBRARIES will guide you to online information including site descriptions and reviews of over 2,000 libraries, including contact information, mainfiles/subfiles, holdings information, subscriptions, services, how to access, information on special collections, OPAC addresses, plus a bibliography, a glossary of Internet terms, White Pages and two indexes. $79. Gale Group, P.O. Box 9187, Farmington Hills, MI 48333-9187. Toll free US and Canada (800) 877-GALE (4253) and (248) 699-GALE, fax (800) 414-5043 and (248) 699-8061, Internet orders galeord@galegroup.com, web site www.galegroup.com or www.gale.com. All Gale Group products are available on approval. Contact Gale for details.

DIRECTORY OF CANADIAN LIBRARY AND INFORMATION SCIENCE CONSULTANTS is a national Canadian directory of library and library related consultants. $29.95. Canada Library Association, 200 Elgin Street, Suite 602, Ottawa, Ontario K2P 1L5 CANADA, (613) 232-9625, fax (613) 563-9895, Internet: bj491@freenet.carleton.ca.

DIRECTORY OF HAZARDOUS WASTE SERVICES contains information on over 1,500 Canadian hazardous waste management companies with information on hazardous waste consultants, waste treatment and disposal outlets, equipment manufacturers, laboratory services, drum reconditioners, spill cleanup firms, hazwaste recyclers, associations, key government contacts, liquid waste haulers, lawyers specializing in environmental law, and environmental libraries. $115. Special discounts available for combined purchases. Published by Southam Information Products Ltd, 1450 Don Mills Road, Don Mills, Ontario M3B 2X7 CANADA, (800) 668-2374. In Toronto 442-2122. Web site www.southam.com.

DIRECTORY OF SPECIAL LIBRARIES AND INFORMATION CENTERS includes over 23,000 libraries and information centers, including libraries associated with the general fields of science and engineering, medicine, law, art, religion and social sciences and humanities, plus expanded international coverage. $815 for 3 volume set. Also available individually.

> Volume 1: Directory of Special Libraries and Information Centers, 2 book set, $580

> Volume 2: Geographic and Personnel Indexes $479. Gale Group, P.O. Box 9187, Farmington Hills, MI 48333-9187. Toll free US and Canada (800) 877-GALE (4253) and (248) 699-GALE, fax (800) 414-5043 and (248) 699-8061, Internet orders galeord@galegroup.com, web site www.galegroup.com or www.gale.com. All Gale Group products are available on approval. Contact Gale for details.

FOREIGN EMBASSIES OR CONSULATES sometimes have library resources from their countries located in foreign countries. For example, there is a superb Canadian library in New York City. For more information, refer to a directory of libraries listed in the "Libraries" section, or ask a librarian. If you do call the embassy or consulate, make sure you speak with a knowledgeable person so as to avoid misinformation. You might ask, "May I please speak to someone who is an expert about libraries?"

FOUNDATION CENTER provides library services and disseminates current information on foundation and corporate giving through their national collections in New York City and Washington, DC, through field offices in Atlanta, Cleveland and San Francisco, and through their network of over 200 libraries in all 50 states and abroad. With these resources, grant seekers have free access to core Center publications and a wide range of books, periodicals and research in connection with foundations and philanthropy. Services include reference librarian assistance, free orientations, and microform and photocopying facilities. For more information call or visit the National Collections in New York (212) 620-4230 or Washington, DC (202) 331-1400. Or contact Field Offices in San Francisco (415) 397-0902, Cleveland (216) 861-1934, or Atlanta (404) 880-0094. The Foundation Center, 79 Fifth Avenue, New York, NY 10003-3076. Web site http://www.fdncenter.org includes their catalog of publications.

HARVARD BUSINESS SCHOOL'S BAKER LIBRARY in Boston provides an outstanding consumer marketing web site at www.library.hbs.edu/. This web site identifies extensive sources of information on consumer marketing, including retail both for job hunters and researchers. It includes associations, membership directories, information on direct mail, public relations, corporate communications, online direct mail and online Dun and Bradstreet Credit Reports.

While the access to the web site itself is free and available to anyone, access to the CAREER ADVISOR database is available only to current Harvard Business School students and Harvard Business School Alumni Advisors (Harvard Business School alumni who have agreed to serve as Career advisors to current students and other alumni). The Advisor Database can be searched by industry, geography, job function, job title, year of graduation and company name. In addition, Reference Librarians at the Harvard Business School can conduct searches for a fee. Hundreds of databases are available. Ask at the Reference Desk for more information. For example, Dun & Bradstreet's Credit Reports are a lucrative source of information about privately held companies.

INDUSTRY CANADA'S Library can be reached at (613) 954-2728. Orders can be placed by calling (613) 947-5194. For more information, see their "Strategis Department" "Canadian Company Capabilities" web site at www.strategis.ic.gc.ca. Strategis's mandate is to print virtually any kind of information you want on Canadian companies. Their Help Desk number is (800) 328-6189. There are virtually no more updated print versions of information as all updates are now online.

INFORMATION IN CANADA—A DIRECTORY OF ELECTRONIC AND SUPPORT RESOURCES provides electronic information on information resources, consultants and information brokers, library based online research services, library automation software, computer accessible library catalogues and a directory of information industry services, plus a large section on databases produced in Canada. Price reduced to $49.95 for 1996 edition. Canada Library Association, 200 Elgin Street, Suite 602, Ottawa, Ontario K2P 1L5 CANADA, (613) 232-9625, fax (613) 563-9895,web site www.cla.amlibs.ca includes an online catalog. Email bj491@freenet.carleton.ca.

MEDICAL AND HEALTH INFORMATION DIRECTORY identifies organizations, agencies, institutions, services and information sources in medicine and health related fields. It includes approximately 20,000 organizations, 11,000 libraries, publications and electronic resources and 27,000 health service providers. Volume 1, Organizations, Agencies and Institutions. Volume 2, Publications, Libraries and Other Information Resources. Volume 3 Health Services. 3 volume set $590. $245 per volume. Gale Group, P.O. Box 9187, Farmington Hills, MI 48333-9187. Toll free US and Canada (800) 877-GALE (4253) and (248) 699-GALE, fax (800) 414-5043 and (248) 699-8061, Internet orders galeord@galegroup.com, web site www.galegroup.com or www.gale.com. All Gale Group products are available on approval. Contact Gale for details.

PUBLISHING MARKET PLACE REFERENCE PLUS CD ROM contains information from the LITERARY MARKET PLACE, INTERNATIONAL LITERARY MARKET PLACE, the AMERICAN LIBRARY DIRECTORY and the WORLD GUIDE TO LIBRARIES, plus 32,000 listings for bookstores and book dealers listed in the AMERICAN BOOK TRADE DIRECTORY, over 100,000 companies listed in PUBLISHERS, DISTRIBUTORS AND WHOLESALERS plus information from the BOWKER ANNUAL LIBRARY AND BOOK TRADE ALMANAC. Includes contact information and the ability to generate customized mailing lists and print labels for publishers, libraries and book dealers. This same mailing list information could be used to develop a list of prospects to contact. Can be searched by keyword, company/institution, personal name, position, subject, titles, conference/meeting, membership, and more. Updated annually. 1 year subscription $895, 3 years $2,551, excluding discounts. For more information visit Bowker Reed Reference's web site at http://www.reedref.com or contact: Bowker Reed Reference Electronic Publishing, 121 Chanlon Road, New Providence, NJ 07974 USA, Phone (800) 323-3288, Fax (908) 665-3528, email info@bowker.com.

SUBJECT DIRECTORY OF SPECIAL LIBRARIES presents the alphabetically organized contents of the DIRECTORY OF SPECIAL LIBRARIES AND INFORMATION CENTERS. It consists of 3 subject volumes and is organized by subject.

> Volume 1, Business, Government and Law Libraries
> Volume 2, Computers, Engineering and Science Libraries
> Volume 3, Health Science Libraries.

$875 for 3 volume set. Available individually at $340 per volume. Gale Group, P.O. Box 9187, Farmington Hills, MI 48333-9187. Toll free US and Canada (800) 877-GALE (4253) and (248) 699-GALE, fax (800) 414-5043 and (248) 699-8061, Internet orders galeord@galegroup.com, web site www.galegroup.com or www.gale.com. All Gale Group products are available on approval. Contact Gale for details.

WORLD DIRECTORY OF BUSINESS INFORMATION LIBRARIES identifies 2,500 major business libraries in 145 countries whose collections are oriented towards consumer markets. $590. Published by Euromonitor (England). Distributed by Gale Group, P.O. Box 9187, Farmington Hills, MI 48333-9187. Toll free US and Canada (800) 877-GALE (4253) and (248) 699-GALE, fax (800) 414-5043 and (248) 699-8061, Internet orders galeord@galegroup.com, web site www.galegroup.com or www.gale.com. All Gale Group products are available on approval. Contact Gale for details.

WORLD GUIDE TO LIBRARIES, from K.G. Saur, $425. R.R. Bowker (a unit of Cahners Business Information), 121 Chanlon Road, New Providence, NJ 07974 USA, Phone (888) BOWKER2 (888-269-5372) & (800) 323-3288, fax (908) 508-7696, email info@bowker.com, web www.bowker.com. Canada—R.R. Bowker, Markham, Ontario, phone (888) BOWKER9 & (905) 415-5837, fax (905) 479-6266. German speaking Europe—K.G. Saur Verlag, Munich, Germany, phone 49-89-76902-232, fax 49-89-76902-250, email 100730.1341@compuserve.com, web www.saur.de/home.htm. Rest of Europe incl. United Kingdom plus Africa & Asia—Bowker-Saur, W. Sussex, UK, phone 44-1342-326-972, fax 44-1342-335-612, email customer@bowker-saur.co.uk, web www.bowker-saur.com/service/. Australia/New Zealand—Thorpe, Port Melbourne, Victoria, Australia, phone 61-03-9-245-7370, fax 61-03-9-245-7395, email customer.service@thorpe.com.au, web www.thorpe.com.au. Technical support for CD ROMs (800) 323-3288, fax 908) 665-3528, email techsupport@bowker.com.

WORLD GUIDE TO SPECIAL LIBRARIES, from K.G. Saur, $400. R.R. Bowker (a unit of Cahners Business Information), 121 Chanlon Road, New Providence, NJ 07974 USA, Phone (888) BOWKER2 (888-269-5372) & (800) 323-3288, fax (908) 508-7696, email info@bowker.com, web www.bowker.com. Canada—R.R. Bowker, Markham, Ontario, phone (888) BOWKER9 & (905) 415-5837, fax (905) 479-6266. German speaking Europe—K.G. Saur Verlag, Munich, Germany, phone 49-89-76902-232, fax 49-89-76902-250, email 100730.1341@compuserve.com, web www.saur.de/home.htm. Rest of Europe incl. United Kingdom plus Africa & Asia—Bowker-Saur, W. Sussex, UK, phone 44-1342-326-972, fax 44-1342-335-612, email customer@bowker-saur.co.uk, web www.bowker-saur.com/service/. Australia/New Zealand—Thorpe, Port Melbourne, Victoria, Australia, phone 61-03-9-245-7370, fax 61-03-9-245-7395, email customer.service@thorpe.com.au, web www.thorpe.com.au. Technical support for CD ROMs (800) 323-3288, fax 908) 665-3528, email techsupport@bowker.com.

www.cweb.com or CareerWeb was ranked as one of the top 5 "Sites Offering the Best Career Resources for Job Seekers" as well as one of the top 5 "General Purpose Sites" by the *National Business Employment Weekly.* Its features include a career resource center and a library. The site was developed by Landmark Communications, Norfolk, Virginia and launched in 1995.

www.fdncenter.org is the web site to the Foundation Center. This site provides grant makers, grant seekers, researchers, policy makers and the general public with 24 hour access to information about the philanthropic community. This site provides links to over 280 foundations, a catalog of their publications you can order online, seminars you can register for, a proposal writing course, an online library with librarians who will respond to your email questions within 48 hours, online orientations to the grant seeking process (both for individuals and for nonprofit organizations), a review of the latest funding trends, the location of the nearest Cooperating Collection where you can use the Foundation Center's publications and CD ROM, and more. The Foundation Center, 79 Fifth Avenue, New York, NY 10003-3076, (212) 620-4230.

www.library.hbs.edu/ is the URL for the Harvard Business School Baker Library, which contains free excellent information on consumer marketing, retail, associations, membership directories, direct mail, public relations, corporate communications, online direct mail and more. Dun and Bradstreet Credit Reports can also be accessed. In addition, for a fee, reference librarians can conduct online searches from any of several hundred databases. See "Harvard Business School's Baker Library" above.

Librarians' References

See References—Librarian. Also refer to Chapter 6, "How to Create an Executive Search Library"

Library and Research Organizations

AMERICAN LIBRARY ASSOCIATION (ALA), 50 East Huron Street, Chicago, IL 60611, (800) 545-2433, in Illinois (800) 545-2444, in Canada (800) 545-2455. Annually publishes the ALA Handbook of Organization and Membership Directory, which provides information about the ALA's divisions, committees, round tables and discussion groups. The major divisions of the ALA are:

* REFERENCE AND ADULT SERVICES DIVISION (RASD) publishes RQ. Committees include Business Reference Sources Committee, Reference Sources Committee, Adult Library Materials Committee, and Reference Tools Advisory Committee (which provides assistance to publishers of reference titles). Other sections include Machine-Assisted Reference Section and History Section.

* ASSOCIATION OF COLLEGE AND RESEARCH LIBRARIES (ACRL) is the largest group within the ALA. It publishes CHOICE, COLLEGE & RESEARCH LIBRARIES, COLLEGE & RESEARCH LIBRARIES NEWS, RARE BOOKS AND MANUSCRIPTS LIBRARIANSHIP.

- PUBLIC LIBRARY ASSOCIATION (PLA) consists of the Metropolitan Libraries Section, Community Information Section, and Armed Forces Library Section. PLA publishes PUBLIC LIBRARIES.

- ASSOCIATION FOR LIBRARY COLLECTIONS AND TECHNICAL SERVICES (ALCTS) publishes LIBRARY RESOURCES AND TECHNICAL SERVICES.

- AMERICAN ASSOCIATION OF SCHOOL LIBRARIANS (AASL) publishes SCHOOL LIBRARY MEDIA QUARTERLY.

See below for International Leads, formerly named the International Relations Roundtable.

AMERICAN SOCIETY FOR INFORMATION SCIENCE, 8720 Georgia Avenue, Suite 501, Silver Springs, MD 20910-3602, (301) 495-0900.

ASSOCIATION OF RESEARCH LIBRARIES, 1527 New Hampshire Avenue, NW, Washington, DC 20036, (202) 232-2466.

CANADIAN ASSOCIATION FOR INFORMATION SCIENCE, University of Toronto, 140 St. George Street, Toronto, ON M5S 1A1 CANADA, (416) 978-8876.

CANADIAN LIBRARY ASSOCIATION is located at Suite 602, 200 Elgin Street, Ottawa, ON K2P 1L5, (613) 232-9625. Their online catalog can be viewed on their web site, www.cla.amlibs.ca and should indicate when an update will be available for their 1992 edition of CANADIAN BUSINESS AND ECONOMICS, A GUIDE TO SOURCES OF INFORMATION.

CANADIAN BUSINESS AND ECONOMICS: A GUIDE TO SOURCES OF INFORMATION lists information by subject, including books, periodicals and services. Fully indexed and thoroughly cross referenced. Price reduced to $39.95 for 1992 edition. Canada Library Association, 200 Elgin Street, Suite 602, Ottawa, Ontario K2P 1L5 CANADA, (613) 232-9625, fax (613) 563-9895, Internet: bj491@freenet.carleton.ca.

EXECUTIVE SEARCH ROUNDTABLE, founded in New York City in 1979, was the first professional association of research professionals established. Their newsletter, ON TARGET, is published quarterly. Members can access a wired capability by email in which they can source each other for ideas, resources, web sites, and names of contacts. For more information contact THE EXECUTIVE SEARCH ROUNDTABLE, P.O. Box 3565, Grand Central Station, New York, NY 10163, phone (212) 439-4630, web site www.esroundtable.org.

HARVARD BUSINESS SCHOOL'S BAKER LIBRARY in Boston provides an outstanding consumer marketing web site at www.library.hbs.edu/. This web site identifies extensive sources of information on consumer marketing, including retail both for job hunters and researchers. It includes associations, membership directories, information on direct mail, public relations, corporate communications, online direct mail and online Dun and Bradstreet Credit Reports.

While the access to the web site itself is free and available to anyone, access to the CAREER ADVISOR database is available only to current Harvard Business School students and Harvard Business School Alumni Advisors (Harvard Business School alumni who have agreed to serve as Career advisors to current students and other alumni). The Advisor Database can be searched by industry, geography, job function, job title, year of graduation and company name. In addition, Reference Librarians at the Harvard Business School can conduct searches for a fee. Hundreds of databases are available. Ask at the Reference Desk for more information. For example, Dun & Bradstreet's Credit Reports are a lucrative source of information about privately held companies.

INTERNATIONAL LEADS reviews works dealing with librarianship in countries other than the USA, with international library and information science agencies and activities. Members $10 per year, non-members $12. Formerly American Library Association, International Relations Round Table. Ordering information: International Leads, International Relations Round Table, International Relations Office, 50 East Huron Street, Chicago, IL 60611, (800) 545-2433, (312) 280-3200, email: robert.p.doyle@ala.org.

MEDICAL LIBRARY ASSOCIATION, 6 North Michigan Avenue, Suite 300, Chicago, IL 60602, (312) 419-9094.

MUSIC LIBRARY ASSOCIATION, Box 487, Canton, MA 02021, (617) 828-8450.

REFERENCE AND RESEARCH BOOK NEWS provides prompt information about new books and CD ROMs of interest to reference librarians and users of reference materials. 8 issues per year, 900 books and CD's reviewed per issue. $100/institutions, $80/individuals US and Canada, $115/foreign. Ordering information: REFERENCE & RESEARCH BOOK NEWS, 5600 NE Hassalo Street, Portland, OR 97213, (503) 281-9230, email: booksnews@booknews. com, http://www.books.com//booknews.

SOCIETY OF AMERICAN ARCHIVISTS, 600 South Federal Street, Suite 504, Chicago, IL 60605, (312) 922-0140.

SPECIAL LIBRARIES ASSOCIATION encompasses business research, among other specialized types of information. It is an important organization which many librarians rely on and a rich source of information. The SLA is located at 1700 18th Street, NW, Washington, DC 20009, (202) 234-4700.

www.library.hbs.edu/ is the URL for the Harvard Business School Baker Library, which contains free excellent information on consumer marketing, retail, associations, membership directories, direct mail, public relations, corporate communications, online direct mail and more. Dun and Bradstreet Credit Reports can also be accessed. In addition, for a fee, reference librarians can conduct online searches from any of several hundred databases. See "Harvard Business School's Baker Library" above.

Lobbying

Also see Associations

AMERICAN MINES HANDBOOK provides information on over 1,000 precious and base metal mining companies working in the US. Includes key contact names plus mining area maps for Alaska, Arizona, California, Colorado, Idaho, Minnesota, Montana, Nevada, South Carolina, Utah. Also includes a Directory of Key Industry Contacts for Government and Support Organizations $52. Special discounts available for combined purchases. For more information on Energy Information Services, call Calgary office (403) 244-6111. Published by Southam Information Products Ltd, 1450 Don Mills Road, Don Mills, Ontario M3B 2X7 CANADA, (800) 668-2374. In Toronto 442-2122. Web site www.southam.com.

ENCYCLOPEDIA OF ASSOCIATIONS: INTERNATIONAL ORGANIZATIONS includes nearly 20,000 multinational and national organizations in foreign countries, including US based associations with multinational membership. Entries also include email addresses, web sites and bulletin board addresses, lobbying activities, and publication and convention information. Indexed by geography, keyword and executives. $595 for 2 volume set. Also available in CD ROM. Database available via commercial online service. Gale Group, P.O. Box 9187, Farmington Hills, MI 48333-9187. Toll free US and Canada (800) 877-GALE (4253) and (248) 699-GALE, fax (800) 414-5043 and (248) 699-8061, Internet orders galeord@galegroup.com, web site www.galegroup.com or www.gale.com. All Gale Group products are available on approval. Contact Gale for details.

NATIONAL DIRECTORY OF CORPORATE PUBLIC AFFAIRS identifies some 14,000 people who manage public affairs and government affairs programs of nearly 2,000 corporations. This directory also includes Washington area offices, corporate foundation/giving programs, federal and state lobbyists and outside contract lobbyists. Indexed by subject and geography. $95. Columbia Books, Inc., 1212 New York Avenue, NW, Suite 330, Washington, DC 20005, (212) 898-0662.

WASHINGTON REPRESENTATIVES—Who Does What For Whom in The Nation's Capital identifies over 17,000 lobbyists, public and government affairs representatives and special interest advocates in Washington, DC. Includes foreign agent registration numbers and federal lobbyist indicators. Listings are organized by client and by representative and are indexed by subject/ industry and foreign interest. $95. Columbia Books, Inc., 1212 New York Avenue, NW, Suite 330, Washington, DC 20005, (212) 898-0662.

Luxembourg

See Europe, International

DIRECTORY OF AMERICAN FIRMS OPERATING IN FOREIGN COUNTRIES, REGIONAL EDITION—EUROPE, WESTERN, $159. Uniworld Business Publications, Inc., 257 Central Park West, Suite 10A, New York, NY 10024-4110, (212) 496-2448, fax (212) 769-0413, email uniworldbp@aol.com. Web site: http://www.uniworldbp.com.

TOP 25,000 COMPANIES OF BELGIUM AND LUXEMBOURG contains information on 25,000 companies. Text in English, Dutch and French. Dun & Bradstreet, Business Reference Solutions, Three Sylvan Way, Parsippany, NJ 07054 USA. (800) 526-0651. Email dnbmdd@mail.dnb.com. Web site http://www.dnbmdd.com.

M

Mailing Lists
See Direct Mail

Management Consulting
Also see Health Care Consulting

CONSULTANTS AND CONSULTING ORGANIZATIONS DIRECTORY identifies consultants in over 400 specialties within 14 general areas. Includes finance, computers, fundraising and others. $620 for 2 volumes. Gale Group, P.O. Box 9187, Farmington Hills, MI 48333-9187. Toll free US and Canada (800) 877-GALE (4253) and (248) 699-GALE, fax (800) 414-5043 and (248) 699-8061, Internet orders galeord@galegroup.com, web site www.galegroup.com or www.gale.com. All Gale Group products are available on approval. Contact Gale for details.

D&B DIRECTORY OF SERVICE COMPANIES is a directory with information on 50,000 US service businesses, including privately held companies, in these sectors: accounting, auditing and bookkeeping, advertising and public relations, architecture and engineering, consumer services, executive search, health, hospitality, management consulting, motion pictures, repair, research, social services and law. Listings include key executives' names and titles, address, phone, sales volume, number of employees, parent company and location, and more. Companies listed employ 50 or more people. Information is listed alphabetically and is cross-referenced geographically and by industry classification. Updated annually. For prices call Dun & Bradstreet at (800) 526-0651. For more information contact Dun & Bradstreet, Business Reference Solutions, Three Sylvan Way, Parsippany, New Jersey 07054. Email dnbmdd@mail.dnb.com. Web site http://www.dnbmdd.com.

DIRECTORY OF CANADIAN LIBRARY AND INFORMATION SCIENCE CONSULTANTS is a national Canadian directory of library and library related consultants. $29.95. Canada Library Association, 200 Elgin Street, Suite 602, Ottawa, Ontario K2P 1L5 CANADA, (613) 232-9625, fax (613) 563-9895, Internet: bj491@freenet.carleton.ca.

DIRECTORY OF MANAGEMENT CONSULTANTS provides accurate information on over 1,300 management consulting firms, specialties, key principals, revenues, fees, geographic information, professional associations, and advice on selecting consultants. $295.95. Published by Kennedy Information, One Kennedy Place, Route 12 South, Fitzwilliam, NH 03447, phone (800) 531-0007 or 603-585-6544, fax 603-585-9555, email bookstore@kennedyinfo.com, web site www.kennedyinfo.com.

HARVARD BUSINESS SCHOOL students gather data and publish it for their own job hunting purposes. The Management Consulting Club publishes one fine book and The Corporate Finance Club publishes another. Basically, the major firms provide descriptions of their businesses, strategic focus, size, contact information and other important data. Since many of these companies are privately held, these resources are unusually valuable because this information could otherwise be very difficult to obtain. It usually requires some detective work to track them down, but it's worth the effort. Call the Harvard Business School in Boston.

Ask the operator for contact information for either the Management Consulting Club or the Corporate Finance Club. If you coax them, you might be able to get more information than a phone number, like a mailing address, an email address or a web site.

LITERARY MARKET PLACE, "The Directory of the American Book Publishing Industry With Industry Yellow Pages" is an excellent 3 volume directory with comprehensive information on US book publishers; imprints, subsidiaries and distributors; book trade acquisitions and mergers, small presses, Canadian book publishers, micropublishers, US electronic publishers, electronic publishing consultants, electronic publishing products and services, editorial services, literary agents, illustrations agents, US agents and offices of foreign publishers, lecture agents, specialized advertising and public relations firms, direct mail specialists, mailing list brokers and services, book review syndicates, book review and index journals and services, book exhibits, book clubs, book lists and catalogs, book importers and exporters, book producers, translators, artists, photographers, stock photo agencies, associations, book trade events and conferences, awards, contents and grants, reference books for the trade, magazines for the trade, a toll free directory of publishers, magazine and newspaper publicity, radio and television publicity, book manufacturing services, book distributors and sales representatives, and wholesalers. $189.95.

LITERARY MARKET PLACE ON DISC, previously titled LITERARY MARKET PLACE PLUS CD ROM, one year subscription $297.00.

LITERARY MARKET PLACE—INTERNET EDITION, www.literarymarketplace.com, is available by subscription.

INTERNATIONAL LITERARY MARKET PLACE Internet database can be directly accessed at www.iliterarymarketplace.com. It is also linked to the US domestic LITERARY MARKET PLACE web site at www.literarymarketplace.com. Contact the publisher for subscription price. INTERNATIONAL LITERARY MARKET PLACE, hard copy $189.95.

R.R. Bowker (a unit of Cahners Business Information), 121 Chanlon Road, New Providence, NJ 07974 USA, Phone (888) BOWKER2 (888-269-5372) & (800) 323-3288, fax (908) 508-7696, email info@bowker.com, web www.bowker.com. Canada—R.R. Bowker, Markham, Ontario, phone (888) BOWKER9 & (905) 415-5837, fax (905) 479-6266. German speaking Europe—K.G. Saur Verlag, Munich, Germany, phone 49-89-76902-232, fax 49-89-76902-250, email 100730.1341@compuserve.com, web www.saur.de/home.htm. Rest of Europe incl. United Kingdom plus Africa & Asia—Bowker-Saur, W. Sussex, UK, phone 44-1342-326-972, fax 44-1342-335-612, email customer@bowker-saur.co.uk, web www.bowker-saur.com/service/. Australia/New Zealand—Thorpe, Port Melbourne, Victoria, Australia, phone 61-03-9-245-7370, fax 61-03-9-245-7395, email customer.service@thorpe.com.au, web www.thorpe.com.au. Technical support for CD ROMs (800) 323-3288, fax 908) 665-3528, email techsupport@bowker.com.

NELSON'S PENSION FUND CONSULTANTS identifies some 2,500 professional consultants at over 300 global pension consulting firms. Listings include names of key executives, phone numbers, services provided, and more. Published annually. $350. Nelson Information, P.O. Box 591, Port Chester, NY 10573 USA. (800) 333-6357, Phone outside the US (914) 937-8400, Fax (914) 937-8590, web site http://www.nelnet.com.

www.americanbanker.com/careerzone or American Banker Online was launched in 1998 by American Banker, New York, New York.

www.kennedyinfo.com is the web site for publisher Kennedy Information. It includes books, newsletters, training materials, directories, and surveys for executive recruiting, human resources, outplacement, management consulting and job seekers. (800) 531-0007 or (603) 585-6544.

Manufacturing

Also see Manufacturing—Plant Locations

APICS, previously the **AMERICAN PRODUCTION AND INVENTORY CONTROL SOCIETY,** now is the EDUCATIONAL SOCIETY FOR RESOURCE MANAGEMENT, a highly respected professional association for manufacturing management. It is a large national organization with local chapters all over the country. They also offer well regarded courses and certifications. While information about the organization may be difficult to obtain, especially membership rosters, it is well worth the effort, especially to locate Fellows, which is like an educational certification. You might need the assistance of a member, who will either lend you a list or will give you permission to use his or her name to receive information. For more information contact the national headquarters, 500 West Annandale Road, Falls Church, VA 22046-4274, (800) 444-2742, (703) 237-8344, web site www.apics.org.

GUIDE TO CANADIAN MANUFACTURERS contains information on Canada's top 44,000 manufacturing companies. Dun & Bradstreet, Business Reference Solutions, Three Sylvan Way, Parsippany, NJ 07054 USA. (800) 526-0651. Email dnbmdd@mail.dnb.com. Web site http://www.dnbmdd.com.

www.ajb.dni.us is the URL for America's Job Bank. It was ranked as one of the top 5 "Sites Offering the Best Job-Search Support" by the *National Business Employment Weekly.* Launched in 1995, the site was developed by the U.S. Department of Labor and state employment/unemployment offices. Most openings were originally listed with a state department of labor and are mainly in the $30,000 to $50,000 range. Many positions are in information technology, administrative and production and manufacturing.

www.thomasregister.com is the URL for Thomas' Register, which provides information Information on US and Canadian manufacturing firms.

Manufacturing—Plant Locations

Annual Reports and 10(k) Reports must be filed each year with the Securities and Exchange Commission by all publicly held companies. Annual reports particularly 10(k) reports often reveal manufacturing plant information and specify all other company locations. If you have not yet familiarized yourself with 10(k) reports, make a point of reviewing several for your next search. You will be astonished at the information available and it's free. Just call the company switchboard and say, "I'd like to request an annual report and a 10(k)." In fact, as long as you're already requesting an annual and a proxy, you might want to ask for a proxy statement, too, because it reveals compensation data of senior management.

CANADIAN MINING JOURNAL is a leading exploration and mining journal in Canada. Published six times a year, it announces executive appointments, provides information on corporate developments, rates Canada's major mining companies, and includes news on mills and metallurgical plants. Annual subscription $34 Canada, $49 US, $34 Foreign. Special discounts available for combined purchases. For more information on Energy Information Services, call Calgary office (403) 244-6111. Published by Southam Information Products Ltd, 1450 Don Mills Road, Don Mills, Ontario M3B 2X7 CANADA, (800) 668-2374. In Toronto 442-2122. Web site www.southam.com.

COMPLETE TWIN PLANT GUIDE is a three volume directory of plants in the $15 billion Mexico Maquila market. Volume 1 covers Baja California, Volume 2 covers the Central Corridor and Volume 3 covers Mexico City, Rio Grande, Gulf, and Lower Pacific regions. This directory includes over 8,000 executive names at some 2,300 plants, plus address, phone numbers, number of employees, SIC or NAICS codes and more. Diskette's available. $170 per volume, $350 for set. CD ROM $650 complete, $220 per single volume on disk. Published annually by Solunet. Distributed by Manufacturers' News, Inc., (888) 752-5200, 1633 Central Street, Evanston, IL 60201-1569. Email info@manufacturersnews.com. Web site www.manufacturersnews.com.

CORPORATE AFFILIATIONS PLUS CD ROM consolidates information in all five volumes of THE DIRECTORY OF CORPORATE AFFILIATIONS, including publicly held and privately held companies in the US and internationally, and AMERICA'S CORPORATE FINANCE DIRECTORY. This CD provides "family tree" overviews for each company with the reporting structure. It also contains information on 15,000 parent companies in the US and abroad, records on over 100,000 subsidiaries, divisions, plants and joint ventures, names and titles of over 250,000 employees, revenue figures and more. Information can be searched by 29 criteria, such as location, SIC or NAICS codes, sales, number of employees, net worth, pension assets and more. Updated quarterly. 1 year subscription $1,995, available for both Windows and Macintosh. If the price is prohibitively high, remember your local library. National Register Publishing, Reed Elsevier-New Providence, 121 Chanlon Road, New Providence, NJ 07974, (800) 521-8110, fax (800) 836-7736, web site www.redbooks.com or www.marquiswhoswho.com. "If, for any reason whatsoever, your order does not fully meet your expectations, simply return the product within 30 days for a prompt, complete, unquestioned

refund," as stated in Catalog of Biographical and Professional References of publisher Marquis Who's Who/National Register Publishing.

D&B INDUSTRIAL GUIDE—THE METAL WORKING DIRECTORY contains information about 75,000 original equipment manufacturers, metalworking plants, metal distributors, machine tools/metalworking machinery distributors for locations with at least 20 people. Listings include plant name, key executives' names and titles, principal manufacturing processes, plant square footage, number of employees and more. Volumes 1 & 2 list plants geographically by state and city. Volume 3 lists companies alphabetically and by industry classification. Updated annually. For prices call Dun & Bradstreet at (800) 526-0651. For more information contact Dun & Bradstreet, Business Reference Solutions, Three Sylvan Way, Parsippany, New Jersey 07054. Email dnbmdd@mail.dnb.com. Web site http://www.dnbmdd.com.

DIRECTORY OF CORPORATE AFFILIATIONS OR WHO OWNS WHOM is a superb directory which can help you decipher the organizational structure of a company. This directory provides detailed information about all parent companies, subsidiaries and divisions, plus plant locations, joint ventures, a brief description of the subsidiary or division, a partial listing of names and titles, location, phone number, and sometimes revenues or number of employees. THE DIRECTORY OF CORPORATE AFFILIATIONS provides a comprehensive "family tree" listing that lays out the corporate hierarchy to provide a picture of the structure of companies, subsidiaries, affiliates & divisions. It includes companies with revenues of at least $10 million and reveals division and subsidiary reporting relationships down to the sixth level. It provides information on 8,500 privately held companies. For US companies it details complex multinational relationships and joint ventures. For additional names and titles of key executives in subsidiaries & divisions, refer to another directory such as Standard & Poors, THE STANDARD DIRECTORY OF ADVERTISERS, or a specialized industry directory. THE DIRECTORY OF CORPORATE AFFILIATIONS consists of 5 volumes, including US Public Companies, US Private Companies, International Companies (both public and private), and indices. It also contains a Brand Name Index. The CD ROM version of this directory is titled Corporate Affiliations Plus.

Note: If THE DIRECTORY OF CORPORATE AFFILIATIONS does not provide all the organization structure information you want and the company is publicly held, there's an abundance of free information available! Check the company's web site or call them for an annual report and 10(k). Even if the company is privately held, they will usually send information if you ask for it. The more specific your request, the more likely you are to get what you need, for example, a list of all company locations, a list of plant locations, or product information.

Ordering information: $1,029.95/5 volumes, excluding discounts. If the price is prohibitively high, remember your local library. National Register Publishing, Reed Elsevier-New Providence, 121 Chanlon Road, New Providence, NJ 07974, (800) 521-8110, fax (800) 836-7736, web site www.redbooks.com or www.marquiswhoswho.com. "If, for any reason whatsoever, your order does not fully meet your expectations, simply return the product within 30 days for a prompt, complete, unquestioned refund," as stated in Catalog of Biographical and Professional References of publisher Marquis Who's Who/National Register Publishing.

HARRIS ELECTRONICS MANUFACTURERS DATABASE, also available as a directory, is published in cooperation with the Electronics Representatives Association and the National Electronic Distributors Association. It contains information on over 20,000 US electronics manufacturing firms and over 2,500 Canadian electronics manufacturers, including names of about 68,000 American executives and 5,500 Canadian executives. Selectory $595. Selectory multi-user (LAN) version $1,190. Directory, updated annually, $255. Ordering information: Harris InfoSource International, 2057 Aurora Road, Twinsburg, OH 44087-1999, (800) 888-5900, fax (800) 643-5997, web site http://www.harrisinfo.com.

ILLINOIS COUNTY BUSINESS DATABASES & DIRECTORIES are published every two years and combine detailed profiles from the ILLINOIS MANUFACTURERS DIRECTORY and the companion ILLINOIS SERVICES DIRECTORY. All directories contains executive names and titles and other information. These editions are available:

• CHICAGO BUSINESS DIRECTORY, $129, Complete CD ROM $545, CD ROM with 100 or more employees $225. CD ROMs with 20 or more employees and 50 or more employees are also available.

- SUBURBAN COOK COUNTY BUSINESS DIRECTORY, $158, Complete CD ROM $695, CD ROM with 100 or more employees $260. CD ROMs with 10 or more employees, 20 or more employees and 50 or more employees are also available.

- DUPAGE COUNTY BUSINESS DIRECTORY, $94, Complete CD ROM $445. Abbreviated CD ROMs are also available.

- KANE COUNTY BUSINESS DIRECTORY, $49, Complete CD ROM $295. Abbreviated CD ROMs are also available.

- LAKE COUNTY BUSINESS DIRECTORY, $59. Complete CD ROM $325. Abbreviated CD ROMs are also available.

- McHENRY COUNTY BUSINESS DIRECTORY, $39, Complete CD ROM $195. Abbreviated CD ROMs are also available.

- WILL COUNTY BUSINESS DIRECTORY, $35, Complete CD ROM $195. Abbreviated CD ROMs are also available.

Distributed by Manufacturers' News, Inc., (888) 752-5200, 1633 Central Street, Evanston, IL 60201-1569. Email info@manufacturersnews.com. Web site www.manufacturersnews.com.

MACRAE'S BLUE BOOK identifies over 42,000 plants but lists no executive names. It is most appropriate for target list research. Distributed by Manufacturers' News, Inc., (888) 752-5200, 1633 Central Street, Evanston, IL 60201-1569. Email info@manufacturersnews.com. Web site www.manufacturersnews.com.

MANUFACTURERS DIRECTORIES and CD ROM'S distributed by Manufacturers' News, Inc. are available for every state of the union plus the metropolitan New York area. They are published by Manufacturers' News, Database Publishing, Commerce Register, Pick Publications. Directory prices generally range between $50 and $165, depending on the size of the directory. Close out prices on old directories are also available. Virtually all directories are published annually. CD ROMs are available with "complete" information, or for 10 or more employees, 20 or more employees, 50 or more employees, or 100 or more employees. CD prices range between $100 for information on plants with over 100 employees for a small state, up to $745 for a complete disk for a large state. Includes names and titles of key executives, plant square footage, number of employees, product, SIC, distribution area. "EZ Select" CD ROMs are another CD ROM option. It allows you to search by 11 fields, including company size, type of industry, and geographic criteria, job function and title. EZ Select CD ROMs cost between approximately $175-$400, depending on the size of the database. EZ Select Disks are also available. For more information contact Manufacturers' News, Inc., (888) 752-5200, 1633 Central Street, Evanston, IL 60201-1569. Email info@manufacturersnews.com. Web site www.manufacturersnews.com.

MAQUILADORAS (TWIN PLANT) GUIDE is a 3 volume directory that covers the $14 billion maquiladora market in Mexico. Volume 1—850 plants in Baja. Volume 2—900 plants in Central Corridor. Volume 3—850 plants in the Rio Grande, Gulf and lower Pacific region. Single volume $140, full set $385, database $720. Database Publishing Company, PO Box 70024, Anaheim, CA 92825, (800) 888-8434, (714) 778-6400, email sales@databasepublishing.com.

MEXICO TWIN PLANT GUIDE is a 3 volume set available as a directory or an electronic database. Directory $385, database $720. Distributed by Harris InfoSource, 2057 East Aurora Road, Twinsburg, OH 44087-1999, (330) 425-9000, (800) 888-5900, www.HarrisInfo.com.

PUERTO RICO INDUSTRIAL DIRECTORY is available for $129 from publisher Harris InfoSource, 2057 East Aurora Road, Twinsburg, OH 44087-1999, (330) 425-9000, (800) 888-5900, www.HarrisInfo.com.

PULP AND PAPER ANNUAL AND DIRECTORY contains an index of companies, divisions and subsidiaries, plus information on 3 sectors: pulp, paper and board manufacturing sector, supply sector and support sector. Includes information on key contacts, mills and recycling companies. Canada $95, USA and foreign $115. Special discounts available for combined purchases. Published by Southam Information Products Ltd, 1450 Don Mills Road, Don Mills, Ontario M3B 2X7 CANADA, (800) 668-2374. In Toronto 442-2122. Web site www.southam.com.

SCOTT'S CANADA DIRECTORIES profile over 60,000 facilities and identify over 120,000 executive names in Canada. The following directories are available and are updated annually:

SCOTT'S ONTARIO MANUFACTURERS, $209

SCOTT'S QUEBEC MANUFACTURERS, $189

SCOTT'S WESTERN INDUSTRIAL EDITION, including Manitoba, Saskatchewan, Alberta and British Columbia, $169

SCOTT'S ATLANTIC INDUSTRIAL EDITION, including Prince Edward Island, Nova Scotia, New Brunswick, $129.

Distributed by Manufacturers' News, Inc., (888) 752-5200, 1633 Central Street, Evanston, IL 60201-1569. Email info@manufacturersnews.com. Web site www.manufacturersnews.com.

STATE MANUFACTURING DIRECTORIES and US regional geographic directories published by Harris are available for all US states as hard copy directories or in electronic Selectory® formats. With Selectory® information is searchable from 25 fields and generates an easy-to-read report containing: company, address, location, county, phone, fax, toll free number, Internet address, a listing of personnel with titles, SIC/NAICS codes, product description, products, number of employees, per cent employment change, sales range, plant size, foreign trade, year established, private or public ownership, and experian credit score. This information could either provide an alternative to "identification research" calls, or offer an excellent place to begin the verification calls of ID research. If time is money, you can access a tremendous amount of precise information quickly with electronic references, such as this one or many others. One attractive feature of Harris's products is that they are relatively inexpensive. Here are a few sample prices: Directories and databases are available for all US states: Alabama $79 directory, $349 database. Arizona $90 directory, $475 database. Arkansas $69 directory, $325 database, Ohio $159 directory, $725 database. New Jersey $99 directory, $595 database. The most expensive is California, $169 directory, $925 database. The least expensive are Delaware and Washington, DC each one at $39 for directory, $149 for database.

Contact Harris for a sample Harris Profile Report. For exact pricing, a catalog and other information, call distributor Scott's Directories, Toronto area: 1450 Don Mills Road, Don Mills, Ontario, M3B 2X7, CANADA, (888) 709-9907, (416) 442-2291, (416) 932-9555. Montréal area: Scott's Directories, 3300 Cote Verde, Suite 410 Ville St.-Laurent, Quebec H4B 2B7 CANADA (514) 339-1397, (800) 363-1327, email scotts@southam.ca. Publisher Harris InfoSource, 2057 East Aurora Road, Twinsburg, OH 44087-1999, (330) 425-9000, (800) 888-5900, www.HarrisInfo.com.

U.S. MANUFACTURERS DATABASE™ ON CD ROM is a comprehensive database that profiles 340,000 manufacturing establishments and contains names and titles of 600,000 CEO's, owners and key executives (This averages to less than 2 names for each of the 340 manufacturing establishments.) This CD ROM can print mailing labels and company profiles. Information can be searched by 24 different fields, including zip code, and 5,500 product categories. National edition (100 or more employees) $1,795. Regional editions (100 or more employees) for the Midwest, South Central and Southeast, $695 each. Northeast regional edition (100 or more employees) $695. West regional edition (100 or more employees) $429. State directories are also available for western states. For more information and a catalog, contact Database Publishing Company, PO Box 70024, Anaheim, CA 92825, (800) 888-8434, (714) 778-6400, email sales@databasepublishing.com.

WORLDWIDE BRANCH LOCATIONS OF MULTINATIONAL COMPANIES focuses on some 500 multinationals and nearly 20,000 plants, branch offices and subsidiaries worldwide and NOT headquartered in the USA. It's organized geographically. Indexes include names of facilities and parent companies, SIC, and a geographic listing of parent companies by country. $200. Ordering information: Gale Research, P.O. Box 33477, Detroit, MI 48232-5477. Phone (800) 877-GALE, Fax (800) 414-5043 will be responded to within 48 hours. Internet orders: galeord@galegroup.com, CompuServe email: 72203.1552, web site http://www.galegroup.com, GaleNet web site address @http://galenet.galegroup.com.

Maritime

JOURNAL OF COMMERCE, published in New York, New York, is a trade journal serving the shipping industry.

Market Research

ASIAN ADVERTISING, MARKETING AND MEDIA HANDBOOK lists information about advertising agencies, newspaper and magazine publishers and market research companies. Published by Euromonitor (England), at $470 (1st edition), it had been exclusively distributed by Gale Group. At the time of this writing, Gale no longer carries it. For more information, contact Euromonitor or Gale or refer to Books in Print. This reference might also be available in the library.

LATIN AMERICAN ADVERTISING, MARKETING & MEDIA SOURCEBOOK, published by Euromonitor (England), at $470 (1st edition), had been exclusively distributed in the USA, Canada and Australia by Gale Group. At the time of this writing, Gale no longer carries it. For more information, contact Euromonitor or Gale or refer to Books in Print or International Books in Print. This reference might also be available in the library.

WORLD DIRECTORY OF BUSINESS INFORMATION WEB SITES provides full details on over 1,500 free business web sites, including information such as online surveys, top company rankings, company information, brand information, market research reports and trade association statistics. $590. Published by Euromonitor (England). Distributed by Gale Group, P.O. Box 9187, Farmington Hills, MI 48333-9187. Toll free US and Canada (800) 877-GALE (4253) and (248) 699-GALE, fax (800) 414-5043 and (248) 699-8061, Internet orders galeord@galegroup.com, web site www.galegroup.com or www.gale.com. All Gale Group products are available on approval. Contact Gale for details.

WORLD DIRECTORY OF MARKETING INFORMATION SOURCES identifies market research companies, online databases, directories and marketing journals for every major consumer market in 75 countries. $595. Published by Euromonitor (England). Distributed by Gale Group, P.O. Box 9187, Farmington Hills, MI 48333-9187. Toll free US and Canada (800) 877-GALE (4253) and (248) 699-GALE, fax (800) 414-5043 and (248) 699-8061, Internet orders galeord@galegroup.com, web site www.galegroup.com or www.gale.com. All Gale Group products are available on approval. Contact Gale for details.

Marketing

Also see Advertising, Commercial Development, Consumer Marketing, Direct Mail, Market Research, Media, Sales

BUSINESS MARKETING is a monthly trade publication. Crain Communications, Inc. is headquartered in Chicago with offices in major cities throughout the US plus London, Tokyo and Frankfurt. New York location: 220 East 42nd Street, New York, NY 10017, (212) 210-0100, Circulation (800) 678-9595. Annual subscription $59, two years $99.

CREATIVITY is a monthly trade publication. Crain Communications, Inc. is headquartered in Chicago with offices in major cities throughout the US plus London, Tokyo and Frankfurt. New York location: 220 East 42nd Street, New York, NY 10017, (212) 210-0100, Circulation (800) 678-9595. Annual subscription $49.

D&B MARKETING INFORMATION BASE contains marketing information on 10,000,000 companies. Every month it is updated, reflecting some 500,000 changes: new business additions, CEO CHANGES and address changes. Information on senior management changes is particularly valuable to job hunters and search firms is an indicator of change, which could mean hiring activity, and/or a need for executive search services. Organizations in transition are generally good places to recruit because quality talent may be unhappy with the politics of the new organization. With respect to the execution of an executive search, this information can be best utilized to develop a list of target companies. Then, names and titles can be identified using another database or through traditional ID research. This technique could be used for an extremely difficult recruiting assignment. For example, finding companies in turmoil could provide a good place to search for candidates eager for a change. Selections are delivered on tape, cartridge, diskette or hard copy. For prices call Dun & Bradstreet at (800) 526-0651. For more information contact Dun & Bradstreet, Business Reference Solutions, Three Sylvan Way, Parsippany, New Jersey 07054. Email dnbmdd@mail.dnb.com. Web site http://www.dnbmdd.com.

D&B MARKETPLACE DISC is a CD ROM that provides access to names, titles, addresses, SIC or NAICS codes, sales volume, number of employees, year the business was founded, phone numbers and marketing information on more than 10 million US businesses. Searches can be conducted by location, size, industry code and by business information. Mailing labels, telemarketing data and full demographic data records can be printed and exported. Available in Windows and Macintosh. Updated quarterly. For prices call Dun & Bradstreet at (800) 526-0651. For more information contact Dun & Bradstreet, Business Reference Solutions, Three Sylvan Way, Parsippany, New Jersey 07054. Email dnbmdd@mail.dnb.com. Web site http://www.dnbmdd.com.

DIRECT MARKETING MARKET PLACE lists over 4,000 direct marketing companies, organized into numerous categories: associations, catalogs, continuity programs, credit card companies, list brokers, market researchers, computer & fulfillment services, creative sources, ad agencies, copywriters, art services and photographers. Also included are geographic indexes, direct marketing publications, telemarketers, printers and lettershops. $239.95. If the price is prohibitively high, remember your local library. National Register Publishing, Reed Elsevier-New Providence, 121 Chanlon Road, New Providence, NJ 07974, (800) 521-8110, fax (800) 836-7736, web site www.redbooks.com or www.marquiswhoswho.com. "If, for any reason whatsoever, your order does not fully meet your expectations, simply return the product within 30 days for a prompt, complete, unquestioned refund," as stated in Catalog of Biographical and Professional References of publisher Marquis Who's Who/National Register Publishing.

ENCYCLOPEDIA OF EMERGING INDUSTRIES provides information on industries that are pioneering new technologies, introducing breakthrough marketing strategies or executing new innovative ways of serving new markets. Each industry profile includes the current size and situation of the industry, a technological overview, leading companies, references to further reading and more. It covers technologies from artificial intelligence to voice recognition systems, marketing initiatives from coffee houses to super-sized movie theater complexes; and service industry ventures from AIDS testing to home health care. $270. Gale Group, P.O. Box 9187, Farmington Hills, MI 48333-9187. Toll free US and Canada (800) 877-GALE (4253) and (248) 699-GALE, fax (800) 414-5043 and (248) 699-8061, Internet orders galeord@galegroup.com, web site www.galegroup.com or www.gale.com. All Gale Group products are available on approval. Contact Gale for details.

EUROPEAN DRINKS MARKETING DIRECTORY provides information on over 1,600 drink manufacturers and over 750 retail and wholesale distributors in Western and Eastern Europe. Includes a directory of 1,500 information sources. $425. Published by Euromonitor (England). Distributed by Gale Group, P.O. Box 9187, Farmington Hills, MI 48333-9187. Toll free US and Canada (800) 877-GALE (4253) and (248) 699-GALE, fax (800) 414-5043 and (248) 699-8061, Internet orders galeord@galegroup.com, web site www.galegroup.com or www.gale.com. All Gale Group products are available on approval. Contact Gale for details.

PHARMACEUTICAL MARKETERS DIRECTORY is a well organized directory that contains many names and titles and other information, including a listing of specialized professional associations. Published annually. $162.50. CPS COMMUNICATIONS, INC., 7200 West Camino Real, Suite 215, Boca Raton, FL 33433, (561) 368-9301, sales office (203) 778-1463, email pmd@cpsnet.com, web site http://www.cpsnet.com.

PHILLIPS BUSINESS INFORMATION provides information in newsletters, magazines, directories and on multiple web sites covering a range of topics, such as magazine products, telecommunications and cable products, satellite products, media, new media and Internet products, marketing and public relations products, financial technology and electronic commerce, aviation and defense products. For more information, contact: Phillips Business Information, Inc., a Phillips Publishing International Company, 120 Seven Locks Road, Potomac, MD 20854, (301) 340-1520, (301) 340-7788, (800) 777-5006, Internet pbi@phillips.com, web site www.phillips.com.

WORLD DIRECTORY OF MARKETING INFORMATION SOURCES identifies market research companies, online databases, directories and marketing journals for every major consumer market in 75 countries. $595. Published by Euromonitor (England). Distributed by Gale Group, P.O. Box 9187, Farmington Hills, MI 48333-9187. Toll free US and Canada (800) 877-GALE (4253) and (248) 699-GALE, fax (800) 414-5043 and (248) 699-8061, Internet orders galeord@galegroup.com, web site www.galegroup.com or www.gale.com. All Gale Group products are available on approval. Contact Gale for details.

WORLD DIRECTORY OF TRADE AND BUSINESS ASSOCIATIONS profiles 3,000 trade and business associations globally, including finance, general business and industry, advertising, marketing and major consumer markets. Entries include web site addresses and publications. $595. Published by Euromonitor (England). Distributed by Gale Group, P.O. Box 9187, Farmington Hills, MI 48333-9187. Toll free US and Canada (800) 877-GALE (4253) and (248) 699-GALE, fax (800) 414-5043 and (248) 699-8061, Internet orders galeord@galegroup.com, web site www.galegroup.com or www.gale.com. All Gale Group products are available on approval. Contact Gale for details.

www.infospace.com is the URL for Classifieds/Jobs at Infospace, Inc., a site with many positions in computers, engineering and marketing, often in the $50,000 to $100,000 range. The site was developed by Infospace, Inc., Redmond, Washington and was launched in 1996.

Media

Also see Cable TV Category, Public Relations Category

ASIA IMAGE is a monthly magazine for creative professionals in broadcast, production and post-production industries in Asia. Contact publisher for price. Cahners Business Information, 58A Smith Street, Singapore 058962, (011) 65 223-8823, fax (011) 65-220-5015, email jonnypim@pacific.net.sg. Headquarters: Cahners Business Information, 275 Washington Street, Newton, MA 02158-1630, (617) 558-4663 or (617) 964-3030, fax (617) 558-4700, email marketaccess@cahners.com. Web sites www.cahners.com or www.chilton.net.

ASIAN ADVERTISING, MARKETING AND MEDIA HANDBOOK lists information about advertising agencies, newspaper and magazine publishers and market research companies. Published by Euromonitor (England), at $470 (1st edition), it had been exclusively distributed by Gale Group. At the time of this writing, Gale no longer carries it. For more information, contact Euromonitor or Gale or refer to Books in Print. This reference might also be available in the library.

BACON'S BUSINESS MEDIA DIRECTORY identifies many financial and business media contacts not found in other Bacon's directories. Media outlets include: major daily newspapers, national, regional, state and city business publications, select business journals, news and general interest magazines, news services and syndicates, freelancers by specialty, and a free midyear update. $275. Ordering information: Call (800) 621-0561, (800) 753-6675. Bacon's Information, Inc., a K-III Communications Company, 332 South Michigan Avenue, Chicago, IL 60604. Satisfaction guaranteed or a full refund within 30 days.

BACON'S CALIFORNIA MEDIA DIRECTORY presents more in-depth coverage than their main directories, including statewide print and broadcast coverage of daily and community newspapers, state bureaus of US dailies, regional business and general interest magazines, broadcast networks, stations, syndicators and programming, detailed editorial staff listings at all outlets, freelance journalists, including "editorial pitching profiles," phone, fax, email and home page. $195. Ordering information: Call (800) 621-0561, (800) 753-6675. Bacon's Information, Inc., a K-III Communications Company, 332 South Michigan Avenue, Chicago, IL 60604. Satisfaction guaranteed or a full refund within 30 days.

BACON'S COMPUTER & HI-TECH MEDIA DIRECTORY identifies 6,500 contacts at 1,900 print and broadcast outlets, serving computers, data management, software, the Internet, electronics, telecommunications and more. $225. Ordering information: Call (800) 621-0561, (800) 753-6675. Bacon's Information, Inc., a K-III Communications Company, 332 South Michigan Avenue, Chicago, IL 60604. Satisfaction guaranteed or a full refund within 30 days.

BACON'S INTERNATIONAL MEDIA DIRECTORY identifies over 28,000 Western European publications and their editors, including business, trade and consumer magazines, national newspapers by country, mailing address, phone, fax and telex, Magazine editorial profiles, and translation requirements by country. $275. Ordering information: Call (800) 621-0561, (800) 753-6675. Bacon's Information, Inc., a K-III Communications Company, 332 South Michigan Avenue, Chicago, IL 60604. Satisfaction guaranteed or a full refund within 30 days.

BACON'S MEDIASOURCE CD ROM is a media database and software with over 250,000 names of contacts at over 48,000 media outlets, including newspapers and their bureaus, magazines and newsletters, news syndicates, wire services, broadcast networks, stations and shows, including phone, fax, email and home page. Updated quarterly. Available for Windows and Macintosh. $1,095 annual subscription. Ordering information: Call (800) 621-0561, (800) 753-6675. Bacon's Information, Inc., a K-III Communications Company, 332 South Michigan Avenue, Chicago, IL 60604.

BACON'S MEDICAL & HEALTH MEDIA DIRECTORY identifies over 6,500 print and broadcast contacts in fitness, personal health, healthcare trade, specialized medicine, nutrition and other categories. $225. Ordering information: Call (800) 621-0561, (800) 753-6675. Bacon's Information, Inc., a K-III Communications Company, 332 South Michigan Avenue, Chicago, IL 60604. Satisfaction guaranteed or a full refund within 30 days.

BACON'S NEW YORK MEDIA DIRECTORY presents more in-depth coverage than their main directories, including statewide print and broadcast coverage of daily and community newspapers, state bureaus of US dailies, regional business and general interest magazines, broadcast networks, stations, syndicators and programming, detailed editorial staff listings at all outlets, freelance journalists, including "editorial pitching profiles," phone, fax, email and home page. $195. Ordering information: Call (800) 621-0561, (800) 753-6675. Bacon's Information, Inc., a K-III Communications Company, 332 South Michigan Avenue, Chicago, IL 60604. Satisfaction guaranteed or a full refund within 30 days.

BACON'S NEWSPAPER/MAGAZINE DIRECTORY is a two volume set that identifies every daily and weekly newspaper in the US, every magazine and newsletter in the US that accepts outside editorial, detailed listings of editorial staffs, with phone, fax and email, publication Internet home pages and other online locations, magazine editorial profiles and types of press materials accepted, syndicated columnists by beat, news services and news syndicates, and indexes of newspapers by market and circulation. Includes names and titles, editors' preferences, like/dislikes and "beat" reporter information to help you find the right contact. $275. Ordering information: Call (800) 621-0561, (800) 753-6675. Bacon's Information, Inc., a K-III Communications Company, 332 South Michigan Avenue, Chicago, IL 60604. Satisfaction guaranteed or a full refund within 30 days.

BACON'S RADIO/TV/CABLE DIRECTORY is a two volume set that identifies all US national and regional networks, all US broadcast stations, management and news executives, radio and TV syndicators, including programming staff, detailed show listings, over 100,000 names of contacts, an index of show subjects and more. $275. Ordering information: Call (800) 621-0561, (800) 753-6675. Bacon's Information, Inc., a K-III Communications Company, 332 South Michigan Avenue, Chicago, IL 60604. Satisfaction guaranteed or a full refund within 30 days.

BROADCASTING AND CABLE YEARBOOK contains information on radio, TV and cable including information about trade associations, trade shows, broadcasting education, awards, industry related books, magazines, videos and more. Also includes information of direct broadcast satellites, Multichannel Multipoint Distribution Services (MMDS), wireless cable companies and more. $179.95.

R.R. Bowker (a unit of Cahners Business Information), 121 Chanlon Road, New Providence, NJ 07974 USA, Phone (888) BOWKER2 (888-269-5372) & (800) 323-3288, fax (908) 508-7696, email info@bowker.com, web www.bowker.com. Canada—R.R. Bowker, Markham, Ontario, phone (888) BOWKER9 & (905) 415-5837, fax (905) 479-6266. German speaking Europe—K.G. Saur Verlag, Munich, Germany, phone 49-89-76902-232, fax 49-89-76902-250, email 100730.1341@compuserve.com, web www.saur.de/home.htm. Rest of Europe incl. United Kingdom plus Africa & Asia—Bowker-Saur, W. Sussex, UK, phone 44-1342-326-972, fax 44-1342-335-612, email customer@bowker-saur.co.uk, web www.bowker-saur.com/service/. Australia/New Zealand—Thorpe, Port Melbourne, Victoria, Australia, phone 61-03-9-245-7370, fax 61-03-9-245-7395, email customer.service@thorpe.com.au, web www.thorpe.com.au. Technical support for CD ROMs (800) 323-3288, fax 908) 665-3528, email techsupport@bowker.com.

CANADIAN ALMANAC AND DIRECTORY includes abbreviations, associations and societies, broadcasting and communications, business statistics, church and religious organizations, commerce and finance, cultural directory, education directory, electoral districts, foreign and international contacts, geographic information, government directory, government quick reference, health and hospitals, historical and general information, legal and judicial directory, postal information, tourism and transportation. The Almanac also includes web sites of significant institutions in business, communications, and the arts, a "Who's Who" of key officials and organizations on the Canadian information highway and up-to-date provincial and territorial election results. Indexed by titles and keyword. $249 US. Inquire about CD ROM availability.

Published by IHS Canada, Micromedia Limited, 20 Victoria Street, Toronto, Ontario M5C 2N8 CANADA, (800) 387-2689, (416) 362-5211, fax (416) 362-6161, email info@micromedia.on.ca. Distributed in the US by the Gale Group, P.O. Box 9187, Farmington Hills, MI 48333-9187. Toll free US and Canada (800) 877-GALE (4253) and (248) 699-GALE, fax (800) 414-5043 and (248) 699-8061, Internet orders galeord@galegroup.com, web site www.galegroup.com or www.gale.com. All Gale Group products are available on approval. Contact Gale for details.

CANADIAN SOURCEBOOK provides listings of libraries, resource centers, associations, societies, labour unions and media outlets, plus names and addresses of government officials, industry associations, financial institutions and social and cultural societies. $197. Special discounts available for combined purchases. Southam Information Products Ltd, 1450 Don Mills Road, Don Mills, Ontario M3B 2X7 CANADA, (800) 668-2374, (416) 445-6641, (416) 442-2122, web site www.southam.com.

GALE DIRECTORY OF PUBLICATIONS AND BROADCAST MEDIA identifies key personnel, feature editors and more at radio and TV stations and cable companies. $615 for 5 volume set. Gale Group, P.O. Box 9187, Farmington Hills, MI 48333-9187. Toll free US and Canada (800) 877-GALE (4253) and (248) 699-GALE, fax (800) 414-5043 and (248) 699-8061, Internet orders galeord@galegroup.com, web site www.galegroup.com or www.gale.com. All Gale Group products are available on approval. Contact Gale for details.

GALE DIRECTORY OF PUBLICATIONS AND BROADCAST MEDIA ONLINE is a GaleNet resource on the Internet that includes information on 64,000 newspapers, periodicals, newsletters, industry directories, television and radio stations, including names of key personnel. Contact the library to access this reference free. For pricing and ordering information, contact: Gale Group, P.O. Box 9187, Farmington Hills, MI 48333-9187. Toll free US and Canada (800) 877-GALE (4253) and (248) 699-GALE, fax (800) 414-5043 and (248) 699-8061, Internet orders galeord@galegroup.com, web site www.galegroup.com or www.gale.com. All Gale Group products are available on approval. Contact Gale for details.

GALE'S READY REFERENCE SHELF ONLINE is a GaleNet Internet resource that provides integrated access to databases covering national, regional, state, local and international associations, publishers, newspapers and periodicals, directories, newsletters, online databases, portable databases, database products and vendors, special libraries and research centers. Information is included from numerous Gale databases, among them THE ENCYCLOPEDIA OF ASSOCIATIONS, PUBLISHERS DIRECTORY, GALE DIRECTORY OF PUBLICATIONS AND BROADCAST MEDIA and several others. If it is prohibitively expensive, locate a library with with this resource. Gale Group, P.O. Box 9187, Farmington Hills, MI 48333-9187. Toll free US and Canada (800) 877-GALE (4253) and (248) 699-GALE, fax (800) 414-5043 and (248) 699-8061, Internet orders galeord@galegroup.com, web site www.galegroup.com or www.gale.com. All Gale Group products are available on approval. Contact Gale for details.

INFOMART DIRECT is a satellite service produced by Infomart Dialog Limited that delivers consolidated news feeds and provides full text print and broadcast sources to the end-user's office computer or LAN. Sources include Canadian daily newspapers, Canadian and international newswire services, including Southam News, Canada NewsWire, and Agence-France Presse, select television broadcast transcripts from major Canadian networks, CBC and CTV, industry trade publications, including Daily Oil Bulletin, Eco/Log Week, Canadian Underwriter, Canadian Business and Marketing Magazine. For Subscriptions and rate information, contact Infomart Dialog Limited at (416) 442-2198 or (800) 668-9215. DIALOG is a service mark of the Dialog Corporation.

INFOMART ON CD is available to CD ROM subscribers from IHS Micromedia Ltd. A full range of Canadian daily newspapers is available on both the KIOSK and VOYAGEUR platforms. KIOSK offers coverage for The Daily News (Halifax), The Gazette (Montréal), Ottawa Citizen, Toronto Star, Toronto Sun, The Spectator (Hamilton), Calgary Herald, Edmonton Journal, The Province (Vancouver), Vancouver Sun, The Financial Post and broadcast news transcripts. On the VOYAGEUR platform, Canadian NewsDisc is available as a complete package, either quarterly or monthly. For Subscriptions and rate information, contact Infomart Dialog Limited at (416) 442-2198 or (800) 668-9215. DIALOG is a service mark of the Dialog Corporation.

LATIN AMERICAN ADVERTISING, MARKETING & MEDIA SOURCEBOOK, published by Euromonitor (England), at $470 (1st edition), had been exclusively distributed in the USA, Canada and

Australia by Gale Group. At the time of this writing, Gale no longer carries it. For more information, contact Euromonitor or Gale or refer to Books in Print or International Books in Print. This reference might also be available in the library.

MEDICAL MARKETING & MEDIA (MM&M) is a trade publication available in hard copy or online. "People on the Move" provides career announcements and sometimes photos. Career & Salary Surveys are also available. www.cpsnet.com. For more information contact CPS COMMUNICATIONS, INC., 7200 West Camino Real, Suite 215, Boca Raton, FL 33433, (561) 368-9301, sales office (203) 778-1463, email webmaster@cpsnet.com, web site http://www.cpsnet.com.

PHILLIPS BUSINESS INFORMATION provides information in newsletters, magazines, directories and on multiple web sites covering a range of topics, such as magazine products, telecommunications and cable products, satellite products, media, new media and Internet products, marketing and public relations products, financial technology and electronic commerce, aviation and defense products. For more information, contact: Phillips Business Information, Inc., a Phillips Publishing International Company, 120 Seven Locks Road, Potomac, MD 20854, (301) 340-1520, (301) 340-7788, (800) 777-5006, Internet pbi@phillips.com, web site www.phillips.com.

RADIO COMMUNICATION REPORT is a weekly trade publication. Crain Communications, Inc. is headquartered in Chicago with offices in major cities throughout the US plus London, Tokyo and Frankfurt. New York location: 220 East 42nd Street, New York, NY 10017, (212) 210-0100, Circulation (800) 678-9595. Annual subscription $49, two years $69. Web site www.rcrnews.com.

STANDARD RATE AND DATA PUBLICATIONS includes "Radio Advertising Source" and "Television and Cable Source" and direct marketing information. $354 annual subscription. Standard Rate and Data Service, Inc., 3004 Glenview Road, Wilmette, IL 60091, (708) 441-2210 in Illinois, (800) 323-4601.

TALK SHOW SELECTS identifies the top 750 local and national TV and radio talk shows. Hard copy $185. Floppy disk and book, $260. Published by Broadcast Interview Source, 2233 Wisconsin Avenue, NW, Suite 540, Washington, DC 20007. (800) 955-0311, (202) 333-4904.

WHO'S WHO IN THE MEDIA AND COMMUNICATIONS, $259.95. National Register Publishing, Reed Elsevier-New Providence, 121 Chanlon Road, New Providence, NJ 07974, (800) 521-8110, fax (800) 836-7736, web site www.marquiswhoswho.com or www.redbooks.com. "If, for any reason whatsoever, your order does not fully meet your expectations, simply return the product within 30 days for a prompt, complete, unquestioned refund," as stated in Catalog of Biographical and Professional References of publisher Marquis Who's Who/National Register Publishing.

WILLINGS PRESS GUIDE identifies UK and international print media, including national and regional newspapers, magazines, and periodicals. It specifies 30,000 titles, contact names, summary of contents, and more. Volume 1, United Kingdom. Volume 2, International. $350 for 2 volume set or $275 per individual volume. Published by Hollis Directories Ltd. Distributed by Gale Group, P.O. Box 9187, Farmington Hills, MI 48333-9187. Toll free US and Canada (800) 877-GALE (4253) and (248) 699-GALE, fax (800) 414-5043 and (248) 699-8061, Internet orders galeord@galegroup.com, web site www.galegroup.com or www.gale.com. All Gale Group products are available on approval. Contact Gale for details.

WORKING PRESS OF THE NATION identifies 180,000 decision makers in newspapers, magazines, newsletters, "hard to find corporate, government and association publications," TV and radio stations and cable networks. Volume 1—Newspapers, Volume 2—Magazines & Internal Publications, Volume 3—TV & Radio. $249 per volume or $439.95 for 3 volume set.

R.R. Bowker (a unit of Cahners Business Information), 121 Chanlon Road, New Providence, NJ 07974 USA, Phone (888) BOWKER2 (888-269-5372) & (800) 323-3288, fax (908) 508-7696, email info@bowker.com, web www.bowker.com. Canada—R.R. Bowker, Markham, Ontario, phone (888) BOWKER9 & (905) 415-5837, fax (905) 479-6266. German speaking Europe—K.G. Saur Verlag, Munich, Germany, phone 49-89-76902-232, fax 49-89-76902-250, email 100730.1341@compuserve.com, web www.saur.de/home.htm. Rest of Europe incl. United Kingdom plus Africa & Asia—Bowker-Saur, W. Sussex, UK, phone 44-1342-326-972, fax 44-1342-335-612, email customer@bowker-saur.co.uk, web www.bowker-saur.com/service/. Australia/New Zealand—Thorpe, Port Melbourne, Victoria, Australia, phone 61-03-9-245-7370, fax 61-03-9-

245-7395, email customer.service@thorpe.com.au, web www.thorpe.com.au. Technical support for CD ROMs (800) 323-3288, fax 908) 665-3528, email techsupport@bowker.com.

www.emheadlines.com is the headline news service for the entertainment business. This Cahners Business Information web site provides information on Film, Television, Books, Technology, Music, Nielsen Ratings, Domestic Box Office, Bestseller List.

YEARBOOK OF EXPERTS, AUTHORITIES & SPOKESPERSONS. $49.95. Free to Journalists. Call for information. Published by Broadcast Interview Source, 2233 Wisconsin Avenue, NW, Suite 540, Washington, DC 20007. (800) 955-0311, (202) 333-4904.

Medical

ABMS MEDICAL SPECIALISTS PLUS CD ROM (American Board of Medical Specialists) is an electronic edition of THE OFFICIAL ABMS DIRECTORY OF BOARD CERTIFIED MEDICAL SPECIALISTS, which is based on the database of the American Board of Medical Specialties (ABMS). Updated annually, it identifies over 500,000 specialists in 37 specialties and 75 sub-specialties. It includes career information, including name, certification and sub-certification, date of birth and place, medical school, year of degree, internship, residency, fellowship, hospital staff appointments, current academic appointment and title, professional associations, type of practice, and addresses and phone numbers, plus address and contact information from US and Canadian medical schools. $1,195 for CD ROM. $499.95 in hard copy. National Register Publishing, Reed Elsevier-New Providence, 121 Chanlon Road, New Providence, NJ 07974, (800) 521-8110, fax (800) 836-7736, web site www.marquiswhoswho.com or www.redbooks.com. "If, for any reason whatsoever, your order does not fully meet your expectations, simply return the product within 30 days for a prompt, complete, unquestioned refund," as stated in Catalog of Biographical and Professional References of publisher Marquis Who's Who/National Register Publishing.

BALTIMORE/ANNAPOLIS is a guide to over 2,000 organizations and institutions. Chapters include government, business, education, medicine/health, arts and culture, community affairs and more. $65. Columbia Books, Inc., 1212 New York Avenue, NW, Suite 330, Washington, DC 20005, (212) 898-0662.

BACON'S MEDICAL & HEALTH MEDIA DIRECTORY identifies over 6,500 print and broadcast contacts in fitness, personal health, healthcare trade, specialized medicine, nutrition and other categories. $225. Ordering information: Call (800) 621-0561, (800) 753-6675. Bacon's Information, Inc., a K-III Communications Company, 332 South Michigan Avenue, Chicago, IL 60604. Satisfaction guaranteed or a full refund within 30 days.

MEDICAL LIBRARY ASSOCIATION, 6 North Michigan Avenue, Suite 300, Chicago, IL 60602, (312) 419-9094.

SciTECH REFERENCE PLUS CD ROM contains directory information, 125,000 biographies of US and Canadian scientists and engineers from AMERICAN MEN AND WOMEN OF SCIENCE, listings for over 8,000 laboratories from the DIRECTORY OF AMERICAN RESEARCH AND TECHNOLOGY, and information from THE DIRECTORY OF CORPORATE AFFILIATIONS (including public, private and international companies) of leading US and international technology firms and their subsidiaries. It also contains 60,000 records on science/technology and medical serials from ULRICH'S INTERNATIONAL PERIODICALS DIRECTORY. Searches can be conducted by SIC, year founded, activity, education, employees, institution/company, city, state or country, memberships/honors, product description, personal statistics, personal title, research area, revenue. Updated annually. 1 year subscription $995, 3 years 2,836, excluding discounts. For more information visit Bowker Reed Reference's web site at http://www.reedref.com or contact: Bowker Reed Reference Electronic Publishing, 121 Chanlon Road, New Providence, NJ 07974 USA, Phone (800) 323-3288, Fax (908) 665-3528, email info@bowker.com.

WASHINGTON identifies 4,500 organizations and institutions in Washington DC and 22,000 key people in them. Includes government, business, education, medicine/health, community affairs, art/culture and others. $85. Columbia Books, Inc., 1212 New York Avenue, NW, Suite 330, Washington, DC 20005, (212) 898-0662.

Medical Devices

PHARMACEUTICAL MARKETERS DIRECTORY is a well organized directory that contains many names and titles and other information, including a listing of specialized professional associations. Published annually. $162.50. CPS COMMUNICATIONS, INC., 7200 West Camino Real, Suite 215, Boca Raton, FL 33433, (561) 368-9301, sales office (203) 778-1463, email pmd@cpsnet.com, web site http://www.cpsnet.com.

Membership Directories and Lists

See Associations Category, Directories

MEMBERSHIP DIRECTORIES FOR PROFESSIONAL ASSOCIATIONS are frequently published, either in hard copy or on an Internet web site. If a membership directory is not accessible on the web site, you might want to purchase a hard copy from the association. However, some associations refuse to sell their membership rosters to non-members. Some even preclude recruiters from becoming members. As a last resort, if an association membership directory is not online, you might need to borrow a copy from a member. Of course, that can be a bit of a "Catch 22," because how can you find a member if you don't have the membership list? Just keep asking everybody you talk to.

If you're having trouble locating an association's web site address (URL), you can always look them up in a directory. If the web site address isn't in the directory, sometimes it's easier to make a phone call and ask for the web site. You can also go to www.web sitez.com to get an organization's URLs.

One way to identify membership directories is to look up associations in a directory, such as Lorna Daniell's BUSINESS INFORMATION SOURCES (University of California Press, Berkeley, Los Angeles and Oxford England/Princeton Fulfillment Services, Newark, NJ), ENCYCLOPEDIA OF ASSOCIATIONS (Gale Group, Farmington Hills, MI) or NATIONAL TRADE AND PROFESSIONAL ASSOCIATIONS (Columbia Books, Washington, DC).

You can call the association and ask them to send information about becoming a member. If you don't want them to know the name of your company, ask them to send the information to your home address. While you're chatting, and before you give your name, make a casual inquiry about whether their membership roster is available for sale to non-members. If it's not, find out their requirements for joining, specifically whether recruiters are precluded.

Merger Summaries

AMERICAN FINANCIAL DIRECTORY consists of five desktop volumes of banks, bank holding companies, savings and Loan Associations and Major Credit Unions in the US, Canada and Mexico. It includes information on head office and branch offices, names of key decision makers, phone and fax numbers, financial summaries, and structural changes such as mergers, name changes and closings. Published twice a year. For more information contact (800) 321-3373, Thomson Financial Publishing, 4709 West Golf Road, Skokie, IL 60076-1253. Web site @ tfp.bankinfo.com.

CORPORATE FINANCE SOURCEBOOK—THE GUIDE TO MAJOR INVESTMENT SOURCES AND RELATED FINANCIAL SERVICES contains over 13,000 names of executives at 3,700 organizations that, broadly speaking, supply growth capital to businesses, such as venture capital lenders, private lenders, commercial finance and factoring, pension managers, master trusts. Names of key management are included. A special section details public offerings of the past 3 years and mergers and acquisitions over $100 million. $499.95 hard copy, excluding discounts. NRP's catalog states, "If you're dissatisfied for any reason, simply return the product within 30 days for a full refund." If the price is prohibitively high, remember your local library. Available in book, online, magnetic tape, and in mailing list formats. For more information contact: National Register Publishing, 121 Chanlon Road, New Providence, NJ 07974 USA, (800) 521-8110, http://www.lexis-nexis.com. For information about online access, call LEXIS®—NEXIS® Online Services, Mountainview, CA at (800) 346-9759; for mailing lists call Cahners Direct Marketing Services at (800) 323-4958; all other inquiries (800) 521-8110.

LITERARY MARKET PLACE, "The Directory of the American Book Publishing Industry With Industry Yellow Pages" is an excellent 3 volume directory with comprehensive information on US book publishers;

imprints, subsidiaries and distributors; book trade acquisitions and mergers, small presses, Canadian book publishers, micropublishers, US electronic publishers, electronic publishing consultants, electronic publishing products and services, editorial services, literary agents, illustrations agents, US agents and offices of foreign publishers, lecture agents, specialized advertising and public relations firms, direct mail specialists, mailing list brokers and services, book review syndicates, book review and index journals and services, book exhibits, book clubs, book lists and catalogs, book importers and exporters, book producers, translators, artists, photographers, stock photo agencies, associations, book trade events and conferences, awards, contents and grants, reference books for the trade, magazines for the trade, a toll free directory of publishers, magazine and newspaper publicity, radio and television publicity, book manufacturing services, book distributors and sales representatives, and wholesalers. $189.95.

LITERARY MARKET PLACE ON DISC, previously titled LITERARY MARKET PLACE PLUS CD ROM, one year subscription $297.00.

LITERARY MARKET PLACE—INTERNET EDITION, www.literarymarketplace.com, is available by subscription.

INTERNATIONAL LITERARY MARKET PLACE Internet database can be directly accessed at www.iliterarymarketplace.com. It is also linked to the US domestic LITERARY MARKET PLACE web site at www.literarymarketplace.com. Contact the publisher for subscription price. INTERNATIONAL LITERARY MARKET PLACE, hard copy $189.95.

R.R. Bowker (a unit of Cahners Business Information), 121 Chanlon Road, New Providence, NJ 07974 USA, Phone (888) BOWKER2 (888-269-5372) & (800) 323-3288, fax (908) 508-7696, email info@bowker.com, web www.bowker.com. Canada—R.R. Bowker, Markham, Ontario, phone (888) BOWKER9 & (905) 415-5837, fax (905) 479-6266. German speaking Europe—K.G. Saur Verlag, Munich, Germany, phone 49-89-76902-232, fax 49-89-76902-250, email 100730.1341@compuserve.com, web www.saur.de/home.htm. Rest of Europe incl. United Kingdom plus Africa & Asia—Bowker-Saur, W. Sussex, UK, phone 44-1342-326-972, fax 44-1342-335-612, email customer@bowker-saur.co.uk, web www.bowker-saur.com/service/. Australia/New Zealand—Thorpe, Port Melbourne, Victoria, Australia, phone 61-03-9-245-7370, fax 61-03-9-245-7395, email customer.service@thorpe.com.au, web www.thorpe.com.au. Technical support for CD ROMs (800) 323-3288, fax 908) 665-3528, email techsupport@bowker.com.

NORTHERN MINER is a weekly newspaper that covers the worldwide activities of all North American Based mining companies. It includes information on company profiles, mergers, career opportunities, a professional directory, a diamond drillers directory, industry news and much more. Annual subscription in Canada $87, US $87, foreign $130 (surface mail or $288 (airmail). Online subscription rates for newspaper subscribers: $60 Canadian, $42 US, $60 Canadian collars for foreign. Online subscription rates for newspaper non-subscribers: $144 Canadian, $108 US, $144 Canadian dollars for foreign. Northern Miner Home Page www.northernminer.com. Special discounts available for combined purchases. For more information on Energy Information Services, call Calgary office (403) 244-6111. Published by Southam Information Products Ltd, 1450 Don Mills Road, Don Mills, Ontario M3B 2X7 CANADA, (800) 668-2374. In Toronto 442-2122. Web site www.southam.com.

POLK NORTH AMERICAN FINANCIAL INSTITUTIONS DIRECTORY includes information on banks, savings and loan associations and major credit unions in North America, including head office and branch offices,names of key decision makers, address, phone and fax, financial summaries, maps, and structural changes such as mergers, name changes, and closings. Published twice a year. For more information contact (800) 321-3373, Thomson Financial Publishing, 4709 West Golf Road, Skokie, IL 60076-1253. Web site @ tfp.bankinfo.com.

POLK WORLD BANK DIRECTORY includes information on worldwide banks, including the top 1,000 banks in the US. Listings include names of key decision makers, address, phone and fax, financial summaries, branch information, maps, and structural changes such as mergers, name changes, and closings, and discontinued banks with explanations. Published annually. For more information contact (800) 321-3373, Thomson Financial Publishing, 4709 West Golf Road, Skokie, IL 60076-1253. Web site @ tfp.bankinfo.com.

THOMSON BANK DIRECTORY is a five volume set of commercial banking directories, worldwide. Listings include head office and branch offices, address, phone, phone and fax, names of key decision makers, the past 2 years of structural changes (such as mergers, name changes and closings), central banks and trade associations. Published twice a year. For more information contact (800) 321-3373, Thomson Financial Publishing, 4709 West Golf Road, Skokie, IL 60076-1253. Web site @ tfp.bankinfo.com.

THOMSON CREDIT UNION DIRECTORY identifies credit unions in the US. Listings include names of key decision makers. addresses. phone and fax numbers, branch offices, number of employees.head office and branch offices,names of key decision makers, address, phone and fax, financial summaries, maps, and structural changes such as mergers, name changes, and closings. Published twice a year. For more information contact (800) 321-3373, Thomson Financial Publishing, 4709 West Golf Road, Skokie, IL 60076-1253. Web site @ tfp.bankinfo.com.

Mergers and Acquisitions

CASES IN CORPORATE ACQUISITIONS, BUYOUTS, MERGERS AND TAKEOVERS includes 300 case studies where at least one participant is a US based company. Each listing contains brief background information, a summary of the major players, and a review of the outcome. $295. Gale Group, P.O. Box 9187, Farmington Hills, MI 48333-9187. Toll free US and Canada (800) 877-GALE (4253) and (248) 699-GALE, fax (800) 414-5043 and (248) 699-8061, Internet orders galeord@galegroup.com, web site www.galegroup.com or www.gale.com. All Gale Group products are available on approval. Contact Gale for details.

CORPORATE FINANCE SOURCEBOOK—THE GUIDE TO MAJOR INVESTMENT SOURCES AND RELATED FINANCIAL SERVICES contains over 13,000 names of executives at 3,700 organizations that, broadly speaking, supply growth capital to businesses, such as venture capital lenders, private lenders, commercial finance and factoring, pension managers, master trusts. Names of key management are included. A special section details public offerings of the past 3 years and mergers and acquisitions over $100 million. $499.95 hard copy, excluding discounts. NRP's catalog states, "If you're dissatisfied for any reason, simply return the product within 30 days for a full refund." If the price is prohibitively high, remember your local library. Available in book, online, magnetic tape, and in mailing list formats. For more information contact: National Register Publishing, 121 Chanlon Road, New Providence, NJ 07974 USA, (800) 521-8110, http://www.lexis-nexis.com. For information about online access, call LEXIS®—NEXIS® Online Services, Mountainview, CA at (800) 346-9759; for mailing lists call Cahners Direct Marketing Services at (800) 323-4958; all other inquiries (800) 521-8110.

GUIDE TO GLOBAL M&A. For more information contact Larry Meranus Professional Publications & Services, 4 Demoray Court, Pine Brook, NJ 07058, (800) MERANUS or (800) 637-2687. Distributed in England by EUROMONEY Books, Plymbridge Distributors Limited, Estover, Plymouth PL6 7PZ, England. Phone 44 (0) 171 779-8955. Fax 44 (0) 171 779-8541.

Metalworking

D&B INDUSTRIAL GUIDE—THE METAL WORKING DIRECTORY contains information about 75,000 original equipment manufacturers, metalworking plants, metal distributors, machine tools/metalworking machinery distributors for locations with at least 20 people. Listings include plant name, key executives' names and titles, principal manufacturing processes, plant square footage, number of employees and more. Volumes 1 & 2 list plants geographically by state and city. Volume 3 lists companies alphabetically and by industry classification. Updated annually. For prices call Dun & Bradstreet at (800) 526-0651. For more information contact Dun & Bradstreet, Business Reference Solutions, Three Sylvan Way, Parsippany, New Jersey 07054. Email dnbmdd@mail.dnb.com. Web site http://www.dnbmdd.com.

Mexico

See Latin America, International

AMERICAN FINANCIAL DIRECTORY consists of five desktop volumes of banks, bank holding companies, savings and Loan Associations and Major Credit Unions in the US, Canada and Mexico. It includes information on head office and branch offices, names of key decision makers, phone and fax numbers, financial summaries, and structural changes such as mergers, name changes and closings. Published twice a year. For more information contact (800) 321-3373, Thomson Financial Publishing, 4709 West Golf Road, Skokie, IL 60076-1253. Web site @ tfp.bankinfo.com.

AMERICAN LIBRARY DIRECTORY is available in hard copy and electronic database formats. It identifies 36,000 general and specialized libraries in the US, Canada and Mexico. Searches can be conducted by 40 general information search criteria, further refined with 50 more fields related to the specific collections and services. **AMERICAN LIBRARY DIRECTORY ON DISC,** one year subscription $423. **AMERICAN LIBRARY DIRECTORY ONLINE** can be accessed by contacting Bowker or Knight-Ridder Information, Inc., Mountainview, California, (800) 334-2564 or (800) 3-DIALOG. Refer to DIALOG file number 460.

LIBRARY RESOURCE GUIDE—INTERNET EDITION is a free Internet directory of library services and suppliers which is drawn from Bowker's American Library Directory. Log on at www.bowker.com or call for more information.

R.R. Bowker (a unit of Cahners Business Information), 121 Chanlon Road, New Providence, NJ 07974 USA, Phone (888) BOWKER2 (888-269-5372) & (800) 323-3288, fax (908) 508-7696, email info@bowker.com, web www.bowker.com. Canada—R.R. Bowker, Markham, Ontario, phone (888) BOWKER9 & (905) 415-5837, fax (905) 479-6266. German speaking Europe—K.G. Saur Verlag, Munich, Germany, phone 49-89-76902-232, fax 49-89-76902-250, email 100730.1341@compuserve.com, web www.saur.de/home.htm. Rest of Europe incl. United Kingdom plus Africa & Asia—Bowker-Saur, W. Sussex, UK, phone 44-1342-326-972, fax 44-1342-335-612, email customer@bowker-saur.co.uk, web www.bowker-saur.com/service/. Australia/New Zealand—Thorpe, Port Melbourne, Victoria, Australia, phone 61-03-9-245-7370, fax 61-03-9-245-7395, email customer.service@thorpe.com.au, web www.thorpe.com.au. Technical support for CD ROMs (800) 323-3288, fax 908) 665-3528, email techsupport@bowker.com.

COMPANIES INTERNATIONAL CD-ROM contains comprehensive financial and contact data for over 300,000 public and privately held companies in 180 countries including the Commonwealth of Independent States, Mexico, Canada and Japan. Companies can be located by company name, product or industry, location, or a combination. This reference can also be used for target lists development for international companies, including privately held companies. $2,995. Gale Group, P.O. Box 9187, Farmington Hills, MI 48333-9187. Toll free US and Canada (800) 877-GALE (4253) and (248) 699-GALE, fax (800) 414-5043 and (248) 699-8061, Internet orders galeord@galegroup.com, web site www.galegroup.com or www.gale.com. All Gale Group products are available on approval. Contact Gale for details.

COMPLETE TWIN PLANT GUIDE is a three volume directory of plants in the $15 billion Mexico Maquila market. Volume 1 covers Baja California, Volume 2 covers the Central Corridor and Volume 3 covers Mexico City, Rio Grande, Gulf, and Lower Pacific regions. This directory includes over 8,000 executive names at some 2,300 plants, plus address, phone numbers, number of employees, SIC or NAICS codes and more. Diskette's available. $170 per volume, $350 for set. CD ROM $650 complete, $220 per single volume on disk. Published annually by Solunet. Distributed by Manufacturers' News, Inc., (888) 752-5200, 1633 Central Street, Evanston, IL 60201-1569. Email info@manufacturersnews.com. Web site www.manufacturersnews.com.

DIRECTORY OF AMERICAN FIRMS OPERATING IN FOREIGN COUNTRIES, REGIONAL EDITION—MEXICO. $49. Ordering information: Uniworld Business Publications, Inc., 257 Central Park West, Suite 10A, New York, NY 10024-4110, (212) 496-2448, fax (212) 769-0413, email uniworldbp@aol.com. Web site: http://www.uniworldbp.com.

DIRECTORY OF FOREIGN FIRMS OPERATING IN THE UNITED STATES, REGIONAL EDITION—NORTH AMERICA. Includes Canada and Mexico. $39. Uniworld Business Publications, Inc., 257 Central Park West, Suite 10A, New York, NY 10024-4110, (212) 496-2448, fax (212) 769-0413, email uniworldbp@aol.com. Web site: http://www.uniworldbp.com.

DIRECTORY OF FOREIGN FIRMS OPERATING IN THE UNITED STATES, REGIONAL EDITION—SOUTH/CENTRAL AMERICA & THE CARIBBEAN. Includes Argentina, Bermuda, Bolivia, Brazil, Chile, Colombia, Costa Rica, Dominican Republic, Guatemala, Mexico, Panama, Paraguay, Peru, Uruguay, Venezuela. $39. Uniworld Business Publications, Inc., 257 Central Park West, Suite 10A, New York, NY 10024-4110, (212) 496-2448, fax (212) 769-0413, email uniworldbp@aol.com. Web site: http://www.uniworldbp.com.

MAQUILADORAS (TWIN PLANT) GUIDE is a 3 volume directory that covers the $14 billion maquiladora market in Mexico. Volume 1—850 plants in Baja. Volume 2—900 plants in Central Corridor. Volume 3—850 plants in the Rio Grande, Gulf and lower Pacific region. Single volume $140, full set $385, database $720. Database Publishing Company, PO Box 70024, Anaheim, CA 92825, (800) 888-8434, (714) 778-6400, email sales@databasepublishing.com.

MEXICO BUSINESS COMMUNICATIONS AND FAX DIRECTORY or CD lists over 11,000 businesses, over 5,000 associations and chambers of commerce, plus a listing of Mexican government departments and Canadian and US embassies and consulates in Mexico. Section 1 lists government offices. Section 2 lists businesses alphabetically by company. Section 3 lists companies by business category. A listing of city codes, maps, historical information and a list of the top 100 companies in Mexico is also included. Published annually. Directory $179.95, CD $229.95. Ordering information: Scott's Directories, Toronto area: 1450 Don Mills Road, Don Mills, Ontario, M3B 2X7, CANADA, (888) 709-9907, (416) 442-2291, (416) 932-9555. Montréal area: Scott's Directories, 3300 Cote Verde, Suite 410 Ville St.-Laurent, Quebec H4B 2B7 CANADA (514) 339-1397, (800) 363-1327, email scotts@southam.ca.

MEXICO CD ROM provides information on over 185,000 companies in Mexico. Dun & Bradstreet, Business Reference Solutions, Three Sylvan Way, Parsippany, NJ 07054 USA. (800) 526-0651. Email dnbmdd@mail.dnb.com. Web site http://www.dnbmdd.com.

MEXICO TWIN PLANT GUIDE is a 3 volume set available as a directory or an electronic database. Directory $385, database $720. Distributed by Harris InfoSource, 2057 East Aurora Road, Twinsburg, OH 44087-1999, (330) 425-9000, (800) 888-5900, www.HarrisInfo.com.

TRADE DIRECTORY OF MEXICO contains information on over 4,500 Mexican manufacturers, agricultural producers and trading companies. Listings include company, address, phone, fax and telex numbers, number of employees, names and titles of key contacts, products and more. $100. Database Publishing Company, PO Box 70024, Anaheim, CA 92825, (800) 888-8434, (714) 778-6400, email sales@databasepublishing.com.

www.kompass.com is the web site for the highly respected Kompass country directories and databases. This web site contains a searchable database that encompasses over 60 countries, 2.5 million executive names, information on 1.5 million companies, 19 million key product references, and 370,000 trade and brand names. At the time of this writing, Kompass is available in English and French. Deutsch, Espanol and Italiano will soon be available.

Middle East

Also see Arab, International, Israel

DIRECTORY OF AMERICAN FIRMS OPERATING IN FOREIGN COUNTRIES, REGIONAL EDITION—NEAR AND MIDDLE EAST. Includes Bahrain, Cyprus, Israel, Jordan, Kuwait, Lebanon, Oman, Qatar, Saudi Arabia, Syria, Turkey, United Arab Emirates, West Bank, Yemen. $49. Uniworld Business Publications, Inc., 257 Central Park West, Suite 10A, New York, NY 10024-4110, (212) 496-2448, fax (212) 769-0413, email uniworldbp@aol.com. Web site: http://www.uniworldbp.com.

DIRECTORY OF AMERICAN FIRMS OPERATING IN FOREIGN COUNTRIES, REGIONAL EDITION—NEAR & MIDDLE EAST & ARABIC COUNTRIES COMBINED, $59. Ordering information: Uniworld Business Publications, Inc., 257 Central Park West, Suite 10A, New York, NY 10024-4110, (212) 496-2448, fax (212) 769-0413, email uniworldbp@aol.com. Web site: http://www.uniworldbp.com.

DIRECTORY OF FOREIGN FIRMS OPERATING IN THE UNITED STATES, REGIONAL EDITION—NEAR & MIDDLE EAST. $39. Uniworld Business Publications, Inc., 257 Central Park West, Suite 10A, New York, NY 10024-4110, (212) 496-2448, fax (212) 769-0413, email uniworldbp@aol.com. Web site: http://www.uniworldbp.com.

MAJOR COMPANIES OF SOUTH WEST ASIA provides names of 39,000 contacts at 6,000 companies, description of business activities, brand names and trademarks, branches and subsidiaries, number of employees, date of establishment, and three indexes. Countries included are Bangladesh, Bhutan, Iran, Nepal, Pakistan, Sri Lanka and Turkey. $530. CD ROM available. US distributor: Larry Meranus Professional Publications & Services, 4 Demoray Court, Pine Brook, NJ 07058, (800) MERANUS or (800) 637-2687. Also distributed by Gale Group, P.O. Box 9187, Farmington Hills, MI 48333-9187. Toll free US and Canada (800) 877-GALE (4253) and (248) 699-GALE, fax (800) 414-5043 and (248) 699-8061, Internet orders galeord@galegroup.com, web site www.galegroup.com or www.gale.com. All Gale Group products are available on approval. Contact Gale for details. Published by Graham & Whiteside Ltd., Tuition House, 5-6 Francis Grove, London SW19 4DT, England. Web site http://www.major-co-data.com. Email sales@major-co-data.com.

WHO'S WHO IN LEBANON contains 2,000 biographies plus essays on economics and demographics. Published by Publitec Publications, Beirut. Distributed exclusively to libraries in the US and Canada by Gale. $168. Gale Group, P.O. Box 9187, Farmington Hills, MI 48333-9187. Toll free US and Canada (800) 877-GALE (4253) and (248) 699-GALE, fax (800) 414-5043 and (248) 699-8061, Internet orders galeord@galegroup.com, web site www.galegroup.com or www.gale.com. All Gale Group products are available on approval. Contact Gale for details.

Military

ENCYCLOPEDIA OF ASSOCIATIONS: INTERNATIONAL ORGANIZATIONS includes nearly 20,000 multinational and national organizations in foreign countries, including US based associations with multinational membership. Entries also include email addresses, web sites and bulletin board addresses, lobbying activities, and publication and convention information. Indexed by geography, keyword and executives. $595 for 2 volume set. Also available in CD ROM. Database available via commercial online service. Gale Group, P.O. Box 9187, Farmington Hills, MI 48333-9187. Toll free US and Canada (800) 877-GALE (4253) and (248) 699-GALE, fax (800) 414-5043 and (248) 699-8061, Internet orders galeord@galegroup.com, web site www.galegroup.com or www.gale.com. All Gale Group products are available on approval. Contact Gale for details.

ENCYCLOPEDIA OF ASSOCIATIONS: NATIONAL ORGANIZATIONS OF THE US. This superb reference is one of the first places you should look when beginning a new recruiting assignment or when looking for specialized references of any type. The keyword index makes this comprehensive reference easy to use, even in hard copy. For over 23,000 nonprofit professional associations with a national scope, this encyclopedia reveals:

* Publications, including membership rosters and newsletters

* Dates and locations of association conferences and conventions

* Names of Executive Directors, who are usually incredible sources of industry information if you call and speak to them

* Committees

* Job and candidate referral banks, which can provide resumes of other industry sources and sometimes candidates

* It includes organizations in these categories: business, trade, environmental, agricultural, legal, govern mental, engineering, technological, scientific, educational, cultural, social welfare, health & medical, public affairs, ethnic, labor unions, chambers of commerce, tourism, & others.

    Volume 1, National Organizations of the US, $505
    Volume 2, Geographic and Executive Indexes, $390
    Volume 3, Supplement, $405

Gale Group, P.O. Box 9187, Farmington Hills, MI 48333-9187. Toll free US and Canada (800) 877-GALE (4253) and (248) 699-GALE, fax (800) 414-5043 and (248) 699-8061, Internet orders galeord@galegroup.com, web site www.galegroup.com or www.gale.com. All Gale Group products are available on approval. Contact Gale for details.

ENCYCLOPEDIA OF ASSOCIATIONS: REGIONAL, STATE AND LOCAL ORGANIZATIONS. The information in this directory is not duplicated anywhere in ENCYCLOPEDIA OF ASSOCIATIONS. Over 100,000 nonprofit organizations are included in this directory. $585 for 5 volume set or $140 per individual volume. Also available on CD ROM and online on the Internet through a GaleNet subscription.

> Volume 1, Great Lakes States (Illinois, Indiana, Michigan, Minnesota, Ohio, Wisconsin)
> Volume 2, Northeastern States (Connecticut, Maine, Massachusetts, New Hampshire, New Jersey, New York, Pennsylvania, Rhode Islands, Vermont)
> Volume 3, Southern and Middle Atlantic States (Including Puerto Rico and the Virgin Islands) (Alabama, Delaware, Washington, DC, Florida, Georgia, Kentucky, Maryland, Mississippi, North Carolina, Puerto Rico, South Carolina, Tennessee, Virginia, West Virginia, Virgin Islands)
> Volume 4, South Central and Great Plains States (Arkansas, Iowa, Kansas, Louisiana, Missouri, Nebraska, North Dakota, Oklahoma, South Dakota, Texas)
> Volume 5, Western States (Alaska, Arizona, California, Colorado, Guam, Hawaii, Idaho, Montana, Nevada, New Mexico, Oregon, Utah, Washington, Wyoming)

Gale Group, P.O. Box 9187, Farmington Hills, MI 48333-9187. Toll free US and Canada (800) 877-GALE (4253) and (248) 699-GALE, fax (800) 414-5043 and (248) 699-8061, Internet orders galeord@galegroup.com, web site www.galegroup.com or www.gale.com. All Gale Group products are available on approval. Contact Gale for details.

RESERVE OFFICERS ASSOCIATION (ROA) is the professional association that represents all officers of the seven uniformed services. Its membership is comprised of active, retired and former reserve, guard and regular commissioned officers and warrant officers. The ROA provides its members with a service that refers resumes of retired career officers to search firms and employers. This is an excellent resource for companies whose corporate culture is a good fit with the military. For more information contact Mr. Kelly Matthews, ROA, One Constitution Avenue NE, Washington DC 20002-5655, (800) 809-9448, (202) 479-2200, web site www.roa.org, email kmatthews@roa.org.

Mining

AMERICAN MINES HANDBOOK provides information on over 1,000 precious and base metal mining companies working in the US. Includes key contact names plus mining area maps for Alaska, Arizona, California, Colorado, Idaho, Minnesota, Montana, Nevada, South Carolina, Utah. Also includes a Directory of Key Industry Contacts for Government and Support Organizations $52. Special discounts available for combined purchases. For more information on Energy Information Services, call Calgary office (403) 244-6111. Published by Southam Information Products Ltd, 1450 Don Mills Road, Don Mills, Ontario M3B 2X7 CANADA, (800) 668-2374. In Toronto 442-2122. Web site www.southam.com.

CANADIAN MINES HANDBOOK contains information on over 2,300 Canadian mining companies, mines and advanced projects, including key contact names, mine and site addresses, and 60 pages of mining area maps. $62. Special discounts available for combined purchases. For more information on Energy Information Services, call Calgary office (403) 244-6111. Published by Southam Information Products Ltd, 1450 Don Mills Road, Don Mills, Ontario M3B 2X7 CANADA, (800) 668-2374. In Toronto 442-2122. Web site www.southam.com.

CANADIAN MINESCAN is a diskette version of the CANADIAN MINES HANDBOOK. Information is available on over 2,500 Canadian mining companies, mines, advanced projects, smelters, refineries and the DIRECTORY OF KEY INDUSTRY CONTACTS. Free demo disk available. $156. Special discounts available for combined purchases. For more information on Energy Information Services, call Calgary office (403) 244-6111. Published by Southam Information Products Ltd, 1450 Don Mills Road, Don Mills, Ontario M3B 2X7 CANADA, (800) 668-2374. In Toronto 442-2122. Web site www.southam.com.

CANADIAN MINING JOURNAL is a leading exploration and mining journal in Canada. Published six times a year, it announces executive appointments, provides information on corporate developments, rates Canada's major mining companies, and includes news on mills and metallurgical plants. Annual subscription $34 Canada, $49 US, $34 Foreign. Special discounts available for combined purchases. For more information on Energy Information Services, call Calgary office (403) 244-6111. Published by Southam

Information Products Ltd, 1450 Don Mills Road, Don Mills, Ontario M3B 2X7 CANADA, (800) 668-2374. In Toronto 442-2122. Web site www.southam.com.

FINANCIAL TIMES ENERGY YEARBOOKS: MINING contains full contact details, financial and operating information, and details about subsidiaries, affiliates, property and operations for about 800 mining companies globally. $320. Published by Financial Times Energy. Distributed by Gale Group, P.O. Box 9187, Farmington Hills, MI 48333-9187. Toll free US and Canada (800) 877-GALE (4253) and (248) 699-GALE, fax (800) 414-5043 and (248) 699-8061, Internet orders galeord@galegroup.com, web site www.galegroup.com or www.gale.com. All Gale Group products are available on approval. Contact Gale for details.

JOBSON'S MINING YEAR BOOK contains information on 600 of Australia and New Zealand's leading mining, petroleum and exploration companies. Dun & Bradstreet, Business Reference Solutions, Three Sylvan Way, Parsippany, NJ 07054 USA. (800) 526-0651. Email dnbmdd@mail.dnb.com. Web site http://www.dnbmdd.com.

NORTHERN MINER is a weekly newspaper that covers the worldwide activities of all North American Based mining companies. It includes information on company profiles, mergers, career opportunities, a professional directory, a diamond drillers directory, industry news and much more. Annual subscription in Canada $87, US $87, foreign $130 (surface mail or $288 (airmail). Online subscription rates for newspaper subscribers: $60 Canadian, $42 US, $60 Canadian collars for foreign. Online subscription rates for newspaper non-subscribers: $144 Canadian, $108 US, $144 Canadian dollars for foreign. Northern Miner Home Page www.northernminer.com. Special discounts available for combined purchases. For more information on Energy Information Services, call Calgary office (403) 244-6111. Published by Southam Information Products Ltd, 1450 Don Mills Road, Don Mills, Ontario M3B 2X7 CANADA, (800) 668-2374. In Toronto 442-2122. Web site www.southam.com.

Minorities

See Diversity

Mortgage Banking

AMERICAN BANKERS ASSOCIATION (ABA) publishes numerous specialized banking journals and otherwise provides a wealth of information, especially lists of leading firms engaged in various banking activities, such as correspondent banking, second mortgages, credit card operations, mortgage servicing, foreign banks in the US, and so forth. AMERICAN BANKERS ASSOCIATION, 1120 Connecticut Ave. NW, Washington, DC 20036, (202) 663-5000, Fax (202) 663-7533, web site www.aba.com.

CORPORATE FINANCE SOURCEBOOK—THE GUIDE TO MAJOR INVESTMENT SOURCES AND RELATED FINANCIAL SERVICES contains over 13,000 names of executives at 3,700 organizations that, broadly speaking, supply growth capital to businesses, such as venture capital lenders, private lenders, commercial finance and factoring, pension managers, master trusts. Names of key management are included. A special section details public offerings of the past 3 years and mergers and acquisitions over $100 million. $499.95 hard copy, excluding discounts. NRP's catalog states, "If you're dissatisfied for any reason, simply return the product within 30 days for a full refund." If the price is prohibitively high, remember your local library. Available in book, online, magnetic tape, and in mailing list formats. For more information contact: National Register Publishing, 121 Chanlon Road, New Providence, NJ 07974 USA, (800) 521-8110, http://www.lexis-nexis.com. For information about online access, call LEXIS®—NEXIS® Online Services, Mountainview, CA at (800) 346-9759; for mailing lists call Cahners Direct Marketing Services at (800) 323-4958; all other inquiries (800) 521-8110.

MEMBERSHIP DIRECTORIES FOR PROFESSIONAL ASSOCIATIONS are frequently published, either in hard copy or on an Internet web site. If a membership directory is not accessible on the web site, you might want to purchase a hard copy from the association. However, some associations refuse to sell their membership rosters to non-members. Some even preclude recruiters from becoming members. As a last resort, if an association membership directory is not online, you might need to borrow a copy from a member.

Of course, that can be a bit of a "Catch 22," because how can you find a member if you don't have the membership list? Just keep asking everybody you talk to.

If you're having trouble locating an association's web site address (URL), you can always look them up in a directory. If the web site address isn't in the directory, sometimes it's easier to make a phone call and ask for the web site. You can also go to www.web sitez.com to get an organization's URLs.

One way to identify membership directories is to look up associations in a directory, such as Lorna Daniell's BUSINESS INFORMATION SOURCES (University of California Press, Berkeley, Los Angeles and Oxford England/Princeton Fulfillment Services, Newark, NJ), ENCYCLOPEDIA OF ASSOCIATIONS (Gale Group, Farmington Hills, MI) or NATIONAL TRADE AND PROFESSIONAL ASSOCIATIONS (Columbia Books, Washington, DC).

You can call the association and ask them to send information about becoming a member. If you don't want them to know the name of your company, ask them to send the information to your home address. While you're chatting, and before you give your name, make a casual inquiry about whether their membership roster is available for sale to non-members. If it's not, find out their requirements for joining, specifically whether recruiters are precluded.

MORTGAGE BANKERS ASSOCIATION OF AMERICA/THE NATIONAL ASSOCIATION OF REAL ESTATE FINANCE, 1125 15th Street NW, Washington, DC 20005, (202) 861-6500, www.mbaa.org.

MORTGAGE BROKER DIRECTORY identifies mortgage brokerage firms in the US. Listings include primary contact names, addresses, phone and fax numbers, market areas, state license information, loan types originated, warehouse line status, FHA correspondent/VA agent status, and branch offices. For more information contact (800) 321-3373, Thomson Financial Publishing, 4709 West Golf Road, Skokie, IL 60076-1253. Web site @ tfp.bankinfo.com.

THOMSON SAVINGS DIRECTORY identifies savings and loan associations and savings banks in the US. Listings include names of key decision makers, address, phone, fax, branch offices, 3 years' information on structural histories, 2 years of financial statistic, breakdown of mortgage portfolio and more. Published twice year. For more information contact (800) 321-3373, Thomson Financial Publishing, 4709 West Golf Road, Skokie, IL 60076-1253. Web site @ tfp.bankinfo.com.

www.realbank.com serves professionals in real estate, mortgages and construction. Many positions are in the $40,000 to $75,000 range. REALBANK was developed by Realbank, Inc., New York, New York and went online in 1996.

Museums

AMERICAN ART DIRECTORY provides information about national and regional art organizations, museums, libraries and associations in the US and Canada, art schools in the US and Canada, plus listings of museums abroad, art schools abroad, state arts councils, state directors and supervisors of art education, art magazines, art editors and critics, scholarships and fellowships, open exhibitions, and traveling exhibition booking agencies, plus a personnel index. $210. If the price is prohibitively high, remember your local library. National Register Publishing, Reed Elsevier-New Providence, 121 Chanlon Road, New Providence, NJ 07974, (800) 521-8110, fax (800) 836-7736, web site www.redbooks.com or www.marquiswhoswho.com. "If, for any reason whatsoever, your order does not fully meet your expectations, simply return the product within 30 days for a prompt, complete, unquestioned refund," as stated in Catalog of Biographical and Professional References of publisher Marquis Who's Who/National Register Publishing.

ENCYCLOPEDIA OF ASSOCIATIONS: NATIONAL ORGANIZATIONS OF THE US. This superb reference is one of the first places you should look when beginning a new recruiting assignment or when looking for specialized references of any type. The keyword index makes this comprehensive reference easy to use, even in hard copy. For over 23,000 nonprofit professional associations with a national scope, this encyclopedia reveals:

- Publications, including membership rosters and newsletters

- Dates and locations of association conferences and conventions

- Names of Executive Directors, who are usually incredible sources of industry information if you call and speak to them

- Committees

- Job and candidate referral banks, which can provide resumes of other industry sources and sometimes candidates

- It includes organizations in these categories: business, trade, environmental, agricultural, legal, govern mental, engineering, technological, scientific, educational, cultural, social welfare, health & medical, public affairs, ethnic, labor unions, chambers of commerce, tourism, & others.

  Volume 1, National Organizations of the US, $505

  Volume 2, Geographic and Executive Indexes, $390

  Volume 3, Supplement, $405

Gale Group, P.O. Box 9187, Farmington Hills, MI 48333-9187. Toll free US and Canada (800) 877-GALE (4253) and (248) 699-GALE, fax (800) 414-5043 and (248) 699-8061, Internet orders galeord@galegroup.com, web site www.galegroup.com or www.gale.com. All Gale Group products are available on approval. Contact Gale for details.

INTERNATIONAL DIRECTORY OF THE ARTS contains information on artists, museums, publishers, conservation authorities, auctioneers, collectors, art dealers, academics, antique dealers and publications. 175 countries are covered. $275. By K.G. Saur. To order contact R.R. Bowker (a unit of Cahners Business Information), 121 Chanlon Road, New Providence, NJ 07974 USA, Phone (888) BOWKER2 (888-269-5372) & (800) 323-3288, fax (908) 508-7696, email info@bowker.com, web www.bowker.com. Canada—R.R. Bowker, Markham, Ontario, phone (888) BOWKER9 & (905) 415-5837, fax (905) 479-6266. German speaking Europe—K.G. Saur Verlag, Munich, Germany, phone 49-89-76902-232, fax 49-89-76902-250, email 100730.1341@compuserve.com, web www.saur.de/home.htm. Rest of Europe incl. United Kingdom plus Africa & Asia—Bowker-Saur, W. Sussex, UK, phone 44-1342-326-972, fax 44-1342-335-612, email customer@bowker-saur.co.uk, web www.bowker-saur.com/service/. Australia/New Zealand—Thorpe, Port Melbourne, Victoria, Australia, phone 61-03-9-245-7370, fax 61-03-9-245-7395, email customer.service@thorpe.com.au, web www.thorpe.com.au. Technical support for CD ROMs (800) 323-3288, fax 908) 665-3528, email techsupport@bowker.com.

INTERNATIONAL DIRECTORY OF ARTS AND MUSEUMS OF THE WORLD CD-ROM, $525. R.R. Bowker (a unit of Cahners Business Information), 121 Chanlon Road, New Providence, NJ 07974 USA, Phone (888) BOWKER2 (888-269-5372) & (800) 323-3288, fax (908) 508-7696, email info@bowker.com, web www.bowker.com. Canada—R.R. Bowker, Markham, Ontario, phone (888) BOWKER9 & (905) 415-5837, fax (905) 479-6266. German speaking Europe—K.G. Saur Verlag, Munich, Germany, phone 49-89-76902-232, fax 49-89-76902-250, email 100730.1341@compuserve.com, web www.saur.de/home.htm. Rest of Europe incl. United Kingdom plus Africa & Asia—Bowker-Saur, W. Sussex, UK, phone 44-1342-326-972, fax 44-1342-335-612, email customer@bowker-saur.co.uk, web www.bowker-saur.com/service/. Australia/New Zealand—Thorpe, Port Melbourne, Victoria, Australia, phone 61-03-9-245-7370, fax 61-03-9-245-7395, email customer.service@thorpe.com.au, web www.thorpe.com.au. Technical support for CD ROMs (800) 323-3288, fax 908) 665-3528, email techsupport@bowker.com.

MUSEUMS OF THE WORLD contains information about 24,000 museums from K.G. Saur. $425. R.R. Bowker (a unit of Cahners Business Information), 121 Chanlon Road, New Providence, NJ 07974 USA, Phone (888) BOWKER2 (888-269-5372) & (800) 323-3288, fax (908) 508-7696, email info@bowker.com, web www.bowker.com. Canada—R.R. Bowker, Markham, Ontario, phone (888) BOWKER9 & (905) 415-5837, fax (905) 479-6266. German speaking Europe—K.G. Saur Verlag, Munich, Germany, phone 49-89-76902-232, fax 49-89-76902-250, email 100730.1341@compuserve.com, web www.saur.de/home.htm. Rest of Europe incl. United Kingdom plus Africa & Asia—Bowker-Saur, W. Sussex, UK, phone 44-1342-326-972, fax 44-1342-335-612, email customer@bowker-saur.co.uk, web www.bowker-saur.com/service/. Australia/New Zealand—Thorpe, Port Melbourne, Victoria, Australia, phone 61-03-9-245-7370, fax 61-03-9-245-7395, email customer.service@thorpe.com.au, web www.thorpe.com.au. Technical support for CD ROMs (800) 323-3288, fax 908) 665-3528, email techsupport@bowker.com.

OFFICIAL MUSEUM DIRECTORY, published in cooperation with the American Association of Museums, provides information about general and history museums, children's museums, historic homes and sites, art museums, parks and visitors' centers, plus science museums, planetariums, wildlife refuges, aquariums, arboretums and zoos. $229. If the price is prohibitively high, remember your local library. National Register Publishing, Reed Elsevier-New Providence, 121 Chanlon Road, New Providence, NJ 07974, (800) 521-8110, fax (800) 836-7736, web site www.redbooks.com or www.marquiswhoswho.com. "If, for any reason whatsoever, your order does not fully meet your expectations, simply return the product within 30 days for a prompt, complete, unquestioned refund," as stated in Catalog of Biographical and Professional References of publisher Marquis Who's Who/National Register Publishing.

STANDARD PERIODICAL DIRECTORY consists of 85,000 American and Canadian periodicals referenced by 250 subjects. Includes new online index and title index. $895. Also available on CD ROM. Published by Oxbridge. Distributed by Gale Group, P.O. Box 9187, Farmington Hills, MI 48333-9187. Toll free US and Canada (800) 877-GALE (4253) and (248) 699-GALE, fax (800) 414-5043 and (248) 699-8061, Internet orders galeord@galegroup.com, web site www.galegroup.com or www.gale.com. All Gale Group products are available on approval. Contact Gale for details.

STANDARD PERIODICAL DIRECTORY ON CD-ROM encompasses 75,000 North American publications, vastly simplifying research in consumer magazines, trade journals, newspapers, yearbooks, museum publications, ethnic publications and more. Contact Gale for prices. Gale Group, P.O. Box 9187, Farmington Hills, MI 48333-9187. Toll free US and Canada (800) 877-GALE (4253) and (248) 699-GALE, fax (800) 414-5043 and (248) 699-8061, Internet orders galeord@galegroup.com, web site www.galegroup.com or www.gale.com. All Gale Group products are available on approval. Contact Gale for details.

Music

See Arts, Entertainment

MUSIC LIBRARY ASSOCIATION, Box 487, Canton, MA 02021, (617) 828-8450.

NATIONAL DIRECTORY OF RECORD LABELS AND MUSIC PUBLISHERS edited by Barbara Taylor, includes over 4,000 major labels, independent labels and music publishers listed, including titles, addresses, phone and fax numbers, with cross references. $24.50, item #B1927. Published by Rising Star Music Publishing. Distributed by SPIN (Songwriter Products, Ideas & Necessities), 345 Sprucewood Road, Lake Mary, FL 32746-5917. (800) 800-487-SPIN, (407) 321-3702. Email rsfspin@aol.com. Web site http://members.aol.com/rsfspin.

SONGWRITERS' MARKET edited by Cindy Laufenberg is a how-to book for songwriters. It includes these chapters: Music Print Publishers comprised of companies that print sheet music; Record Companies; Record Producers; Managers and Booking Agents; Advertising, Audiovisual and Commercial Music Firms; Play Producers and Publishers; and Organizations. $21.95. Published by Writer's Digest. Distributed by SPIN (Songwriter Products, Ideas & Necessities), 345 Sprucewood Road, Lake Mary, FL 32746-5917. (800) 800-487-SPIN, (407) 321-3702. Email rsfspin@aol.com. Web site http://members.aol.com/rsfspin.

www.emheadlines.com is the headline news service for the entertainment business. This Cahners Business Information web site provides information on Film, Television, Books, Technology, Music, Nielsen Ratings, Domestic Box Office, Bestseller List.

Mutual Funds

DIRECTORY OF REGISTERED INVESTMENT ADVISORS identifies over 9,000 CEO's, 7,000 Investment Officers, 10,000 Portfolio Managers, 6,000 Directors of Research and Research Analysts, 2,800 Traders and Trading Managers, and 1,200 Directors of Operations/Chief Financial Officers, plus web sites and personal email addresses. The directory also includes a section on mutual funds for over 4,000 funds at 375 firms, including the name of the person responsible for managing the fund, 1,3 and 5 year returns, benchmark comparisons, and more. DIRECTORY OF REGISTERED INVESTMENT ADVISORS with 4 Regional editions, $475. The Directory with no regional editions, $395. Published by Standard & Poors, a division of

McGraw-Hill, MONEY MARKET DIRECTORIES, INC., 320 East Main Street, Charlottesville, VA 22902, http://www.mmdaccess.com, (800) 446-2810, (804) 977-1450.

FINANCIAL SERVICES CANADA is a handbook of banks, non-depository institutions, stock exchange and brokers, investment management, mutual funds, insurance, accountants, government agencies, financial associations and more, including contact numbers, name, title, organization, phone, fax, email, web site, and cellular. $199 for book, $299 for CD ROM, $399 for both. Ordering information: Copp Clark Professional, 200 Adelaide Street West, 3rd floor, Toronto, ON M5H 1W7 CANADA. Email orders@mail.CanadaInfo.com. Web site http://www.coppclark.com. For additional information contact: IHS Canada, Micromedia Limited, 20 Victoria Street, Toronto, Ontario M5C 2N8 CANADA, (800) 387-2689, (416) 362-5211, fax (416) 362-6161, email info@micromedia.on.ca.

INVESTMENT COMPANIES YEARBOOK is an annual directory that summarizes 12,000 funds, provides performance information, fund address, phone number, advisor, and identifies portfolio manager(s) and tenure, plus minimum investment, sales charges and more. $295. Ordering information: Securities Data Publishing, 1290 Avenue of the Americas, 36th floor, New York, NY 10104, (212) 830-9363.

MUTUAL FUNDS SOURCEBOOK provides information on 1,300 Canadian mutual funds. However, it is impossible to determine from the publisher's catalog whether this directory includes names of personnel. $350 per year, $150 book. Special discounts available for combined purchases. Published by Southam Information Products Ltd, 1450 Don Mills Road, Don Mills, Ontario M3B 2X7 CANADA, (800) 668-2374. In Toronto 442-2122. Web site www.southam.com.

VALUE LINE INVESTMENT SURVEY is considered one of the most respected investment surveys around, particularly for their analysis of future prospects of the publicly held companies they follow. Also analyzes industries. Value Line Investment Survey, 220 East 42nd Street, New York, NY 10017-5891. Available as a Windows® CD ROM or a 3.5" disk covering 1,700 stocks, 2 month trial, $55. 1 year subscription $595. Covering 5,000+ stocks, 2 month trial $95, 1 year subscription $995. Call (800) 535-9648, ext. 2751. Call (800) 634-3583 for pricing about other products, including Mutual Fund Survey, Options, Convertibles, Over-the-Counter Special Situations, and hard copy of the Value Line Investment Survey and Value Line Investment Survey Expanded.

N

Near East

See International

DIRECTORY OF AMERICAN FIRMS OPERATING IN FOREIGN COUNTRIES, REGIONAL EDITION—NEAR AND MIDDLE EAST. Includes Bahrain, Cyprus, Israel, Jordan, Kuwait, Lebanon, Oman, Qatar, Saudi Arabia, Syria, Turkey, United Arab Emirates, West Bank, Yemen. $49. Uniworld Business Publications, Inc., 257 Central Park West, Suite 10A, New York, NY 10024-4110, (212) 496-2448, fax (212) 769-0413, email uniworldbp@aol.com. Web site: http://www.uniworldbp.com.

DIRECTORY OF AMERICAN FIRMS OPERATING IN FOREIGN COUNTRIES, REGIONAL EDITION—NEAR & MIDDLE EAST & ARABIC COUNTRIES COMBINED, $59. Ordering information: Uniworld Business Publications, Inc., 257 Central Park West, Suite 10A, New York, NY 10024-4110, (212) 496-2448, fax (212) 769-0413, email uniworldbp@aol.com. Web site: http://www.uniworldbp.com.

DIRECTORY OF FOREIGN FIRMS OPERATING IN THE UNITED STATES, REGIONAL EDITION—NEAR & MIDDLE EAST. $39. Uniworld Business Publications, Inc., 257 Central Park West, Suite 10A, New York, NY 10024-4110, (212) 496-2448, fax (212) 769-0413, email uniworldbp@aol.com. Web site: http://www.uniworldbp.com.

The Netherlands

See Europe, International

DIRECTORY OF AMERICAN FIRMS OPERATING IN FOREIGN COUNTRIES, REGIONAL EDITION—THE NETHERLANDS, $49. Ordering information: Uniworld Business Publications, Inc., 257 Central Park West, Suite 10A, New York, NY 10024-4110, (212) 496-2448, fax (212) 769-0413, email uniworldbp@aol.com. Web site: http://www.uniworldbp.com.

PENSION FUNDS AND THEIR ADVISERS provides information on the top 2,000 pension funds in the United Kingdom, plus major funds of Japan, Belgium, France, Germany, Ireland, The Netherlands and Switzerland. This Directory is the only source in the US that monitors the growth of assets in the international market. Information includes internal and external fund management contacts, major US and Canadian pension funds and money managers, major European and Japanese pension funds and their advisors. It also includes comprehensive listings of 900 advisors to the pension fund industry including financial advisers, accountants, actuaries and pension fund consultants, pension administrators, insurance companies, attorneys, computer services, global custody, pension trustees, pension /financial recruitment consultants, investment research, associations and professional groups, and publications. $310. Published by A.P. Information Services, Ltd. Marketed exclusively in North America MONEY MARKET DIRECTORIES INC./STANDARD AND POORS, 320 East Main Street, Charlottesville, VA 22902, http://www.mmdaccess.com, (800) 446-2810, (804) 977-1450.

TOP 25,000 COMPANIES—NETHERLANDS contains rankings of the largest industrial, trading, transport, banking, insurance and service companies. Dun & Bradstreet, Business Reference Solutions, Three Sylvan Way, Parsippany, NJ 07054 USA. (800) 526-0651. Email dnbmdd@mail.dnb.com. Web site http://www.dnbmdd.com.

YEARBOOK OF INTERNATIONAL ORGANIZATIONS is a 4 volume directory of non-profit organizations, commercial associations, business groups, conferences, religious orders and intergovernmental bodies. From K.G. Saur. $1,170 for 4 volumes.

YEARBOOK OF INTERNATIONAL ORGANIZATIONS PLUS is a CD ROM which was described by American Reference Books Annual as "The most comprehensive coverage of international organizations." This CD consolidates THE YEARBOOK OF INTERNATIONAL ORGANIZATIONS and WHO'S WHO IN INTERNATIONAL ORGANIZATIONS. It encompasses intergovernmental and national organizations, conferences and religious orders and fraternities. Search criteria include organization name, fields of activity, titles of publications, links to other organizations and more. User languages are English, German, French and Dutch. MS-DOS, Windows and Macintosh compatibility. From K.G. Saur. Updated annually. 1 year subscription $1,318.

R.R. Bowker (a unit of Cahners Business Information), 121 Chanlon Road, New Providence, NJ 07974 USA, Phone (888) BOWKER2 (888-269-5372) & (800) 323-3288, fax (908) 508-7696, email info@bowker.com, web www.bowker.com. Canada—R.R. Bowker, Markham, Ontario, phone (888) BOWKER9 & (905) 415-5837, fax (905) 479-6266. German speaking Europe—K.G. Saur Verlag, Munich, Germany, phone 49-89-76902-232, fax 49-89-76902-250, email 100730.1341@compuserve.com, web www.saur.de/home.htm. Rest of Europe incl. United Kingdom plus Africa & Asia—Bowker-Saur, W. Sussex, UK, phone 44-1342-326-972, fax 44-1342-335-612, email customer@bowker-saur.co.uk, web www.bowker-saur.com/service/. Australia/New Zealand—Thorpe, Port Melbourne, Victoria, Australia, phone 61-03-9-245-7370, fax 61-03-9-245-7395, email customer.service@thorpe.com.au, web www.thorpe.com.au. Technical support for CD ROMs (800) 323-3288, fax 908) 665-3528, email techsupport@bowker.com.

Network Providers

INFORMATION SOURCES was an award winning directory published by the Gale Group in partnership with the Information Industry Association (IIA). At the time of this writing, the IIA has merged with the Software Publishers Association (SPA) to form the newly named Software and Information Industry Association (SIIA).

This directory provides information for the 550 member companies of the Information Industry Association. Entries include company name, address, phone, names of executives, regional offices, trade and brand names and description of products and services. Indexed by product, personal name, trade name, geography, parent company, international, and niche markets. The directory also identifies publishers, database producers, online services, telecommunications and network providers, system integrators and many others. $125. Contact Gale for information as to when an updated directory will be available. In the meantime, visit the Software and Information Industry's web site at www.siia.net to see their membership roster.

Gale Group, P.O. Box 9187, Farmington Hills, MI 48333-9187. Toll free US and Canada (800) 877-GALE (4253) and (248) 699-GALE, fax (800) 414-5043 and (248) 699-8061, Internet orders galeord@galegroup.com, web site www.galegroup.com or www.gale.com. All Gale Group products are available on approval. Contact Gale for details.

Software & Information Industry Association (SIIA), formerly the Software Publishers Association (SPA) and Information Industry Association (IIA) is located at 1730 M Street, NW, Washington, DC 20036, (202) 452-1600, www.siia.net.

TELECOMMUNICATIONS DIRECTORY includes information on over 2,500 national and international communications systems and services, including providers of telephone lines, local area networks, teleconferencing, videotext and teletext, electronic mail, facsimile, Internet access, voicemail, satellite and electronic transactional services. Also includes associations, a glossary, and four indexes. $400. Gale Group, P.O. Box 9187, Farmington Hills, MI 48333-9187. Toll free US and Canada (800) 877-GALE (4253) and (248) 699-GALE, fax (800) 414-5043 and (248) 699-8061, Internet orders galeord@galegroup.com, web site www.galegroup.com or www.gale.com. All Gale Group products are available on approval. Contact Gale for details.

New Business Leads

D&B MARKETING INFORMATION BASE contains marketing information on 10,000,000 companies. Every month it is updated, reflecting some 500,000 changes: new business additions, CEO CHANGES and address changes. Information on senior management changes is particularly valuable to job hunters and search firms is an indicator of change, which could mean hiring activity, and/or a need for executive search services. Organizations in transition are generally good places to recruit because quality talent may be unhappy with the politics of the new organization. With respect to the execution of an executive search, this information can be best utilized to develop a list of target companies. Then, names and titles can be identified using another database or through traditional ID research. This technique could be used for an extremely difficult recruiting assignment. For example, finding companies in turmoil could provide a good place to search for candidates eager for a change. Selections are delivered on tape, cartridge, diskette or hard copy. For prices call Dun & Bradstreet at (800) 526-0651. For more information contact Dun & Bradstreet, Business Reference Solutions, Three Sylvan Way, Parsippany, New Jersey 07054. Email dnbmdd@mail.dnb.com. Web site http://www.dnbmdd.com.

INTERNATIONAL DIRECTORY OF COMPANY HISTORIES. While this directory provides few names and titles, it could be useful as a new business development tool. It provides historical backgrounds of 2,000 companies—potential new clients about whom you should be familiar prior to making a new business presentation. $175 per volume. 25 volumes in print at the time of this writing. If it is not feasible to purchase these reference materials, visit your local library. If they don't have the reference you need, they may have a sharing agreement with another library. Published by Gale Group, P.O. Box 9187, Farmington Hills, MI 48333-9187. Toll free US and Canada (800) 877-GALE (4253) and (248) 699-GALE, fax (800) 414-5043 and (248) 699-8061, Internet orders galeord@galegroup.com, web site www.galegroup.com or www.gale.com. All Gale Group products are available on approval. Contact Gale for details.

WHO'S NEWS in the *Wall Street Journal* and similar columns in other newspapers and trade journals provide a wealth of information about management changes and promotions. A good candidate who has been passed over for promotion might be especially amenable to an overture from a recruiter. Also, organizations in a state of change often have positions to fill, so there could be needs a recruiting firm can address. Even though a company might have a relationship with a large search firm, it could still make sense for a recruiter to nurture a new business relationship for several reasons. First, large companies usually like to dole out business to numerous search firms for off limits reasons, to prevent as many search firms as possible from seeking talent at their companies. Second, since search consultants often say, "You're only as good as your last search," it's smart to stay in touch with a growing company. In other words, how long do you think it will take an arrogant firm to mess up an assignment with an important company? Your next new client might materialize if you happen to be waiting on the sidelines at the right time—and, as they say, "Timing is everything." Who's News and similar columns will give also give you a pulse on where internal change and reorganizations are occurring. Also, from the standpoint of providing important organization information, these columns sometimes clarify that, too.

New England

See Geographic References (USA)

NEW ENGLAND EXECUTIVE RESOURCES COUNCIL, whose URL is http://199.233.99.2/neerc/, is an organization of primarily search consultants. The group meets in Waltham, Mass. The web site includes a listing of members, including some photos.

www.boston.com is the web site for Boston Globe online accesses the Globe's newspaper ads.

www.ma.jobsearch.org Recruiting site for Massachusetts

www.townonline.com/working or Town Online Working is the web site to various community newspapers, including 13 in New England. In addition to job listings, it also has a job profile with the capability of automatically downloading to your Email. Town Online Working was ranked as one of the top 5 "Sites Offering the Best Career Resources for Job Seekers" by the *National Business Employment Weekly.* Many positions are administrative, management and blue collar, often paying in the teens up to $30,000. The site developer is the Community Newspaper Company, Needham, Massachusetts and was established in 1996.

New Jersey

www.jobnet.com was ranked as one of the top 5 "Best Specialty Sites" by the *National Business Employment Weekly.* Jobnet.com specializes in positions located in southeastern Pennsylvania and neighboring areas of New Jersey and Delaware. The site was developed by Online Opportunities, Malvern, Pennsylvania and has been online since 1992.

www.tristatejobs.com is the URL for Tri-State Jobs, a site for positions in New York, New Jersey and Connecticut. Many positions are for programmers, engineers and managers, often in the $50,000 to $100,000 range. The site was developed by Tri-State Jobs, Southbury, Connecticut and went online in 1997.

New Media

See Internet

ELECTRONIC MEDIA is a weekly trade publication. Crain Communications, Inc. is headquartered in Chicago with offices in major cities throughout the US plus London, Tokyo and Frankfurt. New York location: 220 East 42nd Street, New York, NY 10017, (212) 210-0100, Circulation (800) 678-9595. Annual subscription $109, two years $180. Web site www.emonline.

PHILLIPS BUSINESS INFORMATION provides information in newsletters, magazines, directories and on multiple web sites covering a range of topics, such as magazine products, telecommunications and cable products, satellite products, media, new media and Internet products, marketing and public relations products, financial technology and electronic commerce, aviation and defense products. For more information, contact: Phillips Business Information, Inc., a Phillips Publishing International Company, 120 Seven Locks Road, Potomac, MD 20854, (301) 340-1520, (301) 340-7788, (800) 777-5006, Internet pbi@phillips.com, web site www.phillips.com.

TELEVISION INTERNATIONAL is a magazine for cable TV, radio, satellite and interactive multimedia industries around the world. Call publisher for price. Cahners Business Information, 245 West 17th Street, New York, NY 10011-5300, (212) 337-6944, fax (212) 337-6948, email jonnypim@pacific.net.sg and rschatz@cahners.com, URL www.cahners.com/mainmag/bci.htm. Headquarters: Cahners Business Information, 275 Washington Street, Newton, MA 02158-1630, (617) 558-4663 or (617) 964-3030, fax (617) 558-4700, email marketaccess@cahners.com. Web sites www.cahners.com or www.chilton.net.

WHO'S WHO IN UK MULTIMEDIA, Phillips Business Information, Inc., a Phillips Publishing International Company, 120 Seven Locks Road, Potomac, MD 20854, (301) 340-1520, (301) 340-7788, (800) 777-5006, Internet pbi@phillips.com, web site www.phillips.com.

New York

BACON'S NEW YORK MEDIA DIRECTORY presents more in-depth coverage than their main directories, including statewide print and broadcast coverage of daily and community newspapers, state bureaus of US dailies, regional business and general interest magazines, broadcast networks, stations, syndicators and programming, detailed editorial staff listings at all outlets, freelance journalists, including "editorial pitching profiles," phone, fax, email and home page. $195. Ordering information: Call (800) 621-0561, (800) 753-6675. Bacon's Information, Inc., a K-III Communications Company, 332 South Michigan Avenue, Chicago, IL 60604. Satisfaction guaranteed or a full refund within 30 days.

CRAIN NEW YORK is a weekly trade publication. Look for special issues with surveys and lists of top companies by industry. Crain Communications, Inc. is headquartered in Chicago with offices in major cities throughout the US plus London, Tokyo and Frankfurt. New York location: 220 East 42nd Street, New York, NY 10017, (212) 210-0100, Circulation (800) 678-9595. Annual subscription $62, two years $113. Web site www.crainsny.com.

JAPAN FINANCIAL DIRECTORY NEW YORK is published by Nikkin America, Inc., 445 Fifth Avenue, Suite 27D, New York, NY 10016, (212) 679-0196. $195 hard copy. It can also be purchased at Asahiya, the Japanese bookstore at the corner of Vanderbilt and 45th Street, near Grand Central Station in Manhattan. Check other major cities for an Asahiya book store near you.

www.tristatejobs.com is the URL for Tri-State Jobs, a site for positions in New York, New Jersey and Connecticut. Many positions are for programmers, engineers and managers, often in the $50,000 to $100,000 range. The site was developed by Tri-State Jobs, Southbury, Connecticut and went online in 1997.

New Zealand

See Pacific, International, Australia

DIRECTORY OF AMERICAN FIRMS OPERATING IN FOREIGN COUNTRIES, REGIONAL EDITION—AUSTRALIA GROUP. Includes Australia, New Zealand, Fiji French Polynesia, Guam, New Caledonia, New Guinea, North Mariana Island, Palau, Papua, Polynesia. Ordering information: Uniworld Business Publications, Inc., 257 Central Park West, Suite 10A, New York, NY 10024-4110, (212) 496-2448, fax (212) 769-0413, email uniworldbp@aol.com. Web site: http://www.uniworldbp.com.

DIRECTORY OF FOREIGN FIRMS OPERATING IN THE UNITED STATES, REGIONAL EDITION—AUSTRALIA GROUP. Includes Australia and New Zealand. $29. Uniworld Business Publications, Inc., 257 Central Park West, Suite 10A, New York, NY 10024-4110, (212) 496-2448, fax (212) 769-0413, email uniworldbp@aol.com. Web site: http://www.uniworldbp.com.

JOBSON'S MINING YEAR BOOK contains information on 600 of Australia and New Zealand's leading mining, petroleum and exploration companies. Dun & Bradstreet, Business Reference Solutions, Three Sylvan Way, Parsippany, NJ 07054 USA. (800) 526-0651. Email dnbmdd@mail.dnb.com. Web site http://www.dnbmdd.com.

JOBSON'S YEAR BOOK OF PUBLIC COMPANIES OF AUSTRALIA AND NEW ZEALAND contains information on over 2,000 public and private companies and their executives. Dun & Bradstreet, Business Reference Solutions, Three Sylvan Way, Parsippany, NJ 07054 USA. (800) 526-0651. Email dnbmdd@mail.dnb.com. Web site http://www.dnbmdd.com.

KOMPASS is described by the publisher as "the world's most comprehensive global database of companies, products and services for manufacturing and engineering professionals in print, on CD ROM and on the Internet." It contains company and product information for companies in all lines of business, including manufacturing and industrial sectors. Each company listing includes name, address, phone number, management names, business descriptions, and industry and product listings. Kompass's web site is www.kompass.com. Call publisher for prices and information on country directories. Cahners Business Information, 121 Chanlon Road, New Providence, NJ 07974, (908) 771-8785, fax (908) 665-8755, email hholmes@reedref.com. Headquarters: Cahners Business Information, 275 Washington Street, Newton, MA 02158-1630, (617) 558-4663 or (617) 964-3030, fax (617) 558-4700, email marketaccess@cahners.com, web sites www.cahners.com or www.chilton.net.

MAJOR COMPANIES OF THE FAR EAST AND AUSTRALASIA identifies 68,000 senior executives at 12,000 key Asia Pacific companies in 20 countries. Published by Graham & Whiteside Ltd., Tuition House, 5-6 Francis Grove, London SW19 4DT, England. Web site http://www.major-co-data.com. Email sales@major-co-data.com.

$1,450 for all three volumes

Volume 1: South East Asia, $560
Volume 2: East Asia, $560
Volume 3: Australia and New Zealand, $365

CD ROM, updated quarterly, is also available. Distributed by: Larry Meranus Professional Publications & Services, 4 Demoray Court, Pine Brook, NJ 07058, (800) MERANUS or (800) 637-2687. Or by Gale Group, P.O. Box 9187, Farmington Hills, MI 48333-9187. Toll free US and Canada (800) 877-GALE (4253) and (248) 699-GALE, fax (800) 414-5043 and (248) 699-8061, Internet orders galeord@galegroup.com, web site www.galegroup.com or www.gale.com. All Gale Group products are available on approval. Contact Gale for details.

MAJOR COMPANIES SERIES ON CD ROM consists of Graham & Whiteside's annual directories of major international companies. All six directories reside on one disk. After payment, you'll receive a security code to access the region(s) you select. This Windows™ based CD can navigate by company name, company locations, executive names, business activity and more. Free demo CD ROM is available. Regions also available separately for Europe, Central & Eastern Europe, the Far East and Australasia, the Arab World, Africa, and Latin America. For prices and availability, contact the Gale Group, P.O. Box 9187, Farmington Hills, MI 48333-9187. Toll free US and Canada (800) 877-GALE (4253) and (248) 699-GALE, fax (800) 414-5043 and (248) 699-8061, Internet orders galeord@galegroup.com, web site www.galegroup.com or www.gale.com. All Gale Group products are available on approval. Contact Gale for details.

NEW ZEALAND BOOKS IN PRINT, published by Thorpe, $60. Also available on CD ROM. R.R. Bowker (a unit of Cahners Business Information), 121 Chanlon Road, New Providence, NJ 07974 USA, Phone (888) BOWKER2 (888-269-5372) & (800) 323-3288, fax (908) 508-7696, email info@bowker.com, web www.bowker.com. Canada—R.R. Bowker, Markham, Ontario, phone (888) BOWKER9 & (905) 415-5837, fax (905) 479-6266. German speaking Europe—K.G. Saur Verlag, Munich, Germany, phone 49-89-76902-232, fax 49-89-76902-250, email 100730.1341@compuserve.com, web www.saur.de/home.htm. Rest of Europe incl. United Kingdom plus Africa & Asia—Bowker-Saur, W. Sussex, UK, phone 44-1342-326-972, fax 44-1342-335-612, email customer@bowker-saur.co.uk, web www.bowker-saur.com/service/. Australia/New Zealand—Thorpe, Port Melbourne, Victoria, Australia, phone 61-03-9-245-7370, fax 61-03-9-245-7395, email customer.service@thorpe.com.au, web www.thorpe.com.au. Technical support for CD ROMs (800) 323-3288, fax 908) 665-3528, email techsupport@bowker.com.

NEW ZEALAND BUSINESS WHO'S WHO, something like a STANDARD AND POORS Register for New Zealand, provides names and titles of executives. It lists companies by city and includes a "Company Ownership Index" with parent company information, a "Brands Guide," and a "Classified Business Index" which identifies names of companies according to industry. 39th edition is available in the public library in Nelson, New Zealand. Of all the references reviewed in the Nelson library, THE NEW ZEALAND BUSINESS WHO'S WHO was the best.

NEW ZEALAND REGISTER OF ACCREDITED AND CERTIFIED SUPPLIERS lists only one contact name per company and provides a products and services index. It is available in the public library in Nelson, New Zealand. S.P. Publishing Ltd, 59 Victoria Road, Davenport, Auckland, New Zealand, phone (09) 620-1416, fax (09) 620-1417, Wellington (04) 471-2316.

STRATEGIC INFORMATION SERVICE GUIDE TO KEY PERSONNEL IN THE TOP 50 NEW ZEALAND COMPANIES is a superb resource that includes organization charts, an overview of business activities, and contact details. For more information contact the public library in Nelson, New Zealand or the publisher, Strategic Information Service, P.O. Box 33-1039, Takapuna, New Zealand, phone 64-9-309-3657, fax 64-9-309-6828.

NEW ZEALAND'S TOP 200 COMPANIES—REBUILDING AN ECONOMY includes good listings of companies with names and titles of management and sometimes their photos. The first section of the book is a large, impressive Economic Review of various industry sectors with many nice photos. New Zealand's Top 200 Companies, A Division of Profile Publishing Ltd., P.O. Box 5544, Wellesley Street, Auckland, New Zealand, (09) 358-5455 phone, (09) 358-5462 fax. It is available in the public library in Nelson, New Zealand.

www.info@telecom.co.nz is a New Zealand phone book on the Internet.

www.nzjobs.co.nz is a recruiting and jobhunting web site for positions in New Zealand. Email: info@nzjobs.co.nz.

Newsletters

BACON'S MEDIASOURCE CD ROM is a media database and software with over 250,000 names of contacts at over 48,000 media outlets, including newspapers and their bureaus, magazines and newsletters, news syndicates, wire services, broadcast networks, stations and shows, including phone, fax, email and home page. Updated quarterly. Available for Windows and Macintosh. $1,095 annual subscription. Ordering information: Call (800) 621-0561, (800) 753-6675. Bacon's Information, Inc., a K-III Communications Company, 332 South Michigan Avenue, Chicago, IL 60604.

BACON'S NEWSPAPER/MAGAZINE DIRECTORY is a two volume set that identifies every daily and weekly newspaper in the US, every magazine and newsletter in the US that accepts outside editorial, detailed listings of editorial staffs, with phone, fax and email, publication Internet home pages and other online locations, magazine editorial profiles and types of press materials accepted, syndicated columnists by beat, news services and news syndicates, and indexes of newspapers by market and circulation. Includes names and titles, editors' preferences, like/dislikes and "beat" reporter information to help you find the right contact. $275. Ordering information: Call (800) 621-0561, (800) 753-6675. Bacon's Information, Inc., a K-III Communications Company, 332 South Michigan Avenue, Chicago, IL 60604. Satisfaction guaranteed or a full refund within 30 days.

DIRECTORY OF BUSINESS INFORMATION RESOURCES, ASSOCIATIONS, NEWSLETTERS, MAGAZINES AND TRADESHOWS, published by Grey House Publishing, Pocket Knife Square, Lakeville, CT 06039, $199. (800) 562-2139, (860) 435-0868, web site www.greyhouse.com or books@il.com.

ENCYCLOPEDIA OF BUSINESS INFORMATION SOURCES will lead you to specialized directories, professional associations, trade publications, newsletters, databases, Internet resources and more. It's an excellent reference and a great way to find key resources in any industry fast. $330. Gale Group, P.O. Box 9187, Farmington Hills, MI 48333-9187. Toll free US and Canada (800) 877-GALE (4253) and (248) 699-GALE, fax (800) 414-5043 and (248) 699-8061, Internet orders galeord@galegroup.com, web site www.galegroup.com or www.gale.com. All Gale Group products are available on approval. Contact Gale for details.

GALE DIRECTORY OF PUBLICATIONS AND BROADCAST MEDIA ONLINE is a GaleNet resource on the Internet that includes information on 64,000 newspapers, periodicals, newsletters, industry directories, television and radio stations, including names of key personnel. Contact the library to access this reference free. For pricing and ordering information, contact: Gale Group, P.O. Box 9187, Farmington Hills, MI 48333-9187. Toll free US and Canada (800) 877-GALE (4253) and (248) 699-GALE, fax (800) 414-5043 and (248)

699-8061, Internet orders galeord@galegroup.com, web site www.galegroup.com or www.gale.com. All Gale Group products are available on approval. Contact Gale for details.

GALE'S READY REFERENCE SHELF ONLINE is a GaleNet Internet resource that provides integrated access to databases covering national, regional, state, local and international associations, publishers, newspapers and periodicals, directories, newsletters, online databases, portable databases, database products and vendors, special libraries and research centers. Information is included from numerous Gale databases, among them THE ENCYCLOPEDIA OF ASSOCIATIONS, PUBLISHERS DIRECTORY, GALE DIRECTORY OF PUBLICATIONS AND BROADCAST MEDIA and several others. If it is prohibitively expensive, locate a library with with this resource. Gale Group, P.O. Box 9187, Farmington Hills, MI 48333-9187. Toll free US and Canada (800) 877-GALE (4253) and (248) 699-GALE, fax (800) 414-5043 and (248) 699-8061, Internet orders galeord@galegroup.com, web site www.galegroup.com or www.gale.com. All Gale Group products are available on approval. Contact Gale for details.

NEWSLETTERS IN PRINT identifies 12,000 newsletters, cross referenced by six indexes, including title, keyword, and subject. It also identifies online newsletters, free newsletters, and newsletters that accept advertising. $257. Database available via commercial online service. Gale Group, P.O. Box 9187, Farmington Hills, MI 48333-9187. Toll free US and Canada (800) 877-GALE (4253) and (248) 699-GALE, fax (800) 414-5043 and (248) 699-8061, Internet orders galeord@galegroup.com, web site www.galegroup.com or www.gale.com. All Gale Group products are available on approval. Contact Gale for details.

Newspapers

See Periodicals, Associations

Nonprofit

Also see Associations, Chambers of Commerce, Education, Foundations, Government Organizations

ASSOCIATIONS UNLIMITED ONLINE is available on the Internet through GaleNet. You can subscribe to any of the several databases comprising ASSOCIATIONS UNLIMITED, including:

- NATIONAL ORGANIZATIONS OF THE US DATABASE

- REGIONAL, STATE AND LOCAL ORGANIZATIONS DATABASE

- INTERNATIONAL ORGANIZATIONS DATABASE

- ASSOCIATIONS MATERIALS DATABASE

- GOVERNMENT NONPROFIT ORGANIZATIONS DATABASE

For more information on available databases and pricing, contact Gale Group, P.O. Box 9187, Farmington Hills, MI 48333-9187. Toll free US and Canada (800) 877-GALE (4253) and (248) 699-GALE, fax (800) 414-5043 and (248) 699-8061, Internet orders galeord@galegroup.com, web site www.galegroup.com or www.gale.com. All Gale Group products are available on approval. Contact Gale for details.

ENCYCLOPEDIA OF ASSOCIATIONS: INTERNATIONAL ORGANIZATIONS includes nearly 20,000 multinational and national organizations in foreign countries, including US based associations with multinational membership. Entries also include email addresses, web sites and bulletin board addresses, lobbying activities, and publication and convention information. Indexed by geography, keyword and executives. $595 for 2 volume set. Also available in CD ROM. Database available via commercial online service. Gale Group, P.O. Box 9187, Farmington Hills, MI 48333-9187. Toll free US and Canada (800) 877-GALE (4253) and (248) 699-GALE, fax (800) 414-5043 and (248) 699-8061, Internet orders galeord@galegroup.com, web site www.galegroup.com or www.gale.com. All Gale Group products are available on approval. Contact Gale for details.

ENCYCLOPEDIA OF ASSOCIATIONS: NATIONAL ORGANIZATIONS OF THE US. This superb reference is one of the first places you should look when beginning a new recruiting assignment or when looking for specialized references of any type. The keyword index makes this comprehensive reference easy to use, even in hard copy. For over 23,000 nonprofit professional associations with a national scope, this encyclopedia reveals:

• Publications, including membership rosters and newsletters

• Dates and locations of association conferences and conventions

• Names of Executive Directors, who are usually incredible sources of industry information if you call and speak to them

• Committees

• Job and candidate referral banks, which can provide resumes of other industry sources and sometimes candidates

• It includes organizations in these categories: business, trade, environmental, agricultural, legal, govern mental, engineering, technological, scientific, educational, cultural, social welfare, health & medical, public affairs, ethnic, labor unions, chambers of commerce, tourism, & others.

Volume 1, National Organizations of the US, $505
Volume 2, Geographic and Executive Indexes, $390
Volume 3, Supplement, $405

Gale Group, P.O. Box 9187, Farmington Hills, MI 48333-9187. Toll free US and Canada (800) 877-GALE (4253) and (248) 699-GALE, fax (800) 414-5043 and (248) 699-8061, Internet orders galeord@galegroup.com, web site www.galegroup.com or www.gale.com. All Gale Group products are available on approval. Contact Gale for details.

ENCYCLOPEDIA OF ASSOCIATIONS: REGIONAL, STATE AND LOCAL ORGANIZATIONS. The information in this directory is not duplicated anywhere in ENCYCLOPEDIA OF ASSOCIATIONS. Over 100,000 nonprofit organizations are included in this directory. $585 for 5 volume set or $140 per individual volume. Also available on CD ROM and online on the Internet through a GaleNet subscription.

Volume 1, Great Lakes States (Illinois, Indiana, Michigan, Minnesota, Ohio, Wisconsin)
Volume 2, Northeastern States (Connecticut, Maine, Massachusetts, New Hampshire, New Jersey, New York, Pennsylvania, Rhode Islands, Vermont)
Volume 3, Southern and Middle Atlantic States (Including Puerto Rico and the Virgin Islands) (Alabama, Delaware, Washington, DC, Florida, Georgia, Kentucky, Maryland, Mississippi, North Carolina, Puerto Rico, South Carolina, Tennessee, Virginia, West Virginia, Virgin Islands)
Volume 4, South Central and Great Plains States (Arkansas, Iowa, Kansas, Louisiana, Missouri, Nebraska, North Dakota, Oklahoma, South Dakota, Texas)
Volume 5, Western States (Alaska, Arizona, California, Colorado, Guam, Hawaii, Idaho, Montana, Nevada, New Mexico, Oregon, Utah, Washington, Wyoming)

Gale Group, P.O. Box 9187, Farmington Hills, MI 48333-9187. Toll free US and Canada (800) 877-GALE (4253) and (248) 699-GALE, fax (800) 414-5043 and (248) 699-8061, Internet orders galeord@galegroup.com, web site www.galegroup.com or www.gale.com. All Gale Group products are available on approval. Contact Gale for details.

NATIONAL DIRECTORY OF NONPROFIT ORGANIZATIONS lists 80% of the nonprofits required to file 990 returns with the Internal Revenue Service. Volume 1 lists organizations with annual revenues of at least $100,000. Volume 2 covers organizations with revenues up to $99,999. Includes names, addresses and phone numbers at 2250,000 organizations. $505 for 2 volume set. Volume 1 (in 2 parts) $365, Volume 2 (in 2 parts) $235. Gale Group, P.O. Box 9187, Farmington Hills, MI 48333-9187. Toll free US and Canada (800) 877-GALE (4253) and (248) 699-GALE, fax (800) 414-5043 and (248) 699-8061, Internet orders galeord@galegroup.com, web site www.galegroup.com or www.gale.com. All Gale Group products are available on approval. Contact Gale for details.

NON-PROFIT NEWS is a biweekly trade publication. Crain Communications, Inc. is headquartered in Chicago with offices in major cities throughout the US plus London, Tokyo and Frankfurt. New York location: 220 East 42nd Street, New York, NY 10017, (212) 210-0100, Circulation (800) 678-9595. Annual subscription $49 prepaid.

North American Industry Classification System (NAICS)

NORTH AMERICAN INDUSTRY CLASSIFICATION SYSTEM (NAICS) MANUAL now replaces the STANDARD INDUSTRIAL CLASSIFICATION (SIC) MANUAL. Last revised in 1987, The SIC Manual is still available in most business libraries. An SIC is a 4 digit number that serves as a "shorthand" for a specific industry. It identifies in detail the composition of each and every SIC code. Historically this fundamental reference has been important in researching companies by SIC because abbreviated lists of SIC codes, such as those which appear in STANDARD AND POORS or DUN & BRADSTREET'S MILLION DOLLAR DIRECTORY SERIES, didn't always provide the level of detail needed. Until 1998 the SIC Manual had been published by The National Technical Information Service, formerly the US Government Printing Office. NTIS is the central source for government sponsored US and worldwide scientific, engineering and business related information. As a self-supporting agency of the US Department of Commerce's Technology Administration, NTIS covers its business and operating expenses with the sale of its products and services.

HOWEVER, THE 1987 SIC MANUAL IS NO LONGER PUBLISHED because the USA has a new industry classification system. The North American Industry Classification System (NAICS) replaces the US Standard Industrial Classification (SIC) system.

NAICS is the first North American industry classification system. It was developed by the US, Canada and Mexico to provide comparable statistics for all three countries. This will allow government and business analysts to uniformly compare industrial production statistics in the three North American Free Trade Agreement (NAFTA) countries. NAICS also provides for increased comparability with the International Standard Industrial Classification System (ISIC), developed and maintained by the United Nations. Both printed and CD ROM versions of the NAICS Manual are scheduled for availability June, 1998. These official versions include 350 new industries, definitions for each industry, tables correlating the 1997 NAICS and the 1987 SIC codes, an alphabetic list of over 18,000 business activities and the corresponding NAICS code, and a special section on What Small Businesses Need to Know About NAICS. Some new industries include specialized technology niches, such as fiber optic cable manufacturing and satellite communications and other types of businesses, such as bed and breakfast inns, environmental consulting, warehouse clubs, credit card issuing, diet and weight reduction centers. Executive search is also recognized as an industry, as a result of the efforts of Executive Director Emeritus of the Association of Executive Search Consultants, Sheila Avrin McLean.

Unlike the SIC codes, which are 4 digits, the NAICS codes are 6 digits. The first 5 digits are standardized among the US, Canada and Mexico. However, the 6th digit may differ from country to country to accommodate different needs in individual countries. NAICS will be reviewed every five years, so classifications and information will stay current with the economy. For more information, contact the Bureau of the Census Official NAICS web page at www.census.gov/naics or send your questions by email to info@ntis.fedworld.gov.

Ordering information: Softcover version, NTIS Order Number PB98-136187INQ, $28.50, $57 outside the US, Canada and Mexico. Hardcover NTIS Order Number PB98-127293, $32.50, $65 outside the US, Canada and Mexico. CD ROM Order Number PB98-502024, single user $45, 90 outside the US, Canada and Mexico. Up to 5 concurrent network users $120, $240 outside the US, Canada and Mexico. Unlimited concurrent network users $240, $480 outside the US, Canada and Mexico. CD ROM includes a search capability that includes access to more index entries than appear in the manual plus downloadable files. Handling charge is additional.

Phone orders Monday-Friday, 8 am - 8 pm Eastern Time (800) 553-NTIS (6487) or (703) 605-6000.Fax (703) 321-8547. For questions about a product or order, email info@ntis.fedworld.gov. Web site www.ntis.gov/. National Technical Information Service, Technology Administration, US Department of Commerce, 5285 Port Royal Road, Springfield, VA 22161.

Norway

See Scandinavia, Europe, International

NORWAY'S TOP 10,000 contains information organized by line of business. Dun & Bradstreet, Business Reference Solutions, Three Sylvan Way, Parsippany, NJ 07054 USA. (800) 526-0651. Email dnbmdd@mail.dnb.com. Web site http://www.dnbmdd.com.

Nursing

COMPLETE MARQUIS WHO'S WHO ON CD ROM is a compilation of literally all 19 Marquis Who's Who that have appeared in print since 1985, including living and deceased people. WHO'S WHO IN AMERICA®, WHO'S WHO IN THE WORLD®, WHO'S WHO IN AMERICAN EDUCATIONS®, WHO'S WHO IN AMERICAN LAW®, WHO'S WHO IN AMERICAN NURSING®, WHO'S WHO IN MEDICINE AND HEALTHCARE®, WHO'S WHO IN FINANCE AND INDUSTRY®, WHO'S WHO IN SCIENCE AND ENGINEERING®, WHO'S WHO IN THE EAST®, WHO'S WHO IN THE MIDWEST®, WHO'S WHO IN THE SOUTH AND SOUTHWEST®, WHO'S WHO IN THE WEST®, WHO'S WHO OF AMERICAN WOMEN®, WHO'S WHO IN ADVERTISING®, WHO'S WHO OF EMERGING LEADERS IN AMERICA®, WHO'S WHO IN ENTERTAINMENT®, WHO'S WHO AMONG HUMAN SERVICES PROFESSIONALS®. One year subscription with semi-annual updates $995. National Register Publishing, Reed Elsevier-New Providence, 121 Chanlon Road, New Providence, NJ 07974, (800) 521-8110, fax (800) 836-7736, web site www.marquiswhoswho.com or www.redbooks.com. "If, for any reason whatsoever, your order does not fully meet your expectations, simply return the product within 30 days for a prompt, complete, unquestioned refund," as stated in Catalog of Biographical and Professional References of publisher Marquis Who's Who/National Register Publishing.

WHO'S WHO IN AMERICAN NURSING, $149.95, first time standing order, $134.95, Who's Marquis Who's Who, 121 Chanlon Road, New Providence, NJ 07974, (800) 521-8110.

www.medhunters.com is a healthcare jobhunting web site developed by Helen Ziegler and Associates, Inc., Toronto, Canada. Worldwide positions are posted for doctors, nurses and therapists, encompassing a broad range of salaries. The site has been online since 1997.

O

Oil and Gas

See Petroleum

Online References

See CD ROM, Databases, Internet, Online Services

Online Services

R.R. BOWKER and REED REFERENCE PUBLISHING, both located at 121 Chanlon Road, New Providence, New Jersey, offer several online services options such as Knight-Ridder Information's DIALOG and LEXIS®-NEXIS®. These products, with pay-as-you-go charges, can be more economical than an annual subscription to a database. For more information about this and other licensing arrangements, contact Bowker or:

Knight Ridder Information, Inc.
DIALOG Service
Mountain View, CA

(800) 334-2564
(800) 3-DIALOG
(415) 254-7000
www.dialog.com

LEXIS®-NEXIS®
Dayton, Ohio
(800) 227-4908
www.lexis-nexis.com

OVID Technologies, Inc.
New York, New York
(800) 950-2035 (North America)
(44) 1-81-748-3777 (UK)
(31) 20-672-0242 (Europe)
(61) 2-231-5999 (Australia)

Contact Bowker for more information about products from SilverPlatter, Inc. and SilverPlatter ERL™.

R.R. Bowker (a unit of Cahners Business Information), 121 Chanlon Road, New Providence, NJ 07974 USA, Phone (888) BOWKER2 (888-269-5372) & (800) 323-3288, fax (908) 508-7696, email info@bowker.com, web www.bowker.com. Canada—R.R. Bowker, Markham, Ontario, phone (888) BOWKER9 & (905) 415-5837, fax (905) 479-6266. German speaking Europe—K.G. Saur Verlag, Munich, Germany, phone 49-89-76902-232, fax 49-89-76902-250, email 100730.1341@compuserve.com, web www.saur.de/home.htm. Rest of Europe incl. United Kingdom plus Africa & Asia—Bowker-Saur, W. Sussex, UK, phone 44-1342-326-972, fax 44-1342-335-612, email customer@bowker-saur.co.uk, web www.bowker-saur.com/service/. Australia/New Zealand—Thorpe, Port Melbourne, Victoria, Australia, phone 61-03-9-245-7370, fax 61-03-9-245-7395, email customer.service@thorpe.com.au, web www.thorpe.com.au. Technical support for CD ROMs (800) 323-3288, fax 908) 665-3528, email techsupport@bowker.com.

DIALOG® is the oldest and largest online information service, comprised of over 470 databases from an array of disciplines, including business, US and international news, patents and trademarks, science and technology and consumer news. DIALOG SELECT provides a web based guided search service with access to 250 DIALOG databases for people with little or no database search expertise. It is designed to meet the specific information needs of professional end users in the technology, pharmaceutical, legal, consumer product and media industries. DIALOG@SITE is an intranet-based service providing access to the current DIALOG ONDISC™ CD ROM collection, using Internet browser capabilities. Companies will have wide access to an array of fields, such as business, science, technology, medicine and law through their local Intranet. DIALOG is a service mark of the Dialog Corporation and is exclusively distributed in Canada by Infomart Dialog Limited. For subscriptions and rate information for all services in Canada, contact Infomart Dialog Limited at (416) 442-2198 or (800) 668-9215. In the US call Dialog (Knight Ridder Information, Inc.) in Mountain View, California at (800) 3-DIALOG, web site www.dialog.com.

DIRECTORIES IN PRINT identifies over 15,000 directories (local, regional, national and international) which are organized in 26 subject chapters. An alternate formats index includes directories in online databases, CD ROM, diskettes, microfiche and mailing labels and lists. $489 for 2 volumes. Gale Group, P.O. Box 9187, Farmington Hills, MI 48333-9187. Toll free US and Canada (800) 877-GALE (4253) and (248) 699-GALE, fax (800) 414-5043 and (248) 699-8061, Internet orders galeord@galegroup.com, web site www.galegroup.com or www.gale.com. All Gale Group products are available on approval. Contact Gale for details.

GALE DIRECTORY OF DATABASES identifies over 12,000 international databases available in a variety of formats including online, CD ROM, diskette, and others. Entries include producer name, description, subject, language, cost, update frequency, geographic coverage. Volume 1, Online Databases, $260. Volume 2, CD-ROM, Diskette, Magnetic Tape, Handheld and Batch Access Database Products, $170. Both volumes $390. ONLINE MAGAZINE described this as "An excellent directory of online databases." Gale Group, P.O. Box 9187, Farmington Hills, MI 48333-9187. Toll free US and Canada (800) 877-GALE (4253) and (248) 699-GALE, fax (800) 414-5043 and (248) 699-8061, Internet orders galeord@galegroup.com, web site

www.galegroup.com or www.gale.com. All Gale Group products are available on approval. Contact Gale for details.

GALE DIRECTORY OF DATABASES ONLINE is a GaleNet database on the Internet that identifies over 12,000 international databases in various formats, including CD ROM, diskettes, online and others. Check your local library for free access or contact Gale for annual subscription rates. Gale Group, P.O. Box 9187, Farmington Hills, MI 48333-9187. Toll free US and Canada (800) 877-GALE (4253) and (248) 699-GALE, fax (800) 414-5043 and (248) 699-8061, Internet orders galeord@galegroup.com, web site www.galegroup.com or www.gale.com. All Gale Group products are available on approval. Contact Gale for details.

GaleNet is an online resource on the Internet that provides an integrated, one-step access to the most frequently used Gale databases, such as GALE'S READY REFERENCE SHELF ONLINE. As GaleNet's capabilities are constantly changing and being upgraded, contact the publisher for details and prices. Gale Group, P.O. Box 9187, Farmington Hills, MI 48333-9187. Toll free US and Canada (800) 877-GALE (4253) and (248) 699-GALE, fax (800) 414-5043 and (248) 699-8061, Internet orders galeord@galegroup.com, web site www.galegroup.com or www.gale.com. All Gale Group products are available on approval. Contact Gale for details.

HARVARD BUSINESS SCHOOL'S BAKER LIBRARY in Boston provides an outstanding consumer marketing web site at www.library.hbs.edu/. This web site identifies extensive sources of information on consumer marketing, including retail both for job hunters and researchers. It includes associations, membership directories, information on direct mail, public relations, corporate communications, online direct mail and online Dun and Bradstreet Credit Reports.

While the access to the web site itself is free and available to anyone, access to the CAREER ADVISOR database is available only to current Harvard Business School students and Harvard Business School Alumni Advisors (Harvard Business School alumni who have agreed to serve as Career advisors to current students and other alumni). The Advisor Database can be searched by industry, geography, job function, job title, year of graduation and company name. In addition, Reference Librarians at the Harvard Business School can conduct searches for a fee. Hundreds of databases are available. Ask at the Reference Desk for more information. For example, Dun & Bradstreet's Credit Reports are a lucrative source of information about privately held companies.

INFOMART DIRECT is a satellite service produced by Infomart Dialog Limited that delivers consolidated news feeds and provides full text print and broadcast sources to the end-user's office computer or LAN. Sources include Canadian daily newspapers, Canadian and international newswire services, including Southam News, Canada NewsWire, and Agence-France Presse, select television broadcast transcripts from major Canadian networks, CBC and CTV, industry trade publications, including Daily Oil Bulletin, Eco/Log Week, Canadian Underwriter, Canadian Business and Marketing Magazine. For Subscriptions and rate information, contact Infomart Dialog Limited at (416) 442-2198 or (800) 668-9215. DIALOG is a service mark of the Dialog Corporation.

INFOMART ON CD is available to CD ROM subscribers from IHS Micromedia Ltd. A full range of Canadian daily newspapers is available on both the KIOSK and VOYAGEUR platforms. KIOSK offers coverage for The Daily News (Halifax), The Gazette (Montréal), Ottawa Citizen, Toronto Star, Toronto Sun, The Spectator (Hamilton), Calgary Herald, Edmonton Journal, The Province (Vancouver), Vancouver Sun, The Financial Post and broadcast news transcripts. On the VOYAGEUR platform, Canadian NewsDisc is available as a complete package, either quarterly or monthly. For Subscriptions and rate information, contact Infomart Dialog Limited at (416) 442-2198 or (800) 668-9215. DIALOG is a service mark of the Dialog Corporation.

INFORMATION IN CANADA—A DIRECTORY OF ELECTRONIC AND SUPPORT RESOURCES provides electronic information on information resources, consultants and information brokers, library based online research services, library automation software, computer accessible library catalogues and a directory of information industry services, plus a large section on databases produced in Canada. Price reduced to $49.95 for 1996 edition. Canada Library Association, 200 Elgin Street, Suite 602, Ottawa, Ontario K2P 1L5 CANADA, (613) 232-9625, fax (613) 563-9895,web site www.cla.amlibs.ca includes an online catalog. Email bj491@freenet.carleton.ca.

INFORMATION SOURCES was an award winning directory published by the Gale Group in partnership with the Information Industry Association (IIA). At the time of this writing, the IIA has merged with the Software Publishers Association (SPA) to form the newly named Software and Information Industry Association (SIIA).

This directory provides information for the 550 member companies of the Information Industry Association. Entries include company name, address, phone, names of executives, regional offices, trade and brand names and description of products and services. Indexed by product, personal name, trade name, geography, parent company, international, and niche markets. The directory also identifies publishers, database producers, online services, telecommunications and network providers, system integrators and many others. $125. Contact Gale for information as to when an updated directory will be available. In the meantime, visit the Software and Information Industry's web site at www.siia.net to see their membership roster.

Gale Group, P.O. Box 9187, Farmington Hills, MI 48333-9187. Toll free US and Canada (800) 877-GALE (4253) and (248) 699-GALE, fax (800) 414-5043 and (248) 699-8061, Internet orders galeord@galegroup.com, web site www.galegroup.com or www.gale.com. All Gale Group products are available on approval. Contact Gale for details.

Software & Information Industry Association (SIIA), formerly the Software Publishers Association (SPA) and Information Industry Association (IIA) is located at 1730 M Street, NW, Washington, DC 20036, (202) 452-1600, www.siia.net.

www.library.hbs.edu/ is the URL for the Harvard Business School Baker Library, which contains free excellent information on consumer marketing, retail, associations, membership directories, direct mail, public relations, corporate communications, online direct mail and more. Dun and Bradstreet Credit Reports can also be accessed. In addition, for a fee, reference librarians can conduct online searches from any of several hundred databases. See "Harvard Business School's Baker Library" above.

Organization Charts

See Corporate Affiliations and Subsidiaries

ANNUAL REPORTS sometimes contain organization charts. Sometimes organization charts appear in other company publications, such as "fact books," brochures, sales literature and so forth. The way to locate them is to call the company, request an annual report, a 10(k) and a proxy, and "any other information that would help you gain an understanding of how the company is organized." However, do note that org charts nonetheless do appear very rarely. But you never know when one will show up.

CONFERENCE BOARD sells its members organization charts of a select number of companies. The Conference Board, 845 Third Avenue, New York, New York 10022, (212) 339-0345.

INTERVIEWS OF POTENTIAL CANDIDATES (prospects) provide an opportunity to obtain organization chart information. During the interview, ask the person to explain where he or she fits into the organization. You can sketch out the information yourself during the interview, or you can hand the prospect a pad and ask him or her to do so. There are two reasons why you need this information. First, in terms of evaluating the appropriateness of the individual for your search, you have a legitimate need to know the title of the person whom the candidate reports to, as well as that person's boss, plus the number and titles of the candidate's peers, the titles of the candidate's direct reports. Even if you only obtain titles, this is extremely valuable information in helping you ascertain that you're interviewing someone at the right level and in the right part of the organization. Second, this organizational information is extremely useful for conducting additional ID research into that company. Naturally, a skilled interviewer will know "where to draw the line" in asking for sensitive information so as to avoid offending the interviewee.

Once the prospect is already talking about the organization, it will probably be easier to find out if there are other parts of the company where similar business activities occur. If it is large, there may be several places to search for talent. Further, during the course of the interview, if you determine that the prospect is not a good fit and will not proceed further, you could inform the candidate during the interview and then source him or her, asking what other parts of the company are appropriate. Of course, this may not be appropriate with every candidate you close out. Depending on how good a rapport you've established, and how loyal the person feels to the company (perhaps he or she has already left the company), you must exercise good judgment before you start requesting sensitive information. It might be effective to say something like, "Gee, it sure would make my job a lot easier if you would help me understand where else I might look in ABC Enterprises. Of course, your name would be kept totally confidential."

Do note, however, if the interviewee will be presented to the company, then your primary mission is to "handle the candidate." You absolutely should avoid the risk of offending him or her by gathering research that will obviously be used to find more candidates!

ORGANIZATION CHARTS is a working collection of 200 power structures of a diverse range of companies—large and small, international and local, public and private, for profit and not for profit. $150. At the time of this writing, this reference was last published in 1996. Contact the publisher for information about an updated edition. Gale Group, P.O. Box 9187, Farmington Hills, MI 48333-9187. Toll free US and Canada (800) 877-GALE (4253) and (248) 699-GALE, fax (800) 414-5043 and (248) 699-8061, Internet orders galeord@galegroup.com, web site www.galegroup.com or www.gale.com. All Gale Group products are available on approval. Contact Gale for details.

STRATEGIC INFORMATION SERVICE GUIDE TO KEY PERSONNEL IN THE TOP 50 NEW ZEALAND COMPANIES is a superb resource that includes organization charts, an overview of business activities, and contact details. For more information contact the public library in Nelson, New Zealand or the publisher, Strategic Information Service, P.O. Box 33-1039, Takapuna, New Zealand, phone 64-9-309-3657, fax 64-9-309-6828.

WHO'S NEWS in the *Wall Street Journal* and similar columns in other newspapers and trade journals provide a wealth of information about management changes and promotions. A good candidate who has been passed over for promotion might be especially amenable to an overture from a recruiter. Also, organizations in a state of change often have positions to fill, so there could be needs a recruiting firm can address. Even though a company might have a relationship with a large search firm, it could still make sense for a recruiter to nurture a new business relationship for several reasons. First, large companies usually like to dole out business to numerous search firms for off limits reasons, in other words, to prevent as many search firms as possible from seeking talent at their companies. Second, since search consultants often say, "You're only as good as your last search," it's smart to stay in touch with a growing company. In other words, how long do you think it will take an arrogant firm to mess up an assignment with an important company? Your next new client might materialize if you happen to be waiting on the sidelines at the right time—and, as they say, "Timing is everything." Who's News and similar columns will give also give you a pulse on where internal change and reorganizations are occurring. Also, from the standpoint of providing important organization information, these columns sometimes clarify that, too.

Outplacement

DIRECTORY OF OUTPLACEMENT FIRMS provides information on over 200 firms, staff size, revenues, fees, key principals, feature articles and statistics. $74.95. Kennedy Information, One Kennedy Place, Route 12 South, Fitzwilliam, NH 03447, phone (800) 531-0007 or 603-585-6544, fax 603-585-9555, email bookstore@kennedyinfo.com, web site www.kennedyinfo.com.

www.kennedyinfo.com is the web site for publisher Kennedy Information. It includes books, newsletters, training materials, directories, and surveys for executive recruiting, human resources, outplacement, management consulting and job seekers. (800) 531-0007, or (603) 585-6544.

P

Pacific

See Asia, Australia, New Zealand, International

ASIA PACIFIC SATELLITE INDUSTRY DIRECTORY, Phillips Business Information, Inc., a Phillips Publishing International Company, 120 Seven Locks Road, Potomac, MD 20854, (301) 340-1520, (301) 340-7788, (800) 777-5006, Internet pbi@phillips.com, web site www.phillips.com.

DIRECTORY OF AMERICAN FIRMS OPERATING IN FOREIGN COUNTRIES, REGIONAL EDITION—AUSTRALIA GROUP. Includes Australia, New Zealand, Fiji French Polynesia, Guam, New Caledonia, New Guinea, North Mariana Island, Palau, Papua, Polynesia. Ordering information: Uniworld Business Publications, Inc., 257 Central Park West, Suite 10A, New York, NY 10024-4110, (212) 496-2448, fax (212) 769-0413, email uniworldbp@aol.com. Web site: http://www.uniworldbp.com.

DIRECTORY OF CONSUMER BRANDS AND THEIR OWNERS provides information on 50,000 brands in 56 countries and detailed information about the companies that own and manage them. Asia Pacific edition $990. Latin America edition $990. Eastern Europe edition $990. Europe edition $1,190 for 2 volumes. Published by Euromonitor (England). Distributed by Gale Group, P.O. Box 9187, Farmington Hills, MI 48333-9187. Toll free US and Canada (800) 877-GALE (4253) and (248) 699-GALE, fax (800) 414-5043 and (248) 699-8061, Internet orders galeord@galegroup.com, web site www.galegroup.com or www.gale.com. All Gale Group products are available on approval. Contact Gale for details.

KEY BUSINESS DIRECTORY OF INDONESIA/PHILIPPINES/THAILAND contains information on 4,000 companies with more than 50 employees. Dun & Bradstreet, Business Reference Solutions, Three Sylvan Way, Parsippany, NJ 07054 USA. (800) 526-0651. Email dnbmdd@mail.dnb.com. Web site http://www.dnbmdd.com.

MAJOR COMPANIES SERIES ON CD ROM consists of Graham & Whiteside's annual directories of major international companies. All six directories reside on one disk. After payment, you'll receive a security code to access the region(s) you select. This Windows™ based CD can navigate by company name, company locations, executive names, business activity and more. Free demo CD ROM is available. Regions also available separately for Europe, Central & Eastern Europe, the Far East and Australasia, the Arab World, Africa, and Latin America. For prices and availability, contact the Gale Group, P.O. Box 9187, Farmington Hills, MI 48333-9187. Toll free US and Canada (800) 877-GALE (4253) and (248) 699-GALE, fax (800) 414-5043 and (248) 699-8061, Internet orders galeord@galegroup.com, web site www.galegroup.com or www.gale.com. All Gale Group products are available on approval. Contact Gale for details.

MAJOR ENERGY COMPANIES OF THE FAR EAST & AUSTRALASIA provides information on over 500 leading energy companies in the Asia Pacific, $415. US distributor: Larry Meranus Professional Publications & Services, 4 Demoray Court, Pine Brook, NJ 07058, (800) MERANUS or (800) 637-2687. Published by Graham & Whiteside Ltd., Tuition House, 5-6 Francis Grove, London SW19 4DT, England. Web site http://www.major-co-data.com. Email sales@major-co-data.com.

MAJOR FINANCIAL INSTITUTIONS OF THE FAR EAST & AUSTRALASIA contains information on over 1,500 Asia/Pacific financial institutions. $450. US distributor: Larry Meranus Professional Publications & Services, 4 Demoray Court, Pine Brook, NJ 07058, (800) MERANUS or (800) 637-2687. Published by Graham & Whiteside Ltd., Tuition House, 5-6 Francis Grove, London SW19 4DT, England. Web site http://www.major-co-data.com. Email sales@major-co-data.com.

Pakistan

See Asia, International

DIRECTORY OF AMERICAN FIRMS OPERATING IN FOREIGN COUNTRIES, REGIONAL EDITION —ASIA. Includes Bangladesh, Brunei, Cambodia, China, Hong Kong, India, Indonesia, Japan, Korea, Laos, Macau, Malaysia, Mongolia, Myanmar, Nepal, Pakistan, Philippines, Singapore, Sri Lanka, Taiwan, Thailand, Vietnam. $119 Ordering information: Uniworld Business Publications, Inc., 257 Central Park West, Suite 10A, New York, NY 10024-4110, (212) 496-2448, fax (212) 769-0413, email uniworldbp@aol.com. Web site: http://www.uniworldbp.com.

DIRECTORY OF AMERICAN FIRMS OPERATING IN FOREIGN COUNTRIES, REGIONAL EDITION—SOUTH ASIA. Includes Bangladesh, India, Myanmar, Nepal, Pakistan, Sri Lanka. $39. Ordering information: Uniworld Business Publications, Inc., 257 Central Park West, Suite 10A, New York,

NY 10024-4110, (212) 496-2448, fax (212) 769-0413, email uniworldbp@aol.com. Web site: http://www.uniworldbp.com.

MAJOR COMPANIES OF SOUTH WEST ASIA provides names of 39,000 contacts at 6,000 companies, description of business activities, brand names and trademarks, branches and subsidiaries, number of employees, date of establishment, and three indexes. Countries included are Bangladesh, Bhutan, Iran, Nepal, Pakistan, Sri Lanka and Turkey. Hardback directory $450. Standard CD ROM $675. Premium CD ROM $1,150. CD ROMs are published quarterly. US distributor: Larry Meranus Professional Publications & Services, 4 Demoray Court, Pine Brook, NJ 07058, (800) MERANUS or (800) 637-2687. Published by Graham & Whiteside Ltd., Tuition House, 5-6 Francis Grove, London SW19 4DT, England. Web site http://www.major-co-data.com. Email sales@major-co-data.com.

Paper

See Pulp and Paper

Pension Funds

AMERICA'S CORPORATE FINANCE DIRECTORY provides a financial profile of the US's leading 5,000 public and private companies. It includes information about the company's pension plan, names of contacts, and a listing of over 17,000 wholly owned US subsidiaries. The title appears previously to have been The Corporate Finance Bluebook. $585. If the price is prohibitively high, remember your local library. National Register Publishing, Reed Elsevier-New Providence, 121 Chanlon Road, New Providence, NJ 07974, (800) 521-8110, fax (800) 836-7736, web site www.redbooks.com or www.marquiswhoswho.com. "If, for any reason whatsoever, your order does not fully meet your expectations, simply return the product within 30 days for a prompt, complete, unquestioned refund," as stated in Catalog of Biographical and Professional References of publisher Marquis Who's Who/National Register Publishing.

CONSULTANT DIRECTORY profiles the top 400 consulting organizations that specifically serve the pension and investment industries. Includes career biographical information, including education, number of years with the firm, specialties, employment history, direct dial phone number and email address. $295. Published by Standard & Poors, a division of McGraw-Hill, MONEY MARKET DIRECTORIES, INC., 320 East Main Street, Charlottesville, VA 22902, http://www.mmdaccess.com, (800) 446-2810, (804) 977-1450.

CORPORATE FINANCE SOURCEBOOK—THE GUIDE TO MAJOR INVESTMENT SOURCES AND RELATED FINANCIAL SERVICES contains over 13,000 names of executives at 3,700 organizations that, broadly speaking, supply growth capital to businesses, such as venture capital lenders, private lenders, commercial finance and factoring, pension managers, master trusts. Names of key management are included. A special section details public offerings of the past 3 years and mergers and acquisitions over $100 million. $499.95 hard copy, excluding discounts. NRP's catalog states, "If you're dissatisfied for any reason, simply return the product within 30 days for a full refund." If the price is prohibitively high, remember your local library. Available in book, online, magnetic tape, and in mailing list formats. For more information contact: National Register Publishing, 121 Chanlon Road, New Providence, NJ 07974 USA, (800) 521-8110, http://www.lexis-nexis.com. For information about online access, call LEXIS®—NEXIS® Online Services, Mountainview, CA at (800) 346-9759; for mailing lists call Cahners Direct Marketing Services at (800) 323-4958; all other inquiries (800) 521-8110.

DIRECTORY OF PLAN SPONSORS/NELSON S PLAN SPONSORS contains comprehensive information on the pension and endowment industry, including key executives, investment style, level of risk, current investment interest, externally and internally managed funds, investment managers used, consultants and more. Includes 8,500 corporate sponsors, 2,700 endowments and foundations, 1,600 unions, 1,000 hospitals and 900 public /government funds. Available in two versions, alphabetically by sponsor name and geographically by metropolitan area. Published annually. $495. Nelson Information, P.O. Box 591, Port Chester, NY 10573 USA. (800) 333-6357, Phone outside the US (914) 937-8400, Fax (914) 937-8590, web site http://www.nelnet.com.

INSTITUTIONAL INVESTOR publishes excellent surveys of various Wall Street industries. Generally one survey appears in each monthly issue, including names of contacts. Annual subscription $325. INSTITUTIONAL INVESTOR, 488 Madison Avenue, New York, NY 10022, (212) 303-3300.

INSTITUTIONAL MARKETPLACE CD ROM is a relational database the provides information on 14,000 plan sponsors, 3,400 institutional money managers, 400 pension fund consultants, and 80,000 key business executives in those organizations. Updated quarterly, IBM compatible PC required. Free demo disk available. For more information contact Nelson Information, P.O. Box 591, Port Chester, NY 10573 USA. (800) 333-6357, Phone outside the US (914) 937-8400, Fax (914) 937-8590, web site http://www.nelnet.com.

MMD ACCESS for Windows is software exclusively designed for investment management sales and marketing professionals. It identifies over 42,000 Corporate, union and government pension plan sponsors, including over 40,000 defined benefit officers and over 55,000 Defined Contribution Investment Officers and more. Published by Standard & Poors, a division of McGraw-Hill, MONEY MARKET DIRECTORIES, INC., 320 East Main Street, Charlottesville, VA 22902, http://www.mmdaccess.com, (800) 446-2810, (804) 977-1450.

MONEY MARKET DIRECTORY OF PENSION FUNDS AND THEIR INVESTMENT MANAGERS provides plan sponsor profiles, including firm name, address, phone and fax, senior investment officers, names of other key personnel and decision makes including in house asset manager, officer handling inquiries from money managers, officer who evaluates money managers, officer who handles responses to requests for proposals, benefits administrator, chief human resources officer, investor relations officer, corporate cash manager, director of development for endowments some direct dial phone numbers and personal email addresses. The Directory also profiles investment management firms that invest pension assets and investment manager consultant firms. Published by Standard & Poors, a division of McGraw-Hill, MONEY MARKET DIRECTORIES, INC., 320 East Main Street, Charlottesville, VA 22902, http://www.mmdaccess.com, (800) 446-2810, (804) 977-1450. Regional Directories also available. $995 per copy MONEY MARKET DIRECTORY, $150 per additional REGIONAL DIRECTORY.

NELSON FINANCIAL DATABASE provides comprehensive information on the global institutional investment market. Information formatted to your precise needs is available from Nelson Information Mailing List & Customized Database service. The NELSON FINANCIAL DATABASE is comprised of:

    30,000 executives at investment management firms
    11,000 executives at research firms
    100,000 executives at public companies
    40,000 executives at plan sponsors
    3,000 executives at pension fund consulting firms
    24,000 executives at institutional real estate firms
    4,000 executives at technology based vendors

The database also consists of extensive investment information, including money manager performance, peer group analysis, special surveys and more. For customers who with to use Nelson's information in their own systems, Nelson will supply customized data export, using all or any data items. Mailing lists are also available for direct marketers. For more information, contact Nelson Mailing List & Customized Database Services, P.O. Box 591, Port Chester, NY 10573 USA. (800) 333-6357, Phone outside the US (914) 937-8400, Fax (914) 937-8590, web site http://www.nelnet.com.

NELSON'S PENSION FUND CONSULTANTS identifies some 2,500 professional consultants at over 300 global pension consulting firms. Listings include names of key executives, phone numbers, services provided, and more. Published annually. $350. Nelson Information, P.O. Box 591, Port Chester, NY 10573 USA. (800) 333-6357, Phone outside the US (914) 937-8400, Fax (914) 937-8590, web site http://www.nelnet.com.

PENSION AND INVESTMENTS is a biweekly trade publication. Crain Communications, Inc. is headquartered in Chicago with offices in major cities throughout the US plus London, Tokyo and Frankfurt. New York location: 220 East 42nd Street, New York, NY 10017, (212) 210-0100, Circulation (800) 678-9595. Annual subscription $205, two years $365.

PENSION FUNDS AND THEIR ADVISERS provides information on the top 2,000 pension funds in the United Kingdom, plus major funds of Japan, Belgium, France, Germany, Ireland, The Netherlands and

Switzerland. This Directory is the only source in the US that monitors the growth of assets in the international market. Information includes internal and external fund management contacts, major US and Canadian pension funds and money managers, major European and Japanese pension funds and their advisors. It also includes comprehensive listings of 900 advisors to the pension fund industry including financial advisers, accountants, actuaries and pension fund consultants, pension administrators, insurance companies, attorneys, computer services, global custody, pension trustees, pension /financial recruitment consultants, investment research, associations and professional groups, and publications. $310. Published by A.P. Information Services, Ltd. Marketed exclusively in North America MONEY MARKET DIRECTORIES INC./STANDARD AND POORS, 320 East Main Street, Charlottesville, VA 22902, http://www.mmdaccess.com, (800) 446-2810, (804) 977-1450.

PENSIONSCOPE DATASYSTEMS is a database service from MONEY MARKET DIRECTORIES, a division of STANDARD AND POORS. Their database will help you select key decision makers in the pension funds, pension service companies, institutional asset managers, and the nonprofit marketplaces of public and private foundations, endowments and health service organizations. Selections can be based on job function, asset size, type of organization or plan, and geographic location. Selected information available as labels, printouts on index cards or sheets of paper, on magnetic tape, or on disk (minimum $500 order). For more information call Standard & Poors, a division of McGraw-Hill, MONEY MARKET DIRECTORIES, INC., 320 East Main Street, Charlottesville, VA 22902, http://www.mmdaccess.com, (800) 446-2810, (804) 977-1450.

People's Republic of China

See Asia, China, International, Hong Kong

ASIAN HOTELIER is a hospitality trade newspaper with an emphasis on the PRC's hotel development. Produced in English and Chinese. 11 issues per year. Contact publisher for price. Cahners Business Information, 19/F, 8 Commercial Tower, 8 Sun Yip Street, Chaiwan, Hong Kong, (011) 852-2965-1555, fax (011) 852-2976-0706, email hotelier@hk.super.net. Headquarters: Cahners Business Information, 275 Washington Street, Newton, MA 02158-1630, (617) 558-4663 or (617) 964-3030, fax (617) 558-4700, email marketaccess@cahners.com. Web sites www.cahners.com or www.chilton.net.

CHINA: A DIRECTORY AND SOURCEBOOK includes information on 800 of China's and Hong Kong's companies, rankings for the top 50 companies, and over 500 information sources, both national and international. $595. Published by Euromonitor (England). Distributed by Gale Group, P.O. Box 9187, Farmington Hills, MI 48333-9187. Toll free US and Canada (800) 877-GALE (4253) and (248) 699-GALE, fax (800) 414-5043 and (248) 699-8061, Internet orders galeord@galegroup.com, web site www.galegroup.com or www.gale.com. All Gale Group products are available on approval. Contact Gale for details.

DIRECTORY OF AMERICAN FIRMS OPERATING IN FOREIGN COUNTRIES, REGIONAL EDITION—CHINA GROUP. Includes China, Hong Kong, Singapore, Taiwan, Macau. $79. Uniworld Business Publications, Inc., 257 Central Park West, Suite 10A, New York, NY 10024-4110, (212) 496-2448, fax (212) 769-0413, email uniworldbp@aol.com. Web site: http://www.uniworldbp.com.

DIRECTORY OF FOREIGN FIRMS OPERATING IN THE UNITED STATES, REGIONAL EDITION—CHINA GROUP. Includes China, Hong Kong, Singapore, Taiwan. $29. Uniworld Business Publications, Inc., 257 Central Park West, Suite 10A, New York, NY 10024-4110, (212) 496-2448, fax (212) 769-0413, email uniworldbp@aol.com. Web site: http://www.uniworldbp.com.

DUN'S DIRECTORY OF MAJOR CORPORATIONS IN PEOPLE'S REPUBLIC OF CHINA is a two volume set with information on 20,000 major corporations in the PRC. Business categories include financial institutions, foreign invested enterprises, importers/exporters, and manufacturers. Over 80% of the corporations listed have more than 50 employees. Because only one executive name is provided per company, this reference is most suitable for target list development. However, once you've developed a target list, you can consult a business librarian as to the best way to conduct an electronic literature search to obtain names and other information. Better yet, make some telephone inquiries to PRC experts to locate research in English published in Asia. Listings in DUN'S DIRECTORY OF MAJOR CORPORATIONS IN PEOPLE'S REPUBLIC OF CHINA are presented alphabetically within four main business categories and cross-referenced by province, industry and company name in English. In English and Chinese. Published annually. For prices call Dun & Bradstreet at (800) 526-0651. For more information contact Dun & Bradstreet, Business Reference Solutions, Three Sylvan Way, Parsippany, NJ 07054. Email dnbmdd@mail.dnb.com. Web site http://www.dnbmdd.com.

DUN'S GUIDE TO KEY DECISION MAKERS IN HONG KONG identifies some 8,000 directors and senior executives at 1,500 businesses in Hong Kong—an average of two names per company. Also provides information on presence in the People's Republic of China. All companies listed have annual sales of at least $200 million or total employees of 150 or more. Published annually. For prices call Dun & Bradstreet at (800) 526-0651. For more information contact Dun & Bradstreet, Business Reference Solutions, Three Sylvan Way, Parsippany, NJ 07054. Email dnbmdd@mail.dnb.com. Web site http://www.dnbmdd.com.

EDN CHINA is a monthly magazine for China's electronic original equipment manufacturers. Call publisher for price. EDN China/Cahners Business Information, 10th floor, STIP Building, 22 Bai Wan Zhuang Road, Beijing, China, (011) 8610-6832-7920, fax (011) 8610-6832-8356, email ednc@public3.bta.net.cn, URL www.cahners.com/mainmag/ednc.htm. Headquarters: EDN Worldwide Editorial, 275 Washington Street, Newton, MA 02158-1630, (617) 558-4454 or (617) 964-3030, fax (617) 558-4470, URL www.ednmag.com.

Periodicals

ABI GLOBAL and **ABI INFORM** are highly respected databases published by UMI in Ann Arbor, Michigan, a Bell and Howell company. Available in CD ROM and online, ABI allows you to search massive amounts of periodical literature. If you must conduct a literature search for anything, this is one of the first places you should look. Some libraries, such as the New York City Public Library, offer free courses in how to use ABI and other databases. Call your local library for more information.

Ordering information: UMI, 300 North Zeeb Road, Ann Arbor, Michigan 48106 (800) 521-0600, Sales (800) 521-3042, email: pprice@umi.com.

ASAHIYA is a bookstore that specializes in Japanese publications. While most are popular in nature and written in Japanese, there are some directories and business publications in English, such as those from JETRO, the Japan External Trade Organization. A store is located at the corner of Vanderbilt and 45th Street, near Grand Central Station in Manhattan. Check other major cities for an Asahiya book store near you.

BACON'S INFORMATION provides a news clipping and analysis service which can be used to monitor competitive news, to conduct topic research, or to track "pickup" of press releases. For more information, call BACON'S CLIPPING BUREAU to inquire about ExpressClips (same day coverage of top media in key markets), Electronic Clipping (database retrieval of transcripts from a wide selection of publications), International Clipping (coverage for specific countries worldwide) and Clip Analysis Reports (for a review of your own press coverage). (800) 621-0561, (800) 753-6675. Bacon's Information, Inc., a K-III Communications Company, 332 South Michigan Avenue, Chicago, IL 60604.

BACON'S MEDIASOURCE CD ROM is a media database and software with over 250,000 names of contacts at over 48,000 media outlets, including newspapers and their bureaus, magazines and newsletters, news syndicates, wire services, broadcast networks, stations and shows, including phone, fax, email and home page. Updated quarterly. Available for Windows and Macintosh. $1,095 annual subscription. Ordering information: Call (800) 621-0561, (800) 753-6675. Bacon's Information, Inc., a K-III Communications Company, 332 South Michigan Avenue, Chicago, IL 60604.

BACON'S NEWSPAPER/MAGAZINE DIRECTORY is a two volume set that identifies every daily and weekly newspaper in the US, every magazine and newsletter in the US that accepts outside editorial, detailed listings of editorial staffs, with phone, fax and email, publication Internet home pages and other online locations, magazine editorial profiles and types of press materials accepted, syndicated columnists by beat, news services and news syndicates, and indexes of newspapers by market and circulation. Includes names and titles, editors' preferences, like/dislikes and "beat" reporter information to help you find the right contact. $275. Ordering information: Call (800) 621-0561, (800) 753-6675. Bacon's Information, Inc., a K-III Communications Company, 332 South Michigan Avenue, Chicago, IL 60604. Satisfaction guaranteed or a full refund within 30 days.

BUSINESS INFORMATION SOURCES by Lorna Daniells is an outstanding reference at any price. At $39.95 a copy, it's such an extraordinary value, it should have a place in every library. This is clearly one of the top three hard copy references around, and its reasonable price elevates it to first place. Business Information Sources provides a wealth of information routinely needed by search firms, job hunters and corporate recruiters, including general directories, specialized directories, professional associations, periodicals, industry information, international information, and much more. $39.95. Ordering information: Business Information Sources by Lorna Daniells, is published by the University of California Press (Berkeley, CA, Los Angeles, CA & Oxford, England) (510-642-4247). Orders are handled by California Princeton Fulfillment Services, P.O. Box 10769, Newark, NJ 07193-0769. (800-822-6657).

BUSINESS ORGANIZATIONS, AGENCIES AND PUBLICATIONS DIRECTORY contains 32 chapters including information on Canada, business information sources, web sites, and local chambers of commerce. $415. Gale Group, P.O. Box 9187, Farmington Hills, MI 48333-9187. Toll free US and Canada (800) 877-GALE (4253) and (248) 699-GALE, fax (800) 414-5043 and (248) 699-8061, Internet orders galeord@galegroup.com, web site www.galegroup.com or www.gale.com. All Gale Group products are available on approval. Contact Gale for details.

CANADIAN BUSINESS AND ECONOMICS: A GUIDE TO SOURCES OF INFORMATION lists information by subject, including books, periodicals and services. Fully indexed and thoroughly cross referenced. Price reduced to $39.95 for 1992 edition. Canada Library Association, 200 Elgin Street, Suite 602, Ottawa, Ontario K2P 1L5 CANADA, (613) 232-9625, fax (613) 563-9895, Internet: bj491@freenet.carleton.ca.

CANADIAN PERIODICAL INDEX is the standard bilingual resource to over 400 French and English journals, including more than 30 American titles, including 80 business journals. 11 issues per year plus an annual edition. For pricing and ordering information, call Gale Canada at (800) 701-9130.

CRAIN COMMUNICATIONS publishes the following trade journals:

ADVERTISING AGE
CREATIVITY
AUTOMOTIVE NEWS
AUTOWEEK
BUSINESS INSURANCE
BUSINESS MARKETING
CRAIN CHICAGO BUSINESS
CHICAGO BUSINESS WEB SITE
CRAIN CLEVELAND
CRAIN DETROIT
CRAIN NEW YORK
ELECTRONIC MEDIA
GLOBAL WIRELESS
INVESTMENT NEWS
MODERN HEALTHCARE
MODERN PHYSICIAN
NON-PROFIT NEWS
PENSION & INVESTMENTS
PLASTICS NEWS
RADIO COMMUNICATION REPORT
RUBBER & PLASTIC NEWS
TIRE BUSINESS
WASTE NEWS

Crain Communications, Inc. is headquartered in Chicago with offices in major cities throughout the US plus London, Tokyo and Frankfurt. New York location: 220 East 42nd Street, New York, NY 10017, (212) 210-0100, Circulation (800) 678-9595.

CRAIN PUBLICATIONS, headquartered in Chicago, publishes the following web sites for corresponding periodicals:

> www.AdAge.com
> www.autoweek.com
> www.businessinsurance.com
> www.crainschicagobusiness.com
> www.crainscleveland.com
> www.crainsdetroit.com
> www.crainsny.com
> emonline.com
> www.investmentnews.com
> www.modernhealthcare.com
> www.pionline.com
> www.plasticsnews.com
> www.rcrnews.com
> www.rubbernews.com
> www.tirebusiness.com
> www.wastenews.com
> www.globalwirelessnews.com

CYBERHOUND'S® GUIDE TO PUBLICATIONS ON THE INTERNET provides fully indexed information on over 3,000 Internet publications. Covers the World Wide Web, Gopher, Telnet and FTP sites that make online publication available to the public. $79. Gale Group, P.O. Box 9187, Farmington Hills, MI 48333-9187. Toll free US and Canada (800) 877-GALE (4253) and (248) 699-GALE, fax (800) 414-5043 and (248) 699-8061, Internet orders galeord@galegroup.com, web site www.galegroup.com or www.gale.com. All Gale Group products are available on approval. Contact Gale for details.

DIRECTORY OF BUSINESS INFORMATION RESOURCES, ASSOCIATIONS, NEWSLETTERS, MAGAZINES AND TRADESHOWS, published by Grey House Publishing, Pocket Knife Square, Lakeville, CT 06039, $199. (800) 562-2139, (860) 435-0868, web site www.greyhouse.com or books@il.com.

ENCYCLOPEDIA OF ASSOCIATIONS: INTERNATIONAL ORGANIZATIONS includes nearly 20,000 multinational and national organizations in foreign countries, including US based associations with multinational membership. Entries also include email addresses, web sites and bulletin board addresses, lobbying activities, and publication and convention information. Indexed by geography, keyword and executives. $595 for 2 volume set. Also available in CD ROM. Database available via commercial online service. Gale Group, P.O. Box 9187, Farmington Hills, MI 48333-9187. Toll free US and Canada (800) 877-GALE (4253) and (248) 699-GALE, fax (800) 414-5043 and (248) 699-8061, Internet orders galeord@galegroup.com, web site www.galegroup.com or www.gale.com. All Gale Group products are available on approval. Contact Gale for details.

ENCYCLOPEDIA OF ASSOCIATIONS: NATIONAL ORGANIZATIONS OF THE US. This superb reference is one of the first places you should look when beginning a new recruiting assignment or when looking for specialized references of any type. The keyword index makes this comprehensive reference easy to use, even in hard copy. For over 23,000 nonprofit professional associations with a national scope, this encyclopedia reveals:

• Publications, including membership rosters and newsletters

• Dates and locations of association conferences and conventions

• Names of Executive Directors, who are usually incredible sources of industry information if you call and speak to them

• Committees

• Job and candidate referral banks, which can provide resumes of other industry sources and sometimes candidates

- It includes organizations in these categories: business, trade, environmental, agricultural, legal, governmental, engineering, technological, scientific, educational, cultural, social welfare, health & medical, public affairs, ethnic, labor unions, chambers of commerce, tourism, & others.

Volume 1, National Organizations of the US, $505
Volume 2, Geographic and Executive Indexes, $390
Volume 3, Supplement, $405

Gale Group, P.O. Box 9187, Farmington Hills, MI 48333-9187. Toll free US and Canada (800) 877-GALE (4253) and (248) 699-GALE, fax (800) 414-5043 and (248) 699-8061, Internet orders galeord@galegroup.com, web site www.galegroup.com or www.gale.com. All Gale Group products are available on approval. Contact Gale for details.

ENCYCLOPEDIA OF ASSOCIATIONS: REGIONAL, STATE AND LOCAL ORGANIZATIONS. The information in this directory is not duplicated anywhere in ENCYCLOPEDIA OF ASSOCIATIONS. Over 100,000 nonprofit organizations are included in this directory. $585 for 5 volume set or $140 per individual volume. Also available on CD ROM and online on the Internet through a GaleNet subscription.

Volume 1, Great Lakes States (Illinois, Indiana, Michigan, Minnesota, Ohio, Wisconsin)
Volume 2, Northeastern States (Connecticut, Maine, Massachusetts, New Hampshire, New Jersey, New York, Pennsylvania, Rhode Islands, Vermont)
Volume 3, Southern and Middle Atlantic States (Including Puerto Rico and the Virgin Islands) (Alabama, Delaware, Washington, DC, Florida, Georgia, Kentucky, Maryland, Mississippi, North Carolina, Puerto Rico, South Carolina, Tennessee, Virginia, West Virginia, Virgin Islands)
Volume 4, South Central and Great Plains States (Arkansas, Iowa, Kansas, Louisiana, Missouri, Nebraska, North Dakota, Oklahoma, South Dakota, Texas)
Volume 5, Western States (Alaska, Arizona, California, Colorado, Guam, Hawaii, Idaho, Montana, Nevada, New Mexico, Oregon, Utah, Washington, Wyoming)

Gale Group, P.O. Box 9187, Farmington Hills, MI 48333-9187. Toll free US and Canada (800) 877-GALE (4253) and (248) 699-GALE, fax (800) 414-5043 and (248) 699-8061, Internet orders galeord@galegroup.com, web site www.galegroup.com or www.gale.com. All Gale Group products are available on approval. Contact Gale for details.

ENCYCLOPEDIA OF BUSINESS INFORMATION SOURCES will lead you to specialized directories, professional associations, trade publications, newsletters, databases, Internet resources and more. It's an excellent reference and a great way to find key resources in any industry fast. $330. Gale Group, P.O. Box 9187, Farmington Hills, MI 48333-9187. Toll free US and Canada (800) 877-GALE (4253) and (248) 699-GALE, fax (800) 414-5043 and (248) 699-8061, Internet orders galeord@galegroup.com, web site www.galegroup.com or www.gale.com. All Gale Group products are available on approval. Contact Gale for details.

GALE'S READY REFERENCE SHELF ONLINE is a GaleNet Internet resource that provides integrated access to databases covering national, regional, state, local and international associations, publishers, newspapers and periodicals, directories, newsletters, online databases, portable databases, database products and vendors, special libraries and research centers. Information is included from numerous Gale databases, among them THE ENCYCLOPEDIA OF ASSOCIATIONS, PUBLISHERS DIRECTORY, GALE DIRECTORY OF PUBLICATIONS AND BROADCAST MEDIA and several others. If it is prohibitively expensive, locate a library with with this resource. Gale Group, P.O. Box 9187, Farmington Hills, MI 48333-9187. Toll free US and Canada (800) 877-GALE (4253) and (248) 699-GALE, fax (800) 414-5043 and (248) 699-8061, Internet orders galeord@galegroup.com, web site www.galegroup.com or www.gale.com. All Gale Group products are available on approval. Contact Gale for details.

INFOMART DIRECT is a satellite service produced by Infomart Dialog Limited that delivers consolidated news feeds and provides full text print and broadcast sources to the end-user's office computer or LAN. Sources include Canadian daily newspapers, Canadian and international newswire services, including Southam News, Canada NewsWire, and Agence-France Presse, select television broadcast transcripts from major Canadian networks, CBC and CTV, industry trade publications, including Daily Oil Bulletin, Eco/Log Week, Canadian Underwriter, Canadian Business and Marketing Magazine. For Subscriptions and rate information, contact Infomart Dialog Limited at (416) 442-2198 or (800) 668-9215. DIALOG is a service mark of the Dialog Corporation.

INFOMART ON CD is available to CD ROM subscribers from IHS Micromedia Ltd. A full range of Canadian daily newspapers is available on both the KIOSK and VOYAGEUR platforms. KIOSK offers coverage for The Daily News (Halifax), The Gazette (Montréal), Ottawa Citizen, Toronto Star, Toronto Sun, The Spectator (Hamilton), Calgary Herald, Edmonton Journal, The Province (Vancouver), Vancouver Sun, The Financial Post and broadcast news transcripts. On the VOYAGEUR platform, Canadian NewsDisc is available as a complete package, either quarterly or monthly. For Subscriptions and rate information, contact Infomart Dialog Limited at (416) 442-2198 or (800) 668-9215. DIALOG is a service mark of the Dialog Corporation.

INTERNATIONAL DIRECTORY OF BUSINESS INFORMATION SOURCES AND SERVICES contains information on over 4,000 organizations which produce and provide business information in 50 countries. $185. Published by Euromonitor (England). At the time of this writing, while distributor Gale Group was no longer selling this reference, the sales representative indicated it might be available directly from the publisher. For more information check Books in Print or International Books in Print.

LITERARY MARKET PLACE, "The Directory of the American Book Publishing Industry With Industry Yellow Pages" is an excellent 3 volume directory with comprehensive information on US book publishers; imprints, subsidiaries and distributors; book trade acquisitions and mergers, small presses, Canadian book publishers, micropublishers, US electronic publishers, electronic publishing consultants, electronic publishing products and services, editorial services, literary agents, illustrations agents, US agents and offices of foreign publishers, lecture agents, specialized advertising and public relations firms, direct mail specialists, mailing list brokers and services, book review syndicates, book review and index journals and services, book exhibits, book clubs, book lists and catalogs, book importers and exporters, book producers, translators, artists, photographers, stock photo agencies, associations, book trade events and conferences, awards, contents and grants, reference books for the trade, magazines for the trade, a toll free directory of publishers, magazine and newspaper publicity, radio and television publicity, book manufacturing services, book distributors and sales representatives, and wholesalers. $189.95.

LITERARY MARKET PLACE ON DISC, previously titled LITERARY MARKET PLACE PLUS CD ROM, one year subscription $297.00.

LITERARY MARKET PLACE—INTERNET EDITION, www.literarymarketplace.com, is available by subscription.

INTERNATIONAL LITERARY MARKET PLACE Internet database can be directly accessed at www.iliterarymarketplace.com. It is also linked to the US domestic LITERARY MARKET PLACE web site at www.literarymarketplace.com. Contact the publisher for subscription price. INTERNATIONAL LITERARY MARKET PLACE, hard copy $189.95.

R.R. Bowker (a unit of Cahners Business Information), 121 Chanlon Road, New Providence, NJ 07974 USA, Phone (888) BOWKER2 (888-269-5372) & (800) 323-3288, fax (908) 508-7696, email info@bowker.com, web www.bowker.com. Canada—R.R. Bowker, Markham, Ontario, phone (888) BOWKER9 & (905) 415-5837, fax (905) 479-6266. German speaking Europe—K.G. Saur Verlag, Munich, Germany, phone 49-89-76902-232, fax 49-89-76902-250, email 100730.1341@compuserve.com, web www.saur.de/home.htm. Rest of Europe incl. United Kingdom plus Africa & Asia—Bowker-Saur, W. Sussex, UK, phone 44-1342-326-972, fax 44-1342-335-612, email customer@bowker-saur.co.uk, web www.bowker-saur.com/service/. Australia/New Zealand—Thorpe, Port Melbourne, Victoria, Australia, phone 61-03-9-245-7370, fax 61-03-9-245-7395, email customer.service@thorpe.com.au, web www.thorpe.com.au. Technical support for CD ROMs (800) 323-3288, fax 908) 665-3528, email techsupport@bowker.com.

MEDICAL AND HEALTH INFORMATION DIRECTORY identifies organizations, agencies, institutions, services and information sources in medicine and health related fields. It includes approximately 20,000 organizations, 11,000 libraries, publications and electronic resources and 27,000 health service providers. Volume 1, Organizations, Agencies and Institutions. Volume 2, Publications, Libraries and Other Information Resources. Volume 3 Health Services. 3 volume set $590. $245 per volume. Gale Group, P.O. Box 9187, Farmington Hills, MI 48333-9187. Toll free US and Canada (800) 877-GALE (4253) and (248) 699-GALE,

fax (800) 414-5043 and (248) 699-8061, Internet orders galeord@galegroup.com, web site www.galegroup.com or www.gale.com. All Gale Group products are available on approval. Contact Gale for details.

NEW SCIENTIST ON CD ROM contains five years of this science weekly. If you need to conduct a literature search to determine which companies are engaged in cutting edge research, or to locate people who have been quoted, you can conduct full text searches by keyword, author, and publication date and can display either a brief description or full text. Bowker-Saur. Updated quarterly. $795, excluding discounts. For more information visit Bowker Reed Reference's web site at http://www.reedref.com or contact: Bowker Reed Reference Electronic Publishing, 121 Chanlon Road, New Providence, NJ 07974 USA, Phone (800) 323-3288, Fax (908) 665-3528, email info@bowker.com.

PHARMACEUTICAL MARKETERS DIRECTORY is a well organized directory that contains many names and titles and other information, including a listing of specialized professional associations and periodicals. Published annually. $162.50. CPS COMMUNICATIONS, INC., 7200 West Camino Real, Suite 215, Boca Raton, FL 33433, (561) 368-9301, sales office (203) 778-1463, email pmd@cpsnet.com, web site http://www.cpsnet.com.

PHILLIPS BUSINESS INFORMATION provides information in newsletters, magazines, directories and on multiple web sites covering a range of topics, such as magazine products, telecommunications and cable products, satellite products, media, new media and Internet products, marketing and public relations products, financial technology and electronic commerce, aviation and defense products. For more information, contact: Phillips Business Information, Inc., a Phillips Publishing International Company, 120 Seven Locks Road, Potomac, MD 20854, (301) 340-1520, (301) 340-7788, (800) 777-5006, Internet pbi@phillips.com, web site www.phillips.com.

SciTECH REFERENCE PLUS CD ROM contains directory information, 125,000 biographies of US and Canadian scientists and engineers from AMERICAN MEN AND WOMEN OF SCIENCE, listings for over 8,000 laboratories from the DIRECTORY OF AMERICAN RESEARCH AND TECHNOLOGY, and information from THE DIRECTORY OF CORPORATE AFFILIATIONS (including public, private and international companies) of leading US and international technology firms and their subsidiaries. It also contains 60,000 records on science/technology and medical serials from ULRICH'S INTERNATIONAL PERIODICALS DIRECTORY. Searches can be conducted by SIC, year founded, activity, education, employees, institution/company, city, state or country, memberships/honors, product description, personal statistics, personal title, research area, revenue. Updated annually. 1 year subscription $995, 3 years 2,836, excluding discounts. For more information visit Bowker Reed Reference's web site at http://www.reedref.com or contact: Bowker Reed Reference Electronic Publishing, 121 Chanlon Road, New Providence, NJ 07974 USA, Phone (800) 323-3288, Fax (908) 665-3528, email info@bowker.com.

STANDARD PERIODICAL DIRECTORY consists of 85,000 American and Canadian periodicals referenced by 250 subjects. Includes new online index and title index. $895. Also available on CD ROM. Published by Oxbridge. Distributed by Gale Group, P.O. Box 9187, Farmington Hills, MI 48333-9187. Toll free US and Canada (800) 877-GALE (4253) and (248) 699-GALE, fax (800) 414-5043 and (248) 699-8061, Internet orders galeord@galegroup.com, web site www.galegroup.com or www.gale.com. All Gale Group products are available on approval. Contact Gale for details.

STANDARD PERIODICAL DIRECTORY ON CD-ROM encompasses 75,000 North American publications, vastly simplifying research in consumer magazines, trade journals, newspapers, yearbooks, museum publications, ethnic publications and more. Contact Gale for prices. Gale Group, P.O. Box 9187, Farmington Hills, MI 48333-9187. Toll free US and Canada (800) 877-GALE (4253) and (248) 699-GALE, fax (800) 414-5043 and (248) 699-8061, Internet orders galeord@galegroup.com, web site www.galegroup.com or www.gale.com. All Gale Group products are available on approval. Contact Gale for details.

STANDARD RATE AND DATA PUBLICATIONS includes "Radio Advertising Source" and "Television and Cable Source" and direct marketing information. $354 annual subscription. Standard Rate and Data Service, Inc., 3004 Glenview Road, Wilmette, IL 60091, (708) 441-2210 in Illinois, (800) 323-4601.

"THE LIST" is Cahners Business Information catalog. The former Reed Travel Group has merged with Cahners and Chilton to form Cahners Business Information. For every publication in "The List," publishers and editors' names are identified, with address, phone number and email. It also provides a superb description of every periodical they publish—including many serving the travel industry—with local contact information Publications are located throughout the US and in foreign countries. Free. Cahners Business Information, 275 Washington Street, Newton, MA 02158-1630, (617) 558-4663 or (617) 964-3030, fax (617) 558-4700, email marketaccess@cahners.com. Web sites www.cahners.com or www.chilton.net.

THE SOURCE BOOK, "Expert Business Sources from Reed Elsevier Business Information" is a free booklet from the publisher which identifies trade journals published by Reed Elsevier, name of publisher, address, phone and email. Includes a wide variety of industry sources, alphabetically arranged into 23 categories, such as "Broadcasting/cable/communications," "Plant Operations," "Eye Care/Eyewear," "Technology Research." Free. Reed Elsevier Business Information, A Division of Reed Elsevier, Inc., 275 Washington Street, Newton, MA 02158-1630, (617) 964-3030, Fax (617) 558-4700, URLs www.cahners.com, www.chilton.net.

ULRICH'S INTERNATIONAL PERIODICALS DIRECTORY is available in electronic database formats. It contains information on every active and ceased global periodical, annual, irregular publication, plus thousands of newspapers. You can retrieve citations for over 900 subjects. Information is available for current titles of publications, title changes, and translated titles. Contains names, addresses and phone numbers for 80,000 publishers from 200 countries. $469.95 for 5 volume set. ULRICH'S ON DISC encompasses **ULRICH'S INTERNATIONAL PERIODICALS DATABASE** and contains information on over 210,000 periodicals, annuals and irregulars, both active and ceased, plus newspapers, including foreign and US topical newspapers and international general interest dailies and weeklies. It also includes information on over 90,000 publishers in over 200 countries, including the new states of the former Soviet Union, Czechoslovakia and Yugoslavia. One year subscription $650. ULRICH'S INTERNATIONAL PERIODICALS DIRECTORY— INTERNET EDITION, is available by subscription at www.ulrichsweb.com. ULRICH'S ONLINE is available from Bowker or through Knight-Ridder Information, Inc. (DIALOG file 480), OVID Technologies, Inc., LEXIS®—NEXIS® (Library: BUSREF, File Name: ULRICH) and through SilverPlatter Information, Inc. for a subscription online. For more information contact R.R. Bowker (a unit of Cahners Business Information), 121 Chanlon Road, New Providence, NJ 07974 USA, Phone (888) BOWKER2 (888-269-5372) & (800) 323-3288, fax (908) 508-7696, email info@bowker.com, web www.bowker.com. Canada—R.R. Bowker, Markham, Ontario, phone (888) BOWKER9 & (905) 415-5837, fax (905) 479-6266. German speaking Europe—K.G. Saur Verlag, Munich, Germany, phone 49-89-76902-232, fax 49-89-76902-250, email 100730.1341@compuserve.com, web www.saur.de/home.htm. Rest of Europe incl. United Kingdom plus Africa & Asia—Bowker-Saur, W. Sussex, UK, phone 44-1342-326-972, fax 44-1342-335-612, email customer@bowker-saur.co.uk, web www.bowker-saur.com/service/. Australia/New Zealand—Thorpe, Port Melbourne, Victoria, Australia, phone 61-03-9-245-7370, fax 61-03-9-245-7395, email customer.service@thorpe.com.au, web www.thorpe.com.au. Technical support for CD ROMs (800) 323-3288, fax 908) 665-3528, email techsupport@bowker.com.

UMI is a respected publisher (including databases) whose catalog of Books on Demand, Magazines, Newspapers and Collections, consisting of 19,000 titles, is on line. For more information, go to their Home page and then to the Support Center for pricing. www.umi.com. Email: pprice@umi.com. UMI, 300 North Zeeb Road, Ann Arbor, Michigan 48106 (800) 521-0600, Sales (800) 521-3042, email: pprice@umi.com

WORKING PRESS OF THE NATION identifies 180,000 decision makers in newspapers, magazines, newsletters, "hard to find corporate, government and association publications," TV and radio stations and cable networks. Volume 1—Newspapers, Volume 2—Magazines & Internal Publications, Volume 3—TV & Radio. $249 per volume or $439.95 for 3 volume set. R.R. Bowker (a unit of Cahners Business Information), 121 Chanlon Road, New Providence, NJ 07974 USA, Phone (888) BOWKER2 (888-269-5372) & (800) 323-3288, fax (908) 508-7696, email info@bowker.com, web www.bowker.com. Canada—R.R. Bowker, Markham, Ontario, phone (888) BOWKER9 & (905) 415-5837, fax (905) 479-6266. German speaking Europe—K.G. Saur Verlag, Munich, Germany, phone 49-89-76902-232, fax 49-89-76902-250, email 100730.1341@compuserve.com, web www.saur.de/home.htm. Rest of Europe incl. United Kingdom plus Africa & Asia—Bowker-Saur, W. Sussex, UK, phone 44-1342-326-972, fax 44-1342-335-612, email customer@bowker-saur.co.uk, web www.bowker-saur.com/service/. Australia/New Zealand—Thorpe, Port Melbourne, Victoria, Australia, phone 61-03-9-245-7370, fax 61-03-9-245-7395, email customer.service@thorpe.com.au, web www.thorpe.com.au. Technical support for CD ROMs (800) 323-3288, fax 908) 665-3528, email techsupport@bowker.com.

WORLD DIRECTORY OF MARKETING INFORMATION SOURCES identifies market research companies, online databases, directories and marketing journals for every major consumer market in 75 countries. $595. Published by Euromonitor (England). Distributed by Gale Group, P.O. Box 9187, Farmington Hills, MI 48333-9187. Toll free US and Canada (800) 877-GALE (4253) and (248) 699-GALE, fax (800) 414-5043 and (248) 699-8061, Internet orders galeord@galegroup.com, web site www.galegroup.com or www.gale.com. All Gale Group products are available on approval. Contact Gale for details.

www.boston.com is the web site for *Boston Globe* online accesses the Globe's newspaper ads.

www.bowker.com is the web site for this major research publisher. It includes Flagship Products and Services, an online Product Catalog, Electronic Publishing products including CD ROMs, Internet Databases, and Online Subscription and Site Licensing Databases; press releases, career opportunities, and more. Many of their references are accessible through this web site, such as BOOKS IN PRINT PLUS CANADIAN EDITION, ULRICH'S ON DISC, GERMAN BOOKS IN PRINT, GERMAN BOOKS OUT OF PRINT, INTERNATIONAL BOOKS IN PRINT PLUS, ITALIAN BOOKS IN PRINT, YEARBOOK OF INTERNATIONAL ORGANIZATIONS PLUS, ULRICH'S INTERNATIONAL PERIODICALS DIRECTORY, THE SOFTWARE ENCYCLOPEDIA, BOWKER'S COMPLETE VIDEO DIRECTORY, AMERICAN BOOK PUBLISHING RECORD. Visit the web site for more information.

www.careers.wsj.com is the *Wall Street Journal*'s web site. It focuses on positions for middle and senior management including financial positions at $75,000 and up. This web site is among those that encompass senior executive positions. Other features includes Job Seek, Who's Hiring, Career Columnists, Salaries & Profiles, The Salary Calculator™, Job Hunting Advice, Succeeding at Work, HR Issues, Executive Recruiters, Working Globally, College Connection, Starting a Business, Career Bookstore and more. Content from The National Employment Business Weekly is also featured. The site was developed by Dow Jones & Company, Inc., Princeton, New Jersey and was established in 1997.

www.latimes.com is the URL to the comprehensive *Los Angeles Times* web site.

www.nytimes.com is the URL for *The New York Times* web site.

www.townonline.com/working or Town Online Working is the web site to various community newspapers, including 13 in New England. In addition to job listings, it also has a job profile with the capability of automatically downloading to your Email. Town Online Working was ranked as one of the top 5 "Sites Offering the Best Career Resources for Job Seekers" by the *National Business Employment Weekly*. Many positions are administrative, management and blue collar, often paying in the teens up to $30,000. The site developer is the Community Newspaper Company, Needham, Massachusetts and was established in 1996.

Personnel

See Human Resources, Executive Search

Petroleum

DAILY OIL BULLETIN is the leading trade paper for the Canadian oil and gas industry. Includes announcements of staff appointments. $891 annual subscription. Free two week trial subscription is available. Special discounts available for combined purchases. For more information on Energy Information Services, call Calgary office (403) 244-6111. Published by Southam Information Products Ltd, 1450 Don Mills Road, Don Mills, Ontario M3B 2X7 CANADA, (800) 668-2374. In Toronto 442-2122. Web site www.southam.com.

FINANCIAL TIMES ENERGY YEARBOOKS: OIL AND GAS provides narrative, production and financial information for over 800 major oil and gas companies, including full contact details. It also includes major oil and gas brokers and traders, industry associations, and outlines all parent, subsidiary and associate companies. $320. Published by Financial Times Energy. Distributed by Gale Group, P.O. Box 9187,

Farmington Hills, MI 48333-9187. Toll free US and Canada (800) 877-GALE (4253) and (248) 699-GALE, fax (800) 414-5043 and (248) 699-8061, Internet orders galeord@galegroup.com, web site www.galegroup.com or www.gale.com. All Gale Group products are available on approval. Contact Gale for details.

JOBSON'S MINING YEAR BOOK contains information on 600 of Australia and New Zealand's leading mining, petroleum and exploration companies. Dun & Bradstreet, Business Reference Solutions, Three Sylvan Way, Parsippany, NJ 07054 USA. (800) 526-0651. Email dnbmdd@mail.dnb.com. Web site http://www.dnbmdd.com.

MAJOR CHEMICAL & PETROCHEMICAL COMPANIES OF EUROPE contains information on 1,800 companies in 19 western European countries. $450. US distributor: Larry Meranus Professional Publications & Services, 4 Demoray Court, Pine Brook, NJ 07058, (800) MERANUS or (800) 637-2687. Published by Graham & Whiteside Ltd., Tuition House, 5-6 Francis Grove, London SW19 4DT, England. Web site http://www.major-co-data.com. Email sales@major-co-data.com.

MAJOR CHEMICAL & PETROCHEMICAL COMPANIES OF THE FAR EAST & AUSTRALASIA provides information on over 1,100 companies. $415. US distributor: Larry Meranus Professional Publications & Services, 4 Demoray Court, Pine Brook, NJ 07058, (800) MERANUS or (800) 637-2687. Published by Graham & Whiteside Ltd., Tuition House, 5-6 Francis Grove, London SW19 4DT, England. Web site http://www.major-co-data.com. Email sales@major-co-data.com.

MAJOR CHEMICAL & PETROCHEMICAL COMPANIES OF THE WORLD provides information on 6,500 companies. $830. US distributor: Larry Meranus Professional Publications & Services, 4 Demoray Court, Pine Brook, NJ 07058, (800) MERANUS or (800) 637-2687. Published by Graham & Whiteside Ltd., Tuition House, 5-6 Francis Grove, London SW19 4DT, England. Web site http://www.major-co-data.com. Email sales@major-co-data.com.

NICKLE'S CANADIAN OIL REGISTER (COR)—CONTACTS is a diskette on Maximizer, a contact management software. It includes 3,500 companies in 15 business sectors and 17,000 names and titles for over 1,000 product and service categories. COR—CONTACTS (OIL AND GAS PRODUCERS) $395. COR—CONTACTS (SERVICE COMPANIES) $595. COR—CONTACTS (PRODUCTS SOURCING) $495. Special discounts available for combined purchases. For more information on Energy Information Services, call Calgary office (403) 244-6111. Published by Southam Information Products Ltd, 1450 Don Mills Road, Don Mills, Ontario M3B 2X7 CANADA, (800) 668-2374. In Toronto 442-2122. Web site www.southam.com.

NICKLE'S CANADIAN OIL REGISTER is a directory that provides names of key personnel and other information on 4,500 Canadian companies in these industry categories: exploration and production companies, service and supply companies, data processors, consultants, engineers, financial and investment companies, leasebrokers and land agents, geophysical contractors, oil well drilling contractors, oil well servicing contractors, pipeline and power distributors, refiners and processors, transportation and construction companies, government departments, agencies and industry associations. Includes a Who's Who section that identifies over 24,000 key management, engineering and technical personnel. $175. Published annually. Special discounts available for combined purchases. For more information on Energy Information Services, call Calgary office (403) 244-6111. Published by Southam Information Products Ltd, 1450 Don Mills Road, Don Mills, Ontario M3B 2X7 CANADA, (800) 668-2374. In Toronto 442-2122. Web site www.southam.com.

OWNERSHIP STRUCTURES OF PRINCIPAL PETROLEUM COMPANIES IN CANADA documents "who owns whom" in the Canadian Petroleum industry. Includes directors and key officers and a list of major oil patch takeovers since 1976. $177. Special discounts available for combined purchases. For more information on Energy Information Services, call Calgary office (403) 244-6111. Published by Southam Information Products Ltd, 1450 Don Mills Road, Don Mills, Ontario M3B 2X7 CANADA, (800) 668-2374. In Toronto 442-2122. Web site www.southam.com.

www.nickles.com/ is the web site for Nickel's Energy Web site. It provides access to over 18,000 articles published in the DAILY OIL BULLETIN, company profiles linked to news articles, a weekly synopsis of key developments in Canadian energy markets, classified ads, and energy information sources. For more information on Energy Information Services, call Calgary office (403) 244-6111. Published by Southam Information Products Ltd, 1450 Don Mills Road, Don Mills, Ontario M3B 2X7 CANADA, (800) 668-2374. In Toronto 442-2122. Web site www.southam.com.

Pharmaceuticals

ADVERTISER AND AGENCY RED BOOKS PLUS CD ROM combines all the information in THE STANDARD DIRECTORY OF ADVERTISERS, THE STANDARD DIRECTORY OF ADVERTISING AGENCIES and THE STANDARD DIRECTORY OF INTERNATIONAL ADVERTISERS AND AGENCIES. Information is searchable by 25 fields, including company name, personal name, job title/function, product type, product/account name, city, state, zip or country, area code, revenues, number of employees, outside ad agency and even type of computer hardware. Contains professional association information. Available for Windows and Macintosh. Updated quarterly. 1 year subscription $1,295. If the price is prohibitively high, remember your local library. National Register Publishing, Reed Elsevier-New Providence, 121 Chanlon Road, New Providence, NJ 07974, (800) 521-8110, fax (800) 836-7736, web site www.redbooks.com or www.marquiswhoswho.com. "If, for any reason whatsoever, your order does not fully meet your expectations, simply return the product within 30 days for a prompt, complete, unquestioned refund," as stated in Catalog of Biographical and Professional References of publisher Marquis Who's Who/National Register Publishing.

CANADIAN PHARMACISTS DIRECTORY lists over 18,000 Canadian pharmacists, drug information centers, poison control centres, pharmaceutical suppliers, drug wholesalers, related universities, drug store head offices, pharmaceutical associations, chain drug stores, and brand name/generic pharmaceutical companies. $119 prepaid, $149 plus $5 shipping and handling if billed. Special discounts available for combined purchases. Published by Southam Information Products Ltd, 1450 Don Mills Road, Don Mills, Ontario M3B 2X7 CANADA, (800) 668-2374. In Toronto 442-2122. Web site www.southam.com.

DUN & BRADSTREET AND GALE INDUSTRY REFERENCE HANDBOOKS offer a line of industry-specific sourcebooks which include key companies in the industry, ranked lists of companies, professional associations, trade shows and conferences, mergers and acquisitions, consultants who service those industries, information sources, and more. 6 volume set $495. Also available individually for $99: Pharmaceuticals, Health and Medical Services, Computers and Software, Banking and Finance, Telecommunications, Agriculture and Food, Insurance, Construction, Entertainment, Hospitality. First edition available December, 1999. Gale Group, P.O. Box 9187, Farmington Hills, MI 48333-9187. Toll free US and Canada (800) 877-GALE (4253) and (248) 699-GALE, fax (800) 414-5043 and (248) 699-8061, Internet orders galeord@galegroup.com, web site www.galegroup.com or www.gale.com. All Gale Group products are available on approval. Contact Gale for details.

PHARMACEUTICAL MARKETERS DIRECTORY is a well organized directory that contains many names and titles and other information, including a listing of specialized professional associations. Published annually. $162.50. CPS COMMUNICATIONS, INC., 7200 West Camino Real, Suite 215, Boca Raton, FL 33433, (561) 368-9301, sales office (203) 778-1463, email pmd@cpsnet.com, web site http://www.cpsnet.com.

STANDARD DIRECTORY OF ADVERTISERS Business Classifications Edition is an excellent general directory that organizes companies by a wide range of product categories. A few examples include "Apparel 2—Men's and Boys' Wear," "Heating and Air Conditioning," "Cosmetics and Toiletries," and "Aviation and Aerospace." This directory lists names and titles of key officers, revenues and other information. It is available in a geographic edition for the same price. This directory is comprised of over 24,000 companies that annually spend over $200,000 on advertising. It represents a reasonable place to look for hard-to-find information about privately held companies, especially those that heavily advertise their products. It is a good place to look for names if STANDARD AND POORS and the MILLION DOLLAR DIRECTORY fail to yield the names you need. Finally, the Classified Edition of THE STANDARD DIRECTORY OF ADVERTISERS can be a very convenient source of research because both your target list of companies and the corresponding names and titles of management all appear together, in the same Classification. This is important if you still rely on research books in hard copy. THE STANDARD DIRECTORY OF ADVERTISERS also publishes a special volume called THE STANDARD DIRECTORY OF ADVERTISERS TRADENAME INDEX. You can use the TRADENAME INDEX if you know the brand name of a product and need to find the company

that manufactures it. In addition, this directory contains an Associations section which identifies marketing oriented associations.

$599 hard copy. If the price is prohibitively high, remember your local library. THE STANDARD DIRECTORY OF ADVERTISERS is also available on CD ROM under the title ADVERTISER AND AGENCY RED BOOKS PLUS. It is available in Windows® and Macintosh® formats. National Register Publishing, Reed Elsevier-New Providence, 121 Chanlon Road, New Providence, NJ 07974, (800) 521-8110, fax (800) 836-7736, web site www.redbooks.com or www.marquiswhoswho.com. "If, for any reason whatsoever, your order does not fully meet your expectations, simply return the product within 30 days for a prompt, complete, unquestioned refund," as stated in Catalog of Biographical and Professional References of publisher Marquis Who's Who/National Register Publishing.

www.bio.com is the URL for Bio Online. Most positions are for research chemists, biochemists and in clinical development and are usually in the $40,000 to $75,000 range. Developed by Vitadata Corp, Berkeley, California, the site went online in 1993.

www.jobnet.com was ranked as one of the top 5 "Best Specialty Sites" by the *National Business Employment Weekly*. Jobnet.com specializes in positions located in southeastern Pennsylvania and neighboring areas of New Jersey and Delaware. The site was developed by Online Opportunities, Malvern, Pennsylvania and has been online since 1992.

Pharmacists

CANADIAN PHARMACISTS DIRECTORY lists over 18,000 Canadian pharmacists, drug information centers, poison control centres, pharmaceutical suppliers, drug wholesalers, related universities, drug store head offices, pharmaceutical associations, chain drug stores, and brand name/generic pharmaceutical companies. $119 prepaid, $149 plus $5 shipping and handling if billed. Special discounts available for combined purchases. Published by Southam Information Products Ltd, 1450 Don Mills Road, Don Mills, Ontario M3B 2X7 CANADA, (800) 668-2374. In Toronto 442-2122. Web site www.southam.com.

Philadelphia Area

www.jobnet.com was ranked as one of the top 5 "Best Specialty Sites" by the *National Business Employment Weekly*. Jobnet.com specializes in positions located in southeastern Pennsylvania and neighboring areas of New Jersey and Delaware. The site was developed by Online Opportunities, Malvern, Pennsylvania and has been online since 1992.

Philippines

See *Pacific, Asia, International*

KEY BUSINESS DIRECTORY OF INDONESIA/PHILIPPINES/THAILAND contains information on 4,000 companies with more than 50 employees. Dun & Bradstreet, Business Reference Solutions, Three Sylvan Way, Parsippany, NJ 07054 USA. (800) 526-0651. Email dnbmdd@mail.dnb.com. Web site http://www.dnbmdd.com.

Phone Directories

See *Telephone Books*

Physicians

ABMS MEDICAL SPECIALISTS PLUS CD ROM (American Board of Medical Specialists) is an electronic edition of THE OFFICIAL ABMS DIRECTORY OF BOARD CERTIFIED MEDICAL SPECIALISTS, which is based on the database of the American Board of Medical Specialties (ABMS). Updated annually, it identifies over 500,000 specialists in 37 specialties and 75 sub-specialties. It includes career information, including name, certification and sub-certification, date of birth and place, medical school, year of degree, internship, residency, fellowship, hospital staff appointments, current academic appointment and title, professional associations, type of practice, and addresses and phone numbers, plus address and contact information from US and Canadian medical schools. $1,195 for CD ROM. $499.95 in hard copy. National Register Publishing, Reed Elsevier-New Providence, 121 Chanlon Road, New Providence, NJ 07974, (800) 521-8110, fax (800) 836-7736, web site www.marquiswhoswho.com or www.redbooks.com. "If, for any reason whatsoever, your order does not fully meet your expectations, simply return the product within 30 days for a prompt, complete, unquestioned refund," as stated in Catalog of Biographical and Professional References of publisher Marquis Who's Who/National Register Publishing.

CANADIAN DENTAL DIRECTORY provides alphabetical and geographic listings of certified Canadian dentists in Canada. $119. Special discounts available for combined purchases. Published by Southam Information Products Ltd, 1450 Don Mills Road, Don Mills, Ontario M3B 2X7 CANADA, (800) 668-2374. In Toronto 442-2122. Web site www.southam.com.

MD SELECT is an Electronic Canadian Medical Directory endorsed by the Canadian Medical Association. It lists over 50,000 physicians. Information can be searched by these fields: physician name, phone, hospital affiliation, hospital bed size, hospital type, medical specialty, degrees, honors, certified specialty, subspecialty, primary interest, gender, year of graduation, University/Country of graduation, appointments, fellowships, and languages spoken. $495. THE CANADIAN MEDICAL DIRECTORY in hard copy costs $175 Published annually. Special discounts available for combined purchases. Published by Southam Information Products Ltd, 1450 Don Mills Road, Don Mills, Ontario M3B 2X7 CANADA, (800) 668-2374. In Toronto 442-2122. Web site www.southam.com.

MODERN PHYSICIAN is a monthly trade publication. Crain Communications, Inc. is headquartered in Chicago with offices in major cities throughout the US plus London, Tokyo and Frankfurt. New York location: 220 East 42nd Street, New York, NY 10017, (212) 210-0100, Circulation (800) 678-9595. Annual subscription $39.50. Web site www.pionline.com.

Planning

BUSINESS PLANS HANDBOOK is a collection of real business plans prepared by entrepreneurs searching for small business funding in North America. 25 actual plans are presented across a broad spectrum of businesses in manufacturing, retail and service industries. Company identities have been changed to protect confidentiality. $125. Gale Group, P.O. Box 9187, Farmington Hills, MI 48333-9187. Toll free US and Canada (800) 877-GALE (4253) and (248) 699-GALE, fax (800) 414-5043 and (248) 699-8061, Internet orders galeord@galegroup.com, web site www.galegroup.com or www.gale.com. All Gale Group products are available on approval. Previous volumes are available. Contact Gale for details.

CONSULTANTS AND CONSULTING ORGANIZATIONS DIRECTORY identifies consultants in over 400 specialties within 14 general areas. Includes finance, computers, fundraising and others. $620 for 2 volumes. Gale Group, P.O. Box 9187, Farmington Hills, MI 48333-9187. Toll free US and Canada (800) 877-GALE (4253) and (248) 699-GALE, fax (800) 414-5043 and (248) 699-8061, Internet orders galeord@galegroup.com, web site www.galegroup.com or www.gale.com. All Gale Group products are available on approval. Contact Gale for details.

ENCYCLOPEDIA OF SMALL BUSINESS provides entrepreneurs with how-to information on business plan creation, financing, financial planning, market analysis, sales strategy, tax planning, succession plans and more. $395 for 2 volume set. Gale Group, P.O. Box 9187, Farmington Hills, MI 48333-9187. Toll free US and Canada (800) 877-GALE (4253) and (248) 699-GALE, fax (800) 414-5043 and (248) 699-8061, Internet orders galeord@galegroup.com, web site www.galegroup.com or www.gale.com. All Gale Group products are available on approval. Contact Gale for details.

Plants

See Manufacturing—Plant Locations

Politics

BOWKER BIOGRAPHICAL DIRECTORY is comprised of the electronic equivalents of AMERICAN MEN AND WOMEN OF SCIENCE™, WHO'S WHO IN AMERICAN ART™ and WHO'S WHO IN AMERICAN POLITICS™. It is available in electronic database formats from Reed Reference. Entries include past and current career details, publications, education, research interests, languages, personal and family information and more .Available online through Knight-Ridder Information, Inc., (DIALOG file number 236) and on LEXIS™—NEXIS™ (American Men and Women of Science Library: People; busref, file AMSCI). For more information visit Bowker Reed Reference's web site at http://www.reedref.com or contact: Bowker Reed Reference Electronic Publishing, 121 Chanlon Road, New Providence, NJ 07974 USA, Phone (800) 323-3288, Fax (908) 665-3528, email info@bowker.com.

WHO'S WHO IN AMERICAN POLITICS, $259.95. National Register Publishing, Reed Elsevier-New Providence, 121 Chanlon Road, New Providence, NJ 07974, (800) 521-8110, fax (800) 836-7736, web site www.marquiswhoswho.com or www.redbooks.com. "If, for any reason whatsoever, your order does not fully meet your expectations, simply return the product within 30 days for a prompt, complete, unquestioned refund," as stated in Catalog of Biographical and Professional References of publisher Marquis Who's Who/National Register Publishing.

Portfolio Management

See Investment Management

Portugal

See Europe, Spain, International

PRINCIPAL COMPANIES IN PORTUGAL contains information on 3,500 companies, including names of top executives. Dun & Bradstreet, Business Reference Solutions, Three Sylvan Way, Parsippany, NJ 07054 USA. (800) 526-0651. Email dnbmdd@mail.dnb.com. Web site http://www.dnbmdd.com.

Privately Held Companies

ADVERTISER AND AGENCY RED BOOKS PLUS CD ROM combines all the information in THE STANDARD DIRECTORY OF ADVERTISERS, THE STANDARD DIRECTORY OF ADVERTISING AGENCIES and THE STANDARD DIRECTORY OF INTERNATIONAL ADVERTISERS AND AGENCIES. Information is searchable by 25 fields, including company name, personal name, job title/function, product type, product/account name, city, state, zip or country, area code, revenues, number of employees, outside ad agency and even type of computer hardware. Contains professional association information. Available for Windows and Macintosh. Updated quarterly. 1 year subscription $1,295. If the price is prohibitively high, remember your local library. National Register Publishing, Reed Elsevier-New Providence, 121 Chanlon Road, New Providence, NJ 07974, (800) 521-8110, fax (800) 836-7736, web site www.redbooks.com or www.marquiswhoswho.com. "If, for any reason whatsoever, your order does not fully meet your expectations, simply return the product within 30 days for a prompt, complete, unquestioned refund," as stated in Catalog of Biographical and Professional References of publisher Marquis Who's Who/National Register Publishing.

AMERICA'S CORPORATE FINANCE DIRECTORY provides a financial profile of the US's leading 5,000 public and private companies. It includes information about the company's pension plan, names of contacts, and a listing of over 17,000 wholly owned US subsidiaries. The title appears previously to have been The Corporate Finance Bluebook. $585. If the price is prohibitively high, remember your local library. National Register Publishing, Reed Elsevier-New Providence, 121 Chanlon Road, New Providence, NJ 07974, (800) 521-8110, fax (800) 836-7736, web site www.redbooks.com or www.marquiswhoswho.com. "If, for any reason whatsoever, your order does not fully meet your expectations, simply return the product within 30 days for a prompt, complete, unquestioned refund," as stated in Catalog of Biographical and Professional References of publisher Marquis Who's Who/National Register Publishing.

BUSINESS WHO'S WHO OF AUSTRALIA contains 20,000 privately held companies in Australia. Dun & Bradstreet, Business Reference Solutions, Three Sylvan Way, Parsippany, NJ 07054 USA. (800) 526-0651. Email dnbmdd@mail.dnb.com. Web site http://www.dnbmdd.com.

CALIFORNIA PINPOINT DATABASES ON CD ROM use the same information as the CALIFORNIA MANUFACTURERS AND CALIFORNIA WHOLESALERS AND SERVICE COMPANIES REGISTERS. It averages from 2 to slightly over 3 executive names per company, depending on the database. Data includes company name, phone, fax, toll free numbers, web sites, email addresses, sales, plant size, products manufactured, up to 6 SIC or NAICS codes, up to 10 executive names, public or private status.

> NORTHERN CALIFORNIA BUSINESS DATABASE, $595
> SOUTHERN CALIFORNIA BUSINESS DATABASE, $595
> CALIFORNIA MANUFACTURERS DATABASE, $595
> CALIFORNIA MANUFACTURERS, 20+ EMPLOYEES, $429
> CALIFORNIA WHOLESALERS AND SERVICE COMPANIES, $595
> CALIFORNIA TOP COMPANIES, 100+ EMPLOYEES, $429
> CALIFORNIA BUSINESS DATABASE, $995
> CALIFORNIA TECHNOLOGY COMPANIES DATABASE, $425
> CALIFORNIA EXPORTERS AND IMPORTERS, $365
> CALIFORNIA AGRICULTURAL EXPORTERS, $195
> ALAMEDA COUNTY DATABASE, $215
> CONTRA COSTA COUNTY DATABASE, $215
> LOS ANGELES COUNTY DATABASE, $429
> ORANGE COUNTY DATABASE, $235
> SAN DIEGO COUNTY DATABASE, $215
> SAN FRANCISCO COUNTY DATABASE, $215
> SAN MATEO COUNTY DATABASE, $215
> SANTA CLARA COUNTY DATABASE, $215

For more information and a catalog, contact Database Publishing Company, PO Box 70024, Anaheim, CA 92825, (800) 888-8434, (714) 778-6400, email sales@databasepublishing.com.

CD EUROPA contains comprehensive financial and operational data on 130,000 public and private companies in 20 European countries. Dun & Bradstreet, Business Reference Solutions, Three Sylvan Way, Parsippany, NJ 07054 USA. (800) 526-0651. Email dnbmdd@mail.dnb.com. Web site http://www.dnbmdd.com.

COMPANIES INTERNATIONAL CD-ROM contains comprehensive financial and contact data for over 300,000 public and privately held companies in 180 countries including the Commonwealth of Independent States, Mexico, Canada and Japan. Companies can be located by company name, product or industry, location, or a combination. This reference can also be used for target lists development for international companies, including privately held companies. $2,995. Gale Group, P.O. Box 9187, Farmington Hills, MI 48333-9187. Toll free US and Canada (800) 877-GALE (4253) and (248) 699-GALE, fax (800) 414-5043 and (248) 699-8061, Internet orders galeord@galegroup.com, web site www.galegroup.com or www.gale.com. All Gale Group products are available on approval. Contact Gale for details.

CORPORATE AFFILIATIONS PLUS CD ROM consolidates information in all five volumes of THE DIRECTORY OF CORPORATE AFFILIATIONS, including publicly held and privately held companies in the US and internationally, and AMERICA'S CORPORATE FINANCE DIRECTORY. This CD provides "family tree" overviews for each company with the reporting structure. It also contains information on 15,000 parent companies in the US and abroad, records on over 100,000 subsidiaries, divisions, plants and joint ventures, names and titles of over 250,000 employees, revenue figures and more. Information can be searched by 29 criteria, such as location, SIC or NAICS codes, sales, number of employees, net worth, pension assets and more. Updated quarterly. 1 year subscription $1,995, available for both Windows and Macintosh. If the price is prohibitively high, remember your local library. National Register Publishing, Reed Elsevier-New Providence, 121 Chanlon Road, New Providence, NJ 07974, (800) 521-8110, fax (800) 836-7736, web site www.redbooks.com or www.marquiswhoswho.com. "If, for any reason whatsoever, your order does not fully meet your expectations, simply return the product within 30 days for a prompt, complete, unquestioned

refund," as stated in Catalog of Biographical and Professional References of publisher Marquis Who's Who/National Register Publishing.

CORPORATE FINANCE SOURCEBOOK—THE GUIDE TO MAJOR INVESTMENT SOURCES AND RELATED FINANCIAL SERVICES contains over 13,000 names of executives at 3,700 organizations that, broadly speaking, supply growth capital to businesses or are service firms, such as US venture capital lenders, private lenders, commercial finance and factoring, pension managers, master trusts and other sources. Names of key management are included. A special section details public offerings of the past 3 years and mergers and acquisitions over $100 million. $575. If the price is prohibitively high, remember your local library. National Register Publishing, Reed Elsevier-New Providence, 121 Chanlon Road, New Providence, NJ 07974, (800) 521-8110, fax (800) 836-7736, web site www.redbooks.com or www.marquiswhoswho.com. "If, for any reason whatsoever, your order does not fully meet your expectations, simply return the product within 30 days for a prompt, complete, unquestioned refund," as stated in Catalog of Biographical and Professional References of publisher Marquis Who's Who/National Register Publishing.

D&B BUSINESS RANKINGS ranks over 25,000 US companies, both publicly and privately held, from highest to lowest by sales volume and number of employees within a range of different categories. Businesses are listed alphabetically, ranked by size, within state and by industry category. Public companies are ranked by annual sales volume and employee size. Private and foreign owned companies are ranked by sales volume and employee size. The 5,000 largest public companies and private and foreign-owned companies are included in separate ranking sections. As this directory contains no names or titles, it is most appropriate for conducting research to develop a target list of companies. Updated annually. For prices call Dun & Bradstreet at (800) 526-0651. For more information contact Dun & Bradstreet, Business Reference Solutions, Three Sylvan Way, Parsippany, New Jersey 07054. Email dnbmdd@mail.dnb.com. Web site http://www.dnbmdd.com.

D&B CANADIAN KEY BUSINESS DIRECTORY contains information on Canada's top 20,000 companies, both publicly and privately held, with at least $20 million in sales and over 100 employees. Information includes multiple executive names and titles, sales revenue in Canadian dollars, number of employees, address and phone numbers, lines of business, and SIC or NAICS codes. Contains explanations in both English and French. Published annually. For prices call Dun & Bradstreet at (800) 526-0651. For more information contact Dun & Bradstreet, Business Reference Solutions, Three Sylvan Way, Parsippany, NJ 07054. Email dnbmdd@mail.dnb.com. Web site http://www.dnbmdd.com.

D&B DIRECTORY OF SERVICE COMPANIES is a directory with information on 50,000 US service businesses, including privately held companies, in these sectors: accounting, auditing and bookkeeping, advertising and public relations, architecture and engineering, consumer services, executive search, health, hospitality, management consulting, motion pictures, repair, research, social services and law. Listings include key executives' names and titles, address, phone, sales volume, number of employees, parent company and location, and more. Companies listed employ 50 or more people. Information is listed alphabetically and is cross-referenced geographically and by industry classification. Updated annually. For prices call Dun & Bradstreet at (800) 526-0651. For more information contact Dun & Bradstreet, Business Reference Solutions, Three Sylvan Way, Parsippany, New Jersey 07054. Email dnbmdd@mail.dnb.com. Web site http://www.dnbmdd.com.

D&B MILLION DOLLAR DATABASE is an online database on the Internet. Users can access information on more than one million small, mid-sized and large companies, with minimum revenues of $1 million. Searches can be conducted by 22 criteria, including as geographic location, sales volume, number of employees, industry classification. Each company includes up to 30 executive names and titles and biographical data that includes education, work history and birth date. For prices call Dun & Bradstreet at (800) 526-0651. For more information contact Dun & Bradstreet, Business Reference Solutions, Three Sylvan Way, Parsippany, New Jersey 07054. Email dnbmdd@mail.dnb.com. Web site http://www.dnbmdd.com.

D&B MILLION DOLLAR DIRECTORY is a hard copy 5 volume reference that contains profiles on 160,000 public and private US companies. Information is listed alphabetically, geographically and by industry classification. In order to be listed, the company must be a headquarters or single location and must satisfy one of these three requirements: 250 or more employees at that location; $revenues of at least $25 million; tangible net worth of at least $500,000. Entries include key executives' names and titles, parent company and location, sales volume, address, phone number and more. THE D&B MILLION DOLLAR DIRECTORY

TOP 50,000 COMPANIES is an abridged version of the MILLION DOLLAR DIRECTORY. Both are updated annually. For prices call Dun & Bradstreet at (800) 526-0651. For more information contact Dun & Bradstreet, Business Reference Solutions, Three Sylvan Way, Parsippany, New Jersey 07054. Email dnbmdd@mail.dnb.com. Web site http://www.dnbmdd.com.

D&B MILLION DOLLAR DISC is a CD ROM which covers over 240,000 public and private companies, compared to either 160,000 or 50,000 in the two versions of the MILLION DOLLAR DIRECTORY in hard copy. In addition, this CD ROM also contains BIOGRAPHICAL information on key executives. Searches can be conducted by company name, industry, size of company, geography, executive name, key word, and executive business backgrounds. Companies listed have sales of at least $ million or more than 100 employees. Branch locations have more than 500 employees. Both are updated annually. D&B MILLION DOLLAR DISC PLUS is a similar CD ROM with more expansive coverage, including 400,000 companies— both privately held and public—compared to 240,000 in the MILLION DOLLAR DISC. It includes companies with at least 50 employees or revenues of $3 million. For prices call Dun & Bradstreet at (800) 526-0651. For more information contact Dun & Bradstreet, Business Reference Solutions, Three Sylvan Way, Parsippany, New Jersey 07054. Email dnbmdd@mail.dnb.com. Web site http://www.dnbmdd.com.

D&B REGIONAL BUSINESS DIRECTORIES are available for each of fifty-four metropolitan areas. Each three-volume set provides profiles on 20,000 companies, including hard-to-find information on privately held companies. Listings include key executives' names and titles, number of employees at location, sales volume, address, phone number, line of business, parent company, year established, and more. Each directory is cross referenced alphabetically and by industry classification. Updated annually. D&B REGIONAL BUSINESS DISK is a CD ROM which provides up to ten names and titles per company. Searches can be conducted by company name, industry, size of company, geography, executive name and key word. Unmetered and updated bi-annually. For prices call Dun & Bradstreet at (800) 526-0651. For more information contact Dun & Bradstreet, Business Reference Solutions, Three Sylvan Way, Parsippany, New Jersey 07054. Email dnbmdd@mail.dnb.com. Web site http://www.dnbmdd.com.

DIRECTORY OF CORPORATE AFFILIATIONS OR WHO OWNS WHOM is a superb directory which can help you decipher the organizational structure of a company. This directory provides detailed information about all parent companies, subsidiaries and divisions, plus plant locations, joint ventures, a brief description of the subsidiary or division, a partial listing of names and titles, location, phone number, and sometimes revenues or number of employees. THE DIRECTORY OF CORPORATE AFFILIATIONS provides a comprehensive "family tree" listing that lays out the corporate hierarchy to provide a picture of the structure of companies, subsidiaries, affiliates & divisions. It includes companies with revenues of at least $10 million and reveals division and subsidiary reporting relationships down to the sixth level. It provides information on 8,500 privately held companies. For US companies it details complex multinational relationships and joint ventures. For additional names and titles of key executives in subsidiaries & divisions, refer to another directory such as Standard & Poors, THE STANDARD DIRECTORY OF ADVERTISERS, or a specialized industry directory. THE DIRECTORY OF CORPORATE AFFILIATIONS consists of 5 volumes, including US Public Companies, US Private Companies, International Companies (both public and private), and indices. It also contains a Brand Name Index. The CD ROM version of this directory is titled Corporate Affiliations Plus.

Note: If THE DIRECTORY OF CORPORATE AFFILIATIONS does not provide all the organization structure information you want and the company is publicly held, there's an abundance of free information available! Check the company's web site or call them for an annual report and 10(k). Even if the company is privately held, they will usually send information if you ask for it. The more specific your request, the more likely you are to get what you need, for example, a list of all company locations, a list of plant locations, or product information.

Ordering information: $1,029.95/5 volumes, excluding discounts. If the price is prohibitively high, remember your local library. National Register Publishing, Reed Elsevier-New Providence, 121 Chanlon Road, New Providence, NJ 07974, (800) 521-8110, fax (800) 836-7736, web site www.redbooks.com or www.marquiswhoswho.com. "If, for any reason whatsoever, your order does not fully meet your expectations, simply return the product within 30 days for a prompt, complete, unquestioned refund," as stated in Catalog of Biographical and Professional References of publisher Marquis Who's Who/National Register Publishing.

GALE BUSINESS RESOURCES ONLINE provides modules on US Industry (over 200,000 companies) and International Industry (over 200,000 companies), including public and privately held companies, brands, business rankings, trade and professional associations, company histories, merger information, and more. Comprehensive records include company name, officers' names and titles, SIC/NAICS codes and more. GALE BUSINESS RESOURCES is available online on the Internet through GaleNet.

For information on pricing, contact: Gale Group, P.O. Box 9187, Farmington Hills, MI 48333-9187. Toll free US and Canada (800) 877-GALE (4253) and (248) 699-GALE, fax (800) 414-5043 and (248) 699-8061, Internet orders galeord@galegroup.com, web site www.galegroup.com or www.gale.com. All Gale Group products are available on approval. Contact Gale for details.

HARVARD BUSINESS SCHOOL'S BAKER LIBRARY in Boston provides an outstanding consumer marketing web site at www.library.hbs.edu/. This web site identifies extensive sources of information on consumer marketing, including retail both for job hunters and researchers. It includes associations, membership directories, information on direct mail, public relations, corporate communications, online direct mail and online Dun and Bradstreet Credit Reports.

While the access to the web site itself is free and available to anyone, access to the CAREER ADVISOR database is available only to current Harvard Business School students and Harvard Business School Alumni Advisors (Harvard Business School alumni who have agreed to serve as Career advisors to current students and other alumni). The Advisor Database can be searched by industry, geography, job function, job title, year of graduation and company name. In addition, Reference Librarians at the Harvard Business School can conduct searches for a fee. Hundreds of databases are available. Ask at the Reference Desk for more information. For example, Dun & Bradstreet's Credit Reports are a lucrative source of information about privately held companies.

INDUSTRY NORMS & KEY BUSINESS RATIOS is a reference that provides financial performance statistics for over 1 million public and private firms in over 800 lines of business. This statistical reference provides performance benchmarks for over 800 lines of business on over 1 million companies, both publicly and privately held. As this directory contains no names or titles, it is most appropriate for conducting industry research to develop a target list of top performing companies. Published annually. Also available on diskette. For prices call Dun & Bradstreet at (800) 526-0651. For more information contact Dun & Bradstreet, Business Reference Solutions, Three Sylvan Way, Parsippany, New Jersey 07054. Email dnbmdd@mail.dnb.com. Web site http://www.dnbmdd.com.

JOBSON'S YEAR BOOK OF PUBLIC COMPANIES OF AUSTRALIA AND NEW ZEALAND contains information on over 2,000 public and private companies and their executives. Dun & Bradstreet, Business Reference Solutions, Three Sylvan Way, Parsippany, NJ 07054 USA. (800) 526-0651. Email dnbmdd@mail.dnb.com. Web site http://www.dnbmdd.com.

SciTECH REFERENCE PLUS CD ROM contains directory information, 125,000 biographies of US and Canadian scientists and engineers from AMERICAN MEN AND WOMEN OF SCIENCE, listings for over 8,000 laboratories from the DIRECTORY OF AMERICAN RESEARCH AND TECHNOLOGY, and information from THE DIRECTORY OF CORPORATE AFFILIATIONS (including public, private and international companies) of leading US and international technology firms and their subsidiaries. It also contains 60,000 records on science/technology and medical serials from ULRICH'S INTERNATIONAL PERIODICALS DIRECTORY. Searches can be conducted by SIC, year founded, activity, education, employees, institution/company, city, state or country, memberships/honors, product description, personal statistics, personal title, research area, revenue. Updated annually. 1 year subscription $995, 3 years 2,836, excluding discounts. For more information visit Bowker Reed Reference's web site at http://www.reedref.com or contact: Bowker Reed Reference Electronic Publishing, 121 Chanlon Road, New Providence, NJ 07974 USA, Phone (800) 323-3288, Fax (908) 665-3528, email info@bowker.com.

STANDARD DIRECTORY OF ADVERTISERS Business Classifications Edition is an excellent general directory that organizes companies by a wide range of product categories. A few examples include "Apparel 2—Men's and Boys' Wear," "Heating and Air Conditioning," "Cosmetics and Toiletries," and "Aviation and Aerospace." This directory lists names and titles of key officers, revenues and other information. It is available in a geographic edition for the same price. This directory is comprised of over 24,000 companies that annually spend over $200,000 on advertising. It represents a reasonable place to look for hard-to-find information about privately held companies, especially those that heavily advertise their products. It is a good place to look for names if STANDARD AND POORS and the MILLION DOLLAR DIRECTORY fail to yield the names you need. Finally, the Classified Edition of THE STANDARD DIRECTORY OF ADVERTISERS can be a very convenient source of research because both your target list of companies and the corresponding names and titles of management all appear together, in the same Classification. This is important if you still rely on research books in hard copy. THE STANDARD DIRECTORY OF ADVERTISERS also publishes a special volume called THE STANDARD DIRECTORY OF ADVERTISERS TRADENAME INDEX. You can use the TRADENAME INDEX if you know the brand name of a product and need to find the company that manufactures it. In addition, this directory contains an Associations section which identifies marketing oriented associations.

$599 hard copy. If the price is prohibitively high, remember your local library. THE STANDARD DIRECTORY OF ADVERTISERS is also available on CD ROM under the title ADVERTISER AND AGENCY RED BOOKS PLUS. It is available in Windows® and Macintosh® formats. National Register Publishing, Reed Elsevier-New Providence, 121 Chanlon Road, New Providence, NJ 07974, (800) 521-8110, fax (800) 836-7736, web site www.redbooks.com or www.marquiswhoswho.com. "If, for any reason whatsoever, your order does not fully meet your expectations, simply return the product within 30 days for a prompt, complete, unquestioned refund," as stated in Catalog of Biographical and Professional References of publisher Marquis Who's Who/National Register Publishing.

STANDARD DIRECTORY OF ADVERTISING AGENCIES, also referred to as the "Red Book," is a comprehensive directory of the advertising agency business, generally including extensive listings of executives, especially in management, media, account services, creative and production. It also reveals the names of each agency's corporate clients. A CyberAgency Section lists agencies involved with Web design and development and a special "Who Owns Whom" section listing agency subsidiaries. $599. If the price is prohibitively high, remember your local library. THE STANDARD DIRECTORY OF ADVERTISING AGENCIES is also available on CD ROM under the title ADVERTISER AND AGENCY RED BOOKS PLUS. National Register Publishing, Reed Elsevier-New Providence, 121 Chanlon Road, New Providence, NJ 07974, (800) 521-8110, fax (800) 836-7736, web site www.marquiswhoswho.com or www.redbooks.com. "If, for any reason whatsoever, your order does not fully meet your expectations, simply return the product within 30 days for a prompt, complete, unquestioned refund," as stated in Catalog of Biographical and Professional References of publisher Marquis Who's Who/National Register Publishing.

STATE MANUFACTURING DIRECTORIES and US regional geographic directories published by Harris are available for all US states as hard copy directories or in electronic Selectory® formats. With Selectory® information is searchable from 25 fields and generates an easy-to-read report containing: company, address, location, county, phone, fax, toll free number, Internet address, a listing of personnel with titles, SIC/NAICS codes, product description, products, number of employees, per cent employment change, sales range, plant size, foreign trade, year established, private or public ownership, and experian credit score. This information could either provide an alternative to "identification research" calls, or offer an excellent place to begin the verification calls of ID research. If time is money, you can access a tremendous amount of precise information quickly with electronic references, such as this one or many others. One attractive feature of Harris's products is that they are relatively inexpensive. Here are a few sample prices: Directories and databases are available for all US states: Alabama $79 directory, $349 database. Arizona $90 directory, $475 database. Arkansas $69 directory, $325 database, Ohio $159 directory, $725 database. New Jersey $99 directory, $595 database. The most expensive is California, $169 directory, $925 database. The least expensive are Delaware and Washington, DC each one at $39 for directory, $149 for database.

Contact Harris for a sample Harris Profile Report. For exact pricing, a catalog and other information, call distributor Scott's Directories, Toronto area: 1450 Don Mills Road, Don Mills, Ontario, M3B 2X7, CANADA, (888) 709-9907, (416) 442-2291, (416) 932-9555. Montréal area: Scott's Directories, 3300 Cote Verde, Suite 410 Ville St.-Laurent, Quebec H4B 2B7 CANADA (514) 339-1397, (800) 363-1327, email scotts@southam.ca. Publisher Harris InfoSource, 2057 East Aurora Road, Twinsburg, OH 44087-1999, (330) 425-9000, (800) 888-5900, www.HarrisInfo.com.

WARD'S BUSINESS DIRECTORY OF U.S. PRIVATE AND PUBLIC COMPANIES provides information on over 120,000 US companies, over 90% of them privately held. Volumes 1-3 contain company information. Volume 4 lists companies geographically and ranks the top 1,000 privately held companies and the top 1,000 employers. Volume 5 ranks private and public companies by sales within SIC or NAICS code. Volumes 6-7 contain state rankings by sales within SIC or NAICS. Also includes ranking of the top 100 privately held companies, the top publicly held companies and the top 100 employers for each state. Volume 8 ranks sales within the 6 digit NAICS (North American Industry Classification System which replaced the SIC code system). It sorts companies by cross-national agreements between the US, Canada and Mexico. Vols. 1-8, $2,515. Vols. 1-5, $2,125. Vols. 1-4, $1,880. Vol 5, $950. Vols. 6-7, $950. Vol 8, $640. Gale Group, P.O. Box 9187, Farmington Hills, MI 48333-9187. Toll free US and Canada (800) 877-GALE (4253) and (248) 699-GALE, fax (800) 414-5043 and (248) 699-8061, Internet orders galeord@galegroup.com, web site www.galegroup.com or www.gale.com. All Gale Group products are available on approval. Contact Gale for details.

www.library.hbs.edu/ is the URL for the Harvard Business School Baker Library, which contains free excellent information on consumer marketing, retail, associations, membership directories, direct mail, public relations, corporate communications, online direct mail and more. Dun and Bradstreet Credit Reports can also be accessed. In addition, for a fee, reference librarians can conduct online searches from any of several hundred databases. See "Harvard Business School's Baker Library" above.

Professional Associations

See Associations

Public Affairs

ENCYCLOPEDIA OF ASSOCIATIONS: INTERNATIONAL ORGANIZATIONS includes nearly 20,000 multinational and national organizations in foreign countries, including US based associations with multinational membership. Entries also include email addresses, web sites and bulletin board addresses, lobbying activities, and publication and convention information. Indexed by geography, keyword and executives. $595 for 2 volume set. Also available in CD ROM. Database available via commercial online service. Gale Group, P.O. Box 9187, Farmington Hills, MI 48333-9187. Toll free US and Canada (800) 877-GALE (4253) and (248) 699-GALE, fax (800) 414-5043 and (248) 699-8061, Internet orders galeord@galegroup.com, web site www.galegroup.com or www.gale.com. All Gale Group products are available on approval. Contact Gale for details.

ENCYCLOPEDIA OF ASSOCIATIONS: NATIONAL ORGANIZATIONS OF THE US. This superb reference is one of the first places you should look when beginning a new recruiting assignment or when looking for specialized references of any type. The keyword index makes this comprehensive reference easy to use, even in hard copy. For over 23,000 nonprofit professional associations with a national scope, this encyclopedia reveals:

- Publications, including membership rosters and newsletters

- Dates and locations of association conferences and conventions

- Names of Executive Directors, who are usually incredible sources of industry information if you call and speak to them

- Committees

- Job and candidate referral banks, which can provide resumes of other industry sources and sometimes candidates

- It includes organizations in these categories: business, trade, environmental, agricultural, legal, governmental, engineering, technological, scientific, educational, cultural, social welfare, health & medical, public affairs, ethnic, labor unions, chambers of commerce, tourism, & others.

  Volume 1, National Organizations of the US, $505
  Volume 2, Geographic and Executive Indexes, $390
  Volume 3, Supplement, $405

Gale Group, P.O. Box 9187, Farmington Hills, MI 48333-9187. Toll free US and Canada (800) 877-GALE (4253) and (248) 699-GALE, fax (800) 414-5043 and (248) 699-8061, Internet orders galeord@galegroup.com, web site www.galegroup.com or www.gale.com. All Gale Group products are available on approval. Contact Gale for details.

ENCYCLOPEDIA OF ASSOCIATIONS: REGIONAL, STATE AND LOCAL ORGANIZATIONS. The information in this directory is not duplicated anywhere in ENCYCLOPEDIA OF ASSOCIATIONS. Over 100,000 nonprofit organizations are included in this directory. $585 for 5 volume set or $140 per individual volume. Also available on CD ROM and online on the Internet through a GaleNet subscription.

> Volume 1, Great Lakes States (Illinois, Indiana, Michigan, Minnesota, Ohio, Wisconsin)
> Volume 2, Northeastern States (Connecticut, Maine, Massachusetts, New Hampshire, New Jersey, New York, Pennsylvania, Rhode Islands, Vermont)
> Volume 3, Southern and Middle Atlantic States (Including Puerto Rico and the Virgin Islands) (Alabama, Delaware, Washington, DC, Florida, Georgia, Kentucky, Maryland, Mississippi, North Carolina, Puerto Rico, South Carolina, Tennessee, Virginia, West Virginia, Virgin Islands)
> Volume 4, South Central and Great Plains States (Arkansas, Iowa, Kansas, Louisiana, Missouri, Nebraska, North Dakota, Oklahoma, South Dakota, Texas)
> Volume 5, Western States (Alaska, Arizona, California, Colorado, Guam, Hawaii, Idaho, Montana, Nevada, New Mexico, Oregon, Utah, Washington, Wyoming)

Gale Group, P.O. Box 9187, Farmington Hills, MI 48333-9187. Toll free US and Canada (800) 877-GALE (4253) and (248) 699-GALE, fax (800) 414-5043 and (248) 699-8061, Internet orders galeord@galegroup.com, web site www.galegroup.com or www.gale.com. All Gale Group products are available on approval. Contact Gale for details.

NATIONAL DIRECTORY OF CORPORATE PUBLIC AFFAIRS identifies some 14,000 people who manage public affairs and government affairs programs of nearly 2,000 corporations. This directory also includes Washington area offices, corporate foundation/giving programs, federal and state lobbyists and outside contract lobbyists. Indexed by subject and geography. $95. Columbia Books, Inc., 1212 New York Avenue, NW, Suite 330, Washington, DC 20005, (212) 898-0662.

Public Relations

See Corporate Communications

BACON'S BUSINESS MEDIA DIRECTORY identifies many financial and business media contacts not found in other Bacon's directories. Media outlets include: major daily newspapers, national, regional, state and city business publications, select business journals, news and general interest magazines, news services and syndicates, freelancers by specialty, and a free midyear update. $275. Ordering information: Call (800) 621-0561, (800) 753-6675. Bacon's Information, Inc., a K-III Communications Company, 332 South Michigan Avenue, Chicago, IL 60604. Satisfaction guaranteed or a full refund within 30 days.

BACON'S CALIFORNIA MEDIA DIRECTORY presents more in-depth coverage than their main directories, including statewide print and broadcast coverage of daily and community newspapers, state bureaus of US dailies, regional business and general interest magazines, broadcast networks, stations, syndicators and programming, detailed editorial staff listings at all outlets, freelance journalists, including "editorial pitching profiles," phone, fax, email and home page. $195. Ordering information: Call (800) 621-0561, (800) 753-6675. Bacon's Information, Inc., a K-III Communications Company, 332 South Michigan Avenue, Chicago, IL 60604. Satisfaction guaranteed or a full refund within 30 days.

BACON'S COMPUTER & HI-TECH MEDIA DIRECTORY identifies 6,500 contacts at 1,900 print and broadcast outlets, serving computers, data management, software, the Internet, electronics, telecommunications and more. $225. Ordering information: Call (800) 621-0561, (800) 753-6675. Bacon's Information, Inc., a K-III Communications Company, 332 South Michigan Avenue, Chicago, IL 60604. Satisfaction guaranteed or a full refund within 30 days.

BACON'S INFORMATION provides a news clipping and analysis service which can be used to monitor competitive news, to conduct topic research, or to track "pickup" of press releases. For more information, call

BACON'S CLIPPING BUREAU to inquire about ExpressClips (same day coverage of top media in key markets), Electronic Clipping (database retrieval of transcripts from a wide selection of publications), International Clipping (coverage for specific countries worldwide) and Clip Analysis Reports (for a review of your own press coverage). (800) 621-0561, (800) 753-6675. Bacon's Information, Inc., a K-III Communications Company, 332 South Michigan Avenue, Chicago, IL 60604.

BACON'S MEDIASOURCE CD ROM is a media database and software with over 250,000 names of contacts at over 48,000 media outlets, including newspapers and their bureaus, magazines and newsletters, news syndicates, wire services, broadcast networks, stations and shows, including phone, fax, email and home page. Updated quarterly. Available for Windows and Macintosh. $1,095 annual subscription. Ordering information: Call (800) 621-0561, (800) 753-6675. Bacon's Information, Inc., a K-III Communications Company, 332 South Michigan Avenue, Chicago, IL 60604.

BACON'S MEDICAL & HEALTH MEDIA DIRECTORY identifies over 6,500 print and broadcast contacts in fitness, personal health, healthcare trade, specialized medicine, nutrition and other categories. $225. Ordering information: Call (800) 621-0561, (800) 753-6675. Bacon's Information, Inc., a K-III Communications Company, 332 South Michigan Avenue, Chicago, IL 60604. Satisfaction guaranteed or a full refund within 30 days.

BACON'S NEW YORK MEDIA DIRECTORY presents more in-depth coverage than their main directories, including statewide print and broadcast coverage of daily and community newspapers, state bureaus of US dailies, regional business and general interest magazines, broadcast networks, stations, syndicators and programming, detailed editorial staff listings at all outlets, freelance journalists, including "editorial pitching profiles," phone, fax, email and home page. $195. Ordering information: Call (800) 621-0561, (800) 753-6675. Bacon's Information, Inc., a K-III Communications Company, 332 South Michigan Avenue, Chicago, IL 60604. Satisfaction guaranteed or a full refund within 30 days.

BACON'S NEWSPAPER/MAGAZINE DIRECTORY is a two volume set that identifies every daily and weekly newspaper in the US, every magazine and newsletter in the US that accepts outside editorial, detailed listings of editorial staffs, with phone, fax and email, publication Internet home pages and other online locations, magazine editorial profiles and types of press materials accepted, syndicated columnists by beat, news services and news syndicates, and indexes of newspapers by market and circulation. Includes names and titles, editors' preferences, like/dislikes and "beat" reporter information to help you find the right contact. $275. Ordering information: Call (800) 621-0561, (800) 753-6675. Bacon's Information, Inc., a K-III Communications Company, 332 South Michigan Avenue, Chicago, IL 60604. Satisfaction guaranteed or a full refund within 30 days.

BACON'S RADIO/TV/CABLE DIRECTORY is a two volume set that identifies all US national and regional networks, all US broadcast stations, management and news executives, radio and TV syndicators, including programming staff, detailed show listings, over 100,000 names of contacts, an index of show subjects and more. $275. Ordering information: Call (800) 621-0561, (800) 753-6675. Bacon's Information, Inc., a K-III Communications Company, 332 South Michigan Avenue, Chicago, IL 60604. Satisfaction guaranteed or a full refund within 30 days.

D&B DIRECTORY OF SERVICE COMPANIES is a directory with information on 50,000 US service businesses, including privately held companies, in these sectors: accounting, auditing and bookkeeping, advertising and public relations, architecture and engineering, consumer services, executive search, health, hospitality, management consulting, motion pictures, repair, research, social services and law. Listings include key executives' names and titles, address, phone, sales volume, number of employees, parent company and location, and more. Companies listed employ 50 or more people. Information is listed alphabetically and is cross-referenced geographically and by industry classification. Updated annually. For prices call Dun & Bradstreet at (800) 526-0651. For more information contact Dun & Bradstreet, Business Reference Solutions, Three Sylvan Way, Parsippany, New Jersey 07054. Email dnbmdd@mail.dnb.com. Web site http://www.dnbmdd.com.

JACK O'DWYER'S NEWSLETTER is an 8 page weekly public relations newsletter which *The New York Times* says is "the Bible of PR." Annual subscription $250. J.R O'Dwyer Co., Inc., 271 Madison Avenue, New York, New York 10157-0160. Phone (212) 679-2471. Fax (212) 683-2750.

LITERARY MARKET PLACE, "The Directory of the American Book Publishing Industry With Industry Yellow Pages" is an excellent 3 volume directory with comprehensive information on US book publishers; imprints, subsidiaries and distributors; book trade acquisitions and mergers, small presses, Canadian book publishers, micropublishers, US electronic publishers, electronic publishing consultants, electronic publishing products and services, editorial services, literary agents, illustrations agents, US agents and offices of foreign publishers, lecture agents, specialized advertising and public relations firms, direct mail specialists, mailing list brokers and services, book review syndicates, book review and index journals and services, book exhibits, book clubs, book lists and catalogs, book importers and exporters, book producers, translators, artists, photographers, stock photo agencies, associations, book trade events and conferences, awards, contents and grants, reference books for the trade, magazines for the trade, a toll free directory of publishers, magazine and newspaper publicity, radio and television publicity, book manufacturing services, book distributors and sales representatives, and wholesalers. $189.95.

LITERARY MARKET PLACE ON DISC, previously titled LITERARY MARKET PLACE PLUS CD ROM, one year subscription $297.00.

LITERARY MARKET PLACE—INTERNET EDITION, www.literarymarketplace.com, is available by subscription.

INTERNATIONAL LITERARY MARKET PLACE Internet database can be directly accessed at www.iliterarymarketplace.com. It is also linked to the US domestic LITERARY MARKET PLACE web site at www.literarymarketplace.com. Contact the publisher for subscription price. INTERNATIONAL LITERARY MARKET PLACE, hard copy $189.95.

R.R. Bowker (a unit of Cahners Business Information), 121 Chanlon Road, New Providence, NJ 07974 USA, Phone (888) BOWKER2 (888-269-5372) & (800) 323-3288, fax (908) 508-7696, email info@bowker.com, web www.bowker.com. Canada—R.R. Bowker, Markham, Ontario, phone (888) BOWKER9 & (905) 415-5837, fax (905) 479-6266. German speaking Europe—K.G. Saur Verlag, Munich, Germany, phone 49-89-76902-232, fax 49-89-76902-250, email 100730.1341@compuserve.com, web www.saur.de/home.htm. Rest of Europe incl. United Kingdom plus Africa & Asia—Bowker-Saur, W. Sussex, UK, phone 44-1342-326-972, fax 44-1342-335-612, email customer@bowker-saur.co.uk, web www.bowker-saur.com/service/. Australia/New Zealand—Thorpe, Port Melbourne, Victoria, Australia, phone 61-03-9-245-7370, fax 61-03-9-245-7395, email customer.service@thorpe.com.au, web www.thorpe.com.au. Technical support for CD ROMs (800) 323-3288, fax 908) 665-3528, email techsupport@bowker.com.

O'DWYER'S DIRECTORY OF CORPORATE COMMUNICATIONS lists over 10,000 public relations professionals in companies, trade associations and the government, including foreign embassies, cross referenced by industry. $110. J.R O'Dwyer Co., Inc., 271 Madison Avenue, New York, New York 10157-0160. Phone (212) 679-2471. Fax (212) 683-2750.

O'DWYER'S DIRECTORY OF PR EXECUTIVES provides biographical data about over 8,000 public relations professionals, including job and educational backgrounds, plus business addresses and phone numbers, cross referenced by employers. This directory encompasses almost all the organizations in O'DWYER'S DIRECTORY OF PR FIRMS AND O'DWYER'S DIRECTORY OF CORPORATE COMMUNICATIONS. $120. J.R O'Dwyer Co., Inc., 271 Madison Avenue, New York, New York 10157-0160. Phone (212) 679-2471. Fax (212) 683-2750.

O'DWYER'S DIRECTORY OF PR FIRMS lists over 1,700 public relations firms in the US and 500 others in 55 countries. Updated annually. $165. J.R O'Dwyer Co., Inc., 271 Madison Avenue, New York, New York 10157-0160. Phone (212) 679-2471. Fax (212) 683-2750.

O'DWYER'S PR MARKETPLACE is a biweekly publication which lists classified want ads. $24 subscription.J.R O'Dwyer Co., Inc., 271 Madison Avenue, New York, New York 10157-0160. Phone (212) 679-2471. Fax (212) 683-2750.

O'DWYER'S PR SERVICES REPORT is the largest monthly public relations magazine. It is a source of information about databases, among other things. $40 J.R O'Dwyer Co., Inc., 271 Madison Avenue, New York, New York 10157-0160. Phone (212) 679-2471. Fax (212) 683-2750.

PHILLIPS BUSINESS INFORMATION provides information in newsletters, magazines, directories and on multiple web sites covering a range of topics, such as magazine products, telecommunications and cable products, satellite products, media, new media and Internet products, marketing and public relations products, financial technology and electronic commerce, aviation and defense products. For more information, contact: Phillips Business Information, Inc., a Phillips Publishing International Company, 120 Seven Locks Road, Potomac, MD 20854, (301) 340-1520, (301) 340-7788, (800) 777-5006, Internet pbi@phillips.com, web site www.phillips.com.

POWER MEDIA SELECTS includes print, newspapers and magazines. Published by Broadcast Interview Source, 2233 Wisconsin Avenue, NW, Suite 540, Washington, DC 20007. For more information call (800) 955-0311, (202) 333-4904.

PR NEWS ANNUAL SALARY SURVEY AND EXCLUSIVE GUIDE TO EXECUTIVE RECRUITERS, Phillips Business Information, Inc., a Phillips Publishing International Company, 120 Seven Locks Road, Potomac, MD 20854, (301) 340-1520, (301) 340-7788, (800) 777-5006, Internet pbi@phillips.com, web site www.phillips.com.

TALK SHOW SELECTS identifies the top 750 local and national TV and radio talk shows. Hard copy $185. Floppy disk and book, $260. Published by Broadcast Interview Source, 2233 Wisconsin Avenue, NW, Suite 540, Washington, DC 20007. (800) 955-0311, (202) 333-4904.

YEARBOOK OF EXPERTS, AUTHORITIES & SPOKESPERSONS. $49.95. Free to Journalists. Call for information. Published by Broadcast Interview Source, 2233 Wisconsin Avenue, NW, Suite 540, Washington, DC 20007. (800) 955-0311, (202) 333-4904.

Publishers Web Sites

See Publishing Industry

The Publishers Web Sites category identifies web sites for publishers of various types of information covering a broad spectrum of industries and functions, including directories, databases on the Internet and on CD ROM. For example, some listings are www.ambest.com, a publisher of insurance publications, www.dnbmdd.com, the web site for Dun and Bradstreet MILLION DOLLAR DIRECTORY; and www.cpsnet.com, the site for CPS Communications Inc., the healthcare industry publisher of the Pharmaceutical Manufacturers Directory, to name a few. If you wish to locate additional publishers and their web sites, refer to the LITERARY MARKET PLACE, which is described in detail in the Publishing Industry Category. More information on LITERARY MARKET PLACE is available on publisher R.R. Bowker's web site at www.bowker.com.

Remember, another research option is to go to the "Ask Jeeves" web site at www.askjeeves.com

www.amazon.com is a large bookstore web site. At the time of this writing they offer discounts up to 40%.

www.ambest.com is the insurance industry web site for A.M. Best Company. It includes publications and services, a web services resources center, employment, plus sites for Best's Safety Directory, and Attorneys and Adjusters.

www.askjeeves.com or **www.ask.com** or **www.aj.com** or **ask** is an easy site to use. You can ask any type of question in plain English. Visit the site and try it for fun! If you ask Jeeves, "How can I find a job" or "How can I find candidates for an engineering job?" Jeeves has an answer! (Actually, there's very little you CAN'T ask Jeeves.) The Ask Jeeves site includes HOOVER'S CAREER CENTER, which consists of Job Search Tools (monster.com, CareerMosaic,wsj.com careers, hotjobs, Westech's Virtual Job Fair and joboptions), Career Links and Career Research Links. Hoover's Career Center contains much additional information, including extensive RELOCATION data, such as cost of living comparisons, etc. You can also subscribe to Hoover's and access their directories on the Internet.

www.bookwire.com is the web site for *Publishers Weekly*. It is an important web site that serves both publishing industry professionals and consumers with information about publishing and research. Bowker's *Publishers Weekly*'s web site includes a searchable database of current author tour information, links to all book-related web sites, industry classifieds, and Book Wire Insider Direct, a subscription daily e-mail news service, and more.

www.bowker.com is the web site for this major research publisher. It includes Flagship Products and Services, an online Product Catalog, Electronic Publishing products including CD ROMs, Internet Databases, and Online Subscription and Site Licensing Databases; press releases, career opportunities, and more. Many of their references are accessible through this web site, such as BOOKS IN PRINT PLUS CANADIAN EDITION, ULRICH'S ON DISC, GERMAN BOOKS IN PRINT, GERMAN BOOKS OUT OF PRINT, INTERNATIONAL BOOKS IN PRINT PLUS, ITALIAN BOOKS IN PRINT, YEARBOOK OF INTERNATIONAL ORGANIZATIONS PLUS, ULRICH'S INTERNATIONAL PERIODICALS DIRECTORY, THE SOFTWARE ENCYCLOPEDIA, BOWKER'S COMPLETE VIDEO DIRECTORY, AMERICAN BOOK PUBLISHING RECORD. Visit the web site for more information. At this web site you can also search—free—BOOKS OUT OF PRINT database. At this site you can also search free Bowker's LIBRARY RESOURCE GUIDE—INTERNET EDITION, a directory of library services and suppliers which is drawn from Bowker's AMERICAN LIBRARY DIRECTORY. At www.bowker.com you can also access a free online directory from LITERARY MARKET PLACE, including hundreds of services and suppliers to the book publishing community—ad agencies, publicists, typesetters, printers and more.

www.cahners.com is the web site for Cahners Business Information.

www.corptech.com is the site for CorpTech Technology Company Information, including directories, guides, databases, mailing lists, and reports customized from the CorpTech Database.

www.cpsnet.com is the site for the healthcare industry CPS Communications, Inc. They publish the Pharmaceutical Marketers Directory, Healthcare News Net, a daily online publication, and the trade publication Medical Marketing and Media.

www.csgis.com is one of the URLs to Chain Store Guide Information Services. Another is www.d-net.com/csgis.

www.dialog.com is the web site to The Dialog Corporation, "the world's largest online information company."

www.dnbmdd.com is the web site to the DUN & BRADSTREET MILLION DOLLAR DIRECTORY. Their database provides information on over 1 million leading public and private US companies.

www.fairchildpub.com and www.fairchildbooks.com are web sites to Fairchild Publications, publisher of the New York City fashion trade paper Women's Wear Daily and other apparel industry publications.

www.gale.com is the URL to Gale Research's old web site, prior to their merger with Information Access Company and Primary Source Media and the resulting name change to Gale Group.

www.galegroup.com is the web site to publisher Gale Group, one of the largest providers of research references serving the search industry, recruiting and libraries.

www.greyhouse.com is the URL for Grey House Publishing in Lakeville, Connecticut, publisher of The Directory of Business Information Resources, Associations, Newsletters, Magazines and Tradeshows.

www.harrisinfo.com is the URL to the web site of the publisher of technology directories, Harris InfoSource International, 2057 Aurora Road, Twinsburg, OH 44087-1999, (800) 888-5900, fax (800) 643-5997.

www.iliterarymarketplace.com is the URL for International LITERARY MARKET PLACE's Internet database, which is available by subscription from R.R. Bowker. For more information, see Bowker's site at www.bowker.com.

www.kennedyinfo.com is the web site for publisher Kennedy Information. It includes books, newsletters, training materials, directories, and surveys for executive recruiting, human resources, outplacement, management consulting and job seekers. (800) 531-0007 or (603) 585-6544.

www.kompass.com is the URL to Kompass's web site. It contains a searchable database that encompasses over 60 countries, 2.5 million executive names, information on 1.5 million companies, 19 million key product references, and 370,000 trade and brand names. At the time of this writing, Kompass is available in English and French. Inquire to find out when Deutsch, Espanol and Italiano be available.

www.literarymarketplace.com is the URL for LITERARY MARKET PLACE's Internet database, which is available by subscription from R.R. Bowker. Bowker's web site at www.bowker.com also contains a free online directory taken directly from the pages of LITERARY MARKET PLACE.

www.lexis-nexis.com is the URL to the Lexis-Nexis web site.

www.macmillan.com is the URL to Macmillan's web site. It contains sections on science, technical, medical, college academic Professional, School books and ELT, magazines, general Books, electronic publishing and associated companies, including Scientific American.

www.manufacturersnews.com is the web site to Manufacturers' News, Inc., publisher of geographic and manufacturing directories, both US and foreign.

www.mhbizlink.com is the web site address for the major Canadian publisher Maclean Hunter. Among other things, it has links to 30 business publications. For more information call them in Toronto at (416) 596-5000.

www.mmdaccess.com is the web site to financial publisher Money Market Directories, Inc., a division of Standard & Poors, which is a division of McGraw Hill.

www.nelnet.com is the URL to Nelson Information's web site. It includes Manager Hires, Job Bank, Nelson's Products, Investment Manager Listings, World's Best Money Managers, M&A News and more.

www.ntis.gov/ is the web site for National Technical Information Service, formerly called the US Government Printing Office. NTIS published the STANDARD INDUSTRIAL CLASSIFICATION (SIC) MANUAL until it had been replaced by the NORTH AMERICAN INDUSTRY CODE SYSTEM (NAICS) MANUAL in 1997. National Technical Information Service, Technology Administration, US Department of Commerce, Springfield, VA 22161. Phone orders Monday-Friday, 8 am - 8 pm Eastern Time (800) 553-NTIS (6487) or (703) 605-6000. NTIS is the central source for government sponsored US and worldwide scientific, engineering and business related information. As a self-supporting agency of the US Department of Commerce's Technology Administration, NTIS covers its business and operating expenses with the sale of its products and services. For questions about a product or order, email info@ntis.fedworld.gov.

www.oryxpress.com is the web site to Oryx Press, publisher of librarian directories. Browse the site by subject, titles, and authors.

www.phillips.com is the web site to Phillips Business Information, Inc. It contains product catalogs for aviation, defense, electronic commerce, energy/oil and gas, finance, health, marketing/public relations, media, new media/Internet, politics/public policy, satellite, security, telecommunications. Subscription web site to Aviation Today, Communications Today, Defense Daily Network, Electronic Commerce Today, Fabian Investment Resources, Richard E. Bank's Profitable Investing, Telecom Web, Wireless Today. Phillips Subsidiaries are Phillips Publishing Inc., Phillips Business Information, Hart Publications, and Eagle Publishing.

www.reedref.com presents a current catalog for all Reed Reference Publishing companies for both print and electronic references—National Register Publishing, R.R. Bowker, Bowker-Saur, KG Saur, Marquis Who's Who, Martindale-Hubbell and Lexis-Nexis Business Information. At the time of this writing, this catalog is searchable by name, subject, publisher and keyword. To check new offerings, visit individual publisher pages. Free product demos of CD ROM'S can be downloaded for for experimentation and some sample pages—and even entire chapters—and are available for unlimited viewing. The web site also includes a constantly updated menu of special discounts which are available only on the web site. Ask about the growing number of RRP databases accessible via the Internet on subscription or for a usage based price, such as the MARTINDALE-HUBBELL LAW DIRECTORY. For more information visit Bowker Reed Reference's web site at www.reedref.com or www.bowker.com or contact corporate offices, 121 Chanlon Road, New Providence, NJ 07974, (800) 521-8110, (800) 323-3288, Fax (908) 665-3528, email info@bowker.com or webmaster@www.reedref.com.

www.tfp.bankinfo.com is the web site to banking industry publisher Thomson Financial Publishing.

www.thomasregister.com is the web site to Thomas' Register.

www.umi.com is the web site to publisher UMI in Ann Arbor, Michigan, the highly respected publisher of large databases of periodicals and other library references, especially electronic references. UMI publishes the important databases ABI Inform and Books on Demand, Magazines, Newspapers and Collections Online which consists of 19,000 titles.

www.uniworldbp.com is the web site to a publisher of US-International company directories.

www.ziff-davis.com is the web site to computer magazine publisher Ziff-Davis, a Softbank Company.

Publishing Industry

See Publishers Web sites

AMERICAN BOOK TRADE DIRECTORY identifies specialty bookstore, chains, retail & antiquarian book dealers, foreign book dealers, book and magazine wholesalers and distributors and library collection appraisers. Published annually. $249.95. R.R. Bowker (a unit of Cahners Business Information), 121 Chanlon Road, New Providence, NJ 07974 USA, Phone (888) BOWKER2 (888-269-5372) & (800) 323-3288, fax (908) 508-7696, email info@bowker.com, web www.bowker.com. Canada—R.R. Bowker, Markham, Ontario, phone (888) BOWKER9 & (905) 415-5837, fax (905) 479-6266. German speaking Europe—K.G. Saur Verlag, Munich, Germany, phone 49-89-76902-232, fax 49-89-76902-250, email 100730.1341@compuserve.com, web www.saur.de/home.htm. Rest of Europe incl. United Kingdom plus Africa & Asia—Bowker-Saur, W. Sussex, UK, phone 44-1342-326-972, fax 44-1342-335-612, email customer@bowker-saur.co.uk, web www.bowker-saur.com/service/. Australia/New Zealand—Thorpe, Port Melbourne, Victoria, Australia, phone 61-03-9-245-7370, fax 61-03-9-245-7395, email customer.service@thorpe.com.au, web www.thorpe.com.au. Technical support for CD ROMs (800) 323-3288, fax 908) 665-3528, email techsupport@bowker.com.

AMERICAN LIBRARY GUIDE identifies collections, books, library networks, and trade organizations. Published annually. Contact publisher for price. Cahners Business Information, 121 Chanlon Road, New Providence, NJ 07974, (908) 665-2801, 888-269-5372, www.bowker.com. Headquarters: Cahners Business Information, 275 Washington Street, Newton, MA 02158-1630, (617) 558-4663 or (617) 964-3030, fax (617) 558-4700, email marketaccess@cahners.com. Web sites www.cahners.com or www.chilton.net.

ASIAN ADVERTISING, MARKETING AND MEDIA HANDBOOK lists information about advertising agencies, newspaper and magazine publishers and market research companies.

Published by Euromonitor (England), at $470 (1st edition), it had been exclusively distributed by Gale Group. At the time of this writing, Gale no longer carries it. For more information, contact Euromonitor or Gale or refer to Books in Print. This reference might also be available in the library.

BOOKSELLERS DIRECTORY (AUSTRALIAN), from Thorpe, $30. R.R. Bowker (a unit of Cahners Business Information), 121 Chanlon Road, New Providence, NJ 07974 USA, Phone (888) BOWKER2 (888-269-5372) & (800) 323-3288, fax (908) 508-7696, email info@bowker.com, web www.bowker.com. Canada—R.R. Bowker, Markham, Ontario, phone (888) BOWKER9 & (905) 415-5837, fax (905) 479-6266. German speaking Europe—K.G. Saur Verlag, Munich, Germany, phone 49-89-76902-232, fax 49-89-76902-250, email 100730.1341@compuserve.com, web www.saur.de/home.htm. Rest of Europe incl. United Kingdom plus Africa & Asia—Bowker-Saur, W. Sussex, UK, phone 44-1342-326-972, fax 44-1342-335-612, email customer@bowker-saur.co.uk, web www.bowker-saur.com/service/. Australia/New Zealand—Thorpe, Port Melbourne, Victoria, Australia, phone 61-03-9-245-7370, fax 61-03-9-245-7395, email customer.service@thorpe.com.au, web www.thorpe.com.au. Technical support for CD ROMs (800) 323-3288, fax 908) 665-3528, email techsupport@bowker.com.

BOOK TRADE IN CANADA/L'INDUSTRIE DU LIVRE AU CANADA is an annual publication. For further information contact: Ampersand Communications, Inc., 5606 Scobie Crescent, Manotick, ON K4M 1B7, CANADA.

BOOKS IN CANADA is a monthly publication which reviews 300-400 new Canadian books each year. It provides an inexpensive way to learn about new resources in Canada. It is available by subscription ($22.98/year) and is sold at newsstands and in bookstores ($3.95 per issue).

Ordering information:
BOOKS IN CANADA
Canadian Review of Books Ltd.
427 Mt. Pleasant Road
Toronto, ON M4S 2L8 CANADA
(416) 489-4755 Phone

BOOKS IN PRINT ON DISC, CANADIAN EDITION, annual subscription $599. R.R. Bowker (a unit of Cahners Business Information), 121 Chanlon Road, New Providence, NJ 07974 USA, Phone (888) BOWKER2 (888-269-5372) & (800) 323-3288, fax (908) 508-7696, email info@bowker.com, web www.bowker.com. Canada—R.R. Bowker, Markham, Ontario, phone (888) BOWKER9 & (905) 415-5837, fax (905) 479-6266. German speaking Europe—K.G. Saur Verlag, Munich, Germany, phone 49-89-76902-232, fax 49-89-76902-250, email 100730.1341@compuserve.com, web www.saur.de/home.htm. Rest of Europe incl. United Kingdom plus Africa & Asia—Bowker-Saur, W. Sussex, UK, phone 44-1342-326-972, fax 44-1342-335-612, email customer@bowker-saur.co.uk, web www.bowker-saur.com/service/. Australia/New Zealand—Thorpe, Port Melbourne, Victoria, Australia, phone 61-03-9-245-7370, fax 61-03-9-245-7395, email customer.service@thorpe.com.au, web www.thorpe.com.au. Technical support for CD ROMs (800) 323-3288, fax 908) 665-3528, email techsupport@bowker.com.

BOOKS IN PRINT is the only complete record of in-print, out-of-print and forthcoming books published or distributed in the US. For up-to-the-minute current information on INTERNET references and Internet Databases and Internet web sites available, use this reference. It should be available at a public library or in a good book store. Published annually. 9 volume set, $550. BOOKS IN PRINT ON DISC is available in Windows, MS-DOS and Macintosh . Annual subscription $550.

BOOKS IN PRINT INTERNET EDITION at www.booksinprint.com is available by subscription. Log on or call for details.

BOOKS IN PRINT ONLINE is available through the Dialog Corporation, Ovid Technologies, Inc. and LEXIS ®-NEXIS® on a "pay-as-you-go" basis. Contact the publisher for details. BOOKS OUT OF PRINT INTERNET EDITION can be searched free at www.bowker.com. R.R. Bowker (a unit of Cahners Business Information), 121 Chanlon Road, New Providence, NJ 07974 USA, Phone (888) BOWKER2 (888-269-5372) & (800) 323-3288, fax (908) 508-7696, email info@bowker.com, web www.bowker.com. Canada—R.R. Bowker, Markham, Ontario, phone (888) BOWKER9 & (905) 415-5837, fax (905) 479-6266. German speaking Europe—K.G. Saur Verlag, Munich, Germany, phone 49-89-76902-232, fax 49-89-76902-250, email 100730.1341@compuserve.com, web www.saur.de/home.htm. Rest of Europe incl. United Kingdom plus Africa & Asia—Bowker-Saur, W. Sussex, UK, phone 44-1342-326-972, fax 44-1342-335-612, email customer@bowker-saur.co.uk, web www.bowker-saur.com/service/. Australia/New Zealand—Thorpe, Port Melbourne, Victoria, Australia, phone 61-03-9-245-7370, fax 61-03-9-245-7395, email customer.service@thorpe.com.au, web www.thorpe.com.au. Technical support for CD ROMs (800) 323-3288, fax 908) 665-3528, email techsupport@bowker.com. Also see International Books in Print.

BOWKER ANNUAL LIBRARY AND BOOK TRADE ALMANAC is a directory that provides budget, Internet, legislation, industry event and research information. Published annually. Call publisher for price. Cahners Business Information, 121 Chanlon Road, New Providence, NJ 07074, (908) 665-2804, (888) 269-5372, URL www.bowker.com. Headquarters: Cahners Business Information, 275 Washington Street, Newton, MA 02158-1630, (617) 558-4663 or (617) 964-3030, fax (617) 558-4700, email marketaccess@cahners.com. Web sites www.cahners.com or www.chilton.net.

BOWKER/WHITAKER GLOBAL BOOKS IN PRINT ON DISC includes the entire databases of Books in Print (US and Canada), Whitaker's BookBank (UK) and International Books in Print (Continental Europe, Africa, Asia and Latin America), Australian and New Zealand Books in Print (Australia, New Zealand and the Oceanic states). 1 year subscription $2,055.

R.R. Bowker (a unit of Cahners Business Information), 121 Chanlon Road, New Providence, NJ 07974 USA, Phone (888) BOWKER2 (888-269-5372) & (800) 323-3288, fax (908) 508-7696, email info@bowker.com, web www.bowker.com. Canada—R.R. Bowker, Markham, Ontario, phone (888) BOWKER9 & (905) 415-5837, fax (905) 479-6266. German speaking Europe—K.G. Saur Verlag, Munich, Germany, phone 49-89-76902-232, fax 49-89-76902-250, email 100730.1341@compuserve.com, web www.saur.de/home.htm. Rest of Europe incl. United Kingdom plus Africa & Asia—Bowker-Saur, W. Sussex, UK, phone 44-1342-326-972, fax 44-1342-335-612, email customer@bowker-saur.co.uk, web www.bowker-saur.com/service/. Australia/New Zealand—Thorpe, Port Melbourne, Victoria, Australia, phone 61-03-9-245-7370, fax 61-03-9-245-7395, email customer.service@thorpe.com.au, web www.thorpe.com.au. Technical support for CD ROMs (800) 323-3288, fax 908) 665-3528, email techsupport@bowker.com.

CANADIAN PUBLISHERS DIRECTORY is issued semi-annually and includes information about Canadian book publishers in addition to that found in "Canadian Book Publishers" in volume 1 of LITERARY MARKET PLACE. For further information contact: Quill & Quire, Quill & Quire Magazine, 70 The Esplanade, 4th floor, Toronto, ON M5E 1R2, CANADA.

CD-ROM'S IN PRINT contains information on over 11,000 CD's, including subject indexes. It also lists information for nearly 4,000 publishing and distribution companies. LIBRARY JOURNAL'S review describes CD-ROM'S IN PRINT as "The starting point for those who choose CD-ROM titles." $155. Gale Group, P.O. Box 9187, Farmington Hills, MI 48333-9187. Toll free US and Canada (800) 877-GALE (4253) and (248) 699-GALE, fax (800) 414-5043 and (248) 699-8061, Internet orders galeord@galegroup.com, web site www.galegroup.com or www.gale.com. All Gale Group products are available on approval. Contact Gale for details.

GALE'S READY REFERENCE SHELF ONLINE is a GaleNet Internet resource that provides integrated access to databases covering national, regional, state, local and international associations, publishers, newspapers and periodicals, directories, newsletters, online databases, portable databases, database products and vendors, special libraries and research centers. Information is included from numerous Gale databases, among them THE ENCYCLOPEDIA OF ASSOCIATIONS, PUBLISHERS DIRECTORY, GALE DIRECTORY OF PUBLICATIONS AND BROADCAST MEDIA and several others. If it is prohibitively expensive, locate a library with with this resource. Gale Group, P.O. Box 9187, Farmington Hills, MI 48333-9187. Toll free US and Canada (800) 877-GALE (4253) and (248) 699-GALE, fax (800) 414-5043 and (248) 699-8061, Internet orders galeord@galegroup.com, web site www.galegroup.com or www.gale.com. All Gale Group products are available on approval. Contact Gale for details.

INTERNATIONAL BOOK TRADE DIRECTORY contains detailed listings for booksellers, bookstores, and wholesalers worldwide. From K.G. Saur, $360. R.R. Bowker (a unit of Cahners Business Information), 121 Chanlon Road, New Providence, NJ 07974 USA, Phone (888) BOWKER2 (888-269-5372) & (800) 323-3288, fax (908) 508-7696, email info@bowker.com, web www.bowker.com. Canada—R.R. Bowker, Markham, Ontario, phone (888) BOWKER9 & (905) 415-5837, fax (905) 479-6266. German speaking Europe—K.G. Saur Verlag, Munich, Germany, phone 49-89-76902-232, fax 49-89-76902-250, email 100730.1341@compuserve.com, web www.saur.de/home.htm. Rest of Europe incl. United Kingdom plus Africa & Asia—Bowker-Saur, W. Sussex, UK, phone 44-1342-326-972, fax 44-1342-335-612, email customer@bowker-saur.co.uk, web www.bowker-saur.com/service/. Australia/New Zealand—Thorpe, Port Melbourne, Victoria, Australia, phone 61-03-9-245-7370, fax 61-03-9-245-7395, email customer.service@thorpe.com.au, web www.thorpe.com.au. Technical support for CD ROMs (800) 323-3288, fax 908) 665-3528, email techsupport@bowker.com.

INTERNATIONAL BOOKS IN PRINT, from K.G. Saur, $795.

INTERNATIONAL BOOKS IN PRINT PLUS, one year subscription, $1,303. R.R. Bowker (a unit of Cahners Business Information), 121 Chanlon Road, New Providence, NJ 07974 USA, Phone (888) BOWKER2 (888-269-5372) & (800) 323-3288, fax (908) 508-7696, email info@bowker.com, web www.bowker.com. Canada—R.R. Bowker, Markham, Ontario, phone (888) BOWKER9 & (905) 415-5837, fax (905) 479-6266. German speaking Europe—K.G. Saur Verlag, Munich, Germany, phone 49-89-76902-232, fax 49-89-76902-250, email 100730.1341@compuserve.com, web www.saur.de/home.htm. Rest of Europe incl. United Kingdom plus Africa & Asia—Bowker-Saur, W. Sussex, UK, phone 44-1342-326-972, fax 44-1342-335-612, email customer@bowker-saur.co.uk, web www.bowker-saur.com/service/. Australia/New Zealand—Thorpe, Port Melbourne, Victoria, Australia, phone 61-03-9-245-7370, fax 61-03-9-245-7395, email customer.service@thorpe.com.au, web www.thorpe.com.au. Technical support for CD ROMs (800) 323-3288, fax 908) 665-3528, email techsupport@bowker.com.

INTERNATIONAL LITERARY MARKET PLACE contains information on major publishers, book trade organizations, reference books, literary agents, book manufacturers, book clubs, translation agencies and related groups. $189.95 International LITERARY MARKET PLACE can also be accessed on the Internet, directly at www.iliterarymarketplace.com or through a link at the domestic US LITERARY MARKET PLACE site at www.literarymarketplace.com.

R.R. Bowker (a unit of Cahners Business Information), 121 Chanlon Road, New Providence, NJ 07974 USA, Phone (888) BOWKER2 (888-269-5372) & (800) 323-3288, fax (908) 508-7696, email info@bowker.com, web www.bowker.com. Canada—R.R. Bowker, Markham, Ontario, phone (888) BOWKER9 & (905) 415-5837, fax (905) 479-6266. German speaking Europe—K.G. Saur Verlag, Munich, Germany, phone 49-89-76902-232, fax 49-89-76902-250, email 100730.1341@compuserve.com, web www.saur.de/home.htm. Rest of Europe incl. United Kingdom plus Africa & Asia—Bowker-Saur, W. Sussex, UK, phone 44-1342-326-972, fax 44-1342-335-612, email customer@bowker-saur.co.uk, web www.bowker-saur.com/service/. Australia/New Zealand—Thorpe, Port Melbourne, Victoria, Australia, phone 61-03-9-245-7370, fax 61-03-9-245-7395, email customer.service@thorpe.com.au, web www.thorpe.com.au. Technical support for CD ROMs (800) 323-3288, fax 908) 665-3528, email techsupport@bowker.com.

LATIN AMERICAN ADVERTISING, MARKETING & MEDIA SOURCEBOOK, published by Euromonitor (England), at $470 (1st edition), had been exclusively distributed in the USA, Canada and Australia by Gale Group. At the time of this writing, Gale no longer carries it. For more information, contact Euromonitor or Gale or refer to Books in Print or International Books in Print. This reference might also be available in the library.

LITERARY MARKET PLACE, "The Directory of the American Book Publishing Industry With Industry Yellow Pages" is an excellent 3 volume directory with comprehensive information on US book publishers; imprints, subsidiaries and distributors; book trade acquisitions and mergers, small presses, Canadian book publishers, micropublishers, US electronic publishers, electronic publishing consultants, electronic publishing products and services, editorial services, literary agents, illustrations agents, US agents and offices of foreign publishers, lecture agents, specialized advertising and public relations firms, direct mail specialists, mailing list brokers and services, book review syndicates, book review and index journals and services, book exhibits, book clubs, book lists and catalogs, book importers and exporters, book producers, translators, artists, photographers, stock photo agencies, associations, book trade events and conferences, awards, contents and grants, reference books for the trade, magazines for the trade, a toll free directory of publishers, magazine and newspaper publicity, radio and television publicity, book manufacturing services, book distributors and sales representatives, and wholesalers. $189.95.

LITERARY MARKET PLACE ON DISC, previously titled LITERARY MARKET PLACE PLUS CD ROM, one year subscription $297.00.

LITERARY MARKET PLACE—INTERNET EDITION, www.literarymarketplace.com, is available by subscription.

INTERNATIONAL LITERARY MARKET PLACE Internet database can be directly accessed at www.iliterarymarketplace.com. It is also linked to the US domestic LITERARY MARKET PLACE web site at www.literarymarketplace.com. Contact the publisher for subscription price. INTERNATIONAL LITERARY MARKET PLACE, hard copy $189.95.

R.R. Bowker (a unit of Cahners Business Information), 121 Chanlon Road, New Providence, NJ 07974 USA, Phone (888) BOWKER2 (888-269-5372) & (800) 323-3288, fax (908) 508-7696, email info@bowker.com, web www.bowker.com. Canada—R.R. Bowker, Markham, Ontario, phone (888) BOWKER9 & (905) 415-5837, fax (905) 479-6266. German speaking Europe—K.G. Saur Verlag, Munich, Germany, phone 49-89-76902-232, fax 49-89-76902-250, email 100730.1341@compuserve.com, web www.saur.de/home.htm. Rest of Europe incl. United Kingdom plus Africa & Asia—Bowker-Saur, W. Sussex, UK, phone 44-1342-326-972, fax 44-1342-335-612, email customer@bowker-saur.co.uk, web www.bowker-saur.com/service/. Australia/New Zealand—Thorpe, Port Melbourne, Victoria, Australia, phone 61-03-9-245-7370, fax 61-03-9-245-7395, email customer.service@thorpe.com.au, web www.thorpe.com.au. Technical support for CD ROMs (800) 323-3288, fax 908) 665-3528, email techsupport@bowker.com.

NATIONAL DIRECTORY OF RECORD LABELS AND MUSIC PUBLISHERS edited by Barbara Taylor, includes over 4,000 major labels, independent labels and music publishers listed, including titles, addresses, phone and fax numbers, with cross references. $24.50, item #B1927. Published by Rising Star

Music Publishing. Distributed by SPIN (Songwriter Products, Ideas & Necessities), 345 Sprucewood Road, Lake Mary, FL 32746-5917. (800) 800-487-SPIN, (407) 321-3702. Email rsfspin@aol.com. Web site http://members.aol.com/rsfspin.

PUBLISHERS DIRECTORY contains information about 20,000 US and Canadian publishers, including small, independent presses and companies which provide electronic formats. Entries include email addresses. $357. Gale Group, P.O. Box 9187, Farmington Hills, MI 48333-9187. Toll free US and Canada (800) 877-GALE (4253) and (248) 699-GALE, fax (800) 414-5043 and (248) 699-8061, Internet orders galeord@galegroup.com, web site www.galegroup.com or www.gale.com. All Gale Group products are available on approval. Contact Gale for details.

PUBLISHERS, DISTRIBUTORS AND WHOLESALERS OF THE US™ is available in electronic database formats. It identifies over 70,000 publishers, wholesalers, distributors, software firms, museum and association imprints, and trade organizations, covering a variety of media. This database includes discount schedules aimed mainly at libraries, plus compete addresses (for editorial and ordering), toll-free phone numbers. This database is used to identify the outlet(s) offering the best price(s) for books, cassettes and software titles. It is available online through Knight Ridder Information, Inc. (DIALOG File number 450, (800) 334-2564 or (800) 3-DIALOG), through subscription online and on CD-ROM/ hard disk. For more information visit Bowker Reed Reference's web site at http://www.reedref.com or contact: Bowker Reed Reference Electronic Publishing, 121 Chanlon Road, New Providence, NJ 07974 USA, Phone (800) 323-3288, Fax (908) 665-3528, email info@bowker.com.

PUBLISHERS WEEKLY web site "BookWire" is an important publishing industry web site which covers all aspects of the book business. Useful for researchers, librarians, writers, publishers and anyone who likes to read. URL address is www.bookwire.com. Headquarters: Cahners Business Information, 275 Washington Street, Newton, MA 02158-1630, (617) 558-4663 or (617) 964-3030, fax (617) 558-4700, email marketaccess@cahners.com. Web sites www.cahners.com or www.chilton.net.

PUBLISHING MARKET PLACE REFERENCE PLUS CD ROM contains information from the LITERARY MARKET PLACE, INTERNATIONAL LITERARY MARKET PLACE, the AMERICAN LIBRARY DIRECTORY and the WORLD GUIDE TO LIBRARIES, plus 32,000 listings for bookstores and book dealers listed in the AMERICAN BOOK TRADE DIRECTORY, over 100,000 companies listed in PUBLISHERS, DISTRIBUTORS AND WHOLESALERS plus information from the BOWKER ANNUAL LIBRARY AND BOOK TRADE ALMANAC. It includes contact information and the ability to generate customized mailing lists and print labels for publishers, libraries and book dealers. This same mailing list information could be used to develop a list of prospects to contact. Can be searched by keyword, company/institution, personal name, position, subject, titles, conference/meeting, membership, and more. Updated annually. 1 year subscription $895, 3 years $2,551, excluding discounts. For more information visit Bowker Reed Reference's web site at http://www.reedref.com or contact: Bowker Reed Reference Electronic Publishing, 121 Chanlon Road, New Providence, NJ 07974 USA, Phone (800) 323-3288, Fax (908) 665-3528, email info@bowker.com.

SONGWRITERS' MARKET edited by Cindy Laufenberg is a how-to book for songwriters. It includes these chapters: Music Print Publishers comprised of companies that print sheet music; Record Companies; Record Producers; Managers and Booking Agents; Advertising, Audiovisual and Commercial Music Firms; Play Producers and Publishers; and Organizations. $21.95. Published by Writer's Digest. Distributed by SPIN (Songwriter Products, Ideas & Necessities), 345 Sprucewood Road, Lake Mary, FL 32746-5917. (800) 800-487-SPIN, (407) 321-3702. Email rsfspin@aol.com. Web site http://members.aol.com/rsfspin.

SURVEILLANT: ACQUISITIONS & COMMENTARY FOR INTELLIGENCE & SECURITY PROFESSIONALS publishes SURVEILLANT, a book alert newsletter reviews over 250 new books per issue in these areas: competitor and business intelligence, tradecraft, technology-transfer, military intelligence, espionage, covert actions, security and counterintelligence, psychological warfare, propaganda, disinformation, deception, cryptology, guerrilla warfare, terrorism, resistance movements, aerial and space reconnaissance, science, histories or accounts of FBI, CIA, NSA, MOSSAD and other intelligence agencies and personal memoirs. $18 per issue, annual subscription $110 US, $120 Canada, $140 foreign. Ordering information: SURVEILLANT, Suite 165, 2020 Pennsylvania Ave. NW, Washington, DC 20006-1846. (202) 797-1234, email: reviews@surveillant.com.

"**THE LIST**" is Cahners Business Information catalog. The former Reed Travel Group has merged with Cahners and Chilton to form Cahners Business Information. For every publication in "The List," publishers and editors' names are identified, with address, phone number and email. It also provides a superb description of every periodical they publish—including many serving the travel industry—with local contact information Publications are located throughout the US and in foreign countries. Free. Cahners Business Information, 275 Washington Street, Newton, MA 02158-1630, (617) 558-4663 or (617) 964-3030, fax (617) 558-4700, email marketaccess@cahners.com. Web sites www.cahners.com or www.chilton.net.

THE SOURCE BOOK, "Expert Business Sources from Reed Elsevier Business Information" is a free booklet from the publisher which identifies trade journals published by Reed Elsevier, name of publisher, address, phone and email. Includes a wide variety of industry sources, alphabetically arranged into 23 categories, such as "Broadcasting/cable/communications," "Plant Operations," "Eye Care/Eyewear," "Technology Research." Free. Reed Elsevier Business Information, A Division of Reed Elsevier, Inc., 275 Washington Street, Newton, MA 02158-1630, (617) 964-3030, Fax (617) 558-4700, URLs www.cahners.com, www.chilton.net.

WORDS ON CASSETTE is the only complete guide to audio cassette collections with location, ordering and pricing information, running times, content summaries and rental availability, an index to authors, readers and performers. Published annually. Cahners Business Information, 121 Chanlon Road, New Providence, NJ 07974, (908) 777-8669, (888) 269-5372, fax (908) 508-7696, email marin.mixon@bowker.com, URL www.bowker.com. Headquarters: Cahners Business Information, 275 Washington Street, Newton, MA 02158-1630, (617) 558-4663 or (617) 964-3030, fax (617) 558-4700, email marketaccess@cahners.com. Web sites www.cahners.com or www.chilton.net.

Puerto Rico

See Caribbean, International

ENCYCLOPEDIA OF ASSOCIATIONS: REGIONAL, STATE AND LOCAL ORGANIZATIONS. The information in this directory is not duplicated anywhere in ENCYCLOPEDIA OF ASSOCIATIONS. Over 100,000 nonprofit organizations are included in this directory. $585 for 5 volume set or $140 per individual volume. Also available on CD ROM and online on the Internet through a GaleNet subscription.

Volume 1, Great Lakes States (Illinois, Indiana, Michigan, Minnesota, Ohio, Wisconsin)
Volume 2, Northeastern States (Connecticut, Maine, Massachusetts, New Hampshire, New Jersey, New York, Pennsylvania, Rhode Islands, Vermont)
Volume 3, Southern and Middle Atlantic States (Including Puerto Rico and the Virgin Islands) (Alabama, Delaware, Washington, DC, Florida, Georgia, Kentucky, Maryland, Mississippi, North Carolina, Puerto Rico, South Carolina, Tennessee, Virginia, West Virginia, Virgin Islands)
Volume 4, South Central and Great Plains States (Arkansas, Iowa, Kansas, Louisiana, Missouri, Nebraska, North Dakota, Oklahoma, South Dakota, Texas)
Volume 5, Western States (Alaska, Arizona, California, Colorado, Guam, Hawaii, Idaho, Montana, Nevada, New Mexico, Oregon, Utah, Washington, Wyoming)

Gale Group, P.O. Box 9187, Farmington Hills, MI 48333-9187. Toll free US and Canada (800) 877-GALE (4253) and (248) 699-GALE, fax (800) 414-5043 and (248) 699-8061, Internet orders galeord@galegroup.com, web site www.galegroup.com or www.gale.com. All Gale Group products are available on approval. Contact Gale for details.

PUERTO RICO INDUSTRIAL DIRECTORY is available for $129 from publisher Harris InfoSource, 2057 East Aurora Road, Twinsburg, OH 44087-1999, (330) 425-9000, (800) 888-5900, www.HarrisInfo.com.

PUERTO RICO OFFICIAL INDUSTRIAL DIRECTORY identifies over 30,000 names and titles of executives at 8,700 plants, plus phone, fax, SIC, products, number of employees, branch offices and more. Published annually by Direct Marketing & Media Group. $129 hard cover edition. Distributed by Manufacturers' News, Inc., (888) 752-5200, 1633 Central Street, Evanston, IL 60201-1569. Email info@manufacturersnews.com. Web site www.manufacturersnews.com.

Pulp and Paper

PULP AND PAPER ANNUAL AND DIRECTORY contains an index of companies, divisions and subsidiaries, plus information on 3 sectors: pulp, paper and board manufacturing sector, supply sector and support sector. Includes information on key contacts, mills and recycling companies. Canada $95, USA and foreign $115. Special discounts available for combined purchases. Published by Southam Information Products Ltd, 1450 Don Mills Road, Don Mills, Ontario M3B 2X7 CANADA, (800) 668-2374. In Toronto 442-2122. Web site www.southam.com.

R

Radio

BACON'S RADIO/TV/CABLE DIRECTORY is a two volume set that identifies all US national and regional networks, all US broadcast stations, management and news executives, radio and TV syndicators, including programming staff, detailed show listings, over 100,000 names of contacts, an index of show subjects and more. $275. Ordering information: Call (800) 621-0561, (800) 753-6675. Bacon's Information, Inc., a K-III Communications Company, 332 South Michigan Avenue, Chicago, IL 60604. Satisfaction guaranteed or a full refund within 30 days.

BROADCASTING AND CABLE YEARBOOK contains information on radio, TV and cable including information about trade associations, trade shows, broadcasting education, awards, industry related books, magazines, videos and more. Also includes information of direct broadcast satellites, Multichannel Multipoint Distribution Services (MMDS), wireless cable companies and more. $179.95.

R.R. Bowker (a unit of Cahners Business Information), 121 Chanlon Road, New Providence, NJ 07974 USA, Phone (888) BOWKER2 (888-269-5372) & (800) 323-3288, fax (908) 508-7696, email info@bowker.com, web www.bowker.com. Canada—R.R. Bowker, Markham, Ontario, phone (888) BOWKER9 & (905) 415-5837, fax (905) 479-6266. German speaking Europe—K.G. Saur Verlag, Munich, Germany, phone 49-89-76902-232, fax 49-89-76902-250, email 100730.1341@compuserve.com, web www.saur.de/home.htm. Rest of Europe incl. United Kingdom plus Africa & Asia—Bowker-Saur, W. Sussex, UK, phone 44-1342-326-972, fax 44-1342-335-612, email customer@bowker-saur.co.uk, web www.bowker-saur.com/service/. Australia/New Zealand—Thorpe, Port Melbourne, Victoria, Australia, phone 61-03-9-245-7370, fax 61-03-9-245-7395, email customer.service@thorpe.com.au, web www.thorpe.com.au. Technical support for CD ROMs (800) 323-3288, fax 908) 665-3528, email techsupport@bowker.com.

GALE DIRECTORY OF PUBLICATIONS AND BROADCAST MEDIA identifies key personnel, feature editors and more at radio and TV stations and cable companies. $615 for 5 volume set. Gale Group, P.O. Box 9187, Farmington Hills, MI 48333-9187. Toll free US and Canada (800) 877-GALE (4253) and (248) 699-GALE, fax (800) 414-5043 and (248) 699-8061, Internet orders galeord@galegroup.com, web site www.galegroup.com or www.gale.com. All Gale Group products are available on approval. Contact Gale for details.

GALE DIRECTORY OF PUBLICATIONS AND BROADCAST MEDIA ONLINE is a GaleNet resource on the Internet that includes information on 64,000 newspapers, periodicals, newsletters, industry directories, television and radio stations, including names of key personnel. Contact the library to access this reference free. For pricing and ordering information, contact: Gale Group, P.O. Box 9187, Farmington Hills, MI 48333-9187. Toll free US and Canada (800) 877-GALE (4253) and (248) 699-GALE, fax (800) 414-5043 and (248) 699-8061, Internet orders galeord@galegroup.com, web site www.galegroup.com or www.gale.com. All Gale Group products are available on approval. Contact Gale for details.

LITERARY MARKET PLACE, "The Directory of the American Book Publishing Industry With Industry Yellow Pages" is an excellent 3 volume directory with comprehensive information on US book publishers; imprints, subsidiaries and distributors; book trade acquisitions and mergers, small presses, Canadian book publishers, micropublishers, US electronic publishers, electronic publishing consultants, electronic publishing products and services, editorial services, literary agents, illustrations agents, US agents and offices of foreign publishers, lecture agents, specialized advertising and public relations firms, direct mail specialists, mailing list brokers and services, book review syndicates, book review and index journals and services, book exhibits, book clubs, book lists and catalogs, book importers and exporters, book producers, translators, artists, photographers, stock photo agencies, associations, book trade events and conferences, awards, contents and grants, reference books for the trade, magazines for the trade, a toll free directory of publishers, magazine and newspaper publicity, radio and television publicity, book manufacturing services, book distributors and sales representatives, and wholesalers. $189.95.

LITERARY MARKET PLACE ON DISC, previously titled LITERARY MARKET PLACE PLUS CD ROM, one year subscription $297.00.

LITERARY MARKET PLACE—INTERNET EDITION, www.literarymarketplace.com, is available by subscription.

INTERNATIONAL LITERARY MARKET PLACE Internet database can be directly accessed at www.iliterarymarketplace.com. It is also linked to the US domestic LITERARY MARKET PLACE web site at www.literarymarketplace.com. Contact the publisher for subscription price. INTERNATIONAL LITERARY MARKET PLACE, hard copy $189.95.

R.R. Bowker (a unit of Cahners Business Information), 121 Chanlon Road, New Providence, NJ 07974 USA, Phone (888) BOWKER2 (888-269-5372) & (800) 323-3288, fax (908) 508-7696, email info@bowker.com, web www.bowker.com. Canada—R.R. Bowker, Markham, Ontario, phone (888) BOWKER9 & (905) 415-5837, fax (905) 479-6266. German speaking Europe—K.G. Saur Verlag, Munich, Germany, phone 49-89-76902-232, fax 49-89-76902-250, email 100730.1341@compuserve.com, web www.saur.de/home.htm. Rest of Europe incl. United Kingdom plus Africa & Asia—Bowker-Saur, W. Sussex, UK, phone 44-1342-326-972, fax 44-1342-335-612, email customer@bowker-saur.co.uk, web www.bowker-saur.com/service/. Australia/New Zealand—Thorpe, Port Melbourne, Victoria, Australia, phone 61-03-9-245-7370, fax 61-03-9-245-7395, email customer.service@thorpe.com.au, web www.thorpe.com.au. Technical support for CD ROMs (800) 323-3288, fax 908) 665-3528, email techsupport@bowker.com.

RADIO COMMUNICATION REPORT is a weekly trade publication. Crain Communications, Inc. is headquartered in Chicago with offices in major cities throughout the US plus London, Tokyo and Frankfurt. New York location: 220 East 42nd Street, New York, NY 10017, (212) 210-0100, Circulation (800) 678-9595. Annual subscription $49, two years $69. Web site www.rcrnews.com.

STANDARD RATE AND DATA PUBLICATIONS includes "Radio Advertising Source" and "Television and Cable Source" and direct marketing information. $354 annual subscription. Standard Rate and Data Service, Inc., 3004 Glenview Road, Wilmette, IL 60091, (708) 441-2210 in Illinois, (800) 323-4601.

TELEVISION INTERNATIONAL is a magazine for cable TV, radio, satellite and interactive multimedia industries around the world. Call publisher for price. Cahners Business Information, 245 West 17th Street, New York, NY 10011-5300, (212) 337-6944, fax (212) 337-6948, email jonnypim@pacific.net.sg and rschatz@cahners.com, URL www.cahners.com/mainmag/bci.htm. Headquarters: Cahners Business Information, 275 Washington Street, Newton, MA 02158-1630, (617) 558-4663 or (617) 964-3030, fax (617) 558-4700, email marketaccess@cahners.com. Web sites www.cahners.com or www.chilton.net.

WIRELESS WEEK is a weekly newspaper serving the cellular, PCS, paging and mobile radio industry. Also publishes an annual directory. Call for prices. Cahners Business Information, 600 South Cherry Street, Suite 400, Denver CO 80222, (303) 393-7449 ext. 277, fax (303) 399-2034, email tbrooksh@chilton.net, URL www.wirelessweek.com. Headquarters: Cahners Business Information, 275 Washington Street, Newton, MA 02158-1630, (617) 558-4663 or (617) 964-3030, fax (617) 558-4700, email marketaccess@cahners.com. Web sites www.cahners.com or www.chilton.net.

Real Estate

Also see Mortgage Banking

CORPORATE FINANCE SOURCEBOOK—THE GUIDE TO MAJOR INVESTMENT SOURCES AND RELATED FINANCIAL SERVICES contains over 13,000 names of executives at 3,700 organizations that, broadly speaking, supply growth capital to businesses or are service firms, such as US venture capital lenders, private lenders, commercial finance and factoring, pension managers, master trusts and other sources. Names of key management are included. A special section details public offerings of the past 3 years and mergers and acquisitions over $100 million. $575. If the price is prohibitively high, remember your local library. National Register Publishing, Reed Elsevier-New Providence, 121 Chanlon Road, New Providence, NJ 07974, (800) 521-8110, fax (800) 836-7736, web site www.redbooks.com or www.marquiswhoswho.com. "If, for any reason whatsoever, your order does not fully meet your expectations, simply return the product within 30 days for a prompt, complete, unquestioned refund," as stated in Catalog of Biographical and Professional References of publisher Marquis Who's Who/National Register Publishing.

DIRECTORY OF INSTITUTIONAL REAL ESTATE/NELSON'S INSTITUTIONAL REAL ESTATE identifies 5,000 institutions that invest in real estate, including 300 investment managers, 1,700 plan sponsors, 1,000 insurance companies, 2,000 corporations and 380 Real Estate Investment Trusts (REIT's). 2,500 real estate service firms are also listed. Identifies 22,000 key executives. Updated annually. $335. Nelson Information, P.O. Box 591, Port Chester, NY 10573 USA. (800) 333-6357, Phone outside the US (914) 937-8400, Fax (914) 937-8590, web site http://www.nelnet.com.

DUN & BRADSTREET AND GALE INDUSTRY REFERENCE HANDBOOKS offer a line of industry-specific sourcebooks which include key companies in the industry, ranked lists of companies, professional associations, trade shows and conferences, mergers and acquisitions, consultants who service those industries, information sources, and more. 6 volume set $495. Also available individually for $99: Pharmaceuticals, Health and Medical Services, Computers and Software, Banking and Finance, Telecommunications, Agriculture and Food, Insurance, Construction, Entertainment, Hospitality. First edition available December, 1999. Gale Group, P.O. Box 9187, Farmington Hills, MI 48333-9187. Toll free US and Canada (800) 877-GALE (4253) and (248) 699-GALE, fax (800) 414-5043 and (248) 699-8061, Internet orders galeord@galegroup.com, web site www.galegroup.com or www.gale.com. All Gale Group products are available on approval. Contact Gale for details.

MORTGAGE BANKERS ASSOCIATION OF AMERICA/THE NATIONAL ASSOCIATION OF REAL ESTATE FINANCE, 1125 15th Street NW, Washington, DC 20005, (202) 861-6500, www.mbaa.org.

NELSON FINANCIAL DATABASE provides comprehensive information on the global institutional investment market. Information formatted to your precise needs is available from Nelson Information Mailing List & Customized Database service. The NELSON FINANCIAL DATABASE is comprised of:

> 30,000 executives at investment management firms
> 11,000 executives at research firms
> 100,000 executives at public companies
> 40,000 executives at plan sponsors
> 3,000 executives at pension fund consulting firms
> 24,000 executives at institutional real estate firms
> 4,000 executives at technology based vendors

The database also consists of extensive investment information, including money manager performance, peer group analysis, special surveys and more. For customers who with to use Nelson's information in their own systems, Nelson will supply customized data export, using all or any data items. Mailing lists are also available for direct marketers.For more information, contact Nelson Mailing List & Customized Database Services, P.O. Box 591, Port Chester, NY 10573 USA. (800) 333-6357, Phone outside the US (914) 937-8400, Fax (914) 937-8590, web site http://www.nelnet.com.

www.realbank.com serves professionals in real estate, mortgages and construction. Many positions are in the $40,000 to $75,000 range. REALBANK was developed by Realbank, Inc., New York, New York and went online in 1996.

Recruiting

See Campus Recruiting, Databases—Recruiting & Job Matching, Executive Search, Human Resources, Internet Recruitment Training, Jobhunters Resources, Reference Checking, Relocation, Research—Executive Search

If you've identified an electronic database that will make your job easier but the price is prohibitively high, remember your local library. If you're having trouble locating a library with that particular database, perhaps the librarian can check another library for you. Besides a public library, a library at a corporation, embassy, professional association, university or school might be able to help you. Alternatively, maybe the publisher of the database can help locate a library which has it. The publisher should know who their customers are and it is actually to their benefit to help you. After all, as a user of their products, you are creating a demand in the marketplace. If the people at the toll free number can't help you, you're probably calling too low in the organization. Make a point of finding the phone number of corporate headquarters. Call someone senior enough to have the sophistication to understand why demand for their product is a good reason to help you, such as the Vice President or Senior Vice President of Sales and Marketing or even the CEO or Chairman.

AMERICAN COST OF LIVING SURVEY provides cost and expense data for 455 American cities and metropolitan areas. Includes housing, transportation, food, clothing and other consumer goods, utilities, insurance, entertainment, taxes, education and more. $160, 2nd edition, 1995. Contact publisher to find out when next edition will be available. Gale Group, P.O. Box 9187, Farmington Hills, MI 48333-9187. Toll free US and Canada (800) 877-GALE (4253) and (248) 699-GALE, fax (800) 414-5043 and (248) 699-8061, Internet orders galeord@galegroup.com, web site www.galegroup.com or www.gale.com. All Gale Group products are available on approval. Contact Gale for details.

"The Best Web Sites For Job Hunters" was the cover story in the *National Business Employment Weekly* November 15-21, 1998 issue. It surveyed and reviewed 70 web sites which had been profiled in their publication during the previous year. To see a copy, try the library.

Over 60 of the 70 surveyed web sites have been included in this book. Web sites with lower compensation positions have been omitted, and most of those were in computer related areas. However, all the web sites which received top rankings were included, regardless of compensation range, especially sites in out-of-the-ordinary niches.

CANADA EMPLOYMENT WEEKLY'S URL is www.mediacorp2.com/. It features The Career Bookstore for Canadian Career Books, Talent Available to Market Yourself to Canadian Recruiters and Search Firms, Canadian Directory of Search Firms, and Who's Hiring for a list of Canada's top employers. www.mediacorp2.com/cdsf/index.html leads you directly to the Canadian Directory of Search Firms and the Career Bookstore—"Quality Canadian Career Books" including GET WIRED, YOU'RE HIRED, "the definitive Canadian guide to job hunting in Canada."

CAREERXROADS, by Gerry Crispin and Mark Mehler, is an annual directory of job and resume sites. At the time of this writing the number of sites has more than tripled in two years to over 1,000 sites. It includes specialized databases for job seekers and employers. $22.95. Order online or by phone from distributor Kennedy Information, One Kennedy Place, Route 12 South, Fitzwilliam, NH 03447, phone (800) 531-0007 or 603-585-6544, fax 603-585-9555, email bookstore@kennedyinfo.com, web site www.kennedyinfo.com. Also available through from author's web site or at your local book store.

DIRECTORY OF INDEPENDENT RESEARCH CONSULTANTS contains information on 200 contract consultants. Jobhunters who are sending resumes to search firms might also want to include research consultants. They are often indistinguishable from search consultants because the roles of both can be so similar. In addition, at a search firm, a researcher customarily conducts the first screen of a resume, regardless of whom it's addressed to. Further, it's not unusual for these consultants to be directly retained by corporations purchasing "unbundled search" services, which basically means a less expensive "no frills" search product. This means that independent research consultants represent another third party avenue for job hunters, in addition to executive search firms and contingency recruiting firms. $65. Ordering information: Kennedy Information, One Kennedy Place, Route 12 South, Fitzwilliam, NH 03447, phone (800) 531-0007 or 603-585-6544, fax 603-585-9555, email bookstore@kennedyinfo.com, web site www.kennedyinfo.com.

DIRECTORY OF EXECUTIVE RECRUITERS profiles over 5,000 firms in 7,000 locations with over 12,800 individual recruiters listed. It is cross-referenced according to retainer vs. contingency firms, job functions, industries, geography and recruiter specialities. Available in paperback $47.95, hardcover (with more details on each firm) $179.95, on CD as SearchSelect® $245.00, in label or list form for selected categories or on the web. A companion publication, KENNEDY'S POCKET GUIDE TO WORKING WITH EXECUTIVE RECRUITERS is a 150-page assemblage of 30 chapters by the experts themselves, plus a Lexicon of Executive

Recruiting. $9.95. Kennedy Information, One Kennedy Place, Route 12 South, Fitzwilliam, NH 03447, phone (800) 531-0007 or 603-585-6544, fax 603-585-9555, email bookstore@kennedyinfo.com, web site www.kennedyinfo.com.

DIRECTORY OF LEGAL RECRUITERS, $129. Ordering information: Kennedy Information, One Kennedy Place, Route 12 South, Fitzwilliam, NH 03447, phone (800) 531-0007 or 603-585-6544, fax 603-585-9555, email bookstore@kennedyinfo.com, web site www.kennedyinfo.com.

EMPLOYERS' GUIDE TO RECRUITING ON THE INTERNET by Ray Schreyer and John McCarter, Impact Publications. $24.95. Available at bookstores or can be ordered on the web at www.technicalrecruiter.com.

EMPLOYMENT MARKETPLACE is a staffing newsletter for lower and mid level contingency agencies, temporary agencies, and employers who use those services. EMPLOYMENT MARKETPLACE featured several articles on Internet Recruiting in the Winter 1998 issues. While the information is particularly appropriate for contingency recruiters, especially in technology and information systems, there is also valuable information and ideas for the retained search community. Articles include "Evaluating Employment Internet Sites" by William O. Warren, founder and president of Online Career Center, the Internet's first online recruitment site, (317) 293-6499, http://www.occ.com. "Internet Recruiting—Real Possibilities" by Bob Mhoon, President of the Manx Group, Inc., Arlington Texas. Mhoon is an IT recruiter who provides Internet recruiting training programs and IT candidate profile directories. (817) 784-6775, email bobmhoon@onramp.net. "How We Billed an Extra $100,000 by Using the Internet" by Scott Allen, a Technical Recruiter for Emerald Resource Group in Cleveland, (216) 518-4048, email sfa@emeraldresourcegroup.com.

According to Bob Mhoon, President of The Manx Group in Arlington, Texas, "A fundamental problem facing recruiters who want to learn how to effectively use the Internet is simply that no one has a map leading to all of the available resources and tools. Then, even though common Internet tools have user instructions, the tricks to effective recruiting applications must often be learned through trial and error. Difficulties are compounded when generic Internet training programs frustrate recruiters who want sessions focused on their real needs. The Internet is such a new phenomenon that Internet trainers who also have a recruiting background are in short supply." Ordering information: Call to request back issues. $26 annual subscription, 4 issues, Employment Marketplace, PO Box 31112, St. Louis, MO 63131, (314) 569-3095, fax (314) 458-4955

EXECUTIVE SEARCH RESEARCH DIRECTORY (ESRD) provides information on over 350 contract research consultants, including descriptions of research services provided, fees, experience, where trained, areas of concentration, and unusual capabilities, including 26 freelancers with an Internet specialty. Cross referenced by over 300 specialties. $88 postpaid. Ordering information: Kenneth J. Cole, Publisher, The Recruiting & Search Report, P.O. Box 9433, Panama City Beach, FL 32417. (850) 235-3733, fax (850) 233-9695. Email jcole9433@aol.com.

FINANCIAL EXECUTIVES INSTITUTE (FEI) provides a resume matching service for its members, who are senior financial executives, and employers and search firms. The cost is minimal or nil. For more information, contact the Financial Executive Institute. They can be located in the Encyclopedia of Associations or Lorna Daniells' BUSINESS INFORMATION SOURCES or another librarians' reference. Or call your local business librarian. Or ask a senior financial executive, such as a corporate controller or chief financial officer who would likely be a member. The FEI also publishes a membership directory which cross references members by company. However, it is only available to members, so you will have to borrow a copy from a member. It can be used to identify names of contacts, either for recruiting purposes, or for job hunters networking. The FEI is one of many professional associations that provides its members with this type of service.

http://taps.com is a web site for people looking for contract and permanent positions in the United Kingdom and Europe. Positions are mainly in information technology, mostly in the $20,000 to $50,000 range. TAPS.COM was developed by Internet Appointments, Ltd., London, England and was launched in 1996.

INTERNET ADVERTISING BUREAUS (IABs)—According to Warren O. Warren, founder and president of Online Career Center, the Internet's first online recruiting site, careful evaluation of recruiting sites is crucial to the success of your recruiting program. In order to substantiate claims made by commercial sites, ask for third party audits and forms of proof. Make sure the sites you select and and will provide third party audit reports from an Internet Advertising Bureau (IAB) recognized audit firm, such as Nielsen I/PRO, publishers of I/AUDIT™, a trademark of Internet Profiles Corporation. For more information, refer to Warren's article, "Evaluating Employment Internet Sites" which appeared in the Winter 1998 Employment Marketplace. Employment Marketplace, PO Box 31112, St. Louis, MO 63131, (314) 569-3095, fax (314) 458-4955.

INTERNET RECRUITING EDGE by Barbara Ling is a comprehensive collection of research assembled over a two year period. Developed for the novice and experienced Internet recruiter alike, and with a foreword by Tony Byrne, topics include: Where, Oh Where, is my Candidate Now?, Does the Internet Really Benefit Businesses? Phones Still Work, But Don't Buy a Mansion if You Only Need a Cottage, How to Find Candidates on the Internet, Non-Traditional Resources, Before You Begin—A Primer on Internet Culture— Netiquette, Beginner Candidate Location Skill, Resume Banks, Search Engine Basics, The Joy of Bookmarks, The Art of Job Posting, Sleuthing for Company Directories, Finding Employee Directories, Finding Executive Biographies, Alumni Organizations, Forums and Bulletin Boards, Internet Classifieds, Online E-zines (magazines), Professional Organizations, Colleges, Metasearch at Highway 61, Realistic Goals Before You Begin Your Own Recruiter Web site, Perilous Pitfalls, How To Buy Your Recruiter Business Site, Locating Good Web Site Designers, Your Site is Designed—Now What? How To Market A Recruiter Web Site, 14 Killer Web Site Search Engine Visibility Tips, and more. $149. Order by visiting the web site http://www.barbaraling.com or call (732) 563-1464.

JOBHUNTING ON THE INTERNET by Richard Nelson Bolles, Ten Speed Press, P.O. Box 7123, Berkeley, CA 94707. Among other things, this book provides a small but reasonably complete listing of INTERNET URL's (Uniform Resource Locators) with a short description of the contents of each. By the author of the classic WHAT COLOR IS YOUR PARACHUTE?

RECRUITERS' INTERNET SURVIVAL GUIDE by John Sumser, author of the 1996 Electronic Recruiting Index, rated over 500 recruiting web sites and analyzed Internet recruiting issues. The Recruiters' Internet Survival Guide, published by Staffing Industry Resources, $89.50. To view the table of contents or to order a copy, go to web site www.interbiznet.com or contact IBN (Internet Business Network) in Mill Valley, CA.

RITES OF PASSAGE AT $100,000+: The Insider's Lifetime Guide to Executive Job-Changing and Faster Career Progress by John Lucht. Published by Viceroy Press, Inc., New York, NY. Distributed to the trade in the USA by Henry Holt & Company, Inc., 115 West 18th Street, New York, NY 10011. $29.95.

SEARCH ENGINES. Here are the main search engines you can use as a starting point. Some people consider the first four better—Yahoo, Lycos, AltaVista and Excite. The remaining search engines are listed alphabetically.

Yahoo! (http://www.yahoo.com)
Lycos (http://www.lycos.com)
AltaVista (http://www.AltaVista.com)
Excite (http://www.excite.com)

Dejanews (http://www.dejanews.com)
HotBot (http://www.HotBot.com)
Inference (http://www.inference.com/infind)
Infoseek (http://www.infoseek.com)
Nerd World (http://www.NerdWorld.com)
Netfind (http://www.netfind.com)
Northern Light (http://www.northernlight.com)
Opentext (http://www.pinstripe.opentext.com/)
Webcrawler (http://webcrawler.com)

SPECIFICATION SHEET ANALYSIS is a collection of 245 different sets of actual search specifications from senior executive retainer searches. These specifications offer insights into major firm retainer search methodology and specification creation. Especially useful to contingency firms evolving towards retained search. Full catalog of specifications available by fax upon request. $125 for any 25 specifications.

Ordering information: Kenneth J. Cole, Publisher, The Recruiting & Search Report, P.O. Box 9433, Panama City Beach, FL 32417. (850) 235-3733, fax (850) 233-9695 Email jcole9433@aol.com.

UNCOVERING THE TRUTH—HOW TO REALLY CHECK REFERENCES is a cassette by Andrea Jupina that completely covers the art of reference checking in 30 minutes. It's an excellent refresher that really gets your mental juices flowing before you begin to interview references—ideal for line managers, search firms, small business owners, and anyone who needs to know the real story—without a lawsuit. $15.95 plus shipping & handling. Available from Jupina by email order at andreajupina@yahoo.com and from Kennedy Information, One Kennedy Place, Route 12 South, Fitzwilliam, NH 03447, phone (800) 531-0007 or 603-585-6544, fax 603-585-9555, email bookstore@kennedyinfo.com, web site www.kennedyinfo.com.

NOTE: Also refer to "http://" under "H" above for web addresses that omit "www" in the address, such as http://taps.com.

www.accountingjobs.com or Accounting and Finance Jobs, was developed by AccountingNet of Seattle in a joint venture with Career Mosaic. Launched in 1997, this site specializes in accounting and finance positions, mainly in the $30,000-50,000 range.

www.aeps.com/aeps/aepshm.html is the URL for the Aviation Employee Placement Service. Positions generally range from $30,000 to $100,000 and mostly include pilots, mechanics and management. Developed by Sysops, Inc. in Fort Lauderdale, Florida, the site was established in 1995.

www.airsdirectory.com is the URL for AIRS—Advanced Internet Recruitment Strategies. AIRS is a firm which provides training for recruiters who use the Internet as a recruiting tool. For more information contact AIRS, 1790 Franklin Street, Berkeley, CA 94702, phone (800) 336-6360, fax (888) 997-5559. Their web site contains many excellent free helpful resources.

www.ajb.dni.us is the URL for America's Job Bank. It was ranked as one of the top 5 "Sites Offering the Best Job-Search Support" by the *National Business Employment Weekly.* Launched in 1995, the site was developed by the U.S. Department of Labor and state employment/unemployment offices. Most openings were originally listed with a state department of labor and are mainly in the $30,000 to $50,000 range. Many positions are in information technology, administrative and production and manufacturing.

www.amazon.com is a large bookstore web site. At the time of this writing they offer discounts up to 40%.

www.americanbanker.com/careerzone or American Banker Online was launched in 1998 by American Banker, New York, New York.

www.americasemployers.com or America's Employers is a site mainly for positions in technology, finance and sales at approximately $50,000 to $100,000. Launched in 1995, it was developed by Career Relocation Corp of America in Armonk, New York.

www.asianet.com is the address to a web site that matches Pacific Rim positions with individuals who speak Asian languages.

www.askjeeves.com or **www.ask.com** or **www.aj.com** or ask. If you ask Jeeves, "How can I find a job" or "How can I find candidates for an engineering job?" Jeeves has an answer! (Actually, there's very little you CAN'T ask Jeeves.) The Ask Jeeves site includes HOOVER'S CAREER CENTER, which consists of Job Search Tools (monster.com, CareerMosaic,wsj.com careers, hotjobs, westech's virtual job fair and joboptions), Career Links and Career Research Links. Hoover's Career Center contains much additional information, including extensive RELOCATION data, such as cost of living comparisons, etc. You can also subscribe to Hoover's and access their directories on the Internet.

www.asktheheadhunter.com is the web site for the book, ASK THE HEADHUNTER, a book that can effectively be used by both job hunters and interviewers, by Nick Corcodilos, email northbridge@sprintmail.com. According to Tom Peters, it is "a powerful hiring tool.no manager can afford to miss" and it "shreds some of our most basic assumptions about the way to hire top people." Published by Penguin Putnam, New York, $14.95 The book is available from the web site and at bookstores. Corcodilos and his client, Merrill Lynch's Vice President of Global Staffing, were jointly featured in a discussion about changes in corporate recruiting and hiring practices in a segment on "Opportunity Knocks," a CNBC special on Executive Search. To purchase this 5 hour video, contact CNBC or Corcodilos.

www.barnesandnoble.com is the web site for Barnes & Noble Bookstores. Discounts are available.

www.bestjobsusa.com or Best Jobs U.S.A. is a site mainly for information technology, sales and engineering positions usually in the $50,000 to $100,000 range. Launched in 1996, the site was developed by Recourse Communications, Inc., West Palm Beach, Florida.

www.bio.com is the URL for Bio Online. Most positions are for research chemists, biochemists and in clinical development and are usually in the $40,000 to $75,000 range. Developed by Vitadata Corp, Berkeley, California, the site went online in 1993.

www.blackworld.com/careers.htm is the URL for Blackworld Career Center, a site jointly developed by Blackworld Internet Directory in Oakland, California and CareerMosaic. The site, launched in 1998, provides resources for African Americans and other ethnic groups worldwide.

www.boston.com is the web site for *Boston Globe* online accesses the Globe's newspaper ads.

www.businessweek.com/careers/right.htm is the web site for BusinessWeek's Internet Career Center. It offers a free, confidential service for job seekers, advertising that's cheaper than a want ad, and a job posting service if you're an employer.

www.careeravenue.com or Career Avenue lists positions mainly in information technology, management and engineering, mostly in the $50,000 to $100,000 range. The site was established in 1996 and developed by Internet Advertising, Inc., San Antonio, Texas.

www.careerbuilder.com or CareerBuilder Network was ranked as one of the top 5 "Sites Offering the Best Career Resources for Job Seekers" by the *National Business Employment Weekly.* At the time of this writing, CareerBuilder is a network of over 19 different career web sites encompassing diversity, professional, industry and general career sites. Career Builder was established in 1996 and was developed by NetStart, Inc., Reston, Virginia.

www.career.com or Career.com links employers and candidates throughout the world. Heart's goals for www.career.com are to provide free job seeker assistance and to offer employers an effective way to reach qualified job seekers. Most positions are in Engineering, IT and marketing and usually range between $30,000 and $75,000. The site was launched in 1993 and developed by HEART Advertising Network, Los Altos, California.

www.careerexchange.com is a web site for North American job seekers developed by CorpNet InfoHub, Ltd., Vancouver, BC, Canada. Launched in 1996, its People-Match capability notifies the user of jobs through email. Most positions are in high technology, engineering, sales and marketing and are primarily in the $40,000 to $75,000 range.

www.careermosaic.com is the URL for a major recruitment web site that spends millions of dollars in advertising to draw traffic to this site. CareerMosaic features a jobs database; newsgroups for jobs, college connection, online job fairs, employer job postings; company information and more. CareerMosaic was ranked as one of the top 5 "Sites Offering the Best Overall Support for Job Seekers" by the *National Business Employment Weekly.* The site was developed Bernard Hodes Advertising in New York and went online in 1994.

www.careerpath.com was ranked as one of the top 5 "Sites Offering the Best Overall Support for Job-Seekers" by the *National Business Employment Weekly.* CareerPath.com puts the help wanted sections of over 70 US newspapers into one database. Job hunters can post their resumes free. Companies must pay a fee to access resumes. The web site claims, "Powered by the nation's leading newspapers and employers, CareerPath.com has the Web's largest number of the most current job listings." Launched in 1995, the site was developed by a consortium of media companies—Knight-Ridder, *The New York Times,* the Time Mirror Company, the Tribune Company, the Washington Post, Cox Interactive Media, Gannett Company and Hearst Corp.

www.careers.wsj.com is the *Wall Street Journal*'s web site. It focuses on positions for middle and senior management including financial positions at $75,000 and up. This web site is among those that encompass senior executive positions. Other features includes Job Seek, Who's Hiring, Career Columnists, Salaries & Profiles, The Salary Calculator™, Job Hunting Advice, Succeeding at Work, HR Issues, Executive Recruiters,

Working Globally, College Connection, Starting a Business, Career Bookstore and more. Content from The National Employment Business Weekly is also featured. The site was developed by Dow Jones & Company, Inc., Princeton, New Jersey and was established in 1997.

www.careersite.com sends email notification of a job match to job seekers and employers. Most positions are in engineering, marketing and sales and management, mainly in the $40,000 to $75,000 range. CareerSite was developed by CareerSite Corp., Ann Arbor Michigan and was launched in 1995.

www.ceweekly.com is the URL for Contract Employment Weekly, a site for the temporary technical industry. Positions are mainly in information technology, engineering and technical and are mostly in the $40,000 to $75,000 range. The site was developed by C.E. Publications, Inc., Bothell, Washington and has been online since 1994. Contract Employment Weekly Online is a service of C.E. Publications, Inc., P.O. Box 3006, Bothell, WA 98041-3006. (425) 806-5200, Fax (425) 806-5585, email publisher@ceweekly.com.

www.clickit.com is the web site address to "Access Business Online." Its objective is to bring Buyers and Sellers Together on the Internet. Features include Executive Job Network, Capital Sources, Trade Announcements, Professional Services, Top 100 World Business Charts, Company Profiles, International Buyer-Seller, BizWiz! Search Engine, Web Emporium Web Site Development, Classifieds, Corporate News Net, Wall Street and World Wide Finance, Market News & Business Connections, and more. However, a service fee is charged if you wish to access this information.

www.cnn.com is the URL to CNN's impressive comprehensive web site. It contains Big Yellow Search Books to assist in finding businesses and people. It also features global directories, The Directory Store™and a "search the net" capability with InfoSeek. InfoSeek also has a Business Channel with business resources and small businesses, and a Careers Channel.

www.computerwork.com is a specialized site for computer positions with a national web site and sites for Colorado, the Midwest, Minnesota and New England. Developed by Internet Association Group, Inc., Jacksonville, Florida, Computerwork.com has been online since 1996.

www.computerworld.com offers a "Career Search" capability, a free "Resume Database" and posting service for candidates, and various services for recruiters, including workshops and conferences, online and in print.

www.cweb.com or CareerWeb was ranked as one of the top 5 "Sites Offering the Best Career Resources for Job Seekers" as well as one of the top 5 "General Purpose Sites" by the *National Business Employment Weekly*. Its features include a career resource center and a library. The site was developed by Landmark Communications, Norfolk, Virginia and launched in 1995.

www.datamation.com is the web site for IT executives and professionals. It provides targeted daily computer news, IT Executive Job Pavilion, Management Benchmarking Application (MBA), technology workbench, back issues from Datamation and comprehensive links to IT vendors and other online resources. This web site is the winner of the Jesse H. Neal Award and is a Cahners Business Information web site.

www.dbm.com/jobguide is an excellent comprehensive web site if you're either a recruiter looking for candidates or a job seeker. It is the "best Internet recruiting starting point" taught to recruiters by the Tiburon Group, web site http://www.tiburon group.com, a Chicago based firm that provides "Strategic Internet Recruiting Solutions Consultants and Trainers." Tiburon Group, phone (773) 907-8330, Fax (773) 907-9481, email getajob@tiburongroup.com, web site www.tiburongroup.com.

www.decalumni.com is the web site for alumni of Digital Equipment Corp. It includes a directory.

www.dice.com or DICE was ranked as one of the top 5 "Best Specialty Sites" by the *National Business Employment Weekly*. DICE specializes in information technology and high technology positions. One of the oldest employment sites on the Internet, DICE only accepts positions from recruiting firms. The site was developed by is D&L Online, Inc., Des Moines, Iowa and was launched in 1990.

www.eagleview.com is the web site for Eagleview, which presents the Select Candidate™ Network for job seekers and employers, including computer industry positions.

www.emory.edu/CAREER/index.html is Emory University's Career Paradise web site, with modules for alumni, students and employers. It is an excellent resource that should not be missed.

www.employnet-inc.com is the URL for Employnet, a confidential resume database only for recruitment firms, executive search firms and placement agencies. Both recruiters and candidates pay a fee to use this service. It was developed by Employnet, Inc., New York, New York and went online in 1995.

www.EngineeringJobs.com is a web site mainly for mechanical, electrical, industrial and computer engineers. The site was developed by EngineeringJobs, El Cerrito, California and launched in 1996.

www.excite.com/careers or Excite Careers Network was ranked as one of the top 5 "Sites Offering the Best Overall Support for Job Seekers" by the *National Business Employment Weekly.* Many positions are in IT, engineering and management, often in the $50,000 to $100,000 range. The site, online since 1995, was developed by Excite Inc., the search engine, Redwood City, California.

www.execunet.com is the web site for Exec-U-Net. It is a subscription service listing executive level positions by search firms and a few companies for positions at $100,000 or more. Candidates tend to be high quality, perhaps because of the cost. The site was developed by Exec-U-Net, Norwalk, Connecticut and was launched in 1995.

www.executiveagent.com is a web site that helps executive job seekers market their skills and experience to a targeted list of executive recruiters via email. ExecutiveAgent is completely confidential as resumes go directly to the search firms.

www.fedjobs.com provides assistance to people seeking a position with the federal government, including in the Judiciary and Congressional branches, and the United Nations. Many positions are in computers, engineering and medical, with salaries often in the $30,000 to $50,000 range. The site was developed by Federal Research Service, Inc., Vienna, Virginia and was launched in 1996.

www.galegroup.com is the web site to publisher Gale Research, one of the largest providers of research for search, recruiting and libraries.

www.Headhunter.NET was ranked as one of the top 5 "Best General-Purpose Sites" by the *National Business Employment Weekly.* This site claims that no job postings are over 45 days old and that their resume database protects jobhunter confidentiality. Many positions are in computers, engineering and accounting, often in the $50,000 to $100,000 range. The site was developed by HeadHunter.NET, Inc., Norcross, Georgia and went online in 1996.

www.helpwanted.com is a web site for free posting and searching of all content for job seekers, employers and agencies.

www.hospitalitynet.nl is the URL for Hospitality Net, a site developed by Hospitality Net BV in Maastricht, The Netherlands. It connects job hunters and employers in the hospitality and restaurant industries worldwide for positions mostly in the $30,000 to $50,000 range. The site was established in 1995.

www.hotjobs.com was ranked as one of the top 5 "Best General-Purpose Sites" by the *National Business Employment Weekly.* HotJobs.com limits job postings to employers only. They also offer a personal home page to people who store their resume in HotJobs.com's database. Launched in 1996, Hot Jobs was developed by HotJobs.com Ltd., New York, New York.

www.iccweb.com is the web site for Internet Career Connection, an employment matching service with a special section for US Federal Government employment. Internet Career Connection was developed by Gonyea & Associates, Inc., New Port Richey, Florida and launched in 1995. Features include Help Wanted-USA, the Worldwide Resume Bank and Government JOBS Central. Many positions include engineering, computer technology and business. While candidates do pay a fee to post their resumes, employers can view resumes free.

www.infospace.com is the URL for Classifieds/Jobs at Infospace, Inc., a site with many positions in computers, engineering and marketing, often in the $50,000 to $100,000 range. The site was developed by Infospace, Inc., Redmond, Washington and was launched in 1996.

www.interbiznet.com/hrstart.html is the Electronic Recruiting News web site. It features the Recruiters Internet Survival Guide, recruiting seminars and more.

www.it-ta.com is the URL for the ITTA Connection, a site developed by the Information Technology Talent Association in Scottsdale, Arizona. Many positions are in IT, engineering and recruiting, often at the $50,000 to $100,000 range. The site went online in 1995.

www.jobcenter.com is the URL for JobCenter Employment Services, Inc., a site with many job postings in IT, programming and sales and marketing, often in the $30,000 to $100,000 range. The site was developed by JobCenter Employment Services, Inc., Skaneateles, New York and was launched in 1995.

www.jobhunt.com is a Meta-list of On-line Job-Search Resources and Services for recruiters and jobhunters. It includes: The Online Career Center, Career Mosaic, Career Net, Job Web, Standard Job Hunt List, Americas Job Bank, Best Jobs in the USA, Career Web, College Grad Job Hunter, JobOptions (www.joboptions.com, formerly E-span Interactive Employment Network), Job Trak, The Internet Job Locator, The Monster Board, Virtual Job Fair. It also offers the capability of searching by state and local newspapers. New Items (less than a week old) are highlighted, as are "Outstanding Job Resources."

www.job-hunt.org is an on-line job search resources and services that identifies jobs resources and ranks the outstanding ones. It is linked to Career Paradise of Emory University Career Center (www.emory.edu/CAREER/index.html), featuring a "Colossal List" or Career Links and Hiring Express pages. It's given high marks for both its content and humorous presentation.

www.jobnet.com was ranked as one of the top 5 "Best Specialty Sites" by the *National Business Employment Weekly.* Jobnet.com specializes in positions located in southeastern Pennsylvania and neighboring areas of New Jersey and Delaware. The site was developed by Online Opportunities, Malvern, Pennsylvania and has been online since 1992.

www.jobnet.org is a Canadian web site.that features "Looking for a career in financial services?" Scotiabank online recruiting, Jobnet and Alumnet.

www.joboptions.com is the URL for JobOptions, formerly E-Span, a site that has been online since 1991. At the time of this writing, features include "The Right Person For The Job" and "The Right Job For The Person," job listings; post resume edit resume, career library, job match download and more. Many job postings are in sales and marketing, finance and accounting and in technology. The site was developed by Gund Business Group, Indianapolis.

www.jobtrak.com is the web site for the Career service network for college students, alumni, college career staff and employers. JOBTRAK was ranked as one of the top 5 "Best Specialty Sites" by the *National Business Employment Weekly.* JOBTRAK has established relationships with college and university career offices, MBA programs and alumni associations. Most salaries range between $30,000 and $50,000. The site developer is JOBTRAK CORPORATION, Los Angeles, CA, (310) 474-3377, (800) 999-8725, fax (310) 475-7912. The site has been online since 1995.

www.kennedyinfo.com is the web site for publisher Kennedy Information. It includes books, newsletters, training materials, directories, and surveys for executive recruiting, human resources, outplacement, management consulting and job seekers. (800) 531-0007 or (603) 585-6544.

www.latimes.com is the URL to the comprehensive *Los Angeles Times* web site.

www.LatPro.com is the URL for Latin America's Professional Network, a site for experienced Spanish and Portuguese bilingual professionals. Many job postings are for positions in sales and marketing, finance and information technology, often in the $50,000 to $100,000 range. The site was developed by Latin America's Professional Network, Miami, Florida and was launched in 1997.

www.medhunters.com is a healthcare jobhunting site developed by Helen Ziegler and Associates, Inc., Toronto, Canada. Worldwide positions are posted for doctors, nurses and therapists, encompassing a broad range of salaries. The site has been online since 1997.

www.monster.com is the URL for the popular Monster Board web site. The Monster Board was ranked as one of the top 5 "Best General-Purpose Sites" by the *National Business Employment Weekly.* It is a major recruitment web site that spends millions of dollars in advertising to attract traffic to this site. Features include Job search in the US, International or by Companies, Career Center Events, Recruiters' Center, Seminars, Post a Job, free online recruitment seminar. It also offers special links for human resources, health care, technology and entry level positions. Toll free phone number (800) MONSTER. The Monster Board, PO Box 586, Framingham, MA 01704-0586. The site developer is TMP Worldwide, New York, New York and has been online since 1994.

www.monsterhr.com is the URL for The Monster Board: Human Resources careers on the web. Enter your job profile and have job listings automatically downloaded to your Email. International opportunities in Canada are classified by Canada overall, then Alberta, British Columbia, Newfoundland, Ontario and Quebec.

www.nationjob.com is the web site for NationJob Network Online Jobs Database. NationJob, Inc. was ranked as one of the top 5 sites in two different categories by the *National Business Employment Weekly:* "Sites Offering the Best Job-Search Support" and "Best General Purpose Sites." The site offers "Search for a Job Now (no email required)," "Search for a Company" and "Directory of all Companies." P.J. Scout service is a "(P)ersonal (J)ob Scout service that's "like having a friend shop for a job for you." Fill in a form and PJ will send you info on jobs you might be interested in. Information on salary comparisons, moving costs, relocation info, insurance calculator and more. NationJob Inc., 601 SW 9th Street, Suites J&K, Des Moines, IA 50309, (800) 292-7731. The site developer is NationJob, Inc.

www.netjobs.com is the URL to Canada's premiere employment web site. It features Internet Career Centre for employers and job seekers, Overseas Jobs Express, and Personal Computer Training. Email info@netjobs.com. Linked to www.jobnet.org.

www.netshare.com is the URL for NETSHARE 2000, a confidential for-fee career management service designed for executives, companies and recruiters that posts senior level positions on the Internet daily. Salary usually exceeds $100,000 but is sometimes in the $75,000 range. Their ad claims, "A best search site"...FORTUNE Magazine and "Best of the Best"...CareerXRoads. NETSHARE 2000 was developed by Netshare, Inc., Novato, California and went online in 1995. (800) 241-5642, email netshare@netshare.com.

www.net-temps.com or Net-Temps Job Posting Service was ranked as one of the top 5 "Sites Offering the Best Job-Search Support" by the *National Business Employment Weekly.* Many positions are in information systems, engineering, and sales and marketing, often in the $50,000 to $100,000 range. The site was developed by Net-Temps, Inc., Tyngsboro, Massachusetts and went online in 1996.

www.ntes.com is the URL for the Contract Employment Connection, a web site for contract professionals in the temporary professional job market. Most positions are in engineering, computer science and management, mainly in the $50,000 to $100,000 range. The site was developed by National Technical Employment Services, Scottsboro, Alabama and was launched in 1993.

www.nytimes.com is the URL for *The New York Times* web site.

www.nzjobs.co.nz is a recruiting and jobhunting web site for positions in New Zealand. Email: info@nzjobs.co.nz.

www.occ.com is the URL for the On Line Career Center, one of the Internet's first online recruitment sites, launched in 1993. It is a major recruitment web site that spends millions of dollars in advertising to drive traffic to the site. This is a major site that was developed by William O Warren, who has received honors for his pioneering work in the development of Internet Recruiting. This web site allows you to enter your job profile and have job listings automatically downloaded to your Email. Questions to webmaster@occ.com. www.occ.com was rated by the *National Business Employment Weekly* as one of the top 5 sites in 3 different categories: "Sites Offering the Best Overall Support for Job Seekers," "Sites Offering the Best Job-Search Support" and "Sites Offering the Best Career Resources for Job Seekers." Openings are mainly in engineering, information technology and sales and marketing. The site developer is TMP Worldwide, New York, New York.

www.passportaccess.com is a site with many positions in computers and engineering, many of them in the $50,000 to $100,000 range. The site was developed by PassportAccess, Inc., Lafayette, California and was established in 1995.

www.realbank.com serves professionals in real estate, mortgages and construction. Many positions are in the $40,000 to $75,000 range. REALBANK was developed by Realbank, Inc., New York, New York and went online in 1996.

www.recruiterresources.com is the site of Tiburon group, an Internet recruiting training firm who is a certified AIRS and Hire.com Solutions partner.

www.recruitersonline.com is the URL for Recruiters Online Network, a free web site that allows recruiters to post open positions at various online locations and maintain private resume database for members. Most positions are in information technology, management and software. Positions usually range from $50,000 to over $100,000. The site was developed by Recruiters Online Network, Inc., Plano, Texas and was established in 1995.

www.ritesite.com is the web site for the book, RITES OF PASSAGE AT $100,000+ by John Lucht.

www.sciencemag.org is the URL for Science Online, a career site which posts many positions for research scientists, research directors and post-Doctoral positions. Salary often ranges from $50,000 to $100,000. Science Online was developed by the American Association for the Advancement of Science, Washington, DC and was established in 1996.

www.selectjobs.com was ranked as one of the top 5 "Best Specialty Sites" by the *National Business Employment Weekly*. SelectJOBS specializes in computer industry positions. Many job postings are for database administrators, programmer/analysts, and system/network engineers. salary often ranges between $40,000 and $75,000. The site was developed by SelectJOBS, Fort Lauderdale, Florida and was established in 1996.

www.shrm.org/jobs/ is the web site for the Society for Human Resource Management site. It is linked to the major recruitment web site www.career.mosaic./com. It also includes Membership Directory Online, which only can be accessed by members.

www.sireport.com is the web site for the Staffing Industry Report.

www.technicalrecruiter.com is a web site which is a good starting point for a large number of specialized technology sites, such as ProjectManager.com and SoftwareEngineer.com and others.

www.tjobs.com is the URL for Telecommuting Jobs, which connects people to positions at home or otherwise using off site electronic facilities. Most positions are in programming, sales and writing. The site was developed by Levine Communications, Winnetka, Illinois and was launched in 1996.

www.the-dma.org is the web site for the Direct Marketing Association, 1120 Avenue of the Americas, New York, NY 10036-6700, (212) 768-7277, fax (212) 302-6714. It feature the DMA Job Bank, Online Bookstore, Seminars, Conferences. Membership directory is available to members.

www.technicalrecruiter.com is a web site which is an excellent starting point for a large number of specialized technology sites, such as ProjectManager.com and SoftwareEngineer.com and others.

www.tiburon group.com is the web site for the Tiburon Group, Inc., a Chicago based firm that provides "Strategic Internet Recruiting Solutions Consultants and Trainers." They are also a recruiting firm. Phone (773) 907-8330, Fax (773) 907-9481, email getajob@tiburongroup.com.

www.townonline.com/working or Town Online Working is the web site to various community newspapers, including 13 in New England. In addition to job listings, it also has a job profile with the capability of automatically downloading to your Email. Town Online Working was ranked as one of the top 5 "Sites Offering the Best Career Resources for Job Seekers" by the *National Business Employment Weekly*. Many positions are administrative, management and blue collar, often paying in the teens up to $30,000. The site developer is the Community Newspaper Company, Needham, Massachusetts and was established in 1996.

www.tristatejobs.com is the URL for Tri-State Jobs, a site for positions in New York, New Jersey and Connecticut. Many positions are for programmers, engineers and managers, often in the $50,000 to $100,000 range. The site was developed by Tri-State Jobs, Southbury, Connecticut and went online in 1997.

www.umn.edu/apn or Academic Position Network is a web site that lists positions for faculty, professional and administrative staff, including librarians, in academia. The site was developed by Academic Position Network in Blaine, Minnesota and established in 1996.

www.usresume.com is the URL for US Resume, a site that lists many positions in computers, sales and finance, usually in the $50,000 to $100,000 range. The site was developed by Market 2000 Corp, Sparkill, New York and went online in 1996.

www.vjf.com is the URL for Westech Virtual Job Fair. It was ranked as one of the top 5 "Best Specialty Sites" by the *National Business Employment Weekly*. Westech Virtual Job Fair specializes in high tech positions which are listed by the companies. The site developer is Westech Expo Corp in Santa Clara, California, one of the largest sponsors of career fairs in the US. The site went online in 1994.

www.womenconnect.com contains job postings and editorial content from Working Woman and Working Mother magazines. Many positions are in sales, software engineering and general engineering, often in the $30,000 to $75,000 range. The site was developed by womenCONNECT.com, McLean, Virginia and has been online since 1994.

www.worldhire.com is the web site for World Hire. It features a Job profile notification and the Recruiter™ web site product. Some sample recruiter sites include www.coastalcorp.com, www.eds.com, www.ibm.com.

www.world.hire.com is the URL for World Hire Online, a web site with job listings mainly in engineering, information technology and "senior management," usually in the $50,000 to $100,000 range. The site was developed by World.Hire, Austin, Texas and was launched in 1996.

Reference Checking

UNCOVERING THE TRUTH—HOW TO REALLY CHECK REFERENCES is a cassette by Andrea Jupina that completely covers the art of reference checking in 30 minutes. It's an excellent refresher that really gets your mental juices flowing before you begin to interview references—ideal for line managers, search firms, small business owners, and anyone who needs to know the *real* story—without a lawsuit. $15.95 plus shipping & handling. Available from Jupina by email order at andreajupina@yahoo.com and from Kennedy Information, One Kennedy Place, Route 12 South, Fitzwilliam, NH 03447, phone (800) 531-0007 or 603-585-6544, fax 603-585-9555, email bookstore@kennedyinfo.com, web site www.kennedyinfo.com.

References—General

See Chapter 6, "How to Create an Executive Search Library." Also see References—Librarian, Company Research, Periodicals and Publishers Web Sites

While there are many references cited in this section, an asterisk (*) indicates preferred sources that can be used first.

ABI GLOBAL and **ABI INFORM** are highly respected databases published by UMI in Ann Arbor, Michigan, a Bell and Howell company. Available in CD ROM and online, ABI allows you to search massive amounts of periodical literature. If you must conduct a literature search for anything, this is one of the first places you should look. Some libraries, such as the New York City Public Library, offer free courses in how to use ABI and other databases. Call your local library for more information. Ordering information: UMI, 300 North Zeeb Road, Ann Arbor, Michigan 48106 (800) 521-0600, Sales (800) 521-3042, email: pprice@umi.com.

ADVERTISER AND AGENCY RED BOOKS PLUS CD ROM combines all the information in THE STANDARD DIRECTORY OF ADVERTISERS, THE STANDARD DIRECTORY OF ADVERTISING AGENCIES and THE STANDARD DIRECTORY OF INTERNATIONAL ADVERTISERS AND AGENCIES. Information is searchable by 25 fields, including company name, personal name, job title/function, product type, product/account name, city, state, zip or country, area code, revenues, number of employees, outside ad agency and even type of computer hardware. Contains professional association information. Available for Windows and Macintosh. Updated quarterly. 1 year subscription $1,295. If the price is prohibitively high, remember your local library. National Register Publishing, Reed Elsevier-New Providence, 121 Chanlon Road, New Providence, NJ 07974, (800) 521-8110, fax (800) 836-7736, web site www.redbooks.com or www.marquiswhoswho.com. "If, for any reason whatsoever, your order does not fully meet your expectations, simply return the product within 30 days for a prompt, complete, unquestioned

refund," as stated in Catalog of Biographical and Professional References of publisher Marquis Who's Who/National Register Publishing.

AMERICA'S CORPORATE FAMILIES & INTERNATIONAL AFFILIATES is comprised of two volumes of US subsidiaries, divisions and branches and one volume of some 3,000 foreign ultimate parent companies and their 11,000 US subsidiaries and nearly 3,000 US ultimate parent corporations and their 18,000 foreign subsidiaries. Published annually. The International Affiliates (Volume 3) lists US companies with their foreign subsidiaries and foreign ultimates with their US subsidiaries. In addition to listing US and foreign ultimates with their family members alphabetically, all companies are cross-referenced geographically and by industry classification. Updated annually For prices call Dun & Bradstreet at (800) 526-0651. For more information contact Dun & Bradstreet, Business Reference Solutions, Three Sylvan Way, Parsippany, New Jersey 07054. Email dnbmdd@mail.dnb.com. Web site http://www.dnbmdd.com.

AMERICAN LIBRARY ASSOCIATION (ALA), 50 East Huron Street, Chicago, IL 60611, (800) 545-2433, in Illinois (800) 545-2444, in Canada (800) 545-2455. Annually publishes the ALA Handbook of Organization and Membership Directory, which provides information about the ALA's divisions, committees, round tables and discussion groups. The major divisions of the ALA are:

- REFERENCE AND ADULT SERVICES DIVISION (RASD) publishes RQ. Committees include Business Reference Sources Committee, Reference Sources Committee, Adult Library Materials Committee, and Reference Tools Advisory Committee (which provides assistance to publishers of reference titles). Other sections include Machine-Assisted Reference Section and History Section.

- ASSOCIATION OF COLLEGE AND RESEARCH LIBRARIES (ACRL) is the largest group within the ALA. It publishes CHOICE, COLLEGE & RESEARCH LIBRARIES, COLLEGE & RESEARCH LIBRARIES NEWS, RARE BOOKS AND MANUSCRIPTS LIBRARIANSHIP.

- PUBLIC LIBRARY ASSOCIATION (PLA) consists of the Metropolitan Libraries Section, Community Information Section, and Armed Forces Library Section. PLA publishes PUBLIC LIBRARIES.

- ASSOCIATION FOR LIBRARY COLLECTIONS AND TECHNICAL SERVICES (ALCTS) publishes LIBRARY RESOURCES AND TECHNICAL SERVICES.

- AMERICAN ASSOCIATION OF SCHOOL LIBRARIANS (AASL) publishes SCHOOL LIBRARY MEDIA QUARTERLY.

ANNUAL REPORTS. Get the company phone number by calling toll free information (800-555-1212) or looking in a general directory such as STANDARD AND POORS, THE STANDARD DIRECTORY OF ADVERTISERS or NATIONAL DIRECTORY OF ADDRESSES AND TELEPHONE NUMBERS. Say you're calling to request a copy of an Annual Report, a 10(k) Report and a Proxy Statement. This information is FREE and you might as well ask for everything as long as you're on the phone. Note that while publicly held companies are legally required to file these documents with the Securities and Exchange Commission (SEC) every year, privately held companies are not. However, sometimes private companies produce annual reports or other brochures, lists of locations and so forth. You can also ask the Public Affairs department for news clippings or other information. Sales representatives are usually willing to send product information.

While it is possible to review annual reports on line, sometimes on a company's web site or using a specialized database, it may be easier to review hard copy, which is a quick phone call away. Hard copy is easy to mark up and it's portable. You can read it commuting on a bus or train or while you're waiting at the dentist's office.

Annual Reports sometimes contain photos of management, organization charts, lists of all locations, including plants; lists of divisions and subsidiaries, names and titles of management, sometimes at surprisingly junior levels; and almost always provide an explanation of how the company is organized. 10(k) Reports, as a matter of law, are required to identify senior management, their ages and brief background histories; to describe the business activities and products of the company; and to disclose any pending activities which could materially affect the company's financial performance, for example, the potential of an unfavorable outcome in a lawsuit. Proxy Statements are required to reveal the compensation of the four highest paid executives, backgrounds of the Directors of the company, and details about stock ownership and pension plans.

These materials are immensely valuable in analyzing whether you're searching in the part of an organization. This information is often more reliable than anything you will find in a directory or on a CD ROM because the company wrote it themselves and you are obtaining information firsthand, directly from the source. In fact, it could be the same source used by publishers of directories and CD ROMs.

Note: The Securities and Exchange Commission (SEC) legally requires all publicly held companies (that is, any companies that sell their stock) to publish an Annual Report, a 10(k) Report and a Notice of Annual Meeting and Proxy Statement (commonly called the "proxy statement" or just the "proxy.") However, privately held companies are not required to publish such information. Even so, some closely held companies do publish an annual report or an annual review, although they can be difficult to obtain. Sometimes the easiest way to do this is to ask for information from a friend who works there. Or if you work near the company, drop by in person and ask a receptionist for company literature.

BOOKS IN CANADA is a monthly publication which reviews 300-400 new Canadian books each year. It provides an inexpensive way to learn about new resources in Canada. It is available by subscription ($22.98/year) and is sold at newsstands and in bookstores ($3.95 per issue).

Ordering information:

BOOKS IN CANADA
Canadian Review of Books Ltd.
427 Mt. Pleasant Road
Toronto, ON M4S 2L8 CANADA
(416) 489-4755 Phone

BOOKS IN PRINT is the only complete record of in-print, out-of-print and forthcoming books published or distributed in the US. For up-to-the-minute current information on INTERNET references and Internet Databases and Internet web sites available, use this reference. It should be available at a public library or in a good book store. Published annually. 9 volume set, $550. BOOKS IN PRINT ON DISC is available in Windows, MS-DOS and Macintosh . Annual subscription $550.

BOOKS IN PRINT INTERNET EDITION at www.booksinprint.com is available by subscription. Log on or call for details.

BOOKS IN PRINT ONLINE is available through the Dialog Corporation, Ovid Technologies, Inc. and LEXIS ®-NEXIS® on a "pay-as-you-go" basis. Contact the publisher for details. BOOKS OUT OF PRINT INTERNET EDITION can be searched free at www.bowker.com. R.R. Bowker (a unit of Cahners Business Information), 121 Chanlon Road, New Providence, NJ 07974 USA, Phone (888) BOWKER2 (888-269-5372) & (800) 323-3288, fax (908) 508-7696, email info@bowker.com, web www.bowker.com. Canada—R.R. Bowker, Markham, Ontario, phone (888) BOWKER9 & (905) 415-5837, fax (905) 479-6266. German speaking Europe—K.G. Saur Verlag, Munich, Germany, phone 49-89-76902-232, fax 49-89-76902-250, email 100730.1341@compuserve.com, web www.saur.de/home.htm. Rest of Europe incl. United Kingdom plus Africa & Asia—Bowker-Saur, W. Sussex, UK, phone 44-1342-326-972, fax 44-1342-335-612, email customer@bowker-saur.co.uk, web www.bowker-saur.com/service/. Australia/New Zealand—Thorpe, Port Melbourne, Victoria, Australia, phone 61-03-9-245-7370, fax 61-03-9-245-7395, email customer.service@thorpe.com.au, web www.thorpe.com.au. Technical support for CD ROMs (800) 323-3288, fax 908) 665-3528, email techsupport@bowker.com. Also see International Books in Print.

BOWKER/WHITAKER GLOBAL BOOKS IN PRINT ON DISC includes the entire databases of Books in Print (US and Canada), Whitaker's BookBank (UK) and International Books in Print (Continental Europe, Africa, Asia and Latin America), Australian and New Zealand Books in Print (Australia, New Zealand and the Oceanic states). 1 year subscription $2,055.

R.R. Bowker (a unit of Cahners Business Information), 121 Chanlon Road, New Providence, NJ 07974 USA, Phone (888) BOWKER2 (888-269-5372) & (800) 323-3288, fax (908) 508-7696, email info@bowker.com, web www.bowker.com. Canada—R.R. Bowker, Markham, Ontario, phone (888) BOWKER9 & (905) 415-5837, fax (905) 479-6266. German speaking Europe—K.G. Saur Verlag, Munich, Germany, phone 49-89-76902-232, fax 49-89-76902-250, email 100730.1341@compuserve.com, web www.saur.de/home.htm. Rest of Europe incl. United Kingdom plus Africa & Asia—Bowker-Saur, W. Sussex, UK, phone 44-1342-326-972, fax 44-1342-335-612, email customer@bowker-saur.co.uk, web www.bowker-saur.com/service/.

Australia/New Zealand—Thorpe, Port Melbourne, Victoria, Australia, phone 61-03-9-245-7370, fax 61-03-9-245-7395, email customer.service@thorpe.com.au, web www.thorpe.com.au. Technical support for CD ROMs (800) 323-3288, fax 908) 665-3528, email techsupport@bowker.com.

BUSINESS ORGANIZATIONS, AGENCIES AND PUBLICATIONS DIRECTORY contains 32 chapters including information on Canada, business information sources, web sites, and local chambers of commerce. $415. Gale Group, P.O. Box 9187, Farmington Hills, MI 48333-9187. Toll free US and Canada (800) 877-GALE (4253) and (248) 699-GALE, fax (800) 414-5043 and (248) 699-8061, Internet orders galeord@galegroup.com, web site www.galegroup.com or www.gale.com. All Gale Group products are available on approval. Contact Gale for details.

BUSINESSWEEK regularly publishes surveys which are excellent for developing target lists. One of them is the R&D SCOREBOARD, which lists companies by industry and provides various statistics, such as Research and Development expenditures, R&D as a percentage of sales, R&D spending per employee, comparisons to previous year, and so forth.

CD-ROM'S IN PRINT contains information on over 11,000 CD's, including subject indexes. It also lists information for nearly 4,000 publishing and distribution companies. LIBRARY JOURNAL'S review describes CD-ROM'S IN PRINT as "The starting point for those who choose CD-ROM titles." $155. Gale Group, P.O. Box 9187, Farmington Hills, MI 48333-9187. Toll free US and Canada (800) 877-GALE (4253) and (248) 699-GALE, fax (800) 414-5043 and (248) 699-8061, Internet orders galeord@galegroup.com, web site www.galegroup.com or www.gale.com. All Gale Group products are available on approval. Contact Gale for details.

D&B MARKETPLACE DISC is a CD ROM that provides access to names, titles, addresses, SIC or NAICS codes, sales volume, number of employees, year the business was founded, phone numbers and marketing information on more than 10 million US businesses. Searches can be conducted by location, size, industry code and by business information. Mailing labels, telemarketing data and full demographic data records can be printed and exported. Available in Windows and Macintosh. Updated quarterly. For prices call Dun & Bradstreet at (800) 526-0651. For more information contact Dun & Bradstreet, Business Reference Solutions, Three Sylvan Way, Parsippany, New Jersey 07054. Email dnbmdd@mail.dnb.com. Web site http://www.dnbmdd.com.

D&B MILLION DOLLAR DATABASE is an online database on the Internet. Users can access information on more than one million small, mid-sized and large companies, with minimum revenues of $1 million. Searches can be conducted by 22 criteria, including as geographic location, sales volume, number of employees, industry classification. Each company includes up to 30 executive names and titles and biographical data that includes education, work history and birth date. For prices call Dun & Bradstreet at (800) 526-0651. For more information contact Dun & Bradstreet, Business Reference Solutions, Three Sylvan Way, Parsippany, New Jersey 07054. Email dnbmdd@mail.dnb.com. Web site http://www.dnbmdd.com.

D&B MILLION DOLLAR DIRECTORY is a hard copy 5 volume reference that contains profiles on 160,000 public and private US companies. Information is listed alphabetically, geographically and by industry classification. In order to be listed, the company must be a headquarters or single location and must satisfy one of these three requirements: 250 or more employees at that location; $revenues of at least $25 million; tangible net worth of at least $500,000. Entries include key executives' names and titles, parent company and location, sales volume, address, phone number and more. THE D&B MILLION DOLLAR DIRECTORY TOP 50,000 COMPANIES is an abridged version of the MILLION DOLLAR DIRECTORY. Both are updated annually. For prices call Dun & Bradstreet at (800) 526-0651. For more information contact Dun & Bradstreet, Business Reference Solutions, Three Sylvan Way, Parsippany, New Jersey 07054. Email dnbmdd@mail.dnb.com. Web site http://www.dnbmdd.com.

D&B MILLION DOLLAR DISC is a CD ROM which covers over 240,000 public and private companies, compared to either 160,000 or 50,000 in the two versions of the MILLION DOLLAR DIRECTORY in hard copy. In addition, this CD ROM also contains BIOGRAPHICAL information on key executives. Searches can be conducted by company name, industry, size of company, geography, executive name, key word, and executive business backgrounds. Companies listed have sales of at least $ million or more than 100 employees. Branch locations have more than 500 employees. Both are updated annually. D&B MILLION DOLLAR DISC PLUS is a similar CD ROM with more expansive coverage, including 400,000 companies—

both privately held and public—compared to 240,000 in the MILLION DOLLAR DISC. It includes companies with at least 50 employees or revenues of $3 million. For prices call Dun & Bradstreet at (800) 526-0651. For more information contact Dun & Bradstreet, Business Reference Solutions, Three Sylvan Way, Parsippany, New Jersey 07054. Email dnbmdd@mail.dnb.com. Web site http://www.dnbmdd.com.

D&B PRINCIPAL INTERNATIONAL BUSINESSES DIRECTORY is the international companion to the MILLION DOLLAR DIRECTORY SERIES. It provides information on over 50,000 leading companies outside the US. Listings are presented geographically and are cross-referenced alphabetically and by industry classifications. Updated annually. D&B PRINCIPAL INTERNATIONAL BUSINESSES DISC SERIES is a CD ROM is available in three levels of coverage. THE PRINCIPAL INTERNATIONAL BUSINESSES DISC—BASIC provides information on 70,000 leading companies outside the US, based on total number of employees. PRINCIPAL INTERNATIONAL BUSINESSES DISC—EXPANDED covers 220,000 companies outside the US. PRINCIPAL INTERNATIONAL BUSINESSES DISC—EXPANDED PLUS provides information on 450,000 companies outside the US. Searches can be conducted by company name, industry, size of company, geography, chief executive name, key word and line of business. For prices call Dun & Bradstreet at (800) 526-0651. For more information contact Dun & Bradstreet, Business Reference Solutions, Three Sylvan Way, Parsippany, NJ 07054. Email dnbmdd@mail.dnb.com. Web site http://www.dnbmdd.com.

D&B REGIONAL BUSINESS DIRECTORIES are available for each of fifty-four metropolitan areas. Each three-volume set provides profiles on 20,000 companies, including hard-to-find information on privately held companies. Listings include key executives' names and titles, number of employees at location, sales volume, address, phone number, line of business, parent company, year established, and more. Each directory is cross referenced alphabetically and by industry classification. Updated annually. D&B REGIONAL BUSINESS DISK is a CD ROM which provides up to ten names and titles per company. Searches can be conducted by company name, industry, size of company, geography, executive name and key word. Unmetered and updated bi-annually. For prices call Dun & Bradstreet at (800) 526-0651. For more information contact Dun & Bradstreet, Business Reference Solutions, Three Sylvan Way, Parsippany, New Jersey 07054. Email dnbmdd@mail.dnb.com. Web site http://www.dnbmdd.com.

*ENCYCLOPEDIA OF ASSOCIATIONS: NATIONAL ORGANIZATIONS OF THE US. This superb reference is one of the first places you should look when beginning a new recruiting assignment or when looking for specialized references of any type. The keyword index makes this comprehensive reference easy to use, even in hard copy. For over 23,000 nonprofit professional associations with a national scope, this encyclopedia reveals:

- Publications, including membership rosters and newsletters

- Dates and locations of association conferences and conventions

- Names of Executive Directors, who are usually incredible sources of industry information if you call and speak to them

- Committees

- Job and candidate referral banks, which can provide resumes of other industry sources and sometimes candidates

- It includes organizations in these categories: business, trade, environmental, agricultural, legal, govern mental, engineering, technological, scientific, educational, cultural, social welfare, health & medical, public affairs, ethnic, labor unions, chambers of commerce, tourism, & others.

Volume 1, National Organizations of the US, $505
Volume 2, Geographic and Executive Indexes, $390
Volume 3, Supplement, $405

Gale Group, P.O. Box 9187, Farmington Hills, MI 48333-9187. Toll free US and Canada (800) 877-GALE (4253) and (248) 699-GALE, fax (800) 414-5043 and (248) 699-8061, Internet orders galeord@galegroup.com, web site www.galegroup.com or www.gale.com. All Gale Group products are available on approval. Contact Gale for details.

*HOOVER'S HANDBOOK OF AMERICAN BUSINESS provides information on 500 companies, including contacts, products, brand names, key competitors, and a brief history. Published annually. $29.95 softcover, $39.95 hardcover. The Reference Press, Inc., 6448 Highway 209 East, Suite E104, Austin, TX 78723, (512) 454-7778. Hoover's directories can also be accessed on the Internet by going to the Ask Jeeves web site at www.askjeeves.com. A subscription fee is charged for the service.

*HOOVER'S HANDBOOK OF WORLD BUSINESS contains information on 200 companies, including contact information, products, key competitors, and a brief history. Published annually. $27.95 soft cover, $37.95 hard cover. The Reference Press, Inc., 6448 Highway 209 East, Suite E104, Austin, TX 78723, (512) 454-7778. Hoover's directories can also be accessed on the Internet by going to the Ask Jeeves web site at www.askjeeves.com. A subscription fee is charged for the service.

INTERNATIONAL BOOKS IN PRINT, from K.G. Saur, $795.

INTERNATIONAL BOOKS IN PRINT PLUS, one year subscription, $1,303. R.R. Bowker (a unit of Cahners Business Information), 121 Chanlon Road, New Providence, NJ 07974 USA, Phone (888) BOWKER2 (888-269-5372) & (800) 323-3288, fax (908) 508-7696, email info@bowker.com, web www.bowker.com. Canada—R.R. Bowker, Markham, Ontario, phone (888) BOWKER9 & (905) 415-5837, fax (905) 479-6266. German speaking Europe—K.G. Saur Verlag, Munich, Germany, phone 49-89-76902-232, fax 49-89-76902-250, email 100730.1341@compuserve.com, web www.saur.de/home.htm. Rest of Europe incl. United Kingdom plus Africa & Asia—Bowker-Saur, W. Sussex, UK, phone 44-1342-326-972, fax 44-1342-335-612, email customer@bowker-saur.co.uk, web www.bowker-saur.com/service/. Australia/New Zealand—Thorpe, Port Melbourne, Victoria, Australia, phone 61-03-9-245-7370, fax 61-03-9-245-7395, email customer.service@thorpe.com.au, web www.thorpe.com.au. Technical support for CD ROMs (800) 323-3288, fax 908) 665-3528, email techsupport@bowker.com.

*KOMPASS is described by the publisher as "the world's most comprehensive global database of companies, products and services for manufacturing and engineering professionals in print, on CD ROM and on the Internet." It contains company and product information for companies in all lines of business, including manufacturing and industrial sectors. Each company listing includes name, address, phone number, management names, business descriptions, and industry and product listings. Kompass's web site is www.kompass.com. Call publisher for prices and information on country directories. Cahners Business Information, 121 Chanlon Road, New Providence, NJ 07974, (908) 771-8785, fax (908) 665-8755, email hholmes@reedref.com. Headquarters: Cahners Business Information, 275 Washington Street, Newton, MA 02158-1630, (617) 558-4663 or (617) 964-3030, fax (617) 558-4700, email marketaccess@cahners.com, web sites www.cahners.com or www.chilton.net.

NATIONAL DIRECTORY OF ADDRESSES AND TELEPHONE NUMBERS contains addresses and phone numbers for major US companies, arranged alphabetically and by SIC or NAICS codes. Includes special information on hotels, banks, government information, area codes for US cities, transportation, colleges and more. Published annually. $95. Omnigraphics, Inc., Penobscot Building, Detroit, Michigan 48226, (313) 961-1340.

PUBLISHERS WEEKLY web site "BookWire" is an important publishing industry web site which covers all aspects of the book business. Useful for researchers, librarians, writers, publishers and anyone who likes to read. URL address is www.bookwire.com. Headquarters: Cahners Business Information, 275 Washington Street, Newton, MA 02158-1630, (617) 558-4663 or (617) 964-3030, fax (617) 558-4700, email marketaccess@cahners.com. Web sites www.cahners.com or www.chilton.net.

REFERENCE BOOK OF CORPORATE MANAGEMENTS is a three volume directory which details the professional histories of the principal officers and directors of over 12,000 US companies. Listings include key executives' names and titles, present positions, year of birth, colleges attended, degrees earned and dates, prior positions with other companies, titles and dates, military background and more. Information is presented alphabetically by company and is cross referenced geographically and by industry classification. It also lists principal officers and directors alphabetically, as well as by the colleges they attended and their military affiliations. Updated annually. For prices call Dun & Bradstreet at (800) 526-0651. For more information contact Dun & Bradstreet, Business Reference Solutions, Three Sylvan Way, Parsippany, New Jersey 07054. Email dnbmdd@mail.dnb.com. Web site http://www.dnbmdd.com.

SEARCH ENGINES. Here are the main search engines you can use as a starting point. Some people consider the first four better—Yahoo, Lycos, AltaVista and Excite. The remaining search engines are listed alphabetically.

> Yahoo! (http://www.yahoo.com)
> Lycos (http://www.lycos.com)
> AltaVista (http://www.AltaVista.com)
> Excite (http://www.excite.com)
>
> Dejanews (http://www.dejanews.com)
> HotBot (http://www.HotBot.com)
> Inference (http://www.inference.com/infind)
> Infoseek (http://www.infoseek.com)
> Nerd World (http://www.NerdWorld.com)
> Netfind (http://www.netfind.com)
> Northern Light (http://www.northernlight.com)
> Opentext (http://www.pinstripe.opentext.com/)
> Webcrawler (http://webcrawler.com)

SELECTPHONE is a national telephone directory on CD ROM. They offer a range of products at different prices. For more information, call them at (800) 992-3766 or visit their web site at www.infousa.com. SelectPhone is a product of Pro CD, Inc., 5711 South 86th Circle, Omaha, NE 68127.

*STANDARD AND POORS REGISTER OF CORPORATIONS, DIRECTORS AND EXECUTIVES.
Volume 1, Corporations, contains complete listings for 75,000 companies (including large subsidiaries), specifically names, titles, phone numbers, number of employees, annual sales, main products, and SIC/NAICS codes. Volume 2, Directors and Executives alphabetically lists 70,000 key managers with biographical data. Volume 3, Corporate Family Index is useful for locating a company's parent, subsidiaries, divisions and affiliates; also contains an index of companies by state and major cities. Published annually. Hardback directory, $799. Available in CD ROM. Call for price. Published by Standard & Poors Corporation, New York, New York. Distributed by: Larry Meranus Professional Publications & Services, 4 Demoray Court, Pine Brook, NJ 07058, (800) MERANUS or (800) 637-2687.

*STANDARD DIRECTORY OF ADVERTISERS Business Classifications Edition is an excellent general directory that organizes companies by a wide range of product categories. A few examples include "Apparel 2—Men's and Boys' Wear," "Heating and Air Conditioning," "Cosmetics and Toiletries," and "Aviation and Aerospace." This directory lists names and titles of key officers, revenues and other information. It is available in a geographic edition for the same price. This directory is comprised of over 24,000 companies that annually spend over $200,000 on advertising. It represents a reasonable place to look for hard-to-find information about privately held companies, especially those that heavily advertise their products. It is a good place to look for names if STANDARD AND POORS and the MILLION DOLLAR DIRECTORY fail to yield the names you need. Finally, the Classified Edition of THE STANDARD DIRECTORY OF ADVERTISERS can be a very convenient source of research because both your target list of companies and the corresponding names and titles of management all appear together, in the same Classification. This is important if you still rely on research books in hard copy. THE STANDARD DIRECTORY OF ADVERTISERS also publishes a special volume called THE STANDARD DIRECTORY OF ADVERTISERS TRADENAME INDEX. You can use the TRADENAME INDEX if you know the brand name of a product and need to find the company that manufactures it. In addition, this directory contains an Associations section which identifies marketing oriented associations.

$599 hard copy. If the price is prohibitively high, remember your local library. THE STANDARD DIRECTORY OF ADVERTISERS is also available on CD ROM under the title ADVERTISER AND AGENCY RED BOOKS PLUS. It is available in Windows® and Macintosh® formats. National Register Publishing, Reed Elsevier-New Providence, 121 Chanlon Road, New Providence, NJ 07974, (800) 521-8110, fax (800) 836-7736, web site www.redbooks.com or www.marquiswhoswho.com. "If, for any reason whatsoever, your order does not fully meet your expectations, simply return the product within 30 days for a prompt, complete, unquestioned refund," as stated in Catalog of Biographical and Professional References of publisher Marquis Who's Who/National Register Publishing.

STANDARD DIRECTORY OF ADVERTISING AGENCIES, also referred to as the "Red Book," is a comprehensive directory of the advertising agency business, generally including extensive listings of executives, especially in management, media, account services, creative and production. It also reveals the names of each agency's corporate clients. A CyberAgency Section lists agencies involved with Web design and development and a special "Who Owns Whom" section listing agency subsidiaries. $599. If the price is prohibitively high, remember your local library. THE STANDARD DIRECTORY OF ADVERTISING AGENCIES is also available on CD ROM under the title ADVERTISER AND AGENCY RED BOOKS PLUS. National Register Publishing, Reed Elsevier-New Providence, 121 Chanlon Road, New Providence, NJ 07974, (800) 521-8110, fax (800) 836-7736, web site www.marquiswhoswho.com or www.redbooks.com. "If, for any reason whatsoever, your order does not fully meet your expectations, simply return the product within 30 days for a prompt, complete, unquestioned refund," as stated in Catalog of Biographical and Professional References of publisher Marquis Who's Who/National Register Publishing.

THE SOURCE BOOK, "Expert Business Sources from Reed Elsevier Business Information" is a free booklet from the publisher which identifies trade journals published by Reed Elsevier, name of publisher, address, phone and email. Includes a wide variety of industry sources, alphabetically arranged into 23 categories, such as "Broadcasting/cable/communications," "Plant Operations," "Eye Care/Eyewear," "Technology Research." Free. Reed Elsevier Business Information, A Division of Reed Elsevier, Inc., 275 Washington Street, Newton, MA 02158-1630, (617) 964-3030, Fax (617) 558-4700, URLs www.cahners.com, www.chilton.net.

VALUE LINE INVESTMENT SURVEY is considered one of the most respected investment surveys around, particularly for their analysis of future prospects of the publicly held companies they follow. Also analyzes industries. Value Line Investment Survey, 220 East 42nd Street, New York, NY 10017-5891. Available as a Windows® CD ROM or a 3.5" disk covering 1,700 stocks, 2 month trial, $55. 1 year subscription $595. Covering 5,000+ stocks, 2 month trial $95, 1 year subscription $995. Call (800) 535-9648, ext. 2751. Call (800) 634-3583 for pricing about other products, including Mutual Fund Survey, Options, Convertibles, Over-the-Counter Special Situations, and hard copy of the Value Line Investment Survey and Value Line Investment Survey Expanded.

WARD'S BUSINESS DIRECTORY OF U.S. PRIVATE AND PUBLIC COMPANIES provides information on over 120,000 US companies, over 90% of them privately held. Volumes 1-3 contain company information. Volume 4 lists companies geographically and ranks the top 1,000 privately held companies and the top 1,000 employers. Volume 5 ranks private and public companies by sales within SIC or NAICS code. Volumes 6-7 contain state rankings by sales within SIC or NAICS. Also includes ranking of the top 100 privately held companies, the top publicly held companies and the top 100 employers for each state. Volume 8 ranks sales within the 6 digit NAICS (North American Industry Classification System which replaced the SIC code system). It sorts companies by cross-national agreements between the US, Canada and Mexico. Vols. 1-8, $2,515. Vols. 1-5, $2,125. Vols. 1-4, $1,880. Vol 5, $950. Vols. 6-7, $950. Vol 8, $640. Gale Group, P.O. Box 9187, Farmington Hills, MI 48333-9187. Toll free US and Canada (800) 877-GALE (4253) and (248) 699-GALE, fax (800) 414-5043 and (248) 699-8061, Internet orders galeord@galegroup.com, web site www.galegroup.com or www.gale.com. All Gale Group products are available on approval. Contact Gale for details.

www.askjeeves.com or **www.ask.com** or **www.aj.com** or **ask**. If you ask Jeeves, "How can I find a job" or "How can I find candidates for an engineering job?" Jeeves has an answer! (Actually, there's very little you CAN'T ask Jeeves.) The Ask Jeeves site includes HOOVER'S CAREER CENTER, which consists of Job Search Tools (monster.com, CareerMosaic,wsj.com careers, hotjobs, westech's virtual job fair and joboptions), Career Links and Career Research Links. Hoover's Career Center contains much additional information, including extensive RELOCATION data, such as cost of living comparisons, etc. You can also subscribe to Hoover's and access their directories on the Internet.

www.bookwire.com is the web site for *Publishers Weekly*. It serves both publishing industry professionals and consumers with information about publishing and research. Bowker's *Publishers Weekly*'s web site includes a searchable database of current author tour information, links to all book-related Web sites, industry Classifieds, and Book Wire Insider Direct, a subscription daily e-mail news service, and more.

www.bowker.com is the web site for this major research publisher. It includes Flagship Products and Services, an online Product Catalog, Electronic Publishing products including CD ROMs, Internet Databases, and Online Subscription and Site Licensing Databases; press releases, career opportunities, and more. Many of their references are accessible through this web site, such as BOOKS IN PRINT PLUS CANADIAN EDITION, ULRICH'S ON DISC, GERMAN BOOKS IN PRINT, GERMAN BOOKS OUT OF PRINT, INTERNATIONAL BOOKS IN PRINT PLUS, ITALIAN BOOKS IN PRINT, YEARBOOK OF INTERNATIONAL ORGANIZATIONS PLUS, ULRICH'S INTERNATIONAL PERIODICALS DIRECTORY, THE SOFTWARE ENCYCLOPEDIA, BOWKER'S COMPLETE VIDEO DIRECTORY, AMERICAN BOOK PUBLISHING RECORD. Visit the web site for more information.

www.clickit.com is the web site address to "Access Business Online." Its objective is to bring Buyers and Sellers Together on the Internet. Features include Executive Job Network, Capital Sources, Trade Announcements, Professional Services, Top 100 World Business Charts, Company Profiles, International Buyer-Seller, BizWiz! Search Engine, Web Emporium Web Site Development, Classifieds, Corporate News Net, Wall Street and World Wide Finance, Market News & Business Connections, and more. However, a service fee is charged if you wish to access this information.

www.cnn.com is the URL to CNN's impressive comprehensive web site. It contains Big Yellow Search Books to assist in finding businesses and people. It also features global directories, The Directory Store™and a "search the net" capability with InfoSeek. InfoSeek also has a Business Channel with business resources and small businesses, and a Careers Channel.

www.dnbmdd.com is the web site to the DUN & BRADSTREET MILLION DOLLAR DIRECTORY. It provides information on over 1 million leading public and private US companies. The database is available on CD ROM and in print. Key officer biographies are also available. You can also view a sample company record or access a free database trial.

www.galegroup.com is the web site to publisher Gale Research, one of the largest providers of research for search, recruiting and libraries.

www.infousa.com provides free US national directory assistance.

www.latimes.com is the URL to the comprehensive *Los Angeles Times* web site.

www.nytimes.com is the URL for *The New York Times* web site.

www.reedref.com presents a current catalog for all Reed Reference Publishing companies for both print and electronic references—National Register Publishing, R.R. Bowker, Bowker-Saur, KG Saur, Marquis Who's Who, Martindale-Hubbell and Lexis-Nexis Business Information. At the time of this writing, this catalog is searchable by name, subject, publisher and keyword. To check new offerings, visit individual publisher pages. Free product demos of CD ROM'S can be downloaded for for experimentation and some sample pages—and even entire chapters—and are available for unlimited viewing. The web site also includes a constantly updated menu of special discounts which are available only on the web site. Ask about the growing number of RRP databases accessible via the Internet on subscription or for a usage based price, such as the MARTINDALE-HUBBELL LAW DIRECTORY. For more information visit Bowker Reed Reference's web site at www.reedref.com or www.bowker.com or contact corporate offices, 121 Chanlon Road, New Providence, NJ 07974, (800) 521-8110, (800) 323-3288, fax (908) 665-3528, email info@bowker.com or webmaster@www.reedref.com.

References—Librarian

See Chapter 6, "How to Create an Executive Search Library." Also see References—General, Publishers Web sites and Periodicals.

If you like Gale's ENCYCLOPEDIA OF BUSINESS INFORMATION SOURCES or the ENCYCLOPEDIA OF ASSOCIATIONS, you'll love these other librarians' references. They contain an impressive quantity and quality of information, most of it available electronically, too. Librarians' references are some of the best kept secrets around!

While there are many references cited in this section, an asterisk (*) indicates preferred sources that can be used first.

AMERICAN LIBRARY ASSOCIATION (ALA), 50 East Huron Street, Chicago, IL 60611, (800) 545-2433, in Illinois (800) 545-2444, in Canada (800) 545-2455. Annually publishes the ALA Handbook of Organization and Membership Directory, which provides information about the ALA's divisions, committees, round tables and discussion groups. The major divisions of the ALA are:

- REFERENCE AND ADULT SERVICES DIVISION (RASD) publishes RQ. Committees include Business Reference Sources Committee, Reference Sources Committee, Adult Library Materials Committee, and Reference Tools Advisory Committee (which provides assistance to publishers of reference titles). Other sections include Machine-Assisted Reference Section and History Section.

- ASSOCIATION OF COLLEGE AND RESEARCH LIBRARIES (ACRL) is the largest group within the ALA. It publishes CHOICE, COLLEGE & RESEARCH LIBRARIES, COLLEGE & RESEARCH LIBRARIES NEWS, RARE BOOKS AND MANUSCRIPTS LIBRARIANSHIP.

- PUBLIC LIBRARY ASSOCIATION (PLA) consists of the Metropolitan Libraries Section, Community Information Section, and Armed Forces Library Section. PLA publishes PUBLIC LIBRARIES.

- ASSOCIATION FOR LIBRARY COLLECTIONS AND TECHNICAL SERVICES (ALCTS) publishes LIBRARY RESOURCES AND TECHNICAL SERVICES.

- AMERICAN ASSOCIATION OF SCHOOL LIBRARIANS (AASL) publishes SCHOOL LIBRARY MEDIA QUARTERLY.

- ASSOCIATIONS UNLIMITED ONLINE is available on the Internet through GaleNet. You can subscribe to any of the several databases comprising ASSOCIATIONS UNLIMITED, including:

- NATIONAL ORGANIZATIONS OF THE US DATABASE

- REGIONAL, STATE AND LOCAL ORGANIZATIONS DATABASE

- INTERNATIONAL ORGANIZATIONS DATABASE

- ASSOCIATIONS MATERIALS DATABASE

- GOVERNMENT NONPROFIT ORGANIZATIONS DATABASE

For more information on available databases and pricing, contact Gale Group, P.O. Box 9187, Farmington Hills, MI 48333-9187. Toll free US and Canada (800) 877-GALE (4253) and (248) 699-GALE, fax (800) 414-5043 and (248) 699-8061, Internet orders galeord@galegroup.com, web site www.galegroup.com or www.gale.com. All Gale Group products are available on approval. Contact Gale for details.

THE BASIC LIBRARY: CORE RESOURCES by Bernard S. Schlesinger reveals an incredible abundance of information. Oryx Press, Phoenix, Arizona. A tremendous research value at $43.50. Phone (800) 279-6799, email: info@oryxpress.com, web site: www.oryxpress.com.

BOOKS IN CANADA is a monthly publication which reviews 300-400 new Canadian books each year. It provides an inexpensive way to learn about new resources in Canada. It is available by subscription ($22.98/year) and is sold at newsstands and in bookstores ($3.95 per issue).

Ordering information:

BOOKS IN CANADA
Canadian Review of Books Ltd.
427 Mt. Pleasant Road
Toronto, ON M4S 2L8
CANADA
(416) 489-4755 Phone

BOOKS IN PRINT is the only complete record of in-print, out-of-print and forthcoming books published or distributed in the US. For up-to-the-minute current information on INTERNET references and Internet Databases and Internet web sites available, use this reference. It should be available at a public library or in a good book store. Published annually. 9 volume set, $550. BOOKS IN PRINT ON DISC is available in Windows, MS-DOS and Macintosh . Annual subscription $550.

BOOKS IN PRINT INTERNET EDITION at www.booksinprint.com is available by subscription. Log on or call for details.

BOOKS IN PRINT ONLINE is available through the Dialog Corporation, Ovid Technologies, Inc. and LEXIS ®-NEXIS® on a "pay-as-you-go" basis. Contact the publisher for details. BOOKS OUT OF PRINT INTERNET EDITION can be searched free at www.bowker.com. R.R. Bowker (a unit of Cahners Business Information), 121 Chanlon Road, New Providence, NJ 07974 USA, Phone (888) BOWKER2 (888-269-5372) & (800) 323-3288, fax (908) 508-7696, email info@bowker.com, web www.bowker.com. Canada—R.R. Bowker, Markham, Ontario, phone (888) BOWKER9 & (905) 415-5837, fax (905) 479-6266. German speaking Europe—K.G. Saur Verlag, Munich, Germany, phone 49-89-76902-232, fax 49-89-76902-250, email 100730.1341@compuserve.com, web www.saur.de/home.htm. Rest of Europe incl. United Kingdom plus Africa & Asia—Bowker-Saur, W. Sussex, UK, phone 44-1342-326-972, fax 44-1342-335-612, email customer@bowker-saur.co.uk, web www.bowker-saur.com/service/. Australia/New Zealand—Thorpe, Port Melbourne, Victoria, Australia, phone 61-03-9-245-7370, fax 61-03-9-245-7395, email customer.service@thorpe.com.au, web www.thorpe.com.au. Technical support for CD ROMs (800) 323-3288, fax 908) 665-3528, email techsupport@bowker.com. Also see International Books in Print.

BOWKER/WHITAKER GLOBAL BOOKS IN PRINT ON DISC includes the entire databases of BOOKS IN PRINT (US and Canada), WHITAKER'S BOOKBANK (UK) and INTERNATIONAL BOOKS IN PRINT (Continental Europe, Africa, Asia and Latin America), AUSTRALIAN AND NEW ZEALAND BOOKS IN PRINT (Australia, New Zealand and the Oceanic states). 1 year subscription $2,055.

R.R. Bowker (a unit of Cahners Business Information), 121 Chanlon Road, New Providence, NJ 07974 USA, Phone (888) BOWKER2 (888-269-5372) & (800) 323-3288, fax (908) 508-7696, email info@bowker.com, web www.bowker.com. Canada—R.R. Bowker, Markham, Ontario, phone (888) BOWKER9 & (905) 415-5837, fax (905) 479-6266. German speaking Europe—K.G. Saur Verlag, Munich, Germany, phone 49-89-76902-232, fax 49-89-76902-250, email 100730.1341@compuserve.com, web www.saur.de/home.htm. Rest of Europe incl. United Kingdom plus Africa & Asia—Bowker-Saur, W. Sussex, UK, phone 44-1342-326-972, fax 44-1342-335-612, email customer@bowker-saur.co.uk, web www.bowker-saur.com/service/. Australia/New Zealand—Thorpe, Port Melbourne, Victoria, Australia, phone 61-03-9-245-7370, fax 61-03-9-245-7395, email customer.service@thorpe.com.au, web www.thorpe.com.au. Technical support for CD ROMs (800) 323-3288, fax 908) 665-3528, email techsupport@bowker.com.

*BUSINESS INFORMATION SOURCES by Lorna Daniells is an outstanding reference at any price. At $39.95 a copy, it's such an extraordinary value, it should have a place in every library. This is clearly one of the top three hard copy references around, and its reasonable price elevates it to first place. Business Information Sources provides a wealth of information routinely needed by search firms, job hunters and corporate recruiters, including general directories, specialized directories, professional associations, periodicals, industry information, international information, and much more. $39.95. Ordering information: Business Information Sources by Lorna Daniells, is published by the University of California Press (Berkeley, CA, Los Angeles, CA & Oxford, England) (510-642-4247). Orders are handled by California Princeton Fulfillment Services, P.O. Box 10769, Newark, NJ 07193-0769. (800-822-6657).

CANADIAN BUSINESS AND ECONOMICS: A GUIDE TO SOURCES OF INFORMATION lists information by subject, including books, periodicals and services. Fully indexed and thoroughly cross referenced. Price reduced to $39.95 for 1992 edition. Canada Library Association, 200 Elgin Street, Suite 602, Ottawa, Ontario K2P 1L5 CANADA, (613) 232-9625, fax (613) 563-9895, Internet: bj491@freenet.carleton.ca.

CANADIAN LIBRARY ASSOCIATION is located at Suite 602, 200 Elgin Street, Ottawa, ON K2P 1L5, (613) 232-9625. Their online catalog can be viewed on their web site, www.cla.amlibs.ca and should indicate when an update will be available for their 1992 edition of CANADIAN BUSINESS AND ECONOMICS, A GUIDE TO SOURCES OF INFORMATION.

CANADIAN BUSINESS AND ECONOMICS: A GUIDE TO SOURCES OF INFORMATION lists information by subject, including books, periodicals and services. Fully indexed and thoroughly cross referenced. Price reduced to $39.95 for 1992 edition. Canada Library Association, 200 Elgin Street, Suite

602, Ottawa, Ontario K2P 1L5 CANADA, (613) 232-9625, fax (613) 563-9895, Internet: bj491@freenet.carleton.ca.

CD-ROM'S IN PRINT contains information on over 11,000 CD's, including subject indexes. It also lists information for nearly 4,000 publishing and distribution companies. LIBRARY JOURNAL'S review describes CD-ROM'S IN PRINT as "The starting point for those who choose CD-ROM titles." $155. Gale Group, P.O. Box 9187, Farmington Hills, MI 48333-9187. Toll free US and Canada (800) 877-GALE (4253) and (248) 699-GALE, fax (800) 414-5043 and (248) 699-8061, Internet orders galeord@galegroup.com, web site www.galegroup.com or www.gale.com. All Gale Group products are available on approval. Contact Gale for details.

*DIRECTORIES IN PRINT identifies over 15,000 directories (local, regional, national and international) which are organized in 26 subject chapters. An alternate formats index includes directories in online databases, CD ROM, diskettes, microfiche and mailing labels and lists. $489 for 2 volumes. Gale Group, P.O. Box 9187, Farmington Hills, MI 48333-9187. Toll free US and Canada (800) 877-GALE (4253) and (248) 699-GALE, fax (800) 414-5043 and (248) 699-8061, Internet orders galeord@galegroup.com, web site www.galegroup.com or www.gale.com. All Gale Group products are available on approval. Contact Gale for details.

DIRECTORY OF BUSINESS INFORMATION RESOURCES, ASSOCIATIONS, NEWSLETTERS, MAGAZINES AND TRADESHOWS, published by Grey House Pub., Pocket Knife Square, Lakeville, CT 06039, $199. (800) 562-2139, (860) 435-0868, web site www.greyhouse.com or books@il.com.

ENCYCLOPEDIA OF ASSOCIATIONS: INTERNATIONAL ORGANIZATIONS includes nearly 20,000 multinational and national organizations in foreign countries, including US based associations with multinational membership. Entries also include email addresses, web sites and bulletin board addresses, lobbying activities, and publication and convention information. Indexed by geography, keyword and executives. $595 for 2 volume set. Also available in CD ROM. Database available via commercial online service. Gale Group, P.O. Box 9187, Farmington Hills, MI 48333-9187. Toll free US and Canada (800) 877-GALE (4253) and (248) 699-GALE, fax (800) 414-5043 and (248) 699-8061, Internet orders galeord@galegroup.com, web site www.galegroup.com or www.gale.com. All Gale Group products are available on approval. Contact Gale for details.

*ENCYCLOPEDIA OF ASSOCIATIONS: NATIONAL ORGANIZATIONS OF THE US. This superb reference is one of the first places you should look when beginning a new recruiting assignment or when looking for specialized references of any type. The keyword index makes this comprehensive reference easy to use, even in hard copy. For over 23,000 nonprofit professional associations with a national scope, this encyclopedia reveals:

• Publications, including membership rosters and newsletters

• Dates and locations of association conferences and conventions

• Names of Executive Directors, who are usually incredible sources of industry information if you call and speak to them

• Committees

• Job and candidate referral banks, which can provide resumes of other industry sources and sometimes candidates

• It includes organizations in these categories: business, trade, environmental, agricultural, legal, governmental, engineering, technological, scientific, educational, cultural, social welfare, health & medical, public affairs, ethnic, labor unions, chambers of commerce, tourism, & others.

Volume 1, National Organizations of the US, $505
Volume 2, Geographic and Executive Indexes, $390
Volume 3, Supplement, $405

Gale Group, P.O. Box 9187, Farmington Hills, MI 48333-9187. Toll free US and Canada (800) 877-GALE (4253) and (248) 699-GALE, fax (800) 414-5043 and (248) 699-8061, Internet orders

galeord@galegroup.com, web site www.galegroup.com or www.gale.com. All Gale Group products are available on approval. Contact Gale for details.

ENCYCLOPEDIA OF ASSOCIATIONS: REGIONAL, STATE AND LOCAL ORGANIZATIONS. The information in this directory is not duplicated anywhere in ENCYCLOPEDIA OF ASSOCIATIONS. Over 100,000 nonprofit organizations are included in this directory. $585 for 5 volume set or $140 per individual volume. Also available on CD ROM and online on the Internet through a GaleNet subscription.

Volume 1, Great Lakes States (Illinois, Indiana, Michigan, Minnesota, Ohio, Wisconsin)

Volume 2, Northeastern States (Connecticut, Maine, Massachusetts, New Hampshire, New Jersey, New York, Pennsylvania, Rhode Islands, Vermont)

Volume 3, Southern and Middle Atlantic States (Including Puerto Rico and the Virgin Islands) (Alabama, Delaware, Washington, DC, Florida, Georgia, Kentucky, Maryland, Mississippi, North Carolina, Puerto Rico, South Carolina, Tennessee, Virginia, West Virginia, Virgin Islands)

Volume 4, South Central and Great Plains States (Arkansas, Iowa, Kansas, Louisiana, Missouri, Nebraska, North Dakota, Oklahoma, South Dakota, Texas)

Volume 5, Western States (Alaska, Arizona, California, Colorado, Guam, Hawaii, Idaho, Montana, Nevada, New Mexico, Oregon, Utah, Washington, Wyoming)

Gale Group, P.O. Box 9187, Farmington Hills, MI 48333-9187. Toll free US and Canada (800) 877-GALE (4253) and (248) 699-GALE, fax (800) 414-5043 and (248) 699-8061, Internet orders galeord@galegroup.com, web site www.galegroup.com or www.gale.com. All Gale Group products are available on approval. Contact Gale for details.

*ENCYCLOPEDIA OF BUSINESS INFORMATION SOURCES will lead you to specialized directories, professional associations, trade publications, newsletters, databases, Internet resources and more. It's an excellent reference and a great way to find key resources in any industry fast. $330. Gale Group, P.O. Box 9187, Farmington Hills, MI 48333-9187. Toll free US and Canada (800) 877-GALE (4253) and (248) 699-GALE, fax (800) 414-5043 and (248) 699-8061, Internet orders galeord@galegroup.com, web site www.galegroup.com or www.gale.com. All Gale Group products are available on approval. Contact Gale for details.

ENCYCLOPEDIA OF PHYSICAL SCIENCES AND ENGINEERING INFORMATION SOURCES covers over 600 subjects such as chemistry, geology, physics, civil engineering plus new areas of technology such as CD ROM, cybernetics, hazardous material, space shuttle and others. Each subject includes a bibliography of live, print and electronic sources of information. $165. Gale Group, P.O. Box 9187, Farmington Hills, MI 48333-9187. Toll free US and Canada (800) 877-GALE (4253) and (248) 699-GALE, fax (800) 414-5043 and (248) 699-8061, Internet orders galeord@galegroup.com, web site www.galegroup.com or www.gale.com. All Gale Group products are available on approval. Contact Gale for details.

GALE BUSINESS RESOURCES ONLINE provides modules on US Industry (over 200,000 companies) and International Industry (over 200,000 companies), including public and privately held companies, brands, business rankings, trade and professional associations, company histories, merger information, and more. Comprehensive records include company name, officers' names and titles, SIC/NAICS codes and more. GALE BUSINESS RESOURCES is available online on the Internet through GaleNet. For information on pricing, contact: Gale Group, P.O. Box 9187, Farmington Hills, MI 48333-9187. Toll free US and Canada (800) 877-GALE (4253) and (248) 699-GALE, fax (800) 414-5043 and (248) 699-8061, Internet orders galeord@galegroup.com, web site www.galegroup.com or www.gale.com. All Gale Group products are available on approval. Contact Gale for details.

GALE DIRECTORY OF DATABASES identifies over 12,000 international databases available in a variety of formats including online, CD ROM, diskette, and others. Entries include producer name, description, subject, language, cost, update frequency, geographic coverage. Volume 1, Online Databases, $260. Volume 2, CD-ROM, Diskette, Magnetic Tape, Handheld and Batch Access Database Products, $170. Both volumes $390. ONLINE MAGAZINE described this as "An excellent directory of online databases." Gale Group, P.O. Box 9187, Farmington Hills, MI 48333-9187. Toll free US and Canada (800) 877-GALE (4253) and (248) 699-GALE, fax (800) 414-5043 and (248) 699-8061, Internet orders galeord@galegroup.com, web site

www.galegroup.com or www.gale.com. All Gale Group products are available on approval. Contact Gale for details.

GALE DIRECTORY OF DATABASES ONLINE is a GaleNet database on the Internet that identifies over 12,000 international databases in various formats, including CD ROM, diskettes, online and others. Check your local library for free access or contact Gale for annual subscription rates. Gale Group, P.O. Box 9187, Farmington Hills, MI 48333-9187. Toll free US and Canada (800) 877-GALE (4253) and (248) 699-GALE, fax (800) 414-5043 and (248) 699-8061, Internet orders galeord@galegroup.com, web site www.galegroup.com or www.gale.com. All Gale Group products are available on approval. Contact Gale for details.

GaleNet is an online resource on the Internet that provides an integrated, one-step access to the most frequently used Gale databases, such as GALE'S READY REFERENCE SHELF ONLINE. As GaleNet's capabilities are constantly changing and being upgraded, contact the publisher for details and prices. Gale Group, P.O. Box 9187, Farmington Hills, MI 48333-9187. Toll free US and Canada (800) 877-GALE (4253) and (248) 699-GALE, fax (800) 414-5043 and (248) 699-8061, Internet orders galeord@galegroup.com, web site www.galegroup.com or www.gale.com. All Gale Group products are available on approval. Contact Gale for details.

GALE'S READY REFERENCE SHELF ONLINE is a GaleNet Internet resource that provides integrated access to databases covering national, regional, state, local and international associations, publishers, newspapers and periodicals, directories, newsletters, online databases, portable databases, database products and vendors, special libraries and research centers. Information is included from numerous Gale databases, among them THE ENCYCLOPEDIA OF ASSOCIATIONS, PUBLISHERS DIRECTORY, GALE DIRECTORY OF PUBLICATIONS AND BROADCAST MEDIA and several others. If it is prohibitively expensive, locate a library with with this resource. Gale Group, P.O. Box 9187, Farmington Hills, MI 48333-9187. Toll free US and Canada (800) 877-GALE (4253) and (248) 699-GALE, fax (800) 414-5043 and (248) 699-8061, Internet orders galeord@galegroup.com, web site www.galegroup.com or www.gale.com. All Gale Group products are available on approval. Contact Gale for details.

*GUIDE TO AMERICAN DIRECTORIES, $95. B. Klein Publications, P.O. Box 6578, Delray Beach, Florida 33482. Phone (888) 859-8083, (561) 496-3316, fax (561) 496-5546.

INFORMATION IN CANADA—A DIRECTORY OF ELECTRONIC AND SUPPORT RESOURCES provides electronic information on information resources, consultants and information brokers, library based online research services, library automation software, computer accessible library catalogues and a directory of information industry services, plus a large section on databases produced in Canada. Price reduced to $49.95 for 1996 edition. Canada Library Association, 200 Elgin Street, Suite 602, Ottawa, Ontario K2P 1L5 CANADA, (613) 232-9625, fax (613) 563-9895,web site www.cla.amlibs.ca includes an online catalog. Email bj491@freenet.carleton.ca.

INTERNATIONAL BOOKS IN PRINT, from K.G. Saur, $795.

INTERNATIONAL BOOKS IN PRINT PLUS, one year subscription, $1,303. R.R. Bowker (a unit of Cahners Business Information), 121 Chanlon Road, New Providence, NJ 07974 USA, Phone (888) BOWKER2 (888-269-5372) & (800) 323-3288, fax (908) 508-7696, email info@bowker.com, web www.bowker.com. Canada—R.R. Bowker, Markham, Ontario, phone (888) BOWKER9 & (905) 415-5837, fax (905) 479-6266. German speaking Europe—K.G. Saur Verlag, Munich, Germany, phone 49-89-76902-232, fax 49-89-76902-250, email 100730.1341@compuserve.com, web www.saur.de/home.htm. Rest of Europe incl. United Kingdom plus Africa & Asia—Bowker-Saur, W. Sussex, UK, phone 44-1342-326-972, fax 44-1342-335-612, email customer@bowker-saur.co.uk, web www.bowker-saur.com/service/. Australia/New Zealand—Thorpe, Port Melbourne, Victoria, Australia, phone 61-03-9-245-7370, fax 61-03-9-245-7395, email customer.service@thorpe.com.au, web www.thorpe.com.au. Technical support for CD ROMs (800) 323-3288, fax 908) 665-3528, email techsupport@bowker.com.

INTERNATIONAL DIRECTORY OF BUSINESS INFORMATION SOURCES AND SERVICES contains information on over 4,000 organizations which produce and provide business information in 50 countries. $185. Published by Euromonitor (England). At the time of this writing, while distributor Gale Group was no longer selling this reference, the sales representative indicated it might be available directly from the publisher. For more information check BOOKS IN PRINT or INTERNATIONAL BOOKS IN PRINT.

LITERARY MARKET PLACE, "The Directory of the American Book Publishing Industry With Industry Yellow Pages" is an excellent 3 volume directory with comprehensive information on US book publishers; imprints, subsidiaries and distributors; book trade acquisitions and mergers, small presses, Canadian book publishers, micropublishers, US electronic publishers, electronic publishing consultants, electronic publishing products and services, editorial services, literary agents, illustrations agents, US agents and offices of foreign publishers, lecture agents, specialized advertising and public relations firms, direct mail specialists, mailing list brokers and services, book review syndicates, book review and index journals and services, book exhibits, book clubs, book lists and catalogs, book importers and exporters, book producers, translators, artists, photographers, stock photo agencies, associations, book trade events and conferences, awards, contents and grants, reference books for the trade, magazines for the trade, a toll free directory of publishers, magazine and newspaper publicity, radio and television publicity, book manufacturing services, book distributors and sales representatives, and wholesalers. $189.95.

LITERARY MARKET PLACE ON DISC, previously titled LITERARY MARKET PLACE PLUS CD ROM, one year subscription $297.00.

LITERARY MARKET PLACE—INTERNET EDITION, www.literarymarketplace.com, is available by subscription.

INTERNATIONAL LITERARY MARKET PLACE Internet database can be directly accessed at www.iliterarymarketplace.com. It is also linked to the US domestic LITERARY MARKET PLACE web site at www.literarymarketplace.com. Contact the publisher for subscription price. INTERNATIONAL LITERARY MARKET PLACE, hard copy $189.95.

R.R. Bowker (a unit of Cahners Business Information), 121 Chanlon Road, New Providence, NJ 07974 USA, Phone (888) BOWKER2 (888-269-5372) & (800) 323-3288, fax (908) 508-7696, email info@bowker.com, web www.bowker.com. Canada—R.R. Bowker, Markham, Ontario, phone (888) BOWKER9 & (905) 415-5837, fax (905) 479-6266. German speaking Europe—K.G. Saur Verlag, Munich, Germany, phone 49-89-76902-232, fax 49-89-76902-250, email 100730.1341@compuserve.com, web www.saur.de/home.htm. Rest of Europe incl. United Kingdom plus Africa & Asia—Bowker-Saur, W. Sussex, UK, phone 44-1342-326-972, fax 44-1342-335-612, email customer@bowker-saur.co.uk, web www.bowker-saur.com/service/. Australia/New Zealand—Thorpe, Port Melbourne, Victoria, Australia, phone 61-03-9-245-7370, fax 61-03-9-245-7395, email customer.service@thorpe.com.au, web www.thorpe.com.au. Technical support for CD ROMs (800) 323-3288, fax 908) 665-3528, email techsupport@bowker.com.

PUBLISHERS, DISTRIBUTORS AND WHOLESALERS OF THE US™ is available in electronic database formats. It identifies over 70,000 publishers, wholesalers, distributors, software firms, museum and association imprints, and trade organizations, covering a variety of media. This database includes discount schedules aimed mainly at libraries, plus compete addresses (for editorial and ordering), toll-free phone numbers. This database is used to identify the outlet(s) offering the best price(s) for books, cassettes and software titles. It is available online through Knight Ridder Information, Inc. (DIALOG File number 450, (800) 334-2564 or (800) 3-DIALOG), through subscription online and on CD-ROM/ hard disk. For more information visit Bowker Reed Reference's web site at http://www.reedref.com or contact: Bowker Reed Reference Electronic Publishing, 121 Chanlon Road, New Providence, NJ 07974 USA, Phone (800) 323-3288, Fax (908) 665-3528, email info@bowker.com.

REFERENCE AND RESEARCH BOOK NEWS provides prompt information about new books and CD ROMs of interest to reference librarians and users of reference materials. 8 issues per year, 900 books and CD's reviewed per issue. $100/institutions, $80/individuals US and Canada, $115/foreign. Ordering information: REFERENCE & RESEARCH BOOK NEWS, 5600 NE Hassalo Street, Portland, OR 97213, (503) 281-9230, email: booksnews@booknews. com, http://www.books.com//booknews.

REFERENCE CANADA is a comprehensive information source. For more information call (613) 941-4823 or the Reference Librarian at the Ottawa Public Library at (613) 598-4008.

SPECIAL LIBRARIES ASSOCIATION encompasses business research, among other specialized types of information. It is an important organization which many librarians rely on and a rich source of information. The SLA is located at 1700 18th Street, NW, Washington, DC 20009, (202) 234-4700.

WORDS ON CASSETTE is the only complete guide to audio cassette collections with location, ordering and pricing information, running times, content summaries and rental availability, an index to authors, readers and performers. Published annually. Cahners Business Information, 121 Chanlon Road, New Providence, NJ 07974, (908) 777-8669, (888) 269-5372, fax (908) 508-7696, email marin.mixon@bowker.com, URL www.bowker.com. Headquarters: Cahners Business Information, 275 Washington Street, Newton, MA 02158-1630, (617) 558-4663 or (617) 964-3030, fax (617) 558-4700, email marketaccess@cahners.com. Web sites www.cahners.com or www.chilton.net.

WORLD DIRECTORY OF BUSINESS INFORMATION WEB SITES provides full details on over 1,500 free business web sites, including information such as online surveys, top company rankings, company information, brand information, market research reports and trade association statistics. $590. Published by Euromonitor (England). Distributed by Gale Group, P.O. Box 9187, Farmington Hills, MI 48333-9187. Toll free US and Canada (800) 877-GALE (4253) and (248) 699-GALE, fax (800) 414-5043 and (248) 699-8061, Internet orders galeord@galegroup.com, web site www.galegroup.com or www.gale.com. All Gale Group products are available on approval. Contact Gale for details.

WORLD DIRECTORY OF MARKETING INFORMATION SOURCES identifies market research companies, online databases, directories and marketing journals for every major consumer market in 75 countries. $595. Published by Euromonitor (England). Distributed by Gale Group, P.O. Box 9187, Farmington Hills, MI 48333-9187. Toll free US and Canada (800) 877-GALE (4253) and (248) 699-GALE, fax (800) 414-5043 and (248) 699-8061, Internet orders galeord@galegroup.com, web site www.galegroup.com or www.gale.com. All Gale Group products are available on approval. Contact Gale for details.

www.bowker.com is the web site for this major research publisher. It includes Flagship Products and Services, an online Product Catalog, Electronic Publishing products including CD ROMs, Internet Databases, and Online Subscription and Site Licensing Databases; press releases, career opportunities, and more. Many of their references are accessible through this web site, such as BOOKS IN PRINT PLUS CANADIAN EDITION, ULRICH'S ON DISC, GERMAN BOOKS IN PRINT, GERMAN BOOKS OUT OF PRINT, INTERNATIONAL BOOKS IN PRINT PLUS, ITALIAN BOOKS IN PRINT, YEARBOOK OF INTERNATIONAL ORGANIZATIONS PLUS, ULRICH'S INTERNATIONAL PERIODICALS DIRECTORY, THE SOFTWARE ENCYCLOPEDIA, BOWKER'S COMPLETE VIDEO DIRECTORY, AMERICAN BOOK PUBLISHING RECORD. Visit the web site for more information. At this web site you can also search—free—BOOKS OUT OF PRINT database. At this site you can also search free Bowker's LIBRARY RESOURCE GUIDE—INTERNET EDITION, a directory of library services and suppliers which is drawn from Bowker's AMERICAN LIBRARY DIRECTORY. At www.bowker.com you can also access a free online directory from LITERARY MARKET PLACE, including hundreds of services and suppliers to the book publishing community—ad agencies, publicists, typesetters, printers and more.

www.cahners.com is the web site for Cahners Business Information.

www.corptech.com is a web site that contains information about CorpTech Technology Company Information, directories, guides, databases, mailing lists, and reports customized from the CorpTech Database.

www.dnbmdd.com is the web site for the DUN & BRADSTREET MILLION DOLLAR DIRECTORY, which contains information on over 1 million leading public and private US companies. Key officer biographies are also available.

www.galegroup.com is the web site to publisher Gale Research, one of the largest providers of research for search, recruiting and libraries.

Web sites for additional publishers are listed in the Publishers Web Sites category.

Relocation

AMERICAN COST OF LIVING SURVEY provides cost and expense data for 455 American cities and metropolitan areas. Includes housing, transportation, food, clothing and other consumer goods, utilities, insurance, entertainment, taxes, education and more. $160, 2nd edition, 1995. Contact publisher to find out when next edition will be available. Gale Group, P.O. Box 9187, Farmington Hills, MI 48333-9187. Toll free US and Canada (800) 877-GALE (4253) and (248) 699-GALE, fax (800) 414-5043 and (248) 699-8061, Internet orders galeord@galegroup.com, web site www.galegroup.com or www.gale.com. All Gale Group products are available on approval. Contact Gale for details.

CRAIGHEAD'S INTERNATIONAL BUSINESS, TRAVEL AND RELOCATION GUIDE TO 81 COUNTRIES provides information about the business practices, economies, customs, communications, tours and attractions plus maps. $695 for 3 volumes. Data compiled by Craighead Publications. Gale Group, P.O. Box 9187, Farmington Hills, MI 48333-9187. Toll free US and Canada (800) 877-GALE (4253) and (248) 699-GALE, fax (800) 414-5043 and (248) 699-8061, Internet orders galeord@galegroup.com, web site www.galegroup.com or www.gale.com. All Gale Group products are available on approval. Contact Gale for details.

WORLD COST OF LIVING SURVEY includes information such as child care, education, health care, utilities and other areas for major cities around the world. It is a useful resource for companies relocating employees to determine appropriate levels of compensation adjustment and for individuals considering a move abroad. $240. Gale Group, P.O. Box 9187, Farmington Hills, MI 48333-9187. Toll free US and Canada (800) 877-GALE (4253) and (248) 699-GALE, fax (800) 414-5043 and (248) 699-8061, Internet orders galeord@galegroup.com, web site www.galegroup.com or www.gale.com. All Gale Group products are available on approval. Contact Gale for details.

www.askjeeves.com or **www.ask.com** or **www.aj.com** or **ask**. If you ask Jeeves, "How can I find a job" or "How can I find candidates for an engineering job?" Jeeves has an answer! (Actually, there's very little you can't ask Jeeves.) The Ask Jeeves site includes HOOVER'S CAREER CENTER, which consists of Job Search Tools (monster.com, CareerMosaic,wsj.com careers, hotjobs, westech's virtual job fair and joboptions), Career Links and Career Research Links. Hoover's Career Center contains much additional information, including extensive RELOCATION data, such as cost of living comparisons, etc. You can also subscribe to Hoover's and access their directories on the Internet.

www.careers.wsj.com is the *Wall Street Journal*'s web site. It focuses on positions for middle and senior management including financial positions at $75,000 and up. This web site is among those that encompass senior executive positions. Other features includes Job Seek, Who's Hiring, Career Columnists, Salaries & Profiles, The Salary Calculator™, Job Hunting Advice, Succeeding at Work, HR Issues, Executive Recruiters, Working Globally, College Connection, Starting a Business, Career Bookstore and more. Content from The National Employment Business Weekly is also featured. The site was developed by Dow Jones & Company, Inc., Princeton, New Jersey and was established in 1997.

www.nationjob.com is the web site for NationJob Network Online Jobs Database. NationJob, Inc. was ranked as one of the top 5 sites in two different categories by the *National Business Employment Weekly:* "Sites Offering the Best Job-Search Support" and "Best General Purpose Sites." The site offers "Search for a Job Now (no email required)," "Search for a Company" and "Directory of all Companies." P.J. Scout service is a "(P)ersonal (J)ob Scout service that's "like having a friend shop for a job for you." Fill in a form and PJ will send you info on jobs you might be interested in. Information on salary comparisons, moving costs, relocation info, insurance calculator and more. NationJob Inc., 601 SW 9th Street, Suites J&K, Des Moines, IA 50309, (800) 292-7731. The site developer is NationJob, Inc.

Research—General

See References—General

Research and Development

AMERICAN MEN AND WOMEN OF SCIENCE provides detailed biographical information on over 100,000 US and Canadian scientists. This information is very useful for searches in research and development and other areas, because you can review the individual's background, titles, and degrees with dates,before you ever place a phone call. 8 volume set $900. AMERICAN MEN & WOMEN OF SCIENCE (AMWS Online) is also available online on a "pay as you go" basis through The Dialog Corporation, DIALOG file no. 236, Subfile: AMWS, or through LEXIS-NEXIS using NEXIS Library : BUSREF, File Name: AMSCI. Call Bowker for more information including availability of American Men and Women of Science on CD ROM.

R.R. Bowker (a unit of Cahners Business Information), 121 Chanlon Road, New Providence, NJ 07974 USA, Phone (888) BOWKER2 (888-269-5372) & (800) 323-3288, fax (908) 508-7696, email info@bowker.com, web www.bowker.com. Canada—R.R. Bowker, Markham, Ontario, phone (888) BOWKER9 & (905) 415-5837, fax (905) 479-6266. German speaking Europe—K.G. Saur Verlag, Munich, Germany, phone 49-89-76902-232, fax 49-89-76902-250, email 100730.1341@compuserve.com, web www.saur.de/home.htm. Rest of Europe incl. United Kingdom plus Africa & Asia—Bowker-Saur, W. Sussex, UK, phone 44-1342-326-972, fax 44-1342-335-612, email customer@bowker-saur.co.uk, web www.bowker-saur.com/service/. Australia/New Zealand—Thorpe, Port Melbourne, Victoria, Australia, phone 61-03-9-245-7370, fax 61-03-9-245-7395, email customer.service@thorpe.com.au, web www.thorpe.com.au. Technical support for CD ROMs (800) 323-3288, fax 908) 665-3528, email techsupport@bowker.com.

BOWKER BIOGRAPHICAL DIRECTORY is comprised of the electronic equivalents of AMERICAN MEN AND WOMEN OF SCIENCE™, WHO'S WHO IN AMERICAN ART™ and WHO'S WHO IN AMERICAN POLITICS™. It is available in electronic database formats from Reed Reference. Entries include past and current career details, publications, education, research interests, languages, personal and family information and more .Available online through Knight-Ridder Information, Inc., (DIALOG file number 236) and on LEXIS™—NEXIS™ (American Men and Women of Science Library: People; busref, file AMSCI). For more information visit Bowker Reed Reference's web site at http://www.reedref.com or contact: Bowker Reed Reference Electronic Publishing, 121 Chanlon Road, New Providence, NJ 07974 USA, Phone (800) 323-3288, Fax (908) 665-3528, email info@bowker.com.

BUSINESSWEEK regularly publishes surveys which are excellent for developing target lists. One of them is the R&D SCOREBOARD, which lists companies by industry and provides various statistics, such as Research and Development expenditures, R&D as a percentage of sales, R&D spending per employee, comparisons to previous year, and so forth.

COMPLETE MARQUIS WHO'S WHO ON CD ROM is a compilation of literally all 19 Marquis Who's Who that have appeared in print since 1985, including living and deceased people. WHO'S WHO IN AMERICA®, WHO'S WHO IN THE WORLD®, WHO'S WHO IN AMERICAN EDUCATIONS®, WHO'S WHO IN AMERICAN LAW®, WHO'S WHO IN AMERICAN NURSING®, WHO'S WHO IN MEDICINE AND HEALTHCARE®, WHO'S WHO IN FINANCE AND INDUSTRY®, WHO'S WHO IN SCIENCE AND ENGINEERING®, WHO'S WHO IN THE EAST®, WHO'S WHO IN THE MIDWEST®, WHO'S WHO IN THE SOUTH AND SOUTHWEST®, WHO'S WHO IN THE WEST®, WHO'S WHO OF AMERICAN WOMEN®, WHO'S WHO IN ADVERTISING®, WHO'S WHO OF EMERGING LEADERS IN AMERICA®, WHO'S WHO IN ENTERTAINMENT®, WHO'S WHO AMONG HUMAN SERVICES PROFESSIONALS®. One year subscription with semi-annual updates $995. National Register Publishing, Reed Elsevier-New Providence, 121 Chanlon Road, New Providence, NJ 07974, (800) 521-8110, fax (800) 836-7736, web site www.marquiswhoswho.com or www.redbooks.com. "If, for any reason whatsoever, your order does not fully meet your expectations, simply return the product within 30 days for a prompt, complete, unquestioned refund," as stated in Catalog of Biographical and Professional References of publisher Marquis Who's Who/National Register Publishing.

DIRECTORY OF AMERICAN RESEARCH AND TECHNOLOGY™ (DART) is available in electronic database formats from Reed Reference. It covers over 11,000 labs in over 1,500 research fields. Searches can be conducted by R&D field, doctoral disciplines, staff size, names and titles of executive and research personnel, location and more. Available Online through NEXIS®—NEXIS® and on CD ROM/Hard Disk. For more information visit Bowker Reed Reference's web site at http://www.reedref.com or contact: Bowker Reed Reference Electronic Publishing, 121 Chanlon Road, New Providence, NJ 07974 USA, Phone (800) 323-3288, Fax (908) 665-3528, email info@bowker.com.

EUROPEAN R&D PLUS DATABASE ON CD ROM is a consolidation of the DIRECTORY OF EUROPEAN RESEARCH AND DEVELOPMENT and WHO'S WHO IN EUROPEAN RESEARCH AND DEVELOPMENT. It covers over 20,000 labs, both commercial and academic, in 36 countries including all the European former Soviet Republics. Searches can be conducted by over 20 fields in over 600 scientific disciplines. Information is available about over 100,000 people, including senior researchers, research managers and consultants, including: name, career data, current position, education, publications, research scope, current activities, nationality, languages and more. From Bowker-Saur. Updated annually. 1 year subscription $1,595, excluding discounts. For more information visit Bowker Reed Reference's web site at http://www.reedref.com or contact: Bowker Reed Reference Electronic Publishing, 121 Chanlon Road, New Providence, NJ 07974 USA, Phone (800) 323-3288, Fax (908) 665-3528, email info@bowker.com.

GOVERNMENT RESEARCH DIRECTORY identifies over 4,300 research labs and programs of the U.S. and Canadian federal governments. $510. Gale Group, P.O. Box 9187, Farmington Hills, MI 48333-9187. Toll free US and Canada (800) 877-GALE (4253) and (248) 699-GALE, fax (800) 414-5043 and (248) 699-8061, Internet orders galeord@galegroup.com, web site www.galegroup.com or www.gale.com. All Gale Group products are available on approval. Contact Gale for details.

INTERNATIONAL RESEARCH CENTERS DIRECTORY identifies government, university, independent, nonprofit and commercial research and development facilities in nearly 125 countries. Entries include English and foreign name of center, email addresses, personal contact, organizational affiliates, staff, description of research program, publications, services and more. Master, subject and country indexes are included. Booklist 's review described this as "A useful contribution to the reference shelf of international directories." $470. Database also available via commercial online service. Gale Group, P.O. Box 9187, Farmington Hills, MI 48333-9187. Toll free US and Canada (800) 877-GALE (4253) and (248) 699-GALE, fax (800) 414-5043 and (248) 699-8061, Internet orders galeord@galegroup.com, web site www.galegroup.com or www.gale.com. All Gale Group products are available on approval. Contact Gale for details.

R&D CONTRACTS MONTHLY is the monthly counterpart of the annual UNIQUE THREE-IN-ONE RESEARCH AND DEVELOPMENT DIRECTORY. $49.50 on CD ROM. Ordering Information: Government Data Publications, Inc., 1155 Connecticut Avenue, NW, Washington, DC 20077-6106.

R&D RATIOS AND BUDGETS provides R&D budgets, R&D to sales ratios and R&D to gross margin ratios for over 6,000 companies in some 400 industries. It also includes industry and R&D budgets on over 150 major foreign companies. This information can be used to develop a fine-honed target list of preeminent organizations for a research and development search. Further, a target list which incorporates these ratios can provide "added value" competitive information to a company. $345 book, $495 book and diskette database. Updated annually. Ordering information: Schonfeld & Associates, Inc., One Sherwood Drive, Lincolnshire, IL 60069, (800) 205-0030, Fax (847) 948-8096, email schonassoc@aol.com, http://www.saibooks.com. Catalog available online.

RESEARCH CENTERS AND SERVICES DIRECTORY ONLINE is a GaleNet database on the Internet which includes three types of R&D centers around the world—US research centers, international research centers and government research centers, including nonprofit research centers, commercial labs, international institutes, government experiment stations, university research parks, in the areas of agriculture, environment, engineering, physical and earth sciences, labor and industrial relations, and education. Available by subscription or at a library. 1 user $1,575 per year, 2 users $2,835 annually. Call publisher for additional pricing information. Gale Group, P.O. Box 9187, Farmington Hills, MI 48333-9187. Toll free US and Canada (800) 877-GALE (4253) and (248) 699-GALE, fax (800) 414-5043 and (248) 699-8061, Internet orders galeord@galegroup.com, web site www.galegroup.com or www.gale.com. All Gale Group products are available on approval. Contact Gale for details.

RESEARCH CENTERS DIRECTORY describes programs, facilities, publications,educational efforts and services of North America's leading nonprofit research institutes. It includes a personal name index that lists center directors and other contacts. Subject, geographic and master indexes are also included. Booklist's review described this as "an extremely valuable reference tool." $548 for a two volume set. Database also available via commercial online service. Gale Group, P.O. Box 9187, Farmington Hills, MI 48333-9187. Toll free US and Canada (800) 877-GALE (4253) and (248) 699-GALE, fax (800) 414-5043 and (248) 699-8061, Internet orders galeord@galegroup.com, web site www.galegroup.com or www.gale.com. All Gale Group products are available on approval. Contact Gale for details.

RESEARCH SERVICES DIRECTORY contains information on commercial research and development companies in the USA. Entries contain contact information, company description, principal clients, description of services, patents, licenses, publications and more. This directory includes firms conducting in-house research and contract or fee-for services. Alphabetical, geographic, personal name and subject indexes are provided. Previously distributed by Gale Group for $340 (6th edition), at the time of this writing Gale had sold this directory to Grey House Publishing in Lakeville, Connecticut, (800) 562-2139, (860) 435-0868, www.greyhouse.com or books@il.com.

SciTECH REFERENCE PLUS CD ROM contains directory information, 125,000 biographies of US and Canadian scientists and engineers from AMERICAN MEN AND WOMEN OF SCIENCE, listings for over 8,000 laboratories from the DIRECTORY OF AMERICAN RESEARCH AND TECHNOLOGY, and information from THE DIRECTORY OF CORPORATE AFFILIATIONS (including public, private and international companies) of leading US and international technology firms and their subsidiaries. It also contains 60,000 records on science/technology and medical serials from ULRICH'S INTERNATIONAL PERIODICALS DIRECTORY. Searches can be conducted by SIC, year founded, activity, education, employees, institution/company, city, state or country, memberships/honors, product description, personal statistics, personal title, research area, revenue. Updated annually. 1 year subscription $995, 3 years 2,836, excluding discounts. For more information visit Bowker Reed Reference's web site at http://www.reedref.com or contact: Bowker Reed Reference Electronic Publishing, 121 Chanlon Road, New Providence, NJ 07974 USA, Phone (800) 323-3288, Fax (908) 665-3528, email info@bowker.com.

U.S. SOURCEBOOK OF R&D SPENDERS is a directory of publicly owned corporations that spend on research and development. Information includes names and titles of three senior executives, R&D budgets, sales, and more. Organized by state and zip code. $345 book, $495 book and diskette database. Updated annually. Ordering information: Schonfeld & Associates, Inc., One Sherwood Drive, Lincolnshire, IL 60069, (800) 205-0030, Fax (847) 948-8096, email schonassoc@aol.com, http://www.saibooks.com. Catalog available online.

UNIQUE THREE-IN-ONE RESEARCH AND DEVELOPMENT DIRECTORY, details research and development government contracts awarded over the prior 12 months. Each listing includes awardee, address, agency, description of work, amount of contract, and more. Directory I contains alphabetical information by awardee. Directory II contains geographical information by awarding agency. Directory III is organized by the nature of the research. It identifies the latest developments in materials, techniques and processes in every field of industrial and scientific endeavor, programs whose production contracts are likely to expire, areas where advanced research is being conducted, and the names of organizations specializing in specific technical areas. Published annually since 1959. $49.50 ON CD ROM. Ordering Information: Government Data Publications, Inc., 1155 Connecticut Avenue, NW, Washington, DC 20077-6106.

www.bio.com is the URL for Bio Online. Most positions are for research chemists, biochemists and in clinical development and are usually in the $40,000 to $75,000 range. Developed by Vitadata Corp, Berkeley, California, the site went online in 1993.

www.rtp.org is the home page for Research Triangle Park, North Carolina . It includes a directory of companies in the Park and listing of companies according to research specialization, appropriate for target list development.

www.sciencemag.org is the URL for Science Online, a career site which posts many positions for research scientists, research directors and post-Doctoral positions. Salary often ranges from $50,000 to $100,000. Science Online was developed by the American Association for the Advancement of Science, Washington, DC and was established in 1996.

Research—Executive Search

See Recruiting

DIRECTORY OF INDEPENDENT RESEARCH CONSULTANTS contains information on 200 contract consultants. Jobhunters who are sending resumes to search firms might also want to include research consultants. They are often indistinguishable from search consultants because the roles of both can be so similar. In addition, at a search firm, a researcher customarily conducts the first screen of a resume, regardless of whom it's addressed to. Further, it's not unusual for these consultants to be directly retained by corporations purchasing "unbundled search" services, which basically means a less expensive "no frills" search product. This means that independent research consultants represent another third party avenue for job hunters, in addition to executive search firms and contingency recruiting firms. $65. Ordering information: Kennedy Information, One Kennedy Place, Route 12 South, Fitzwilliam, NH 03447, phone (800) 531-0007 or 603-585-6544, fax 603-585-9555, email bookstore@kennedyinfo.com, web site www.kennedyinfo.com.

EXECUTIVE SEARCH RESEARCH DIRECTORY (ESRD) provides information on over 350 contract research consultants, including descriptions of research services provided, fees, experience, where trained, areas of concentration, and unusual capabilities, including 26 freelancers with an Internet specialty. Cross referenced by over 300 specialties. $88 postpaid. Ordering information: Kenneth J. Cole, Publisher, The Recruiting & Search Report, P.O. Box 9433, Panama City Beach, FL 32417. (850) 235-3733, fax (850) 233-9695. Email jcole9433@aol.com.

EXECUTIVE SEARCH ROUNDTABLE, founded in New York City in 1979, was the first professional association of research professionals established. Their newsletter, ON TARGET, is published quarterly. Members can access a wired capability by Email in which they can source each other for ideas, resources, web sites, and names of contacts. For more information contact THE EXECUTIVE SEARCH ROUNDTABLE, P. O. Box 3565, Grand Central Station, New York, NY 10163, phone (212) 439-4630, web site www.esroundtable.org.

INTERNET RECRUITING EDGE by Barbara Ling is a comprehensive collection of research assembled over a two year period. Developed for the novice and experienced Internet recruiter alike, and with a foreword by Tony Byrne, topics include: Where, Oh Where, is my Candidate Now?, Does the Internet Really Benefit Businesses? Phones Still Work, But Don't Buy a Mansion if You Only Need a Cottage, How to Find Candidates on the Internet, Non-Traditional Resources, Before You Begin—A Primer on Internet Culture—Netiquette, Beginner Candidate Location Skill, Resume Banks, Search Engine Basics, The Joy of Bookmarks, The Art of Job Posting, Sleuthing for Company Directories, Finding Employee Directories, Finding Executive Biographies, Alumni Organizations, Forums and Bulletin Boards, Internet Classifieds, Online E-zines (magazines), Professional Organizations, Colleges, Metasearch at Highway 61, Realistic Goals Before You Begin Your Own Recruiter Web site, Perilous Pitfalls, How To Buy Your Recruiter Business Site, Locating Good Web Site Designers, Your Site is Designed—Now What? How To Market A Recruiter Web Site, 14 Killer Web Site Search Engine Visibility Tips, and more. $149. Order by visiting the web site http://www.barbaraling.com or call (732) 563-1464.

Professional Associations are listed in chapter 25, "Professional Associations and Roundtables — Including Research, Recruitment and an Array of Human Resources Activities."

UNCOVERING THE TRUTH—HOW TO REALLY CHECK REFERENCES is a cassette by Andrea Jupina that completely covers the art of reference checking in 30 minutes. It's an excellent refresher that really gets your mental juices flowing before you begin to interview references—ideal for line managers, search firms, small business owners, and anyone who needs to know the real story—without a lawsuit. $15.95 plus shipping & handling. Available from Jupina by email order at andreajupina@yahoo.com and from Kennedy Information, One Kennedy Place, Route 12 South, Fitzwilliam, NH 03447, phone (800) 531-0007 or 603-585-6544, fax 603-585-9555, email bookstore@kennedyinfo.com, web site www.kennedyinfo.com.

Research Mini-Case Study

CRAIN PUBLICATIONS—Here's how we conducted phone research about Crain's, whose publications have always been superb. First, we called Crain's headquarters office in Chicago and told the operator what we were looking for. Specifically, we wanted to do research on certain topics and needed to know whether Crain's published an index of the articles it had published, (similar to that done by the Harvard Business Review, for example). The operator connected us to the Editorial Department, where we found out that each of the 20 or so individual Crain publications determines whether to produce its own index.

The man we spoke to very helpfully suggested that if we had any questions about particular types of articles in the future, if we called the editorial office, someone would probably be willing to give an answer "off the top of his head." He also said that if the question was simple and they weren't insanely busy, someone might even be willing to check NEXUS for us. This is a classic example of why telephone research can be so effective. There are a lot of really nice people out there who are willing to help, especially if they have the time.

Next, we called the switchboard again to ask for a list of Crain's various periodicals. Surprisingly, we were connected to the Personnel Department, proving once again that you never know where your information will come from! The lady mailed a brochure which named officers and directors, provided circulation figures and a list of their publications.

At a later date, we called to verify that our list of publications was current. We also needed web site addresses for the publications. However, the person we called was too busy to help. But she was nice enough update our list of publications—and web site addresses—by mailing us a handwritten list. Where there's a will, there's a way.

Note: Whenever you have someone on the phone, you can ask if it's easier to provide this type of industry information by fax or email. If the person is too busy, sometimes I ask if he or she will read it to me over the phone and I'll write it down very quickly. That way I don't have to wait. I also don't have to wonder if he or she will ever follow up. There's a very basic psychological motivation at work here. Everybody is most interested in his or her own survival. I know that my need for information is not nearly as important to someone else as it is to me. So I must make a point of getting the information I need. It's simply a question of nicely being persistent and tenacious. In fact, if you're persistent, sometimes people will give you the information just to get off the phone.

Restaurants

See Retail

CHAIN STORE GUIDE'S CHAIN RESTAURANT OPERATORS CD-ROM. allows you to conduct data searches from five topic screens: 1. Personnel by title, 2. Personnel by functional area, 3. Restaurant type (cafeteria, dinnerhouse, fast food, family restaurant, in-store feeder, table cloth), 4. Menu type (Greek, German, health food, ice cream, etc.) You can also make selections based on geography or the size of a company (number of units and/or sales). Contains information about professional associations. Several output options are available, including mailing labels, and electronic formats (such as DBASE, ASCII, text) for mail merge customization. $995 including companion directory. If the price is prohibitively high, remember your local library. Ordering information: Chain Store Guide Information Services, 3922 Coconut Palm Drive, Tampa, FL 33619. (800) 927-9292, (813) 664-6800, (813) 627-6822, (800) 289-6822. http://www.d-net.com/csgis or http://www.csgis.com.

DIRECTORY OF CHAIN RESTAURANT OPERATORS describes 3-or-more unit chain restaurant companies in the U.S. and Canada operating or franchising restaurants, cafeterias, contract and industrial feeders. Hotel/motel companies controlling three or more restaurants within hotels and 3 or more foodservice operations are profiled, as well as food units in drug chains, general merchandise chains and discount stores. Key personnel, a listing of major trade associations and a trade show calendar are also included. An index to the top 100 restaurants is also included and is a valuable tool for target list development. An industry profile as provided by the National Restaurant Association is also included. Updated annually. $290. Chain Store Guide Information Services, 3922 Coconut Palm Drive, Tampa, FL 33619. (800) 927-9292, (813) 664-6800, (813) 627-6822, (800) 289-6822. http://www.d-net.com/csgis or http://www.csgis.com.

DIRECTORY OF HIGH VOLUME INDEPENDENT RESTAURANTS lists nearly 6,000 independent restaurants in the U.S. with at least $1 million in annual sales. A companion to the Chain Restaurant Operators directory, this guide identifies independent restaurants with one or two units that are part of a national chain but purchase separately. This directory lists key executives and buyers, major trade associations and a trade show calendar. $290. Chain Store Guide Information Services, 3922 Coconut Palm Drive, Tampa, FL 33619. (800) 927-9292, (813) 664-6800, (813) 627-6822, (800) 289-6822. http://www.d-net.com/csgis or http://www.csgis.com.

MAJOR FOOD & DRINK COMPANIES OF EUROPE provides information on 2,100 major companies in food and beverages (alcoholic and non-alcoholic) in Western Europe. $450. US distributor: Larry Meranus Professional Publications & Services, 4 Demoray Court, Pine Brook, NJ 07058, (800) MERANUS or (800)

637-2687. Published by Graham & Whiteside Ltd., Tuition House, 5-6 Francis Grove, London SW19 4DT, England. Web site http://www.major-co-data.com. Email sales@major-co-data.com.

MAJOR FOOD & DRINK COMPANIES OF THE FAR EAST & AUSTRALASIA provides information on over 1,100 top food and beverage (alcoholic and non-alcoholic) organizations in the Asia Pacific region. $415. US distributor: Larry Meranus Professional Publications & Services, 4 Demoray Court, Pine Brook, NJ 07058, (800) MERANUS or (800) 637-2687. Published by Graham & Whiteside Ltd., Tuition House, 5-6 Francis Grove, London SW19 4DT, England. Web site http://www.major-co-data.com. Email sales@major-co-data.com.

MAJOR FOOD & DRINK COMPANIES OF THE WORLD provides information on nearly 6,000 major food and drink companies in the world. $830 or 460 pounds sterling. US distributor: Larry Meranus Professional Publications & Services, 4 Demoray Court, Pine Brook, NJ 07058, (800) MERANUS or (800) 637-2687. Published by Graham & Whiteside Ltd., Tuition House, 5-6 Francis Grove, London SW19 4DT, England. Web site http://www.major-co-data.com. Email sales@major-co-data.com.

NATION'S RESTAURANT NEWS is a 30 year old newsweekly of the foodservice industry. For info about subscriptions and customer service, call 800-447-7133. URL: www.nrn.com or http://www.d-net.com/csgis or http://www.csgis.com. Chain Store Guide Information Services, 3922 Coconut Palm Drive, Tampa, FL 33619.

www.hospitalitynet.nl is the URL for Hospitality Net, a site developed by Hospitality Net BV in Maastricht, The Netherlands. It connects job hunters and employers in the hospitality and restaurant industries worldwide for positions mostly in the $30,000 to $50,000 range. The site was established in 1995.

Resume Databases

See Jobhunters' Resources, Web Sites, Recruiting and Chapter 7, "Major Internet Web Sites"

Retail

See Restaurants

ADVERTISER AND AGENCY RED BOOKS PLUS CD ROM combines all the information in THE STANDARD DIRECTORY OF ADVERTISERS, THE STANDARD DIRECTORY OF ADVERTISING AGENCIES and THE STANDARD DIRECTORY OF INTERNATIONAL ADVERTISERS AND AGENCIES. Information is searchable by 25 fields, including company name, personal name, job title/function, product type, product/account name, city, state, zip or country, area code, revenues, number of employees, outside ad agency and even type of computer hardware. Contains professional association information. Available for Windows and Macintosh. Updated quarterly. 1 year subscription $1,295. If the price is prohibitively high, remember your local library. National Register Publishing, Reed Elsevier-New Providence, 121 Chanlon Road, New Providence, NJ 07974, (800) 521-8110, fax (800) 836-7736, web site www.redbooks.com or www.marquiswhoswho.com. "If, for any reason whatsoever, your order does not fully meet your expectations, simply return the product within 30 days for a prompt, complete, unquestioned refund," as stated in Catalog of Biographical and Professional References of publisher Marquis Who's Who/National Register Publishing.

CANADIAN PHARMACISTS DIRECTORY lists over 18,000 Canadian pharmacists, drug information centers, poison control centres, pharmaceutical suppliers, drug wholesalers, related universities, drug store head offices, pharmaceutical associations, chain drug stores, and brand name/generic pharmaceutical companies. $119 prepaid, $149 plus $5 shipping and handling if billed. Special discounts available for combined purchases. Published by Southam Information Products Ltd, 1450 Don Mills Road, Don Mills, Ontario M3B 2X7 CANADA, (800) 668-2374. In Toronto 442-2122. Web site www.southam.com.

CHAIN STORE GUIDE'S DATABASE MARKETING DIVISION can customize databases in these industries: Supermarket, department stores, discount department stores, drug stores. Your made-to-order database can include one or several of the named industries and the criteria of your ideal "customer" or search prospect. Information is available on a 3.5" diskette for IBM-PC, Apple Macintosh and DBF, ASCII, comma delimited and others. Mailing labels are also available or you can generate your own labels from a 3.5" diskette. For pricing or ordering information contact Chain Store Guide Information Services, 3922 Coconut Palm Drive, Tampa, FL 33619. (800) 927-9292, (813) 664-6800, (813) 627-6822, (800) 289-6822. http://www.d-net.com/csgis or http://www.csgis.com.

DIRECTORY OF DRUG STORE AND HBC CHAINS identifies over 1,800 drug retailers in the U.S. and Canada operating over 45,000 stores including drug, HBC, cosmetic, deep discount, home health care, discount, and grocery stores/supermarket chains with pharmacies, mass merchants with pharmacies, deep discount chains, and wholesale drug companies. It includes names and titles of key personnel, a listing of major trade associations and a trade show calendar. It also provides indexes to top drug retailers, top drug wholesalers, top grocery chains and top discount chains. $290. Chain Store Guide Information Services, 3922 Coconut Palm Drive, Tampa, FL 33619. (800) 927-9292, (813) 664-6800, (813) 627-6822, (800) 289-6822. http://www.d-net.com/csgis or http://www.csgis.com.

DIRECTORY OF SINGLE UNIT SUPERMARKET OPERATORS lists 7,000 independent (single unit) supermarket operators/grocery retailers with sales of at least $1 million. names and titles of key personnel. It also identifies major trade associations and a trade show calendar. $280. Chain Store Guide Information Services, 3922 Coconut Palm Drive, Tampa, FL 33619. (800) 927-9292, (813) 664-6800, (813) 627-6822, (800) 289-6822. http://www.d-net.com/csgis or http://www.csgis.com.

DIRECTORY OF SUPERMARKET, GROCERY AND CONVENIENCE STORE CHAINS describes and indexes over 2,300 supermarket chains with $2 million in annual sales. It covers supermarkets, superstores, club stores, gourmet supermarkets and combo stores in the U.S. and Canada, plus a special section profiling 1,700 convenience store chains. It includes an index to the top 200 supermarket chains and the top 100 convenience store chains, which is a valuable tool for target list development. It also lists over 29,000 key executives, buyers and administrative personnel. The directory also lists major trade associations and a trade show calendar. $300. Chain Store Guide Information Services, 3922 Coconut Palm Drive, Tampa, FL 33619. (800) 927-9292, (813) 664-6800, (813) 627-6822, (800) 289-6822. http://www.d-net.com/csgis or http://www.csgis.com.

EUROPEAN DIRECTORY OF RETAILERS AND WHOLESALERS includes information on some 3,000 European retailers and wholesalers, including a directory of information sources. $790. Published by Euromonitor (England). Distributed by Gale Group, P.O. Box 9187, Farmington Hills, MI 48333-9187. Toll free US and Canada (800) 877-GALE (4253) and (248) 699-GALE, fax (800) 414-5043 and (248) 699-8061, Internet orders galeord@galegroup.com, web site www.galegroup.com or www.gale.com. All Gale Group products are available on approval. Contact Gale for details.

FAIRCHILD PUBLICATIONS publishes a number of fashion and retail publications, such as FAIRCHILD'S TEXTILE AND APPAREL FINANCIAL DIRECTORY, which provides information about a range of textile and garment manufacturers. Published annually. $85. Fairchild also publishes industry trade publications, such as WOMEN'S WEAR DAILY (www.wwd.com) and numerous specialized apparel industry directories, such as FASHION RESOURCE DIRECTORY, DIRECTORY OF BRAND NAME APPAREL MANUFACTURERS (which includes buyers), and APPAREL INDUSTRY SOURCEBOOK (which also includes buyers). Fairchild also publishes material for specialized retail niches, such as supermarkets, shoes, etc. For more information, contact Fairchild Books, 7 West 34th Street, New York, NY 10001, (212) 630-3880, (800) 247 6622, email fpwebmaster@fairchildpub.com, web site www.fairchildpub.com or www.fairchildbooks.com.

HARVARD BUSINESS SCHOOL'S BAKER LIBRARY in Boston provides an outstanding consumer marketing web site at www.library.hbs.edu/. This web site identifies extensive sources of information on consumer marketing, including retail both for job hunters and researchers. It includes associations, membership directories, information on direct mail, public relations, corporate communications, online direct mail and online Dun and Bradstreet Credit Reports.

While the access to the web site itself is free and available to anyone, access to the CAREER ADVISOR database is available only to current Harvard Business School students and Harvard Business School Alumni Advisors (Harvard Business School alumni who have agreed to serve as Career advisors to current students and other alumni). The Advisor Database can be searched by industry, geography, job function, job title, year of graduation and company name. In addition, Reference Librarians at the Harvard Business School can conduct searches for a fee. Hundreds of databases are available. Ask at the Reference Desk for more information. For example, Dun & Bradstreet's Credit Reports are a lucrative source of information about privately held companies.

SHELDON'S RETAIL DIRECTORY OF THE US AND CANADA is published by Phelon, Sheldon & Marsar, 1364 Georgetowne Circle, Sarasota, FL 34232-2048, (941) 342-7990, fax (941) 342-7994, who also publish numerous retail and apparel directories. For more information contact the Reference Desk at the Baker Library, Harvard Business School in Boston, in connection with the Advisor Database. Web site www.library.hbs.edu/.

STANDARD DIRECTORY OF ADVERTISERS Business Classifications Edition is an excellent general directory that organizes companies by a wide range of product categories. A few examples include "Apparel 2—Men's and Boys' Wear," "Heating and Air Conditioning," "Cosmetics and Toiletries," and "Aviation and Aerospace." This directory lists names and titles of key officers, revenues and other information. It is available in a geographic edition for the same price. This directory is comprised of over 24,000 companies that annually spend over $200,000 on advertising. It represents a reasonable place to look for hard-to-find information about privately held companies, especially those that heavily advertise their products. It is a good place to look for names if STANDARD AND POORS and the MILLION DOLLAR DIRECTORY fail to yield the names you need. Finally, the Classified Edition of THE STANDARD DIRECTORY OF ADVERTISERS can be a very convenient source of research because both your target list of companies and the corresponding names and titles of management all appear together, in the same Classification. This is important if you still rely on research books in hard copy. THE STANDARD DIRECTORY OF ADVERTISERS also publishes a special volume called THE STANDARD DIRECTORY OF ADVERTISERS TRADENAME INDEX. You can use the TRADENAME INDEX if you know the brand name of a product and need to find the company that manufactures it. In addition, this directory contains an Associations section which identifies marketing oriented associations.

$599 hard copy. If the price is prohibitively high, remember your local library. THE STANDARD DIRECTORY OF ADVERTISERS is also available on CD ROM under the title ADVERTISER AND AGENCY RED BOOKS PLUS. It is available in Windows® and Macintosh® formats. National Register Publishing, Reed Elsevier-New Providence, 121 Chanlon Road, New Providence, NJ 07974, (800) 521-8110, fax (800) 836-7736, web site www.redbooks.com or www.marquiswhoswho.com. "If, for any reason whatsoever, your order does not fully meet your expectations, simply return the product within 30 days for a prompt, complete, unquestioned refund," as stated in Catalog of Biographical and Professional References of publisher Marquis Who's Who/National Register Publishing.

SUPERMARKET BUSINESS is a monthly trade magazine provides information about key trade events, trends, and research findings. Supermarket Business Week is a weekly news fax with highlights of the week's key developments in the supermarket business. Call (201) 833-1900 for subscription information. Remember to find out if there are any back issues with the specific information you need—or an annual index. Ordering information: Chain Store Guide Information Services, 3922 Coconut Palm Drive, Tampa, FL 33619. (800) 927-9292, (813) 664-6800, (813) 627-6822, (800) 289-6822. http://www.d-net.com/csgis or http://www.csgis.com.

SUPERMARKET, GROCERY AND CONVENIENCE STORE CHAINS CD-ROM can conduct data searches from five topic screens: 1. Personnel by title, 2. Personnel by functional area, 3. Listing type (branch office, corporate office, divisional office, headquarters, location, managed care div, regional office, subsidiary, warehouse), 4. Stores operated (superstores, supermarkets, convenience, warehouse, combo stores, gourmet supermarkets, stores w/gas), 5. Specialty departments (e.g., auto supplies, automatic teller machines, beer, books/magazines, floral/horticulture,gourmet/specialty foods, greeting cards, in-store bakeries, in-store banking, in-store restaurant, lawn & garden, liquor, nutrition center, et al.). You can also make selections based on geography or the size of a company (number of units and/or sales). Several output options are available, including mailing labels, and electronic formats (such as DBASE, ASCII, text) for mail merge customization. $795, including companion directory. If the price is prohibitively high, remember your local library. Chain Store Guide Information Services, 3922 Coconut Palm Drive, Tampa, FL 33619. (800) 927-9292, (813) 664-6800, (813) 627-6822, (800) 289-6822. http://www.d-net.com/csgis or http://www.csgis.com.

WORLD RETAIL DIRECTORY profiles over 2,600 retailers in 15 sectors, including in Latin America, Eastern Europe and Asia. $990. Published by Euromonitor (England). Distributed by Gale Group, P.O. Box 9187, Farmington Hills, MI 48333-9187. Toll free US and Canada (800) 877-GALE (4253) and (248) 699-GALE, fax (800) 414-5043 and (248) 699-8061, Internet orders galeord@galegroup.com, web site www.galegroup.com or www.gale.com. All Gale Group products are available on approval. Contact Gale for details.

www.library.hbs.edu/ is the URL for the Harvard Business School Baker Library, which contains free excellent information on consumer marketing, retail, associations, membership directories, direct mail, public relations, corporate communications, online direct mail and more. Dun and Bradstreet Credit Reports can also be accessed. In addition, for a fee, reference librarians can conduct online searches from any of several hundred databases. See "Harvard Business School's Baker Library" above.

www.nrf.com is the URL for the excellent NATIONAL RETAIL FEDERATION (NRF) web site. It includes information about publications such as ANNUAL SPECIALTY STORE WAGE AND BENEFIT SURVEY, SMALL STORE SURVIVAL by Arthur Andersen, COOPERS AND LYBRAND SOFTWARE DIRECTORY FOR RETAILERS, ERNST AND YOUNG NATIONAL RETAIL FEDERATION'S INTERNET STUDY.

Russia

See Commonwealth of Independent States, International

S

Sales

See Marketing

www.americasemployers.com or America's Employers is a site mainly for positions in technology, finance and sales at approximately $50,000 to $100,000. Launched in 1995, it was developed by Career Relocation Corp of America in Armonk, New York.

www.bestjobsusa.com or Best Jobs U.S.A. is a site mainly for information technology, sales and engineering positions usually in the $50,000 to $100,000 range. Launched in 1996, the site was developed by Recourse Communications, Inc., West Palm Beach, Florida.

www.careerexchange.com is a web site for North American job seekers developed by CorpNet InfoHub, Ltd., Vancouver, BC, Canada. Launched in 1996, its People-Match capability notifies the user of jobs through email. Most positions are in high technology, engineering, sales and marketing and are primarily in the $40,000 to $75,000 range.

www.careersite.com sends email notification of a job match to job seekers and employers. Most positions are in engineering, marketing and sales and management, mainly in the $40,000 to $75,000 range. CareerSite was developed by CareerSite Corp., Ann Arbor Michigan and was launched in 1995.

www.jobcenter.com is the URL for JobCenter Employment Services, Inc., a site with many job postings in IT, programming and sales and marketing, often in the $30,000 to $100,000 range. The site was developed by JobCenter Employment Services, Inc., Skaneateles, New York and was launched in 1995.

www.joblynx.com is a site that connects recruiters with people seeking full time, part time and contract positions at all levels, starting at $50,000 and exceeding $100,000. Many positions are posted in IT, management and sales and marketing. The site was developed by JobLynx, Green Bay, Wisconsin. It was launched in 1996.

www.joboptions.com is the URL for JobOptions, formerly E-Span, a site that has been online since 1991. At the time of this writing, features include "The Right Person For The Job" and "The Right Job For The

Person," job listings; post resume edit resume, career library, job match download and more. Many job postings are in sales and marketing, finance and accounting and in technology. The site was developed by Gund Business Group, Indianapolis.

www.LatPro.com is the URL for Latin America's Professional Network, a site for experienced Spanish and Portuguese bilingual professionals. Many job postings are for positions in sales and marketing, finance and information technology, often in the $50,000 to $100,000 range. The site was developed by Latin America's Professional Network, Miami, Florida and was launched in 1997.

www.net-temps.com or Net-Temps Job Posting Service was ranked as one of the top 5 "Sites Offering the Best Job-Search Support" by the *National Business Employment Weekly*. Many positions are in information systems, engineering, and sales and marketing, often in the $50,000 to $100,000 range. The site was developed by Net-Temps, Inc., Tyngsboro, Massachusetts and went online in 1996.

www.occ.com is the URL for the On Line Career Center, one of the Internet's first online recruitment sites, launched in 1993. It is a major recruitment web site that spends millions of dollars in advertising to drive traffic to the site. This is a major site that was developed by William O Warren, who has received honors for his pioneering work in the development of Internet Recruiting. This web site allows you to enter your job profile and have job listings automatically downloaded to your Email. Questions to webmaster@occ.com. www.occ.com was rated by the *National Business Employment Weekly* as one of the top 5 sites in 3 different categories: "Sites Offering the Best Overall Support for Job Seekers," "Sites Offering the Best Job-Search Support" and "Sites Offering the Best Career Resources for Job Seekers." Openings are mainly in engineering, information technology and sales and marketing. The site developer is TMP Worldwide, New York, New York.

www.tjobs.com is the URL for Telecommuting Jobs, which connects people to positions at home or otherwise using off site electronic facilities. Most positions are in programming, sales and writing. The site was developed by Levine Communications, Winnetka, Illinois and was launched in 1996.

www.usresume.com is the URL for US Resume, a site that lists many positions in computers, sales and finance, usually in the $50,000 to $100,000 range. The site was developed by Market 2000 Corp, Sparkill, New York and went online in 1996.

www.womenconnect.com contains job postings and editorial content from Working Woman and Working Mother magazines. Many positions are in sales, software engineering and general engineering, often in the $30,000 to $75,000 range. The site was developed by womenCONNECT.com, McLean, Virginia and has been online since 1994.

Satellites

ASIA PACIFIC SATELLITE INDUSTRY DIRECTORY, Phillips Business Information, Inc., a Phillips Publishing International Company, 120 Seven Locks Road, Potomac, MD 20854, (301) 340-1520, (301) 340-7788, (800) 777-5006, Internet pbi@phillips.com, web site www.phillips.com.

BROADCASTING AND CABLE YEARBOOK contains information on radio, TV and cable including information about trade associations, trade shows, broadcasting education, awards, industry related books, magazines, videos and more. Also includes information of direct broadcast satellites, Multichannel Multipoint Distribution Services (MMDS), wireless cable companies and more. $179.95.

R.R. Bowker (a unit of Cahners Business Information), 121 Chanlon Road, New Providence, NJ 07974 USA, Phone (888) BOWKER2 (888-269-5372) & (800) 323-3288, fax (908) 508-7696, email info@bowker.com, web www.bowker.com. Canada—R.R. Bowker, Markham, Ontario, phone (888) BOWKER9 & (905) 415-5837, fax (905) 479-6266. German speaking Europe—K.G. Saur Verlag, Munich, Germany, phone 49-89-76902-232, fax 49-89-76902-250, email 100730.1341@compuserve.com, web www.saur.de/home.htm. Rest of Europe incl. United Kingdom plus Africa & Asia—Bowker-Saur, W. Sussex, UK, phone 44-1342-326-972, fax 44-1342-335-612, email customer@bowker-saur.co.uk, web www.bowker-saur.com/service/. Australia/New Zealand—Thorpe, Port Melbourne, Victoria, Australia, phone 61-03-9-245-7370, fax 61-03-9-245-7395, email customer.service@thorpe.com.au, web www.thorpe.com.au. Technical support for CD ROMs (800) 323-3288, fax 908) 665-3528, email techsupport@bowker.com.

GPS DIRECTORY is a satellite industry directory published by Phillips Business Information, Inc., a Phillips Publishing International Company, 120 Seven Locks Road, Potomac, MD 20854, (301) 340-1520, (301) 340-7788, (800) 777-5006, Internet pbi@phillips.com, web site www.phillips.com.

LATIN AMERICAN SATELLITE DIRECTORY, Phillips Business Information, Inc., a Phillips Publishing International Company, 120 Seven Locks Road, Potomac, MD 20854, (301) 340-1520, (301) 340-7788, (800) 777-5006, Internet pbi@phillips.com, web site www.phillips.com.

PHILLIPS BUSINESS INFORMATION provides information in newsletters, magazines, directories and on multiple web sites covering a range of topics, such as magazine products, telecommunications and cable products, satellite products, media, new media and Internet products, marketing and public relations products, financial technology and electronic commerce, aviation and defense products. For more information, contact: Phillips Business Information, Inc., a Phillips Publishing International Company, 120 Seven Locks Road, Potomac, MD 20854, (301) 340-1520, (301) 340-7788, (800) 777-5006, Internet pbi@phillips.com, web site www.phillips.com.

SATELLITE INDUSTRY DIRECTORY, Phillips Business Information, Inc., a Phillips Publishing International Company, 120 Seven Locks Road, Potomac, MD 20854, (301) 340-1520, (301) 340-7788, (800) 777-5006, Internet pbi@phillips.com, web site www.phillips.com.

WHO'S WHO IN CABLE & SATELLITE EUROPE, Phillips Business Information, Inc., a Phillips Publishing International Company, 120 Seven Locks Road, Potomac, MD 20854, (301) 340-1520, (301) 340-7788, (800) 777-5006, Internet pbi@phillips.com, web site www.phillips.com.

WHO'S WHO IN CABLE & SATELLITE (UK), Phillips Business Information, Inc., a Phillips Publishing International Company, 120 Seven Locks Road, Potomac, MD 20854, (301) 340-1520, (301) 340-7788, (800) 777-5006, Internet pbi@phillips.com, web site www.phillips.com.

Savings and Loan Associations

See Thrift Institutions

Scandinavia

Also see Europe, International, Denmark, Norway and Sweden

DIRECTORY OF AMERICAN FIRMS OPERATING IN FOREIGN COUNTRIES, REGIONAL EDITION—SCANDINAVIA. Includes Denmark, Finland, Iceland, Norway, Sweden, $59. Ordering information: Uniworld Business Publications, Inc., 257 Central Park West, Suite 10A, New York, NY 10024-4110, (212) 496-2448, fax (212) 769-0413, email uniworldbp@aol.com. Web site: http://www.uniworldbp.com.

DIRECTORY OF FOREIGN FIRMS OPERATING IN THE UNITED STATES, REGIONAL EDITION—SCANDINAVIA. $49.Ordering information: Uniworld Business Publications, Inc., 257 Central Park West, Suite 10A, New York, NY 10024-4110, (212) 496-2448, fax (212) 769-0413, email uniworldbp@aol.com. Web site: http://www.uniworldbp.com.

MAJOR COMPANIES OF SCANDINAVIA, includes names of key decision makers. $480. US distributor: Larry Meranus Professional Publications & Services, 4 Demoray Court, Pine Brook, NJ 07058, (800) MERANUS or (800) 637-2687. Published by Graham & Whiteside Ltd., Tuition House, 5-6 Francis Grove, London SW19 4DT, England. Web site http://www.major-co-data.com. Email sales@major-co-data.com.

Scotland

See England, Europe, International

DIRECTORY OF AMERICAN FIRMS OPERATING IN FOREIGN COUNTRIES, REGIONAL EDITION—EUROPE, WESTERN, $159. Uniworld Business Publications, Inc., 257 Central Park West,

Suite 10A, New York, NY 10024-4110, (212) 496-2448, fax (212) 769-0413, email uniworldbp@aol.com. Web site: http://www.uniworldbp.com.

DIRECTORY OF FOREIGN FIRMS OPERATING IN THE UNITED STATES, REGIONAL EDITION—EUROPE, ALL. Includes Austria, Belgium, Czech Republic, Denmark, England, Finland, France, Germany, Greece, Iceland, Ireland, Italy, Luxembourg, Netherlands, Norway, Poland, Portugal, Romania, Russia, Scotland, Slovenia, Spain, Sweden, Switzerland. $119. Uniworld Business Publications, Inc., 257 Central Park West, Suite 10A, New York, NY 10024-4110, (212) 496-2448, fax (212) 769-0413, email uniworldbp@aol.com. Web site: http://www.uniworldbp.com.

DIRECTORY OF FOREIGN FIRMS OPERATING IN THE UNITED STATES, REGIONAL EDITION—BRITISH ISLES. Includes England, Ireland, Scotland. $59. Ordering information: Uniworld Business Publications, Inc., 257 Central Park West, Suite 10A, New York, NY 10024-4110, (212) 496-2448, fax (212) 769-0413, email uniworldbp@aol.com. Web site: http://www.uniworldbp.com.

Search Engines

In addition to proper search engines *per se,* other quasi-search engine resources are included here, too.

SEARCH ENGINES. Here are the main search engines you can use as a starting point. By using a search engine, you can locate all kinds of information about anything. Some people consider the first four better—Yahoo, Lycos, AltaVista and Excite. The remaining search engines are listed alphabetically.

Yahoo! (http://www.yahoo.com)
Lycos (http://www.lycos.com)
AltaVista (http://www.AltaVista.com)
Excite (http://www.excite.com)

Dejanews (http://www.dejanews.com)
HotBot (http://www.HotBot.com)
Inference (http://www.inference.com/infind)
Infoseek (http://www.infoseek.com)
Nerd World (http://www.NerdWorld.com)
Netfind (http://www.netfind.com)
Northern Light (http://www.northernlight.com)
Opentext (http://www.pinstripe.opentext.com/)
Webcrawler (http://webcrawler.com)

Here's additional summary information on the major search engines on the Internet:

Yahoo
www.yahoo.com is excellent for searching broad general topics. It is a human-compiled directory of web sites—in fact, the only directory done by humans, rather than a computer program. Yahoo cannot help you search for the contents of individual web pages. It may locate too many results and some may be irrelevant.

Hotbot
www.hotbot.com is excellent for finding specific information. It's the search site of WIRED magazine, whose search engine Inktomi also powers Yahoo and Snap.com's web searches.

Alta Vista
www.altavista.net is an excellent to for thorough, precise searches. However, Hotbot is probably easier for beginners, especially in writing precise queries. However, results sometimes include duplicates.

Excite
www.excite.com is good for broad general topics. It also includes company information, news headlines, and sports scores. However, sometimes search results aren't relevant.

Infoseek
www.infoseek.com search results are generally accurate and relevant. But according to search Engine Watch (www.searchenginewatch.com), it has a much smaller index of web pages.

Lycos	www.lycos.com offer a good advanced search capability, for example to search for certain media (like Java scripts or JPEG files). Lycos Pro offers even greater capability. But results for general web searches may be less satisfying.
Metacrawler	www.metacrawler.com is a metasearch site. It searches Yahoo, Excite and 5 other engines, then consolidates the results. It's very good for a quick overview. However, its limited search capabilities make precise queries difficult.
Dogpile	www.dogpile.com is a metasearch site which reviews 13 Web search engines and over 24 online news agencies and other services. Results are presented by search engine. This information can help you assess which search engine best meets your needs.
Ask Jeeves	www.askjeeves.com is an excellent beginner's site. It's also good for general questions. It prompts you with questions that help narrow your search and searches 6 other sites.
Northern Light	www.nlsearch.com searches both its index of web pages plus pay-per-view articles from books and publications not usually available on the web. It presents results according to topic heading.
Internet Sleuth	www.isleuth.com is a metasearch site of 3,000 specialized on-line databases plus it searches up to 6 other sites for web pages, news and other information. It's excellent for highly specialized searches. It has a detailed directory, but it does not present findings intuitively.

SEARCH ENGINE "OPERATORS" are sometimes called Boolean operators, so named after the man who invented them. Here's a short explanation of how to use "operators" from *The New York Times* (September 3, 1998):

" " (quotation marks) enclose words to search for a phrase, such as "Strawberry Fields Forever"

AND connects two or more words, all which must appear in the results: Strawberry AND Fields AND Forever

OR connects two or more search words. Any of them can appear in the results: Strawberry Fields OR Strawberryfields

NOT excludes the word after it from the results: Strawberry Fields NOT W.C.

- (minus sign), like NOT, excludes the word that follows it: Strawberry Fields -W.C.

+ (plus sign) precedes a word that must appear: +Strawberry +Fields

Note that it's possible to string together several operators to construct a precise query. As an example, to exclude certain cover versions of a certain song, you could use: "Strawberry Fields" AND "The Beatles" NOT "Sandy Farina" NOT "Nashville Superpickers."

SEARCH ENGINE WATCH, located on the web at www.searchenginewatch.com, is a newsletter edited by Danny Sullivan that monitors the web searching universe. "The first step in creating more effective searches is picking the right search site for the job," says Matt Lake, author of a *New York Times* article on how to successfully search the web (page D1, September 3, 1998). Search engines are important if you need to use the Internet to find information anything for which you don't already have the web site.

www.clickit.com is the web site address to "Access Business Online." Its objective is to bring Buyers and Sellers Together on the Internet. Features include Executive Job Network, Capital Sources, Trade Announcements, Professional Services, Top 100 World Business Charts, Company Profiles, International Buyer-Seller, BizWiz! Search Engine, Web Emporium Web Site Development, Classifieds, Corporate News Net, Wall Street and World Wide Finance, Market News & Business Connections, and more. However, a service fee is charged if you wish to access this information.

www.cnn.com is the URL to CNN's impressive comprehensive web site. It contains Big Yellow Search Books to assist in finding businesses and people. It also features global directories, The Directory Store™and a "search the net" capability with InfoSeek. InfoSeek also has a Business Channel with business resources and small businesses, and a Careers Channel.

www.web sitez.com is the URL to a web site that assists in finding any web address in the world.

www.whois.net is the URL to a capability that allows you to find your own domain or look up a web site.

Securities (Wall Street)

See Investment Management, Investment Research, Mutual Funds, Trading

CORPORATE FINANCE SOURCEBOOK—THE GUIDE TO MAJOR INVESTMENT SOURCES AND RELATED FINANCIAL SERVICES contains over 13,000 names of executives at 3,700 organizations that, broadly speaking, supply growth capital to businesses or are service firms, such as US venture capital lenders, private lenders, commercial finance and factoring, pension managers, master trusts and other sources. Names of key management are included. A special section details public offerings of the past 3 years and mergers and acquisitions over $100 million.

$575. If the price is prohibitively high, remember your local library. National Register Publishing, Reed Elsevier-New Providence, 121 Chanlon Road, New Providence, NJ 07974, (800) 521-8110, fax (800) 836-7736, web site www.redbooks.com or www.marquiswhoswho.com. "If, for any reason whatsoever, your order does not fully meet your expectations, simply return the product within 30 days for a prompt, complete, unquestioned refund," as stated in Catalog of Biographical and Professional References of publisher Marquis Who's Who/National Register Publishing.

EUROMONEY BANK REGISTER is a detailed directory of the world's leading financial institutions and a comprehensive guide to "who's who" in global capital markets. This directory lists senior executives, investment and commercial bankers, traders, analysts, support and legal staff. Expanded coverage of Asia, central Europe and eastern Europe and Latin America is provided. Available in print or CD ROM. The print version of The EUROMONEY Bank Register is comprehensively indexed alphabetically and by city. It also contains rankings of the top banks. The read only version of the CD ROM provides full access to the entire database. However, by disabling the print and export functions, the result is a lower cost alternative to the full version. A 14 day free trial is available with the CD ROM.

    Print Directory, USA, US $493 or 297 pounds sterling
    Print Directory, UK, Europe, Rest of World US $493 or 297 pounds sterling
    Read Only Version CD ROM 750 pounds or US $1,250
    Full Version CD ROM 1,750 pounds or US $3,000

Ordering information: Larry Meranus Professional Publications & Services, 4 Demoray Court, Pine Brook, NJ 07058, (800) MERANUS or (800) 637-2687. Distributed in England by EUROMONEY Books, Plymbridge Distributors Limited, Estover, Plymouth PL6 7PZ, England. Phone 44 (0) 171 779-8955 for a free demo disk. Fax 44 (0) 171 779-8541.

DIRECTORY OF REGISTERED INVESTMENT ADVISORS identifies over 9,000 CEO's, 7,000 Investment Officers, 10,000 Portfolio Managers, 6,000 Directors of Research and Research Analysts, 2,800 Traders and Trading Managers, and 1,200 Directors of Operations/Chief Financial Officers, plus web sites and personal email addresses. The directory also includes a section on mutual funds for over 4,000 funds at 375 firms, including the name of the person responsible for managing the fund, 1,3 and 5 year returns, benchmark comparisons, and more. DIRECTORY OF REGISTERED INVESTMENT ADVISORS with 4 Regional editions, $475. The Directory with no regional editions, $395. Published by Standard & Poors, a division of McGraw-Hill, MONEY MARKET DIRECTORIES, INC., 320 East Main Street, Charlottesville, VA 22902, http://www.mmdaccess.com, (800) 446-2810, (804) 977-1450.

FINANCIAL SERVICES CANADA is a handbook of banks, non-depository institutions, stock exchange and brokers, investment management, mutual funds, insurance, accountants, government agencies, financial associations and more, including contact numbers, name, title, organization, phone, fax, email, web site, and cellular. $199 for book, $299 for CD ROM, $399 for both. Ordering information: Copp Clark Professional, 200 Adelaide Street West, 3rd floor, Toronto, ON M5H 1W7 CANADA. Email orders@mail.CanadaInfo.com. Web site http://www.coppclark.com. For additional information contact: IHS Canada, Micromedia Limited, 20 Victoria Street, Toronto, Ontario M5C 2N8 CANADA, (800) 387-2689, (416) 362-5211, fax (416) 362-6161, email info@micromedia.on.ca.

INSTITUTIONAL INVESTOR publishes excellent surveys of various Wall Street industries. Generally one survey appears in each monthly issue, including names of contacts. Annual subscription $325. INSTITUTIONAL INVESTOR, 488 Madison Avenue, New York, NY 10022, (212) 303-3300.

INVESTMENT COMPANIES YEARBOOK is an annual directory that summarizes 12,000 funds, provides performance information, fund address, phone number, advisor, and identifies portfolio manager(s) and tenure, plus minimum investment, sales charges and more. $295. Ordering information: Securities Data Publishing, 1290 Avenue of the Americas, 36th floor, New York, NY 10104, (212) 830-9363.

RETAIL BROKER-DEALER DIRECTORY identifies key personnel, number of employees and representatives, product sales mix, areas of specialization, commission payout levels, clearing firm, technology providers, total revenues, and capital. It is indexed by company, by distribution channel and by geographic location. $270. Ordering information: Securities Data Publishing, 40 West 57th Street, 11th Floor, New York, NY 10019, (212) 765-5311, (800) 455-5844. At the time of this writing, Investment Dealers Digest has been purchased by Securities Data Publishing, a division of Thomson Financial Publishers.

SECURITIES INDUSTRY YEARBOOK provides names and titles and other information for Wall Street firms. Published annually. $75 for members, $115 for non-members. Securities Industry Association, 120 Broadway, New York, NY 10271, (212) 608-1500).

www.mmdaccess.com is the URL for Money Market Directories, Inc., 320 East Main Street, Charlottesville, VA 22902, (800) 446-2810, (804) 977-1450. Owned by Standard & Poors, a division of McGraw Hill.

www.nelnet.com is the URL for Wall Street and financial publisher Nelson Information, P.O. Box 591, Port Chester, NY 10573 USA. (800) 333-6357, phone outside the US (914) 937-8400, fax (914) 937-8590.

www.sec.gov/edgarhp.htm is the URL to the EDGAR Database of corporate information from the Securities & Exchange Commission, a database of corporate information. Features include: About the SEC, Investor Assistance & Complaints, EDGAR Database, SEC Digest & Statements, Current SEC Rulemaking, Enforcement Division, Small Business Information, Other sites to visit.

Security Industry

SECURITY INDUSTRY BUYERS GUIDE, Phillips Business Information, Inc., a Phillips Publishing International Company, 120 Seven Locks Road, Potomac, MD 20854, (301) 340-1520, (301) 340-7788, (800) 777-5006, Internet pbi@phillips.com, web site www.phillips.com.

SURVEILLANT: ACQUISITIONS & COMMENTARY FOR INTELLIGENCE & SECURITY PROFESSIONALS publishes SURVEILLANT, a book alert newsletter reviews over 250 new books per issue in these areas: competitor and business intelligence, tradecraft, technology-transfer, military intelligence, espionage, covert actions, security and counterintelligence, psychological warfare, propaganda, disinformation, deception, cryptology, guerrilla warfare, terrorism, resistance movements, aerial and space reconnaissance, science, histories or accounts of FBI, CIA, NSA, MOSSAD and other intelligence agencies and personal memoirs. $18 per issue, annual subscription $110 US, $120 Canada, $140 foreign. Ordering information: SURVEILLANT, Suite 165, 2020 Pennsylvania Ave. NW, Washington, DC 20006-1846. (202) 797-1234, email: reviews@surveillant.com.

Singapore

See Asia, International

DIRECTORY OF AMERICAN FIRMS OPERATING IN FOREIGN COUNTRIES, REGIONAL EDITION—CHINA GROUP. Includes China, Hong Kong, Singapore, Taiwan, Macau. $79. Uniworld Business Publications, Inc., 257 Central Park West, Suite 10A, New York, NY 10024-4110, (212) 496-2448, fax (212) 769-0413, email uniworldbp@aol.com. Web site: http://www.uniworldbp.com.

DIRECTORY OF FOREIGN FIRMS OPERATING IN THE UNITED STATES, REGIONAL EDITION—CHINA GROUP. Includes China, Hong Kong, Singapore, Taiwan. $29. Uniworld Business

Publications, Inc., 257 Central Park West, Suite 10A, New York, NY 10024-4110, (212) 496-2448, fax (212) 769-0413, email uniworldbp@aol.com. Web site: http://www.uniworldbp.com.

KEY BUSINESS DIRECTORY OF SINGAPORE contains information on 3,200 companies with at least 50 employees and revenues over $12 million. Dun & Bradstreet, Business Reference Solutions, Three Sylvan Way, Parsippany, NJ 07054 USA. (800) 526-0651. Email dnbmdd@mail.dnb.com. Web site http://www.dnbmdd.com.

SINGAPORE INDUSTRIAL DIRECTORY identifies 5,000 executives by name and title at 6,000 companies. Companies are listed by product/service, by trade name, and alphabetically by company name. All three sections contain phone numbers. Published annually by Promedia International. $60. Distributed by Manufacturers' News, Inc., (888) 752-5200, 1633 Central Street, Evanston, IL 60201-1569. Email info@manufacturersnews.com. Web site www.manufacturersnews.com.

Social Services

THE ADOPTION DIRECTORY provides the names of agencies and individuals to contact and a range of other information and three indexes. $65.00. Gale Group, P.O. Box 9187, Farmington Hills, MI 48333-9187. Toll free US and Canada (800) 877-GALE (4253) and (248) 699-GALE, fax (800) 414-5043 and (248) 699-8061, Internet orders galeord@galegroup.com, web site www.galegroup.com or www.gale.com. All Gale Group products are available on approval. Contact Gale for details.

BALTIMORE/ANNAPOLIS is a guide to over 2,000 organizations and institutions. Chapters include government, business, education, medicine/health, arts and culture, community affairs and more. $65. Columbia Books, Inc., 1212 New York Avenue, NW, Suite 330, Washington, DC 20005, (212) 898-0662.

COMPLETE MARQUIS WHO'S WHO ON CD ROM is a compilation of literally all 19 Marquis Who's Who that have appeared in print since 1985, including living and deceased people. WHO'S WHO IN AMERICA®, WHO'S WHO IN THE WORLD®, WHO'S WHO IN AMERICAN EDUCATIONS®, WHO'S WHO IN AMERICAN LAW®, WHO'S WHO IN AMERICAN NURSING®, WHO'S WHO IN MEDICINE AND HEALTHCARE®, WHO'S WHO IN FINANCE AND INDUSTRY®, WHO'S WHO IN SCIENCE AND ENGINEERING®, WHO'S WHO IN THE EAST®, WHO'S WHO IN THE MIDWEST®, WHO'S WHO IN THE SOUTH AND SOUTHWEST®, WHO'S WHO IN THE WEST®, WHO'S WHO OF AMERICAN WOMEN®, WHO'S WHO IN ADVERTISING®, WHO'S WHO OF EMERGING LEADERS IN AMERICA®, WHO'S WHO IN ENTERTAINMENT®, WHO'S WHO AMONG HUMAN SERVICES PROFESSIONALS®. One year subscription with semi-annual updates $995. National Register Publishing, Reed Elsevier-New Providence, 121 Chanlon Road, New Providence, NJ 07974, (800) 521-8110, fax (800) 836-7736, web site www.marquiswhoswho.com or www.redbooks.com. "If, for any reason whatsoever, your order does not fully meet your expectations, simply return the product within 30 days for a prompt, complete, unquestioned refund," as stated in Catalog of Biographical and Professional References of publisher Marquis Who's Who/National Register Publishing.

D&B DIRECTORY OF SERVICE COMPANIES is a directory with information on 50,000 US service businesses, including privately held companies, in these sectors: accounting, auditing and bookkeeping, advertising and public relations, architecture and engineering, consumer services, executive search, health, hospitality, management consulting, motion pictures, repair, research, social services and law. Listings include key executives' names and titles, address, phone, sales volume, number of employees, parent company and location, and more. Companies listed employ 50 or more people. Information is listed alphabetically and is cross-referenced geographically and by industry classification. Updated annually. For prices call Dun & Bradstreet at (800) 526-0651. For more information contact Dun & Bradstreet, Business Reference Solutions, Three Sylvan Way, Parsippany, New Jersey 07054. Email dnbmdd@mail.dnb.com. Web site http://www.dnbmdd.com.

DIVORCE HELP SOURCEBOOK provides information on organizations, publications, and professional associations, plus information, advice, references to books and articles and a State-by-State Information Section. $44.95. Gale Group, P.O. Box 9187, Farmington Hills, MI 48333-9187. Toll free US and Canada (800) 877-GALE (4253) and (248) 699-GALE, fax (800) 414-5043 and (248) 699-8061, Internet orders galeord@galegroup.com, web site www.galegroup.com or www.gale.com. All Gale Group products are available on approval. Contact Gale for details.

HEALTH CARE SERVICES DIRECTORY provides information on over 65,000 US providers of health and rehabilitation services in 50 different categories. Includes homecare, rehab, eldercare, addiction, hospice, mental health, AIDS and more. Available in regional editions and a national edition. For pricing and more information, contact Database Publishing Company, PO Box 70024, Anaheim, CA 92825, (800) 888-8434, (714) 778-6400, email sales@databasepublishing.com.

WASHINGTON identifies 4,500 organizations and institutions in Washington DC and 22,000 key people in them. Includes government, business, education, medicine/health, community affairs, art/culture and others. $85. Columbia Books, Inc., 1212 New York Avenue, NW, Suite 330, Washington, DC 20005, (212) 898-0662.

WHO'S WHO IN MEDICINE AND HEALTHCARE, $249.95. National Register Publishing, Reed Elsevier-New Providence, 121 Chanlon Road, New Providence, NJ 07974, (800) 521-8110, fax (800) 836-7736, web site www.marquiswhoswho.com or www.redbooks.com. "If, for any reason whatsoever, your order does not fully meet your expectations, simply return the product within 30 days for a prompt, complete, unquestioned refund," as stated in Catalog of Biographical and Professional References of publisher Marquis Who's Who/National Register Publishing.

Software

See Information Technology

AV MARKET PLACE is a directory of companies that create, apply or distribute a range of AV equipment and services for business, education, science and government. It includes multi-media, virtual reality, digital audio, presentation software and interactive video, plus a Products, Services and Companies Index and a Company Directory with contact information.

R.R. Bowker (a unit of Cahners Business Information), 121 Chanlon Road, New Providence, NJ 07974 USA, Phone (888) BOWKER2 (888-269-5372) & (800) 323-3288, fax (908) 508-7696, email info@bowker.com, web www.bowker.com. Canada—R.R. Bowker, Markham, Ontario, phone (888) BOWKER9 & (905) 415-5837, fax (905) 479-6266. German speaking Europe—K.G. Saur Verlag, Munich, Germany, phone 49-89-76902-232, fax 49-89-76902-250, email 100730.1341@compuserve.com, web www.saur.de/home.htm. Rest of Europe incl. United Kingdom plus Africa & Asia—Bowker-Saur, W. Sussex, UK, phone 44-1342-326-972, fax 44-1342-335-612, email customer@bowker-saur.co.uk, web www.bowker-saur.com/service/. Australia/New Zealand—Thorpe, Port Melbourne, Victoria, Australia, phone 61-03-9-245-7370, fax 61-03-9-245-7395, email customer.service@thorpe.com.au, web www.thorpe.com.au. Technical support for CD ROMs (800) 323-3288, fax 908) 665-3528, email techsupport@bowker.com.

CORPTECH DIRECTORY OF TECHNOLOGY COMPANIES is available in hard copy, Regional Guides, on PC disk, and on CD ROM. CorpTech EXPLORE Database is an outstanding reference that was awarded Best CD-ROM Directory by the National Directory Publishing Association. One click moves you from the CD ROM Database to Internet information on the same company. CorpTech also provides other sophisticated but reasonably priced automated services. You can save a tremendous amount of time researching relatively small, emerging new companies in various high technology niches and obtain names, titles and mailing address labels. CorpTech EXPLORE Database CD ROM $2,450 (including free soft cover CorpTech Directory worth $545). Ordering Information: CorpTech, Corporate Technology Information Services, Inc., 12 Alfred Street, Suite 200, Woburn, MA 01801-1915. (800) 333-8036, (781) 932-3100, (781) 932-3939. Fax (781) 932-6335. Email sales@corptech.com. Web site http://www.corptech.com.

CYBERHOUND'S® GUIDE TO COMPANIES ON THE INTERNET reviews over 2,000 corporate sites, including major companies as well as those in the information industry, software and hardware developers and networking and telecommunications companies. It also includes a user's guide, a directory of specialized business we sites, a bibliography of Internet products, and a glossary of Internet terms. At the time of this writing 1st edition (1996) available from Gale for $79, reduced from $95. Published by Euromonitor (England). Distributed by Gale Group, P.O. Box 9187, Farmington Hills, MI 48333-9187. Toll free US and Canada (800) 877-GALE (4253) and (248) 699-GALE, fax (800) 414-5043 and (248) 699-8061, Internet orders galeord@galegroup.com, web site www.galegroup.com or www.gale.com. All Gale Group products are available on approval. Contact Gale for details.

DATA SOURCES. Volume 1, "Hardware" is comprised of 11,000 manufacturers of computers systems, graphics equipment, PC expansion boards, modems, LAN products, multiplexers, printers, disk and tape equipment, and terminals. Volume 2, :Software" is comprised of over 70,000 products including data communications and telecommunications software, database management systems software, software utilities and other application software packages. Listings include corporate officers, company name, address, phone, gross revenues, number of employees, products, and year established. Information is presented by function, then alphabetically with indexes by company, product, and a master subject index. Published semi-annually. $495 per year. Also available on CD ROM. DATA SOURCES, Information Access Company, One Park Avenue, New York, NY 10016, (800) 546-1223 and (212) 503-5398, fax (212) 502 5800.

DIRECTORY OF CALIFORNIA TECHNOLOGY COMPANIES identifies over 33,000 executive names and titles at over 12,000 companies, including research labs, telecommunications, biotechnology and software. Published annually by Database Publishing, PO Box 70024, Anaheim, CA 92825/1590 South Lewis Street, Anaheim, CA 92805. (800) 888-8434, (714) 778-6400, web site www.databasepublishing.com, email sales@databasepublishing.com. Directory $145, complete CD ROM $645, CD ROM one-year lease $425. Also distributed by Manufacturers' News, Inc., (888) 752-5200, 1633 Central Street, Evanston, IL 60201-1569. Email info@manufacturersnews.com. Web site www.manufacturersnews.com.

DIRECTORY OF CALIFORNIA WHOLESALERS AND SERVICE COMPANIES identifies over 85,000 names and titles of executives at some 34,000 non-manufacturing firms, such as wholesalers, transportation, telecommunications, video production and software, including web sites and email addresses. Annual directory published by Database Publishing, $169. Complete CD ROM $925, One year CD ROM lease, $595. Distributed by Manufacturers' News, Inc., (888) 752-5200, 1633 Central Street, Evanston, IL 60201-1569. Email info@manufacturersnews.com. Web site www.manufacturersnews.com.

DUN & BRADSTREET AND GALE INDUSTRY REFERENCE HANDBOOKS offer a line of industry-specific sourcebooks which include key companies in the industry, ranked lists of companies, professional associations, trade shows and conferences, mergers and acquisitions, consultants who service those industries, information sources, and more. 6 volume set $495. Also available individually for $99: Pharmaceuticals, Health and Medical Services, Computers and Software, Banking and Finance, Telecommunications, Agriculture and Food, Insurance, Construction, Entertainment, Hospitality. First edition available December, 1999. Gale Group, P.O. Box 9187, Farmington Hills, MI 48333-9187. Toll free US and Canada (800) 877-GALE (4253) and (248) 699-GALE, fax (800) 414-5043 and (248) 699-8061, Internet orders galeord@galegroup.com, web site www.galegroup.com or www.gale.com. All Gale Group products are available on approval. Contact Gale for details.

INFORMATION INDUSTRY ASSOCIATION (IIA) merged with the Software Publishers Association (SPA) to form the Software and Information Industry Association (SIIA). As with many other professional associations, you can access their membership directory online free by going to their web site, www.siia.net. Software and Information Industry Association, 1730 M Street, NW, Washington, DC 20036, (202) 452-1600, www.siia.net.

INFORMATION SOURCES was an award winning directory published by the Gale Group in partnership with the Information Industry Association (IIA). At the time of this writing, the IIA has merged with the Software Publishers Association (SPA) to form the newly named Software and Information Industry Association (SIIA).

This directory provides information for the 550 member companies of the Information Industry Association. Entries include company name, address, phone, names of executives, regional offices, trade and brand names and description of products and services. Indexed by product, personal name, trade name, geography, parent company, international, and niche markets. The directory also identifies publishers, database producers, online services, telecommunications and network providers, system integrators and many others. $125. Contact Gale for information as to when an updated directory will be available. In the meantime, visit the Software and Information Industry's web site at www.siia.net to see their membership roster.

Gale Group, P.O. Box 9187, Farmington Hills, MI 48333-9187. Toll free US and Canada (800) 877-GALE (4253) and (248) 699-GALE, fax (800) 414-5043 and (248) 699-8061, Internet orders galeord@galegroup.com, web site www.galegroup.com or www.gale.com. All Gale Group products are available on approval. Contact Gale for details.

Software & Information Industry Association (SIIA), formerly the Software Publishers Association (SPA) and Information Industry Association (IIA) is located at 1730 M Street, NW, Washington, DC 20036, (202) 452-1600, www.siia.net.

INFORMATION TECHNOLOGY ASSOCIATION OF AMERICA (ITAA) MEMBERSHIP DIRECTORY) is an annual directory which covers 11,000 members, mainly in the US with limited international coverage. Listings include, company name, address, phone, fax, names of executives, number of employees, company descriptions, products and services. Indexed geographically, by services provided, software application, hardware, and vertical markets served. It is available to non-members for $100. For more information contact Information Technology Association of America (ITAA), 1616 North Fort Myer Drive, Suite 1300, Arlington, VA 22209, (703) 522-5055, Fax (525-2279. Email can be accessed through their web site, www.itaa.org.

PUBLISHERS, DISTRIBUTORS AND WHOLESALERS OF THE US™ is available in electronic database formats. It identifies over 70,000 publishers, wholesalers, distributors, software firms, museum and association imprints, and trade organizations, covering a variety of media. This database includes discount schedules aimed mainly at libraries, plus compete addresses (for editorial and ordering), toll-free phone numbers. This database is used to identify the outlet(s) offering the best price(s) for books, cassettes and software titles. It is available online through Knight Ridder Information, Inc. (DIALOG File number 450, (800) 334-2564 or (800) 3-DIALOG), through subscription online and on CD-ROM/ hard disk. For more information visit Bowker Reed Reference's web site at http://www.reedref.com or contact: Bowker Reed Reference Electronic Publishing, 121 Chanlon Road, New Providence, NJ 07974 USA, Phone (800) 323-3288, Fax (908) 665-3528, email info@bowker.com.

SOFTWARE AND INFORMATION INDUSTRY ASSOCIATION (SIIA), 1730 M Street NW, Washington, DC 20036 was formed by a merger with the Information Industry Association (IIA) and the Software Publishers Association (SPA). (202) 452-1600. Visit their web site at www.siia.net to access their online membership directory free.

SOFTWARE ENCYCLOPEDIA—A Guide for Personal, Professional and Business Users identifies over 27,000 new and established programs on every format including disk and CD ROM. Search capability allows you to search by application, hardware, memory requirements, machine version, operating system, programming language and more. This resource can best be used either for your systems needs, or to do target list research in the software industry. $265 for 2 volume set. R.R. Bowker (a unit of Cahners Business Information), 121 Chanlon Road, New Providence, NJ 07974 USA, Phone (888) BOWKER2 (888-269-5372) & (800) 323-3288, fax (908) 508-7696, email info@bowker.com, web www.bowker.com. Canada—R.R. Bowker, Markham, Ontario, phone (888) BOWKER9 & (905) 415-5837, fax (905) 479-6266. German speaking Europe—K.G. Saur Verlag, Munich, Germany, phone 49-89-76902-232, fax 49-89-76902-250, email 100730.1341@compuserve.com, web www.saur.de/home.htm. Rest of Europe incl. United Kingdom plus Africa & Asia—Bowker-Saur, W. Sussex, UK, phone 44-1342-326-972, fax 44-1342-335-612, email customer@bowker-saur.co.uk, web www.bowker-saur.com/service/. Australia/New Zealand—Thorpe, Port Melbourne, Victoria, Australia, phone 61-03-9-245-7370, fax 61-03-9-245-7395, email customer.service@thorpe.com.au, web www.thorpe.com.au. Technical support for CD ROMs (800) 323-3288, fax 908) 665-3528, email techsupport@bowker.com.

www.bowker.com is the web site for this major research publisher. It includes Flagship Products and Services, an online Product Catalog, Electronic Publishing products including CD ROMs, Internet Databases, and Online Subscription and Site Licensing Databases; press releases, career opportunities, and more. Many of their references are accessible through this web site, such as BOOKS IN PRINT PLUS CANADIAN EDITION, ULRICH'S ON DISC, GERMAN BOOKS IN PRINT, GERMAN BOOKS OUT OF PRINT, INTERNATIONAL BOOKS IN PRINT PLUS, ITALIAN BOOKS IN PRINT, YEARBOOK OF INTERNATIONAL ORGANIZATIONS PLUS, ULRICH'S INTERNATIONAL PERIODICALS DIRECTORY, THE SOFTWARE ENCYCLOPEDIA, BOWKER'S COMPLETE VIDEO DIRECTORY, AMERICAN BOOK PUBLISHING RECORD. Visit the web site for more information.

www.recruitersonline.com is the URL for Recruiters Online Network, a free web site that allows recruiters to post open positions at various online locations and maintain private resume database for members. Most positions are in information technology, management and software. Positions usually range from $50,000 to

---

over $100,000. The site was developed by Recruiters Online Network, Inc., Plano, Texas and was established in 1995.

www.technicalrecruiter.com is a web site which is an excellent starting point for a large number of specialized technology sites, such as ProjectManager.com and SoftwareEngineer.com and others.

www.womenconnect.com contains job postings and editorial content from Working Woman and Working Mother magazines. Many positions are in sales, software engineering and general engineering, often in the $30,000 to $75,000 range. The site was developed by womenCONNECT.com, McLean, Virginia and has been online since 1994.

South Africa

See International, Africa

MAJOR COMPANIES OF AFRICA SOUTH OF THE SAHARA identifies 22,000 contacts at over 6,000 companies in 42 countries, including 1,700 in South Africa alone. $530. CD ROMs available. Published by Graham & Whiteside Ltd., Tuition House, 5-6 Francis Grove, London SW19 4DT, England. Web site http://www.major-co-data.com. Email sales@major-co-data.com. Distributed by: Larry Meranus Professional Publications & Services, 4 Demoray Court, Pine Brook, NJ 07058, (800) MERANUS or (800) 637-2687. Also distributed by Gale Group, P.O. Box 9187, Farmington Hills, MI 48333-9187. Toll free US and Canada (800) 877-GALE (4253) and (248) 699-GALE, fax (800) 414-5043 and (248) 699-8061, Internet orders galeord@galegroup.com, web site www.galegroup.com or www.gale.com. All Gale Group products are available on approval. Contact Gale for details.

Countries include: Angola, Benin, Botswana, Burkina Faso, Burundi, Cameroon, Cape Verde, Central Africa Republic, Chad, Comoros, The Congo, Democratic Republic of the Congo, Equatorial Guinea, Ethiopia, Gabon, The Gambia, Ghana, Guinea, Guinea Bissau, Ivory Coast, Kenya, Lesotho, Liberia, Madagascar, Malawi, Mali, Mauritius, Mozambique, Namibia, Niger, Nigeria, Rwanda, Sao Tome & Principe, Senegal, Seychelles, Sierra Leone, Swaziland, Tanzania, Togo, Uganda, Zambia, Zimbabwe.

South America

See Latin America, International

DIRECTORY OF AMERICAN FIRMS OPERATING IN FOREIGN COUNTRIES, REGIONAL EDITION—CARIBBEAN ISLANDS. Includes Anguilla, Antigua, Aruba, Bahamas, Barbados, Bermuda, British West Indies, Cayman Islands, Dominican Republic, Grenada, Haiti, Jamaica, Netherlands Antilles, Trinidad & Tobago, Turks & Caicos. $39. Uniworld Business Publications, Inc., 257 Central Park West, Suite 10A, New York, NY 10024-4110, (212) 496-2448, fax (212) 769-0413, email uniworldbp@aol.com. Web site: http://www.uniworldbp.com.

DIRECTORY OF FOREIGN FIRMS OPERATING IN THE UNITED STATES, REGIONAL EDITION—SOUTH/CENTRAL AMERICA & THE CARIBBEAN. Includes Argentina, Bermuda, Bolivia, Brazil, Chile, Colombia, Costa Rica, Dominican Republic, Guatemala, Mexico, Panama, Paraguay, Peru, Uruguay, Venezuela. $39. Uniworld Business Publications, Inc., 257 Central Park West, Suite 10A, New York, NY 10024-4110, (212) 496-2448, fax (212) 769-0413, email uniworldbp@aol.com. Web site: http://www.uniworldbp.com.

KOMPASS is described by the publisher as "the world's most comprehensive global database of companies, products and services for manufacturing and engineering professionals in print, on CD ROM and on the Internet." It contains company and product information for companies in all lines of business, including manufacturing and industrial sectors. Each company listing includes name, address, phone number, management names, business descriptions, and industry and product listings. Kompass's web site is www.kompass.com. Call publisher for prices and information on country directories. Cahners Business Information, 121 Chanlon Road, New Providence, NJ 07974, (908) 771-8785, fax (908) 665-8755, email hholmes@reedref.com. Headquarters: Cahners Business Information, 275 Washington Street, Newton, MA

02158-1630, (617) 558-4663 or (617) 964-3030, fax (617) 558-4700, email marketaccess@cahners.com, web sites www.cahners.com or www.chilton.net.

MAJOR COMPANIES OF LATIN AMERICA AND THE CARIBBEAN lists information on 7,500 companies in Latin America and South America and the Caribbean, including description of company activities, brand names, over 35,000 names of key executives and financial data, plus three indexes, mainly for target list development. $765. Available in CD ROM. Distributed by Larry Meranus Professional Publications & Services, 4 Demoray Court, Pine Brook, NJ 07058, (800) MERANUS or (800) 637-2687. Also distributed by Gale Group, P.O. Box 9187, Farmington Hills, MI 48333-9187. Toll free US and Canada (800) 877-GALE (4253) and (248) 699-GALE, fax (800) 414-5043 and (248) 699-8061, Internet orders galeord@galegroup.com, web site www.galegroup.com or www.gale.com. All Gale Group products are available on approval. Contact Gale for details. Published by Graham & Whiteside Ltd., Tuition House, 5-6 Francis Grove, London SW19 4DT, England. Web site http://www.major-co-data.com. Email sales@major-co-data.com.

Soviet Union

See Commonwealth of Independent States, International

Spain

See Europe, International

DIRECTORY OF AMERICAN FIRMS OPERATING IN FOREIGN COUNTRIES, REGIONAL EDITION—SPAIN, $39. Ordering information: Uniworld Business Publications, Inc., 257 Central Park West, Suite 10A, New York, NY 10024-4110, (212) 496-2448, fax (212) 769-0413, email uniworldbp@aol.com. Web site: http://www.uniworldbp.com.

SPAIN'S TOP 30,000 contains information on companies with annual sales of over $250,000 US Dollars. Dun & Bradstreet, Business Reference Solutions, Three Sylvan Way, Parsippany, NJ 07054 USA. (800) 526-0651. Email dnbmdd@mail.dnb.com. Web site http://www.dnbmdd.com.

www.europages.com is a web site of a business directory of over 500,000 European firms. In Deutsch, English, Espanol, Français & Italiano. Features include Search for Companies, Company Catalogues, Business Information, Yellow Pages in Europe. Search by Product/Service, Thematic Search or by Company Name. Address, phone, fax, products, turnover. Europages' Daily Business News, European Trade Fairs, Chambers of Commerce in Europe, European Patent Offices, Official International Organisations, European Standardization Bodies.

www.kompass.com is the web site for the highly respected Kompass country directories and databases. This web site contains a searchable database that encompasses over 60 countries, 2.5 million executive names, information on 1.5 million companies, 19 million key product references, and 370,000 trade and brand names. At the time of this writing, Kompass is available in English and French. Deutsch, Espanol and Italiano will soon be available.

Standard Industrial Classification (SIC)

NORTH AMERICAN INDUSTRY CLASSIFICATION SYSTEM (NAICS) MANUAL now replaces the STANDARD INDUSTRIAL CLASSIFICATION (SIC) MANUAL. Last revised in 1987, The SIC Manual is still available in most business libraries. An SIC is a 4 digit number that serves as a "shorthand" for a specific industry. It identifies in detail the composition of each and every SIC code. Historically this fundamental reference has been important in researching companies by SIC because abbreviated lists of SIC codes, such as those which appear in STANDARD AND POORS or DUN & BRADSTREET'S MILLION DOLLAR DIRECTORY SERIES, didn't always provide the level of detail needed. Until 1998 the SIC Manual had been published by The National Technical Information Service, formerly the US Government Printing Office. NTIS is the central source for government sponsored US and worldwide scientific, engineering and business related information. As a self-supporting agency of the US Department of Commerce's Technology Administration, NTIS covers its business and operating expenses with the sale of its products and services.

However, the 1987 SIC manual is no longer being published because the USA has a new industry classification system. The North American Industry Classification System (NAICS) replaces the US Standard Industrial Classification (SIC) system.

NAICS is the first North American industry classification system. It was developed by the US, Canada and Mexico to provide comparable statistics for all three countries. This will allow government and business analysts to uniformly compare industrial production statistics in the three North American Free Trade Agreement (NAFTA) countries. NAICS also provides for increased comparability with the International Standard Industrial Classification System (ISIC), developed and maintained by the United Nations. Both printed and CD ROM versions of the NAICS Manual are scheduled for availability June, 1998. These official versions include 350 new industries, definitions for each industry, tables correlating the 1997 NAICS and the 1987 SIC codes, an alphabetic list of over 18,000 business activities and the corresponding NAICS code, and a special section on What Small Businesses Need to Know About NAICS. Some new industries include specialized technology niches, such as fiber optic cable manufacturing and satellite communications and other types of businesses, such as bed and breakfast inns, environmental consulting, warehouse clubs, credit card issuing, diet and weight reduction centers. Executive search is also recognized as an industry, as a result of the efforts of Executive Director Emeritus of the Association of Executive Search Consultants, Sheila Avrin McLean.

Unlike the SIC codes, which are 4 digits, the NAICS codes are 6 digits. The first 5 digits are standardized among the US, Canada and Mexico. However, the 6th digit may differ from country to country to accommodate different needs in individual countries. NAICS will be reviewed every five years, so classifications and information will stay current with the economy. For more information, contact the Bureau of the Census Official NAICS web page at www.census.gov/naics or send your questions by email to info@ntis.fedworld.gov.

Ordering information: Softcover version, NTIS Order Number PB98-136187INQ, $28.50, $57 outside the US, Canada and Mexico. Hardcover NTIS Order Number PB98-127293, $32.50, $65 outside the US, Canada and Mexico. CD ROM Order Number PB98-502024, single user $45, 90 outside the US, Canada and Mexico. Up to 5 concurrent network users $120, $240 outside the US, Canada and Mexico. Unlimited concurrent network users $240, $480 outside the US, Canada and Mexico. CD ROM includes a search capability that includes access to more index entries than appear in the manual plus downloadable files.

Phone orders Monday-Friday, 8 am - 8 pm Eastern Time (800) 553-NTIS (6487) or (703) 605-6000.Fax (703) 321-8547. For questions about a product or order, email info@ntis.fedworld.gov. Web site www.ntis.gov/. National Technical Information Service, Technology Administration, US Department of Commerce, 5285 Port Royal Road, Springfield, VA 22161.

Subsidiaries

See Corporate Affiliations and Organization Charts

AMERICA'S CORPORATE FAMILIES & INTERNATIONAL AFFILIATES is comprised of two volumes of US subsidiaries, divisions and branches and one volume of some 3,000 foreign ultimate parent companies and their 11,000 US subsidiaries and nearly 3,000 US ultimate parent corporations and their 18,000 foreign subsidiaries. Published annually. The International Affiliates (Volume 3) lists US companies with their foreign subsidiaries and foreign ultimates with their US subsidiaries. In addition to listing US and foreign ultimates with their family members alphabetically, all companies are cross-referenced geographically and by industry classification. Updated annually For prices call Dun & Bradstreet at (800) 526-0651. For more information contact Dun & Bradstreet, Business Reference Solutions, Three Sylvan Way, Parsippany, New Jersey 07054. Email dnbmdd@mail.dnb.com. Web site http://www.dnbmdd.com.

AMERICA'S CORPORATE FINANCE DIRECTORY provides a financial profile of the US's leading 5,000 public and private companies. It includes information about the company's pension plan, names of contacts, and a listing of over 17,000 wholly owned US subsidiaries. The title appears previously to have been The Corporate Finance Bluebook. $585. If the price is prohibitively high, remember your local library. National Register Publishing, Reed Elsevier-New Providence, 121 Chanlon Road, New Providence, NJ 07974, (800) 521-8110, fax (800) 836-7736, web site www.redbooks.com or www.marquiswhoswho.com. "If, for any reason whatsoever, your order does not fully meet your expectations, simply return the product within 30 days for a prompt, complete, unquestioned refund," as stated in Catalog of Biographical and Professional References of publisher Marquis Who's Who/National Register Publishing.

ANNUAL REPORTS. Get the company phone number by calling toll free information (800-555-1212) or looking in a general directory such as STANDARD AND POORS, THE STANDARD DIRECTORY OF ADVERTISERS or NATIONAL DIRECTORY OF ADDRESSES AND TELEPHONE NUMBERS. Say you're calling to request a copy of an Annual Report, a 10(k) Report and a Proxy Statement. This information is FREE and you might as well ask for everything as long as you're on the phone. Note that while publicly held companies are legally required to file these documents with the Securities and Exchange Commission (SEC) every year, privately held companies are not. However, sometimes private companies produce annual reports or other brochures, lists of locations and so forth. You can also ask the Public Affairs department for news clippings or other information. Sales representatives are usually willing to send product information.

While it is possible to review annual reports on line, sometimes on a company's web site or using a specialized database, it may be easier to review hard copy, which is a quick phone call away. Hard copy is easy to mark up and it's portable. You can read it commuting on a bus or train or while you're waiting at the dentist's office.

Annual Reports sometimes contain photos of management, organization charts, lists of all locations, including plants; lists of divisions and subsidiaries, names and titles of management, sometimes at surprisingly junior levels; and almost always provide an explanation of how the company is organized. 10(k) Reports, as a matter of law, are required to identify senior management, their ages and brief background histories; to describe the business activities and products of the company; and to disclose any pending activities which could materially affect the company's financial performance, for example, the potential of an unfavorable outcome in a lawsuit. Proxy Statements are required to reveal the compensation of the four highest paid executives, backgrounds of the Directors of the company, and details about stock ownership and pension plans.

These materials are immensely valuable in analyzing whether you're searching in the part of an organization. This information is often more reliable than anything you will find in a directory or on a CD ROM because the company wrote it themselves and you are obtaining information firsthand, directly from the source. In fact, it could be the same source used by publishers of directories and CD ROMs.

Note: The Securities and Exchange Commission (SEC) legally requires all publicly held companies (that is, any companies that sell their stock) to publish an Annual Report, a 10(k) Report and a Notice of Annual Meeting and Proxy Statement (commonly called the "proxy statement" or just the "proxy.") However, privately held companies are not required to publish such information. Even so, some closely held companies do publish an annual report or an annual review, although they can be difficult to obtain. Sometimes the easiest way to do this is to ask for information from a friend who works there. Or if you work near the company, drop by in person and ask a receptionist for company literature.

CORPORATE AFFILIATIONS PLUS CD ROM consolidates information in all five volumes of THE DIRECTORY OF CORPORATE AFFILIATIONS, including publicly held and privately held companies in the US and internationally, and AMERICA'S CORPORATE FINANCE DIRECTORY. This CD provides "family tree" overviews for each company with the reporting structure. It also contains information on 15,000 parent companies in the US and abroad, records on over 100,000 subsidiaries, divisions, plants and joint ventures, names and titles of over 250,000 employees, revenue figures and more. Information can be searched by 29 criteria, such as location, SIC or NAICS codes, sales, number of employees, net worth, pension assets and more. Updated quarterly. 1 year subscription $1,995, available for both Windows and Macintosh. If the price is prohibitively high, remember your local library. National Register Publishing, Reed Elsevier-New Providence, 121 Chanlon Road, New Providence, NJ 07974, (800) 521-8110, fax (800) 836-7736, web site www.redbooks.com or www.marquiswhoswho.com. "If, for any reason whatsoever, your order does not fully meet your expectations, simply return the product within 30 days for a prompt, complete, unquestioned refund," as stated in Catalog of Biographical and Professional References of publisher Marquis Who's Who/National Register Publishing.

DIRECTORY OF CORPORATE AFFILIATIONS OR WHO OWNS WHOM is a superb directory which can help you decipher the organizational structure of a company. This directory provides detailed information about all parent companies, subsidiaries and divisions, plus plant locations, joint ventures, a brief description of the subsidiary or division, a partial listing of names and titles, location, phone number, and sometimes revenues or number of employees. THE DIRECTORY OF CORPORATE AFFILIATIONS provides a comprehensive "family tree" listing that lays out the corporate hierarchy to provide a picture of the structure of companies, subsidiaries, affiliates & divisions. It includes companies with revenues of at least $10 million and reveals division and subsidiary reporting relationships down to the sixth level. It provides information on 8,500 privately held companies. For US companies it details complex multinational relationships and joint ventures. For additional names and titles of key executives in subsidiaries & divisions, refer to another directory such as Standard & Poors, THE STANDARD DIRECTORY OF ADVERTISERS, or a specialized industry directory. THE DIRECTORY OF CORPORATE AFFILIATIONS consists of 5 volumes, including US Public Companies, US Private Companies, International Companies (both public and private), and indices. It also contains a Brand Name Index. The CD ROM version of this directory is titled Corporate Affiliations Plus.

Note: If THE DIRECTORY OF CORPORATE AFFILIATIONS does not provide all the organization structure information you want and the company is publicly held, there's an abundance of free information available! Check the company's web site or call them for an annual report and 10(k). Even if the company is privately held, they will usually send information if you ask for it. The more specific your request, the more likely you are to get what you need, for example, a list of all company locations, a list of plant locations, or product information.

Ordering information: $1,029.95/5 volumes, excluding discounts. If the price is prohibitively high, remember your local library. National Register Publishing, Reed Elsevier-New Providence, 121 Chanlon Road, New Providence, NJ 07974, (800) 521-8110, fax (800) 836-7736, web site www.redbooks.com or www.marquiswhoswho.com. "If, for any reason whatsoever, your order does not fully meet your expectations, simply return the product within 30 days for a prompt, complete, unquestioned refund," as stated in Catalog of Biographical and Professional References of publisher Marquis Who's Who/National Register Publishing.

EUROPE'S MAJOR COMPANIES DIRECTORY provides information on 6,000 leading companies in 16 European countries, including banking, retail and utilities. Details ownership, subsidiaries, key personnel, main operations, main products and brand names, and when available retail outlets and number of employees. $590. Published by Euromonitor (England). Distributed by Gale Group, P.O. Box 9187, Farmington Hills, MI 48333-9187. Toll free US and Canada (800) 877-GALE (4253) and (248) 699-GALE, fax (800) 414-5043 and (248) 699-8061, Internet orders galeord@galegroup.com, web site www.galegroup.com or www.gale.com. All Gale Group products are available on approval. Contact Gale for details.

EUROPE'S MEDIUM SIZED COMPANIES DIRECTORY profiles 6,500 of the "next largest" companies, beginning where EUROPE'S MAJOR COMPANIES DIRECTORY leaves off. It includes key personnel, ownership, subsidiaries, main products and brands, revenues, outlets and trading names, number of employees and more. $590. Published by Euromonitor (England). Distributed by Gale Group, P.O. Box 9187, Farmington Hills, MI 48333-9187. Toll free US and Canada (800) 877-GALE (4253) and (248) 699-GALE, fax (800) 414-5043 and (248) 699-8061, Internet orders galeord@galegroup.com, web site www.galegroup.com or www.gale.com. All Gale Group products are available on approval. Contact Gale for details.

FINANCIAL TIMES ENERGY YEARBOOKS: OIL AND GAS provides narrative, production and financial information for over 800 major oil and gas companies, including full contact details. It also includes major oil and gas brokers and traders, industry associations, and outlines all parent, subsidiary and associate companies. $320. Published by Financial Times Energy. Distributed by Gale Group, P.O. Box 9187, Farmington Hills, MI 48333-9187. Toll free US and Canada (800) 877-GALE (4253) and (248) 699-GALE, fax (800) 414-5043 and (248) 699-8061, Internet orders galeord@galegroup.com, web site www.galegroup.com or www.gale.com. All Gale Group products are available on approval. Contact Gale for details.

MAJOR COMPANIES OF SOUTH WEST ASIA provides names of 39,000 contacts at 6,000 companies, description of business activities, brand names and trademarks, branches and subsidiaries, number of employees, date of establishment, and three indexes. Countries included are Bangladesh, Bhutan, Iran, Nepal,

Pakistan, Sri Lanka and Turkey. $530. CD ROM available. US distributor: Larry Meranus Professional Publications & Services, 4 Demoray Court, Pine Brook, NJ 07058, (800) MERANUS or (800) 637-2687. Also distributed by Gale Group, P.O. Box 9187, Farmington Hills, MI 48333-9187. Toll free US and Canada (800) 877-GALE (4253) and (248) 699-GALE, fax (800) 414-5043 and (248) 699-8061, Internet orders galeord@galegroup.com, web site www.galegroup.com or www.galc.com. All Gale Group products are available on approval. Contact Gale for details. Published by Graham & Whiteside Ltd., Tuition House, 5-6 Francis Grove, London SW19 4DT, England. Web site http://www.major-co-data.com. Email sales@major-co-data.com.

STANDARD AND POORS REGISTER OF CORPORATIONS, DIRECTORS AND EXECUTIVES. Volume 1, Corporations, contains complete listings for 75,000 companies (including large subsidiaries), specifically names, titles, phone numbers, number of employees, annual sales, main products, and SIC/NAICS codes. Volume 2, Directors and Executives alphabetically lists 70,000 key managers with biographical data. Volume 3, Corporate Family Index is useful for locating a company's parent, subsidiaries, divisions and affiliates; also contains an index of companies by state and major cities. Published annually. Hardback directory, $799. Available in CD ROM. Call for price. Published by Standard & Poors Corporation, New York, New York. Distributed by: Larry Meranus Professional Publications & Services, 4 Demoray Court, Pine Brook, NJ 07058, (800) MERANUS or (800) 637-2687.

SciTECH REFERENCE PLUS CD ROM contains directory information, 125,000 biographies of US and Canadian scientists and engineers from AMERICAN MEN AND WOMEN OF SCIENCE, listings for over 8,000 laboratories from the DIRECTORY OF AMERICAN RESEARCH AND TECHNOLOGY, and information from THE DIRECTORY OF CORPORATE AFFILIATIONS (including public, private and international companies) of leading US and international technology firms and their subsidiaries. It also contains 60,000 records on science/technology and medical serials from ULRICH'S INTERNATIONAL PERIODICALS DIRECTORY. Searches can be conducted by SIC, year founded, activity, education, employees, institution/company, city, state or country, memberships/honors, product description, personal statistics, personal title, research area, revenue. Updated annually. 1 year subscription $995, 3 years 2,836, excluding discounts. For more information visit Bowker Reed Reference's web site at http://www.reedref.com or contact: Bowker Reed Reference Electronic Publishing, 121 Chanlon Road, New Providence, NJ 07974 USA, Phone (800) 323-3288, Fax (908) 665-3528, email info@bowker.com.

WORLDWIDE BRANCH LOCATIONS OF MULTINATIONAL COMPANIES focuses on some 500 multinationals and nearly 20,000 plants, branch offices and subsidiaries worldwide and NOT headquartered in the USA. It's organized geographically. Indexes include names of facilities and parent companies, SIC, and a geographic listing of parent companies by country. $200. Ordering information: Gale Research, P.O. Box 33477, Detroit, MI 48232-5477. Phone (800) 877-GALE, Fax (800) 414-5043 will be responded to within 48 hours. Internet orders: galeord@galegroup.com, CompuServe email: 72203.1552, web site http://www.galegroup.com, GaleNet web site address @http://galenet.galegroup.com.

Supermarkets

See Retail Category

CHAIN STORE GUIDE'S DATABASE MARKETING DIVISION can customize databases in these industries: Supermarket, department stores, discount department stores, drug stores. Your made-to-order database can include one or several of the named industries and the criteria of your ideal "customer" or search prospect. Information is available on a 3.5" diskette for IBM-PC, Apple Macintosh and DBF, ASCII, comma delimited and others. Mailing labels are also available or you can generate your own labels from a 3.5" diskette. For pricing or ordering information contact Chain Store Guide Information Services, 3922 Coconut Palm Drive, Tampa, FL 33619. (800) 927-9292, (813) 664-6800, (813) 627-6822, (800) 289-6822. http://www.d-net.com/csgis or http://www.csgis.com.

DIRECTORY OF SINGLE UNIT SUPERMARKET OPERATORS lists 7,000 independent (single unit) supermarket operators/grocery retailers with sales of at least $1 million. names and titles of key personnel. It also identifies major trade associations and a trade show calendar. $280. Chain Store Guide Information Services, 3922 Coconut Palm Drive, Tampa, FL 33619. (800) 927-9292, (813) 664-6800, (813) 627-6822, (800) 289-6822. http://www.d-net.com/csgis or http://www.csgis.com.

DIRECTORY OF SUPERMARKET, GROCERY AND CONVENIENCE STORE CHAINS describes and indexes over 2,300 supermarket chains with $2 million in annual sales. It covers supermarkets, superstores, club stores, gourmet supermarkets and combo stores in the U.S. and Canada, plus a special section profiling 1,700 convenience store chains. It includes an index to the top 200 supermarket chains and the top 100 convenience store chains, which is a valuable tool for target list development. It also lists over 29,000 key executives, buyers and administrative personnel. The directory also lists major trade associations and a trade show calendar. $300. Chain Store Guide Information Services, 3922 Coconut Palm Drive, Tampa, FL 33619. (800) 927-9292, (813) 664-6800, (813) 627-6822, (800) 289-6822. http://www.d-net.com/csgis or http://www.csgis.com.

FAIRCHILD PUBLICATIONS publishes a number of fashion and retail publications, such as FAIRCHILD'S TEXTILE AND APPAREL FINANCIAL DIRECTORY, which provides information about a range of textile and garment manufacturers. Published annually. $85. Fairchild also publishes industry trade publications, such as WOMEN'S WEAR DAILY (www.wwd.com) and numerous specialized apparel industry directories, such as FASHION RESOURCE DIRECTORY, DIRECTORY OF BRAND NAME APPAREL MANUFACTURERS (which includes buyers), and APPAREL INDUSTRY SOURCEBOOK (which also includes buyers). Fairchild also publishes material for specialized retail niches, such as supermarkets, shoes, etc. For more information, contact Fairchild Books, 7 West 34th Street, New York, NY 10001, (212) 630-3880, (800) 247 6622, email fpwebmaster@fairchildpub.com, web site www.fairchildpub.com or www.fairchildbooks.com.

SUPERMARKET BUSINESS is a monthly trade magazine provides information about key trade events, trends, and research findings. Supermarket Business Week is a weekly news fax with highlights of the week's key developments in the supermarket business. Call (201) 833-1900 for subscription information. Remember to find out if there are any back issues with the specific information you need—or an annual index. Ordering information: Chain Store Guide Information Services, 3922 Coconut Palm Drive, Tampa, FL 33619. (800) 927-9292, (813) 664-6800, (813) 627-6822, (800) 289-6822. http://www.d-net.com/csgis or http://www.csgis.com.

SUPERMARKET, GROCERY AND CONVENIENCE STORE CHAINS CD-ROM can conduct data searches from five topic screens: 1. Personnel by title, 2. Personnel by functional area, 3. Listing type (branch office, corporate office, divisional office, headquarters, location, managed care div, regional office, subsidiary, warehouse), 4. Stores operated (superstores, supermarkets, convenience, warehouse, combo stores, gourmet supermarkets, stores w/gas), 5. Specialty departments (e.g., auto supplies, automatic teller machines, beer, books/magazines, floral/horticulture,gourmet/specialty foods, greeting cards, in-store bakeries, in-store banking, in-store restaurant, lawn & garden, liquor, nutrition center, et al.). You can also make selections based on geography or the size of a company (number of units and/or sales). Several output options are available, including mailing labels, and electronic formats (such as DBASE, ASCII, text) for mail merge customization. $795, including companion directory. If the price is prohibitively high, remember your local library. Chain Store Guide Information Services, 3922 Coconut Palm Drive, Tampa, FL 33619. (800) 927-9292, (813) 664-6800, (813) 627-6822, (800) 289-6822. http://www.d-net.com/csgis or http://www.csgis.com.

Sweden

See Scandinavia, Europe, International

DIRECTORY OF AMERICAN FIRMS OPERATING IN FOREIGN COUNTRIES, REGIONAL EDITION—SWEDEN, $39. Ordering information: Uniworld Business Publications, Inc., 257 Central Park West, Suite 10A, New York, NY 10024-4110, (212) 496-2448, fax (212) 769-0413, email uniworldbp@aol.com. Web site: http://www.uniworldbp.com.

DIRECTORY OF FOREIGN FIRMS OPERATING IN THE UNITED STATES, REGIONAL EDITION—SWEDEN. $39. Ordering information: Uniworld Business Publications, Inc., 257 Central Park West, Suite 10A, New York, NY 10024-4110, (212) 496-2448, fax (212) 769-0413, email uniworldbp@aol.com. Web site: http://www.uniworldbp.com.

SWEDEN'S TOP 8,000 COMPANIES contains company and business profiles, including county listings. Dun & Bradstreet, Business Reference Solutions, Three Sylvan Way, Parsippany, NJ 07054 USA. (800) 526-0651. Email dnbmdd@mail.dnb.com. Web site http://www.dnbmdd.com.

Switzerland

See Europe, International

DIRECTORY OF AMERICAN FIRMS OPERATING IN FOREIGN COUNTRIES, REGIONAL EDITION—SWITZERLAND, $39. Ordering information: Uniworld Business Publications, Inc., 257 Central Park West, Suite 10A, New York, NY 10024-4110, (212) 496-2448, fax (212) 769-0413, email uniworldbp@aol.com. Web site: http://www.uniworldbp.com.

DIRECTORY OF FOREIGN FIRMS OPERATING IN THE UNITED STATES, REGIONAL EDITION—SWITZERLAND. $39. Ordering information: Uniworld Business Publications, Inc., 257 Central Park West, Suite 10A, New York, NY 10024-4110, (212) 496-2448, fax (212) 769-0413, email uniworldbp@aol.com. Web site: http://www.uniworldbp.com.

PENSION FUNDS AND THEIR ADVISERS provides information on the top 2,000 pension funds in the United Kingdom, plus major funds of Japan, Belgium, France, Germany, Ireland, The Netherlands and Switzerland. This Directory is the only source in the US that monitors the growth of assets in the international market. Information includes internal and external fund management contacts, major US and Canadian pension funds and money managers, major European and Japanese pension funds and their advisors. It also includes comprehensive listings of 900 advisors to the pension fund industry including financial advisers, accountants, actuaries and pension fund consultants, pension administrators, insurance companies, attorneys, computer services, global custody, pension trustees, pension /financial recruitment consultants, investment research, associations and professional groups, and publications. $310. Published by A.P. Information Services, Ltd. Marketed exclusively in North America MONEY MARKET DIRECTORIES INC./STANDARD AND POORS, 320 East Main Street, Charlottesville, VA 22902, http://www.mmdaccess.com, (800) 446-2810, (804) 977-1450.

T

Taiwan

See Asia, International, China

DIRECTORY OF AMERICAN FIRMS OPERATING IN FOREIGN COUNTRIES, REGIONAL EDITION—CHINA GROUP. Includes China, Hong Kong, Singapore, Taiwan, Macau. $79. Uniworld Business Publications, Inc., 257 Central Park West, Suite 10A, New York, NY 10024-4110, (212) 496-2448, fax (212) 769-0413, email uniworldbp@aol.com. Web site: http://www.uniworldbp.com.

DIRECTORY OF FOREIGN FIRMS OPERATING IN THE UNITED STATES, REGIONAL EDITION—CHINA GROUP. Includes China, Hong Kong, Singapore, Taiwan. $29. Uniworld Business Publications, Inc., 257 Central Park West, Suite 10A, New York, NY 10024-4110, (212) 496-2448, fax (212) 769-0413, email uniworldbp@aol.com. Web site: http://www.uniworldbp.com.

TAIWAN'S LEADING CORPORATIONS profiles 8,000 companies in Taiwan, both publicly and privately held. Information is listed alphabetically by company name and is cross referenced by district and five industries: Computers, Electrical & Electronics, Financial Services, Textiles and Machinery. Listings include multiple executive names are provided, address, phone number, SIC or NAICS codes, year established, sales volume, number of employees and more. For prices call Dun & Bradstreet at (800) 526-0651. For more information contact Dun & Bradstreet, Business Reference Solutions, Three Sylvan Way, Parsippany, NJ 07054. Email dnbmdd@mail.dnb.com. Web site http://www.dnbmdd.com.

Target List Development

As a point of clarification, a target list, by its very definition, is a list of companies only. Target lists never list names of people. A list comprised of names of people is called something else, such as a list of sources and prospects, a list of contacts, or a list of candidates. For further discussion about target lists, refer to the Glossary and the Research Check List in Chapter 1.

ADVERTISER AND AGENCY RED BOOKS PLUS CD ROM combines all the information in THE STANDARD DIRECTORY OF ADVERTISERS, THE STANDARD DIRECTORY OF ADVERTISING AGENCIES and the STANDARD DIRECTORY OF INTERNATIONAL ADVERTISERS AND AGENCIES. Information is searchable by 25 fields, including company name, personal name, job title/function, product type, product/account name, city, state, zip or country, area code, revenues, number of employees, outside ad agency and even type of computer hardware. Contains professional association information. Available for Windows and Macintosh. Updated quarterly. 1 year subscription $1,295. If the price is prohibitively high, remember your local library. National Register Publishing, Reed Elsevier-New Providence, 121 Chanlon Road, New Providence, NJ 07974, (800) 521-8110, fax (800) 836-7736, web site www.redbooks.com or www.marquiswhoswho.com. "If, for any reason whatsoever, your order does not fully meet your expectations, simply return the product within 30 days for a prompt, complete, unquestioned refund," as stated in Catalog of Biographical and Professional References of publisher Marquis Who's Who/National Register Publishing.

AMERICAN BANKERS ASSOCIATION (ABA) publishes numerous specialized banking journals and otherwise provides a wealth of information, especially lists of leading firms engaged in various banking.activities, such as correspondent banking, second mortgages, credit card operations, mortgage servicing, foreign banks in the US, and so forth. AMERICAN BANKERS ASSOCIATION, 1120 Connecticut Ave. NW, Washington, DC 20036, (202) 663-5000, Fax (202) 663-7533, web site www.aba.com.

AMERICAN JOBS ABROAD is a guide to over 800 US firms and organizations that employ Americans abroad in 110 countries. While this directory provides considerable information for a job seeker, it can also be used to identify American target companies operating in foreign countries. Regardless of whether the ideal candidate will be a local or an American, once you have identified who the target companies are, you can then conduct ID research to identify sources and prospects. $65. Gale Group, P.O. Box 9187, Farmington Hills, MI 48333-9187. Toll free US and Canada (800) 877-GALE (4253) and (248) 699-GALE, fax (800) 414-5043 and (248) 699-8061, Internet orders galeord@galegroup.com, web site www.galegroup.com or www.gale.com. All Gale Group products are available on approval. Contact Gale for details.

BEST HOSPITALS IN AMERICA describes nearly 400 top rated medical facilities in the USA. Written from the patient's point of view, it includes a history of each institution, highly rated services, special programs and facilities, well-known specialists, admissions policies and contact information. Best utilized for target list development or possibly a search in hospital admissions. $40. Gale Group, P.O. Box 9187, Farmington Hills, MI 48333-9187. Toll free US and Canada (800) 877-GALE (4253) and (248) 699-GALE, fax (800) 414-5043 and (248) 699-8061, Internet orders galeord@galegroup.com, web site www.galegroup.com or www.gale.com. All Gale Group products are available on approval. Contact Gale for details.

BUSINESS RANKINGS ANNUAL tracks the leading US businesses through 3,800 "top 10" business lists in over 1,500 subject areas. $275.00. Also available on CD ROM. Gale Group, P.O. Box 9187, Farmington Hills, MI 48333-9187. Toll free US and Canada (800) 877-GALE (4253) and (248) 699-GALE, fax (800) 414-5043 and (248) 699-8061, Internet orders galeord@galegroup.com, web site www.galegroup.com or www.gale.com. All Gale Group products are available on approval. Contact Gale for details.

BUSINESSWEEK regularly publishes surveys which are excellent for developing target lists. One of them is the R&D SCOREBOARD, which lists companies by industry and provides various statistics, such as Research and Development expenditures, R&D as a percentage of sales, R&D spending per employee, comparisons to previous year, and so forth.

CANADIAN BUSINESS MAGAZINE publishes an Annual Top 500.

CATALOG OF INSTITUTIONAL RESEARCH REPORTS (GLOBAL EDITION) tracks over 15,000 monthly investment research reports published by Wall Street's European and Pacific counterparts in over 500 research firms worldwide. Reports are listed alphabetically by company and by research firm. This information is best used for target list research, or your own personal investing. Published ten times per year. $125 per year. Nelson Information, P.O. Box 591, Port Chester, NY 10573 USA. (800) 333-6357, Phone outside the US (914) 937-8400, Fax (914) 937-8590, web site http://www.nelnet.com.

COMPANIES INTERNATIONAL CD-ROM contains comprehensive financial and contact data for over 300,000 public and privately held companies in 180 countries including the Commonwealth of Independent States, Mexico, Canada and Japan. Companies can be located by company name, product or industry, location, or a combination. This reference can also be used for target lists development for international companies, including privately held companies. $2,995. Gale Group, P.O. Box 9187, Farmington Hills, MI 48333-9187. Toll free US and Canada (800) 877-GALE (4253) and (248) 699-GALE, fax (800) 414-5043 and (248) 699-8061, Internet orders galeord@galegroup.com, web site www.galegroup.com or www.gale.com. All Gale Group products are available on approval. Contact Gale for details.

CONSUMER SOURCEBOOK includes over 15,000 programs and services available to the general public at little or no cost. Services are provided by federal, state, county and local governments, agencies, and organizations and associations. Consumer affairs and customer service departments for corporations are also listed as well as publications. $265.00. Gale Group, P.O. Box 9187, Farmington Hills, MI 48333-9187. Toll free US and Canada (800) 877-GALE (4253) and (248) 699-GALE, fax (800) 414-5043 and (248) 699-8061, Internet orders galeord@galegroup.com, web site www.galegroup.com or www.gale.com. All Gale Group products are available on approval. Contact Gale for details.

CRAIN PUBLICATIONS publishes specialized industry newspapers across a wide range of industries and functions (including marketing and advertising.) Contact the editorial office of the appropriate publication to find out if any surveys have been published. Or try their corporate library. Some surveys, such as top business lists, will be suitable for target list research, while others, such as Advertising Age's annual "100 Leading Advertisers" issue identifies names and titles of employees at those consumer products companies.

CRAIN CHICAGO BUSINESS is a weekly trade publication. Look for special issues with surveys and lists of top companies by industry. Crain Communications, Inc. is headquartered in Chicago with offices in major cities throughout the US plus London, Tokyo and Frankfurt. New York location: 220 East 42nd Street, New York, NY 10017, (212) 210-0100, Circulation (800) 678-9595. Annual subscription $89, two years $155.

CRAIN CLEVELAND is a weekly trade publication. Look for special issues with surveys and lists of top companies by industry. Crain Communications, Inc. is headquartered in Chicago with offices in major cities throughout the US plus London, Tokyo and Frankfurt. New York location: 220 East 42nd Street, New York, NY 10017, (212) 210-0100, Circulation (800) 678-9595. Annual subscription $49, two years $87. Web site www.crainscleveland.com.

CRAIN DETROIT is a weekly trade publication. Look for special issues with surveys and lists of top companies by industry. Crain Communications, Inc. is headquartered in Chicago with offices in major cities throughout the US plus London, Tokyo and Frankfurt. New York location: 220 East 42nd Street, New York, NY 10017, (212) 210-0100, Circulation (800) 678-9595. Annual subscription $49, two years $84. Web site www.crainsdetroit.com.

CRAIN NEW YORK is a weekly trade publication. Look for special issues with surveys and lists of top companies by industry. Crain Communications, Inc. is headquartered in Chicago with offices in major cities throughout the US plus London, Tokyo and Frankfurt. New York location: 220 East 42nd Street, New York, NY 10017, (212) 210-0100, Circulation (800) 678-9595. Annual subscription $62, two years $113. Web site www.crainsny.com.

D&B BUSINESS RANKINGS ranks over 25,000 US companies, both publicly and privately held, from highest to lowest by sales volume and number of employees within a range of different categories. Businesses are listed alphabetically, ranked by size, within state and by industry category. Public companies are ranked by annual sales volume and employee size. Private and foreign owned companies are ranked by sales volume and employee size. The 5,000 largest public companies and private and foreign-owned companies are included in separate ranking sections. As this directory contains no names or titles, it is most appropriate for conducting research to develop a target list of companies. Updated annually. For prices call Dun & Bradstreet at (800) 526-0651. For more information contact Dun & Bradstreet, Business Reference Solutions, Three

Sylvan Way, Parsippany, New Jersey 07054. Email dnbmdd@mail.dnb.com. Web site http://www.dnbmdd.com.

D&B MARKETING INFORMATION BASE contains marketing information on 10,000,000 companies. Every month it is updated, reflecting some 500,000 changes: new business additions, CEO CHANGES and address changes. Information on senior management changes is particularly valuable to job hunters and search firms is an indicator of change, which could mean hiring activity, and/or a need for executive search services. Organizations in transition are generally good places to recruit because quality talent may be unhappy with the politics of the new organization. With respect to the execution of an executive search, this information can be best utilized to develop a list of target companies. Then, names and titles can be identified using another database or through traditional ID research. This technique could be used for an extremely difficult recruiting assignment. For example, finding companies in turmoil could provide a good place to search for candidates eager for a change. Selections are delivered on tape, cartridge, diskette or hard copy. For prices call Dun & Bradstreet at (800) 526-0651. For more information contact Dun & Bradstreet, Business Reference Solutions, Three Sylvan Way, Parsippany, New Jersey 07054. Email dnbmdd@mail.dnb.com. Web site http://www.dnbmdd.com.

DUN'S DIRECTORY OF MAJOR CORPORATIONS IN PEOPLE'S REPUBLIC OF CHINA is a two volume set with information on 20,000 major corporations in the PRC. Business categories include financial institutions, foreign invested enterprises, importers/exporters, and manufacturers. Over 80% of the corporations listed have more than 50 employees. Because only one executive name is provided per company, this reference is most suitable for target list development. However, once you've developed a target list, you can consult a business librarian as to the best way to conduct an electronic literature search to obtain names and other information. Better yet, make some telephone inquiries to PRC experts to locate research in English published in Asia. Listings in DUN'S DIRECTORY OF MAJOR CORPORATIONS IN PEOPLE'S REPUBLIC OF CHINA are presented alphabetically within four main business categories and cross-referenced by province, industry and company name in English. In English and Chinese. Published annually. For prices call Dun & Bradstreet at (800) 526-0651. For more information contact Dun & Bradstreet, Business Reference Solutions, Three Sylvan Way, Parsippany, NJ 07054. Email dnbmdd@mail.dnb.com. Web site http://www.dnbmdd.com.

DUN'S MARKET GUIDE: SMALL TO MEDIUM SIZE BUSINESSES IN HONG KONG identifies 30,000 companies in Hong Kong with 50 or fewer employees in seven industries: Construction, Finance, Insurance and Real Estate, Manufacturing, Retail Trade, Services, Transportation, and Wholesale Trade. However, as the only name this directory provides is that of the CEO, this reference is best used for Target List Development. For prices call Dun & Bradstreet at (800) 526-0651. For more information contact Dun & Bradstreet, Business Reference Solutions, Three Sylvan Way, Parsippany, NJ 07054. Email dnbmdd@mail.dnb.com. Web site http://www.dnbmdd.com.

EDUCATIONAL RANKINGS ANNUAL presents 3,500 national, regional, local and international lists and complete source citations if you need additional research. $199. Gale Group, P.O. Box 9187, Farmington Hills, MI 48333-9187. Toll free US and Canada (800) 877-GALE (4253) and (248) 699-GALE, fax (800) 414-5043 and (248) 699-8061, Internet orders galeord@galegroup.com, web site www.galegroup.com or www.gale.com. All Gale Group products are available on approval. Contact Gale for details.

ENCYCLOPEDIA OF EMERGING INDUSTRIES provides information on industries that are pioneering new technologies, introducing breakthrough marketing strategies or executing new innovative ways of serving new markets. Each industry profile includes the current size and situation of the industry, a technological overview, leading companies, references to further reading and more. It covers technologies from artificial intelligence to voice recognition systems, marketing initiatives from coffee houses to super-sized movie theater complexes; and service industry ventures from AIDS testing to home health care. $270. Gale Group, P.O. Box 9187, Farmington Hills, MI 48333-9187. Toll free US and Canada (800) 877-GALE (4253) and (248) 699-GALE, fax (800) 414-5043 and (248) 699-8061, Internet orders galeord@galegroup.com, web site www.galegroup.com or www.gale.com. All Gale Group products are available on approval. Contact Gale for details.

EUROMONITOR DIRECTORY OF ASIAN COMPANIES provides information about 5,000 major companies in Asia and a ranking of the top 100 companies, excluding financial institutions. Each country chapter includes a listing of the top 50 companies. $550. Published by Euromonitor (England). Distributed by Gale Group, P.O. Box 9187, Farmington Hills, MI 48333-9187. Toll free US and Canada (800) 877-GALE (4253) and (248) 699-GALE, fax (800) 414-5043 and (248) 699-8061, Internet orders galeord@galegroup.com, web site www.galegroup.com or www.gale.com. All Gale Group products are available on approval. Contact Gale for details.

FINANCIAL TIMES ENERGY YEARBOOKS: MINING contains full contact details, financial and operating information, and details about subsidiaries, affiliates, property and operations for about 800 mining companies globally. $320. Published by Financial Times Energy. Distributed by Gale Group, P.O. Box 9187, Farmington Hills, MI 48333-9187. Toll free US and Canada (800) 877-GALE (4253) and (248) 699-GALE, fax (800) 414-5043 and (248) 699-8061, Internet orders galeord@galegroup.com, web site www.galegroup.com or www.gale.com. All Gale Group products are available on approval. Contact Gale for details.

FINANCIAL TIMES TOP BANKS list can be obtained by calling the FINANCIAL TIMES in London, England (from the USA) at (011) 44 171 896-2274, (011) 44 171 873-4211. Faxes (011) 44 171 896-2371 & (011) 44 171 873-3595. Web site www.ft.com.

FORTUNE MAGAZINE, "THE FORTUNE GLOBAL 500" ISSUE. Published by Time, Inc. Fortune Single Copy Desk, PO Box 60001, Tampa, FL 33660, (800) 621-8000). $5 plus $3 shipping and handling.

FT 500 Expanded Book Version is a listing of the top 500 UK and European companies, ranked by market capitalization and published by the FINANCIAL TIMES. It contains the names of the CEO or Chairman, address, phone and fax. 29.95 pounds sterling. Also available on disk, 171 896-2744. For more information contact FT 500, FT Publishing, Financial Times, Number One Southwark Bridge, London SE1 9HL, England. Phone from the US (011) 44 171 873-3000 or (011) 44 171 873-4211. Fax from US (011) 44 171 873 3595, web site http://www.FT.com.

GALE BUSINESS RESOURCES ONLINE provides modules on US Industry (over 200,000 companies) and International Industry (over 200,000 companies), including public and privately held companies, brands, business rankings, trade and professional associations, company histories, merger information, and more. Comprehensive records include company name, officers' names and titles, SIC/NAICS codes and more. GALE BUSINESS RESOURCES is available online on the Internet through GaleNet.

For information on pricing, contact: Gale Group, P.O. Box 9187, Farmington Hills, MI 48333-9187. Toll free US and Canada (800) 877-GALE (4253) and (248) 699-GALE, fax (800) 414-5043 and (248) 699-8061, Internet orders galeord@galegroup.com, web site www.galegroup.com or www.gale.com. All Gale Group products are available on approval. Contact Gale for details.

HOOVER'S HANDBOOK OF AMERICAN BUSINESS provides information on 500 companies, including contacts, products, brand names, key competitors, and a brief history. Published annually. $29.95 softcover, $39.95 hardcover. The Reference Press, Inc., 6448 Highway 209 East, Suite E104, Austin, TX 78723, (512) 454-7778. Hoover's directories can also be accessed on the Internet by going to the Ask Jeeves web site at www.askjeeves.com. A subscription fee is charged for the service.

HOOVER'S HANDBOOK OF WORLD BUSINESS contains information on 200 companies, including contact information, products, key competitors, and a brief history. Published annually. $27.95 soft cover, $37.95 hard cover. The Reference Press, Inc., 6448 Highway 209 East, Suite E104, Austin, TX 78723, (512) 454-7778. Hoover's directories can also be accessed on the Internet by going to the Ask Jeeves web site at www.askjeeves.com. A subscription fee is charged for the service.

INDUSTRY NORMS & KEY BUSINESS RATIOS is a reference that provides financial performance statistics for over 1 million public and private firms in over 800 lines of business. This statistical reference provides performance benchmarks for over 800 lines of business on over 1 million companies, both publicly and privately held. As this directory contains no names or titles, it is most appropriate for conducting industry research to develop a target list of top performing companies. Published annually. Also available on diskette. For prices call Dun & Bradstreet at (800) 526-0651. For more information contact Dun & Bradstreet, Business Reference Solutions, Three Sylvan Way, Parsippany, New Jersey 07054. Email dnbmdd@mail.dnb.com. Web site http://www.dnbmdd.com.

INC. is a magazine written for entrepreneurs and small businesses. Their INC. 500 list of the 500 most rapidly growing businesses is an excellent resource. INC. Magazine, 38 Commercial Wharf, Boston, MA 02110, (800) 978-1800, (617) 248-8000, www.inc.com. To search for articles, go to www.inc.com/search.

JOBSEEKERS GUIDE TO SOCIALLY RESPONSIBLE COMPANIES, $59.95. If this directory is not available from the publisher, you might find it in the library. Gale Group, P.O. Box 9187, Farmington Hills, MI 48333-9187. Toll free US and Canada (800) 877-GALE (4253) and (248) 699-GALE, fax (800) 414-5043 and (248) 699-8061, Internet orders galeord@galegroup.com, web site www.galegroup.com or www.gale.com. All Gale Group products are available on approval. Contact Gale for details.

MACRAE'S BLUE BOOK identifies over 42,000 plants but lists no executive names. It is most appropriate for target list research. Distributed by Manufacturers' News, Inc., (888) 752-5200, 1633 Central Street, Evanston, IL 60201-1569. Email info@manufacturersnews.com. Web site www.manufacturersnews.com.

R&D RATIOS AND BUDGETS provides R&D budgets, R&D to sales ratios and R&D to gross margin ratios for over 6,000 companies in some 400 industries. It also includes industry and R&D budgets on over 150 major foreign companies. This information can be used to develop a fine-honed target list of preeminent organizations for a research and development search. Further, a target list which incorporates these ratios can provide "added value" competitive information to a company. $345 book, $495 book and diskette database. Updated annually. Ordering information: Schonfeld & Associates, Inc., One Sherwood Drive, Lincolnshire, IL 60069, (800) 205-0030, Fax (847) 948-8096, email schonassoc@aol.com, http://www.saibooks.com. Catalog available online.

SOFTWARE ENCYCLOPEDIA—A GUIDE FOR PERSONAL, PROFESSIONAL AND BUSINESS USERS identifies over 27,000 new and established programs on every format including disk and CD ROM. Search capability allows you to search by application, hardware, memory requirements, machine version, operating system, programming language and more. This resource can best be used either for your systems needs, or to do target list research in the software industry. $265 for 2 volume set.

R.R. Bowker (a unit of Cahners Business Information), 121 Chanlon Road, New Providence, NJ 07974 USA, Phone (888) BOWKER2 (888-269-5372) & (800) 323-3288, fax (908) 508-7696, email info@bowker.com, web www.bowker.com. Canada—R.R. Bowker, Markham, Ontario, phone (888) BOWKER9 & (905) 415-5837, fax (905) 479-6266. German speaking Europe—K.G. Saur Verlag, Munich, Germany, phone 49-89-76902-232, fax 49-89-76902-250, email 100730.1341@compuserve.com, web www.saur.de/home.htm. Rest of Europe incl. United Kingdom plus Africa & Asia—Bowker-Saur, W. Sussex, UK, phone 44-1342-326-972, fax 44-1342-335-612, email customer@bowker-saur.co.uk, web www.bowker-saur.com/service/. Australia/New Zealand—Thorpe, Port Melbourne, Victoria, Australia, phone 61-03-9-245-7370, fax 61-03-9-245-7395, email customer.service@thorpe.com.au, web www.thorpe.com.au. Technical support for CD ROMs (800) 323-3288, fax 908) 665-3528, email techsupport@bowker.com.

STANDARD AND POOR'S INDUSTRY SURVEYS provides a brief review of an industry and the major companies. Published twice a year. $1,475 annual subscription. Standard and Poor's Corporation, 25 Broadway, New York, NY 10004, (212) 438-2000, (800) 221-5277. Distributor Larry Meranus Professional Publications & Services, 4 Demoray Court, Pine Brook, NJ 07058, (800) MERANUS or (800) 637-2687.

STANDARD DIRECTORY OF ADVERTISERS Business Classifications Edition is an excellent general directory that organizes companies by a wide range of product categories. A few examples include "Apparel 2—Men's and Boys' Wear," "Heating and Air Conditioning," "Cosmetics and Toiletries," and "Aviation and Aerospace." This directory lists names and titles of key officers, revenues and other information. It is available in a geographic edition for the same price. This directory is comprised of over 24,000 companies that annually spend over $200,000 on advertising. It represents a reasonable place to look for hard-to-find information about privately held companies, especially those that heavily advertise their products. It is a good place to look for names if STANDARD AND POORS and the MILLION DOLLAR DIRECTORY fail to yield the names you need. Finally, the Classified Edition of THE STANDARD DIRECTORY OF ADVERTISERS can be a very convenient source of research because both your target list of companies and the corresponding names and titles of management all appear together, in the same Classification. This is important if you still rely on research books in hard copy. THE STANDARD DIRECTORY OF ADVERTISERS also publishes a special volume called THE STANDARD DIRECTORY OF ADVERTISERS TRADENAME INDEX. You can use the TRADENAME INDEX if you know the brand name of a product and need to find the company

that manufactures it. In addition, this directory contains an Associations section which identifies marketing oriented associations.

$599 hard copy. If the price is prohibitively high, remember your local library. THE STANDARD DIRECTORY OF ADVERTISERS is also available on CD ROM under the title ADVERTISER AND AGENCY RED BOOKS PLUS. It is available in Windows® and Macintosh® formats. National Register Publishing, Reed Elsevier-New Providence, 121 Chanlon Road, New Providence, NJ 07974, (800) 521-8110, fax (800) 836-7736, web site www.redbooks.com or www.marquiswhoswho.com. "If, for any reason whatsoever, your order does not fully meet your expectations, simply return the product within 30 days for a prompt, complete, unquestioned refund," as stated in Catalog of Biographical and Professional References of publisher Marquis Who's Who/National Register Publishing.

WARD'S BUSINESS DIRECTORY OF U.S. PRIVATE AND PUBLIC COMPANIES provides information on over 120,000 US companies, over 90% of them privately held. Volumes 1-3 contain company information. Volume 4 lists companies geographically and ranks the top 1,000 privately held companies and the top 1,000 employers. Volume 5 ranks private and public companies by sales within SIC or NAICS code. Volumes 6-7 contain state rankings by sales within SIC or NAICS. Also includes ranking of the top 100 privately held companies, the top publicly held companies and the top 100 employers for each state. Volume 8 ranks sales within the 6 digit NAICS (North American Industry Classification System which replaced the SIC code system). It sorts companies by cross-national agreements between the US, Canada and Mexico. Vols. 1-8, $2,515. Vols. 1-5, $2,125. Vols. 1-4, $1,880. Vol 5, $950. Vols. 6-7, $950. Vol 8, $640. Gale Group, P.O. Box 9187, Farmington Hills, MI 48333-9187. Toll free US and Canada (800) 877-GALE (4253) and (248) 699-GALE, fax (800) 414-5043 and (248) 699-8061, Internet orders galeord@galegroup.com, web site www.galegroup.com or www.gale.com. All Gale Group products are available on approval. Contact Gale for details.

WORLD BUSINESS RANKINGS ANNUAL is modeled after Gale's award-winning BUSINESS RANKINGS ANNUAL. It provides 2,500 "top 10" ranked lists and references the sources of information. $189. Gale Group, P.O. Box 9187, Farmington Hills, MI 48333-9187. Toll free US and Canada (800) 877-GALE (4253) and (248) 699-GALE, fax (800) 414-5043 and (248) 699-8061, Internet orders galeord@galegroup.com, web site www.galegroup.com or www.gale.com. All Gale Group products are available on approval. Contact Gale for details.

WORLD DIRECTORY OF BUSINESS INFORMATION WEB SITES provides full details on over 1,500 free business web sites, including information such as online surveys, top company rankings, company information, brand information, market research reports and trade association statistics. $590. Published by Euromonitor (England). Distributed by Gale Group, P.O. Box 9187, Farmington Hills, MI 48333-9187. Toll free US and Canada (800) 877-GALE (4253) and (248) 699-GALE, fax (800) 414-5043 and (248) 699-8061, Internet orders galeord@galegroup.com, web site www.galegroup.com or www.gale.com. All Gale Group products are available on approval. Contact Gale for details.

WORLDWIDE BRANCH LOCATIONS OF MULTINATIONAL COMPANIES focuses on some 500 multinationals and nearly 20,000 plants, branch offices and subsidiaries worldwide and NOT headquartered in the USA. It's organized geographically. Indexes include names of facilities and parent companies, SIC, and a geographic listing of parent companies by country. $200. Ordering information: Gale Research, P.O. Box 33477, Detroit, MI 48232-5477. Phone (800) 877-GALE, Fax (800) 414-5043 will be responded to within 48 hours. Internet orders: galeord@galegroup.com, CompuServe email: 72203.1552, web site http://www.galegroup.com, GaleNet web site address @http://galenet.galegroup.com.

www.rtp.org is the home page for Research Triangle Park, North Carolina . It includes a directory of companies in the Park and listing of companies according to research specialization, appropriate for target list development.

Technology

See Biotechnology, Electronics, Information Technology, Software, Telecommunications

AMERICAN ELECTRONICS ASSOCIATION annually publishes the AEA DIRECTORY for $175. With 18 regional groups, this association conducts networking programs for industry executives, and provides information on compensation surveys and employee benefits plans, among other things. For more information contact: American Electronics Association (AEA), 5201 Great America Parkway, Suite 520, PO Box 54990, Santa Clara, CA 95056, (408) 987-4200.

AMERICAN MEN AND WOMEN OF SCIENCE provides detailed biographical information on over 100,000 US and Canadian scientists. This information is very useful for searches in research and development and other areas, because you can review the individual's background, titles, and degrees with dates,before you ever place a phone call. 8 volume set $900. AMERICAN MEN & WOMEN OF SCIENCE (AMWS Online) is also available online on a "pay as you go" basis through The Dialog Corporation, DIALOG file no. 236, Subfile: AMWS, or through LEXIS-NEXIS using NEXIS Library : BUSREF, File Name: AMSCI. Call Bowker for more information including availability of American Men and Women of Science on CD ROM.

R.R. Bowker (a unit of Cahners Business Information), 121 Chanlon Road, New Providence, NJ 07974 USA, Phone (888) BOWKER2 (888-269-5372) & (800) 323-3288, fax (908) 508-7696, email info@bowker.com, web www.bowker.com. Canada—R.R. Bowker, Markham, Ontario, phone (888) BOWKER9 & (905) 415-5837, fax (905) 479-6266. German speaking Europe—K.G. Saur Verlag, Munich, Germany, phone 49-89-76902-232, fax 49-89-76902-250, email 100730.1341@compuserve.com, web www.saur.de/home.htm. Rest of Europe incl. United Kingdom plus Africa & Asia—Bowker-Saur, W. Sussex, UK, phone 44-1342-326-972, fax 44-1342-335-612, email customer@bowker-saur.co.uk, web www.bowker-saur.com/service/. Australia/New Zealand—Thorpe, Port Melbourne, Victoria, Australia, phone 61-03-9-245-7370, fax 61-03-9-245-7395, email customer.service@thorpe.com.au, web www.thorpe.com.au. Technical support for CD ROMs (800) 323-3288, fax 908) 665-3528, email techsupport@bowker.com.

ASSOCIATION OF HIGH TECH DISTRIBUTORS (AHTD) publishes a quarterly newsletter and periodically a MEMBERSHIP DIRECTORY comprised of about 175 high technology distributors and 110 manufacturing affiliates. For more information contact Association of High Tech Distributors, 1900 Arch Street, Philadelphia, PA 19103, (215) 564-3484, web site www.ahtd.org.

BACON'S COMPUTER & HI-TECH MEDIA DIRECTORY identifies 6,500 contacts at 1,900 print and broadcast outlets, serving computers, data management, software, the Internet, electronics, telecommunications and more. $225. Ordering information: Call (800) 621-0561, (800) 753-6675. Bacon's Information, Inc., a K-III Communications Company, 332 South Michigan Avenue, Chicago, IL 60604. Satisfaction guaranteed or a full refund within 30 days.

CORPTECH DIRECTORY OF TECHNOLOGY COMPANIES is available in hard copy, Regional Guides, on PC disk, and on CD ROM. CorpTech EXPLORE Database is an outstanding reference that was awarded Best CD-ROM Directory by the National Directory Publishing Association. One click moves you from the CD ROM Database to Internet information on the same company. CorpTech also provides other sophisticated but reasonably priced automated services. You can save a tremendous amount of time researching relatively small, emerging new companies in various high technology niches and obtain names, titles and mailing address labels. CorpTech EXPLORE Database CD ROM $2,450 (including free soft cover CorpTech Directory worth $545). Ordering Information: CorpTech, Corporate Technology Information Services, Inc., 12 Alfred Street, Suite 200, Woburn, MA 01801-1915. (800) 333-8036, (781) 932-3100, (781) 932-3939. Fax (781) 932-6335. Email sales@corptech.com. Web site http://www.corptech.com.

CTI PLUS (CURRENT TECHNOLOGY INDEX) is a technology index database enhanced with the SUPERTECH ABSTRACTS database. CTI PLUS covers 320 technical and applied science journals from the US and the UK. Topics covered include general technology, industrial health and safety, ergonomics, electronics, applied optics, heat, machine vision, natural language processing, pattern recognition, computer architecture, neural networks, computer integrated manufacturing, computer graphics, simulation, robot research, engineering, applied acoustics, power transmission, civil engineering, town planning, transport technology, military technology, fishing, mining, chemical engineering, radiochemistry, photochemistry, inorganic and organic chemistry, coatings, textile manufacturing, photography, packaging and more. If you're doing a search in an exotic new area of technology, this library index will lead you to the right organizations. You can conduct a literature search to determine which companies are engaged in cutting edge research, or to locate people who have been quoted. From Bowker-Saur. Updated quarterly. 1 year subscription $1,495, excluding discounts. For more information visit Bowker Reed Reference's web site at http://www.reedref.com

or contact: Bowker Reed Reference Electronic Publishing, 121 Chanlon Road, New Providence, NJ 07974 USA, Phone (800) 323-3288, Fax (908) 665-3528, email info@bowker.com.

DIRECTORY OF CALIFORNIA TECHNOLOGY COMPANIES identifies over 33,000 executive names and titles at over 12,000 companies, including research labs, telecommunications, biotechnology and software. Published annually by Database Publishing, PO Box 70024, Anaheim, CA 92825/1590 South Lewis Street, Anaheim, CA 92805. (800) 888-8434, (714) 778-6400, web site www.databasepublishing.com, email sales@databasepublishing.com. Directory $145, complete CD ROM $645, CD ROM one-year lease $425. Also distributed by Manufacturers' News, Inc., (888) 752-5200, 1633 Central Street, Evanston, IL 60201-1569. Email info@manufacturersnews.com. Web site www.manufacturersnews.com.

ELSEVIER ADVANCED TECHNOLOGY is a leading supplier of Electronics industry information. They publish a CD-ROM of a complete database of electronic companies in Europe, developed in conjunction with THE EUROPEAN ELECTRONICS DIRECTORY: COMPONENTS AND SUB-ASSEMBLIES AND SYSTEMS AND APPLICATIONS. Elsevier also publishes yearbooks, directories, market research reports and industrial journals, technical handbooks and newsletters, such as PROFILE OF THE WORLDWIDE TELECOMMUNICATIONS INDUSTRY, PROFILE OF THE WORLDWIDE CAPACITOR INDUSTRY, PROFILE OF THE WORLDWIDE SEMICONDUCTOR INDUSTRY, and PROFILE OF THE EUROPEAN CONNECTOR INDUSTRY. For more information contact: Elsevier Advanced Technology, P.O. Box 150, Kidlington, Oxford, OX5 1AS, England. Phone (44) (0) 1865 843-848, fax (44) (0) 1865 843-971.

ENCYCLOPEDIA OF ASSOCIATIONS: INTERNATIONAL ORGANIZATIONS includes nearly 20,000 multinational and national organizations in foreign countries, including US based associations with multinational membership. Entries also include email addresses, web sites and bulletin board addresses, lobbying activities, and publication and convention information. Indexed by geography, keyword and executives. $595 for 2 volume set. Also available in CD ROM. Database available via commercial online service. Gale Group, P.O. Box 9187, Farmington Hills, MI 48333-9187. Toll free US and Canada (800) 877-GALE (4253) and (248) 699-GALE, fax (800) 414-5043 and (248) 699-8061, Internet orders galeord@galegroup.com, web site www.galegroup.com or www.gale.com. All Gale Group products are available on approval. Contact Gale for details.

ENCYCLOPEDIA OF ASSOCIATIONS: NATIONAL ORGANIZATIONS OF THE US. This superb reference is one of the first places you should look when beginning a new recruiting assignment or when looking for specialized references of any type. The keyword index makes this comprehensive reference easy to use, even in hard copy. For over 23,000 nonprofit professional associations with a national scope, this encyclopedia reveals:

- Publications, including membership rosters and newsletters

- Dates and locations of association conferences and conventions

- Names of Executive Directors, who are usually incredible sources of industry information if you call and speak to them

- Committees

- Job and candidate referral banks, which can provide resumes of other industry sources and sometimes candidates

- It includes organizations in these categories: business, trade, environmental, agricultural, legal, governmental, engineering, technological, scientific, educational, cultural, social welfare, health & medical, public affairs, ethnic, labor unions, chambers of commerce, tourism, & others.

  Volume 1, National Organizations of the US, $505
  Volume 2, Geographic and Executive Indexes, $390
  Volume 3, Supplement, $405

Gale Group, P.O. Box 9187, Farmington Hills, MI 48333-9187. Toll free US and Canada (800) 877-GALE (4253) and (248) 699-GALE, fax (800) 414-5043 and (248) 699-8061, Internet orders galeord@galegroup.com, web site www.galegroup.com or www.gale.com. All Gale Group products are available on approval. Contact Gale for details.

ENCYCLOPEDIA OF ASSOCIATIONS: REGIONAL, STATE AND LOCAL ORGANIZATIONS. The information in this directory is not duplicated anywhere in ENCYCLOPEDIA OF ASSOCIATIONS. Over 100,000 nonprofit organizations are included in this directory. $585 for 5 volume set or $140 per individual volume. Also available on CD ROM and online on the Internet through a GaleNet subscription.

Volume 1, Great Lakes States (Illinois, Indiana, Michigan, Minnesota, Ohio, Wisconsin)

Volume 2, Northeastern States (Connecticut, Maine, Massachusetts, New Hampshire, New Jersey, New York, Pennsylvania, Rhode Islands, Vermont)

Volume 3, Southern and Middle Atlantic States (Including Puerto Rico and the Virgin Islands) (Alabama, Delaware, Washington, DC, Florida, Georgia, Kentucky, Maryland, Mississippi, North Carolina, Puerto Rico, South Carolina, Tennessee, Virginia, West Virginia, Virgin Islands)

Volume 4, South Central and Great Plains States (Arkansas, Iowa, Kansas, Louisiana, Missouri, Nebraska, North Dakota, Oklahoma, South Dakota, Texas)

Volume 5, Western States (Alaska, Arizona, California, Colorado, Guam, Hawaii, Idaho, Montana, Nevada, New Mexico, Oregon, Utah, Washington, Wyoming)

Gale Group, P.O. Box 9187, Farmington Hills, MI 48333-9187. Toll free US and Canada (800) 877-GALE (4253) and (248) 699-GALE, fax (800) 414-5043 and (248) 699-8061, Internet orders galeord@galegroup.com, web site www.galegroup.com or www.gale.com. All Gale Group products are available on approval. Contact Gale for details.

ENCYCLOPEDIA OF EMERGING INDUSTRIES provides information on industries that are pioneering new technologies, introducing breakthrough marketing strategies or executing new innovative ways of serving new markets. Each industry profile includes the current size and situation of the industry, a technological overview, leading companies, references to further reading and more. It covers technologies from artificial intelligence to voice recognition systems, marketing initiatives from coffee houses to super-sized movie theater complexes; and service industry ventures from AIDS testing to home health care. $270. Gale Group, P.O. Box 9187, Farmington Hills, MI 48333-9187. Toll free US and Canada (800) 877-GALE (4253) and (248) 699-GALE, fax (800) 414-5043 and (248) 699-8061, Internet orders galeord@galegroup.com, web site www.galegroup.com or www.gale.com. All Gale Group products are available on approval. Contact Gale for details.

ENCYCLOPEDIA OF PHYSICAL SCIENCES AND ENGINEERING INFORMATION SOURCES covers over 600 subjects such as chemistry, geology, physics, civil engineering plus new areas of technology such as CD ROM, cybernetics, hazardous material, space shuttle and others. Each subject includes a bibliography of live, print and electronic sources of information. $165. Gale Group, P.O. Box 9187, Farmington Hills, MI 48333-9187. Toll free US and Canada (800) 877-GALE (4253) and (248) 699-GALE, fax (800) 414-5043 and (248) 699-8061, Internet orders galeord@galegroup.com, web site www.galegroup.com or www.gale.com. All Gale Group products are available on approval. Contact Gale for details.

EUROPEAN R&D PLUS DATABASE ON CD ROM is a consolidation of the DIRECTORY OF EUROPEAN RESEARCH AND DEVELOPMENT and WHO'S WHO IN EUROPEAN RESEARCH AND DEVELOPMENT. It covers over 20,000 labs, both commercial and academic, in 36 countries including all the European former Soviet Republics. Searches can be conducted by over 20 fields in over 600 scientific disciplines. Information is available about over 100,000 people, including senior researchers, research managers and consultants, including: name, career data, current position, education, publications, research scope, current activities, nationality, languages and more. From Bowker-Saur. Updated annually. 1 year subscription $1,595, excluding discounts. For more information visit Bowker Reed Reference's web site at http://www.reedref.com or contact: Bowker Reed Reference Electronic Publishing, 121 Chanlon Road, New Providence, NJ 07974 USA, Phone (800) 323-3288, Fax (908) 665-3528, email info@bowker.com.

HARRIS ELECTRONICS MANUFACTURERS DATABASE, also available as a directory, is published in cooperation with the Electronics Representatives Association and the National Electronic Distributors Association. It contains information on over 20,000 US electronics manufacturing firms and over 2,500 Canadian electronics manufacturers, including names of about 68,000 American executives and 5,500 Canadian executives. Selectory $595. Selectory multi-user (LAN) version $1,190. Directory, updated annually, $255. Ordering information: Harris InfoSource International, 2057 Aurora Road, Twinsburg, OH 44087-1999, (800) 888-5900, fax (800) 643-5997, web site http://www.harrisinfo.com.

NATIONAL CORPORATE TECHNOLOGY DIRECTORY is a 4 volume set that profiles over 35,000 technology manufacturers. Includes information on 3,000 product categories, details of operating units, and toll free phone numbers. Most of these companies are "small," with under 1,000 employees. $545 soft cover, $595 hard cover. Regional Directories are also available, although the national directory does contain more detailed information. Regional directories are available for: Northern New England, Eastern Lakes, New York Metro, New Jersey & the Delaware Valley, Mid-Atlantic, Southeast, Central, Great Lakes, Midwest, Southwest, Northwest, Northern California, Southern California. $175 per regional directory. Diskettes are also available. Call for price and availability. Ordering information: Harris InfoSource International, 2057 Aurora Road, Twinsburg, OH 44087-1999, (800) 888-5900, fax (800) 643-5997, web site http://www.harrisinfo.com.

NELSON FINANCIAL DATABASE provides comprehensive information on the global institutional investment market. Information formatted to your precise needs is available from Nelson Information Mailing List & Customized Database service. The NELSON FINANCIAL DATABASE is comprised of:

30,000 executives at investment management firms

11,000 executives at research firms

100,000 executives at public companies

40,000 executives at plan sponsors

3,000 executives at pension fund consulting firms

24,000 executives at institutional real estate firms

4,000 executives at technology based vendors

The database also consists of extensive investment information, including money manager performance, peer group analysis, special surveys and more. For customers who with to use Nelson's information in their own systems, Nelson will supply customized data export, using all or any data items. Mailing lists are also available for direct marketers.For more information, contact Nelson Mailing List & Customized Database Services, P.O. Box 591, Port Chester, NY 10573 USA. (800) 333-6357, Phone outside the US (914) 937-8400, Fax (914) 937-8590, web site http://www.nelnet.com.

NEW SCIENTIST ON CD ROM contains five years of this science weekly. If you need to conduct a literature search to determine which companies are engaged in cutting edge research, or to locate people who have been quoted, you can conduct full text searches by keyword, author, and publication date and can display either a brief description or full text. Bowker-Saur. Updated quarterly. $795, excluding discounts. For more information visit Bowker Reed Reference's web site at http://www.reedref.com or contact: Bowker Reed Reference Electronic Publishing, 121 Chanlon Road, New Providence, NJ 07974 USA, Phone (800) 323-3288, Fax (908) 665-3528, email info@bowker.com.

SciTECH REFERENCE PLUS CD ROM contains directory information, 125,000 biographies of US and Canadian scientists and engineers from AMERICAN MEN AND WOMEN OF SCIENCE, listings for over 8,000 laboratories from the DIRECTORY OF AMERICAN RESEARCH AND TECHNOLOGY, and information from THE DIRECTORY OF CORPORATE AFFILIATIONS (including public, private and international companies) of leading US and international technology firms and their subsidiaries. It also contains 60,000 records on science/technology and medical serials from ULRICH'S INTERNATIONAL PERIODICALS DIRECTORY. Searches can be conducted by SIC, year founded, activity, education, employees, institution/company, city, state or country, memberships/honors, product description, personal statistics, personal title, research area, revenue. Updated annually. 1 year subscription $995, 3 years 2,836, excluding discounts. For more information visit Bowker Reed Reference's web site at http://www.reedref.com or contact: Bowker Reed Reference Electronic Publishing, 121 Chanlon Road, New Providence, NJ 07974 USA, Phone (800) 323-3288, Fax (908) 665-3528, email info@bowker.com.

SOFTWARE AND INFORMATION INDUSTRY ASSOCIATION (SIIA), 1730 M Street NW, Washington, DC 20036 was formed by a merger with the Information Industry Association (IIA) and the Software Publishers Association (SPA). (202) 452-1600. Visit their web site at www.siia.net to access their online membership directory free.

WHO'S WHO IN SCIENCE AND ENGINEERING, $259.95. National Register Publishing, Reed Elsevier-New Providence, 121 Chanlon Road, New Providence, NJ 07974, (800) 521-8110, fax (800) 836-7736, web site www.marquiswhoswho.com or www.redbooks.com. "If, for any reason whatsoever, your order does not fully meet your expectations, simply return the product within 30 days for a prompt, complete, unquestioned refund," as stated in Catalog of Biographical and Professional References of publisher Marquis Who's Who/National Register Publishing.

WORLD AVIATION DIRECTORY AND BUYER'S GUIDE is available as a hard copy directory, on CD ROM and as an Internet database. Some companies on the Internet even have email and web site links. Print directory $275, 2 issues per year; CD ROM $995. Published by Aviation Week, a Division of The McGraw-Hill Companies. McGraw Hill, Print Division, PO Box 629, Hightstown, NJ 08520, (800) 525-5003. McGraw Hill, Other Media Division (202) 383-2420, (800) 551-2015, extension 4. Web site: www.wadaviation.com.

WORLD GUIDE TO SCIENTIFIC ASSOCIATIONS AND LEARNED SOCIETIES encompasses international, national and regional associations in science, culture and technology. From K.G. Saur, $300. R.R. Bowker (a unit of Cahners Business Information), 121 Chanlon Road, New Providence, NJ 07974 USA, Phone (888) BOWKER2 (888-269-5372) & (800) 323-3288, fax (908) 508-7696, email info@bowker.com, web www.bowker.com. Canada—R.R. Bowker, Markham, Ontario, phone (888) BOWKER9 & (905) 415-5837, fax (905) 479-6266. German speaking Europe—K.G. Saur Verlag, Munich, Germany, phone 49-89-76902-232, fax 49-89-76902-250, email 100730.1341@compuserve.com, web www.saur.de/home.htm. Rest of Europe incl. United Kingdom plus Africa & Asia—Bowker-Saur, W. Sussex, UK, phone 44-1342-326-972, fax 44-1342-335-612, email customer@bowker-saur.co.uk, web www.bowker-saur.com/service/. Australia/New Zealand—Thorpe, Port Melbourne, Victoria, Australia, phone 61-03-9-245-7370, fax 61-03-9-245-7395, email customer.service@thorpe.com.au, web www.thorpe.com.au. Technical support for CD ROMs (800) 323-3288, fax 908) 665-3528, email techsupport@bowker.com.

www.americasemployers.com or America's Employers is a site mainly for positions in technology, finance and sales at approximately $50,000 to $100,000. Launched in 1995, it was developed by Career Relocation Corp of America in Armonk, New York.

www.career.com or Career.com links employers and candidates throughout the world. Heart's goals for www.career.com are to provide free job seeker assistance and to offer employers an effective way to reach qualified job seekers. Most positions are in Engineering, IT and marketing and usually range between $30,000 and $75,000. The site was launched in 1993 and developed by HEART Advertising Network, Los Altos, California.

www.ceweekly.com is the URL for Contract Employment Weekly, a site for the temporary technical industry. Positions are mainly in information technology, engineering and technical and are mostly in the $40,000 to $75,000 range. The site was developed by C.E. Publications, Inc., Bothell, Washington and has been online since 1994. Contract Employment Weekly Online is a service of C.E. Publications, Inc., P.O. Box 3006, Bothell, WA 98041-3006. (425) 806-5200, Fax (425) 806-5585, email publisher@ceweekly.com.

www.dice.com or DICE was ranked as one of the top 5 "Best Specialty Sites" by the *National Business Employment Weekly*. DICE specializes in information technology and high technology positions. One of the oldest employment sites on the Internet, DICE only accepts positions from recruiting firms. The site was developed by is D&L Online, Inc., Des Moines, Iowa and was launched in 1990.

www.emheadlines.com is the headline news service for the entertainment business. This Cahners Business Information web site provides information on Film, Television, Books, Technology, Music, Nielsen Ratings, Domestic Box Office, Bestseller List.

www.executiveagent.com is a web site that helps executive job seekers market their skills and experience to a targeted list of executive recruiters via email. ExecutiveAgent is completely confidential as resumes go directly to the search firms.

www.monster.com is the URL for the popular Monster Board web site. The Monster Board was ranked as one of the top 5 "Best General-Purpose Sites" by the *National Business Employment Weekly*. It is a major recruitment web site that spends millions of dollars in advertising to attract traffic to this site. Features include Job search in the US, International or by Companies, Career Center Events, Recruiters' Center, Seminars, Post a Job, free online recruitment seminar. It also offers special links for human resources, health care, technology and entry level positions. Toll free phone number (800) MONSTER. The Monster Board, PO Box 586, Framingham, MA 01704-0586. The site developer is TMP Worldwide, New York, New York and has been online since 1994.

www.rtp.org is the home page for Research Triangle Park, North Carolina . It includes a directory of companies in the Park and listing of companies according to research specialization, appropriate for target list development.

www.technicalrecruiter.com is a web site which is an excellent starting point for a large number of specialized technology sites, such as ProjectManager.com and SoftwareEngineer.com and others.

www.vjf.com is the URL for Westech Virtual Job Fair. It was ranked as one of the top 5 "Best Specialty Sites" by the *National Business Employment Weekly*. Westech Virtual Job Fair specializes in high tech positions which are listed by the companies. The site developer is Westech Expo Corp in Santa Clara, California, one of the largest sponsors of career fairs in the US. The site went online in 1994.

Telecommunications
See Information Technology, Satellites, Radio

BACON'S COMPUTER & HI-TECH MEDIA DIRECTORY identifies 6,500 contacts at 1,900 print and broadcast outlets, serving computers, data management, software, the Internet, electronics, telecommunications and more. $225. Ordering information: Call (800) 621-0561, (800) 753-6675. Bacon's Information, Inc., a K-III Communications Company, 332 South Michigan Avenue, Chicago, IL 60604. Satisfaction guaranteed or a full refund within 30 days.

CABLE TV & TELECOM YEARBOOK (UK), Phillips Business Information, Inc., a Phillips Publishing International Company, 120 Seven Locks Road, Potomac, MD 20854, (301) 340-1520, (301) 340-7788, (800) 777-5006, Internet pbi@phillips.com, web site www.phillips.com.

CED is a monthly magazine of broadband communications with an editorial focus on the new technologies shaping broadband and communications networks of the 21st century. Call publisher for price. Cahners Business Information, 600 South Cherry Street, Suite 400, Denver, CO 80222, (303) 393-7449 ext. 221, URL www.cedmagazine.com. Headquarters: Cahners Business Information, 275 Washington Street, Newton, MA 02158-1630, (617) 558-4663 or (617) 964-3030, fax (617) 558-4700, email marketaccess@cahners.com. Web sites www.cahners.com or www.chilton.net.

CELLULAR WORLDWIDE DIRECTORY, Phillips Business Information, Inc., a Phillips Publishing International Company, 120 Seven Locks Road, Potomac, MD 20854, (301) 340-1520, (301) 340-7788, (800) 777-5006, Internet pbi@phillips.com, web site www.phillips.com.

COMMUNICATIONS INDUSTRY BUYERS GUIDE, Phillips Business Information, Inc., a Phillips Publishing International Company, 120 Seven Locks Road, Potomac, MD 20854, (301) 340-1520, (301) 340-7788, (800) 777-5006, Internet pbi@phillips.com, web site www.phillips.com.

COMMUNICATIONS INDUSTRY DIRECTORY, Phillips Business Information, Inc., a Phillips Publishing International Company, 120 Seven Locks Road, Potomac, MD 20854, (301) 340-1520, (301) 340-7788, (800) 777-5006, Internet pbi@phillips.com, web site www.phillips.com.

COMPUTING, HI-TECH AND TELECOMMUNICATIONS CAREER HANDBOOK, published by Canadian publisher Marskell. Web site www.marskell.com.

CORPTECH DIRECTORY OF TECHNOLOGY COMPANIES is available in hard copy, Regional Guides, on PC disk, and on CD ROM. CorpTech EXPLORE Database is an outstanding reference that was awarded Best CD-ROM Directory by the National Directory Publishing Association. One click moves you from the CD ROM Database to Internet information on the same company. CorpTech also provides other sophisticated but reasonably priced automated services. You can save a tremendous amount of time researching relatively small, emerging new companies in various high technology niches and obtain names, titles and mailing address labels. CorpTech EXPLORE Database CD ROM $2,450 (including free soft cover

CorpTech Directory worth $545). Ordering Information: CorpTech, Corporate Technology Information Services, Inc., 12 Alfred Street, Suite 200, Woburn, MA 01801-1915. (800) 333-8036, (781) 932-3100, (781) 932-3939. Fax (781) 932-6335. Email sales@corptech.com. Web site http://www.corptech.com.

CYBERHOUND'S® GUIDE TO COMPANIES ON THE INTERNET reviews over 2,000 corporate sites, including major companies as well as those in the information industry, software and hardware developers and networking and telecommunications companies. It also includes a user's guide, a directory of specialized business we sites, a bibliography of Internet products, and a glossary of Internet terms. At the time of this writing 1st edition (1996) available from Gale for $79, reduced from $95. Published by Euromonitor (England). Distributed by Gale Group, P.O. Box 9187, Farmington Hills, MI 48333-9187. Toll free US and Canada (800) 877-GALE (4253) and (248) 699-GALE, fax (800) 414-5043 and (248) 699-8061, Internet orders galeord@galegroup.com, web site www.galegroup.com or www.gale.com. All Gale Group products are available on approval. Contact Gale for details.

DATA SOURCES. Volume 1, "Hardware" is comprised of 11,000 manufacturers of computers systems, graphics equipment, PC expansion boards, modems, LAN products, multiplexers, printers, disk and tape equipment, and terminals. Volume 2, :Software" is comprised of over 70,000 products including data communications and telecommunications software, database management systems software, software utilities and other application software packages. Listings include corporate officers, company name, address, phone, gross revenues, number of employees, products, and year established. Information is presented by function, then alphabetically with indexes by company, product, and a master subject index. Published semi-annually. $495 per year. Also available on CD ROM. Ordering information: DATA SOURCES, Information Access Company, One Park Avenue, New York, NY 10016, (800) 546-1223 and (212) 503-5398, fax (212) 502 5800.

DIRECTORY OF CALIFORNIA TECHNOLOGY COMPANIES identifies over 33,000 executive names and titles at over 12,000 companies, including research labs, telecommunications, biotechnology and software. Published annually by Database Publishing, PO Box 70024, Anaheim, CA 92825/1590 South Lewis Street, Anaheim, CA 92805. (800) 888-8434, (714) 778-6400, web site www.databasepublishing.com, email sales@databasepublishing.com. Directory $145, complete CD ROM $645, CD ROM one-year lease $425. Also distributed by Manufacturers' News, Inc., (888) 752-5200, 1633 Central Street, Evanston, IL 60201-1569. Email info@manufacturersnews.com. Web site www.manufacturersnews.com.

DIRECTORY OF CALIFORNIA WHOLESALERS AND SERVICE COMPANIES identifies over 85,000 names and titles of executives at some 34,000 non-manufacturing firms, such as wholesalers, transportation, telecommunications, video production and software, including web sites and email addresses. Annual directory published by Database Publishing, $169. Complete CD ROM $925, One year CD ROM lease, $595. Distributed by Manufacturers' News, Inc., (888) 752-5200, 1633 Central Street, Evanston, IL 60201-1569. Email info@manufacturersnews.com. Web site www.manufacturersnews.com.

DUN & BRADSTREET AND GALE INDUSTRY REFERENCE HANDBOOKS offer a line of industry-specific sourcebooks which include key companies in the industry, ranked lists of companies, professional associations, trade shows and conferences, mergers and acquisitions, consultants who service those industries, information sources, and more. 6 volume set $495. Also available individually for $99: Pharmaceuticals, Health and Medical Services, Computers and Software, Banking and Finance, Telecommunications, Agriculture and Food, Insurance, Construction, Entertainment, Hospitality. First edition available December, 1999. Gale Group, P.O. Box 9187, Farmington Hills, MI 48333-9187. Toll free US and Canada (800) 877-GALE (4253) and (248) 699-GALE, fax (800) 414-5043 and (248) 699-8061, Internet orders galeord@galegroup.com, web site www.galegroup.com or www.gale.com. All Gale Group products are available on approval. Contact Gale for details.

ELSEVIER ADVANCED TECHNOLOGY is a leading supplier of Electronics industry information. They publish a CD-ROM of a complete database of electronics companies in Europe, developed in conjunction with THE EUROPEAN ELECTRONICS DIRECTORY: COMPONENTS AND SUB-ASSEMBLIES AND SYSTEMS AND APPLICATIONS.

Elsevier also publishes yearbooks, directories, market research reports and industrial journals, technical handbooks and newsletters, such as PROFILE OF THE WORLDWIDE TELECOMMUNICATIONS INDUSTRY, PROFILE OF THE WORLDWIDE CAPACITOR INDUSTRY, PROFILE OF THE WORLDWIDE SEMICONDUCTOR INDUSTRY, and PROFILE OF THE EUROPEAN CONNECTOR

INDUSTRY. For more information contact: Elsevier Advanced Technology, P.O. Box 150, Kidlington, Oxford, OX5 1AS, England. Phone (44) (0) 1865 843-848, fax (44) (0) 1865 843-971.

EUROPEAN TELECOMMUNICATIONS, Phillips Business Information, Inc., a Phillips Publishing International Company, 120 Seven Locks Road, Potomac, MD 20854, (301) 340-1520, (301) 340-7788, (800) 777-5006, Internet pbi@phillips.com, web site www.phillips.com.

GLOBAL WIRELESS is a trade publication which comes out 6 times a year. trade publication. Crain Communications, Inc. is headquartered in Chicago with offices in major cities throughout the US plus London, Tokyo and Frankfurt. New York location: 220 East 42nd Street, New York, NY 10017, (212) 210-0100, Circulation (800) 678-9595. Annual subscription $39. Web site www.globalwirelessnews.com.

INFORMATION SOURCES was an award winning directory published by the Gale Group in partnership with the Information Industry Association (IIA). At the time of this writing, the IIA has merged with the Software Publishers Association (SPA) to form the newly named Software and Information Industry Association (SIIA).

This directory provides information for the 550 member companies of the Information Industry Association. Entries include company name, address, phone, names of executives, regional offices, trade and brand names and description of products and services. Indexed by product, personal name, trade name, geography, parent company, international, and niche markets. The directory also identifies publishers, database producers, online services, telecommunications and network providers, system integrators and many others. $125. Contact Gale for information as to when an updated directory will be available. In the meantime, visit the Software and Information Industry's web site at www.siia.net to see their membership roster.

Gale Group, P.O. Box 9187, Farmington Hills, MI 48333-9187. Toll free US and Canada (800) 877-GALE (4253) and (248) 699-GALE, fax (800) 414-5043 and (248) 699-8061, Internet orders galeord@galegroup.com, web site www.galegroup.com or www.gale.com. All Gale Group products are available on approval. Contact Gale for details.

Software & Information Industry Association (SIIA), formerly the Software Publishers Association (SPA) and Information Industry Association (IIA) is located at 1730 M Street, NW, Washington, DC 20036, (202) 452-1600, www.siia.net.

MAJOR TELECOMMUNICATIONS COMPANIES OF EUROPE contains information and contacts for 1,100 major telecommunications companies and their equipment suppliers in western Europe, central Europe and eastern Europe. $415. US distributor: Larry Meranus Professional Publications & Services, 4 Demoray Court, Pine Brook, NJ 07058, (800) MERANUS or (800) 637-2687. Published by Graham & Whiteside Ltd., Tuition House, 5-6 Francis Grove, London SW19 4DT, England. Web site http://www.major-co-data.com. Email sales@major-co-data.com.

MAJOR TELECOMMUNICATIONS COMPANIES OF THE FAR EAST & AUSTRALASIA contains information on 1,000 top telecommunications companies and their Asia Pacific equipment suppliers. $415. US distributor: Larry Meranus Professional Publications & Services, 4 Demoray Court, Pine Brook, NJ 07058, (800) MERANUS or (800) 637-2687. Published by Graham & Whiteside Ltd., Tuition House, 5-6 Francis Grove, London SW19 4DT, England. Web site http://www.major-co-data.com. Email sales@major-co-data.com.

MAJOR TELECOMMUNICATIONS COMPANIES OF THE WORLD—INCLUDING MAJOR INTERNET COMPANIES provides information on 3,700 companies, including 600 international companies involved in the Internet. $830. US distributor: Larry Meranus Professional Publications & Services, 4 Demoray Court, Pine Brook, NJ 07058, (800) MERANUS or (800) 637-2687. Published by Graham & Whiteside Ltd., Tuition House, 5-6 Francis Grove, London SW19 4DT, England. Web site http://www.major-co-data.com. Email sales@major-co-data.com.

PHILLIPS BUSINESS INFORMATION provides information in newsletters, magazines, directories and on multiple web sites covering a range of topics, such as magazine products, telecommunications and cable products, satellite products, media, new media and Internet products, marketing and public relations products, financial technology and electronic commerce, aviation and defense products. For more information, contact: Phillips Business Information, Inc., a Phillips Publishing International Company, 120 Seven Locks Road,

Potomac, MD 20854, (301) 340-1520, (301) 340-7788, (800) 777-5006, Internet pbi@phillips.com, web site www.phillips.com.

TELECOMMUNICATIONS DIRECTORY includes information on over 2,500 national and international communications systems and services, including providers of telephone lines, local area networks, teleconferencing, videotext and teletext, electronic mail, facsimile, Internet access, voicemail, satellite and electronic transactional services. Also includes associations, a glossary, and four indexes. $400. Gale Group, P.O. Box 9187, Farmington Hills, MI 48333-9187. Toll free US and Canada (800) 877-GALE (4253) and (248) 699-GALE, fax (800) 414-5043 and (248) 699-8061, Internet orders galeord@galegroup.com, web site www.galegroup.com or www.gale.com. All Gale Group products are available on approval. Contact Gale for details.

WIRELESS WEEK is a weekly newspaper serving the cellular, PCS, paging and mobile radio industry. Also publishes an annual directory. Call for prices. Cahners Business Information, 600 South Cherry Street, Suite 400, Denver CO 80222, (303) 393-7449 ext. 277, fax (303) 399-2034, email tbrooksh@chilton.net, URL www.wirelessweek.com. Headquarters: Cahners Business Information, 275 Washington Street, Newton, MA 02158-1630, (617) 558-4663 or (617) 964-3030, fax (617) 558-4700, email marketaccess@cahners.com. Web sites www.cahners.com or www.chilton.net.

www.ceweekly.com is the URL for Contract Employment Weekly, a site for the temporary technical industry. Positions are mainly in information technology, engineering and technical and are mostly in the $40,000 to $75,000 range. The site was developed by C.E. Publications, Inc., Bothell, Washington and has been online since 1994. Contract Employment Weekly Online is a service of C.E. Publications, Inc., P.O. Box 3006, Bothell, WA 98041-3006. (425) 806-5200, Fax (425) 806-5585, email publisher@ceweekly.com.

www.technicalrecruiter.com is a web site which is an excellent starting point for a large number of specialized technology sites, such as ProjectManager.com and SoftwareEngineer.com and others.

Telecommuting Positions

www.tjobs.com is the URL for Telecommuting Jobs, which connects people to positions at home or otherwise using off site electronic facilities. Most positions are in programming, sales and writing. The site was developed by Levine Communications, Winnetka, Illinois and was launched in 1996.

Telephone Books

CYBERHOUND'S® GUIDE TO PEOPLE ON THE INTERNET is organized into three sections. (1) Who's Who Online identifies 1,000 online directories, databases and membership listings. For example, it lists Architects in Canada, Attorney Finder, Famous Left-Handers, and The Missing Persons Pages. (2) White Pages provides and alphabetical listing of 3,000 business professionals who are accessible by email. Other information includes area of expertise, personal and professional affiliation and company information. (3) Personal Web Sites are organized alphabetically by name. 1,500 pages of people in the news in business, entertainment, and sports. $79. Gale Group, P.O. Box 9187, Farmington Hills, MI 48333-9187. Toll free US and Canada (800) 877-GALE (4253) and (248) 699-GALE, fax (800) 414-5043 and (248) 699-8061, Internet orders galeord@galegroup.com, web site www.galegroup.com or www.gale.com. All Gale Group products are available on approval. Contact Gale for details.

ELECTRONICS INDUSTRY TELEPHONE DIRECTORY (EITD) is an industry phone directory that lists over 30,000 company locations and 3,000 product types in the electronics industry. Published annually. Available in hard copy for $55 from Harris InfoSource, 2057 East Aurora Road, Twinsburg, OH 44087-1999, (330) 425-9000, (800) 888-5900, www.HarrisInfo.com. Also available from Cahners Business Information, 201 King of Prussia Road, Radnor, PA 19089, (610) 964-4345, fax (610) 964-4348, email jbreck@chilton.net, URL www.ecnmag.com/eitd. Headquarters: Cahners Business Information, 275 Washington Street, Newton, MA 02158-1630, (617) 558-4663 or (617) 964-3030, fax (617) 558-4700, email marketaccess@cahners.com. Web sites www.cahners.com or www.chilton.net.

MEXICO BUSINESS COMMUNICATIONS AND FAX DIRECTORY or CD lists over 11,000 businesses, over 5,000 associations and chambers of commerce, plus a listing of Mexican government departments and Canadian and US embassies and consulates in Mexico. Section 1 lists government offices. Section 2 lists businesses alphabetically by company. Section 3 lists companies by business category. A listing of city codes, maps, historical information and a list of the top 100 companies in Mexico is also included. Published annually. Directory $179.95, CD $229.95. Ordering information: Scott's Directories, Toronto area: 1450 Don Mills Road, Don Mills, Ontario, M3B 2X7, CANADA, (888) 709-9907, (416) 442-2291, (416) 932-9555. Montréal area: Scott's Directories, 3300 Cote Verde, Suite 410 Ville St.-Laurent, Quebec H4B 2B7 CANADA (514) 339-1397, (800) 363-1327, email scotts@southam.ca.

NATIONAL DIRECTORY OF ADDRESSES AND TELEPHONE NUMBERS contains addresses and phone numbers for major US companies, arranged alphabetically and by SIC or NAICS codes. Includes special information on hotels, banks, government information, area codes for US cities, transportation, colleges and more. Published annually. $95. Omnigraphics, Inc., Penobscot Building, Detroit, Michigan 48226, (313) 961-1340.

NATIONAL E-MAIL AND FAX DIRECTORY provides over 180,000 fax numbers for US companies, organizations and government agencies, cross referenced by subject. $126. Gale Group, P.O. Box 9187, Farmington Hills, MI 48333-9187. Toll free US and Canada (800) 877-GALE (4253) and (248) 699-GALE, fax (800) 414-5043 and (248) 699-8061, Internet orders galeord@galegroup.com, web site www.galegroup.com or www.gale.com. All Gale Group products are available on approval. Contact Gale for details.

PHONE BOOKS can be terrific research tools. Remember the yellow pages, the white pages, and toll free directories, which can minimize the phone bill.

SELECTPHONE is a national telephone directory on CD ROM. They offer a range of products at different prices. For more information, call them at (800) 992-3766 or visit their web site at www.infousa.com. SelectPhone is a product of Pro CD, Inc., 5711 South 86th Circle, Omaha, NE 68127.

www.info@telecom.co.nz is a New Zealand phone book on the Internet.

www.infousa.com provides free US national directory assistance.

www.websitez.com is the URL to a web site that assists in finding any web address in the world.

www.whitepages.com.au/ is the web site address for Australian white pages. I found it by first going to www.askjeeves.com and asking "How can I find someone in Australia?"

Television

See Cable

BACON'S RADIO/TV/CABLE DIRECTORY is a two volume set that identifies all US national and regional networks, all US broadcast stations, management and news executives, radio and TV syndicators, including programming staff, detailed show listings, over 100,000 names of contacts, an index of show subjects and more. $275. Ordering information: Call (800) 621-0561, (800) 753-6675. Bacon's Information, Inc., a K-III Communications Company, 332 South Michigan Avenue, Chicago, IL 60604. Satisfaction guaranteed or a full refund within 30 days.

BROADCASTING AND CABLE YEARBOOK contains information on radio, TV and cable including information about trade associations, trade shows, broadcasting education, awards, industry related books, magazines, videos and more. Also includes information of direct broadcast satellites, Multichannel Multipoint Distribution Services (MMDS), wireless cable companies and more. $179.95.

R.R. Bowker (a unit of Cahners Business Information), 121 Chanlon Road, New Providence, NJ 07974 USA, Phone (888) BOWKER2 (888-269-5372) & (800) 323-3288, fax (908) 508-7696, email info@bowker.com, web www.bowker.com. Canada—R.R. Bowker, Markham, Ontario, phone (888) BOWKER9 & (905) 415-5837, fax (905) 479-6266. German speaking Europe—K.G. Saur Verlag, Munich, Germany, phone 49-89-76902-232, fax 49-89-76902-250, email 100730.1341@compuserve.com, web www.saur.de/home.htm. Rest of Europe incl. United Kingdom plus Africa & Asia—Bowker-Saur, W. Sussex, UK, phone 44-1342-326-972, fax 44-1342-335-612, email customer@bowker-saur.co.uk, web www.bowker-saur.com/service/. Australia/New Zealand—Thorpe, Port Melbourne, Victoria, Australia, phone 61-03-9-245-7370, fax 61-03-9-

245-7395, email customer.service@thorpe.com.au, web www.thorpe.com.au. Technical support for CD ROMs (800) 323-3288, fax 908) 665-3528, email techsupport@bowker.com.

GALE DIRECTORY OF PUBLICATIONS AND BROADCAST MEDIA identifies key personnel, feature editors and more at radio and TV stations and cable companies. $615 for 5 volume set. Gale Group, P.O. Box 9187, Farmington Hills, MI 48333-9187. Toll free US and Canada (800) 877-GALE (4253) and (248) 699-GALE, fax (800) 414-5043 and (248) 699-8061, Internet orders galeord@galegroup.com, web site www.galegroup.com or www.gale.com. All Gale Group products are available on approval. Contact Gale for details.

GALE DIRECTORY OF PUBLICATIONS AND BROADCAST MEDIA ONLINE is a GaleNet resource on the Internet that includes information on 64,000 newspapers, periodicals, newsletters, industry directories, television and radio stations, including names of key personnel. Contact the library to access this reference free. For pricing and ordering information, contact: Gale Group, P.O. Box 9187, Farmington Hills, MI 48333-9187. Toll free US and Canada (800) 877-GALE (4253) and (248) 699-GALE, fax (800) 414-5043 and (248) 699-8061, Internet orders galeord@galegroup.com, web site www.galegroup.com or www.gale.com. All Gale Group products are available on approval. Contact Gale for details.

KEMPS FILM, TV & VIDEO HANDBOOK is a directory for the production and post production sectors of the industry. Published annually. Call publisher for price. Cahners Business Information, 34-35 Newman Street, London W1P 3PD England. (011) 44 171 637-3663, fax (011) 44 171 580-5559. Headquarters: Cahners Business Information, 275 Washington Street, Newton, MA 02158-1630, (617) 558-4663 or (617) 964-3030, fax (617) 558-4700, email marketaccess@cahners.com. Web sites www.cahners.com or www.chilton.net.

LITERARY MARKET PLACE, "The Directory of the American Book Publishing Industry With Industry Yellow Pages" is an excellent 3 volume directory with comprehensive information on US book publishers; imprints, subsidiaries and distributors; book trade acquisitions and mergers, small presses, Canadian book publishers, micropublishers, US electronic publishers, electronic publishing consultants, electronic publishing products and services, editorial services, literary agents, illustrations agents, US agents and offices of foreign publishers, lecture agents, specialized advertising and public relations firms, direct mail specialists, mailing list brokers and services, book review syndicates, book review and index journals and services, book exhibits, book clubs, book lists and catalogs, book importers and exporters, book producers, translators, artists, photographers, stock photo agencies, associations, book trade events and conferences, awards, contents and grants, reference books for the trade, magazines for the trade, a toll free directory of publishers, magazine and newspaper publicity, radio and television publicity, book manufacturing services, book distributors and sales representatives, and wholesalers. $189.95.

LITERARY MARKET PLACE ON DISC, previously titled LITERARY MARKET PLACE PLUS CD ROM, one year subscription $297.00.

LITERARY MARKET PLACE—INTERNET EDITION, www.literarymarketplace.com, is available by subscription.

INTERNATIONAL LITERARY MARKET PLACE Internet database can be directly accessed at www.iliterarymarketplace.com. It is also linked to the US domestic LITERARY MARKET PLACE web site at www.literarymarketplace.com. Contact the publisher for subscription price. INTERNATIONAL LITERARY MARKET PLACE, hard copy $189.95.

R.R. Bowker (a unit of Cahners Business Information), 121 Chanlon Road, New Providence, NJ 07974 USA, Phone (888) BOWKER2 (888-269-5372) & (800) 323-3288, fax (908) 508-7696, email info@bowker.com, web www.bowker.com. Canada—R.R. Bowker, Markham, Ontario, phone (888) BOWKER9 & (905) 415-5837, fax (905) 479-6266. German speaking Europe—K.G. Saur Verlag, Munich, Germany, phone 49-89-76902-232, fax 49-89-76902-250, email 100730.1341@compuserve.com, web www.saur.de/home.htm. Rest of Europe incl. United Kingdom plus Africa & Asia—Bowker-Saur, W. Sussex, UK, phone 44-1342-326-972, fax 44-1342-335-612, email customer@bowker-saur.co.uk, web www.bowker-saur.com/service/. Australia/New Zealand—Thorpe, Port Melbourne, Victoria, Australia, phone 61-03-9-245-7370, fax 61-03-9-245-7395, email customer.service@thorpe.com.au, web www.thorpe.com.au. Technical support for CD ROMs (800) 323-3288, fax 908) 665-3528, email techsupport@bowker.com.

STANDARD RATE AND DATA PUBLICATIONS includes "Radio Advertising Source" and "Television and Cable Source" and direct marketing information. $354 annual subscription. Standard Rate and Data Service, Inc., 3004 Glenview Road, Wilmette, IL 60091, (708) 441-2210 in Illinois, (800) 323-4601.

TALK SHOW SELECTS identifies the top 750 local and national TV and radio talk shows. Hard copy $185. Floppy disk and book, $260. Published by Broadcast Interview Source, 2233 Wisconsin Avenue, NW, Suite 540, Washington, DC 20007. (800) 955-0311, (202) 333-4904.

TELEVISION ASIA is a Singapore based publication that covers the Asian television industry. Call publisher for prices. Cahners Business Information, 58A Smith Street, Singapore 058962, (011) 65-223-8823, fax (011) 65-220-5015, email jonnypim@pacific.net.sg and rschatz@cahners.com, URL home1.pacific.net.sg/~tvasia. Headquarters: Cahners Business Information, 275 Washington Street, Newton, MA 02158-1630, (617) 558-4663 or (617) 964-3030, fax (617) 558-4700, email marketaccess@cahners.com. Web sites www.cahners.com or www.chilton.net.

TELEVISION EUROPE is a London based publication that covers the European television industry. Call publisher for price. Cahners Business Information, 6 Bell Yard, London WC2 A1EJ, England, (011) 44 171 520-5285, fax (011) 44 171 520-5226, email jonnypim@pacific.net.sg and rschatz@cahners.com. Headquarters: Cahners Business Information, 275 Washington Street, Newton, MA 02158-1630, (617) 558-4663 or (617) 964-3030, fax (617) 558-4700, email marketaccess@cahners.com. Web sites www.cahners.com or www.chilton.net.

TELEVISION INTERNATIONAL is a magazine for cable TV, radio, satellite and interactive multimedia industries around the world. Call publisher for price. Cahners Business Information, 245 West 17th Street, New York, NY 10011-5300, (212) 337-6944, fax (212) 337-6948, email jonnypim@pacific.net.sg and rschatz@cahners.com, URL www.cahners.com/mainmag/bci.htm. Headquarters: Cahners Business Information, 275 Washington Street, Newton, MA 02158-1630, (617) 558-4663 or (617) 964-3030, fax (617) 558-4700, email marketaccess@cahners.com. Web sites www.cahners.com or www.chilton.net.

www.emheadlines.com is the headline news service for the entertainment business. This Cahners Business Information web site provides information on Film, Television, Books, Technology, Music, Nielsen Ratings, Domestic Box Office, Bestseller List.

Temporary

DIRECTORY OF TEMPORARY PLACEMENT FIRMS for Executives, Managers & Professionals profiles over 1,900 firms that focus on placing high-level talent. Arranged geographically and indexed by job functions, industries, and key principals. $39.95. Published by Kennedy Information, One Kennedy Place, Route 12 South, Fitzwilliam, NH 03447, phone (800) 531-0007 or 603-585-6544, fax 603-585-9555, email bookstore@kennedyinfo.con, web site www.kennedyinfo.com.

www.ceweekly.com is the URL for Contract Employment Weekly, a site for the temporary technical industry. Positions are mainly in information technology, engineering and technical and are mostly in the $40,000 to $75,000 range. The site was developed by C.E. Publications, Inc., Bothell, Washington and has been online since 1994. Contract Employment Weekly Online is a service of C.E. Publications, Inc., P.O. Box 3006, Bothell, WA 98041-3006. (425) 806-5200, Fax (425) 806-5585, email publisher@ceweekly.com.

www.joblynx.com is a site that connects recruiters with people seeking full time, part time and contract positions at all levels, starting at $50,000 and exceeding $100,000. Many positions are posted in IT, management and sales and marketing. The site was developed by JobLynx, Green Bay, Wisconsin. It was launched in 1996.

www.ntes.com is the URL for the Contract Employment Connection, a web site for contract professionals in the temporary professional job market. Most positions are in engineering, computer science and management, mainly in the $50,000 to $100,000 range. The site was developed by National Technical Employment Services, Scottsboro, Alabama and was launched in 1993.

Thailand

See Asia, International

KEY BUSINESS DIRECTORY OF INDONESIA/PHILIPPINES/THAILAND contains information on 4,000 companies with more than 50 employees. Dun & Bradstreet, Business Reference Solutions, Three Sylvan Way, Parsippany, NJ 07054 USA. (800) 526-0651. Email dnbmdd@mail.dnb.com. Web site http://www.dnbmdd.com.

Thrift Institutions

AMERICAN FINANCIAL DIRECTORY consists of five desktop volumes of banks, bank holding companies, savings and Loan Associations and Major Credit Unions in the US, Canada and Mexico. It includes information on head office and branch offices, names of key decision makers, phone and fax numbers, financial summaries, and structural changes such as mergers, name changes and closings. Published twice a year. For more information contact (800) 321-3373, Thomson Financial Publishing, 4709 West Golf Road, Skokie, IL 60076-1253. Web site @ tfp.bankinfo.com.

AMERICAN FINANCIAL DIRECTORY CUSTOMIZED DIRECTORIES are available for any state of combination of states for banks, bank holding companies, savings and loans and major credit unions. For more information contact (800) 321-3373, Thomson Financial Publishing, 4709 West Golf Road, Skokie, IL 60076-1253. Web site @ tfp.bankinfo.com.

AMERICAN FINANCIAL DIRECTORY REGIONAL DIRECTORIES include banks, bank holding companies, savings and loan associations and major credit unions. Published twice a year. One volume:

- SOUTHERN BANKERS DIRECTORY covers Alabama, Arkansas, District of Columbia, Florida, Georgia, Kentucky, Louisiana, Maryland, Mississippi, North Carolina, South Carolina, Tennessee, Virginia and West Virginia. Published twice a year.

- GOLDEN STATES FINANCIAL DIRECTORY includes Alaska, Arizona, California, Colorado, Hawaii, Idaho, Montana, Nevada, New Mexico, Oregon, Utah, Washington, and Wyoming. Published twice a year.

- UPPER MIDWEST FINANCIAL DIRECTORY includes Michigan, Minnesota, Montana, North Dakota, South Dakota and Wisconsin. Published once a year.

- SOUTHWESTERN FINANCIAL DIRECTORY includes Arkansas, Louisiana, New Mexico, Oklahoma and Texas. Published twice a year.

For more information contact (800) 321-3373, Thomson Financial Publishing, 4709 West Golf Road, Skokie, IL 60076-1253. Web site @ tfp.bankinfo.com.

POLK NORTH AMERICAN FINANCIAL INSTITUTIONS DIRECTORY includes information on banks, savings and loan associations and major credit unions in North America, including head office and branch offices,names of key decision makers, address, phone and fax, financial summaries, maps, and structural changes such as mergers, name changes, and closings. Published twice a year. For more information contact (800) 321-3373, Thomson Financial Publishing, 4709 West Golf Road, Skokie, IL 60076-1253. Web site @ tfp.bankinfo.com.

THOMSON SAVINGS DIRECTORY identifies savings and loan associations and savings banks in the US. Listings include names of key decision makers, address, phone, fax, branch offices, 3 years' information on structural histories, 2 years of financial statistic, breakdown of mortgage portfolio and more. Published twice year. For more information contact (800) 321-3373, Thomson Financial Publishing, 4709 West Golf Road, Skokie, IL 60076-1253. Web site @ tfp.bankinfo.com.

Toiletries

See Consumer Marketing

ADVERTISER AND AGENCY RED BOOKS PLUS CD ROM combines all the information in THE STANDARD DIRECTORY OF ADVERTISERS, THE STANDARD DIRECTORY OF ADVERTISING AGENCIES and THE STANDARD DIRECTORY OF INTERNATIONAL ADVERTISERS AND AGENCIES. Information is searchable by 25 fields, including company name, personal name, job title/function, product type, product/account name, city, state, zip or country, area code, revenues, number of employees, outside ad agency and even type of computer hardware. Contains professional association information. Available for Windows and Macintosh. Updated quarterly. 1 year subscription $1,295. If the price is prohibitively high, remember your local library. National Register Publishing, Reed Elsevier-New Providence, 121 Chanlon Road, New Providence, NJ 07974, (800) 521-8110, fax (800) 836-7736, web site www.redbooks.com or www.marquiswhoswho.com. "If, for any reason whatsoever, your order does not fully meet your expectations, simply return the product within 30 days for a prompt, complete, unquestioned refund," as stated in Catalog of Biographical and Professional References of publisher Marquis Who's Who/National Register Publishing.

ADVERTISING AGE is a weekly trade paper. Inquire about their 100 Leading National Advertisers issue, an annual survey which identifies names and titles of employees at large consumer marketing companies. 1 year subscription $109, 2 years $175. web site www.adage.com. Crain Communications, Inc. is headquartered in Chicago with offices in major cities throughout the US plus London, Tokyo and Frankfurt. New York location: 220 East 42nd Street, New York, NY 10017, (212) 210-0100, Circulation (800) 678-9595.

STANDARD DIRECTORY OF ADVERTISERS Business Classifications Edition is an excellent general directory that organizes companies by a wide range of product categories. A few examples include "Apparel 2—Men's and Boys' Wear," "Heating and Air Conditioning," "Cosmetics and Toiletries," and "Aviation and Aerospace." This directory lists names and titles of key officers, revenues and other information. It is available in a geographic edition for the same price. This directory is comprised of over 24,000 companies that annually spend over $200,000 on advertising. It represents a reasonable place to look for hard-to-find information about privately held companies, especially those that heavily advertise their products. It is a good place to look for names if STANDARD AND POORS and the MILLION DOLLAR DIRECTORY fail to yield the names you need. Finally, the Classified Edition of THE STANDARD DIRECTORY OF ADVERTISERS can be a very convenient source of research because both your target list of companies and the corresponding names and titles of management all appear together, in the same Classification. This is important if you still rely on research books in hard copy. THE STANDARD DIRECTORY OF ADVERTISERS also publishes a special volume called THE STANDARD DIRECTORY OF ADVERTISERS TRADENAME INDEX. You can use the TRADENAME INDEX if you know the brand name of a product and need to find the company that manufactures it. In addition, this directory contains an Associations section which identifies marketing oriented associations.

$599 hard copy. If the price is prohibitively high, remember your local library. THE STANDARD DIRECTORY OF ADVERTISERS is also available on CD ROM under the title ADVERTISER AND AGENCY RED BOOKS PLUS. It is available in Windows® and Macintosh® formats. National Register Publishing, Reed Elsevier-New Providence, 121 Chanlon Road, New Providence, NJ 07974, (800) 521-8110, fax (800) 836-7736, web site www.redbooks.com or www.marquiswhoswho.com. "If, for any reason whatsoever, your order does not fully meet your expectations, simply return the product within 30 days for a prompt, complete, unquestioned refund," as stated in Catalog of Biographical and Professional References of publisher Marquis Who's Who/National Register Publishing.

WORLD COSMETICS AND TOILETRIES DIRECTORY includes products in fragrances, skincare, oral hygiene, shower additives, baby care and more. $990. Published by Euromonitor (England). Distributed by Gale Group, P.O. Box 9187, Farmington Hills, MI 48333-9187. Toll free US and Canada (800) 877-GALE (4253) and (248) 699-GALE, fax (800) 414-5043 and (248) 699-8061, Internet orders galeord@galegroup.com, web site www.galegroup.com or www.gale.com. All Gale Group products are available on approval. Contact Gale for details.

Toronto

See Canada

GREATER TORONTO BUSINESS DIRECTORY is a 2 volume directory which identifies over 56,000 executive names and titles at some 30,000 companies. Volume 1 is comprised of Metropolitan Toronto engaged in contracting, jobbers, transportation, law, finance and retail. Volume 2, Metro Toronto Boundary covers surrounding Toronto from Brampton to Richmond Hill to Whitby. $249 for both volumes, $141 apiece. Published annually by Scott's Directories. Distributed by Manufacturers' News, Inc., (888) 752-5200, 1633 Central Street, Evanston, IL 60201-1569. Email info@manufacturersnews.com. Web site www.manufacturersnews.com.

Tourism

See Travel

AMERICAN SOCIETY OF TRAVEL AGENTS (ASTA) is a major professional association which can provide information about surveys, directories and so forth. For more information about this and other travel organizations, refer to one of the references listed under "References—Librarian" such as BUSINESS INFORMATION SOURCES by Lorna Daniells, ENCYCLOPEDIA OF BUSINESS INFORMATION SOURCES, and the ENCYCLOPEDIA OF ASSOCIATIONS.

CANADIAN ALMANAC AND DIRECTORY includes abbreviations, associations and societies, broadcasting and communications, business statistics, church and religious organizations, commerce and finance, cultural directory, education directory, electoral districts, foreign and international contacts, geographic information, government directory, government quick reference, health and hospitals, historical and general information, legal and judicial directory, postal information, tourism and transportation. The Almanac also includes web sites of significant institutions in business, communications, and the arts, a "Who's Who" of key officials and organizations on the Canadian information highway and up-to-date provincial and territorial election results. Indexed by titles and keyword. $249 US. Inquire about CD ROM availability. Published by IHS Canada, Micromedia Limited, 20 Victoria Street, Toronto, Ontario M5C 2N8 CANADA, (800) 387-2689, (416) 362-5211, fax (416) 362-6161, email info@micromedia.on.ca. Distributed in the US by the Gale Group, P.O. Box 9187, Farmington Hills, MI 48333-9187. Toll free US and Canada (800) 877-GALE (4253) and (248) 699-GALE, fax (800) 414-5043 and (248) 699-8061, Internet orders galeord@galegroup.com, web site www.galegroup.com or www.gale.com. All Gale Group products are available on approval. Contact Gale for details.

CONSUMER REPORTS TRAVEL LETTER is published by Consumers Union, a nonprofit independent organization providing consumers with information and advice on goods, services, health and personal finance. No advertising is accepted. $39/year subscription. Single copy $5. Flash By Fax releases late breaking news that would otherwise miss Consumer Reports Travel Letter. It also reveals short term deals on travel, especially airfare. To order Flash By Fax, call 800-559-8905 for 12 issues @ $25 per year. For more information contact Consumer Reports Travel Letter, Ed Perkins, Editor, Consumers Union, 101 Truman Avenue, Yonkers, NY 10703-1057, (800) 234-1970, (914) 378-2740.

ENCYCLOPEDIA OF ASSOCIATIONS: INTERNATIONAL ORGANIZATIONS includes nearly 20,000 multinational and national organizations in foreign countries, including US based associations with multinational membership. Entries also include email addresses, web sites and bulletin board addresses, lobbying activities, and publication and convention information. Indexed by geography, keyword and executives. $595 for 2 volume set. Also available in CD ROM. Database available via commercial online service. Gale Group, P.O. Box 9187, Farmington Hills, MI 48333-9187. Toll free US and Canada (800) 877-GALE (4253) and (248) 699-GALE, fax (800) 414-5043 and (248) 699-8061, Internet orders galeord@galegroup.com, web site www.galegroup.com or www.gale.com. All Gale Group products are available on approval. Contact Gale for details.

ENCYCLOPEDIA OF ASSOCIATIONS: NATIONAL ORGANIZATIONS OF THE US. This superb reference is one of the first places you should look when beginning a new recruiting assignment or when looking for specialized references of any type. The keyword index makes this comprehensive reference easy to use, even in hard copy. For over 23,000 nonprofit professional associations with a national scope, this encyclopedia reveals:

- Publications, including membership rosters and newsletters

- Dates and locations of association conferences and conventions

- Names of Executive Directors, who are usually incredible sources of industry information if you call and speak to them

- Committees

- Job and candidate referral banks, which can provide resumes of other industry sources and sometimes candidates

- It includes organizations in these categories: business, trade, environmental, agricultural, legal, governmental, engineering, technological, scientific, educational, cultural, social welfare, health & medical, public affairs, ethnic, labor unions, chambers of commerce, tourism, & others.

> Volume 1, National Organizations of the US, $505
> Volume 2, Geographic and Executive Indexes, $390
> Volume 3, Supplement, $405

Gale Group, P.O. Box 9187, Farmington Hills, MI 48333-9187. Toll free US and Canada (800) 877-GALE (4253) and (248) 699-GALE, fax (800) 414-5043 and (248) 699-8061, Internet orders galeord@galegroup.com, web site www.galegroup.com or www.gale.com. All Gale Group products are available on approval. Contact Gale for details.

ENCYCLOPEDIA OF ASSOCIATIONS: REGIONAL, STATE AND LOCAL ORGANIZATIONS. The information in this directory is not duplicated anywhere in ENCYCLOPEDIA OF ASSOCIATIONS. Over 100,000 nonprofit organizations are included in this directory. $585 for 5 volume set or $140 per individual volume. Also available on CD ROM and online on the Internet through a GaleNet subscription.

> Volume 1, Great Lakes States (Illinois, Indiana, Michigan, Minnesota, Ohio, Wisconsin)
> Volume 2, Northeastern States (Connecticut, Maine, Massachusetts, New Hampshire, New Jersey, New York, Pennsylvania, Rhode Islands, Vermont)
> Volume 3, Southern and Middle Atlantic States (Including Puerto Rico and the Virgin Islands) (Alabama, Delaware, Washington, DC, Florida, Georgia, Kentucky, Maryland, Mississippi, North Carolina, Puerto Rico, South Carolina, Tennessee, Virginia, West Virginia, Virgin Islands)
> Volume 4, South Central and Great Plains States (Arkansas, Iowa, Kansas, Louisiana, Missouri, Nebraska, North Dakota, Oklahoma, South Dakota, Texas)
> Volume 5, Western States (Alaska, Arizona, California, Colorado, Guam, Hawaii, Idaho, Montana, Nevada, New Mexico, Oregon, Utah, Washington, Wyoming)

Gale Group, P.O. Box 9187, Farmington Hills, MI 48333-9187. Toll free US and Canada (800) 877-GALE (4253) and (248) 699-GALE, fax (800) 414-5043 and (248) 699-8061, Internet orders galeord@galegroup.com, web site www.galegroup.com or www.gale.com. All Gale Group products are available on approval. Contact Gale for details.

TRAVEL LETTER, published by Consumer Reports, reports that substantial savings on hotels are available by using a hotel broker or by joining a half-price hotel program. Each program offers varying additional discounts (if any) on airfares, car rentals, cruises, admissions to visitor attractions, and so forth. One large hotel broker and six discount hotel programs are listed below, ranked by quality and value:

- HRN is a large hotel broker. There's no need to join a program to use their services. (800) 380-7666.

- Entertainment Publications, publisher of HOTEL & TRAVEL ULTIMATE SAVINGS DIRECTORY ranks number 1 in total North American and worldwide locations. $62.95. (800) 445-4137.

- ENCORE, (800) 444-9800. $49.95

- ITC-50, (800) 987-6216, $49.00

- PRIVILEGE CARD, (800) 236-9732, www.privilegecard.com $80.90.

• AMERICAN TRAVELER also offers discounts on condominium rentals through Condolink and 50% off greens fees at golf courses through its Golf Access program. (800) 548-2812. Web site www.memberweb.com. Portfolio Package $99.95 for the first year, $49.95 for renewals.

• QUEST is sometimes available at a discount through associations, charge cards and so forth. (800) 742-3543, $99.00

For more information, contact Consumer Reports Travel Letter, Ed Perkins, Editor, Consumers Union, 101 Truman Avenue, Yonkers, NY 10703-1057, (800) 234-1970, (914) 378-2740. Refer to March, 1997 issue, pages 52-56.

Trade Shows

See Associations, Conferences

CHAIN STORE GUIDE'S CHAIN RESTAURANT OPERATORS CD-ROM. allows you to conduct data searches from five topic screens: 1. Personnel by title, 2. Personnel by functional area, 3. Restaurant type (cafeteria, dinnerhouse, fast food, family restaurant, in-store feeder, table cloth), 4. Menu type (Greek, German, health food, ice cream, etc.) You can also make selections based on geography or the size of a company (number of units and/or sales). Contains information about professional associations. Several output options are available, including mailing labels, and electronic formats (such as DBASE, ASCII, text) for mail merge customization. $995 including companion directory. If the price is prohibitively high, remember your local library. Ordering information: Chain Store Guide Information Services, 3922 Coconut Palm Drive, Tampa, FL 33619. (800) 927-9292, (813) 664-6800, (813) 627-6822, (800) 289-6822. http://www.d-net.com/csgis or http://www.csgis.com.

DIRECTORY OF BUSINESS INFORMATION RESOURCES, ASSOCIATIONS, NEWSLETTERS, MAGAZINES AND TRADESHOWS, published by Grey House Publishing, Pocket Knife Square, Lakeville, CT 06039, $199. (800) 562-2139, (860) 435-0868, web site www.greyhouse.com or books@il.com.

DIRECTORY OF CHAIN RESTAURANT OPERATORS describes 3-or-more unit chain restaurant companies in the U.S. and Canada operating or franchising restaurants, cafeterias, contract and industrial feeders. Hotel/motel companies controlling three or more restaurants within hotels and 3 or more foodservice operations are profiled, as well as food units in drug chains, general merchandise chains and discount stores. Key personnel, a listing of major trade associations and a trade show calendar are also included. An index to the top 100 restaurants is also included and is a valuable tool for target list development. An industry profile as provided by the National Restaurant Association is also included. Updated annually. $290. Chain Store Guide Information Services, 3922 Coconut Palm Drive, Tampa, FL 33619. (800) 927-9292, (813) 664-6800, (813) 627-6822, (800) 289-6822. http://www.d-net.com/csgis or http://www.csgis.com.

DIRECTORY OF DRUG STORE AND HBC CHAINS identifies over 1,800 drug retailers in the U.S. and Canada operating over 45,000 stores including drug, HBC, cosmetic, deep discount, home health care, discount, and grocery stores/supermarket chains with pharmacies, mass merchants with pharmacies, deep discount chains, and wholesale drug companies. It includes names and titles of key personnel, a listing of major trade associations and a trade show calendar. It also provides indexes to top drug retailers, top drug wholesalers, top grocery chains and top discount chains. $290. Chain Store Guide Information Services, 3922 Coconut Palm Drive, Tampa, FL 33619. (800) 927-9292, (813) 664-6800, (813) 627-6822, (800) 289-6822. http://www.d-net.com/csgis or http://www.csgis.com.

DIRECTORY OF FOODSERVICE DISTRIBUTORS lists U.S. and Canadian companies with at least $500,000 in sales to foodservice, food equipment, supply and full-line distributors. Each offers more than one product line and no more than 95% of its food distribution sales volume comes from self-manufactured merchandise. Key personnel and major buying/marketing groups, trade associations and a trade show calendar are also included. $290. Chain Store Guide Information Services, 3922 Coconut Palm Drive, Tampa, FL 33619. (800) 927-9292, (813) 664-6800, (813) 627-6822, (800) 289-6822. http://www.d-net.com/csgis or http://www.csgis.com.

DIRECTORY OF HIGH VOLUME INDEPENDENT RESTAURANTS lists nearly 6,000 independent restaurants in the U.S. with at least $1 million in annual sales. A companion to the Chain Restaurant

Operators directory, this guide identifies independent restaurants with one or two units that are part of a national chain but purchase separately. This directory lists key executives and buyers, major trade associations and a trade show calendar. $290. Chain Store Guide Information Services, 3922 Coconut Palm Drive, Tampa, FL 33619. (800) 927-9292, (813) 664-6800, (813) 627-6822, (800) 289-6822. http://www.d-net.com/csgis or http://www.csgis.com.

DIRECTORY OF SINGLE UNIT SUPERMARKET OPERATORS lists 7,000 independent (single unit) supermarket operators/grocery retailers with sales of at least $1 million. names and titles of key personnel. It also identifies major trade associations and a trade show calendar. $280. Chain Store Guide Information Services, 3922 Coconut Palm Drive, Tampa, FL 33619. (800) 927-9292, (813) 664-6800, (813) 627-6822, (800) 289-6822. http://www.d-net.com/csgis or http://www.csgis.com.

DIRECTORY OF SUPERMARKET, GROCERY AND CONVENIENCE STORE CHAINS describes and indexes over 2,300 supermarket chains with $2 million in annual sales. It covers supermarkets, superstores, club stores, gourmet supermarkets and combo stores in the U.S. and Canada, plus a special section profiling 1,700 convenience store chains. It includes an index to the top 200 supermarket chains and the top 100 convenience store chains, which is a valuable tool for target list development. It also lists over 29,000 key executives, buyers and administrative personnel. The directory also lists major trade associations and a trade show calendar. $300. Chain Store Guide Information Services, 3922 Coconut Palm Drive, Tampa, FL 33619. (800) 927-9292, (813) 664-6800, (813) 627-6822, (800) 289-6822. http://www.d-net.com/csgis or http://www.csgis.com.

DIRECTORY OF WHOLESALE GROCERY lists wholesale grocers' headquarters, divisions and branches, both in the US and Canada. All companies listed are required to sell a multi-line of products to the supermarket, convenience store, discount and drug industries. It includes names and titles of personnel, a listing of major trade associations and a trade show calendar. It also provides an index to the top 100 wholesale grocers, which is a valuable tool for target list development. $300. Chain Store Guide Information Services, 3922 Coconut Palm Drive, Tampa, FL 33619. (800) 927-9292, (813) 664-6800, (813) 627-6822, (800) 289-6822. http://www.d-net.com/csgis or http://www.csgis.com.

NATION'S RESTAURANT NEWS is a 30 year old newsweekly of the foodservice industry. For info about subscriptions and customer service, call 800-447-7133. URL: www.nrn.com or http://www.d-net.com/csgis or http://www.csgis.com. Chain Store Guide Information Services, 3922 Coconut Palm Drive, Tampa, FL 33619.

TRADE SHOWS WORLDWIDE—AN INTERNATIONAL DIRECTORY OF EVENTS, FACILITIES AND SUPPLIERS profiles over 8,000 trade shows, some 5,000 trade show organizers, over 1,200 convention centers plus exhibit builders, transportations firms industry suppliers, professional associations, consultants, and published sources of industry information. Three sections cover hotel/motel systems, visitor and convention bureaus and world trade centers. $277. Gale Group, P.O. Box 9187, Farmington Hills, MI 48333-9187. Toll free US and Canada (800) 877-GALE (4253) and (248) 699-GALE, fax (800) 414-5043 and (248) 699-8061, Internet orders galeord@galegroup.com, web site www.galegroup.com or www.gale.com. All Gale Group products are available on approval. Contact Gale for details.

Trading

DIRECTORY OF REGISTERED INVESTMENT ADVISORS identifies over 9,000 CEO's, 7,000 Investment Officers, 10,000 Portfolio Managers, 6,000 Directors of Research and Research Analysts, 2,800 Traders and Trading Managers, and 1,200 Directors of Operations/Chief Financial Officers, plus web sites and personal email addresses. The directory also includes a section on mutual funds for over 4,000 funds at 375 firms, including the name of the person responsible for managing the fund, 1,3 and 5 year returns, benchmark comparisons, and more. DIRECTORY OF REGISTERED INVESTMENT ADVISORS with 4 Regional editions, $475. The Directory with no regional editions, $395. Published by Standard & Poors, a division of McGraw-Hill, MONEY MARKET DIRECTORIES, INC., 320 East Main Street, Charlottesville, VA 22902, http://www.mmdaccess.com, (800) 446-2810, (804) 977-1450.

EUROMARKETS ISSUERS DIRECTORY. For more information contact Larry Meranus Professional Publications & Services, 4 Demoray Court, Pine Brook, NJ 07058, (800) MERANUS or (800) 637-2687. Distributed in England by EUROMONEY Books, Plymbridge Distributors Limited, Estover, Plymouth PL6 7PZ, England. Phone 44 (0) 171 779-8955. Fax 44 (0) 171 779-8541.

EUROMONEY BANK REGISTER is a detailed directory of the world's leading financial institutions and a comprehensive guide to "who's who" in global capital markets. This directory lists senior executives, investment and commercial bankers, traders, analysts, support and legal staff. Expanded coverage of Asia, central Europe and eastern Europe and Latin America is provided. Available in print or CD ROM. The print version of The EUROMONEY Bank Register is comprehensively indexed alphabetically and by city. It also contains rankings of the top banks. The read only version of the CD ROM provides full access to the entire database. However, by disabling the print and export functions, the result is a lower cost alternative to the full version. A 14 day free trial is available with the CD ROM.

Print Directory, USA, US $493 or 297 pounds sterling
Print Directory, UK, Europe, Rest of World US $493 or 297 pounds sterling
Read Only Version CD ROM 750 pounds or US $1,250
Full Version CD ROM 1,750 pounds or US $3,000

Ordering information: Larry Meranus Professional Publications & Services, 4 Demoray Court, Pine Brook, NJ 07058, (800) MERANUS or (800) 637-2687. Distributed in England by EUROMONEY Books, Plymbridge Distributors Limited, Estover, Plymouth PL6 7PZ, England. Phone 44 (0) 171 779-8955 for a free demo disk. Fax 44 (0) 171 779-8541.

Training

Also see Internet Recruitment Training

AMERICAN SOCIETY FOR TRAINING AND DEVELOPMENT (ASTD) is a major professional association which can provide information about surveys, directories and so forth. AMERICAN SOCIETY FOR TRAINING AND DEVELOPMENT, 1640 King Street, Box 1443, Alexandria, VA 22313-2043, (703) 683-8100, Fax (703) 683-8103, web site www.astd.org. For more information about other training organizations, refer to one of the references listed under "References—Librarian" such as BUSINESS INFORMATION SOURCES by Lorna Daniells, ENCYCLOPEDIA OF BUSINESS INFORMATION SOURCES, or ENCYCLOPEDIA OF ASSOCIATIONS.

SMALL BUSINESS SOURCEBOOK encompasses comprehensive information on small businesses, including professional associations, training sources, small business investment companies, over 400 Internet databases, publications, awards and honors, company and personal email addresses. $325 for 2 vol. set. Gale Group, P.O. Box 9187, Farmington Hills, MI 48333-9187. Toll free US and Canada (800) 877-GALE (4253) and (248) 699-GALE, fax (800) 414-5043 and (248) 699-8061, Internet orders galeord@galegroup.com, web site www.galegroup.com or www.gale.com. All Gale Group products are available on approval. Contact Gale for details.

VIDEO SOURCEBOOK lists nearly 150,000 video programs in business, medicine, entertainment, education and culture. Indexes include subject, credits, program distributors, alternate title, and special formats. $325 for 2 volume set. Also available on commercial online service. Gale Group, P.O. Box 9187, Farmington Hills, MI 48333-9187. Toll free US and Canada (800) 877-GALE (4253) and (248) 699-GALE, fax (800) 414-5043 and (248) 699-8061, Internet orders galeord@galegroup.com, web site www.galegroup.com or www.gale.com. All Gale Group products are available on approval. Contact Gale for details.

WORDS ON CASSETTE is the only complete guide to audio cassette collections with location, ordering and pricing information, running times, content summaries and rental availability, an index to authors, readers and performers. Published annually. Cahners Business Information, 121 Chanlon Road, New Providence, NJ 07974, (908) 777-8669, (888) 269-5372, fax (908) 508-7696, email marin.mixon@bowker.com, URL www.bowker.com. Headquarters: Cahners Business Information, 275 Washington Street, Newton, MA 02158-1630, (617) 558-4663 or (617) 964-3030, fax (617) 558-4700, email marketaccess@cahners.com. Web sites www.cahners.com or www.chilton.net.

www.asktheheadhunter.com is the web site for the book, ASK THE HEADHUNTER, a book that can effectively be used by both job hunters and interviewers, by Nick Corcodilos, email northbridge@sprintmail.com. According to Tom Peters, it is "a powerful hiring tool.no manager can afford to miss" and it "shreds some of our most basic assumptions about the way to hire top people." Published by

Penguin Putnam, New York, $14.95   The book is available from the web site and at bookstores. Corcodilos and his client, Merrill Lynch's Vice President of Global Staffing, were jointly featured in a discussion about changes in corporate recruiting and hiring practices in a segment on "Opportunity Knocks," a CNBC special on Executive Search. To purchase this 5 hour video, contact CNBC or Corcodilos.

www.kennedyinfo.com is the web site for publisher Kennedy Information. It includes books, newsletters, training materials, directories, and surveys for executive recruiting, human resources, outplacement, management consulting and job seekers. (800) 531-0007 or (603) 585-6544.

www.netjobs.com is the URL to Canada's premiere employment web site. It features Internet Career Centre for employers and job seekers, Overseas Jobs Express, and Personal Computer Training. Email info@netjobs.com. Linked to www.jobnet.org.

Transportation

ADVERTISER AND AGENCY RED BOOKS PLUS CD ROM combines all the information in THE STANDARD DIRECTORY OF ADVERTISERS, THE STANDARD DIRECTORY OF ADVERTISING AGENCIES and THE STANDARD DIRECTORY OF INTERNATIONAL ADVERTISERS AND AGENCIES. Information is searchable by 25 fields, including company name, personal name, job title/function, product type, product/account name, city, state, zip or country, area code, revenues, number of employees, outside ad agency and even type of computer hardware. Contains professional association information. Available for Windows and Macintosh. Updated quarterly. 1 year subscription $1,295. If the price is prohibitively high, remember your local library. National Register Publishing, Reed Elsevier-New Providence, 121 Chanlon Road, New Providence, NJ 07974, (800) 521-8110, fax (800) 836-7736, web site www.redbooks.com or www.marquiswhoswho.com. "If, for any reason whatsoever, your order does not fully meet your expectations, simply return the product within 30 days for a prompt, complete, unquestioned refund," as stated in Catalog of Biographical and Professional References of publisher Marquis Who's Who/National Register Publishing.

BUSINESS INFORMATION SOURCES by Lorna Daniells is an outstanding reference at any price. At $39.95 a copy, it's such an extraordinary value, it should have a place in every library. This is clearly one of the top three hard copy references around, and its reasonable price elevates it to first place. Business Information Sources provides a wealth of information routinely needed by search firms, job hunters and corporate recruiters, including general directories, specialized directories, professional associations, periodicals, industry information, international information, and much more. $39.95. Ordering information: Business Information Sources by Lorna Daniells, is published by the University of California Press (Berkeley, CA, Los Angeles, CA & Oxford, England) (510-642-4247). Orders are handled by California Princeton Fulfillment Services, P.O. Box 10769, Newark, NJ 07193-0769. (800-822-6657).

CALIFORNIA INTERNATIONAL TRADE REGISTER identifies 24,000 contacts at over 7,000 companies engaged in import/export, manufacturing, wholesaling, freight forwarding, custom brokerage and trading companies. Published annually by Database Publishing. Directory $129. Complete CD ROM $545, CD ROM one year lease $365. Distributed by Manufacturers' News, Inc., (888) 752-5200, 1633 Central Street, Evanston, IL 60201-1569. Email info@manufacturersnews.com. Web site www.manufacturersnews.com.

ENCYCLOPEDIA OF ASSOCIATIONS: INTERNATIONAL ORGANIZATIONS includes nearly 20,000 multinational and national organizations in foreign countries, including US based associations with multinational membership. Entries also include email addresses, web sites and bulletin board addresses, lobbying activities, and publication and convention information. Indexed by geography, keyword and executives. $595 for 2 volume set. Also available in CD ROM. Database available via commercial online service. Gale Group, P.O. Box 9187, Farmington Hills, MI 48333-9187. Toll free US and Canada (800) 877-GALE (4253) and (248) 699-GALE, fax (800) 414-5043 and (248) 699-8061, Internet orders galeord@galegroup.com, web site www.galegroup.com or www.gale.com. All Gale Group products are available on approval. Contact Gale for details.

ENCYCLOPEDIA OF ASSOCIATIONS: NATIONAL ORGANIZATIONS OF THE US. This superb reference is one of the first places you should look when beginning a new recruiting assignment or when looking for specialized references of any type. The keyword index makes this comprehensive reference easy to use, even in hard copy. For over 23,000 nonprofit professional associations with a national scope, this encyclopedia reveals:

- Publications, including membership rosters and newsletters

- Dates and locations of association conferences and conventions

- Names of Executive Directors, who are usually incredible sources of industry information if you call and speak to them

- Committees

- Job and candidate referral banks, which can provide resumes of other industry sources and sometimes candidates

- It includes organizations in these categories: business, trade, environmental, agricultural, legal, govern mental, engineering, technological, scientific, educational, cultural, social welfare, health & medical, public affairs, ethnic, labor unions, chambers of commerce, tourism, & others.

   Volume 1, National Organizations of the US, $505
   Volume 2, Geographic and Executive Indexes, $390
   Volume 3, Supplement, $405

Gale Group, P.O. Box 9187, Farmington Hills, MI 48333-9187. Toll free US and Canada (800) 877-GALE (4253) and (248) 699-GALE, fax (800) 414-5043 and (248) 699-8061, Internet orders galeord@galegroup.com, web site www.galegroup.com or www.gale.com. All Gale Group products are available on approval. Contact Gale for details.

ENCYCLOPEDIA OF BUSINESS INFORMATION SOURCES will lead you to specialized directories, professional associations, trade publications, newsletters, databases, Internet resources and more. It's an excellent reference and a great way to find key resources in any industry fast. $330. Gale Group, P.O. Box 9187, Farmington Hills, MI 48333-9187. Toll free US and Canada (800) 877-GALE (4253) and (248) 699-GALE, fax (800) 414-5043 and (248) 699-8061, Internet orders galeord@galegroup.com, web site www.galegroup.com or www.gale.com. All Gale Group products are available on approval. Contact Gale for details.

JOURNAL OF COMMERCE, published in New York, New York, is a trade journal serving the shipping industry.

STANDARD DIRECTORY OF ADVERTISERS Business Classifications Edition is an excellent general directory that organizes companies by a wide range of product categories. A few examples include "Apparel 2—Men's and Boys' Wear," "Heating and Air Conditioning," "Cosmetics and Toiletries," and "Aviation and Aerospace." This directory lists names and titles of key officers, revenues and other information. It is available in a geographic edition for the same price. This directory is comprised of over 24,000 companies that annually spend over $200,000 on advertising. It represents a reasonable place to look for hard-to-find information about privately held companies, especially those that heavily advertise their products. It is a good place to look for names if STANDARD AND POORS and the MILLION DOLLAR DIRECTORY fail to yield the names you need. Finally, the Classified Edition of THE STANDARD DIRECTORY OF ADVERTISERS can be a very convenient source of research because both your target list of companies and the corresponding names and titles of management all appear together, in the same Classification. This is important if you still rely on research books in hard copy. THE STANDARD DIRECTORY OF ADVERTISERS also publishes a special volume called THE STANDARD DIRECTORY OF ADVERTISERS TRADENAME INDEX. You can use the TRADENAME INDEX if you know the brand name of a product and need to find the company that manufactures it. In addition, this directory contains an Associations section which identifies marketing oriented associations.

$599 hard copy. If the price is prohibitively high, remember your local library. THE STANDARD DIRECTORY OF ADVERTISERS is also available on CD ROM under the title ADVERTISER AND AGENCY RED BOOKS PLUS. It is available in Windows® and Macintosh® formats. National Register Publishing, Reed Elsevier-New Providence, 121 Chanlon Road, New Providence, NJ 07974, (800) 521-8110, fax (800) 836-7736, web site www.redbooks.com or www.marquiswhoswho.com. "If, for any reason whatsoever, your order does not fully meet your expectations, simply return the product within 30 days for a prompt, complete, unquestioned refund," as stated in Catalog of Biographical and Professional References of publisher Marquis Who's Who/National Register Publishing.

SUPPLY CHAIN MANAGEMENT REVIEW is a new journal dedicated to movement of materials and products. Published 4 times a year. Call publisher for price. Cahners Business Information, 275 Washington Street, Newton, MA 02158-1630, (617) 558-4474 fax (617) 558-4327, email memac@cahners.com. Headquarters: Cahners Business Information, 275 Washington Street, Newton, MA 02158-1630, (617) 558-4663 or (617) 964-3030, fax (617) 558-4700, email marketaccess@cahners.com. Web sites www.cahners.com or www.chilton.net.

Travel

See Tourism Category

AMERICAN SOCIETY OF TRAVEL AGENTS (ASTA) is a major professional association which can provide information about surveys, directories and so forth. For more information about this and other travel organizations, refer to one of the references listed under "References—Librarian" such as BUSINESS INFORMATION SOURCES by Lorna Daniells, ENCYCLOPEDIA OF BUSINESS INFORMATION SOURCES, and the ENCYCLOPEDIA OF ASSOCIATIONS.

CONSUMER REPORTS TRAVEL LETTER is published by Consumers Union, a nonprofit independent organization providing consumers with information and advice on goods, services, health and personal finance. No advertising is accepted. $39/year subscription. Single copy $5. Flash By Fax releases late breaking news that would otherwise miss Consumer Reports Travel Letter. It also reveals short term deals on travel, especially airfare. To order Flash By Fax, call 800-559-8905 for 12 issues @ $25 per year. For more information contact Consumer Reports Travel Letter, Ed Perkins, Editor, Consumers Union, 101 Truman Avenue, Yonkers, NY 10703-1057, (800) 234-1970, (914) 378-2740.

CRAIGHEAD'S INTERNATIONAL BUSINESS, TRAVEL AND RELOCATION GUIDE TO 81 COUNTRIES provides information about the business practices, economies, customs, communications, tours and attractions plus maps. $695 for 3 volumes. Data compiled by Craighead Publications. Gale Group, P.O. Box 9187, Farmington Hills, MI 48333-9187. Toll free US and Canada (800) 877-GALE (4253) and (248) 699-GALE, fax (800) 414-5043 and (248) 699-8061, Internet orders galeord@galegroup.com, web site www.galegroup.com or www.gale.com. All Gale Group products are available on approval. Contact Gale for details.

"THE LIST" is Cahners Business Information catalog. The former Reed Travel Group has merged with Cahners and Chilton to form Cahners Business Information. For every publication in "The List," publishers and editors' names are identified, with address, phone number and email. It also provides a superb description of every periodical they publish—including many serving the travel industry—with local contact information Publications are located throughout the US and in foreign countries. Free. Cahners Business Information, 275 Washington Street, Newton, MA 02158-1630, (617) 558-4663 or (617) 964-3030, fax (617) 558-4700, email marketaccess@cahners.com. Web sites www.cahners.com or www.chilton.net.

TRAVEL LETTER, published by Consumer Reports, reports that substantial savings on hotels are available by using a hotel broker or by joining a half-price hotel program. Each program offers varying additional discounts (if any) on airfares, car rentals, cruises, admissions to visitor attractions, and so forth. One large hotel broker and six discount hotel programs are listed below, ranked by quality and value:

- HRN is a large hotel broker. There's no need to join a program to use their services. (800) 380-7666.

- Entertainment Publications, publisher of HOTEL & TRAVEL ULTIMATE SAVINGS DIRECTORY ranks number 1 in total North American and worldwide locations. $62.95. (800) 445-4137.

- ENCORE, (800) 444-9800. $49.95

- ITC-50, (800) 987-6216, $49.00

- PRIVILEGE CARD, (800) 236-9732, www.privilegecard.com $80.90.

- GREAT AMERICAN TRAVELER also offers discounts on condominium rentals through Condolink and 50% off greens fees at golf courses through its Golf Access program. (800) 548-2812. Web site www.memberweb.com. Portfolio Package $99.95 for the first year, $49.95 for renewals.

- QUEST is sometimes available at a discount through associations, charge cards and so forth. (800) 742-3543, $99.00

For more information, contact Consumer Reports Travel Letter, Ed Perkins, Editor, Consumers Union, 101 Truman Avenue, Yonkers, NY 10703-1057, (800) 234-1970, (914) 378-2740. Refer to March, 1997 issue, pages 52-56.

Trusts

CORPORATE FINANCE SOURCEBOOK—THE GUIDE TO MAJOR INVESTMENT SOURCES AND RELATED FINANCIAL SERVICES contains over 13,000 names of executives at 3,700 organizations that, broadly speaking, supply growth capital to businesses or are service firms, such as US venture capital lenders, private lenders, commercial finance and factoring, pension managers, master trusts and other sources. Names of key management are included. A special section details public offerings of the past 3 years and mergers and acquisitions over $100 million. $575. If the price is prohibitively high, remember your local library. National Register Publishing, Reed Elsevier-New Providence, 121 Chanlon Road, New Providence, NJ 07974, (800) 521-8110, fax (800) 836-7736, web site www.redbooks.com or www.marquiswhoswho.com. "If, for any reason whatsoever, your order does not fully meet your expectations, simply return the product within 30 days for a prompt, complete, unquestioned refund," as stated in Catalog of Biographical and Professional References of publisher Marquis Who's Who/National Register Publishing.

DIRECTORY OF INSTITUTIONAL REAL ESTATE/NELSON'S INSTITUTIONAL REAL ESTATE identifies 5,000 institutions that invest in real estate, including 300 investment managers, 1,700 plan sponsors, 1,000 insurance companies, 2,000 corporations and 380 Real Estate Investment Trusts (REIT's). 2,500 real estate service firms are also listed. Identifies 22,000 key executives. Updated annually. $335. Nelson Information, P.O. Box 591, Port Chester, NY 10573 USA. (800) 333-6357, Phone outside the US (914) 937-8400, Fax (914) 937-8590, web site http://www.nelnet.com.

DIRECTORY OF TRUST BANKING, an official publication of the American Bankers Association, is a one volume directory that identifies banks and private trust companies in the Unites States. Listings include trust officer names and functional responsibilities, address, fax and phone, financial information outlining scope and amount of trust activity in collective investment funds, investment instruments used, discretionary and non-discretionary assets and corporate funds, plus national and state rankings and a summary of mergers. Published annually. For more information contact (800) 321-3373, Thomson Financial Publishing, 4709 West Golf Road, Skokie, IL 60076-1253. Web site @ tfp.bankinfo.com.

U

Unions

ENCYCLOPEDIA OF ASSOCIATIONS: NATIONAL ORGANIZATIONS OF THE US. This superb reference is one of the first places you should look when beginning a new recruiting assignment or when looking for specialized references of any type. The keyword index makes this comprehensive reference easy to use, even in hard copy. For over 23,000 nonprofit professional associations with a national scope, this encyclopedia reveals:

- Publications, including membership rosters and newsletters

- Dates and locations of association conferences and conventions

- Names of Executive Directors, who are usually incredible sources of industry information if you call and speak to them

- Committees

- Job and candidate referral banks, which can provide resumes of other industry sources and sometimes candidates

- It includes organizations in these categories: business, trade, environmental, agricultural, legal, governmental, engineering, technological, scientific, educational, cultural, social welfare, health & medical, public affairs, ethnic, labor unions, chambers of commerce, tourism, & others.

> Volume 1, National Organizations of the US, $505
> Volume 2, Geographic and Executive Indexes, $390
> Volume 3, Supplement, $405

Gale Group, P.O. Box 9187, Farmington Hills, MI 48333-9187. Toll free US and Canada (800) 877-GALE (4253) and (248) 699-GALE, fax (800) 414-5043 and (248) 699-8061, Internet orders galeord@galegroup.com, web site www.galegroup.com or www.gale.com. All Gale Group products are available on approval. Contact Gale for details.

ENCYCLOPEDIA OF ASSOCIATIONS: REGIONAL, STATE AND LOCAL ORGANIZATIONS. The information in this directory is not duplicated anywhere in ENCYCLOPEDIA OF ASSOCIATIONS. Over 100,000 nonprofit organizations are included in this directory. $585 for 5 volume set or $140 per individual volume. Also available on CD ROM and online on the Internet through a GaleNet subscription.

> Volume 1, Great Lakes States (Illinois, Indiana, Michigan, Minnesota, Ohio, Wisconsin)
> Volume 2, Northeastern States (Connecticut, Maine, Massachusetts, New Hampshire, New Jersey, New York, Pennsylvania, Rhode Islands, Vermont)
> Volume 3, Southern and Middle Atlantic States (Including Puerto Rico and the Virgin Islands) (Alabama, Delaware, Washington, DC, Florida, Georgia, Kentucky, Maryland, Mississippi, North Carolina, Puerto Rico, South Carolina, Tennessee, Virginia, West Virginia, Virgin Islands)
> Volume 4, South Central and Great Plains States (Arkansas, Iowa, Kansas, Louisiana, Missouri, Nebraska, North Dakota, Oklahoma, South Dakota, Texas)
> Volume 5, Western States (Alaska, Arizona, California, Colorado, Guam, Hawaii, Idaho, Montana, Nevada, New Mexico, Oregon, Utah, Washington, Wyoming)

Gale Group, P.O. Box 9187, Farmington Hills, MI 48333-9187. Toll free US and Canada (800) 877-GALE (4253) and (248) 699-GALE, fax (800) 414-5043 and (248) 699-8061, Internet orders galeord@galegroup.com, web site www.galegroup.com or www.gale.com. All Gale Group products are available on approval. Contact Gale for details.

PROFILES OF AMERICAN LABOR UNIONS, formerly titled American Directory of Organized Labor, outlines nearly 300 national labor unions. It includes information on bargaining agreements and biographies of over 170 past and present union officials, nearly 800 current bargaining agreements and over 500 employers and their addresses. It is indexed by industry, geography and key officials. $285. Gale Group, P.O. Box 9187, Farmington Hills, MI 48333-9187. Toll free US and Canada (800) 877-GALE (4253) and (248) 699-GALE, fax (800) 414-5043 and (248) 699-8061, Internet orders galeord@galegroup.com, web site www.galegroup.com or www.gale.com. All Gale Group products are available on approval. Contact Gale for details.

United Nations

www.fedjobs.com provides assistance to people seeking a position with the federal government, including in the Judiciary and Congressional branches, and the United Nations. Many positions are in computers, engineering and medical, with salaries often in the $30,000 to $50,000 range. The site was developed by Federal Research Service, Inc., Vienna, Virginia and was launched in 1996.

University Alumni

ALUMNI DIRECTORIES. Sometimes school directories (graduate and undergraduate) cross-reference names of people according to company. When the directory is so organized, it can be a useful recruiting tool, for example, if you're looking for an MSEE employed by a certain company. If you want to buy a directory, you will usually need the help of a graduate because most schools will only sell directories to their alumni. If you work for a big company, there's usually a graduate around willing to either lend you a directory, or will help you buy one. Actually, it's usually as simple as getting the graduate's permission to use his or her name to order the directory. Then YOU can order the directory, send a company check with your order, and have the directory mailed to the company, to your office address c/o the graduate. This way the graduate doesn't have to go to any trouble. Historically the alumni directories for the graduate schools of business at Harvard and Wharton have been well organized, from a recruiting research standpoint. To find out if an alumni directory is available in a CD ROM, ask a graduate, or call the alumni office directly.

HARVARD BUSINESS SCHOOL'S BAKER LIBRARY in Boston provides an outstanding consumer marketing web site at www.library.hbs.edu/. This web site identifies extensive sources of information on consumer marketing, including retail both for job hunters and researchers. It includes associations, membership directories, information on direct mail, public relations, corporate communications, online direct mail and online Dun and Bradstreet Credit Reports.

While the access to the web site itself is free and available to anyone, access to the CAREER ADVISOR database is available only to current Harvard Business School students and Harvard Business School Alumni Advisors (Harvard Business School alumni who have agreed to serve as Career advisors to current students and other alumni). The Advisor Database can be searched by industry, geography, job function, job title, year of graduation and company name. In addition, Reference Librarians at the Harvard Business School can conduct searches for a fee. Hundreds of databases are available. Ask at the Reference Desk for more information. For example, Dun & Bradstreet's Credit Reports are a lucrative source of information about privately held companies.

www.jobtrak.com is the web site for the Career service network for college students, alumni, college career staff and employers. JOBTRAK was ranked as one of the top 5 "Best Specialty Sites" by the *National Business Employment Weekly*. JOBTRAK has established relationships with college and university career offices, MBA programs and alumni associations. Most salaries range between $30,000 and $50,000. The site developer is JOBTRAK CORPORATION, Los Angeles, CA, (310) 474-3377, (800) 999-8725, fax (310) 475-7912. The site has been online since 1995.

V

Venezuela

See Latin America, South America, International

DIRECTORY OF AMERICAN FIRMS OPERATING IN FOREIGN COUNTRIES, REGIONAL EDITION—VENEZUELA, $29. Uniworld Business Publications, Inc., 257 Central Park West, Suite 10A, New York, NY 10024-4110, (212) 496-2448, fax (212) 769-0413, email uniworldbp@aol.com. Web site: http://www.uniworldbp.com.

Venture Capital

BUSINESS PLANS HANDBOOK is a collection of real business plans prepared by entrepreneurs searching for small business funding in North America. 25 actual plans are presented across a broad spectrum of businesses in manufacturing, retail and service industries. Company identities have been changed to protect confidentiality. $125. Gale Group, P.O. Box 9187, Farmington Hills, MI 48333-9187. Toll free US and Canada (800) 877-GALE (4253) and (248) 699-GALE, fax (800) 414-5043 and (248) 699-8061, Internet orders galeord@galegroup.com, web site www.galegroup.com or www.gale.com. All Gale Group products are available on approval. Previous volumes are available. Contact Gale for details.

CORPORATE FINANCE SOURCEBOOK—THE GUIDE TO MAJOR INVESTMENT SOURCES AND RELATED FINANCIAL SERVICES contains over 13,000 names of executives at 3,700 organizations that, broadly speaking, supply growth capital to businesses or are service firms, such as US venture capital lenders, private lenders, commercial finance and factoring, pension managers, master trusts and other sources.

Names of key management are included. A special section details public offerings of the past 3 years and mergers and acquisitions over $100 million. $575. If the price is prohibitively high, remember your local library. National Register Publishing, Reed Elsevier-New Providence, 121 Chanlon Road, New Providence, NJ 07974, (800) 521-8110, fax (800) 836-7736, web site www.redbooks.com or www.marquiswhoswho.com. "If, for any reason whatsoever, your order does not fully meet your expectations, simply return the product within 30 days for a prompt, complete, unquestioned refund," as stated in Catalog of Biographical and Professional References of publisher Marquis Who's Who/National Register Publishing.

THE GOLD BOOK OF VENTURE CAPITAL FIRMS provides detailed listings of 869 venture capital firms with full contact data, fund and preferred investment sizes, paragraph descriptions, industry focus and unique samplings of portfolio companies. Arranged geographically, the directory features four extensive indexes by industry specialties, preferred stages of financing, firms names and key principals. $37.95. Published by Kennedy Information, One Kennedy Place, Route 12 South, Fitzwilliam, NH 03447, phone (800) 531-0007 or 603-585-6544, fax 603-585-9555, email bookstore@kennedyinfo.com, web site www.kennedyinfo.com.

PRATT'S GUIDE TO VENTURE CAPITAL SOURCES, published annually, $225. Venture Economics, Inc., 40 West 57th St., 11th floor, New York, NY 10019, (212) 765-5311.

Video

AV MARKET PLACE is a directory of companies that create, apply or distribute a range of AV equipment and services for business, education, science and government. It includes multi-media, virtual reality, digital audio, presentation software and interactive video, plus a Products, Services and Companies Index and a Company Directory with contact information.

R.R. Bowker (a unit of Cahners Business Information), 121 Chanlon Road, New Providence, NJ 07974 USA, Phone (888) BOWKER2 (888-269-5372) & (800) 323-3288, fax (908) 508-7696, email info@bowker.com, web www.bowker.com. Canada—R.R. Bowker, Markham, Ontario, phone (888) BOWKER9 & (905) 415-5837, fax (905) 479-6266. German speaking Europe—K.G. Saur Verlag, Munich, Germany, phone 49-89-76902-232, fax 49-89-76902-250, email 100730.1341@compuserve.com, web www.saur.de/home.htm. Rest of Europe incl. United Kingdom plus Africa & Asia—Bowker-Saur, W. Sussex, UK, phone 44-1342-326-972, fax 44-1342-335-612, email customer@bowker-saur.co.uk, web www.bowker-saur.com/service/. Australia/New Zealand—Thorpe, Port Melbourne, Victoria, Australia, phone 61-03-9-245-7370, fax 61-03-9-245-7395, email customer.service@thorpe.com.au, web www.thorpe.com.au. Technical support for CD ROMs (800) 323-3288, fax 908) 665-3528, email techsupport@bowker.com.

DIRECTORY OF CALIFORNIA WHOLESALERS AND SERVICE COMPANIES identifies over 85,000 names and titles of executives at some 34,000 non-manufacturing firms, such as wholesalers, transportation, telecommunications, video production and software, including web sites and email addresses. Annual directory published by Database Publishing, $169. Complete CD ROM $925, One year CD ROM lease, $595. Distributed by Manufacturers' News, Inc., (888) 752-5200, 1633 Central Street, Evanston, IL 60201-1569. Email info@manufacturersnews.com. Web site www.manufacturersnews.com.

KEMPS FILM, TV & VIDEO HANDBOOK is a directory for the production and post production sectors of the industry. Published annually. Call publisher for price. Cahners Business Information, 34-35 Newman Street, London W1P 3PD England. (011) 44 171 637-3663, fax (011) 44 171 580-5559. Headquarters: Cahners Business Information, 275 Washington Street, Newton, MA 02158-1630, (617) 558-4663 or (617) 964-3030, fax (617) 558-4700, email marketaccess@cahners.com. Web sites www.cahners.com or www.chilton.net.

VIDEO SOURCEBOOK lists nearly 150,000 video programs in business, medicine, entertainment, education and culture. Indexes include subject, credits, program distributors, alternate title, and special formats. $325 for 2 volume set. Also available on commercial online service. Gale Group, P.O. Box 9187, Farmington Hills, MI 48333-9187. Toll free US and Canada (800) 877-GALE (4253) and (248) 699-GALE, fax (800) 414-5043 and (248) 699-8061, Internet orders galeord@galegroup.com, web site www.galegroup.com or www.gale.com. All Gale Group products are available on approval. Contact Gale for details.

www.bowker.com is the web site for this major research publisher. It includes Flagship Products and Services, an online Product Catalog, Electronic Publishing products including CD ROMs, Internet Databases, and Online Subscription and Site Licensing Databases; press releases, career opportunities, and more. Many of their references are accessible through this web site, such as BOOKS IN PRINT PLUS CANADIAN EDITION, ULRICH'S ON DISC, GERMAN BOOKS IN PRINT, GERMAN BOOKS OUT OF PRINT, INTERNATIONAL BOOKS IN PRINT PLUS, ITALIAN BOOKS IN PRINT, YEARBOOK OF INTERNATIONAL ORGANIZATIONS PLUS, ULRICH'S INTERNATIONAL PERIODICALS DIRECTORY, THE SOFTWARE ENCYCLOPEDIA, BOWKER'S COMPLETE VIDEO DIRECTORY, AMERICAN BOOK PUBLISHING RECORD. Visit the web site for more information.

Virgin Islands

See Caribbean, International, Bermuda

ENCYCLOPEDIA OF ASSOCIATIONS: REGIONAL, STATE AND LOCAL ORGANIZATIONS. The information in this directory is not duplicated anywhere in ENCYCLOPEDIA OF ASSOCIATIONS. Over 100,000 nonprofit organizations are included in this directory. $585 for 5 volume set or $140 per individual volume. Also available on CD ROM and online on the Internet through a GaleNet subscription.

Volume 1, Great Lakes States (Illinois, Indiana, Michigan, Minnesota, Ohio, Wisconsin)

Volume 2, Northeastern States (Connecticut, Maine, Massachusetts, New Hampshire, New Jersey, New York, Pennsylvania, Rhode Islands, Vermont)

Volume 3, Southern and Middle Atlantic States (Including Puerto Rico and the Virgin Islands) (Alabama, Delaware, Washington, DC, Florida, Georgia, Kentucky, Maryland, Mississippi, North Carolina, Puerto Rico, South Carolina, Tennessee, Virginia, West Virginia, Virgin Islands)

Volume 4, South Central and Great Plains States (Arkansas, Iowa, Kansas, Louisiana, Missouri, Nebraska, North Dakota, Oklahoma, South Dakota, Texas)

Volume 5, Western States (Alaska, Arizona, California, Colorado, Guam, Hawaii, Idaho, Montana, Nevada, New Mexico, Oregon, Utah, Washington, Wyoming)

Gale Group, P.O. Box 9187, Farmington Hills, MI 48333-9187. Toll free US and Canada (800) 877-GALE (4253) and (248) 699-GALE, fax (800) 414-5043 and (248) 699-8061, Internet orders galeord@galegroup.com, web site www.galegroup.com or www.gale.com. All Gale Group products are available on approval. Contact Gale for details.

W

Washington, D.C.

See Baltimore/Annapolis

WASHINGTON identifies 4,500 organizations and institutions in Washington DC and 22,000 key people in them. Includes government, business, education, medicine/health, community affairs, art/culture and others. $85. Columbia Books, Inc., 1212 New York Avenue, NW, Suite 330, Washington, DC 20005, (212) 898-0662.

Wealth

WHO'S WEALTHY IN AMERICA provides information on nearly 110,000 of the richest Americans. Information includes address and sometimes phone, plus data on political contributions, real estate holdings, insider stock holdings, education and lifestyle indicators. $460 for 2 volume set. Gale Group, P.O. Box 9187, Farmington Hills, MI 48333-9187. Toll free US and Canada (800) 877-GALE (4253) and (248) 699-GALE, fax (800) 414-5043 and (248) 699-8061, Internet orders galeord@galegroup.com, web site www.galegroup.com or www.gale.com. All Gale Group products are available on approval. Contact Gale for details.

Web Sites

See Publishers Web Sites, Search Engines and Chapter 7, "Major Internet Web Sites"

NOTE: Web sites for various publishers are listed in the Publishers Web sites Category. It identifies web sites for publishers of various types of information covering a broad spectrum of industries and functions, including directories, databases on the Internet and on CD ROM. For example, some listings are www.ambest.com, a publisher of insurance publications, www.dnbmdd.com, the web site for Dun and Bradstreet MILLION DOLLAR DIRECTORY; and www.cpsnet.com, the site for CPS Communications Inc., the healthcare industry publisher of the Pharmaceutical Manufacturers Directory, to name a few. If you wish to locate additional publishers and their web sites, refer to the LITERARY MARKET PLACE, which is described in detail in the Publishing Industry Category. More information on LITERARY MARKET PLACE is available on publisher R.R. Bowker's web site at www.bowker.com.

Remember, another research option is to go to the "Ask Jeeves" web site at www.askjeeves.com

"The Best Web Sites For Job Hunters" was the cover story in the *National Business Employment Weekly* November 15-21, 1998 issue. It surveyed and reviewed 70 web sites which had been profiled in their publication during the previous year. To see a copy, try the library.

Over 60 of the 70 surveyed web sites have been included in this book. Web sites with lower compensation positions have been omitted, and most of those were in computer related areas. However, all the web sites which received top rankings were included, regardless of compensation range, especially sites in out-of-the-ordinary niches.

CRAIN PUBLICATIONS, headquartered in Chicago, publishes the following web sites for corresponding periodicals:

> www.AdAge.com
> www.autoweek.com
> www.businessinsurance.com
> www.crainschicagobusiness.com
> www.crainscleveland.com
> www.crainsdetroit.com
> www.crainsny.com
> emonline.com
> www.investmentnews.com
> www.modernhealthcare.com
> www.pionline.com
> www.plasticsnews.com
> www.rcrnews.com
> www.rubbernews.com
> www.tirebusiness.com
> www.wastenews.com
> www.globalwirelessnews.com

CYBERHOUND® ONLINE is a guide to finding and retrieving significant sites on the Internet. It has a search engine and 75 search delimiters. It adds thousands of site reviews monthly. To try it out free, go to the world wide web at http://www.cyberhound.com. For pricing and ordering information, call Gale Research at (800) 877-GALE.

CYBERHOUND'S® GUIDE TO PEOPLE ON THE INTERNET is organized into three sections. (1) Who's Who Online identifies 1,000 online directories, databases and membership listings. For example, it lists Architects in Canada, Attorney Finder, Famous Left-Handers, and The Missing Persons Pages. (2) White Pages provides and alphabetical listing of 3,000 business professionals who are accessible by email. Other information includes area of expertise, personal and professional affiliation and company information. (3) Personal Web Sites are organized alphabetically by name. 1,500 pages of people in the news in business, entertainment, and sports. $79. Gale Group, P.O. Box 9187, Farmington Hills, MI 48333-9187. Toll free US and Canada (800) 877-GALE (4253) and (248) 699-GALE, fax (800) 414-5043 and (248) 699-8061, Internet orders galeord@galegroup.com, web site www.galegroup.com or www.gale.com. All Gale Group products are available on approval. Contact Gale for details.

PRIME COMPUTER AND COMPUTERVISION'S COMPANY ALUMNI WEB SITE URL'S are http://member.aol.com/uncleroy22/prime.htm and http://members.xoom.com/uncleroy/prime.htm.

PUBLISHERS' WEB SITES—Remember to check the web sites of the PUBLISHERS of your favorite directories, magazines and newspapers for the latest information on their new products, electronic and otherwise. Publishers' URL's are identified in each listing in this chapter. At the time of this writing, most publishers had web sites, but not all. You can make a phone call to find out if that's changed, or to receive a copy of their latest catalog. See Publishers Web Sites category.

SEARCH ENGINES. Here are the main search engines you can use as a starting point. Some people consider the first four better—Yahoo, Lycos, AltaVista and Excite. The remaining search engines are listed alphabetically.

> Yahoo! (http://www.yahoo.com)
> Lycos (http://www.lycos.com)
> AltaVista (http://www.AltaVista.com)
> Excite (http://www.excite.com)
>
> Dejanews (http://www.dejanews.com)
> HotBot (http://www.HotBot.com)
> Inference (http://www.inference.com/infind)
> Infoseek (http://www.infoseek.com)
> Nerd World (http://www.NerdWorld.com)
> Netfind (http://www.netfind.com)
> Northern Light (http://www.northernlight.com)
> Opentext (http://www.pinstripe.opentext.com/)
> Webcrawler (http://webcrawler.com)

URL'S—Here is a good cross section of URL's (Uniform Resource Locator) for jobhunters, company recruiters, executive search professionals and personnel agencies. These web sites are also individually listed under the appropriate categories.

http://199.233.99.2/neerc/ This is the URL for the New England Executive Resources Council. It is an organization mainly comprised of search consultants. Meetings are held in Waltham, Mass. This site includes a listing of members, including some photos.

http://member.aol.com/uncleroy22/prime.htm This is the URL to the Prime Computer/Computervision alumni web site.

www.abbott.com/career/index.htm This is the URL for the Career Pages for Abbott Laboratories. Their main web site is http://www.abbot.com. Check the sites of other companies for additional career opportunities.

www.airsdirectory.com This is the URL for AIRS—Advanced Internet Recruitment Strategies. AIRS is a firm which provides training for recruiters who use the Internet as a recruiting tool. For more information contact AIRS, 1790 Franklin Street, Berkeley, CA 94702, phone (800) 336-6360, fax (888) 997-5559. Their web site contains many excellent free helpful resources.

www.amazon.com This is the web site for a large online bookstore which gives discounts.

www.asianet.com This site matches Pacific Rim positions with individuals who speak Asian languages.

www.askjeeves.com or **www.ask.com** or **www.aj.com** or **ask**. Ask Jeeves a question. For example, if you ask Jeeves, "How can I find a job" or "How can I find candidates for an engineering job?" Jeeves has an answer! Actually, there's very little you can't ask Jeeves. This web site can also be used for targeted email. How-to details are discussed in The Internet Recruiting Edge by Barbara Ling @ http://www.barbaraling.com.

www.asktheheadhunter.com This is the web site for the book, Ask The Headhunter, a book that can effectively be used by both job hunters and interviewers, by Nick Corcodilos, email northbridge@sprintmail.com. According to Tom Peters, it is "a powerful hiring tool no manager can afford to miss" and it "shreds some of our most basic assumptions about the way to hire top people." Published by Penguin Putnam, New York, $14.95, the book is available from the web site and at bookstores. Corcodilos and his client, Merrill Lynch's Vice President of Global Staffing, were jointly featured in a discussion about changes in corporate recruiting and hiring practices in a segment on "Opportunity Knocks," a CNBC special on Executive Search. To purchase this 5 hour video, contact CNBC or Corcodilos.

www.aviationtoday.com This is the web site for PHILLIPS AVIATION TODAY, published by Phillips Business Information, Inc., a Phillips Publishing International Company, 120 Seven Locks Road, Potomac, MD 20854, (301) 340-1520, (301) 340-7788, (800) 777-5006, Internet pbi@phillips.com, web site www.phillips.com.

www.barbaraling.com This is the web site for the book The Internet Recruiting Edge by Barbara Ling. Linked to this site is AIRS, a collection of Internet Recruiting tools and recruiting seminars; and author Bill Radin's site.

www.bookwire.com For information about publishing and research, the *Publishers Weekly* web site at http://www.bookwire.com serves consumers & publishing professionals. Bowker's *Publishers Weekly*'s web site includes a searchable database of current author tour information, links to all book-related Web sites, industry Classifieds, and Book Wire Insider Direct, a subscription daily e-mail news service, and more.

www.boston.com This is the site for the *Boston Globe*'s online access to their newspaper ads.

www.bowker.com This large research publisher's web site includes an online product catalog, ordering information, electronic publishing, Internet databases, CD ROMs, online subscription and site licensing databases, press releases, career opportunities, and more. Many of their references are accessible through this web site, such as Books in Print Plus Canadian Edition, Ulrich's on Disc, German Books In Print, German Books Out of Print, International Books in Print PLUS, Italian Books in Print, Yearbook of International Organizations PLUS, Ulrich's International Periodicals Directory, The Software Encyclopedia, Bowker's Complete Video Directory, American Book Publishing Record. Visit the web site for more information.

www.businessweek.com/careers/right.htm *BusinessWeek*'s Internet Career Center offers a free, confidential service for job seekers, advertising that's cheaper than a want ad, and a job posting service if you're an employer.

www.career.com Career.com links employers and candidates throughout the world. Heart's goals for www.career.com are to provide free job seeker assistance and to offer employers an effective way to reach qualified job seekers. Most positions are in Engineering, IT and marketing and usually range between $30,000 and $75,000. The site was launched in 1993 and developed by Heart Advertising Network, Los Altos, California.

www.careermosaic.com Career Mosaic is a major recruitment web site that spends millions of dollars in advertising to draw traffic to this site. CareerMosaic features a jobs database; newsgroups for jobs, college connection, online job fairs, employer job postings; company information and more. CareerMosaic was ranked as one of the top 5 "Sites Offering the Best Overall Support for Job Seekers" by the *National Business Employment Weekly.* The site was developed Bernard Hodes Advertising in New York and went online in 1994.

www.careerpath.com This site was ranked as one of the top 5 "Sites Offering the Best Overall Support for Job-Seekers" by the *National Business Employment Weekly.* CareerPath.com puts the help wanted sections of over 70 US newspapers into one database. Job hunters can post their resumes free. Companies must pay a fee to access resumes. The web site claims, "Powered by the nation's leading newspapers and employers, CareerPath.com has the Web's largest number of the most current job listings." Launched in 1995, the site was developed by a consortium of media companies—Knight-Ridder, *The New York Times,* the Time Mirror Company, the Tribune Company, the Washington Post, Cox Interactive Media, Gannett Company and Hearst Corp.

www.careers.computerworld.com This is a computer industry career web site.

www.careers.wsj.com/ This *Wall Street Journal* web site includes Job Seek, Who's Hiring, Career Columnists, Salaries & Profiles, The Salary Calculator™, Job Hunting Advice, Succeeding at Work, HR Issues, Executive Recruiters, Working Globally, College Connection, Starting a Business, Career Bookstore and more. Content from The National Employment Business Weekly is also featured.

www.careerxroads.com This is the web site for the book CareerXroads by Gerry Crispin and Mark Mehler. It is a directory to the best job, resume and career management sites on the world wide web.

www.ceweekly.com This site for Contract Employment Weekly lists engineering and information systems positions, for both recruiters and job seekers. Contract Employment Weekly Online is a service of C.E. Publications, Inc., P.O. Box 3006, Bothell, WA 98041-3006. (425) 806-5200, Fax (425) 806-5585, email publisher@ceweekly.com.

www.clickit.com "Access Business Online" Brings Buyers and Sellers Together on the Internet, including Executive Job Network, Capital Sources, Trade Announcements, Professional Services, Top 100 World Business Charts, International Buyer-Seller, Company Profiles, BizWiz! Search Engine, Web Emporium Web Site Development, Classifieds, Corporate News Net, Wall Street and World Wide Finance, Market News & Business Connections, and more.

www.cnn.com CNN's impressive web site contains Big Yellow Search Books to find Businesses, people, global directories and The Directory Store™. It also contains a "search the net" capability with InfoSeek. InfoSeek has a Business Channel with business resources and small businesses and a Careers Channel.

www.datamation.com This winner of the Jesse H. Neal Award is a web site for IT executives and professionals. Provides targeted daily computer news, IT Executive Job Pavilion, Management Benchmarking Application (MBA), technology workbench, back issues from Datamation and comprehensive links to IT vendors and other online resources. A Cahners Business Information web site.

www.dbm.com/jobguide This is the web site of DBM, an outplacement firm. It is "the best Internet recruiting starting point" according to the Tiburon Group, a Chicago based firm that provides "Strategic Internet Recruiting Solutions Consultants and Trainers." Tiburon Group, phone (773) 907-8330, Fax (773) 907-9481, email getajob@tiburongroup.com, web site www.tiburongroup.com.

www.decalumni.com This is the web site for alumni of Digital Equipment Corp. It includes a directory.

www.the-dma.org This is the site of the Direct Marketing Association, 1120 Avenue of the Americas, New York, NY 10036-6700, (212) 768-7277, fax (212) 302-6714. It features the DMA Job Bank, Online Bookstore, Seminars, Conferences. Their membership directory is available to members.

www.eagleview.com Eagleview presents Select Candidate™ Network for job seekers and employers and other information for Data General alumni.

www.ectoday.com This is the web site that contains the latest electronic commerce industry news. For more information, contact: Phillips Business Information, Inc., a Phillips Publishing International Company, 120 Seven Locks Road, Potomac, MD 20854, (301) 340-1520, (301) 340-7788, (800) 777-5006, Internet pbi@phillips.com, web site www.phillips.com.

emheadlines.com This site is an entertainment business headline news service from Cahners Business Information. It covers Film, Television, Books, Technology, Music. Nielsen Ratings, Domestic Box Office, Bestseller List.

www.emory.edu/CAREER/index.html This is Emory University's Career Paradise web site, with modules for alumni, students and employers.

www.europages.com This is the site to a business directory of over 500,000 European firms.n Deutsch, English, Espanol, Français & Italiano. Search for Companies, Company Catalogues, Business Information, Yellow Pages in Europe. Search by Product/Service, Thematic Search or by Company Name. Address, phone, fax, products, turnover. Europages' Daily Business News, European Trade Fairs, Chambers of Commerce in Europe, European Patent Offices, Official International Organisations, European Standardization Bodies.

www.execunet.com Exec-U-Net is a subscription service, listing executive level positions by search firms and a few companies for positions at $100,000 or more. Candidates tend to be high quality, perhaps because of the cost.

www.executiveagent.com is a web site that helps executive job seekers market their skills and experience to a targeted list of executive recruiters via email. ExecutiveAgent is completely confidential as resumes go directly to the search firms.

www.galegroup.com This is the web site to publisher Gale Group, formerly Gale Research. Also see the Gale Research web site at www.gale.com.

www.helpwanted.com This is a web site for free posting and searching of all content for job seekers, employers and agencies.

www.iccweb.com This is the site to Internet Career Connection, an employment matching service, including Federal Government employment.

www.interbiznet.com/hrstart.html This is the URL to the Electronic Recruiting News web site. It includes the Recruiters Internet Survival Guide and recruiting seminars information.

www.jobhunt.com is a Meta-list of On-line Job-Search Resources and Services for recruiters and jobhunters. It includes: The Online Career Center, Career Mosaic, Career Net, Job Web, Standard Job Hunt List, Americas Job Bank, Best Jobs in the USA, Career Web, College Grad Job Hunter, JobOptions (www.joboptions.com, formerly E-span Interactive Employment Network), Job Trak, The Internet Job Locator, The Monster Board, Virtual Job Fair. It also offers the capability of searching by state and local newspapers. New Items (less than a week old) are highlighted, as are "Outstanding Job Resources."

www.job-hunt.org This site provides on-line job search resources and services identifies jobs resources and ranks the outstanding ones. Is linked to Career Paradise of Emory University Career Center (www.emory.edu/CAREER/index.html), featuring a "Colossal List" or Career Links and Hiring Express pages. It's given high marks for both its content and humorous presentation.

www.jobnet.org This Canadian web site includes "Looking for a career in financial services?" Scotiabank online recruiting, Jobnet and Alumnet.

www.jobtrak.com Jobtrak is a career service network for college students, alumni, college career staff and employers. JOBTRAK CORPORATION, Los Angeles, CA, (310) 474-3377, (800) 999-8725, fax (310) 475-7912.

www.kennedyinfo.com Publisher Kennedy Information's web site includes books, newsletters, training materials, directories, and surveys for executive recruiting, human resources, outplacement, management consulting and job seekers. (800) 531-0007 or (603) 585-6544.

www.kompass.com Kompass's web site contains a searchable database that encompasses over 60 countries, 2.5 million executive names, information on 1.5 million companies, 19 million key product references, and 370,000 trade and brand names. At the time of this writing, Kompass is available in English and French. Deutsch, Espanol and Italiano will soon be available.

www.latimes.com This is the URL to the comprehensive *Los Angeles Times* web site.

www.mediacorp2.com/ This is the site to Canada Employment Weekly. It includes The Career Bookstore for Canadian career books, Talent Available to market yourself to Canadian recruiters and search firms, Canadian Directory of Search Firms, and Who's Hiring for a list of Canada's top employers.

www.mediacorp2.com/cds/findex.html This site sells the Canadian Directory of Search Firms, in French and English. It contains over 1,700 search firms and 3,000 recruitment professionals, 70 occupational categories, a geographic index, and a Who's Who Index. $39.95, ISBN 0-9681447-1-3. To locate the Canadian Directory of Search Firms, go to www.netjobs.com. Send questions or comments to info@netjobs.com, NetJobs Information Services @JOBNET, 103 Wright Street, Richmond Hill, ON L4C 4A3, CANADA, (800) 367-6563 or (905) 770-0829, fax (905) 770-5024

www.monster.com This is the URL for the popular Monster Board web site. The Monster Board was ranked as one of the top 5 "Best General-Purpose Sites" by the *National Business Employment Weekly.* It is a major recruitment web site that spends millions of dollars in advertising to attract traffic to this site. Features include Job search in the US, International or by Companies, Career Center Events, Recruiters' Center, Seminars, Post a Job, free online recruitment seminar. It also offers special links for human resources, health care, technology and entry level positions. Toll free phone number (800) MONSTER. The Monster Board, PO Box 586, Framingham, MA 01704-0586. The site developer is TMP Worldwide, New York, New York and has been online since 1994.

www.monsterhr.com This is the site to the Monster Board: Human Resources careers on the web. Enter your job profile and have job listings automatically downloaded to your Email. International opportunities in Canada are classified by Canada overall, then Alberta, British Columbia, Newfoundland, Ontario and Quebec.

www.nationjob.com Nationjob Network Online Jobs Database offers "Search for a Job Now (no email required)," "Search for a Company" and "Directory of all Companies." P.J. Scout service is a "(P) ersonal (J)ob Scout service that's "like having a friend shop for a job for you." Fill in a form and PJ will send you info on jobs you might be interested in. Information on salary comparisons, moving costs, relocation info, insurance calculator and more. NationJob Inc., 601 SW 9th Street, Suites J&K, Des Moines, IA 50309, (800) 292-7731.

www.nehra.com This is the URL to the Northeast Human Resources Association's web site.

www.netjobs.com This site is reportedly Canada's premiere employment web site. It includes Internet Career Centre for employers and job seekers. Overseas Jobs Express, Personal Computer Training. Email info@netjobs.com. Linked to www.jobnet.org.

www.netshare.com This is the URL for NETSHARE 2000, a confidential for-fee career management service designed for executives, companies and recruiters that posts senior level positions on the Internet daily. Salary usually exceeds $100,000 but is sometimes in the $75,000 range. Their ad claims, "A best search site"...FORTUNE Magazine and "Best of the Best"...CareerXRoads. NETSHARE 2000 was developed by Netshare, Inc., Novato, California and went online in 1995. (800) 241-5642, email netshare@netshare.com.

www.nytimes.com This is *The New York Times* web site

www.occ.com This is the URL for the On Line Career Center, one of the Internet's first online recruitment sites, launched in 1993. It is a major recruitment web site that spends millions of dollars in advertising to drive traffic to the site. This is a major site that was developed by William O Warren, who has received honors for his pioneering work in the development of Internet Recruiting. This web site allows you to enter your job profile and have job listings automatically downloaded to your Email. Questions to webmaster@occ.com. www.occ.com was rated by the *National Business Employment Weekly* as one of the top 5 sites in 3 different categories: "Sites Offering the Best Overall Support for Job Seekers," "Sites Offering the Best Job-Search Support" and "Sites Offering the Best Career Resources for Job Seekers." Openings are mainly in engineering, information technology and sales and marketing. The site developer is TMP Worldwide, New York, New York.

www.reedref.com This site presents a current catalog for all Reed Reference Publishing companies for both print and electronic references—National Register Publishing, R.R. Bowker, Bowker-Saur, KG Saur, Marquis Who's Who, Martindale-Hubbell and Lexis-Nexis Business Information. At the time of this writing, this catalog is searchable by name, subject, publisher and keyword. To check new offerings, visit individual publisher pages. Free product demos of CD ROM'S can be downloaded for for experimentation and some sample pages—and even entire chapters—and are available for unlimited viewing. The web site also includes a constantly updated menu of special discounts which are available only on the web site. Ask about the growing number of RRP databases accessible via the Internet on subscription or for a usage based price, such as the Martindale-Hubbell Law Directory. For more information visit Bowker Reed Reference's web site at www.reedref.com or www.bowker.com or contact corporate offices, 121 Chanlon Road, New Providence, NJ 07974, (800) 521-8110, (800) 323-3288, fax (908) 665-3528, email info@bowker.com or webmaster@www.reedref.com.

www.ritesite.com This is the web site to the book, Rites of Passage at $100,000+ by John Lucht.

www.rtp.org This is the home page for Research Triangle Park, North Carolina including a directory of companies in the Park. Includes listing of companies according to research specialization, appropriate for target list development.

www.sec.gov/edgarhp.htm   This is the site to the EDGAR Database of corporate information from the Securities & Exchange Commission database of corporate information. It contains About the SEC, Investor Assistance & Complaints, EDGAR Database, SEC Digest & Statements, Current SEC Rulemaking, Enforcement Division, Small Business Information, Other sites to visit.

www.shrm.org/jobs/   The Society for Human Resource Management site is linked to www.career.mosaic./com. It also includes Membership Directory Online, which only can be accessed by members.

www.sireport.com   This is the site to the Staffing Industry Report.

www.technicalrecruiter.com   This is an excellent starting point for a large number of specialized sites, such as ProjectManager.com and SoftwareEngineer.com.

www.thomasregister.com This site provides information on US and Canadian manufacturing firms.

www.tiburongroup.com   This is the web site to the Tiburon Group in Chicago, an Internet Recruitment Training and Strategy firm. They are also a recruiting firm. Phone (773) 907-8330, Fax (773) 907-9481, email getajob@tiburongroup.com.

www.townline.com/working/   This site encompasses job listings from 113 community newspapers. It also has job profiles to automatically download to your email.

www.wageweb.com   This is the site to the Salary Survey Data Online.

www.world.hire.com   World Hire Online is a web site with job listings mainly in engineering, information technology and "senior management," usually in the $50,000 to $100,000 range. The site was developed by World.Hire, Austin, Texas and was launched in 1996. World Hire also features a Job profile notification and the Recruiter™ web site product. Some sample recruiter sites include www.coastalcorp.com, www.eds.com, www.ibm.com.

www.websitez.com   This is the URL to a web site that assists in finding any web address in the world.

www.whois.net This site can help you find your own domain or look up a web site.

www.555-1212.com   This is the Internet Domain name registration service and directory of phone and email listings for businesses and individuals.

Web Sites—Books of URL's for Recruiters & Jobhunters

CAREERXROADS, by Gerry Crispin and Mark Mehler, is an annual directory of job and resume sites. At the time of this writing the number of sites has more than tripled in two years to over 1,000 sites. It includes specialized databases for job seekers and employers. $22.95. Order online or by phone from distributor Kennedy Information, One Kennedy Place, Route 12 South, Fitzwilliam, NH 03447, phone (800) 531-0007 or 603-585-6544, fax 603-585-9555, email bookstore@kennedyinfo.com, web site www.kennedyinfo.com. Also available through from author's web site or at your local book store.

CYBERHOUND® ONLINE is a guide to finding and retrieving significant sites on the Internet. It has a search engine and 75 search delimiters. It adds thousands of site reviews monthly. To try it out free, go to the world wide web at http://www.cyberhound.com. For pricing and ordering information, call Gale Research at (800) 877-GALE.

CYBERHOUND'S® GUIDE TO COMPANIES ON THE INTERNET reviews over 2,000 corporate sites, including major companies as well as those in the information industry, software and hardware developers and networking and telecommunications companies. It also includes a user's guide, a directory of specialized business we sites, a bibliography of Internet products, and a glossary of Internet terms. At the time of this writing 1st edition (1996) available from Gale for $79, reduced from $95. Published by Euromonitor (England). Distributed by Gale Group, P.O. Box 9187, Farmington Hills, MI 48333-9187. Toll free US and Canada (800) 877-GALE (4253) and (248) 699-GALE, fax (800) 414-5043 and (248) 699-8061, Internet orders galeord@galegroup.com, web site www.galegroup.com or www.gale.com. All Gale Group products are available on approval. Contact Gale for details.

CYBERHOUND'S® GUIDE TO INTERNET DISCUSSION GROUPS contains over 4,000 Internet listservs and news groups and a subject and master index, such as computer know-how groups, such as the virus Computer Newsgroup (comp.virus), health information groups, and social interaction groups. $79. Gale Group, P.O. Box 9187, Farmington Hills, MI 48333-9187. Toll free US and Canada (800) 877-GALE (4253) and (248) 699-GALE, fax (800) 414-5043 and (248) 699-8061, Internet orders galeord@galegroup.com, web site www.galegroup.com or www.gale.com. All Gale Group products are available on approval. Contact Gale for details.

CYBERHOUND'S® GUIDE TO INTERNET LIBRARIES will guide you to online information including site descriptions and reviews of over 2,000 libraries, including contact information, mainfiles/subfiles, holdings information, subscriptions, services, how to access, information on special collections, OPAC addresses, plus a bibliography, a glossary of Internet terms, White Pages and two indexes. $79. Gale Group, P.O. Box 9187, Farmington Hills, MI 48333-9187. Toll free US and Canada (800) 877-GALE (4253) and (248) 699-GALE, fax (800) 414-5043 and (248) 699-8061, Internet orders galeord@galegroup.com, web site www.galegroup.com or www.gale.com. All Gale Group products are available on approval. Contact Gale for details.

CYBERHOUND'S® GUIDE TO PEOPLE ON THE INTERNET is organized into three sections. (1) Who's Who Online identifies 1,000 online directories, databases and membership listings. For example, it lists Architects in Canada, Attorney Finder, Famous Left-Handers, and The Missing Persons Pages. (2) White Pages provides and alphabetical listing of 3,000 business professionals who are accessible by email. Other information includes area of expertise, personal and professional affiliation and company information. (3) Personal Web Sites are organized alphabetically by name. 1,500 pages of people in the news in business, entertainment, and sports. $79. Gale Group, P.O. Box 9187, Farmington Hills, MI 48333-9187. Toll free US and Canada (800) 877-GALE (4253) and (248) 699-GALE, fax (800) 414-5043 and (248) 699-8061, Internet orders galeord@galegroup.com, web site www.galegroup.com or www.gale.com. All Gale Group products are available on approval. Contact Gale for details.

CYBERHOUND'S® GUIDE TO PUBLICATIONS ON THE INTERNET provides fully indexed information on over 3,000 Internet publications. Covers the World Wide Web, Gopher, Telnet and FTP sites that make online publication available to the public. $79. Gale Group, P.O. Box 9187, Farmington Hills, MI 48333-9187. Toll free US and Canada (800) 877-GALE (4253) and (248) 699-GALE, fax (800) 414-5043 and (248) 699-8061, Internet orders galeord@galegroup.com, web site www.galegroup.com or www.gale.com. All Gale Group products are available on approval. Contact Gale for details.

GALE GUIDE TO INTERNET DATABASES, formerly titled CYBERHOUND'S GUIDE TO INTERNET DATABASES, identifies over 5,000 Internet databases. $115. Gale Group, P.O. Box 9187, Farmington Hills, MI 48333-9187. Toll free US and Canada (800) 877-GALE (4253) and (248) 699-GALE, fax (800) 414-5043 and (248) 699-8061, Internet orders galeord@galegroup.com, web site www.galegroup.com or www.gale.com. All Gale Group products are available on approval. Contact Gale for details.

INTERNET RECRUITING EDGE by Barbara Ling is a comprehensive collection of research assembled over a two year period. Developed for the novice and experienced Internet recruiter alike, and with a foreword by Tony Byrne, topics include: Where, Oh Where, is my Candidate Now?, Does the Internet Really Benefit Businesses? Phones Still Work, But Don't Buy a Mansion if You Only Need a Cottage, How to Find Candidates on the Internet, Non-Traditional Resources, Before You Begin—A Primer on Internet Culture—Netiquette, Beginner Candidate Location Skill, Resume Banks, Search Engine Basics, The Joy of Bookmarks, The Art of Job Posting, Sleuthing for Company Directories, Finding Employee Directories, Finding Executive Biographies, Alumni Organizations, Forums and Bulletin Boards, Internet Classifieds, Online E-zines (magazines), Professional Organizations, Colleges, Metasearch at Highway 61, Realistic Goals Before You Begin Your Own Recruiter Web site, Perilous Pitfalls, How To Buy Your Recruiter Business Site, Locating Good Web Site Designers, Your Site is Designed—Now What? How To Market A Recruiter Web Site, 14 Killer Web Site Search Engine Visibility Tips, and more. $149. Order by visiting the web site http://www.barbaraling.com or call (732) 563-1464.

JOBHUNTING ON THE INTERNET by Richard Nelson Bolles, Ten Speed Press, P.O. Box 7123, Berkeley, CA 94707. Among other things, this book provides a small but reasonably complete listing of INTERNET URL's (Uniform Resource Locators) with a short description of the contents of each. By the author of the classic WHAT COLOR IS YOUR PARACHUTE?

RECRUITERS' INTERNET SURVIVAL GUIDE by John Sumser, author of the 1996 Electronic Recruiting Index, rated over 500 recruiting web sites and analyzed Internet recruiting issues. The Recruiters' Internet Survival Guide, published by Staffing Industry Resources, $89.50. To view the table of contents or to order a copy, go to web site www.interbiznet.com or contact IBN (Internet Business Network) in Mill Valley, CA.

WORLD DIRECTORY OF BUSINESS INFORMATION WEB SITES provides full details on over 1,500 free business web sites, including information such as online surveys, top company rankings, company information, brand information, market research reports and trade association statistics. $590. Published by Euromonitor (England). Distributed by Gale Group, P.O. Box 9187, Farmington Hills, MI 48333-9187. Toll free US and Canada (800) 877-GALE (4253) and (248) 699-GALE, fax (800) 414-5043 and (248) 699-8061, Internet orders galeord@galegroup.com, web site www.galegroup.com or www.gale.com. All Gale Group products are available on approval. Contact Gale for details.

Wholesale Drugs

DIRECTORY OF DRUG STORE AND HBC CHAINS identifies over 1,800 drug retailers in the U.S. and Canada operating over 45,000 stores including drug, HBC, cosmetic, deep discount, home health care, discount, and grocery stores/supermarket chains with pharmacies, mass merchants with pharmacies, deep discount chains, and wholesale drug companies. It includes names and titles of key personnel, a listing of major trade associations and a trade show calendar. It also provides indexes to top drug retailers, top drug wholesalers, top grocery chains and top discount chains. $290. Chain Store Guide Information Services, 3922 Coconut Palm Drive, Tampa, FL 33619. (800) 927-9292, (813) 664-6800, (813) 627-6822, (800) 289-6822. http://www.d-net.com/csgis or http://www.csgis.com.

Who's Who

See Biographies

CANADIAN DIRECTORY OF SEARCH FIRMS, in French and English, lists over 1,700 search firms and 3,000 recruitment professionals. 70 occupational categories, geographic index, and a Who's Who Index. $39.95, ISBN 0-9681447-1-3. To locate the CANADIAN DIRECTORY OF SEARCH FIRMS, go to www.netjobs.com or ask your favorite bookstore to look it up in BOOKS IN PRINT.

COMPLETE MARQUIS WHO'S WHO ON CD ROM is a compilation of literally all 19 Marquis Who's Who that have appeared in print since 1985, including living and deceased people. WHO'S WHO IN AMERICA®, WHO'S WHO IN THE WORLD®, WHO'S WHO IN AMERICAN EDUCATIONS®, WHO'S WHO IN AMERICAN LAW®, WHO'S WHO IN AMERICAN NURSING®, WHO'S WHO IN MEDICINE AND HEALTHCARE®, WHO'S WHO IN FINANCE AND INDUSTRY®, WHO'S WHO IN SCIENCE AND ENGINEERING®, WHO'S WHO IN THE EAST®, WHO'S WHO IN THE MIDWEST®, WHO'S WHO IN THE SOUTH AND SOUTHWEST®, WHO'S WHO IN THE WEST®, WHO'S WHO OF AMERICAN WOMEN®, WHO'S WHO IN ADVERTISING®, WHO'S WHO OF EMERGING LEADERS IN AMERICA®, WHO'S WHO IN ENTERTAINMENT®, WHO'S WHO AMONG HUMAN SERVICES PROFESSIONALS®. One year subscription with semi-annual updates $995. National Register Publishing, Reed Elsevier-New Providence, 121 Chanlon Road, New Providence, NJ 07974, (800) 521-8110, fax (800) 836-7736, web site www.marquiswhoswho.com or www.redbooks.com. "If, for any reason whatsoever, your order does not fully meet your expectations, simply return the product within 30 days for a prompt, complete, unquestioned refund," as stated in Catalog of Biographical and Professional References of publisher Marquis Who's Who/National Register Publishing.

CYBERHOUND'S® GUIDE TO PEOPLE ON THE INTERNET is organized into three sections. (1) Who's Who Online identifies 1,000 online directories, databases and membership listings. For example, it lists Architects in Canada, Attorney Finder, Famous Left-Handers, and The Missing Persons Pages. (2) White Pages provides and alphabetical listing of 3,000 business professionals who are accessible by email. Other information includes area of expertise, personal and professional affiliation and company information. (3) Personal Web Sites are organized alphabetically by name. 1,500 pages of people in the news in business, entertainment, and sports. $79. Gale Group, P.O. Box 9187, Farmington Hills, MI 48333-9187. Toll free US and Canada (800) 877-GALE (4253) and (248) 699-GALE, fax (800) 414-5043 and (248) 699-8061, Internet orders galeord@galegroup.com, web site www.galegroup.com or www.gale.com. All Gale Group products are available on approval. Contact Gale for details.

INDEX TO MARQUIS WHO'S WHO PUBLICATIONS provides a complete list of Who's Who names and the volume(s) in which they appear. $105. First time standing order $94.50. Marquis Who's Who, 121 Chanlon Road, New Providence, NJ 07974, (800) 521-8110.

INTERNATIONAL WHO'S WHO contains 20,000 biographies. $340. Published by Europa. Distributed in the US and Canada by Gale Group, P.O. Box 9187, Farmington Hills, MI 48333-9187. Toll free US and Canada (800) 877-GALE (4253) and (248) 699-GALE, fax (800) 414-5043 and (248) 699-8061, Internet orders galeord@galegroup.com, web site www.galegroup.com or www.gale.com. All Gale Group products are available on approval. Contact Gale for details.

INTERNATIONAL WHO'S WHO OF WOMEN lists 4,000 women, including well known figures and women who have recently come to the forefront of their fields. Information includes woman's nationality, date and place of birth, education, family, career history and present position, honors, awards, publications, and contact information. $390. Published by Europa. Distributed by Gale Group, P.O. Box 9187, Farmington Hills, MI 48333-9187. Toll free US and Canada (800) 877-GALE (4253) and (248) 699-GALE, fax (800) 414-5043 and (248) 699-8061, Internet orders galeord@galegroup.com, web site www.galegroup.com or www.gale.com. All Gale Group products are available on approval. Contact Gale for details.

NICKLE'S CANADIAN OIL REGISTER is a directory that provides names of key personnel and other information on 4,500 Canadian companies in these industry categories: exploration and production companies, service and supply companies, data processors, consultants, engineers, financial and investment companies, leasebrokers and land agents, geophysical contractors, oil well drilling contractors, oil well servicing contractors, pipeline and power distributors, refiners and processors, transportation and construction companies, government departments, agencies and industry associations. Includes a Who's Who section that identifies over 24,000 key management, engineering and technical personnel. $175. Published annually. Special discounts available for combined purchases. For more information on Energy Information Services, call Calgary office (403) 244-6111. Published by Southam Information Products Ltd, 1450 Don Mills Road, Don Mills, Ontario M3B 2X7 CANADA, (800) 668-2374. In Toronto 442-2122. Web site www.southam.com.

WHO'S WHO AMONG AFRICAN AMERICANS contains information on 20,000 people including figures in business, the arts, sports, and religion. Includes geographic and occupational indexes. $165. Gale Group, P.O. Box 9187, Farmington Hills, MI 48333-9187. Toll free US and Canada (800) 877-GALE (4253) and (248) 699-GALE, fax (800) 414-5043 and (248) 699-8061, Internet orders galeord@galegroup.com, web site www.galegroup.com or www.gale.com. All Gale Group products are available on approval. Contact Gale for details.

WHO'S WHO AMONG ASIAN AMERICANS contains information including career information and addresses for nearly 6,000 people. Also includes occupation, geographic and ethnic/cultural heritage indexes and and obituary section. $85. Gale Group, P.O. Box 9187, Farmington Hills, MI 48333-9187. Toll free US and Canada (800) 877-GALE (4253) and (248) 699-GALE, fax (800) 414-5043 and (248) 699-8061, Internet orders galeord@galegroup.com, web site www.galegroup.com or www.gale.com. All Gale Group products are available on approval. Contact Gale for details.

WHO'S WHO IN AMERICA, $525. National Register Publishing, Reed Elsevier-New Providence, 121 Chanlon Road, New Providence, NJ 07974, (800) 521-8110, fax (800) 836-7736, web site www.marquiswhoswho.com or www.redbooks.com. "If, for any reason whatsoever, your order does not fully meet your expectations, simply return the product within 30 days for a prompt, complete, unquestioned refund," as stated in Catalog of Biographical and Professional References of publisher Marquis Who's Who/National Register Publishing.

WHO'S WHO IN AMERICAN ART, $210. National Register Publishing, Reed Elsevier-New Providence, 121 Chanlon Road, New Providence, NJ 07974, (800) 521-8110, fax (800) 836-7736, web site www.marquiswhoswho.com or www.redbooks.com. "If, for any reason whatsoever, your order does not fully meet your expectations, simply return the product within 30 days for a prompt, complete, unquestioned refund," as stated in Catalog of Biographical and Professional References of publisher Marquis Who's Who/National Register Publishing.

WHO'S WHO IN AMERICAN EDUCATION, $159.95, first time standing order $143.95, Marquis Who's Who, 121 Chanlon Road, New Providence, NJ 07974, (800) 521-8110.

WHO'S WHO IN AMERICAN LAW, $285. WHO'S WHO IN AMERICAN LAW ON CD ROM is also available. Call publisher for price. National Register Publishing, Reed Elsevier-New Providence, 121 Chanlon Road, New Providence, NJ 07974, (800) 521-8110, fax (800) 836-7736, web site www.marquiswhoswho.com or www.redbooks.com. "If, for any reason whatsoever, your order does not fully meet your expectations, simply return the product within 30 days for a prompt, complete, unquestioned refund," as stated in Catalog of Biographical and Professional References of publisher Marquis Who's Who/National Register Publishing.

WHO'S WHO IN AMERICAN NURSING, $149.95, first time standing order, $134.95, Who's Marquis Who's Who, 121 Chanlon Road, New Providence, NJ 07974, (800) 521-8110.

WHO'S WHO IN AMERICAN POLITICS, $259.95. National Register Publishing, Reed Elsevier-New Providence, 121 Chanlon Road, New Providence, NJ 07974, (800) 521-8110, fax (800) 836-7736, web site www.marquiswhoswho.com or www.redbooks.com. "If, for any reason whatsoever, your order does not fully meet your expectations, simply return the product within 30 days for a prompt, complete, unquestioned refund," as stated in Catalog of Biographical and Professional References of publisher Marquis Who's Who/National Register Publishing.

WHO'S WHO IN ART contains 3,000 brief biographies. $120 Published by Art Trade Press. Distributed by Gale Group, P.O. Box 9187, Farmington Hills, MI 48333-9187. Toll free US and Canada (800) 877-GALE (4253) and (248) 699-GALE, fax (800) 414-5043 and (248) 699-8061, Internet orders galeord@galegroup.com, web site www.galegroup.com or www.gale.com. All Gale Group products are available on approval. Contact Gale for details.

WHO'S WHO IN CABLE & SATELLITE EUROPE, Phillips Business Information, Inc., a Phillips Publishing International Company, 120 Seven Locks Road, Potomac, MD 20854, (301) 340-1520, (301) 340-7788, (800) 777-5006, Internet pbi@phillips.com, web site www.phillips.com.

WHO'S WHO IN CABLE & SATELLITE (UK), Phillips Business Information, Inc., a Phillips Publishing International Company, 120 Seven Locks Road, Potomac, MD 20854, (301) 340-1520, (301) 340-7788, (800) 777-5006, Internet pbi@phillips.com, web site www.phillips.com.

WHO'S WHO IN ENTERTAINMENT, $259.95. National Register Publishing, Reed Elsevier-New Providence, 121 Chanlon Road, New Providence, NJ 07974, (800) 521-8110, fax (800) 836-7736, web site www.marquiswhoswho.com or www.redbooks.com. "If, for any reason whatsoever, your order does not fully meet your expectations, simply return the product within 30 days for a prompt, complete, unquestioned refund," as stated in Catalog of Biographical and Professional References of publisher Marquis Who's Who/National Register Publishing.

WHO'S WHO IN FINANCE AND INDUSTRY, $279.95. National Register Publishing, Reed Elsevier-New Providence, 121 Chanlon Road, New Providence, NJ 07974, (800) 521-8110, fax (800) 836-7736, web site www.marquiswhoswho.com or www.redbooks.com. "If, for any reason whatsoever, your order does not fully meet your expectations, simply return the product within 30 days for a prompt, complete, unquestioned refund," as stated in Catalog of Biographical and Professional References of publisher Marquis Who's Who/National Register Publishing.

WHO'S WHO IN INSURANCE provides biographical information. $115. Underwriter Printing and Publishing Company, 50 East Palisades Avenue, Englewood, NJ 07631, (201) 569-8808, (800) 526-4700.

WHO'S WHO IN INTERNATIONAL AFFAIRS contains over 7,000 biographies of individuals in politics, trade, diplomats, international academics, civil servants, delegates to international bodies, judges, elected officials, bankers and scientists. $425. Published by Europa. Distributed by the Gale Group, P.O. Box 9187, Farmington Hills, MI 48333-9187. Toll free US and Canada (800) 877-GALE (4253) and (248) 699-GALE, fax (800) 414-5043 and (248) 699-8061, Internet orders galeord@galegroup.com, web site www.galegroup.com or www.gale.com. All Gale Group products are available on approval. Contact Gale for details.

WHO'S WHO IN LEBANON contains 2,000 biographies plus essays on economics and demographics.

Published by Publitec, Beirut. Distributed exclusively to libraries in the US and Canada by Gale. $160. Gale Research, P.O. Box 33477, Detroit, MI 48232-5477. Phone (800) 877-GALE, Fax (800) 414-5043 will be responded to within 48 hours. Internet orders: galeord@galegroup.com, CompuServe email: 72203.1552, web site http://www.galegroup.com, GaleNet web site address @http://galenet.galegroup.com.

WHO'S WHO IN MEDICINE AND HEALTHCARE, $249.95. National Register Publishing, Reed Elsevier-New Providence, 121 Chanlon Road, New Providence, NJ 07974, (800) 521-8110, fax (800) 836-7736, web site www.marquiswhoswho.com or www.redbooks.com. "If, for any reason whatsoever, your order does not fully meet your expectations, simply return the product within 30 days for a prompt, complete, unquestioned refund," as stated in Catalog of Biographical and Professional References of publisher Marquis Who's Who/National Register Publishing.

WHO'S WHO IN RISK MANAGEMENT. $65. Underwriter Printing and Publishing Company, 50 East Palisades Avenue, Englewood, NJ 07631, (201) 569-8808, (800) 526-4700.

WHO'S WHO IN SCIENCE AND ENGINEERING, $259.95. National Register Publishing, Reed Elsevier-New Providence, 121 Chanlon Road, New Providence, NJ 07974, (800) 521-8110, fax (800) 836-7736, web site www.marquiswhoswho.com or www.redbooks.com. "If, for any reason whatsoever, your order does not fully meet your expectations, simply return the product within 30 days for a prompt, complete, unquestioned refund," as stated in Catalog of Biographical and Professional References of publisher Marquis Who's Who/National Register Publishing.

WHO'S WHO IN TESTING & MONITORING, Phillips Business Information, Inc., a Phillips Publishing International Company, 120 Seven Locks Road, Potomac, MD 20854, (301) 340-1520, (301) 340-7788, (800) 777-5006, Internet pbi@phillips.com, web site www.phillips.com.

WHO'S WHO IN THE ARAB WORLD contains 6,000 biographies from 19 Arab countries. $340. Published by Publitec Publications, Beirut. Distributed to libraries in the US and Canada by Gale Group, P.O. Box 9187, Farmington Hills, MI 48333-9187. Toll free US and Canada (800) 877-GALE (4253) and (248) 699-GALE, fax (800) 414-5043 and (248) 699-8061, Internet orders galeord@galegroup.com, web site www.galegroup.com or www.gale.com. All Gale Group products are available on approval. Contact Gale for details.

WHO'S WHO IN THE EAST, $289.95. National Register Publishing, Reed Elsevier-New Providence, 121 Chanlon Road, New Providence, NJ 07974, (800) 521-8110, fax (800) 836-7736, web site www.marquiswhoswho.com or www.redbooks.com. "If, for any reason whatsoever, your order does not fully meet your expectations, simply return the product within 30 days for a prompt, complete, unquestioned refund," as stated in Catalog of Biographical and Professional References of publisher Marquis Who's Who/National Register Publishing.

WHO'S WHO IN THE MEDIA AND COMMUNICATIONS, $259.95. National Register Publishing, Reed Elsevier-New Providence, 121 Chanlon Road, New Providence, NJ 07974, (800) 521-8110, fax (800) 836-7736, web site www.marquiswhoswho.com or www.redbooks.com. "If, for any reason whatsoever, your order does not fully meet your expectations, simply return the product within 30 days for a prompt, complete, unquestioned refund," as stated in Catalog of Biographical and Professional References of publisher Marquis Who's Who/National Register Publishing.

WHO'S WHO IN THE MIDWEST, $269.95. National Register Publishing, Reed Elsevier-New Providence, 121 Chanlon Road, New Providence, NJ 07974, (800) 521-8110, fax (800) 836-7736, web site www.marquiswhoswho.com or www.redbooks.com. "If, for any reason whatsoever, your order does not fully meet your expectations, simply return the product within 30 days for a prompt, complete, unquestioned refund," as stated in Catalog of Biographical and Professional References of publisher Marquis Who's Who/National Register Publishing.

WHO'S WHO IN THE SOUTH AND SOUTHWEST, $259.95. National Register Publishing, Reed Elsevier-New Providence, 121 Chanlon Road, New Providence, NJ 07974, (800) 521-8110, fax (800) 836-7736, web site www.marquiswhoswho.com or www.redbooks.com. "If, for any reason whatsoever, your order does not fully meet your expectations, simply return the product within 30 days for a prompt, complete, unquestioned refund," as stated in Catalog of Biographical and Professional References of publisher Marquis Who's Who/National Register Publishing.

WHO'S WHO IN THE WEST, $272.95. National Register Publishing, Reed Elsevier-New Providence, 121 Chanlon Road, New Providence, NJ 07974, (800) 521-8110, fax (800) 836-7736, web site www.marquiswhoswho.com or www.redbooks.com. "If, for any reason whatsoever, your order does not fully meet your expectations, simply return the product within 30 days for a prompt, complete, unquestioned refund," as stated in Catalog of Biographical and Professional References of publisher Marquis Who's Who/National Register Publishing.

WHO'S WHO IN THE WORLD, $379.95. National Register Publishing, Reed Elsevier-New Providence, 121 Chanlon Road, New Providence, NJ 07974, (800) 521-8110, fax (800) 836-7736, web site www.marquiswhoswho.com or www.redbooks.com. "If, for any reason whatsoever, your order does not fully meet your expectations, simply return the product within 30 days for a prompt, complete, unquestioned refund," as stated in Catalog of Biographical and Professional References of publisher Marquis Who's Who/National Register Publishing.

WHO'S WHO IN UK MULTIMEDIA, Phillips Business Information, Inc., a Phillips Publishing International Company, 120 Seven Locks Road, Potomac, MD 20854, (301) 340-1520, (301) 340-7788, (800) 777-5006, Internet pbi@phillips.com, web site www.phillips.com.

WHO'S WHO OF AMERICAN WOMEN, $259.00. National Register Publishing, Reed Elsevier-New Providence, 121 Chanlon Road, New Providence, NJ 07974, (800) 521-8110, fax (800) 836-7736, web site www.marquiswhoswho.com or www.redbooks.com. "If, for any reason whatsoever, your order does not fully meet your expectations, simply return the product within 30 days for a prompt, complete, unquestioned refund," as stated in Catalog of Biographical and Professional References of publisher Marquis Who's Who/National Register Publishing.

WHO'S WHOM AMONG HISPANIC AMERICANS contains biographical data on over 11,000 people from a broad range of professions. Includes occupation, geographic and ethnic/cultural heritage indexes. $100. Gale Group, P.O. Box 9187, Farmington Hills, MI 48333-9187. Toll free US and Canada (800) 877-GALE (4253) and (248) 699-GALE, fax (800) 414-5043 and (248) 699-8061, Internet orders galeord@galegroup.com, web site www.galegroup.com or www.gale.com. All Gale Group products are available on approval. Contact Gale for details.

Wisconsin

WISCONSIN BUSINESS SERVICE DIRECTORY identifies over 24,000 names and titles of executives at 16,000 companies. Annual directory published by Wisconsin Manufacturers & Commerce, $139. CD ROM $610. Distributed by Manufacturers' News, Inc., (888) 752-5200, 1633 Central Street, Evanston, IL 60201-1569. Email info@manufacturersnews.com. Web site www.manufacturersnews.com.

Women

COMPLETE MARQUIS WHO'S WHO ON CD ROM is a compilation of literally all 19 Marquis Who's Who that have appeared in print since 1985, including living and deceased people. WHO'S WHO IN AMERICA®, WHO'S WHO IN THE WORLD®, WHO'S WHO IN AMERICAN EDUCATIONS®, WHO'S WHO IN AMERICAN LAW®, WHO'S WHO IN AMERICAN NURSING®, WHO'S WHO IN MEDICINE AND HEALTHCARE®, WHO'S WHO IN FINANCE AND INDUSTRY®, WHO'S WHO IN SCIENCE AND ENGINEERING®, WHO'S WHO IN THE EAST®, WHO'S WHO IN THE MIDWEST®, WHO'S WHO IN THE SOUTH AND SOUTHWEST®, WHO'S WHO IN THE WEST®, WHO'S WHO OF AMERICAN WOMEN®, WHO'S WHO IN ADVERTISING®, WHO'S WHO OF EMERGING LEADERS IN AMERICA®, WHO'S WHO IN ENTERTAINMENT®, WHO'S WHO AMONG HUMAN SERVICES PROFESSIONALS®. One year subscription with semi-annual updates $995. National Register Publishing, Reed Elsevier-New Providence, 121 Chanlon Road, New Providence, NJ 07974, (800) 521-8110, fax (800) 836-7736, web site www.marquiswhoswho.com or www.redbooks.com. "If, for any reason whatsoever, your order does not fully meet your expectations, simply return the product within 30 days for a prompt, complete, unquestioned refund," as stated in Catalog of Biographical and Professional References of publisher Marquis Who's Who/National Register Publishing.

ENCYCLOPEDIA OF ASSOCIATIONS—NATIONAL ORGANIZATIONS OF THE US provides a comprehensive listing of hundreds of women's associations. To look them up, refer to the Keyword Index. If you don't want to buy the directory, it should be in virtually any business library.

> Volume 1, National Organizations of the US, in 3 parts, $505
> Volume 2, Geographic and Executive Indexes, $390
> Volume 3, Supplement, $405

Gale Group, P.O. Box 9187, Farmington Hills, MI 48333-9187. Toll free US and Canada (800) 877-GALE (4253) and (248) 699-GALE, fax (800) 414-5043 and (248) 699-8061, Internet orders galeord@galegroup.com, web site www.galegroup.com or www.gale.com. All Gale Group products are available on approval. Contact Gale for details.

INTERNATIONAL WHO'S WHO OF WOMEN lists 4,000 women, including well known figures and women who have recently come to the forefront of their fields. Information includes woman's nationality, date and place of birth, education, family, career history and present position, honors, awards, publications, and contact information. $390. Published by Europa. Distributed by Gale Group, P.O. Box 9187, Farmington Hills, MI 48333-9187. Toll free US and Canada (800) 877-GALE (4253) and (248) 699-GALE, fax (800) 414-5043 and (248) 699-8061, Internet orders galeord@galegroup.com, web site www.galegroup.com or www.gale.com. All Gale Group products are available on approval. Contact Gale for details.

NATIONAL DIRECTORY OF WOMAN-OWNED BUSINESS FIRMS includes government contracting experience and other information. $275. Gale Group, P.O. Box 9187, Farmington Hills, MI 48333-9187. Toll free US and Canada (800) 877-GALE (4253) and (248) 699-GALE, fax (800) 414-5043 and (248) 699-8061, Internet orders galeord@galegroup.com, web site www.galegroup.com or www.gale.com. All Gale Group products are available on approval. Contact Gale for details.

WHO'S WHO OF AMERICAN WOMEN, $259.00. National Register Publishing, Reed Elsevier-New Providence, 121 Chanlon Road, New Providence, NJ 07974, (800) 521-8110, fax (800) 836-7736, web site www.marquiswhoswho.com or www.redbooks.com. "If, for any reason whatsoever, your order does not fully meet your expectations, simply return the product within 30 days for a prompt, complete, unquestioned refund," as stated in Catalog of Biographical and Professional References of publisher Marquis Who's Who/National Register Publishing.

www.womenconnect.com contains job postings and editorial content from Working Woman and Working Mother magazines. Many positions are in sales, software engineering and general engineering, often in the $30,000 to $75,000 range. The site was developed by womenCONNECT.com, McLean, Virginia and has been online since 1994.

READER'S FORUM

We want to hear from you! We want to know what works for you about this book and what we can do to make it better.

Please let us know if we should add to the next edition any other resources, such as directories, CD ROM's, Internet web sites, databases, special editions of magazines or newspapers, alumni directories, company directories, directories of company alumni, membership directories, trade journals or other periodicals, professional associations, libraries, and so forth:

_____

_____

_____

_____

_____

_____

_____

_____

_____

_____

Comments:_____

_____

_____

_____

_____

_____

_____

_____

_____

Use additional pages if needed.

From (Name, Title, Company, Address, Phone, Fax, Email): _____

_____

_____

_____

Respond to:

andreajupina@yahoo.com
or
Carolyn Edwards
Director of Marketing
Kennedy Information, Inc.
One Kennedy Place
Route 12 South
Fitzwilliam, NH 03447
cedwards@kennedyinfo.com